MW01057014

Criminal Law

Criminal Law

Cases and Materials

FOURTH EDITION

Arnold H. Loewy

GEORGE KILLAM PROFESSOR OF CRIMINAL LAW
TEXAS TECH UNIVERSITY SCHOOL OF LAW

CAROLINA ACADEMIC PRESS
Durham, North Carolina

Copyright © 2020
Arnold H. Loewy
All Rights Reserved

ISBN 978-1-5310-1495-7
eISBN 978-1-5310-1496-4
LCCN 2020937444

Carolina Academic Press
700 Kent Street
Durham, North Carolina 27701
Telephone (919) 489-7486
Fax (919) 493-5668
E-mail: cap@cap-press.com
www.cap-press.com

Printed in the United States of America

To my family

Contents

Table of Cases

Preface to the Fourth Edition

This 2020 edition is primarily an update of the prior editions. I have added minor theft crimes to the book. The bulk of the book can still be completed in forty two hours and the entire book can be completed in fifty hours, although those with the luxury of a four (fifty-six) hour course should find plenty of material to keep you busy.

I was assisted in preparing this book by my research assistant Elliott O'Day and with the support of the Texas Tech School of Law, for which I am most grateful.

Criminal Law

Criminal Law

Chapter 1

Punishment

The concept of punishment is central to the criminal law. Although aspects of punishment appear elsewhere in the law (e.g., punitive damages in civil law), nowhere else is it so central. Indeed, were simple compensation to the victim sufficient, it would be unnecessary to bring down the full moral force of the criminal law on the criminal.

In asking whether a particular activity ought to be criminal, we are asking whether it ought to be punished. In creating a hierarchy of crimes from the most to the least serious, we are asking how severe the punishment should be. These questions cannot be answered unless we have a sense of the purposes of punishment. Consequently, we begin our study of the criminal law by attempting to ascertain these purposes.

Traditionally, most courts have allowed trial judges almost unfettered discretion in sentencing, subject only to the sentence being between the statutory minimum and maximum prescribed by the legislature. Because this system tends to make one's sentence largely dependent upon the philosophical biases of the judge in a particular case, a number of states and the federal government have attempted to cabin this discretion by providing for presumptive sentencing that can only be altered by a finding of aggravating and/or mitigating circumstances.

Alaska has adopted a more comprehensive scheme of sentence review than most of the other 49 states. Under its scheme, the Alaska Supreme Court is empowered to review sentences at either the behest of the defendant or the State. Consequently, it has developed a punishment jurisprudence more explicit than most other states. For this reason, we will focus our attention on cases from Alaska.

As you read *Chaney* and *Leuch*, think about how you would have sentenced them if you had been the trial judge, how you would have altered the actual sentences if you had been on the Alaska Supreme Court, and what factors would be most significant in your decision.

State v. Chaney
477 P.2d 441 (Alaska 1970)

RABINOWITZ, J.

Appellee Donald Scott Chaney was indicted on two counts of forcible rape and one count of robbery. After trial by jury, appellee was found guilty on all three counts. The superior court imposed concurrent one-year terms of imprisonment and provided for parole in the discretion of the parole board. The State of Alaska has appealed from the judgment and commitment which was entered by the trial court.

In 1969, the Alaska legislature enacted legislation providing for appellate review of criminal sentences. The 1969 act, codified as AS 12.55.120, states in part that:

(a) A sentence of imprisonment lawfully imposed by the superior court for a term or for aggregate terms exceeding one year may be appealed to the supreme court by the defendant on the ground that the sentence is excessive. By appealing a sentence under this section, the defendant waives the right to plead that by a revision of the sentence resulting from the appeal he has been twice placed in jeopardy for the same offense.

(b) A sentence of imprisonment lawfully imposed by the superior court may be appealed to the supreme court by the state on the ground that the sentence is too lenient; however, when a sentence is appealed by the state and the defendant has not appealed the sentence, the court is not authorized to increase the sentence but may express its approval or disapproval of the sentence and its reasons in a written opinion.

In the case at bar, the state has appealed from the sentence imposed. In such circumstances, the provisions of subsection (b) of AS 12.55.120 prohibit any increase in the sentence which was passed by the trial court although this court may express its approval or disapproval of the sentence in a written opinion.

This appeal is the first by the state under the 1969 act. Since this legislation is of great significance to the administration of criminal justice in the State of Alaska, we deem it important to express our approval or disapproval of sentences within this category of sentence appeal. For in our view, the 1969 sentence appeal statute manifests the legislature's awareness of existing deficiencies in sentencing practices throughout Alaska's entire court system and the compelling necessity of developing appropriate sentencing criteria. The primary goal of such legislation is an attempt to implement Alaska's constitutional mandate that "Penal administration shall be based on the principle of reformation and upon the need for protecting the public."

In the case at bar, appellant, the State of Alaska, claims that the one-year concurrent sentences were too lenient in view of the severity of the crimes of forcible rape and robbery, the need to deter others from such brutal behavior, and in view of the presentence recommendations, all of which called for significantly greater sentences than those which were imposed by the superior court.

The objectives of sentence review have been said to be:

(i) To correct the sentence which is excessive in length, having regard to the nature of the offense, the character of the offender, and the protection of the public interest;

(ii) To facilitate the rehabilitation of the offender by affording him an opportunity to assert grievances he may have regarding his sentence;

(iii) To promote respect for law by correcting abuses of the sentencing power and by increasing the fairness of the sentencing process; and

(iv) To promote the development and application of criteria for sentencing which are both rational and just.[10]

We think this a fair statement of some of the general objectives of sentencing review. Sentencing is a discretionary judicial function. When a sentence is appealed, we will make our own examination of the record and will modify the sentence if we are convinced that the sentencing court was clearly mistaken in imposing the sanction it did. Under Alaska's Constitution, the principles of reformation and necessity of protecting the public constitute the touchstones of penal administration.[13] Multiple goals are encompassed within these broad constitutional standards. Within the ambit of this constitutional phraseology are found the objectives of rehabilitation of the offender into a noncriminal member of society, isolation of the offender from society to prevent criminal conduct during the period of confinement, deterrence of the offender himself after his release from confinement or other penological treatment, as well as deterrence of other members of the community who might possess tendencies toward criminal conduct similar to that of the offender, and community condemnation of the individual offender, or in other words, reaffirmation of societal norms for the purpose of maintaining respect for the norms themselves.

In *Faulkner v. State*,[15] it was said, determination of an appropriate sentence involves the judicious balancing of many and ofttimes competing factors ... (of which) primacy cannot be ascribed to any particular factor.[16]

We now turn to the facts of the case at bar. At the time appellee committed the crimes of forcible rape and robbery, he was an unmarried member of the United States Armed Forces stationed at Fort Richardson, near Anchorage, Alaska.[17] Appellee was born in 1948, the youngest of eight children. His youth was spent on the family's dairy farm in Washington County, Maryland. He played basketball on the

---

10. *ABA Project on Minimum Standards for Criminal Justice, Standards Relating to Appellate Review of Sentences*, Standard 1.2 (Approved Draft, 1968). Under the 1969 act, codified as AS 12.55.120(b), the state was given the right of appeal on the ground that the sentence imposed was too lenient. Thus, one of the objectives of sentence review under our statute is to express our disapproval of the sentence which is too lenient, having regard to the nature of the offense, the character of the offender, protection of the public.

13. ALASKA CONST., art I, § 12.

15. 445 P.2d 815, 823 (Alaska 1968).

16. In *Bear v. State*, 439 P.2d 432, 436 (Alaska 1968) (footnote omitted), we said: The determination of the exact period of time that a convicted defendant should serve is basically a sociological problem to be resolved by a careful weighing of the principle of reformation and the need for protecting the public. In *Appellate Review of Primary Sentencing Decisions: A Connecticut Case Study*, 69 YALE L.J. 1454 (1960), it is stated in part: [T]o determine the appropriate type and degree of sanction to be applied, the sentencing authority must decide which aim is primarily to be implemented and the relative weight to be assigned to secondary aims.

17. Appellee's commanding officer stated, prior to sentencing, that appellee was an excellent soldier, takes orders well, and was on the promotion list before his crimes.

Boonsboro High School team, was a member of Future Farmers of America and the Boy Scouts. Appellee did not complete high school, having dropped out one month prior to graduation.[18] After a series of varying types of employment, appellee was drafted into the United States Army in 1968. At sentencing, it was disclosed that appellee did not have any prior criminal record, was not a user of drugs, and was only a social drinker.

From the record that has been furnished, it appears that appellee and a companion picked up the prosecutrix at a downtown location in Anchorage. After driving the victim around in their car, appellee and his companion beat her and forcibly raped her four times.[19] During this same period of time, the victim's money was removed from her purse. Upon completion of these events, the prosecutrix was permitted to leave the vehicle to the accompaniment of dire threats of reprisals if she attempted to report the incident to the police.

The presentence report which was furnished to the trial court prior to sentencing contains appellee's version of the rapes. According to appellee, he felt "that it wasn't rape as forcible and against her will on my part." As to his conviction of robbery, appellee states: "I found the money on the floor of the car afterwards and was planning on giving it back, but didn't get to see the girl." At the time of sentencing, appellee told the court that he "didn't direct any violence against the girl."

The Division of Corrections, in its presentence report, recommended appellee be incarcerated and parole be denied. The assistant district attorney who appeared for the state at the time of sentencing recommended that appellee receive concurrent seven-year sentences with two years suspended on the two rape convictions, and that the appellee be sentenced to a consecutive five-year term of imprisonment on the robbery conviction, and that this sentence be suspended and appellee be placed on probation during this period of time. At the time of sentencing, a representative of the Division of Corrections recommended that appellee serve two years on each of the rape convictions and that appellee be sentenced to two years suspended with probation as to the robbery conviction. In his opinion, there was "an excellent possibility of ... early parole." Counsel for appellee concurred in the Division of Corrections' recommendation. As was indicated at the outset, the trial court imposed concurrent one-year terms of imprisonment and provided for parole at the discretion of the parole board.[21] The trial judge further recommended that appellee be placed in a minimum-security facility.

In imposing this sentence, the trial judge remarked that he was "sorry that the [military] regulations would not permit keeping [appellee] ... in the service if he

---

18. Appellee asserts he was forced to take this action because his father needed his help on the family dairy farm.

19. The prosecutrix was also forced to perform an act of fellatio with appellee's companion.

21. These were minimum sentences under the applicable statutes. Rape carries a potential range of imprisonment from 1 to 20 years while a conviction of robbery can result in imprisonment from 1 to 15 years.

wanted to stay because it seems to me that is . . . a better setup for everybody concerned than putting him in the penitentiary."[22] At a later point in his remarks, the trial judge said:

> Now as a matter of fact, I have sentenced you to a minimum on all 3 counts here but there will be no problem as far as I'm concerned for you to be paroled at the first day, the Parole Board says that you're eligible for parole. . . . [If] the Parole Board should decide 10 days from now that you're eligible for parole and parole you, it's entirely satisfactory with the court.[23]

Exercising the appellate jurisdiction vested in this court by virtue of the provisions of AS 12.55.120(b), we express our disapproval of the sentence which was imposed by the trial court in the case at bar. In our opinion, the sentence was too lenient considering the circumstances surrounding the commission of these crimes. It further appears that several significant goals of our system of penal justice were accorded little or no weight by the sentencing court.

Forcible rape and robbery rank among the most serious crimes. In the case at bar, the record reflects that the trial judge explicitly stated, on several occasions, that he disbelieved appellee and believed the prosecutrix's version of what happened after she entered the vehicle which was occupied by appellee and his companion. Considering both the jury's and the trial judge's resolution of this issue of credibility, and the violent circumstances surrounding the commission of these dangerous crimes, we have difficulty in understanding why one-year concurrent sentences were thought appropriate.

Review of the sentencing proceedings leads to the impression that the trial judge was apologetic in regard to his decision to impose a sanction of incarceration. Much was made of appellee's fine military record and his potential eligibility for early parole.[24] On the one hand, the record is devoid of any trace of remorse on appellee's part. Seemingly all but forgotten in the sentencing proceedings is the victim of appellee's rapes and robbery. On the other hand, the record discloses that the trial judge properly considered the mitigating circumstance that the prosecutrix,

---

22. Collateral consequences flowing from an accused's conviction may be considered by the trial judge in arriving at an appropriate sentence. In addition to giving weight to the fact that military regulations prohibited appellee's retention in the service, the record further indicates that the trial judge also took into consideration the fact that appellee's conviction would result in his receiving an undesirable discharge from the military service.

23. Supreme Ct. R. 21(f) requires that: At the time of imposition of sentence the judge shall make a statement on the record explaining his reasons for imposition of the sentence. The basic reasons for this requirement are that a statement of the reasons by the sentencing judge should greatly increase the rationality of sentences, such a statement can be of therapeutic value to the defendant, and the statement can be of significance to an appellate court faced with the prospect of reviewing the sentence. *ABA Project on Minimum Standards for Criminal Justice, Sentencing Alternatives and Procedures*, Standard 5.6(ii) 269, 270–71 (Approved Draft, 1968).

24. A military spokesman represented to the sentencing court that: An occurrence such as the one concerned is very common and happens many times each night in Anchorage. Needless to say, Donald Chaney was the unlucky 'G.I.' that picked a young lady who told.

who at the time did not know either appellee or his companion, voluntarily entered appellee's car. But the crux of our disapproval of the sentence stems from what we consider to be the trial judge's de-emphasis of several important goals of criminal justice.

In view of the circumstances of this record, we think the sentence imposed is not well calculated to achieve the objective of reformation of the accused. Considering the apologetic tone of the sentencing proceedings, the court's endorsement of an extremely early parole, and the concurrent minimum sentences which were imposed for these three serious felonies, we fail to discern how the objective of reformation was effectuated. At most, appellee was told that he was only technically guilty and minimally blameworthy, all of which minimized the possibility of appellee's comprehending the wrongfulness of his conduct. We also think that the sentence imposed falls short of effectuating the goal of community condemnation, or the reaffirmation of societal norms for the purpose of maintaining respect for the norms themselves. In short, knowledge of the calculated circumstances involved in the commission of these felonies and the sentence imposed could lead to the conclusion that forcible rape and robbery are not reflective of serious antisocial conduct. Thus, respect for society's condemnation of forcible rape and robbery is eroded and reaffirmation of these societal norms negated.[25]

We believe that a concurrent sentence calling for a substantially longer period of incarceration on each count was appropriate in light of the particular facts of this record and the goals of penal administration. A sentence of imprisonment for a substantially longer period of imprisonment than the one-year sentence which was imposed would unequivocally bring home to appellee the seriousness of his dangerously unlawful conduct, would reaffirm society's condemnation of forcible rape and robbery, and would provide the Division of Corrections of the State of Alaska with the opportunity of determining whether appellee required any special treatment prior to his return to society.

Questions and Notes

1. Would (should) the trial judge's ruling have been upheld if he had given the minimum sentence without the apologetic overtones?

2. Were the judge's apologetic overtones motivated by his belief in the general disutility of prison, or by his depreciating the seriousness of rape? Should it matter?

3. Could the judge have impressed the seriousness of rape and robbery upon the defendant without substantial imprisonment?

4. Assuming the technology (e.g., electronic bracelets, etc.) exists to meaningfully enforce house arrest, might lengthy house arrest, coupled with substantial

---

25. We also doubt whether the sentence in the case at bar mitigates the persistent problem of disparity in sentences. What is sought is reasonable differentiation among sentences.

community service, victim compensation (for medical and psychiatric care, if necessary) and a substantial rehabilitation program have been more effective?

5. Is the problem the lack of severity of punishment or the lack of certainty? Reconsider footnote 24. If Chaney's conduct is really that commonplace, don't we need to convict a lot more people rather than give more time to the people we convict?

6. On the other hand, if Chaney's conduct is typical, should a lengthy sentence be endorsed by the court as an example to others? Ideally, such an opinion could be posted on every bulletin board in the Anchorage barracks. This would convey a clear message that such behavior will not be tolerated but would not apply to Chaney because he did not appeal his sentence.

7. Why did the judges (trial and appellate) consider the victim's voluntarily entering Chaney's car to be a mitigating circumstance? Didn't that simply eliminate the aggravating circumstance of kidnapping? Or did the judges assume that the victim should have been aware of the behavior described in footnote 24?

8. Should the defendant's background have been a mitigating circumstance? If so, to what degree?

9. Is (should) the absence of remorse (be) relevant? If Chaney denies his guilt, how can he be expected to be remorseful? Does making remorse relevant lead to phony professions of remorse?

Leuch v. State

633 P.2d 1006 (Alaska 1981)

RABINOWITZ, CHIEF JUSTICE.

David Leuch pled guilty to two counts of grand larceny. The superior court imposed concurrent sentences of eight years with four suspended. Leuch now appeals this sentence, claiming it is excessive. The offenses to which Leuch and his co-defendant, Michael Darr, pled guilty involved the theft of two motorcycles from the Fairbanks Harley-Davidson dealership and the theft of a safe, a dolly, and approximately $12,000 from the Healy Roadhouse on the Parks Highway.[1]

The presentence report on Leuch's background shows that he grew up in a "stable, loving environment" with his adoptive parents in California. During that time, he graduated from high school, having participated in the tennis and music programs and served as class president. He attended college for a time, but his grades show that he was a poor student at this level. In 1975, having taken a three-month

---

1. Both were also charged with an additional count of grand larceny, three counts of burglary not in a dwelling, and one count of concealing stolen property, and Darr was charged with an additional count of receiving stolen property. The state argues that these additional counts "cannot be overlooked," forcing us to repeat once again that, absent a conviction, an indictment is absolutely no evidence of guilty conduct. *Waters v. State*, 483 P.2d 199 (Alaska 1971).

course in truck driving, Leuch began to drive a truck cross-country. In 1976, he worked for a few months for a Manpower program in Denver, Colorado, then came to Anchorage in June of 1976 to find a trucking job. For three months in 1977, he was employed as a driller's helper. From June of 1977 to February of 1979 he worked as a cab driver, leasing his own taxi for the last nine months of that time.

His criminal record up to that point consisted only of several traffic offenses. On February 14, 1979, however, he was convicted of twenty-six counts of unemployment fraud, for which he was given a ninety-day sentence with all but fifty-four suspended, together with a fine of $260, and was required to make restitution in the amount of $1,274.[2]

It was during this initial incarceration on the unemployment fraud charges that he met his co-defendant Michael Darr. After their release, the two traveled to Fairbanks together purportedly intending to file on a gold claim of Darr's. Upon their arrival in Fairbanks, their truck broke down. They tried to spend the night in the truck until it got too cold, according to Leuch, and then they entered a church (unlocked, by Leuch's account) which apparently led to their conviction in Fairbanks on June 12 of petty larceny and unauthorized entry.[3] Leuch was given ten days in jail. During that time, he apparently injured his knee, was hospitalized for surgery on some torn cartilage in that knee, and later convalesced at Careage North a convalescent home in Fairbanks.

There he met a health care assistant who, presumably concerned about the fact that he knew few people in Fairbanks apart from Darr, allowed Leuch to reside with her until he was able to find suitable work.

The theft of the motorcycles was, in Leuch's words, sheer impulse on his part; he indicated that Darr, who had been considering the act for a couple of weeks, suggested it. They went to the motorcycle store; Leuch broke a window with a rock; Darr climbed through the window and opened the door; and each removed a motorcycle which they stored at a friend's cabin.

The Healy Roadhouse theft was to get money to ship the motorcycles out of the state. The health care assistant with whom Leuch was residing had a friend who had formerly been employed at the Roadhouse and apparently had a grudge against its owner. This friend supplied Darr and Leuch with the floor plans of the Roadhouse to enable them to locate the safe. Darr and Leuch, having planned the venture for two weeks in advance, broke in by unscrewing a single bolt lock on the back door. They then found a dolly and used it to remove the safe, taking both safe and dolly in a station wagon to a dirt road off Chena Pump Road. They broke into the safe and

---

2. On November 15, 1979, Leuch admitted failure to make restitution on this charge, and was sentenced to an additional 30 days in jail.

3. We cannot tell from the record whether these convictions were based on the entry into the church or on another incident.

found about $7500 cash, along with numerous checks and notes which they burned. They then dumped the safe into the river.

Leuch's letter explaining the incidents expressed his remorse over the harm caused the victims by his actions.[5] He stated that he had been in a depressed state of mind during his recuperation, and that he was too easily influenced by his companions.

Letters on Leuch's behalf were submitted from Leuch's girlfriend, opining that Leuch, being new to Fairbanks, had been unduly influenced by his relationship with Darr, whom she had known for a long time and regarded as "bad company"; from his girlfriend's mother, stressing that she would continue to accept him into her home and endeavor to provide a positive influence; and from Leuch's parents, stating that Leuch's criminal activity came as a shock to them and that they were sure he would never engage in criminal behavior again. An institutional counselor in Anchorage indicated that Leuch had adjusted well to incarceration and was in the less secure section of the jail.

The probation officer preparing the presentence report noted that Leuch was the product of a stable home environment; that he appeared to be a dependable worker; that he was cooperative during the interview; and that he appeared to feel remorse for his actions. Although Leuch used alcohol and drugs (marijuana and occasionally cocaine), they were not a factor in the offenses. The probation officer attributed Leuch's criminal conduct to several factors: the fact that Leuch was an impulsive individual[6] with poor judgment, especially with respect to choosing his associates; his lack of employment and poor financial situation; his lack of discipline and structure in goal orientation; and his lack of familial ties in Alaska, where he apparently plans to reside. The probation officer noted that Leuch stated he had two job offers, one as a trucker north of Fairbanks and the other as a laborer in a cannery in Dutch Harbor. The probation officer did not, however, regard either of these opportunities as a viable job plan. The presentence report concluded by recommending incarceration, in view of the seriousness of the offenses and the large amounts of money involved, and the fact that Leuch had apparently not learned from his prior contacts with the criminal justice system.

At the sentencing hearing, the prosecutor apparently ignored his agreement with Leuch's defense counsel to bring to the court's attention Leuch's cooperation with the state in offering to testify against Darr, and this was pointed out by defense

---

5. His letter said:
   I know that when I had the money and the motorcycles I felt guilty and trapped and had the empty and insecure feeling of knowing they didn't belong to me. It feels good to have something that you make for yourself and pretty bad if someone takes it away from you. I can assure you that I am truly sorry about the events that took place and to the people I offended!
6. Although the theft of the motorcycles was apparently impulsive on the part of Leuch, the theft of the safe, as the probation officer pointed out, was a deliberately planned act.

counsel. It was also brought out that Darr, learning of Leuch's cooperation, had made statements indicating that he intended to retaliate physically against Leuch.

The superior court did not find Leuch to be the worst offender within the class, but found the question a close one. The court stated that although this was Leuch's first felony offense, his misdemeanor convictions showed extreme dishonesty, and that he was on his way to becoming a professional criminal. But the court also noted that, to Leuch's credit, he had admitted his participation and that his attitude in jail appeared to be good. The superior court assessed the *Chaney* factors as follows: Leuch's chances of rehabilitation were greater than those of Darr, which were described as "slim;" there was also a little higher likelihood that Leuch would be deterred by a sentence than in the case of Darr, where the likelihood was "not that good;" the necessity of isolation for the protection of the community was high; and the extent of community condemnation was also high. The superior court also expressed the view that the deterrent effect of a sentence on the general community is negligible in practically any case because, in the superior court's view, sentences are not sufficiently publicized to have any significant impact. The court's main concern was the proximity of this offense to Leuch's two prior jail sentences, which precluded a suspended sentence. The court then imposed the concurrent eight year sentences with four years suspended.

We will modify a sentence only if, after an independent review of the record, we conclude that the superior court was clearly mistaken. In reviewing a sentence, a portion of which is suspended, the period of suspension as well as the period of incarceration must be weighed. It would, of course, be unrealistic to consider the suspended time to be as harsh a sanction as time to be served in prison. However, it would also be incorrect to consider suspended time as a nugatory or insignificant sanction. Thus, this appeal involves concurrent eight-year sentences four years of which have been suspended. We have previously indicated that, except for cases involving particularly serious offenses, dangerous offenses, and professional criminals, maximum sentences ought not to exceed five years.

We are in general agreement with the position of the ABA Standards that, in the absence of affirmative reasons to the contrary, a sentence not involving confinement is to be preferred. "Affirmative reasons to the contrary" should be found on the basis of a showing that probation, or some other alternative to incarceration, is inadequate to serve one or more of the *Chaney* criteria. The ABA Standards list the following legitimate reasons for the selection of total confinement:

(i) Confinement is necessary in order to protect the public from further criminal activity by the defendant; or

(ii) The defendant is in need of correctional treatment which can most effectively be provided if he is placed in total confinement; or

(iii) It would unduly depreciate the seriousness of the offense to impose a sentence other than total confinement.

ABA Standards Relating to Sentencing Alternatives and Procedures §2.5(c) (Approved Draft 1968).

The Standards go on to specify that "[o]n the other hand, community hostility to the defendant is not a legitimate basis for imposing a sentence of total confinement." *Id.* We read these considerations as corresponding to the *Chaney* criteria of isolation, rehabilitation, and community condemnation. We also think that a finding that a non-custodial sentence would fail to deter the defendant and/or others to the requisite degree, the other factors in the *Chaney* list, justifies a sentence of incarceration. These "affirmative reasons to the contrary" should have some basis in the record.

A significant indication that a non-custodial sentence is inappropriate would be a past history of unsuccessful attempts at such sentences. If an individual has not proven amenable to parole or probation in the past, it is likely that, absent some change, he will not prove to be so in the future.

A lack of information which stems from the absence of any experience as to how the offender will perform on probation renders it especially difficult to make any judgment as to three of the *Chaney* factors: the need to deter the offender, the need to isolate the offender, and the offender's amenability to the rehabilitative process. On the other hand, it is clear from Leuch's record that a pattern of short incarcerations followed by unsupervised release has been insufficient to protect the public, to deter Leuch himself, or to assist him in rehabilitating himself.

The preference for non-incarcerative sanctions may be overridden, even if information is lacking regarding their past use in terms of the above three factors, by the other *Chaney* considerations, general deterrence and community condemnation, which are not as closely tied to information regarding past performance on probation programs.

Here, the superior court opined that the general deterrence factor played little or no role. The community condemnation factor, however, was regarded as significant by the superior court.

In light of the fact that the community condemnation factor has been the cause of some concern in this and other recent cases, we think a discussion of this sentencing factor is appropriate. We recently discussed the community condemnation factor in *Kelly v. State*, 622 P.2d 432, 435–36 (Alaska 1981). There we emphasized that community condemnation is a different concept from general deterrence, a separate sentencing goal under *Chaney*, and from retribution, an impermissible consideration in sentencing.

Many theoretical explanations of this concept have been put forward, all of which are useful in understanding why this aspect of *Chaney* is to be retained in sentencing decisions. The Kantian view is that each member of society is granted certain benefits, and agrees to subject himself to certain restraints so that other members of society may enjoy these same benefits. When an individual ignores these restraints, he achieves an unfair advantage over other members of society by avoiding his obligations while continuing to enjoy his benefits. According to Kant, restoration of the balance on which society depends requires that such an individual be deprived of those benefits to some extent.[13] Oliver Wendell Holmes believed that, since society has required individual victims to set aside their tendency toward private vengeful action in favor of societal remedies against the offender, society must punish the offender on behalf of the victim or else risk a return to private methods of forcing the offender to suffer.[14] More recently, concern over the disparity in sentences under rehabilitation-oriented systems has led to the conclusion that some notion of just punishment must be included in sentencing considerations.

Theoretical justifications are of limited value in the difficult sentencing decision itself in a particular case. Our decisions have not provided the internal structure which is necessary to implement this concept in sentencing decisions. We have been reluctant to provide this structure ourselves because judgments as to the extent to which the community condemns a particular offense are more properly made in the legislative area than by the judiciary. The new criminal code with its sentencing provisions provides this structure for most crimes, and should be of immense guidance to sentencing courts. One principle which emerges, both from our prior case law and from the new criminal code, is that offenses which are committed solely against property or the public order are, on the whole, less severe than offenses involving threats, injuries, or death, or other invasions of another's person.

This is congruent, not only with the theoretical justifications noted above, but also with common-sense notions of reprehensibility. In Kantian terms, the imbalance which is solely one person's wrongful loss of property and another's wrongful gain is more easily righted than the imbalance which involves the victim's loss of life, limb or dignity. Under the Holmes view, society can fulfill its obligation to the victim of a purely financial loss with less drastic means (ideally, restitution) than in the case of a victim of a physical assault. In common-sense terms, the harm imposed on the victim of a financial loss is generally much less injurious, degrading and painful than the harm stemming from a personal threat or physical injury. Yet another relevant aspect of purely property crime is that the remedy of restitution can approximate the "making whole" of a victim in this context in a way which it

---

13. *See* J. MURPHY, KANT: THE PHILOSOPHY OF RIGHT 109–12, 140–44 (1970).

14. O.W. HOLMES, THE COMMON LAW 36 (Howe ed. 1963). *See also* Weiler, *Why Do We Punish? The Case for Retributive Justice*, 12 U. B.C. L. REV. 295, 308 (1978). Sir James Stephen, the famed Victorian jurist and historian of criminal law once said, "[t]he criminal law stands to the passion of revenge in much the same relation as marriage to the sexual appetite." He believed that authoritative punishment of criminals was a desirable institution because it provided an orderly outlet for emotions that would otherwise express themselves in socially less acceptable ways. If the state did nothing about punishing an offender, the natural and potentially destructive feelings of resentment aroused in victims of the offence or other interested parties would no doubt result in attempts at private vengeance.

cannot in the context of crimes involving physical threats or invasions of a victim's person.[19]

This is not meant to indicate that the loss occasioned by property crimes is an insignificant one, or that it should be disregarded, or that it can never result in incarceration. We do think, however, that the extent of harm visited upon the victim by the offender is a proper consideration at sentencing, and that the proper *Chaney* vehicle for this consideration is the community condemnation factor.

Taking all these factors into account, we think that where an offense is against only property, involving no physical threats or violence; where it is the offender's first felony conviction; and where there is no background of unsuccessful paroles or probations which would indicate that probation is unsuitable to protect the public, to deter the offender, and to further his rehabilitative progress, probation, coupled with restitution,[20] is the appropriate sentence unless other factors militate against it.[21] Naturally, this is not to be construed as a hard and fast rule.

Here, several factors are present which would justify a departure from this general rule. Although these were Leuch's first felony convictions, he had a record of

---

19. Again, we find significance in the new legislative enactments which give a greater role to restitution in the sentencing provisions: The Code gives greater emphasis to restitution than is the case under existing law. Restitution is available in all cases and in connection with most kinds of sentences. As it now stands, only passing reference is made to restitution in AS 12.55.100(a)(2), where it is listed as a possible condition of probation. . . . Further, because restitution is the one sanction which has the potential for making a victim 'whole,' or nearly so, and because the victim is the most frequently ignored party in the justice system, the Subcommission felt that restitution should be given more extended treatment as a complementary sanction in the Revised Code. *Criminal Code Revision Subcommission, Alaska Criminal Code Revision*, Commentary to ch. 36, art. 6, at 54 (Tent. Draft, Part 6, 1978).

20. The probation officer in the instant case noted that Leuch did not have the financial resources to make restitution. We do note that, generally, an offender will be in a better position to make restitution while in the community than while incarcerated.

21. It was while serving his initial sentence for his prior misdemeanors that Leuch met Darr, striking up a relationship which has led to nothing but trouble for both and for their innocent victims. Given the probation officer's opinion that there was a direct correlation between Leuch's criminal behavior and his peer group association, Leuch's own admission that he was unduly influenced by Darr, and Leuch's girlfriend's statements that Leuch, who was new to Fairbanks, had erred in regarding as his friend such "bad company" as Darr, the only possible conclusion is that Leuch's prior incarceration had a net impact of furthering his criminal career. This is a classic illustration of the counter-productive effect which incarceration can have. *Cf.* G.B. SHAW, THE CRIME OF IMPRISONMENT 32–33 (Citadel ed. 1961):

> He is, at the expiration of his sentence, flung out of the prison into the streets to earn his living in a labor market where nobody will employ an ex-prisoner. . . . He seeks the only company in which he is welcome: the society of criminals; and sooner or later, according to his luck, he finds himself in prison again. . . . The criminal, far from being deterred from crime, is forced into it; and the citizen whom his punishment was meant to protect suffers from his depredations.

Obviously, we do not mean to intimate that incarceration always has this effect, or that the end result is solely caused by the incarceration rather than by the offender's exercise of free will. The pattern here, however, is too striking for us not to notice it.

numerous misdemeanors which the sentencing judge found had involved "extreme dishonesty"; although there was no background of supervised probation, there was a failure to make restitution for the prior offenses; and although the offenses in question here were solely against property, one of the felonies was a large-scale crime and had a severe impact on the uninsured victim. Consequently, the community condemnation factor must be placed on the upper end of the spectrum for property crimes. Thus, we are unwilling to hold that the general rule articulated above must be applied literally in the case at bar. Therefore, we think the sentencing court was correct in concluding that some period of incarceration was appropriate. We think the court was clearly mistaken, however, in imposing concurrent sentences of eight years with four suspended. Given the circumstances of this case we think the superior court was clearly mistaken in imposing a total sentence which exceeded five years.[22] In short, we hold the sentence is excessive and that upon remand appellant should receive concurrent sentences which, including any period of suspension and probation, do not exceed five years in total length.

MATTHEWS, J, with whom BURKE, J, joins, dissenting.

In view of the fact that the defendant had been twice incarcerated for two separate crimes not long before he committed the two felonies of which he now stands convicted, and in view of the premeditated nature of the theft of the safe, I am unable to say that the trial court was clearly mistaken in imposing concurrent eight year sentences with four years suspended.

Questions and Notes

1. The court purports to draw a sharp distinction between community condemnation, which it considers legitimate, and retribution, which it considers illegitimate. Do you see the distinction? Is community condemnation essentially expiation, that is, a cleansing of society whereas retribution is hatred for the criminal? Examine footnote 14 and the accompanying text. If that is not retribution, what on earth is?

2. Should retribution, however defined, be a (the principal) factor in punishment?

---

22. Under the new criminal code, Leuch's offenses would be classified as Theft in the Second Degree, a class C felony. AS 11.46.130. Under that statute, no presumptive sentence is given for first offenders, but we note that the maximum sentence would be five years, the presumptive sentence for a second offender two years, and the presumptive sentence for a third offender three years. AS 12.55.125(e). The Sentencing Guidelines Committee's current recommendations as to first offenses, which had not been promulgated as of the time sentence was imposed in this case, coordinate well with this statutory scheme. For this particular class C felony, the presumptive sentence under those recommendations for a first offender is probation, with up to sixty days incarceration. The presence of aggravating factors (including a history of misdemeanor convictions involving fraud, theft, or violence), to be specified by the sentencing judge, may support any sentence between sixty days and two years. A sentence in excess of two years (which would exceed the presumptive sentence for second offenders) should not be imposed unless the court finds on the basis of clear and convincing evidence that manifest injustice would result from the imposition of a sentence of two years or less, and the "extraordinary" circumstances necessary to support this finding are to be specified in the record.

3. Did Alaska use bad judgment in initially sending Leuch to prison for his first misdemeanor offenses without having attempted probation or house arrest? (*See* footnote 21.) Is it now appropriate to assume that because brief incarceration didn't work, more substantial incarceration is appropriate? Isn't that just more of the wrong approach?

4. Do you agree with the trial court's rejection of general deterrence? If sentence publicity were necessary for general deterrence to be relevant, would it not be limited to the most sensational trials?

5. Is this a good case for victim compensation? How should a sentence be structured to maximize this opportunity? Should restitution beyond the defendant's ability to pay ever be ordered? The Alaska Supreme Court has said no. *Karr v. State*, 686 P.2d 1192 (Alaska 1984).

6. What factors should determine severity of sentence? Should the happenstance of a victim being uninsured and therefore suffering greater harm be relevant as *Leuch* says it is? (*See generally* Arnold H. Loewy, *Culpability, Dangerousness, and Harm: Balancing the Factors on Which Our Criminal Law is Predicated*, 66 N.C. L. Rev. 283 (1988) [hereinafter *Culpability, Dangerousness, and Harm*] reprinted in Appendix B, *infra*.) Should the amount stolen be relevant? In the *Karr* case (Question 5 above), the court upheld a 10-year sentence (five suspended) for a woman who embezzled more than $350,000 from her employer despite the absence of violence or any prior criminal record. The court concluded that the magnitude of the theft was so great that considerations of condemnation and general deterrence justified the penalty.

Problems

Jones, a 35-year-old married man, pleaded guilty to three counts of indecent assault. The victims were young girls aged six, seven, and eight, respectively. This was Jones' first offense, and the evidence indicated that theretofore he was a person of good character. Furthermore, psychiatric testimony at his trial indicated that he was not a true sexual deviant, that the incident that led to these convictions was unlikely to recur, and that imprisonment would definitely be detrimental to his recovery. The crimes for which he was convicted each carry a maximum of five years' imprisonment.

Assume that you are the trial judge. Would you sentence him to prison? If so, for how long? Why? What are the costs and benefits of the sentence you have chosen? *See Regina v. Jones*, 115 Can. Crim. Cas. Ann. 273 (1956).

See discussion in Criminal Law in a Nutshell § 1.03 A (5th ed.) (West 2009) [hereinafter Nutshell]. For collateral reading, see Nutshell §§ 1.01–1.05, and *Culpability, Dangerousness, and Harm*, Section IV (Appendix B).

Chapter 2

Homicide

The study of criminal homicide involves an evaluation of a complex common law and statutory scheme of gradations. At common law, there were only two forms of homicide: murder, which was subject to capital punishment, and manslaughter, which was not. The grand criterion distinguishing murder from manslaughter was malice aforethought. The most important thing to remember about malice aforethought is that courts do not normally employ it in its dictionary sense. That is, the defendant need be neither malicious nor preparatory as the terms imply. Rather, she must kill with one of the requisite states of mind necessary for murder.

These states of mind include intent to kill, intent to inflict serious bodily injury (or in some jurisdictions assault with a deadly weapon), outrageous recklessness amounting to a depraved heart, and, in most jurisdictions, a killing committed while perpetrating a felony. We will examine these states of mind separately, but for now it is important that you understand that each will ordinarily suffice for murder.

A. Premeditation

Most legislatures have chosen to divide murder into degrees. First degree murder is generally punishable by life imprisonment or death. Second degree murder is punishable by life or, in some jurisdictions, a term of years. A few jurisdictions have more than two degrees of murder. States are not required to divide murder into degrees, and those that do sometimes have different criteria.

One of the most common sets of criteria derives from Pennsylvania, which first adopted it in 1794: "All murder which shall be perpetrated by means of poison, or by lying in wait, or by any other kind of willful, deliberate or premeditated killing . . . shall be deemed murder in the first degree." Although a less common formulation than it used to be, this or a similar formulation remains a typical means of distinguishing first degree murder from second degree murder.

Some courts have tried to define "premeditation." Others have virtually read it out of existence. As you read the majority and concurring opinions in *Ollens* and the Questions and Notes following them, think about which approach makes more sense.

State v. Ollens

733 P.2d 984 (Wash. 1987)

GOODLOE, Justice.

This case involves a brutal killing inflicted by multiple stabs and slashes with a knife. We address whether, as a matter of law, there is sufficient evidence to allow the issue of premeditation to go to a jury. We answer in the affirmative.

Respondent Lawrence C. Ollens was charged with the crime of aggravated murder in the first degree for the November 9, 1985 robbery/stabbing death of William Tyler, a Tacoma taxicab driver. Before trial respondent moved that the trial court review and dismiss the aggravated first-degree murder charge because of lack of evidence to prove the element of premeditation. The State acquiesced to pretrial review.

The State relied on the testimony of Dr. Emmanuel Lacsina, the Pierce County Medical Examiner. Dr. Lacsina testified that Tyler died from multiple stab wounds and resulting blood loss. One stab perforated the left lung and the right ventricle of the heart. Dr. Lacsina indicated that this was one of the first wounds inflicted. A second stab perforated the right lobe of the liver and the soft tissues around the right kidney. A third stab entered between Tyler's ribs penetrating the right lobe of the liver. These wounds were not immediately fatal. However, all three wounds were potentially fatal if not treated shortly after their infliction. A fourth stab penetrated Tyler's right thigh.

In addition, Dr. Lacsina testified that Tyler's throat had been slit. More than one slashing motion was needed to complete the 6-inch gash which nearly transected the voice box and jugular vein. This injury was also capable of causing death. Dr. Lacsina testified, however, that Tyler could have been alive and struggling for 2 to 3 minutes after the neck wound.

Dr. Lacsina stated that the stab wounds preceded the slashing of Tyler's throat. Dr. Lacsina also noted that there were numerous defensive wounds. These wounds were inflicted when the victim was alive and indicate that the assailant and victim struggled.

At the hearing, the defense asserted that the State's main witness, Lawrence Haney, would testify that Ollens supposedly admitted to him that he had killed the victim when the victim made a move as if to reach for a weapon and "[Ollens] cut the man because he felt it was either the man's life or his." Citing to *State v. Bingham*, 105 Wash. 2d 820, 719 P.2d 109 (1986), and *Austin v. United States*, 382 F.2d 129 (D.C. Cir. 1967), the Superior Court removed the question of premeditation from the trial. The Superior Court concluded that the "use of a knife to inflict more than one wound, in and of itself, is not probative of premeditation, but . . . can only be probative of intent to kill." The State appealed to this court seeking review as a matter of right. Superior Court proceedings have been stayed pending a further order of this court.

The issue we address is: Given multiple stab and slash wounds, is there sufficient evidence to send the question of premeditation to a jury?

Specific intent to kill and premeditation are not synonymous, but separate and distinct elements of the crime of first-degree murder. *See* RCW 9A.32.030(1)(a), .050(1)(a). Premeditation has been defined as "the deliberate formation of and reflection upon the intent to take a human life," and involves "the mental process of thinking beforehand, deliberation, reflection, weighing or reasoning for a period of time, however short." Premeditation must involve more than a moment in point of time.

The State argues that *Bingham* is limited to its facts. In *Bingham*, we held that manual strangulation alone shows only an opportunity to deliberate and is insufficient to sustain the element of premeditation. *Bingham*, 105 Wash. 2d at 828, 719 P.2d 109. The State points out, however, that *Bingham* recognizes that "[t]he planned presence of a weapon necessary to facilitate a killing has been held to be adequate evidence to allow the issue of premeditation to go to the jury." *Bingham*, at 827, 719 P.2d 109. *State v. Lanning*, 5 Wash. App. 426, 439, 487 P.2d 785 (1971), in which the victim's neck had been slashed, states: *Some premeditation was necessarily involved in order to have available a knife edged, lethal instrument* capable of nearly severing the victim's neck. (Italics ours.)

The State argues that Ollens necessarily planned the presence of a weapon, the double-edged knife used to inflict the fatal wounds. The State posits that the evidence suggests that Ollens carried such a knife in another robbery approximately 1 week earlier. The State concludes that the presence of a knife, as distinguished from no weapon, suffices to allow the issue of premeditation to go to a jury.

The State argues that as evidenced by the multiple stab wounds to the chest and heart, respondent intended to kill Tyler. It further argues that the multiple slashing of the victim's neck, which occurred after the stabbings, conclusively demonstrates a deliberation—however short—on the previously formed and demonstrated intent to kill. The State concludes that the physical evidence of manner and method of death, as a matter of law, sustains the element of premeditation.

Ollens disputes that the evidence in this case permits the inference that premeditation occurred. He argues that some time did pass during the struggle, however, this passage of time is inherent in the manner of a multiple stabbing death and is mere passage of time, not evidence of premeditation.

Respondent also asserts that the manner of death, *i.e.*, violence and multiple wounds, does not support an inference of deliberation actually occurring or of a calmly calculated plan to kill which is requisite for premeditation and deliberation. *Austin v. United States*, 382 F.2d 129, 139 (D.C. Cir. 1967), provides:

> [V]iolence and multiple wounds, while more than ample to show an intent to kill, cannot standing alone support an inference of a calmly calculated plan to kill requisite for premeditation and deliberation, as contrasted with an impulsive and senseless, albeit sustained, frenzy. *See also People v.*

Anderson, 70 Cal. 2d 15, 73 Cal. Rptr. 550, 447 P.2d 942 (1968). Respondent argues that the evidence may indicate an intent to kill in the frenzy of the struggle, but it provides no basis from which a jury could infer that premeditation occurred.

Ollens argues that *Bingham* is not limited to manual strangulation, as *Bingham* emphasizes the application of its analysis to other methods of death.

Having the opportunity to deliberate is not evidence the defendant did deliberate, which is necessary for a finding of premeditation. Otherwise, any form of killing which took more than a moment could result in a finding of premeditation, without some additional evidence showing reflection. *Bingham*, 105 Wash. 2d at 826, 719 P.2d 109. *Austin v. United States, supra*, which is quoted in *Bingham*, involved a homicide committed with a knife, wherein the victim was stabbed 26 times and the knife left imbedded in the victim's skull. The *Austin* court held this evidence was insufficient to prove the elements of premeditation and deliberation, concluding that:

> [T]he Government was not able to show any motive for the crime or any prior threats or quarrels between appellant and deceased which might support an inference of premeditation and deliberation. Thus, the jury could only speculate and surmise, without any basis in the testimony or evidence, that appellant acted with premeditation and deliberation.

Austin, at 139.

This is distinguished from the present case where a possible motive is present—that Ollens killed Tyler in order to effectuate the robbery. We also note that *Bingham* quotes *Austin* solely to caution against letting "[t]he facts of a savage murder generate a powerful drive . . . to crush the crime with the utmost condemnation available." *Bingham*, 105 Wash. 2d at 827–28, 719 P.2d 109. *Austin* was not quoted as part of *Bingham*'s analysis on the issue of premeditation.

The issue before this court is whether *Bingham* is controlling in this situation such that given the evidence no trier of fact could find premeditation beyond a reasonable doubt. *See Jackson v. Virginia*, 443 U.S. 307, 319 (1979); *State v. Green*, 94 Wash. 2d 216, 221, 616 P.2d 628 (1980). We hold that *Bingham* is distinguishable. First, manual strangulation involves one continuous act. In the case at hand, not only did Ollens stab the victim numerous times, he thereafter slashed the victim's throat. This subsequent slashing is an indication that respondent did premeditate on his already formed intent to kill. Second, a knife was used in the killing. The strangulation in Bingham did not involve the procurement of a weapon. Third, from the evidence a jury could find that Ollens struck Tyler from behind, a further indication of premeditation. Finally, as indicated above, a jury could find the presence of a motive and, therefore, it would not be left to speculate or surmise only as to the existence of premeditation.

We hold that there is sufficient evidence to submit to a jury the issue of whether Ollens not only intended to kill the victim, but also premeditated. It is properly the function of a jury to determine whether Ollens deliberated, formed and reflected upon the intent to take Tyler's life in order to effectuate the robbery.

We reverse the Superior Court's dismissal of the premeditation charge and remand for the continuation of proceedings consistent with this opinion.

Pearson, C.J., and Utter, Dore, Brachtenbach and Dolliver, JJ., concur.

Callow, Justice.

I concur in the result. The majority states that "the planned presence of a weapon necessary to facilitate a killing" is adequate evidence to allow the issue of premeditation to go to the jury. The majority poses the issue as being whether under the evidence no trier of fact could find premeditation beyond a reasonable doubt. The majority distinguishes *State v. Bingham*, 105 Wash. 2d 820, 719 P.2d 109 (1986), by stating that (1) *Bingham* involved one continuous act while Ollens involves stabbings and a final throat slashing; (2) the strangulation used in *Bingham* did not involve the procurement of a weapon, while the stabbing in Ollens does; (3) the jury could have found that Ollens struck the defendant from behind as evidence of premeditation; and (4) the jury in Ollens could find a motive which would eliminate speculation as to the existence of premeditation. The majority then concludes that it is the function of the jury to determine whether Ollens "deliberated, formed and reflected upon the intent to take Tyler's life in order to effectuate the robbery."

Premeditated means thought over beforehand. When a person, after any deliberation, forms an intent to take human life, the killing may follow immediately after the formation of the settled purpose and it will still be premeditated. Premeditation must involve more than a moment in point of time. The law requires some time, however long or short, in which a design to kill is deliberately formed. WPIC 26.01.

When the four justifications for finding sufficient evidence for the issue of premeditation to go to the jury set forth in the majority are compared with *Bingham*, we find: (1) both attacks were prolonged, continued for an appreciable period of time and concluded with the death of the victim; (2) the absence of a weapon in *Bingham* is more than compensated for by the physical advantage of a man over a retarded female. I recognize that the procurement of a knife is a conscious act, but when a person habitually carries a knife as a tool this may not be evidence of premeditation, while, on the other hand, the physically powerful man who can kill a smaller woman at will without a weapon may well have premeditated. Is the evidence of the first fact evidence of premeditation and of the latter fact not for consideration by a jury on the question of premeditation? I submit the presence of the knife in the first situation might not prove premeditation, while evidence of a dominant, physically strong man with a motive to kill to silence a potential witness reflects a situation which could establish premeditation. I submit that in either situation the evaluation of the totality of the evidence in the light of all of the surrounding circumstances is for the jury. (3) The jury in *Ollens*, because they could have found that the defendant struck the victim from behind, is permitted to find that this was evidence of premeditation. The jury in *Bingham* had before it the conclusive evidence that the defendant had violently raped and then strangled his victim. This latter fact is surely as probative as speculation as to which stab wound was inflicted first and from what direction. (4) While the jury in *Ollens* is permitted to find a motive ("could find") to eliminate speculation as to premeditation, the jury in *Bingham* had before it as strong a reason to find a motive from the evidence as exists in this case.

I do not concur for the purpose of rehashing the result in *Bingham*; I concur to point out that no basis exists to make homicide by strangulation an isolated crime where premeditation cannot be proven. The majority's rationale forces this conclusion when only the defendant and the victim were present in a one-on-one situation yet allows proof of premeditation in a one-on-one situation when a weapon is present. Sufficiency of the evidence of premeditation to allow the issue to go to the jury is present in this case, and I submit the evidence was sufficient to pass that test in the *Bingham* circumstances.

The only question for this court is whether we can evaluate from the record the sufficiency of the evidence to take the question to the jury.

As stated by the court in both *State v. Green*, 94 Wash. 2d 216, 221, 616 P.2d 628 (1980) and in *State v. Bingham, supra*, 105 Wash. 2d at 823, 719 P.2d 109, quoting *Jackson v. Virginia*, 443 U.S. 307, 319 (1979), the standard for reviewing the sufficiency of evidence is "whether, after viewing the evidence in the light most favorable to the prosecution, any rational trier of fact could have found the essential elements . . . beyond a reasonable doubt."

The decision of the majority in this case does not violate that standard of review, while the decision in *Bingham* does. A special area has been carved out and removed from jury consideration. This is a dangerous precedent and it is for this reason that I concur in the result.

DURHAM AND ANDERSEN, JJ., concur.

Questions and Notes

1. At what point did Ollens arguably premeditate? (A) When he brought the knife into the cab? (B) When he inflicted the second stab wound? (C) When he slit Tyler's throat?

2. Do you agree with Justice Callow that *Bingham* involved at least as much premeditation as *Ollens*? In *Bingham*, Justice Callow dissented, emphasizing that it took Bingham five minutes to strangle his victim, during at least four of which she was unconscious.

3. Is the *Ollens* court retreating from *Bingham*?

4. Does the fact that Ollens thought it was necessary to kill Tyler or be killed by him cut for or against premeditation?

5. Does deliberation mean something different from premeditation? If so, what does it mean?

6. If you were Ollens' lawyer at retrial, how would you defend him?

7. The California Supreme Court has probably tried harder than any other court to ascribe meaning to the concept of premeditation. In *People v. Wolff*, 394 P.2d 959 (1964), it defined premeditation to require mature and meaningful reflection upon the gravity of the act. Under that standard, the court reversed the conviction of a 15-year-old mentally disturbed boy who premeditated his mother's death, but not maturely and meaningfully. In 1981, the California legislature explicitly negated this meaningful and mature requirement.

In 1968, the same court suggested three factors to be noted in ascertaining premeditation: (1) facts about how and what defendant did prior to the actual killing that show that the defendant was engaged in activity directed toward, and explicable as intended to result in, the killing—what may be characterized as "planning" activity; (2) facts about the defendant's prior relationship and/or conduct with the victim from which the jury could reasonably infer a 'motive' to kill the victim, and (3) facts about the nature of the killing from which the jury could infer that the manner of killing was so particular and exacting that the defendant must have intentionally killed according to a "preconceived design" to take his victim's life in a particular way for a "reason" that the jury can reasonably infer from facts of type (1) or (2). Applying those standards to the case before it, the court found that a man who had brutally stabbed his roommate's 10-year-old daughter (functionally, his stepdaughter) more than 60 times could not be convicted of first degree murder. The absence of planning or proven motive, coupled with the randomness of the 60 stab wounds (as opposed to one in the heart or the jugular vein) failed to present a jury question of premeditation, according to the court, which ruled that the defendant could be guilty of nothing more than second degree murder. *People v. Anderson*, 447 P.2d 942.

Dissatisfaction with opinions like *Anderson* has caused some courts to require only nominal premeditation. For example, in *State v. Misenhimer*, 282 S.E.2d 791 (N.C. 1981), the court held that "some period of time, however short, before the actual killing" will suffice. One court went even further, holding that any intentional killing qualified as a willful, deliberate, and premeditated killing. *See Commonwealth v. O'Searo*, 352 A.2d 30 (Pa. 1976). In response to *O'Searo*, the Pennsylvania Legislature, which first created the premeditation deliberation formula, now defines "an intentional killing" as first degree murder (although the Legislature [somewhat circularly] defined intentional as willful, deliberate, and premeditated).

8. We now turn to *Thompson*, where the Supreme Court of Arizona not only took premeditation seriously, but did so in the face of a contrary legislative determination.

State v. Thompson
65 P.3d 420 (Ariz. 2003)

BERCH, Justice.

Defendant Larry Thompson challenges the constitutionality of Arizona's first-degree murder statute, Ariz. Rev. Stat. ("A.R.S.") § 13-1105(A)(1) (2001). He argues that the definition of premeditation, which provides that "[p]roof of actual reflection is not required," eliminates any meaningful distinction between first and second-degree murder and renders the first-degree murder statute unconstitutionally vague.

Background

On May 17, 1999, Thompson shot and killed his wife, Roberta Palma.[1] Several days before the shooting, Palma had filed for divorce, and Thompson had discovered that she was seeing someone else. Just a week before the shooting, Thompson moved out of the couple's home. As he did so, Thompson threatened Palma that, "[i]f you divorce me, I will kill you."

Thompson returned to the couple's neighborhood the morning of May 17. He was seen walking on the sidewalk near the home and his car was spotted in a nearby alley. Two witnesses reported that a man dragged a woman by the hair from the front porch into the home. That same morning, police received and recorded a 9-1-1 call from the house. The tape recorded a woman's screams and four gunshots. The four gunshots span nearly twenty-seven seconds. Nine seconds elapse between the first shot and the third, and there is an eighteen-second delay between the third shot and the fourth.

At trial, Thompson did not deny killing his wife, but claimed that he did so in the heat of passion, making the killing manslaughter or, at most, second degree murder. During closing arguments, Thompson's counsel argued that the crime had occurred in the heat of passion and that Thompson had "simply snapped."

In her closing arguments, the prosecutor argued that the evidence that Thompson premeditated the murder was "overwhelming." She emphasized the timing of the shots and the delay between them. The prosecutor also reminded the jury of Thompson's threat, made a week before the murder, to kill his wife. The prosecutor then argued that Thompson need not actually have reflected, but only had the time to reflect: "But the main point to remember about premeditation is that premeditation is time to permit reflection. The instruction also tells you that actual reflection is not necessary, [only] the time to permit reflection." Nonetheless, the prosecutor referred to circumstantial evidence suggesting that Thompson actually had reflected, but then told the jury it need only decide that Thompson had the time to reflect, not that he actually had reflected.

After closing arguments, the judge instructed the jury regarding premeditation as follows:

> "Premeditation" means that the defendant acts with either the intention or the knowledge that he will kill another human being, when such intention or knowledge precedes the killing by any length of time to permit reflection.

---

1. We review the facts in the light most favorable to sustaining the verdict. *State v. Gallegos*, 178 Ariz. 1, 9, 870 P.2d 1097, 1105 (1994).

Proof of actual reflection is not required, but an act is not done with pre-meditation if it is the instant effect of a sudden quarrel or heat of passion.

The jury found Thompson guilty of first-degree murder and the judge sentenced him to life in prison without the possibility of parole. Thompson appealed, arguing that the definition of premeditation, particularly the clause stating that "[p]roof of actual reflection is not required," unconstitutionally relieved the State of the burden of proving the element of premeditation.

Discussion

Thompson challenges the constitutionality of the statute, arguing that it renders first degree murder indistinguishable from second degree murder. A person commits second degree murder in Arizona "if *without* premeditation . . . [s]uch person intentionally causes the death of another person." (emphasis added). Thus, for the purposes of this appeal, first and second degree murder are indistinguishable except that first degree murder requires premeditation.

According to the definition adopted by the legislature,

"[p]remeditation" means that the defendant acts with either the intention or the knowledge that he will kill another human being, when such intention or knowledge precedes the killing by any length of time to permit reflection. *Proof of actual reflection is not required*, but an act is not done with premeditation if it is the instant effect of a sudden quarrel or heat of passion.[2]

The question before us is whether this definition of premeditation abolishes the requirement of actual reflection altogether, whether it eliminates the requirement of direct proof of actual reflection, or whether it substitutes for the necessary proof of actual reflection the mere passage of enough time to permit reflection. The State asserts the third interpretation, that the legislature intended to relieve the State of the burden of proving a defendant's hidden thought processes, and that this definition of premeditation establishes that the passage of time may serve as a proxy for reflection. The court of appeals agreed with this interpretation.

Thompson maintains that reducing premeditation to the mere passage of time renders the statute vague and unenforceable because courts have held that actual reflection can occur as quickly as "successive thoughts of the mind." Thus, he argues and the court of appeals agreed, the difference between first and second degree murder has been eliminated.

Although the legislature may classify crimes as it sees fit, it must do so in a way that is not arbitrary or capricious. Laws must provide explicit standards for those charged with enforcing them and may not "impermissibly delegate[ ] basic policy matters to policemen, judges, and juries for resolution on an *ad hoc* and subjective

---

2. We know of no other state, nor have the parties alerted us to one, that includes the clause "[p]roof of actual reflection is not required" in its definition of premeditation.

basis." Accordingly, for the first-degree murder statute to be constitutional, the definition of premeditation must provide a meaningful distinction between first and second degree murder. We turn now to a review of how premeditation has provided that distinction in Arizona.

A. History of the First Degree Murder Statute in Arizona

For most of this state's history, first degree murder explicitly required proof of "premeditation," or actual reflection by the defendant. Despite these cautions, however, litigants over time have injected confusion into the analysis of premeditation through inappropriate emphasis on the time element in cases in which there was evidence, whether direct or circumstantial, of actual reflection. To stem the confusion, the court of appeals decided *State v. Ramirez*, 190 Ariz. 65, 945 P.2d 376 (App. 1997), explicitly holding that premeditation requires actual reflection. The appeals court reasoned that defining premeditation as a length of time that can be instantaneous "obliterates any meaningful difference between first and second degree murder-other than the penalties." It concluded that "[i]f the difference between first and second degree murder is to be maintained, premeditation has to be understood as reflection."

But other courts in this state disagreed with *Ramirez*. In *State v. Haley*, for example, the court of appeals found that "premeditated murder requires only that the defendant's intent to kill . . . precede the killing by a sufficient period of time to permit reflection, and does not require actual reflection."

B. The Current Definition of Premeditation

To resolve the conflict and clarify the distinction between first and second degree murder, the legislature amended the definition of premeditation in 1998 to include the clause "[p]roof of actual reflection is not required." This amendment, however, has not eliminated the confusion regarding the interpretation of premeditation. Indeed, it may have compounded it. In this case, the court of appeals interpreted the legislature's 1998 amendment of as ensuring "that premeditation was defined solely as the passage of a period of time, . . . eliminat[ing] actual reflection as part of the definition, and . . . overrul[ing] the case law to the contrary."

Nonetheless, the court concluded that the statute was not constitutionally infirm because it determined that "a fair reading of the statute, combined with a common-sense consideration of how jurors perform their function, demonstrates that the time period employed by the statute to describe premeditation has enough substance to provide a workable method for distinguishing between degrees of murder." The court reasoned that only when the phrase "any length of time to permit reflection" is understood in light of the cases allowing the "time to permit reflection" to be as "instantaneous as successive thoughts of the mind" that the statute became unconstitutionally standardless. Thus, the court of appeals concluded that the statute is constitutional in the case now before us, but is unconstitutional when a jury is instructed that reflection can occur as quickly as successive thoughts of the mind, for "when premeditation is just an instant of time and nothing more, irrebuttable evidence of premeditation will exist in every case of intentional or knowing murder."

We have not, until this case, had the opportunity to address the confusion surrounding the issue of premeditation. Thompson urges us to overturn his conviction on the ground that the statute is unconstitutionally vague. The State, on the other hand, argues that the statute is constitutional and that the current definition of premeditation meaningfully distinguishes between first and second-degree murder.

We conclude, as did the court of appeals, that if the only difference between first and second degree murder is the mere passage of time, and that length of time can be "as instantaneous as successive thoughts of the mind," then there is no meaningful distinction between first and second degree murder. Such an interpretation would relieve the state of its burden to prove actual reflection and would render the first-degree murder statute impermissibly vague and therefore unconstitutional under the United States and Arizona Constitutions.

We are, however, mindful of our duty to construe this statute, if possible, in a way that not only gives effect to the legislature's intent, but also in a way that maintains its constitutionality. As a starting point, we note that the words chosen by the legislature do not say that actual reflection is no longer required to distinguish first from second degree murder. Rather, the legislature provided that "*[p]roof of actual reflection is not required.*" (emphasis added). Recognizing that direct proof of a defendant's intent to kill often does not exist, the legislature sought to relieve the state of the often impossible burden of proving premeditation through direct evidence. But by this act the legislature did not intend to eliminate the requirement of reflection altogether or to allow the state to substitute the mere passing of time for the element of premeditation. While the phrase "proof of actual reflection is not required" can be interpreted in a way that relieves the state of the burden of proving reflection, such an interpretation would not pass constitutional scrutiny, and the legislature could not have intended such a result. Accordingly, we conclude that the legislature intended to relieve the state of the burden of proving a defendant's thought processes by direct evidence. It intended for premeditation, and the reflection that it requires, to mean more than the mere passage of time.

We find support for our interpretation in the admonition that "an act is not done with premeditation if it is the instant effect of a sudden quarrel or heat of passion." This language distinguishes impulsive killings from planned or deliberated killings and confirms the legislature's intent that premeditation be more than just a snap decision made in the heat of passion.

Our decision today distinguishes the *element* of premeditation from the *evidence* that might establish that element. Although the mere passage of time suggests that a defendant premeditated-and the state might be able to convince a jury to make that inference-the passage of time is not, in and of itself, premeditation.[3] To allow the state to establish the element of premeditation by merely proving that sufficient time passed to permit reflection would be to essentially relieve the state of its burden to establish the sole element that distinguishes between first and second degree murder.

C. Jury Instruction

Our review of the case law in this area uncovered various jury instructions relating to the definition of premeditation. These instructions are intended to inform jurors of the law applicable to the case in terms that the jurors can readily understand. We recognize that premeditation should be defined for the jury. But we also recognize that the statutory definition of premeditation may not explain it in an easily understandable way and, indeed, might mislead the jury. Thus, we disapprove of the use of the phrase "proof of actual reflection is not required" in a jury instruction. As we explained above, that phrase merely relieves the state of the burden of proving with direct evidence that a defendant reflected; it does not relieve the state of its burden of proving reflection. We also discourage the use of the phrase "as instantaneous as successive thoughts of the mind." We continue to be concerned that juries could be misled by instructions that needlessly emphasize the rapidity with which reflection may occur. Accordingly, trial judges should, in future cases, instruct juries as follows:

> "Premeditation" means that the defendant intended to kill another human being [knew he/she would kill another human being], and that after forming that intent [knowledge], reflected on the decision before killing. It is this reflection, regardless of the length of time in which it occurs, that distinguishes first degree murder from second degree murder. An act is not done with premeditation if it is the instant effect of a sudden quarrel or heat of passion.

Only when the facts of a case require it should a trial judge instruct the jury, or may the state argue, that "the time needed for reflection is not necessarily prolonged, and the space of time between the intent [knowledge] to kill and the act of killing may be very short." It is the act of premeditation and not the length of time available that determines the question.

This instruction does not mean that the state must rely on direct evidence of premeditation; as we have noted, such evidence is rarely available. Nor does this instruction mean that the state cannot rely on the passage of time between the formation of intent and the act of killing as a fact tending to show premeditation. This instruction merely clarifies that the state may not use the passage of time as a proxy

---

3. Part of the confusion, we believe, stems from the unfortunate use of the adjective "actual" to describe reflection. It is unquestioned that the state must prove the defendant's "actual" intent or knowledge in a first degree murder case, yet there is no suggestion nor could one reasonably be made that the state must prove with direct evidence the element of intent or knowledge. We allow the state to satisfy its burden with circumstantial evidence of intent or knowledge. The state's burden is the same when establishing the element of premeditation.

for premeditation. The state may argue that the passage of time *suggests* premeditation, but it may not argue that the passage of time *is* premeditation.

In the case before us, the jury was instructed that "proof of actual reflection is not required." We hold that, without further clarification, this instruction was erroneous. The State also argued that it did not have to prove actual reflection but had to prove only that enough time had elapsed to allow reflection. This, too, was in error. However, the jury was not instructed that actual reflection can occur as instantaneously as successive thoughts of the mind. Moreover, the State presented overwhelming evidence that Thompson actually reflected on his decision to kill his wife, including evidence of threats to kill her a week before the murder, the time that elapsed between each gunshot, and the victim's screams as recorded on the 9-1-1 tape between each gunshot. We conclude beyond a reasonable doubt that the flawed jury instruction and the State's reliance on that instruction did not affect the jury's verdict, and we will not overturn Thompson's conviction and sentence.

Conclusion

As we have interpreted it, we find the definition of premeditation in Arizona's first-degree murder statute, constitutional. We vacate the opinion of the court of appeals but affirm Thompson's conviction and sentence for first degree murder.

Concurring: Charles E. Jones, Chief Justice, Ruth V. McGregor, Vice Chief Justice, and Stanley G. Feldman, Justice (retired).

Ryan, Justice, Concurring in Part and Dissenting in Part:

The court of appeals in *State v. Ramirez*, held that the 1978 statutory definition of premeditation, along with the instruction that premeditation may be as instantaneous as successive thoughts of the mind, "obliterates any meaningful difference between first and second-degree murder-other than the penalties." The *Ramirez* court concluded that juries should be instructed that "premeditation requires actual reflection." In obvious disagreement with the *Ramirez* decision, the legislature responded in 1998 by amending the definition of premeditation. Yet, today this court adds to the definition of premeditation that which the legislature expressly excluded. Therefore, while I agree with affirming the conviction here, I disagree with the majority's conclusion that the statutory definition of premeditation requires evidence of actual reflection. Accordingly, I respectfully dissent from those portions of the opinion holding that actual reflection must be proven.

I begin with several principles of statutory construction. First, it is the province of the legislature to define crimes. Second, a statute must not be written so vaguely that it "impermissibly delegates basic policy matters to policemen, judges, and juries for resolution on an ad hoc and subjective basis, with the attendant dangers of arbitrary and discriminatory application." However, "[d]ue process requires neither perfect notice, absolute precision nor impossible standards" when defining a crime. Third, a statute's language is "the best and most reliable index" of its meaning. Finally, it is not the province of the judiciary to add language to a statute that the legislature expressly excluded.

With these principles in mind, I turn to the first-degree murder statute at issue here and the definition of premeditation. Thompson was convicted of violating A.R.S. section 13-1105(A)(1), which defines first degree murder as an intentional or knowing killing of another person with premeditation. Premeditation is defined as follows:

> "Premeditation" means that the defendant acts with either the intention or the knowledge that he will kill another human being, when such intention or knowledge precedes the killing by any length of time to permit reflection. Proof of actual reflection is not required, but an act is not done with premeditation if it is the instant effect of a sudden quarrel or heat of passion.

The majority finds that when the legislature added the phrase "[p]roof of actual reflection is not required" to the definition of premeditation, "the legislature did not intend to eliminate the requirement of reflection altogether or to allow the state to substitute the mere passing of time for the element of premeditation." *Supra*, at ¶ 27. This finding is based on the assumption that "the legislature sought to relieve the state of the often impossible burden of proving premeditation through *direct* evidence." *Id.* (emphasis added).

But there can be no doubt that the legislature intended to eliminate any requirement that the state prove actual reflection, whether by direct or circumstantial evidence. First, the plain language of the definition of premeditation specifically excludes any requirement that the state prove a defendant actually reflected. Second, the Senate Fact Sheet on the proposed amendment states that the amended statute "[e]liminates the requirement that the prosecution show proof of actual reflection in order to establish premeditation in homicide cases." Third, "[w]e presume that the legislature knows the existing case law when it . . . modifies a statute. Additionally, we presume that by amending a statute, the legislature intend[ed] to change the existing case law." The *Ramirez* court specifically stated that reflection "may be proved by *direct* or circumstantial evidence." (emphasis added). When the legislature added the phrase, "[p]roof of actual reflection is not required," it unmistakably intended to change "existing case law" and relieve the state of proving reflection, whether by direct or circumstantial evidence. Legislative intent could not have been more clearly expressed.

Despite this clear expression of legislative intent, the majority concludes that the state must produce evidence, "whether direct or circumstantial," that a defendant "actually reflected." Such evidence is required, the majority claims, for the statute to "pass constitutional scrutiny."

Unlike my colleagues, I do not find the legislature's decision to eliminate proof of actual reflection and instead rely, in part, on the passage of enough "time to permit reflection," makes the statute unconstitutional. The definition of premeditation must be read as a whole. And read as a whole, I think the statute adequately distinguishes between an intentional or knowing second degree murder and an intentional or knowing first degree murder.

To prove the element of premeditation, the state must satisfy three statutory factors. First, there must be proof that the defendant acted "with either the intention or the knowledge that he [would] kill another human being." Second, there must be proof that such intention or knowledge preceded the killing "by any length of time to permit reflection." Third, while "[p]roof of actual reflection is not required," there must be evidence that the killing was not the result of a "sudden quarrel or heat of passion." These three factors combine to define a cold-blooded killing. By requiring proof that a defendant had sufficient time to permit reflection, coupled with requiring proof that a defendant did not act under the influence of a sudden quarrel or heat of passion, the legislature established a discernible standard for determining whether a killing is first degree murder. If the facts demonstrate that the murder occurred during a quarrel, or as a result of impulsive behavior, it necessarily follows that the defendant's accompanying state of mind was such that he had insufficient time in which he could have reflected. Consequently, the definition of premeditation merely requires jurors to apply a reasonable person standard to the facts and circumstances of the case. "This is not dissimilar to asking jurors to determine whether an individual acted 'reasonably' or to resolve other conflicts similarly elusive but dependent upon the human experience."

The majority, however, concludes that "if the only difference between first and second degree murder is the mere passage of time, and that length of time can be 'as instantaneous as successive thoughts of the mind,' then there is no meaningful distinction between first and second degree murder." But as discussed above, the mere passage of time is not the only distinction between first and second degree murder. The state must also prove that the killing was not done under the influence of a quarrel or heat of passion. This latter requirement focuses the jury's assessment of the facts relating to the time factor; it requires the jury to find that a defendant's accompanying state of mind be such that the killing is not the result of an impulsive act. If the facts support such a finding, a conviction for first degree murder is neither arbitrary nor capricious.

Perhaps as one commentator contends, premeditation fails "as the dividing line between degrees of murder." Matthew A. Pauley, *Murder by Premeditation*, 36 Am.Crim. L.Rev. 145, 169 (1999). Nonetheless, our legislature has chosen to use premeditation as that dividing line. By using the passage of time as a substitute for actual reflection, while at the same time requiring that a killing not be "the instant effect of a sudden quarrel or heat of passion," A.R.S. section 13-1101(1), the legislature has drawn a discernible line between intentional or knowing first degree murder and intentional or knowing second degree murder. That is all the constitution requires. *See Fuenning*, 139 Ariz. at 598, 680 P.2d at 129.

In sum, I conclude the definition of premeditation as statutorily defined is not unconstitutionally vague. As such, I see no need to rewrite the statute to require the state prove a defendant actually reflected, whether by direct or circumstantial evidence. Finally, I would approve an instruction that tracks the statutory language of A.R.S. section 13-1101(1) and suggest that trial courts refrain from instructing juries that the time to reflect may be "as instantaneous as successive thoughts of the mind."

For the foregoing reasons, I concur with the majority in affirming the conviction in this case, but dissent from the majority's interpretation of A.R.S. section 13-1101(1).

Questions and Notes

1. Did the majority really interpret legislative intent, or did it interpret its own intent and attribute that to the legislature?

2. If it did not really interpret legislative intent, why didn't it?

3. Did you find the majority or concurrence more persuasive? Why? Does it matter whether you are answering that question on constitutional grounds or policy grounds?

4. Given the majority's analysis, why didn't it reverse the conviction and remand for a new trial?

5. How would *Ollens* have been decided under the majority's rule? What about *Bingham*?

6. Are premeditated and deliberated murders really the worst? The MPC thought not, eschewing the concept for a series of aggravating and mitigating circumstances. *See* MPC §§ 210.2(2), 210.6 (Appendix A). The concept of aggravating and mitigating circumstances will be discussed in Chapter 15, *infra*.

7. We now turn to *Johnson*, which shows how, in some cases, premeditation and even specific intent to kill can be removed from the definition of first degree murder.

State v. Johnson
344 S.E.2d 775 (N.C. 1986)

MEYER, J.

The State's evidence tended to show that the defendant and his wife, Brenda Johnson, separated in March 1984, and the defendant retained custody of the two children born of the marriage. The separation was less than amicable. At one point, the defendant and Mrs. Johnson engaged in a heated confrontation concerning Mrs. Johnson's access to the children. On that occasion, the defendant asked Mrs. Johnson if she "remembered Jim Ward and what he done to his family." Mrs. Johnson testified that, approximately ten years earlier, Ward had killed his children and then committed suicide. Mrs. Johnson stated that the defendant threatened to do the same thing.

In June 1984, the defendant lived in Hot Springs, North Carolina, with his eleven-year old son, Christopher, and his five-year-old daughter, Joyce. In early June 1984, Christopher Johnson was brought to Asheville Memorial Mission Hospital. At the time of the admission, Christopher was sweating profusely, his pupils were pin-pointed, his chest muscles were fluctuating violently, and his speech was slurred. He was diagnosed as suffering from organophosphate poisoning. An antidote was administered, and Christopher soon began to recover. He was released the following day.

On 15 June, Joyce Johnson was brought to Asheville Memorial Mission Hospital suffering from nausea, abdominal pain, headaches, and pain during urination. She was diagnosed as suffering from a urinary tract infection, and the doctor prescribed an antibiotic which was described as a sweet-odored, dark-orange liquid.

On the morning of 17 June 1984, the defendant told Christopher to look after Joyce while he went into town. The defendant then gave Joyce a teaspoon of white liquid.

Christopher testified at trial that the liquid which the defendant administered to Joyce had an odor similar to bug poison. The defendant then proceeded to town. A few minutes after the defendant's departure, Joyce became very ill. White foam was coming from her mouth, her stomach was growling, she was staggering, and her conversation made no sense at all. Christopher stated that Joyce eventually laid down on the bed and stopped moving.

Meanwhile, the defendant went to the cafe in Hot Springs and ate breakfast. As he was leaving, he approached a local emergency medical technician (E.M.T.) who was also in the cafe. The defendant asked the E.M.T. where the town ambulance was located. The E.M.T. responded that the ambulance was in the garage next to the ambulance hut in order to be painted. The E.M.T. then inquired as to why the defendant was concerned about the whereabouts of the ambulance. The defendant simply responded, "I might need it later." The defendant then left the café.

Upon his return home, the defendant was made aware of Joyce's illness. He immediately took her to the ambulance hut in Hot Springs. The E.M.T.s placed Joyce in the ambulance and proceeded to Asheville. The defendant and Christopher followed in a pickup truck. Near the Madison County-Buncombe County line, Joyce was transferred to a Buncombe County ambulance which took her to Asheville Memorial Mission Hospital.

The ambulance arrived at the hospital shortly before 10:00 a.m. Dr. Thomas Howald testified that upon arrival Joyce was not breathing and had no pulse. She was foaming at the mouth, and her pupils were pinpointed. Dr. Howald stated that the bubblous secretions or foam had an odor which he associated with an organophosphate insecticide such as Malathion or Diazinon. He detected the same odor in her vomitus. Dr. Howald further testified that an organophosphate poison is the only type of poison that would cause the symptoms which he observed. He also opined that the poison was introduced into Joyce's system orally as opposed to being absorbed through the skin. Dr. Howald was also of the opinion that in order for Joyce to exhibit the symptoms that he observed, she would have had to orally ingest the poison within thirty minutes to two hours of the onset of the symptoms.

He also stated that the symptoms he observed could not have been the result of a periodic, chronic exposure to organophosphate poisoning.

Despite a valiant effort by medical personnel to reverse the effects of the poison, Joyce suffered irreversible brain death. Life support systems were withdrawn on the afternoon of 20 June 1984, and Joyce died approximately thirty minutes later without ever regaining consciousness.

Tim Ramsey, a friend of the defendant, testified that he had a conversation with the defendant at the hospital on 20 June 1984. He testified that the defendant told him that the doctors had said Joyce "had got in some kind of poisoning." Ramsey stated that the defendant offered to take him to his house and show him what Joyce "had gotten into." He also testified that the defendant said half a teaspoon of the poison would kill a person. Ramsey further testified that approximately one month after the defendant and his wife separated, the defendant told him that he "would rather see the kids in hell as his wife have them."

The defendant testified on his own behalf. He stated that in early June 1984, he sprayed his house with Malathion in order to alleviate an insect problem. The insecticide which was left over was placed in a container and left on the back porch.

The defendant further testified that on the morning of 17 June 1984, he woke up his two children and prepared to go into town to get some gas. When Joyce acted as though she was not feeling well, the defendant was reminded that she was on medication. The defendant stated that he went to the refrigerator, got the bottle of medicine, and gave Joyce a teaspoonful. He then proceeded to town. He admitted asking the E.M.T. in the cafe about the whereabouts of the ambulance, but he indicated that he did so merely out of curiosity after observing that it was not parked in its usual location. The defendant denied telling Tim Ramsey that he had any poison at his house. He also denied making the statement attributed to him by his wife in which he threatened to kill his children and himself. The defendant testified that he loved Joyce and Christopher, and he denied administering poison to Joyce.

Leroy Johnson, the defendant's father, testified that he took Christopher to the hospital when he became sick in early June. Mr. Johnson told the doctor that Christopher had entered the house immediately after it had been sprayed for insects. The doctor asked if there was any of the insecticide remaining. Mr. Johnson said yes and brought the container to the hospital. He testified that he never saw the container again. The defendant's mother testified that after Christopher was poisoned, the defendant scrubbed the entire house in an effort to remove all traces of the poison. Carol Johnson, the defendant's sister-in-law, testified that she was present during the confrontation during which the defendant was alleged to have threatened to kill his children. Carol Johnson testified that the defendant made no statement with regard to a "Ward man from Hot Springs." The defense also produced several witnesses who testified that the defendant had a good relationship with his children.

The jury found the defendant guilty of first-degree murder.

The defendant's next argument relates to the instructions given to the jury by the trial court. The trial judge instructed the jury in pertinent part:

> Now, Members of the Jury, I charge that for you to find the Defendant guilty of first degree murder by means of poison, the State must prove three things beyond a reasonable doubt: FIRST, that the Defendant intentionally caused poison to be placed into or to enter the body of Joyce Johnson. A poison is a substance which is likely to cause death by a chemical reaction when placed into or caused to enter the body of a human being.

Intent is a mental attitude which is seldom provable by direct evidence. It must ordinarily be proved by circumstances from which it may be inferred. You arrive at the intent of a person by such just and reasonable deductions from the circumstances proven as a reasonably prudent person would ordinarily draw therefrom.

SECOND, the State must prove that the Defendant did this with malice. Malice means not only hatred, ill-will or spite as it is ordinarily understood, to be sure that is malice, but it also means that condition of mind which prompts a person to take the life of another intentionally or to intentionally inflict serious injury upon another, which proximately results in her death without just cause, excuse or justification. Or to wantonly act in such a manner as to manifest depravity of mind, a heart devoid of sense of social duty and a callous disregard for human life.

And THIRD, the State must prove that the poisoning was a proximate cause of Joyce Johnson's death. A proximate cause is a real cause, a cause without which Joyce Johnson's death would not have occurred.

So, I finally charge you, Members of the Jury, that if you find from the evidence beyond a reasonable doubt that on or about June 17th, 1984, Richard Johnson intentionally administered Diazinon to Joyce Johnson by mouth, thereby proximately causing her death, and that he acted with malice, it would be your duty to return a verdict of guilty of first degree murder by means of poison.

The defendant contends that the trial court committed reversible error by failing to specifically instruct the jury that in order to return a conviction for first-degree murder, it was required to find that he possessed the specific intent to kill Joyce at the time the poison was administered. In order to resolve this issue, we find it necessary to review certain fundamental principles concerning first-degree murder.

N.C.G.S. § 14-17 provides:

> § 14-17. Murder in the first and second degree defined; Punishment. A murder which shall be perpetrated by means of poison, lying in wait, imprisonment, starving, torture, or by any other kind of willful, deliberate, and premeditated killing, or which shall be committed in the perpetration or attempted perpetration of any arson, rape or a sex offense, robbery, kidnapping, burglary, or other felony committed or attempted with the use of a deadly weapon shall be deemed to be murder in the first degree, and any person who commits such murder shall be punished with death or

imprisonment in the State's prison for life as the court shall determine pursuant to G.S. 15A-2000. All other kinds of murder, including that which shall be proximately caused by the unlawful distribution of opium or any synthetic or natural salt, compound, derivative, or preparation of opium when the ingestion of such substance causes the death of the user, shall be deemed murder in the second degree, and any person who commits such murder shall be punished as a Class C felon.

In *State v. Strickland*, 307 N.C. 274, 298 S.E.2d 645 (1983), we interpreted this statute as separating first-degree murder into four distinct classes as determined by the proof: (1) murder perpetrated by means of poison, lying in wait, imprisonment, starving, or torture; (2) murder perpetrated by any other kind of willful, deliberate, and premeditated killing; (3) murder committed in the perpetration or attempted perpetration of certain enumerated felonies; and (4) murder committed in the perpetration or attempted perpetration of any other felony committed or attempted with the use of a deadly weapon.

First-degree murder has been historically defined in this State as the unlawful killing of a human being with malice and with premeditation and deliberation. However, this definition is not entirely correct, as it is well established that the prosecution need not show premeditation and deliberation in order to obtain a conviction for first-degree murder under the felony-murder rule.

Numerous cases also hold that a specific intent to kill is an essential element of first-degree murder. Once again, this is not completely correct, as it is well established that a homicide committed during the perpetration or attempted perpetration of a felony is first-degree murder without regard to whether the death was "intended."

In *State v. Strickland*, 307 N.C. 274, 298 S.E.2d 645, we stated that when a homicide is perpetrated by means of poison, lying in wait, imprisonment, starving, or torture, the law conclusively presumes that the murder was committed with premeditation and deliberation. In a concurring opinion, Justice Mitchell took issue with this statement. He felt that "when a homicide is perpetrated by means of poison, lying in wait, imprisonment, starving or torture, the law does not presume, conclusively or otherwise, that the murder was carried out with premeditation and deliberation. Instead, the presence or absence of premeditation and deliberation is irrelevant." *Id.* at 306, 298 S.E.2d at 663. We belatedly conclude that Justice Mitchell's well-reasoned view was correct and now hold that premeditation and deliberation is not an element of the crime of first-degree murder perpetrated by means of poison, lying in wait, imprisonment, starving, or torture. Likewise, a specific intent to kill is equally irrelevant when the homicide is perpetrated by means of poison, lying in wait, imprisonment, starving, or torture; and we hold that an intent to kill is not an element of first-degree murder where the homicide is carried out by one of these methods. Cases from other jurisdictions support this view. *See People v. Thomas*, 41 Cal. 2d 470, 261 P.2d 1 (1953); *State v. Thomas*, 135 Iowa 717, 109 N.W. 900 (1906); *State v. Wagner*, 78 Mo. 644, 47 Am. Rep. 131 (1883); *Rupe v. State*, 61 S.W. 929, 42

Tex. Cr. R. 477 (1901). *But see State v. Farmer*, 156 Ohio St. 214, 102 N.E.2d 11 (1951). Since the intent to kill is not an element of the crime of first-degree murder when the murder is perpetrated by means of poison, the trial court was not required to instruct the jury on intent to kill.

We acknowledge that there is language in several prior opinions of this Court which intimates that in cases involving death by means of poison, the prosecution is still required to come forward with evidence showing an intent to kill in order to obtain a conviction for first-degree murder. *See, e.g.,* State v. Barfield, 298 N.C. 306, 259 S.E.2d 510 (1979). In *Barfield*, the defendant was charged with first-degree murder by poison. We held that evidence that the defendant had poisoned other individuals was admissible on the basis that "[s]uch evidence is clearly relevant in a prosecution for first-degree murder in that the state must prove a specific intent to kill if it is to win a conviction." We also note that the pattern jury instruction for first-degree murder by means of poison includes a specific instruction requiring the jury to find that the defendant administered the poison with the intent to kill the victim. N.C.P.I.-Crim. 206.12 at 3 (1978). Nevertheless, we hold that when the State proceeds upon a theory of first-degree murder perpetrated by means of poison, the State is not required to come forward with evidence tending to show that the defendant possessed the intent to kill the victim, and the trial judge should not instruct the jury that it is required to find such an intent as a prerequisite for returning a conviction for first-degree murder.

When a murder is committed during the commission of a felony, the murder is first-degree even if all of the evidence presented tends to show only an intent to injure. The rule is no different when the murder is committed by means of poison— the murder is first degree even if all the evidence presented tends to show only an intent to make the victim ill. In the case before us, the only contention of the defendant is that he did not administer the poisonous substance at all.

The defendant also contends that the trial court erred by failing to instruct the jury on second-degree murder based on the possibility that the jury could have found that he administered the poison with the intent to injure the victim but without an intent to kill. However, as discussed above, an intent to kill is not necessary to constitute the crime of first-degree murder when the murder was allegedly committed by means of poison. Any murder committed by means of poison is automatically first-degree murder. Furthermore, a defendant is entitled to have a lesser-included offense submitted to the jury only when there is evidence to support it. The defendant emphatically and repeatedly testified that on the morning of 17 June, he gave Joyce a teaspoon of medicine and that at no time did he administer Diazinon to his daughter. If the State's evidence is sufficient to fully satisfy its burden of proving each element of the greater offense and there is no evidence to negate these elements other than the defendant's denial that he committed the offense, the defendant is not entitled to an instruction on a lesser offense. *See State v. Strickland*, 307 N.C. 274, 298 S.E.2d 645. The evidence in this case supported each element of the charged crime of first-degree murder. The only evidence to negate these elements was the defendant's denial that he had committed the offense. The trial court did not err by refusing to instruct the jury on second-degree murder.

Finally, the defendant argues that the trial court erred by failing to instruct the jury on the lesser-included offense of involuntary manslaughter. We do not agree.

Involuntary manslaughter is a lesser-included offense of murder. As noted above, a defendant is entitled to have a lesser-included offense submitted to the jury only when there is evidence to support it. Involuntary manslaughter has been defined as the unlawful and unintentional killing of another without malice which proximately results from an unlawful act not amounting to a felony nor naturally dangerous to human life, or by an act or omission constituting culpable negligence. The defendant notes that a great deal of evidence was elicited as to the differences in the odor and appearance of organophosphate poison and the medicine which had been prescribed for Joyce. He argues that based on this evidence, the jury could find that he was culpably negligent in administering the insecticide instead of the medicine. This contention, however, ignores the fact, alluded to above, that the defendant testified that he gave the victim medicine and did not at any time either by design or by mistake administer insecticide to his daughter. Since the State's evidence was sufficient to fully satisfy its burden of proving each element of first-degree murder and there was no other evidence to negate these elements other than the defendant's denial that he committed the offense, the defendant was not entitled to an instruction on the lesser-included offense of involuntary manslaughter. This assignment of error is overruled.

The defendant received a fair trial, free from prejudicial error.

NO ERROR.

Questions and Notes

1. Is there any way that the North Carolina statute (N.C.G.S. § 14-17) could have been read to limit first degree murder by poison to willful, deliberate, and premeditated murders? Or is the court's construction of the statute the only reasonable one?

2. Should a person who poisons another intending to sicken her be treated the same as another who poisons his victim intending to kill her?

3. Is death by poison, like death by torture, sufficiently painful that no further aggravation, such as premeditation, should be necessary?

4. Is the *Johnson* result largely attributable to the court's lack of sympathy for a man who would poison his children?

5. Isn't it possible that Johnson thought that he had given medicine to his daughter, but in fact had given her poison? If so, shouldn't he have been entitled to an involuntary manslaughter instruction on the theory of culpable negligence? Does the court's failure to demand such an instruction indicate that the court believed that he got what he deserved? *See* NUTSHELL §§ 2.01–2.02.

B. Heat of Passion

Killings, which would otherwise constitute murder, that are committed during the heat of passion will sometimes be reduced to voluntary manslaughter. Manslaughter is usually defined as the unlawful killing of another human being without malice aforethought. Consequently, the primary function of the heat of passion defense is to negate what would otherwise be malice aforethought.

Under traditional law, malice aforethought will be negated if, but only if, the provocation was legally sufficient, and was determined by a jury to be adequate to cause a reasonable person to act rashly and without due consideration.

As you read the material, consider the following extreme propositions: (1) Heat of passion should always negate malice aforethought because a person who kills in the heat of passion, regardless of the cause, is not as culpable as one who kills in cold blood; (2) Heat of passion should never mitigate murder to manslaughter because the reasonable person does not kill no matter how provoked he or she becomes. Virtually all courts reject both of these propositions in the form stated above. Why?

Some courts have fixed categories of justifiable passion, usually called categories of "legally sufficient" provocation. Others simply require that the provocation be such that a reasonable jury could find it adequate. But as you read *Oropeza*, it will be clear that even those that do not have fixed categories of legally sufficient provocation will not allow all kinds of anger to be considered by the jury.

People v. Oropeza
59 Cal. Rptr. 3d 653 (Cal. App. 4 Dist. 2007)

Benke, Acting P.J.

Jorge Diego Oropeza was convicted of first degree murder, attempted murder first degree murder, shooting at an inhabited vehicle and discharging a firearm from a vehicle.

Oropeza was sentenced to a prison term of 80 years to life.

Facts

A. Prosecution Case

1. Crimes

In the early morning of March 6, 2004, Eglen Coss, his cousin Moraima Coss (Moraima) and her boyfriend Noah Johnson were driving home on Interstate 805 after an evening in Tijuana. Coss was driving, Johnson was in the passenger seat and Moraima was sitting between them. As they drove north, a confrontation occurred between Coss and the occupants of a silver Ford F150 pickup truck who apparently believed Coss had "cut them off." At first there was yelling and an exchange of offensive hand gestures. Then as the vehicles drove side by side, with a lane between the two vehicles, a person wearing a red shirt and sitting in the front passenger seat of the Ford stuck his arm out the window and fired a handgun. The bullet passed through Coss's arm, striking Moraima in the head and killing her. Coss stopped to summon help. The Ford pickup truck drove away.

Jose Lopez, who as part of a plea bargain pled guilty to voluntary manslaughter regarding the death of Moraima, testified that in the early morning of March 7, 2004, he and appellant were returning from Tijuana in a silver Ford F150 pickup truck. Because appellant was drunk, Lopez drove. Lopez stated that after entering the United States they were "cut off" by another vehicle. The cars continued up the freeway with the occupants exchanging abusive words and gestures. Eventually, appellant drew a gun and fired a shot. Lopez drove away.

B. Voluntary Manslaughter

Appellant argues the trial court erred when it refused to instruct on voluntary manslaughter based on sudden quarrel and heat of passion. Appellant notes there was evidence the incident began when Coss's truck cut off the truck in which appellant was a passenger, that Coss continued to provoke appellant with his aggressive driving, his yelling and his obscene gestures. Appellant argues he clearly acted in the heat of passion; and because there was adequate provocation by Coss and those in his truck, the trial court was required to instruct concerning the lesser included offense of voluntary manslaughter based on sudden quarrel or heat of passion.

A defendant commits voluntary manslaughter and not murder when he or she intentionally and unlawfully kills "upon a sudden quarrel or heat of passion." Voluntary manslaughter has both a subjective and an objective requirement. The defendant must kill while actually in the heat of passion. That heat of passion, however, must be aroused by sufficient provocation judged objectively. "[T]his heat of passion must be such a passion as would naturally be aroused in the mind of an ordinarily reasonable person under the given facts and circumstances," because' "no defendant may set up his own standard of conduct and justify or excuse himself because in fact his passions were aroused, unless further the jury believe that the facts and circumstances were sufficient to arouse the passions of the ordinarily reasonable man."

Because the test of sufficient provocation is an objective one based on a reasonable person standard, the fact the defendant is intoxicated or suffers from a mental abnormality or has particular susceptibilities to events is irrelevant in determining whether the claimed provocation was sufficient.

A defendant may not provoke a fight, become the aggressor, and, without first seeking to withdraw from the conflict, kill an adversary and expect to reduce the crime to manslaughter by merely asserting that it was accomplished upon a sudden quarrel or in the heat of passion. The claim of provocation cannot be based on events for which the defendant is culpably responsible.

As was stated in *People v. Hurtado* (1883) 63 Cal. 288, 292: "In an abstract sense anger is never reasonable, but the law, in consideration of human weakness, makes the offense manslaughter when it is committed under the influence of passion caused by an insult or provocation sufficient to excite an irresistible passion in a reasonable person; one of ordinary self-under the influence of passion caused by an insult or provocation sufficient to excite an irresistible passion in a reasonable person; one of ordinary self-control."

There is certainly evidence appellant acted in the heat of passion. The question is whether the claimed provocation for his impassioned state of mind was sufficient, i.e., the provocation was sufficient to arouse such passion in an ordinarily reasonable person and the provocation was not based on events for which appellant was responsible. Viewed in a manner most favorable to appellant, this incident began when Coss intentionally cut off the truck in which appellant was riding. While an ordinarily reasonable person might be angered by the act, such a person would not pursue or encourage the driver of a vehicle in which he or she was a passenger to follow the offending vehicle at a high rate of speed and engage in highly aggressive driving and abusive personal behavior. Coss departed after cutting off Lopez. Had Lopez, with appellant's encouragement, not made extraordinary efforts to catch up to him and then engage in an alcohol-infused, ego-inspired act of mutual road rage, the shooting would never have occurred.

While appellant showed an abundance of human weakness, it was not of a type such that the law is willing to declare his acts less culpable. The trial court acted properly in not instructing the jury concerning voluntary manslaughter based on sudden quarrel or heat of passion.

Questions and Notes

1. Should the relative commonality of road rage in recent years have been relevant to the resolution of this case?

2. If so, how? (A) Does it make Oropeza's anger more reasonable because of its commonality, or (B) Is it important for the court to come down hard on road rage killers to avoid appearing to partially condone it?

3. Should Oropeza's intoxication have been relevant? If so, how?

4. In *Freddo*, the court considered a common limitation to voluntary manslaughter, the rule that "mere words" will not suffice. The rule troubled a court that felt constrained to apply it.

Freddo v. State

155 S.W. 170 (Tenn. 1913)

WILLIAMS, J.

The plaintiff in error, Raymond Freddo, was indicted in the criminal court of Davidson County for the crime of murder in the first degree, alleged to have been committed on the body of James Higginbotham on December 22, 1911, and was found by the jury guilty of murder in the second degree; his punishment being fixed at ten years imprisonment. After the verdict, a motion for a new trial was overruled, and appeal prayed to this court, where errors are assigned.

Two of the assigned errors go to lack of due support of the verdict by the evidence; and it is earnestly and ably urged in behalf of plaintiff in error that the facts adduced did not warrant a verdict of guilty of a crime of degree greater than voluntary manslaughter, if guilt of any crime be shown.

By the preponderance of the proof, we deem the record to establish the facts to be: That in the roundhouse department of the shops of the Nashville & Chattanooga Railway Company, at Nashville, from 50 to 60 men were employed, among them being plaintiff in error, Freddo, and the deceased, Higginbotham. Freddo was at the time about 19 years of age; he had been from the age of 4 years an orphan; he had been reared thereafter in an orphanage, and yet later in the family of a Nashville lady, with result that he had been morally well trained. The proof shows him to have been a quiet, peaceable, high-minded young man of a somewhat retiring disposition. Due, perhaps, to the loss of his mother in his infancy, and to his gratitude to his foster mother, he respected womanhood beyond the average young man, and had a decided antipathy to language of obscene trend or that reflected on womanhood.

Deceased, Higginbotham, was about 6 years older than Freddo, and was one of a coterie of the roundhouse employees, few in number in comparison with the whole, given to the use of obscene language, and to the frequent application to those of the coterie, and at times to others not of their set who would permit of it, of the expression "son of a bitch"—meant to be taken as an expression of good fellowship or of slight depreciation. Deceased, prior to the date of difficulty, had applied this epithet to plaintiff in error, Freddo, without meaning offense, but was requested by the latter to discontinue it, as it was not appreciated, but resented. It was not discontinued, but repeated, and Freddo so chafed under it that he again warned deceased not to repeat it; and the fact of Freddo's sensitiveness being noted by the mechanic, J.J. Lynch, under whom Freddo served as helper, Lynch sought out deceased in Freddo's behalf and warned him to desist. On Lynch's telling deceased of the offense given to plaintiff in error, and that "he will hurt you some day," deceased replied, "The son of a bitch, he won't do nothing of the kind."

By a strong preponderance of the evidence, deceased is shown to have been habitually foul-mouthed, overbearing, and "nagging and tormenting" in language, and at times in conduct.

On the afternoon of the tragedy, Higginbotham and Freddo were engaged, as parts of a small force of men under Foreman Lynch, in the packing of a locomotive cylinder—putting a pin in the crosshead. Deceased, so engaged, was in a squatting posture, holding a pinch bar. It appears that someone, thought by deceased to have been Freddo, had spilled oil on deceased's tool box, and as he proceeded with his work the latter, in hearing of the crew, remarked: "Freddo, what in the hell did you want to spill that oil on that box for. If someone spilled oil on your box, you would be raising hell, wouldn't you, you son of a bitch?" Freddo asked Higginbotham if he meant to call the former a son of a bitch and was replied to in an angry and harsh tone: "Yes, you are a son of a bitch." The plaintiff in error, standing to the left of and about eight feet away from deceased, seeing deceased preparing to rise or rising from his squatting posture, seized a steel bar, one yard long and one inch thick, lying immediately at hand, and advancing struck deceased a blow on the side of his head, above the left ear, and extending slightly to the front and yet more to the rear of the head, but not shown to have been delivered from the rear.

Higginbotham fell on the pinch bar, from which his body suspended, until he was removed to a hospital, where, shortly he died from the effects of the wound.

It is apparent to the court that the blow was struck by plaintiff in error in sudden anger and passion, aroused by the epithet repeated and emphasized in a tone that made it opprobrious, and the more so in view of the repeated warnings that had preceded. Theretofore plaintiff in error had entertained neither friendship nor hostility towards deceased; and the proof indicates that after the warnings and before the killing the two had been on amicable, but not familiar, terms.

As had been indicated above, we deem the facts sufficient to show that plaintiff in error killed deceased under the impulse of sudden heat of passion; but, no matter how strong his passionate resentment was, it did not suffice to reduce the grade of the crime from murder to voluntary manslaughter, unless that passion were due to a provocation such as the law deemed reasonable and adequate—that is, a provocation of such a character as would, in the mind of an average reasonable man, stir resentment likely to cause violence, obscuring the reason, and leading to action from passion rather than judgment.

While the testimony indicates that plaintiff in error was peculiarly sensitive in respect of the use by another, as applied to him, of the opprobrious epithet used by deceased, yet we believe the rule to be firmly fixed on authority to the effect that the law proceeds in testing the adequacy of the provocation upon the basis of a mind ordinarily constituted—of the fair average mind and disposition.

The rule in this state is, as it was at common law, that the law regards no mere epithet or language, however violent or offensive, as sufficient provocation for taking life.

Affirmed.

In view of the very good character of the young plaintiff in error, as disclosed in the record, and of the peculiar motive and the circumstances under which he acted, we feel constrained to and do recommend to the Governor of the state that his sentence be commuted to such punishment as the executive may, in the light of this record and opinion, in his discretion think proper. To allow time for such application, execution of sentence is ordered stayed for 10 days from this date.

Judgment Affirmed.

GOLDBERG, P.J., and BURKE, J., concur.

Questions and Notes

1. Why shouldn't Freddo's good character have been relevant?

2. More generally, to what extent should the defendant's personal characteristics be relevant to an assessment of reasonableness, i.e., should the question in *Freddo*

have been the reaction of a reasonable person, or of a reasonable man who abhors profanity? Consider the following: V kicks one-legged D's crutch, D kills V. Should D be judged by the standard of the reasonable person whose personal property is attacked, or the reasonable one-legged person whose crutch is kicked? *See Rex v. Raney*, 29 C.A. 12 (1942). V, a prostitute, jeers at and kicks D, an impotent man, in the crotch upon D's inability to perform, whereupon D kills V. Should D be judged by the standard of a reasonable man or a reasonable impotent man? *See Bedder v. D.P.P.*, [1954] 2 All E.R. 801 (H.L.). Do *Freddo, Raney*, and *Bedder* raise the same question or different questions?

3. Is the theory of voluntary manslaughter that the victim is less worthy of protection than some other victim? Put differently, didn't Higginbotham ask for trouble?

4. Why did the court take the extraordinary step of recommending gubernatorial leniency for Freddo? As it is, he only received 10 years. Did the court want him to literally get away with murder?

5. Of jurisdictions retaining categories of legally sufficient provocation, the "mere words will not suffice" rule is probably the most common.

6. Should it matter if the words are threatening (e.g., "I'll kill you") or informational ("I just raped your wife") rather than merely insulting?

7. The Tennessee Supreme Court, as we shall see from the *Toler* case, cited in *Thornton*, treats informational words differently from insulting words. Not all courts agree.

State v. Thornton

730 S.W.2d 309 (Tenn. 1987)

Harbison, Justice.

Appellant was convicted of murder in the first degree as a result of shooting his wife's paramour in the home of appellant and his wife on May 3, 1983. Appellant found his wife and the victim, Mark McConkey, engaged in sexual relations in the front bedroom of appellant's home. He fired a single shot which struck McConkey in the left hip. The victim died sixteen days later as a result of a massive infection resulting from the bullet wound. Before the night in question appellant had never been acquainted with McConkey or had any previous contact with him.

Appellant and his wife had been married just under four years, and their three-year old son was in the home in an upstairs bedroom when the shooting occurred in a downstairs bedroom. Appellant and his wife had been separated for about six weeks, but no divorce action had been filed and appellant had been making a serious effort toward reconciliation with his wife.

Under these undisputed facts, in our opinion, the case does not warrant a conviction of homicide greater than that of voluntary manslaughter. The charges accordingly will be reduced to that offense, and the cause will be remanded to the trial court for sentencing and disposition on that basis.

In several previous decisions from this Court and in the almost unanimous course of judicial authority from other states, the encountering by a spouse of the situation which occurred here has been held, as a matter of law, to constitute sufficient provocation to reduce a charge of homicide from one of the degrees of murder to manslaughter absent actual malice, such as a previous grudge, revenge, or the like. Every case, of course, must be decided upon its own facts, but the facts in the present case were entirely undisputed. Appellant's wife testified at the trial and admitted her unfaithfulness to her husband and simply sought to excuse it upon the view that she was separated from him, and that she had told him earlier on the evening of the homicide that she had met someone else and planned to "date" him. In fact she had met McConkey on the evening of Saturday, April 30, 1983, and had had intimate sexual relations with him on that night and on each of the succeeding three nights, including the night of May 3 just before appellant burst into the bedroom and found both of them nude and in bed together.

Appellant, James Clark Thornton, III, was thirty-one years of age at the time of the trial of this case in June 1984. His wife, Lavinia, was twenty-seven years of age; they had been married on May 19, 1979, and at the time of the homicide had one child, a son about three years of age. Appellant was a second-year law student at Memphis State University, having previously received his undergraduate degree from the University of Tennessee at Chattanooga. His wife had not completed her undergraduate work when the parties married, but at the time of the homicide she was taking some additional class work toward her undergraduate degree. The victim, Mark McConkey, was twenty-five years of age, single, and a third-year student at the University of Tennessee Medical School in Memphis.

As stated, appellant had never met McConkey and did not even know his name. Mrs. Thornton had met him four days before the homicide and had engaged in sexual relations with him in the home belonging to her and appellant every night since that time, including the night of the homicide. She testified that she thought that when she told her husband that she might want to "date" someone else, that this, in modern society, indicated that she intended to have sexual relations. In that manner she sought to mitigate her infidelity and misconduct toward a husband who had never been unfaithful to her insofar as disclosed by the record.

The marriage of the parties was in some difficulty, apparently as a result of dissatisfaction of Mrs. Thornton. She had advised her husband in March 1983 that she wanted to be separated from him for a time, and he had voluntarily taken an apartment about two miles away from their home. He visited the home almost daily, however, and there has been no suggestion that he was ever guilty of violence, physical misconduct or mistreatment toward his wife or son. He was particularly devoted to the child, and frequently kept the child with him at his apartment on weekends or in the evenings.

Appellant had graduated from a public high school in Chattanooga, after having taken his first three years of high school at a private institution, Baylor. During his junior year at Baylor it was discovered that he had developed a severe case of scoliosis, or curvature of the spine, and he had undergone surgery to correct that condition. He was disabled to the point that he received a vocational rehabilitation grant which enabled him to attend undergraduate school at the University of Tennessee at Chattanooga. He was slightly built, being only five feet six inches in height and weighing about 125 to 130 pounds. McConkey was an athlete, a former basketball and football player in high school. He was five feet nine inches in height and weighed about 183 pounds.

Mrs. Thornton testified that she told McConkey when she first met him that she was married but separated from her husband. She had consulted an attorney and had signed a divorce petition, but the same apparently had not been filed on the date of the homicide.

Appellant, according to uncontradicted testimony, was deeply disturbed over the separation of the parties. He had sought assistance from a marriage counselor, and had persuaded his wife to go with him to the marriage counselor on several occasions. They had a joint meeting scheduled with the counselor on May 4, the day after the homicide. Appellant testified that the parties had agreed to a separation of six months, and both he and the marriage counselor testified that the parties had agreed that they would not have sexual relations with each other or with anyone else during that period. Mrs. Thornton denied making that agreement, but she did admit meeting with the marriage counselor on several occasions.

Mrs. Thornton was from a very wealthy family and had a generous trust fund which enabled the parties to live on a much more elaborate scale than most graduate students. Appellant, however, had also inherited some property through his family. This had been sold at a profit, and all of his assets had been invested in the home which the parties had purchased in Memphis, together with substantial additions from Mrs. Thornton. It was suggested by the State throughout the trial that appellant was insincere in his concern for the marriage, and that his principal concern was for his financial security.

The record indicates that as early as May 1, two days before the homicide, Mrs. Thornton had stated to her husband that she did not think that the parties would ever be reconciled. On the evening of May 3, appellant picked her and their child up at their home, and the three went to dinner. Again, on that occasion, Mrs. Thornton reiterated that she thought that the marriage was over, and on this occasion, she told appellant that she planned to date someone else whom she had met. Appellant was concerned over the situation, but on a previous occasion his wife had told him that she had had sexual relations with another student, and this had proved to be false.

He returned his wife and child to their home at about 7:30 p.m. and then went to his apartment to study for a final examination in the law school. He called two close friends of the parties, however, and discussed his marital situation with them. Both of them verified that he was very concerned about the situation, but both told him that they believed that his wife was serious about going through with a divorce.

One of them advised him that his wife apparently did not believe his feelings about a reconciliation were sincere.

Acting on that suggestion, appellant returned to the home of the parties in his automobile, stating that he wanted to try once more to convince his wife that he was indeed sincere. When he arrived at the home, he saw an automobile parked in the driveway. He did not recognize the car as being one belonging to any of his wife's friends. Accordingly, he parked around the corner and walked back to the house. Observing from the rear of the house, he saw his wife and McConkey in the kitchen with the child. He observed as Mrs. Thornton washed some laundry for McConkey and as they were eating dinner. Thereafter, they sat and read. They drank wine and smoked some marijuana, and appellant saw them kissing.

He decided to go home to get his camera, but before doing so he let the air out of one of the tires on McConkey's car. He went to his apartment and obtained his camera and an old pistol which had belonged to his father. He visited a convenience store in an attempt to find film for the camera, and finally obtained some at a drugstore. He then returned to the marital residence, arriving at about 9:30 p.m. He testified that he intended to take pictures for the purpose of showing them to the marriage counselor on the next day and possibly also for use in evidence if divorce proceedings did ensue.

Appellant spent more than an hour in the backyard of his home observing his wife and McConkey in the den and kitchen. Thereafter they left the den area, but appellant remained behind the house, thinking that McConkey was about to leave. When he went around the house, however, he found that McConkey's car was still in the driveway and saw the drapes in the front guest bedroom downstairs had been closed. He listened near the window and heard unmistakable sounds of sexual intercourse. He then burst through the front door and into the bedroom where he found the nude couple and attempted to take some pictures. At that point he testified that he thought McConkey was attempting to attack him. In all events he drew his pistol and fired a single shot, striking McConkey in the left hip. Appellant did not harm either his wife or child, although Mrs. Thornton said that he did make some threats against her. He went upstairs and brought down the little boy, who had been awakened and who was crying. He assisted in giving directions to enable an ambulance to bring aid to McConkey, and he remained at the house until the police arrived.

Appellant testified that he simply lost control and "exploded" when he found his wife in bed with the victim. He testified that he had armed himself because McConkey was much larger than he, and he felt that he needed protection if there was trouble when he returned to the residence with the camera.

Appellant testified that he did not intend to kill McConkey, but simply to shoot him in order to disable him and also because of his outrage at the situation which he had found. The single shot was not aimed at a vital organ, but the victim ultimately died because of the spread of a massive infection from the wound.

The marriage counselor who had been seeing appellant and his wife examined appellant on a number of occasions after the shooting. When McConkey died sixteen days later, appellant attempted to take his own life. The psychologist, Dr. Hunsacker, testified that appellant was under severe emotional pressure at the time of shooting to the point that he believed appellant had a brief period of temporary insanity and was not legally responsible for his actions. An expert on behalf of the State testified to the contrary with respect to the issue of temporary insanity, but she testified that appellant was undoubtedly under severe emotional stress on the evening in question both before and at the time of the shooting.

Appellant attempted to interpose alternative defenses of self-defense and insanity. The jury rejected both of these defenses, and we agree with the Court of Criminal Appeals that this was entirely within their province. We further agree with the Court of Criminal Appeals that the State is entitled to the strongest legitimate view of the evidence on appeal.

There are, however, legal principles with respect to the sufficiency of provocation to reduce charges of homicide from murder to manslaughter, and, in our opinion, these principles are controlling here.

One of the leading cases in this jurisdiction is *Toler v. State*, 152 Tenn. 1, 260 S.W. 134 (1924). There the defendant learned during a noon hour that on a previous occasion the victim had seduced his teenage daughter and had attempted to molest his nine-year-old daughter. The defendant immediately armed himself, walked a quarter of a mile to a field in which the unarmed victim was working, and shot him several times, killing him instantly.

There, as here, the jury rejected a theory of self-defense. It returned a verdict of murder in the second degree. Reversing and remanding for a new trial, this Court said:

> "We are, however, of the opinion that the facts did not warrant a verdict of murder in the second degree. It is undisputed that within less than an hour before he killed the deceased defendant had been informed of the outrage by the deceased of his young daughter. He was convinced of its truth, and, in all probability, it was true. This greatly shocked him and greatly aroused his passion, as it was calculated to do. Defendant, no doubt, from the time he was informed of this assault upon his young daughter until the shooting was done, was greatly agitated and was not capable of cool and deliberate thinking and reasoning, and killed the deceased while in this state of mind; in fact, we think the record fairly shows that this was the state of the defendant's mind at the time he did the shooting. He says that he was greatly shocked and so bothered that he did not know what to do. At any rate his mental stress must have been great, and in view of the fact that less than an hour had elapsed between the time he received information of the assault by deceased upon his daughter and the shooting, there was hardly time for his passion to subside or cool. There could therefore have been

neither malice, express or implied, in the killing of deceased under such circumstances."

The Court further stated:

"It is not necessary to reduce killing to manslaughter that the passion should be so great as to render the defendant incapable of deliberation or premeditation. If the circumstances be such as are calculated to produce such excitement and passion as would obscure the reason of an ordinary man and induce him, under such excitement and passion, to strike the blow that causes the death of the deceased, this will reduce the killing to manslaughter."

The Court pointed out that if there had been sufficient time for the passion or emotion of the defendant to cool before the shooting, then a verdict of murder might be sustained. It found no such time in that case, nor, in our opinion, was there any such showing in the present case.

The facts of the present case are far stronger. Appellant actually discovered his wife *in flagrante delicto* with a man who was a total stranger to him, and at a time when appellant was trying to save his marriage and was deeply concerned about both his wife and his young child. He did not fire a shot or in any way harm the victim until he actually discovered the victim and his wife engaged in sexual intercourse in appellant's own home. In our opinion the passions of any reasonable person would have been inflamed and intensely aroused by this sort of discovery, given the factual background of this case. Even though he was not legally insane, so as to relieve him of all criminal responsibility for the tragic death which occurred, in our opinion this was a classic case of voluntary manslaughter and no more.

We are of the opinion that the necessary elements of malice and premeditation were not demonstrated in this case and that the appellant acted under legally sufficient provocation. The conviction of murder in the first degree is set aside, and the cause will be remanded to the trial court for sentencing of the defendant for voluntary manslaughter and for such other disposition as may be appropriate in view of the time already served by the appellant. Costs of the appeal are taxed to the State. All other costs will be fixed by the trial court.

DROWOTA, Justice, concurring in part and dissenting in part.

While I concur with the result of the majority opinion insofar as the evidence in this case will not sustain the jury's finding that Defendant, James C. Thornton, III, is guilty of murder in the first degree, I must respectfully dissent from the holding of the majority that the conviction should be reduced to voluntary manslaughter. Because the evidence clearly establishes that Defendant acted with sufficient malice, the killing constitutes murder in the second degree.

In this case, the facts demonstrate that the events on the evening of May 3, 1983, took place over about a four hour period between approximately 7:30 and 11:30 p.m. Without reciting the evidence extensively, I summarize the evidence here to emphasize the sequence and timing of the events and Defendant's state of mind during this period. After returning to the marital home following dinner with his estranged wife and son, Defendant went to his apartment several miles away, arriving there sometime close to 7:30 p.m. He was tense, distraught, and depressed and decided to make telephone calls to mutual friends of his and his wife to discuss his problems. These telephone conversations continued until about 8:30 p.m. In his desperation, Defendant returned to the marital home to talk to his wife again and upon arriving discovered an unfamiliar car parked in the driveway. Aware that his wife might be dating someone, Defendant parked some distance away and stealthily made his way to the rear of the house to see who was visiting his wife. Defendant's wife testified that the victim, Mark A. McConkey, had arrived at the house close to 8:30 p.m., her date with him having been pre-arranged earlier that same day. Defendant saw his son playing in the den while his wife and the victim, whom he did not recognize, were kissing and embracing. He described his emotional state as one of shock and a sickening fear. He was upset at seeing his wife being embraced by another man in front of his child. Not unreasoning, however, in view of a pending divorce, Defendant determined to return to his apartment to get his camera to take photographs of his wife's adulterous rendezvous. Before departing, Defendant deflated the left rear tire of the victim's car.

At about 9:00 p.m., according to the wife's testimony, their son was put to bed in the master bedroom on the second floor of the house. She testified that for about two hours after putting her son to bed, she and Mr. McConkey ate, read, and did laundry in the kitchen and den area on the first floor of the house. Evidently, Defendant left before his son was put to bed. At his apartment, Defendant changed clothes, obtained his camera, which had flash and telescopic lens attachments, and his loaded .45 caliber service automatic pistol. Having no film for the camera, Defendant was required to stop at two places before finding film, purchasing some at a Walgreen's Drugstore at about 9:30 p.m. He loaded the camera and drove back to his wife's neighborhood, parked around the corner from the house, and again walked to the marital home. The first photograph he took was of the license plate on the rear of the victim's car. Defendant then went behind the house to look into the windows of the kitchen and den. His wife and Mr. McConkey were in the den reading. Defendant watched this scene for some time, feeling despondent. Eventually, he saw his wife go to Mr. McConkey and lie down on top of him on the couch; they became affectionate, kissing and talking. At this point he started taking a series of twelve to fifteen photographs. Anger started welling up in him, yet he did nothing more than make photographs. They got up to complete Mr. McConkey's laundry. After folding the laundry, Defendant's wife and Mr. McConkey turned off the lights in the kitchen and den and carried the laundry to the front of the house. Believing or hoping that the victim would then be leaving, Defendant waited at the rear of the house for a short time and then walked around to the front; he saw Mr. McConkey's car still parked in the driveway. Noticing that the curtains to the guest bedroom were drawn, Defendant feared that his wife and the victim had retired to this bedroom. He drew closer to the window to listen and heard the sounds of two persons engaged in sexual relations. Defendant testified that his head started to swim and that he felt sickened.

Suddenly, at approximately 11:15 p.m., Defendant, a small man, kicked through the locked front doors of the house and went directly to the guest room. The room was dark, but the door was open. His camera ready to take photographs, Defendant switched the lights on; the first thing he saw was his nude wife. Mr. McConkey, nude but covered with a sheet, was on the side of the bed nearest to the door. Defendant's first reaction was to attempt to take photographs, but he could not focus the camera. He then reached down and jerked the sheet off of Mr. McConkey. Again, he attempted to take a photograph but without success. While trying to work the camera, thinking that he saw the victim's hands reaching towards him in his peripheral vision, Defendant drew the loaded pistol from his coat pocket. Defendant testified that at this moment he lost control and began screaming, the pistol in his hand, saying to Mr. McConkey: "I ought to teach you screwing around with somebody else's wife. I ought to shoot you in the ass." He further testified that he intentionally pointed the muzzle of the pistol at the victim's lower body. He didn't remember cocking the single action pistol, but the pistol discharged, the bullet striking Mr. McConkey in the left rear hip, passing completely through the abdomen to lodge in a wall. Defendant also testified that when he pulled the pistol, Mr. McConkey had retreated and turned away from him, exposing his left rear side to him. After being shot, the victim pulled himself off of the bed and tried to push the bed between himself and Defendant, who again was trying to take a photograph. When he realized that Mr. McConkey was injured, Defendant regained sufficient control of himself to disarm the weapon. He subsequently gave instructions on the telephone to assist an ambulance in locating the address. At about 11:41 p.m., the first police officers arrived on the scene. Asked what had happened, Defendant stated: "He was in bed with my wife and I shot him. I don't know what came over me." Defendant was then arrested.

None of the evidence in this case is sufficient to sustain a verdict of first-degree murder. As this Court observed in *State v. Bullington*, 532 S.W.2d 556, 559–560 (Tenn. 1976):

> "The premeditation-deliberation element of first-degree murder requires that the act be performed with a cool purpose. ... In order to constitute murder in the first degree, the cool purpose must be formed, and the deliberate intention conceived in the mind of the accused, in the absence of passion, to take the life of the person slain. ... If the purpose to kill is first formed during the heat of passion, the accused, to be guilty of first-degree murder, must have committed the act after the passion has subsided. 'Passion' as here used means any of the human emotions known as anger, rage, sudden resentment or terror which renders the mind incapable of cool reflection."

I think that Defendant did not act after a cooling off period and thus a conviction of first-degree murder cannot be supported on these facts. Although the State argues with force and logic that these facts demonstrate premeditation and sustain the jury's verdict, as this Court observed in *Drye v. State*, 181 Tenn. 637, 646, 184 S.W.2d 10, 13 (1944):

> "That [defendant's] actions in procuring the weapon and seeking contact with his wife appeared deliberate and determined, is not persuasive that his passion had cooled. Suppressed anger is a common accompaniment of passion, the deepest and most powerful emotion, and of a determination beyond control to carry through a design formed in passion. Nor is the fact that he was relatively calm after the event inconsistent. Having discharged the weapon, his mind recoiled into calm. . . ."

The law is well established that the presence and amount of passion will affect the degree of a homicide; however, "[i]n order to reduce second degree murder to voluntary manslaughter, it must be shown that the defendant acted upon a sudden heat of passion, *without malice*." Malice is evident on the facts of this case and "is an essential element of both murder in the first degree and murder in the second degree."

"Malice is not necessarily confined to an intention to take the life of the deceased but includes an intention to do any unlawful act which may probably result in depriving the party of life. It is not so much spite or malevolence to the individual in particular as an evil design in general, the dictates of a wicked and depraved and malignant heart."

Aside from the use of a firearm, which in itself permits an inference of malice, Defendant threatened the victim immediately before the weapon discharged, striking the victim precisely where Defendant threatened to shoot. Defendant intentionally aimed the weapon at the victim to avoid a fatal wound, but this inadequate precaution was insufficient to prevent the foreseeable consequence of death from a serious wound at close range with a large caliber weapon. The use of a firearm coupled, with threatening statements, supported the finding of malice to sustain a conviction for second degree murder. Other evidence of malice exists in this record as well,[1] but these two facts are sufficient to negate the majority's conclusions that no malice exists, and that Defendant is guilty of voluntary manslaughter.

Furthermore, assuming that Defendant was provoked to act when he heard the sounds of sexual relations emanating from the guest room and was provoked to such an extent that he was able to break through the locked front doors, he did not fire immediately upon entering the bedroom but instead attempted to take photographs and then threatened the victim before the gun discharged. These actions preceding the shooting do not indicate that Defendant's reason had been so overcome by passion and excitement to make him incapable of malice. For a killing to be considered voluntary manslaughter, absence of malice as well as sufficient provocation are

---

1. For instance, Mr. McConkey asked Defendant not to shoot; he was retreating at the time the Defendant's weapon discharged and was shot from the rear. That Defendant deflated one of Mr. McConkey's tires may also be some evidence of malice.

among the required elements of the offense. Any killing that is not first-degree murder but cannot constitute a lesser offense of manslaughter is second degree murder. Defendant acted in passion and without any previously formed design to kill, but he didn't act without malice at the time of the shooting. The reasoning of the Court in *Drye v. State, supra*, is applicable here:

> "[I]f the killing is done in passion, the offense is not murder in the first degree; if in passion adequately provoked and acted on before the passion has cooled, it is voluntary manslaughter; and, if in passion in fact, although the provocation be insufficient to reduce the offense to manslaughter, it will nevertheless be murder in the second degree only."

Similarly, as in this case, if a killing is provoked but committed *with malice*, it will constitute second degree murder because not every element of voluntary manslaughter is shown but every element of second degree murder is shown on the facts. Consequently, I would reduce the conviction to second degree murder.

Questions and Notes

1. Why do you suppose that the jury found Thornton guilty of first degree murder? Is there any justification for that? Explain.

2. What is Justice Drowota's theory for finding Thornton guilty of second degree murder? Is there another theory for reaching the same conclusion? What is it?

3. Adultery seems to be the paradigm example of an acceptable invocation of provocation. How justifiable is that? Was Thornton more justifiably provoked than Oropeza? Than Freddo?

4. In thinking about Question 3, consider this classic justification from old England: "[W]hen a man is taken in adultery with another man's wife, if the husband shall stab the adulterer, or knock out his brains, that is bare manslaughter: for jealousy is the rage of man, and adultery is the highest invasion of *property*." (Emphasis added).

5. Do you think that Thornton was more concerned with his "property" interest in his wife's virtue or his property interest in her inheritance? What did the jury probably think? What did the Supreme Court of Tennessee think?

6. How would you have voted had you been on the jury? The Tennessee Supreme Court?

7. In 2002, Maryland enacted the following statute: 2-207 (b): "The discovery of one's spouse in sexual intercourse does not constitute legally adequate provocation for the purpose of mitigating a killing from the crime of murder to voluntary manslaughter even though the killing was provoked by that discovery." Is this statute a good idea or a bad idea? Explain.

8. In *Berry*, we see a court that has eliminated the concept of legally sufficient provocation.

People v. Berry

556 P.2d 777 (Cal. 1976)

SULLIVAN, Justice.

Defendant Albert Joseph Berry was charged by indictment with one count of murder and one count of assault by means of force likely to produce great bodily injury. The assault was allegedly committed on July 23, 1974, and the murder on July 26, 1974. In each count, the alleged victim was defendant's wife, Rachel Pessah Berry. A jury found defendant guilty as charged and determined that the murder was of the first degree. Defendant was sentenced to state prison for the term prescribed by law. He appeals from the judgment of conviction.

Defendant contends that there is sufficient evidence in the record to show that he committed the homicide while in a state of uncontrollable rage caused by provocation and therefore that it was error for the trial court to fail to instruct the jury on voluntary manslaughter as indeed he had requested. He claims that he was entitled to an instruction on voluntary manslaughter as since the killing was done upon a sudden quarrel or heat of passion. We agree with defendant.

Defendant, a cook, 46 years old, and Rachel Pessah, a 20-year-old girl from Israel, were married on May 27, 1974. Three days later Rachel went to Israel by herself, returning on July 13, 1974. On July 23, 1974, defendant choked Rachel into unconsciousness. She was treated at a hospital where she reported her strangulation by defendant to an officer of the San Francisco Police Department. On July 25, Inspector Sammon, who had been assigned to the case, met with Rachel and as a result of the interview a warrant was issued for defendant's arrest.

While Rachel was at the hospital, defendant removed his clothes from their apartment and stored them in a Greyhound Bus Depot locker. He stayed overnight at the home of a friend, Mrs. Jean Berk, admitting to her that he had choked his wife. On July 26, he telephoned Mrs. Berk and informed her that he had killed Rachel with a telephone cord on that morning at their apartment. The next day Mrs. Berk and two others telephoned the police to report a possible homicide and met Officer Kelleher at defendant's apartment. They gained entry and found Rachel on the bathroom floor. A pathologist from the coroner's office concluded that the cause of Rachel's death was strangulation. Defendant was arrested on August 1, 1974 and confessed to the killing.

At trial, defendant did not deny strangling his wife, but claimed through his own testimony and the testimony of a psychiatrist, Dr. Martin Blinder, that he was provoked into killing her because of a sudden and uncontrollable rage so as to reduce the offense to one of voluntary manslaughter. He testified that upon her return from Israel, Rachel announced to him that while there she had fallen in love with another man, one Yako, and had enjoyed his sexual favors, that he was coming to this country to claim her and that she wished a divorce. Thus, commenced a tormenting two weeks in which Rachel alternately taunted defendant with her involvement with Yako and at the same time sexually excited defendant, indicating her desire to remain with him. Defendant's detailed testimony, summarized below, chronicles this strange course of events.

After their marriage, Rachel lived with defendant for only three days and then left for Israel. Immediately upon her return to San Francisco she told defendant about her relationship with and love for Yako. This brought about further argument and a brawl that evening in which defendant choked Rachel and she responded by scratching him deeply many times. Nonetheless they continued to live together. Rachel kept taunting defendant with Yako and demanding a divorce. She claimed she thought she might be pregnant by Yako. She showed defendant pictures of herself with Yako. Nevertheless, during a return trip from Santa Rosa, Rachel demanded immediate sexual intercourse with defendant in the car, which was achieved; however, upon reaching their apartment, she again stated that she loved Yako and that she would not have intercourse with defendant in the future.

On the evening of July 22d defendant and Rachel went to a movie where they engaged in heavy petting. When they returned home and got into bed, Rachel announced that she had intended to make love with defendant, 'But I am saving myself for this man Yako, so I don't think I will.' Defendant got out of bed and prepared to leave the apartment whereupon Rachel screamed and yelled at him. Defendant choked her into unconsciousness.

Two hours later defendant called a taxi for his wife to take her to the hospital. He put his clothes in the Greyhound bus station and went to the home of his friend Mrs. Berk for the night. The next day he went to Reno and returned the day after. Rachel informed him by telephone that there was a warrant for his arrest as a result of her report to the police about the choking incident. On July 25th defendant returned to the apartment to talk to Rachel, but she was out. He slept there overnight. Rachel returned around 11 a.m. the next day. Upon seeing defendant there, she said, 'I suppose you have come here to kill me.' Defendant responded, 'yes,' changed his response to 'no,' and then again to 'yes,' and finally stated 'I have really come to talk to you.' Rachel began screaming. Defendant grabbed her by the shoulder and tried to stop her screaming. She continued. They struggled and finally defendant strangled her with a telephone cord.

Dr. Martin Blinder, a physician and psychiatrist, called by the defense,[3] testified that Rachel was a depressed, suicidally inclined girl and that this suicidal impulse led her to involve herself ever more deeply in a dangerous situation with defendant. She did this by sexually arousing him and taunting him into jealous rages in an unconscious desire to provoke him into killing her and thus consummating her desire for suicide. Throughout the period commencing with her return from Israel until her death, that is from July 13 to July 26, Rachel continually provoked defendant with sexual taunts and incitements, alternating acceptance and rejection of him. This conduct was accompanied by repeated references to her involvement with another

---

3. Dr. Blinder was appointed by the court to examine defendant pursuant to Evidence Code sections 730 and 1017. The defense called only two witnesses—Dr. Blinder and defendant himself.

man; it led defendant to choke her on two occasions, until finally she achieved her unconscious desire and was strangled. Dr. Blinder testified that as a result of this cumulative series of provocations, defendant at the time he fatally strangled Rachel, was in a state of uncontrollable rage, completely under the sway of passion.

We first take up defendant's claim that on the basis of the foregoing evidence he was entitled to an instruction on voluntary manslaughter as defined by statute which is 'the unlawful killing of a human being, without malice . . . upon a sudden quarrel or heat of passion.' (§ 192.) In *People v. Valentine* (1946) 28 Cal. 2d 121, 169 P.2d 1, this court, in an extensive review of the law of manslaughter, specifically approved the following quotation as a correct statement of the law: 'In the present condition of our law *it is left to the jurors* to say whether or not the facts and circumstances in evidence are sufficient to lead them to believe that the defendant did, or to create a reasonable doubt in their minds as to whether or not he did, commit his offense under a heat of passion. The jury is further to be admonished and advised by the court that this heat of passion must be such a passion as would naturally be aroused in the mind of an ordinarily reasonable person under the given facts and circumstances, and that, consequently, no defendant may set up his own standard of conduct and justify or excuse himself because in fact his passions were aroused, unless further the jury believe that the facts and circumstances were sufficient to arouse the passions of the ordinarily reasonable man. . . . For the fundamental of the inquiry is whether or not the defendant's reason was, at the time of his act, so disturbed or obscured by some passion — not necessarily fear and never, of course, the passion for revenge — to such an extent as would render ordinary men of average disposition liable to act rashly or without due deliberation and reflection, and from this passion rather than from judgment.' (169 P.2d at p. 12, italics in original.)

We further held in *Valentine* that there is no specific type of provocation required by section 192 and that verbal provocation may be sufficient. (28 Cal. 2d at pp. 141–144, 169 P.2d 1.) In *People v. Borchers* (1958) 50 Cal. 2d 321, 329, 325 P.2d 97 in the course of explaining the phrase 'heat of passion' used in the statute defining manslaughter we pointed out that 'passion' need not mean 'rage' or 'anger' but may be any '(v)iolent, intense, high-wrought or enthusiastic emotion' and concluded there 'that defendant was aroused to a heat of 'passion' by a series of events over a considerable period of time. . . .' (50 Cal. 2d at p. 328, 329, 325 P.2d at p. 102.) Accordingly, we there declared that evidence of admissions of infidelity by the defendant's paramour, taunts directed to him and other conduct, 'supports a finding that defendant killed in wild desperation induced by (the woman's) long continued provocatory conduct.' (50 Cal. 2d at p. 329, 325 P.2d at p. 102.) We find this reasoning persuasive in the case now before us. Defendant's testimony chronicles a two-week period of provocatory conduct by his wife Rachel that could arouse a passion of jealousy, pain and sexual rage in an ordinary man of average disposition such as to cause him to act rashly from this passion. It is significant that both defendant and Dr. Blinder testified that the former was in the heat of passion under an uncontrollable rage when he killed Rachel.

The Attorney General contends that the killing could not have been done in the heat of passion because there was a cooling period, defendant having waited in the apartment for 20 hours. However, the long course of provocatory conduct, which had resulted in intermittent outbreaks of rage under specific provocation in the past, reached its final culmination in the apartment when Rachel began screaming. Both defendant and Dr. Blinder testified that defendant killed in a state of uncontrollable rage, of passion, and there is ample evidence in the record to support the conclusion that this passion was the result of the long course of provocatory conduct by Rachel.

As to the first degree murder conviction, judgment is reversed.

WRIGHT, C.J., and MCCOMB, TOBRINER, MOSK, CLARK and RICHARDSON, JJ., concur.

Questions and Notes

1. Is the court saying that Berry should have been convicted of voluntary manslaughter? If not, what is the court saying?

2. If you represented the State on retrial, would you have much hope for a murder conviction? What would you argue?

3. Does the court attribute unreal omniscience to Dr. Blinder? How does he know that Berry was "completely under the sway of passion" when he killed Rachel? How did he know that "Rachel was a depressed, suicidally inclined girl"?

4. Would defendant's case have been stronger if he had killed Rachel on the night that he assaulted her, or following one of her earlier taunts?

5. Shouldn't Berry's passion have cooled by the time Rachel returned to the apartment? Assuming that passion can be rekindled, what did Rachel do to rekindle it?

6. In *State v. Gounagias*, 153 P. 9 (Wash. 1915), V sodomized D, his then-roommate, while D was semi-conscious. V bragged about it for several days, causing D to become the laughingstock of the community. Despite D's requests to desist, V continued to brag about it. Some days later, when D entered a tavern to the taunts of his compatriots, D became angry, sought out V, and killed him. What result? Is this a stronger or weaker case for the defendant than *Berry*? *Thornton*?

7. The MPC has refocused the heat of passion defense as explained in *Casassa*. As you read *Casassa*, consider how *Oropeza, Freddo, Thornton, Berry*, and *Gounagias* would have been decided under it.

People v. Casassa
404 N.E.2d 1310 (N.Y. 1980)

JASEN, Judge.

The significant issue on this appeal is whether the defendant, in a murder prosecution, established the affirmative defense of "extreme emotional disturbance" which would have reduced the crime to manslaughter in the first degree.

On February 28, 1977, Victoria Lo Consolo was brutally murdered. Defendant Victor Casassa and Miss Lo Consolo had been acquainted for some time prior to the latter's tragic death. They met in August, 1976 as a result of their residence in the same apartment complex. Shortly thereafter, defendant asked Miss Lo Consolo to accompany him to a social function and she agreed. The two apparently dated casually on other occasions until November, 1976 when Miss Lo Consolo informed defendant that she was not "falling in love" with him. Defendant claims that Miss Lo Consolo's candid statement of her feelings "devastated him." Miss Lo Consolo's rejection of defendant's advances also precipitated a bizarre series of actions on the part of defendant which, he asserts, demonstrate the existence of extreme emotional disturbance upon which he predicates his affirmative defense. Defendant, aware that Miss Lo Consolo maintained social relationships with others, broke into the apartment below Miss Lo Consolo's on several occasions to eavesdrop. These eavesdropping sessions allegedly caused him to be under great emotional stress. Thereafter, on one occasion, he broke into Miss Lo Consolo's apartment while she was out. Defendant took nothing, but, instead, observed the apartment, disrobed and lay for a time in Miss Lo Consolo's bed. During this break-in, defendant was armed with a knife which, he later told police, he carried "because he knew that he was either going to hurt Victoria or Victoria was going to cause him to commit suicide."

Defendant's final visit to his victim's apartment occurred on February 28, 1977. Defendant brought several bottles of wine and liquor with him to offer as a gift. Upon Miss Lo Consolo's rejection of this offering, defendant produced a steak knife which he had brought with him, stabbed Miss Lo Consolo several times in the throat, dragged her body to the bathroom and submerged it in a bathtub full of water to "make sure she was dead."

The defendant did not contest the underlying facts of the crime. Instead, the sole issue presented to the trial court was whether the defendant, at the time of the killing, had acted under the influence of "extreme emotional disturbance". (Penal Law, § 125.25, subd. 1, par. (a).) The defense presented only one witness, a psychiatrist, who testified, in essence, that the defendant had become obsessed with Miss Lo Consolo and that the course which their relationship had taken, combined with several personality attributes peculiar to defendant, caused him to be under the influence of extreme emotional disturbance at the time of the killing.

In rebuttal, the People produced several witnesses. Among these witnesses was a psychiatrist who testified that although the defendant was emotionally disturbed, he was not under the influence of "extreme emotional disturbance" within the meaning of section 125.25 (subd. 1, par. (a)) of the Penal Law because his disturbed state was not the product of external factors but rather was "a stress he created from within himself, dealing mostly with a fantasy, a refusal to accept the reality of the situation."

The trial court in resolving this issue noted that the affirmative defense of extreme emotional disturbance may be based upon a series of events, rather than a single precipitating cause. In order to be entitled to the defense, the court held, a defendant must show that his reaction to such events was reasonable. In determining whether defendant's emotional reaction was reasonable, the court considered the appropriate test to be whether in the totality of the circumstances the finder of fact could understand how a person might have his reason overcome. Concluding that the test was not to be applied solely from the viewpoint of defendant, the court found that defendant's emotional reaction at the time of the commission of the crime was so peculiar to him that it could not be considered reasonable so as to reduce the conviction to manslaughter in the first degree. Accordingly, the trial court found defendant guilty of the crime of murder in the second degree. The Appellate Division affirmed, without opinion.

On this appeal defendant contends that the trial court erred in failing to afford him the benefit of the affirmative defense of "extreme emotional disturbance". It is argued that the defendant established that he suffered from a mental infirmity not arising to the level of insanity which disoriented his reason to the extent that his emotional reaction, from his own subjective point of view, was supported by a reasonable explanation or excuse. Defendant asserts that by refusing to apply a wholly subjective standard the trial court misconstrued section 125.25 (subd. 1, par. (a)) of the Penal Law. We cannot agree.

Section 125.25 (subd. 1, par. (a)) of the Penal Law provides that it is an affirmative defense to the crime of murder in the second degree where "(t)he defendant acted under the influence of extreme emotional disturbance for which there was a reasonable explanation or excuse." This defense allows a defendant charged with the commission of acts which would otherwise constitute murder to demonstrate the existence of mitigating factors which indicate that, although he is not free from responsibility for his crime, he ought to be punished less severely by reducing the crime upon conviction to manslaughter in the first degree.

In enacting section 125.25 (subd. 1, par. (a)) of the Penal Law, the Legislature adopted the language of the manslaughter provisions of the Model Penal Code (see § 201.3, subd. (1), par. (b) (Tent Draft No. 9)). The Model Penal Code formulation, as enacted by the Legislature, represented a significant departure from the prior law of this State.

The "extreme emotional disturbance" defense is an outgrowth of the "heat of passion" doctrine which had for some time been recognized by New York as a distinguishing factor between the crimes of manslaughter and murder. However, the new formulation is significantly broader in scope than the "heat of passion" doctrine which it replaced. (People v. Patterson, 39 N.Y.2d 288, 302–303, 383 N.Y.S.2d 573, 347 N.E.2d 898.)

For example, the "heat of passion" doctrine required that a defendant's action be undertaken as a response to some provocation which prevented him from reflecting upon his actions. Moreover, such reaction had to be immediate. The existence of a "cooling off" period completely negated any mitigating effect which the provocation might otherwise have had. In Patterson, however, this court recognized that "(a)n action influenced by an extreme emotional disturbance is not one that is necessarily so spontaneously undertaken. Rather, it may be that a significant mental trauma has affected a defendant's mind for a substantial period of time, simmering in the unknowing subconscious and then inexplicably coming to the fore." (39 N.Y.2d at p. 303, 383 N.Y.S.2d at p. 582, 347 N.E.2d at p. 908.) This distinction between the past and present law of mitigation, enunciated in *Patterson*, was expressly adopted by the trial court and properly applied in this case.

The thrust of defendant's claim, however, concerns a question arising out of another perceived distinction between "heat of passion" and "extreme emotional disturbance" which was not directly addressed in *Patterson*, to wit: whether, assuming that the defense is applicable to a broader range of circumstances, the standard by which the reasonableness of defendant's emotional reaction is to be tested must be an entirely subjective one. Defendant relies principally upon our decision in *Patterson* and upon the language of the statute to support his claim that the reasonableness of his "explanation or excuse" should be determined solely with reference to his own subjective viewpoint. Such reliance is misplaced.

In *Patterson*, we noted that "(t)he purpose of the extreme emotional disturbance defense is to permit the defendant to show that his actions were caused by a mental infirmity not arising to the level of insanity, and that he is less culpable for having committed them." We also noted that "(t)he differences between the present New York statute and its predecessor . . . can be explained by the tremendous advances made in psychology since 1881 and a willingness on the part of the courts, legislators, and the public to reduce the level of responsibility imposed on those whose capacity has been diminished by mental trauma."

Defendant, however, would read *Patterson* as holding that all mental infirmity, short of insanity, must constitute "extreme emotional disturbance" if such infirmity causes the defendant to become emotionally disturbed and the defendant subjectively believed his disturbance had a reasonable explanation or excuse. While it is true that the court in *Patterson* recognized that "extreme emotional disturbance" as contemplated by the statute is a lesser form of mental infirmity than insanity,[1] the court did not hold that all mental infirmities not arising to the level of insanity constitute "extreme emotional disturbance" within the meaning of the statute. This question was not presented to us in *Patterson* and we did not decide it.

---

1. Defendant also notes that the People's expert witness stated that a mental disease not arising to the level of insanity could not be considered to be "extreme emotional disturbance" within the meaning of the statute. Of course, to the extent that the witness' comments can be interpreted as being in conflict with our decision in *Patterson*, the witness is in error. However, the trial court did not fully adopt this view and, in fact, predicated its decision upon a finding that the emotional disturbance which defendant experienced had no reasonable explanation or excuse. We would note that the trial court could have completely disregarded the witness' testimony and still have denied the defendant the benefit of the defense. (*People v. Solari*, 43 A.D.2d 610, 612, 349 N.Y.S.2d 31, *aff'd.*, 35 N.Y.2d 876, 363 N.Y.S.2d 953, 323 N.E.2d 191.)

Having determined that our decision in *Patterson* does not require that reasonableness be tested with a completely subjective standard, we must now determine whether the language of the statute or the legislative history of the statute indicates that such a standard is required.

Section 125.25 (subd. 1, par. (a)) of the Penal Law states it is an affirmative defense to the crime of murder that "(t)he defendant acted under the influence of extreme emotional disturbance for which there was a reasonable explanation or excuse, the reasonableness of which is to be determined from the viewpoint of a person in the defendant's situation under the circumstances as the defendant believed them to be." Whether the language of this statute requires a completely subjective evaluation of reasonableness is a question that has never been decided by this court, although it has been raised in our lower courts with diverse results.

Consideration of the Comments to the Model Penal Code, from which the New York statute was drawn, are instructive. (Model Penal Code, §201.3, Comment (Tent Draft No. 9 (1959)).) The defense of "extreme emotional disturbance" has two principal components (1) the particular defendant must have "acted under the influence of extreme emotional disturbance," and (2) there must have been "a reasonable explanation or excuse" for such extreme emotional disturbance, "the reasonableness of which is to be determined from the viewpoint of a person in the defendant's situation under the circumstances as the defendant believed them to be." The first requirement is wholly subjective, *i.e.*, it involves a determination that the particular defendant did in fact act under extreme emotional disturbance, that the claimed explanation as to the cause of his action is not contrived or sham.

The second component is more difficult to describe, *i.e.*, whether there was a reasonable explanation or excuse for the emotional disturbance. It was designed to sweep away "the rigid rules that have developed with respect to the sufficiency of particular types of provocation, such as the rule that words alone can never be enough," and "avoids a merely arbitrary limitation on the nature of the antecedent circumstances that may justify a mitigation." "The ultimate test, however, is objective; there must be 'reasonable' explanation or excuse for the actor's disturbance." In light of these comments and the necessity of articulating the defense in terms comprehensible to jurors, we conclude that the determination whether there was reasonable explanation or excuse for a particular emotional disturbance should be made by viewing the subjective, internal situation in which the defendant found himself and the external circumstances as he perceived them at the time, however inaccurate that perception may have been, and assessing from that standpoint whether the explanation or excuse for his emotional disturbance was reasonable, so as to entitle him to a reduction of the crime charged from murder in the second degree to manslaughter in the first degree.[2] We recognize that even such a description of the defense provides no precise guidelines and necessarily leaves room for

---

2. We emphasize that this test is to be applied to determine whether defendant's emotional disturbance, and not the act of killing, was supported by a reasonable explanation or excuse.

the exercise of judgmental evaluation by the jury. This, however, appears to have been the intent of the draftsmen. "The purpose was explicitly to give full scope to what amounts to a plea in mitigation based upon a mental or emotional trauma of significant dimensions, with the jury asked to show whatever empathy it can." (Wechsler, *Codification of Criminal Law in the United States: The Model Penal Code*, 68 COLO. L. REV. 1425, 1446.)

By suggesting a standard of evaluation which contains both subjective and objective elements, we believe that the drafters of the code adequately achieved their dual goals of broadening the "heat of passion" doctrine to apply to a wider range of circumstances while retaining some element of objectivity in the process. The result of their draftsmanship is a statute which offers the defendant a fair opportunity to seek mitigation without requiring that the trier of fact find mitigation in each case where an emotional disturbance is shown or as the drafters put it, to offer "room for argument as to the reasonableness of the explanations or excuses offered."

We note also that this interpretation comports with what has long been recognized as the underlying purpose of any mitigation statute. In the words of Mr. Justice Cardozo, referring to an earlier statute: "What we have is merely a privilege offered to the jury to find the lesser degree when the suddenness of the intent, the vehemence of the passion, seems to call irresistibly for the exercise of mercy. I have no objection to giving them this dispensing power, but it should be given to them directly and not in a mystifying cloud of words." (CARDOZO, LAW AND LITERATURE, pp. 100–101.) In the end, we believe that what the Legislature intended in enacting the statute was to allow the finder of fact the discretionary power to mitigate the penalty when presented with a situation which, under the circumstances, appears to them to have caused an understandable weakness in one of their fellows. Perhaps the chief virtue of the statute is that it allows such discretion without engaging in a detailed explanation of individual circumstances in which the statute would apply, thus avoiding the "mystifying cloud of words" which Mr. Justice Cardozo abhorred.

We conclude that the trial court, in this case, properly applied the statute. The court apparently accepted, as a factual matter, that defendant killed Miss Lo Consolo while under the influence of "extreme emotional disturbance," a threshold question which must be answered in the affirmative before any test of reasonableness is required. The court, however, also recognized that in exercising its function as trier of fact, it must make a further inquiry into the reasonableness of that disturbance. In this regard, the court considered each of the mitigating factors put forward by defendant, including his claimed mental disability, but found that the excuse offered by defendant was so peculiar to him that it was unworthy of mitigation. The court obviously made a sincere effort to understand defendant's "situation" and "the circumstances as defendant believed them to be," but concluded that the murder in this case was the result of defendant's malevolence rather than an understandable human response deserving of mercy. We cannot say, as a matter of law, that the court erred in so concluding. Indeed, to do so would subvert the purpose of the statute.

In our opinion, this statute would not require that the jury or the court as trier of fact find mitigation on any particular set of facts, but, rather, allows the finder of fact the opportunity to do so, such opportunity being conditional only upon a finding of extreme emotional disturbance in the first instance. In essence, the statute requires mitigation to be afforded an emotionally disturbed defendant only when the trier of fact, after considering a broad range of mitigating circumstances, believes that such leniency is justified. Since the trier of fact found that defendant failed to establish that he was acting "under the influence of extreme emotional disturbance for which there was a reasonable explanation or excuse," defendant's conviction of murder in the second degree should not be reduced to the crime of manslaughter in the first degree.

Accordingly, the order of the Appellate Division should be affirmed.

Cooke, C.J., and Gabrielli, Jones, Wachtler, Fuchsberg and Meyer, JJ., concur.

Questions and Notes

1. Did the appellate court find that Casassa was guilty of murder rather than manslaughter, or only that a reasonable judge or jury could so conclude? Does the court's statement: "On February 27, 1977, Victoria Lo Consolo was brutally *murdered*" answer the question?

2. Why do you suppose that the trial judge found against Casassa? If you were a juror in this case, what result do you think you would have reached?

3. What constitutes "extreme" emotional disturbance? In *State v. Ott*, 686 P.2d 1001 (Or. 1984), the trial court defined extreme as meaning "outermost." Under that definition, the prosecutor could defeat the defense by showing that there are more extreme emotional disturbances than that possessed by the defendant. For obvious reasons, the Oregon Supreme Court opted for a more relativistic definition. On the other hand, most killers are emotionally disturbed. Consequently, it is easy to raise the defense in a large number of murder cases. The New York Court of Appeals seems to have assumed that Casassa suffered from an "extreme emotional disturbance." Is it clear to you that his disturbance was extreme? Is the court saying that it is better to assume "extreme emotional disturbance" and focus on "reasonable explanation or excuse"?

4. Although *Casassa* made it clear that extreme emotional disturbance is not a carte blanche for every angry man to reduce his conviction to manslaughter, *Harris* indicates that it may well be easier than under the common law.

People v. Harris
740 N.E.2d 227 (N.Y. 2000)

Levine, J.

Defendant was convicted after a jury trial of murder in the second degree. The evidence established that defendant killed his long-time friend, Larry Amorose, with a machete. With the help of his girlfriend, defendant decapitated and dismembered Amorose's body, put the body parts in garbage bags and discarded the bags in the ocean off Coney Island.

The trial court rejected defendant's request for a charge on extreme emotional disturbance on the ground that the evidence was insufficient to justify submission of that affirmative defense to the jury. We now reverse.

The Legislature has recognized that some intentional homicides may result from "an understandable human response deserving of mercy." *Casassa*. Thus, the fact "that [a] homicide was committed under the influence of extreme emotional disturbance constitutes a mitigating circumstance reducing murder to manslaughter in the first degree." Mitigation is not limited to circumstances associated with the traditional "heat of passion" doctrine, but may be considered with respect to a broad range of situations where the trier of fact believes that such leniency should be afforded an emotionally disturbed defendant (*see, People v. Casassa*).

Hence, Penal Law § 125.25(1)(a) provides that it is an affirmative defense to the crime of murder in the second degree that "[t]he defendant acted under the influence of extreme emotional disturbance for which there was a reasonable explanation or excuse, the reasonableness of which is to be determined from the viewpoint of a person in the defendant's situation under the circumstances as the defendant believed them to be." The determination whether a defendant is entitled to a charge on extreme emotional disturbance requires the trial court to assess whether sufficient evidence was presented "for the jury to find by a preponderance of the evidence that the elements of the affirmative defense are satisfied."

The extreme emotional disturbance defense requires proof of both subjective and objective elements. The subjective element focuses on the defendant's state of mind at the time of the crime and requires sufficient evidence that the defendant's conduct was actually influenced by an extreme emotional disturbance. This element is generally associated with a loss of self-control.

The objective element requires proof of a reasonable explanation or excuse for the emotional disturbance. *Casassa*. Whether such a reasonable explanation or excuse exists must be determined by viewing the subjective mental condition of the defendant and the external circumstances as the defendant perceived them to be at the time, "however inaccurate that perception may have been, and assessing from that standpoint whether the explanation or excuse for [the] emotional disturbance was reasonable." *Casassa*.

People v. Moye, 66 N.Y.2d 887, 498 N.Y.S.2d 767, 489 N.E.2d 736, provides an apt illustration of proof warranting the submission to the jury of the extreme emotional disturbance defense. The defendant in that case admitted, in statements to the police and District Attorney's Office, that he decapitated and eviscerated a woman who teased and ridiculed him for his inability to perform sexual intercourse with her. Addressing the subjective element of the extreme emotional disturbance defense, we held that the defendant's "savage acts of mutilating and decapitating his victim, coupled with his statements to the police and District Attorney that 'something snapped' inside him when she mocked and taunted him, that he went 'bananas' and he needed help, were evidence of a loss of self-control associated with the defense." As for the objective element, we held that "there was sufficient evidence for submission to the jury-which a rational jury might have accepted or rejected-of an explanation or excuse for defendant's emotional state, in his recounting of the victim's continued ridicule and taunting about his impotence."

In our view, the present case is analytically indistinguishable from *Moye*. Thus, viewing the evidence in the light most favorable to the defendant, as we must in considering whether the extreme emotional disturbance defense should have been charged to the jury, we conclude that defendant presented sufficient evidence with respect to both elements of the defense of extreme emotional disturbance so as to be entitled to the charge.

Defendant confessed to the murder. His handwritten and videotaped statements to the police and District Attorney's Office were introduced into evidence by the People. Defendant explained that he was in love with his live-in girlfriend, Monique Lloyd, and that Amorose started talking to her. Lloyd had been unfaithful to defendant with Amorose in the past. Indeed, she once left defendant for Amorose. When Lloyd went to another room, Amorose began taunting defendant by expressing in crude terms that he could still have sex with Lloyd at anytime and that Lloyd would leave defendant for him merely at his beck and call.

Like the statements in *Moye*, defendant's confessions explained that he completely lost control over his actions in response to Amorose's taunts. Defendant related that he started hitting Amorose and that "it was like [he] was looking at a movie [and] didn't have any control" at the time. He admitted that he just "couldn't stop" his attack on Amorose. He stated that he started crying and vomiting after he killed Amorose with the machete. He then related how he cut his victim to pieces.

Additional evidence relevant to both elements of the defense was introduced in the form of psychiatric testimony. Based upon diagnostic analysis and review of pertinent records, defendant's psychiatric expert opined that defendant was acting under "extreme stress' at the time of the incident and that he satisfied the criteria equated with "the legal terminology' of extreme emotional disturbance. The expert also explained that defendant's comment-that he felt as if he were looking at a movie when he lost control over his actions-described a psychological phenomenon known as derealization, which often occurs "in extreme stress situations." The expert further testified that defendant suffered from post-traumatic stress disorder as a result of previous traumatic incidents involving extreme violence, including defendant's presence as an eyewitness to a murder. The expert relied upon this diagnosis, and other psychological factors that shaped how defendant perceived the world and events leading up to the slaying of Amorose, to explain why, in his opinion, a reasonable explanation existed for defendant's disturbed state of mind.

Based upon the foregoing evidence, a rational jury could conclude that defendant exhibited the severe loss of self-control normally associated with the subjective element of the extreme emotional disturbance defense. A rational jury could also determine that defendant satisfied the objective element of the defense. The jury could reasonably infer that he was provoked to rage over the emotionally charged subject of his lover's past and potentially future infidelity with Amorose.

Relying upon other portions of defendant's statements and expert testimony, the People argue that defendant did not suffer from any extreme emotional disturbance but acted solely out of anger and jealousy and then in self-defense. However, this merely presented conflicts in the evidence that raised issues of fact for the jury to resolve in determining whether to accept or reject the affirmative defense of extreme emotional disturbance.

Where, as here, the defendant's request for submission of the extreme emotional disturbance defense to the jury should have been granted, the trial court's failure to charge the defense requires a reversal and new trial. In light of our determination, we need not consider defendant's remaining arguments.

Accordingly, the order of the Appellate Division should be reversed and a new trial ordered.

Chief Judge KAYE and Judges SMITH, CIPARICK, WESLEY and ROSENBLATT concur.

Order reversed, etc.

Questions and Notes

1. Is the New York court retreating from *Casassa*, or are *Moye* and *Harris* just different? If different, how are they different?

2. Does the gruesome nature of the killings (interestingly called "murder" by the court) help or hurt the defendant (A) with the the appellate court, (B) with the jury?

3. If you were on the jury on remand, do you think that you would find the defendant guilty of murder or manslaughter?

4. If New York law were followed in California, would the jury in *Oropeza* have been given the opportunity to find him guilty of only manslaughter? Would that have been a good option?

5. A growing minority of jurisdictions have adopted the MPC standard. Probably a majority have either adopted the MPC or a liberal version of the common law, such as *Berry*. Not all have followed *Harris*, however.

For additional reading on the issues raised in this section, see S.J. Morse, *Undiminished Confusion in Diminished Capacity*, 75 J. CRIM. L. & CRIMINOLOGY 1, 28–37 (1984); J. Dressler, *Rethinking Heat of Passion: A Defense in Search of a Rationale*, 73 J. CRIM. L. & CRIMINOLOGY 421 (1982); and *Culpability, Dangerousness and Harm*, Section III.F (Appendix B).

Problem

Defendant was charged with the first degree murder of his father, Clyde Forrest. The facts of this case are essentially uncontested, and the evidence presented at trial tended to show the following series of events. On December 22, 1985, defendant John Forrest admitted his critically ill father, Clyde Forrest Sr., to Moore Memorial Hospital. Defendant's father, who had previously been hospitalized, was suffering from numerous serious ailments, including severe heart disease, hypertension, a thoracic aneurysm, numerous pulmonary emboli, and a peptic ulcer. By the morning of December 23, 1985, his medical condition was determined to be untreatable and terminal. Accordingly, he was classified as "No Code," meaning that no extraordinary measures would be used to save his life, and he was moved to a more comfortable room.

On December 24, 1985, defendant went to the hospital to visit his ailing father. No other family members were present in his father's room when he arrived. While one of the nurse's assistants was tending to his father, defendant told her, "There is no need in doing that. He's dying." She responded, "Well, I think he's better." The nurse's assistant noticed that defendant was sniffing as though crying and that he kept his hand in his pocket during their conversation. She subsequently went to get the nurse.

When the nurse's assistant returned with the nurse, defendant once again stated his belief that his father was dying. The nurse tried to comfort defendant, telling him, "I don't think your father is as sick as you think he is." Defendant, very upset, responded, "Go to hell. I've been taking care of him for years. I'll take care of him." Defendant was then left alone in the room with his father.

Alone at his father's bedside, defendant began to cry and to tell his father how much he loved him. His father began to cough, emitting a gurgling and rattling noise. Extremely upset, defendant pulled a small pistol from his pants pocket, put it to his father's temple, and fired. He subsequently fired three more times and walked out into the hospital corridor, dropping the gun to the floor just outside his father's room.

Following the shooting, defendant, who was crying and upset, neither ran nor threatened anyone. Moreover, he never denied shooting his father and talked openly with law enforcement officials. Specifically, defendant made the following oral statements: "You can't do anything to him now. He's out of his suffering." "I killed my daddy." "He won't have to suffer anymore." "I know they can burn me for it, but my dad will not have to suffer anymore." "I know the doctors couldn't do it, but I could." "I promised my dad I wouldn't let him suffer."

Defendant's father was found in his hospital bed, with several raised spots and blood on the right side of his head. Blood and brain tissue were found on the bed, the floor, and the wall. Though defendant's father had been near death as a result of his medical condition, the exact cause of the deceased's death was determined to be the four point-blank bullet wounds to his head. Defendant's pistol was a single-action .22-caliber five-shot revolver. The weapon, which had to be cocked each time it was fired, contained four empty shells and one live round.

At the close of the evidence, defendant's case was submitted to the jury for one of four possible verdicts: first degree murder, second degree murder, voluntary manslaughter, or not guilty.

1. If you were the prosecution, how would you establish premeditation? If you were the defense counsel, how could you negate it?

2. Is there any way to reduce the crime to voluntary manslaughter? Would it matter whether your jurisdiction followed *Oropeza, Freddo, Berry,* or *Harris*? Explain.

3. Think about whether there is any basis for exculpating Forrest entirely? This question can be better discussed in conjunction with the material on necessity, *infra*.

4. For two different perspectives, see the majority and dissenting opinions in *State v. Forrest,* 362 S.E.2d 252 (N.C. 1987).

C. Assisted Suicide

Distinguishing assisted suicide from murder or manslaughter is not always easy. In the *Forrest* Problem, *supra*, it was clear that the defendant was 100% responsible for the death of the victim. Consequently, assisted suicide was not an option. At minimum, to be guilty of assisted suicide rather than murder or manslaughter, the decedent must have requested help in terminating his life.

The issue of assisted suicide has been largely the domain of Dr. Jack Kevorkian, one of whose cases appears below. As you read *Kevorkian*, think about how (or whether) assisted suicide should be distinguished from murder, or whether it should be punishable at all.

There was a separate issue raised in *Kevorkian* about the constitutional right of a patient to physician-assisted suicide. In a deleted portion of *Kevorkian*, the Michigan Supreme Court rejected such a right. Without getting into too much detail, the United States Supreme Court appears to substantially concur. (For those who want more detail, see *Washington v. Glucksberg,* 521 U.S. 702 (1997).) Consequently, for purposes of analysis, you may assume that the victims in *Kevorkian*, or the case cited therein, have no constitutional right to assisted suicide.

People v. Kevorkian

527 N.W.2d 714 (Mich. 1994)

MICHAEL F. CAVANAGH, Chief Justice, and BRICKLEY and ROBERT P. GRIFFIN, Justices.

VI

A

[W]e turn to the issue presented in the Oakland County case involving the deaths of Sherry Miller and Marjorie Wantz. Their deaths occurred before the enactment of Michigan's ban on assisted suicide, and the question is whether defendant Kevorkian can be prosecuted for his role in the deaths.

Each woman was said to be suffering from a condition that caused her great pain or was severely disabling. Each separately had sought defendant Kevorkian's assistance in ending her life. The women and several friends and relatives met the defendant at a cabin in Oakland County on October 23, 1991.

According to the testimony presented at the defendant's preliminary examination, the plan was to use his "suicide machine." The device consisted of a board to which one's arm is strapped to prevent movement, a needle to be inserted into a blood vessel and attached to IV tubing, and containers of various chemicals that are to be released through the needle into the bloodstream. Strings are tied to two of the fingers of the person who intends to die. The strings are attached to clips on the IV tubing that control the flow of the chemicals. As explained by one witness, the person raises that hand, releasing a drug called methohexital, which was described by expert witnesses as a fast-acting barbiturate that is used under controlled circumstances to administer anesthesia rapidly.[61] When the person falls asleep, the hand drops, pulling the other string, which releases another clip and allows potassium chloride to flow into the body in concentrations sufficient to cause death.

The defendant tried several times, without success, to insert the suicide-machine needle into Ms. Miller's arm and hand. He then left the cabin, returning several hours later with a cylinder of carbon monoxide gas and a mask apparatus. He attached a screwdriver to the cylinder, and showed Ms. Miller how to use the tool as a lever to open the gas valve.

The defendant then turned his attention to Ms. Wantz. He was successful in inserting the suicide-machine needle into her arm. The defendant explained to Ms. Wantz how to activate the device so as to allow the drugs to enter her bloodstream. The device was activated,[62] and Ms. Wantz died.[63]

---

61. A large enough dose can cause the recipient to stop breathing.

62. No one who testified at the preliminary examination actually witnessed the activation of the device. The only persons in the cabin at that time were the decedents, the defendant, and the defendant's sister, who since has died. Ms. Wantz' husband was walking away from the cabin. He testified as follows:

Q. You don't know who pulled the string?
A. I have no idea. She knew that she had to pull the string when I left.
Q. You don't know if she tried to pull the string and it didn't work and Kevorkian pushed her hand at all, do you?
A. I can say this, when I left the room, she was in the process of trying to pull the string.
Q. You don't know who pulled the string? That's what you're telling me?
A. I can tell you she was in the process of trying to pull the string when I left the room, but I did not see her pull the string. The only thing I can take and tell you is once I left the room, Dr. Kevorkian did—I heard Dr. Kevorkian say, "Marj, you have to hold your hand up," and that is the only thing I know.

63. The pathologist who performed the autopsy testified that there was a lethal level of methohexital in Ms. Wantz' blood, but that because of the body's release of potassium on death, no conclusions could be drawn regarding potassium chloride.

The defendant then placed the mask apparatus on Ms. Miller. The only witness at the preliminary examination who was present at the time said that Ms. Miller opened the gas valve by pulling on the screwdriver. The cause of her death was determined to be carbon monoxide poisoning.

The defendant was indicted on two counts of open murder. He was bound over for trial following a preliminary examination. However, in circuit court, the defendant moved to quash the information and dismiss the charges, and the court granted the motion.

B

A divided Court of Appeals reversed. The Court of Appeals majority relied principally on *People v. Roberts*, 211 Mich. 187, 178 N.W. 690 (1920).

In *Roberts*, the defendant's wife was suffering from advanced multiple sclerosis and in great pain. She previously had attempted suicide and, according to the defendant's statements at the plea proceeding, requested that he provide her with poison. He agreed and placed a glass of poison within her reach. She drank the mixture and died. The defendant was charged with murder. He pleaded guilty, and the trial court determined the crime to be murder in the first degree.

The defendant appealed. He argued, among other things, that because suicide is not a crime in Michigan, and his wife thus committed no offense, he committed none in acting as an accessory before the fact. The Court rejected that argument, explaining:

> If we were living in a purely common-law atmosphere with a strictly common law practice, and defendant were charged with being guilty as an accessory of the offense of suicide, counsel's argument would be more persuasive than it is. But defendant is not charged with that offense. He is charged with murder and the theory of the people was that he committed the crime by means of poison. He has come into court and confessed that he mixed poison with water and placed it within her reach, but at her request. The important question, therefore, arises as to whether what defendant did constitutes murder by means of poison.

After discussing a similar Ohio case, *Blackburn v. State*, 23 Ohio. St. 146 (1872), the *Roberts* Court concluded:

> We are of the opinion that when defendant mixed the Paris green with water and placed it within reach of his wife to enable her to put an end to her suffering by putting an end to her life, he was guilty of murder by means of poison within the meaning of the statute, even though she requested him to do so. By this act he deliberately placed within her reach the means of taking her own life, which she could have obtained in no other way by reason of her helpless condition.

In the instant case, defendant Kevorkian had argued that the discussion of this issue in *Roberts* was dicta because the defendant in that case had pleaded guilty of murder, and thus the controlling authority was *People v. Campbell*, 124 Mich. App. 333, 335 N.W.2d 27 (1983).[64] The Court of Appeals majority rejected that view and said that *Roberts* controlled the issue presented in the instant case.

C

We agree with the Court of Appeals that the holding in *Roberts* was not dicta. While it is true that defendant Roberts pleaded guilty of placing a poisonous mixture at the bedside of his sick wife, knowing that she intended to use it to commit suicide, nothing in the opinion indicates that this Court based its affirmance of the conviction of first-degree murder on the fact that the conviction stemmed from a guilty plea.

However, it is not sufficient in the instant case to decide simply that the holding in *Roberts* was not dicta. We must determine further whether *Roberts* remains viable, because, as noted in *People v. Stevenson*, 416 Mich. 383, 390, 331 N.W.2d 143 (1982):

This Court has often recognized its authority, and indeed its duty, to change the common law when change is required.

The crime of murder has been classified and categorized by the Legislature, but the definition of murder has been left to the common law.

Under the common-law definition, "[m]urder is where a person of sound memory and discretion unlawfully kills any reasonable creature in being, in peace of the state, with malice prepense or aforethought, either express or implied." Implicit in this definition is a finding that the defendant performed an act that caused the death of another. To convict a defendant of criminal homicide, it must be proven that death occurred as a direct and natural result of the defendant's act.

Early decisions indicate that a murder conviction may be based on merely providing the means by which another commits suicide.[67] However, few jurisdictions, if any, have retained the early common-law view that assisting in a suicide is murder. The modern statutory scheme in the majority of states treats assisted suicide as a

---

64. In *Campbell*, the decedent and the defendant had been drinking heavily at the decedent's home. The decedent had been talking about suicide, and the fact that he did not have a gun. The defendant offered to sell the decedent a gun. At first, the decedent did not accept the offer. However, defendant Campbell persisted in alternately encouraging and ridiculing him. Eventually, the defendant provided the decedent with a gun and five shells. The defendant and the decedent's girlfriend left, and some time later, the decedent shot himself. The defendant was charged with open murder. Although the defendant failed to persuade the circuit court to quash the information, the Court of Appeals reversed. Among other things, the Court said that more recent Supreme Court decisions had "cast doubt" that *Roberts* remained good law. The Court also noted that the trial judge in *Roberts* had "assumed that a murder had occurred and considered only the degree of that crime." The *Campbell* panel further found that the defendant did not have the required "present intention to kill." He only "hoped" that the decedent would kill himself, and "hope" is not the degree of intent required to sustain a charge of murder.

67. *See Marzen, supra* at 79–81.

separate crime, with penalties less onerous than those for murder. *See, e.g.,* 1993 P.A. 3, which was enacted by our own Legislature.[68]

Recent decisions draw a distinction between active participation in a suicide and involvement in the events leading up to the suicide, such as providing the means. Frequently, these cases arise in the context of a claim by the defendant that the prosecution should have been brought under an assisted suicide statute. The courts generally have held that a person may be prosecuted for murder if the person's acts went beyond the conduct that the assisted suicide statute was intended to cover.

For example, in *People v. Cleaves,* 229 Cal. App. 3d 367, 280 Cal. Rptr. 146 (1991), the defendant was charged with first-degree murder in the strangulation death of another man. The trial court had refused a defense request to instruct the jury on the statutory offense of aiding and abetting a suicide, and the jury convicted him of second-degree murder.

In deciding whether an instruction on the statutory offense of aiding and abetting suicide should have been given, the appellate court accepted the defendant's detailed version of the events. The decedent in *Cleaves* was suffering from AIDS and wanted the defendant's assistance in strangling himself. With the defendant's help, the decedent trussed his body in an arched position, with his face down on a pillow. The defendant's role, when the decedent "pulled down" on the truss to effect strangulation, was to put his hand on the decedent's back to steady him. At one point, when the sash slipped from the decedent's neck, the defendant rewrapped it at the decedent's request and retied it to the decedent's hands. By straightening out his body with his feet, the decedent was in sole control of how tight the sash was around

---

68. In addition, the Model Penal Code incorporates this view:

(1) Causing Suicide as Criminal Homicide. A person may be convicted of criminal homicide for causing another to commit suicide only if he purposely causes such suicide by force, duress or deception.

(2) Aiding or Soliciting Suicide as an Independent Offense. A person who purposely aids or solicits another to commit suicide is guilty of a felony of the second degree if his conduct causes such suicide or an attempted suicide, and otherwise of a misdemeanor. [Model Penal Code, § 210.5.]

In commentary to its provision detailing sanctions against suicide assistance, the drafters of the Model Penal Code discussed the rationale supporting its recommendations, as well as expressing concern over the severity of the penalty imposed in *Roberts*:

The fact that penal sanctions will prove ineffective to deter the suicide itself does not mean that the criminal law is equally powerless to influence the behavior of those who would aid or induce another to take his own life. Moreover, in principle it would seem that the interests in the sanctity of life that are represented by the criminal homicide laws are threatened by one who expresses a willingness to participate in taking the life of another, even though the act may be accomplished with the consent, or at the request, of the suicide victim. On the other hand, cases such as *People v. Roberts*, where a husband yielded to the urging of his incurably sick wife to provide her with the means of self-destruction, sorely test the resiliency of a principle that completely fails to take account of the claim for mitigation that such a circumstance presents.

[ALA, Model Penal Code, § 210.5, commentary at 100.]

his neck. In holding that the trial judge properly refused to instruct the jury under the assisted suicide statute, the appeals court said:

> [The statute] provides: "Every person who deliberately aids, or advises, or encourages another to commit suicide, is guilty of a felony." As explained by our Supreme Court, the "key to distinguishing between the crimes of murder and of assisting suicide is the active or passive role of the defendant in the suicide. If the defendant merely furnishes the means, he is guilty of aiding a suicide; if he actively participates in the death of the suicide victim, he is guilty of murder." The statute providing for a crime less than murder "does not contemplate active participation by one in the overt act directly causing death. It contemplates some participation in the events leading up to the commission of the final overt act, such as furnishing the means for bringing about death, the gun, the knife, the poison, or providing the water, for the use of the person who himself commits the act of self-murder. But where a person actually performs, or actively assists in performing, the overt act resulting in death, such as shooting or stabbing the victim, administering the poison, or holding one under water until death takes place by drowning, his act constitutes murder, and it is wholly immaterial whether this act is committed pursuant to an agreement with the victim. . . ."

In *Cleaves*, viewing the evidence most favorably for the defense, the court said there were no facts to support the requested instruction on aiding and abetting an assisted suicide. Although the defendant may not have applied pressure to the ligature itself, he admitted that his act of holding the decedent to keep him from falling off the bed was designed to assist the decedent in completing an act of strangulation. "This factual scenario indisputably shows active assistance in the overt act of strangulation," the court said.

Similarly, in *State v. Sexson*, 117 N.M. 113, 869 P.2d 301 (N.M. App. 1994), *cert. denied*, 117 N.M. 215, 870 P.2d 753 (1994), the defendant was charged with first-degree murder in connection with the fatal shooting of his wife. He was convicted of second-degree murder following a bench trial and argued on appeal that he should have been prosecuted under the state's assisted suicide statute.

The only fact in dispute in *Sexson* was whether it was the defendant or the decedent who actually pulled the trigger of the rifle that killed her. It was not disputed that there was a suicide agreement between the two, and that the pact was genuine. The defendant claimed simply to have held the rifle in position while the decedent pulled the trigger, and that he had failed to then kill himself because he "freaked out" when the decedent continued to breathe after being shot.

The appellate court rejected the defendant's argument that he could not be prosecuted under the more general murder statute because of the specific assisted suicide statute. In so doing, the court emphasized that the two statutes proscribed different conduct:

The wrongful act triggering criminal liability for the offense of assisting suicide is "aiding another" in the taking of his or her own life. It is well accepted that "aiding," in the context of determining whether one is criminally liable for their involvement in the suicide of another, is intended to mean providing the means to commit suicide, not actively performing the act which results in death. . . .

There are three different views about the criminal liability of one who, whether pursuant to a suicide pact or not, solicits (by talk) or aids (as by providing the means of self-destruction) another to commit suicide. Occasionally aiding or soliciting suicide has been held to be no crime at all on the ground that suicide is not criminal. That view is most certainly unsound. At one time many jurisdictions held it to be murder, but a great many states now deal specifically with causing or aiding suicide by statute, treating it either as a form of manslaughter or as a separate crime. Such statutes typically do "not contemplate active participation by one in the overt act directly causing death," and thus their existence is not barrier to a murder conviction in such circumstances.

In contrast, the wrongful act triggering criminal liability for second degree murder is "kill[ing]" or "caus[ing] the death" of another. In the context of the instant case, the second degree murder statute is aimed at preventing an individual from actively causing the death of someone contemplating suicide, whereas the assisting suicide statute is aimed at preventing an individual from providing someone contemplating suicide with the means to commit suicide. Thus, the two statutes do not condemn the same offense. . . .

Turning to the evidence presented in *Sexson*, the court reiterated that the distinction accepted in other jurisdictions between murder and aiding suicide "generally hinges upon whether the defendant actively participates in the overt act directly causing death, or whether he merely provides the means of committing suicide." This distinction applies even where the decedent has given consent or requested that actual assistance be provided. In *Sexson*, the defendant admitted holding the rifle in a position calculated to assure the decedent's death. The court concluded: "That action transcends merely providing Victim a means to kill herself and becomes active participation in the death of another."

As noted, this Court has modified the common law when it perceives a need to tailor culpability to fit the crime more precisely than is achieved through application of existing interpretations of the common law. For the reasons given, we perceive such a need here. Accordingly, we would overrule *Roberts* to the extent that it can be read to support the view that the common-law definition of murder encompasses the act of intentionally providing the means by which a person commits suicide. Only where there is probable cause to believe that death was the direct and natural result of a defendant's act can the defendant be properly bound over on a charge of murder.[70] Where a defendant merely is involved in the events leading up to the death, such as providing the means, the proper charge is assisting in a suicide.

However, even absent a statute that specifically proscribes assisted suicide, prosecution and punishment for assisting in a suicide would not be precluded. Rather, such conduct may be prosecuted as a separate common-law offense under the saving clause of M.C.L. § 750.505; M.S.A. § 28.773:

> Any person who shall commit any indictable offense at the common law, for the punishment of which no provision is expressly made by any statute of this state, shall be guilty of a felony, punishable by imprisonment in the state prison not more than 5 years or by a fine of not more than $10,000.00, or both in the discretion of the court.[72]

Our reinterpretation of the common law does not enlarge the scope of criminal liability for assisted suicide, but rather reduces liability where a defendant merely is involved in the events leading up to the suicide, such as providing the means. Therefore, there is no violation of the prohibition on ex post facto laws. U.S. Const., art. I, § 9; Const. 1963, art. 1, § 10.

D

The decision regarding whether an examining magistrate erred in binding a defendant over for trial is one that should be made in the first instance by the trial court. In this case, the lower courts did not have the benefit of the analysis set forth in this opinion for evaluating the degree of participation by defendant Kevorkian

---

70. However, there may be circumstances where one who recklessly or negligently provides the means by which another commits suicide could be found guilty of a lesser offense, such as involuntary manslaughter. There are a number of cases in which providing a gun to a person known to the defendant to be intoxicated and despondent or agitated has constituted sufficient recklessness to support such a conviction. For example, in *People v. Duffy*, 79 N.Y.2d 611, 79 N.Y.2d 611, 613, 595 N.E.2d 814 (1992), the defendant provided a gun to the intoxicated and despondent decedent, who had said he wanted to kill himself, and urged him to "blow his head off." The decedent proceeded to shoot himself. Duffy was indicted for two counts of manslaughter in the second degree. The first count alleged that he had intentionally caused or aided the deceased in committing suicide (N.Y. Penal Law, § 125.15[3]), and the second alleged that he had recklessly caused the death (N.Y. Penal Law, § 125.15[1]). After a jury trial, the defendant was acquitted of the first count, but convicted of the second. The New York Court of Appeals concluded:
> [T]he conduct with which defendant was charged clearly fell within the scope of section 125.15(1)'s proscription against recklessly causing the death of another person. As the People aptly observe, a person who, knowing that another is contemplating immediate suicide, deliberately prods that person to go forward and furnishes the means of bringing about death may certainly be said to have "consciously disregard[ed] a substantial and unjustifiable risk" that his actions would result in the death of that person. . . .

72. See *State v. Carney*, 69 N.J.L. 478, 480, 55 A. 44 (1903) (concluding that a failed attempt at suicide was criminal under the New Jersey saving clause, which made all "offenses of an indictable nature at common law," not otherwise provided for, misdemeanors); *State v. Willis*, 255 N.C. 473, 121 S.E.2d 854 (1961) (finding an attempt to commit suicide to be an indictable misdemeanor under North Carolina's saving clause).

in the events leading to the deaths of Ms. Wantz and Ms. Miller. Accordingly, we remand this matter to the circuit court for reconsideration of the defendant's motion to quash in light of the principles discussed in this opinion.

MICHAEL F. CAVANAGH, BRICKLEY and ROBERT P. GRIFFIN, JJ., concur.

BOYLE, Justice (concurring in part and dissenting in part).

I agree with the lead opinion that §7 of 1993 P.A. 3 does not violate the Title-Object Clause of the Michigan Constitution[1] in its entirety. I also agree with the lead opinion's result and rationale finding that the act is not violative of a fundamental right protected by the Due Process Clause of the state or federal constitution. In addition, as stated in the observations of Justice Harlan[2] quoted approvingly in *Planned Parenthood of Southeastern Pennsylvania v. Casey*, 505 U.S. 833, ___, 112 S. Ct. 2791, 2805–06, 120 L.Ed.2d 674, 697–698 (1992), and the expansion on those principles that follow, the task of the judiciary is to strike a balance between the respect for the liberty of the individual and the demands of organized society. Such balance should be struck with due respect to history and rationally evolving tradition. Thus, in the present context, the process of rational evolution must focus on a determination whether the question of assisted suicide can be left to the political process without intrusion on a protected liberty interest, eschewing either a radical departure from tradition or the moral code of individual judges. I agree that it can.

I do not agree with the lead opinion's redefinition of the statutory offense of murder to exclude participation in the events leading up to the death, including, without limitation, providing the means and all other acts save that of the final act precipitating death. A person who participates in the death of another may be charged with murder, irrespective of the consent of the deceased. Nor do I agree with the lead opinion's conclusion or rationale justifying a charge of assisted suicide under the saving clause.[3] The saving clause recognizes only unprovided-for common-law crimes; it does not authorize this Court to create new crimes. If assisting a suicide is a common-law crime and not murder under the common-law definition incorporated in our murder statutes, it may be penalized as another crime under the saving clause. The Court, however, cannot simply exclude from the common-law definition of murder that which is murder under our statutes and then hold that the Legislature intended in the saving clause to authorize the Court to say that that which was murder at the common law is now a new crime.

Finally, I disagree with the conclusion that one who provides the means for suicides and participates in the acts leading up to death may not be charged with murder as long as the final act is that of the decedent. In stating this conclusion, the lead opinion has parsed the definition of participation to permit involvement that

---

1. CONST. 1963, art. 4, §24.
2. *Poe v. Ullman*, 367 U.S. 497, 542 (1961) (Harlan, J., dissenting from dismissal on jurisdictional grounds).
3. M.C.L. §750.505; M.S.A. §28.773.

is dangerously overinclusive. Absent standards established to distinguish between those who are in fact terminally ill or suffering in agony and rationally wish to die and those who are not, there is no principled vehicle in the judicial arsenal to protect against abuse, save the jury's evaluation of a given defendant's conduct. The acts shown in the Oakland County case establish causation as a matter of law for purposes of bindover. Thus, the trial court erred in quashing the information, and the decision of the Court of Appeals should be affirmed.

I

Criminal homicide has been a statutory offense in Michigan since 1846. The crime is not defined by reference to its elements but by reference to the common law. There is no dispute that at the time these offenses were committed, the Legislature had shown no disposition to depart from the common-law definition of murder as including assisted suicide. The lead opinion today would alter the definition of murder by changing the causation requirement in the context of suicide to exclude from liability for criminal homicide those who intentionally participate in the events that directly cause death with the intention that death occur.

However, the intended results of the plaintiff's acts were the results actually obtained, and the acts were both the cause in fact and the proximate or foreseeable cause of the decedents' deaths. The lead opinion would thus redefine murder as it is defined in our statutes and has created a special causation standard, unknown in any other jurisdiction.

The detailed account of the preliminary examination testimony describing the assisted suicides of Ms. Miller and Ms. Wantz belies the notion that the degree of participation by the defendant in these events was insufficient to permit a charge of murder even in those states that have adopted separate penalties for soliciting or assisting suicide. Testimony at the preliminary examination presented evidence that the defendant, inter alia, inserted IV needles into Ms. Wantz' arm, tied strings to her fingers so she could release chemicals into her bloodstream, and placed a mask over Ms. Miller's face so that she could breathe carbon monoxide gas. The mask was secured so tightly that without intervention that fact alone would have caused death. It cannot be said, as a matter of law, that these actions did not establish probable cause to believe that the defendant committed murder.

The decedents' alleged desire in the present case that they die with the defendant's assistance does not absolve the defendant of criminal liability. The request by the decedents does not provide justification or excuse. The magistrate's decision to bind over the defendant for trial should be upheld.

II

The lead opinion invites the circuit court on remand to draw a distinction between acts of participation that are merely "the events leading up to" the deaths of the decedents and "*the* final overt act that causes death" that, as a matter of law, will constitute probable cause for the charge of murder. Such a "test" transfers the responsibility for the outcome from the shoulders of this Court to the trial court and effectively converts every criminal homicide accomplished by participation into assisting suicide.

It could be argued that this solution does no more than what the assisted suicide law does. But the assisted suicide law is still only a temporary measure, and the Legislature has never indicated that it would not follow the model of other states and continue to apply the law of criminal homicide despite the existence of statutes specifically directed to suicide.

The lead opinion's "solution" is in fact an invitation to continue participation until the level of participation assumes a level of proof for bind over suggesting that the defendant intended to kill a decedent for impure reasons. In pragmatic terms, the force of the law is to discourage conduct on the margins. What the lead opinion would do in setting new margins is permitting a new range of activity and thus increase the potential for abuse of the vulnerable by the active participant.

As the Canadian Supreme Court recently and aptly observed in upholding a blanket prohibition against assisted suicide:

> The basis for this refusal is twofold it seems — first, the active participation by one individual in the death of another is intrinsically morally and legally wrong, and secondly, there is no certainty that abuses can be prevented by anything less than a complete prohibition.

[*Rodriguez v. British Columbia*, 107 DLR 4th 342; 1993 LEXIS/Canada 51 (1993).]

A

People v. Roberts correctly held that the homicide statute had incorporated the common-law definition of assisted suicide as murder. The question presented is whether we have the authority to modify that definition and, granting that we have the power to do so, whether we should. The latter question involves the issue whether the judiciary can devise an acceptable formula advancing the autonomy of those who deem their lives not worthy to be lived, without jeopardizing the lives of those whose further existence society might deem not worthy of protection. That the Court is unable to do so is illustrated by today's decision that alters the law of causation in all suicide settings, not just those of the terminally ill or acutely suffering.

As Justice Jackson observed in a famous dissent, a judicial decision has a force all its own. "The principle then lies about like a loaded weapon. . . . Every repetition imbeds that principle more deeply in our law and thinking and expands it to new purposes." *Korematsu v. United States*, 323 U.S. 214, 246.

The fact that an active participant in the death of another risks jury determination that the circumstances are not so compelling as to benefit from their mercy-dispensing power tests the situation and the actions by the only repository of authority within the judicial reach. Whether death has been caused for good, bad, or mixed reasons, or whether the person is in fact presently incurable or suffering intolerable and unmanageable pain, and has a fixed and rational desire to die, are issues that should be addressed by a jury or the Legislature, not by this Court as a matter of law.

Today the Court purports to approve only a mild deviation from the common law by moving the line of protection the murder statute affords from participation to pulling the trigger. But the law that condemns such killings as murder has a substantially greater deterrent effect, imposing a substantially greater responsibility on those who would violate it than the penalty for assisted suicide.

While the Court's redefinition of causation is presumably correctable, the lead opinion would reduce the deterrent potential without any assurance that the line it draws will not marginally increase the risk of death for those who would have a reason to live had society and the participant in their demise valued their continued existence.

The lead opinion's distrust of the jury and its dislike for the severity of the punishment imposed by the law of criminal homicide has caused it to draw a line that crosses a dangerous threshold. The risk of irreversible mistake, however "minimal," should not be borne by those no longer able to protest — it should rest on those who assume the authority and wisdom to extinguish human life.

B

To the extent that this Court reduces culpability for those who actively participate in acts that produce death, we do so at the risk of the most vulnerable members of our society — the elderly, the ill, the chronically depressed, those suffering from a panoply of stressful situations: adolescence, loss of employment, the death of a child or spouse, divorce, alcoholism, the abuse of other mind-altering substances, and the burden of social stigmatization.

The lead opinion's solution assumes the actor is a sufficient buffer between the patient and the family, that the actor knows enough about the disease to assure its terminal course and enough about the sanity of the deceased to evaluate the rationality of suicide. The lead opinion thus ignores the distinction between a voluntary act carried out if the victim is sane, and the inquiry into whether the victim's mental state is compromised by disease, depression, or medication.

C

The Model Penal Code recognizes the inherent difficulty of objective management of an assisted suicide law to separate proper from improper motivations of a participant. The code classifies purposely causing, that is, engaging in conduct "but for which the result in question would not have occurred," Model Penal Code, §210.5, comment 4, p. 98, suicide by force, duress, or deception as criminal homicide. Aiding or assisting another to commit suicide is a felony at the level of manslaughter if the defendant's conduct causes, that is, was a "significantly contributing factor" to a suicide or attempted suicide. The same distinctions are drawn in statutory schemes. States that have enacted assisted suicide statutes continue to permit prosecutions for criminal homicides out of recognition that underinclusive line drawing by the judiciary may, as here, permit dangerously overinclusive activity.

In fact, as the excerpts from the cases cited by the lead opinion indicate, it has not aligned itself with other states. Thus, in *People v. Cleaves*, the court found that a defendant who held the decedent's back so the decedent could strangle himself was not merely a passive participant in a suicide, stating that the murder statute applies "where a person actively assists in performing the overt act resulting in death. . . ." Likewise, *State v. Sexson* does not support the lead opinion's revisionist view of causation. In *Sexson*, the court found that defendant could be charged with murder on evidence that he merely held a gun in place because "[t]hat action transcends merely providing the Victim a means to kill herself and becomes active participation in the death of another."

Although these distinctions are irrelevant in this context because we did not have an assisted suicide statute at the time of the deaths of Ms. Wantz and Ms. Miller, the referenced discussion establishes that, in these states, participation in the overt acts causing death is chargeable as murder. Thus, the cases cited do not support the lead opinion's conclusion that if the defendant did not participate "in *the* act that . . . directly cause[s] death," (emphasis added) he cannot be bound over on a charge of murder.[7] Sexson did not pull the trigger, he held up the gun, and Cleaves did not strangle the decedent, he assisted the decedent in completing the act. Likewise, defendant Kevorkian did not pull the trigger for Ms. Miller, but he assisted Ms. Miller in completing the act. In Ms. Wantz' case, his involvement was even more direct. Defendant inserted the needle and Ms. Wantz sedated herself. When her hand dropped involuntarily, the trigger was pulled and the needle inserted by defendant was activated carrying potassium chloride in sufficient quantities to cause death.

III

Finally, the lead opinion finds that one who has only participated in a suicide but has not done the final act causing death may be prosecuted under the saving clause. The statute is applicable only when two conditions obtain: the conduct is not otherwise punishable by statute and the conduct was indictable at common law. If suicide is not criminal, the lead opinion has attempted by judicial fiat to create a new crime of assisting suicide. Culpability for persons assisting in suicide at common law was based on participation as parties to the crime of suicide. The saving clause furnishes no basis for the Court's creation of a new crime. The usurpation of legislative authority in the lead opinion's approach is evident if one considers the reach of its rationale. The lead opinion suggests an ability to exclude certain factual settings from the reach of the homicide statutes and then, as it were, find

---

7. The lead opinion is willing to recognize that one who negligently furnishes the means by which another commits suicide could be found guilty of manslaughter. Thus, one who is only criminally careless and does not participate at all may be found guilty of a fifteen-year felony, while one who is present and participates in the events leading up to the act that directly caused death with the intent to cause death can only be charged with assisted suicide, punishable by a maximum penalty of five years. Moreover, since an act of suicide is innocent, it would follow that one who attempts and fails but kills others in the process may not be charged with any offense.

legislative authorization of a free-standing authority to recognize newly evolving crimes punishable under the saving clause. If such conduct were permissible, the Court could simply reorder the punishment for any felony by concluding that conduct falls outside a given statute but within the saving clause. Contrary to the lead opinion's conclusion, the saving clause is not a delegation of legislative authority to this Court to create new crimes. The Legislature intended to save only what had not otherwise been covered in 1846.

RILEY, J., concurs.

LEVIN, Justice (concurring in part and dissenting in part).

I agree with the lead opinion that the common-law offense of murder should be redefined to preclude conviction for murder on evidence that the accused was merely involved in the events leading up to the death, such as providing the means, and that in such a case the proper charge is assisted suicide under the saving clause of the Penal Code providing that it is a five-year felony to commit a common-law offense for which no provision is made by statute.

IV

Dr. Kevorkian is not a murderer. The evidence in the instant *Kevorkian* cases, in contrast with the record in *Roberts*, which depended substantially on the possibly self-serving testimony of the defendant, who had pleaded guilty, establishes that Dr. Kevorkian did no more than provide the physical means by which the decedents took their own lives. That evidence establishes no more than criminal assistance of suicide or a common-law assisted suicide offense for which no provision is made by statute.

I agree with the lead opinion that *Roberts* should be overruled insofar as it can be read as holding that a person who does no more than assist another in committing suicide has acted with the requisite malice to establish that element of the crime of murder.[8]

Because the evidence adduced in the murder prosecutions showed no more than criminal assistance to suicide or such a common-law assisted suicide offense, I see no need for a remand to determine whether Dr. Kevorkian should be bound over on a charge of murder. I join in part VI of the lead opinion to join in overruling *Roberts* to the extent that it can be read to support the view that the common-law definition of murder encompasses intentionally providing the means by which a person commits suicide.

Questions and Notes

1. Should Kevorkian have been found guilty of murder for either of the two deaths? Why? Why not?

---

8. A person who purposely causes another to commit suicide by force, duress or deception may be prosecuted for murder. *See* ALA, Model Penal Code, §210.5(1), pp. 91ff.

2. Should Kevorkian have been acquitted in either of the two cases? Is it relevant that at the time of those deaths, Michigan had not yet enacted an assisted suicide law?

3. Should *Roberts* have been overruled? Why? Why not?

4. How would you have resolved the *Campbell* case (footnote 64)?

5. Why were Cleaves and Sexson guilty of murder? How was Kevorkian different?

See NUTSHELL § 2.05.

Problem

Joseph G., a minor, was charged in a juvenile court petition to declare him a ward of the court with murder and aiding and abetting a suicide. At the contested adjudication hearing, the court sustained the petition as to the murder count but dismissed the aiding and abetting charge as inapplicable; the court further found that the murder was in the first degree.

The minor and his friend, Jeff W., both 16 years old, drove to the Fillmore library one evening and joined a number of their friends who had congregated there. During the course of the two hours they spent at the library talking, mention was made of a car turnout on a curve overlooking a 300- to 350-foot precipice on a country road known as "the cliff." Both the minor and Jeff declared that they intended to "fly off the cliff" and that they meant to kill themselves. The others were skeptical, but the minor affirmed their seriousness, stating "You don't believe us that we are going to do it. We are going to do it. You can read it in the paper tomorrow." The minor gave one of the girls his baseball hat, saying firmly that this was the last time he would see her. Jeff repeatedly encouraged the minor by urging, "let's go, let's go" whenever the minor spoke. One other youth attempted to get in the car with Jeff and the minor, but they refused to allow him to join them "because we don't want to be responsible for you." Jeff and the minor shook hands with their friends and departed.

The pair then drove to a gas station and put air in a front tire of the car, which had been damaged earlier in the evening; the fender and passenger door were dented, and the tire was very low in air pressure, nearly flat. Two of their fellow students, Keith C. and Craig B., drove up and spoke with Jeff and the minor. The minor said, "Shake my hand and stay cool." Jeff urged, "Let's go," shook their hands and said, "Remember you shook my hand." The minor then drove off in the direction of the cliff with Jeff in the passenger seat; Keith and Craig surreptitiously followed them out of curiosity. The minor and Jeff proceeded up the hill past the cliff, turned around and drove down around the curve and over the steep cliff.

Two other vehicles were parked in the turnout, from which vantage point their occupants watched the minor's car plummeting down the hill at an estimated 50 miles per hour. The car veered off the road without swerving or changing course; the witnesses heard the car accelerate and then drive straight off the cliff. No one saw brake lights flash. The impact of the crash killed Jeff and caused severe injuries to the minor, resulting in the amputation of a foot.

Investigations following the incident revealed there were no defects in the steering or brake mechanisms. There were no skid marks at the scene, but a gouge in the pavement apparently caused by the frame of a motor vehicle coming into contact with the asphalt at high speed indicated that the car had gone straight over the cliff without swerving or skidding.

A few weeks after the crash, another friend of the minor discussed the incident with him. The minor declared he had "a quart" before driving over the cliff; the friend interpreted this to mean a quart of beer. The minor told his friend that he had "no reason" to drive off the cliff, that it was "stupid" but that he "did it on purpose." Just before the car went over the cliff, the minor told Jeff, "I guess this is it [Jeff]. Take it easy." The minor maintains that, under the peculiar circumstances presented here, he can be convicted only of aiding and abetting a suicide and not of murder.

How should this case be resolved? Why? Would it matter if Joseph had been the passenger rather than the driver? For one court's solution, see *In re Joseph G.*, 667 P.2d 1176 (Cal. 1983).

D. Unintentional Killings

To begin this section, one might question why unintentional killings should be criminal at all. Indeed, where a careful individual accidentally kills another, a successful homicidal prosecution would be extremely rare. On the other hand, because the harm of death is so great, governments are unwilling to overlook liability for people whose culpable and dangerous behavior has unnecessarily caused innocent people to die.

Several factors differentiate unintentional killings from one another. Among these are: (1) the extent of the defendant's awareness of the homicidal risk he has created, (2) the magnitude of the risk, (3) the number of people subjected to the risk, and (4) the reasons for taking the risk. Factors (1) and (2) are especially important in involuntary manslaughter cases — that is, criminal, but unintentional, killings without malice aforethought.

The first issue that we shall explore is whether a criminal defendant must be aware of the risk that he is creating, and if so, how aware must he be, and why. Think about that as you read the *Goodman* and *Welansky* cases.

Goodman v. State

190 S.W.3d 823 (Tex. App.-Fort Worth 2006)

ANNE GARDNER, Justice.

I. Introduction

A jury convicted Appellant Louis Earl Goodman of manslaughter and assessed his punishment at eighteen years' confinement. Appellant contends: the trial court erred by failing to submit the lesser included offense of criminally negligent homicide to the jury; and the evidence is insufficient to support his conviction. We affirm.

II. Background

On November 25, 2003, Appellant, Ted Garland, Henry Quinten Clay, and Shawn Davis were working the evening shift on a gas drilling rig in Denton County, Texas. Appellant, as the driller, was in charge of the crew that evening. At about 8:00 p.m., Clay went into the top doghouse 1 where Appellant, Garland, and Davis were sitting around and talking. At some point, the conversation turned to initiating Davis since he was a new member of the crew. Several initiation techniques were mentioned, including hoisting Davis up with either the "cat line" or the "boom line." A "cat line" consists of a rope, a cable, and a chain with a hook on it. One end of the rope is wrapped around the cathead for traction, and the other end of the rope is attached to the cable that runs through a shiv on the derrick. The cable is then attached to the chain, which is wrapped around whatever needs to be lifted. Generally, a cat line is used to pick up pipe and put it in the "mousehole" on the rig floor.

The "top doghouse" is an upstairs building where the drillers change their clothes and take care of necessary paperwork. Appellant, Clay, and J.C. "Bud" Wells, a long-time drilling contractor, all testified that initiating new crew members is common on drilling rigs. Davis had worked with the crew for approximately one week.

After Clay had gone downstairs, Appellant and Garland suggested to Davis that they put a derrick belt on him. A derrick belt is a belt or harness that a crew member wears to help him climb the derrick. In the front of the belt are two "D-rings," or pieces of metal woven into the belt, where a chain attaches. Davis replied that he did not want to put a belt on and that they would have to put it on him. The three men wrestled, and Appellant and Garland succeeded in putting the belt on Davis. Appellant then retrieved the cat line.

Clay was making his way back up the stairs when he saw Appellant walking into the top doghouse with the chain end of the cat line. Clay testified that he began shaking his head because he thought that "wasn't very smart." He stated that the kelly, the device located on the rig floor that is used to drill into the ground and rotates at seventy rounds per minute, was turning and, based on his experience, he knew that any slack in the cat line could get caught on the kelly as it turned. Clay saw the end of the cat line going up the backside of the derrick, indicating that it either had slack in it and the weight of the chain on the cable was pulling it up or that it had gotten caught in something. Clay then saw that the chain part of the cat line was tight and was being pulled in reverse out of the top doghouse; therefore, he knew that the cat line was wrapping around the kelly.

Meanwhile, inside of the top doghouse, Appellant hooked the cat line onto the belt Davis was wearing and said, "I got you." Without taking his hand off the cat line, Appellant immediately tried to unhook it. However, Appellant stated that he felt something start to pull the cat line, and he was unable to unhook the cat line as it pulled Davis out of the door of the top doghouse.

Clay saw Davis being dragged, face first, out of the building. Clay testified that Davis hit the bottom half of the doghouse door, taking it off the hinges. Davis was then dragged to the kelly bushing where he was spun around approximately ten to twenty times as his body hit several different pieces of equipment and surfaces. Clay testified that Davis was getting beaten to death; therefore, he yelled for Appellant so that Appellant would shut down the equipment. Appellant shut down the rotary table, and Clay "kicked the pumps out" to stop the rotary table from spinning backwards.

Appellant, Garland, and Clay checked on Davis. Appellant tried to use the company rig phone to call 911, but the phone would not work. Clay went to his truck, called 911 on his cell phone, and drove to a convenience store to meet the ambulance. While Clay was gone, Appellant removed the belt from Davis and hung it back up in the top doghouse. Clay returned to the rig with the ambulance. The paramedics checked Davis for a pulse, but he was dead.

While they waited for the police officers to arrive, Appellant, Garland, and Clay talked about what had happened. Clay testified that Appellant wanted him to tell the police officers that the cat line had come loose from a pipe, that Davis was then showing the cat line to Appellant, and that Davis accidentally got too close to the kelly, causing the cat line to wrap around it. When Troy Mac Hohenberger, the fire chief for the Argyle Fire District and a paramedic, arrived on the scene, Appellant told him this story five or six times. Additionally, when Appellant spoke with Deputy David Brawner that night about how Davis had died, he told Deputy Brawner a similar story.

In Clay's written statement that he gave to the police that night, he simply wrote down what he had seen-that he had seen Davis getting wrapped up in the kelly. He testified that he did not put everything in the statement because Garland was standing right behind him when he wrote it. The following morning, however, Clay called Investigator Don Britt of the Denton County Sheriff's Office. Investigator Britt testified that based on his conversation with Clay that morning, he was no longer looking at the incident as an accident.

After obtaining the owner's permission to go back out to the drilling rig, Investigator Britt, Investigator Larry Kish, and Lieutenant Terry Kimbell returned to the scene. They collected several belts that were hanging on a hook inside the top doghouse. Investigator Britt also located both halves of the top doghouse door that had been taken off the doghouse and placed behind a shed. Investigator Britt noticed that on one of the door halves, the hinge was bent off and there was blood on it. Carolyn Van Winkle, a senior DNA analyst with the Tarrant County Medical Examiner's Office, later testified that the blood on the belt was a "positive match" to Davis's blood and that it was "highly likely" that the blood on the door was Davis's blood.

While the officers were investigating at the drilling rig, Appellant arrived for work. Investigator Britt asked Appellant to come to the sheriff's office with him so that he could interview Appellant about what happened. Appellant agreed to do so. When they first arrived at Investigator Britt's office, Appellant related the same story to Investigator Britt that he had told the law enforcement officers on the previous night. Investigator Britt told Appellant that they had reason to believe the incident happened differently than Appellant's story. Appellant then gave the following statement, which Investigator Britt typed as Appellant related the facts to him:

> All four of us was in the dog house talking about Thanksgiving: me, Quintin, Ted and Shawn. Quintin left, down onto the ground, to do some work. The three of us was sitting in there drinking coke and coffe [sic], talking.

Ted said something about initiating Shawn. He was the new hand on the crew. It is something that normally happens with the new guy. I said we were too far away from the pits. Normally we would throw someone in the pit for initiation. We said we would put the derrick belt on Shawn. Me and Ted put it on him. We wrestled around, getting it on him. We sat around for about 15–20 minutes afterward, smoking cigarettes.

I said I would just hook a chain on him. Then Ted said, "No, grab the catline." The catline is a cable that picks up pipe and puts it in the mouse hole. It was outside. I brung it through the door. I hooked it on Shawn, on the derrick belt. As I reached down to take it off, it was too late. The cat line got wrapped around the kelly. It is a bushing that is always turning. It drug both of us out the door. Shawn was pulled through the door. I run over and started kicking everything out of gear. It stopped. I rolled him over and tried to get all the cable off to see if I could help him. I tried to dial 9-1-1 but it wouldn't work. Quintin ran down and got his phone and dialed 911.

I took the belt off him, trying to help him.

Appellant admitted at trial that he lied in this statement when he said that they sat around for about fifteen to twenty minutes after putting the belt on Davis.

III. Lesser Included Offense

In his first issue, Appellant contends that the trial court erred by failing to submit the lesser included offense of criminally negligent homicide to the jury. We disagree.

We use a two-pronged test to determine whether a defendant is entitled to an instruction on a lesser included offense. First, the lesser included offense must be included within the proof necessary to establish the offense charged. "An offense is a lesser included offense if . . . it differs from the offense charged only in the respect that a less culpable mental state suffices to establish its commission."

Second, some evidence must exist in the record that would permit a jury to rationally find that if Appellant is guilty, he is guilty only of the lesser offense. There must be some evidence from which a rational jury could acquit the defendant of the greater offense while convicting him of the lesser included offense. The court may not consider whether the evidence is credible, controverted, or in conflict with other evidence. If there is evidence from any source that negates or refutes the element establishing the greater offense, or if the evidence is so weak that it is subject to more than one reasonable inference regarding the aggravating element, the jury should be charged on the lesser included offense. The State does not challenge Appellant's contention that criminally negligent homicide is a lesser included offense of manslaughter. The issue here is whether there is some evidence in the record that would permit a jury to rationally find that if Appellant is guilty, he is guilty only of the lesser included offense of criminally negligent homicide.

A person commits manslaughter if he recklessly causes the death of another.

[a] person acts recklessly, or is reckless, with respect to circumstances surrounding his conduct or the result of his conduct when he is aware of but consciously disregards a substantial and unjustifiable risk that the circumstances exist or the result will occur. The risk must be of such a nature and degree that its disregard constitutes a gross deviation from the standard of care that an ordinary person would exercise under all the circumstances as viewed from the actor's standpoint.

A person commits criminally negligent homicide if he causes the death of another by criminal negligence.

[a] person acts with criminal negligence, or is criminally negligent, with respect to circumstances surrounding his conduct or the result of his conduct when he ought to be aware of a substantial and unjustifiable risk that the circumstances exist or the result will occur. The risk must be of such a nature and degree that the failure to perceive it constitutes a gross deviation from the standard of care that an ordinary person would exercise under all the circumstances as viewed from the actor's standpoint.

The difference between criminally negligent homicide and manslaughter is the culpable mental state. The offense of manslaughter "involves conscious risk creation, that is, the actor is aware of the risk surrounding his conduct or the results thereof, but consciously disregards it." On the other hand, the offense of criminally negligent homicide "involves inattentive risk creation, that is, the wactor ought to be aware of the risk surrounding his conduct or the results thereof [but fails] to perceive the risk." Therefore, before a charge on criminally negligent homicide is required, the record must contain evidence showing an unawareness of the risk.

Here, Appellant supports his contention that he acted with criminal negligence by pointing us to evidence showing that he was unaware that the cat line had tangled when he hooked it to Davis. The dissent likewise focuses on this evidence. However, even accepting that fact as true, it does not raise an issue of unawareness of the *risk*.

We cannot ignore that Appellant testified that he was the supervisor of the crew of four men that evening and had worked on drilling rigs for approximately twenty-five years. Appellant stated that he began working in the oil field as soon as he was old enough, age eighteen, and had continued to work in the oil field ever since. Through those years, he had worked as a roustabout, a floor hand, a derrick hand, and a chain hand while working his way up to the position of driller.

Furthermore, during cross-examination, Appellant testified as follows:

Q. In fact, people have gotten hurt on drilling rigs, haven't they?

A. Yes, sir.

Q. I mean, people have gotten seriously injured, haven't they?

A. Yes, sir.

Q. And some of those injuries that you're aware of have involved cat lines, right?

A. A couple of them.

Q. So-and you were aware of that. You knew about that prior to Shawn being killed didn't you?

A. Yes, sir.

Q. So you knew that cat lines were risky business.

A. Yes, sir.

Q. You knew that they were dangerous enough that someone could get seriously hurt.

A. At-yes, sir.

Q. I mean, isn't it even possible-I mean, in your mind, someone could get killed with a cat line. You knew that, right?

A. Yes, sir.

Q. I mean, cat lines, catheads, they sometimes get, I think the phrase is, fouled up, right?

A. If you wrap the rope around, yes, sir, it can get fouled up.

Q. And you knew that?

A. Yes, sir. But the rope never did touch it.

Q. But getting fouled up, was that a possibility?

A. Not at that time.

Q. It wasn't a possibility?

A. Not at that time.

Q. You'd seen cat lines get fouled up in the past, hadn't you?

A. Yes, sir.

Q. In fact, there had been a prior incident on that particular rig, hadn't there?

A. Yes, sir.

Q. Where the cat line had gotten tangled up while it was attached to a pipe that was suspended in the air.

A. Yes, sir.

Q. And that situation was a situation that you were well aware of going into the night that you hooked Shawn up to that cat line.

A. That was the night that-the cat line got fouled up was when the guy was picking it up with the rope around the head.

Q. And so you knew about that.

A. Yes, sir.

Q. Before you put the cat line onto Shawn.

A. Yes, sir.

Appellant also testified that he still had his hand on the cable after he had hooked it to Davis's belt because he *knew* that it was not something he should have done. This testimony is evidence that Appellant himself was aware of a risk of death involving a cat line.

Appellant's contention that he was entitled to a charge on the lesser-included offense of criminally negligent homicide because he was unaware that the cat line had tangled in this particular instance is misplaced. The State did not bear the burden to prove that Appellant knew the rope was actually tangling, just that Appellant was aware of the *risk*. In fact, as the State points out, if Appellant had known that the cat line was tangling as he attached it to Davis, Appellant would more likely have been charged with murder for his actions than with manslaughter.

We find no evidence in the record that would permit a jury to rationally find that Appellant is guilty only of the lesser included offense of criminally negligent homicide. We hold that Appellant was not entitled to an instruction on the lesser included offense of criminally negligent homicide and that the trial court did not err in refusing to grant his requested charge. We overrule Appellant's first issue.

Sue Walker, Justice, dissenting.

I respectfully dissent. Because some evidence exists in the record that would permit a jury to rationally find that if Appellant was guilty, he is guilty only of criminally negligent homicide, I would hold that the trial court erred by refusing to submit this lesser included offense to the jury. Accordingly, I would reverse the trial court's judgment, and remand this case for a new trial.

I agree with the majority's recitation of the law concerning the two-pronged test we apply to determine whether a defendant is entitled to an instruction on a lesser included offense and with the majority's holding that criminally negligent homicide is a lesser included offense of manslaughter. I also agree with the majority's explanation of the legal distinction between criminally negligent homicide and manslaughter, the culpable mental state required. I cannot agree, however, with the majority that no evidence exists in the record that would permit a jury to rationally find that if Appellant is guilty, he is guilty only of the lesser offense.

The record contains the following testimony, in addition to the testimony recited by the majority. Drilling rigs are inherently dangerous. They are dangerous even when everyone is doing exactly what they are supposed to be doing. The State's expert, Mr. J.C. Bud Wells, testified that he had over forty-five years of experience in the drilling industry in various capacities. When asked whether it was common or uncommon for the cat line to get "fouled up," Mr. Wells testified that "it is not an everyday occurrence" and that in his forty-five years of experience working rigs, he has known about a half-dozen people who have been injured by the cat line.

Mr. Wells testified that initiations and horseplay are common on rigs and that the participants are "not intending to hurt anybody." Mr. Wells was asked what types of things would occur if a "new guy" was being initiated. He responded, "Well, there's a number of things: You know, taking a dope brush and doping them up; blindfolding them, letting them take a sledgehammer to hit an X and stick their hard hat under it where they hit their hardhat with a sledgehammer; letting them walk a plank on the pit or something and move the plank out of the way and let them fall in the pit."

Mr. Wells described "doping" as taking the worker's "britches down and dope them between their legs with pipe dope." Appellant likewise testified that it was common practice for new work hands to be initiated on a rig. Appellant had initiated new workers by "greasing their boots," "throwing them in the pits," and "putting them on the cat line." In fact, these initiations and "pranks" had likewise been done to Appellant "many times" during his twenty-five years of working on rigs, and he was never injured, except for minor "bumps and bruises." Appellant also testified that he had been "picked up a bunch of times" by the cat line "to work on things" on the rig.

Concerning the incident at issue, Appellant testified that he never took his hand off of the cat line; he hooked it on the derrick belt and attempted to immediately unhook it. Additionally, Appellant who was in the top doghouse did not have the same vantage point as Clay who was on his way up the stairs to the doghouse when Clay saw that the cat line was wrapping around the kelly.

Finally, Appellant possessed only a sixth-grade education. He cannot read or write, except to mark his name.

Keeping in mind that this court cannot consider whether the above evidence is credible, controverted, or in conflict with other evidence, the evidence recited above refutes the intent element required for the offense of manslaughter, that is recklessness. A person acts recklessly with respect to circumstances surrounding his conduct when he is aware of but consciously disregards a substantial and unjustifiable risk that the circumstances exist or the result will occur. The risk must be of such a nature and degree that its disregard constitutes a gross deviation from the standard of care that an ordinary person would exercise under all the circumstances *as viewed from the actor's standpoint.*

Testimony exists that Appellant himself had been hoisted on the cat line "a bunch of times" with only minor bumps and bruises, thus showing that from Appellant's standpoint, the risk of hooking the cat line to Shawn for a couple of seconds did not constitute a substantial and unjustifiable risk that was a gross deviation from the standard of care that an ordinary rig worker would exercise. Likewise, Mr. Wells's testimony-that in forty-five years he was aware of approximately six injuries from the cat line-is evidence that Appellant's perceived risk from hooking the cat line to Shawn's derrick belt for a few seconds was not so substantial and unjustifiable that its disregard would constitute a gross deviation from the standard of care that an ordinary rig worker would exercise. The admittedly pervasive practice on rigs of horseplay and of initiating new workers with physical pranks also refutes the requirement for "recklessness" that viewed from Appellant's standpoint, by performing the initiation prank here, he consciously disregarded a substantial and unjustifiable risk of Shawn's death. The sheer frequency of these "pranks" lessens risk perception from Appellant's standpoint. Moreover, the evidence showed that on the day in question, Appellant was not aware that while he was in the top doghouse the cat line was wrapping around the kelly. Finally, Appellant possessed a sixth-grade education, had no training beyond sixth grade, and had worked on rigs since he was eighteen. Appellant was steeped in the life and culture of working on a rig that was dangerous even when everyone was doing his job. Viewed from Appellant's standpoint, not the standpoint of the judges on this court, the above constitutes some evidence that by hooking the cat line to Shawn's derrick belt, Appellant did not consciously disregard a substantial and unjustifiable risk, but instead only should have been aware of the risk surrounding his conduct but failed to perceive it.

In my view, the majority focuses on evidence of Appellant's knowledge of the dangerousness of cat lines in general, instead of determining whether evidence exists that Appellant was not, but should have been, aware of the risk of his conduct, viewed from his standpoint, in clipping the cat line on Shawn's derrick belt for a few seconds. I cannot agree that Appellant's general knowledge that cat lines are dangerous equates to a specific knowledge by Appellant that by performing the initiation act of clipping the cat line to Shawn's derrick belt for a few seconds he was consciously disregarding a substantial and unjustifiable risk that the cat line was or would become "fouled up" or that Shawn would be injured or killed.

For the reasons set forth above, I dissent.

Questions and Notes

1. Given that Goodman's conduct was just as dangerous and caused the same harm whether or not he perceived the risk involved, why should his perception of the risk, or lack thereof, matter?

2. Conversely, if Goodman didn't perceive the risk, why should he be punished at all?

3. Suppose that Goodman fully perceived the risk, took it anyway, but Davis was not injured (apparently the usual result of similar horseplay)? Should he be punished at all? Why? The MPC has a statute punishing reckless endangerment (§ 211.2, Appendix A), but some states do not.

4. How could the defendant *not* have been aware of the risk?

5. How much of the risk must the defendant perceive in order to be reckless? Is he reckless if he perceived any risk at all, only if he perceived the risk accurately, or something else? If something else, what would that be?

6. What is the core of the difference between the majority and the dissent?

7. With which opinion (if either) do you agree? Why? Is (should it be) relevant that Goodman was sentenced to 18 years in prison as a penalty?

8. Texas, adopting the MPC standard (*see* MPC § 211.2, Appendix A), defines one who knowingly runs a risk as reckless, and one who should be, but is not, aware of a risk as negligent. As you read *Welansky*, consider whether Massachusetts employs the same definitions. If not, how do they differ?

Commonwealth v. Welansky
55 N.E.2d 902 (Mass. 1944)

[The defendant, Barnett Welansky, owned and operated a night club called the Cocoanut Grove in Boston. One night while Welansky was in the hospital recovering from an illness, a fire raged out of control at the night club. Several people were killed, allegedly because Welansky provided inadequate exits in the event of fire. On that basis he was charged with involuntary manslaughter.]

LUMMUS, Justice.

The Commonwealth disclaimed any contention that the defendant intentionally killed or injured the persons named in the indictments as victims. It based its case on involuntary manslaughter through wanton or reckless conduct. The judge instructed the jury correctly with respect to the nature of such conduct.

Usually wanton or reckless conduct consists of an affirmative act, like driving an automobile or discharging a firearm, in disregard of probable harmful consequences to another. But where as in the present case there is a duty of care for the safety of business visitors invited to premises which the defendant controls, wanton or reckless conduct may consist of intentional failure to take such care in disregard of the probable harmful consequences to them or of their right to care.

To define wanton or reckless conduct so as to distinguish it clearly from negligence and gross negligence is not easy. Sometimes the word "willful" is prefaced to the words "wanton" and "reckless" in expressing the concept. That only blurs it. Willful means intentional. In the phrase "willful, wanton or reckless conduct," if "willful" modifies "conduct" it introduces something different from wanton or reckless conduct, even though the legal result is the same. Willfully causing harm is a wrong, but a different wrong from wantonly or recklessly causing harm. If "willful" modifies "wanton or reckless conduct" its use is accurate. What must be intended is the conduct, not the resulting harm. The words "wanton" and "reckless" are practically synonymous in this connection, although the word "wanton" may contain a suggestion of arrogance or insolence or heartlessness that is lacking in the word "reckless." But intentional conduct to which either word applies is followed by the same legal consequences as though both words applied.

The standard of wanton or reckless conduct is at once subjective and objective. Knowing facts that would cause a reasonable man to know the danger is equivalent to knowing the danger. The judge charged the jury correctly when he said,

To constitute wanton or reckless conduct, as distinguished from mere negligence, grave danger to others must have been apparent and the defendant
must have chosen to run the risk rather than alter his conduct so as to
avoid the act or omission which caused the harm. If the grave danger was
in fact realized by the defendant, his subsequent voluntary act or omission
which caused the harm amounts to wanton or reckless conduct, no matter
whether the ordinary man would have realized the gravity of the danger or
not. But even if a particular defendant is so stupid [or] so heedless . . . that
in fact he did not realize the grave danger, he cannot escape the imputation
of wanton or reckless conduct in his dangerous act or omission, if an ordinary normal man under the same circumstances would have realized the
gravity of the danger. A man may be reckless within the meaning of the law
although he himself thought he was careful.

The essence of wanton or reckless conduct is intentional conduct, by way either
of commission or of omission where there is a duty to act, which conduct involves
a high degree of likelihood that substantial harm will result to another. Wanton or
reckless conduct amounts to what has been variously described as indifference to or
disregard of probable consequences to that other.

The words "wanton" and "reckless" are thus not merely rhetorical or vituperative
expressions used instead of negligent or grossly negligent. They express a difference
in the degree of risk and in the voluntary taking of risk so marked, as compared with
negligence, as to amount substantially and in the eyes of the law to a difference in kind.

Notwithstanding language used commonly in earlier cases, and occasionally in
later ones, it is now clear in this Commonwealth that at common law conduct does
not become criminal until it passes the borders of negligence and gross negligence
and enters into the domain of wanton or reckless conduct. There is in Massachusetts at common law no such thing as "criminal negligence." "Wanton or reckless
conduct is the legal equivalent of intentional conduct."

To convict the defendant of manslaughter, the Commonwealth was not required
to prove that he caused the fire by some wanton or reckless conduct. Fire in a place
of public resort is an ever present danger. It was enough to prove that death resulted
from his wanton or reckless disregard of the safety of patrons in the event of fire
from any cause.

Judgments Affirmed.

Questions and Notes

1. The prevailing use of the word "reckless," in line with the MPC, includes subjective awareness of the risk. Some courts, however, use it to describe gross negligence—that is, an extremely unjustified failure to appreciate the risk. Which
definition did Massachusetts adopt in *Welansky*?

2. In assessing Question 1, how do you square the approved jury instruction ("A
man may be reckless within the law although he himself thought he was careful.")

with the court's unequivocal declaration ("There is in Massachusetts at common law no such thing as 'criminal negligence.'")?

3. If "the words 'wanton' and 'reckless' are not merely rhetorical or vituperative expressions used instead of negligently or grossly negligently," what are they?

4. If Goodman had been tried under the *Welansky* standard, do you think that he would have been convicted of manslaughter? Why?

5. As you read *Conrad*, think about whether it adopts the same standard as *Welansky*, or a different standard.

Conrad v. Commonwealth
521 S.E.2d 321 (Va. App. 1999)

FITZPATRICK, Chief Judge.

Christopher Scott Conrad (appellant) appealed the trial court's conviction for involuntary manslaughter. Appellant argued that the evidence was insufficient to prove he acted in a criminally negligent manner. A panel of this Court agreed and reversed his conviction. We granted the Commonwealth's request for rehearing en banc, and upon rehearing, we affirm appellant's conviction.

I.

Under familiar principles of appellate review, we examine the evidence in the light most favorable to the Commonwealth, the prevailing party below, granting to it all reasonable inferences fairly deducible therefrom. So viewed, the evidence established that on May 11, 1997, at about 9:00 a.m., on Gayton Road in Henrico County, appellant fell asleep at the wheel of his automobile and drove off the road, striking and killing Judy Dahlkemper, who was jogging on the side of the road. Officer R.J. Smith (Smith) responded to the scene. Shortly after 11:00 a.m., after examining the physical evidence, Smith took appellant's statement. Smith described appellant as "extremely tired" with bloodshot eyes and a faint odor of alcohol about his person.

Appellant told Smith that he had last slept on May 10, the day before the accident, arising at 11:00 a.m. after six hours of sleep. It was not unusual for appellant to stay up for long periods of time because he had been working an irregular schedule at a retail store and playing in a band. On May 10, appellant worked a shift at the retail store, ran errands, practiced with his band and went to the home of a friend in Richmond. While at his friend's home, between about 11:00 p.m. and 1:30 a.m., appellant consumed about fifty ounces of beer.1 He remained at his friend's home, awake and watching television, until about 8:45 a.m. on May 11, at which time he left to drive home. Appellant testified that he was not sleepy before he left for home and that it had not occurred to him that he might fall asleep on the drive home.

When Officer Smith first asked appellant whether he had consumed any alcohol, appellant said he had not. However, when Smith asked appellant for consent to test his blood for alcohol, appellant admitted his alcohol consumption. A blood test performed "a little after noon" on May 11 was negative for drugs or alcohol. During argument, the trial court commented, "[T]here's no evidence that his drinking ... was the cause of [the accident]," and the court made no mention of appellant's drinking in finding him guilty.

Appellant traveled about twenty minutes on Interstate 64 to Gaskins Road. As appellant exited Interstate 64, "he really got tired and felt himself going to sleep." Because he was only about five minutes or four-and-one-half miles from home, "he did not really want to stop." He reported to Officer Smith that "he ran off the road only after dozing off for a half second, caught himself drifting four or five times, still nodding, but said he would catch himself and said [he] would snap out of it." On Gayton Road, a little over one-half mile from his home, he fell asleep and heard a loud noise. He initially thought someone had hit his car with a bottle, but then he saw the body and stopped his vehicle.

Another driver on the road, Mary Elizabeth Harris (Harris), testified that she had been driving behind appellant, who was traveling at the forty-five mile-per-hour speed limit. Appellant traveled approximately two-tenths of a mile before Harris saw his car veer right into a turn lane and strike the jogger, Ms. Dahlkemper, who had been running, facing traffic, on the edge of the turn lane near the adjacent grass. Appellant's vehicle displayed no turn indicator and did not brake prior to impact. Officer Smith determined that Ms. Dahlkemper had been jogging eighteen inches from the edge of the pavement when she was struck, and he confirmed that appellant had not applied his brakes prior to impact.

At trial, appellant testified to substantially the same version of events that he had given to Officer Smith at the scene. Appellant stated that when he turned onto Gayton Road, he began to yawn, was "incredibly close to dozing off," and "was starting to kind of drift ... in the road." However, he "[did not] recall" telling Officer Smith that he had caught himself about to doze off on four to five occasions prior to the accident and said he believed that he told Officer Smith he had done so only one or two times. He also said he had not gone off the road prior to the accident but had "com[e] [within] about ... an inch [of] the line."

At the conclusion of the presentation of evidence by both parties, the trial court found that appellant's actions constituted a gross, wanton disregard for human life, stating the following: What I feel I have to do is look at the evidence under the law and see if ... the conduct rises to the level of reckless driving or involuntary manslaughter. And I think the situation is this:

> You've got the fact that Mr. Conrad had been up for 22 hours. He chose to drive the car some distance, ... a fairly long distance, and did okay, under the evidence, until he got off of [Interstate] 64. But I think that's where the problem comes. He got off of 64, and at that point, as described both to Officer Smith, as well as his own testimony today, ... he felt himself just about going to sleep. And to an extent, as he very well described, his car just drifted over to the right, but he was able to catch it on *four or five different occasions*, as he told Officer Smith, and that he was, in fact, *nodding in and out.*

... And under those circumstances, he's driving after he's been up for 22 hours, after he knows that he is about to fall asleep to an extent that it's affecting his operation of the motor vehicle. He chose to continue to drive for 45 miles an hour in the residential area, not that that's exceeding the speed limit, because it is not, but driving at that speed to try to get home.

And I think from the evidence that, at that time, that he was operating that motor vehicle in a state that he knew very well or should have known very well that he may, in fact, fall asleep. . . . (Emphasis added). The trial court concluded that appellant's conduct was "gross, wanton, and culpable, [and] showed a disregard for human life." Accordingly, the trial court convicted appellant of involuntary manslaughter.

II.

"[I]nvoluntary manslaughter in the operation of a motor vehicle [is defined] as an 'accidental killing which, although unintended, is the proximate result of negligence so gross, wanton, and culpable as to show a reckless disregard of human life.' '[A] higher degree of negligence in the operation of a motor vehicle is required to establish criminal liability for involuntary manslaughter than to establish liability in a civil action for ordinary or even gross negligence. This higher degree of negligence has come to be known as 'criminal negligence.'"*Keech v. Commonwealth*, 9 Va.App. 272, 277, 386 S.E.2d 813, 816 (1989).

"[Criminal negligence] must be more than mere inadvertence or misadventure. It is a recklessness or indifference incompatible with a proper regard for human life." Criminal negligence has also been defined as conduct "so gross, wanton, and culpable as to show a reckless disregard of human life," and conduct "so flagrant, culpable, and wanton as to show utter disregard of the safety of others under circumstances likely to cause injury," and conduct "so gross and culpable as to indicate a callous disregard of human life."

As we stated in *Keech*, "[t]hese various definitions make clear that the distinction between the negligence which will support a conviction of involuntary manslaughter involving the operation of a motor vehicle and the negligence that will merely support a civil action is one of degree." "The law recognizes three degrees of negligence, (1) ordinary or simple, (2) gross, and (3) willful, wanton and reckless." Ordinary negligence is "failure to use "that degree of care which an ordinarily prudent person would exercise under the same or similar circumstances to avoid injury to another." Gross negligence "is a manifestly smaller amount of watchfulness and circumspection than the circumstances require of a person of ordinary prudence. . . . It falls short of being such reckless disregard of probable consequence as is equivalent to a willful and intentional wrong." Finally, criminal or willful and wanton negligence "involves a greater degree of negligence than gross negligence, particularly in the sense that in the former an actual or constructive consciousness of the danger involved is an essential ingredient of the act or omission."

Criminal negligence as the basis for involuntary manslaughter is judged under an objective standard and, therefore, may be found to exist where the offender either knew or should have known the probable results of his acts. Thus, criminal negligence "is acting consciously in disregard of another person's rights or acting with reckless indifference to the consequences, with the defendant aware, from his knowledge of existing circumstances and conditions, that his conduct *probably* would cause injury to another." (emphasis added).

We have not addressed whether a driver who *previously* has fallen asleep while driving and who *subsequently*, during that same trip, again falls asleep causing an injury or death is guilty of involuntary manslaughter. However, our decision in *Hargrove v. Commonwealth*, 10 Va.App. 618, 394 S.E.2d 729 (1990), provides some guidance. In *Hargrove*, the defendant fell asleep while driving home after working the midnight-to-8:00-a.m. shift, striking and killing a pedestrian who was walking across the highway. The defendant made a statement at the accident scene that he was "extremely tired," he dozed off "for one second" and the accident occurred.

We noted in *Hargrove* that courts in other states have found that "when a driver falls asleep and causes death a jury issue is created on the issue of whether it constituted involuntary manslaughter." However, in reversing Hargrove's conviction for involuntary manslaughter, we concluded that the evidence failed to show that he should have known that his conduct constituted a reckless disregard for human life. We wrote:

> In this case, all the record shows about Hargrove is that he had worked the previous night and was "extremely tired" and in need of sleep. We do not know . . . that Hargrove should have known that it was not improbable that he would fall asleep during his travel from the workplace to home. . . . In this case, the record is devoid of evidence as to the distance or time it would have required Hargrove to drive from work to home. . . . The evidence does not exclude the reasonable hypothesis that, although Hargrove had worked all night, *he had not fallen asleep, had not previously dozed during the trip before the accident*, and, although tired and in need of sleep and having only a short distance or a trip of a few minutes to reach his home, he could reasonably have believed that he could negotiate his vehicle a short distance without endangering human life. (emphasis added).

Thus, we recognized in *Hargrove* that if the defendant "had been operating his vehicle for a number of hours in a tired and sleepy condition, or while in such a state undertook a trip of such a substantial distance or time that he should have known he might fall asleep, the evidence might support a finding that he was acting in reckless disregard for human life."

Our Supreme Court has recently enunciated the following principles of appellate review in a voluntary manslaughter case:

> When a defendant challenges on appeal the sufficiency of the evidence to sustain his conviction, it is the duty of an appellate court to examine the evidence that tends to support the conviction and to permit the conviction to stand unless the conviction is plainly wrong or without

evidentiary support. If there is evidence to support the conviction, an appellate court is not permitted to substitute its own judgment for that of the finder of fact, even if the appellate court might have reached a different conclusion.

Additionally, upon appellate review, the evidence and all inferences reasonably deducible therefrom must be examined in the light most favorable to the Commonwealth, the prevailing party in the trial court. Any evidence properly admitted at trial is subject to this review. *Commonwealth v. Presley*, 256 Va. 465, 466–67, 507 S.E.2d 72, 72 (1998).

Adhering to these well established principles, we conclude the evidence was sufficient to prove criminal negligence on appellant's part. Indeed, the facts of the instant case were almost presciently stated in *Hargrove*, where we noted that had the evidence in that case shown a propensity to fall asleep or nod off while driving, such evidence could support a finding that the accused was "acting in reckless disregard for human life." Here, appellant had been up for twenty-two hours without sleep and chose to drive his vehicle "a fairly long distance" to his home in the early morning. After he exited the interstate onto Gaskins Road, he "really got tired" and "felt himself going to sleep" but did not want to stop because he was only five minutes from home. Appellant told Officer Smith that "he nodded in and out, . . . he ran off the road only after dozing off for a half second, caught himself drifting four or five times, still nodding, but . . . he would catch himself and . . . he would snap out of it." The trier of fact accepted the Commonwealth's evidence that appellant had dozed off four or five times prior to the impact with the victim.

Under the circumstances of this case, we conclude that sufficient evidence supports the trial court's finding that appellant should have known that his "dozing off" four or five times affected his driving abilities and, therefore, should have known of the risks that his driving conduct created. *See Keech*, 9 Va.App. at 279, 386 S.E.2d at 817 (noting that criminal negligence is framed "in terms of *a great risk of injury* coupled with an objective awareness of that risk on the part of the offender"). We also conclude that appellant's decision to continue driving in such an impaired state was a callous act of indifference to the safety of others. Accordingly, appellant's involuntary manslaughter conviction is affirmed.

Affirmed.

ELDER, Judge, with whom BENTON, COLEMAN and ANNUNZIATA, Judges, join, dissenting.

I disagree with the majority's legal conclusion. I would hold that the evidence is insufficient, as a matter of law, to support an involuntary manslaughter conviction. I believe the evidence fails to support a finding that appellant knew or should have known that driving no more than five minutes to his home once he became sleepy was "likely to cause injury" and that his failure to stop under such circumstances was "so gross and culpable as to indicate a callous disregard of human life." Therefore, I respectfully dissent.

The Virginia Supreme Court has acknowledged that "the application of distinctions between [the various] degrees of negligence [recognized by the law] is frequently difficult to apply." Although the majority correctly sets forth the general principles of law governing the crime of involuntary manslaughter, I consider it helpful to further clarify the distinctions. Ordinary negligence is "failure to use that degree of care which an ordinarily prudent person would exercise under the same or similar circumstances to avoid injury to another." Gross negligence "is a manifestly smaller amount of watchfulness and circumspection than the circumstances require of a person of ordinary prudence." It is "that degree of negligence which shows indifference to others as constitutes an utter disregard of prudence. . . . It must be such a degree of negligence as would *shock* fair minded men although something less than willful recklessness[, i.e., criminal negligence]." (emphasis added). Finally, criminal or willful and wanton negligence is "[m]arked by or manifesting arrogant recklessness of justice, of the rights or feelings of others, . . . *merciless; inhumane.*" *Forbes v. Commonwealth*, 27 Va.App. 304, 310, 498 S.E.2d 457, 459 (1998) (citation omitted) (emphasis added).

These distinctions establish that criminal responsibility cannot be predicated upon every act carelessly performed merely because the carelessness results in the death of another. Rather, the negligence must be of such a high degree of "carelessness or recklessness" that the act of commission or "'omission must be one *likely* to cause death.'" "*Goodman v. Commonwealth*, 153 Va. 943, 948, 151 S.E. 168, 169 (1930) (emphasis added). For example, it is settled law in Virginia that "[a]nyone who falls asleep while operating an automobile on a public road is guilty of a degree of negligence exceeding lack of ordinary care." Such behavior also may be "sufficient to find the operator guilty of the offense of reckless driving." *Kennedy*, 1 Va.App. at 473, 339 S.E.2d at 907–08 (upholding reckless driving conviction where driver admitted he had been sleepy fifteen minutes before unexplained accident and evidence established that family had been on the road for eight hours and that vehicle left no skid marks or other evidence of braking prior to running off the road). However, such evidence, standing alone, proves no more than ordinary negligence or reckless driving and will not support a finding of criminal negligence required for an involuntary manslaughter conviction.

A conviction for reckless driving requires proof of driving "on a highway recklessly or at a speed or in a manner so as to endanger the life, limb, or property of any person." Violation of this statute "is insufficient to bring the negligent act within the common law definition of manslaughter unless it is so flagrant, culpable, and wanton as to show utter disregard of the safety of others under circumstances likely to cause injury." *King*, 217 Va. at 605–06, 231 S.E.2d at 316. *King* clearly distinguishes between acts which constitute reckless driving and acts of recklessness which constitute involuntary manslaughter.

Some states provide by statute that certain acts proximately causing death are crimes. Virginia's legislature has enacted such a statute, providing that an unintentional death which results from an act of driving under the influence in violation of specified portions of Code § 18.2-266 constitutes involuntary manslaughter. *See* Code § 18.2-36.1. Such a conviction requires no proof that "the conduct of the defendant was so gross, wanton and culpable as to show a reckless disregard for human life," and if the Commonwealth makes such a showing, the defendant is subject to greater punishment for "aggravated involuntary manslaughter." The legislature, however, has not provided that death resulting from falling asleep while driving constitutes involuntary manslaughter as a matter of law.

To make such a finding, a court must conclude that the act of negligence proximately causing the death would do *more* than "shock fair minded men," the language of the standard for gross negligence. Instead, it must be negligence "so flagrant, culpable, and wanton as to show utter disregard of the safety of others under circumstances *likely* to cause injury." *King*, 217 Va. at 605–06, 231 S.E.2d at 316 (emphasis added). As quoted above, we have previously characterized criminal negligence as "manifesting [an] arrogant recklessness of justice" and rising to the level of being "*merciless*" or "*inhumane*." *Forbes*, 27 Va.App. at 310, 498 S.E.2d at 459 (citation omitted) (emphasis added). In assessing the degree of negligence involved, a court must consider all "existing circumstances and conditions."

I do not believe the evidence supports a finding that appellant acted mercilessly or inhumanely when he concluded, albeit incorrectly, that he could safely complete his trip to his home, which was only four-and-one-half miles away when he first became sleepy. In affirming appellant's conviction, the majority relies in part on this Court's decision in *Hargrove v. Commonwealth*. It observes that the facts of appellant's case "were almost presciently stated in *Hargrove*, where we noted that had the evidence . . . shown a propensity to fall asleep or nod off while driving, such evidence could support a finding that the accused was "acting in reckless disregard for human life." In reversing the involuntary manslaughter conviction in *Hargrove*, we held:

> [T]he evidence does not exclude the reasonable hypothesis that, although Hargrove had worked all night, he had not fallen asleep, had not previously dozed during the trip before the accident, and, although tired and in need of sleep and having only a short distance or a trip of a few minutes to reach his home, he could reasonably have believed that he could negotiate his vehicle a short distance without endangering human life.

I believe the majority erroneously utilizes *Hargrove* to support its holding. First, we did not hold in *Hargrove* that a driver's "[having] previously dozed during the trip before the accident" mandated a finding, or even was sufficient to support a finding, that the driver was on notice that he would fall asleep again, causing injury to another, before reaching his destination. Even if we purported to make such a finding in *Hargrove*, it would have been dicta, for no evidence indicated that Hargrove, in fact, had previously fallen asleep during his travel from work to home. The facts in *Hargrove* proved only that Hargrove knew he was sleepy before leaving for home, which we found insufficient to prove the criminal negligence necessary to support an involuntary manslaughter conviction.

Second, *Hargrove* erroneously attempted to distinguish the events in *Hargrove* from those in *Kennedy v. Commonwealth*, 1 Va.App. 469, 339 S.E.2d 905 (1986). *See Hargrove*, 10 Va.App. at 621–22, 394 S.E.2d at 731–32. In *Kennedy*, we affirmed a conviction for reckless driving upon evidence establishing that Kennedy knew he was tired and subsequently fell asleep at the wheel, running off the road. However, no death resulted from Kennedy's reckless driving, and we had no occasion to consider whether Kennedy's acts amounted to criminal negligence. *See King*, (holding that reckless driving conviction does not require proof of criminal negligence). Therefore, *Hargrove's* attempt to distinguish *Kennedy* also is dicta and does not control the outcome of this case.

Third, the language in *Hargrove* necessary to the decision in that case does not support the result the majority reaches. Had appellant fallen asleep and struck the jogger immediately after exiting Interstate 64 onto Gaskins Road before becoming tired, he would have been no more culpable than Hargrove and perhaps even less so. Hargrove *knew* he was tired before he dozed off and struck the pedestrian, and the record did not establish how far he had to drive. Appellant, however, was not tired until he reached a point only five minutes from home. Therefore, when appellant exited Interstate 64, "he could reasonably have believed that he could negotiate his vehicle a short distance without endangering human life." Of course, the evidence establishes that, after appellant exited the interstate, he became sleepy and felt himself "[run] off the road . . . after dozing off for [only] a half second." However, to conclude that appellant acted mercilessly or inhumanely in failing to pull over the instant he felt himself doze would be to ignore other "existing circumstances and conditions" in the case. Those other circumstances indicate that appellant, who was *less* than five minutes from home at that point, "caught himself drifting four or five times" but was able to "catch himself and . . . snap out of it" on each occasion. Thereafter, for about two-tenths of a mile before leaving the road and striking the jogger, appellant maintained the speed limit and engaged in no weaving or other erratic driving.

Although appellant testified he was not sleepy before he left his friend's home, the trial court was entitled to disbelieve and reject appellant's testimony. However, rejecting that explanation did not provide affirmative evidence that appellant was, in fact, sleepy before he left his friend's home. Therefore, the evidence, viewed in the light most favorable to the Commonwealth, did not exclude the reasonable hypothesis that appellant became sleepy, as he told Officer Smith, only after leaving Interstate 64, when he was only five minutes from home. Under all these circumstances, I cannot conclude that appellant knew or should have known that his conduct in proceeding the short distance to his home "likely would cause injury to another" or that he acted mercilessly or inhumanely in failing to stop. That his conduct did, in fact, result in death is tragic and may constitute ordinary or even gross negligence, but it does not, without more, support a finding of criminal negligence.

For these reasons, I would reverse appellant's conviction.

Questions and Notes

1. Is criminal negligence as defined by Virginia an easier standard for the State than recklessness as defined in *Goodman*, the same standard, or a harder standard? How does it compare to the *Welansky* standard?

2. Do terms like "callous disregard of life" (majority) or "merciless or inhumane" (dissent) overstate what ought to be the standard? Does it depend on how severely involuntary manslaughter is punished?

3. Given the standard, would you agree with the majority or dissent? Why?

4. Does *Porter* reflect a different standard? If so, is it better or worse?

Porter v. State

88 So. 2d 924 (Fla. 1956)

ROBERTS, Justice.

Appellant was convicted of manslaughter for causing the death of a human being by culpable negligence in the operation of his automobile, and has appealed from the judgment of conviction. The point for determination on this appeal is the sufficiency of the evidence to support the conviction.

The accident resulting in the death of the decedent occurred at 9:30 a.m. on a Saturday morning at a street intersection on the outskirts of the city of Bradenton, but apparently outside the city limits. The appellant was proceeding north on a street which was well marked with 'stop' signs prior to its intersection with the street upon which the decedent was travelling in a westerly direction, and which was marked only with a "slow" sign. The right front of appellant's car collided with the left front and side of the decedent's car. There was ample evidence from which the jury could find that the appellant was driving at the rate of 60 or 65 miles per hour and did not stop before entering the intersection.

"Culpable negligence," within the meaning of our manslaughter statute, Section 782.07, Fla. Stat.1953, F.S.A., means negligence of "a gross and flagrant character, evincing reckless disregard of human life or of the safety of persons exposed to its dangerous effects; or that entire want of care which would raise the presumption of indifference to consequences; or such wantonness or recklessness or grossly careless disregard of the safety and welfare of the public, or that reckless indifference to the rights of others, which is equivalent to an intentional violation of them."

While excessive speed alone is not sufficient to support a conviction of manslaughter by culpable negligence, *Maxey v. State*, Fla., 64 So. 677; *Smith v. State*, Fla., 65 So. 303, we think that appellant's action in "running" a stop sign at a high rate of speed was, in the circumstances shown by this record, negligence of a "gross and flagrant character" within the definition of culpable negligence, quoted above.

Accordingly, the verdict and judgment of guilty of manslaughter should be and it is hereby.

Affirmed.

Terrell, Thomas and O'Connell, J.J., concur.

Drew, C.J., and Hobson and Thornal, J.J., dissent.

Drew, Chief Justice (dissenting).

I cannot agree that the evidence in this cause sustains the verdict of manslaughter.

The accident occurred outside the city limits on a county road in the daylight. There is no evidence in the record establishing the speed limit in this area so we must presume that it was sixty miles per hour. The evidence in the light most favorable to the State establishes the speed of the car at about sixty miles per hour. The driver was perfectly sober and there is no suggestion to the contrary. The sole evidence of reckless driving is that he failed to stop or slow down at a stop street which crossed the highway on which he was travelling. The record shows there was a stop sign on the right side of the road 112 feet from the intersection but there is no evidence in the record that the defendant had ever traversed this road before or was familiar with the locality.

To sustain the conviction of the defendant in this case is tantamount to a holding that if a person is killed because of the failure of a driver of an automobile to stop at a stop sign, such conduct constitutes in itself negligence of such a gross and flagrant character that it evinces a reckless disregard of human life.

There are few, if any, of us who have not through momentary lapse of attention — particularly on strange roads — been guilty of traversing stop streets without slowing down. Such, no doubt, constitutes such negligence as to support a damage action, but I do not think it was ever intended that negligence of that kind was sufficient to support a verdict of manslaughter. It is exceedingly doubtful that such negligence would be sufficient to support an action for punitive damages.

Hobson and Thornal, J.J., concur.

On Rehearing Granted.

O'Connell, Justice.

This cause is before us now on petition for rehearing of our opinion affirming the verdict and judgment of guilty of manslaughter.

From the evidence in this cause it appears that the only evidence of culpable negligence is that the appellant failed to stop at an intersection which was marked by (1) a perpendicular "stop" sign on the side of the road defendant was traveling and by (2) the word "stop" painted on the road. There is no evidence of heavy traffic, weather conditions or other unusual circumstances surrounding the accident or its locale, which was not in the corporate limits of any municipality. There is no evidence of or suggestion that the defendant was drinking or intoxicated. The accident happened in broad daylight. The speed limit we assume to be 60 miles per hour, and the evidence shows that the jury could have found the defendant to have been going between 60–65 miles per hour.

We feel that to sustain the conviction of the defendant under the facts in this cause will be tantamount to a holding that the death of a human being caused by the failure of the driver to stop at an intersection marked by a stop sign constitutes, in and of itself, negligence of such a gross and flagrant character that it evinces a reckless disregard of human life. We do not believe that such was the intent of the legislature in enacting the statute in question. Section 782.07, F.S.A.

True the jury was entitled to consider as evidence, all inferences which would logically flow from the proven facts. It does not follow logically, that one who runs a "stop sign on a country road while traveling at a speed at or near the limit prescribed by law has exercised the entire want of care which would raise the presumption of a conscious indifference to consequences." Defendant was required to be proved guilty of culpable negligence beyond and to the exclusion of a reasonable doubt.

We feel that the evidence before the jury, taken with all inferences to be logically drawn therefrom, was insufficient to meet the required proof and to overcome the presumption of innocence of the defendant. The verdict and judgment appealed from is—reversed, on rehearing granted, and we recede from the majority opinion on April 18, 1956.

DREW, C.J., and TERRELL, HOBSON and THORNAL, J.J., concur.

THOMAS and ROBERTS, JJ., dissent.

Questions and Notes

1. Is Justice Roberts' original majority's definition of culpable negligence any different from the *Welansky* definition of recklessness?

2. Is the concept of gross negligence more attractive than recklessness because of the difficulty of proving subjective intent? For example, in *Porter*, it might be difficult for the prosecution to deny Porter's claim that he didn't see the stop sign. How would the prosecution prove that Porter saw the stop sign?

3. Was it necessary for Justice Roberts to have concluded that Porter's conduct was "negligence of a gross and flagrant character" or would it have been sufficient to have concluded that a jury could have so found? Might this unnecessary endorsement of the jury's conclusion have contributed to the defection of Justices O'Connell and Terrell on rehearing?

4. Under the supposedly more stringent standard of recklessness in Texas, do you think that a prosecutor could have gotten a manslaughter conviction on the facts of *Porter*? How?

5. Is it accurate to describe Porter's negligence as limited to failure to stop for a stop sign?

6. Do most drivers, at one time or another, do what Porter did? Do they occasionally drive when sleepy?

7. Decisions like *Porter* have encouraged many states to enact vehicular homicide statutes, which permit convictions of a lesser degree of homicide than involuntary manslaughter under standards less stringent than those enunciated in *Porter*.

8. Some states will permit a manslaughter conviction for ordinary negligence. Why would a state want to do this? Consider that in conjunction with *Williams.*

State v. Williams

484 P.2d 1167 (Wash. App. 1971)

HOROWITZ, Chief Judge.

Defendants, husband and wife, were charged by information filed October 3, 1968, with the crime of manslaughter for negligently failing to supply their 17-month child with necessary medical attention, as a result of which he died on September 12, 1968. Upon entry of findings, conclusions and judgment of guilty, sentences were imposed on April 22, 1969. Defendants appeal.

The defendant husband, Walter Williams, is a 24-year old full-blooded Sheshone Indian with a sixth-grade education. His sole occupation is that of laborer. The defendant wife, Bernice Williams, is a 20-year-old part Indian with an 11th grade education. At the time of the marriage, the wife had two children, the younger of whom was a 14-month son. Both parents worked and the children were cared for by the 85-year-old mother of the defendant husband. The defendant husband assumed parental responsibility with the defendant wife to provide clothing, care and medical attention for the child. Both defendants possessed a great deal of love and affection for the defendant wife's young son.

The court expressly found:

That both defendants were aware that William Joseph Tabafunda was ill during the period September 1, 1968 to September 12, 1968. The defendants were ignorant. They did not realize how sick the baby was. They thought that the baby had a toothache and no layman regards a toothache as dangerous to life. They loved the baby and gave it aspirin in hopes of improving its condition. They did not take the baby to a doctor because of fear that the Welfare Department would take the baby away from them. They knew that medical help was available because of previous experience. They had no excuse that the law will recognize for not taking the baby to a doctor.

The defendants Walter L. Williams and Bernice J. Williams were negligent in not seeking medical attention for William Joseph Tabafunda. As a proximate result of this negligence, William Joseph Tabafunda died.

On the question of the quality or seriousness of breach of the duty, at common law, in the case of involuntary manslaughter, the breach had to amount to more than mere ordinary or simple negligence — gross negligence was essential. In Washington, however, RCW 9.48.060[6] (since amended by Laws of 1970, ch. 49, §2) and

---

6. RCW 9.48.060 provided in part: "In any case other than those specified in RCW 9.48.030, 9.48.040 and 9.48.050, homicide, not being excusable or justifiable, is manslaughter."

RCW 9.48.150[7] supersede both voluntary and involuntary manslaughter as those crimes were defined at common law. Under these statutes the crime is deemed committed even though the death of the victim is the proximate result of only simple or ordinary negligence. *State v. Brubaker*, 385 P.2d 318 (1963); *State v. Ramser*, 136 P.2d 1013 (1943); *State v. Hedges*, 113 P.2d 530 (1941).

The concept of simple or ordinary negligence describes a failure to exercise the "ordinary caution' necessary to make out the defense of excusable homicide." RCW 9.48.150. Ordinary caution is the kind of caution that a man of reasonable prudence would exercise under the same or similar conditions. If, therefore, the conduct of a defendant, regardless of his ignorance, good intentions and good faith, fails to measure up to the conduct required of a man of reasonable prudence, he is guilty of ordinary negligence because of his failure to use 'ordinary caution.' If such negligence proximately causes the death of the victim, the defendant, as pointed out above, is guilty of statutory manslaughter.

We quite agree that the Code does not contemplate the necessity of calling a physician for every trifling complaint with which the child may be afflicted, which in most instances may be overcome by the ordinary household nursing by members of the family; that a reasonable amount of discretion is vested in parents, charged with the duty of maintaining and bringing up infant children; and that the standard is at what time would an ordinarily prudent person, solicitous for the welfare of his child and anxious to promote its recovery, deem it necessary to call in the services of a physician.

It remains to apply the law discussed to the facts of the instant case.

Dr. Gale Wilson, the autopsy surgeon and chief pathologist for the King County Coroner, testified that the child died because an abscessed tooth had been allowed to develop into an infection of the mouth and cheeks, eventually becoming gangrenous. This condition, accompanied by the child's inability to eat, brought about malnutrition, lowering the child's resistance and eventually producing pneumonia, causing the death. Dr. Wilson testified that in his opinion the infection had lasted for approximately 2 weeks, and that the odor generally associated with gangrene would have been present for approximately 10 days before death. He also expressed the opinion that had medical care been first obtained in the last week before the baby's death, such care would have been obtained too late to have saved the baby's life. Accordingly, the baby's apparent condition between September 1 and September 5, 1968 became the critical period for the purpose of determining whether in the exercise of ordinary caution defendants should have provided medical care for the minor child.

The testimony concerning the child's apparent condition during the critical period is not crystal clear, but is sufficient to warrant the following statement of the matter.

---

7. RCW 9.48.150 provides: "Homicide is excusable when committed by accident or misfortune in doing any lawful act by lawful means, with ordinary caution and without any unlawful intent."

The defendant husband testified that he noticed the baby was sick about 2 weeks before the baby died. The defendant wife testified that she noticed the baby was ill about a week and a half or 2 weeks before the baby died. The evidence showed that in the critical period the baby was fussy; that he could not keep his food down; and that a cheek started swelling up. The swelling went up and down but did not disappear. In that same period, the cheek turned "a bluish color like." The defendants, not realizing that the baby was as ill as it was or that the baby was in danger of dying, attempted to provide some relief to the baby by giving the baby aspirin during the critical period and continued to do so until the night before the baby died. The defendants thought the swelling would go down and were waiting for it to do so; and defendant husband testified, that from what he had heard, neither doctors nor dentists pull out a tooth "when it's all swollen up like that." There was an additional explanation for not calling a doctor given by each defendant. Defendant husband testified that "the way the cheek looked, . . . and that stuff on his hair, they would think we were neglecting him and take him away from us and not give him back." Defendant wife testified that the defendants were "waiting for the swelling to go down," and also that they were afraid to take the child to a doctor for fear that the doctor would report them to the welfare department, who, in turn, would take the child away. "It's just that I was so scared of losing him." They testified that they had heard that the defendant husband's cousin lost a child that way. The evidence showed that the defendants did not understand the significance or seriousness of the baby's symptoms. However, there is no evidence that the defendants were physically or financially unable to obtain a doctor, or that they did not know an available doctor, or that the symptoms did not continue to be a matter of concern during the critical period. Indeed, the evidence shows that in April 1968 defendant husband had taken the child to a doctor for medical attention.

In our opinion, there is sufficient evidence from which the court could find, as it necessarily did, that applying the standard of ordinary caution, *i.e.*, the caution exercisable by a man of reasonable prudence under the same or similar conditions, defendants were sufficiently put on notice concerning the symptoms of the baby's illness and lack of improvement in the baby's apparent condition in the period from September 1 to September 5, 1968 to have required them to have obtained medical care for the child. The failure so to do in this case is ordinary or simple negligence, and such negligence is sufficient to support a conviction of statutory manslaughter.

The judgment is affirmed.

UTTER and WILLIAMS, JJ., concur.

Questions and Notes

1. As a policy matter, why would a state want to allow ordinary negligence to suffice for manslaughter?

2. As District Attorney, would you have prosecuted the Williamses? Haven't they suffered enough? Do you view their fear of the welfare department as an aggravating or mitigating circumstance?

3. Do the Washington statutes clearly mandate ordinary negligence as the test for manslaughter? If you represented the defendants, how could you argue that the statutes merely incorporate the common law rule?

4. Part of the court's rationale was *stare decisis*. That is, prior decisions had construed the Washington statute to permit a manslaughter conviction based on ordinary negligence. If the court were now convinced that its prior decisions were erroneous, to what extent should it feel bound by them? Would it matter if the legislature reenacted the statute after the court's decision?

5. Few, if any, other states regularly permit ordinary negligence to suffice for manslaughter. Several states, however, permit ordinary negligence to suffice for the handling of inherently dangerous instrumentalities, such as vicious dogs. *See, e.g., People v. Sandgren*, 98 N.E.2d 460 (N.Y. 1951).

6. However, occasionally it will be theoretically possible to find a totally blameless individual guilty of involuntary manslaughter. Consider *Weitbrecht*.

State v. Weitbrecht
715 N.E.2d 167 (Ohio 1999)

FRANCIS E. SWEENEY, SR., J.

The issue certified for our review is, "Does Ohio's involuntary manslaughter statute [R.C. 2903.04(B)] as applied to a minor misdemeanor traffic offense which results in a vehicular homicide violate the Eighth Amendment to the United States Constitution and Section 9, Article [I] of the Ohio Constitution?" For the reasons that follow, we answer the certified question in the negative.

R.C. 2903.04 provides, in relevant part:

"(B) No person shall cause the death of another as a proximate result of the offender's committing or attempting to commit a misdemeanor of the first, second, third, or fourth degree or a minor misdemeanor.

"(C) Whoever violates this section is guilty of involuntary manslaughter. Violation of division (B) of this section is a felony of the third degree."

A third degree felony carries the potential penalty of one to five years in prison and a fine of up to $10,000.

Appellee successfully argued to the lower courts that the potential penalty imposed for a violation of R.C. 2903.04(B) is disproportionate to the crime committed (a minor misdemeanor) and is violative of the constitutional prohibition against cruel and unusual punishments. We are now asked to decide whether the lower courts were correct in finding that R.C. 2903.04(B) violates the Eighth Amendment to the United States Constitution and Section 9, Article I of the Ohio Constitution. In resolving this issue, we are mindful that legislative enactments are to be afforded a strong presumption of constitutionality. Any reasonable doubt regarding the constitutionality of a statute must be resolved in favor of the legislature's power to enact the law. Thus, the legislation will not be struck down unless the challenger establishes that it is unconstitutional beyond a reasonable doubt.

The Eighth Amendment to the Constitution of the United States provides: "Excessive bail shall not be required, nor excessive fines imposed, nor cruel and unusual punishments inflicted." Section 9, Article I of the Ohio Constitution is couched in identical language. Historically, the Eighth Amendment has been invoked in extremely rare cases, where it has been necessary to protect individuals from inhumane punishment such as torture or other barbarous acts. *Robinson v. California* (1962), 370 U.S. 660, 676, 768. Over the years, it has also been used to prohibit punishments that were found to be disproportionate to the crimes committed. In *McDougle v. Maxwell* (1964), 1 Ohio St.2d 68, 203 N.E.2d 334, 30 O.O.2d 38, this court stressed that Eighth Amendment violations are rare. We stated that "[c]ases in which cruel and unusual punishments have been found are limited to those involving sanctions which under the circumstances would be considered shocking to any reasonable person." Furthermore, "the penalty must be so greatly disproportionate to the offense as to shock the sense of justice of the community."

The United States Supreme Court has also discussed the concept of whether the Eighth Amendment requires that sentences be proportionate to the offenses committed. An Eighth Amendment challenge on these grounds was initially applied only in cases involving the death penalty or unusual forms of imprisonment. Then, in *Solem v. Helm* (1983), 463 U.S. 277, 290, 103 S.Ct. 3001, 3009, 77 L.Ed.2d 637, 649, the court applied the Eighth Amendment to reverse a felony sentence on proportionality grounds, finding that "a criminal sentence must be proportionate to the crime for which the defendant has been convicted." In so holding, the *Solem* court set forth the following tripartite test to review sentences under the Eighth Amendment:

> "First, we look to the gravity of the offense and the harshness of the penalty. Second, it may be helpful to compare the sentences imposed on other criminals in the same jurisdiction. If more serious crimes are subject to the same penalty, or to less serious penalties, that is some indication that the punishment at issue may be excessive. Third, courts may find it useful to compare the sentences imposed for commission of the same crime in other jurisdictions."

More recently, in *Harmelin v. Michigan* (1991), 501 U.S. 957, the United States Supreme Court revisited the issue of proportionality as it relates to the Eighth Amendment. In *Harmelin*, the court was asked to decide whether a mandatory term of life imprisonment without possibility of parole for possession of six hundred seventy-two grams of cocaine violated the prohibition against cruel and unusual punishments. In finding no constitutional violation, the lead opinion rejected earlier statements made in *Solem v. Helm* and stated that the Eighth Amendment contains no proportionality guarantee. However, this statement failed to garner a majority. The three Justices who concurred in part would refine the *Solem* decision to an analysis of "gross disproportionality" between sentence and crime. As stated by Justice Kennedy in his opinion concurring in part, "The Eighth Amendment does not require strict proportionality between crime and sentence. Rather, it forbids only extreme sentences that are 'grossly disproportionate' to the crime."

With these principles in mind, we now turn to the case at hand. Appellant contends that R.C. 2903.04(B), as applied to a minor misdemeanor traffic offense, does not constitute cruel and unusual punishment because its potential penalty for causing the death of another is not disproportionate to the offense committed and does not shock the community's sense of justice. Appellant relies on *State v. Garland* (1996), 116 Ohio App.3d 461, 688 N.E.2d 557, to support its position. The *Garland* court did fully consider the issue. In *Garland*, the defendant was convicted of involuntary manslaughter with the underlying minor misdemeanor of failure to stop at a stop sign and was sentenced to a term of five to ten years. The court held that "[t]he sentence imposed by the trial court falls within the range of punishments contained within the sentencing statute for this offense. There is no evidence to suggest that appellant's sentence would shock the conscience of the community. Accordingly, the punishment imposed cannot be deemed cruel and unusual."

In contrast, appellee argues that the court of appeals' decision was correct and urges us to follow the appellate decision of *State v. Campbell* (1997), 117 Ohio App.3d 762, 691 N.E.2d 711, which used the tripartite test set forth in *Solem* to find that R.C. 2903.04(B) violates the Cruel and Unusual Punishment Clauses of the United States and Ohio Constitutions. In these decisions, the courts found that the potential punishment for committing a minor misdemeanor traffic offense is grossly disproportionate to the crime. Furthermore, the courts found that the potential sentence under R.C. 2903.04(B) was excessive when compared to similar related Ohio crimes that require a greater degree of culpability (such as negligent homicide, vehicular homicide, and aggravated vehicular homicide), and when compared with other jurisdictions. These decisions also relied, in part, on dictum from our decision in *State v. Collins* (1993), 67 Ohio St.3d 115, 117, 616 N.E.2d 224, 225, which questioned the policy behind applying the involuntary manslaughter statute to include minor misdemeanors as predicate offenses.

At the outset, we reject appellee's reliance on the *Collins* decision. In *Collins*, we interpreted the statutory language of former R.C. 2903.04(B), which stated that it applied to "misdemeanors." Under the principles of statutory construction, and in reviewing various sections of R.C. Title 29 that differentiate between misdemeanors and minor misdemeanors, we found that the statute as written did not include minor misdemeanors. Thus, we held that offenses classified as minor misdemeanors could not serve as a predicate offense for a charge of involuntary manslaughter.[FN2] Since the General Assembly has amended R.C. 2903.04 so that Ohio's involuntary manslaughter statute now encompasses minor misdemeanors as predicate offenses, the current version of R.C. 2903.04 differs from that which we interpreted in *Collins*. Thus, our decision in *Collins* has no bearing on our decision today.[2]

We also reject the reasoning employed by those courts, which found that R.C. 2903.04(B) violates the prohibition against cruel and unusual punishments. Although the potential maximum penalty of five years' imprisonment may be somewhat severe, it is not tantamount to cruel and unusual punishment. Unfortunately, lives were lost as a result of the traffic accident. Where human lives are lost, the gravity of the crime is serious and is not lessened by the fact that the underlying crime consists of a minor misdemeanor. Furthermore, we note that the trial court has the option of imposing a less stringent punishment than actual incarceration.[3] For instance, an offender can be sentenced to a term of probation (R.C. 2929.15 to R.C. 2929.17) or, if incarcerated, can file an application for judicial release after six months (R.C. 2929.20[A]; [B][2]). Under these circumstances, we cannot say that the potential penalty for violating R.C. 2903.04(B) is "so greatly disproportionate to the offense as to shock the sense of justice of the community." *McDougle v. Maxwell*, where the court held that severe, mandatory penalties may be cruel, but they are not unusual in the constitutional sense, and do not violate the Eighth Amendment.[4]

In reaching this decision, we are cognizant of the fact that reviewing courts should grant substantial deference to the broad authority that legislatures possess in determining the types and limits of punishments for crimes. We find that the General Assembly acted within its discretion in setting forth the penalties it did when the commission of minor misdemeanors results in the deaths of individuals.

Accordingly, we hold that R.C. 2903.04(B), as applied to a minor misdemeanor traffic offense which results in a vehicular homicide, does not violate the Eighth Amendment to the United States Constitution or Section 9, Article I of the Ohio Constitution.

The judgment of the court of appeals is reversed, and the cause is remanded to the trial court.

PFEIFER, J., dissenting.

Dispassionate dissection of a legal conundrum is often required to achieve the correct result in matters that come before this court. In those instances, the facts of

---

2. Former R.C. 2903.04(B) provided that "[n]o person shall cause the death of another as a proximate cause result of the offender's committing or attempting to commit a misdemeanor."

3. Although appellee has not been sentenced, or even been found guilty we find that the potential maximum sentence is not grossly disproportionate to the underlying crimes.

4. The court of appeals compared the potential sentence in this case with similar Ohio crimes and with those of other jurisdictions. However, we decline to make these comparisons. Instead, we agree with Justice Kennedy's concurrence in *Harmelin v. Michigan*, in which he stated that a comparative analysis within the state where the crime was committed and between jurisdictions (the second and third prongs in *Solem*) is "appropriate only in the rare case in which a threshold comparison of the crime committed and the sentence imposed lead to an inference of gross disproportionality."

the case are secondary to the legal analysis. Here, where we are considering whether the sentence at issue would "shock the sense of justice of the community," the facts must stand at the center of our consideration. The facts in this case tell the whole story.

While driving on Highway 62 on April 27, 1997, Nancy Weitbrecht apparently suffered a cardiac event, lost consciousness, crossed left of center, and collided with the Carroll vehicle. She lost her husband and a friend in the accident, and must live with the fact that she also caused the death of Vera Carroll. The state stipulated that there was no evidence of criminal recklessness or criminal negligence on her part. Nancy Weitbrecht now faces a potential five-year prison term. It would be hard to conjure up a situation more shocking to the community's sense of justice, or a more inappropriate exercise of prosecutorial discretion. I accordingly dissent.

Questions and Notes

1. Did Justices Sweeney and Pfifer answer the same question or a different question? If different, how were they different?

2. If the facts were as described by Justice Pfifer and the trial court actually imposed a five-year sentence on Nancy Weitbrecht, would the court have upheld that sentence? Why? Why not? Is footnote 3 relevant to this question? Should the court have upheld such a sentence? Do you believe that was the legislative intent?

3. In Chapters 8 and 9, we will see that occasionally one may be liable for a minor misdemeanor without intentionally or negligently doing anything wrong (or even being in bodily control). Should a legislature be able to raise that type of misdemeanor to a serious felony? Compare *Thompson*, where the court insisted on a meaningful definition of premeditation to pass constitutional muster.

4. If you were in a position to adopt the involuntary manslaughter rule for your jurisdiction, would you adopt *Goodman, Welansky, Conrad, Porter, Williams, Weitbrect* or something else? Explain.

See NUTSHELL §§ 2.06, 2.07, and 2.10; *Culpability, Dangerousness, and Harm*, Section III G (Appendix B).

E. Depraved Heart Murder

Depraved heart murder bears a surface resemblance to involuntary manslaughter but differs in that depraved heart murder requires "malice aforethought." Ascertaining which unexcused but unintentional killings are so bad as to be malicious, and which are not, is no easy task.

Some, but not all, courts that do not require subjective appreciation of the risk for involuntary manslaughter, do require it for depraved heart murder. All courts require that the risk be more outrageous to qualify for murder. Most courts consider the number of people subjected to the risk to be relevant, and a few will not even permit a murder conviction unless more than one person is subjected to the risk. (*See Northington, infra.*) Finally, the extent of the social disutility in taking the risk seems to be a factor for at least some of the courts.

The MPC employs the word "extreme" to distinguish the reckless disregard necessary for murder as opposed to manslaughter. (*See* Appendix A.) As you read *Essex* and *Pears*, try to explain the factors that the court thinks are relevant in drawing this elusive distinction.

Essex v. Commonwealth

322 S.E.2d 216 (Va. 1984)

RUSSELL, Justice.

In this case of first impression, we must determine whether driving under the influence of alcohol, resulting in a fatal collision, can supply the requisite element of implied malice to support a conviction of second-degree murder. The appeal also raises questions concerning the application of the statutory presumption of intoxication in a prosecution for both homicide and driving under the influence.

A jury convicted Warren Wesley Essex of one count of driving under the influence of alcohol (defined as a misdemeanor in Code § 18.2-266) and three counts of second-degree murder for deaths resulting from injuries sustained in an automobile collision. By final order entered November 22, 1982, the trial court entered judgment on the four verdicts.

The collision occurred about 10:45 p.m. on November 20, 1981, at a point on State Route 28 south of its intersection with State Route 17. Essex, driving a Plymouth Duster automobile, entered Route 28, a two-lane, hard-surfaced highway, north of the intersection and headed south. Linda Bates, who was traveling south on Route 28, testified that the Duster entered the highway behind her, passed her across a solid center line, almost struck her car as it returned to the right lane, and ran onto the shoulder of the road, nearly striking a mailbox before it reentered the southbound lane. She said that the Duster passed another vehicle across a solid line and returned to the right lane just in time to avoid a northbound pickup truck. Later, it crossed double solid lines on a curve to pass yet another vehicle. For a distance of six miles, Mrs. Bates watched the car as it swerved from one lane to the other and off the edge of the hard surface.

Although there were "speed bumps" in the pavement north of the intersection, the Duster ran through a red traffic signal at a speed Mrs. Bates estimated at 55 m.p.h. A tractor-trailer truck moving through the intersection on Route 17 "nearly hit the back end of the Plymouth." A mile and a half south of the intersection, the Duster collided with a northbound pickup truck driven by John Gouldthorpe.

Gouldthorpe testified that "[t]he last thing I remember was seeing four headlights, one set in one lane and one in the other." State Trooper Donald Johnson, the investigating officer, testified that when he asked Essex what had happened, the defendant replied, "I was in his lane because my steering had gone. . . . I had been having trouble with it all night." An expert mechanic who inspected the Duster at the officer's request testified that "there was nothing loose" and "no failures" in any part of the steering linkage, and that the only damage he found was a break in the steering column which he said was "due to the impact where the front end had been shoved back about a foot."

Debra Gouldthorpe and Nora Neale, passengers in the pickup, and James Carter, a passenger in the defendant's car, died from injuries sustained in the collision.

Essex was treated at Fauquier Hospital for "a large laceration on his knee" and "a small laceration of the tongue." Dr. Steven Von Elton, the attending physician in the emergency room who examined Essex about 12:30 a.m., testified that Essex was in a "stuperous condition" and that although "the lady next to him was screaming very intensely . . . he was totally unaware of that." Because he could "very easily . . . smell the odor of alcohol . . . at that bedside," Dr. Elton ordered a blood alcohol content test. The test, conducted about two and a half hours after the collision, disclosed an alcohol content of .144 percent.

Where death proximately results from the want of ordinary care as practiced by a reasonably prudent person, the causative negligence is actionable as a tort. If the negligence is so gross, wanton, and culpable as to show a reckless disregard of human life, a killing resulting therefrom, although unintentional, is both a tort and a crime, punishable as involuntary manslaughter.

Criminal homicides in Virginia are classified as follows:

1. Capital murder,

2. First-degree murder,

3. Second-degree murder,

4. Voluntary manslaughter, and

5. Involuntary manslaughter.

Malice, a requisite element for murder of any kind, is unnecessary in manslaughter cases and is the touchstone by which murder and manslaughter cases are distinguished.

The authorities are replete with definitions of malice, but a common theme running through them is a requirement that a wrongful act be done "wilfully or purposefully." This requirement of volitional action is inconsistent with inadvertence. Thus, if a killing results from negligence, however gross or culpable, and the killing is contrary to the defendant's intention, malice cannot be implied. In order to evaluate the crime to second-degree murder, the defendant must be shown to have wilfully or purposefully, rather than negligently, embarked upon a course of wrongful conduct likely to cause death or great bodily harm.

A motor vehicle, wrongfully used, can be a weapon as deadly as a gun or a knife. Circumstances can be imagined in which a killing caused by the wrongful use of a motor vehicle might fit any one of the five categories of homicide known to our law. We recognized in *Harrison v. Commonwealth*, 183 Va. 394, 401, 32 S.E.2d 136, 139–40 (1944), that the premeditated use of an automobile to kill can be first-degree murder. If such an act fits within the statutory categories of Code § 18.2-31, such a killing could be capital murder. A killing in sudden heat of passion, upon reasonable provocation, by the use of a motor vehicle, could be voluntary manslaughter. Killings caused by the grossly negligent operation of motor vehicles, showing a reckless disregard of human life, have frequently resulted in convictions of involuntary manslaughter.

We have not, heretofore, had occasion to review a second-degree murder conviction based upon the use of an automobile, but the governing principles are the same as those which apply to any other kind of second-degree murder: the victim must be shown to have died as a result of the defendant's conduct, and the defendant's conduct must be shown to be malicious. In the absence of express malice, this element may only be implied from conduct likely to cause death or great bodily harm, willfully or purposefully undertaken. Thus, for example, one who deliberately drives a car into a crowd of people at a high speed, not intending to kill or injure any particular person, but rather seeking the perverse thrill of terrifying them and causing them to scatter, might be convicted of second-degree murder if death results. One who accomplishes the same result inadvertently, because of grossly negligent driving, causing him to lose control of his car, could be convicted only of involuntary manslaughter. In the first case the act was volitional; in the second it was inadvertent, however reckless and irresponsible.

In some jurisdictions, drunken driving is held to be *malum in se*, and where death is the proximate result of any degree of negligence attributable to intoxication, malice may be inferred by the fact-finder. *See, e.g., Shiflet v. State*, 216 Tenn. 365, 392 S.W.2d 676 (1965). We do not follow that view because of our distinction between volitional and inadvertent conduct.

We hold that the defendant's degree of intoxication, however great, neither enhances nor impairs the set of facts relied upon to establish implied malice. In making the determination whether malice exists, the factfinder must be guided by the quality of the defendant's conduct, its likelihood of causing death or great bodily harm, and whether it was volitional or inadvertent; not by the defendant's blood-alcohol level.

In *Baker v. Marcus*, 201 Va. 905, 114 S.E.2d 617 (1960), we considered, in a civil context, whether malice could be inferred from drunken driving so as to support an award of punitive damages. There we said: "One who knowingly drives his automobile on the highway under the influence of intoxicants, in violation of statute, is, of course, negligent. It is a wrong, reckless and unlawful thing to do; but it is not necessarily a malicious act." A sober driver may be eminently malicious, while a drunken driver may be merely reckless.[3]

Even though the fact of the defendant's intoxication, and its degree, are irrelevant to the determination whether his conduct was volitional or inadvertent, and thus whether it was malicious or merely negligent, the question remains whether such evidence is relevant for any other purpose.

Drunken driving is not only unlawful in itself, but it tends to make the defendant's dangerous conduct more dangerous. A sober but reckless driver may rely on his skill and prompt reflexes to extricate himself from any emergency created by his reckless driving. A drunken driver has dulled his perceptions, blunted his skill, and slowed his reflexes in advance. The same reckless driving is more dangerous at his hands than it would be if he were sober, and his conduct is therefore more culpable. Intoxication, therefore, is relevant as an aggravating factor, increasing with its degree, bearing upon the relative culpability of the defendant's conduct, even though it is irrelevant to the determination of malice.

Intoxication is, accordingly, relevant to a determination of the degree of the defendant's negligence: whether ordinary, gross, or wanton. It may serve to elevate the defendant's conduct to the level of "negligence so gross, wanton, and culpable as to show a reckless disregard of human life," a requisite element for a conviction of involuntary manslaughter.

The defendant's degree of intoxication is also relevant to a determination of the appropriate quantum of punishment. In Virginia, the factfinder, whether judge or jury, has the duty, if it convicts the defendant, of fixing his punishment, usually within wide limits. The principal criterion for the discharge of the responsibility must be the relative seriousness of the offense, within its grade. All aggravating and mitigating factors shown by the evidence must be taken into account. Voluntary intoxication, in the case of a driver, is an aggravating factor properly considered for this purpose.

Applying these principles to the record before us, we find the evidence, viewed in the light most favorable to the Commonwealth, insufficient to support a finding of implied malice. The defendant was intoxicated and guilty of an appalling degree of reckless driving. His multiple tortious acts conjoined as proximate causes of three tragic deaths, and clearly met the standard for proof of involuntary manslaughter: an "accidental killing which, although unintended, is the proximate result of negligence so gross, wanton, and culpable as to show a reckless disregard of human life." The Commonwealth, however, has the burden of proving malice beyond a

---

3. Some courts reason that one who deliberately drives a car to a place remote from home for the purpose of drinking, knowing that he will have to drive home under the influence of alcohol, then, after becoming intoxicated, drives recklessly, thereby acts so wantonly, and with such a disregard of human life as to supply an inference of malice. *See, e.g., People v. Watson*, 30 Cal. 3d 290, 179 Cal. Rptr. 43, 637 P.2d 279 (1981). We do not think the premises support the conclusion reached.

reasonable doubt. The jury could only speculate, upon this evidence, whether the defendant embarked upon his ill-fated course of conduct willfully and with a malicious purpose. No facts were proved from which such a purpose can be inferred. The distinction is close but crucial.

> [T]he intent to do an act in wanton and willful disregard of the *obvious likelihood* of causing death or great bodily injury is a malicious intent. . . . [A] motorist who attempts to pass another car on a "blind curve" may be acting with such criminal negligence that if he causes the death of another in a resulting traffic accident he will be guilty of manslaughter. And such a motorist may be creating fully as great a human hazard as one who shoots into a house or train "just for kicks," who is guilty of murder if loss of life results. The difference is that in the act of the shooter there is an element of *viciousness*—an extreme indifference to the value of human life—that is not found in the act of the motorist.

Because the evidence was insufficient to support a finding of malice, it was error to instruct the jury that it might find the defendant guilty of second-degree murder.

For the foregoing reasons, the convictions of second-degree murder will be vacated and the three homicide cases remanded for further proceedings, consistent with this opinion, wherein the Commonwealth may, if it be so advised, retry the defendant for offenses no greater than involuntary manslaughter.

Reversed and Remanded.

POFF, J., concurring in part and dissenting in part.

The level of culpability of criminal negligence determines the grade of the offense. Between the class of deliberate deeds committed with premeditated intent to kill, which is the essence of murder of the first degree, and the type of negligence inherent in the definition of involuntary manslaughter there is a species of reckless behavior so willful and wanton, so heedless of foreseeable consequences, and so indifferent to the value of human life that it supplies the element of malice which distinguishes murder of the second degree from manslaughter. More than a century and a half ago, this court observed that a killing caused by "criminal carelessness" could constitute "murder in the second degree."" *Whiteford v. Commonwealth*, 27 Va. (6 Rand.) 721, 724–25 (1828).

While, as the majority notes, we have never, until now, had occasion to review a second-degree murder conviction based upon malice inferred from the negligent operation of a motor vehicle, we have commented upon the question in rather unmistakable language.

> When men, while drunk or sober, drive automobiles along highways and through crowded streets recklessly, the killing of human beings is a natural and probable result to be anticipated. When a homicide follows as a consequence of such conduct, a criminal intent is imputed to the offender and he may be punished for his crime. The precise grade of such a homicide,

whether murder or manslaughter, depends upon the facts of the particular case.

Goodman v. Commonwealth, 153 Va. 943, 952, 151 S.E. 168, 171 (1930).

I acknowledge that the language in *Goodman* is *dicta.* But it is in harmony with the common law in most jurisdictions. The great weight of authority holds that a motorist's negligence may be so gross and culpable as to imply a malicious intent to kill and that, in determining whether the homicide is manslaughter or murder, intoxication is an aggravating factor.

The vehicular homicide statutes adopted by some states abandon the definitional differences the common law makes between manslaughter and murder and define homicide resulting from the criminal negligence of the driver of a motor vehicle as a unique offense, graded according to the nature and extent of the driver's negligence. *See* Traffic Laws Annotated § 11-903. *See also* Model Penal Code § 210.4, at 88. Virginia has no such statute, and as defined by the majority opinion, vehicular homicide is hereafter relegated to the lowest grade of criminal homicide. The degree of culpability is immaterial.

Reaffirming what we said in *Whiteford* and *Goodman* and adopting what appears to be the judicial consensus, I would hold that where the evidence is sufficient to show that the driver of a motor vehicle, whether drunk or sober, is guilty of criminal negligence which is the sole proximate cause of a homicide, such evidence raises a question of fact whether the offense is manslaughter or murder of the second degree. Unless the finding made by the trier of fact is plainly wrong or without evidence to support it, the finding should be upheld by this Court.

I am of opinion that the evidence of record in this case is fully sufficient to justify the jury's finding that the defendant's negligence was the sole proximate cause of three deaths and that such negligence was so willful and wanton, so heedless of foreseeable consequences, and so indifferent to the value of human life as to imply the element of malice charged in the homicide counts of the indictment.

Questions and Notes

1. How could death by an automobile be first degree murder?

2. What does the court mean by the statement: "A sober driver may be eminently malicious, while a drunken driver may be merely reckless"?

3. Why is one who shoots into a house more malicious than one who passes on a blind curve (assuming that the odds of causing death are equal)?

4. What additional evidence would the court need to uphold a depraved heart murder conviction?

5. Is Justice Poff saying that mere negligence could support a murder verdict? If not, what is he saying?

6. In *Pears*, consider whether Alaska applies the same test as Virginia, or a different one to distinguish murder from manslaughter.

Pears v. State

672 P.2d 903 (Alaska App. 1983)

COATS, Judge.

While driving while intoxicated, Richard Pears caused an automobile accident in which two people died and one was injured. The state charged Pears with two counts of murder in the second degree, and one count of assault in the second degree. A jury convicted Pears on all three counts, and Judge Jay Hodges sentenced Pears to twenty years for the murder convictions and five years for the assault. The sentences are concurrent. Judge Hodges also revoked Pears' driver's license permanently. Pears has appealed his conviction and sentence to this court. We affirm Pears' conviction and sentence.

Pears first argues that Judge Hodges should have dismissed the grand jury indictment for second degree murder. The second-degree murder statute under which Pears was charged, AS 11.41.110(a)(2), provides:

> A person commits the crime of murder in the second degree if (2) he intentionally performs an act that results in the death of another person under circumstances manifesting an extreme indifference to the value of human life.

Pears argues that the legislature did not intend to have a motor vehicle homicide prosecuted as murder and that his offense should only have been charged as manslaughter. Manslaughter is defined in AS 11.41.120(a) and provides:

> A person commits the crime of manslaughter if he (1) intentionally, knowingly, or recklessly causes the death of another person under circumstances not amounting to murder in the first or second degree.

We find unpersuasive Pears' argument that the legislature did not intend for any motor vehicle homicide which was caused by an intoxicated driver to be charged as murder. This court discussed the relationship between second-degree murder and manslaughter in *Neitzel v. State*, 655 P.2d 325, 335–38 (Alaska App. 1982). In that case we indicated that the difference between second-degree murder and manslaughter was one of degree which was a question for the jury under proper instructions:

> Under the Revised Code, negligent homicide and reckless manslaughter are satisfied by conduct creating a significant risk of death absent justification or excuse. They differ only in the actor's knowledge of the risk. In differentiating reckless murder from reckless manslaughter, the jury is asked to determine whether the recklessness manifests an extreme indifference to human life.
>
> [T]he jury must consider the nature and gravity of the risk, including the harm to be foreseen and the likelihood that it will occur. For both murder and manslaughter, the harm to be foreseen is a death. Therefore, the

significant distinction is in the likelihood that a death will result from the
defendant's act. Where the defendant's act has limited social utility, a very
slight though significant and avoidable risk of death may make him guilty
of manslaughter if his act causes death. Driving an automobile has some
social utility although substantially reduced when the driver is intoxicated.
The odds that a legally intoxicated person driving home after the bars close
will hit and kill or seriously injure someone may be as low as one chance
in a thousand and still qualify for manslaughter. Where murder is charged,
however, an act must create a much greater risk that death or serious physical injury will result.

The legislature has not indicated that no motor vehicle homicide could be
charged as second-degree murder. It is certainly clear that an automobile can be as
dangerous a weapon as a gun or a knife and the results of its misuse just as deadly. It
seems clear to us from the Revised Criminal Code that where a driver's recklessness
manifests an extreme indifference to human life he can be charged with murder
even though the instrument by which he causes death is an automobile. We conclude Judge Hodges did not err in refusing to dismiss the indictment charging Pears
with murder in the second degree.[4]

In determining whether to grant a motion for a judgment of acquittal, the trial
court must view the evidence and the inferences therefrom in the light most favorable to the state and decide whether reasonable minds could conclude that guilt had
been established beyond a reasonable doubt. When we look at the evidence in the
light most favorable to the state, we conclude that a jury could find that Pears committed second-degree murder. The evidence produced at trial indicated that Pears
voluntarily drank in a bar to the point of intoxication. After becoming intoxicated
he drove recklessly, speeding, running through stop signs and stop lights and failing to slow for yield signs. His passenger at the time, Kathy Hill, told him that his
driving scared her. Pears and Kathy Hill then went to another bar and had more
drinks. Pears and Hill then left the bar and while they were approaching his truck
on foot, Pears was stopped by two uniformed police officers in a patrol car. One of
the officers told Pears not to drive because he was too intoxicated. Pears and Hill
walked back toward the bar until the officers were out of sight. They then returned
to his truck and drove away. Once again, with Hill protesting, Pears drove over the
speed limit and ran red lights and stop signs. Pears then dropped Kathy Hill off and
continued to drive around. Shortly before the fatal collision Pears was seen by Steve
Call, who was turning his car onto the four-lane Steese Highway. According to Call,
Pears' car ran a red light on the highway, going through the light at a high rate of
speed and passing two cars which were stopped at the light. Call said he was going
about forty-five miles per hour, the speed limit, but Pears was going faster. As they

---

4. We emphasize that a charge of second-degree murder should only rarely be appropriate in a
motor vehicle homicide. The murder charge in this case is supported by the extreme facts which are
set out more fully later in the opinion.

approached the next intersection Call could clearly see the red light against them and the cars stopping. Pears got around the cars which were stopping by passing them in the right turn lane, going into the intersection without breaking or slowing down. Pears collided with one of the cars entering the intersection on the green light, an orange Datsun. The impact of the collision knocked the Datsun 146 feet, killing two of the three people in the car and seriously injuring the third.

We believe that a jury could have found that Pears' driving constituted circumstances manifesting an extreme indifference to human life. He was made abundantly aware of the dangerous nature of his driving by both his passenger, Kathy Hill, and the police officers who warned him not to drive. The fact that Pears drove recklessly and ran stop signs and red lights several times before the fatal collision supports the theory that he did not inadvertently run the red light when the collision occurred but that he was intentionally running the red light at high speed without regard for the fact that other cars were crossing the intersection.[3] We believe this evidence would support a second degree murder conviction and conclude that Judge Hodges did not err in refusing to grant Pears' motion for judgment of acquittal.

Pears also contends that his sentence of twenty years' imprisonment is excessive. There is little question from the extreme recklessness which resulted in the collision that Pears' offense was particularly serious and that Judge Hodges did not err in imposing a substantial sentence of imprisonment. On the other hand, Pears' sentence appears to be substantially greater than other sentences that courts have imposed in this state for homicides caused by intoxicated drivers.

Of course, one problem with relying on these former cases in deciding whether Pears' sentence is appropriate is that the former sentences were imposed for either negligent homicide or manslaughter. Pears is the first person in this state to be convicted of murder for a motor vehicle homicide.[5]

---

3. Pears claims that he was passed out when he entered the intersection. Under the instructions given by the court the jury apparently rejected this contention and concluded that Pears intended to drive while intoxicated in a manner constituting extreme indifference to human life. The court charged:

> Our law provides that voluntary intoxication is generally not a defense to a prosecution for an offense. However, in the crime of murder in the second degree for which the defendant is charged in Counts I and II, the necessary element is the existence in the mind of the defendant of the intent to drive a motor vehicle while intoxicated in a manner constituting extreme indifference for the value of human life.
>
> If the evidence shows that the defendant was intoxicated at the time of the alleged offense, the jury should consider the state of intoxication in determining if defendant had such intent.
>
> If from all the evidence you have a reasonable doubt whether the defendant was capable of forming such intent, you must find that he did not have such intent. "Intoxication" includes intoxication from the use of a drug or alcohol.

5. It has been generally recognized that the mere fact that a motor vehicle has been the instrumentality of death does not preclude a murder charge where the evidence also discloses the requisite elements of murder. *Commander v. State*, 374 So. 2d 910 (Ala. Cr. App. 1978); *People v. Watson*, 30 Cal.3d 290, 179 Cal. Rptr. 43, 637 P.2d 279 (1981); *Hamilton v. Commonwealth*, 560 S.W.2d 539

The jury found that Pears' conduct was extreme; it manifested an extreme indifference to human life. In addition, Pears' conduct resulted in two deaths and severe
injury to a third person.

The question of whether the sentence imposed in this case is excessive is a close
one. Balanced on one side is Pears' conduct and the result of that conduct. Balanced on the other side is the fact that Pears' sentence appears to be the most severe
ever imposed for a vehicular homicide in the State of Alaska. Pears was only nineteen at the time of this offense and had no prior record of alcohol related driving
offenses. We conclude that the former Alaska cases which involved sentences for
motor vehicle homicide can and should be distinguished because those sentences
were imposed for negligent homicide and manslaughter. The instant case involves a
charge of murder. If Pears' sentence is looked at as a sentence for murder, we do not
believe that we can find that it was clearly mistaken. In *Page v. State*, 657 P.2d 850,
855 (Alaska App. 1983) we said:

> A review of the sentences for second-degree murder considered by the
> supreme court and this court since [1980] indicate that the typical sentence
> is twenty to twenty-five years. It is possible that the reported cases over-
> state sentences, since someone receiving less than twenty years may not be
> strongly motivated to appeal. Twenty years is therefore a proper benchmark
> to measure sentences for this crime. Any sentence substantially exceed-
> ing that amount would appear at least provisionally suspect. It would
> appear appropriate, therefore, in light of AS 12.55.125(b) and experience
> in sentencing second-degree murderers, both before and after enacting the
> revised code, that one convicted of that offense should receive a sentence
> of from twenty to thirty years. Naturally, mitigating circumstances could
> reduce the sentence down to the five-year minimum and aggravating cir-
> cumstances could enhance it up to the ninety-nine year maximum. [Foot-
> note omitted.]

Thus, Pears' twenty-year sentence does not appear to be out of line with other
sentences which have been imposed for murder. We conclude that although Pears'

(Ky. 1978); *People v. France*, 57 A.D.2d 432, 394 N.Y.S.2d 891 (N.Y. App. Div. 1977); *Farr v. State*,
591 S.W.2d 449 (Tenn. Cr. App. 1979); *Wagner v. State*, 76 Wis. 2d 30, 250 N.W.2d 331 (1977); *See
also State v. Boone*, 294 Or. 630, 661 P.2d 917 (1983). However, other courts have recognized that it
is difficult to establish the element of malice, or its equivalent, and to apply the general statutes or
doctrines governing murder. In two of the above listed cases it is certainly arguable that the courts
would not have allowed a murder charge for Pears' conduct. In *Wagner v. State*, the court decided
that the defendant could not be convicted of murder for killing a person while drag racing down
the main street of a town at 11:00 p.m. while intoxicated. 250 N.W.2d at 336. In *People v. France*,
the defendant killed a person during a high speed automobile chase at 3 a.m. while attempting to
escape from the police. The defendant apparently ran through several traffic signals while attempting to elude the police. 394 N.Y.S.2d at 892. In the other cases cited it appears that Pears' conduct
would fall within the murder statutes. *See generally Homicide by Automobile as Murder*, 21 A.L.R.3d
116 (1968).

sentence is severe and certainly appears to be significantly greater than any sentence which has formerly been imposed in a case in this state involving a motor vehicle homicide, the sentence is not clearly mistaken.

The conviction and sentence are AFFIRMED.

SINGLETON, Judge, with whom BRYNER, Chief Judge, joins concurring.

Richard Pears argues that as a matter of statutory construction vehicular homicide cannot equal second-degree murder regardless of the facts. AS 11.41.110(a)(2). He separately argues that the evidence presented during his trial was insufficient to support a conviction of second-degree murder and that the court erred in denying his motion for judgment of acquittal. The court rejects both of these arguments. I agree with that result, first, because I am convinced that there are certain limited circumstances under which vehicular homicide can constitute second-degree murder and, second, because I am convinced that this is one of those rare cases. I believe it is important to stress, however, that a prima facie case for manslaughter is not automatically a prima facie case for second-degree murder. A trial judge faced with a prosecution for vehicular homicide must carefully evaluate the prosecution's case-in-chief in deciding whether to permit a jury to deliberate on the issue of second-degree murder. An automobile clearly constitutes a "dangerous instrument" as that term is defined in the Revised Code. "'Dangerous instrument' means anything which, under the circumstances in which it is used, attempted to be used, or threatened to be used, is capable of causing death or serious physical injury." AS 11.81.900(b)(11). Certainly, an intoxicated person in control of a dangerous instrument in a place where others are present creates a substantial and unjustifiable risk that death or serious injury will occur, see AS 11.81.900(a)(3) (defining recklessly). A person commits the crime of manslaughter if he recklessly causes the death of another person under circumstances not amounting to murder in the first or second degree. AS 11.41.120(a)(1). Consequently, a prosecutor showing that an intoxicated person drove a car and caused a death probably makes a prima facie case of manslaughter as defined in AS 11.41.120(a). Before recklessness can meet the test of second-degree murder, however, it must "manifest an extreme indifference to the value of human life." As we noted in *Neitzel v. State*, 655 P.2d 325, 335–38 (Alaska App. 1982), murder, which is defined based upon the Model Penal Code, requires a finding of recklessness virtually amounting to purpose or knowledge:

> In a prosecution for murder, however, the Code calls for the further judgment whether the actor's conscious disregard of the risk, under the circumstances, manifests extreme indifference to the value of human life. The significance of purpose or knowledge as a standard of culpability is that, cases of provocation or other mitigation apart, purposeful or knowing homicide demonstrates precisely such indifference to the value of human life. Whether recklessness is so extreme that it demonstrates similar indifference is not a question, it is submitted, that can be further clarified. It must be left directly to the trier of fact under instructions which make it clear that recklessness that can fairly be assimilated to purpose or knowledge should

be treated as murder and that less extreme recklessness should be punished as manslaughter. 655 P.2d at 335–36, quoting A.L.I., Model Penal Code and Commentaries, Part II, § 210.2, at 21–23 (1980) (footnote omitted).

In summary, reckless murder occupies the middle ground between (1) mere recklessness, creating a substantial risk of death, and (2) knowledge, creating a virtual certainty of death. Before Pears could be found guilty of murder, his recklessness must be found to approach knowledge that his acts were practically certain to cause death or serious physical injury.

Three factors, in my opinion, distinguish this case from the typical drunk driver homicide. First, Pears drove despite the fact that his companion, Kathy Hill, warned him that his driving was endangering her and other people. Second, Pears was stopped by two uniformed police officers and told not to drive and by his conduct led the police officers to believe that he would not drive. Finally, the evidence supports a finding that Pears just missed colliding with a number of other vehicles on the road prior to the eventual homicide. Given these factors, I think a prima facie case of murder was made. It was therefore a jury question as to whether Pears' conduct manifested extreme indifference to the value of human life.

Questions and Notes

1. The Supreme Court of Alaska refused to reconsider the Court of Appeals' decision in regard to liability for murder. It did, however, reconsider Pears' sentence and rejected it as disproportionately harsh. The court emphasized that Alaska had recently changed its murder law to encompass extreme recklessness (previously only intentional killings could be categorized as murder). At the same time, it reduced the minimum sentence for second degree murder from 15 years to five years. Consequently, the Alaska Supreme Court concluded that some of the previous drunk driving manslaughter cases might now qualify for murder. It also concluded that Pears was considerably less culpable than most second degree murderers. Therefore, the court (3-2) determined that prior drunk driving manslaughter cases rather than other second degree murder cases were the appropriate benchmark from which to measure Pears' sentence. Two of the Justices thought that more than 10 years would be inappropriate. A third simply thought that 20 years was too long. Of course, the two dissenters would have upheld the 20-year sentence.

Which court got it right? Why?

2. On that score, were *Essex* and *Pears* all that different? Essex was convicted of manslaughter with a recommendation for a high sentence because of his intoxication. Pears was convicted of murder with a low sentence. Should there be an "in between" crime?

3. Would Pears have been guilty of murder or manslaughter in Virginia? Explain.

4. What was so extreme about Pears' recklessness? The court stresses the warnings from Kathy Hill and from the police officer. Didn't those warnings simply put

Pears on notice, i.e., make his conduct reckless, rather than grossly negligent? What, if anything, did they have to do with the extremity of his recklessness?

5. Is footnote 3 more favorable to the defendant than he deserves? Should he really be acquitted if he had passed out prior to entering the intersection? Compare *People v. Decina*, and Questions and Notes following, Chapter 9, *infra*.

6. Is Pears as culpable as an intentional killer? If not, why should he be treated as if he were? Does it have anything to do with the number of people that he put at risk? *Compare Northington.*

7. In *Jeffries*, one could argue that the Alaska Supreme Court appears to be widening the scope of killings that can qualify as murder. Do you agree, and if so, is that a good idea?

Jeffries v. State

169 P.3d 913 (Alaska, 2007)

EASTAUGH, Justice.

Facts and Proceedings

While grossly intoxicated, Michael Jeffries drove an automobile and caused a February 7, 2000 traffic accident that fatally injured his front seat passenger, Beulah Dean. The two were eastbound on DeBarr Road in Anchorage, driving home at 8 P.M. from a social club where alcohol had been served, when Jeffries made an abrupt left turn—but at slow speed—directly in front of Mark Bergeron's oncoming westbound car. The posted speed on the five-lane street where the collision occurred was forty-five miles per hour and Bergeron was driving at about thirty-five miles per hour. There was a thin layer of packed snow in the center lane from which Jeffries turned. There was a sheen of ice in the traffic lanes and the road was icy and slippery. It was dark, but the street was "well-lit" with streetlights. Bergeron and the investigating detective believed that headlights of Bergeron's car were on at the time of the collision. The right front corner of Bergeron's car struck the passenger door beside Beulah Dean, penetrating more than twelve inches into the passenger compartment and fatally injuring Dean. She was taken to a hospital but died soon after.

Jeffries's blood alcohol content was 0.27 percent when it was tested about seventy minutes after the accident. There was evidence that Jeffries had been drinking alcoholic beverages before noon on the day of his accident, that after drinking in the morning, he drove to a social club, where he consumed at least six more beers before he drove home and caused the fatal accident.

There was also evidence that Jeffries may have been drinking while he was driving home. A police officer found an empty beer can on the floor on the driver's side of the car. As the court of appeals later observed, "[v]iewing the evidence presented at trial in the light most favorable to the State, Jeffries downed approximately twenty beers over the course of several hours."

Jeffries was indicted on a charge of second-degree murder under for engaging in conduct that resulted in death under circumstances manifesting extreme indifference to the value of human life. He was also charged with manslaughter, negligent homicide, driving while intoxicated (DWI), and driving with a suspended license.

At trial, the prosecution introduced evidence of Jeffries's long history of driving while intoxicated. The jury heard evidence that Jeffries had six prior DWI convictions, that his license had been suspended since 1989, that he had four times failed to participate in court-ordered substance abuse programs, and that as a condition of probation he had been ordered to abstain from drinking alcohol. Jeffries objected to the admission of this evidence as irrelevant, unfairly prejudicial, and improper character evidence.

After the close of evidence Jeffries moved for a judgment of acquittal on the second-degree murder count. He argued that the state had failed to present sufficient evidence that he was driving in a manner that exhibited extreme indifference to the value of human life. The superior court denied Jeffries's motion; in doing so, it relied in part on Jeffries's history of driving while intoxicated. The jury found Jeffries guilty of second-degree murder, driving while intoxicated, and driving with a suspended license.

Jeffries appealed, arguing that extreme-indifference murder should be reserved for cases in which an intoxicated driver operates his vehicle in a particularly dangerous or heedless manner. After a thorough review of Alaska and nationwide case law, the court of appeals agreed with the superior court that Jeffries's past convictions for driving while intoxicated, his repeated refusal to participate in court-ordered treatment for alcohol abuse, his decision to drive despite his license suspension or revocation for prior DWI convictions, as well as his "extreme intoxication" on the night of the accident were sufficient to allow the murder charge to go to the jury, even if the defendant did not engage in "egregiously dangerous driving."

Given this holding, the court also rejected Jeffries's contention that the evidence of the DWI convictions and Jeffries's failure to comply with court-ordered substance abuse treatment and abstinence from alcohol was irrelevant and unduly prejudicial.

We granted Jeffries's petition for hearing.

Discussion

A. The Evidence of Jeffries's Extreme Indifference to the Value of Human Life Was Sufficient To Allow a Reasonable Jury To Convict Him of Second-Degree Murder.

Jeffries challenges the superior court's denial of his motion to acquit. In reviewing the denial of a motion to acquit, we must determine whether there is "such relevant evidence which is adequate to support a conclusion by a reasonable mind that there was no reasonable doubt as to [the defendant's] guilt." In making this determination, we "will consider only those facts in the record most favorable to the prosecution and such reasonable inferences as a jury may have drawn from them."

The court of appeals identified four factors the jury must consider in determining whether a defendant has displayed extreme indifference to the value of human life:

(1) the social utility of the actor's conduct;

(2) the magnitude of the risk his conduct creates including both the nature of foreseeable harm and the likelihood that the conduct will result in that harm;

(3) the actor's knowledge of the risk; and

(4) any precautions the actor takes to minimize the risk.

These factors have been in use in Alaska since 1982 and provide a proper framework to distinguish extreme-indifference murder from manslaughter.

The commentaries to the Model Penal Code suggest that extreme-indifference murder is intended to allow actors to be convicted of murder if their actions, while not purposeful or knowing with regard to the resulting death, demonstrate equivalent indifference to the value of human life. According to the commentaries, "there is a kind of reckless homicide that cannot fairly be distinguished in grading terms from homicides committed purposely or knowingly." Recklessness is defined as "an awareness of the creation of substantial homicidal risk, a risk too great to be deemed justifiable by any valid purpose that the actor's conduct served." For a reckless homicide to be classified as murder instead of manslaughter, the factfinder must find that "the actor's conscious disregard of the risk, under the circumstances, manifests extreme indifference to the value of human life." The commentaries advise that the factfinder must determine whether "extreme indifference to the value of human life" exists:

> Whether recklessness is so extreme that it demonstrates similar indifference [as to purposeful or knowing homicide] is not a question, it is submitted, that can be further clarified. It must be left directly to the trier of fact under instructions which make it clear that recklessness that can fairly be assimilated to purpose or knowledge should be treated as murder and that less extreme recklessness should be punished as manslaughter.

Because the question whether an actor's conduct demonstrates extreme indifference to the value of human life is primarily one for the factfinder, only rarely will evidence favorable to the defendant as to a single factor in the *Neitzel* analysis prevent the case from going to a jury. *Neitzel*'s four factors provide a test in which particularly convincing evidence as to one factor may compensate for lack of evidence as to another. Thus, although attempting to drive normally while intoxicated usually renders the driver who causes a death culpable of only manslaughter, such conduct might be found to demonstrate the requisite extreme indifference if the other *Neitzel* factors all point strongly towards greater culpability. The court may only intervene if the evidence, viewed as a whole, cannot be reasonably interpreted as demonstrating the type of heightened recklessness that is equivalent to purposeful or knowing homicide.

Jeffries contends that the only way to ensure a clear distinction between man-slaughter and extreme-indifference murder is to reserve murder for cases in which the objective risk of death or serious physical injury posed by the defendant's actions is "very high." This is a correct statement of the law, but we do not agree with his implicit contention that the objective risk posed by his conduct was not "very high."

Jeffries correctly notes that many intoxicated drivers whose convictions of extreme-indifference murder were affirmed on appeal in Alaska operated their vehicles in an exceptionally dangerous manner over an extended period of time. In *Ratliff v. State*, for example, the intoxicated defendant swerved across the road, caus-ing an accident and a near-miss, and then drove at an excessive speed on the wrong side of a divided highway for two miles until he collided head-on with another car. In *Stiegele v. State*, the intoxicated defendant drove on the left side of the road at eighty-five miles per hour with passengers in the back of his truck who were scream-ing for him to stop, and finally crashed when he could not negotiate a corner. And in *Pears v. State*, the intoxicated defendant ran stop signs and red lights and eventually collided with another car when he ran a red light without even slowing.

Although the defendants in those cases engaged in more egregious driving con-duct than Jeffries, this does not mean that his driving was not in fact egregious.

When viewed in the light most favorable to the state, the evidence at trial— including the expert testimony concerning the impairing effects of a .27 blood alco-hol level and the testimony describing the accident itself—would have enabled a reasonable jury to find not just that Jeffries was extremely intoxicated, but also that his intoxication extremely impaired his ability to drive, so that he lacked the ability to identify and react to common and easily avoidable hazards of everyday driving. In other words, the evidence tended to show that he was literally "blind" drunk to oncoming cars, not merely distracted or somewhat slowed down. Severe impair-ment of his kind would pose a grave danger at every intersection Jeffries crossed, not just at the place where his (and Dean's) luck happened to run out; and the danger of driving while blind to surrounding hazards is no less egregious merely because it poses a covert rather than an overt risk.

Nor is prolonged driving misconduct over an extended period of time inherently necessary for an extreme-indifference murder conviction. Jeffries has not identified any case in which this court or the court of appeals has overturned a jury verdict of extreme-indifference murder because the evidence of objective risk was insufficient.

Furthermore, Alaska defendants who have driven while severely intoxicated and who have engaged in driving conduct comparable to Jeffries's have been convicted of extreme-indifference murder.[23] In two such reported cases, *Richardson v. State*

---

23. We use "driving conduct" here to refer to the conduct in manipulating the controls-such as steering the wheel, accelerator, and brake pedal-that affect transient operation of a vehicle, and thus its speed and direction, as distinguished from the conduct of choosing to drive while gravely impaired.

and *Puzewicz v. State*, the defendants did not challenge their convictions on appeal, and indeed both pleaded no contest to charges of extreme-indifference murder. Both defendants unintentionally crossed the center line and collided with oncoming vehicles. Both were convicted of extreme-indifference murder for driving conduct that essentially involved fatal lapses of attention or control by very intoxicated drivers who, like Jeffries, knew or should have known they should not be driving. Neither engaged in inherently reckless or intentional gravely dangerous driving conduct, such as swerving in and out of traffic or driving at high speed, that might have justified extreme-indifference murder charges even against sober drivers. Both collisions seem to have occurred relatively soon after the defendants began or resumed driving. Thus, neither case involved prolonged or overtly "egregious" driving misconduct apart from erratic driving resulting from each defendant's severe intoxication.

Although both appellate decisions were only sentence appeals, it is significant that no party or court in either case appears to have detected any obvious legal or evidentiary flaw in basing an extreme-indifference murder conviction on a death attributable to this sort of driving conduct. No one seems to have thought that prolonged and overtly "egregious" driving conduct was necessary to support either conviction under all the circumstances in each case. Indeed, the absence of such driving conduct did not generate much mitigating force with respect to sentencing in either case. These cases illustrate that Jeffries's proposed restrictions on extreme-indifference murder would be a sharp break from the long-accepted view of the offense in Alaska. And as a practical matter, that only a few such appellate cases have arisen during the past decades refutes Jeffries's claim that his proposed restrictions are needed to avoid some sort of an endless slippery slope that threatens to swallow all repeat DWI offenders.

Jeffries cites cases from outside Alaska that purportedly demonstrate that extreme-indifference murder is not an appropriate charge for intoxicated drivers attempting to drive normally. Several of these cases, such as *Park v. State*,[28] *State v. Jensen*,[29] and *Blackwell v. State*,[30] were decided some years ago, when public awareness of the dangers of driving while intoxicated was far less than it is today. Other cases cited by Jeffries hold that a typical drunk driving accident should not be grounds for extreme indifference murder, but appear to leave open the possibility that aggravating factors that could justify a murder conviction are not limited to especially

28. *Park v. State*, 204 Ga. 766, 51 S.E.2d 832, 834–35 (Ga. 1949) (holding that vehicular homicide by intoxicated driver can only be murder if "concomitant circumstances" showed that act "naturally tended to destroy human life").

29. *State v. Jensen*, 197 Kan. 427, 417 P.2d 273, 288 (Kan. 1966) (holding that more must be shown than that defendant was driving while intoxicated to prove reckless murder).

30. *Blackwell v. State*, 34 Md. App. 547, 369 A.2d 153, at 156, 158 (Md. App. 1977) (holding that, in vehicular homicide case where defendant was intoxicated but driving within speed limit, "an inference of 'viciousness' or 'extreme indifference to the value of human life' may [not] be drawn from the past, although persistent, drinking habits of an accused").

egregious driving over a long period of time. For example, in *Allen v. State*, the Alabama Court of Criminal Appeals held that "the 'situation' that will support a conviction for reckless murder must involve something more than simply driving after having consumed alcohol and becoming involved in a collision." "[S]ome shocking, outrageous, or special heinousness must be shown." But nothing in that opinion suggests that operation at a very high level of intoxication and driving directly in front of oncoming traffic at such a slow speed that a passenger-side collision is sure to happen could not prove "special heinousness." Furthermore, the Alabama Supreme Court upheld Allen's murder conviction although his driving was no more egregious than Jeffries's. Allen was not speeding at the time of the crash and had a much lower blood alcohol content than Jeffries.[35] The accident resulted from his inability to keep his car in the proper lane of travel.

Similarly, in *United States v. Fleming*, the Fourth Circuit held that a conviction for reckless murder was appropriate because "the facts show a deviation from established standards of regard for life and the safety of others that is markedly different in degree from that found in most vehicular homicides." Although Fleming engaged in a series of dangerous maneuvers, this does not mean that Jeffries's conduct did not meet the legal standard set forth in Fleming.[38] Like *Allen*, *Fleming* leaves open the possibility that a "deviation from established standards" may be found on the basis of factors other than a prolonged period of egregious driving.

Jeffries also relies on scholarly authority as theoretical support for his argument. He cites a student note in the American Criminal Law Review that argues "the average drunk driver who drives poorly simply because of alcohol-induced sense distortion" cannot be found guilty of extreme-indifference murder. The note reasons that extreme indifference "can only be proven from inferences drawn from the defendant's conduct." In *Neitzel*, the court of appeals took a different view of "sense distortion," when it concluded that "recklessness may be found despite unawareness of a risk where intoxication accounts for the failure to perceive the risk."

We agree with the court of appeals' holding that drunk drivers are responsible for their actions when their intoxication prevents them from perceiving dangers that a sober driver would notice. Indeed, this holding is dictated by the plain language of the Alaska Criminal Code, which defines the culpable mental state "knowingly" to require a finding of knowing conduct when the defendant's failure to perceive surrounding circumstances results from voluntary intoxication: "[A] person who is unaware of conduct or a circumstance of which the person would have been aware had that person not been intoxicated acts knowingly with respect to the conduct or circumstance." In our view, the circumstances present here, including the defendant's extreme intoxication, his knowledge based on prior convictions that

35. Allen's blood alcohol content was 0.163 percent. *Id.* at 1189.
38. The defendant swerved in and out of oncoming traffic at seventy to 100 miles per hour for several miles, ultimately losing control on a curve and crashing into another car at seventy to eighty miles per hour in a thirty-mile-per-hour zone.

such intoxication was unjustifiably dangerous, and his conduct in driving directly in front of an oncoming car that had no opportunity to stop allow a jury to infer a defendant's disregard for the lives of others. The student note concedes the point that previous drunk driving convictions should be "placed in the scales" in determining whether a murder charge is appropriate.

Jeffries also argues that Professor LaFave has stated that extreme-indifference murder requires conduct creating a "very high degree of risk." We agree. But Jeffries neglects to mention that Professor LaFave concedes that the precise degree of objective risk necessary to support a charge of extreme-indifference murder varies depending on the circumstances. "[I]t is what the defendant should realize to be the degree of risk, in the light of the surrounding circumstance which he knows, which is important, rather than the amount of risk as an abstract proposition of the mathematics of chance."[45] Furthermore, Professor LaFave states that "the social utility of [the defendant's] conduct is a fact to be considered."[46] Our approach is consistent with Professor LaFave's reasoning. As did Professor LaFave, we consider the concrete facts at play in each case, not merely the abstract risk of driving while intoxicated. We hold that, in a case such as Jeffries's, in which the *Neitzel* factors weigh heavily against the defendant when taken together, the actual degree of risk required for murder has been met.

A review of the evidence in this case in light of the four *Neitzel* factors demonstrates that the jury acted reasonably in finding that Jeffries acted with extreme indifference to the value of human life. We consider each factor in turn.

1. Social utility

The state argues that driving with a blood alcohol content of two-and-a-half times the legal limit has "no social utility." Jeffries concedes that the utility of driving a vehicle home from a bar while intoxicated is "limited," but apparently does not agree it is nonexistent. In the past, the court of appeals has held that the utility of driving while intoxicated is "marginal, at best" and "substantially reduced" from the utility of driving sober.

We disagree with those decisions insofar as they suggest that driving home while intoxicated necessarily has some social utility. As the state points out, public awareness of the dangers of drunk driving has increased in recent years, as have penalties. While there is certainly utility in driving, that utility is, except in rare circumstances, completely negated by the grave danger posed to society by an extremely intoxicated driver. In this case, there was no evidence of extenuating circumstances, such as the need to take a critically ill friend or family member to the hospital or the lack of any alternative means of getting home (e.g., taxis buses, or friends) that might require a conclusion that Jeffries's driving had some limited social utility. In addition, there was evidence in the record that Jeffries had been drinking on the

---

45. *Id.* at 439.
46. *Id.*

morning of the accident and that after drinking he drove to a social club where he consumed at least six more beers before attempting to drive home. Also, Jeffries may have continued to drink while he was driving. A witness to the accident testified that "the entire vehicle smelled like alcohol," and one of the responding police officers discovered a beer can on the floor on the driver's side of the vehicle. A reasonable jury is not obliged to give an extremely drunk driver any credit for the social utility of "merely attempting to drive home." This is especially so after he has chosen to consume alcohol in the morning at home, gets behind the wheel of a car, and drives to a social club to continue his drinking, before rolling the dice by trying to drive home, perhaps drinking in the car while driving despite already being grossly intoxicated.[49]

2. Magnitude of the risk; nature and likelihood of foreseeable harm

Jeffries argues that his actual driving was not particularly egregious and did not create "a very high risk of death." He minimizes the riskiness of his behavior by characterizing it as a "poorly executed left turn." We are unpersuaded by this characterization. Jeffries's conduct was much more risky than the conduct in a typical drunk-driving accident for two reasons.

First, the evidence suggests that Jeffries's error in judgment was severe. Jeffries was attempting to make a left-hand turn across DeBarr Road, a five-lane street with a speed limit of forty-five miles per hour, against oncoming traffic. Jeffries was traveling as slowly as ten miles per hour when he pulled directly in front of Bergeron's oncoming car. Bergeron's headlights were on, and although it was dark, streetlights lit the street well. Bergeron was traveling at or below the posted speed limit, probably at about thirty-five miles per hour. The street was icy and slippery. Bergeron "had about enough warning to take [his] foot off the gas" before the collision, but not enough time to stop or swerve to avoid the accident. Bergeron's car hit Jeffries's passenger door—almost the center of the car. The point of impact demonstrates that Jeffries either badly misjudged the speed of the oncoming car or altogether failed to see it. His speed of ten miles per hour was too slow to permit him to cross safely in front of Bergeron's oncoming car and left Jeffries's passenger gravely and predictably vulnerable to a side impact.

Second, Jeffries was highly intoxicated on the night of the accident. Jeffries's apartment maintenance supervisor testified that Jeffries smelled of beer during an encounter with Jeffries between 10:30 A.M. and noon on the day of the crash. In response to the supervisor's concerned inquiry about Jeffries's ability to drive,

---

49. Our holding should not be understood as suggesting that there could be no drunk driving conduct that demonstrates less social utility than driving home from a bar. Just as driving a critically ill family member to the hospital might require a conclusion that a defendant's drunk driving had at least some social utility, one might also imagine circumstances in which a defendant's drunk driving requires a finding of extraordinary disutility. For example, racing while intoxicated is even more indicative of a disregard for human life than attempting to drive home from a bar while extremely intoxicated.

Dean commented that "he's been worse than this." At roughly 3:30 P.M. Jeffries and Dean arrived at the Veterans of Foreign Wars (VFW) club in MountainView. The bartender testified that Jeffries drank "only" six beers there and left with Dean at 8:00 P.M. After the crash, an empty beer can was found on the passenger floorboard of the car. Police investigating the crash testified that Jeffries smelled strongly of alcohol and failed a field sobriety test. A blood test performed at 9:25 P.M., an hour and ten minutes after the accident, measured Jeffries's blood alcohol content at 0.27 percent. The state's expert testified that had Jeffries begun drinking at noon, he would have had to consume 23.6 drinks to reach a blood alcohol content of 0.27 percent by 9:25 P.M.

The evidence established that Jeffries's blood alcohol content made it highly dangerous for him to drive. An expert witness for the state testified about a study that demonstrated that the probability of causing an accident increases "exponentially" as blood alcohol content increases. While a driver with a .08 percent blood alcohol content is three times more likely to cause an accident than a sober driver,[50] a driver with a 0.15 percent blood alcohol content is twelve times more likely to cause an accident than a sober person. Jeffries's blood alcohol content was nearly twice the highest level discussed by the expert. Thus, there was evidence that the probability Jeffries would cause an accident was at least twelve—and probably many more—times that for a sober driver. The fact that the roads were "icy" and "slick" on the night of the accident probably increased the risk even more because the condition of the road made it more difficult for oncoming drivers to altogether avoid a collision by stopping or swerving or to minimize the consequences by slowing down.

At least one court, the Kentucky Supreme Court, has upheld murder convictions of intoxicated drivers based primarily on their extreme intoxication at the time of the accident. Although we do not decide here whether a murder conviction might be warranted on the basis of extreme intoxication alone, we do conclude that Jeffries's intoxication, at over two-and-a-half times the legal limit, was extreme. The jury could properly find the objective risk posed by a driver with Jeffries's level of intoxication to be significantly higher than that of a typical drunk driver.

Likewise, the nature of the harm—the risk of death or serious bodily injury—inherent in abruptly turning and driving slowly across the path of oncoming traffic on slippery streets is both great and readily foreseeable. And it is very likely, and foreseeable, under such circumstances that the conduct will cause that harm.

3. Awareness of the risk

Jeffries's heightened awareness of the risks of drinking and driving differentiates this case from other deaths involving drunk drivers. The evidence relevant to his awareness was strong. The parties stipulated that Jeffries had six prior DWI

---

50. It appears from the testimony that the expert considered a "sober" driver to be a driver with no alcohol in his or her bloodstream.

convictions between 1981 and 1996, four of them occurring in the 1990s. The parties also stipulated that Jeffries's license had been continuously revoked since 1989, that it would remain revoked until 2018, and that Jeffries was aware that his license had been revoked.[53] They also stipulated that a DWI conviction was the basis for the 2000 revocation. The state presented evidence that four times between 1989 and 1994 Alaska courts had ordered Jeffries as a condition of his probation to report to a probation program that screens offenders and assigns them to alcohol treatment programs and that he failed to comply with each order despite the possibility that he could be sent to prison for noncompliance. Finally, the state presented evidence that as a condition of his probation Jeffries was forbidden from drinking alcohol at the time of the most recent accident. There is no claim Jeffries did not have actual knowledge of his past drunk driving convictions and of the court orders requiring him to get treatment. In short, there was significant evidence that Jeffries had a heightened awareness of the dangerousness of his conduct, the need to refrain completely from any driving and to refrain completely from any drinking, and of the danger of driving intoxicated.

As Superior Court Judge Dan A. Hensley explained in determining that evidence of Jeffries's past problems with alcohol was relevant to this inquiry:

> [A] person who drinks, drives, causes an accident, gets arrested, goes to jail, is ordered to alcohol treatment, ordered not to drink and then drinks and drives again, and then drinks and drives again, and then drinks and drives again, not only has the intellectual understanding of the risks associated with drinking and driving but also has the very real understanding. Which in my view is relevant to show the heightened awareness of those risks. Experience is the best teacher.

The superior court was correct in its assessment. An intoxicated driver with a record as long as Jeffries's cannot possibly be unaware of the significant threat that his actions pose in the eyes of society. A reasonable jury could have inferred from this evidence that Jeffries had a heightened awareness of the risk of drinking and driving and could have given this factor substantial weight in its analysis under *Neitzel.*

4. Precautions to minimize the risk

The state argues correctly that there is no evidence that Jeffries took any precautions to minimize the risk of his conduct. In fact, Jeffries's past failures to follow orders to participate in substance abuse programs and to refrain from either driving or drinking demonstrate a willful refusal to take precautions to minimize the risk. A reasonable jury could have properly taken Jeffries's refusal into account in evaluating whether he exhibited extreme indifference to the value of human life.

---

53. The stipulation does not establish that Jeffries knew that his license was revoked until 2018.

5. A reasonable jury weighing these factors could convict Jeffries of murder

We agree with the admonition in *Pears* that "a charge of second-degree murder should only rarely be appropriate in a motor vehicle homicide." But Jeffries is distinguishable from the typical intoxicated driver by his heightened awareness of the risk resulting from his past history of drunk driving offenses and the revocation of his license, his extreme level of intoxication, and his inherently dangerous conduct in driving his car directly in front of an oncoming car that had no opportunity to react.[56] The evidence allowed a reasonable jury to conclude that Jeffries's conduct was not only reckless, but also demonstrated extreme indifference to the value of human life.

B. The Superior Court Did Not Abuse Its Discretion by Admitting Evidence of Jeffries's Failure To Complete Alcohol Treatment and His Probation Condition that He Not Consume Alcohol.

Jeffries argues that evidence of his failures to complete court-ordered alcohol treatment and his probation condition which prohibited him from drinking alcohol on the night in question was irrelevant and prejudicial. The court of appeals reasoned that this evidence demonstrated Jeffries's heightened awareness of the risks of his conduct.[57]

Because it is usually impossible to present direct evidence of a defendant's mental state, indirect evidence that establishes that the defendant was informed of the dangerousness of his actions is often essential to establish the defendant's awareness of the risk. In this case, the challenged evidence is highly probative.

IV. Conclusion

We hold that an intoxicated driver may be guilty of extreme-indifference murder if all four *Neitzel* factors, taken together, permit a reasonable jury to find extreme indifference to the value of human life. Evidence of extreme intoxication, inherently dangerous conduct while driving, and heightened awareness of the dangers of driving while intoxicated is highly relevant to this determination. Because a reasonable jury could find Jeffries guilty of extreme-indifference murder on the evidence presented, we AFFIRM the decision of the court of appeals that affirmed his judgment and commitment.

MATTHEWS, Justice, with whom FABE, Justice, joins, dissenting.

---

56. The dissenting opinion asserts that "[a] prosecutor now will be able to charge murder whenever a repeat offender with a high blood alcohol reading causes a fatal accident." This overstates the holding we reach today, and readers should not assume that the dissent accurately describes the effect of our holding. Our conclusion that there was sufficient evidence to sustain the verdict turns not just on Jeffries's prior record and his extremely high level of intoxication but also on case-specific evidence including both crime-scene evidence and expert testimony that Jeffries was extremely incapacitated when he drove and actually did engage in egregiously dangerous driving.

57. *Jeffries v. State*, 90 P.3d 185, 194 (Alaska App. 2004).

Today's opinion holds that a drunken driver who causes a fatal accident can be guilty of reckless murder if he has a high blood alcohol content and a prior record of driving while intoxicated. I do not join in this conclusion.

The legislative history of our reckless murder statute makes it clear that the statute was meant to be confined to cases in which reckless conduct closely resembles an intentional or knowing murder. Conduct was contemplated that is similar in degree of risk to that which is encompassed in the phrase that governs knowing or intentional second-degree murder: "substantially certain to cause death or serious physical injury." The examples of such conduct offered by the senate committee which recommended the adoption of the statute were shooting into a tent or persuading a person to play Russian roulette.

In my view, drinking too much—even way too much—and then attempting to drive safely is not substantially certain to cause death, nor is it comparable in terms of risk, or in terms of utility or anti-social mind-set, with these examples. As the court of appeals observed in *Neitzel v. State*:

> For both murder and manslaughter, the harm to be foreseen is a death. Therefore, the significant distinction is in the likelihood that a death will result from the defendant's act. Where the defendant's act has limited social utility, a very slight though significant and avoidable risk of death may make him guilty of manslaughter if his act causes death. Driving an automobile has some social utility although substantially reduced when the driver is intoxicated. The odds that a legally intoxicated person driving home after the bars close will hit and kill or seriously injure someone may be as low as one chance in a thousand and still qualify for manslaughter. Where murder is charged, however, an act must create a much greater risk that death or serious physical injury will result.

I agree with those cases and authorities that suggest that if a fatality caused by a drunken driver is to be murder rather than manslaughter, the driver must have engaged in egregiously unsafe maneuvers such as extreme speeding, wrong-way driving, or running stop lights.[4] Merely being drunk and attempting without success to drive normally can be manslaughter, but not murder.

Today's opinion may generate an unintended result. A prosecutor now will be able to charge murder whenever a repeat offender with a high blood alcohol reading causes a fatal accident. The murder charge will go to the jury and the jury will be instructed that it may consider the defendant's prior DWI record. But the defendant's record might not be admissible if the charge were merely manslaughter rather

---

4. *See Pears v. State*, (intoxicated defendant "drove recklessly, speeding, running through stop signs and stop lights and failing to slow for yield signs"; court "emphasize[d] that a charge of second-degree murder should only rarely be appropriate in a motor vehicle homicide. The murder charge in this case is supported by the[se] extreme facts").

than murder.[6] Given the likely impact on the jury's deliberations of a prior history of DWI convictions, it may turn out to be easier in such cases to obtain a conviction of murder than a conviction of manslaughter.

For the reasons stated, I would reverse Jeffries's second-degree murder conviction.

Questions and Notes

1. *Ex ante*, do you think that it was highly likely that Jeffries would kill somebody?

2. In assessing that question, is it relevant that for all of his prior drunkenness he never previously killed, and so far as the record shows, never seriously injured anybody with his drunk driving?

3. Is (should it be) relevant that his passenger (victim) had said that she'd seen him worse?

4. Is the Alaska standard for murder essentially the same as the Virginia (*Conrad*) standard for involuntary manslaughter?

5. Is there, or can there be, a meaningful standard to distinguish murder from manslaughter?

6. Is there in Alaska after *Jeffries*?

7. Should an unlicensed multiple recidivist drunk driver who causes a death be per se guilty of murder?

8. If not, what, if anything, was different about *Jeffries*?

9. In *Northington*, we see a court that will not consider depraved heart murder unless the outrageous recklessness created a grave risk of death to more than one individual.

Northington v. State

413 So. 2d 1169 (Ala. App. 1981)

Bowen, Judge.

The defendant was indicted and convicted for the murder of her five-month-old daughter. Sentence was life imprisonment.

The indictment contained two counts. Count 2 charged that the defendant intentionally killed Dana Northington by suffocation. The jury found the defendant guilty of Count 1 which charged that the defendant

> "did recklessly engage in conduct which manifested extreme indifference to human life and created grave risk of death to the person of Dana Northington, and the said conduct did hereby cause the death of Dana

---

6. *E.g.* The superior court in this case exercised its discretion under Evidence Rule 403 by ruling the defendant's prior record would not be admitted on the manslaughter charge because the defendant's prior record would be more prejudicial than probative.

Northington, by withholding food and medical attention from the said
Dana Northington. . . ."

Under Alabama Code 1975, Section 13A-6-2(a)(2) (Amended 1977), a person
commits the crime of murder if:

"Under circumstances manifesting extreme indifference to human life, he
recklessly engages in conduct which creates a grave risk of death to a person
other than himself, and thereby causes the death of another person."

Essentially, this section is a restatement of Alabama law which defined murder
in the first degree to include every homicide "perpetrated by any act greatly dangerous to the lives of others and evincing a depraved mind regardless of human
life, although without any preconceived purpose to deprive any particular person
of life." Alabama Code 1975, Section 13-1-70. The commentary to Section 13A-6-2
makes this clear.

"Section 13A-6-2(a)(2) also retains as murder the recklessly engaging in
conduct which creates a grave risk of death under circumstances 'manifesting extreme indifference to human life', which is different from a positive
intent to kill, and which essentially restates existing law. Section 13-1-70."

The new statute, 13A-6-2(a)(2), removes the requirement that more than one
person be endangered by the reckless conduct of the accused. Compare the phrase
"any act greatly dangerous to the *lives* of others" with "conduct which creates a
grave risk of death to a *person* other than himself." (Emphasis added.) However, the
statute still requires conduct which manifests an extreme indifference to *human life*
and not to a particular person only.

At the close of the State's evidence defense counsel requested the trial judge to
exclude Count 1 of the indictment from the consideration of the jury. The defendant
argued that he could not be convicted of a count charging "universal malice" where
the criminal acts of the accused were directed solely at the deceased and where the
method of death alleged in the indictment (starvation) required a specific intent.

Reckless homicide manifesting extreme indifference to human life (13A-6-2(a)
(2)) must be distinguished from purposeful or knowing murder (13A-6-2(a)(1)). *See*
American Law Institute, Model Penal Code and Commentaries, Part II, Section 210.2
(1980). Under whatever name, the doctrine of universal malice, depraved heart murder, or reckless homicide manifesting extreme indifference to human life is intended
to embrace those cases where a person has no deliberate intent to kill or injure any
particular individual. "The element of 'extreme indifference to human life', by definition, does not address itself to the life of the victim, but to human life generally."

The evidence in this case, even when viewed in the light most favorable to the
prosecution, reveals that the defendant's acts and omissions were specifically
directed at a particular victim and no other.

The State presented no evidence that the defendant engaged in conduct "under
circumstances manifesting extreme indifference to human life" for, while the

defendant's conduct did indeed evidence an extreme indifference to the life of her child, there was nothing to show that the conduct displayed an extreme indifference to human life generally. Although the defendant's conduct created a grave risk of death to another and thereby caused the death of that person, the acts of the defendant were aimed at the particular victim and no other. Not only did the defendant's conduct create a grave risk of death to only her daughter and no other, but the defendant's actions (or inactions) were directed specifically against the young infant. This evidence does not support a conviction of murder as charged under Section 13A-6-2(a)(2). The function of this section is to embrace those homicides caused by such acts as driving an automobile in a grossly wanton manner, shooting a firearm into a crowd or moving train, and throwing a timber from a roof onto a crowded street.

In order that a person who withholds food or medical attention from another to whom a legal duty is owed may be found guilty of murder it is necessary to show that the conduct of the accused was willful or done with malicious intent. In *Bliley v. State*, 42 Ala. App. 261, 262, 160 So. 2d 507 (1964), the court held: "To prove murder by starvation, under the established cases, the prosecution must prove that with malice aforethought the person charged (1) is under a duty to feed, (2) has control of the food, and (3) denies food to the deceased."

The jury's verdict found the defendant guilty as charged in Count 1 of the indictment. Our review of the record convinces us that the evidence was insufficient to sustain the conviction of reckless homicide manifesting extreme indifference to human life. A long and diligent search has revealed no case where an accused was either indicted or convicted for murder by the denial of food or medical attention under an indictment involving universal malice or reckless homicide manifesting indifference to human life.

Because of the revolting and heart sickening details of this case, this Court is extremely reluctant to reverse the conviction of the defendant. Yet, because our system is one of law and not of men, we have no other choice. The judgment of the Circuit Court is reversed and the cause remanded.

Questions and Notes

1. If Northington had intended the death of her child (or presumably her serious illness), she would have been guilty of murder. How could she have been extremely indifferent to human life without having intended death or serious illness?

2. If the prosecutor had simply alleged that Northington had intentionally withheld food, do you think that a conviction for murder could have been sustained?

3. Is there a sensible construction of the statute by which a court (in a system of law and not of persons) could have construed the statute to apply to Northington's conduct? Should the court have done so?

4. How would *Jeffries* have been decided under the *Northington* rule? Did he create a grave risk of death to anyone other than his passenger?

5. In a law review article, Professor Alan Michaels suggested that the vague concept of depraved heart murder should be replaced by a standard of murder liability if, but only if, the defendant would have acted as he did even if he had known that a death would have occurred. *See* Michaels, *Acceptance: The Missing Mental State*, 71 S.C. L. REV. 953 (1998). Do you agree with that test? Why? Why not? Under that test, what result in *Essex, Pears, Jeffries*, and *Northington*?

See NUTSHELL § 2.06; *Culpability, Dangerousness, and Harm*, Section III G (Appendix B).

Problem

On June 13, 1987, James Soto, then aged two years and eight months, was killed by a pit bulldog named "Willy," owned by defendant. The animal was tethered near defendant's house but no obstacle prevented access to the dog's area. The victim and his family lived in a house that stood on the same lot, sharing a common driveway.

The Soto family had four young children, then aged 10, 4½, 2½, and one year. On the day of the child's death, his mother, Yvonne Nunez, left the child playing on the patio of their home for a minute or so while she went into the house, and when she came out the child was gone. She was looking for him when within some three to five minutes her brother-in-law, Richard Soto, called her and said defendant's dog had attacked James. Meanwhile the father, Arthur Soto, had come upon the dog Willy mauling his son. He screamed for defendant to come get the dog off the child; defendant did so. The child was bleeding profusely. Although an on-call volunteer fireman with paramedical training who lived nearby arrived within minutes and attempted to resuscitate the child, James died before an emergency crew arrived at the scene.

There was no evidence that Willy had ever before attacked a human being, but there was considerable evidence that he was bred and trained to be a fighting dog and that he posed a known threat to people. Defendant bought Willy from a breeder of fighting dogs, who informed defendant of the dog's fighting abilities, his gameness, wind, and exceptionally hard bite. The breeder told defendant that in a dog fight "a dog won't go an hour with Willy and live."

The police searched defendant's house after the death of James and found many underground publications about dog fighting; a pamphlet titled "42 day keep" which set out the six-week conditioning procedures used to prepare a dog for a match; a treadmill used to condition a dog and increase its endurance; correspondence with Willy's breeder, Gene Smith; photographs of dog fights; and a "break stick," used to pry fighting dogs apart since they will not release on command. One of Smith's letters dated December 7, 1984, described Willy as having an exceptionally hard bite.

Two women who knew defendant testified he told them he had raised dogs for fighting purposes and had fought pit bulls.

Richard Soto testified that the defendant told him he used the treadmill to increase the strength and endurance of his dogs. Defendant also told both Arthur and Richard Soto that he would not fight his dogs for less than $500 and he told Richard that Willy had had matches as far away as South Carolina.

The victim's mother testified defendant had several dogs. He told her not to be concerned about the dogs, that they would not bother her children, except for "one that he had on the side of the house" which was behind a six-foot fence. Defendant further said this dangerous dog was Willy but that she need not be concerned since he was behind a fence. There was a fence where the dog was tethered on the west side of defendant's house, but the fence was not an enclosure and did not prevent access to the area the dog could reach.

The police found some 243 marijuana plants growing behind defendant's house. Willy was tethered in such location that anyone wanting to approach the plants would have to cross the area the dog could reach. That area was readily accessible to anyone.

An animal control officer qualified as an expert on fighting dogs testified. He said pit bull dogs are selectively bred to be aggressive toward other animals. They give no warning of their attack, attack swiftly, silently, and tenaciously. Although many recently bred pit bulls have good dispositions near human beings and are bred and raised to be pets, there are no uniform breeding standards for temperament and the animal control officers consider a pit bull dangerous unless proved otherwise. When testifying, Arthur Soto denied having told any investigator that defendant had warned him about Willy. Counsel interrogating him insinuated that he was afraid to testify about prior warnings because he might jeopardize his civil lawsuit against defendant. Later an officer who had investigated the death and had interviewed Arthur testified pursuant to Evidence Code section 1237 that Arthur had told the officer defendant had warned Arthur to "keep the kids away from the killer dog," meaning Willy.

1. If you represented Berry and the prosecutor offered you the choice of pleading guilty to involuntary manslaughter, or going to trial for depraved heart murder, which would you choose? Why?

2. As the prosecutor, upon what factors would you focus to establish murder? As defense counsel, what factors would you emphasize to negate the "depraved heart" claim?

3. In terms of culpability and dangerousness, how does *Berry* compare to *Pears*, *Jeffries*, and *Northington*?

4. See *Berry v. Superior Court*, 256 Cal. Rptr. 344 (1989), in which the court permitted the case to be tried on a theory of "depraved heart" murder.

F. Felony-Murder

Under the felony-murder rule, in its strictest form, all killings perpetrated in the course of a felony constitute murder. Although the doctrine is rarely enforced so starkly, in many states, one can be convicted of murder for a death resulting from a felony that would not be murder apart from the felony-murder rule.

This section focuses on the claimed rationales for the rule, the varying scope and limitations imposed upon the rule, and, ultimately, the question of whether the rule should be retained. Think about these questions as you read the cases.

People v. Gladman
359 N.E.2d 420 (N.Y. 1976)

JASEN, Judge.

On this appeal, defendant argues that his shooting of a police officer did not occur, as a matter of law, in immediate flight from a robbery and that, therefore, his conviction for felony murder should be set aside. We hold that, under the circumstances presented, the issue of whether the homicide was committed in immediate flight from the robbery was properly presented to the jury as a question of fact. The order of the Appellate Division, therefore, should be affirmed.

At trial, the People submitted overwhelming evidence that on the night of December 29, 1971, the defendant shot and killed Nassau County Police Officer Richard Rose in a bowling alley parking lot. The events of that evening can be briefly recited. At approximately 8:00 p.m., defendant obtained a ride to the County Line Shopping Center in Amityville, New York. Ten minutes later, he entered a delicatessen, produced a gun, and demanded money from the clerk. The clerk turned over about $145 in cash and checks. After the robbery, Gladman left the shopping center and walked through the surrounding neighborhood, eventually arriving at the County Line Bowling Alley. In the meantime, the robbery had been reported to the Nassau County Police Department and an alert was transmitted over the police radio. Two officers arrived at the delicatessen at 8:16 p.m., just minutes after the defendant had left. A description of the robber was obtained and broadcast over the police radio. Normal police procedure required that unassigned patrol cars proceed to the vicinity of the crime area and any nearby major intersections in an effort to seal off potential avenues of escape. As Gladman walked onto the parking lot of the bowling alley, he saw a police car turn and enter the lot. He hid under a parked car. Patrolman Rose, the lone officer in the car, emerged from his vehicle and walked over to defendant's hiding place. The defendant got up from underneath the car with his gun concealed between his legs. The officer ordered the defendant to put his weapon on the car hood; instead, the defendant turned and fired. Patrolman Rose, mortally wounded, struggled to his police car and attempted to use the radio to summon the assistance of brother officers. He collapsed on the seat. The defendant commandeered the automobile of a bowling alley patron and made good his escape. An off-duty New York City police officer used Rose's radio to broadcast a signal for help. The report of the shooting went over the police radio at 8:24 p.m. Eyewitnesses fixed the time of the altercation at approximately 8:25 p.m. The bowling alley was located less than one-half mile from the robbed delicatessen.

After a jury trial, the defendant was convicted of manslaughter in the first degree, felony murder, robbery in the first degree and grand larceny in the third degree. The Appellate Division unanimously affirmed the judgment of conviction, without opinion. The principal issue on this appeal is whether the jury was properly permitted to conclude that the shooting of Officer Rose occurred in the immediate flight from the delicatessen robbery.

A felony murder is committed when a person, acting alone or in concert with others, commits or attempts to commit one of nine predicate felonies, of which robbery is one, and "in the course of and in furtherance of such crime or of immediate flight therefrom, he, or another participant, if there be any, causes the death of a person other than one of the participants." (Penal Law, § 125.25, subd. 3.) By operation of law, the intent necessary to sustain a murder conviction is inferred from the intent to commit a specific, serious, felonious act, even though the defendant, in truth, may not have intended to kill. Here, the jury, by its verdict, found that the defendant did not possess a murderous intent.* The question is whether the jury could properly find that the killing of Officer Rose was in the immediate area from the robbery, thus triggering the application of the felony murder doctrine. To resolve the issue, it is first necessary to refer to the checkered case law in this State, applying the felony murder concepts to cases, such as this one, where the fatal wounds were inflicted in the course of escape.

Under older statutes which did not specifically address the issue, it was early held that a killing committed during an escape could, under some circumstances, constitute a felony murder. In *People v. Giro*, 197 N.Y. 152, 90 N.E. 432, burglars aroused a slumbering family, the son struggled with one intruder and when the mother went to the aid of her child, she was shot dead. In affirming subsequent convictions, the court stated that the defendants committed actions in furtherance of their design to rob the house and "escape was as much a part thereof as breaking in with the jimmy or stealing the pocketbook. When they armed themselves to enter upon a felonious undertaking, shooting was the natural and probable result in order to get away if discovered, and if either fired the fatal shot both are responsible." *Giro*, however, was a case where the defendants got away with some loot. A different result was reached in *People v. Huter*, 184 N.Y. 237, 77 N.E. 6, where the defendant broke into a bake shop and, when discovered, was in the act of removing egg crates from the store and placing them in his wagon. On discovery, defendant and his companion abandoned the wagon and fled on foot. A watchman summoned a police officer, the officer chased the defendant, and was fatally shot. The court held that a felony murder conviction could not be sustained. The hot pursuit of the watchman and the police officer "did not operate to continue the burglary

---

* Under New York law, unlike most other states, assault with intent to inflict serious injury resulting in death constitutes manslaughter in the first degree. Because the jury found Gladman guilty of manslaughter in the first degree rather than nonfelony murder (which does require an intent to kill), the court could assume that the jury found an absence of murderous intent. — Ed.

after the defendant had abandoned the property that he undertook to carry away and had escaped from the premises burglarized. In all of the cases to which our attention has been called, in which persons have been convicted of murder in the first degree by reason of the killing of a person while the accused was engaged in the commission of a burglary, the killing took place upon the premises." Although the defendant had armed himself in preparation of a possible escape, this did not serve to continue an "abandoned" crime. Rather, this was a factor that the jury could consider in finding that the defendant had intended to kill anyone who crossed his criminal path, thereby justifying conviction for an intentional killing. These kinds of analyses soon led to the development of some rather arbitrary rules. If the defendant left the premises without the loot, the criminal action was deemed either terminated or abandoned and a subsequent homicide would not be a felony murder. "The very meaning of flight is desistance or abandonment, unless, indeed, in special circumstances as in cases where a thief is fleeing with his loot." On the other hand, both presence on the premises and retention of loot were not regarded as conclusive proof of felony continuation, but were merely evidence that the felony was continuing. The term premises was rather strictly confined to "within the four walls of the building" and a killing on an immediately adjoining public street would not be a killing on the "premises." (*People v. Collins*, 234 N.Y. 355, 363, 137 N.E. 753 (warehouse burglar was discovered and hid under railway car; when the watchman flushed him out, the watchman was killed by burglar's accomplices)).

The later New York cases indicate some dissatisfaction with the strict legal rules that had developed and tended to leave the question of escape killings to the jury as a question of fact, under appropriate instructions. The change was to point out

> "generally that the killing to be felony murder must occur while the actor or one or more of his confederates is engaged in securing the plunder or in doing something immediately connected with the underlying crime; that escape may, under certain unities of time, manner and place, be a matter so immediately connected with the crime as to be part of its commission; but that, where there is no reasonable doubt of a complete intervening desistance from the crime, as by the abandonment of the loot and running away, the subsequent homicide is not murder in the first degree without proof of deliberation and intent." The question of termination of the underlying felony was then left to the jury as a fact question.

The New York approach was more rigid than that developed in other jurisdictions. The majority of the States tended to follow the "*res gestae*" theory—*i.e.*, whether the killing was committed in, about and as a part of the underlying transaction. California had adopted the *res gestae* theory, at least insofar as robbery is concerned, holding that a robbery is not complete if the

> "conspirators have not won their way even momentarily to a place of temporary safety and the possession of the plunder is nothing more than a scrambling possession. In such a case the continuation of the use of arms

which was necessary to aid the felon in reducing the property to possession is necessary to protect him in its possession and in making good his
escape. . . . The escape of the robbers with the loot, by means of arms, necessarily is as important to the execution of the plan as gaining possession
of the property. Without revolvers to terrify, or, if occasion requires, to kill
any person who attempts to apprehend them at the time of or immediately
upon gaining possession of said property, their plan would be childlike."

(*People v. Boss*, 210 Cal. 245, 250–251, 290 P. 881 (1930).) Subsequent case law indicates that, in California, the robbery is ongoing simply if the culprit had failed to
reach a place of temporary safety. (*People v. Salas*, 7 Cal.3d 812, 103 Cal. Rptr. 431,
500 P.2d 7.) The comparative rigidity of the New York approach has been explained
as stemming from the fact that, at the time, New York, with a minority of other
States, provided that all felonies would support a conviction for felony murder. Of
course, felony murder was also a capital offense and the cases attempted to narrow
the scope of liability particularly where it was an accomplice that did the actual
killing.

The 1967 Penal Law limited the application of the felony murder concept to nine
serious and violent predicate felonies. At the same time, it was provided that the
doctrine would apply to a killing committed in "immediate flight." This change was
intended to do away with many of the old technical distinctions relating to "abandonment" or "completion."

Under the new formulation, the issue of whether the homicide occurred in
"immediate flight" from a felony is only rarely to be considered as a question of law
for resolution by the court. Only where the record compels the inference that the
actor was not in "immediate flight" may a felony murder conviction be set aside on
the law. Rather, the question is to be submitted to the jury, under an appropriate
charge. The jury should be instructed to give consideration to whether the homicide and the felony occurred at the same location or, if not, to the distance separating the two locations. Weight may also be placed on whether there is an interval of
time between the commission of the felony and the commission of the homicide.
The jury may properly consider such additional factors as whether the culprits had
possession of the fruits of criminal activity, whether the police, watchmen or concerned citizens were in close pursuit, and whether the criminals had reached a place
of temporary safety. These factors are not exclusive; others may be appropriate in
differing factual settings. If anything, past history demonstrates the fruitlessness
of attempting to apply rigid rules to virtually limitless factual variations. No single
factor is necessarily controlling; it is the combination of several factors that leads to
a justifiable inference.

In this case, the jury could properly find, as a question of fact, that the killing
of Officer Rose occurred in immediate flight from the delicatessen robbery. The
shooting occurred less than 15 minutes after the robbery and less than a half mile
away. The defendant had made off with cash proceeds and was attempting to secure
his possession of the loot. The police had reason to believe that the robber was still

in the immediate vicinity and had taken steps to seal off avenues of escape. In this regard, the absence of proof as to why Officer Rose turned into the bowling alley parking lot is no deficiency. The standard is not whether the police officer subjectively believed that the defendant was the robber. Indeed, the defendant's own apprehension may be more valuable. The defendant's response to the observation of the police car was to seek an immediate hiding place. This indicates that the defendant perceived that the police were on his trail. The record does not indicate that the officer knew or supposed, that defendant committed a crime; it does indicate that the defendant feared that the officer possessed such knowledge. Additionally, the defendant had not reached any place of temporary safety. In short, there is evidence from which the jury could conclude, as it did, that the defendant was in immediate flight from the robbery and that he shot the officer in order to make good his escape with the loot. The jury was properly charged as to the relevant considerations and we see no basis for disturbing its findings.

The order of the Appellate Division should be affirmed.

BREITEL, C.J., and GABRIELLI, JONES, WACHTLER, FUCHSBERG and COOKE, JJ., concur.

Order Affirmed.

Questions and Notes

1. Is it important that Gladman shot Rose to avoid detection for the felony? Suppose Gladman had driven away from the robbery and crashed into a car driven by Officer Rose, killing him? See *Whitman v. People*, 420 P.2d 416 (Colo. 1966), upholding a felony-murder conviction.

2. Why should temporal or spatial considerations matter? Suppose that three days after the robbery, Officer Rose rang Gladman's doorbell to discuss the robbery with him and was met by a hail of gunfire from Gladman, who feared being arrested for the crime.

3. Same as Question 2, except that Officer Rose rang Gladman's doorbell to sell him tickets to the policeman's ball.

4. Most states would not impose felony-murder liability in either Question 2 or 3, *but cf. State v. Metalski*, 185 A. 351 (N.J. 1936), upholding a felony-murder conviction for the killing of a police officer during a traffic stop, two hours, several miles, and one state away from the robbery.

5. If you had represented Gladman at trial, how would you have argued that he was not in the process of "immediate flight"?

6. Should the court have found that this was not "immediate flight" as a matter of law?

7. The next two cases, *Phillips* and *Sears*, focus on the attributes that a felony must possess in order to qualify for felony-murder.

People v. Phillips

414 P.2d 353 (Cal. 1966)

TOBRINER, Justice.

Defendant, a doctor of chiropractic, appeals from a judgment of the Superior Court of Los Angeles County convicting him of second degree murder in connection with the death from cancer of one of his patients. We reverse solely on the ground that the trial court erred in giving a felony murder instruction.

Linda Epping died on December 29, 1961, at the age of 8, from a rare and fast-growing form of eye cancer. Linda's mother first observed a swelling over the girl's left eye in June of that year. The doctor whom she consulted recommended that Linda be taken to Dr. Straatsma, an ophthalmologist at the UCLA Medical Center. On July 10th Dr. Straatsma first saw Linda; on July 17th the girl, suffering great pain, was admitted to the center. Dr. Straatsma performed an exploratory operation and the resulting biopsy established the nature of the child's affliction.

Dr. Straatsma advised Linda's parents that her only hope for survival lay in immediate surgical removal of the affected eye. The Eppings were loath to permit such surgery, but on the morning of July 21st Mr. Epping called the hospital and gave his oral consent. The Eppings arrived at the hospital that afternoon to consult with the surgeon. While waiting they encountered a Mrs. Eaton who told them that defendant had cured her son of a brain tumor without surgery.

Mrs. Epping called defendant at his office. According to the Eppings, defendant repeatedly assured them that he could cure Linda without surgery. They testified that defendant urged them to take Linda out of the hospital, claiming that the hospital was "an experimental place," that the doctors there would use Linda as "a human guinea pig" and would relieve the Eppings of their money as well.

The Eppings testified that in reliance upon defendant's statements they took Linda out of the hospital and placed her under defendant's care. They stated that if defendant had not represented to them that he could cure the child without surgery and that the UCLA doctors were only interested in experimentation, they would have proceeded with the scheduled operation. The prosecution introduced medical testimony which tended to prove that if Linda had undergone surgery on July 21st her life would have been prolonged or she would have been completely cured.

Defendant treated Linda from July 22 to August 12, 1961. He charged an advance fee of $500 for three months' care as well as a sum exceeding $200 for pills and medicines. On August 13th Linda's condition had not improved; the Eppings dismissed defendant.

Later the Eppings sought to cure Linda by means of a Mexican herbal drug known as yerba mansa and, about the 1st of September, they placed her under the care of the Christian Science movement. They did not take her back to the hospital for treatment.

Defendant testified that he knew that he could not cure cancer, that he did not represent to the Eppings that he could do so, that he urged them to return Linda to the hospital and that he agreed to treat her only when it became clear that the Eppings would never consent to surgery. He further testified that in administering treatment he sought to build up Linda's general health and so prolong her life. He insisted that he had never purported to "treat" cancer as such, but only to give "supportive" care to the body as a whole. He variously described his purpose as being "to build up her resistance," "assisting the body to overcome its own deficiencies" and "supporting the body defenses."

Defendant challenges the propriety of the trial court's instructions to the jury. The court gave the following tripartite instruction on murder in the second degree:[4]

> "(T)he unlawful killing of a human being with malice aforethought, but without a deliberately formed and premeditated intent to kill, is murder of the second degree:

> "(1) If the killing proximately results from an unlawful act, the natural consequences of which are dangerous to life, which act is deliberately performed by a person who knows that his conduct endangers the life of another, or;

> "(2) If the circumstances proximately causing the killing show an abandoned and malignant heart, or;

> "(3) If the killing is done in the perpetration or attempt to perpetrate a felony such as Grand Theft. If a death occurs in the perpetration of a course of conduct amounting to Grand Theft, which course of conduct is a proximate cause of the unlawful killing of a human being, such course of conduct constitutes murder in the second degree, even though the death was not intended."

---

4. The record suggests that the evidence would have supported a finding of involuntary manslaughter. The jury might, for example, have found that defendant sincerely, though unreasonably, believed that the removal of Linda from the hospital and treatment according to the principles of chiropractic would be in her best interests. Having so found, the jury could have concluded that in causing Linda's removal from the hospital and so endangering her life defendant acted "without due caution and circumspection." (Pen. Code, § 192, subd. 2.) Accordingly, the trial court should have given a manslaughter instruction. (*People v. Modesto* (1963) 59 Cal. 2d 722, 729–730, 31 Cal. Rptr. 225, 382 P.2d 33; *People v. Henderson* (1963) 60 Cal. 2d 482, 489–491, 35 Cal. Rptr. 77, 386 P.2d 677.) The record reveals, however, that defendant's counsel strongly opposed the manslaughter instruction and indicated to the trial court that he considered it "tactically" to defendant's advantage to confront the jury with the limited choice between murder and acquittal. Thus, the failure of the trial court to instruct on manslaughter, though erroneous, was invited error; defendant may not properly complain of such error on appeal. (*People v. Wright* (1914) 167 Cal. 1, 7, 138 P. 349; *People v. Hite* (1901) 135 Cal. 76, 79–80, 67 P. 57; *People v. Jones* (1965) 232 Cal. App. 2d 379, 390, 42 Cal. Rptr. 714; *People v. Johnson* (1962) 203 Cal. App. 2d 624, 629–630, 21 Cal. Rptr. 650.)

The third part of this instruction rests upon the felony murder rule and reflects the prosecution's theory that defendant's conduct amounted to grand theft by false pretenses in violation of Penal Code section 484.

Despite defendant's contention that the Penal Code does not expressly set forth any provision for second degree felony murder and that, therefore, we should not follow any such doctrine here, the concept lies imbedded in our law. We have stated in *People v. Williams* (1965) 63 A.C. 471, 47 Cal. Rptr. 7, 406 P.2d 647, that the cases hold that the perpetration of some felonies, exclusive of those enumerated in Penal Code section 189, may provide the basis for a murder conviction under the felony murder rule.*

We have held, however, that only such felonies as are in themselves "inherently dangerous to human life" can support the application of the felony murder rule. We have ruled that in assessing such peril to human life inherent in any given felony "we look to the elements of the felony in the abstract, not the particular 'facts' of the case." (*People v. Williams, supra.*)

We have thus recognized that the felony murder doctrine expresses a highly artificial concept that deserves no extension beyond its required application.[5] Indeed the rule itself has been abandoned by the courts of England, where it had its inception. It has been subjected to severe and sweeping criticism. No case to our knowledge in any jurisdiction has held that because death results from a course of conduct involving a felonious perpetration of a fraud, the felony murder doctrine can be invoked.

Admitting that grand theft is not inherently dangerous to life, the prosecution asks us to encompass the entire course of defendant's conduct so that we may incorporate such elements as would make his crime inherently dangerous. In so framing the definition of a given felony for the purpose of assessing its inherent peril to life the prosecution would abandon the statutory definition of the felony as such and substitute the factual elements of defendant's actual conduct. In the present case the Attorney General would characterize that conduct as "grand theft medical fraud," and this newly created "felony," he urges, clearly involves danger to human life and supports an application of the felony murder rule.

To fragmentize the "course of conduct" of defendant so that the felony murder rule applies if any segment of that conduct may be considered dangerous to life would widen the rule beyond calculation. It would then apply not only to the

---

* The California statute explicitly lists certain felonies as qualifying for first degree murder under the felony-murder rule. Phillips is arguing that because there is no statutory authorization for applying the felony-murder rule for other felonies that there is no second-degree felony-murder rule. The court rejects this argument, holding that the perpetrator of certain other felonies will be liable for second degree murder for all deaths attributable thereto.—Ed.

5. Although it is the law in this state (Pen. Code, § 189), it should not be extended beyond any rational function that it is designed to serve.

commission of specific felonies, which are themselves dangerous to life, but to the perpetration of any felony during which defendant may have acted in such a manner as to endanger life.

The proposed approach would entail the rejection of our holding in *Williams*. That case limited the felony murder doctrine to such felonies as were themselves inherently dangerous to life. That decision eschews the prosecution's present sweeping concept because, once the Legislature's own definition is discarded, the number or nature of the contextual elements which could be incorporated into an expanded felony terminology would be limitless. We have been, and remain, unwilling to embark on such an uncharted sea of felony murder.

The felony murder instruction should not, then, have been given; its rendition, further, worked prejudice upon defendant. It withdrew from the jury the issue of malice, permitting a conviction upon the bare showing that Linda's death proximately resulted from conduct of defendant amounting to grand theft. The instruction as rendered did not require the jury to find either express malice or the implied malice which is manifested in an "intent with conscious disregard for life to commit acts likely to kill."

The instruction thus relieved the jury of the necessity of finding one of the elements of the crime of murder. Even if the evidence could have supported a finding of implied malice, the instruction failed to require the jury so to determine.

The prosecution does not deny that the giving of a felony murder instruction engendered the possibility of a conviction of murder in the absence of a finding of malice. It contends, however, that even if the jury acted on the erroneous instruction it must necessarily have found facts which establish, as a matter of law, that defendant acted with conscious disregard for life and hence with malice. The prosecution thus asks us to dissect the jury's verdict, setting the facts of the case against the instructions in an attempt to isolate the facts which the jury necessarily found in reaching its verdict. From these facts it further asks us to infer the existence of others which the jury was never asked to find.

Examination of the record suggests that even this doubtful enterprise would not enable us to overcome the effect of the erroneous instruction. The prosecution urges that the jury could not have convicted defendant under the felony murder instruction without having found that he made representations to the Eppings which he knew to be false or which he recklessly rendered without information which would justify a reasonable belief in their truth. Such a finding does not, however, establish as a matter of law the existence of an "intent with conscious disregard for life to commit acts likely to kill." (*People v. Washington.*) In the absence of a finding that defendant subjectively appreciated the peril to which his conduct exposed the girl, we cannot determine that he acted with conscious disregard for life. The record contains evidence from which a trier of fact could reasonably have concluded that although defendant made false representations concerning his ability to cure, he nevertheless believed that the treatment which he proposed to give would be as efficacious in relieving pain and prolonging life as the scheduled surgery.[10]

Of course, the jury could have concluded from some of the evidence that defendant did not entertain any such belief in the relative efficacy of his proposed treatment. We cannot, however, undertake to resolve this evidentiary conflict without invading the province of the trier of fact. We cannot predicate a finding of conscious disregard of life upon a record that would as conclusively afford a basis for the opposite conclusion.

The judgment is reversed.

Traynor, C.J., and Peters and Peek, J.J., concur.

Questions and Notes

1. At its inception, which felony is most likely to result in death: robbery (as in *Gladman*) or grand theft medical fraud, as in *Phillips*? If it is grand theft medical fraud, why should that crime be excluded from the list of qualifying crimes?

2. Why should the courts care if the felony is inherently dangerous, so long as the method of committing it is?

3. The issue of which crimes are inherently dangerous depends a lot on the particular judge's view of felony-murder. (*See, e.g.,* footnote 5 in *Phillips*.) There is hardly any crime that couldn't be committed in a non-life-threatening way. For example, robbery could be committed with a toy gun. Deciding whether the crime is inherently dangerous has split the courts on several different crimes. Two of the most troubling are an ex-felon's carrying a concealed weapon is an inherently dangerous crime (see *State v. Underwood*, 615 P.2d 153 (Kan. 1980)), and the sale of dangerous drugs (see *People v. Patterson*, 778 P.2d 549 (Cal. 1989)). How would you resolve those issues?

4. Quite apart from the felony-murder rule, why wouldn't the crassly financial motives of one who accepts money from the parents of a dying girl with knowledge that he cannot deliver on his promise to cure her constitute malice? (Justice Burke dissented on substantially that ground.)

---

10. For example, defendant testified that he believed the girl's cancer to be incurable and understood that surgery might stimulate the spread of the disease to other parts of the body and thus hasten death. To some extent this evidence was contradicted by defendant's further testimony that he repeatedly urged the Eppings to return Linda to the hospital. The jury, however, was not bound to accept all of defendant's testimony, and substantial evidence supported a reasonable conclusion that defendant believed that he was not endangering Linda's life by persuading her parents to put her under his care. Proof that defendant entertained such a belief would only establish a defense to murder. If the jury found that defendant acted "without due caution and circumspection" in forming and entertaining this belief he would be subject to conviction for involuntary manslaughter. (Pen. Code, § 192, subd. 2.)

5. Why do you suppose that the defense attorney elected not to submit the theory of involuntary manslaughter to the jury? Would you have concurred in that strategy?

6. As you read *Sears*, try to imagine a more dangerous felony than the one that the court says does not qualify for felony-murder.

People v. Sears
465 P.2d 847 (Cal. 1970)

PETERS, Justice.

In 1963, a jury found defendant guilty of the first-degree murder of his step-daughter Elizabeth Olives, the attempted murder of his wife Clara Sears, and the attempted murder of his mother-in-law Frances Montijo. The penalty for the murder was fixed as death. On appeal this judgment was reversed, largely because of the erroneous admission of a confession. A second trial started on September 28, 1966, but this ended with a mistrial on October 11 because the prosecutor asked defendant a palpably improper question. Defendant's third trial commenced on October 18, 1966. The jury returned the same verdict as the jury in the first trial, and again fixed death as the penalty for the murder. This appeal is automatic.

Defendant married Clara Sears in 1960. The spouses agreed that Clara and her three children by a former marriage would continue living in a cottage which she and the children had occupied before the marriage, while defendant would sleep in a nearby garage until he completed an addition to the cottage. Defendant never completed the addition, and Clara refused to let defendant sleep in the cottage even after one of her daughters married and moved out. Defendant had his meals and watched television in the cottage.

Around the end of April 1963 defendant moved to a hotel. On Sunday, May 12, defendant visited his wife. According to her testimony, defendant threatened that he would kill her and the children if she got a divorce.

On May 16, 1963, defendant completed his work for the day and went to a neighborhood tavern where he drank beer with friends until about 7:30 p.m. Defendant then returned to his hotel and went to dinner with one Robert Kjaerbye. At 10 p.m. the two went to a tavern where defendant was a regular customer. After each man had drunk a beer, they drove approximately one block to the cottage occupied by Mrs. Sears.

Defendant and Kjaerbye entered the cottage through the unlocked front door. While Kjaerbye stayed in the living room, defendant went into the bedroom. Elizabeth was asleep and Clara was reading. Defendant told Clara that he wanted to talk with her, and she put on a robe and accompanied defendant to the kitchen. Because the floor was cold, Clara returned to the bedroom to get a pair of slippers. As she reentered the kitchen, defendant grabbed her robe and said, "If you won't want to come back to me. . . ." Then defendant unbuttoned his shirt and drew out an iron bar that he had stuck in his pants before entering the cottage. He struck Clara about the head until she lost consciousness. Elizabeth awakened and approached the kitchen. As she cried out for defendant to leave her mother alone, defendant turned on her with the iron bar. Clara regained consciousness and unsuccessfully tried to place herself between defendant and Elizabeth, but she again became unconscious.

Clara's mother, Frances Montijo, who lived next door with Clara's brother Patrick Montijo, heard the noise from her daughter's home and decided to investigate. As she approached the cottage Kjaerbye was leaving. He told her that he knew nothing of what was happening inside. Frances entered to find defendant on top of the screaming child. When defendant saw Frances, he attacked her with a knife he had taken from Clara's kitchen. After cutting her face, defendant threw Frances into a chair, rolled the iron bar against her throat and chest, and stabbed her with a barbecue fork, also taken from the kitchen.

Patrick's wife, Dolores, became concerned when Frances did not return from Clara's, and decided to investigate. As she arrived at the cottage, the injured Frances was making her escape. Dolores took Frances to a neighbor's house and went back to her own house for Patrick.

Patrick went over to the cottage. As he entered, defendant was standing over Clara with the barbecue fork in his raised hand. Patrick asked defendant what he was doing; defendant did not reply, but lunged at Patrick with the fork. A fight ensued, and defendant stabbed Patrick in the neck and chest. Defendant then ran to his car and drove away.

Elizabeth died from a knife wound that punctured her jugular vein. She also suffered numerous other cuts and bruises. Clara suffered multiple lacerations as well as a fractured jaw and a fractured arm. Frances received several wounds on her face, neck, and hands.

Defendant testified that he returned to the cottage to discuss their marital situation and effect a reconciliation; that he particularly wanted to ask her to accompany him that weekend to inspect some rental units he hoped to move to; that before entering the cottage, he saw an iron bar, picked it up and stuck it in his pants; that he intended only that his wife see the bar, hoping that she would then sit down and talk with him; and that he did not have any intent to use it on Clara or to scare her.[1]

---

1. Q. Did you intend to use the bar on your wife when you walked in the door?
   A. I didn't have no intention to use the bar on anyone. . . .
   Q. Did you intend that she see the bar?
   A. Yes, sir, I did. . . .
   Q. What did you intend when you picked up the iron bar, wherever you got it, you put it in your, on your person?
   A. When I picked, when I seen that bar laying on the concrete wall, I stuck it in my pants there just to figure she would see it and would listen to me. . . .
   Q. In going to the house to talk about the reconciliation, you were going to talk about moving to different places and what was your reason that you assign now for taking the iron bar into the cottage with you?

Whether the bar was visible is disputed. Clara testified that she did not see it until defendant pulled it out from beneath his shirt.

In his argument to the jury, the prosecutor urged at some length that the first degree felony-murder doctrine was applicable, urging that defendant committed a burglary in entering the cottage. He emphasized repeatedly that burglary included an entry with an intent to commit any felony, not merely theft, and he repeatedly asserted that defendant entered with intent to assault.

The jury was instructed on first and second-degree murder. In connection with the felony-murder rule, the trial judge instructed the jury:

> "I will now instruct you on the law concerning first degree murder in the perpetration of burglary. The unlawful killing of a human being, whether intentional, unintentional, or accidental, which is committed in the perpetration or attempt to perpetrate burglary, the commission of which crime itself must be proved beyond a reasonable doubt, is murder of the first degree.

> "Every person who enters any structure such as is shown by the evidence in this case, with intent to commit theft or any felony is guilty of burglary. The essence of a burglary is entering a place such as I have mentioned with such specific intent; and the crime is complete as soon as the entry is made, regardless of whether the intent thereafter is carried out."

Subsequently, the jury returned to the courtroom and asked the judge the following question. "Does assault on wife constitute a felony regardless of intent upon entering and if so, does felony murder doctrine dictating first degree murder apply?"

The court reread the felony-murder instruction, and the instruction on burglary. It did not instruct on assault with a deadly weapon or assault. The court also stated: "In answer to the specific inquiry, the court would advise that the specific intent to commit the assault must exist at the time of entry, otherwise the felony-murder rule does not apply. Does that answer your question?" Whereupon the foreman of the jury stated that he believed it did.

A   I figured when she seen that she'd go around and sit down and listen to what I had to say.
Q.   You figured you were going to use it on her if you didn't like what she said?
A.   No, sir, I did not.
Q.   You thought you'd scare her a little bit?
A.   No, sir.
Q.   You thought you'd frighten her a teeny-weeny bit?
A.   No, sir.
Q.   Just put it where you say you put it so she could see it?
A.   Yes, sir.
Q.   What did you expect her to do when she saw the iron bar?
A.   I figured she'd go around and sit down and listen to what I had to say.

The jurors continued their deliberations for six hours after the above instruction before retiring for the night. The jury returned its verdict the following morning, apparently one and a half hours after resuming deliberations.

In *People v. Ireland*, 70 Cal.2d 522, 537 et seq., 75 Cal. Rptr. 188, 450 P.2d 580, we considered the applicability of the second degree felony-murder rule to a situation where the claimed felony in the course of which the homicide occurred was an assault with a deadly weapon. We explained the felony-murder doctrine as follows:

> "The felony-murder rule operates (1) to posit the existence of malice aforethought in homicides which are the direct causal result of the perpetration or attempted perpetration of *all* felonies inherently dangerous to human life, and (2) to posit the existence of malice aforethought and to classify the offense as murder of the first degree in homicides which are the direct causal result of those six felonies specifically enumerated in section 189 of the Penal Code."

We further stated:

> "We have concluded that the utilization of the felony-murder rule in circumstances such as those before us extends the operation of that rule 'beyond any rational function that it is designed to serve.' (*People v. Washington.*) To allow such use of the felony-murder rule would effectively preclude the jury from considering the issue of malice aforethought in all cases wherein homicide has been committed as a result of a felonious assault—a category which includes the great majority of all homicides. This kind of bootstrapping finds support neither in logic nor in law. We therefore hold that a second degree felony-murder instruction may not properly be given when it is based upon a felony which is an integral part of the homicide and which the evidence produced by the prosecution shows to be an offense included in fact within the offense charged."

We also pointed out that other jurisdictions, through a so-called "merger" doctrine, had applied similar limitations on the felony-murder doctrine and that, although it was not clear whether we would adopt the entire doctrine, "we believe that the reasoning underlying that doctrine is basically sound and should be applied to the extent that it is consistent with the laws and policies of this state."

Ireland was followed in our recent decision of *People v. Wilson*, 1 Cal.3d 431, 82 Cal. Rptr. 494, 462 P.2d 22, where the jury was instructed on the first-degree felony-murder rule on the theory that the homicide was committed in the course of a burglary because the defendant entered the premises with intent to commit a felonious assault. In *Wilson*, the defendant forcibly entered his estranged wife's apartment carrying a shotgun. He shot one man on the stairs of the apartment, shot William Washington in the living room of the apartment, broke into the bathroom, and killed Mrs. Wilson. The defendant was convicted of the second degree murder of Washington and the first degree murder of his wife. We held that there was error in instructing the jury on both the second degree and the first degree felony-murder rules.

In reversing the judgment convicting defendant of first and second degree murder, we stated with respect to the first degree felony-murder instruction: "Here the prosecution sought to apply the felony-murder rule on the theory that the homicide occurred in the course of a burglary, but the only basis for finding a felonious entry is the intent to commit an assault with a deadly weapon. When, as here, the entry would be nonfelonious but for the intent to commit the assault, and the assault is an integral part of the homicide and is included in fact in the offense charged, utilization of the felony-murder rule extends that doctrine 'beyond any rational function that it is designed to serve.' We have heretofore emphasized "that the felony-murder doctrine expresses a highly artificial concept that deserves no extension beyond its required application." (*People v. Phillips.*)

"The purpose of the felony-murder rule is to deter felons from killing negligently or accidentally by holding them strictly responsible for killings they commit." (*People v. Washington.*) Where a person enters a building with an intent to assault his victim with a deadly weapon, he is not deterred by the felony-murder rule. That doctrine can serve its purpose only when applied to a felony independent of the homicide. In *Ireland*, we reasoned that a man assaulting another with a deadly weapon could not be deterred by the second degree felony-murder rule, since the assault was an integral part of the homicide. Here, the only distinction is that the assault and homicide occurred inside a dwelling so that the underlying felony is burglary based on an intention to assault with a deadly weapon, rather than simply assault with a deadly weapon.

> "We do not suggest that no relevant differences exist between crimes committed inside and outside dwellings. We have often recognized that persons within dwellings are in greater peril from intruders bent on stealing or engaging in other felonious conduct. Persons within dwellings are more likely to resist and less likely to be able to avoid the consequences of crimes committed inside their homes. However, this rationale does not justify application of the felony murder rule to the case at bar. Where the intended felony of the burglar is an assault with a deadly weapon, the likelihood of homicide from the lethal weapon is not significantly increased by the site of the assault. Furthermore, the burglary statute in this state includes within its definition numerous structures other than dwellings as to which there can be no conceivable basis for distinguishing between an assault with a deadly weapon outdoors and a burglary in which the felonious intent is solely to assault with a deadly weapon.[2]

> "In *Ireland*, we rejected the bootstrap reasoning involved in taking an element of a homicide and using it as the underlying felony in a second degree felony-murder instruction. We conclude that the same bootstrapping is

---

2. Included are any "shop, warehouse, store, mill, barn, stable, outhouse or other building, tent, vessel, railroad car, trailer coach . . . , vehicle . . . , aircraft . . . , mine or any underground portion thereof. . . ." (Pen. Code, § 459.)

involved in instructing a jury that the intent to assault makes the entry burglary and that the burglary raises the homicide resulting from the assault to first degree murder without proof of malice aforethought and premeditation. To hold otherwise, we would have to declare that because burglary is not technically a lesser offense included within a charge of murder, burglary constitutes an independent felony which can support a felony-murder instruction. However, in *Ireland* itself we did not assert that assault with a deadly weapon was a lesser included offense in murder; we asserted only that it was 'included in fact' in the charge of murder, in that the elements of the assault were necessary elements in the homicide. In the same sense, a burglary based on intent to assault with a deadly weapon is included in fact within a charge of murder, and cannot support a felony-murder instruction."

(*People v. Wilson, supra,* 1 Cal.3d 431, 440–441, 82 Cal. Rptr. 494, 499–500, 462 P.2d 22, 28–29.)

[Cases holding otherwise] were overruled insofar as they held that a felony-murder instruction could be predicated upon a burglary based on an entry with intent to assault the victim of the homicide with a deadly weapon.

Under *Ireland* and *Wilson*, the instructions of the court on the first degree felony-murder rule and the court's answer to the question asked by the jury must be held erroneous. Those instructions and the answer could reasonably be understood to mean that if defendant entered with intent to assault his wife and stepdaughter, he was guilty of burglary and that the first degree felony-murder rule was applicable. To apply the felony-murder rule to such a situation would extend the doctrine "beyond any rational function that it is designed to serve." As pointed out in *Wilson*, that doctrine can serve its purpose only when applied to a felony independent of the homicide, and where a person enters a building with intent to assault his victims with a deadly weapon, he is not deterred by the felony-murder rule.

The Attorney General, pointing out that there is evidence from which the jury might have concluded that defendant entered with intent to assault his wife with a deadly weapon but not his stepdaughter, urges that the felony-murder rule is applicable on the theory that the burglary based on the intent to assault the wife was independent of and collateral to the killing of the stepdaughter. It may be noted in this connection that in New York it has been held that, although the felony-murder rule does not apply where a defendant intentionally assaults each of his two victims who die as a result of the assaults, the rule is applicable if the defendant assaulted one person but killed another who came to the first's defense. (*People v. Moran,* 246 N.Y. 100, 158 N.E. 35, 36–37 (1927); *People v. Wagner* (1927) 245 N.Y. 143, 156 N.E. 644, 646.)

However, the instructions given to the jury did not posit the applicability of the felony-murder rule upon any such theory. Moreover, we are satisfied that the distinction made by the New York cases is untenable in the light of ordinary principles of culpability. It would be anomalous to place the person who intends to attack one person and in the course of the assault kills another inadvertently or in the heat of battle in a worse position than the person who from the outset intended to attack both persons and killed one or both.

Where a defendant assaults one or more persons killing one, his criminal responsibility for the homicide should not depend upon which of the victims died.

The judgment is reversed.

Questions and Notes

1. If *Ireland* were decided the other way, presumably most voluntary manslaughter cases could be elevated to murder on the ground that they included the inherently dangerous felony of assault with a deadly weapon. Consequently, one would think that *Ireland* would be the law everywhere. Although it is the majority rule, it is not universally accepted, *see, e.g., State v. Thompson*, 558 P.2d 202 (Wash. 1977).

2. Is there a better argument for rejecting *Wilson*?

3. Assuming that *Wilson* were correctly decided, shouldn't Sears be convicted nonetheless on the theory that his intent was to attack Mrs. Sears, not Elizabeth? The court says: "It would be anomalous to place the person who intends to attack one person and in the course of the assault kills another inadvertently or in the heat of battle in a worse position than the person who from the outset intended to attack both persons and killed one or both." On the other hand, if Sears had entered to steal the television set, and Elizabeth had tried to protect it, Sears' killing her while stealing the television would clearly be felony-murder. Is the court saying that televisions are entitled to more protection than people? What should the law say in cases like this?

4. Could part of the court's reluctance to affirm the conviction in *Sears* be its aversion to the death penalty?

5. In most states, Sears' conduct probably would not have constituted burglary because his entry wasn't trespassory. In California, however, an entry is deemed trespassory if, unbeknownst to the homeowner, the defendant intended to commit a felony when he entered. Perhaps the technical nature of the felony influenced the court. (*See* footnote 2.)

6. In conjunction with footnote 2, you should note that a felony specifically enumerated in the statute need not be inherently dangerous. (*Compare Phillips*.)

7. Determining which felonies merge with the killings and which have not always been easy. In *People v. Burton*, 491 P.2d 793 (Cal. 1971), the court rejected an argument that robbery includes an assault, which is part of murder, rendering robbery ineligible for felony-murder. The court reasoned that robbery also includes theft, which is independent of the homicide. In *People v. Smith*, 678 P.2d 886 (Cal. 1984), the court held that felonious child abuse was not a crime upon which felony-murder could be predicated.

Problem

On May 3, 1998, the following editorial, written by the author of your casebook, appeared in the Raleigh, North Carolina, *News and Observer*:

Better Paths to Justice for Drunken Drivers' Victims
Arnold H. Loewy

The Triangle area still mourns the loss of four-year-old Megan Dail, a beautiful child cut down by a hopelessly irresponsible drunken driver, Timothy Blackwell, who had no business being free to inflict such carnage. But why was he?

Evidently because North Carolina law does not compel the lengthy incarceration of habitual drunken drivers.

Suppose that Blackwell had been stopped for weaving prior to the fatal accident, and the officer stopping him had determined that he was driving drunk with a revoked license and seven prior convictions. Would he have served a lengthy prison term? Not likely. Should he? Absolutely.

I am not suggesting that prison terms generally are too light (quite the contrary), but I do think that dangerous people who have proven unrestrainable on the outside need to be incarcerated for a very long time. Quite frankly, drunken drivers pose a danger to ourselves and our children that is more difficult to protect against than even drug dealers. In an ideal world, Timothy Blackwell would have received 10 years minimum in prison after his seventh DWI (assuming that we allowed him even that many chances, which I would not), and would have been incarcerated in prison rather than intoxicated on the highway on that tragic fateful day in Durham County.

Another positive step that the legislature could take is to require a Breathalyzer attached to the engine of all automobiles regularly driven by a convicted drunken driver. This procedure (which is in use in other states) would preclude a drunk from starting his car in the first place. Although such a device could presumably be disabled or circumvented, I would make such conduct a serious felony punishable by several years in prison.

What should not have been done was to convolute the felony murder rule to serve as an instrument of community outrage.

First of all, it was not necessary. Although highway deaths are usually punishable as vehicular homicide and sometime involuntary manslaughter, there are exceptions. In some cases of extreme recklessness, second degree murder convictions have been sustained.

The theory of these cases is that the outrageously out-of-control driver is like a person who shoots a gun into a crowd without intending to kill anybody, but hits and kills someone in the crowd. Both the shooter and the driver are so heedless of human life that we can say that they acted with malice and are guilty of second degree murder. Second degree murder in North Carolina is punishable by life imprisonment. That is all Blackwell got anyway, and surely it is adequate.

Felony murder, on the other hand, does not comfortably fit. Drunken driving does not qualify as the underlying felony under the statute, and nobody claimed that it did. Rather, the prosecution claimed that the underlying felony was assault with a deadly weapon (Blackwell's truck) inflicting serious injury on another person in the car, resulting in Megan's death. (If the assault were just on Megan, it would have been part of the killing and could not have qualified as a separate felony for purposes of the felony-murder rule.)

Thus, because, and only because, of the fortuity of someone other than the victim being seriously injured, the state was able to make a case for felony-murder.

If this and the similar Winston-Salem case a year earlier are upheld by our appellate courts (and I sincerely hope that they will not be), the following cases could arise:

CASE A. Joe Boozehound, a hopelessly and repeatedly intoxicated driver (in the Blackwell mold) is swerving down the road, loses control of his car, crashes through a fence, and kills a little child playing therein. He is not guilty of felony-murder because there is no underlying felony. He did not assault another person with a deadly weapon, and the assault on the victim doesn't count.

CASE B. Johnny Reckless, an overly exuberant teenager, is out driving with three of his buddies. They urge him to pass a car on a curve, which he does even though he knows that he can't see what is up ahead. He has a head-on crash with another car in which Ms. Victim is killed, and Mr. Victim is seriously injured. Because assault can be committed unintentionally, but recklessly, Johnny is guilty of assault with a deadly weapon inflicting serious injury on Mr. Victim, and consequently of felony-murder of Ms. Victim. Furthermore, under aiding and abetting principles, all of Johnny's buddies are guilty of felony-murder.

If you don't like the dichotomy suggested by my hypothetical (and I don't), you shouldn't like the rationale of the Blackwell verdict (and I don't).

I have no quarrel with the Blackwell jury that absolutely performed its duty by following instructions to the letter. I do, however, quarrel with the trial court's willingness to treat an unintentional felony (reckless assault with a deadly weapon inflicting serious injury) as the functional equivalent of an intentional felony (e.g., rape, robbery, kidnaping, etc.) If one is going to be convicted of first degree murder for a killing that he did not intend, the state should at least have to prove that he intended the underlying felony.

Short-sighted jurisprudence is an inappropriate monument to the memory of a child. Surely our legislature can do better. Legislation keeping otherwise unrestrainable drunken drivers in prison where they can't kill other children would surely be the most beautiful possible monument to Megan.

The North Carolina Court of Appeals, in the above referenced Winston-Salem case, upheld the felony-murder conviction by a 2-1 vote. (*State v. Jones*, 516 S.E.2d 405 (N.C. App. 1999).) Should the North Carolina Supreme Court uphold the Court of Appeals, decide the case in accordance with Professor Loewy's editorial, or reach some other resolution? Explain. See *State v. Jones*, 353 N.C. 159 (2000), 538 S.E.2d 917 (N.C. 2000) .

Sometimes the felony is clearly sufficient to qualify for felony murder (e.g., robbery), but the death was not part of, or was even contrary to, the robbers' plan (e.g., a policeman kills one of the robbers). *Sophophone* explores the extent to which the remaining robber can be held liable for felony-murder.

State v. Sophophone

19 P.3d 70 (Kan. 2001)

The opinion of the court was delivered by LARSON, J.

This is Sanexay Sophophone's direct appeal of his felony-murder conviction for the death of his co-felon during flight from an aggravated burglary in which both men participated.

The facts are not in dispute. Sophophone and three other individuals conspired to and broke into a house in Emporia. The resident reported the break-in to the police.

Police officers responded to the call, saw four individuals leaving the back of the house, shined a light on the suspects, identified themselves as police officers, and ordered them to stop. The individuals, one being Sophophone, started to run away. One officer ran down Sophophone, hand-cuffed him, and placed him in a police car.

Other officers arrived to assist in apprehending the other individuals as they were running from the house. An officer chased one of the suspects later identified as Somphone Sysoumphone. Sysoumphone crossed railroad tracks, jumped a fence, and then stopped. The officer approached with his weapon drawn and ordered Sysoumphone to the ground and not to move. Sysoumphone was lying face down but raised up and fired at the officer, who returned fire and killed him. It is not disputed that Sysoumphone was one of the individuals observed by the officers leaving the house that had been burglarized.

Sophophone was charged with conspiracy to commit aggravated burglary, K.S.A. 21-3302; aggravated burglary, K.S.A. 21-3716; obstruction of official duty, K.S.A. 21-3808; and felony murder, K.S.A. 21-3401(b).

Sophophone moved to dismiss the felony-murder charges, contending the complaint was defective because it alleged that he and not the police officer had killed Sysoumphone and further because he was in custody and sitting in the police car when the deceased was killed and therefore not attempting to commit or even fleeing from an inherently dangerous felony. His motion to dismiss was denied by the trial court.

Sophophone was convicted by a jury of all counts. His motion for judgment of acquittal was denied. He was sentenced on all counts. He appeals only his conviction of felony murder.

Sophophone does not dispute that aggravated burglary is an inherently danger-ous felony which given the right circumstances would support a felony-murder charge. His principal argument centers on his being in custody at the time his co-felon was killed by the lawful act of the officer which he contends was a "break in circumstances" sufficient to insulate him from further criminal responsibility.

This "intervening cause" or "break in circumstances" argument has no merit under the facts of this case. We have held in numerous cases that "time, distance, and the causal relationship between the underlying felony and a killing are factors to be considered in determining whether the killing occurs in the commission of the underlying felony and the defendant is therefore subject to the felony-murder rule."

Based on the uncontroverted evidence in this case, the killing took place during flight from the aggravated burglary, and it is only because the act which resulted in the killing was a lawful one by a third party that a question of law exists as to whether Sophophone can be convicted of felony murder.

In *State v. Branch & Bussey*, 223 Kan. 381, 383–84, 573 P.2d 1041 (1978), where a killing was accidental but committed by Bussey during a robbery incidental to a drug deal, and we broadly stated:

> "We conclude that any participant in a life-endangering felony is guilty of first degree murder when a life is taken in the course of committing or attempting to commit the felony, whether the death was intentional or acci-dental, or whether the participant directly caused it to occur."

We have also stated that another purpose for the felony-murder doctrine "is to relieve the state of the burden of proving premeditation and malice when the vic-tim's death is caused by the killer while he is committing another felony."'" *State v. Clark*, 204 Kan. 38, 43, 460 P.2d 586 (1969).

Our cases are legion in interpreting the felony-murder statute, but we have not previously decided a case where the killing was not by the direct acts of the felon but rather where a co-felon was killed during his flight from the scene of the felony by the lawful acts of a third party (in our case, a law enforcement officer).

Although there were clearly different facts, we held in *Hoang*, 243 Kan. at 42–46, 755 P.2d 7 that felony murder may include the accidental death of a co-felon during the commission of arson. The decedents had conspired with Hoang to burn down a building housing a Wichita restaurant/club but died when they were trapped inside the building while starting the fire. Hoang was an active participant in the felony and present at the scene, although he remained outside the building while his three accomplices entered the building with containers of gasoline to start the fire.

We held, in a split decision, that the decedents were killed during the perpetra-tion of a felony inherently dangerous to human life and there was nothing in the statute to exclude the killing of co-felons from its application. It must be pointed out that the facts in *Hoang* involved the wrongful acts of a co-felon which were directly responsible for the deaths of his co-felons.

The dissent in *Hoang* noted that in previous cases the felony-murder rule had been applied only to the deaths of innocents and not to the deaths of co-felons. The result was deemed by the dissent to be contrary to legislative intent and the strict construction of criminal statutes that is required.

With this brief background of our prior Kansas cases, we look to the prevailing views concerning the applicability of the felony-murder doc-trine where the killing has been caused by the acts of a third party. The two different approaches applicable are succinctly set forth in Comment *Kansas Felony Murder: Agency or Proximate Cause?* 48 KAN. L. REV. 1047, 1051–52 (2000), in the following manner:

> "There are two basic approaches to application of the felony-murder doc-trine: the agency and proximate cause theories. The agency approach, which is the majority view, limits application of the doctrine to those homicides committed by the felon or an agent of the felon. Under such an approach, 'the identity of the killer becomes the threshold requirement for finding liability under the felony-murder doctrine.'

> "The proximate cause approach provides that 'liability attaches 'for *any* death proximately resulting from the unlawful activity — even the death of a co-felon — notwithstanding the killing was by one resisting the crime." Under the proximate cause approach, felony murder may preclude consid-eration of the deceased's identity, which would make a defendant liable for all deaths caused by others during the crime. Application of the proximate cause varies greatly by jurisdiction because the statutes differ substantially. The proximate cause approach becomes controversial when the homicide is committed by someone other than the felons, but only a minority of juris-dictions follow this approach."

As we noted in *Hoang*, it is not very helpful to review case law from other states because of differences in statutory language; however, the high courts which have considered this precise question are divided between the agency approach and the proximate cause approach.

The leading case adopting the agency approach is *Commonwealth v. Redline*, 391 Pa. 486, 495, 137 A.2d 472 (1958), where the underlying principle of the agency theory is described as follows:

> "In adjudging a felony-murder, it is to be remembered at all times that the thing which is imputed to a felon for a killing incidental to his felony is malice and not the act of killing. The mere coincidence of homicide and felony is not enough to satisfy the felony-murder doctrine."

The following statement from *Redline* is more persuasive for Sophophone:

> "In the present instance, the victim of the homicide was one of the rob-bers who, while resisting apprehension in his effort to escape, was shot and killed by a policeman in the performance of his duty. Thus, the homicide was justifiable and, obviously, could not be availed of, on any rational legal

theory, to support a charge of murder. How can anyone, no matter how much of an outlaw he may be, have a criminal charge lodged against him for the consequences of the lawful conduct of another person? The mere question carries with it its own answer."

The minority of the states whose courts have adopted the proximate cause theory believe their legislatures intended that any person, co-felon, or accomplice who commits an inherently dangerous felony should be held responsible for any death which is a direct and foreseeable consequence of the actions of those committing the felony. These courts apply the civil law concept of proximate cause to felony-murder situations.

We have not adopted the proximate cause approach because of our holding and language in *State v. Shaw*, 260 Kan. 396, 405, 921 P.2d 779 (1990), where we held that a defendant who bound and gagged a 86-year-old robbery victim with duct tape was liable for the victim's death when he died of a heart attack while so bound and gagged. Although we may speak of causation in such a case, our ruling in *Shaw* is better described by quoting syllabus ¶ 2: "The victim must be taken as the defendant finds him. Death resulting from a heart attack will support a felony-murder conviction if there is a causal connection between the heart attack and the felonious conduct of the defendant." This is not the embracing of a proximate cause approach under the facts we face.

An additional argument has been made that when we approved the language of PIK Crim. 3d 56.02 relating to the causation required by the law for felony murder in *State v. Lamae*, 268 Kan. 544, 555, 998 P.2d 106 (2000), we recognized that the killing could be perpetrated by the defendant *or another*. (Emphasis added). The case involved the death of a participant in a methamphetamine fire. Our opinion did state: "It is true that there must be a direct causal connection between the commission of the felony and the homicide to invoke the felony-murder rule. *See State v. Underwood*, 228 Kan. 294, 302, 615 P.2d 153 (1980). *However, the general rules of proximate cause used in civil actions do not apply.*" (Emphasis added.) This language, if taken in isolation, is much more favorable to Sophophone's position. However, we believe that neither this statement nor the "or another" language in *Lamae* should be given undue consideration when we resolve the different question we face here.

There is language in K.S.A. 21-3205(2) that predicates criminal responsibility to an aider or abettor for "any other crime committed in pursuance of the intended crime if reasonably foreseeable by such person as a probable consequence of committing or attempting to commit the crime intended." This wording does not assist us for the killing of the co-felon in our case where it was the lawful act by a law enforcement officer who was in no manner subject to these aider and abettor provisions.

The overriding fact which exists in our case is that neither Sophophone nor any of his accomplices "killed" anyone. The law enforcement officer acted lawfully in committing the act which resulted in the death of the co-felon. This does not fall within the language of K.S.A. 21-3205 since the officer committed no crime.

Of more assistance to us is our long-time rule of statutory interpretation:

> "Criminal statutes must be strictly construed in favor of the accused. Any reasonable doubt about the meaning is decided in favor of anyone subjected to the criminal statute. The rule of strict construction, however, is subordinate to the rule that judicial interpretation must be reasonable and sensible to effect legislative design and in-tent." *State v. Vega-Fuentes*, 264 Kan. 10, 14, 955 P.2d 1235 (1998).

It appears to the majority that to impute the act of killing to Sophophone when the act was the lawful and courageous one of a law enforcement officer acting in the line of his duties is contrary to the strict construction we are required to give criminal statutes. There is considerable doubt about the meaning of K.S.A. 21-3401(b) as applied to the facts of this case, and we believe that making one criminally responsible for the lawful acts of a law enforcement officer is not the intent of the felony-murder statute as it is currently written. Cf. *State v. Murphy*, 19 P.3d 80, 2001 Kan. LEXIS 159, this day decided (felon may not be convicted of felony murder for the killing of his co-felon caused not by his acts or actions but by the lawful acts of a victim of aggravated robbery and kidnapping acting in self-defense for the protection of his residence and the property thereof).

It does little good to suggest one construction over another would prevent the commission of dangerous felonies or that it would deter those who engage in dangerous felonies from killing purposely, negligently, or accidentally. Actually, innocent parties and victims of crimes appear to be those who are sought to be protected rather than co-felons.

We hold that under the facts of this case where the killing resulted from the lawful acts of a law enforcement officer in attempting to apprehend a co-felon, Sophophone is not criminally responsible for the resulting death of Somphone Sysoumphone, and his felony-murder conviction must be reversed.

This decision is in no manner inconsistent with our rulings in *Hoang* or *Lamae*, which are based on the direct acts of a co-felon and are simply factually different from our case. Sophophone's request that *State v. Hoang*, 243 Kan. 40, 755 P.2d 7 (1988), be overruled is denied.

Reversed.

ABBOTT, J., dissenting:

The issue facing the court in this case is whether Sophophone may be legally convicted under the felony-murder statute when he did not pull the trigger and where the victim was one of the co-felons. The majority holds that Sophophone cannot be convicted of felony murder. I dissent.

An analysis of this issue must begin with an examination of the murder statute. K.S.A. 21-3401 provides:

"Murder in the first degree is the killing of a human being committed:

"(b) in the commission of, attempt to commit, or flight from an inherently dangerous felony as defined in K.S.A. 21-3436 and amendments thereto."

When an issue requires statutory analysis and the statute is unambiguous, we are limited by the wording chosen by the legislature. We are not free to alter the statutory language, regardless of the result. In the present case, the felony-murder statute does not require us to adopt the "agency" theory favored by the majority. Indeed, there is nothing in the statute which establishes an agency approach. The statute does not address the issue at all. The requirements, according to the statute, are: (1) there must be a killing, and (2) the killing must be committed in the commission, attempt to commit, or flight from an inherently dangerous felony. The statute simply does not contain the limitations discussed by the majority. There is nothing in K.S.A. 21-3401 which requires us to adopt the agency approach or that requires Sophophone to be the shooter in this case. The facts in this case, in my opinion, satisfy all of the requirements set forth in K.S.A. 21-3401(b).

Moreover, there are sound reasons to adopt the proximate cause approach described in the majority opinion. In *State v. Hoang*, 243 Kan. 40, 755 P.2d 7 (1988), this court took such an approach, although never referring to it by name. In *Hoang*, Chief Justice McFarland, writing for the court, discussed at length the requirements of the felony-murder rule in Kansas and stated:

"In felony-murder cases, the elements of malice, deliberation, and premeditation which are required for murder in the first degree are deemed to be supplied by felonious conduct alone *if a homicide results*. To support a conviction for felony murder, *all that is required is* to prove that a felony was being committed, which felony was inherently dangerous to human life, and that the homicide which followed *was a direct result of the commission of that felony. In a felony-murder case, evidence of who the triggerman is irrelevant and all participants are principals.* [Citations omitted.]

"The purpose of the felony-murder doctrine is to deter all those engaged in felonies from killing negligently or accidentally. . . .

"It is argued in the case before us that felony murder applies only to the deaths of 'innocents' rather than co-felons. There is nothing in our statute on which to base such a distinction. . . .

"Dung and Thuong, the decedents herein, were human beings who were killed in the perpetration of a felony. . . . Defendant was an active participant in the felony and present on the scene during all pertinent times. *There is nothing in the statute excluding the killing of the co-felons herein from its application.* For this court to exclude the co-felons would constitute judicial amendment of a statute on philosophic rather than legal grounds. This would be highly improper. The legislature has defined felony murder. If this definition is to be amended to exclude the killing of co-felons therefrom under circumstances such as are before us, it is up to the legislature to make such an amendment." (Emphasis added.)

The majority states that the decision in this case is not inconsistent with the ruling in *Hoang*. I disagree. The language in *Hoang* warns of the dangers of judicial reconstruction and statutory revisionism; however, the majority has taken that approach regardless. Although the facts in *Hoang* are not identical to the facts in this case, the differences are inconsequential. In my opinion, *Hoang* is still good law and provides ample justification to apply the felony-murder rule to Sophophone.

The majority in this case points out that the majority of states have adopted the agency approach when faced with the death of a co-felon. They acknowledge, however, that because statutes vary significantly from state to state, reference to a "majority" rule and a "minority" rule is meaningless. Indeed, an in-depth analysis of the current case law in this area leads me to the following conclusions: (1) While a majority of states would agree with the majority opinion in this case, the margin is slim; (2) many of the states that have adopted the so-called "agency" approach have done so because the statutory language in their state *requires* them to do so; and (3) several of the states that have adopted the "proximate cause" approach have done so because their statutes are silent on the is-sue, like Kansas.

Some courts have been forced to take an agency approach because of the statutory language contained within their felony-murder statutes. *See Weick v. State*, 420 A.2d 159, 161–63 (Del. 1980) (reversing second-degree murder conviction where victim killed co-felon because statute requires that "he, with criminal negligence, causes the death of another person")); *State v. Jones*, 859 P.2d 514, 515 (Okla. Crim. 1993) (taking an agency approach because statute provides that the person committing the felony must "take the life of a human being"); *State v. Hansen*, 734 P.2d 421, 427 (Utah 1986) (holding that state law precluded second-degree felony-murder conviction where co-felon is killed because language in statute requires the death to be "other than a party" to the crime).

As noted in *Hoang*, references to cases from other jurisdictions, regardless of the "majority" or "minority" rule, is unnecessary because the statutory language, if unambiguous, should control the outcome.

In my opinion, our statute is unambiguous and simply does not re-quire the defendant to be the direct cause of the victim's death, nor does it limit application of the felony-murder rule to the death of "innocents."

In *People v. Lowery*, 178 Ill. 2d 462, 227 Ill. Dec. 491, 687 N.E.2d 973 (1997), the Illinois Supreme Court discussed the public policy reasons justifying application of a proximate cause approach, stating:

It is equally consistent with reason and sound public policy to hold that when a felon's attempt to commit a forcible felony sets in motion a chain of events which were or should have been within his contemplation when the motion was initiated, he should be held responsible for any death which by direct and almost inevitable sequence results from the initial criminal act. Thus, there is no reason why the principle underlying the doctrine of proximate cause should not apply to criminal cases. Moreover, we believe that the intent behind the felony-murder doctrine would be thwarted if we did not hold felons responsible for the foreseeable consequences of their actions.

Here, Sophophone set in motion acts which would have resulted in the death or serious injury of a law enforcement officer had it not been for the highly alert law enforcement officer. This set of events could have very easily resulted in the death of a law enforcement officer, and in my opinion, this is exactly the type of case the legislature had in mind when it adopted the felony-murder rule.

The majority has opened a Pandora's box and left the law grossly un-settled. It does not take much imagination to see a number of situations where a death is going to result from an inherently dangerous felony and the majority's opinion is going to prevent the accused from being charged with felony murder.

If there is to be a change in the law, it should be by the legislature and not by this court adopting a statutory scheme set forth by the legislatures of other states. I would continue to follow the proximate cause theory of liability for felony murder which holds that criminal liability attaches for any death proximately resulting from the unlawful activity notwithstanding the fact that the killing was by one resisting the crime.

I would affirm the conviction based upon the statutory language found in K.S.A. 21-3401, the decision in *Hoang*, and the cases cited from other jurisdictions.

McFARLAND, C.J., and DAVIS, J., join in the foregoing dissenting opinion.

Questions and Notes

1. What is the difference between the proximate cause theory of felony-murder liability and the agency theory? Which theory is more sound? Does your answer depend on whether you think that the felony-murder rule is a good idea or a bad idea in principle?

2. Should it matter whether the victim is a co-felon or an innocent bystander? Explain.

3. Was the officer justified in killing Sysoumphone? If your answer is "yes," was the majority necessarily correct because of the impossibility of Sophophone being deemed a first degree murderer because of another's justifiable homicide?

4. Suppose Sysoumphone had laid down his weapons and surrendered, but the officer killed him anyway. Under the dissent's rationale, could Sophophone have been guilty of felony-murder? Why? Why not?

5. Is *Houng* really distinguishable? If so, how?

6. In view of some of the anomalies surrounding felony-murder and the criticisms of it, some have recommended its abolition. The Michigan Supreme Court was persuaded in *People v. Aaron*.

People v. Aaron

299 N.W.2d 304 (Mich. 1979)

FITZGERALD, Justice.

The existence and scope of the felony-murder doctrine have perplexed generations of law students, commentators and jurists in the United States and England, and have split our own Court of Appeals. In these cases, we must decide whether Michigan has a felony murder rule which allows the element of malice required for murder to be satisfied by the intent to commit the underlying felony or whether malice must be otherwise found by the trier of fact. We must also determine what is the *mens rea* required to support a conviction under Michigan's first-degree murder statute.

Our review of Michigan case law persuades us that we should abolish the rule which defines malice as the intent to commit the underlying felony. Abrogation of the felony-murder rule is not a drastic move in light of the significant restrictions this Court has already imposed. Further, it is a logical extension of our decisions.

We believe that it is no longer acceptable to equate the intent to commit a felony with the intent to kill, intent to do great bodily harm, or wanton and willful disregard of the likelihood that the natural tendency of a person's behavior is to cause death or great bodily harm.

Accordingly, we hold today that malice is the intention to kill, the intention to do great bodily harm, or the wanton and willful disregard of the likelihood that the natural tendency of defendant's behavior is to cause death or great bodily harm. We further hold that malice is an essential element of any murder, as that term is judicially defined, whether the murder occurs in the course of a felony or otherwise. The facts and circumstances involved in the perpetration of a felony may evidence an intent to kill, an intent to cause great bodily harm, or a wanton and willful disregard of the likelihood that the natural tendency of defendant's behavior is to cause death or great bodily harm; however, the conclusion must be left to the jury to infer from all the evidence. Otherwise, "juries might be required to find the fact of malice where they were satisfied from the whole evidence it did not exist."

From a practical standpoint, the abolition of the category of malice arising from the intent to commit the underlying felony should have little effect on the result of the majority of cases. In many cases where felony murder has been applied, the use of the doctrine was unnecessary because the other types of malice could have been inferred from the evidence.

Abrogation of this rule does not make irrelevant the fact that a death occurred in the course of a felony. A jury can properly infer malice from evidence that a defendant intentionally set in motion a force likely to cause death or great bodily harm. Thus, whenever a killing occurs in the perpetration or attempted perpetration of an inherently dangerous felony, in order to establish, malice the jury may consider the "nature of the underlying felony and the circumstances surrounding its commission." If the jury concludes that malice existed, they can find murder and, if they determine that the murder occurred in the perpetration or attempted perpetration of one of the enumerated felonies, by statute the murder would become first-degree murder.

The difference is that the jury may not find malice from the intent to commit the underlying felony alone. The defendant will be permitted to assert any of the applicable defenses relating to mens rea which he would be allowed to assert if charged with premeditated murder. The latter result is reasonable in light of the fact that felony murder is certainly no more heinous than premeditated murder. The prosecution will still be able to prove first-degree murder without proof of premeditation when a homicide is committed with malice, as we have defined it, and the perpetration or attempted perpetration of an enumerated felony is established. Hence, our first-degree murder statute continues to elevate to first-degree murder a murder which is committed in the perpetration or attempted perpetration of one of the enumerated felonies.

As previously noted, in many circumstances the commission of a felony, particularly one involving violence or the use of force, will indicate an intention to kill, an intention to cause great bodily harm, or wanton or willful disregard of the likelihood that the natural tendency of defendant's behavior is to cause death or great bodily harm. Thus, the felony-murder rule is not necessary to establish *mens rea* in these cases. In the past, the felony-murder rule has been employed where unforeseen or accidental deaths occur and where the state seeks to prove vicarious liability of co-felons. In situations involving the vicarious liability of co-felons, the individual liability of each felon must be shown. It is fundamentally unfair and in violation of basic principles of individual criminal culpability to hold one felon liable for the unforeseen and unagreed-to results of another felon. In cases where the felons are acting intentionally or recklessly in pursuit of a common plan, the felony-murder rule is unnecessary because liability may be established on agency principles.

Finally, in cases where the death was purely accidental, application of the felony-murder doctrine is unjust and should be precluded. The underlying felony, of course, will still be subject to punishment. The draftsmen of the Model Penal Code report that juries are not disposed to accept unfounded claims of accident in Ohio where all first-degree murder requires a purpose to kill.

Thus, in the three situations in which the felony-murder doctrine typically has applied, the rule is either unnecessary or contrary to fundamental principles of our criminal law.

"It is submitted that this is one of the most persuasive arguments in favor of abolition of the doctrine: it is not necessary to the establishment of criminal liability in the majority of cases in which it has been applied, and its application to those cases in which death occurred wholly by accident — *i.e.*, without intent or likelihood of harm — is contrary to the modern trend toward establishment of culpability as the basis of criminal liability."

"(I)t is unsatisfactory and inelegant to have a rule of law which, whenever it is applied, is either unnecessary (as in the case where dangerous violence is knowingly used) or unjust (as in the case where the risk of death is not foreseen)."

The Pennsylvania Supreme Court has called the felony-murder rule "nonessential," and the commentators to the Hawaii statute abolishing felony murder concluded that "(t)he rule certainly is not an indispensable ingredient in a system of criminal justice." The penal code of India has done away with felony murder and the doctrine "is also unknown as such in continental Europe." England, the birthplace of the felony-murder doctrine, has been without the rule for over 20 years and "its passing apparently has not been mourned."

One writer suggests that the experience in England demonstrates that its demise would have little effect on the rate of convictions for murders occurring in the perpetration of felonies.

We are in full agreement with the following conclusion of the Model Penal Code draftsmen:

> "We are, in any case, entirely clear that it is indefensible to use the sanctions that the law employs to deal with murder, unless there is at least a finding that the actor's conduct manifested an extreme indifference to the value of human life. The fact that the actor was engaged in a crime of the kind that is included in the usual first-degree felony-murder enumeration or was an accomplice in such crime will frequently justify such a finding. . . . But liability depends, as we believe it should, upon the crucial finding. The result may not differ often under such a formulation from that which would be reached under the present rule. But what is more important is that a conviction on this basis rests upon sound ground."

Questions and Notes

1. How would *Gladman, Phillips, Sears,* and *Sophophone* be decided in Michigan?

2. Is there any substantial argument in favor of punishing accidental homicides committed in the perpetration of robbery, rape, burglary, arson, or kidnapping as first degree murder?

3. In addition to the collateral reading suggested by the cases in this section, see Crump & Crump, *In Defense of the Felony Murder Doctrine*, 9 HARV. J.L. & PUB. POL. 359 (1985); *Culpability, Dangerousness, and Harm*, Section III H (Appendix B); and NUTSHELL § 2.09.

4. Despite the logic of *Aaron*, there has been no significant move away from the felony-murder rule. (*See, e.g., Dekens.*) Indeed, in concluding with *Ervin*, we see an endorsement for its expansion.

State v. Ervin

577 A.2d 1273 (N.J. Super. A.D. 1990)

Brochin, J.A.D.

N.J.S.A. 2C:35-9 declares that any person who illegally manufactures, distributes or dispenses any of a list of illegal drugs "is strictly liable for a death which results from the injection, inhalation or ingestion of that substance, and is guilty of a crime of the first degree." In this case, the defendant challenges the constitutionality of that statute. We disagree with his argument and therefore affirm.

Defendant Joseph R. Ervin procured cocaine which he and his girlfriend shared. She died as the result. He was indicted for possessing cocaine contrary to N.J.S.A. 2C:35-10a(1) and N.J.S.A. 2C:35-10a(3), possessing cocaine with the intent of distributing it contrary to N.J.S.A. 2C:35-5b(3), distributing cocaine contrary to N.J.S.A. 2C:35-5b(3), causing a drug induced death contrary to N.J.S.A. 2C:35-9 and for manslaughter contrary to N.J.S.A. 2C:11-4b.

On the ground that N.J.S.A. 2C:35-9 is unconstitutional, defendant moved before the trial court to dismiss the charge of having caused a drug induced death. His motion was denied. Pursuant to a plea bargain, he pleaded guilty to the charge of violating N.J.S.A. 2C:35-9, and the remaining counts of the indictment were dismissed. He was sentenced to ten years' imprisonment.

Having reserved his right to appeal from the denial of his motion to dismiss the count of the indictment against him which charged him with having caused a drug induced death in violation of N.J.S.A. 2C:35-9, defendant now pursues his argument against the constitutionality of the statute before this court. He contends that the strict or absolute liability feature of the statute violates due process of law and exceeds the Legislature's power to create a strict liability crime, and the law also violates the State and Federal constitutional prohibitions against cruel and unusual punishments, U.S. Const., Amend. VIII and N.J. Const. (1947), Art. I, par. 12.

N.J.S.A. 2C:35-9 was adopted as part of the Comprehensive Drug Reform Act of 1987, N.J.S.A. 2C:35-1 et seq. and following. The absolute liability or "transferred intent" feature of the criminal homicide which it created was modeled on and is similar to the same element in felony murder law.[2] Because of the similarity, cases which have considered constitutional challenges to felony murder statutes on grounds similar to those posed by the defendant in the present case are relevant to our decision. The Official Commentary to the Comprehensive Drug Reform Act describes the felony murder model and its similarities to the crime proscribed by N.J.S.A. 2C:35-9 as follows:

---

2. "At common law . . . the intent to commit the felony, even in the absence of an intent to kill, was transferred to the death of the victim. [Citations omitted.] More recently, felony murder has been viewed not as a crime of transferred intent but as one of absolute or strict liability."

The offense defined in this section is somewhat similar to the 'felony murder' provisions developed at common law and which are now codified in Chapter 11 of the penal code. The penal code currently provides, for example, that criminal homicide constitutes murder when the defendant, acting either alone or with one or more other persons, is engaged in the commission of, attempt to commit or immediate flight after committing certain enumerated crimes, and in the course of such crime or flight therefrom causes the death of a person other than one of the participants. It is well-established that the State need not prove in such a prosecution that the death was purposely, knowingly or recklessly committed.

Rather a wholly unintended killing constitutes murder if it results from the commission of the underlying felony.[7] It is equally well-settled that a participant may be convicted of murder under this theory even if the victim dies as a consequence of a shot fired by a police officer who was attempting to apprehend the fleeing felon. In other words, it is generally not a defense to a prosecution for felony murder that the death was directly caused by the volitional act of another. Current law thus establishes an unambiguous warning for accountability for even unintended deaths which are closely connected with the commission of certain inherently dangerous crimes. The offense defined in this section posts a similar warning to all drug manufacturers and dealers.

No reported New Jersey case has expressly considered the argument that because conviction of felony murder does not require the perpetrator of the crime to have acted "purposely" or "knowingly," *cf.* N.J.S.A. 2C:11-3a(1) and (2), our felony murder statute violates the due process clause or some other constitutional provision. However, the numerous reported cases which have affirmed convictions for felony murder have implicitly assumed the constitutionality of the statute. But in jurisdictions where the constitutionality of a felony murder statute has been questioned on the ground that it required no mental culpability other than that which is a prerequisite for conviction of the predicate felony, the argument has been rejected. In view of these decisions and of the long history and wide prevalence of felony murder statutes which dispense with the need to prove that homicides which they proscribe were committed willfully or purposely, we can proceed confidently from the premise that the constitutionality of the "transferred intent" or absolute liability feature of such statutes is not in doubt.

---

7. Conviction of felony murder "requires only a showing that a death was caused during the commission of (or attempted commission or flight from) one of the crimes designated in the statute. The State need not prove that the death was purposely or knowingly committed; a wholly unintended killing is murder if it results from the commission of the underlying felony." *State v. Darby*, 200 N.J. Super. 327, 331, 491 A.2d 733 (App. Div. 1984), *certif. den.*, 101 N.J. 226, 501 A.2d 905 (1985). *See State v. Madden*, 61 N.J. 377, 384–385, 294 A.2d 609 (1972).

The New Jersey Legislature has determined that manufacturing, distributing and dispensing certain illegal drugs, including cocaine which is the substance involved in the present case, are criminal activities which, like the crimes enumerated in the felony murder statute, pose inherent dangers to others including those who use the drugs.[9] Defendant has shown us no basis upon which to conclude that that determination is irrational. N.J.S.A. 2C:35-9b limits criminal liability to cases in which the defendant has illegally manufactured, distributed or dispensed a prohibited substance, death results which would not have occurred but for the injection, inhalation or ingestion of that substance, and "the death was not (a) too remote in its occurrence as to have a just bearing on the defendant's liability; or (b) too dependent upon conduct of another person which was unrelated to the injection, inhalation or ingestion of the substance or its effect as to have a just bearing on the defendant's liability." N.J.S.A. 2C:35-9. These limitations on liability are similar to those imposed on criminal liability for felony murder. By analogy to the felony murder rule, we hold that the absolute or strict liability feature of N.J.S.A. 2C:35-9, limited as it is to deaths which are the proximate consequences of inherently dangerous illegal activities, does not violate due process of law.[10]

In *State v. Ramseur*, 106 N.J. 123, 169, 524 A.2d 188 (1987), the Supreme Court described as follows the tests for determining whether a statute violates the constitutional prohibition against cruel and unusual punishments:

> Three inquiries are required. First, does the punishment for the crime conform with contemporary standards of decency? Second, is the punishment grossly disproportionate to the offense? Third, does the punishment go beyond what is necessary to accomplish any penological objective? We

---

9. In the Comprehensive Drug Reform Act of 1987, the Legislature made the following declaration of policy and legislative findings:
> Despite the impressive efforts and gains of our law enforcement agencies, the unlawful use, manufacture and distribution of controlled dangerous substances continues to pose a serious and pervasive threat to the health, safety and welfare of the citizens of this State. New Jersey continues to experience an unacceptably high rate of drug-related crime, and continues to serve as conduit for the illegal trafficking of drugs to and from other jurisdictions.

In addition to the harm suffered by the victims of drug abuse and drug-related crime, the incidence of such offenses is directly related to the rate of other violent and non-violent crimes, including murder, assault, robbery, theft, burglary and organized criminal activities. For this reason, enhanced and coordinated efforts designed specifically to curtail drug related offenses will lead inexorably to a reduction in the rate of crime generally, and is therefore decidedly in the public interest. N.J.S.A. 2C:35-1.1b.

10. Even before adoption of N.J.S.A. 2C:35-9, this court held that a defendant who sold heroin to a drug user who died from an overdose could be convicted of manslaughter because the court was "satisfied that there can be imputed to defendant either knowledge or reckless disregard of the consequence of his act, and that the jury could have reasonably found from the proofs that beyond a reasonable doubt the regular, natural and likely consequence of the sale of heroin was the user's death." *State v. Thomas*, 118 N.J. Super. 377, 380, 288 A.2d 32 (App. Div.), *certif. den.*, 60 N.J. 513, 291 A.2d 374 (1972).

have also been told that the requisite showing to sustain a claim of cruel and unusual punishment is substantial. *State v. Des Marets*, 92 N.J. 62, 82, 455 A.2d 1074 (1983). Absent that showing, a reviewing court must respect the legislative will. *State v. Muessig*, 198 N.J. Super. 197, 201, 486 A.2d 924 (App. Div.), *certif. den.*, 101 N.J. 234, 501 A.2d 912 (1985).

With respect to *Ramseur's* first two tests, whether the punishment prescribed by N.J.S.A. 2C:35-9 "conform[s] with contemporary standards of decency" and whether "the punishment [is] grossly disproportionate to the offense," we agree with the State's argument that the strongest indicator that the penalties at issue here conform with contemporary standards of decency and are not gross disproportionate to the offense is that the Legislature passed the Act only three years ago, in 1987.

Felony murder statutes have been held to impose "cruel and unusual punishment[s]" when they prescribed the death penalty or life imprisonment with or without the possibility of parole. *See, e.g., Enmund v. Florida*, 458 U.S. 782, 102 S. Ct. 3368, 73 L.Ed.2d 1140 (1982); *People v. Dillon*, 34 Cal.3d 441, 194 Cal. Rptr. 390, 668 P. 2d 697 (1983). On the other hand, a sentence of incarceration for two consecutive twenty-year terms and $20,000 in fines for possession of marijuana with intent to distribute and distribution of marijuana was held not to violate the federal constitutional prohibition against cruel and unusual punishments.

Hutto v. Davis, 454 U.S. 370, 102 S. Ct. 703, 70 L.Ed.2d 556 (1982). Because N.J.S.A. 2C:35-9 creates a first degree crime, the ordinary custodial sentence for its violation is from ten to twenty years' imprisonment. N.J.S.A. 2C:43-6a (1). Even if no user is shown to have died as a result, the manufacture, distribution or dispensing of designated controlled dangerous substances, including cocaine, is a first degree offense if the quantity involved is five ounces or more and is a second degree offense if the quantity is between one-half ounce and five ounces. N.J.S.A. 2C:35-5b(1) and (2). Before the effective date of the current law, the penalties for similar offenses were up to twelve years' imprisonment for one ounce or more of a mixture including less than 3.5 grams of the illegal drug in its pure form and up to life imprisonment for larger amounts. In view of these penalties and the Legislature's declaration and findings of fact, we hold that the penalties prescribed for violation of N.J.S.A. 2C:35-9 do not fail to "conform with contemporary standards of decency" and are not "grossly disproportionate to the offense."

The third *Ramseur* test is whether "the punishment go[es] beyond what is necessary to accomplish any penological objective." The rationale for the strict or absolute liability established by N.J.S.A. 2C:35-9 and for its categorizing a violation as first degree offense is similar to that offered for the felony murder rule:

> The historical justification for the rule [in the case of felony murder] is that it serves as a general deterrent against the commission of violent crimes. [Citation omitted.] The rationale is that if potential felons realize that they will be culpable as murderers for a death that occurs during the commission of a felony, they will be less likely to commit the felony. From this

perspective, the imposition of strict liability without regard to the intent to kill serves to deter the commission of serious crimes.

Similarly, the justification for N.J.S.A. 2C:35-9 is that it serves as a general deterrent against manufacturing, distributing and dispensing illegal drugs which the Legislature has found "pose a serious and pervasive threat to the health, safety and welfare of the citizens of this State." N.J.S.A. 2C:35-1.1b Consequently, we are of the view that the Legislature was not unreasonable in determining that the punishment which it prescribed does not "go beyond what is necessary to accomplish any penological objective." We therefore hold that N.J.S.A. 2C:35-9 does not violate the prohibitions against cruel and unusual punishments contained in our State and Federal Constitutions.

The judgment appealed from is therefore affirmed.

Questions and Notes

1. Do you think that felony-murder, if it is justified at all, is more justified on the theory of "transferred intent" or "strict liability"? We will study both of those concepts later in the materials.

2. Assuming the abstract propriety of the statute, was Ervin a drug distributer within the meaning of the statute? Wasn't he just a consumer sharing the drugs with another consumer?

3. Assume that it was a crime to distribute contaminated meat. Assume further that Alvin buys a roast that turns out to be contaminated. He serves it to his family, who all become ill. Is Alvin liable for violating the statute relating to the distribution of contaminated meat?

4. If your answer to Question 3 was "no," how is *Ervin* different?

Chapter 3

Causation

Although issues of causation can arise whenever harm is relevant, they most frequently occur in homicide cases. Consequently, we will focus on causation in the context of homicide. We have already considered causation issues in conjunction with *Dekens* as part of our felony-murder analysis.

Causation issues focus on the relevance of harm to the criminal law. Some commentators believe that as between two equally culpable and equally dangerous defendants, no distinction based on the happenstance of one causing harm should be drawn.[1] That, however, is not (and in my judgment should not be)[2] the law. So long as causing a particular harm is relevant to criminal liability, causation issues will periodically recur.

Any given crime, generally, has a great many "but for" causes, e.g., if the victim hadn't been born, she wouldn't have died. The underlying issue facing a court in a causation case is whether, given the defendant's culpability and the way the death occurred, it is fair to hold the defendant criminally liable for the death. Although clouded in mystifying terms such as "proximate cause," it all seems to boil down to fairness.

Think about whether it is fair to hold the defendants liable for homicide in the cases that follow.

A. Intentional Killings (or Killings Resulting from Intentional Assaults)

Oxendine v. State

528 A.2d 870 (Del. 1987)

Before HORSEY, MOORE, and WALSH, JJ.

HORSEY, Justice:

Defendant, Jeffrey Oxendine, Sr., appeals his conviction in trial by jury in Superior Court of manslaughter[1] in the beating death of his six-year-old son, Jeffrey

---

1. *See, e.g.,* Schulhofer, *Harm and Punishment: A Critique of Emphasis on the Results of Conduct in the Criminal Law,* 122 U. PA. L. REV. 1497 (1974); Dan Cohen, *Causation, in* 1 ENCY. OF CRIME & JUSTICE 165 (S. Kadish, ed. 1983).

2. *See Culpability, Dangerousness, and Harm,* Section I C (Appendix B).

1. 11 *Del.C.* §632(1) states: "A person is guilty of manslaughter when: (1) He recklessly causes the death of another person."

Oxendine, Jr. Oxendine was sentenced to twelve years' imprisonment.[2] On appeal, Oxendine's principal argument is that the Trial Court committed reversible error by denying his motion for a judgment of acquittal on the issue of causation. Specifically, he argues that the State's medical testimony, relating to which of the codefendants' admittedly repeated beatings of the child was the cause of death, was so vague and uncertain as to preclude his conviction of any criminal offense.

We conclude that the evidence upon causation was insufficient to sustain Oxendine's conviction of manslaughter, but that the evidence was sufficient to sustain his conviction of the lesser included offense of assault in the second degree.[3]

The facts may be summarized as follows: On the morning of January 18, 1984, Leotha Tyree, Oxendine's girlfriend, who lived with him, pushed Jeffrey into the bathtub causing microscopic tears in his intestines which led to peritonitis. During a break at work that evening, Oxendine telephoned home and talked to Jeffrey, who complained of stomach pains. When Oxendine returned home from work, he saw bruises on Jeffrey and knew that Tyree had beaten the child during the day. Although Jeffrey continued to complain of a stomachache, he apparently did not tell his father how or when he received the bruises.

The next morning at approximately 7:30 a.m., Oxendine went into Jeffrey's bedroom and began screaming at him to get up. A neighbor in the same apartment building testified to hearing sounds coming from the room of blows being struck, obscenities uttered by a male voice, and cries from a child saying, "Please stop, Daddy, it hurts." After hearing these sounds continue for what seemed like five to ten minutes, the witness heard a final noise consisting of a loud thump, as if someone had been kicked or punched "with a great blow."

Later that day, Jeffrey's abdomen became swollen. When Oxendine arrived home from work at about 5:00 p.m., Tyree told him of Jeffrey's condition and urged him to take Jeffrey to the hospital. Oxendine, apparently believing that Jeffrey was exaggerating his discomfort, went out, bought a newspaper, and returned home to read it. Upon his return, Tyree had prepared to take Jeffrey to the hospital. En route, Jeffrey stopped breathing; and was pronounced dead shortly after his arrival at the hospital.

I

In order to convict Oxendine of manslaughter, the State had to show that his conduct caused Jeffrey's death. 11 *Del.C.* § 261 defines causation as the "antecedent but for which the result in question would not have occurred." At trial, the State's

---

2. Codefendant, Leotha Tyree, was also convicted in the same trial of manslaughter in the death of Jeffrey Oxendine, Jr. and was sentenced to nine years' imprisonment. On direct appeal, this Court has affirmed her conviction. *Tyree v. State, Del.Supr.,* 510 A.2d 222 (1986).

3. 11 *Del.C.* § 612(1) states: "A person is guilty of assault in the second degree when: (1) He intentionally causes serious physical injury to another person." Assault in the Second Degree is a Class C felony for which the range of punishment is 2 to 20 years.

original theories of causation were, alternatively, (1) a "combined direct effect," or (2) an "aggravation" theory.

During its case-in-chief, the State called medical examiners Dr. Inguito and Dr. Hameli, who both testified that Jeffrey's death was caused by intra-abdominal hemorrhage and acute peritonitis, occurring as a result of blunt force trauma to the front of the abdomen. Similarly, each pathologist identified two distinct injuries, one caused more than twenty-four hours before death, and one inflicted less than twenty-four hours before death.

Dr. Inguito could not separate the effects of the two injuries. In his view, it was possible that both the older and more recent hemorrhage could have contributed to the death of the child, but he was unable to tell which of the hemorrhages caused the death of the child. Dr. Inguito could not place any quantitative value on either of the hemorrhages nor could he state whether the fresh hemorrhage or the older hemorrhage caused the death. The prosecutor never asked, nor did Dr. Inguito give, an opinion on whether the second hemorrhage accelerated Jeffrey's death.

Dr. Hameli, on the other hand, was of the opinion that the earlier injury was the underlying cause of death. According to him, the later injury, *i.e.*, the second hemorrhage, "was an aggravating, and probably some factors [sic] contributing," but it was the earlier injury that was the plain underlying cause of death.

The prosecutor, however, did explicitly ask Dr. Hameli if the second injury accelerated Jeffrey's death. The relevant portion of the testimony is as follows:

> **Prosecutor:** Dr. Hameli, within a reasonable degree of medical certainty and in your expert opinion, did the second hemorrhage accelerate this child's death?
>
> **Hameli:** I do not know. If you are talking about timewise-I assume that's what you are talking about, exploration.
>
> **Prosecutor:** You cannot give an opinion of that area; is that correct?
>
> **Hameli:** No.

Oxendine moved for judgment of acquittal at the end of the State's case-in-chief. The Trial Court, however, denied his motion.

As part of her case, codefendant Tyree called Dr. Hofman, a medical examiner, who disagreed about the number of injuries. He perceived only one injury inflicted about twelve hours before death.

Subsequently, the prosecutor asked Hofman the following hypothetical question that assumed two blows when Hofman only testified as to one blow:

> **Prosecutor:** In your expert medical opinion within a reasonable degree of medical certainty, if this child, given his weakened state as a result of the significant trauma to his abdominal cavity, suffered subsequently another blunt force trauma to the same area, would it accelerate this child's death?

Hofman: My opinion, as in a general statement, not knowing this child, it certainly would have an impact on shortening this child's life.

Prosecutor: Is then, therefore, your answer yes?

Hofman: Yes.

At the end of trial, Oxendine again moved for judgment of acquittal. The Trial Court denied the motion and instructed the jury on the elements of recklessness, causation and on various lesser included offenses. The ultimate and only theory of causation on which the jury was charged was based on "acceleration." The Trial Court instructed the jury that "[a] defendant who causes the death of another . . . is not relieved of responsibility for causing the death if another later injury accelerates, that is, hastens the death of the other person. Contribution without acceleration is not sufficient." As previously noted, the jury returned verdicts of manslaughter against Oxendine and Tyree.

II

In this case, the evidence established that Oxendine inflicted a nonlethal injury upon Jeffrey after his son had, twenty-four hours earlier, sustained a lethal injury from a previous beating inflicted by Tyree. Thus, for Oxendine to be convicted of manslaughter in this factual context, the State was required to show for purposes of causation under 11 *Del.C.* § 261 that Oxendine's conduct hastened or accelerated the child's death. The Superior Court correctly instructed the jury that "[c]ontribution [or aggravation] without acceleration is insufficient to establish causation." We do not equate aggravation with acceleration. It is possible to make the victim's pain more intense, *i.e.*, aggravate the injury, without accelerating the time of the victim's death. Thus, in terms of section 261, and as applied to defendant, the relevant inquiry is: but for his infliction of the second injury, would the victim have died when he died? If the second injury caused his son to die *any* sooner, then defendant, who inflicted the second injury, would be deemed to have caused his son's death within the definition of section 261.

A finding of medical causation may not be based on speculation or conjecture. A doctor's testimony that a certain thing is possible is no evidence at all. His opinion as to what is possible is no more valid than the jury's own speculation as to what is or is not possible. Almost anything is possible, and it is improper to allow a jury to consider and base a verdict upon a "possible" cause of death. Therefore, a doctor's testimony can only be considered evidence when his conclusions are based on reasonable medical certainty that a fact is true or untrue.

The State's expert medical testimony, even when viewed in the light most favorable to the State, was (1) insufficient to sustain the State's original theories of causation (a "combined direct effect" or an "aggravation" theory); and (2) insufficient to sustain the State's ultimate theory of causation ("acceleration") on which the court instructed the jury. Both of the State's expert witnesses, Dr. Inguito and Dr. Hameli, were unable to state with any degree of medical certainty that the second injury contributed to the death of the child. Dr. Inguito could only testify that it was possible that both the older and more recent hemorrhage could have contributed to the death of the child. As for Dr. Hameli, he testified that the second injury independent of the first injury could have caused death but probably would not cause death. Furthermore, Dr. Hameli explicitly stated that he could not give an opinion as to whether the second injury accelerated Jeffrey's death. Similarly, Dr. Inguito was neither asked nor did he offer an opinion about acceleration.

The record establishes that the only theory of causation under which the State submitted the case to the jury was the acceleration theory. The State apparently abandoned its initial theories of causation and adopted the acceleration theory as the cause of death, based on the testimony of Dr. Hofman, a witness for codefendant Tyree, recalled by the State on rebuttal. That was too late to sustain the State's case-in-chief for manslaughter.

The State concedes that when it closed its case-in-chief it did not have a prima facie case to support acceleration. Therefore, even though the State could, based on Dr. Hofman's testimony, establish a prima facie case of acceleration at the end of the trial, Oxendine's conviction of manslaughter must be set aside for insufficiency of the evidence to establish that his conduct accelerated Jeffrey's death.

Furthermore, even if the State's evidence was sufficient to sustain its original theories of causation, we could not affirm Oxendine's conviction because the jury was not instructed on either of these theories. Although the State may submit alternate theories of causation to the jury, if supported by the evidence, it must establish in its case-in-chief a prima facie basis for each theory that goes to the jury.[4] In this case, the State did not maintain alternate theories throughout the trial. The State abandoned and completely changed its section 261 theories of causation after it closed its case-in-chief. The ultimate and only theory ("acceleration") on which the court instructed the jury was different and not compatible with the State's original theories of causation that it attempted to establish during its case-in-chief. As previously noted, acceleration is not synonymous with either aggravation or the combined effects of two injuries. Thus, when the State was unable to establish at the end of its case-in-chief a prima facie case for acceleration, its case for manslaughter failed.

It is extremely "difficult to be objective about the death of a child.... Those responsible ought to be punished. Nevertheless, there must be proof as to who, if anyone, inflicted the injuries that resulted in death." "Reprehensible and repulsive as the conduct of the defendant is, nevertheless it is not proof of manslaughter."

The Trial Court, however, properly denied Oxendine's motion for judgment of acquittal at the close of the State's case because its medical testimony was sufficient for a rational trier of fact to conclude beyond a reasonable doubt that Oxendine was guilty of the lesser included offense of assault in the second degree, 11 *Del.C.* §612(1). Therefore, we reverse Oxendine's conviction of manslaughter and remand

---

4. This practice is often employed in murder cases when the State is unsure as to what type of murder, *i.e.*, intentional, second degree, felony murder, etc., has taken place.

the case to Superior Court for entry of a judgment of conviction and resentence of defendant for the lesser included offense of assault in the second degree.

REVERSED AND REMANDED.

Questions and Notes

1. Why did the State lose this manslaughter conviction?

2. Can you see a way to win this case if you were the prosecutor?

3. If all three doctors had testified, should both Tyree and Oxendine have been convicted? Should they have both been acquitted? Recall that Dr. Inguito wasn't sure which injury caused the death. Dr. Hameli thought that Tyree's beating caused the death, and Dr. Hofman thought that Oxendine's beating caused the death.

4. Are you satisfied with the result in this case? Why? Why not?

5. In *Brackett*, the court seemed a bit more willing to attribute causation to the batterer.

People v. Brackett
510 N.E.2d 877 (Ill. 1987)

Justice RYAN delivered the opinion of the court:

On the evening of October 20, 1981, defendant Randy Brackett, age 21, entered the home of Elizabeth Winslow, an 85-year-old widow, for whom he had previously done yard work. During the course of that evening, he raped and severely beat Mrs. Winslow, forced her to write him a check for $125, cooked himself some food and fell asleep for a time in an arm chair. He finally left in the early hours of the morning. The first policeman on the scene found Mrs. Winslow lying naked on the living room hide-a-bed. She was severely bruised about the face and appeared to have a broken arm and various other injuries to her body. She said she had been raped, choked and beaten.

She was admitted to the hospital, where medical examinations revealed she had a broken arm, broken rib, bruises on her face, neck, arms, trunk and inner thighs. There are no issues on appeal to this court involving the rape and aggravated battery convictions; therefore, it is unnecessary to recite the details of the physical and medical evidence involved in the proof of those charges. That evidence will be germane only to the extent that it may be involved in the issue on appeal concerning the cause of death.

Dr. Robert William Elliott was one of the doctors who treated Mrs. Winslow while she was hospitalized. Dr. Elliott had been Mrs. Winslow's physician for 20 years. He testified that prior to the events of October 21, 1981, Mrs. Winslow was a "feisty" old woman who lived alone and took care of herself. He further stated that during her stay in the hospital Mrs. Winslow became depressed and resisted efforts to feed her, and her condition progressively weakened. After receiving maximum benefit from hospital treatment, Mrs. Winslow was transferred to a nursing home on November 13, 1981. Her prognosis was poor, according to Dr. Elliott, even though her injuries were healing. Dr. Elliott accounted for the poor prognosis by relating the effects of trauma to elderly patients and the depression of elderly patients when they are removed from their homes for any type of hospitalization.

The nursing home staff noted Mrs. Winslow's continuing declining condition and reported to Dr. Elliott her refusal to eat. He, in turn, ordered a nasal gastric tube to be used to try to feed her. The staff reported back that they could not use the tube because Mrs. Winslow's nasal passages were too small, and her facial injuries made it too painful to insert. Dr. Elliott withdrew the order because he did not want to cause Mrs. Winslow any further pain. It was his medical opinion that her death was imminent. He testified that, to a reasonable medical certainty, the tube could not be inserted because of her injuries. Two days later Mrs. Winslow's family was called to the nursing home because her condition had worsened, she had become cyanotic (a condition where the extremities turn blue and the blood pressure drops) and they expected her to die.

The next day, November 24, 1981, Mrs. Winslow's family was with her in the nursing home while she was being served lunch. For approximately 20 minutes a nurse's aide was feeding her small portions of pureed food on a spoon, which Mrs. Winslow was accepting without choking or gagging in any way. She eventually spit out some vegetables, which the aide interpreted to mean that Mrs. Winslow did not want any more. The aide tried to give Mrs. Winslow ice cream, but she noticed Mrs. Winslow had stopped moving her mouth. The nurse's aide went to summon the nurses, who determined Mrs. Winslow had died.

There was an autopsy conducted by Dr. Steven Neurenberger. He determined her immediate cause of death to be asphyxiation, which resulted from six ounces of food being aspirated into her trachea. He found evidence of the internal abdominal bruises around the colon and kidney, a broken rib, and facial bruises. He testified that none of these injuries of themselves caused her death. He also testified as to the mechanics of clearing the trachea when food enters it. This requires a sufficient volume of air to be present in the lungs, which, when expelled, pushes the food out of the trachea and back into the mouth, thus preventing asphyxiation. He also testified that the pain associated with a broken rib generally inhibits deep breathing, which limits the amount of air available to the lungs. He further testified that the volume of food lodged in Mrs. Winslow's trachea was very large and would have been difficult for a normal, healthy person to expel. He stated the amount of food in her trachea would have led to her unconsciousness within 30 seconds, and death would have soon followed.

In this appeal, the defendant first contends he was not proved guilty of murder beyond a reasonable doubt because there was insufficient evidence to prove a criminal agency caused Mrs. Winslow's death. He also contends that even if there was sufficient proof of causation, he had no intent to kill, nor did he know his acts created a strong probability of death, nor could he have foreseen that death was a likely consequence of blows from his bare fists. We disagree and affirm the decisions of the circuit court of Madison County and the appellate court.

The State must prove that death was caused by a criminal agency. The defendant contends the State did not meet its burden of proof on this issue of causation. Briefly stated, the defendant claims that death was caused by an intervening event, namely asphyxiation, which was totally unrelated to the crimes of rape and aggravated battery, which the defendant acknowledges he perpetrated against Mrs. Winslow five weeks before she died.

It is a matter of common knowledge that a person can accidentally choke to death while eating. Moreover, that type of accidental death could be the type of intervening cause which would relieve a defendant of criminal responsibility for death. The courts in Illinois have repeatedly held that an intervening cause completely unrelated to the acts of the defendant does relieve a defendant of criminal liability. The converse of this is also true: when criminal acts of the defendant have contributed to a person's death, the defendant may be found guilty of murder. It is not the law in this State that the defendant's acts must be the sole and immediate cause of death.

In this case, the initial trier of fact was the circuit judge. He ruled on the issue of causation. His findings of fact and judgment specifically held that the defendant's acts were a contributing cause of Mrs. Winslow's death, in that the defendant, through his criminal acts, set in motion a chain of events which culminated in her death. The appellate court affirmed his ruling on causation. We have held that when presented with a challenge to the sufficiency of the evidence, it is not the function of this court to retry the defendant. Rather, the relevant question is whether, after viewing the evidence in the light most favorable to the prosecution, any rational trier of fact could have found the essential elements of the crime beyond a reasonable doubt.

Cases concerning unrelated, intervening causes of death have been problematic in the law for hundreds of years. By the mid-1700's the doctrine was well established that

"if a man receives a wound, which is not in itself mortal, but either for want of helpful applications, or neglect thereof, it turns to a gangrene, or a fever, and that gangrene or fever be the immediate cause of his death, yet, this is murder or manslaughter in him that gave the stroke or wound, for that wound, tho [sic] it were not the immediate cause of his death, yet, if it were the mediate cause thereof, and the fever or gangrene was the immediate cause of his death, yet the wound was the cause of the gangrene or fever, and so consequently is causa causati."

(1 Hale, Pleas of the Crown 428 (S. Emlyn Ed.).) In our technological age, we have come to expect scientific explanations for all types of physical phenomena. In cases such as this, where the causal links are not immediately apparent, we frequently look to medical experts to assist the trier of fact in determining whether the defendant's acts constitute a contributing factor to the victim's death.

Here there was uncontradicted evidence that the ability to expel food lodged in the trachea is directly related to the volume of air present in the lungs. The victim, due to her broken rib, was not able to breathe deeply, nor would she have had the capacity to expel the food. There was further uncontradicted evidence that the nasal feeding tube could not be used because of the beating the victim had received. Consequently, the nursing home staff was unable to use a feeding method that would have avoided the possibility of choking. Also, the victim's depressed, weakened, debilitated state was the direct result of the trauma associated with the attack upon her, and there was uncontradicted evidence to that effect. It was Dr. Elliott's opinion that she became too weak even to swallow.

Contrary to the defendant's contentions, we believe this is precisely the kind of case where the defendant takes his victim as he finds him. There are many cases in this State where the victim's existing health condition contributed to the victim's death. However, so long as the defendant's acts contribute to the death there is still sufficient proof of causation, despite the preexisting health condition. It appears to this court that a person's advanced age is as significant a part of his existing health condition as diabetes or hardening of the arteries.

The trial court placed great weight on the testimony of Dr. Elliott, as it was entitled to do. It was his testimony that this victim's advanced age affected her recuperative powers. Viewing all the evidence in a light most favorable to the prosecution, there was no reversible error on the issue of causation. The trier of fact was entitled to find that the defendant, a 21-year-old male, 6 feet 3 inches tall and 170 pounds, who battered and raped an 85-year-old woman, set in motion a chain of events which contributed to her death.

The defendant argues that the appellate court ignored a long-standing principle in this State, that death is not ordinarily contemplated as a natural consequence of blows from bare fists. He therefore asserts he could not know that blows from his bare fists created a strong probability of death or great bodily harm. We do not see that the appellate court ignored this principle. While Illinois cases do stand for the proposition the defendant recites, these same cases also stand for the proposition that death may be the natural consequence of blows with bare fists where there is great disparity in size and strength between the two parties. Given the disparity in size and strength between the defendant and Mrs. Winslow, we find it difficult to give credibility to this argument that the defendant, who battered this victim with enough force to break bones, did not know that his acts created a strong probability of death or great bodily harm.

Finally, the defendant argues that Mrs. Winslow's death by asphyxiation was not a foreseeable consequence of his felonious acts. There are often cases in which the precise manner of death will not be foreseeable to the defendant while he is committing a felony. This does not relieve the defendant of responsibility. There are cases where the immediate cause of death was meningitis (*People v. Paulson* (1967), 80 Ill. App. 2d 44, 225 N.E.2d 424), or pneumonia (*People v. Gulliford* (1980), 86 Ill. App. 3d 237, 41 Ill. Dec. 596, 407 N.E.2d 1094), or a heart condition (*People v. Fuller*

(1986), 141 Ill. App. 3d 737, 95 Ill. Dec. 885, 490 N.E.2d 977). In each of these cases the defendant's felonious acts contributed to the victim's demise, and in each of these cases the defendant could not foresee the exact manner in which the victim would die. We hold here that the defendant did not have to foresee that this victim would die from asphyxiation in order to be guilty of felony murder.

For the reasons stated, the defendant's conviction is affirmed.

Questions and Notes

1. Other than being deemed a murderer, Brackett was not hurt by the conviction. He had previously received 60 years for raping Mrs. Winslow. The intermediate court of appeals, however, had held that under Illinois law Brackett could not be sentenced for both rape and murder of the same person resulting from the same transaction. This doctrine, at least as applied to felony-murder, is fairly common, thereby mollifying much of the harshness (some would say draining much of the utility) of the felony-murder rule.

2. Did Mrs. Winslow die because: (1) her broken rib precluded expulsion of the food, (2) her face was beaten too much to use a feeding tube, (3) she was too weak to swallow, (4) she was too depressed to care about eating, (5) she was aged, (6) she became cyanotic, or (7) something else?

3. If she died because she was too weak to swallow, should the negligence of the nurse's aide in feeding her exculpate Brackett?

4. Typically, courts will not allow negligent treatment to exculpate unless the negligence is so extreme as to render the defendant's conduct no longer a meaningful cause. (E.g., V's wound is nonmortal, but he dies from either an unnecessary operation performed during his hospitalization, or from gross negligence on the part of the doctor.) If the wound is mortal, only a totally supervening cause such as V's being decapitated by a maniac would likely exculpate D. If another stabs or shoots V while he is languishing near death, most courts would say that both wounds contributed to the death and the original D is still liable. *Cf., People v. Lewis*, 57 P. 470 (Cal. 1899).

5. If she had not been fed, but died from her cyanotic condition, would Brackett still have been convicted? Why or why not?

6. If her refusal to eat was reflective of a desire to die, would (should) Brackett be exculpated?

7. Would this case have been different if Mrs. Winslow were depressed and suicidal before the rape and battery? If your answer is yes, are you saying that feisty old women get more protection than those who are depressed and suicidal? If not, what are you saying?

8. The suicide following crime cases are among the more difficult for the courts. The courts seem to look for causal links in such cases, however, probably because it seems unjust to exculpate a criminal whose outrageous act has driven a victim to kill herself. *See, e.g., Stephenson v. State*, 179 N.E. 633 (Ind. 1932).

Problem

The following Associated Press newspaper story appeared in several newspapers in May 1999:

Woman whose mother shot her dies after removal of life support

Orlando, Fla.—A woman paralyzed from the neck down by a bullet was taken off life support at her request and died Wednesday, clearing the way for prosecutors to bring murder charges against the person who shot her—her mother.

Georgette Smith, 42, had won a judge's ruling a day earlier forcing doctors at Lucerne Medical Center to disconnect her ventilator. She argued that she couldn't bear to live in such a condition.

Even though Smith made the decision to die, prosecutors planned to charge her mother with murder, creating a highly unusual—and perhaps unprecedented—case that will be watched closely by legal experts.

Smith's mother, Shirley Egan, 68, has already been charged with attempted murder. Egan, a frail, 85-pound woman who is blind in one eye, allegedly shot Smith in March after overhearing Smith and her boyfriend talking about putting Egan in a nursing home.

The bullet struck Smith in the neck, tearing through her spinal cord. The former Sears merchandise stocker was left unable to speak without effort, incapable of swallowing and unable to control her bladder. She was fed through a tube and ran a high risk of pneumonia, infections, ulcers and bedsores.

"All I can do is wink my eyes and wiggle my nose, wiggle my tongue. I can't move any other part of my body," she said in court papers. "I can't live like this."

On Tuesday, judge Richard Conrad, who had met with Smith and studied her medical history, ruled that she was mentally competent to make the decision to die. He said she could have life support removed at 5:00 p.m. Wednesday. Smith was sedated before the ventilator was disconnected and was pronounced dead at 5:46 p.m. A hospital spokeswoman refused to say what time she was taken off life support.

The same day she won in court, Smith gave prosecutors a video-taped deposition from her hospital bed, and it will be among the pieces of evidence against Egan, who was in jail Wednesday.

Egan's attorney has said she did not mean to shoot her daughter and didn't want to see her suffer. But he argued against removing Smith from the ventilator because prosecutors had said they would seek a murder indictment against Egan.

Prosecutors have upgraded charges to murder when comatose victims have died after family members decided to take them off life support. But Robert Moffat, a law professor at the University of Florida, said this case is unique because Smith made the choice herself.

That could make murder charges harder to prove, because a strong case could be made that the cause of Smith's death was the removal of life support, not being shot, said Andrew Kayton, legal director of the American Civil Liberties Union of Florida.

"It would be an important legal issue—whether the mother's shooting was the legal cause of death," Kayton said.

Smith's daughters, Candace Smith, 22, and Joeleen Hill, 19, supported their mother's decision.

"She's prepared herself," Candace Smith said in court last week, "because she knows she's lived a good life and she doesn't want to finish her life in this way."

How should the Florida Court rule? Why? For another state's solution to a similar problem, see *People v. Caldwell*, 692 N.E.2d 448 (Ill. App. 1998).

B. Unintentional Killings

People v. Russell

693 N.E.2d 193 (N.Y. 1998)

KAYE, Chief Judge

Shortly before noon on December 17, 1992, Shamel Burroughs engaged in a gun battle with Jermaine Russell and Khary Bekka on Centre Mall of the Red Hook Housing Project in Brooklyn. During the course of the battle, Patrick Daly, a public school principal looking for a child who had left school, was fatally wounded by a single stray nine millimeter bullet that struck him in the chest. Burroughs, Bekka and Russell—defendants on this appeal—were all charged with second degree murder.

Two separate juries, one for Burroughs and another for Russell and Bekka, were impanelled contemporaneously and heard the evidence presented at trial. Although ballistics tests were inconclusive in determining which defendant actually fired the bullet that killed Daly, the theory of the prosecution was that each of them acted with the mental culpability required for commission of the crime, and that each "intentionally aided" the defendant who fired the fatal shot. Both juries convicted defendants of second degree, depraved indifference murder.

On appeal, each defendant challenges the sufficiency of the evidence. Because the evidence, viewed in the light most favorable to the prosecution, could have led a rational trier of fact to find, beyond a reasonable doubt, that each defendant was guilty of depraved indifference murder as charged, we affirm the order of the Appellate Division sustaining all three convictions.

A depraved indifference murder conviction requires proof that defendant, under circumstances evincing a depraved indifference to human life, recklessly engaged in conduct creating a grave risk of death to another person, and thereby caused the death of another person. Reckless conduct requires awareness and conscious disregard of a substantial and unjustifiable risk that such result will occur or that such circumstance exists "The risk must be of such nature and degree that disregard thereof constitutes a gross deviation from the standard of conduct that a reasonable person would observe in the situation" [*id.*]. To constitute "depraved indifference," conduct must be "'so wanton, so deficient in a moral sense of concern, so devoid of regard of the life or lives of others, and so blameworthy as to warrant the same criminal liability as that which the law imposes upon a person who intentionally causes the death of another.'"

Although defendants underscore that only one bullet killed Patrick Daly and it is uncertain which of them fired that bullet, the prosecution was not required to prove which defendant fired the fatal shot when the evidence was sufficient to establish that each defendant acted with the mental culpability required for the commission of depraved indifference murder, and each defendant "intentionally aided" the defendant who fired the fatal shot. Defendants urge, however, that the evidence adduced at trial did not support a finding that they—as adversaries in a deadly gun battle—shared the "community of purpose" necessary for accomplice liability. We disagree. The fact that defendants set out to injure or kill one another does not rationally preclude a finding that they intentionally aided each other to engage in the mutual combat that caused Daly's death.

People v Abbott, 84 A.D.2d 11, 445 N.Y.S.2D 344, provides an apt illustration. That case involved two defendants—Abbott and Moon—who were engaged in a "drag race" on a residential street when Abbott lost control and smashed into another automobile, killing the driver and two passengers. Both defendants were convicted of criminally negligent homicide, but Moon asserted that he was not responsible for Abbott's actions and that his conviction should be set aside. Rejecting this argument, the court found that, although Moon did not strike the victim's car and was Abbott's adversary in a competitive race, he intentionally participated with Abbott in an inherently dangerous and unlawful activity and therefore shared Abbott's culpability. Moon's "conduct made the race possible" in the first place, as there would not have been a race had Moon not "accepted Abbott's challenge" *see also, People v. Fabian*, 154 Misc.2d 957, 962, 586 N.Y.S.2d 468 [although defendants were trying to harm each other, at the same time they acted in concert to create an explosive condition that resulted inevitably in the victims' death and injuries]; *Alston v State*, 339 Md. 306, 320, 662 A.2d 247, 254 [there was sufficient evidence to support a jury finding that rival groups tacitly agreed, pursuant to an "unwritten code of macho honor," that there would be mutual combat and that each group aided, abetted and encouraged its adversary to engage in urban warfare].

In the present case, the jurors were instructed: "If you find that the People have proven beyond a reasonable doubt that [defendants] *took up each other's challenge*, shared in the venture and unjustifiably, voluntarily and jointly created a zone of danger, then each is responsible for his own acts and the acts of the others ... [and] it makes no difference whether it was a bullet from Mr. Bekka's gun, Mr. Russell's gun or Mr. Burrough's gun that penetrated Mr. Daly and caused his death" (emphasis added).

The trial evidence was sufficient to support each jury's findings in accordance with this charge. Although Burroughs was shooting at Russell and Bekka, and Russell and Bekka were shooting at Burroughs, there was adequate proof to justify the finding that the three defendants tacitly agreed to engage in the gun battle that placed the life of any innocent bystander at grave risk and ultimately killed Daly. Indeed, unlike an unanticipated ambush or spontaneous attack that might have taken defendants by surprise, the gunfight in this case only began after defendants acknowledged and accepted each others' challenge to engage in a deadly battle on a public concourse.

As defendants approached one another on Centre Mall, a grassy open area that serves as a thoroughfare for the 7,000 residents of the 28-building housing complex, it was evident that an encounter between them would be violent and would endanger others. There was trial evidence that when Burroughs first saw Bekka and Russell walking toward him, he immediately recognized the danger, instructing the two female friends accompanying him, one of them pregnant, to "run" or "go." They too plainly sensed the danger because, without hesitation, they turned and ran.

Despite the palpable threat, Burroughs, armed with a nine-millimeter Glock, did not flee with his friends. Rather, he continued toward Russell and Bekka, tacitly accepting their invitation and issuing one of his own. In turn, Russell and Bekka, also armed with automatic weapons, continued walking toward Burroughs, challenging him and accepting his challenge. As they drew nearer, defendants each began firing their high-powered guns, capable of shooting bullets at an average rate of 1,100 feet per second, across the pedestrian thoroughfare.

The dozen or more people in the area, as well as those with windows overlooking the Mall, were put at grave risk as defendants unleashed a hail of bullets. Witnesses testified that the battle sounded "like a war" and that anywhere from nine to 20 shots were fired.

Although Centre Mall is surrounded by buildings affording refuge, defendants chose instead to run through the area aggressively pursuing one another. Indeed, even after exchanging an initial volley of shots, they continued to wage their private war, issuing taunts and ducking back and forth behind buildings and trees, seeking tactical advantage. As a result of defendants' deadly gun battle, Patrick Daly was shot in the chest and killed almost instantly.

The evidence adduced at trial was also sufficient for the jury to determine that all three defendants acted with the mental culpability required for depraved indifference murder, and that they intentionally aided and encouraged each other to create the lethal crossfire that caused the death of Patrick Daly.

Accordingly, in each case the order of the Appellate Division should be affirmed.

Questions and Notes

1. Assuming that Burroughs fired the fatal shot, how can we say that Russell caused it? Is *Sophophone* relevant in any way? If so, how?

2. If Burroughs had killed Bekka, would (should) Russell be liable? Explain.

3. Is the theory of the case that Russell is responsible for Burroughs' conduct or that Russell is responsible for his own conduct? Explain.

4. In *McFadden*, we see similar reasoning applied to less egregious conduct.

State v. McFadden

320 N.W.2d 608 (Iowa 1982)

ALLBEE, Justice.

This case stems from a drag race between defendant Michael Dwayne McFadden and another driver, Matthew Sulgrove, which occurred on a Des Moines city street in April 1980. During the course of the two vehicles' southbound progression, Sulgrove lost control of his automobile and swerved into a lane of oncoming traffic, where he struck a lawfully operated northbound vehicle. This third vehicle contained a six-year-old passenger, Faith Ellis, who was killed in the collision along with Sulgrove. Defendant's automobile did not physically contact either of the two colliding vehicles. Further details concerning the race and the accident will be related as necessary for treatment of the issues raised by defendant. Preliminarily, we note that the fact that defendant's automobile did not physically contact either of the other two vehicles does not, standing alone, preclude his conviction. This rule was established in Iowa in another drag-racing case, *State v. Youngblut*, 257 Iowa 343, 132 N.W.2d 486 (1965), where a defendant was held to have been properly charged with involuntary manslaughter under similar facts. Having taken initial note of *Youngblut*, we proceed to address defendant's legal arguments concerning causation.

Defendant asserts that because Sulgrove was a competitor in the drag race, he assumed the risk of his own death, and therefore defendant could not be convicted or sentenced for that death. This question was not raised in *Youngblut* because the only victim there was an innocent third party who had been traveling in a nonracing vehicle.

Defendant's position finds some support in *State v. Petersen*, 270 Or. 166, 167–68, 526 P.2d 1008, 1009 (1974), a drag-racing case in which the court held that Oregon's involuntary manslaughter statute "should not be interpreted to extend to those cases in which the victim is a knowing and voluntary participant in the course of reckless conduct." Drag-racing cases from other jurisdictions, however, have held defendants liable for manslaughter in the death of a co-participant. *Commonwealth v. Peak*, 12 Pa. D. & C. 2d 379, 381–82 (1957) [other citations omitted]. Although *Peak* appears to have been effectively overruled by *Commonwealth v. Root*, 403 Pa. 571, 170 A.2d 310 (1961), a case we will discuss further below, we find ourselves in agreement with *Peak* rather than with *Root*. Therefore, we quote with approval the following discussion from *Peak* which is pertinent to the issue at hand:

"Defendants by participating in the unlawful racing initiated a series of events resulting in the death of Young. Under these circumstances, decedent's own unlawful conduct does not absolve defendants from their guilt. The acts of defendants were contributing and substantial factors in bringing about the death of Young. The acts and omissions of two or more persons may work concurrently as the efficient cause of an injury and in such case each of the participating acts or omissions is regarded in law as a proximate cause."

12 Pa. D. & C. 2d at 382.

We hold that the fact of Sulgrove's voluntary and reckless participation in the drag race does not of itself bar defendant from being convicted of involuntary manslaughter for Sulgrove's death. Next, defendant contends trial court erred in applying the civil standard of proximate cause in a criminal prosecution, rather than adopting the more stringent standard of "direct causal connection" used by the Pennsylvania court in *Commonwealth v. Root*, 403 Pa. 571, 580, 170 A.2d 310, 314 (1961). In *Root*, the court held that "the tort liability concept of proximate cause has no proper place in prosecutions for criminal homicide and more direct causal connection is required for conviction." The court cited the facts of another Pennsylvania case as an example of such direct causation: In *Commonwealth v. Levin*, 184 Pa. Super. 436, 135 A.2d 764 (1957)] two cars were racing on the streets of Philadelphia at speeds estimated at from 85 to 95 miles per hour. The defendant's car, in the left hand lane, was racing alongside of the car in which the deceased was a passenger when the defendant turned his automobile sharply to the right in front of the other car thereby causing the driver of the latter car to lose control and smash into a tree, the passenger being thrown to the road and killed as a result of the impact. . . . Levin's act of cutting his automobile sharply in front of the car in which the deceased was riding directly forced that car off of the road and into the tree. The defendant's reckless and unlawful maneuver was the direct cause of the crucial fatality. *Id.* at 576, 170 A.2d at 312.

We had occasion to consider a similar standard-of-causation issue in *State v. Marti*, 290 N.W.2d 570, 584–85 (Iowa 1980), which upheld the involuntary manslaughter conviction of a man who provided an obviously intoxicated, suicidal woman with the means to shoot herself by loading a gun for her and placing it within her reach. As here, the defendant in *Marti* argued that the trial court "inappropriately adopted the standards of proximate cause applied in civil cases." Unlike the Pennsylvania court in *Root*, however, we said in *Marti* that we were "unwilling to hold as a blanket rule of law that instructions used in civil trials regarding proximate cause are inappropriate for criminal trials."

We explained:

One reason for this is the similar functions that the requirement of proximate cause plays in both sorts of trials. The element of proximate cause in criminal prosecutions serves as a requirement that there be a sufficient causal relationship between the defendant's conduct and a proscribed harm to hold him criminally responsible. Similarly, in the law of torts it is the element that requires there to be a sufficient causal relationship between the defendant's conduct and the plaintiff's damage to hold the defendant civilly liable.

We did note in *Marti*, however, that legal causation (as opposed to factual causation) is "essentially a question of whether the policy of the law will extend the responsibility for the conduct to the consequences which have in fact occurred." *Id.* at 585 (quoting W. PROSSER, HANDBOOK OF THE LAW OF TORTS § 42, at 244 (4th ed. (1971)). Further, we recognized "that different policy considerations may come into play in criminal prosecutions than in civil trials," and that an "argument could be made that these differences should be reflected in the proximate cause instructions used in the different kinds of trials." Nevertheless, we had no occasion to consider whether such differences existed in that case because the defendant there failed to indicate any differences in policy considerations relevant to his case, much less how such differences might have prejudicially affected any particular instruction given here.

We [now] address the standard-of-causation question on its merits. First, although defendant does not cite or appear to rely on *State v. Rullestad*, 259 Iowa 209, 212–13, 143 N.W.2d 278, 280 (1966), we are aware of *Rullestad's* holding that to sustain an involuntary manslaughter conviction based on the public offense of drunk driving, it is necessary to show a "direct causal connection" between the drunk driving and the death. *Rullestad* cites *Root* among a list of cases "having some bearing" on the point. While *Rullestad* does use the phrase "direct causal connection," the case contains no discussion of the distinction between the ordinary concept of proximate cause and the more stringent standard adopted in *Root*. Elsewhere in *Rullestad*, the term "proximate cause" is used repeatedly in referring to the appropriate legal standard. 259 Iowa at 212–14, 143 N.W.2d at 280–81. Thus, we believe *Rullestad's* use of the phrase "direct causal connection" was intended to convey nothing more than the ordinary notion of proximate cause.

This view is reinforced by the fact that *Youngblut* implicitly rejects the causation standard adopted in *Root*. The facts outlined in the minutes of testimony attached to the indictment in *Youngblut* did not include any specific act by defendant which directly caused his fellow racer to collide with the hapless third vehicle. Thus, those facts would not have met the direct causation test of *Root*. Yet this court held that those facts were legally sufficient to satisfy the elements of involuntary manslaughter.

Furthermore, of all the involuntary manslaughter cases we have studied which involve drag racing, we have found only one that applies a standard of causation as stringent as that in *Root: Thacker v. State*, 103 Ga. App. 36, 37–39, 117 S.E.2d 913, 914–15 (1961). Other cases, when not based on a theory of vicarious liability, appear to apply a proximate cause standard similar to that in tort cases. *E.g., State v. Melcher*, 15 Ariz. App. 157, 161–62, 487 P.2d 3, 7–8 (1971); *Campbell v. State*, 285 So. 2d 891, 893–95 (Miss. 1973). Finally, defendant has suggested no specific policy differences, nor can we think of any, that would justify a different standard of proximate causation under our involuntary manslaughter statute than under our tort law. The *Root* court opined that "[l]egal theory which makes guilt or innocence of criminal homicide depend upon such accidental and fortuitous circumstances as are now embraced by modern tort law's encompassing concept of proximate cause is too harsh to be just." We do not agree. Proximate cause is based on the concept of foreseeability. We believe the foreseeability requirement, coupled with the requirement of recklessness, will prevent the possibility of harsh or unjust results in involuntary manslaughter cases. We disagree with the *Root* court's apparent opinion that drag racing on a public street is "not generally considered to present the likelihood of a resultant death."

Accordingly, we hold that trial court did not err in applying ordinary proximate cause principles to determine whether the causation element of section 707.5(1) had been met, and in declining to adopt the more stringent "direct causal connection" standard of *Root*.

Defendant argues that trial court erred in failing to find that defendant had withdrawn from the drag race prior to the collision between the Sulgrove and Ellis vehicles. [T]he notion of withdrawal is pertinent only insofar as it relates to the element of proximate cause. For example, if one drag racer were to abandon the race by slowing down to normal speeds or stopping, and his competitor became aware of the defendant's withdrawal but still chose to continue driving fast and recklessly, that fact might have a bearing on whether the defendant's drag racing was a proximate cause of a subsequent collision between his competitor and a third party; it might also bear on whether the competitor's decision to continue his reckless driving was an intervening, superseding cause. Thus, the point we wish to make here is that under the theory of direct liability we are considering, a defendant's asserted withdrawal should not be viewed as an absolute defense, but only as a factor affecting the determination of proximate cause. We will so consider it when we review the sufficiency of the evidence of proximate causation.

With the foregoing principles in mind, we review the evidence in this case. Testifying for the State were three witnesses who were driving in the vicinity on the morning of the accident, and two police department accident reconstruction experts who had been called to the scene. Defendant's only witness was a private investigator who, as a former police officer, also had accident reconstruction training and experience. In addition, the trial judge viewed the scene of the drag race and accident under the stipulation of both parties that anything he observed could be evidence in either the State's or defendant's case.

On Saturday morning, April 5, 1980, a green car driven by Sulgrove was observed moving at a high rate of speed off the exit ramp of the MacVicar Freeway onto Southeast Fourteenth Street, a multi-lane city street. In making his exit, Sulgrove hit a curb, "fishtailed," and then entered the southbound traffic on Southeast Fourteenth. Traffic was fairly heavy at this point, and Sulgrove moved from one southbound lane to another trying unsuccessfully to pass cars and get ahead. Farther down the street, which had narrowed to two northbound and two southbound lanes,

Sulgrove's car was seen traveling at a "fairly high" rate of speed; it came up behind a red car driven by defendant, an acquaintance of Sulgrove's, just past the Gratis Street intersection. Defendant, traveling at an estimated speed of 40–47 m.p.h., had been in the left southbound lane until just before Sulgrove came up behind him; at that time, defendant pulled his car into the right southbound lane alongside a car in the left lane, thereby preventing Sulgrove from passing. Defendant's maneuver forced Sulgrove to brake suddenly, and Sulgrove's car again "fishtailed." After getting past the vehicle which blocked the left lane, the red and green vehicles were observed engaging in what a witness described as a "cat-and-mouse" game: Defendant's red car, traveling generally in the right lane just ahead of Sulgrove's green car, repeatedly blocked Sulgrove's attempts to pass by moving partially into the left lane and then back to the right again when Sulgrove would change lanes. Starting at the Pioneer Street intersection, where the speed limit is 40 m.p.h., a witness who had some experience in drag racing under controlled conditions saw the two cars traveling "head to head" at an estimated speed of 70–75 m.p.h., with defendant in the right lane and Sulgrove in the left. The witness testified that when the two cars came upon a gold car in the left lane near the Lacona Street intersection, "neither driver was willing to give up the [competitive] edge in order to negotiate the gold car until at the very last second," when Sulgrove braked, swerved into the right lane behind defendant, bounced off a curb, and passed the gold car. Sulgrove then got back into the left lane and the two cars continued southward at a high rate of speed. Because the two vehicles were "traveling as a pair" in a competitive manner, the witness concluded they were drag racing.

Beyond the Lacona intersection, Southeast Fourteenth slopes upward and crests twice, the first crest being between Creston and King streets and the second crest being 1126 feet beyond the first. A witness named Jamison who was traveling behind the red and green vehicles testified that he watched both vehicles continue to speed and participate in "cat-and-mouse" activity up to the top of the second crest, where they dropped out of his sight.

Just beyond the second crest, a pickup truck was traveling in the left southbound lane at a normal speed. The pickup driver testified that Sulgrove's car "came around" her truck at a high rate of speed in the right lane, lost control and skidded across the left lane in front of her. Sulgrove then crossed over the median and struck the northbound Ellis vehicle at a point 263 feet beyond the second crest. The pickup driver did not recall seeing defendant's red car.[2]

When the police arrived, they found 84 feet of skid marks left by Sulgrove's vehicle. It was determined from physical evidence that Sulgrove had been going about 80 m.p.h. just before he went into the skid. Defendant was present at the accident site, and his car was parked in the lot of Godfather's Pizza, which is located on the

2. This same witness, who was traveling with a small child, had the erroneous impression that the Ellis vehicle was traveling in the left southbound lane just ahead of her, rather than in the center northbound lane.

west side of the street. The southernmost driveway to this lot is 351 feet beyond the second crest. There were no skid marks left by defendant's car anywhere in the vicinity.

Defendant challenges the sufficiency of the foregoing evidence under both perspectives of causation, factual and legal. Factual causation is determined under the *sine qua non* test: but for the defendant's conduct, the harm or damage would not have occurred. Defendant argues that because Sulgrove was driving fast and recklessly even before defendant entered the picture, the accident would have occurred even without defendant's participation in the drag race. Viewing the evidence in the light most favorable to the State, however, we find there was substantial evidence from which trial court could conclude that Sulgrove's speed and recklessness both increased once he entered the heat of competition with defendant,[4] and that the accident would not have occurred but for their joint racing.

Defendant next asserts that proof of proximate or legal causation was lacking because there was no credible evidence that defendant continued to race beyond the first crest of the hill. Witness Jamison, mentioned earlier, testified unequivocally that he observed the red and green cars go over both crests of the hill. He said: "Well, there is two small hills there as you are going up that hill, and I never lost sight of them over the first hill because it is high enough up that I could see them, and the last hill, whichever one it is where they go over the crest was where I saw them last." Jamison was the only witness who claimed to have observed defendant's activity between the first and second crests. Defendant attempted to discredit that testimony by proving that Jamison could not have observed the cars once they passed over the first crest. It was shown that a person sitting in a stationary vehicle at the Lacona intersection can see only the first crest, and that traffic disappears from sight as it goes over that crest. When a person in a moving vehicle comes within 150 feet of the first crest, however, he can see over that crest all the way to the second crest. Thus, adding 150 feet to the distance between the crests, it can be seen that Jamison would have had to be no more than 1,276 feet behind the red and green cars in order to watch them go over the second crest. Jamison estimated that he was roughly 1/4 to 1/2 mile (1320 to 2640 feet) behind the two cars when they went over the second crest, but he also disclaimed any ability to estimate distance accurately. Indications that the distance was not great included Jamison's testimony that he saw dust rise over the hill ahead of him when the collision occurred, and that he arrived at the accident site just as defendant was getting out of his car in the Godfather's lot.

Even if Jamison did only see the cars go over the first crest, the evidence of proximate causation would not be insufficient. As noted earlier, the distance between the two crests is 1126 feet. Evidence presented at trial concerning the number of feet per second traveled at various speeds indicates to us that it would take less than 10

---

4. The defense expert's attempt to prove that Sulgrove was traveling 80 m.p.h. before he came up to defendant's car could have been discredited by trial court on the ground that the expert's calculations were based on erroneous or imprecise assumptions.

seconds to go from crest to crest at 80 m.p.h. and less than 13 seconds at 60 m.p.h. There was substantial evidence that defendant and Sulgrove were traveling in the 60–80 m.p.h. range when they topped the first crest. Based on this evidence, trial court could find that it would have been impossible for defendant, in such a short period of time, to effect a timely withdrawal which would have allowed Sulgrove an opportunity to slow down and avoid the accident. As stated in a civil drag-racing case: [R]acing on a highway is hazardous to all other persons upon the highway and . . . the actor participates at his peril. . . . One who does participate in setting in motion such hazardous conduct cannot thereafter turn his liability off like a light switch.

From the authorities cited we conclude that one who participates in setting such hazardous conduct in motion cannot later be heard to say: "Oh! I withdrew before harm resulted even though no one else was aware of my withdrawal." It would be a reasonable probability that the excitement and stimulus created by this race of several miles had not dissipated nor, in fact, terminated at all, in the fraction of a minute in time between the act of passing and the accident. The state of mind of the participants was material. We cannot gauge that state of mind to the point of saying that the stimulus or intent had ended. The evidence warrants a finding that it did continue. It would be for the jury to decide if the racing were the cause of the accident. Thus, even if defendant had started to slow down between the first and second crests, as his counsel argues he did, trial court could find that any such last-minute effort to withdraw would not break the chain of causation set in motion by the drag race.

For the same reason, trial court could find that the lack of skid marks from defendant's car into the Godfather's parking lot failed to create a reasonable doubt as to defendant's guilt. A defense expert testified that it would have been impossible for defendant to turn into that lot without leaving skid marks if he, like Sulgrove, was traveling 80 m.p.h. as he came over the second crest. From what we have said in the preceding paragraph, however, it was not necessary for the State to prove that defendant was going 80 m.p.h. when he topped that hill. One of the accident reconstruction experts who testified for the State theorized that defendant and Sulgrove continued to race almost side-by-side until they neared the second crest and saw the pickup truck ahead blocking Sulgrove's path, at which point defendant slowed down to allow Sulgrove into the right lane. This theory would explain why the pickup driver did not notice defendant's car, and would also be one explanation for the lack of skid marks from defendant's car.[5]

Viewing the evidence in the light most favorable to the State, we hold that the record contains substantial evidence that defendant's participation in a drag race

---

5. Another possible explanation for the lack of skid marks, suggested by the same expert, was that defendant could have turned into the next drive past Godfather's and driven back to the God-father's lot across a stretch of grass between the two drives. Under this theory, defendant's initial braking need not have occurred before the second crest.

with Sulgrove was a concurring proximate cause of the accident in which Sulgrove and Faith Ellis were killed. We therefore affirm defendant's convictions.

Questions and Notes

1. Should it matter whether the victim was a fellow participant (Sulgrove) or an innocent third party (Faith Ellis)?

2. Could Sulgrove's estate have successfully sued McFadden in tort? If not, is the criminal law *more* stringent than tort law? Why should that be?

3. If Faith Ellis were not wearing her seatbelt, and the evidence showed that she would not have been killed if she were wearing it, should McFadden be exculpated? Would it matter whether failure to wear a seatbelt was a crime in Iowa?

4. If McFadden had slowed down on the second hill to allow Sulgrove to safely avoid the pickup truck as the state's witness theorized (*see* text accompanying footnote 5), why shouldn't that exculpate him?

5. Do you prefer the *Root* rule, the *McFadden* rule, or some other alternative? If the last, what other alternative might there be?

6. Do you think that the jury would have reached the same result in this case if only Sulgrove had been killed? Or might it have been influenced by the death of six-year-old Faith Ellis?

7. Is *McFadden* a harder case than *Russell* or is it essentially the same case? Explain.

8. The *Rullestad* case, discussed in *McFadden*, holds that to convict a drunk driver of involuntary manslaughter, the state must prove that the intoxication caused the death. Consider whether this is a wise burden to place on the State as you read the majority and dissenting opinions in *Caibaiosai*.

State v. Caibaiosai

363 N.W.2d 574 (Wis. 1985)

STEINMETZ, Justice.

The issue in this case [is] whether sec. 940.09(1)(a), Stats.,[1] proscribing the crime of homicide by an intoxicated operation of a motor vehicle is unconstitutional in that it does not require a causal connection between the intoxicated condition of the operator and the death of another person.

---

1. Sec. 940.09(1)(a), Stats., provides as follows:
   "940.09 Homicide by intoxicated use of vehicle or firearm. (1) Any person who does either of the following under par. (a) or (b) is guilty of a Class D felony:
   "(a) Causes the death of another by the operation or handling of a vehicle, firearm or airgun and while under the influence of an intoxicant or a controlled substance or a combination of an intoxicant and a controlled substance. . . ."

The defendant, Gary Caibaiosai, was charged with violating sec. 940.09(1)(a), Stats., by operating a motor vehicle while under the influence of an intoxicant which resulted in the death of Janet M. Tunkieicz. He was tried by a jury, found guilty and on February 24, 1983, was sentenced to serve a term of imprisonment not to exceed three years.

On June 6, 1982, at approximately 8:04 p.m., defendant was driving his 1977 Harley-Davidson motorcycle eastbound on Highway 142 in the vicinity of county Highway "MB" with Janet Tunkieicz as his passenger. Ahead of the defendant was David Dickinson operating a motorcycle with his passenger Yvonne Mink in the side-car. At the trial, Mink testified the defendant and Tunkieicz pulled into the oncoming lane and passed them. She estimated that the defendant was driving somewhere between 60 and 65 miles per hour at the moment that he passed her. After the defendant completed the pass and pulled back into the right lane, Mink observed his brake light flash and then his motorcycle go into the gravel along a curve in the road and skid into the three to four foot deep ditch along the side of the road. She did not identify the location of the gravel in reference to the pavement or the shoulder of the highway. Defendant's motorcycle traveled approximately 180 to 200 feet, struck a utility pole and flipped over causing Tunkieicz to strike a tree approximately 80 feet from the utility pole. Janet Tunkieicz was killed instantly. Upon impact the defendant was thrown clear, remained conscious and was not seriously injured.

Evidence was admitted that at approximately 10:09 p.m., a blood sample was taken from the defendant and later tested for alcohol content which registered at 0.13 percent. At 10:39 p.m. defendant was tested on a breathalyzer, and his blood alcohol level was listed as 0.11 percent.

The defense presented one witness, David Dickinson, the operator of the motorcycle on which Mink was a passenger. He testified he was a motorcycle mechanic and had a long history of owning and operating motorcycles. He testified he had lost control of motorcycles on numerous occasions and that a passenger riding on the back of a motorcycle could easily affect the controllability of the motorcycle. He also testified that road conditions could also cause a motorcyclist to lose control. Dickinson stated he was operating his motorcycle at around the speed limit on Highway 142 when the defendant's motorcycle passed his. He described the accident by saying that it looked like the defendant's motorcycle had gone "towards the gravel" and a cloud of dust was raised. Dickinson testified he saw "a cloud of dust and it looked like the defendant recovered for a second and then the bike went down in the ditch." The defendant presented no other evidence and did not testify in his own behalf.

Section 940.09, Stats., was designed to protect the public from a particular type of risk and harm, namely to hold accountable persons who become intoxicated, operate a motor vehicle and cause the death of another person. In the preface to the latest revisions of the drunk driving laws, the legislature expressly stated that its purpose was to "provide maximum safety for all users of the highway of this state" from the harm threatened by "[o]peration of motor vehicles by persons who are under the influence of an intoxicant."

Laws of 1981, ch. 20, secs. 2051(13)(a)1 and 2051(13)(b)1.

From the creation of sec. 940.09, Stats., to 1955 there were only two elements of the offense: causing the death of another person by the operation of a vehicle and being under the influence of an intoxicant at the time of the accident. *State v. Peckham*, 263 Wis. 239, 242, 56 N.W.2d 835 (1953). The *Peckham* court held that there was negligence in "the driving of an automobile while under the influence of intoxicating liquor. *Id.* at 243, 56 N.W.2d 835. One intoxicated is without proper control of all those faculties the exercise of which is necessary to avoid danger to others while driving a car upon a public highway. The driving of a car by one in such condition betrays an absence of any care and indicates such recklessness and wantonness as evinces an utter disregard of consequences.

As this court stated in *State v. Resler*, 262 Wis. 285, 290, 55 N.W.2d 35 (1952):

> "[T]o require that facts be shown to prove that defendant's operation of the car was so affected by his intoxication that the accident would not have happened if he had been sober, would be to impose an impossible burden upon the state in the prosecution of such a case." Moreover, "If it can also be shown that the defendant was intoxicated when he so operated his vehicle, it must be assumed that there existed a causal connection between the intoxication and the death."

In 1955 the legislature revised the statute to provide that a person was guilty of homicide by an intoxicated use of a vehicle if he caused the death of another "by the negligent operation . . . of a vehicle . . . while under the influence of an intoxicant." Sec. 940.09, 1955.

The only change in the elements of the offense was the requirement of "proof of causal negligence in addition to [the] operation or handling [of a vehicle] while under the influence of an intoxicant." There was still no requirement that the defendant's intoxication cause the victim's death.

Section 940.09(1)(a), Stats.,[2] in its present form clearly states that a person commits a Class D felony who:

(1) causes the death of another,

(2) by the operation of a vehicle,

(3) while under the influence of an intoxicant.

The legislature has determined that combining the operation of a motor vehicle with being in an intoxicated state is conduct which is pervasively antisocial. Since the conduct is considered inherently evil, it conceptually cannot be divided into portions which are bad and portions which are not bad. Section 346.63, Stats., entitled "Operating under the influence of intoxicants" is violated by a person who, one, operates a

---

2. Laws of 1981, ch. 20, sec. 1817g, effective May 1, 1978, and amended in Laws of 1983, Act 459, sec. 26, effective May 18, 1984.

motor vehicle, and two, is at the time under the influence of an intoxicant. The commission of the offense does not require any erratic or negligent driving.

Section 940.09, Stats., requires that the prosecution prove and the jury find beyond a reasonable doubt a causal connection between the defendant's unlawful conduct, operation of a motor vehicle while intoxicated, and the victim's death. The statute does not include as an element of the crime a direct causal connection between the fact of defendant's intoxication, conceptualized as an isolated act, and the victim's death. Under this statute there is an inherently dangerous activity in which it is reasonably foreseeable that driving while intoxicated may result in the death of an individual. The legislature has determined this activity so inherently dangerous that proof of it need not require causal connection between the defendant's intoxication and the death.

What punishment is to be related to a particular crime is within the province of the legislature and the relating process is governed by the constitution to the extent no cruel and inhuman punishment is permitted and due process and equal protection are afforded. We think the consequences of the act and their seriousness may be a proper consideration in fixing the severity of the punishment. Acts which result in death frequently carry increased penalties over the same act which does not result in death, *i.e.*, sec. 940.03, Stats., felony murder.

So, when a person chooses to operate an automobile while under the influence of intoxicants and has done so deliberately knowing that society has through its legislature established such combined activities as dangerous and when such operation results in death, it may be punished as a felony.

It is negligence per se to operate a motor vehicle while under the influence of intoxicants. Experience has established this conclusion and the legislature has accepted it as a fact in sec. 346.63(1)(a), Stats., and has made such combined activities a class D felony when the operation of the vehicle results in death in sec. 940.09(1)(a). The substantial factor in the cause of the death is the cause in fact of the operation of the vehicle while intoxicated.

Section 940.09(1)(a) accepts that the conduct of operating under the influence of intoxicants plus the consequences of death will result in a felony charge. The people of this state through their legislature have determined in sec. 940.09(1)(a) that the operation of a motor vehicle by one who is under the influence of intoxicants is a risk that will not be tolerated.

The order of the circuit court is affirmed.

ABRAHAMSON, Justice (dissenting).

Driving while under the influence of an intoxicant is deplorable, antisocial, dangerous behavior which the legislature can — and should — penalize severely. Providing for a maximum five years' imprisonment and a $10,000 fine, sec. 940.09(1)(a), Stats. 1981–82, punishes any person who causes the death of another by the operation or handling of a vehicle while under the influence of an intoxicant.

While an initial reading of the statute suggests that sec. 940.09(1)(a) is a valid legislative response to the problem of drunk driving, careful consideration of the majority's interpretation of the statute—an interpretation which apparently is in harmony with legislative intent—demonstrates that the statute violates basic concepts of due process and is unconstitutional.

Sec. 940.09 dispenses with the state's burden of proving beyond a reasonable doubt a causal connection between the wrongful conduct (here, the intoxication or faulty operation of a vehicle while under the influence of an intoxicant) and the particular result of the wrongful conduct (here, death). Under sec. 940.09 the state need prove only that the operation of the vehicle caused the death. Thus sec. 940.09(1)(a) provides that when a person operates a vehicle while intoxicated and a death results, the defendant is guilty of a felony, even if there is no causal connection between the intoxication and the death and even if the defendant's actual operation of the vehicle is in no way faulty.

Accordingly, the jury in this case was instructed regarding causation as follows:

> "The third element of this offense requires that the relation of cause and effect exists between the death of [the victim] and the defendant's operation of a vehicle. Before such relation of cause and effect can be found to exist, it must appear that the defendant's operation of his vehicle was a substantial factor in producing the death. That is, the defendant's operation must have been a factor which had substantial effect in producing the death as a natural result.

> "*It is not required that the death was caused by any drinking of alcohol or by any negligent or improper operation of the vehicle. What is required is that the injury was caused by the defendant's operation of the vehicle.*" Wis. J.I.–Cr. No. 1885.

Because the state need prove only the three statutory elements of the crime beyond a reasonable doubt—(1) the driver was operating a vehicle; (2) the driver was operating the vehicle while under the influence of an intoxicant; and (3) the operation of the vehicle, but not necessarily the driver's faulty operation of the vehicle or the driver's intoxicated condition, "caused" the death—the following drivers can be convicted of homicide under sec. 940.09(1)(a):

1. A driver under the influence of an intoxicant kills a child who darts into the path of the car (Vehicle A) from between parked cars.

2. A driver under the influence of an intoxicant stops the car (Vehicle A) at a red light. His passenger is killed when Car B rear-ends Vehicle A.

3. A driver under the influence of an intoxicant stops the car (Vehicle A) at a red light and proceeds through the intersection after the light turns green. His passenger is killed when Car B strikes Vehicle A.

4. A driver under the influence of an intoxicant loses control of the motorcycle (Vehicle A) when it skids on an oil slick. The passenger in Vehicle A is killed when she hits a tree.

In these four examples, "but for" the operation of Vehicle A, the victim would not have died. The operation of Vehicle A was a substantial factor causing the victim's death.

In short, in each of the four examples sec. 940.09(1)(a) would allow the state to prosecute and convict the driver of homicide by proving that the death was caused by the mere operation of the vehicle. True, the driver must be operating the vehicle while under the influence of an intoxicant, and operation in that condition is unlawful conduct. The fact is, however, that in each of the four examples set forth above, the driver was (except for driving while under the influence of an intoxicant) obeying the rules of the road, and no driver operating Vehicle A (intoxicated or sober) could have prevented the incident or the death. In each of the four examples, the unlawful conduct as such (operating while under the influence of an intoxicant) did not cause the death. Nevertheless, because the state does not have to prove that the unlawful conduct caused the death, a conviction results.

Requiring the state to prove causation between the wrongful conduct and the harm is a basic principle of criminal jurisprudence. In my opinion this statute which punishes a driver for homicide without requiring the state to prove the causal connection between wrongful conduct (that is, the driver's intoxication or the driver's faulty operation of the vehicle while under the influence of an intoxicant) and the harm (death) is unconstitutional.

Proof of this causal connection is so critical to culpability for homicide that if a conviction for homicide may be obtained without proof of this causality the statute violates basic notions of what is right and fair. As the four examples illustrate, the driver is blameless of homicide unless there is proof of a causal connection between the wrongful conduct and the harm; without this connection, the culpability necessary to justify a conviction for homicide is missing. From those examples it is clear that causal culpability, not the culpability associate with driving while intoxicated, is required to convict of homicide.

I conclude that in enacting sec. 940.09 the Wisconsin legislature has gone beyond its constitutional powers. The person who drives while intoxicated should be punished. The driver is blameworthy. A person convicted of operating a vehicle while intoxicated is punished under Wisconsin law with a civil forfeiture or a criminal penalty depending on whether it is a first offense. The drunk driver may be convicted of homicide if the state proves beyond a reasonable doubt that his intoxication or faulty driving while under the influence of an intoxicant caused the death. In summary, I conclude that this statute providing for imprisonment of up to 5 years without requiring the state to prove a causal connection between a defendant's wrongful conduct (that is, intoxication or faulty operation of the vehicle while under the influence of an intoxicant) and the resulting harm (death) violates basic notions of fairness embodied in the due process clause and is unconstitutional.

Drunk driving is reprehensible conduct. Anyone who operates a vehicle while under the influence of an intoxicant should be punished, whether or not there is injury to person or property. When the drunk driver causes injury, the punishment should be increased. The drunk driver should not, however, be punished for homicide unless the driver's intoxication or faulty operation while under the influence of an intoxicant caused the death.

Because sec. 940.09(1)(a) permits the state to punish a driver for homicide with 5 years' imprisonment when death occurs by chance, I conclude the statute is unconstitutional.

Accordingly, I must dissent from the court's opinion.

Questions and Notes

1. Most states require proof that the defendant's intoxication caused the accident. Is that such a difficult burden? Why? (Note that even under the old Wisconsin statute, it was not necessary to prove that intoxication caused the accident, only that negligent driving while intoxicated caused the accident.)

2. Focus on Justice Abrahamson's four hypotheticals. Are there any that you think would *not* support a verdict of involuntary manslaughter? Explain.

3. If Justice Abrahamson is wrong about the liability of the drivers in her first three hypotheticals, but right about the liability of the driver in hypothetical four (a case that looks suspiciously like a possible version of the case at bar), are her constitutional arguments weakened?

4. Do you see anything inherently unfair about convicting the driver in the fourth hypothetical?

Problem

Alan and Barbara are a happily married, deeply-in-love couple who enjoy playing practical jokes on one another. Carolyn is a former lover of Alan, who was rejected by him five years ago. Since then, she has been looking for an opportunity to murder him.

One day, Alan announced to Barbara that he was going to spend a week in the desert to prove that he could survive it. He calculated that one 10-gallon drum of water would be adequate to sustain him for the week. Nevertheless, he decided to take two 10-gallon drums as a precautionary measure. Barbara suggested that one would do just fine, but Alan insisted on taking two.

At the appointed time, Barbara drove Alan to the appropriate spot on the desert where she left him with his two 10-gallon drums filled with water. He kept one inside the tent and one outside.

During Alan's first night on the desert while he was asleep, Carolyn (who had heard of his plans) drove to his tent on the desert and stealthily emptied the 10-gallon drum outside of his tent (which she assumed to be the only water he had). Next to the empty drum, she left a note saying: "Vengeance is mine. — Carolyn."

When he awoke the next day, Alan picked up the note, put it in his pocket and said to himself: "Oh well, we'll see if Barbara was right."

The next night, Barbara drove to the tent, noticed the drum outside the tent, but did not notice that it was empty. She stealthily entered the tent and emptied the other drum. She left a note saying: "You'll make it on one drum just fine. See you in a week. Love, Barbara."

At the end of the week, Barbara drove to the tent where she found Alan dead from lack of water.

You are the District Attorney. Who should you prosecute for what? What are your chances of getting a conviction? Would your answer be any different if Barbara had come the first night and Carolyn had come on the second night?

For an attempt to codify causation, see MPC § 2.03 (Appendix A). For collateral reading, see NUTSHELL Ch. III.

Chapter 4

Assault and Kidnapping

A. Assault

In most jurisdictions, it is possible to assault another by attempting a battery, or by putting the victim in fear of being battered. To understand the difference, consider *Harrod v. State*.

Harrod v. State

499 A.2d 959 (Md. App. 1985)

ALPERT, Judge.

We are called upon in this appeal to decide, *inter alia*, whether a person can be convicted of assaulting another who has suffered no harm and was never aware of the alleged assault. Appellant John G. Harrod was charged with two counts of assault and two counts of carrying a deadly weapon openly with intent to injure. He was convicted of these offenses on December 11, 1984, following a trial without a jury in the Circuit Court for Carroll County, and sentenced on January 21, 1985, to two terms of two years' imprisonment for the assault convictions and two terms of one year's imprisonment for the weapons convictions, all sentences to run concurrently. On appeal to this court, appellant presents three questions:

I. Was the evidence sufficient to sustain the charge of assault upon James Christopher Harrod?

II. [Omitted.]

III. Was the sentence imposed based upon an improper factor?

It will be of little solace to appellant that we answer the first question in his favor, for our response to the third questions leave his ultimate period of incarceration unchanged.

I.

The common law crime of assault encompasses two definitions: (1) an attempt to commit a battery or (2) an unlawful intentional act which places another in reasonable apprehension of receiving an immediate battery. The facts in the instant case present this court with an excellent opportunity to explain the distinctions between these two different types of assault. The assault charges arose out of a confrontation among appellant, his wife Cheryl, and her friend Calvin Crigger. The only two witnesses at trial were appellant and Cheryl Harrod. Cheryl testified that on September 15, 1983, Calvin Crigger came over to visit when she thought appellant had gone to work; that "all of a sudden [appellant] came out of the bedroom with a hammer in his hand, swinging it around, coming after me and my friend [Calvin]"; that Calvin ran out of the house and down the steps; that appellant "had thrown the hammer over top of [Christopher's] port-a-crib in the living room, and it went into the wall"; that appellant then reentered the bedroom and returned with a five-inch blade hunting knife; that appellant told Cheryl that he was going to kill her and that, if she took his daughter away from him, he was going to kill Christopher; that appellant put the knife into the bannister near Cheryl's arm; that appellant followed Cheryl out to Calvin's car and "went after Calvin, going around and around the car."

Appellant testified that he missed his ride to work that day; that he came back home around 10:00 a.m. and went to sleep in a back room; that he was awakened by Calvin's deep voice; that appellant picked up his hammer and, walking into the living room, told Calvin to leave; that Cheryl told Calvin he didn't have to leave; that he then told Calvin, "Buddy, if you want your head busted in, stand here; if you want to be healthy and leave, go." Appellant said that Calvin just stood there, so he swung the hammer, Calvin moved his head back, and the hammer struck the wall over Christopher's crib, which was near the door. In rendering its verdict, the court stated:

> And, the Court finds beyond a reasonable doubt and to a moral certainty that Mr. Harrod . . . came after [Cheryl] and . . . Calvin; and that Mr. Harrod came out of his room swinging a . . . hammer, and ultimately threw it, not too far from the child, Christopher, and that he went after both Cheryl and Calvin, down the steps with a knife, with a blade of about four to five inches. The Court finds that he is guilty of two counts of Carrying a Deadly Weapon; that is the knife and the hammer; and, also two counts of Assault; one against Cheryl and one against the minor child.

Defense counsel inquired of the court: "On the second count of the Information, is the Court finding specific intent on behalf of the Defendant to injure his child?" The court responded, "Yes. Threw that hammer within a very short distance— sticking it—it was still sticking in the wall."

A. Two Types of Assault

Appellant contends that there was insufficient evidence to demonstrate that he harbored a specific intent to injure Christopher when he threw the hammer. Further, he notes that there was no evidence that Christopher was injured by the hammer or that he was even aware that a hammer was thrown. Therefore, appellant claims that the trial court's finding that he committed a criminal assault upon Christopher was clearly erroneous. We agree for the reasons set forth below.

In reviewing a criminal conviction, we must affirm if, after viewing the evidence in the light most favorable to the prosecution, any rational trier of fact could have found the essential elements of the crime beyond a reasonable doubt. It is necessary, therefore, that the essential elements of assault be determined. As we noted *supra*, an assault "is committed when there is either an attempt to commit a battery or when, by an unlawful act, a person is placed in reasonable apprehension of receiving an immediate battery." These two types of assaults—*attempted battery and putting another in fear*—are indeed two distinct crimes that have been inadvertently overlapped and confused. One commentator explained this confusion:

> "In the early law the word 'assault' represented an entirely different concept in criminal law than it did in the law of torts. As an offense it was an attempt to commit a battery; as a basis for a civil action for damages it was an intentional act wrongfully placing another in apprehension of receiving an immediate battery. The distinction has frequently passed unnoticed because a misdeed involving either usually involves both. If, with the intention of hitting X, D wrongfully threw a stone that X barely managed to dodge, then D would have been guilty of a criminal assault because he had attempted to commit a battery, and he would also have been liable in a civil action of trespass for assault because he had wrongfully placed X in apprehension of physical harm. Some commentators have been so imbued with the tort theory of assault that they have had difficulty in realizing that in the early law a criminal assault was an attempt to commit a battery and that only."

PERKINS & BOYCE, CRIMINAL LAW 159 (footnote omitted).

This confusion is apparent in the State's brief. There, appellee, quoting from *Taylor v. State*, 52 Md. App. 500, 505, 450 A.2d 1312 (1982) that "[i]t is not necessary to constitute an assault that any actual violence be done to the person. If the party threatening the assault has the ability, means, and apparent intention to carry his threat into execution, it may in law constitute an assault." [Emphasis removed.] Appellee then goes on to cite dictum from this court's decision in *Woods v. State*, 14 Md. App. 627, 288 A.2d 215 (1972). There, we stated in a footnote:

> "Whether apprehension of impending harm on the part of the potential victim is a necessary ingredient of assault in tort law, we need not and do not decide. And while such apprehension may be present in most criminal assaults, it is not always present, and therefore it cannot be a required element."

Id. at 630 n.3, 288 A.2d 215 215. The problem here is that the language in Taylor derived from an examination of tort theories of assault, while the language in Woods is based on the criminal attempted battery theory.

B. Attempted Battery

The language in *Woods* supports the proposition that in an attempted battery-type assault, the victim need not be aware of the perpetrator's intent or threat.

If a person be struck from behind, or by stealth or surprise, or while asleep, he is certainly the victim of a battery. But if we accept the oft-repeated statement that every battery included or is preceded by an assault, and if there could be no assault without premonitory apprehension in the victim, then it could be argued that there was no battery. That is not the law. In other words, because there may be committed a battery without the victim first being aware of the attack, an attempted battery-type assault cannot include a requirement that the victim be aware.

The facts in the case *sub judice* do not support a finding that appellant committed an attempted battery towards the infant, Christopher. An attempt to commit any crime requires a specific intent to commit that crime. An attempted battery-type assault thus requires that the accused harbor a specific intent to cause physical injury to the victim, and take a substantial step towards causing that injury.

Nowhere does the record indicate that appellant threw the hammer with the specific intent to injure Christopher. The court expressly stated that it found specific intent on behalf of appellant because he "[t]hrew that hammer within a very short distance" of the child. The court here is merely inferring a criminal intent from reckless or negligent acts of the appellant. This is not sufficient especially where all of the evidence tends to the contrary: that appellant's intent was to injure Calvin.

C. Assault by Placing One in Fear

There is likewise insufficient evidence that appellant, by an unlawful intentional act, placed Christopher in reasonable apprehension of receiving an immediate battery. By definition the victim must be aware of the impending contact. This is consistent with the tort theory of assault. "Since the interest involved is the mental one of apprehension of contact, it should follow that the plaintiff must be aware of the defendant's act at the time, and that it is not an assault to aim a gun at one who is unaware of it." *See* Restatement (Second) of Torts §§ 21–22 (1966).

There is no evidence in the record before us that Christopher was in fact aware of the occurrences in his home on the morning in question. Therefore, there was insufficient evidence to find appellant guilty of the putting victim in fear-type assault.

Because the trial court was clearly erroneous in finding appellant guilty of an assault on Christopher, we must reverse that conviction.

III.

Anticipating that we would find the conviction on one count of assault to be erroneous, appellant asks that we remand for new sentencing on the grounds that the trial court clearly considered the alleged assault on Christopher in determining sentence.

In Maryland, a sentencing judge is vested with "virtually boundless discretion" in deciding what factors to consider on the issue of punishment. A review of the sentencing hearing reveals that the trial court here considered several factors including appellant's relationship with the victims of the assaults (or alleged assaults), his employment situation, and his prior criminal record. In addition, the trial court emphasized the proximity of the hammer to Christopher and the "special vulnerability of the victim, because it was a child." This however was not error. It is well settled in Maryland that a trial court may properly consider reliable evidence concerning the details and circumstances surrounding a criminal charge of which a person has been acquitted. The trial judge's concern about potential injury to the child was not an impermissible consideration.

JUDGMENT OF CONVICTION OF ASSAULT UPON JAMES CHRISTOPHER HARROD REVERSED AND SENTENCE VACATED; ALL OTHER JUDGMENTS AFFIRMED.

Questions and Notes

1. Why should the trial judge have been permitted to consider potential injury to the child in sentencing Harrod, when the appellate court found that he was not guilty of that crime?

2. Is there any way that a prosecutor could have successfully brought two counts of assault? If so, why do you suppose he didn't?

3. Attempted battery assault punishes primarily the culpability of the defendant, and to some extent his dangerousness. If the victim is unaware of and uninjured by the assault, definitionally she has suffered no harm. Tort assault, on the other hand, focuses largely on the harm caused to the victim. To the extent that he might not have really been trying to injure her, his culpability is diminished.

4. Assault can be aggravated in a variety of ways. *See, Culpability, Dangerousness, and Harm,* Introduction (Appendix B). In addition to the illustrations presented therein, assaults are sometimes aggravated by the characteristics of the victim. Among those victims sometimes given heightened protection are women, children, the elderly, and police officers in the line of duty.

B. Kidnapping

Kidnapping, which was only a misdemeanor at common law, is regarded today as one of the most heinous felonies. Definitionally, it can subsume or supplement many lesser crimes because most crimes require some movement of the victim. Exacerbating the problem is the possibility of convicting of one of kidnapping by fraud, i.e., a false representation of purpose, such as a rapist inviting his victim into the woods to see the flowers.

Because of the potential for prosecutorial overcharging and double charging, states have adopted various limitations on the crime. Consider the desirability and effectiveness of these limitations as you read *Beatty*.

State v. Beatty

495 S.E.2d 367 (N.C. 1998)

WHICHARD, Justice.

On 23 May 1994 a Mecklenburg County grand jury indicted defendant Edward Ronald Beatty for robbery with a dangerous weapon, assault with a deadly weapon with intent to kill inflicting serious injury, felonious breaking and entering, safe-cracking, first degree kidnapping, two counts of second-degree kidnapping, and possession of a firearm by a convicted felon. The trial court severed the charge of possession of a firearm by a convicted felon and later dismissed the charge of safe-cracking. The remaining charges were tried during the 22 May 1995 Mixed Session of Superior Court, Mecklenburg County.

The jury found defendant guilty as charged, except that assault with a deadly weapon with intent to kill was reduced to assault with a deadly weapon inflicting serious injury, and breaking and entering was submitted and found as entering only. The trial court arrested judgment on the conviction for first-degree kidnapping and sentenced defendant to imprisonment of thirty years for the robbery with a dangerous weapon, ten years for felonious assault, ten years for entering, and fifteen years for each of the second-degree kidnappings, all sentences to be served consecutively.

Defendant appealed to the Court of Appeals asserting, *inter alia*, that his kidnapping convictions should be vacated because there was insufficient evidence of restraint separate and apart from that inherent in the crime of robbery with a dangerous weapon to support those convictions. The Court of Appeals majority disagreed. Judge Wynn dissented in part on the ground that "the restraint in this case was an inherent and inevitable feature of the commission of the armed robbery" and thus could not support a conviction for second-degree kidnapping. Defendant appeals based upon Judge Wynn's dissent. For reasons that follow, we affirm with regard to defendant's conviction for the second-degree kidnapping of victim Koufaloitis, and we reverse with regard to defendant's conviction for the second-degree kidnapping of victim Poulos.

The State's evidence tended to show that on 19 March 1994 defendant met a group of men at a party. They decided to rob South 21, a drive-in restaurant in Charlotte, North Carolina. When they approached the restaurant, the owner, Nicholas Copsis, stood just outside near an open door. The robbers approached this door, put a gun to Copsis' head, and told him to go inside and open the safe.

Once inside, the robbers saw restaurant employees Hristos Poulos and Tom Koufaloitis. Poulos was on his knees washing the floor at the front, and Koufaloitis stood three to four feet from the safe cleaning the floor in the back. One robber put a gun to Poulos' head and stood beside him during the robbery. An unarmed robber put duct tape around Koufaloitis' wrists and told him to lie on the floor.

Copsis did not open the safe on his first attempt. One robber said, "Let's go. We're taking too long. Hurry up." Another shot Copsis twice in the legs. Copsis then opened the safe. The robbers took more than $2,000 and fled. The robbery took approximately three to four minutes.

Defendant contends that his convictions for second-degree kidnapping must be vacated because the State presented insufficient evidence of restraint separate from that inherent in the robbery. He asserts that such evidence is necessary to satisfy the requirements of N.C.G.S. § 14-39, the kidnapping statute, as interpreted by this Court in *State v. Fulcher*, 294 N.C. 503, 523, 243 S.E.2d 338, 351 (1978).

N.C.G.S. § 14-39(a) provides in pertinent part that a person is guilty of kidnapping if he or she shall unlawfully confine, restrain, or remove from one place to another, any other person 16 years of age or over without the consent of such person . . . if such confinement, restraint or removal is for the purpose of:

> (2) Facilitating the commission of any felony or facilitating flight of any person following the commission of a felony. . . .

In *Fulcher* this Court recognized that certain felonies, such as robbery with a dangerous weapon, cannot be committed without some restraint of the victim; and it held that "restraint, which is an inherent, inevitable feature of such other felony," could not form the basis of a kidnapping conviction. The Court stated that the legislature did not intend N.C.G.S. § 14-39 "to permit the conviction and punishment of the defendant for both crimes." The Court further noted that "to hold otherwise would violate the constitutional prohibition against double jeopardy."

The State contends that *Fulcher* was based upon a now-outmoded understanding of the Double Jeopardy Clause of the United States Constitution. It argues that under modern double jeopardy analysis, this Court's interpretation and application of N.C.G.S. § 14-39 in *Fulcher* is unnecessary and should be overruled. This Court did not decide Fulcher solely on constitutional grounds, however. Rather, it interpreted the kidnapping statute under the "cardinal principle of statutory construction . . . that the intent of the Legislature is controlling," stating:

> We are of the opinion, and so hold, that G.S. 14-39 was *not intended by the Legislature* to make a restraint, which is an inherent, inevitable feature of such other felony, also kidnapping so as to permit the conviction and punishment of the defendant for both crimes. (emphasis added).

"The key question . . . is whether the kidnapping charge is supported by evidence from which a jury could reasonably find that the necessary restraint for kidnapping 'exposed [the victim] to greater danger than that inherent in the armed robbery itself.'" Here, the robbers, including defendant, restrained two victims, Koufaloitis and Poulos, and defendant was convicted of one count of second-degree kidnapping for each restraint. We address each in turn.

The evidence of defendant's restraint of victim Koufaloitis supports a finding that the robbers, including defendant, put duct tape around the victim's wrists, forced him to lie on the floor, and kicked him in the back twice. Because the binding and kicking were not inherent, inevitable parts of the robbery, these forms of restraint "exposed [the victim to a] greater danger than that inherent in the armed robbery itself." *State v. Pigott*, 331 N.C. at 199, 210, 415 S.E.2d 555, 561 (holding that when the defendant bound the victim's hands and feet, he exposed the victim to a greater danger than that inherent in the armed robbery and therefore upholding the defendant's kidnapping conviction); Fulcher (holding that binding of victims' hands was not an inherent and inevitable feature of rape and therefore upholding the defendant's kidnapping convictions based upon that restraint). When defendant bound this victim's wrists and kicked him in the back, he increased the victim's helplessness and vulnerability beyond what was necessary to enable him and his comrades to rob the restaurant. Such actions constituted sufficient additional restraint to satisfy the restraint element of kidnapping under N.C.G.S. § 14-39, and the Court of Appeals properly found no error in defendant's conviction for the second-degree kidnapping of victim Koufaloitis.

With regard to victim Poulos, the evidence shows only that one of the robbers approached the victim, pointed a gun at him, and stood guarding him during the robbery. The victim did not move during the robbery, and the robbers did not injure him in any way. In order to commit a robbery with a dangerous weapon under N.C.G.S. § 14-87(a), defendant had to possess, use, or threaten to use a firearm while taking personal property from a place of business where persons were in attendance. The only evidence of restraint of this victim was the threatened use of a firearm. This restraint is an essential element of robbery with a dangerous weapon under N.C.G.S. § 14-87, and defendant's use of this restraint exposed the victim to no greater danger than that required to complete the robbery with a dangerous weapon. We thus hold that threatening victim Poulos with a gun was an inherent, inevitable feature of the robbery and is insufficient to support a conviction for kidnapping under N.C.G.S. § 14-39. The Court of Appeals therefore erred in finding no error in defendant's conviction for the second-degree kidnapping of victim Poulos.

For the reasons stated, we affirm the Court of Appeals with regard to defendant's conviction for the second-degree kidnapping of victim Koufaloitis, and we reverse the Court of Appeals with regard to defendant's conviction for the second-degree kidnapping of victim Poulos. We remand the case to the Court of Appeals for further remand to the Superior Court, Mecklenburg County, for entry of an order arresting judgment on defendant's conviction for the second-degree kidnapping of victim Poulos.

Questions and Notes

1. Is there really a difference between the amount of restraint to which victim Koufaloitis, as opposed to victim Poulos, was subjected?

2. Would you feel safer with a gun pointed at you and orders not to move, or an unarmed man guarding you with duct tape on your wrist? If you would feel safer with the duct tape, was the court's decision perverse?

3. If the injury was the key, why wasn't there a charge for kidnapping Copsis, who was actually shot? Presumably, the assault with a deadly weapon charge was predicated on that shooting. Kidnapping is a considerably more serious charge than assault with a deadly weapon inflicting serious injury.

4. Could there have also been a charge for assault with a deadly weapon against Poulos? Why? Why not?

5. How limited (expansive) should kidnapping be in an ideal system of jurisprudence?

6. Should assault, kidnapping, and robbery all be possible from the same transaction? Always? Sometimes? Never?

Chapter 5

Rape

A. The Traditional View

State v. Rusk

424 A.2d 720 (Md. 1981)

Murphy, Chief Judge.

Edward Rusk was found guilty by a jury in the Criminal Court of Baltimore of second degree rape in violation of the Maryland Code which provides in pertinent part:

> "A person is guilty of rape in the second degree if the person engages in vaginal intercourse with another person:
>
> (1) By force or threat of force against the will and without the consent of the other person . . ."

On appeal, the Court of Special Appeals, sitting en banc, reversed the conviction; it concluded by an 8-5 majority that insufficient evidence of Rusk's guilt had been adduced at the trial to permit the case to go to the jury.

At the trial, the 21-year-old prosecuting witness, Pat, testified that on the evening of September 21, 1977, she attended a high school alumnae meeting where she met a girl friend, Terry. After the meeting, Terry and Pat agreed to drive in their respective cars to Fells Point to have a few drinks. On the way, Pat stopped to telephone her mother, who was baby sitting for Pat's two-year-old son; she told her mother that she was going with Terry to Fells Point and would not be late in arriving home.

The women arrived in Fells Point about 9:45 p.m. They went to a bar where each had one drink. After staying approximately one hour, Pat and Terry walked several blocks to a second bar, where each of them had another drink. After about thirty minutes, they walked two blocks to a third bar known as E.J. Buggs. The bar was crowded and a band was playing in the back. Pat ordered another drink and as she and Terry were leaning against the wall, Rusk approached and said "hello" to Terry. Terry, who was then conversing with another individual, momentarily interrupted her conversation and said "Hi, Eddie." Rusk then began talking with Pat and during their conversation both of them acknowledged being separated from their respective spouses and having a child. Pat told Rusk that she had to go home because it was a weeknight and she had to wake up with her baby early in the morning.

Rusk asked Pat the direction in which she was driving and after she responded, Rusk requested a ride to his apartment. Although Pat did not know Rusk, she thought that Terry knew him. She thereafter agreed to give him a ride. Pat cautioned Rusk on the way to the car that "I'm just giving a ride home, you know, as a friend, not anything to be, you know, thought of other than a ride," and he said, "Oh, okay." They left the bar between 12:00 and 12:20 a.m.

Pat testified that on the way to Rusk's apartment, they continued the general conversation that they had started in the bar. After a twenty-minute drive, they arrived at Rusk's apartment in the 3100 block of Guilford Avenue. Pat testified that she was totally unfamiliar with the neighborhood. She parked the car at the curb on the opposite side of the street from Rusk's apartment but left the engine running. Rusk asked Pat to come in, but she refused. He invited her again, and she again declined. She told Rusk that she could not go into his apartment even if she wanted to because she was separated from her husband and a detective could be observing her movements. Pat said that Rusk was fully aware that she did not want to accompany him to his room. Notwithstanding her repeated refusals, Pat testified that Rusk reached over and turned off the ignition to her car and took her car keys. He got out of the car, walked over to her side, opened the door and said, "Now, will you come up?" Pat explained her subsequent actions: "At that point, because I was scared, because he had my car keys. I didn't know what to do. I was someplace I didn't even know where I was. It was in the city. I didn't know whether to run. I really didn't think at that point, what to do. Now, I know that I should have blown the horn. I should have run. There were a million things I could have done. I was scared, at that point, and I didn't do any of them."

Pat testified at this moment she feared that Rusk would rape her. She said: "[I]t was the way he looked at me, and said 'Come on up, come on up;' and when he took the keys, I knew that was wrong."

It was then about 1 a.m. Pat accompanied Rusk across the street into a totally dark house. She followed him up two flights of stairs. She neither saw nor heard anyone in the building. Once they ascended the stairs, Rusk unlocked the door to his one-room apartment, and turned on the light. According to Pat, he told her to sit down. She sat in a chair beside the bed. Rusk sat on the bed. After Rusk talked for a few minutes, he left the room for about one to five minutes. Pat remained seated in the chair. She made no noise and did not attempt to leave. She said that she did not notice a telephone in the room. When Rusk returned, he turned off the light and sat down on the bed. Pat asked if she could leave; she told him that she wanted to go home and "didn't want to come up." She said, "Now, [that] I came up, can I go?" Rusk, who was still in possession of her car keys, said he wanted her to stay.

Rusk then asked Pat to get on the bed with him. He pulled her by the arms to the bed and began to undress her, removing her blouse and bra. He unzipped her slacks and she took them off after he told her to do so. Pat removed the rest of her clothing, and then removed Rusk's pants because "he asked me to do it." After they were both undressed Rusk started kissing Pat as she was lying on her back. Pat explained what happened next: "I was still begging him to please let, you know, let me leave. I said, 'you can get a lot of other girls down there, for what you want,' and he just kept saying, 'no;' and then I was really scared, because I can't describe, you know, what was said. It was more the look in his eyes; and I said, at that point—I didn't know what to say; and I said, 'If I do what you want, will you let me go without killing me?' Because I didn't know, at that point, what he was going to do; and I started to cry; and when I did, he put his hands on my throat, and started lightly to choke me; and I said, 'If I do what you want, will you let me go?' And he said, yes, and at that time, I proceeded to do what he wanted me to." Pat testified that Rusk made her perform oral sex and then vaginal intercourse.

Immediately after the intercourse, Pat asked if she could leave. She testified that Rusk said, "Yes," after which she got up and got dressed and Rusk returned her car keys. She said that Rusk then "walked me to my car, and asked if he could see me again; and I said, 'Yes;' and he asked me for my telephone number; and I said, 'No, I'll see you down Fells Point sometime,' just so I could leave." Pat testified that she "had no intention of meeting him again." She asked him for directions out of the neighborhood and left.

On her way home, Pat stopped at a gas station, went to the ladies room, and then drove "pretty much straight home and pulled up and parked the car." At first, she was not going to say anything about the incident. She explained her initial reaction not to report the incident: "I didn't want to go through what I'm going through now [at the trial]." As she sat in her car reflecting on the incident, Pat said she began to "wonder what would happen if I hadn't of done what he wanted me to do. So I thought the right thing to do was to report it, and I went from there to Hillendale to find a police car." She reported the incident to the police at about 3:15 a.m. Subsequently, Pat took the police to Rusk's apartment, which she located without any great difficulty.

Pat's girlfriend Terry corroborated her testimony concerning the events which occurred up to the time that Pat left the bar with Rusk. Questioned about Pat's alcohol consumption, Terry said she was drinking screwdrivers that night but normally did not finish a drink. Terry testified about her acquaintanceship with Rusk: "I knew his face, and his first name, but I honestly couldn't tell you—apparently I ran into him sometime before. I couldn't tell you how I know him. I don't know him very well at all."

Officer Hammett of the Baltimore City Police Department acknowledged receiving Pat's complaint at 3:15 a.m. on September 22, 1977. He accompanied her to the 3100 block of Guilford Avenue where it took Pat several minutes to locate Rusk's apartment. Officer Hammett entered Rusk's multi-dwelling apartment house, which contained at least six apartments, and arrested Rusk in a room on the second floor.

Hammett testified that Pat was sober, and she was taken to City Hospital for an examination. The examination disclosed that seminal fluid and spermatozoa were detected in Pat's vagina, on her underpants, and on the bedsheets recovered from Rusk's bed.

At the close of the State's case-in-chief, Rusk moved for a judgment of acquittal. In denying the motion, the trial court said: "There is evidence that there is a taking of automobile keys forcibly, a request that the prosecuting witness accompany the Defendant to the upstairs apartment. She described a look in his eye which put her in fear. Now, you are absolutely correct that there was no weapon, no physical threatening testified to. However, while she was seated on a chair next to the bed, the Defendant excused himself, and came back in five minutes; and then she testified, he pulled her on to the bed by reaching over and grabbing her wrists, and/or had her or requested, that she disrobe, and assist him in disrobing. Again, she said she was scared, and then she testified to something to the effect that she said to him, she was begging him to let her leave. She was scared. She started to cry. He started to strangle her softly she said. She asked the Defendant, that if she'd submit, would he not kill her, at which point he indicated that he would not; and she performed oral sex on him, and then had intercourse."

Rusk and two of his friends, Michael Trimp and David Carroll, testified on his behalf. According to Trimp, they went in Carroll's car to Buggs' bar to dance, drink and "tr[y] to pick up some ladies." Rusk stayed at the bar, while the others went to get something to eat.

Trimp and Carroll next saw Rusk walking down the street arm-in-arm with a lady whom Trimp was unable to identify. Trimp asked Rusk if he needed a ride home. Rusk responded that the woman he was with was going to drive him home. Trimp testified that at about 2:00–2:30 a.m. he returned to the room he rented with Rusk on Guilford Avenue and found Rusk to be the only person present. Trimp said that as many as twelve people lived in the entire building and that the room he rented with Rusk was referred to as their "pit stop." Both Rusk and Trimp actually resided at places other than the Guilford Avenue room. Trimp testified that there was a telephone in the apartment.

Carroll's testimony corroborated Trimp's. He saw Rusk walking down the street arm-in-arm with a woman. He said "[s]he was kind of like, you know, snuggling up to him like. . . . She was hanging all over him then." Carroll was fairly certain that Pat was the woman who was with Rusk.

Rusk, the 31-year-old defendant, testified that he was in the Buggs Tavern for about thirty minutes when he noticed Pat standing at the bar. Rusk said: "She looked at me, and she smiled. I walked over and said, hi, and started talking to her." He did not remember either knowing or speaking to Terry. When Pat mentioned that she was about to leave, Rusk asked her if she wanted to go home with him. In response, Pat said that she would like to, but could not because she had her car. Rusk then suggested that they take her car. Pat agreed and they left the bar arm-in-arm.

Rusk testified that during the drive to her apartment, he discussed with Pat their similar marital situations and talked about their children. He said that Pat asked him if he was going to rape her. When he inquired why she was asking, Pat said that she had been raped once before. Rusk expressed his sympathy for her. Pat then asked if he planned to beat her. He inquired why she was asking, and Pat explained that her husband used to beat her. Rusk again expressed his sympathy. He testified that at no time did Pat express a fear that she was being followed by her separated husband.

According to Rusk, when they arrived in front of his apartment Pat parked the car and turned the engine off. They sat for several minutes "petting each other." Rusk denied switching off the ignition and removing the keys. He said that they walked to the apartment house and proceeded up the stairs to his room. Rusk testified that Pat came willingly to his room and that at no time did he make threatening facial expressions. Once inside his room, Rusk left Pat alone for several minutes while he used the bathroom down the hall. Upon his return, he switched the light on but immediately turned it off because Pat, who was seated in the dark in a chair next to the bed, complained it was too bright. Rusk said that he sat on the bed across from Pat and reached out "and started to put my arms around her, and started kissing her; and we fell back into the bed, and she—we were petting, kissing, and she stuck her hand down in my pants and started playing with me; and I undid her blouse, and took off her bra; and then I sat up and I said 'Let's take our clothes off;' and she said, 'Okay;' and I took my clothes off, and she took her clothes off; and then we proceeded to have intercourse."

Rusk explained that after the intercourse, Pat "got uptight." "Well, she started to cry. She said that—she said, 'You guys are all alike,' she says, 'just out for,' you know, 'one thing.' She started talking about—I don't know, she was crying and all. I tried to calm her down and all; and I said, 'What's the matter?' And she said, that she just wanted to leave; and I said, 'Well, okay;' and she walked out to the car. I walked out to the car. She got in the car and left."

Rusk denied placing his hands on Pat's throat or attempting to strangle her. He also denied using force or threats of force to get Pat to have intercourse with him.

In reversing Rusk's second degree rape conviction, the Court of Special Appeals, noted that: "Force is an essential element of the crime [of rape] and to justify a conviction, the evidence must warrant a conclusion either that the victim resisted and her resistance was overcome by force or that she was prevented from resisting by threats by her safety." Writing for the majority, Judge Thompson said: "In all of the victim's testimony we have been unable to see any resistance on her part to the sex acts and certainly can we see no fear as would overcome her attempt to resist or escape. Possession of the keys by the accused may have deterred her vehicular escape but hardly a departure seeking help in the rooming house or in the street. We must say that 'the way he looked' fails utterly to support the fear required."

The Court of Special Appeals required a showing of a reasonable apprehension of fear in instances where the prosecutrix did not resist. It concluded: "we find the evidence legally insufficient to warrant a conclusion that appellant's words or actions

---

created in the mind of the victim a reasonable fear that if she resisted, he would have harmed her, or that faced with such resistance, he would have used force to overcome it. The prosecutrix stated that she was afraid, and submitted because of 'the look in his eyes.' After both were undressed and in the bed, and she pleaded to him that she wanted to leave, he started to lightly choke her. At oral argument it was brought out that the 'lightly choking' could have been a heavy caress. We do not believe that 'lightly choking' along with all the facts and circumstances in the case, were sufficient to cause a reasonable fear which overcame her ability to resist. In the absence of any other evidence showing force used by appellant, we find that the evidence was insufficient to convict appellant of rape."

The issue was whether there was evidence before the jury legally sufficient to prove beyond a reasonable doubt that the intercourse was "[b]y force or threat of force against the will and without the consent" of the victim. The applicable standard is "whether, after viewing the evidence in the light most favorable to the prosecution, *any* rational trier of fact could have found the essential elements of the crime beyond a reasonable doubt." *Jackson v. Virginia*, 443 U.S. 307, 319 (emphasis in original).

The terms "force," "threat of force," "against the will" and "without the consent" are not defined in the statute, but are to be afforded their "judicially determined meaning" as applied in cases involving common law rape.

In this regard, it is well settled that the terms "against the will" and "without the consent" are synonymous in the law of rape. In an earlier case, *State v. Hazel*, 157 A.2d 922, the Court said: "Force is an essential element of the crime and to justify a conviction, the evidence must warrant a conclusion either that the victim resisted and her resistance was overcome by force or that she was prevented from resisting by threats to her safety. But no particular amount of force, either actual or constructive, is required to constitute rape. Necessarily, that fact must depend upon the prevailing circumstances. As in this case force may exist without violence. If the acts and threats of the defendant were reasonably calculated to create in the mind of the victim—having regard to the circumstances in which she was placed—a real apprehension, due to fear, of imminent bodily harm, serious enough to impair or overcome her will to resist, then such acts and threats are the equivalent of force." *Id.* at 469, 157, A.2d 922.

> "[I]t is true, of course, that however reluctantly given, consent to the act at any time prior to penetration deprives the subsequent intercourse of its criminal character. There is, however, a wide difference between consent and a submission to the act. Consent may involve submission, but submission does not necessarily imply consent. Furthermore, submission to a compelling force, or as a result of being put in fear, is not consent." *Id.*

The Court noted that lack of consent is generally established through proof of resistance or by proof that the victim failed to resist because of fear. The degree of fear necessary to obviate the need to prove resistance, and thereby establish lack of consent, was defined in the following manner:

"The kind of fear which would render resistance by a woman unnecessary to support a conviction of rape includes, but is not necessarily limited to, a fear of death or serious bodily harm, or a fear so extreme as to preclude resistance, or a fear which would well nigh render her mind incapable of continuing to resist, or a fear that so overpowers her that she does not dare resist." *Id.* at 470, 157 A.2d 922.

Hazel thus made it clear that lack of consent could be established through proof that the victim submitted as a result of fear of imminent death or serious bodily harm. In addition, if the actions and conduct of the defendant were reasonably calculated to induce this fear in the victim's mind, then the element of force is present ... the same kind of evidence may be used in establishing both force and non-consent, particularly when a threat rather than actual force is involved.

Hazel did not expressly determine whether the victim's fear must be "reasonable." Its only reference to reasonableness related to whether "the acts and threats of the defendant were reasonably calculated to create in the mind of the victim ... a real apprehension, due to the fear, of imminent bodily harm. . . ." 221 Md. at 469, 157 A.2d 922. Manifestly, the Court was there referring to the calculations of the accused, not to the fear of the victim. While *Hazel* made it clear that the victim's fear had to be genuine, it did not pass upon whether a real but unreasonable fear of imminent death or serious bodily harm would suffice. The vast majority of jurisdictions have required that the victim's fear be reasonably grounded in order to obviate the need for either proof of actual force on the part of the assailant or physical resistance on the part of the victim. We think that, generally, this is the correct standard.

As earlier indicated, the Court of Special Appeals held that a showing of a reasonable apprehension of fear was essential under *Hazel* to establish the elements of the offense where the victim did not resist. The Court did not believe, however, that the evidence was legally sufficient to demonstrate the existence of "a reasonable fear" which overcame Pat's ability to resist. In support of the Court's conclusion, Rusk maintains that the evidence showed that Pat voluntarily entered his apartment without being subjected to a "single threat nor a scintilla of force;" that she made no effort to run away nor did she scream for help; that she never exhibited a will to resist; and that her subjective reaction of fear to the situation in which she had voluntarily placed herself was unreasonable and exaggerated. Rusk claims that his acts were not reasonably calculated to overcome a will to resist; that Pat's verbal resistance was not resistance within the contemplation of *Hazel*; that his alleged menacing look did not constitute a threat of force; and that even had he pulled Pat to the bed, and lightly choked her, as she claimed, these actions, viewed in the context of the entire incident—no prior threats having been made—would be insufficient to constitute force or threat of force or render the intercourse non-consensual.

We think the reversal of Rusk's conviction by the Court of Special Appeals was in error for the fundamental reason so well expressed in the dissenting opinion by Judge Wilner when he observed that the majority had "trampled upon the first principle of appellate restraint ... [because it had] substituted [its] own view of the evidence (and the inferences that may fairly be drawn from it) for that of the judge and jury . . . [and had thereby] improperly invaded the province allotted to those tribunals." . . . Applying the constitutional standards of review articulated in *Jackson v. Virginia, supra, i.e.,* — whether after considering the evidence in the light most favorable to the prosecution, *any* rational trier of fact could have found the essential elements of the crime beyond a reasonable doubt — it is readily apparent to us that the trier of fact could rationally find that the elements of force and non-consent had been established and that Rusk was guilty of the offense beyond a reasonable doubt. Of course, it was for the jury to observe the witnesses and their demeanor, and to judge their credibility and weigh their testimony. Quite obviously, the jury disbelieved Rusk and believed Pat's testimony. From her testimony, the jury could have reasonably concluded that the taking of her car keys was intended by Rusk to immobilize her alone, late at night, in a neighborhood with which she was not familiar; that after Pat had repeatedly refused to enter his apartment, Rusk commanded in firm tones that she do so; that Pat was badly frightened and feared that Rusk intended to rape her; that unable to think clearly and believing that she had no other choice in the circumstances, Pat entered Rusk's apartment; that once inside Pat asked permission to leave but Rusk told her to stay; that he then pulled Pat by the arms to the bed and undressed her; that Pat was afraid that Rusk would kill her unless she submitted; that she began to cry and Rusk then put his hands on her throat and began "lightly to choke" her; that Pat asked him if he would let her go without killing her if she complied with his demands; that Rusk gave an affirmative response, after which she finally submitted.

Just where persuasion ends and force begins in cases like the present is essentially a factual issue, to be resolved in light of the controlling legal precepts. That threats of force need not be made in any particular manner in order to put a person in fear of bodily harm is well established. Indeed, conduct, rather than words, may convey the threat. That a victim did not scream out for help or attempt to escape, while bearing on the question of consent, is unnecessary where she is restrained by fear of violence.

Considering all of the evidence in the case, with particular focus upon the actual force applied by Rusk to Pat's neck, we conclude that the jury could rationally find that the essential elements of second degree rape had been established and that Rusk was guilty of that offense beyond a reasonable doubt.

COLE, Judge, dissenting.

I agree with the Court of Special Appeals that the evidence adduced at the trial of Edward Salvatore Rusk was insufficient to convict him of rape. I, therefore, respectfully dissent.

The standard of appellate review in deciding a question of sufficiency, as the majority correctly notes, is "whether, after viewing the evidence in the light most favorable to the prosecution, *any* rational trier of fact could have found the essential elements of the crime beyond a reasonable doubt." *Jackson v. Virginia*, 443 U.S. 307,

319 (1979) (emphasis in original). However, it is equally well settled that when one of the essential elements of a crime is not sustained by the evidence, the conviction of the defendant cannot stand as a matter of law.

The majority, in applying this standard, concludes that "[i]n view of the evidence adduced at the trial, the reasonableness of Pat's apprehension of fear was plainly a question of fact for the jury to determine." In so concluding, the majority has skipped over the crucial issue. It seems to me that whether the prosecutrix's fear is reasonable becomes a question only after the court determines that the defendant's conduct under the circumstances was reasonably calculated to give rise to a fear on her part to the extent that she was unable to resist. In other words, the fear must stem from his articulable conduct, and equally, if not more importantly, cannot be inconsistent with her own contemporaneous reaction to that conduct. The conduct of the defendant, in and of itself, must clearly indicate force or the threat of force such as to overpower the prosecutrix's ability to resist or will to resist. In my view, there is no evidence to support the majority's conclusion that the prosecutrix was forced to submit to sexual intercourse, certainly not fellatio.

". . ."Force is an essential element of the crime and to justify a conviction, the evidence must warrant a conclusion either that the victim resisted and her resistance was overcome by force or that she was prevented from resisting by threats to her safety." "No particular amount of force, either actual or constructive, is required to constitute rape. Necessarily that fact must depend upon the prevailing circumstances." However, we hastened to add that "[i]f the acts and threats of the defendant [are] reasonably calculated to create in the mind of the victim—having regard to the circumstances in which she [is] placed—a real apprehension, due to fear, of imminent bodily harm, serious enough to impair or overcome her will to resist, then such acts and threats are the equivalent of force."

The authorities are by no means in accord as to what degree of resistance is necessary to establish the absence of consent . . . the generally accepted doctrine seems to be that a female—who was conscious and possessed her natural, mental and physical powers when the attack took place—must have resisted to the extent of her ability at the time, unless it appears that she was overcome by numbers or so terrified by threats as to overcome her will to resist.

Hazel intended to require clear and cognizable evidence of force or threat of force sufficient to overcome or prevent resistance by the female before there would arise a jury question of whether the prosecutrix had a reasonable apprehension of harm. The majority today departs from this requirement and places its imprimatur on the female's conclusory statements that she was in fear, as sufficient to support a conviction of rape.

In *Goldberg v. State*, 41 Md. App. 58, 395 A.2d 1213, and *Winegan v. State*, 10 Md. App. 196, 268 A.2d 585 (1970), the convictions were reversed by the Court of Special Appeals. *Goldberg* concerned a student, professing to be a talent agent, who lured a young woman to an apartment upon the pretext of offering her a modeling job. She freely accompanied him, and though she protested verbally, she did not physically resist his advances. The Court of Special Appeals held:

> "The prosecutrix swore that the reasons for her fear of being killed if she did not accede to appellant's advances were two-fold: 1) she was alone with the appellant in a house with no buildings close by and no one to help her if she resisted, and 2) the appellant was much larger than she was. In the complete absence of any threatening words or actions by the appellant, these two factors, as a matter of law, are simply not enough to have created a reasonable fear of harm so as to preclude resistance and be 'the equivalent of force.' Without proof of force, actual or constructive, evidenced by words or conduct of the defendant or those acting in consort with him, sexual intercourse is not rape."

In *Winegan*, the appellant's conviction was reversed because, although the prosecutrix accompanied him to a boarding house and had sexual intercourse only because she thought he had a gun, *he had no gun nor at any time claimed to have one*. It was on this basis, coupled with the facts that (1) the complainant at no time made outcry and (2) *she followed him up the steps to his room*, that the court concluded that her fear, if actually present, was so unreasonable as to preclude a conviction of rape.

In each case in which there was a conviction there was either physical violence or specific threatening words or conduct which were calculated to create a very real and specific fear of *immediate* physical injury to the victim if she did not comply, coupled with the apparent power to execute those threats in the event of non-submission.

While courts no longer require a female to resist to the utmost or to resist where resistance would be foolhardy, they do require her acquiescence in the act of intercourse to stem from fear generated by something of substance. She may not simply say, "I was really scared," and thereby transform consent or mere unwillingness into submission by force. These words do not transform a seducer into a rapist. She must follow the natural instinct of every proud female to resist, by more than mere words, the violation of her person by a stranger or an unwelcomed friend. She must make it plain that she regards such sexual acts as abhorrent and repugnant to her natural sense of pride. She must resist unless the defendant has objectively manifested his intent to use physical force to accomplish his purpose. The law regards rape as a crime of violence. The majority today attenuates this proposition. It declares the innocence of an at best distraught young woman. It does not demonstrate the defendant's guilt of the crime of rape.

My examination of the evidence in light most favorably to the State reveals no conduct by the defendant reasonably calculated to cause the prosecutrix to be so fearful that she should fail to resist and thus, the element of force is lacking in the State's proof.

Here we have a full grown married woman who meets the defendant in a bar under friendly circumstances. They drink and talk together. She agrees to give him a ride home in her car. When they arrive at his house, located in an area with which she was unfamiliar but which was certainly not isolated, he invites her to come up to his apartment and she refuses. According to her testimony he takes her keys, walks around to her side of the car, and says "Now will you come up?" She answers, "yes." The majority suggests that "from her testimony the jury could have reasonably concluded that the taking of her keys was intended by Rusk to immobilize her alone, late at night, in a neighborhood with which she was unfamiliar. . . ." But on what facts does the majority so conclude? There is no evidence descriptive of the tone of his voice; her testimony indicates only the bare statement quoted above. How can the majority extract from this conduct a threat reasonably calculated to create a fear of imminent bodily harm? There was no weapon, no threat to inflict physical injury.

She also testified that she was afraid of "the way he looked," and afraid of his statement, "come on up, come on up." But what can the majority conclude from this statement coupled with a "look" that remained undescribed? There is no evidence whatsoever to suggest that this was anything other than a pattern of conduct consistent with the ordinary seduction of a female acquaintance who at first suggests her disinclination.

After reaching the room she described what occurred as follows:

> I was still begging him to please let, you know, let me leave. I said, "you can get a lot of other girls down there, for what you want,' and he just kept saying, "no," and then I was really scared, because I can't describe, you know, what was said. It was more the look in his eyes; and I said, at that point—I didn't know what to say; and I said, "If I do what you want, will you let me go without killing me?" Because I didn't know, at that point, what he was going to do; and I started to cry; and when I did, he put his hands on my throat, and started lightly to choke me; and I said, 'If I do what you want, will you let me go?' And he said, yes, and at that time, I proceeded to do what he wanted me to.

The majority relies on the trial court's statement that the defendant responded affirmatively to her question "If I do what you want, will you let me go without killing me?" The majority further suggests that the jury could infer the defendant's affirmative response. The facts belie such inferences since the prosecutrix's own testimony the defendant made *no* response. *He said nothing!*

She then testified that she started to cry and he "started lightly to choke" her, whatever that means. Obviously, the choking was not of any persuasive significance. During this "choking" she was able to talk. She said "If I do what you want will you let me go?" It was at this point that the defendant said yes.

I find it incredible for the majority to conclude that on these facts, without more, a woman was *forced* to commit oral sex upon the defendant and then to engage in vaginal intercourse. In the absence of any verbal threat to do her grievous bodily harm or the display of any weapon and threat to use it, I find it difficult to understand how a victim could participate in these sexual activities and not be willing.

What was the nature and extent of her fear anyhow? She herself testified she was "fearful that maybe I had someone following me." She was afraid because she didn't know him, and she was afraid he was going to "rape" her. But there are no acts or conduct on the part of the defendant to suggest that these fears were created by the defendant or that he made any objective, identifiable threats to her which would give rise to this woman's failure to flee, summon help, scream, or make physical resistance.

As the defendant well knew, this was not a child. This was a married woman with children, a woman familiar with the social setting in which these two actors met. It was an ordinary city street, not an isolated spot. He had not forced his way into her car; he had not taken advantage of a difference in years or any state of intoxication or mental or physical incapacity on her part. He did not grapple with her. She got out of the car, *walked with him* across the street and *followed* him up the stairs to his room. She certainly had to realize that they were not going upstairs to play *Scrabble*.

Once in the room she waited while he went to the bathroom where he stayed for five minutes. In his absence, the room was lighted but she did not seek a means of escape. She did not even "try the door" to determine if it was locked. She waited.

Upon his return, he turned off the lights and pulled her on the bed. There is no suggestion or inference to be drawn from her testimony that he yanked her on the bed or in any manner physically abused her by this conduct. As a matter of fact there is no suggestion by her that he bruised or hurt her in any manner, or that the "choking" was intended to be disabling.

He then proceeded to unbutton her blouse and her bra. He did not rip her clothes off or use any greater force than was necessary to unfasten her garments. He did not even complete this procedure but requested that she do it, which she did "because he asked me to." However, she not only removed her clothing but took his clothes off, too.

Then for a while they lay together on the bed kissing, though she says she did not return his kisses. However, without protest she then proceeded to perform oral sex and later submitted to vaginal intercourse. After these activities were completed, she asked to leave. They dressed and he walked her to her car and asked to see her again. She indicated that perhaps they might meet at Fells Point. He gave her directions home and returned to his apartment where the police found him later that morning.

The record does not disclose the basis for this young woman's misgivings about her experience with the defendant. The only substantive fear she had was that she would be late arriving home. The objective facts make it inherently improbable that the defendant's conduct generated any fear for her physical well-being.

In my judgment the State failed to prove the essential element of force beyond a reasonable doubt and, therefore, the judgment of conviction should be reversed.

Judges Smith and Digges have authorized me to state that they concur in the views expressed herein.

Questions and Notes

1. Are you more comfortable with the majority or dissenting opinion in *Rusk*? Why?

2. Even if the dissent were correct as a matter of law, did it not owe an obligation to refrain from endorsing Rusk's behavior (at least as described by Pat). The statement that "(t)here is no evidence whatsoever to suggest that this was anything other than a pattern of conduct consistent with the ordinary seduction of a female acquaintance who at first suggests her disinclination" hardly seems apt for a man who took a woman's car keys in a strange neighborhood early in the morning.

3. Should there be a lesser offense that makes force irrelevant? *See Berkowitz, infra.*

4. Would violation of such a statute be a more appropriate charge for Rusk?

5. In general, do you think that rape should be divided into degrees? If so, how would you distinguish degrees of rape? *Compare* MPC § 2.03 (Appendix A).

6. If you had unbridled discretion as a judge, what sentence would you impose on Rusk? Why?

7. If Pat had testified that she didn't want to have sex with Rusk, but preferred having sex with him to being stranded in the neighborhood, of what, if any, crime should Rusk be convicted?

8. In either the immediately preceding hypothetical, or in *Rusk* itself, would kidnapping (by taking the keys) have been a more appropriate crime than rape?

9. For a view of the appropriate resolution of cases like *Rusk* from the perspective of a former rape victim, see Estrich, *Rape*, 95 YALE L.J. 1087 (1986).

B. Legislative Reform
Commonwealth v. Berkowitz
641 A.2d 1161 (Pa. 1994)

CAPPY, Justice

We granted allocatur in this case to address the question of the precise degree of force necessary to prove the "forcible compulsion" element of the crime of rape. In addition, our disposition of this case further defines the scope of the Rape Shield Law.

The Commonwealth appeals from an order of the Superior Court which overturned the conviction by a jury of Appellee, Robert A. Berkowitz, of one count of rape and one count of indecent assault. The judgment of the Superior Court discharged Appellee as to the charge of rape and reversed and remanded for a new trial on the charge of indecent assault because it found that evidence was improperly excluded under the Rape Shield Law. For the reasons that follow, we affirm the

Superior Court's reversal of the conviction for rape, vacate its decision reversing and remanding the charge of indecent assault for a new trial, and reinstate the verdict of the jury as to indecent assault.

The relevant facts of this case are as follows. The complainant, a female college student, left her class, went to her dormitory room where she drank a martini, and then went to a lounge to await her boyfriend. When her boyfriend failed to appear, she went to another dormitory to find a friend, Earl Hassel. She knocked on the door, but received no answer. She tried the doorknob and, finding it unlocked, entered the room and discovered a man sleeping on the bed. The complainant originally believed the man to be Hassel, but it turned out to be Hassel's roomate [sic], Appellee. Appellee asked her to stay for a while and she agreed. He requested a back-rub and she declined. He suggested that she sit on the bed, but she declined and sat on the floor.

Appellee then moved to the floor beside her, lifted up her shirt and bra and massaged her breasts. He then unfastened his pants and unsuccessfully attempted to put his penis in her mouth. They both stood up, and he locked the door. He returned to push her onto the bed, and removed her undergarments from one leg. He then penetrated her vagina with his penis. After withdrawing and ejaculating on her stomach, he stated, "Wow, I guess we just got carried away," to which she responded, "No, we didn't get carried away, you got carried away."

In reviewing the sufficiency of the evidence, this Court must view the evidence in the light most favorable to the Commonwealth as verdict winner, and accept as true all evidence and reasonable inferences that may be reasonably drawn therefrom, upon which, if believed, the jury could have relied in reaching its verdict. If, upon such review, the Court concludes that the jury could not have determined from the evidence adduced that all of the necessary elements of the crime were established, then the evidence will be deemed insufficient to support the verdict.

The crime of rape is defined as follows:

§ 3121. Rape

A person commits a felony of the first degree when he engages in sexual intercourse with another person not one's spouse:

(1) by forcible compulsion;

(2) by threat of forcible compulsion that would prevent resistance by a person of reasonable resolution;

(3) who is unconscious; or

(4) who is so mentally deranged or deficient that such person is incapable of consent.

The victim of a rape need not resist. "The force necessary to support a conviction of rape . . . need only be such as to establish lack of consent and to induce the [victim] to submit without additional resistance. . . . The degree of force required to constitute rape is relative and depends on the facts and particular circumstance of the case."

In regard to the critical issue of forcible compulsion, the complainant's testimony is devoid of any statement which clearly or adequately describes the use of force or the threat of force against her. In response to defense counsel's question, "Is it possible that [when Appellee lifted your bra and shirt] you took no physical action to discourage him," the complainant replied, "It's possible." When asked, "Is it possible that [Appellee] was not making any physical contact with you . . . aside from attempting to untie the knot [in the drawstrings of complainant's sweatpants]," she answered, "It's possible." She testified that "He put me down on the bed. It was kind of like—He didn't throw me on the bed. It's hard to explain. It was kind of like a push but not—I can't explain what I'm trying to say." She concluded that "it wasn't much" in reference to whether she bounced on the bed, and further detailed that their movement to the bed "wasn't slow like a romantic kind of thing, but it wasn't a fast shove either. It was kind of in the middle." She agreed that Appellee's hands were not restraining her in any manner during the actual penetration, and that the weight of his body on top of her was the only force applied. She testified that at no time did Appellee verbally threaten her. The complainant did testify that she sought to leave the room and said "no" throughout the encounter. As to the complainant's desire to leave the room, the record clearly demonstrates that the door could be unlocked easily from the inside, that she was aware of this fact, but that she never attempted to go to the door or unlock it.

As to the complainant's testimony that she stated "no" throughout the encounter with Appellee, we point out that, while such an allegation of fact would be relevant to the issue of consent, it is not relevant to the issue of force. In *Commonwealth v. Mlinarich*, 518 Pa. 247, 542 A.2d 1335 (1988) (plurality opinion), this Court sustained the reversal of a defendant's conviction of rape where the alleged victim, a minor, repeatedly stated that she did not want to engage in sexual intercourse, but offered no physical resistance and was compelled to engage in sexual intercourse under threat of being recommitted to a juvenile detention center. The Opinion in Support of Affirmance acknowledged that physical force, a threat of force, or psychological coercion may be sufficient to support the element of "forcible compulsion", if found to be enough to "prevent resistance by a person of reasonable resolution." However, under the facts of *Mlinarich*, neither physical force, the threat of physical force, nor psychological coercion were found to have been proven, and this Court held that the conviction was properly reversed by the Superior Court. Accordingly, the ruling in *Mlinarich* implicitly dictates that where there is a lack of consent, but no showing of either physical force, a threat of physical force, or psychological coercion, the "forcible compulsion" requirement under 18 Pa. C.S. § 3121 is not met.[4]

---

4. The Opinion in Support of Reversal in *Mlinarich* did not take issue with the implicit holding of the Opinion in Support of Affirmance that something more than a lack of consent is required to prove "forcible compulsion." The Opinion in Support of Reversal acknowledged a general

Moreover, we find it instructive that in defining the related but distinct crime of "indecent assault" under 18 Pa. C.S § 3126, the Legislature did not employ the phrase "forcible compulsion" but rather chose to define indecent assault as "indecent contact with another . . . *without the consent of the other person.*" (Emphasis added.) The phrase "forcible compulsion" is explicitly set forth in the definition of rape under 18 Pa. C.S. § 3121, but the phrase "*without the consent of the other person,*" is conspicuously absent. The choice by the Legislature to define the crime of indecent assault utilizing the phrase "without the consent of the other" and to not so define the crime of rape indicates a legislative intent that the term "forcible compulsion" under 18 Pa. C.S. § 3121, be interpreted as something more than a lack of consent. Moreover, we note that penal statutes must be strictly construed to provide fair warning to the defendant of the nature of the proscribed conduct.

Reviewed in light of the above described standard, the complainant's testimony simply fails to establish that the Appellee forcibly compelled her to engage in sexual intercourse. Thus, even if all of the complainant's testimony was believed, the jury, as a matter of law, could not have found Appellee guilty of rape. Accordingly, we hold that the Superior Court did not err in reversing Appellee's conviction of rape.

As to the indecent assault charge, the Superior Court reversed the trial court's judgment of sentence and remanded for a new trial, holding that the trial court had erred by excluding evidence proffered by Appellee. Defense counsel attempted to admit evidence of the jealous nature of the victim's boyfriend. Defense counsel wanted to argue before the jury that the boyfriend was jealous because he believed that the victim had been unfaithful to him, that the victim and her boyfriend had argued over the issue of her alleged infidelity, and that it was the victim's fear of her boyfriend's jealousy which motivated her to accuse Appellee of rape. The trial court allowed defense counsel to offer evidence of frequent fights between the victim and her boyfriend but excluded any mention that the content or subject matter of these fights involved the victim's alleged infidelity, citing the Rape Shield Law.

The Superior Court held that the trial court had erred in its application of the Rape Shield Law, finding that because the proffered evidence was *not that the victim had, in fact, been unfaithful,* but rather only that the victim and her boyfriend had argued over *whether or not she had been unfaithful,* the Rape Shield Law was not seriously implicated. In this Court's view, the Rape Shield Law does not recognize such a distinction.

The Rape Shield Law provides in pertinent part as follows:

---

legislative intent to introduce an objective standard regarding the degree of physical force, threat of physical force, or psychological coercion required under 18 Pa. C.S. § 3121, in that it must be sufficient to "prevent resistance by a person of reasonable resolution," but argued that the "peculiar situation" of the victim and other subjective factors should be considered by the court in determining "resistance," "assent," and "consent," and that under the specific circumstances in *Mlinarich* sufficient facts were set forth to allow a finding of the requisite degree of psychological coercion to support the forcible compulsion element of 18 Pa. C.S. § 3121.

§ 3104. Evidence of victim's sexual conduct

(a) General rule.—Evidence of specific instances of the alleged victim's past sexual conduct, opinion evidence of the alleged victim's past sexual conduct, and reputation evidence of the alleged victim's past sexual conduct shall not be admissible in prosecutions under this chapter except evidence of the alleged victim's past sexual conduct with the defendant where consent of the alleged victim is at issue and such evidence is otherwise admissible pursuant to the rules of evidence.

18 Pa. C.S. § 3104 (a). The purpose of the Rape Shield Law is to prevent a sexual assault trial from degenerating into an attack upon the victim's reputation for chastity. The allegation that the victim and her boyfriend had argued over the issue of her infidelity is so closely tied to the issue of the victim's fidelity itself that, for the purposes of the Rape Shield Law, they are one and the same. This is precisely the type of allegation regarding past sexual conduct from which the Rape Shield Law is specifically designed to protect victims.

Furthermore, the evidence presented at trial was sufficient to support Appellee's conviction of indecent assault. The crime of indecent assault is defined as follows:

§ 3126. Indecent Assault

A person who has indecent contact with another not his spouse, or causes such other to have indecent contact with him is guilty of indecent assault, a misdemeanor of the second degree, if:

(1) He does so without the consent of the other person;

(2) He knows that the other person suffers from a mental disease or defect which renders him or her incapable of appraising the nature of his or her conduct;

(3) He knows that the other person is unaware that an indecent contact is being committed;

(4) He has substantially impaired the other person's power to appraise or control his or her conduct, by administering or employing without knowledge of the other drugs, intoxicants or other means for the purpose of preventing resistance; or

(5) The other person is in custody of law or detained in a hospital or other institution and the actor has supervisory or disciplinary authority over him.

As discussed earlier, the crime of indecent assault does not include the element of "forcible compulsion" as does the crime of rape. The evidence described above is clearly sufficient to support the jury's conviction of indecent assault. "Indecent contact" is defined as "any touching of the sexual or other intimate parts of the person for the purpose of arousing or gratifying sexual desire, in either person." Appellee himself testified to the "indecent contact." The victim testified that she repeatedly said "no" throughout the encounter. Viewing that testimony in the light most favorable to the Commonwealth as verdict winner, the jury reasonably could have inferred that the victim did not consent to the indecent contact. Thus, the evidence was sufficient to support the jury's verdict finding Appellee guilty of indecent assault.

We hold that the trial court's application of the Rape Shield Law, excluding the proffered evidence under the instant facts, was not error, that the evidence was sufficient to support a conviction of indecent assault, and that the Superior Court's reversal of the trial court's order with regard to the indecent assault charge was error.

Accordingly, the order of the Superior Court reversing the rape conviction is affirmed. The order of the Superior Court reversing Appellee's conviction of indecent assault and remanding for a new trial is vacated. The conviction and the trial court's sentence on the indecent assault charge are reinstated.

Questions and Notes

1. Explain how Berkowitz can be not guilty of rape, but guilty of indecent assault. Do you agree with that dichotomy?

2. Would Rusk have been convicted of rape under Pennsylvania law?

3. How did the Pennsylvania Supreme Court differ from the Superior Court in its assessment of the rape shield law? Which court got it right? Why?

4. In *MTS*, we see that under some modern rape laws, "force" can be very narrowly defined.

State of New Jersey in the Interest of M.T.S.

609 A.2d 1266 (N.J. 1992)

HANDLER, J.

Under New Jersey law a person who commits an act of sexual penetration using physical force or coercion is guilty of second-degree sexual assault. The sexual assault statute does not define the words "physical force." The question posed by this appeal is whether the element of "physical force" is met simply by an act of non-consensual penetration involving no more force than necessary to accomplish that result.

That issue is presented in the context of what is often referred to as "acquaintance rape." The record in the case discloses that the juvenile, a seventeen-year-old boy, engaged in consensual kissing and heavy petting with a fifteen-year-old girl and thereafter engaged in actual sexual penetration of the girl to which she had not consented. There was no evidence or suggestion that the juvenile used any unusual or extra force or threats to accomplish the act of penetration.

The trial court determined that the juvenile was delinquent for committing a sexual assault. The Appellate Division reversed the disposition of delinquency, concluding that non-consensual penetration does not constitute sexual assault unless it is accompanied by some level of force more than that necessary to accomplish the penetration. We granted the State's petition for certification.

I.

The issues in this case are perplexing and controversial. We must explain the role of force in the contemporary crime of sexual assault and then define its essential features. We then must consider what evidence is probative to establish the commission of a sexual assault. The factual circumstances of this case expose the complexity and sensitivity of those issues and underscore the analytic difficulty of those seemingly-straight-forward legal questions.

On Monday, May 21, 1990, fifteen-year-old C.G. was living with her mother, her three siblings, and several other people, including M.T.S. and his girlfriend. A total of ten people resided in the three-bedroom townhome at the time of the incident. M.T.S., then age seventeen, was temporarily residing at the home with the permission of the C.G.'s mother; he slept downstairs on a couch. C.G. had her own room on the second floor. At approximately 11:30 p.m. on May 21, C.G. went upstairs to sleep after having watched television with her mother, M.T.S., and his girlfriend. When C.G. went to bed, she was wearing underpants, a bra, shorts, and a shirt. At trial, C.G. and M.T.S. offered very different accounts concerning the nature of their relationship and the events that occurred after C.G. had gone upstairs. The trial court did not credit fully either teenager's testimony.

C.G. stated that earlier in the day, M.T.S. had told her three or four times that he "was going to make a surprise visit up in [her] bedroom." She said that she had not taken M.T.S. seriously and considered his comments a joke because he frequently teased her. She testified that M.T.S. had attempted to kiss her on numerous other occasions and at least once had attempted to put his hands inside of her pants, but that she had rejected all of his previous advances.

C.G. testified that on May 22, at approximately 1:30 a.m., she awoke to use the bathroom. As she was getting out of bed, she said, she saw M.T.S., fully clothed, standing in her doorway. According to C.G., M.T.S. then said that "he was going to tease [her] a little bit." C.G. testified that she "didn't think anything of it"; she walked past him, used the bathroom, and then returned to bed, falling into a "heavy" sleep within fifteen minutes. The next event C.G. claimed to recall of that morning was waking up with M.T.S. on top of her, her underpants and shorts removed. She said "his penis was into [her] vagina." As soon as C.G. realized what had happened, she said, she immediately slapped M.T.S. once in the face, then "told him to get off [her], and get out." She did not scream or cry out. She testified that M.T.S. complied in less than one minute after being struck; according to C.G., "he jumped right off of [her]." She said she did not know how long M.T.S. had been inside of her before she awoke.

C.G. said that after M.T.S. left the room, she "fell asleep crying" because "[she] couldn't believe that he did what he did to [her]." She explained that she did not immediately tell her mother or anyone else in the house of the events of that morning because she was "scared and in shock." According to C.G., M.T.S. engaged in intercourse with her "without [her] wanting it or telling him to come up [to her bedroom]." By her own account, C.G. was not otherwise harmed by M.T.S.

At about 7:00 a.m., C.G. went downstairs and told her mother about her encounter with M.T.S. earlier in the morning and said that they would have to "get [him] out of the house." While M.T.S. was out on an errand, C.G.'s mother gathered his clothes and put them outside in his car; when he returned, he was told that "[he] better not even get near the house." C.G. and her mother then filed a complaint with the police.

According to M.T.S., he and C.G. had been good friends for a long time, and their relationship "kept leading on to more and more." He had been living at C.G.'s home for about five days before the incident occurred; he testified that during the three days preceding the incident they had been "kissing and necking" and had discussed having sexual intercourse. The first time M.T.S. kissed C.G., he said, she "didn't want him to, but she did after that." He said C.G. repeatedly had encouraged him to "make a surprise visit up in her room."

M.T.S. testified that at exactly 1:15 a.m. on May 22, he entered C.G.'s bedroom as she was walking to the bathroom. He said C.G. soon returned from the bathroom, and the two began "kissing and all," eventually moving to the bed. Once they were in bed, he said, they undressed each other and continued to kiss and touch for about five minutes. M.T.S. and C.G. proceeded to engage in sexual intercourse. According to M.T.S., who was on top of C.G., he "stuck it in" and "did it [thrust] three times, and then the fourth time [he] stuck it in, that's when [she] pulled [him] off of her." M.T.S. said that as C.G. pushed him off, she said "stop, get off," and he "hopped off right away."

According to M.T.S., after about one minute, he asked C.G. what was wrong; she replied with a backhand to his face. He recalled asking C.G. what was wrong a second time, and her replying, "how can you take advantage of me or something like that." M.T.S. said that he proceeded to get dressed and told C.G. to calm down, but that she then told him to get away from her and began to cry. Before leaving the room, he told C.G., "I'm leaving . . . I'm going with my real girlfriend, don't talk to me . . . I don't want nothing to do with you or anything, stay out of my life . . . don't tell anybody about this . . . it would just screw everything up." He then walked downstairs and went to sleep.

On May 23, 1990, M.T.S. was charged with conduct that if engaged in by an adult would constitute second-degree sexual assault of the victim, contrary to N.J.S.A. 2C:14-2c (1).

Following a two-day trial on the sexual assault charge, M.T.S. was adjudicated delinquent. After reviewing the testimony, the court concluded that the victim had consented to a session of kissing and heavy petting with M.T.S. The trial court did not find that C.G. had been sleeping at the time of penetration, but nevertheless found that she had not consented to the actual sexual act. Accordingly, the court concluded that the State had proven second-degree sexual assault beyond a reasonable doubt. On appeal, following the imposition of suspended sentences on the sexual assault and the other remaining charges, the Appellate Division determined that the absence of force beyond that involved in the act of sexual penetration precluded a finding of second-degree sexual assault. It therefore reversed the juvenile's adjudication of delinquency for that offense.

II.

The New Jersey Code of Criminal Justice defines "sexual assault" as the commission "of sexual penetration" "with another person" with the use of "physical force or coercion."[1] An unconstrained reading of the statutory language indicates that both the act of "sexual penetration" and the use of "physical force or coercion" are separate and distinct elements of the offense. *See Medical Soc. v. Department of Law & Pub. Safety*, 120 N.J. 18, 26, 575 A.2d 1348 (1990) (declaring that no part of a statute should be considered meaningless or superfluous). Neither the definitions section of N.J.S.A. 2C:14-1 to -8, nor the remainder of the Code of Criminal Justice provides assistance in interpreting the words "physical force." The initial inquiry is, therefore, whether the statutory words are unambiguous on their face and can be understood and applied in accordance with their plain meaning. The answer to that inquiry is revealed by the conflicting decisions of the lower courts and the arguments of the opposing parties. The trial court held that "physical force" had been established by the sexual penetration of the victim without her consent. The Appellate Division believed that the statute requires some amount of force more than that necessary to accomplish penetration.

The parties offer two alternative understandings of the concept of "physical force" as it is used in the statute. The State would read "physical force" to entail any

---

1. The sexual assault statute, N.J.S.A.: 2C:14-2c (1), reads as follows:
c. An actor is guilty of sexual assault if he commits an act of sexual penetration with another person under any one of the following circumstances:
(1) The actor *uses physical force or coercion*, but the victim does not sustain severe personal injury;
(2) The victim is one whom the actor knew or should have known was physically helpless, mentally defective or mentally incapacitated;
(3) The victim is on probation or parole, or is detained in a hospital, prison or other institution and the actor has supervisory or disciplinary power over the victim by virtue of the actor's legal, professional or occupational status;
(4) The victim is at least 16 but less than 18 years old and:
(a) The actor is related to the victim by blood or affinity to the third degree; or
(b) The actor has supervisory or disciplinary power over the victim; or
(c) The actor is a foster parent, a guardian, or stands in loco parentis within the household;
(5) The victim is at least 13 but less than 16 years old and the actor is at least 4 years older than the victim.
Sexual assault is a crime of the second degree.

amount of sexual touching brought about involuntarily. A showing of sexual penetration coupled with a lack of consent would satisfy the elements of the statute. The Public Defender urges an interpretation of "physical force" to mean force "used to overcome lack of consent." That definition equates force with violence and leads to the conclusion that sexual assault requires the application of some amount of force in addition to the act of penetration.

Current judicial practice suggests an understanding of "physical force" to mean "any degree of physical power or strength used against the victim, even though it entails no injury and leaves no mark." MODEL JURY CHARGES, CRIMINAL 3 (revised Mar. 27, 1989). Resort to common experience or understanding does not yield a conclusive meaning. The dictionary provides several definitions of "force," among which are the following: (1) "power, violence, compulsion, or constraint exerted upon or against a person or thing," (2) "a general term for exercise of strength or power, esp. physical, to overcome resistance," or (3) "strength or power of any degree that is exercised without justification or contrary to law upon a person or thing." WEBSTER'S THIRD NEW INTERNATIONAL DICTIONARY 887 (1961).

Thus, as evidenced by the disagreements among the lower courts and the parties, and the variety of possible usages, the statutory words "physical force" do not evoke a single meaning that is obvious and plain. Hence, we must pursue avenues of construction in order to ascertain the meaning of that statutory language. Those avenues are well charted. When a statute is open to conflicting interpretations, the court seeks the underlying intent of the legislature, relying on legislative history and the contemporary context of the statute. With respect to a law, like the sexual assault statute, that "alters or amends the previous law or creates or abolishes types of actions, it is important, in discovering the legislative intent, to ascertain the old law, the mischief and the proposed remedy." We also remain mindful of the basic tenet of statutory construction that penal statutes are to be strictly construed in favor of the accused. Nevertheless, the construction must conform to the intent of the Legislature.

The provisions proscribing sexual offenses found in the Code of Criminal Justice, became effective in 1979, and were written against almost two hundred years of rape law in New Jersey. The origin of the rape statute that the current statutory offense of sexual assault replaced can be traced to the English common law. Under the common law, rape was defined as "carnal knowledge of a woman against her will." American jurisdictions generally adopted the English view, but over time states added the requirement that the carnal knowledge have been forcible, apparently in order to prove that the act was against the victim's will. As of 1796, New Jersey statutory law defined rape as "carnal knowledge of a woman, forcibly and against her will." Those three elements of rape—carnal knowledge, forcibly, and against her will—remained the essential elements of the crime until 1979.

Under traditional rape law, in order to prove that a rape had occurred, the state had to show both that force had been used and that the penetration had been against the woman's will. Force was identified and determined not as an independent factor but in relation to the response of the victim, which in turn implicated the victim's own state of mind. "Thus, the perpetrator's use of force became criminal only if the victim's state of mind met the statutory requirement. The perpetrator could use all the force imaginable and no crime would be committed if the state could not prove additionally that the victim did not consent." Although the terms "non-consent" and "against her will" were often treated as equivalent, under the traditional definition of rape, both formulations squarely placed on the victim the burden of proof and of action. Effectively, a woman who was above the age of consent had actively and affirmatively to withdraw that consent for the intercourse to be against her will. As a Delaware court stated, "If sexual intercourse is obtained by milder means, or with the consent or silent submission of the female, it cannot constitute the crime of rape."

The presence or absence of consent often turned on credibility. To demonstrate that the victim had not consented to the intercourse, and also that sufficient force had been used to accomplish the rape, the state had to prove that the victim had resisted. According to the oft-quoted Lord Hale, to be deemed a credible witness, a woman had to be of good fame, disclose the injury immediately, suffer signs of injury, and cry out for help. Courts and commentators historically distrusted the testimony of victims, "assuming that women lie about their lack of consent for various reasons: to blackmail men, to explain the discovery of a consensual affair, or because of psychological illness." Evidence of resistance was viewed as a solution to the credibility problem; it was the "outward manifestation of nonconsent, [a] device for determining whether a woman actually gave consent."

The resistance requirement had a profound effect on the kind of conduct that could be deemed criminal and on the type of evidence needed to establish the crime. *See, e.g., State v. Brown*, 127 Wis. 193, 106 N.W. 536 (1906) (overturning forcible rape conviction based on inadequate resistance by the victim); *People v. Dohring*, 59 N.Y. 374 (1874).Courts assumed that any woman who was forced to have intercourse against her will necessarily would resist to the extent of her ability. *People v. Barnes*, 42 Cal.3d 284, 228 Cal. Rptr. 228, 721 P.2d 110, 117 (1986) (observing that "[h]istorically, it was considered inconceivable that a woman who truly did not consent to sexual intercourse would not meet force with force"). In many jurisdictions the requirement was that the woman have resisted to the utmost. "Rape is not committed unless the woman oppose the man to the utmost limit of her power." *People v. Carey*, 223 N.Y. 519, 119 N.E. 83 (N.Y. 1918). "[A] mere tactical surrender in the face of an assumed superior physical force is not enough. Where the penalty for the defendant may be supreme, so must resistance be unto the uttermost." *Moss v. State*, 208 Miss. 531, 45 So. 2d 125, 126 (1950). Other states followed a "reasonableness" standard, while some required only sufficient resistance to make non-consent reasonably manifest.

At least by the 1960s courts in New Jersey followed a standard for establishing resistance that was somewhat less drastic than the traditional rule. In *State v. Harris*, 70 N.J. Super. 9, 174 A.2d 645 (1961), the Appellate Division recognized that the "to the uttermost" test was obsolete. "The fact that a victim finally submits does not necessarily imply that she consented. Submission to a compelling force, or as a result of being put in fear, is not consent." Nonetheless, the "resistance" requirement remained an essential feature of New Jersey rape law. Thus, in 1965 the Appellate Division stated: "[W]e have rejected the former test that a woman must resist 'to the uttermost.' We only require that she resist as much as she possibly can under the circumstances."

Under the prereform law, the resistance offered had to be "in good faith and without pretense, with an active determination to prevent the violation of her person, and must not be merely passive and perfunctory." That the law put the rape victim on trial was clear.

The resistance requirement had another untoward influence on traditional rape law. Resistance was necessary not only to prove non-consent but also to demonstrate that the force used by the defendant had been sufficient to overcome the victim's will. The amount of force used by the defendant was assessed in relation to the resistance of the victim. In New Jersey the amount of force necessary to establish rape was characterized as "'the degree of force sufficient to overcome any resistance that had been put up by the female.'" Resistance, often demonstrated by torn clothing and blood, was a sign that the defendant had used significant force to accomplish the sexual intercourse. Thus, if the defendant forced himself on a woman, it was her responsibility to fight back, because force was measured in relation to the resistance she put forward. Only if she resisted, causing him to use more force than was necessary to achieve penetration, would his conduct be criminalized. Indeed, the significance of resistance as the proxy for force is illustrated by cases in which victims were unable to resist; in such cases the force incident to penetration was deemed sufficient to establish the "force" element of the offense.

The importance of resistance as an evidentiary requirement set the law of rape apart from other common-law crimes, particularly in the eyes of those who advocated reform of rape law in the 1970s.

To refute the misguided belief that rape was not real unless the victim fought back, reformers emphasized empirical research indicating that women who resisted forcible intercourse often suffered far more serious injury as a result. That research discredited the assumption that resistance to the utmost or to the best of a woman's ability was the most reasonable or rational response to a rape.

The research also helped demonstrate the underlying point of the reformers that the crime of rape rested not in the overcoming of a woman's will or the insult to her chastity but in the forcible attack itself—the assault on her person. Reformers criticized the conception of rape as a distinctly sexual crime rather than a crime of violence. They emphasized that rape had its legal origins in laws designed to protect the property rights of men to their wives and daughters. Although the crime had evolved into an offense against women, reformers argued that vestiges of the old law remained, particularly in the understanding of rape as a crime against the purity or chastity of a woman. The burden of protecting that chastity fell on the woman, with the state offering its protection only after the woman demonstrated that she had resisted sufficiently.

That rape under the traditional approach constituted a sexual rather than an assaultive crime is underscored by the spousal exemption. According to the traditional reasoning, a man could not rape his wife because consent to sexual intercourse was implied by the marriage contract. Therefore, sexual intercourse between spouses was lawful regardless of the force or violence used to accomplish it.

[W]ith regard to force, rape law reform sought to give independent significance to the forceful or assaultive conduct of the defendant and to avoid a definition of force that depended on the reaction of the victim. Traditional interpretations of force were strongly criticized for failing to acknowledge that force may be understood simply as the invasion of "bodily integrity." In urging that the "resistance" requirement be abandoned, reformers sought to break the connection between force and resistance.

III

The history of traditional rape law sheds clearer light on the factors that became most influential in the enactment of current law dealing with sexual offenses. The circumstances surrounding the actual passage of the current law reveal that it was conceived as a reform measure reconstituting the law to address a widely-sensed evil and to effectuate an important public policy. Those circumstances are highly relevant in understanding legislative intent and in determining the objectives of the current law.

In October 1971, the New Jersey Criminal Law Revision Commission promulgated a Final Report and Commentary on its proposed New Jersey Penal Code. The proposed Code substantially followed the American Law Institute's Model Penal Code (MPC) with respect to sexual offenses. See M.P.C. §§ 213.1 to 213.4. The proposed provisions did not present a break from traditional rape law. They would have established two principal sexual offenses: aggravated rape, a first-degree or second-degree crime involving egregious circumstances; and rape, a crime of the third-degree. 1971 Penal Code, § 2C:14-1(a)(1). Rape was defined as sexual intercourse with a female to which she was compelled to submit by any threat that would prevent resistance by a woman of ordinary resolution. Id. at § 14-1(b)(1). The comments to the MPC, on which the proposed Code was based, state that "[c]ompulsion plainly implies non-consent," and that the words "compels to submit" require more than "a token initial resistance." A.L.I., MPC, § 213.1, comments at 306 (revised commentary 1980).

The Legislature did not endorse the Model Penal Code approach to rape. Rather, it passed a fundamentally different proposal in 1978 when it adopted the Code of Criminal Justice. The new statutory provisions covering rape were formulated by a coalition of feminist groups assisted by the National Organization of Women (NOW) National Task Force on Rape. Both houses of the Legislature adopted the NOW bill, as it was called, without major changes and Governor Byrne signed it

into law on August 10, 1978. The NOW bill had been modeled after the 1976 Philadelphia Center for Rape Concern Model Sex Offense Statute. The stated intent of
the drafters of the Philadelphia Center's Model Statute had been to remove all features found to be contrary to the interests of rape victims. According to its proponents the statute would "'normalize the law. We are no longer saying rape victims
are likely to lie. What we are saying is that rape is just like other violent crimes.'"

Since the 1978 reform, the Code has referred to the crime that was once known as
"rape" as "sexual assault." The crime now requires "penetration," not "sexual intercourse." It requires "force" or "coercion," not "submission" or "resistance." It makes
no reference to the victim's state of mind or attitude, or conduct in response to the
assault. It eliminates the spousal exception based on implied consent. It emphasizes
the assaultive character of the offense by defining sexual penetration to encompass
a wide range of sexual contacts, going well beyond traditional "carnal knowledge."[2]
Consistent with the assaultive character, as opposed to the traditional sexual character, of the offense, the statute also renders the crime gender-neutral: both males
and females can be actors or victims. The reform replaced the concept of carnal
abuse, which was limited to vaginal intercourse, with specific kinds of sexual acts
contained in a broad definition of penetration: The reform statute defines sexual
assault as penetration accomplished by the use of "physical force" or "coercion,"
but it does not define either "physical force" or "coercion" or enumerate examples
of evidence that would establish those elements. Some reformers had argued that
defining "physical force" too specifically in the sexual offense statute might have the
effect of limiting force to the enumerated examples. The task of defining "physical
force" therefore was left to the courts.

The Legislature's concept of sexual assault and the role of force was significantly
colored by its understanding of the law of assault and battery. As a general matter,
criminal battery is defined as "the unlawful application of force to the person of
another." The application of force is criminal when it results in either (a) a physical
injury or (b) an offensive touching. Any "unauthorized touching of another [is] a
battery." Thus, by eliminating all references to the victim's state of mind and conduct, and by broadening the definition of penetration to cover not only sexual intercourse between a man and a woman but a range of acts that invade another's body
or compel intimate contact, the Legislature emphasized the affinity between sexual
assault and other forms of assault and battery.

The intent of the Legislature to redefine rape consistent with the law of assault
and battery is further evidenced by the legislative treatment of other sexual crimes
less serious than and derivative of traditional rape. The Code redefined the offense
of criminal sexual contact to emphasize the involuntary and personally-offensive
nature of the touching. Sexual contact is criminal under the same circumstances

2. Sexual penetration means vaginal intercourse, cunnilingus, fellatio or anal intercourse
between persons or insertion of the hand, finger or object into the anus or vagina either by the
actor or upon the actor's instruction. [N.J.S.A. 2C:14-1.]

that render an act of sexual penetration a sexual assault, namely, when "physical force" or "coercion" demonstrates that it is unauthorized and offensive. Thus, just as any unauthorized touching is a crime under traditional laws of assault and battery, so is any unauthorized sexual contact a crime under the reformed law of criminal sexual contact, and so is any unauthorized sexual penetration a crime under the reformed law of sexual assault.

The understanding of sexual assault as a criminal battery, albeit one with especially serious consequences, follows necessarily from the Legislature's decision to eliminate nonconsent and resistance from the substantive definition of the offense. Under the new law, the victim no longer is required to resist and therefore need not have said or done anything in order for the sexual penetration to be unlawful. The alleged victim is not put on trial, and his or her responsive or defensive behavior is rendered immaterial. We are thus satisfied that an interpretation of the statutory crime of sexual assault to require physical force in addition to that entailed in an act of involuntary or unwanted sexual penetration would be fundamentally inconsistent with the legislative purpose to eliminate any consideration of whether the victim resisted or expressed non-consent.

We note that the contrary interpretation of force—that the element of force need be extrinsic to the sexual act—would not only reintroduce a resistance requirement into the sexual assault law, but also would immunize many acts of criminal sexual contact short of penetration. The characteristics that make a sexual contact unlawful are the same as those that make a sexual penetration unlawful. An actor is guilty of criminal sexual contact if he or she commits an act of sexual contact with another using "physical force" or "coercion." That the Legislature would have wanted to decriminalize unauthorized sexual intrusions on the bodily integrity of a victim by requiring a showing of force in addition to that entailed in the sexual contact itself is hardly possible.

Because the statute eschews any reference to the victim's will or resistance, the standard defining the role of force in sexual penetration must prevent the possibility that the establishment of the crime will turn on the alleged victim's state of mind or responsive behavior. We conclude, therefore, that any act of sexual penetration engaged in by the defendant without the affirmative and freely-given permission of the victim to the specific act of penetration constitutes the offense of sexual assault. Therefore, physical force in excess of that inherent in the act of sexual penetration is not required for such penetration to be unlawful. The definition of "physical force" is satisfied under N.J.S.A. 2C:14-2c(1) if the defendant applies any amount of force against another person in the absence of what a reasonable person would believe to be affirmative and freely-given permission to the act of sexual penetration.

Under the reformed statute, permission to engage in sexual penetration must be affirmative and it must be given freely, but that permission may be inferred either from acts or statements reasonably viewed in light of the surrounding circumstances. Persons need not, of course, expressly announce their consent to engage in intercourse for there to be affirmative permission. Permission to engage in an act of sexual penetration can be and indeed often is indicated through physical actions rather than words. Permission is demonstrated when the evidence, in whatever form, is sufficient to demonstrate that a reasonable person would have believed that the alleged victim had affirmatively and freely given authorization to the act.

Our understanding of the meaning and application of "physical force" under the sexual assault statute indicates that the term's inclusion was neither inadvertent nor redundant. The term "physical force," like its companion term "coercion," acts to qualify the nature and character of the "sexual penetration." Sexual penetration accomplished through the use of force is unauthorized sexual penetration. That functional understanding of "physical force" encompasses the notion of "unpermitted touching" derived from the Legislature's decision to redefine rape as a sexual assault. As already noted, under assault and battery doctrine, any amount of force that results in either physical injury or offensive touching is sufficient to establish a battery. Hence, as a description of the method of achieving "sexual penetration," the term "physical force" serves to define and explain the acts that are offensive, unauthorized, and unlawful.

That understanding of the crime of sexual assault fully comports with the public policy sought to be effectuated by the Legislature. In redefining rape law as sexual assault, the Legislature adopted the concept of sexual assault as a crime against the bodily integrity of the victim. Although it is possible to imagine a set of rules in which persons must demonstrate affirmatively that sexual contact is unwanted or not permitted, such a regime would be inconsistent with modern principles of personal autonomy. The Legislature recast the law of rape as sexual assault to bring that area of law in line with the expectation of privacy and bodily control that long has characterized most of our private and public law. In interpreting "physical force" to include any touching that occurs without permission we seek to respect that goal.

Today the law of sexual assault is indispensable to the system of legal rules that assures each of us the right to decide who may touch our bodies, when, and under what circumstances. The decision to engage in sexual relations with another person is one of the most private and intimate decisions a person can make. Each person has the right not only to decide whether to engage in sexual contact with another, but also to control the circumstances and character of that contact. No one, neither a spouse, nor a friend, nor an acquaintance, nor a stranger, has the right or the privilege to force sexual contact. *See Definition of Forcible Rape, supra,* 61 Va. L. Rev. at 1529 (arguing that "forcible rape is viewed as a heinous crime primarily because it is a violent assault on a person's bodily security, particularly degrading because that person is forced to submit to an act of the most intimate nature").

We emphasize as well that what is now referred to as "acquaintance rape" is not a new phenomenon. Nor was it a "futuristic" concept in 1978 when the sexual assault law was enacted. Current concern over the prevalence of forced sexual intercourse between persons who know one another reflects both greater awareness of the extent of such behavior and a growing appreciation of its gravity. Notwithstanding the stereotype of rape as a violent attack by a stranger, the vast majority of sexual assaults are perpetrated by someone known to the victim. One respected study indicates that more than half of all rapes are committed by male relatives, current or former husbands, boyfriends or lovers. Similarly, contrary to common myths, perpetrators generally do not use guns or knives and victims generally do not suffer external bruises or cuts. Although this more realistic and accurate view of rape only recently has achieved widespread public circulation, it was a central concern of the proponents of reform in the 1970s.

The insight into rape as an assaultive crime is consistent with our evolving understanding of the wrong inherent in forced sexual intimacy. It is one that was appreciated by the Legislature when it reformed the rape laws, reflecting an emerging awareness that the definition of rape should correspond fully with the experiences and perspectives of rape victims. Although reformers focused primarily on the problems associated with convicting defendants accused of violent rape, the recognition that forced sexual intercourse often takes place between persons who know each other and often involves little or no violence comports with the understanding of the sexual assault law that was embraced by the Legislature. Any other interpretation of the law, particularly one that defined force in relation to the resistance or protest of the victim, would directly undermine the goals sought to be achieved by its reform.

IV

In a case such as this one, in which the State does not allege violence or force extrinsic to the act of penetration, the factfinder must decide whether the defendant's act of penetration was undertaken in circumstances that led the defendant reasonably to believe that the alleged victim had freely given affirmative permission to the specific act of sexual penetration. Such permission can be indicated either through words or through actions that, when viewed in the light of all the surrounding circumstances, would demonstrate to a reasonable person affirmative and freely-given authorization for the specific act of sexual penetration.

In applying that standard to the facts in these cases, the focus of attention must be on the nature of the defendant's actions. The role of the factfinder is not to decide whether reasonable people may engage in acts of penetration without the permission of others. The Legislature answered that question when it enacted the reformed sexual assault statute: reasonable people do not engage in acts of penetration without permission, and it is unlawful to do so. The role of the factfinder is to decide not whether engaging in an act of penetration without permission of another person is reasonable, but only whether the defendant's belief that the alleged victim had freely given affirmative permission was reasonable.

In these cases neither the alleged victim's subjective state of mind nor the reasonableness of the alleged victim's actions can be deemed relevant to the offense. The alleged victim may be questioned about what he or she did or said only to determine whether the defendant was reasonable in believing that affirmative permission had been freely given. To repeat, the law places no burden on the alleged victim to have expressed non-consent or to have denied permission, and no inquiry is made into what he or she thought or desired or why he or she did not resist or protest.

In short, in order to convict under the sexual assault statute in cases such as these, the State must prove beyond a reasonable doubt that there was sexual penetration and that it was accomplished without the affirmative and freely-given permission of the alleged victim. As we have indicated, such proof can be based on evidence of conduct or words in light of surrounding circumstances and must demonstrate beyond a reasonable doubt that a reasonable person would not have believed that there was affirmative and freely-given permission. If there is evidence to suggest that the defendant reasonably believed that such permission had been given, the State must demonstrate either that defendant did not actually believe that affirmative permission had been freely-given or that such a belief was unreasonable under all of the circumstances. Thus, the State bears the burden of proof throughout the case.

In the context of a sexual penetration not involving unusual or added "physical force," the inclusion of "permission" as an aspect of "physical force" effectively subsumes and obviates any defense based on consent. *See* N.J.S.A. 2C:2-10c(3). The definition of "permission" serves to define the "consent" that otherwise might allow a defendant to avoid criminal liability. Because "physical force" as an element of sexual assault in this context requires the absence of affirmative and freely-given permission, the "consent" necessary to negate such "physical force" under a defense based on consent would require the *presence* of such affirmative and freely-given permission. Any lesser form of consent would render the sexual penetration unlawful and cannot constitute a defense.

In this case, the Appellate Division concluded that non-consensual penetration accomplished with no additional physical force or coercion is not criminalized under the sexual assault statute. It acknowledged that its conclusion was "anomalous" because it recognized that "a woman has every right to end [physically intimate] activity without sexual penetration." Thus, it added to its holding that "[e]ven the force of penetration might . . . be sufficient if it is shown to be employed to overcome the victim's unequivocal expressed desire to limit the encounter."

The Appellate Division was correct in recognizing that a woman's right to end intimate activity without penetration is a protectable right the violation of which can be a criminal offense. However, it misperceived the purpose of the statute in believing that the only way that right can be protected is by the woman's unequivocally-expressed desire to end the activity. The effect of that requirement would be to import into the sexual assault statute the notion that an assault occurs only if the victim's will is overcome, and thus to reintroduce the requirement of non-consent and victim-resistance as a constituent material element of the crime. Under the reformed statute, a person's failure to protest or resist cannot be considered or used as justification for bodily invasion.

We acknowledge that cases such as this are inherently fact sensitive and depend on the reasoned judgment and common sense of judges and juries. The trial court concluded that the victim had not expressed consent to the act of intercourse, either through her words or actions. We conclude that the record provides reasonable support for the trial court's disposition.

Accordingly, we reverse the judgment of the Appellate Division and reinstate the disposition of juvenile delinquency for the commission of second-degree sexual assault.

Questions and Notes

1. If the facts were as CG described them, would MTS have been guilty of rape in a traditional jurisdiction? Why? Why not?

2. One of the criticisms of traditional rape law is that "no" should mean "no." *MTS* seems to go a step beyond that and hold that the absence of "yes" should mean "no." Is that a positive change in the law? Explain.

3. Should it have been relevant (determinative) that (even according to CG's testimony), MTS desisted as soon as he was asked to do so?

4. The court holds that the only force required to satisfy the "force" element of the crime is the amount of force necessary to establish penetration. Is that a sound reading of the statute? Explain. Is it sound policy? Explain.

5. A question suggested but not resolved in *M.T.S.* is the liability of one who initially engages in consensual sexual intercourse but persists in the intercourse after consent is withdrawn. That question was explored in the *Bunyard* case.

State v. Bunyard

133 P.3d 14 (Kan. 2006)

The opinion of the court was delivered by Davis, J.:

The defendant was 21 years old when he met E.N. at a pool party at the home of a mutual friend. E.N., who was 17 years old, flirted with the defendant. She thought the defendant was "cool" so she invited him to a party at her friend's house the following night.

The defendant and friends attended the party the next night. After talking with E.N. for awhile, the defendant invited her to watch a movie in his car with another one of his friends. The defendant drove a Chrysler Sebring two-door convertible with a DVD player built in the dash. The defendant put the car's convertible top up before they began watching the movie.

After the defendant's friend left the car, the defendant and E.N. began kissing. E.N. did not object when the defendant removed her clothing. Likewise, she did not object when the defendant removed his clothing and placed a condom on his penis. However, after the defendant laid E.N. back in the seat and penetrated her vagina with his penis, E.N. said, "I don't want to do this." The defendant did not stop, replying, "Just a little bit longer." E.N. again stated that she did not "want to do this," but the defendant did not stop. E.N. testified that she unsuccessfully tried to sit up and roll over on her stomach to get away from the defendant. After 5 or 10 minutes had passed, E.N. began to cry, and the defendant stopped having sexual intercourse with her. The defendant told her she had given him "blue balls," and E.N. declined his request for her to perform oral sex.

The defendant testified that E.N. was on top of him during consensual intercourse and they were talking. E.N. asked him if he wanted a relationship and if he planned on calling her the next day. When the defendant said he was not interested in a relationship, E.N. became upset, got off of him, and told him about how she had been hurt by other guys in the past. E.N. wanted to continue kissing and wanted him to stay in the car and hold her, but the defendant did not stay in the car and told her to get dressed.

E.N. went back into the house visibly upset and told K.B. that she had been taken advantage of, that the defendant had gotten inside of her, and that she had said "no" more than once. M.B. also spoke with E.N., who was crying. M.B. testified that E.N. said, "I was raped. We had sex. I said no." E.N. did not want to report the incident to the police at that time because she did not want her parents to find out that she had been drinking.

Four days later, E.N. reported the incident to the police, and she was examined at the local hospital. The sexual assault examiner detected a cluster of abrasions consistent with blunt force trauma in E.N.'s vagina. The examiner testified that the location of the abrasions was consistent with mounting injuries. Although consensual sex could not be ruled out, the examiner testified that mounting injuries are more commonly found after nonconsensual sexual intercourse.

The defendant appealed his conviction for one count of rape to the Court of Appeals. In a divided opinion, the majority affirmed the defendant's conviction.

Prosecutorial Misconduct

The defendant complains that the prosecutor misstated the law when she advised the jury that the force of the penis entering the woman's vagina was sufficient to constitute rape.

The Court of Appeals found that the prosecutor's remark ("The force of his penis in her vagina is enough under the law of the State of Kansas.") was an incorrect statement of the law in Kansas, reasoning: "K.S.A.2002 Supp. 21-3502(a)(1)(A) clearly contemplates that in addition to sexual intercourse (the penetration portion of the equation), the victim must be overcome by force or fear. It is inaccurate to say that the crime of rape is completed with penetration."

We agree with the panel's conclusion that the prosecutor misstated the law. Relevant to this case, rape is "sexual intercourse with a person who does not consent to the sexual intercourse" "[w]hen the victim is overcome by force or fear." K.S.A.2004 Supp. 21-3502(a)(1)(A). The prosecutor misstated the law during closing argument by equating the "overcome by force or fear" element of rape with the act of sexual intercourse/penetration. Misstating the law is not within the wide latitude given to prosecutors in closing arguments. We do not agree, however, that this misconduct constituted harmless error under the second prong of the prosecutorial misconduct test.

Consent Withdrawn After Penetration

The defendant argues that the Kansas rape statute does not include circumstances where consent is revoked after intercourse has begun. The defendant interprets the rape statute to apply only to the initial entry into the vagina and argues that if the woman consents to the initial entry, there can be no rape even if consent is withdrawn before the act of coitus is completed. According to the defendant, the sexual battery statutes, K.S.A. 21-3517 for sexual battery or K.S.A. 21-3518 for aggravated sexual battery, or another criminal statute should apply if intercourse is continued after the woman revokes her consent, but the rape statute is not violated.

Penal statutes are to be construed strictly in favor of the accused. Ordinary words are given their ordinary meanings. A court should not read a statute to add something that is not found in the language of the statute or to delete something that is clearly found in the language of the statute.

K.S.A.2004 Supp. 21-3502(a)(1)(A) defines rape as "[s]exual intercourse with a person who does not consent to the sexual intercourse . . . [w]hen the victim is overcome by force or fear." "'Sexual intercourse' means any penetration of the female sex organ by a finger, the male sex organ or any object. Any penetration, however slight, is sufficient to constitute sexual intercourse."

The defendant focuses on the phrase "[a]ny penetration, however slight, is sufficient to constitute sexual intercourse," claiming that the statute limits penetration to the initial entry of the penis or other object into the woman's vagina. While we disagree with the defendant's narrow definition of penetration, he finds support in at least two states.

Maryland and North Carolina have concluded that consent may only be withdrawn prior to the initial penetration. If consent is withdrawn after the initial penetration, the defendant cannot be convicted of rape even if the sexual acts are continued against the victim's will by force or fear. *Battle v. State*, 287 Md. 675, 684, 414 A.2d 1266 (1980); *State v. Way*, 297 N.C. 293, 296–97, 254 S.E.2d 760 (1979) (limiting the withdrawal of consent to multiple acts of intercourse). Neither of these courts provide any analysis or citation to authority to support their conclusions. We decline to follow Maryland and North Carolina.

The defendant's narrow definition of penetration fails to comport with the ordinary meaning and understanding of sexual intercourse, which includes the entire sexual act. Under the defendant's definition of penetration, intercourse begins and ends at the same time. Rather than limiting the definition of intercourse, the phrase "[a]ny penetration, however slight, is sufficient to constitute sexual intercourse" establishes the threshold of evidence necessary to prove that intercourse has occurred. See *State v. Siering*, 35 Conn.App. 173, 182, 644 A.2d 958 (1994) (concluding that the phrase "[p]enetration, however slight, [is sufficient] to complete . . .

intercourse" in the statutes did not mean that intercourse was completed upon the initial penetration). When K.S.A.2004 Supp. 21-3502(a)(1)(A) is construed in accordance with the ordinary meanings of its words, the defendant's argument fails. K.S.A.2004 Supp. 21-3502(a)(1)(A) proscribes *all* nonconsensual sexual intercourse that is accomplished by force or fear, not just the initial penetration. Thus, a person may be convicted of rape if consent is withdrawn after the initial penetration but intercourse is continued by the use of force or fear.

Our conclusion that rape may occur after the initial penetration is aligned with the majority of states that have addressed the issue of post-penetration rape. See *McGill v. State*, 18 P.3d 77, 82–84 (Alaska App.2001) (affirming the trial court's instruction that consent could be withdrawn after the initial penetration); *In re John Z.*, 29 Cal.4th 756, 761–63, 128 Cal.Rptr.2d 783, 60 P.3d 183 (2003) (overruling prior California appellate court decision of *People v. Vela*, 172 Cal.App.3d 237, 218 Cal.Rptr. 161 [1985], which held that consent may only be withdrawn before the initial penetration); *Siering*, 35 Conn.App. at 180–83, 644 A.2d 958; *State v. Robinson*, 496 A.2d 1067, 1069–71 (Me.1985) (analyzing a definition for sexual intercourse like K.S.A. 21 3501[1]); *State v. Crims*, 540 N.W.2d 860, 865 (Minn.App.1995) (concluding that rape does not become a legal impossibility if the victim initially consents to penetration); *State v. Jones*, 521 N.W.2d 662, 672 (S.D.1994) (declining to adopt the *Vela* analysis); see also Ill. Comp. Stat. ch. 720 5/12-17(c) (2004 Supp.) ("A person who initially consents to sexual penetration or sexual conduct is not deemed to have consented to any sexual penetration or conduct that occurs after he or she withdraws consent during the course of that sexual penetration or sexual conduct.").

A Reasonable Time to Withdraw

The defendant contends that even if rape can occur after consensual penetration, the State failed to prove that he did not cease sexual intercourse within a reasonable time after E.N. withdrew her consent. Relying upon *In re John Z*, 29 Cal.4th 756, 128 Cal.Rptr.2d 783, 60 P.3d 183, the Court of Appeals found that "[w]hen consent is withdrawn, continuing sexual intercourse for 5 to 10 minutes is not reasonable and constitutes rape." 31 Kan.App.2d at 859, 75 P.3d 750. The majority opinion and the defendant's argument presume the issue we must decide-whether a defendant is entitled to a reasonable time to act on the victim's withdrawal of consent after consensual penetration.

In *In re John Z*, the victim told the defendant three times that she "needed to go home," but the intercourse continued for an estimated 4 to 5 minutes after the victim first told the defendant she needed to go home. 29 Cal.4th at 763, 128 Cal. Rptr.2d 783, 60 P.3d 183. The defendant argued that in cases involving an initial consent to intercourse, the male should be permitted a reasonable amount of time in which to withdraw once the female raises an objection to intercourse. The defendant reasoned:

> "'By essence of the act of sexual intercourse, a male's primal urge to reproduce is aroused. It is therefore unreasonable for a female and the law to

expect a male to cease having sexual intercourse immediately upon her withdrawal of consent. It is only natural, fair and just that the male be given a reasonable amount of time in which to quell his primal urge. . . .'"

In disagreeing with this argument, the California Supreme Court found that apart from the apparent lack of supporting authority for the "primal urge" theory, nothing in the language of its statute suggested that the defendant was entitled to persist in intercourse once his victim withdrew her consent. The court went on to find that even if it was to accept the "reasonable time" argument, the defendant was given ample time to withdraw but refused despite the victim's resistance and objections. The court declined to explore or recommend instructional language governing the point in time at which a defendant must cease intercourse once consent is withdrawn.

The dissenting opinion questioned the majority's reluctance to flesh out what constitutes a reasonable time: "The majority relies heavily on John Z.'s failure to desist immediately. But it does not tell us how soon would have been soon enough. Ten seconds? Thirty? A minute? Is persistence the same thing as force?"

The Court of Appeals' decision in this case seems to assume that a defendant should be given a reasonable amount of time to desist but concludes that continuation for an additional 5 to 10 minutes once consent is withdrawn was unreasonable. A recent law review article suggests the California Supreme Court's failure in *In re John Z* to suggest what constitutes a "reasonable time" leads to the disturbing result that men are expected to control their sexual urges eventually, although not immediately, upon withdrawal of consent. Palmer, *Antiquated Notions of Womanhood and the Myth of the Unstoppable Male: Why Post-penetration Rape Should Be a Crime in North Carolina*, 82 N.C. L.Rev. 1258, 1277 (2004).

The majority opinion in this case relied upon *In re John Z* in finding that the defendant did not stop within a reasonable time after the withdrawal of consent, but failed to discuss the California Supreme Court's clear rejection of John Z's argument that he was entitled to a reasonable time in which to act after consent was withdrawn. Although the majority did not explicitly state that a defendant is entitled to a reasonable period to continue intercourse, the idea was implied through its ruling. See note, *Acquaintance Rape and Degrees of Consent: "No" Means "No," But What Does "Yes" Mean?*, 117 Harv. L.Rev. 2341, 2359 (2004).

In the case of consensual intercourse and withdrawn consent, we agree that the defendant should be entitled to a reasonable time in which to act after consent is withdrawn and communicated to the defendant. However, we conclude that the jury should determine whether the time between withdrawal of consent and the interruption of intercourse was reasonable. This determination must be based upon the particular facts of each case, taking into account the manner in which consent was withdrawn. We believe this conclusion balances our rejection of the primal urge theory per se with our recognition of the unique facts and circumstances of each individual case.

While the facts of this case may establish that the defendant's continuation of intercourse by placing the victim in fear or by forcing the victim to continue for 5 to 10 minutes was well beyond a reasonable time, we reiterate that this is a jury determination and not for the trial court or the appellate courts to decide. We, thus, conclude that the trial court had a duty to instruct the jury that post-penetration rape can occur under Kansas law and that the defendant has a "reasonable time" to respond to the withdrawal of consent.

Although we have strongly advised trial judges to follow PIK instructions, we have also advised that when faced with a novel question such as the one in this case, a trial court "should not hesitate to make such modification or addition" as is not covered by the PIK instructions. The trial court in this case was presented with a question of first impression by the appellate courts of this state. Under these circumstances, the trial judge did the best he could by following the PIK instructions. However, the PIK committee had not considered the question raised in this case, and the response by the trial court, therefore, did not directly address the question raised by the jury.

We note that other courts have approved additional instructions such as the following in response to similar juror questions:

> "[I]f a couple consensually engages in sexual intercourse and one or the other changes his or her mind, and communicates the revocation or change of mind of the consent, and the other partner continues the sexual intercourse by compulsion of the party who changes his or her mind, then it would be rape. The critical element there is the continuation under compulsion." *Robinson*, 496 A.2d at 1069.

> "If there exists consensual sexual intercourse and the alleged victim changes her mind and communicates the revocation or change of mind of consent and the other person continues the sexual intercourse by compelling the victim through the use of force then it would be sexual assault in the first degree.

> "This is not just someone withdrawing their consent but it's a withdrawal of consent communicated to the other and then sexual intercourse continues by compelling the victim through the use of force. So it's not just a withdrawal of consent, it's also a withdrawal of consent communicated to the other person and then a compelling use of force to continue sexual intercourse." *Siering*, 35 Conn.App. at 179 n. 4, 644 A.2d 958.

The answer given by the trial court in this case was partially correct by referring to the elements of rape. However, the complete answer in addition to setting forth the elements of rape should have indicated to the jury that rape may occur even though consent was given to the initial penetration, but only if the consent is withdrawn and communicated to the defendant, the defendant does not respond within a reasonable time, and the sexual intercourse continues where the victim is overcome by force or fear. A reasonable time depends upon the circumstances of each case and is judged by an objective reasonable person standard to be applied by the trier of fact on a case-by-case basis.

Judgment of the Court of Appeals affirming the district court is reversed. The district court is reversed, and the case is remanded for a new trial.

LUCKERT, J., dissenting in part and concurring in part:

I dissent from the majority's conclusion that a defendant who is charged with rape under K.S.A.2004 Supp. 21-3502(a)(1)(A)"is entitled to a reasonable time in which to act after consent is withdrawn."

The majority does not explain how a jury should interpret "reasonable time" when a defendant is charged with rape under K.S.A.2004 Supp. 21-3502(a)(1)(A), which requires the State to prove the victim was overcome by force or fear. There are two possible readings of the majority holding. The presence of an ambiguity is, in itself, troubling. Additionally, both of the potential interpretations are problematic.

Under one interpretation, the majority, by allowing a reasonable time to act, may be implicitly recognizing that persistence is sufficient to satisfy the requirement of force after penetration has occurred. Yet, the majority would reverse the conviction in this case because the prosecutor stated, "The force of his penis in her vagina is enough under the law of the State of Kansas." Does this mean that the physical contact inherent in intercourse cannot satisfy the element of force when there is no consent before penetration but may be sufficient force to constitute rape when the consent is withdrawn post-penetration? The potential dichotomy is troubling.

The alternative reading is even more troubling. If the majority opinion is read to require more force than mere persistence, the effect of the ruling is to grant a defendant a safe harbor of "reasonable time" during which the defendant may exert this higher degree of force or strike fear in the victim.

I would hold that a defendant has committed rape if, after consent is withdrawn, the act of intercourse continues as the result of force or fear. This holding is consistent with the elements defined by K.S.A.2004 Supp. 21-3502(a)(1)(A). The court should not judicially add a defense allowing a reasonable time in which to commit rape.

Questions and Notes

1. The Kansas Supreme Court clearly rejects the New Jersey rule in regard to force. Which position is more logical? Which is better policy? Explain.

2. Do you agree that continuation of initially consensual intercourse should constitute rape when one of the parties changes her (his) mind after the initiation of intercourse? Why? Why not? Note: Maryland has changed its rule since *Bunyard* was decided, and now allows rape to be committed when initial consent has been withdrawn. *See State v. Baby*, 404 Md. 220 (Md. App. 2008).

3. Assuming the correctness of the rule, should the defendant be given a reasonable time to withdraw?

4. If a reasonable amount of time is to be given, should the Court have explained what it meant? "Primal urge to reproduce"? Hardly, given that the defendant was wearing a condom. Primal urge to ejaculate? Did the Court really mean to endorse that? If not, what did it mean? What's a jury to do?

5. In the next section, we look at sex obtained by undue influence (perhaps even extortion).

C. Undue Influence
State v. Thompson
792 P.2d 1103 (Mont. 1990)

The defendant, Gerald Roy Thompson, the principal and boys basketball coach at Hobson High School, was accused of two counts of sexual intercourse without consent, and one count of sexual assault. This appeal only concerns the two counts of sexual intercourse without consent. The information, filed with the District Court, alleged the defendant committed the crime of sexual intercourse without consent, and stated the following:

Count I

On or between September, 1986 and January, 1987, the defendant knowingly had sexual intercourse without consent with a person of the opposite sex; namely Jane Doe, by threatening Jane Doe that she would not graduate from high school and forced Jane Doe to engage in an act of oral sexual intercourse.

Count II

On or between February, 1987 and June, 1987, the defendant knowingly had sexual intercourse without consent with a person of the opposite sex; namely Jane Doe, by threatening Jane Doe that she would not graduate from high school and forced Jane Doe to engage in act of oral sexual intercourse."

The affidavits filed in support of this information contained facts and allegations supporting the two counts of sexual intercourse without consent. In essence, they alleged that the threats "caused Jane Doe great psychological pain and fear."

The State contended that fear of the power of Thompson and his authority to keep her from graduating forced Jane Doe into silence until after she graduated from high school in June of 1987. On November 25, 1988, Jane Doe filed a letter with the Hobson School Board describing the activities against her by Thompson. After investigations by both the school board and the Judith Basin County prosecutor's office, the prosecutor filed an information on May 25, 1989. The information charged Thompson with two counts of sexual intercourse without consent, both felonies in violation of sec. 45-5-503, MCA, and with one count of attempted sexual assault, a felony.

Defendant filed a number of motions, requesting, among other things, a motion to dismiss Counts I and II of the information for lack of probable cause in the supporting affidavit. The District Court granted Thompson's motion, due to the fact the State failed to meet the element of "without consent" under sec. 45-5-501, MCA.

We agree with the District Court that the facts in the information, in regards to Counts I and II, fail to state offenses. The allegations in the affidavit, however, do not indicate a probability that Thompson committed the crime of sexual intercourse without consent.

Thompson was charged with two counts of alleged sexual intercourse without consent under sec. 45-5-503, MCA. Section 45-5-503, MCA, states the following:

> "A person who knowingly has sexual intercourse without consent with a person of the opposite sex commits the offense of sexual intercourse without consent. . . ."

The phrase "without consent" the key element of the crime has a very specific definition in Montana's criminal code. This phrase is defined in sec. 45-5-501, MCA, which states in pertinent part:

> "As used in 45-5-503 and 45-5-505, the term 'without consent' means:

> "(i) the victim is compelled to submit by force or by threat of imminent death, bodily injury, or kidnapping to be inflicted on anyone; . . ."

Section 45-5-501, MCA, makes it clear that the element of "without consent" is satisfied if submission of the victim is obtained either by force or by threat of imminent death, bodily injury, or kidnapping. No other circumstances relating to force or threat eliminate consent under the statute.

Thompson challenged the probable cause affidavit in the District Court, contending it failed to state any fact or circumstance showing that Jane Doe's submission to an alleged act of sexual intercourse was obtained by force or by any of the threats listed in sec. 45-5-501, MCA. In contrast, the State argues that Thompson's actions constitute sexual intercourse through force or threats. The District Court, in its opinion and order, agreed with Thompson's contentions, and found that the facts in the affidavit supporting the information failed to show the element of "without consent." In reaching this conclusion, the District Court first considered whether or not there were facts or circumstances in the probable cause affidavit to indicate that submission to the alleged act of sexual intercourse without consent was obtained "by force." In order to determine whether Thompson forced Jane Doe to submit to the sexual act, the District Court had to define the phrase "by force" since there is no definition contained in the Montana Criminal Code.

The District Court in its order defined force as follows:

> "The word 'force' is used in its ordinary and normal connotation: physical compulsion, the use or immediate threat of bodily harm, injury."

Next, the District Court examined the information and probable cause affidavit to determine if there were any facts or circumstances constituting force. The District Court found that "force was not alleged in the information nor in the affidavit in support of it."

In contrast, the State argues the District Court's definition of force is too limited. The State, relying on *Raines v. State* (1989), 191 Ga. App. 743, 382 S.E.2d 738, 739, argues that intimidation and fear may constitute force. The State also contends that Thompson, in his position of authority as the principal, intimidated Jane Doe into the alleged acts. Furthermore, the State argues the fear and apprehension of Jane Doe show Thompson used force against her. We agree with the State that Thompson intimidated Jane Doe; however, we cannot stretch the definition of force to include intimidation, fear, or apprehension. Rather, we adopt the District Court's definition of force.

Other jurisdictions, such as California, have expanded the definition of force, beyond its physical connotation. *People v. Cicero* (1984), 157 Cal. App. 3d 465, 204 Cal. Rptr. 582. The California Supreme Court adopted the following reasoning to expand the word force:

> "... the fundamental wrong at which the law of rape is aimed is not the application of physical force that causes physical harm. Rather, the law of rape primarily guards the integrity of a woman's will and the privacy of her sexuality from an act of intercourse undertaken without her consent. Because the fundamental wrong is the violation of a woman's will and sexuality, the law of rape does not require that 'force' cause physical harm. Rather, in this scenario, 'force' plays merely a supporting evidentiary role, as necessary only to ensure an act of intercourse has been undertaken against a victim's will."

Cicero, 204 Cal. Rptr. at 590.

The California Supreme Court's definition of the word force is too broad under Montana's definition of the crime. Until the legislature adopts a definition for the word "force," we must adopt the ordinary and normal definition of the word "force" as set forth by the District Court.

The State in its information and accompanying affidavit complain that Thompson deprived Jane Doe of consent to the sexual act by threatening that he would prevent her from graduating from high school. The threat required in sec. 45-5-501, MCA, is a "threat of imminent death, bodily injury, or kidnapping to be inflicted on anyone...." The District Court found that something more than a threat is necessary to satisfy the statutory requirement. A threat one will not graduate from high school is not one of the threats listed under sec. 45-5-501, MCA. The State argues that the definition "threat of bodily injury" includes psychological impairment. Unfortunately, the statute sets forth bodily injury, not psychological impairment. A threat that eventually leads to psychological impairment is not sufficient under the statute. The statute only addresses the results of three specific kinds of threats, and psychological impairment is not one of them.

The State urges this Court to adopt the definitions of threat set forth in sec. 45-2-101(68), MCA. Section 45-2-101(68), MCA, has no application in regard to the crime of sexual intercourse without consent. Section 45-5-501, MCA, plainly and succinctly lays out the types of threats necessary to make the victim act "without consent."

Under sec. 45-5-501, MCA, the threat also must be of "imminent death, bodily injury, or kidnapping." Thompson's threats cannot be considered imminent. The alleged sexual act and threat occurred in December of 1986. Jane Doe graduated from Hobson High School in June of 1987. Clearly, Thompson's alleged threats were not imminent.

Peppered throughout the State's brief is the contention that "under Montana law the issue of consent is a fact question, and therefore a question for the jury to decide." The State is correct, the jury is the proper trier of facts in regard to issues such as consent. However, in this case, the State's information and probable cause affidavit have failed to set forth any facts or circumstances to show that the alleged act of sexual intercourse were within the statute defining the elements of the crime. So, the issue in this case is not whether the jury was denied its role as trier of the facts, but whether the State sufficiently set forth facts or circumstances to show the element of "without consent." The court properly granted defendant's motion to dismiss for lack of probable cause.

This case is one of considerable difficulty for us, as indeed it must have been for the District Court judge. The alleged facts, if true, show disgusting acts of taking advantage of a young person by an adult who occupied a position of authority over the young person. If we could rewrite the statutes to define the alleged acts here as sexual intercourse without consent, we would willingly do so. The business of courts, however, is to interpret statutes, not to rewrite them, nor to insert words not put there by the legislature. With a good deal of reluctance, and with strong condemnation of the alleged acts, we affirm the District Court.

Questions and Notes

1. Did the court correctly construe the Montana statute? How free do you think that the court should have felt to construe the statute in accordance with what almost everybody believes is sound public policy?

2. Is there a serious argument to made for a construction of the statute that would have upheld the conviction? What might it be?

3. How would *Thompson* have been decided in New Jersey (*MTS*)? Pennsylvania (*Berkowitz*)?

4. In the next section, we examine sex by fraud.

D. Fraud

Boro v. Superior Court

210 Cal. Rptr. 122 (Cal. App. 1985)

NEWSOM, Associate Justice

In relevant part the factual background may be summarized as follows. Ms. R., the rape victim, was employed as a clerk at the Holiday Inn in South San Francisco when, on March 30, 1984, at about 8:45 a.m., she received a telephone call from a person who identified himself as "Dr. Stevens" and said that he worked at Peninsula Hospital.

"Dr. Stevens" told Ms. R. that he had the results of her blood test and that she had contracted a dangerous, highly infectious and perhaps fatal disease; that she could be sued as a result; that the disease came from using public toilets; and that she would have to tell him the identity of all her friends who would then have to be contacted in the interest of controlling the spread of the disease.

"Dr. Stevens" further explained that there were only two ways to treat the disease. The first was a painful surgical procedure—graphically described—costing $9,000, and requiring her uninsured hospitalization for six weeks. A second alternative, "Dr. Stevens" explained, was to have sexual intercourse with an anonymous donor who had been injected with a serum which would cure the disease. The latter, nonsurgical procedure would only cost $4,500. When the victim replied that she lacked sufficient funds the "doctor" suggested that $1,000 would suffice as a down payment. The victim thereupon agreed to the nonsurgical alternative and consented to intercourse with the mysterious donor, believing "it was the only choice I had."

After discussing her intentions with her work supervisor, the victim proceeded to the Hyatt Hotel in Burlingame as instructed, and contacted "Dr. Stevens" by telephone. The latter became furious when he learned Ms. R. had informed her employer of the plan, and threatened to terminate his treatment, finally instructing her to inform her employer she had decided not to go through with the treatment. Ms. R. did so, then went to her bank, withdrew $1,000 and, as instructed, checked into another hotel and called "Dr. Stevens" to give him her room number.

About a half hour later the defendant "donor" arrived at her room. When Ms. R. had undressed, the "donor," petitioner, after urging her to relax, had sexual intercourse with her.

At the time of penetration, it was Ms. R.'s belief that she would die unless she consented to sexual intercourse with the defendant: as she testified, "My life felt threatened, and for that reason and that reason alone did I do it."

Petitioner was apprehended when the police arrived at the hotel room, having been called by Ms. R.'s supervisor. Petitioner was identified as "Dr. Stevens" at a police voice lineup by another potential victim of the same scheme.

Upon the basis of the evidence just recounted, petitioner was charged with five crimes, as follows: Count I: section 261, subdivision (2)—rape: accomplished against a person's will by means of force or fear of immediate and unlawful bodily injury on the person or another. Count II: section 261, subdivision (4)—rape "[where] a person is at the time unconscious of the nature of the act, and this is known to the accused." Count III: section 266—procuring a female to have illicit carnal connection with a man "by any false pretenses, false representation, or other fraudulent means. . . .' Count IV: section 664/487—attempted grand theft. Count V: section 459—burglary (entry into the hotel room with intent to commit theft).

A section 995 motion to set aside the information was granted as to counts I and III—the latter by concession of the district attorney. Petitioner's sole challenge is to denial of the motion to dismiss count II.

The People's position is stated concisely: "We contend, quite simply, that at the time of the intercourse Ms. R., the victim, was 'unconscious of the nature of the act': because of [petitioner's] misrepresentation she believed it was in the nature of a medical treatment and not a simple, ordinary act of sexual intercourse." Petitioner, on the other hand, stresses that the victim was plainly aware of the nature of the act in which she voluntarily engaged, so that her motivation in doing so (since it did not fall within the proscription of section 261, subdivision (2)) is irrelevant.

Our research discloses sparse California authority on the subject. A victim need not be totally and physically unconscious in order that section 261, subdivision (4) apply. In *People v. Minkowski* (1962) 204 Cal. App. 2d 832, 23 Cal. Rptr. 92, the defendant was a physician who "treated" several victims for menstrual cramps. Each victim testified that she was treated in a position with her back to the doctor, bent over a table, with feet apart, in a dressing gown. And in each case the "treatment" consisted of the defendant first inserting a metal instrument, then substituting an instrument which "felt different"—the victims not realizing that the second instrument was in fact the doctor's penis. The precise issue before us was never tendered in *People v. Minkowski* because the petitioner there conceded the sufficiency of evidence to support the element of consciousness.

The decision is useful to this analysis, however, because it exactly illustrates certain traditional rules in the area of our inquiry. Thus, as a leading authority has written, "if deception causes a misunderstanding as to the fact itself (fraud in the factum) there is no legally-recognized consent because what happened is not that for which consent was given; whereas consent induced by fraud is as effective as any other consent, so far as direct and immediate legal consequences are concerned, if the deception relates not to the thing done but merely to some collateral matter (fraud in the inducement)."

The victims in *Minkowski* consented, not to sexual intercourse, but to an act of an altogether different nature, penetration by medical instrument. The consent was to a pathological, and not a carnal, act, and the mistake was, therefore, in the factum and not merely in the inducement.

Another relatively common situation in the literature on this subject is the fraudulent obtaining of intercourse by impersonating a spouse. As Professor Perkins observes, the courts are not in accord as to whether the crime of rape is thereby committed. "[The] disagreement is not in regard to the underlying principle but only as to its application. Some courts have taken the position that such a misdeed is fraud in the inducement on the theory that the woman consents to exactly what is done (sexual intercourse) and hence there is no rape; other courts, with better reason it would seem, hold such a misdeed to be rape on the theory that it involves fraud in the factum since the woman's consent is to an innocent act of marital intercourse while what is actually perpetrated upon her is an act of adultery. Her innocence seems never to have been questioned in such a case and the reason she is not guilty of adultery is because she did not consent to adulterous intercourse.

In California, of course, we have by statute[3] adopted the majority view that such fraud is in the factum, not the inducement, and have thus held it to vitiate consent. It is otherwise, however, with respect to the conceptually much murkier statutory offense with which we here deal, and the language of which has remained essentially unchanged since its enactment in 1872.

The language itself could not be plainer. It defines rape to be "an act of sexual intercourse" with a nonspouse, accomplished where the victim is "at the time unconscious of the nature of the act. . . ." (§261, subd. (4).) Nor, as we have just seen, can we entertain the slightest doubt that the Legislature well understood how to draft a statute to encompass fraud in the factum and how to specify certain fraud in the inducement as vitiating consent.[4] Moreover, courts of this state have previously confronted the general rule that fraud in the inducement does not vitiate consent. *Mathews v. Superior Court* found section 266 (fraudulent procurement of a female for illicit carnal connection) inapplicable where the facts showed that the defendant, impersonating an unmarried woman's paramour, made sexual advances to the victim with her consent. While the facts demonstrate classic fraud in the factum, a concurring opinion in *Mathews* specifically decried the lack of a California statutory prohibition against fraudulently induced consent to sexual relations in circumstances other than those specified in section 261, subdivision (5) and then-section 268.

The People, however, direct our attention to Penal Code section 261.6, which in their opinion has changed the rule that fraud in the inducement does not vitiate consent. That provision reads as follows: "In prosecutions under sections 261, 286,

---

3. Section 261, subdivision (5) reads as follows: "Where a person submits under the belief that the person committing the act is the victim's spouse, and this belief is induced by any artifice, pretense, or concealment practiced by the accused, with intent to induce the belief."

4. Prior to its repeal by Statutes 1984, chapter 438, section 2, section 268 provided that: "Every person who, under promise of marriage, seduces and has sexual intercourse with an unmarried female of previous chaste character, is punishable by imprisonment in the state prison, or by a fine of not more than five thousand dollars [$5,000], or by both such fine and imprisonment."

288a or 289, in which consent is at issue, 'consent' shall be defined to mean positive cooperation in act or attitude pursuant to an act of free will. The person must act freely and voluntarily and have knowledge of the nature of the act or transaction involved."

We find little legislative history for this section. Section 261.6 was enacted as a part of Chapter 1111, Statutes of 1982, which amended various substantive sex crime statutes and created the crime of sexual battery. (§ 243.4.)

If the Legislature at that time had desired to correct the apparent oversight decried in *Mathews, supra*,[5] — it could certainly have done so. But the Attorney General's strained reading of section 261.6 would render section 261, subdivision (5) meaningless surplusage; and we are "'exceedingly reluctant to attach an interpretation to a particular statute which renders other existing provisions unnecessary.'"

Finally, the Attorney General cites *People v. Howard* (1981) 117 Cal. App. 3d 53 [172 Cal. Rptr. 539]. There, the court dealt with section 288a, subdivision (f) and section 286, subdivision (f) making criminal oral copulation or sodomy between adults where one person is "unconscious of the nature of the act." But in *Howard, supra* the victim was a 19-year-old with the mental capacity of a 6-to-8-year-old, who "simply [did] not understand the nature of the act in which he [participated]." Whether or not we agree with the *Howard* court's analysis, we note that here, in contrast, there is not a shred of evidence on the record before us to suggest that as the result of mental retardation Ms. R. lacked the capacity to appreciate the nature of the sex act in which she engaged. On the contrary, her testimony was clear that she precisely understood the "nature of the act," but, motivated by a fear of disease, and death, succumbed to petitioner's fraudulent blandishments.

To so conclude is not to vitiate the heartless cruelty of petitioner's scheme, but to say that it comprised crimes of a different order than a violation of section 261, subdivision (4).

RACANELLI, P.J., concurs

HOLMDAHL, Associate Justice, dissenting.

I respectfully dissent.

All concerned with this case are handicapped by what my colleagues call "sparse California authority on the subject" before us. Neither are we aided by the "little legislative history" concerning the 1982 enactment of Penal Code section 261.6.

I agree with my colleagues' conclusion that in enacting section 261.6 the Legislature could have corrected, but did not, "the apparent oversight decried in

---

5. It is not difficult to conceive of reasons why the Legislature may have consciously wished to leave the matter where it lies. Thus, as a matter of degree, where consent to intercourse is obtained by promises of travel, fame, celebrity and the like — ought the liar and seducer to be chargeable as a rapist? Where is the line to be drawn?

Mathews. . . ." I disagree, however, with their apparent conclusion that section 261.6 does not apply in the present case.

While *Mathews* did involve alleged false pretenses, that opinion was concerned solely with an interpretation of section 266. The new section 261.6 does not apply to prosecutions under section 266. Section 261.6 does, however, expressly apply to "prosecutions under Section 261, 286, 288a, or 289, in which consent is at issue. . . ."

The case before us concerns a prosecution under section 261, subd. (4), and "consent is at issue." Consequently, section 261.6, defining "consent" applies in this case. It is apparent from the abundance of appropriate adjectives and adverbs in the statute that the Legislature intended to the point of redundancy to limit "consent" to that which is found to have been truly free and voluntary, truly unrestricted and knowledgeable. Thus, section 261.6 provides: "In prosecutions under Section 261, 286, 288a, or 289, in which consent is at issue, 'consent' shall be defined to mean positive cooperation in act or attitude pursuant to an exercise of *free* will. The person must act *freely* and *voluntarily* and *have knowledge* of the nature of the act or transaction involved." (Italics added.)

[Courts] are bound to give effect to statutes according to the usual, ordinary import of the language employed in framing them. Recourse to the Oxford English Dictionary (1978) indicates that the "positive" of "positive cooperation" is that which is "free from qualifications, conditions, or reservations; absolute, unconditional; opposed to *relative* and *comparative*." (*Id.* vol. 4, p. 1152, italics in original.)

"Free will" is defined as "[spontaneous] will, unconstrained choice (to do or act) . . . left to or depending upon one's choice or election." (*Id.* vol. 4, "F.," p. 528.)

"Freely" is defined as "[of] one's own accord, spontaneously; without constraint or reluctance; unreservedly, without stipulation; readily, willingly." (*Id.* vol. 4, "F.," p. 526.)

"Voluntarily" is defined as "[of] one's own free will or accord; without compulsion, constraint, or undue influence by others; freely, willingly. . . . Without other determining force than natural character or tendency; naturally, spontaneously."

Further, I take the statute's use of "act or attitude" and "act or transaction" to mean more than an alleged victim's knowledge that she would be engaging in the physical act of sexual intercourse and more than that she intended to do so. Those phrases, in combination with the adjectives and adverbs discussed, lead me to conclude that while the Legislature in section 261.6 did not expressly repeal the legalisms distinguishing "fraud in the *factum*" and "fraud in the inducement," its intention certainly was to restrict "consent" to cases of true, good faith consent, obtained without substantial fraud or deceit.

I believe there is a sufficient basis for prosecution of petitioner pursuant to section 261, subd. (4). I would deny the writ.

Questions and Notes

1. How do the majority and dissent differ in their reading of the statute? With whom would you have agreed? Why?

2. Should the defendant have been guilty under counts I and/or III, which were dismissed? Explain.

3. Is the distinction between fraud in the inducement and fraud in the factum sound?

4. Accepting that distinction, was *Mathews* properly decided?

5. An explanation for cases like *Mathews* and much else in the law of rape can be found in an insightful law review article by Professor Anne Coughlin titled *Sex and Guilt*, 84 U. Va. L. Rev. 1 (1998). Professor Coughlin contends that rape laws were originally designed to protect chastity, not sexual autonomy. Consequently, one who was willing to give up chastity without a major fight was guilty of adultery or fornication and had no defense that she was raped. Similarly, one who obtained sex by impersonating a husband was deceiving a woman into having lawful sex whereas one, like Mathews, who deceived another into thinking he was her lover was simply substituting one form of illegal sex for another. Some, but not all, modern courts reject *Mathews*. (*Compare United States v. Hughes*, 48 M.J. 214 (1998) *with People v. Hough*, 607 N.Y.S. 2d 884 (1994).)

6. Interestingly, accepting Professor Coughlin's historical analysis, Boro should have been guilty of rape because having extramarital sexual relations to save one's life should qualify under the necessity defense. *See* Chapter 12, *infra*.

7. Should the fact that Boro presented a threat to only the most gullible among us be relevant in assessing his liability?

8. We close our analysis of rape with a study of traditional juridical limitations.

E. Juridical Limitations

At common law, it was legally impossible for a husband to rape his wife (except when he aided another man to forcibly have sexual intercourse with her). Most modern jurisdictions have repealed that limitation when the parties are legally separated. A smaller number have repealed it for all marriages.

Another common law doctrine required that the perpetrator be male and the victim female. Most, but not all, jurisdictions have repealed this doctrine. However, some of these jurisdictions retain the rule that only forcible penile/vaginal contact can be punished as rape.

The MPC retained the marital exemption, gender discrimination, and the penile/vaginal requirement (although it has a lesser offense of deviate sexual intercourse). *See* MPC § 213.1 (Appendix A). Consider whether there are good reasons for retaining any of these rules as you read *People v. Liberta*.

People v. Liberta

474 N.E.2d 567 (N.Y. 1984)

WACHTLER, Judge.

The defendant, while living apart from his wife pursuant to a Family Court order, forcibly raped and sodomized her in the presence of their 21/2 year old son. Under the New York Penal Law a married man ordinarily cannot be prosecuted for raping or sodomizing his wife. The defendant, however, though married at the time of the incident, is treated as an unmarried man under the Penal Law because of the Family Court order. On this appeal, he contends that because of the exemption for married men, the statutes for rape in the first degree (Penal Law, § 130.35) and sodomy in the first degree (Penal Law, § 130.50), violate the equal protection clause of the Federal Constitution (U.S. CONST., 14th Amdt.). The defendant also contends that the rape statute violates equal protection because only men, and not women, can be prosecuted under it.

Defendant Mario Liberta and Denise Liberta were married in 1978. Shortly after the birth of their son, in October of that year, Mario began to beat Denise. In early 1980 Denise brought a proceeding in the Family Court in Erie County seeking protection from the defendant. On April 30, 1980, a temporary order of protection was issued to her by the Family Court. Under this order, the defendant was to move out and remain away from the family home, and stay away from Denise. The order provided that the defendant could visit with his son once each weekend.

On the weekend of March 21, 1981, Mario, who was then living in a motel, did not visit his son. On Tuesday, March 24, 1981, he called Denise to ask if he could visit his son on that day. Denise would not allow the defendant to come to her house, but she did agree to allow him to pick up their son and her and take them both back to his motel after being assured that a friend of his would be with them at all times. The defendant and his friend picked up Denise and their son and the four of them drove to defendant's motel.

When they arrived at the motel the friend left. As soon as only Mario, Denise, and their son were alone in the motel room, Mario attacked Denise, threatened to kill her, and forced her to perform fellatio on him and to engage in sexual intercourse with him. The son was in the room during the entire episode, and the defendant forced Denise to tell their son to watch what the defendant was doing to her.

The defendant allowed Denise and their son to leave shortly after the incident. Denise, after going to her parents' home, went to a hospital to be treated for scratches on her neck and bruises on her head and back, all inflicted by her husband. She also went to the police station, and on the next day she swore out a felony complaint against the defendant. On July 15, 1981, the defendant was indicted for rape in the first degree and sodomy in the first degree.

The defendant's constitutional challenges to the rape and sodomy statutes are premised on his being considered "not married" to Denise and are the same

challenges as could be made by any unmarried male convicted under these statutes. The defendant's claim is that both statutes violate equal protection because
they are underinclusive classifications which burden him, but not others similarly
situated.

A. The Marital Exemption

[U]nder the Penal Law a married man ordinarily cannot be convicted of forcibly
raping or sodomizing his wife. Although a marital exemption was not explicit in
earlier rape statutes, an 1852 treatise stated that a man could not be guilty of raping
his wife. The assumption, even before the marital exemption was codified, that a
man could not be guilty of raping his wife, is traceable to a statement made by the
17th century English jurist Lord Hale, who wrote: "[T]he husband cannot be guilty
of a rape committed by himself upon his lawful wife, for by their mutual matri-
monial consent and contract the wife hath given up herself in this kind unto her
husband, which she cannot retract." (1 HALE, HISTORY OF PLEAS OF THE CROWN,
p. 629.) Although Hale cited no authority for his statement, it was relied on by State
Legislatures which enacted rape statutes with a marital exemption and by courts
which established a common-law exemption for husbands.

Presently, over 40 States still retain some form of marital exemption for rape.[6]
While the marital exemption is subject to an equal protection challenge, because it
classifies unmarried men differently than married men, the equal protection clause
does not prohibit a State from making classifications, provided the statute does not
arbitrarily burden a particular group of individuals. Where a statute draws a distinction based upon marital status, the classification must be reasonable and must
be based upon "some ground of difference that rationally explains the different
treatment." (*Eisenstadt v. Baird*, 405 U.S. 438, 447.)

We find that there is no rational basis for distinguishing between marital rape
and nonmarital rape. The various rationales which have been asserted in defense
of the exemption are either based upon archaic notions about the consent and

---

6. Statutes in nine States provide a complete exemption to rape as long as there is a valid marriage (Alabama, Arkansas, Kansas, Montana, South Dakota, Texas, Vermont, Washington, West
Virginia). In 26 other States, statutes provide for a marital exemption but with certain exceptions,
most typically where the spouses are living apart pursuant to either a court order or a separation
agreement (Alaska, Arizona, Colorado, Idaho, Indiana, Kentucky, Louisiana, Maine, Maryland,
Michigan, Minnesota, Missouri, Nevada, New Mexico, New York, North Carolina, North Dakota,
Ohio, Oklahoma, Pennsylvania, Rhode Island, South Carolina, Tennessee, Utah, Wyoming, Wisconsin). In three other States (Georgia, Mississippi, Nebraska) and the District of Columbia the
exemption appears to still exist as a common-law doctrine, and it may still have a limited application in Virginia (see *Weishaupt v. Commonwealth*, 227 Va. 389, 315 S.E.2d 847). Finally, in Connecticut, Delaware, Hawaii, and Iowa, there is a marital exemption for some, but not all degrees
of forcible rape (see, generally, for statutory references, Schwartz, *Spousal Exemption for Criminal
Rape Prosecution*, 7 VT. L. REV. 33, 38–41 [hereafter cited as "Rape Prosecution"]; Note, Clancy,
Equal Protection Considerations of the Spousal Sexual Assault Exclusion, 16 N. ENG. L. REV. 1, 2–3,
n.4 [hereafter cited as "Equal Protection Considerations"]; "Abolishing the Marital Exemption",
supra, at n.4, at pp. 203–205).

property rights incident to marriage or are simply unable to withstand even the slightest scrutiny. We therefore declare the marital exemption for rape in the New York statute to be unconstitutional.

[The court then considered and rejected two ancient justifications (irrevocable consent predicated on the marriage, and the wife's being the property of the husband) and two more modern arguments predicated on disruption of the marriage and difficulties of proof.]

The final argument in defense of the marital exemption is that marital rape is not as serious an offense as other rape and is thus adequately dealt with by the possibility of prosecution under criminal statutes, such as assault statutes, which provide for less severe punishment. The fact that rape statutes exist, however, is a recognition that the harm caused by a forcible rape is different, and more severe, than the harm caused by an ordinary assault. Under the Penal Law, assault is generally a misdemeanor unless either the victim suffers "serious physical injury" or a deadly weapon or dangerous instrument is used. N.Y. Penal Law §§ 120.00, 120.05, 120.1010.) Thus, if the defendant had been living with Denise at the time he forcibly raped and sodomized her he probably could not have been charged with a felony, let alone a felony with punishment equal to that for rape in the first degree.[9]

Moreover, there is no evidence to support the argument that marital rape has less severe consequences than other rape. On the contrary, numerous studies have shown that marital rape is frequently quite violent and generally has more severe, traumatic effects on the victim than other rape. (*See, generally,* Russell, *Rape In Marriage,* pp. 190–199.)

Among the recent decisions in this country addressing the marital exemption, only one court has concluded that there is a rational basis for it. We agree with the other courts which have analyzed the exemption, which have been unable to find any present justification for it. Justice Holmes wrote: "It is revolting to have no better reason for a rule of law than that so it was laid down in the time of Henry IV. It is still more revolting if the grounds upon which it was laid down have vanished long since, and the rule simply persists from blind imitation of the past." (Holmes, *The Path of the Law,* 10 HARV. L. REV. 457, 469.) This statement is an apt characterization of the marital exemption; it lacks a rational basis, and therefore violates the equal protection clauses of both the Federal and State Constitutions. (U.S. CONST., 14th Amdt., § 1; N.Y. CONST., art. I, § 11.)

---

9. Rape in the first degree and sodomy in the first degree are "Class B violent felony offenses", the minimum sentence for which is a jail term of 2–6 years, and the maximum sentence for which is a jail term of 81/3-25 years (Penal Law, § 70.02). The defendant possibly could have been charged with coercion in the first degree, a class D felony (Penal Law, § 135.65), but not all forcible rapes meet all the elements of the coercion statute (see *People v. Greer,* 42 N.Y.2d 170, 174–175, 397 N.Y.S.2d 613, 366 N.E.2d 273), and thus if a husband cannot be prosecuted under the rape statute when he forcibly rapes his wife he may be able to escape prosecution for any felony.

B. The Exemption for Females

Under the Penal Law only males can be convicted of rape in the first degree.[11] Insofar as the rape statute applies to acts of "sexual intercourse", which, as defined in the Penal Law (*see* N.Y. Penal Law § 130.0000) can only occur between a male and a female, it is true that a female cannot physically rape a female and that therefore there is no denial of equal protection when punishing only males for forcibly engaging in sexual intercourse with females. The equal protection issue, however, stems from the fact that the statute applies to males who forcibly rape females but does not apply to females who forcibly rape males.

Rape statutes historically applied only to conduct by males against females, largely because the purpose behind the proscriptions was to protect the chastity of women and thus their property value to their fathers or husbands. New York's rape statute has always protected only females, and has thus applied only to males. (*See* Penal Law, § 130.35; 1909 Penal Law, § 2010; 1881 Penal Code, tit. X, ch. II, § 278). Presently New York is one of only 10 jurisdictions that does not have a gender-neutral statute for forcible rape.[13]

A statute which treats males and females differently violates equal protection unless the classification is substantially related to the achievement of an important governmental objective. This burden is not met in the present case, and therefore the gender exemption also renders the statute unconstitutional.

The first argument advanced by the People in support of the exemption for females is that because only females can become pregnant the State may constitutionally differentiate between forcible rapes of females and forcible rapes of males. This court and the United States Supreme Court have upheld statutes which subject males to criminal liability for engaging in sexual intercourse with underage females without the converse being true. (*See Michael M. v. Sonoma County Superior Ct.*, 450 U.S. 464.) The rationale behind these decisions was that the primary purpose of such "statutory rape" laws is to protect against the harm caused by teenage pregnancies, there being no need to provide the same protection to young males.

There is no evidence, however, that preventing pregnancies is a primary purpose of the statute prohibiting forcible rape, nor does such a purpose seem likely. Rather, the very fact that the statute proscribes "forcible compulsion" shows that its overriding purpose is to protect a woman from an unwanted, forcible, and often violent sexual intrusion into her body. Thus, due to the different purposes behind forcible rape laws and "statutory" (consensual) rape laws, the cases upholding the gender discrimination in the latter are not decisive with respect to the former, and

---

11. The sodomy statute applies to any "person" and is thus gender neutral. Defendant's gender-based equal protection challenge is therefore addressed only to the rape statute.

13. The other nine jurisdictions are Alabama, Delaware, District of Columbia, Georgia, Idaho, Kansas, Mississippi, Oregon, and Virginia. Some of these other States, like New York (see Penal Law, § 130.65), have other statutes which proscribe conduct including the forcible rape of a male by a female and which have less severe punishments than for forcible rape of a female by a male.

the People cannot meet their burden here by simply stating that only females can become pregnant.

The People also claim that the discrimination is justified because a female rape victim "faces the probability of medical, sociological, and psychological problems unique to her gender." This same argument, when advanced in support of the discrimination in the statutory rape laws, was rejected by this court, and it is no more convincing in the present case. "[A]n "'archaic and overbroad" generalization' ... which is evidently grounded in long-standing stereotypical notions of the differences between the sexes, simply cannot serve as a legitimate rationale for a penal provision that is addressed only to adult males." (*Craig v. Boren*, 429 U.S. at 198.)

Finally, the People suggest that a gender-neutral law for forcible rape is unnecessary, and that therefore the present law is constitutional, because a woman either cannot actually rape a man or such attacks, if possible, are extremely rare. Although the "physiologically impossible" argument has been accepted by several courts, it is simply wrong. The argument is premised on the notion that a man cannot engage in sexual intercourse unless he is sexually aroused, and if he is aroused then he is consenting to intercourse. "Sexual intercourse" however, "occurs upon any penetration, however slight" (Penal Law, § 130.00); this degree of contact can be achieved without a male being aroused and thus without his consent.

As to the "infrequency" argument, while forcible sexual assaults by females upon males are undoubtedly less common than those by males upon females this numerical disparity cannot by itself make the gender discrimination constitutional. Women may well be responsible for a far lower number of all serious crimes than are men, but such a disparity would not make it permissible for the State to punish only men who commit, for example, robbery.

Accordingly, we find that section 130.35 of the Penal Law violates equal protection because it exempts females from criminal liability for forcible rape.

[The court then found that the best way to preserve the statute, given its equal protection holding, was to invalidate the exemptions. Consequently, it upheld Liberta's conviction while announcing that all future rapes committed by husbands against their wives and women against men would be subject to the rape statute.]

Problem

George and Martha are a happily married couple living in New York after the *Liberta* case. One night, while Martha was sleeping, George made love to her. When Martha awoke, the following conversation transpired:

Martha: I like it when you make love to me while I'm sleeping.

George: I thought you would, but I want you to know something. I do not want you to ever make love to me while I'm sleeping. I don't like it.

Martha thought about that conversation for a week and concluded that George would like it more than he thought and decided to make love to him the next time that he was asleep. The next night she executed her plan. This angered George who told her that he was going to have her prosecuted for rape (active resistance is not required when the victim is unconscious or asleep). Because George is the local District Attorney, he had no difficulty getting Martha prosecuted.

Martha has appealed her conviction to the New York Court of Appeals. Under *Liberta*, how should the court resolve the case? In an ideal system of jurisprudence, should Martha be guilty of rape? If your answer to the first question is "conviction affirmed" and your answer to the second question is "no," was *Liberta* wrongly decided?

Questions and Notes

1. *Liberta* should not be regarded as a mainstream constitutional decision. The other cases that have rejected a marital exemption have done so as a matter of statutory or common law construction. Nevertheless, *Liberta* is valuable as an analytical starting point for weighing the arguments in favor of and against a special rule for marital rape and rape perpetrated by women.

2. Is it clear that the harm of unwanted sexual intercourse in an ongoing marriage is more significant than other types of assaults? Unquestionably the presence of rape laws indicates that this is true outside of the marital setting. On the other hand, the very presence of the marital exemption (including in some fairly recently rethought codes, such as the MPC, *see* § 2.03) is some evidence that assault might more nearly reflect the severity of the harm imposed on the victim. It is also worth noting that the assault involved in a case like *Liberta*, involving married people, has always been subject to punishment. An unseparated, married Liberta would be criminally liable for assaulting his wife. He just wouldn't be liable for rape.

3. In assessing whether spouses should be treated differently from other rapists, are any of the following considerations relevant: (a) a spouse has a duty, usually enforceable by the criminal law, to support his or her spouse, (b) sex outside of marriage by a spouse is frequently criminal, or at least a factor in setting the financial terms of a divorce, (c) an aggrieved spouse can be legally separated at will? In regard to the latter, how relevant should it be that attempting to separate from a battering spouse frequently increases the level of violence? *See Weiand v. State*, Chapter 6, *infra*.

4. Is there any good reason for punishing a woman who forces a man to have intercourse with her less seriously than a man who does the same thing to a woman?

5. Is statutory rape (carnal knowledge of a minor with consent) really designed to prevent unwanted pregnancy? Any more than forcible rape?

6. Does a statute that punishes sex with a female under 18 discriminate against males, females, or both? Explain. *See* Loewy, *Returned to the Pedestal*, 60 N.C. L. Rev. 87, 97–102 (1981).

For more reading on this section, see MPC 2.13 (Appendix A); Nutshell Chapter IV.

Problem

Assume that all seven of the defendants in this chapter had been convicted. Assume further that you were free to sentence them based on the reprehensibility of their conduct. Rank the seven defendants—Rusk, Berkowitz, MTS, Bunyard, Thompson, Boro, and Liberta—in descending order of reprehensibility, indicating how you would sentence each one, and why.

Chapter 6

Self-Defense

A. In General

Although self-defense and related defenses (defense of others, defense of property, prevention of crime) are analytically similar to defenses such as insanity, intoxication, necessity, and duress, which will be studied later, self-defense is so closely related to crimes against the person that it is appropriate to study it in conjunction with those crimes. Indeed, almost definitionally, a defendant raising the defense will be defending against an assault or murder charge. Usually, she will be defending against an assault, attempted murder, or attempted rape.

It is blackletter law everywhere that a person may use no more force than she thinks is necessary to defend herself. Most jurisdictions add that the danger defended against must be either real or apparent to a reasonable person. A further issue is proportionality. A person may not ordinarily use deadly force to prevent a minor beating or to prevent the theft of personal property. The law deems it better that a person suffer minor harm than that another (albeit minor criminal) have his life needlessly spent.

As you read *Schroeder*, think about whether and when it was appropriate to use deadly force.

State v. Schroeder

261 N.W.2d 759 (Neb. 1978)

BOSLAUGH, Justice.

The defendant, Mark Schroeder, appeals from a sentence to imprisonment for 2 to 3 years for assault with intent to inflict great bodily injury. The defendant has assigned as error the trial court's refusal to instruct on the defense of justification, or choice of evils, as provided in section 28-834, R.R.S.1943.

The assault took place in a cell at the Reformatory Unit near Lincoln, Nebraska. The defendant was confined in the cell with three other prisoners, one of whom was Gary Riggs, the victim.

The defendant was 19 years of age at the time of the offense. Riggs was 24 years of age. Riggs had a reputation among the other prisoners for sex and violence and the defendant was afraid of Riggs. In its brief the State concedes that Riggs had unquestionably placed the defendant in a position of general subservience.

The evidence shows that the defendant and Riggs had been gambling and that the defendant owed Riggs approximately $3,000. Riggs had threatened to make a "punk" out of the defendant by selling the debt to some other prisoner. A punk is defined in the record as a prisoner who commits homosexual acts with other prisoners.

The defendant testified that he did not want to gamble with Riggs, but Riggs made the defendant continue to play cards and gamble. On the day before the incident, the defendant and the other two prisoners in the cell submitted a written request that Riggs be moved to another cell.

On the night the assault occurred the defendant and Riggs played cards until about 10 p.m. The defendant testified Riggs said that he might walk in his sleep that night and "collect some of this money I got owed to me tonight."

The defendant went to bed about 10 p.m. but, apparently, was unable to sleep because of what Riggs had said. The defendant got up about 1 a.m., and stabbed Riggs in the back with a knife made from a table knife. Riggs was asleep at the time but awakened when he was stabbed. When Riggs tried to remove the knife from his back, the defendant struck Riggs in the face several times with a metal ashtray. The guard was called, and Riggs was taken to the hospital.

Section 28-834, R.R.S.1943, which is a part of the self-defense statute enacted in 1972, provides as follows:

"(1) Conduct which the actor believes to be necessary to avoid a harm or evil to himself or to another is justifiable if:

"(a) The harm or evil sought to be avoided by such conduct is greater than that sought to be prevented by the law defining the offense charged;

"(b) Neither sections 28-833 to 28-843 nor other law defining the offense provides exceptions or defenses dealing with the specific situation involved; and

"(c) A legislative purpose to exclude the justification claimed does not otherwise plainly appear.

"(2) When the actor was reckless or negligent in bringing about the situation requiring a choice of harms or evils or in appraising the necessity for his conduct, the justification afforded by this section is unavailable in a prosecution for any offense for which recklessness or negligence, as the case may be, suffices to establish culpability."

The defendant submitted a requested instruction based upon section 28-834, R.R.S.1943, and NJI No. 14.33, as revised, which the trial court refused. The defendant contends the refusal was erroneous. The State contends the request was properly refused because the harm or evil sought to be avoided was not greater than that sought to be prevented and there was no specific and imminent threat or injury to the defendant's person at the time he stabbed Riggs.

The defendant was charged with stabbing with intent to kill, wound, or maim but the jury found the defendant guilty of the lesser offense of assault with intent to inflict great bodily injury. The State argues that the determination as to which harm or evil is greater is to be made by a comparison of the punishment prescribed by law for the acts in question. This does not appear to be a correct interpretation of the statute.

Under section 28-836(4), R.R.S.1943, the use of deadly force may be justifiable if the actor believes such force is necessary to protect himself against sexual intercourse compelled by force or threat. The defendant's evidence was such that the jury could have found that the defendant believed he would be forced by Riggs to submit to sodomy if he did not kill or disable Riggs that night.

The circumstance of confinement is an important factor in this case. Under ordinary circumstances the actor has a duty to retreat if he can with complete safety avoid the necessity of using force by retreating. The duty to retreat was not applicable here because the defendant could not retreat.

The State further contends that the defense was not applicable because there was no specific and imminent threat of injury to the defendant. Riggs was asleep when the defendant stabbed him, and Riggs had made no overt act or assault upon the defendant. Section 28-836(1), R.R.S.1943, provides that the use of force may be justifiable if the actor believes that such force is immediately necessary for the purpose of protecting himself against the use of unlawful force by the other person on the present occasion.

The rule in this state has been that in order to excuse or justify a killing in self-defense the defendant must have reasonably believed that his life was in imminent danger or that he was in imminent danger of suffering great bodily harm.

The present statutory requirement is that the actor believe such force is immediately necessary to protect himself against the use of unlawful force by the other person on the present occasion. Although the term "present occasion" may have relaxed somewhat the former requirement of imminent danger, the present statutory requirement is essentially the same requirement as existed prior to the enactment of section 28-836, R.R.S.1943.

The problem in this case is that there was no evidence to sustain a finding that the defendant could believe an assault was imminent except the threat that Riggs had made before he went to bed. The general rule is that words alone are not sufficient justification for an assault.

There is a very real danger in a rule which would legalize preventive assaults involving the use of deadly force where there has been nothing more than threats. We conclude that the trial court did not err in refusing to instruct the jury as requested by the defendant.

This is a difficult case and we are of the opinion there are extenuating circumstances which justify a reduction in the sentence. The judgment is modified by reducing the term of imprisonment to 1 year, the statutory minimum. As modified, the judgment is affirmed.

AFFIRMED AS MODIFIED.

CLINTON, Justice, dissenting.

I respectfully dissent because I believe the defendant was entitled to an instruction under the provisions of section 28-834(1)(a), R.R.S.1943, which provides: "(1) Conduct which the actor believes to be necessary to avoid a harm or evil to himself or to another is justifiable if: "(a) The harm or evil sought to be avoided by such conduct is greater than that sought to be prevented by the law defining the offense charged"; insofar as that such an instruction would relate to the lesser-included offense of assault with intent to commit great bodily harm. That is the offense of which the defendant was found guilty. I do not believe he was entitled to such an instruction insofar as the offense of stabbing with intent to kill was concerned.

Section 28-834(1)(a) and section 28-836(1), R.R.S.1943, must be read together. Section 28-836(1), R.R.S.1943, provides that the use of force may be justifiable if the actor believes that such force is immediately necessary for the purpose of protecting himself against the use of unlawful force by the other person "on the present occasion."

The comments to section 3.04 of the Model Penal Code, from which section 28-836, R.R.S.1943, was taken, contain the following: "Nor does the draft limit the privilege of using defensive force to cases where the danger of unlawful violence is 'imminent', as many formulations of the rule now do. The actor must believe that his defensive action is immediately necessary and the unlawful force against which he defends must be force that he apprehends will be used on the present occasion, but he need not apprehend that it will be immediately used. There would, for example, be a privilege to use defensive force to prevent an assailant from going to summon reinforcements, given belief and reason to believe that it is necessary to disable him to prevent an attack by overwhelming numbers so long as the attack is apprehended on the 'present occasion.' The latter words are used in preference to 'imminent' or 'immediate' to introduce the necessary latitude for the attainment of a just result in cases of this kind."

In this case the defendant was faced with a threat by Riggs that he would "collect some of this money I got owed to me tonight." The defendant could not be expected to remain awake all night, every night, waiting for the attack that Riggs had threatened to make. The defendant's evidence here was such that the jury could have found the defendant was justified in believing the use of force was necessary to protect himself against an attack by Riggs "on the present occasion."

Under the evidence in this case, which the majority opinion fairly states, I think that a factual question was presented for the jury to determine whether evil of forcible sodomy was greater than the evil of the assault with intent to commit great bodily harm, where the assault was made to avoid a forcible sexual attack by Riggs. Forcible sodomy is surely a great wrong to the victim. Our statute recognizes the common law rule that one may use deadly force to protect oneself from a forcible sexual assault. § 28-836(4), R.R.S.1943. The evidence would justify the conclusion and permit the jury to find that defendant could not have waited and protected himself by the use of deadly force. With the weapon, which was available to him, he seemingly could not have exercised such deadly force had he waited. Without much doubt, the jury, in finding the defendant guilty of the lesser crime considered the nature of the weapon which he had available and which he used. That weapon may have been inadequate to protect him had he waited until the actual assault commenced.

I would remand for a new trial.

C. Thomas White, Justice, dissenting.

I join in the dissent of Clinton, J., except for that portion which suggests that the instruction was not required to be given with respect to the charge of assault with intent to kill. As stated in the dissent, "one may use deadly force to protect oneself from a forcible sexual assault." § 28-836(4), R.R.S.1943.

Questions and Notes

1. Did Schroeder lose because the harm that he feared was not serious enough to justify deadly force, or because it was not imminent enough to justify any force?

2. Does the statute require that the harm be imminent or only that the need to use force be immediate? If the latter, why wasn't it immediately necessary to use force? Consider the following hypothetical: While Ashley is visiting Burt at Burt's house, Burt locks Ashley in the basement. He tells her that he will keep her there for seven days and on the seventh night, he will kill her with his gun. (Assume that this does not constitute kidnapping or any other crime for which a deadly response would be appropriate.) Suppose that Ashley finds a knife in the basement. Suppose further that there is no place to hide the knife so that Burt will discover it the first time he comes down to feed Ashley. Ashley's choices are to stab Burt the first time he comes down to feed her, or to let Burt discover the knife and remove Ashley's only means of defense.

Under *Schroeder*'s standard of "imminence," is Ashley forbidden to use the knife because death is not threatened for a week? Under a rational system of jurisprudence, should she be denied use of the knife? Should the "imminence" question relate to the harm or the need to use force? (*Cf.* MPC commentaries.) If *Schroeder* had viewed the "imminence" question in terms of the need to use force, would it have reached a different result?

3. Is Justice Clinton speaking out of both sides of his mouth? He contends: (1) that deadly force is appropriate to defend oneself from forcible sodomy, (2) that the defendant could not have waited and safely defended himself, and (3) that he would not have had the right of anticipatory self-defense if he had used a deadly weapon with the intent to kill, wound, or maim. How can one maintain all of those things at the same time?

4. With which justice, if any, would you have agreed? Why?

5. In *Norman*, we again see the conflict between "imminent" and "immediate" in the context of a battered wife.

State v. Norman

378 S.E.2d 8 (N.C. 1989)

MITCHELL, JUSTICE.

The defendant was tried at the 16 February 1987 Criminal Session of Superior Court for Rutherford County upon a proper indictment charging her with the first degree murder of her husband. The jury found the defendant guilty of voluntary manslaughter. The defendant appealed from the trial court's judgment sentencing her to six years imprisonment.

The Court of Appeals granted a new trial, citing as error the trial court's refusal to submit a possible verdict of acquittal by reason of self-defense. Notwithstanding the uncontroverted evidence that the defendant shot her husband three times in the back of the head as he lay sleeping in his bed, the Court of Appeals held that the defendant's evidence that she exhibited what has come to be called "the battered wife syndrome" entitled her to have the jury consider whether the homicide was an act of self-defense and, thus, not a legal wrong.

We conclude that the evidence introduced in this case would not support a finding that the defendant killed her husband due to a reasonable fear of imminent death or great bodily harm, as is required before a defendant is entitled to jury instructions concerning self-defense. Therefore, the trial court properly declined to instruct the jury on the law relating to self-defense. Accordingly, we reverse the Court of Appeals.

At trial, the State presented the testimony of Deputy Sheriff R.H. Epley of the Rutherford County Sheriff's Department, who was called to the Norman residence on the night of 12 June 1985. Inside the home, Epley found the defendant's husband, John Thomas Norman, lying on a bed in a rear bedroom with his face toward the wall and his back toward the middle of the room. He was dead, but blood was still coming from wounds to the back of his head. A later autopsy revealed three gunshot wounds to the head, two of which caused fatal brain injury. The autopsy also revealed a .12 percent blood alcohol level in the victim's body.

Later that night, the defendant related an account of the events leading to the killing, after Epley had advised her of her constitutional rights and she had waived her right to remain silent. The defendant told Epley that her husband had been beating her all day and had made her lie down on the floor while he slept on the bed. After her husband fell asleep, the defendant carried her grandchild to the defendant's mother's house. The defendant took a pistol from her mother's purse and walked the short distance back to her home. She pointed the pistol at the back of her sleeping husband's head, but it jammed the first time she tried to shoot him. She fixed the gun and then shot her husband in the back of the head as he lay sleeping.

After one shot, she felt her husband's chest and determined that he was still breathing and making sounds. She then shot him twice more in the back of the head. The defendant told Epley that she killed her husband because "she took all she was going to take from him, so she shot him."

The defendant presented evidence tending to show a long history of physical and mental abuse by her husband due to his alcoholism. At the time of the killing, the thirty-nine-year-old defendant and her husband had been married almost twenty-five years and had several children. The defendant testified that her husband had started drinking and abusing her about five years after they were married. His physical abuse of her consisted of frequent assaults that included slapping, punching and kicking her, striking her with various objects, and throwing glasses, beer bottles and other objects at her. The defendant described other specific incidents of abuse, such as her husband putting her cigarettes out on her, throwing hot coffee on her, breaking glass against her face and crushing food on her face. Although the defendant did not present evidence of ever having received medical treatment for any physical injuries inflicted by her husband, she displayed several scars about her face which she attributed to her husband's assaults.

The defendant's evidence also tended to show other indignities inflicted upon her by her husband. Her evidence tended to show that her husband did not work and forced her to make money by prostitution, and that he made humor of that fact to family and friends. He would beat her if she resisted going out to prostitute herself or if he was unsatisfied with the amounts of money she made. He routinely called the defendant "dog," "bitch" and "whore," and on a few occasions made her eat pet food out of the pets' bowls and bark like a dog. He often made her sleep on the floor. At times, he deprived her of food and refused to let her get food for the family. During those years of abuse, the defendant's husband threatened numerous times to kill her and to maim her in various ways.

The defendant said her husband's abuse occurred only when he was intoxicated, but that he would not give up drinking. She said she and her husband "got along very well when he was sober," and that he was "a good guy" when he was not drunk. She had accompanied her husband to the local mental health center for sporadic counseling sessions for his problem, but he continued to drink.

In the early morning hours on the day before his death, the defendant's husband, who was intoxicated, went to a rest area off I-85 near Kings Mountain where the defendant was engaging in prostitution and assaulted her. While driving home, he was stopped by a patrolman and jailed on a charge of driving while impaired. After the defendant's mother got him out of jail at the defendant's request later that morning, he resumed his drinking and abuse of the defendant.

The defendant's evidence also tended to show that her husband seemed angrier than ever after he was released from jail and that his abuse of the defendant was more frequent. That evening, sheriff's deputies were called to the Norman residence, and the defendant complained that her husband had been beating her all day and she could not take it anymore. The defendant was advised to file a complaint, but she said she was afraid her husband would kill her if she had him arrested. The deputies told her they needed a warrant before they could arrest her husband, and they left the scene.

The deputies were called back less than an hour later after the defendant had taken a bottle of pills. The defendant's husband cursed her and called her names as she was attended by paramedics, and he told them to let her die. A sheriff's deputy finally chased him back into his house as the defendant was put into an ambulance. The defendant's stomach was pumped at the local hospital, and she was sent home with her mother.

While in the hospital, the defendant was visited by a therapist with whom she discussed filing charges against her husband and having him committed for treatment. Before the therapist left, the defendant agreed to go to the mental health center the next day to discuss those possibilities. The therapist testified at trial that the defendant seemed depressed in the hospital, and that she expressed considerable anger toward her husband. He testified that the defendant threatened a number of times that night to kill her husband and that she said she should kill him "because of the things he had done to her."

The next day, the day she shot her husband, the defendant went to the mental health center to talk about charges and possible commitment, and she confronted her husband with that possibility. She testified that she told her husband later that day: "J.T., straighten up. Quit drinking. I'm going to have you committed to help you." She said her husband then told her he would "see them coming" and would cut her throat before they got to him.

The defendant also went to the social services office that day to seek welfare benefits, but her husband followed her there, interrupted her interview and made her go home with him. He continued his abuse of her, threatening to kill and to maim her, slapping her, kicking her, and throwing objects at her. At one point, he took her cigarette and put it out on her, causing a small burn on her upper torso. He would not let her eat or bring food into the house for their children.

That evening, the defendant and her husband went into their bedroom to lie down, and he called her a "dog" and made her lie on the floor when he lay down on the bed. Their daughter brought in her baby to leave with the defendant, and the defendant's husband agreed to let her baby-sit. After the defendant's husband fell asleep, the baby started crying and the defendant took it to her mother's house so it would not wake up her husband. She returned shortly with the pistol and killed her husband.

The defendant testified at trial that she was too afraid of her husband to press charges against him or to leave him. She said that she had temporarily left their home on several previous occasions, but he had always found her, brought her home and beaten her. Asked why she killed her husband, the defendant replied: "Because I was scared of him and I knowed when he woke up, it was going to be the same thing, and I was scared when he took me to the truck stop that night it was going to be worse than he had ever been. I just couldn't take it no more. There ain't no way, even if it means going to prison. It's better than living in that. That's worse hell than anything."

The defendant and other witnesses testified that for years her husband had frequently threatened to kill her and to maim her. When asked if she believed those threats, the defendant replied: "Yes. I believed him; he would, he would kill me if he got a chance. If he thought he wouldn't a had to went to jail, he would a done it."

Two expert witnesses in forensic psychology and psychiatry who examined the defendant after the shooting, Dr. William Tyson and Dr. Robert Rollins, testified that the defendant fit the profile of battered wife syndrome. This condition, they testified, is characterized by such abuse and degradation that the battered wife comes to believe she is unable to help herself and cannot expect help from anyone else. She believes that she cannot escape the complete control of her husband and that he is invulnerable to law enforcement and other sources of help.

Dr. Tyson, a psychologist, was asked his opinion as to whether, on 12 June 1985, "it appeared reasonably necessary for Judy Norman to shoot J. T. Norman?" He replied: "I believe that . . . Mrs. Norman believed herself to be doomed . . . to a life of the worst kind of torture and abuse, degradation that she had experienced over the years in a progressive way; that it would only get worse, and that death was inevitable. . . . Dr. Tyson later added: "I think Judy Norman felt that she had no choice, both in the protection of herself and her family, but to engage, exhibit deadly force against Mr. Norman, and that in so doing, she was sacrificing herself, both for herself and for her family."

Dr. Rollins, who was the defendant's attending physician at Dorothea Dix Hospital when she was sent there for evaluation, testified that in his opinion the defendant was a typical abused spouse and that "[s]he saw herself as powerless to deal with the situation, that there was no alternative, no way she could escape it." Dr. Rollins was asked his opinion as to whether "on June 12th, 1985, it appeared reasonably necessary that Judy Norman would take the life of J.T. Norman?" Dr. Rollins replied that in his opinion, "that course of action did appear necessary to Mrs. Norman."

Based on the evidence that the defendant exhibited battered wife syndrome, that she believed she could not escape her husband nor expect help from others, that her husband had threatened her, and that her husband's abuse of her had worsened in the two days preceding his death, the Court of Appeals concluded that a jury reasonably could have found that her killing of her husband was justified as an act of perfect self-defense. The Court of Appeals reasoned that the nature of battered wife syndrome is such that a jury could not be precluded from finding the defendant killed her husband lawfully in self-defense, even though he was asleep when she killed him. We disagree.

The right to kill in self-defense is based on the necessity, real or reasonably apparent, of killing an unlawful aggressor to save oneself from imminent death or great bodily harm at his hands. Our law has recognized that self-preservation under such circumstances springs from a primal impulse and is an inherent right of natural law.

In North Carolina, a defendant is entitled to have the jury consider acquittal by reason of perfect self-defense when the evidence, viewed in the light most favorable to the defendant, tends to show that at the time of the killing it appeared to the defendant and she believed it to be necessary to kill the decedent to save herself from imminent death or great bodily harm. That belief must be reasonable, however, in that the circumstances as they appeared to the defendant would create such a belief in the mind of a person of ordinary firmness. *Id.* Further, the defendant must not have been the initial aggressor provoking the fatal confrontation. *Id.* A killing in the proper exercise of the right of perfect self-defense is always completely justified in law and constitutes no legal wrong.

The defendant in the present case was not entitled to a jury instruction on self-defense. The trial court was not required to instruct self-defense unless evidence was introduced tending to show that at the time of the killing the defendant reasonably believed herself to be confronted by circumstances which necessitated her killing her husband to save herself from imminent death or great bodily harm. No such evidence was introduced in this case.

The killing of another human being is the most extreme recourse to our inherent right of self-preservation and can be justified in law only by the utmost real or apparent necessity brought about by the decedent. For that reason, our law of self-defense has required that a defendant claiming that a homicide was justified and, as a result, inherently lawful by reason of perfect self-defense must establish that she reasonably believed at the time of the killing she otherwise would have immediately suffered death or great bodily harm. Only if defendants are required to show that they killed due to a reasonable belief that death or great bodily harm was imminent can the justification for homicide remain clearly and firmly rooted in necessity. The Imminence requirement ensures that deadly force will be used only where it is necessary as a last resort in the exercise of the inherent right of self-preservation. It also ensures that before a homicide is justified and, as a result, not a legal wrong, it will be reliably determined that the defendant reasonably believed that absent the use of deadly force, not only would an unlawful attack have occurred, but also that the attack would have caused death or great bodily harm. The law does not sanction the use of deadly force to repel simple assaults.

The term "imminent," as used to describe such perceived threats of death or great bodily harm as will justify a homicide by reason of self-defense, has been defined as "immediate danger, such as must be instantly met, such as cannot be guarded against by calling for the assistance of others or the protection of the law." BLACK's LAW DICTIONARY 676 (5th ed. 1979). Our cases have sometimes used the phrase "about to suffer" interchangeably with "imminent" to describe the immediacy of threat that is required to justify killing in self-defense.

The evidence in this case did not tend to show that the defendant reasonably believed that she was confronted by a threat of imminent death or great bodily harm. The evidence tended to show that no harm was "imminent" or about to happen to the defendant when she shot her husband. The uncontroverted evidence was that her husband had been asleep for some time when she walked to her mother's house, returned with the pistol, fixed the pistol after it jammed and then shot her husband three times in the back of the head. The defendant was not faced with an instantaneous choice between killing her husband or being killed or seriously injured. Instead, all of the evidence tended to show that the defendant had ample time and opportunity to resort to other means of preventing further abuse by her husband. There was no action underway by the decedent from which the jury could have found that the defendant had reasonable grounds to believe either that a felonious assault was imminent or that it might result in her death or great bodily injury. Additionally, no such action by the decedent had been underway immediately prior to his falling asleep.

Faced with somewhat similar facts, we have previously held that a defendant who believed himself to be threatened by the decedent was not entitled to a jury instruction on self-defense when it was the defendant who went to the decedent and initiated the final, fatal confrontation. *State v. Mize*, 316 N.C. 48, 340 S.E.2d 439 (1986). In *Mize*, the decedent Joe McDonald was reported to be looking for the defendant George Mize to get revenge for Mize's alleged rape of McDonald's girlfriend, which had exacerbated existing animosity between Mize and McDonald. After hiding from McDonald for most of the day, Mize finally went to McDonald's residence, woke him up and then shot and killed him. Mize claimed that he feared McDonald was going to kill him and that his killing of McDonald was in self-defense. Rejecting Mize's argument that his jury should have been instructed on self-defense, we stated: Here, although the victim had pursued defendant during the day approximately eight hours before the killing, defendant Mize was in no imminent danger while McDonald was at home asleep. When Mize went to McDonald's trailer with his shotgun, it was a new confrontation. Therefore, even if Mize believed it was necessary to kill McDonald to avoid his own imminent death, that belief was unreasonable. The same reasoning applies in the present case.

Additionally, the lack of any belief by the defendant—reasonable or otherwise—that she faced a threat of imminent death or great bodily harm from the drunk and sleeping victim in the present case was illustrated by the defendant and her own expert witnesses when testifying about her subjective assessment of her situation at the time of the killing. The psychologist and psychiatrist replied affirmatively when asked their opinions of whether killing her husband "appeared reasonably necessary" to the defendant at the time of the homicide. That testimony spoke of no imminent threat nor of any fear by the defendant of death or great bodily harm, imminent or otherwise. Testimony in the form of a conclusion that a killing "appeared reasonably necessary" to a defendant does not tend to show all that must be shown to establish self-defense. More specifically, for a killing to be in self-defense, the perceived necessity must arise from a reasonable fear of imminent death or great bodily harm.

Dr. Tyson additionally testified that the defendant "believed herself to be doomed . . . to a life of the worst kind of torture and abuse, degradation that she had experienced over the years in a progressive way; that it would only get worse, and that death was inevitable." Such evidence of the defendant's speculative beliefs concerning her remote and indefinite future, while indicating she had felt generally threatened, did not tend to show that she killed in the belief—reasonable or otherwise—that her husband presented a threat of imminent death or great bodily harm. Under our law of self-defense, a defendant's subjective belief of what might be "inevitable" at some indefinite point in the future does not equate to what she believes to be "imminent." Dr. Tyson's opinion that the defendant believed it was necessary to kill her husband for "the protection of herself and her family" was similarly indefinite and devoid of time frame and did not tend to show a threat or fear of imminent harm.

The defendant testified that, "I knowed when he woke up, it was going to be the same thing, and I was scared when he took me to the truck stop that night it was going to be worse than he had ever been." She also testified, when asked if she believed her husband's threats: "Yes. . . . [H]e would kill me if he got a chance. If he thought he wouldn't a had to went to jail, he would a done it." Testimony about such indefinite fears concerning what her sleeping husband might do at some time in the future did not tend to establish a fear—reasonable or otherwise—of imminent death or great bodily harm at the time of the killing.

We are not persuaded by the reasoning of our Court of Appeals in this case that when there is evidence of battered wife syndrome, neither an actual attack nor threat of attack by the husband at the moment the wife uses deadly force is required to justify the wife's killing of him in perfect self-defense. The Court of Appeals concluded that to impose such requirements would ignore the "learned helplessness," meekness and other realities of battered wife syndrome and would effectively preclude such women from exercising their right of self-defense. Other jurisdictions which have addressed this question under similar facts are divided in their views, and we can discern no clear majority position on facts closely similar to those of this case. *Compare, e.g., Commonwealth v. Grove*, 363 Pa. Super. 328, 526 A.2d 369, *appeal denied*, 517 Pa. 630, 539 A.2d 810 (1987) (abused wife who killed her sleeping husband not entitled to self-defense instruction as no immediate threat was posed by the decedent), *with State v. Gallegos*, 104 N.M. 247, 719 P.2d 1268 (1986) (abused wife could claim self-defense where she walked into bedroom with gun and killed husband who was awake but lying on the bed).

The reasoning of our Court of Appeals in this case proposes to change the established law of self-defense by giving the term "imminent" a meaning substantially more indefinite and all-encompassing than its present meaning. This would result in a substantial relaxation of the requirement of real or apparent necessity to justify homicide. Such reasoning proposes justifying the taking of human life not upon the reasonable belief it is necessary to prevent death or great bodily harm—which the imminence requirement ensures—but upon purely subjective speculation that the decedent probably would present a threat to life at a future time and that the defendant would not be able to avoid the predicted threat.

The Court of Appeals suggests that such speculation would have been particularly reliable in the present case because the jury, based on the evidence of the decedent's intensified abuse during the thirty-six hours preceding his death, could have found that the decedent's passive state at the time of his death was "but a momentary hiatus in a continuous reign of terror by the decedent [and] the defendant merely took advantage of her first opportunity to protect herself." Requiring jury instructions on perfect self-defense in such situations, however, would still tend to make opportune homicide lawful as a result of mere subjective predictions of indefinite future assaults and circumstances. Such predictions of future assaults to justify the defendant's use of deadly force in this case would be entirely speculative, because there was no evidence that her husband had ever inflicted any harm upon her that approached life-threatening injury, even during the "reign of terror." It is far from clear in the defendant's poignant evidence that any abuse by the decedent had ever involved the degree of physical threat required to justify the defendant in using deadly force, even when those threats were imminent. The use of deadly force in self-defense to prevent harm other than death or great bodily harm is excessive as a matter of law.

As we have stated, stretching the law of self-defense to fit the facts of this case would require changing the "imminent death or great bodily harm" requirement to something substantially more indefinite than previously required and would weaken our assurances that justification for the taking of human life remains firmly rooted in real or apparent necessity. That result in principle could not be limited to a few cases decided on evidence as poignant as this. The relaxed requirements for self-defense proposed by our Court of Appeals would tend to categorically legalize the opportune killing of abusive husbands by their wives solely on the basis of the wives' testimony concerning their subjective speculation as to the probability of future felonious assaults by their husbands. Homicidal self-help would then become a lawful solution, and perhaps the easiest and most effective solution, to this problem. *See generally* Rosen, *The Excuse of Self-Defense: Correcting a Historical Accident on Behalf of Battered Women Who Kill*, 36 Am. U. L. Rev. 11 (1986) (advocating changing the basis of self-defense acquittals to excuse rather than justification, so that excusing battered women's killing of their husbands under circumstances not fitting within the traditional requirements of self-defense would not be seen as justifying and therefore encouraging such self-help killing). It has even been suggested that the relaxed requirements of self-defense found in what is often called the "battered woman's defense" could be extended in principle to any type of case in which a defendant testified that he or she subjectively believed that killing was necessary and proportionate to any perceived threat.

In conclusion, we decline to expand our law of self-defense beyond the limits of immediacy and necessity which have heretofore provided an appropriately narrow but firm basis upon which homicide may be justified and, thus, lawful by reason of self-defense.

For the foregoing reasons, we conclude that the defendant's conviction for voluntary manslaughter and the trial court's judgment sentencing her to a six-year term of imprisonment were without error. Therefore, we must reverse the decision of the Court of Appeals which awarded the defendant a new trial.

REVERSED

MARTIN, J. dissenting:

At the heart of the majority's reasoning is its unsubstantiated concern that to find that the evidence presented by defendant would support an instruction on self-defense would "expand our law of self-defense beyond the limits of immediacy and necessity." Defendant does not seek to expand or relax the requirements of self-defense and thereby "legalize the opportune killing of allegedly abusive husbands by their wives," as the majority overstates. Rather, defendant contends that the evidence as gauged by the existing laws of self-defense is sufficient to require the submission of a self-defense instruction to the jury. The proper issue for this Court is to determine whether the evidence, viewed in the light most favorable to the defendant, was sufficient to require the trial court to instruct on the law of self-defense. I conclude that it was.

> A defendant is entitled to an instruction on self-defense when there is evidence, viewed in the light most favorable to the defendant, that these four elements existed at the time of the killing:
>
> (1) it appeared to defendant and he believed it to be necessary to kill the deceased in order to save himself from death or great bodily harm; and
>
> (2) defendant's belief was reasonable in that the circumstances as they appeared to him at the time were sufficient to create such a belief in the mind of a person of ordinary firmness; and
>
> (3) defendant was not the aggressor in bringing on the affray, i.e., he did not aggressively and willingly enter into the fight without legal excuse or provocation; and
>
> (4) defendant did not use excessive force, i.e., did not use more force than was necessary or reasonably appeared to him to be necessary under the circumstances to protect himself from death or great bodily harm. The first element requires that there be evidence that the defendant believed it was necessary to kill in order to protect herself from serious bodily harm or death; the second requires that the circumstances as defendant perceived them were sufficient to create such a belief in the mind of a person of ordinary firmness. Both elements were supported by evidence at defendant's trial.

Evidence presented by defendant described a twenty-year history of beatings and other dehumanizing and degrading treatment by her husband. In his expert testimony a clinical psychologist concluded that defendant fit "and exceed[ed]" the profile of an abused or battered spouse, analogizing this treatment to the dehumanization process suffered by prisoners of war under the Nazis during the Second World War and the brainwashing techniques of the Korean War. The psychologist described the defendant as a woman incarcerated by abuse, by fear, and by her conviction that her husband was invincible and inescapable: Mrs. Norman didn't leave because she believed, fully believed that escape was totally impossible. There was no place to go. She had left before; he had come and gotten her. She had gone to the Department of Social Services. He had come and gotten her. The law, she believed the law could not protect her; no one could protect her, and I must admit, looking over the records, that there was nothing done that would contradict that belief. She fully believed that he was invulnerable to the law and to all social agencies that were available; that nobody could withstand his power. As a result, there was no such thing as escape. When asked if he had an opinion whether it appeared reasonably necessary for Judy Norman to shoot her husband, this witness responded: "Yes. . . . I believe that in examining the facts of this case and examining the psychological data, that Mrs. Norman believed herself to be doomed . . . to a life of the worst kind of torture and abuse, degradation that she had experienced over the years in a progressive way; that it would only get worse, and that death was inevitable; death of herself, which was not such, I don't think was such an issue for her, as she had attempted to commit suicide, and in her continuing conviction of J.T. Norman's power over her, and even failed at that form of escape. I believe she also came to the point of beginning to fear for family members and her children, that were she to commit suicide that the abuse and the treatment that was heaped on her would be transferred onto them." This testimony describes defendant's perception of circumstances in which she was held hostage to her husband's abuse for two decades and which ultimately compelled her to kill him. This testimony alone is evidence amply indicating the first two elements required for entitlement to an instruction on self-defense.

In addition to the testimony of the clinical psychologist, defendant presented the testimony of witnesses who had actually seen defendant's husband abuse her. These witnesses described circumstances that caused not only defendant to believe escape was impossible, but that also convinced them of its impossibility. Defendant's isolation and helplessness were evident in testimony that her family was intimidated by her husband into acquiescing in his torture of her. Witnesses also described defendant's experience with social service agencies and the law, which had contributed to her sense of futility and abandonment through the inefficacy of their protection and the strength of her husband's wrath when they failed. Where torture appears interminable and escape impossible, the belief that only the death of the oppressor can provide relief is reasonable in the mind of a person of ordinary firmness, let alone in the mind of the defendant, who, like a prisoner of war of some years, has been deprived of her humanity and is held hostage by fear.

In *State v. Mize*, this Court noted that if the defendant was in "no imminent danger" at the time of the killing, then his belief that it was necessary to kill the man who had pursued him eight hours before was unreasonable. The second element of self-defense was therefore not satisfied. In the context of the doctrine of self-defense, the definition of "imminent" must be informed by the defendant's perceptions. It is not bounded merely by measurable time, but by all of the facts and circumstances. Its meaning depends upon the assessment of the facts by one of "ordinary firmness" with regard to whether the defendant's perception of impending death or injury was so pressing as to render reasonable her belief that it was necessary to kill.

Evidence presented in the case *sub judice* revealed no letup of tension or fear, no moment in which the defendant felt released from impending serious harm, even while the decedent slept. This, in fact, is a state of mind common to the battered spouse, and one that dramatically distinguishes Judy Norman's belief in the imminence of serious harm from that asserted by the defendant in *Mize*. Psychologists have observed and commentators have described a "constant state of fear" brought on by the cyclical nature of battering as well as the battered spouse's perception that her abuser is both "omnipotent and unstoppable." Constant fear means a perpetual anticipation of the next blow, a perpetual expectation that the next blow will kill. "[T]he battered wife is constantly in a heightened state of terror because she is certain that one day her husband will kill her during the course of a beating. . . . Thus, from the perspective of the battered wife, the danger is constantly 'immediate.'" Eber, *The Battered Wife's Dilemma: To Kill or To Be Killed*, 32 HASTINGS L.J. 895, 928–29 (1981). For the battered wife, if there is no escape, if there is no window of relief or momentary sense of safety, then the next attack, which could be the fatal one, is imminent. In the context of the doctrine of self-defense, "imminent" is a term the meaning of which must be grasped from the defendant's point of view. Properly stated, the second prong of the question is not whether the threat was in fact imminent, but whether defendant's belief in the impending nature of the threat, given the circumstances as she saw them, was reasonable in the mind of a person of ordinary firmness.[1]

Defendant's intense fear, based on her belief that her husband intended not only to maim or deface her, as he had in the past, but to kill her, was evident in the testimony of witnesses who recounted events of the last three days of the decedent's life. This testimony could have led a juror to conclude that defendant reasonably perceived a threat to her life as "imminent," even while her husband slept. Over these three days, her husband's anger was exhibited in an unprecedented crescendo

---

1. This interpretation of the meaning of "imminent" is reflected in the Comments to the Model Penal Code: "The actor must believe that his defensive action is immediately necessary and the unlawful force against which he defends must be force that he apprehends will be used on the present occasion, but he need not apprehend that it will be immediately used." Model Penal Code § 3.04 comment (ALI 1985).

of violence. The evidence showed defendant's fear and sense of hopelessness similarly intensifying, leading to an unsuccessful attempt to escape through suicide and culminating in her belief that escape would be possible only through her husband's death.

Defendant testified that on 10 June, two days before her husband's death, he had again forced her to go to a rest stop near Kings Mountain to make money by prostitution. Her daughter Phyllis and Phyllis's boyfriend Mark Navarra accompanied her on this occasion because, defendant said, whenever her husband took her there, he would beat her. Phyllis corroborated this account. She testified that her father had arrived sometime later and had begun beating her mother, asking how much money she had. Defendant said they all then drove off. Shortly afterwards an officer arrested defendant's husband for driving under the influence.

Defendant testified that her husband was argumentative and abusive all through the next day, 11 June. Mark Navarra testified that at one point, defendant's husband threw a sandwich that defendant had made for him on the floor. She made another; he threw it on the floor, as well, then insisted she prepare one without touching it. Defendant's husband had then taken the third sandwich, which defendant had wrapped in paper towels, and smeared it on her face. Both Navarra and Phyllis testified that they had later watched defendant's husband seize defendant's cigarette and put it out on her neck, the scars from which defendant displayed to the jury.

A police officer testified that he arrived at defendant's home at 8:00 that evening in response to a call reporting a domestic quarrel. Defendant, whose face was bruised, was crying, and she told the officer that her husband had beaten her all day long and that she could not take it any longer. The officer told her that he could do nothing for her unless she took out a warrant on her husband. She responded that if she did, her husband would kill her. The officer left but was soon radioed to return because defendant had taken an overdose of pills. The officer testified that defendant's husband was interfering with ambulance attendants, saying "Let the bitch die." When he refused to respond to the officer's warning that if he continued to hinder the attendants, he would be arrested, the officer was compelled to chase him into the house.

Defendant's mother testified that her son-in-law had reacted to the discovery that her daughter had taken the pills with cursing and obscenities and threats such as, "Now, you're going to pay for taking those pills," and "I'll kill you, your mother and your grandmother." His rage was such that defendant's mother feared he might kill the whole family, and knowing defendant's sister had a gun in her purse, she took the gun and placed it in her own.

Defendant was taken to the hospital, treated, and released at 2:30 a.m. She spent the remainder of the night at her grandmother's house. Defendant testified that the next day, 12 June, she felt dazed all day long. She went in the morning to the county mental health center for guidance on domestic abuse. When she returned home, she tried to talk to her husband, telling him to "straighten up. Quit drinking. . . . I'm going to have you committed to help you." Her husband responded, "If you do, I'll see them coming and before they get here, I'll cut your throat."

Later, her husband made her drive him and his friend to Spartanburg to pick up the friend's paycheck. On the way, the friend testified, defendant's husband "started slapping on her" when she was following a truck too closely, and he periodically poured his beer into a glass, then reached over and poured it on defendant's head. At one point, defendant's husband lay down on the front seat with his head on the arm rest, "like he was going to go to sleep," and kicked defendant, who was still driving, in the side of the head.

Mark Navarra testified that in the year and a half he had lived with the Normans, he had never seen defendant's husband madder than he was on 12 June, opining that it was the DUI arrest two days before that had ignited J.T.'s fury. Phyllis testified that her father had beaten her mother "all day long." She testified that this was the third day defendant's husband had forbidden her to eat any food. Phyllis said defendant's family tried to get her to eat, but defendant, fearing a beating, would not. Although Phyllis's grandmother had sent over a bag of groceries that day, defendant's husband had made defendant put them back in the bag and would not let anyone eat them.

Early in the evening of 12 June, defendant's husband told defendant, "Let's go to bed." Phyllis testified that although there were two beds in the room, her father had forbidden defendant from sleeping on either. Instead, he had made her lie down on the concrete floor between the two beds, saying, "Dogs don't lay in the bed. They lay in the floor." Shortly afterward, defendant testified, Phyllis came in and asked her father if defendant could take care of her baby while she went to the store. He assented and eventually went to sleep. Defendant was still on the floor, the baby on the small bed. The baby started to cry and defendant "snuck up and took him out there to [her] mother's [house]." She asked her mother to watch the baby, then asked if her mother had anything for headache, as her head was "busting." Her mother responded that she had some pain pills in her purse. Defendant went in to get the pills, "and the gun was in there, and I don't know, I just seen the gun, and I took it out, and I went back there and shot him."

From this evidence of the exacerbated nature of the last three days of twenty years of provocation, a juror could conclude that defendant believed that her husband's threats to her life were viable, that serious bodily harm was imminent, and that it was necessary to kill her husband to escape that harm. And from this evidence a juror could find defendant's belief in the necessity to kill her husband not merely reasonable but compelling.

Finally, the fourth element of self-defense poses the question of whether there was any evidence tending to show that the force used by defendant to repel her husband was not excessive, that is, more than reasonably appeared to be necessary under the circumstances. This question is answered in part by abundant testimony describing defendant's immobilization by fear caused by abuse by her husband. Three witnesses, including the decedent's best friend, all recounted incidents in which defendant passively accepted beating, kicks, commands, or humiliating affronts without striking back. From such evidence that she was paralyzed by her husband's presence, a jury could infer that it reasonably appeared to defendant to be necessary to kill her husband in order ultimately to protect herself from the death he had threatened and from severe bodily injury, a foretaste of which she had already experienced.

In *State v. Wingler*, 184 N.C. 747, 115 S.E. 59 (1922), in which the defendant was found guilty for the murder of his wife, Justice Stacy recognized the pain and oppression under which a woman suffers at the hands of an abusive husband: "The supreme tragedy of life is the immolation of woman. With a heavy hand, nature exacts from her a high tax of blood and tears." By his barbaric conduct over the course of twenty years, J.T. Norman reduced the quality of the defendant's life to such an abysmal state that, given the opportunity to do so, the jury might well have found that she was justified in acting in self-defense for the preservation of her tragic life.

If the evidence in support of self-defense is sufficient to create a reasonable doubt in the mind of a rational juror whether the state has proved an intentional killing without justification or excuse, self-defense must be submitted to the jury. This is such a case.

Questions and Notes

1. Is the court's concern about letting self-defense go to the jury predicated on: (1) the subjective rather than objective nature of her fears, (2) the lack of imminence, or (3) insufficient severity of harm?

2. If the concern was subjectivity, did defense counsel exacerbate the problem by focusing on "the battered woman's syndrome"?

3. Should the standard of reasonableness be the person of ordinary firmness or the ordinary battered woman? What would the court say? What would Justice Martin say?

4. What would a person of ordinary firmness have thought necessary in Mrs. Norman's situation?

5. Assuming that Ms. Norman did not reasonably fear death, did she fear any harm against which she could use deadly force?

6. Are there any points in the chronology of events leading up to Mr. Norman's death when Ms. Norman would have been justified in using deadly force?

7. How would *Norman* have been decided under the Nebraska statute in *Schroeder*? If the case arose in Nebraska and you represented Ms. Norman, could you have distinguished *Schroeder*? How?

8. Do people like J.T. Norman deserve to be killed? In what sense? Should their crimes be punishable by death?

9. If you think that Ms. Norman should have prevailed on her self-defense claim, do you think that she was justified (society is glad she killed him) or merely excused (society would have preferred that she had not killed him, but is sufficiently understanding to not impose penal sanctions)?

10. We will shortly turn to *Weiand*, a case raising the issue of retreat in a context somewhat similar to *Norman*. We will see that the Florida court takes a very different view of battered spouse syndrome from that of the North Carolina court. But first, we reexamine another aspect of the *Russell* case.

B. Retreat Rule

People v. Russell
693 N.E.2d 193 (N.Y. 1998)

[The facts of this case are reprinted at page 190, *supra*—Ed.]

CHIEF JUDGE KAYE.

At trial, all three defendants sought to exonerate themselves by arguing self-defense—each claiming that their opponent shot first and they were justified in firing back. Under New York law, however, a person who reasonably believes that another is about to use deadly physical force is not free to reciprocate with "deadly physical force if he knows that he can with complete safety as to himself and others avoid the necessity of so doing by retreating" (Penal Law § 35.15[2][a]; *People v. Goetz*, 68 NY2d 96, 106.) Here, there was evidence that defendants did not avail themselves of opportunities for safe retreat, choosing instead to use deadly force against each other. As such, there was adequate support for each jury's rejection of defendants' justification defense.

Questions and Notes

1. Does the retreat rule reward bullies and encourage cowardice?

2. Does the retreat rule comport with reality in the Brooklyn projects? Assume that Russell and Bekka really were coming after Burroughs, but that Burroughs, like his female friends who were with him, could have retreated. Would it be realistic to expect Borroughs to run and hide? Even if your answer is "no," is the result nevertheless justifiable in that the law wants to create an incentive for people to retreat to prevent what happened in this case?

3. Most jurisdictions that have recently considered the question seem to have adopted some form of the retreat rule, although it may still not be the majority view in this country. In *Weiand*, we see an application of the retreat rule in the context of a battered spouse.

Weiand v. State

24 Fla. L. Weekly S124 (1999)

Pariente, J.

II. Facts

Kathleen Weiand was charged with first-degree murder for the 1994 shooting death of her husband Todd Weiand. Weiand shot her husband during a violent argument in the apartment where the two were living together with their seven-week-old daughter. At trial Weiand claimed self-defense and presented battered spouse syndrome[3] evidence pursuant to *Hickson* in support of her claim. Weiand testified that her husband had beaten and choked her throughout the course of their three-year relationship and had threatened further violence if she left him.

Two experts, including Dr. Lenore Walker, a nationally recognized expert on battered women, testified that Weiand suffered from "battered woman's syndrome." Dr. Walker detailed Weiand's history of abuse by her husband and testified about the effect of the abusive relationship on Weiand. Based on her studies, her work with Weiand and Weiand's history of abuse, Dr. Walker concluded that when Weiand shot her husband she believed that he was going to seriously hurt or kill her.

Dr. Walker opined that there were several reasons why Weiand did not leave the apartment that night during the argument, despite apparent opportunities to do so: she felt that she was unable to leave because she had just given birth seven weeks earlier; she had been choked unconscious; she was paralyzed with terror; and experience had taught her that threats of leaving only made her husband more violent.

At the charge conference following the close of the evidence, defense counsel requested that the following standard jury instruction be given:

> If the defendant was attacked in [his][her] own home or on [his][her] own premises, [he][she] had no duty to retreat and had the lawful right to stand [his][her] ground and meet force with force, even to the extent of using force likely to cause death or great bodily harm if it was necessary to prevent either death or great bodily harm.

In accordance with this Court's opinion in *Bobbitt*, the trial court refused the request to give this "defense of home" instruction. Instead, the trial court only gave the instruction applicable in all self-defense cases regarding the duty to retreat:

---

3. The *amicus curiae* criticizes the use of the term "battered woman's syndrome," which is often used interchangeably with the term "battered spouse syndrome," arguing that the terms "do[ ] not fully capture all the material presented through expert testimony on domestic violence." Brief of *Amicus Curiae* at 7. We have used the terms in this opinion because the experts, including Dr. Lenore Walker, used them when testifying in this trial. We express no view on the criticism raised by the *amicus curiae*.

The fact that the defendant was wrongfully attacked cannot justify her use of force likely to cause death or great bodily harm if by retreating she could have avoided the need to use that force.

During closing arguments, the prosecutor used this standard instruction to the State's advantage by emphasizing Weiand's duty to retreat. The prosecutor stressed as "critical" that the killing could not be considered justifiable homicide unless Weiand had exhausted every reasonable means to escape the danger, including fleeing her home:

She had to exhaust every reasonable means of escape prior to killing him. Did she do that? No. Did she use the phone that was two feet away? No. Did she go out the door where her baby was sitting next to? No. Did she get in the car that she had driven all over town drinking and boozing it up all day? No.

The jury found Weiand guilty of second-degree murder and the trial court sentenced her to eighteen years' imprisonment. The Second District affirmed her conviction and sentence, see *Weiand*, 701 So. 2d at 565, but on rehearing certified the question of whether this Court should recede from *Bobbitt*.

III. The Privilege of Nonretreat from The Residence

Under Florida statutory and common law, a person may use deadly force in self-defense if he or she reasonably believes that deadly force is necessary to prevent imminent death or great bodily harm. Even under those circumstances, however, a person may not resort to deadly force without first using every reasonable means within his or her power to avoid the danger, including retreat. The duty to retreat emanates from common law, rather than from our statutes.[4]

There is an exception to this common law duty to retreat "to the wall," which applies when an individual claims self-defense in his or her own residence. An individual is not required to retreat from the residence before resorting to deadly force in self-defense, so long as the deadly force is necessary to prevent death or great bodily harm.

The privilege of nonretreat from the home, part of the "castle doctrine,"[5] has early common law origins. In [*People v.*] *Tomlins*, the defendant claimed self-defense when attacked in his home by his son. In reversing the defendant's conviction because the

---

4. Presently, however, a majority of jurisdictions do not impose a duty to retreat before a defendant may resort to deadly force when threatened with death or great bodily harm. There is no duty to retreat recognized when the defendant uses non-deadly force in self-defense.

5. The "castle doctrine" has also been defined as including:

the proposition that a person's dwelling house is a castle of defense for himself and his family, and an assault on it with intent to injure him or any lawful inmate of it may justify the use of force as protection, and even deadly force if there exist reasonable and factual grounds to believe that unless so used, a felony would be committed.

Falco v. State, 407 So. 2d 203, 208 (Fla. 1981).

duty to retreat instruction was given, Justice Cardozo explained the historical basis of the privilege of nonretreat from the home:

> It is not now and never has been the law that a man assailed in his own dwelling is bound to retreat. If assailed there, he may stand his ground and resist the attack. He is under no duty to take to the fields and the highways, a fugitive from his own home. More than 200 years ago it was said by Lord Chief Justice Hale: In case a man "is assailed in his own house, he need not flee as far as he can, as in other cases of *se defendendo*,[6] for he hath the protection of his house to excuse him from flying, as that would be to give up the protection of his house to his adversary by flight." Flight is for sanctuary and shelter, and shelter, if not sanctuary, is in the home. . . . The rule is the same whether the attack proceeds from some other occupant or from an intruder.

In *Hedges*, this Court applied the privilege of nonretreat from the residence where the attacker was not an intruder but an invitee with the defendant's permission to be on the premises. In that case, the defendant and the victim had maintained a long-term intimate relationship, and on the morning of the shooting the victim was an invitee, lawfully in the defendant's home. In instructing the jury on the law of self-defense, the trial court informed the jury that the defendant was required to use "all reasonable means within his power and consistent with his own safety to avoid the danger and avert the necessity of taking human life." The trial court failed to instruct the jury that the defendant was under no duty to retreat from her residence.

In reversing the conviction of manslaughter, our Court held:

> The instruction correctly stated the law as far as it went but again it was not complete. The quoted language placed upon the accused the duty to use all reasonable means consistent with her own safety to avoid the danger and avert the necessity of taking human life. To the lay mind this well could be construed to mean the duty to run or to get out of the way. There is no such duty when one is assaulted in his own home, despite the common law duty to "retreat to the wall" when one is attacked elsewhere. *Pell v. State*, 97 Fla. 650, 122 So. 110 [(1929)]. While *Pell* involved a trespasser, it clearly states the rule to be that when one is violently assaulted in his own house or immediately surrounding premises, he is not obliged to retreat but may stand his ground and use such force as prudence and caution would dictate as necessary to avoid death or great bodily harm. When in his home he has "retreated to the wall." *Pell* further decides that such an instruction should be an element of the charge on self-defense where the evidence supports it. Other courts have held that a man is under no duty to retreat when attacked in his own home. His home is his ultimate sanctuary.

---

6. Self defense. *See* BLACK'S LAW DICTIONARY 1357 (6th ed. 1990).

Eighteen years later, in *Bobbitt*, this Court considered whether the privilege of nonretreat from the home should also apply where the defendant killed her co-occupant husband in self-defense, after being attacked without provocation. This Court rejected the extension of Hedges under those circumstances:

> [T]he privilege not to retreat, premised on the maxim that every man's home is his castle which he is entitled to protect from invasion, does not apply here where both Bobbitt and her husband had equal rights to be in the "castle" and neither had the legal right to eject the other.

Justice Overton, in a strongly-worded dissent, disagreed with the majority's decision because it was contrary to a "basic premise in our law that the home is a special place of protection and security." He further criticized the distinction made by the majority that authorized the privilege of nonretreat instruction in cases like *Hedges*, where the aggressor was an invitee with a legal right to be on the premises, but not where the aggressor was a co-occupant.

At the time we rendered our decision in *Bobbitt* in 1982, we were in a minority of jurisdictions that refused to extend the privilege of nonretreat from the residence where the aggressor was a co-occupant. Since our decision in *Bobbitt*, an even greater number of jurisdictions have declined to impose a duty to retreat from the residence.

IV. Reconsideration of Our Decision in *Bobbitt*

We now conclude that it is appropriate to recede from *Bobbitt* and adopt Justice Overton's well-reasoned dissent in that case. We join the majority of jurisdictions that do not impose a duty to retreat from the residence when a defendant uses deadly force in self-defense, if that force is necessary to prevent death or great bodily harm from a co-occupant.

There are two distinct reasons for our conclusion. First, we can no longer agree with *Bobbitt*'s minority view that relies on concepts of property law and possessory rights to impose a duty to retreat from the residence. Second, based on our increased understanding of the plight of victims of domestic violence in the years since our decision in *Bobbitt*, we find that there are sound policy reasons for not imposing a duty to retreat from the residence when a defendant resorts to deadly force in self-defense against a co-occupant. The more recent decisions of state supreme courts confronting this issue have recognized that imposing a duty to retreat from the residence has a potentially damaging effect on victims of domestic violence claiming self-defense.

A. *Bobbitt*'s Possessory Rights Distinction

In refusing to extend the privilege of nonretreat in *Bobbitt*, we held that the privilege not to retreat . . . does not apply here where both Bobbitt and her husband had equal rights to be in the "castle" and neither had the legal right to eject the other.

Thus, our decision in *Bobbitt* appears to have been grounded upon the sanctity of property and possessory rights, rather than the sanctity of human life.

In light of our decision in *Hedges*, our holding in *Bobbitt* created a distinction that resulted in the privilege of nonretreat applying when the defendant is defending herself against an invitee, with a legal right to be on the premises, but not when defending herself against a co-occupant, who also had a legal right to be on the premises. Justice Overton illustrated the effect of this "illogical distinction" in his dissenting opinion in *Bobbitt*:

> Under the majority opinion, a woman killing her paramour in her home has more protection under the law than a woman who kills her husband in her home. More difficult still to understand is the application of the majority's rule to the situation where a mother is attacked in her home by a nineteen-year-old son. If the son is living in the home, the mother has a duty to retreat before she can use deadly force, but, if the son is not residing in the home, the mother has no duty to retreat before such force is used.

Bobbitt's distinction based on possessory rights may be important in the context of defending the home. However, the privilege of nonretreat from the home stems not from the sanctity of property rights, but from the time-honored principle that the home is the ultimate sanctuary. As has been asked rhetorically, if the duty to retreat from the home is applied to a defendant attacked by a co-occupant in the home, "whither shall he flee, and how far, and when may he be permitted to return?" *Jones v. Alabama*, 76 Ala. 8, 16 (1884).

The omission of the jury instruction on the privilege of nonretreat from the home is not cured by the jury instruction given in all self-defense cases that there is no legal duty to retreat if retreating would increase the danger of death or great bodily harm. *See* Fla. Std. Jury Instr. (Crim.), "Justifiable Use of Deadly Force," §3.04(d) at 48. In *Hedges*, the jury was instructed that the defendant had to use all reasonable means consistent with her own safety to avoid the danger before resorting to deadly force in self-defense. 172 So. 2d at 826–27. We found that the instructions were incomplete because, without the privilege of nonretreat instruction, the jury may have believed that the defendant had a duty to retreat from her home. *See id.* at 827. For the same reason, we find that in circumstances where the nonretreat instruction is applicable, the instructions are incomplete and misleading if the nonretreat instruction is not given. *See id.*

B. Implications for Victims of Domestic Violence

1. Imposing a duty to retreat from the home may adversely impact victims of domestic violence.

Although the State argues that nothing has changed in the intervening years since *Bobbitt* to require us to recede from that decision, to the contrary, much has changed in the public policy of this State, based on increased knowledge about the plight of domestic violence victims. It is now widely recognized that domestic violence "attacks are often repeated over time, and escape from the home is rarely possible without the threat of great personal violence or death." As quoted by the New Jersey Supreme Court:

Imposition of the duty to retreat on a battered woman who finds herself the target of a unilateral, unprovoked attack in her own home is inherently unfair. During repeated instances of past abuse, she has "retreated," only to be caught, dragged back inside, and severely beaten again. If she manages to escape, other hurdles confront her. Where will she go if she has no money, no transportation, and if her children are left behind in the "care" of an enraged man?

What [the duty to retreat] exception means for a battered woman is that as long as it is a stranger who attacks her in her home, she has a right to fight back and labors under no duty to retreat. If the attacker is her husband or live-in partner, however, she must retreat. The threat of death or serious bodily injury may be just as real (and, statistically, is more real) when her husband or partner attacks her in home, but still she must retreat.

Studies show that women who retreat from the residence when attacked by their cooccupant spouse or boyfriend may, in fact, increase the danger of harm to themselves due to the possibility of attack after separation. According to Dr. Lenore Walker, "[t]he batterer would often rather kill, or die himself, than separate from the battered woman." Lenore E. Walker, Terrifying Love: Why Battered Women Kill and How Society Responds 65 (1989).

Experts in the field explain that separation or retreat can be the most dangerous time in the relationship for the victims of domestic violence because "[v]iolence increases dramatically when a woman leaves an abusive relationship." A leading expert in the field cites one study which revealed that forty-five percent of the murders of women "were generated by the man's 'rage over the actual or impending estrangement from his partner.'" Another study found that the murder of the battered victim was often "triggered by a walkout, a demand, a threat of separation [which] were taken by the men to represent intolerable desertion, rejection and abandonment. Thus . . . the threat of separation is usually the trigger for violence."

The imposition of a duty to retreat from one's residence when faced with a violent aggressor has the most significant impact on women because an overwhelming majority of victims of domestic violence are women. According to the statistics compiled by the Governor's Task Force on Domestic Violence, seventy-three percent of domestic violence victims are women. Domestic violence is the single major cause of injury to women, more frequent than auto accidents, rapes, and muggings combined. "Over four thousand women die annually at the hands of their abuser," and in 1995, of all female homicide victims, thirty-nine percent were killed during domestic violence incidents.[10] These studies and other similar findings in the intervening years since *Bobbitt* provide proof of Justice Overton's observation that

---

10. According to one commentator, "even conservative estimates suggest that women are abused in twelve percent of marriages, and . . . up to fifty percent of women will be victims of abuse during their lives." Joan H. Krause, *Of Merciful Justice and Justified Mercy: Commuting the Sentences of Battered Women Who Kill*, 46 Fla. L. Rev. 699, 702 (1994).

retaining a duty to retreat from the home "clearly penalizes spouses, and particularly wives, in defending themselves from an aggressor spouse."

2. A jury instruction on the duty to retreat may reinforce common myths about domestic violence.

There is a common myth that the victims of domestic violence are free to leave the battering relationship any time they wish to do so, and that the "'beatings' could not have been too bad for if they had been, she certainly would have left." This stereotypical view may extend beyond the jurors deciding the case. One commentator quotes a Maryland judge expressing disbelief of the defendant's claimed defense:

> The reason I don't believe it is because I don't believe anything like this could happen to me. If I was you and someone had threatened me with a gun, there is no way that I could continue to stay with them.

A jury instruction placing a duty to retreat from the home on the defendant may serve to legitimize the common myth and allow prosecutors to capitalize upon it. The prosecutor capitalized on the jury instruction and the common myth in this case when she questioned the believability of Weiand's claims and asked the jury why Weiand did not "go out the door?" and why she did not "get in the car?" before resorting to violence.

In *Hickson* we authorized the admission of battered spouse syndrome evidence to rebut the common myths concerning battered women and explained the very real dangers faced by women in these relationships. As the expert evidence demonstrates, there are many reasons battered women do not feel free to leave a battering relationship. The woman might have been isolated from her family by the abuser, she may not be able to afford to go, or she may realize that leaving is more dangerous than staying. To re-affirm *Bobbitt* with its duty to retreat from the home would undermine our reasons in *Hickson* for approving expert testimony on battered woman's syndrome.

C. The Evolution of Public Policy

In tandem with the increased understanding of domestic violence, there has been a substantial evolution in the public policy of this state since *Bobbitt*. A decision to recede from *Bobbitt* at this time is an evolution of the common law consistent with this evolution in public policy.[12]

Developments in all three branches of government since *Bobbitt* reflect the public's concern regarding the plight of victims of domestic violence. For example, recognizing that "violence against women in their own homes is epidemic in our

---

12. Although *stare decisis* is fundamentally important in our system of justice, it is not "an iron-clad and unwavering rule" so that we must bend to the "voice of the past, however outmoded or meaningless that voice may have become." The doctrine of *stare decisis* must bend when there has been a significant change in circumstances since the adoption of the legal rule. The changes in the public policy of this state, and our awareness of the plight of victims of domestic violence provides additional justification for receding from *Bobbitt*.

society," the executive branch has established a task force on domestic violence, whose purpose is the issuance of reports and recommendations which document "the extent of our awareness, and the responsiveness of our resources to battered women and their families."

Since the *Bobbitt* decision, the Legislature has enacted numerous laws in response to the plight of the victims of domestic violence. For example, the law now requires that a person arrested for domestic violence must be held until first appearance, and the court must consider the safety of the victim in determining whether the defendant should be released and in setting the defendant's bail.

Likewise, since our decision in *Bobbitt*, the judiciary has focused judicial resources on the plight of victims of spousal abuse. Eight domestic violence courts have been organized within the twenty judicial circuits of Florida. As of 1997, more than half of the twenty judicial circuits had domestic violence task forces. To further the goal of proper judicial response to incidents of domestic violence, this Court has been active in providing educational opportunities for judges throughout the state, and circuit and county court judges now have training available specifically addressing domestic violence and its related issues.

D. The Jury Instruction on the Privilege of Nonretreat

The public policy of this State is clearly directed at reducing domestic violence. We have thus considered the views of jurists in the minority position, who have expressed a concern that eliminating a duty to retreat from the residence will increase violence because "[t]here are dramatically more opportunities for deadly violence in the domestic setting than in the intrusion setting."

While there may be more opportunities for violence in the domestic setting, no empirical data has been presented, either through expert testimony or studies, demonstrating any correlation between eliminating a duty to retreat from the home and an increase in incidents of domestic violence. In contrast, a duty to retreat from the home adversely affects victims of domestic violence by placing them at greater risk of death or great bodily harm. In addition, failing to inform the jurors that the defendant had no duty to retreat from the residence when attacked by a co-occupant may actually reinforce commonly held myths concerning domestic violence victims.

As Florida's Standard Jury Instructions on self-defense make clear, a defendant is entitled to resort to deadly force in self-defense only if that force is necessary to protect himself or herself from death or great bodily harm. Furthermore, the jury is instructed in all cases—even those cases where the privilege of nonretreat instruction is given—that:

> The defendant cannot justify the use of force likely to cause death or great bodily harm unless [he][she] used every reasonable means within [his] [her] power and consistent with [his][her] own safety to avoid the danger before resorting to that force.

Thus, the availability of the nonretreat instruction does not "invite" violence.

Nonetheless, we conclude that Justice Overton's "middle ground" instruction, as set forth in his dissent in *Bobbitt*, satisfies any concern that eliminating a duty to retreat might invite violence. This instruction imposes a limited duty to retreat within the residence to the extent reasonably possible, but no duty to flee the residence. Accordingly, we adopt the following instruction:

> If the defendant was attacked in [his/her] own home, or on [his/her] own premises, by a co-occupant [or any other person lawfully on the premises] [he/she] had a duty to retreat to the extent reasonably possible without increasing [his/her] own danger of death or great bodily harm. However, the defendant was not required to flee [his/her] home and had the lawful right to stand [his/her] ground and meet force with force even to the extent of using force likely to cause death or great bodily harm if it was necessary to prevent death or great bodily harm to [himself/herself].

It is our increased knowledge of the complexities of domestic violence that provides the impetus for reconsidering our decision in *Bobbitt*. However, in deciding whether the privilege of nonretreat instruction is available we consider it inappropriate to distinguish between victims of domestic violence and other defendants who have been attacked by a co-occupant in the residence. This was the position espoused in Justice Overton's dissent.

As Justice Kogan stated in his concurring opinion in *Perkins v. State*, 576 So. 2d 1310, 1314 (Fla. 1991), "[t]he right to fend off an unprovoked and deadly attack is nothing less than the right to life itself, which [article I, section 2] of our Constitution declares to be a basic right." Thus, the privilege of nonretreat instruction should be equally available to all those lawfully residing in the premises, provided, of course, that the use of deadly force was necessary to prevent death or great bodily harm.[16] Because this instruction will apply to both invitees and co-occupants alike, we recede from *Hedges* to the extent that *Hedges* does not require a middle-ground instruction for invitees.

V. Exclusion of Defense Witnesses

Because we have jurisdiction to answer the certified question, we have jurisdiction to review other alleged errors raised in the appellate court.

We first emphasize that expert testimony about domestic violence, as authorized by *Hickson*, does not replace the value of eyewitness testimony to corroborate the claim of prior acts of abuse. We approved the admission of battered spouse syndrome testimony in Hickson as an aid to the jury in understanding the characteristics of

---

16. Most studies refer to victims of domestic violence as women because the overwhelming majority of the victims are women. However, because men can also be victims of domestic violence, our opinion applies to males and females alike. See Art. XI, §5(c), FLA. CONST.

victims of domestic violence and to help dispel common myths and stereotypes associated with them. However, expert testimony on battered spouse syndrome, even when it contains details of alleged incidents of abuse that have been related by the defendant to the expert, does not replace the importance of eyewitness testimony to corroborate the defense.

As the Second District correctly acknowledged, the trial court improperly excluded three defense witnesses, all of whom would have provided eyewitness testimony to corroborate Weiand's assertion of prior acts of abuse by her husband. None of the other witnesses who testified at trial gave eyewitness testimony of Weiand's abuse by her husband. Thus, the excluded witnesses would have provided the only direct testimony to support Weiand's claims of prior abuse and to corroborate the basis for the experts' opinions.

Nonetheless, the Second District found that the exclusion of the witnesses was harmless error in light of the testimony of the defendant herself, that of the two experts who explained the battered-spouse syndrome from which defendant suffered, and the history of abuse in the relationship. We disagree.

By excluding the witnesses in this case, the trial court deprived the defendant of eyewitness testimony. Furthermore, the exclusion of the three witnesses to prior incidents of domestic violence enabled the prosecutor to discredit Weiand's claims of abuse by arguing that no one had ever witnessed any injuries on Weiand or seen evidence of her husband's abuse of her:

> Nobody saw any injuries to [Kathy] then. Nobody saw anything. . . . And how do we know that she's not [a battered woman]? All we have to back her up is her own statements. . . . Nobody saw any injuries to her then. Nobody saw anything. . . . Co-workers didn't see injuries to her. Her mother-in-law didn't see injuries to her. Her father-in-law didn't see the injuries to her. . . . Nobody sees any injuries to her. Nobody, nobody, ever.

Thus, we find that the Second District erred by concluding that the exclusion of the witnesses was harmless beyond a reasonable doubt.

VI. Conclusion

In conclusion, we hold that there is no duty to retreat from the residence before resorting to deadly force against a co-occupant or invitee, if necessary, to prevent death or great bodily harm, although there is a limited duty to retreat within the residence to the extent reasonably possible. Thus, we answer the certified question, as rephrased, in the negative, recede from *Bobbitt*, recede in part from *Hedges*, and adopt the middle-ground jury instruction proposed by Justice Overton in his dissent in *Bobbitt*.

This opinion and the instruction will be applicable in all future cases, and all cases that are pending on direct review, or not yet final. This opinion will not, however, apply retroactively to convictions that have become final. The decision of the Second District is quashed.

Questions and Notes

1. The dissenting opinion agreed with the majority on the merits, but dissented on jurisdictional grounds, in part because the governor had granted executive clemency to the defendant, and the case will not be retried.

2. Is battered woman's syndrome evidence admissible in Florida to excuse the defendant from acting reasonably, or to prove that she did act reasonably?

3. Would Norman have been convicted in Florida? Explain.

4. Does the partial retreat rule make sense (i.e., one must retreat within the confines of one's residence, if attacked by a cotenant or invitee, but not outside of the residence)?

5. Should *Weiand* be limited to battered spouses? Suppose that in *Russell*, Russell and Burroughs were roommates, and one challenged the other, who could safely retreat. Should he be required to do so? Note that in *Schroeder*, the court would have required retreat but for the impossibility of a prisoner retreating from his cell.

6. Sometimes a person exercising defensive force is not protecting himself but is protecting another. In some of those instances, the other person may not have been justified in using defensive force, but the defendant reasonably thinks that he was. Under those circumstances, should the defendant's justification be measured by how the situation reasonably appeared to him, or by the scope of the other person's right? Think about that as you read *Young*.

C. Defense of Others

People v. Young

183 N.E.2d 319 (N.Y. 1962)

PER CURIAM.

Whether one, who in good faith aggressively intervenes in a struggle between another person and a police officer in civilian dress attempting to effect the lawful arrest of the third person, may be properly convicted of assault in the third degree is a question of law of first impression here. The opinions in the court below in the absence of precedents in this State carefully expound the opposing views found in other jurisdictions. The majority in the Appellate Division have adopted the minority rule in the other States that one who intervenes in a struggle between strangers under the mistaken but reasonable belief that he is protecting another who[m] he assumes is being unlawfully beaten is thereby exonerated from criminal liability. The weight of authority holds with the dissenters below that one who goes to the aid of a third person does so at his own peril.

While the doctrine espoused by the majority of the court below may have support in some States, we feel that such a policy would not be conducive to an orderly society. We agree with the settled policy of law in most jurisdictions that the right of a person to defend another ordinarily should not be greater than such person's right to defend himself. Whatever may be the public policy where the felony charged requires proof of a specific intent and the issue is justifiable homicide (*cf. People v. Maine*, 166 N.Y. 50, 59 N.E. 696 (N.Y. 1906)), it is not relevant in a prosecution for assault in the third degree where it is only necessary to show that the defendant knowingly struck a blow.

In this case there can be no doubt that the defendant intended to assault the police officer in civilian dress. The resulting assault was forceful. Hence motive or mistake of fact is of no significance as the defendant was not charged with a crime requiring such intent or knowledge. To be guilty of third-degree assault (i)t is sufficient that the defendant voluntarily intended to commit the unlawful act of touching. Since in these circumstances the aggression was inexcusable the defendant was properly convicted.

Accordingly, the order of the Appellate Division should be reversed, and the information reinstated.

FROESSEL, Judge (dissenting).

The law is clear that one may kill in defense of another when there is reasonable, though mistaken, ground for believing that the person slain is about to commit a felony or to do some great personal injury to the apparent victim; yet the majority now hold, for the first time, that in the event of a simple assault under similar circumstances, the mistaken belief, no matter how reasonable, is no defense.

Briefly, the relevant facts are these: On a Friday afternoon at about 3:40, Detectives Driscoll and Murphy, not in uniform, observed an argument taking place between a motorist and one McGriff in the street in front of premises 64 West 54th Street, in midtown Manhattan. Driscoll attempted to chase McGriff out of the roadway in order to allow traffic to pass, but McGriff refused to move back; his actions caused a crowd to collect. After identifying himself to McGriff, Driscoll placed him under arrest. As McGriff resisted, defendant, "came out of the crowd" from Driscoll's rear and struck Murphy about the head with his fist. In the ensuing struggle Driscoll's right kneecap was injured when defendant fell on top of him. At the station house, defendant said he had not known or thought Driscoll and Murphy were police officers.

Defendant testified that while he was proceeding on 54th Street he observed two white men, who appeared to be 45 or 50 years old, pulling on a "colored boy" (McGriff), who appeared to be a lad about 18, whom he did not know. The men had nearly pulled McGriff's pants off, and he was crying. Defendant admitted he knew nothing of what had transpired between the officers and McGriff and made no inquiry of anyone; he just came there and pulled the officer away from McGriff. Defendant was convicted of assault third degree. In reversing upon the law and dismissing the information, the Appellate Division held that on is not "criminally liable for assault in the third degree if he goes to the aid of another who he mistakenly, but *reasonably*, believes is being unlawfully beaten, and thereby injures one of the apparent assaulters" (emphasis supplied). While in my opinion the majority below correctly stated the law, I would reverse here and remit so that the Appellate Division may pass on the question of whether or not defendant's conduct was reasonable in light of the circumstances presented at the trial.

As the majority below pointed out, assault is a crime derived from the common law. Basic to the imposition of criminal liability both at common law and under our statutory law is the existence in the one whom committed the prohibited act of what has been variously termed a guilty mind, a *mens rea* or a criminal intent.

It is undisputed that defendant did not known that Driscoll and Murphy were detectives in plain clothes engaged in lawfully apprehending an alleged disorderly person. If, therefore, defendant reasonably believed he was lawfully assisting another, he would not have been guilty of a crime. Subdivision 3 of section 246 of the Penal Law provides that it is not unlawful to use force "When committed either by the party about to be injured or *by another person in his aid or defense, in preventing or attempting to prevent an offense against his person,* . . . if the force or violence used is not more than sufficient to prevent such offense" (emphasis supplied). The law is thus clear that if defendant entertained an "honest and reasonable belief" that the facts were as he perceived them to be, he would be exonerated from criminal liability.

There is no need, in my opinion, to consider the law of other States, for New York policy clearly supports the view that one may act on appearances reasonably ascertained. Our Penal Law, to which I have already alluded, is a statement of that policy. The same policy was expressed by this court in *People v. Maine*, 166 N.Y. 50, 59 N.E. 696. There, the defendant observed his brother fighting in the street with two other men; he stepped in and stabbed to death one of the latter. The defense was justifiable homicide under the predecessor of section 1055. The court held it reversible error to admit into evidence the declarations of the defendant's brother, made before defendant happened upon the scene, which tended to show that the brother was the aggressor. We said (p. 52, 59 N.E. p. 696): "Of course, the acts and conduct of the defendant must be judged solely with reference to the situation as it was when he first and afterwards saw it." Mistake of relevant fact, reasonably entertained, is thus a defense to homicide, and one who kills in defense of another and proffers this defense of justification is to be judged according to the circumstances as they appeared to him.

The mistaken belief, however, must be one which is reasonably entertained, and the question of reasonableness is for the trier of the facts. The question is not, merely, what did the accused believe? but also, what did he have the right to believe? Without passing on the facts of the instant case, the Appellate Division had no right to assume that defendant's conduct was reasonable, and to dismiss the information as a matter of law. Nor do we have the right to reinstate the verdict without giving the Appellate Division the opportunity to pass upon the facts.

Although the majority of our courts are now purporting to fashion a policy "conducive to an orderly society," by their decision they have defeated their avowed purpose. What public interest is promoted by a principle which would deter one from coming to the aid of a fellow citizen who he has reasonable ground to apprehend is in imminent danger of personal injury at the hands of assailants? Is it reasonable to denominate, as justifiable homicide, a slaying committed under a mistaken but reasonably held belief, and deny this same defense of justification to one using less force? Logic, as well as historical background and related precedent, dictates that the rule and policy expressed by our Legislature in the case of homicide, which is an assault resulting in death, should likewise be applicable to a much less serious assault not resulting in death.

I would reverse the order appealed from and remit the case to the Appellate Division for determination upon the questions of fact raised in that court.

Questions and Notes

1. Is the majority or dissenting opinion more conducive to a civilized society?

2. Was it reasonable for Young to punch Murphy first and ask questions later? Assuming that it was, would the majority have allowed Young a defense?

3. How does the majority distinguish *People v. Maine*, the homicide case? As a policy matter, is there more or less reason to allow one to enter a fray at his peril when he intends to use deadly force (*Maine*) or when he intends to use nondeadly force (*Young*)?

4. The court says: "In this case there can be no doubt that the defendant intended to assault the police officer in civilian dress." Do you agree?

5. Is the court more concerned with harm than with culpability? Which is the dissent more concerned about? From a perspective of dangerousness, which rule serves us better?

6. Subsequent to the *Young* decision, the legislature codified the rule advocated by the dissent. What do you suppose motivated the legislature to do so?

7. Suppose that the defendant's right to defend another or himself is not perfect (either because he used excessive force or because he — or his cohort — started the fight). Suppose further that the result of the confrontation is the death of the victim. Is there (should there be) a theory under which the defendant might be convicted of manslaughter rather than murder? Consider this problem in conjunction with *Shuck*.

D. Imperfect Self-Defense

Shuck v. State

349 A.2d 378 (Md. App. 1975)

MOYLAN, Judge.

The appellant, Mark A. Shuck, was convicted in the Circuit Court for Anne Arundel County by a jury, a presided over by Judge Matthew S. Evans, of both murder in the second degree and assault with intent to murder.

[The court concluded that there was sufficient evidence to go to the jury on the two charges, and further concluded that there was insufficient evidence to present to the jury on perfect self-defense.]

From the evidence, the jury could fairly deduce the following picture. The appellant and his companion, John Jackman, were two young men and co-workers who had been visiting a bar and a party and consuming a number of beers from the early evening of June 28 through approximately midnight. At shortly after midnight, Jackman was driving his Corvette sports car. The appellant was a passenger in the car and they were both returning to a bar to pick up the appellant's girlfriend, who worked there. As they stopped for a light, a GTO sports car pulled up beside them. When the light turned green, the GTO pulled off suddenly, spinning its wheels and throwing up gravel. Interpreting this as an invitation to a race, Jackman and the appellant took off in pursuit. It was at that point that George Parker, a 48-year-old man, was returning home in his pickup truck from his own evening of drinking at his own bar. The pickup truck pulled onto the highway and ended up between the GTO and the pursuing Corvette. The GTO pulled onto a side road. The Corvette, occupied by the appellant and his companion, pulled off after it, cutting off in the process [but] not hitting the pickup truck driven by Parker. In slamming on his brakes, Parker hit his head on his own windshield and became angry. Rather than let the matter rest, Parker then took off in pursuit.

The GTO soon pulled to a stop in a small court with a single entrance. Its occupant, the ultimate homicide victim, Buddy Voelker, alighted. The appellant and his companion, who were strangers to Voelker, pulled to a stop behind the GTO. Apparently because of their shared common interest in automobiles, Voelker and Jackman began a friendly conversation. At that moment, Parker arrived in his pickup truck, still red with anger. He parked his truck across the entrance to the court so as to block any vehicular exit therefrom. He approached the Corvette, in which the appellant and Jackman were still seated. (Voelker had walked up to the window and was carrying on the conversation from that vantage point.) Parker ordered Jackman out of the car. He shouted several obscenities. According to the appellant, Parker reached into the car and hit Jackman at least once in the face with his fist. After repeatedly being challenged by Parker in angry words, Jackman got out of his own vehicle. At one point, apparently, Jackman and the appellant attempted to get back in Jackman's car and leave the area. Parker, with Voelker trying to restrain him, shouted several obscenities at them and they stopped the car and got out. According to the appellant, at one point, Parker and Jackman were struggling with each other when Voelker leaped onto both of them, knocking everyone to the ground in the process. The appellant testified that he attempted to pull Voelker from the pile. At that point, Voelker turned to the appellant and ultimately was on his back, gripping him about the shoulders. The appellant stated that Voelker hit him several times. At this point, the appellant ran and got the bat from his companion's automobile and swung at least twice. One blow hit Parker, injuring him slightly. The other hit Voelker in the head and ultimately resulted in his death.

At Voelker's autopsy, the blood alcohol level was revealed to be 0.14%. A girl-friend of Jackman's Terri Jones, testified that when she saw Jackman shortly after the incident, he was bleeding from the mouth and nose and had strangulation marks on his neck.

Mitigation by Way of "Imperfect" Self-Defense.

Although by far the most common form of mitigation is that of a hot-blooded response to legally adequate provocation, this is not the only form of mitigation that will negate malice and will reduce what might otherwise be murder to manslaughter. Perkins described this legal phenomenon of "Mitigation Other Than Provocation":

> "Since manslaughter is a 'catch-all' concept, covering all homicides which are neither murder nor innocent, it logically includes some killings involving other types of mitigation, and such is the rule of the common law. For example, if one man kills another intentionally, under circumstances beyond the scope of innocent homicide, the facts may come so close to justification or excuse that the killing will be classed voluntary manslaughter rather than murder. 'It is not always necessary to show that the killing was done in the heat of passion, to reduce the crime to manslaughter;' said the Arkansas court, 'for, where the killing was done because the slayer believes that he is in great danger, but the facts do not warrant such a belief, it may be murder or manslaughter according to the circumstances, even though there be no passion.' To give another illustration, the intentional taking of human life to prevent crime may fall a little short of complete justification or excuse and still be without malice aforethought."

One of these other forms of mitigation is "imperfect" self-defense. Looking at the facts in a light most favorable to the appellant, his companion was neither an aggressor nor a mutual combatant. He was under unprovoked attack from at least one and possibly two persons. Under the circumstances, the appellant was entitled to intervene in defense of his friend.

Even granting the unreasonableness of his excessive escalation to the deadly level of what had been a non-deadly combat, he had nonetheless generated the issue that even this "imperfect" right of self-defense might mitigate his guilt for the felonious homicide to the manslaughter level and might, thereby, totally exculpate him on the assault with intent to murder charge. With respect to this less common form of mitigation, we are highly persuaded by LaFave and Scott, at 583–584:

> "In order for a killer to have a 'perfect' defense of self-defense to homicide, (1) he must be free from fault in bringing on the difficulty with his adversary; and (2) he must reasonably believe (though he need not correctly believe) both (a) that his adversary will, unless forcibly prevented, immediately inflict upon him a fatal or serious bodily injury, and (b) that he must use deadly force upon the adversary to prevent him from inflicting such an injury. If one who is not the aggressor kills his adversary with these

two actual and reasonable beliefs in his mind, his homicide is justified, and he is guilty of no crime-not murder, not manslaughter, but no crime.

> What if a defendant who did not initiate the difficulty honestly but unreasonably believes either that he is in danger of the injury or that killing is the only way to prevent it; or, even though he reasonably believes these things, he was at fault in bringing about the difficulty? He cannot have the defense of self-defense, for that requires both freedom from fault in the inception of the difficulty and the entertainment of beliefs which are reasonable. But is murder the only alternative? Or should the matter fall into the category of manslaughter, consisting of those homicides which lie in between murder and no crime. Some cases so hold, whether the reason for the "imperfection" of the defense is the defendant's own fault in bringing on the difficulty or the unreasonableness of the honest but erroneous beliefs which he entertains. On principle, the same rule should apply to a killing done in the case of a homicide under an "imperfect" right to defend others, as applies in the case of the homicide under an "imperfect" right of self-defense. The manslaughter provisions of two of the latest comprehensive criminal codes—those of Illinois and Wisconsin—recognize the existence of this imperfect-right-of-self-defense or defense-of-others type of voluntary manslaughter."

Under the circumstances, the convictions must be reversed.

Questions and Notes

1. A type of imperfect defense alluded to but not developed in *Shuck* occurs when the instigator of a nondeadly attack is forced to use deadly force to defend himself. For example, if Parker had killed Shuck after the baseball bat attack, he would not have been totally exculpated because of his initiation of the violence. On the other hand, because his initial attack was nondeadly, malice would have been negated and he would have been guilty of voluntary manslaughter. Under those circumstances, the MPC would convict him of his initial assault, but allow him a right of perfect self-defense.

2. In a case like *Shuck*, where the defendant honestly but unreasonably believes that deadly force is necessary, should his crime be voluntary manslaughter or involuntary manslaughter? Why? Most states say voluntary manslaughter, but the MPC would convict him of negligent or reckless homicide.

3. Does imperfect self-defense unnecessarily complicate things? Would a better rule be to either acquit the defendant because of perfect self-defense, mitigate to manslaughter if the provocation is adequate, or convict the defendant of murder?

4. The next issue we will explore is the right of an unlawfully arrested person to use force to frustrate the arrest. At common law, the arrestee could use moderate, but not deadly force to frustrate the arrest. As we see in *Curtis*, the modern trend is to deny this right? Why?

E. Resisting Arrest

People v. Curtis
450 P.2d 33 (Cal. 1969)

Mosk, Justice.

Defendant Albert Allen Curtis appeals from a conviction of battery upon a peace officer, a felony. We conclude that the proper construction of these sections requires a reversal of defendant's conviction.

Defendant was arrested on the night of July 9, 1966, by Lt. Riley of the Stockton Police Department. Riley was investigating a report of a prowler and had received a cursory description of the suspect as a male Negro, about six feet tall, wearing a white shirt and tan trousers. While cruising the neighborhood in his patrol car, the officer observed defendant, who matched the foregoing general description, walking along the street. Riley pulled up next to defendant and called to him to stop; defendant complied. The officer then emerged from his patrol car in full uniform and told defendant he was under arrest and would have to come along with him. Riley reached for the arm of defendant, and the latter attempted to back away. A violent struggle ensued, during which both men were injured, and defendant was finally subdued and taken into custody by several officers.

Defendant was subsequently acquitted of a charge of burglary but was convicted of battery upon a peace officer. He challenges this conviction on several grounds.

I

Defendant initially contends that his arrest was unlawful due to a lack of probable cause and that it was accomplished by the use of excessive force, and therefore his resistance was justified. Under the general common law rule prevailing in most states, an unlawful arrest may be resisted reasonably, and excessive force used by an officer in effecting an arrest may be countered lawfully. Until 1957, this rule prevailed in California. However, as we shall first discuss, Penal Code section 834a, enacted in 1957, revised the first aspect of that rule.

Section 834a provides: "If a person has knowledge, or by the exercise to reasonable care, should have knowledge, that he is being arrested by a peace officer, it is the duty of such person to refrain from using force or any weapon to resist such arrest." [I]t has been consistently held that section 834a prohibits forceful resistance to unlawful as well as lawful arrests. The legislative history of section 834a strongly supports this construction. General acceptance of this apparent intent and its adoption by courts without serious question for more than a decade cannot be ignored at this late date. We find no reason to reject the firmly established judicial construction of section 834a.

While defendant's rights are no doubt violated when he is arrested and detained a matter of days or hours without probable cause, we conclude the state in removing the right to resist does not contribute to or effectuate this deprivation of liberty. In a day when police are armed with lethal and chemical weapons and possess scientific communication and detection devices readily available for use, it has become highly unlikely that a suspect, using Reasonable force, can escape from or effectively deter an arrest, whether lawful or unlawful. His accomplishment is generally limited to temporary evasion, merely rendering the officer's task more difficult or prolonged. Thus, self-help as a practical remedy is anachronistic, whatever may have been its original justification or efficacy in an era when the common law doctrine permitting resistance evolved. Indeed, self-help not infrequently causes far graver consequences for both the officer and the suspect than does the unlawful arrest itself. Accordingly, the state, in deleting the right to resist, has not actually altered or diminished the remedies available against the illegality of an arrest without probable cause, it has merely required a person to submit peacefully to the inevitable and to pursue his available remedies through the orderly judicial process.

We are not unmindful that under present conditions the available remedies for unlawful arrest—release followed by civil or criminal action against the offending officer—may be deemed inadequate. However, this circumstance does not elevate physical resistance to anything other than the least effective and desirable of all possible remedies; as such its rejection, particularly when balanced against the state's interest in discouraging violence, cannot realistically be considered an affirmative "seizure" or deprivation of liberty.

II

Our task, however, is by no means completed with the foregoing construction of section 834a. Defendant was charged not with simply battery, a misdemeanor, but with battery upon a peace officer "engaged in the performance of his duties," a felony under Penal Code, section 243. Unlike section 834a, which had no predecessor when enacted in 1957, the language of section 243, speaking in terms of the officer's "duty," has been incorporated in section 148 of the Penal Code since 1872. The latter section makes it a misdemeanor to resist, delay or obstruct an officer in the discharge of "any duty of his office." Section 148 has long been construed by the courts as applying only to lawful arrests, because "An officer is under no duty to make an unlawful arrest." Even if section 834a now makes it a Citizen's duty not to resist an unlawful arrest, this change in the law in no way purports to include an unlawful arrest within the performance of an Officer's duty.

Moreover, simply as a matter of statutory construction, it is clear that section 834a was meant at most to eliminate the common law defense of resistance to unlawful arrest, and not to make such resistance a new substantive crime. This interpretation is borne out by reference to legislative hearings at which there were discussions on the purpose of section.[5]

---

5. Robert Burns, Assistant City Attorney of Los Angeles, testified as follows regarding the application of section 834a to section 148: "We took away the right to resist (an unlawful arrest), but we didn't make it a new kind of crime, resisting. It's still the same old crime. However, let's take you

Significantly, both the Uniform Arrest Act, from which the language of section 834a was drawn, and the Model Penal Code take the approach of eliminating the defense but declining to make resistance a separate and additional crime. When section 834a was enacted in 1957, the Legislature amended the penalty provisions but did not change the "duty" language of section 148, thereby impliedly adopting the prior judicial interpretation of "duty." Therefore we must construe section 243, like section 148, as excluding unlawful arrests from its definition of "duty." This in no way thwarts the legislative purpose to consign to the courtroom all controversies over legality. We confirm that a resisting defendant commits a public offense; but if the arrest is ultimately determined factually to be unlawful, the defendant can be validly convicted only of simple assault or battery. Cases holding or implying the contrary are disapproved.

The above construction of sections 148 and 243 as not applying to unlawful arrests makes it unnecessary to reach a potentially difficult constitutional question. Unlike section 834a, which applies only to forceful resistance, section 148 penalizes even passive delay or obstruction of an arrest, such as refusal to cooperate. The United States Supreme Court has made it clear that "one cannot be punished for failing to obey the command of an officer if that command is itself violative of the Constitution." (*Wright v. Georgia* (1963) 373 U.S. 284, 291–292.) Yet this would be the result if "duty" were construed to include unlawful arrests, since an arrest without probable cause is by definition an "unreasonable seizure" within the Fourth Amendment.

III

Defendant contends that his arrest was not only lacking in probable cause and thus unlawful, but also was accomplished with excessive force and hence he was justified in employing counterforce in self-defense. Some courts appear to have incorrectly treated these two problems unitarily, as if a technically unlawful arrest were identical with an overly forceful arrest.

There are, however, two distinct and separate rights at stake. The common law rule allowing resistance to technically unlawful arrests protects a person's freedom from unreasonable seizure and confinement; the rule allowing resistance to excessive force, which applies during a technically lawful *or* unlawful arrest, protects a person's right to bodily integrity and permits resort to self-defense. Liberty can be restored through legal processes, but life and limb cannot be repaired in a courtroom. Therefore, any rationale, pragmatic or constitutional, for outlawing resistance to unlawful arrests and resolving the dispute over legality in the courts has no determinative application to the right to resist excessive force. The commentators are unanimous on this point, and the Model Penal Code states it explicitly.[7]

---

example—the officer's absolutely wrong. He hasn't probable cause—you're not guilty of resisting an officer in the performance of his duty because he has no duty to make."

7. Model Penal Code (Tent. Draft No. 8, 1958) section 3.04. The comments thereto state, at page 19:

Under Penal Code, sections 835 and 835a, an officer may lawfully use only Reasonable force to make an arrest or to overcome resistance. Sections 692 and 693 set forth the basic privilege one has to defend against unlawful force. In the absence of unequivocal language, we cannot ascribe to the Legislature an intention to penalize the exercise of a right it has specifically bestowed.

To summarize, then, construing sections 834a and 243, it is now the law of California that a person may not use force to resist any arrest, lawful or unlawful, except that he may use reasonable force to defend life and limb against excessive force; but if it should be determined that resistance was not thus justified, the felony provisions of section 243 apply when the arrest is lawful, and if the arrest is determined to be unlawful the defendant may be convicted only of a misdemeanor.

Thus, if the peace officer was acting unlawfully, only the lesser penalty would apply.

IV

We now apply the foregoing principles to the facts before us. First, as to the lawfulness of the arrest, it appears that the officer lacked probable cause when he arrested defendant. The only information the officer possessed was a description of the suspect's race, the color of his clothing, and the general area of the alleged burglary. No doubt he had sufficient grounds to detain and question defendant (*People v. Mickelson* (1963) 59 Cal. 2d 448, 30 Cal. Rptr. 18, 380 P.2d 658); but it is evident that he lacked probable cause to arrest him. As in *Mickelson* "There could have been more than one tall white man with dark hair wearing a red sweater abroad at night in such a metropolitan area" (*id.* at p. 454, 30 Cal. Rptr. at 22, 380 P.2d at 662), so there could have been more than one Negro in white shirt and tan trousers in the neighborhood on the night defendant was arrested. Defendant made no furtive or suspicious movements; he stopped on command and was cooperative until the officer attempted to detain him physically; he had a plausible explanation for his whereabouts, since he lived a block from where he was arrested. This is not "such a state of facts as would lead a man of ordinary care and prudence to believe and conscientiously entertain an honest and strong suspicion" that defendant was guilty of the crime.

The question of the exercise of reasonable force and the right to self-defense, which we emphasize is distinct from that of the lawfulness of the arrest, is for the trier of fact to determine. Here the jury had before it evidence which could justify a finding either way, depending upon the credibility of witnesses and the weight of the evidence. The court's instructions merely quoted or paraphrased the Penal Code sections regarding the privilege of self-defense, the duty not to resist an arrest, and an officer's privilege to use reasonable force in effecting an arrest. In view of our

---

"The paragraph, it should be noted, forbids the use of force for the purpose of preventing an arrest; it has *no application when the actor apprehends bodily injury*, as when the arresting officer unlawfully employs or threatens deadly force, unless the actor knows that he is in no peril greater than arrest if he submits to the assertion of authority." (Italics added.)

conclusions on the law, we must hold that the jury was not adequately instructed as to the rights and duties of the respective parties.

The judgment is reversed.

Questions and Notes

1. Why does the court permit defensive force to be used against an arrest effectuated with excessive force, but not against one perpetrated in contravention of the Constitution? Isn't the Constitution supposed to be the supreme law of the land?

2. Although a minority decision when rendered, the *Curtis*/MPC rule now seems to be the predominant rule. Why do you suppose that legislatures have denied the right of self-defense to those unlawfully arrested? Do you concur with that judgment?

3. The next series of cases deals with the force that may be used to effectuate an arrest. Here, too, the right to use force seems to be diminishing.

F. Crime Prevention

Tennessee v. Garner

471 U.S. 1 (1985)

Justice WHITE delivered the opinion of the Court.

This case requires us to determine the constitutionality of the use of deadly force to prevent the escape of an apparently unarmed suspected felon. We conclude that such force may not be used unless it is necessary to prevent the escape and the officer has probable cause to believe that the suspect poses a significant threat of death or serious physical injury to the officer or others.

I

At about 10:45 p.m. on October 3, 1974, Memphis Police Officers Elton Hymon and Leslie Wright were dispatched to answer a "prowler inside call." Upon arriving at the scene they saw a woman standing on her porch and gesturing toward the adjacent house. She told them she had heard glass breaking and that "they" or "someone" was breaking in next door. While Wright radioed the dispatcher to say that they were on the scene, Hymon went behind the house. He heard a door slam and saw someone run across the backyard. The fleeing suspect, who was appellee-respondent's decedent, Edward Garner, stopped at a 6-feet-high chain link fence at the edge of the yard. With the aid of a flashlight, Hymon was able to see Garner's face and hands. He saw no sign of a weapon, and, though not certain, was "reasonably sure" and "figured" that Garner was unarmed. He thought Garner was 17 or 18 years old and about 5'5" or 5'7" tall.[2] While Garner was crouched at the base of

---

2. In fact, Garner, an eighth-grader, was 15. He was 5'4" tall and weighed somewhere around 100 or 110 pounds.

the fence, Hymon called out "police, halt" and took a few steps toward him. Garner then began to climb over the fence. Convinced that if Garner made it over the fence, he would elude capture, Hymon shot him. The bullet hit Garner in the back of the head. Garner was taken by ambulance to a hospital, where he died on the operating table. Ten dollars and a purse taken from the house were found on his body.

In using deadly force to prevent the escape, Hymon was acting under the authority of a Tennessee statute and pursuant to Police Department policy. The statute provides that "[i]f, after notice of the intention to arrest the defendant, he either flee or forcibly resist, the officer may use all the necessary means to effect the arrest."[3] The Department policy was slightly more restrictive than the statute, but still allowed the use of deadly force in cases of burglary. The incident was reviewed by the Memphis Police Firearm's Review Board and presented to a grand jury. Neither took any action.

Garner's father then brought this action in the Federal District Court for the Western District of Tennessee, seeking damages under 42 U.S.C. § 1983 for asserted violations of Garner's constitutional rights. The District Court considered whether the use of deadly force and hollow point bullets in these circumstances was constitutional. The District Court concluded that Hymon's actions, were constitutional.

The Court of Appeals reversed and remanded. 710 F.2d 240 (1983). It reasoned that the killing of a fleeing suspect is a "seizure" under the Fourth Amendment, and is therefore constitutional only if "reasonable." The Tennessee statute failed as applied to this case because it did not adequately limit the use of deadly force by distinguishing between felonies of different magnitudes—"the facts, as found, did not justify the use of deadly force under the Fourth Amendment." Officers cannot resort to deadly force unless they "have probable cause . . . to believe that the suspect [has committed a felony and] poses a threat to the safety of the officers or a danger to the community if left at large."[7] The State of Tennessee, which had intervened to defend the statute, appealed to this Court. The city filed a petition for certiorari. We noted probable jurisdiction in the appeal and granted the petition.

---

3. Although the statute does not say so explicitly, Tennessee law forbids the use of deadly force in the arrest of a misdemeanant. *See Johnson v. State*, 173 Tenn. 134, 114 S.W.2d 819 (1938).

7. The Court of Appeals concluded that the rule set out in the Model Penal Code "accurately states Fourth Amendment limitations on the use of deadly force against fleeing felons." 710 F.2d at 247. The relevant portion of the Model Penal Code provides:
"The use of deadly force is not justifiable . . . unless (i) the arrest is for a felony; and (ii) the person effecting the arrest is authorized to act as a peace officer; or is assisting a person whom he believes to be authorized to act as a peace officer, and (iii) the actor believes that the force employed creates no substantial risk of injury to innocent persons; and (iv) the actor believes that (1) the crime for which the arrest is made involved conduct including the use or threatened use of deadly force; or (2) there is a substantial risk that the person to be arrested will cause death or serious bodily harm if his apprehension is delayed." American Law Institute, MODEL PENAL CODE § 3.07(2)(b) (Proposed Official Draft 1962).

Whenever an officer restrains the freedom of a person to walk away, he has seized that person. While it is not always clear just when minimal police interference becomes a seizure, there can be no question that apprehension by the use of deadly force is a seizure subject to the reasonableness requirement of the Fourth Amendment.

A

A police officer may arrest a person if he has probable cause to believe that person committed a crime. Petitioners and appellant argue that if this requirement is satisfied the Fourth Amendment has nothing to say about *how* that seizure is made. This submission ignores the many cases in which this Court, by balancing the extent of the intrusion against the need for it, has examined the reasonableness of the manner in which a search or seizure is conducted. To determine the constitutionality of a seizure "[w]e must balance the nature and quality of the intrusion, on the individual's Fourth Amendment interests against the importance if the governmental interests alleged to justify the intrusion." We have described "the balancing of competing interests" as "the key principle of the Fourth Amendment." *Michigan v. Summers*, 452 U.S. 692, 700, n.12. Because one of the factors is the extent of the intrusion, it is plain that reasonableness depends on not only when a seizure is made, but also how it is carried out.

B

The balancing process applied in our cases demonstrates that, notwithstanding probable cause to seize a suspect, an officer may not always do so by killing him. The intrusiveness of a seizure by means of deadly force is unmatched. The suspect's fundamental interest in his own life need not be elaborated upon. The use of deadly force also frustrates the interest of the individual, and of society, in judicial determination of guilt and punishment. Against these interests are ranged governmental interests in effective law enforcement. It is argued that overall violence will be reduced by encouraging the peaceful submission of suspects who know that they may be shot if they flee. Effectiveness in making arrests requires the resort to deadly force, or at least the meaningful threat thereof. "Being able to arrest such individuals is a condition precedent to the state's entire system of law enforcement."

Without in any way disparaging the importance of these goals, we are not convinced that the use of deadly force is a sufficiently productive means of accomplishing them to justify the killing of nonviolent suspects. The use of deadly force is a self-defeating way of apprehending a suspect and so setting the criminal justice mechanism in motion. If successful, it guarantees that that mechanism will not be set in motion. And while the meaningful threat of deadly force might be thought to lead to the arrest of more live suspects by discouraging escape attempts, the presently available evidence does not support this thesis. The fact is that a majority of police departments in this country have forbidden the use of deadly force against nonviolent suspects. If those charged with the enforcement of the criminal law have abjured the use of deadly force in arresting nondangerous felons, there is a substantial basis for doubting that the use of such force is an essential attribute of the arrest power in all felony cases. Petitioners and appellant have not persuaded us that shooting nondangerous fleeing suspects is so vital as to outweigh the suspect's interest in his own life.

The use of deadly force to prevent the escape of all felony suspects, whatever the circumstances, is constitutionally unreasonable. It is not better that all felony suspects die than that they escape. Where the suspect poses no immediate threat to the officer and no threat to others, the harm resulting from failing to apprehend him does not justify the use of deadly force to do so. It is no doubt unfortunate when a suspect who is in sight escapes, but the fact that the police arrive a little late or are a little slower afoot does not always justify killing the suspect. A police officer may not seize an unarmed, nondangerous suspect by shooting him dead. The Tennessee statute is unconstitutional insofar as it authorizes the use of deadly force against such fleeing suspects.

It is not, however, unconstitutional on its face. Where the officer has probable cause to believe that the suspect poses a threat of serious physical harm, either to the officer or to others, it is not constitutionally unreasonable to prevent escape by using deadly force. Thus, if the suspect threatens the officer with a weapon or there is probable cause to believe that he has committed a crime involving the infliction or threatened infliction of serious physical harm, deadly force may be used if necessary to prevent escape, and if, where feasible, some warning has been given. As applied in such circumstances, the Tennessee statute would pass constitutional muster.

III

A

It is insisted that the Fourth Amendment must be construed in light of the common law rule, which allowed the use of whatever force was necessary to effect the arrest of a fleeing felon, though not a misdemeanant. As stated in Hale's posthumously published Pleas of the Crown:

> "[I]f persons that are pursued by these officers for felony or the just suspicion thereof . . . shall not yield themselves to these officers, but shall either resist or fly before they are apprehended or being apprehended shall rescue themselves and resist or fly, so that they cannot be otherwise apprehended, and are upon necessity slain therein, because they cannot be otherwise taken, it is no felony."

2 M. Hale, Historia Placitorum Coronae 85 (1736). See also 4 W Blackstone, Commentaries. Most American jurisdictions also imposed a flat prohibition against the use of deadly force to stop a fleeing misdemeanant, coupled with a general privilege to use such force to stop a fleeing felon.

The State and city argue that because this was the prevailing rule at the time of the adoption of the Fourth Amendment and for some time thereafter, and is still in force in some States, use of deadly force against a fleeing felon must be "reasonable"

It is true that this Court has often looked to the common law in evaluating the reasonableness, for Fourth Amendment purposes, of police activity. On the other hand, it "has not simply frozen into constitutional law those law enforcement practices that existed at the time of the Fourth Amendment's passage." Because of sweeping change in the legal and technological context, reliance on the common-law rule in this case would be a mistaken literalism that ignores the purposes of a historical inquiry.

B

It has been pointed out many times that the common-law rule is best understood in light of the fact that it arose at a time when virtually all felonies were punishable by death. "Though effected without the protections and formalities of an orderly trial and conviction, the killing of a resisting or fleeing felon resulted in no greater consequences than those authorized for punishment of the felony of which the individual was charged or suspected." American Law Institute, Model Penal Code § 3.07, Comment 3, p. 56 (Tentative Draft No. 8, 1958) (hereinafter Model Penal Code Comment). Courts have also justified the common-law rule by emphasizing the relative dangerousness of felons. And while in earlier times "the gulf between the felonies and the minor offences was broad and deep," today the distinction is minor and often arbitrary. Many crimes classified as misdemeanors, or nonexistent, at common law are now felonies. These changes have undermined the concept, which was questionable to begin with, that use of deadly force against a fleeing felon is merely a speedier execution of someone who has already forfeited his life. They have also made the assumption that a "felon" is more dangerous than a misdemeanant untenable. Indeed, numerous misdemeanors involve conduct more dangerous than many felonies.[12]

There is an additional reason why the common-law rule cannot be directly translated to the present day. The common-law rule developed at a time when weapons were rudimentary. Deadly force could be inflicted almost solely in a hand-to-hand struggle during which, necessarily, the safety of the arresting officer was at risk. Handguns were not carried by police officers until the latter half of the last century. Only then did it become possible to use deadly force from a distance as a means of apprehension. As a practical matter, the use of deadly force under the standard articulation of the common-law rule has an altogether different meaning—and harsher consequences—now than in past centuries. One other aspect of the common-law rule bears emphasis. It forbids the use of deadly force to apprehend a misdemeanant, condemning such action as disproportionately severe.

In short, though the common-law pedigree of Tennessee's rule is pure on its face, changes in the legal and technological context mean the rule is distorted almost beyond recognition when literally applied.

---

12. White-collar crime, for example, poses a less significant physical threat than, say, drunken driving.

C

In evaluating the reasonableness of police procedures under the Fourth Amendment, we have also looked to prevailing rules in individual jurisdictions. Some 19 States have codified the common-law rule, though in two of these, the courts have significantly limited the statute. Four States, though without a relevant statute, apparently retain the common-law rule. Two States have adopted the Model Penal Code's provision verbatim. Eighteen others allow, in slightly varying language, the use of deadly force only if the suspect has committed a felony involving the use or threat of physical or deadly force, or is escaping with a deadly weapon, or is likely to endanger life or inflict serious physical injury if not arrested. Louisiana and Vermont, though without statutes or case law on point, do forbid the use of deadly force to prevent any but violent felonies. The remaining States either have no relevant statute or case law or have positions that are unclear.

It cannot be said that there is a constant or overwhelming trend away from the common-law rule. In recent years, some States have reviewed their laws and expressly rejected abandonment of the common-law rule. Nonetheless, the long-term movement has been away from the rule that deadly force may be used against any fleeing felon, and that remains the rule in less than half the States.

This trend is more evident and impressive when viewed in light of the policies adopted by the police departments themselves. Overwhelmingly, these are more restrictive than the common-law rule. The Federal Bureau of Investigation and the New York City Police Department, for example, both forbid the use of firearms except when necessary to prevent death or grievous bodily harm. A 1974 study reported that the police department regulations in a majority of the large cities of the United States allowed the firing of a weapon only when a felon presented a threat of death or serious bodily harm. In light of the rules adopted by those who must actually administer them, the older and fading common-law view is a dubious indicium of the constitutionality of the Tennessee statute now before us.

D

Actual departmental policies are important for an additional reason. We would hesitate to declare a police practice of long standing "unreasonable" if doing so would severely hamper effective law enforcement. But the indications are to the contrary. There has been no suggestion that crime has worsened in any way in jurisdictions that have adopted, by legislation or departmental policy, rules similar to that announced today. Amici noted that "[a]fter extensive research and consideration, [they] have concluded that laws permitting police officers to use deadly force to apprehend unarmed, nonviolent fleeing felony suspects actually do not protect citizens or law enforcement officers, do not deter crime or alleviate problems caused by crime, and do not improve the crime-fighting ability of law enforcement agencies." The submission is that the obvious state interests in apprehension are not sufficiently served to warrant the use of lethal weapons against all fleeing felons.

The dissent argues that the shooting was justified by the fact that Officer Hymon had probable cause to believe that Garner had committed a nighttime burglary. While we agree that burglary is a serious crime, we cannot agree that it is so dangerous as automatically to justify the use of deadly force. The FBI classifies burglary as a "property" rather than a "violent" crime. *See* Federal Bureau of Investigation, Uniform Crime Reports, Crime in the United States 1 (1984).[22] Although the armed burglar would present a different situation, the fact that an unarmed suspect has broken into a dwelling at night does not automatically mean he is physically dangerous. This case demonstrates as much. In fact, the available statistics demonstrate that burglaries only rarely involve physical violence. During the 10-year period from 1973–1982, only 3.8% of all burglaries involved violent crime.[23]

The judgment of the Court of Appeals is affirmed, and the case is remanded for further proceedings consistent with this opinion.

Justice O'CONNOR, with whom THE CHIEF JUSTICE and Justice REHNQUIST join, dissenting.

The Court today holds that the Fourth Amendment prohibits a police officer from using deadly force as a last resort to apprehend a criminal suspect who refuses to halt when fleeing the scene of a nighttime burglary. This conclusion rests on the majority's balancing of the interests of the suspect and the public interest in effective law enforcement. Notwithstanding the venerable common-law rule authorizing the use of deadly force if necessary to apprehend a fleeing felon, and continued acceptance of this rule by nearly half the States, the majority concludes that Tennessee's statute is unconstitutional inasmuch as it allows the use of such force to apprehend a burglary suspect who is not obviously armed or otherwise dangerous. Although the circumstances of this case are unquestionably tragic and unfortunate, our constitutional holdings must be sensitive both to the history of the Fourth Amendment and to the general implications of the Court's reasoning. By disregarding the serious and dangerous nature of residential burglaries and the longstanding practice of many States, the Court effectively creates a Fourth Amendment right allowing a burglary suspect to flee unimpeded from a police officer who has probable cause to

---

22. In a recent report, the Department of Corrections of the District of Columbia also noted that "there is nothing inherently dangerous or violent about the offense," which is a crime against property. D.C. Department of Corrections, Prisoner Screening Project 2 (1985).

23. The dissent points out that three-fifths of all rapes in the home, three-fifths of all home robberies, and about a third of home assaults are committed by burglars. *Post*, at 1709. These figures mean only that if one knows that a suspect committed a rape in the home, there is a good chance that the suspect is also a burglar. That has nothing to do with the question here, which is whether the fact that someone has committed a burglary indicates that he has committed, or might commit, a violent crime. The dissent also points out that this 3.8% adds up to 2.8 million violent crimes over a 10-year period, as if to imply that today's holding will let loose 2.8 million violent burglars. The relevant universe is, of course, far smaller. At issue is only that tiny fraction of cases where violence has taken place and an officer who has no other means of apprehending the suspect is unaware of its occurrence.

arrest, who has ordered the suspect to halt, and who has no means short of firing his weapon to prevent escape. I do not believe that the Fourth Amendment supports such a right, and I accordingly dissent.

I

The facts below warrant brief review because they highlight the difficult, split-second decisions police officers must make in these circumstances. Memphis Police Officers Elton Hymon and Leslie Wright responded to a late-night call that a burglary was in progress at a private residence. When the officers arrived at the scene, the caller said that "they" were breaking into the house next door. The officers found the residence had been forcibly entered through a window and saw lights on inside the house. Officer Hymon testified that when he saw the broken window he realized "that something was wrong inside," but that he could not determine whether anyone either a burglar or a member of the household was within the residence. As Officer Hymon walked behind the house, he heard a door slam. He saw Edward Eugene Garner run away from the house through the dark and cluttered backyard. Garner crouched next to a 6-foot-high fence. Officer Hymon thought Garner was an adult and was unsure whether Garner was armed because Hymon "had no idea what was in the hand [that he could not see] or what he might have had on his person." In fact, Garner was 15 years old and unarmed. Hymon also did not know whether accomplices remained inside the house. The officer identified himself as a police officer and ordered Garner to halt. Garner paused briefly and then sprang to the top of the fence. Believing that Garner would escape if he climbed over the fence, Hymon fired his revolver and mortally wounded the suspected burglar.

The Court affirms on the ground that application of the Tennessee statute to authorize Officer Hymon's use of deadly force constituted an unreasonable seizure in violation of the Fourth Amendment. The precise issue before the Court deserves emphasis, because both the decision below and the majority Obscure what must be decided in this case. The issue is not the constitutional validity of the Tennessee statute on its face or as applied to some hypothetical set of facts. Instead, the issue is whether the use of deadly force by Officer Hymon under the circumstances of this case violated Garner's constitutional rights. Thus, the majority's assertion that a police officer who has probable cause to seize a suspect "may not always do so by killing him" is unexceptionable but also of little relevance to the question presented here. The same is true of the rhetorically stirring statement that "[t]he use of deadly force to prevent the escape of all felony suspects, whatever the circumstances, is constitutionally unreasonable." The question we must address is whether the Constitution allows the use of such force to apprehend a suspect who resists arrest by attempting to flee the scene of a nighttime burglary of a residence.

II

For purposes of Fourth Amendment analysis, I agree with the Court that Officer Hymon "seized" Garner by shooting him. Whether that seizure was reasonable and therefore permitted by the Fourth Amendment requires a careful balancing of the important public interest in crime prevention and detection and the nature and quality of the intrusion upon legitimate interests of the individual. In striking this balance here, it is crucial to acknowledge that police use of deadly force to apprehend a fleeing criminal suspect falls within the "rubric of police conduct . . . necessarily [involving] swift action predicated upon the on-the-spot observations of the officer on the beat. The clarity of hindsight cannot provide the standard for judging the reasonableness of police decisions made in uncertain and often dangerous circumstances. Moreover, I am far more reluctant than is the Court to conclude that the Fourth Amendment proscribes a police practice that was accepted at the time of the adoption of the Bill of Rights and has continued to receive the support of many state legislatures. Although the Court has recognized that the requirements of the Fourth Amendment must respond to the reality of social and technological change, fidelity to the notion of constitutional—as opposed to purely judicial—limits on governmental action requires us to impose a heavy burden on those who claim that practices accepted when the Fourth Amendment was adopted are now constitutionally impermissible.

The public interest involved in the use of deadly force as a last resort to apprehend a fleeing burglary suspect relates primarily to the serious nature of the crime. Household burglaries not only represent the illegal entry into a person's home, but also "pos[e] real risk of serious harm to others." According to recent Department of Justice statistics, "[t]hree-fifths of all rapes in the home, three-fifths of all home robberies, and about a third of home aggravated and simple assaults are committed by burglars." During the period 1973–1982, 2.8 million such violent crimes were committed in the course of burglaries. Victims of a forcible intrusion into their home by a nighttime prowler will find little consolation in the majority's confident assertion that "burglaries only rarely involve physical violence." Moreover, even if a particular burglary, when viewed in retrospect, does not involve physical harm to others, the "harsh potentialities for violence" inherent in the forced entry into a home preclude characterization of the crime as "innocuous, inconsequential, minor, or 'nonviolent.'"

Because burglary is a serious and dangerous felony, the public interest in the prevention and detection of the crime is of compelling importance. Where a police officer has probable cause to arrest a suspected burglar, the use of deadly force as a last resort might well be the only means of apprehending the suspect. With respect to a particular burglary, subsequent investigation simply cannot represent a substitute for immediate apprehension of the criminal suspect at the scene. Indeed, the Captain of the Memphis Police Department testified that in his city, if apprehension is not immediate, it is likely that the suspect will not be caught. Although some law enforcement agencies may choose to assume the risk that a criminal will remain at large, the Tennessee statute reflects a legislative determination that the use of deadly force in prescribed circumstances will serve generally to protect the public. Such statutes assist the police in apprehending suspected perpetrators of serious crimes and provide notice that a lawful police order to stop and submit to arrest may not be ignored with impunity.

The Court unconvincingly dismisses the general deterrence effects by stating that "the presently available evidence does not support [the] thesis" that the threat of force discourages escape and that "there is a substantial basis for doubting that the use of such force is an essential attribute to the arrest power in all felony cases." Moreover, the fact that police conduct pursuant to a state statute is challenged on constitutional grounds does not impose a burden on the State to produce social science statistics or to dispel any possible doubts about the necessity of the conduct. This observation, I believe, has particular force where the challenged practice both predates enactment of the Bill of Rights and continues to be accepted by a substantial number of the States.

Against the strong public interests justifying the conduct at issue here must be weighed the individual interests implicated in the use of deadly force by police officers. The majority declares that "[t]he suspect's fundamental interest in his own life need not be elaborated upon." This blithe assertion hardly provides an adequate substitute for the majority's failure to acknowledge the distinctive manner in which the suspect's interest in his life is even exposed to risk. For purposes of this case, we must recall that the police officer, in the course of investigating a nighttime burglary, had reasonable cause to arrest the suspect and ordered him to halt. The officer's use of force resulted because the suspected burglar refused to heed this command and the officer reasonably believed that there was no means short of firing his weapon to apprehend the suspect. Without questioning the importance of a person's interest in his life, I do not think this interest encompasses a right to flee unimpeded from the scene of a burglary. The policeman's hands should not be tied merely because of the possibility that the suspect will fail to cooperate with legitimate actions by law enforcement personnel. The legitimate interests of the suspect in these circumstances are adequately accommodated by the Tennessee statute: to avoid the use of deadly force and the consequent risk to his life, the suspect need merely obey the valid order to halt.

A proper balancing of the interests involved suggests that use of deadly force as a last resort to apprehend a criminal suspect fleeing from the scene of a nighttime burglary is not unreasonable within the meaning of the Fourth Amendment. Admittedly, the events giving rise to this case are in retrospect deeply regrettable. No one can view the death of an unarmed and apparently nonviolent 15-year-old without sorrow, much less disapproval. Nonetheless, the reasonableness of Officer Hymon's conduct for purposes of the Fourth Amendment cannot be evaluated by what later appears to have been a preferable course of police action. The officer pursued a suspect in the darkened backyard of a house that from all indications had just been burglarized. The police officer was not certain whether the suspect was alone or unarmed; nor did he know what had transpired inside the house. He ordered the suspect to halt, and when the suspect refused to obey and attempted to flee into the night, the officer fired his weapon to prevent escape. The reasonableness of this action for purposes of the Fourth Amendment is not determined by the unfortunate nature of this particular case; instead, the question is whether it is constitutionally impermissible for police officers, as a last resort, to shoot a burglary suspect fleeing the scene of the crime.

I cannot accept the majority's creation of a constitutional right to flight for burglary suspects seeking to avoid capture at the scene of the crime. Whatever the constitutional limits on police use of deadly force in order to apprehend a fleeing felon, I do not believe they are exceeded in a case in which a police officer has probable cause to arrest a suspect at the scene of a residential burglary, orders the suspect to halt, and then fires his weapon as a last resort to prevent the suspect's escape into the night. I respectfully dissent.

Questions and Notes

1. Is Justice O'Connor correct in categorizing the Court's holding as the "creation of a constitutional right to flight?" In what sense? Could a state make it a crime to refuse to yield to a lawful command of a police officer? Had Garner lived, could he have been convicted of such a crime?

2. A newspaper cartoon following *Garner* depicted a policeman watching a bank robber running away from the scene of his crime, shouting: "Stop, or I'll uh ... um ... blow my whistle." Is that fair commentary on the case?

3. Assuming that deadly force can only be used to arrest dangerous felons, do you agree with the court that apparently unarmed burglars do not fall in that category?

4. Was there a more reasonable way by which Officer Hymon could have arrested (seized) Garner?

5. Given that the burglar could avoid the cruel societal choice of death or escape by simply yielding to the officer's command, why should society have to tolerate the option of escape, thereby letting (if not encouraging) him to do it again?

6. Because *Garner is* a constitutional decision emanating from the Supreme Court, it is binding in all states and federal courts in the United States. As you read *Clothier,* consider whether *Garner* would have been decided differently if the homeowner rather than Officer Hymon had shot Garner. Before doing that, however, consider the following problem:

Problem

In March 2001, a Georgia county deputy clocked respondent's vehicle traveling at 73 miles per hour on a road with a 55-mile-per-hour speed limit. The deputy activated his blue flashing lights indicating that respondent should pull over. Instead, respondent sped away, initiating a chase down what is in most portions a two-lane road, at speeds exceeding 85 miles per hour. The deputy radioed his dispatch to report that he was pursuing a fleeing vehicle, and broadcast its license plate number. Petitioner, Deputy Timothy Scott, heard the radio communication and joined the pursuit along with other officers. In the midst of the chase, respondent pulled into the parking lot of a shopping center and was nearly boxed in by the various police vehicles. Respondent evaded the trap by making a sharp turn, colliding with Scott's police car, exiting the parking lot, and speeding off once again down a two-lane highway.

Following respondent's shopping center maneuvering, which resulted in slight damage to Scott's police car, Scott took over as the lead pursuit vehicle. Six minutes and nearly 10 miles after the chase had begun, Scott decided to attempt to terminate the episode by employing a "Precision Intervention Technique ('PIT') maneuver, which causes the fleeing vehicle to spin to a stop." Having radioed his supervisor for permission, Scott was told to "[g]o ahead and take him out." Instead, Scott applied his push bumper to the rear of respondent's vehicle.[1] As a result, respondent lost control of his vehicle, which left the roadway, ran down an embankment, overturned, and crashed. Respondent was badly injured and was rendered a quadriplegic.

Respondent filed suit against Deputy Scott and others under Rev. Stat. § 1979, 42 U.S.C. § 1983, alleging *inter alia*, a violation of his federal constitutional rights, viz. use of excessive force resulting in an unreasonable seizure under the Fourth Amendment.

How should the Supreme Court resolve this case? Why? For the Court's resolution, see *Scott v. Harris*, 127 S. Ct. 468 (2007).

State v. Clothier
753 P.2d 1267 (Kan. 1988)

PRAGER, Chief Justice:

This is an appeal by the State on a question reserved following the acquittal of the defendant, Lloyd D. Clothier, on a charge of involuntary manslaughter (K.S.A. 1987 Supp. 21-3404).

The evidence presented at the trial was essentially as follows: Defendant Clothier was awakened by his barking dog at his home around 3:30 a.m. on November 23, 1986. He got up and let the dog out of the house. A few minutes later, the dog returned. Defendant returned to bed, but the dog continued snarling. Defendant got up, took a revolver from his night stand, and went to the dining room. He looked out the window and observed someone reaching in the window of his automobile parked on the driveway. The person had not only broken the window but had actually opened the door of the vehicle. Defendant was scared and concerned, because his garage door opener was located inside the vehicle. Defendant testified that he wanted to scare the person away so he fired a warning shot through the window, not

---

1. Scott says he decided not to employ the PIT maneuver because he was "concerned that the vehicles were moving too quickly to safely execute the maneuver." Respondent agrees that the PIT maneuver could not have been safely employed. It is irrelevant to our analysis whether Scott had permission to take the precise action he took.

intending to hurt anyone. He then saw someone run behind the car and across the yard. He fired another shot, aiming down at the ground, to warn the person not to return. Defendant told his girl friend to call the police. He then stepped outside of the house and saw 15-year-old Seanan Picard lying injured on the driveway. Picard later died from a gunshot wound to the head. Defendant was acquitted by the jury on the theory that he acted in defense of his property.

The State appealed on a question reserved. The question presented is whether the district court erred in instructing the jury that a person may use deadly force to defend a dwelling or property other than a dwelling, without limiting such instruction to situations in which human life and safety are imminently endangered. The court instructed the jury as follows:

"INSTRUCTION 6

"Use of force in the defense of a dwelling. A person is justified in the use of force against another when and to the extent that it appears to him and he reasonably believes that such conduct is necessary to prevent or terminate such other's unlawful entry into or attack upon his dwelling. Such justification requires both a belief on the part of defendant and the existence of facts that would persuade a reasonable person to that belief.

"Use of force in defense of property other than a dwelling. A person who is lawfully in possession of property other than a dwelling is justified in the threat, or use of force against another for the purpose of preventing or terminating an unlawful interference with such property. Only such degree of force or threat of force thereof as a reasonable man would deem necessary to prevent or terminate the interference may be intentionally used."

At the close of the evidence the State submitted to the court a proposed jury instruction which stated:

"A person is justified in using force likely to cause death or great bodily harm in defense of property not a dwelling only when he reasonably believes that such force is necessary to prevent death or great bodily harm to [himself] [another]."

The instruction, as actually given by the court, followed the language of K.S.A. 21-3212 and K.S.A. 21-3213, as well as PIK Crim. 2d 54.18 and 54.19. K.S.A. 21-3212 and K.S.A. 22-3213 provide as follows:

"21-3212. Use of force in defense of dwelling. A person is justified in the use of force against another when and to the extent that it appears to him and he reasonably believes that such conduct is necessary to prevent or terminate such other's unlawful entry into or attack upon his dwelling."

"21-3213. Use of force in defense of property other than a dwelling. A person who is lawfully in possession of property other than a dwelling is justified in the threat or use of force against another for the purpose of preventing or terminating an unlawful interference with such property. Only such degree

of force or threat thereof as a reasonable man would deem necessary to prevent or terminate the interference may intentionally be used."

The State argues that these statutes are in derogation of the common law which
prohibits the use of deadly force in defense of property unless there is a threat of
imminent bodily harm prior to the use of such force. At the time of the adoption
of the Kansas Criminal Code in 1969, the proposal by the Kansas judicial Council
included the following concluding sentence to the proposed K.S.A. 21-3213:

> "It is not reasonable to intentionally use force intended or likely to cause
> death or great bodily harm for the sole purpose of defending property other
> than a dwelling."

That sentence was deleted by the legislature, demonstrating an intent to avoid
limitation, thus leaving this section apparently as broad as K.S.A. 21-3212. In adopting that position, the Kansas legislature joined a minority of jurisdictions which
permit the use of all reasonably necessary force in the defense of property other
than a dwelling.

It is the position of the State on this appeal that the jury instructions on the use
of force in defense of a dwelling and in defense of property other than a dwelling (K.S.A. 21-3212 and 213213) are unconstitutional as a violation of the Fourth
Amendment to the United States Constitution. The State bases its argument on the
case of *Tennessee v. Garner*, 471 U.S. 1 (1985), where the United States Supreme Court
ruled that the Fourth Amendment prohibits the use of deadly force by a police officer to prevent the escape of a suspected felon unless it is necessary to prevent the
escape and the pursuing police officer has probable cause to believe that the suspect
poses a significant threat of death or serious physical injury to the officer or others.

The State on this appeal has taken the position that, if the police cannot use
deadly force to stop a 15-year-old burglary suspect without probable cause, why
should a private citizen have that privilege? The State maintains that the defenses
created by K.S.A. 21-3212 and 21-3213 constitute state action which violates the
Fourth Amendment.

The State's argument in this case presents essentially a quarrel with the legislative wisdom of deciding to grant the defenses set forth in K.S.A. 21-3212 and K.S.A.
21-3213. In asking this court to change the rule of self-defense provided by statute,
the State is in effect asking this court to exercise a legislative prerogative. The legislature has made a determination that juries in Kansas should be allowed to determine whether the action of a person was reasonable or unreasonable in the use of
force in defense of his property.

As to the claim of unconstitutionality based upon *Tennessee v. Garner*, we hold that
the rule of that case has no application in a criminal case. *Tennessee v. Garner* must
be followed in determining the rights of an injured victim in a civil action where
he claims that excessive force was used by a police officer or by a private individual.
The rule, however, has no application where an owner of property who used force
in defense of his property is charged with the crime of involuntary manslaughter.

In the opinion in *Tennessee v. Garner,* the Supreme Court of the United States does not at any place state that a criminal defense such as we have in K.S.A. 21-3212 and K.S.A. 21-3213 would be a violation of the United States Constitution.

As pointed out by counsel for the defendant in his brief, the law in Kansas is clear that the legislature has determined by statute that a jury should determine whether or not the application of force in defense of property was reasonable under all the circumstances existing. The trial court in this case had no right to exercise its judgment in determining the reasonableness of the defendant's actions, for to do so would be an intrusion into the function of the jury. Based upon the reasoning set forth above, we hold that the trial court did not err in its instructions to the jury on the issue of the reasonableness of the force used by defendant in defense of his property.

The appeal of the State is denied.

Questions and Notes

1. At common law, the right of a citizen to use deadly force to protect property or arrest a felon was considerably more circumscribed than that of a police officer. Do *Garner* and *Clothier* suggest that the respective rights of citizens and police may soon be inverted?

2. Despite the opinion of the court, could you argue that *Garner* would *not* apply, even to a civil suit against Clothier? On what basis?

3. Do you think that the Kansas statute is an improvement in the common law or a step in the wrong direction? Why?

4. At common law, a citizen could not arrest a felon unless the felony had actually been committed. Consider whether the common law rule is too harsh as you read *Hillsman.*

United States v. Hillsman

522 F.2d 454 (7th Cir. 1975)

PELL, Circuit Judge.

The defendants James Hillsman and Clinton Bush were convicted by a jury of assaulting a federal officer, in violation of 18 U.S.C. § 111. On appeal, the defendants contend that the district court erred in refusing to instruct the jury that if the defendants reasonably believed the federal officer to be a fleeing felon, the defendants should be acquitted.

On February 8, 1974, the defendants, along with two to three hundred other persons, attended a funeral in Gary, Indiana. Several agents of the Drug Enforcement Administration were conducting undercover surveillance at the funeral home for the purpose of observing and identifying suspected narcotics dealers. All of the agents involved in the surveillance wore ordinary "street" clothes and drove unmarked cars.

Agent David Munson, who was equipped with a video tape camera, stationed himself outside the funeral home alongside photographers from a Gary newspaper and began filming the mourners as they left the funeral home. Most of the several hundred mourners at the funeral home (including the defendants) were black and a group of the black mourners demanded that Munson, who is white, cease taking pictures and leave the area. One member of the crowd, William Hanyard, began shoving and hitting Munson when he continued to film the mourners. The defendants Hillsman and Bush were not identified as being in any way involved in the verbal or physical exchange with Munson.

Agent Kenneth Rhodes, the acting agent in charge of the DEA in the area, was approximately six feet from Munson at this time and observed Hanyard's attack on the agent. Intending to shoot Hanyard, Rhodes, who is black, drew his revolver and began to assume the "combat" position. However, before he was able to get into this position, Rhodes either stepped back or was pushed from the rear and his gun discharged prematurely. The bullet merely grazed Hanyard but struck and killed Albert Griffin, an innocent bystander.

Immediately after the shot was fired, Rhodes announced that he was a federal agent and told Munson, "Let's get out of here." Although Munson heard the latter statement, he did not hear Rhodes announce that he was a federal officer. Rhodes and Munson then moved to their cars. Munson jumped into a car with several other agents and Rhodes stopped to talk briefly with one of these agents. Rhodes then began walking toward his own car. At no time did Rhodes or Munson approach the body of Griffin.

As Rhodes was moving toward his car, a woman in the crowd pointed at him and said, "He is the one; there he goes." A group of the mourners then began running after Rhodes. As Rhodes drove away, shots were fired at his car. One bullet struck the car but Rhodes himself was not injured.

Hillsman and Bush were identified as being members of the group that chased Rhodes and were observed firing weapons at Rhodes' car.

The defendants argue that the district court erred in failing to instruct the jury that if the defendants reasonably believed Rhodes to be a fleeing felon, the jury should find the defendants not guilty.

The undisputed evidence indicated that neither Bush nor Hillsman was involved in the Munson-Hanyard skirmish. Both defendants testified that although they saw the altercation, they, like Agent Munson, did not hear Rhodes announce that he was a federal officer. According to their testimony, the defendants pursued Rhodes because they believed him to be a felon fleeing from the scene of the crime and they wanted to catch and hold him until the police arrived. If Hillsman and Bush did fire at Rhodes' car, a point which the defense did not concede, they did so, according to one theory of the defense, only because of their mistaken belief that Rhodes was a fleeing felon.

[T]he district court gave a lengthy instruction concerning the right of a private citizen to make an arrest. The court however, refused to give a defense instruction which provided:

"There has been evidence that the Defendants, James Hillsman and Clinton Bush, gave chase to Kenneth Rhodes, as he was leaving the scene of the funeral of Van Lott in the vicinity of 23rd Avenue and Washington Street in Gary, Indiana, and that at the time the Defendants gave chase they did not have knowledge that Kenneth Rhodes was a Federal Agent.

"If you find from the evidence that the Defendants, James Hillsman and Clinton Bush, acted out of reasonable belief that Kenneth Rhodes was not a Federal Agent but instead was a private citizen who the Defendants, James Hillsman and Clinton Bush, had reasonable cause to believe had committed a felony and was fleeing the scene in order to avoid apprehension, and that the Defendants, James Hillsman and Clinton Bush, chased Kenneth Rhodes in order to stop his flight and detain him then you must find the Defendants, James Hillsman and Clinton Bush not guilty."

We turn to the question of whether, assuming *arguendo*, that Hillsman and Bush were attempting to make a citizen's arrest, the actions of the defendants would have been justified had Rhodes been, as they allegedly believed, a private citizen. Since the incident would have been governed by Indiana law if Rhodes had been a private citizen, we look to the law of that state in making this determination.

Indiana follows the general common law rule that "a private citizen has the right to arrest one who has committed a felony in his presence, and may even arrest one he reasonably believes to have committed a felony, so long as the felony was in fact committed." Where a felony of violence has been committed, moreover, a private citizen may use reasonable force, including deadly force, to prevent the felon's escape from the scene.

The private citizen's right to make an arrest, however, is limited by the fact that he, unlike a police officer, acts at his own peril. A police officer has the right to arrest without a warrant where he reasonably believes that a felony has been committed and that the person arrested is guilty, even if, in fact, no felony has occurred. A private citizen, on the other hand, is privileged to make an arrest only when he has reasonable grounds for believing in the guilt of the person arrested and a felony has in fact been committed.

In the present case, the proffered defense instruction in question contained an incomplete statement of the law regarding a citizen's arrest. The instruction tendered by the defendants stated that Hillsman and Bush should be found not guilty if they reasonably believed Rhodes to be a private citizen and reasonably believed that he had committed a felony. And, as explained, Hillsman and Bush would have been justified in making a citizen's arrest only if they reasonably believed that Rhodes had committed a felony *and* a felony had in fact been committed.

The trial court did instruct the jury in detail with regard to the right of a private citizen to make an arrest without a warrant. This instruction accurately stated that although deadly force could be used to effect such an arrest in an appropriate case, no citizen's arrest would be valid unless a felony had in fact been committed.

In addition, the district court instructed the jury with respect to the question of whether a felony had occurred when Rhodes shot Hanyard and Griffin. The jury was expressly told that if they found that a felony had occurred, then they could apply the law of citizen's arrest. The court admittedly instructed the jury with respect to only one type of felony, voluntary manslaughter. This, however, was the only felony for which the defense requested an instruction and the defense does not contend on appeal that instructions on other felonies were necessary. Although it may be argued that a jury could have found that Rhodes committed a felony other than voluntary manslaughter, we cannot say that the district court's failure to instruct on other felonies, in the absence of any request by the defendants, was plain error requiring reversal.

Affirmed.

Questions and Notes

1. Is there any good reason for relying so much on harm and so little on culpability or objective dangerousness in regard to citizen's arrest? Don't we want to encourage citizen involvement in enforcing the criminal law?

2. Are there any policy differences between the *Hillsman* issue and the issue raised by *People v. Young* (page 303, *supra*)? Which case is stronger for allowing the intervenor (intermeddler?) to act in appearances?

See NUTSHELL §§ 6.08, 6.09; and MPC § 3.07 (Appendix A).

Problem

On Saturday afternoon, December 22, 1984, Troy Canty, Darryl Cabey, James Ramseur, and Barry Allen boarded an IRT express subway train in The Bronx and headed south toward lower Manhattan. The four youths rode together in the rear portion of the seventh car of the train. Two of the four, Ramseur and Cabey, had screwdrivers inside their coats, which they said were to be used to break into the coin boxes of video machines.

Defendant Bernhard Goetz boarded this subway train at 14th Street in Manhattan and sat down on a bench toward the rear section of the same car occupied by the four youths. Goetz was carrying an unlicensed .38 caliber pistol loaded with five rounds of ammunition in a waistband holster. The train left the 14th Street station and headed toward Chambers Street.

It appears from the evidence before the grand jury that Canty approached Goetz, possibly with Allen beside him, and stated "give me five dollars." Neither Canty nor any of the other youths displayed a weapon. Goetz responded by standing up, pulling out his handgun and firing four shots in rapid succession. The first shot hit Canty in the chest; the second struck Allen in the back; the third went through Ramseur's arm and into his left side; the fourth was fired at Cabey, who apparently was then standing in the corner of the car, but missed, deflecting instead off of a wall of the conductor's cab. After Goetz briefly surveyed the scene around him, he fired another shot at Cabey, who then was sitting on the end bench of the car. The bullet entered the rear of Cabey's side and severed his spinal cord.

All but two of the other passengers fled the car when, or immediately after, the shots were fired. The conductor, who had been in the next car, heard the shots and instructed the motorman to radio for emergency assistance. The conductor then went into the car where the shooting occurred and saw Goetz sitting on a bench, the injured youths lying on the floor or slumped against a seat, and two women who had apparently taken cover, also lying on the floor. Goetz told the conductor that the four youths had tried to rob him.

While the conductor was aiding the youths, Goetz headed toward the front of the car. The train had stopped just before the Chambers Street station and Goetz went between two of the cars, jumped onto the tracks and fled. Police and ambulance crews arrived at the scene shortly thereafter. Ramseur and Canty, initially listed in critical condition, have fully recovered. Cabey remains paralyzed and has suffered some degree of brain damage.

On December 31, 1984, Goetz surrendered to police in Concord, New Hampshire, identifying himself as the gunman being sought for the subway shootings in New York nine days earlier. Later that day, after receiving *Miranda* warnings, he made two lengthy statements, both of which were tape-recorded with his permission. In the statements, which are substantially similar, Goetz admitted that he had been illegally carrying a handgun in New York City for three years. He stated that he had first purchased a gun in 1981 after he had been injured in a mugging. Goetz also revealed that twice between 1981 and 1984 he had successfully warded off assailants simply by displaying the pistol.

According to Goetz' statement, the first contact he had with the four youths came when Canty, sitting or lying on the bench across from him, asked "how are you," to which he replied "fine." Shortly thereafter, Canty, followed by one of the other youths, walked over to the defendant and stood to his left, while the other two youths remained to his right, in the corner of the subway car. Canty then said "give me five dollars." Goetz stated that he knew from the smile on Canty's face that they wanted to "play with me." Although he was certain that none of the youths had a gun, he had a fear, based on prior experiences, of being "maimed."

In assessing Goetz' criminal liability, should it matter whether the victims were in fact trying to rob him, what Goetz' prior experience had taught him, and/or what motivated Goetz to act as he did? Is there a good case to be made for justifying his behavior? For excusing it?

See People v. Goetz, 497 N.E.2d 41 (N.Y. 1986).

Chapter 7

Theft

A. Larceny

At common law, larceny was defined as the trespassory taking and carrying away of the personal property of another with the intent to deprive the person entitled to possession of that property. Because the most important (and difficult) litigation concerns the concept of trespass to possession, our primary focus will be on that issue. The entire definition, however, is important and has occasioned litigation.

For example, because the property must be carried away (asportation), courts must determine whether one who starts another's automobile, but is arrested before he can drive it off, has satisfied the asportation element. *See People v. Alamo,* 315 N.E.2d 446 (N.Y. 1974). Similarly, because only personal property is subject to theft, stealing things such as trade secrets or computer time (which is not uncommon) do not subject the thief to a larceny prosecution unless a statute so provides. The "of another" requirement has caused courts to acquit husbands who steal from their wives (husband and wives are one) and partners who steal from the partnership. *See People v. Zinke,* 555 N.E.2d 263 (N.Y. 1990). Finally, because larceny protects the person entitled to possession, it is even possible to steal one's own property if another has a superior possessory interest in it, such as a lien.

The first four cases in this section — *Topolewski, Pruitt, Rogers,* and *Blackburn* — focus primarily on the question of "trespass." As you read the cases, try to ascertain where the prosecutor thinks there is a trespass to possession, and why the court agrees or disagrees.

Topolewski v. State

109 N.W. 1037 (Wis. 1906)

[Mat Dolan, an employee of the Plankinton Meat Company, was indebted to John Topolewski. Topolewski suggested that Dolan discharge his debt by placing four barrels of Plankinton meat on the loading platform with instructions to the loading foreman to deliver the meat to Topolewski. Dolan reported the plan to his superiors, who instructed him to go along with it for the purpose of catching Topolewski. The scheme progressed as suggested. Topolewski was arrested shortly after driving away with the meat. He appeals his conviction for larceny.]

Marshall, J.

It will be noted that the plan for depriving the packing company of its property originated with the accused, but that it was wholly impracticable of accomplishment

333

without the property being placed on the loading platform and the accused not being interfered with when he attempted to take it. When Dolan agreed to procure such placing the packing company in legal effect agreed thereto. Dolan did not expressly consent nor did the agreement he had with the packing company authorize him to do so, to the misappropriation of the property. Did the agreement with the accused to place the property of the packing company on the loading platform, where it could be appropriated by the accused, constitute consent to such appropriation?

The case is very near the border line, if not across it, between consent and non-consent to the taking of the property. *Reg. v. Lawrence*, 4 Cox C. C. 438, it was held that if the property was delivered by a servant to the defendant by the master's direction the offense cannot be larceny, regardless of the purpose of the defendant. In this case the property was not only placed on the loading platform, as was usual in delivering such goods to customers, with knowledge that the accused would soon arrive, having a formed design to take it, but the packing company's employee in charge of the platform, Ernst Klotz, was instructed that the property was placed there for a man who would call for it. Klotz from such statement had every reason to infer, when the accused arrived and claimed the right to take the property, that he was the one referred to and that it was proper to make delivery to him and he acted accordingly. While he did not physically place the property, or assist in doing so, in the wagon, his standing by, witnessing such placing by the accused, and then assisting him in arranging the wagon, as the evidence shows he did, and taking the order, in the usual way, from the accused as to the disposition of the fourth barrel, and his conduct in respect thereto amounted, practically, to a delivery of the three barrels to the accused.

In *Rex v. Egginton*, 2 P. & P. 508, we have a very instructive case on the subject under discussion here. A servant informed his master that he had been solicited to aid in robbing the latter's house. By the master's discretion the servant opened the house, gave the would-be thieves access thereto and took them to the place where the intended subject of the larceny had been laid in order that they might take it. All this was done with a view to the apprehension of the guilty parties after the accomplishment of their purpose. The servant by direction of the master not only gave access to the house but afforded the would-be thieves every facility for taking the property, and yet the court held that the crime of larceny was complete, because there was no direction to the servant to deliver the property to the intruders or consent to their taking it. They were left free to commit the larceny, as they had purposed doing, and the way was made easy for them to do so, but they were neither induced to commit the crime, nor was any act essential to the offense done by anyone but themselves.

In the case before us the owner of the property through its agent, Dolan, did not suggest the plan for committing the offense of larceny, which was finally adopted, but the evidence shows, conclusively, that by the consent or direction of the packing company, through words or otherwise, he suggested the commission of such an offense and invited from the accused plans to that end. The fair construction of the evidence is that in the finality the plan was a joint creation of the two and that it required each to be an active participant in its consummation.

We cannot well escape the conclusion that this case falls under the condemnation of the rule that where the owner of property by himself or his agent, actually or constructively, aids in the commission of the offense, as intended by the wrongdoer, by performing or rendering unnecessary some act in the transaction essential to the offense, the would-be criminal is not guilty of all the elements of the offense. Here the owner of the property packed or superintended the packing of the four barrels of meat, and caused the same to be placed on the platform, knowing that the accused would soon arrive to take them, and directed its platform boss [to] "Let them go; They are for some man and he will call for them." He substantially made such delivery, by treating the accused when he arrived upon the scene as having a right to take the property. In that the design to trap a criminal went a little too far, at least, in that it included the doing of an act, in effect preventing the taking of the property from being characterized by any element of trespass.

The logical basis for the doctrine above discussed is that there can be no larceny without a trespass. So if one procures his property to be taken by another intending to commit larceny, or delivers his property to such other, the latter purposing to commit such crime, the element of trespass is wanting and the crime not fully consummated however plain may be the guilty purpose of the one possessing himself of such property. That does not militate against a person's being free to set a trap to catch one whom he suspects of an intention to commit the crime of larceny, but the setting of such trap must not go further than to afford the would-be thief the amplest opportunity to carry out his purpose, formed without such inducement on the part of the owner of the property, as to put him in the position of having consented to the taking. If I induce one to come and take my property and then place it before him to be taken, and he takes it with criminal intent, or if knowing that one intends to take my property I deliver it to him and he takes it with such intent, the essential element of trespass involving non-consent requisite to a completed offense of larceny does not characterize the transaction, regardless of the fact that the moral turpitude involved is no less than it would be if such essential were present.

The judgment is reversed, and the cause remanded for a new trial.

Questions and Notes

1. What is the difference between *Topolewski* and *Egginton*? How does that difference relate to the trespass element in larceny?

2. If you had represented the Plankinton Meat Company and one of their officials had come to you for advice prior to Topolewski's taking the meat, what would you have advised the Company? Is there a way that they could have captured Topolewski without effectively giving him the meat, thereby negating the trespass element?

3. Try to identify the trespass in *Pruitt*.

United States v. Pruitt
446 F.2d 513 (6th Cir. 1971)

PHILLIPS, Chief Judge.

The issue on this appeal is whether a bank messenger entrusted with funds of his employer for delivery to a branch bank may be prosecuted under 18 U.S.C. 2113(b) for appropriating such funds to his own use. We answer this question in the affirmative and uphold the conviction of Dennis Ray Pruitt under 2113(b) for larceny of bank funds.

Pruitt was employed as a messenger by the Second National Bank of Lexington, Kentucky. His duties included the transportation and delivery of money to branch banks. In March of 1969 Pruitt developed an acquaintance with Hargis Trusty, an employee of a local garage. These two men devised a plan to steal bank funds entrusted to Pruitt for delivery by making it appear that Pruitt had been robbed. On March 21, 1969, while on a delivery run, Pruitt met Trusty at a rendezvous and turned over to him $16,000 in bank funds. Pruitt was shot in the arm and bullets were fired into the bank vehicle. Shortly thereafter Pruitt reported to police that he had been robbed by three masked men.

On March 30, 1969, after being confronted with certain statements made by Trusty, Pruitt admitted that his robbery report was not true and that Trusty had actually taken the money. Pruitt was subsequently tried and convicted for stealing bank funds in contravention of 18 U.S.C. 2113(b).

18 U.S.C. 2113(b) provides in pertinent part:

> "Whoever takes and carries away, with intent to steal or purloin, any property or money or any other thing of value exceeding $100 belonging to, or in the care, custody, control, management, or possession of any bank, or any savings and loan association, shall be fined not more than $5,000 or imprisoned not more than ten years, or both. . . ."

The legislative history of 2113(b) shows that Congress intended to outlaw larceny from a federally insured bank. H.R. Rep. No. 732, 75th Cong., 1st Sess. (1937). We have no hesitation in holding that Pruitt's crime constituted larceny.

"The common-law courts also drew a distinction, which is recognized in most jurisdictions at the present day, between possession and mere custody. Where one having only the bare charge or custody of property for the owner converts it *animo furandi*, he commits a trespass and is guilty of larceny; the possession, in judgment of law, remains in the owner until the conversion. This is the rule at common law and under statutes declaratory of the common law." 50 AM. JUR. 2d, *Larceny*, 89.

Further, employees receiving property from their employers for the limited purpose of delivery of the property to another were considered at common law and under statutes declaratory of the common law to have a mere custody of the property, so that their wrongful conversion of the property constituted the crime of larceny. 50 AM. JUR. 2d, *Larceny*, 93; Annotation, 125 A.L.R. 367, 375.

We hold that Pruitt's crime falls within this category and is punishable under 2113(b). Paraphrasing the language of the statute, he took and carried away money exceeding $100 belonging to the bank with the intent to steal it. We need not decide on this appeal to what extent 2113(b) proscribes crimes other than larceny as argued by the Government.

Questions and Notes

1. Explain how Pruitt trespassed against the bank's possession.

2. Why do you suppose the common law created such a fiction?

3. If a customer gave money to a bank teller and the teller kept it without ever turning it over to the bank, the common law courts held that the trespass element was not satisfied. *See Bazely's Case*, 168 Eng. Rep. 517 (Cr. Cas. Res. 1799). Because of *Bazely's Case*, the crime of embezzlement was developed. *See* Section B, *infra*. What is the difference between *Pruitt* and *Bazely*?

4. Would (should) *Bazely* be decided differently if he had put the money in the drawer when he obtained it, and stole it at the end of the day? *Compare State v. Nolan*, 131 A.2d 851 (Md. App. 1957), *with Commonwealth v. Ryan*, 30 N.E. 364 (Mass. 1892).

5. Look for the "trespass" as you read *Rogers*.

United States v. Rogers

289 F.2d 433 (4th Cir. 1961)

HAYNSWORTH, Circuit Judge.

The defendant has appealed from his conviction under the "bank robbery statute," complaining that the proof did not show the commission of larceny* and that the verdict of the jury was coerced by the Court's instructions. We think the proof did support the conviction, but that a new trial should be granted because of the possibly coercive effect of the Court's instructions designed to produce agreement of the jurors upon a verdict.

There was testimony showing that, at the request of his brother, the defendant took a payroll check, payable to the brother in the face amount of $97.92, to a bank where the brother maintained an account. In accordance with the brother's request, he asked the teller to deposit $80 to the credit of the brother's account and to deliver to him the balance of the check in cash. The teller was inexperienced. She first inquired of another teller whether the check could be credited to an account in part and cashed in part. Having been told that this was permissible, she required the defendant's endorsement on the check, and, misreading its date (12-06-59) as the amount payable, she deducted the $80 deposit and placed $1,126.59 on the counter. There were two strapped packages, each containing $500, and $126.59 in

---

* Despite its name, the "bank robbery statute" also punishes larceny. — Ed.

miscellaneous bills and change. The defendant took the $1,126.59 in cash thus placed upon the counter and departed.

There was also testimony that when the day's business was done, the teller who handled the transaction was found to be short in her accounts by $1,108.67, the exact amount of the difference between the $1,206.59, for which she had supposed the check to have been drawn, and $97.92, its actual face amount, and that her adding machine tape showed that she had accepted the check as having been drawn for $1,206.59.

There was corroboration from other witnesses of some phases of this story as told by the tellers and the bookkeeper.

The defendant agreed that he took the check to the bank for his brother, asked that $80 be credited to his brother's account, and that the excess be paid to him in cash. He stated, however, that he received in cash only the $17.92, to which he was entitled, denying that he had received the larger sum.

The case was submitted to the jury under instructions that they should find the defendant guilty if they found the much larger sum was placed upon the counter and was taken by the defendant with the intention to appropriate the overpayment, or if he thereafter formed the intention to, and did, appropriate the overpayment to his own use.

After it had deliberated for approximately four hours, the jury reported at 4:15 o'clock in the afternoon that it was unable to reach an agreement upon a verdict. Thereupon, the Court instructed the jury regarding its duty to agree, but without the ameliorating admonition that no juror should yield his conscientious conviction. The jury again retired and, in a few minutes, at 4:32 o'clock in the afternoon, reported it had reached an agreement upon a verdict.

Since the other questions, directed to the nature of the offense, will arise necessarily upon a retrial, we address ourselves to them.

We accept the defendant's premise that paragraph (b) of the bank robbery act reaches only the offense of larceny as that crime has been defined by the common law. It does not encompass the crimes of embezzlement from a bank, reached by another statute, or obtaining goods by false pretense. That this is so is indicated by the use of the words, "whoever takes and carries away, with intent to steal and purloin, . . ." borrowed from the Act of April 30, 1790, which had been construed as a larceny statute. It is further indicated by the title of the act and its legislative history.

An essential element of the crime of larceny, the "'felonious taking and carrying' away the personal goods of another," is that the taking must be trespassory. It is an invasion of the other's right to possession, and therein is found the principal distinction between larceny and other related offenses.

It has long been recognized, however, that when the transferor acts under a unilateral mistake of fact, his delivery of a chattel may be ineffective to transfer title or his right to possession. If the transferee, knowing of the transferor's mistake, receives the goods with the intention of appropriating them, his receipt and removal of them is a trespass and his offense is larceny.

Such a situation was presented in *Regina v. Middleton*, 28 Law Times (N.S.) 777, 12 Cox C.C. 417 (1873). There it appeared that the defendant had a credit balance of 11 s. in a postal savings account. He obtained a warrant for the withdrawal of 10 s. which he presented to the postal clerk. The clerk mistakenly referred to the wrong letter of advice, one which had been received in connection with the prospective withdrawal of a much larger sum by another depositor. The clerk then placed upon the counter a 5 £ note, 3 sovereigns, a half crown and silver and copper amounting altogether to 8 £ 16 s. 10 d. The defendant gathered up the money and departed. The jury found that the defendant was aware of the clerk's mistake and took the money with intent to steal it. His conviction of larceny was affirmed by the Court of Criminal Appeals.

Subsequently, it appears to have become settled in England that, if the initial receipt of the chattel is innocent, its subsequent conversion cannot be larceny, but, if the recipient knows at the time he is receiving more than his due and intends to convert it to his own use, he is guilty of larceny. *See Regina v. Flowers*, 16 Q.B. 643 (1886). That is the established rule of the American cases.

The District Court went too far, however, when it told the jury it might convict if, though his initial receipt of the overpayment was innocent, the defendant thereafter formed the intention to, and did, convert the overpayment.[19]

Upon the retrial, therefore, the jury should be instructed that among the essential elements of the offense are (1) that the defendant knew when he received the money from the teller or picked it up from the counter that it was more than his due and (2) that he took it from the bank with the intention of converting it.

The judgment is reversed and the case remanded for further proceedings not inconsistent with this opinion.

Questions and Notes

1. Why should it matter whether the defendant initially knew of the mistake? Isn't a defendant who discovered the mistake when he got home and immediately decided to keep the money as dishonest as Rogers?

2. Why do you suppose that the jury had so much difficulty reaching a verdict in such an obvious case?

3. In *Blackburn*, once again, find the trespass.

---

19. Since the overpayment was so large and obvious to one who knew the amount of the check, the error may have been harmless. Upon the retrial, however, the jury should be properly instructed.

Blackburn v. Commonwealth

89 S.W. 160 (Ky. 1905)

PAYNTER, J.

On Monday, January 30, 1905, the appellant hired from A. E. Marcum, at Catlettsburg, a horse and buggy to drive to his uncle's on Laurel creek, in Boyd county. He asked for the horse he had hired on the previous Saturday. The evidence tends to show that, in company with a woman, he drove beyond Laurel creek to Bear creek, in Lawrence, an adjoining county, where he left the horse in charge of one Cornutte, who agreed to take care of it; the appellant promising to return in a day or two. Cornutte says that the appellant borrowed $2 from him, representing to him that the horse and buggy belonged to him. The appellant, accompanied by the woman, crossed over into West Virginia, where he was arrested on Wednesday on the charge of having stolen the horse. The appellant claims that he had been on a spree at the time he hired the horse, and carried a lot of whisky with him, and after leaving Catlettsburg, he being a one-armed man, the woman did the driving; that he went to sleep from the effects of the drinking, and that she drove him beyond his destination to the place where the horse was found; and that he was drinking, and did not remember what he said to Cornutte with reference to the horse and buggy. He denied that he had any purpose to steal the horse or any intention to deprive the owner of it. He also testified that, when arrested, he had money to pay Cornutte the borrowed money and for the care of the horse. The foregoing is the substance of the evidence upon which the jury found him guilty of stealing the horse.

If one obtains the possession of property for a particular purpose, and at the time he does so he had a fraudulent intent to use the possession as the means of converting the property to his own use, and does so convert it, he is guilty of larceny. In discussing the question it is said in 1 WHARTON CRIMINAL LAW (8th Ed.) § 886: "It is essential that there should be an intent to deprive the owner permanently of the property; but, if the original intent was felonious, then on conversion the larceny is completed." In the instructions which the court gave the jury it followed the principles of law announced, except that it did not give an instruction requiring the jury to believe, before it convicted the defendant, that there had been a conversion of the property. To have been guilty of the offense of horse stealing, it was just as essential to show a conversion of the property as it was to show that at the time of obtaining possession of it he had the fraudulent intent to use the possession as a means of converting it to his own use. The court seems to have been of the opinion that, if the appellant obtained the possession of the property with the fraudulent intent to convert it to his own use, the offense had been established. This we do not think is the law. The question should have been submitted to the jury under appropriate instructions as to whether there had been a conversion of the property.

There is a question as to whether the property was actually pledged for the $2 to Cornutte. If he did so, then the further question arises whether he did so with the intention of redeeming and restoring it to the owner; for, if he had a fair and reasonable expectation of doing so, he was not guilty of larceny. In *Regina v. Phetheon*, 9 Car. & P. 225, it was held that while a defense to a charge of stealing, that the prisoner pawned the property with the intention of redeeming, was not a defense to be generally encouraged, yet, if clearly made out in proof, it should prevail; but, to make such a defense available, there must not only be the intent, but the ability, to redeem. We are of the opinion that, in addition to the instructions given, the court should have submitted the question to the jury as to whether the property was pledged to Cornutte for the $2, and in addition to that told the jury in substance that if he did so with the intention of redeeming and restoring it to the owner and had a fair and reasonable expectation of doing so, the jury should find him not guilty.

The judgment is reversed, for proceedings consistent with this opinion.

Questions and Notes

1. When did the trespass occur? Was it when the horse was hired or when the horse was sold?

2. If it occurred when the horse was hired, why should it matter whether or not the horse was subsequently sold?

3. On the other hand, if it didn't occur until the sale, didn't Blackburn have rightful possession?

4. Would a larceny conviction have been possible if Blackburn had intended to return the horse at the time it was hired, but subsequently decided to pledge him for $2 in order to continue his spree, intending at that time to never redeem the pledge? Why? Why not?

5. The type of larceny described in *Blackburn* is usually called "larceny by trick" and was first recognized at common law in *Pear's Case*, 168 Eng. Rep. 208 (1779), a case also involving a fraudulent horse renter.

6. No discussion of the rules of trespass in larceny would be complete without referring to the fifteenth-century *Carrier's Case*, Y.B. 13 Edw. IV, fo. 9, pl. 5 (1473), in which a bailee broke open a package and stole the contents. As the case was subsequently construed, it held that the carrier's act of "breaking the bulk" caused possession to revert to the bailor, thereby rendering the carrier's taking trespassory. Hardly anybody takes that case seriously today. *But see* Fletcher, *The Metamorphosis of Larceny*, 89 Harv. L. Rev. 469 (1976).

7. Why should it matter whether Blackburn intended to redeem the horse? Is the court saying that a permanent deprivation of the property (or at least risk of permanent deprivation) should be required? Why? If somebody takes my car for an hour, haven't I been deprived of my property?

8. As you read *Butler*, consider whether a claim of right can negate the element of trespass in larceny. If so, what else can it negate?

People v. Butler

421 P.2d 703 (Cal. 1967)

Traynor, Chief Justice.

Defendant was charged by information with the murder of Joseph H. Anderson and with assault with intent to murder William Russell Locklear. A jury convicted defendant of first-degree felony murder and of assault with a deadly weapon; it fixed the penalty for the murder at death. This appeal is automatic. (Pen. Code, § 1239, subd. (b).)

We have determined that error in the guilt phase of the trial deprived defendant of his primary defense to the charge of first-degree felony murder. The judgment of conviction of murder must therefore be reversed.

Joseph H. Anderson operated a catering service in Los Angeles at the time of his death, and William Locklear assisted him. On the evening of May 18, 1965, Locklear was at Anderson's home where he planned to remain for the night. He testified that the doorbell rang shortly after midnight while he was in the bedroom. He heard little for 20 to 30 minutes after that because he was in the shower. When he returned to the bedroom he heard Anderson call, "Bill, he's got a gun." Anderson then entered the bedroom followed by defendant, whose hand was in his coat pocket. Locklear did not see a gun until two or three minutes later when defendant produced one from "someplace." Anderson attempted to seize the gun, it fired and Anderson fell. Locklear tried to apprehend defendant but was himself shot and lost consciousness.

Defendant was gone when Locklear regained consciousness. Defendant testified that he met Anderson several weeks before the killing and that Anderson employed him on one occasion to do catering work. Anderson did not pay him for the work, and when he requested payment Anderson asked him to wait a few days. On the evening of May 18th, defendant went to Anderson's home to obtain payment. While the two were sitting in the living room discussing the debt, Anderson made an indecent proposal and, when defendant rejected it, offered to double the money he owed defendant. Defendant also refused this offer telling Anderson he needed his money and wished only to be paid.

Defendant also testified that at this point Anderson agreed to pay him, but they had two or three drinks together before Anderson started toward the bedroom to get the money. Anderson apparently changed his mind and returned to discuss his earlier proposition. Defendant persisted in his refusal, and Anderson again went to the bedroom. Defendant testified that when he entered the bedroom a few seconds later, Anderson approached him with a pistol. He had not previously been aware of Locklear's presence, but he then saw Locklear lying on the bed. Defendant stated that he had armed himself before going to Anderson's home because he had heard stories about Anderson's brutality, and that when he saw a gun in Anderson's hand, he brought out his own to defend himself. Anderson called to Locklear that defendant had a gun and threw a towel or bathrobe at defendant. Defendant testified that he did not intend to shoot, but as the towel was thrown at him, Anderson grabbed his arm and the gun fired. After Anderson was shot, Locklear jumped up and as he came forward defendant shot him too. Defendant then ran to the living room and back to the bedroom where he looked for money. Finding none, he took a wallet and ran from the house.

No evidence of premeditation or deliberation was adduced by the prosecution. The court instructed the jury that since these elements were not present, it could find first degree murder only if defendant committed the killing in the perpetration of a robbery.

Defendant testified that he did not intend to rob Anderson when he went to the house, but intended only to recover money owed to him. Over his objection, the prosecutor argued to the jury, "If you think a man owes you a hundred dollars, or fifty dollars, or five dollars, or a dollar, and you go over with a gun to try to get his money, it's robbery." And, "If you go into a man's home and merely because he's supposed to owe you some money, you take money from him at gunpoint, you have robbed him." Again objecting to further argument by the prosecutor that a robbery was committed even if defendant believed Anderson owed him money, defendant suggested that a necessary element of theft, the intent to steal, was requisite to robbery, but was overruled by the court.

Defendant's objection was well taken. "Robbery is the felonious taking of personal property in the possession of another, from his person or immediate presence, and against his will, accomplished by means of force or fear." (Pen. Code, § 211.) An essential element of robbery is the felonious intent or *Animus furandi* that accompanies the taking. Since robbery is but larceny aggravated by the use of force or fear to accomplish the taking of property from the person or presence of the possessor, the felonious intent requisite to robbery is the same intent common to those offenses that, like larceny, are grouped in the Penal Code designation of "theft." The taking of property is not theft in the absence of an intent to steal, and a specific intent to steal, *i.e.*, an intent to deprive an owner permanently of his property, is an essential element of robbery.

Although an intent to steal may ordinarily be inferred when one person takes the property of another, particularly if he takes it by force, proof of the existence of a state of mind incompatible with an intent to steal precludes a finding of either theft or robbery. It has long been the rule in this state and generally throughout the country that a bona fide belief, even though mistakenly held, that one has a right or claim to the property negates felonious intent. A belief that the property taken belongs to the taker, or that he had a right to retake goods sold is sufficient to preclude felonious intent. Felonious intent exists only if the actor intends to take the property of another without believing in good faith that he has a right or claim to it.[2]

---

2. Defendant concedes, as he must, that although the offense could not constitute robbery absent an intent to steal, an unprovoked assault accompanying an attempt to collect a debt may

The judgment of conviction of murder is reversed.

Mosk, Justice.

I dissent.

The question here is whether the defendant may assert *Ipse dixit* his belief that he was entitled to an unpaid debt taken from another by force or fear as a defense to a charge of robbery, and by extrapolation as a defense to a charge of murder committed in the course of a robbery. While there is some authority suggesting this query be answered in the affirmative, there has been no explicit holding of this court on the issue.

Thus, the question is ultimately one of basic public policy, which unequivocally states that the proper forum for resolving debt disputes is a court of law, pursuant to legal process—not the street, at the business end of a lethal weapon. To hold otherwise would be to constitute him judge and jury in his own cause.

It is significant that the basic cases permitting forcible recaption of property one believes his own were decided before the turn of the century. In a bucolic western scene or in the woolly atmosphere of the frontier in the nineteenth century, the six-shooter may have been an acceptable device for do-it-yourself debt collection. If the law permitted a might-makes-right doctrine in that milieu, it is of dubious adaptability to urban society in this final third of the twentieth century.

I would affirm the judgment.

Questions and Notes

1. Recall that Butler was charged with first degree murder. Is the court saying that claim of right to property is a defense to murder?

2. Although most courts accept claim of right to larceny where the claim is for particular property, a growing number reject the defense for robbery, or for larceny where the claim is for a debt allegedly owed (e.g., $50) as opposed to specific property (e.g., a borrowed teapot). *See, e.g., People v. Reid*, 508 N.E.2d 661 (N.Y. 1987).

3. Did the court, per Chief Justice Traynor, or the dissent, per Justice Mosk, reach the better result? Why? In *People v. Barnett*, 954 P.2d 384 (Cal. 1998), the California Supreme Court spoke approvingly of Justice Mosk's dissent, indicating that, in an appropriate case, it might be prepared to reconsider *Butler*.

4. The next series of cases focuses on legislative attempts to fill in the gaps created by the common law development of larceny. You will recall that after *Bazely's Case*, discussed after *Pruitt*, legislatures enacted various embezzlement statutes. Their breadth varied widely. As you read *Riggins* and *Mitchneck*, consider when legislatures and courts ought to criminalize dishonest breaches of contract.

---

be a crime other than robbery. Among the range of offenses that might have been committed are: assault (Pen. Code, § 240), assault with a deadly weapon (Pen. Code, § 245), assault with intent to commit murder (Pen. Code, § 217).

B. Embezzlement

People v. Riggins

132 N.E.2d 519 (Ill. 1956)

HERSHEY, Chief Justice.

The defendant, Marven E. Riggins, was indicted in the circuit court of Winnebago County for embezzlement. (Ill. Rev. Stat. 1953, chap. 38, par. 210.) After a verdict of guilty by a jury, the court sentenced him to a term in the penitentiary of not less than two nor more than seven years.

The defendant argues for reversal on the ground that as operator of a collection agency he was an independent businessman, who at no time acted as "agent" for the complaining witness, Dorothy Tarrant, within the meaning of this embezzlement statute.

At the time of the indictment (January, 1955), the defendant was the owner and operator of a collection agency in Rockford called the Creditors Collection Service, and had been so engaged for about five years. He maintained an office, had both full and part-time employees, and during 1953 and 1954 had a clientele of some 500 persons and firms for whom he collected delinquent accounts.

In February 1953, he called on the complaining witness, Dorothy Tarrant, who operated a firm known as Cooper's Music and jewelry. He said he was in the collection business and asked to collect the firm's delinquent accounts. As a result, they reached an oral agreement whereby the defendant was to undertake the collections.

By this agreement, the defendant was to receive one third on city accounts and one half on out-of-city accounts. It was further agreed that he need not account for the amounts collected until a bill was paid in full, at which time he was to remit by check.

The parties operated under this agreement for almost two years. During that time the complaining witness exercised no control over the defendant as to the time or manner of collecting the accounts, and with her knowledge he commingled funds collected for all his clients in a single bank account. He also used this as a personal account, from which he drew for business, family and personal expenses.

In October 1954, the complaining witness became aware that the defendant had collected several accounts for her in full, but had not accounted to her. She discussed the matter with him, and he assured her that he would bring his records up to date and pay what was due. After the defendant defaulted on this promise, she made further investigations and discovered new breaches of the agreement. She had further discussions with him and received additional promises to pay up, none of which were kept. Negotiations were terminated December 14, 1954, when the defendant filed a bankruptcy petition listing Coopers jewelry and Music, among others, as a creditor. Thereafter, the complaining witness preferred the charges against the defendant which resulted in his indictment and conviction for embezzlement.

To decide whether the defendant, a collection agent, can be guilty of embezzlement in Illinois, it is helpful to consider our embezzlement statutes in the historical context of this crime.

Embezzlement, unknown at common law, is established by statute, and its scope, therefore, is limited to those persons designated therein. The general objective of embezzlement statutes is to meet and obviate certain defects in the law of larceny through which many persons who misappropriated another's property escaped criminal prosecution. Thus, the Illinois statutes which make embezzlement a felony state that the violator "shall be deemed guilty of larceny."

Viewed in their entirety, our laws relating to embezzlement are broad and comprehensive. The following persons are included in those statutes making the crime of embezzlement a felony: "Whoever embezzles or fraudulently converts to his own use" (Ill. Rev. Stat. 1953, chap. 38, par. 207); "a clerk, agent, servant or apprentice of any person" (par. 208); "any banker or broker, or his agent or servant, or any officer, agent or servant of any banking company, or incorporated bank" (par. 209); "any clerk, agent, servant, solicitor, broker, apprentice or officer ... receiving any money ... in his fiduciary capacity" (par. 210); public officers (par. 214); administrators, guardians, conservators and other fiduciaries (par. 216); and certain members and officers of fraternal societies (par. 218).

In addition, certain sections of the Criminal Code make the crime of embezzlement a misdemeanor and cover the following: "any warehouseman, storage, forwarding or commission merchant, or other person selling on commission, or his agent, clerk or servant" (par. 212); "any attorney at law, justice of the peace, constable, clerk of a court, or other person authorized by law to collect money." (par. 213).

[I]t can hardly be disputed but that the defendant acted as agent for the complaining witness in collecting her accounts. He undertook the collections on her behalf by virtue of authority which she delegated to him. He had no right to collect from anyone except as authorized by her and was required to render a full account of all matters entrusted to him, the same as any agent. Likewise, it is apparent that in so acting he assumed other duties ordinarily attendant upon that relationship, such as the duty to exercise good faith, make full disclosure, etc. The prevailing view of the courts in construing embezzlement statutes is succinctly expressed in 18 AM. JUR., *Embezzlement*, sec. 30, as follows: "The term 'agent' as used in embezzlement statutes is construed in its popular sense as meaning a person who undertakes to transact some business or to manage some affair for another by the latter's authority and to render an account of such business or affair. The term 'agent' as employed in such statutes imports a principal and implies employment, service and delegated authority to do something in the name and stead of the principal—an employment by virtue of which the money or property embezzled came into the agent's possession. The employment, however, need not be permanent. It may be temporary, occasional, general, or special."

[I]t is clear that the defendant received the funds in his fiduciary capacity. In Illinois, as in other jurisdictions, the relationship of principal and agent is a fiduciary one. 1 I.L.P., Agency, sec. 4. One acts in a fiduciary capacity where special confidence is reposed in one who is bound in equity and good conscience to act in good faith with due regard to the interest of the person reposing the confidence.

We conclude that the defendant was an "agent" of the complaining witness, receiving money in a "fiduciary capacity" and, therefore, within the purview of said embezzlement statute.

SCHAEFER, Justice (dissenting).

The critical question is whether the defendant was the agent of the complaining witness. Upon the record it seems to me that he was not. He maintained his own office, had his own employees, and collected accounts for approximately 500 other individuals and firms. He was subject to no control whatsoever by any of his customers in making his collections. His customers knew that he kept all of his collections in a single account. That the defendant was not an agent would be clear, I think, if vicarious liability was sought to be asserted against Dorothy Tarrant on account of the defendant's conduct in the course of his collection activities.

The conclusion of the majority that the defendant was an agent rests upon the assertion that "[t]he term 'agent' as used in embezzlement statutes is construed in its popular sense. . . ." That generalization runs counter to the basic rule that criminal statutes are strictly construed.

More important than generalized statements as to the proper approach to the problem of construction, however, is the language to be construed. The statute under which the defendant was indicted (Ill. Rev. Stat. 1953, chap. 38, par. 210), refers to "any clerk, agent, servant, solicitor, broker, apprentice or officer." If "agent" has the broad meaning which the majority gives it, each of the other terms is superfluous because all are embraced within the single term "agent."

Many of the specific enumerations in the other statutes referred to by the majority likewise become largely, if not entirely, meaningless, for the particular relationships they seek to reach are also swallowed up in the expanded definition of the term "agent." It is arguable of course that the conduct of the defendant in this case should be regarded as criminal. The General Assembly might wish to make it so. But it might not. It might regard the collection agency as a desirable service enterprise which should not be made unduly perilous. If the defendant in this case, with his little agency, is guilty of one embezzlement, he is guilty of 500. The General Assembly might not want to make the enterprise so hazardous. It has not done so, in my opinion, by the statute before us.

Questions and Notes

1. Why couldn't Riggins have been convicted of common law larceny?

2. Who has the better of the "agency" argument, Chief Justice Hershey or Justice Schaefer? Under the court's decision, could an attorney (who is explicitly listed in the misdemeanor section) be charged with a felony on the theory that, in addition to being an attorney, he is also an agent?

3. In what sense did Riggins hold the funds in a fiduciary capacity? Doesn't the fact that his creditors knew that he commingled funds make him simply a substituted debtor? Assume that Riggins went bankrupt because he was involved in an automobile accident for which he was underinsured, and the person he injured in the accident caused his bankruptcy by a successful lawsuit. Would Riggins be guilty of one count of embezzlement? 500 counts? Is this like the debtor's prisons against which Charles Dickens protested?

4. Some states, such as Pennsylvania, have fraudulent conversion statutes, which are essentially generic embezzlement statutes applicable to all who have rightful possession. As you will see in *Mitchneck*, even those statutes are not free of "fiduciary"-type issues.

Commonwealth v. Mitchneck

198 A. 463 (Pa. Super. Ct. 1938)

KELLER, President Judge

The appellant was convicted of the offense of fraudulently converting the money of another person to his own use, contrary to the provisions of the Act of May 18, 1917, PL. 241, 188 PS. § 2486 et seq.[1]

The evidence produced on the part of the commonwealth would have warranted the jury in finding that the defendant, Mitchneck, operated a coal mine in Beaver township, Columbia county; that he employed certain persons, Hunsinger, Derr, Steeley, and others, as workers in and about his mine; that these employees dealt at the store of A. Vagnom and signed orders directing their employer to deduct from their wages the amounts of their respective store bills and pay the same to Vagnom; that the defendant agreed to do so, and pursuant to said agreement work deducted

---

1. Section 1. Be it enacted, etc. that "any person having received or having possession, in any capacity or by any means or manner whatever, of any money or property, of any kind whatsoever, of or belonging to any other person, firm, or corporation, or which any other person, firm, or corporation is entitled to receive and have, who fraudulently withholds, converts, or applies the same, or any part thereof, or the proceeds or any part of the proceeds, derived, from the sale or other disposition thereof, to and for his own use and benefit, or to and for the use and benefit of any other person, shall be guilty of a misdemeanor, and upon conviction thereof shall be sentenced to pay a fine not exceeding one thousand dollars, and to undergo an imprisonment not exceeding five years, or either or both, in the discretion of the court." 18 P.S. § 2486.

from the wages due the eleven workmen, named in the indictment, an aggregate $259.26, which he agreed to pay Vagnoni, but had failed and neglected to do so.

We are of opinion that this evidence was insufficient to support a conviction under the Fraudulent Conversion Act of 1917, and that the court erred in refusing the defendant's point for a directed verdict of acquittal.

The gist of the offense of fraudulent conversion is that the defendant has received into his possession the money or property of another person, firm, or corporation, and fraudulently withholds, converts or applies the same to or for his own use and benefit, or to the use and benefit of any person other than the one to whom the money or property belonged. If the property so withheld or applied to the defendant's use and benefit, etc., did not belong to some other person, etc., but was the defendant's own money or property, even though obtained by borrowing the money, or by a purchase or credit of the property, the offense has not been committed. Whatever may have been the intention of the legislature in the enactment of the statute under which the indictment in this case was drawn, it was clearly not intended to make criminal the act of one who sells his own property, and it is not to be so applied as to make it an effective substitute for an action at law in the collection of a debt.

The act of May 18, 1917 makes the fraudulent conversion of property a misdemeanor, but it is essential that the property at the time of sale or conversion shall have belonged to another. The words of the statute, "money or property . . . which any other person, firm, or corporation is entitled to receive and have," do not refer to money owing another, but to money or property the title to and ownership of which is in another; it is another form of expressing money or property belonging to another.

The defendant in the present case had not received, nor did he have in his possession, any money belonging to his employees. True he owed them money, but that did not transfer to them the title to and ownership of the money. His deduction from their wages of the amounts of the store bills which they had assigned to Vagnoni did not change the title and ownership of the money thus withheld, nor did his agreement to pay to Vagnoni the amounts thus deducted constitute the latter the owner of the money. It effected only a change of creditors. The money, if Mitchneck actually had it, of which there was no proof, was still his own, but, after he accepted the assignments, he owed the amount due his employees to Vagnoni instead of to them. A novation had been effected. The defendant had been discharged of his liability to his employees by contracting a new obligation in favor of Vagnoni. But failure to pay the amount due the new creditor was not fraudulent conversion within the Act of 1917. Otherwise it would be a very dangerous thing to agree to a novation. Defendant's liability for the unpaid wages due his employees was, and remained, civil, not criminal. His liability for the amount due Vagnoni after his agreement to accept or honor the assignments of his employees' wages was likewise civil and not criminal.

The judgment is reversed, and the appellant is discharged.

Questions and Notes

1. In the commentary to Model Penal Code § 223.8, the framers of that document wrote harshly of *Mitchneck:* "If the miners in the *Mitchneck* case had drawn their pay at one window and passed part of it back to Mitchneck's cashier at the next window, conviction for embezzlement or fraudulent conversion could have been obtained . . . the bookkeeping shortcut actually used hardly serves as a rational basis for exculpating Mitchneck from criminal liability." Do you agree?

2. Suppose that on payday, Mitchneck had told his miners: "I lost the money that I owe you; I bet on the wrong horse at the racetrack." Would (should) Mitchneck be liable for fraudulent conversion? Why? Why not?

3. If your answer to the Question 2 hypothetical is "no," do you think that that hypothetical or the Model Penal Code hypothetical in Question 1 is closer to the actual *Mitchneck* case? Why? *See* Nutshell § 7.04.

4. Just as embezzlement (fraudulent conversion) was necessary to fill some of the gaps in larceny, the crime of obtaining property by false pretenses was necessary to deal with the situation in which the defendant obtained "title," as opposed to merely possession, by a false representation. When the defendant obtains title, there is no opportunity for a subsequent misappropriation. One cannot misappropriate what one owns, consequently there can be no larceny. Some of the potential limits on obtaining property by false pretenses are developed in *Ashley* and *Nelson.*

C. False Pretenses

People v. Ashley

267 P.2d 271 (Cal. 1954)

[Ashley was convicted of California's statutory offense called "theft," which will be explained in Justice Traynor's opinion. He made false representations to two elderly women that he owned certain property and wished to borrow money from them to develop the properties. He neither owned the properties nor intended to use the money to improve them.]

Traynor, Justice.

Although the crimes of larceny by trick and device and obtaining property by false pretenses are much alike, they are aimed at different criminal acquisitive techniques. Larceny by trick and device is the appropriation of property, the possession of which was fraudulently acquired; obtaining property by false pretenses is the fraudulent or deceitful acquisition of both title and possession. In this state, these two offenses, with other larcenous crimes, have been consolidated into the single crime of theft, but their elements have not been changed thereby. The elements of the several types of theft included within section 484 have not been changed, however, and a judgment of conviction of theft, based on a general verdict of guilty, can be sustained only if the evidence discloses the elements of one of the consolidated offenses. In the present case, it is clear from the record that each of the prosecuting witnesses intended to pass both title and possession, and that the type of theft, if any, in each case, was that of obtaining property by false pretenses.

To support a conviction of theft for obtaining property by false pretenses, it must be shown that the defendant made a false pretense or representation with intent to defraud the owner of his property, and that the owner was in fact defrauded. It is unnecessary to prove that the defendant benefitted personally from the fraudulent acquisition. The false pretense or representation must have materially influenced the owner to part with his property, but the false pretense need not be the sole inducing cause. If the conviction rests primarily on the testimony of a single witness that the false pretense was made, the making of the pretense must be corroborated.

The crime of obtaining property by false pretenses was unknown in the early common law, see *Young v. The King*, 3 T.R. 98, 102 (1789), and our statute, like those of most American states, is directly traceable to 30 Geo. 11, ch. 24, section 1 (22 Statutes-at-Large 114 (1757)). In an early Crown Case Reserved, *Rex v. Goodhall, Russ. & Ry.* 461 (1821), the defendant obtained a quantity of meat from a merchant by promising to pay at a future day. The jury found that the promise was made without intention to perform. The judges concluded, however, that the defendant's conviction was erroneous because the pretense "was merely a promise of future conduct, and common prudence and caution would have prevented any injury arising from it." *Russ. & Ry.* at 463. The correctness of this decision is questionable in light of the reasoning in an earlier decision of the King's Bench, *Young v. The King, supra*, not mentioned in *Rex v. Goodhall*. By stating that the "promise of future conduct" was such that "common prudence and caution" could prevent any injury arising therefrom, the new offense was confused with the old common law "cheat.[A] The decision also seems contrary to the plain meaning of the statute, and was so interpreted by two English writers on the law of crimes. ARCHBOLD, PLEADING AND EVIDENCE IN CRIMINAL CASES 183 (3rd ed., 1828); ROSCOE, DIGEST OF THE LAW OF EVIDENCE IN CRIMINAL CASES 418 (2d Amer. ed., 1840). Wharton formulated the following generalization: the false pretense to be within the statute, must relate to a state of things averred to be at the time existing, and not to a state of things thereafter to exist." WHARTON, AMERICAN CRIMINAL LAW 542 (1st ed., 1846). The generalization has been followed in the majority of American cases. The rule has not been followed in all jurisdictions, however. Some courts have avoided the problems created by the rule by blurring the distinctions between larceny by trick and device and obtaining property by false pretenses.

A. Common law "cheats" occurred when a merchant intentionally used false weights and measures. The indiscriminate character of the dishonesty, coupled with the inability of one to protect herself by ordinary prudence, was enough to persuade the common law judges to punish this activity.

The Court of Appeals for the District of Columbia has advanced the following reasons in defense of the majority rule:

> "It is of course true that then, (at the time of the early English cases cited by Wharton, *supra*) as now, the intention to commit certain crimes was ascertained by looking backward from the act and finding that the accused intended to do what he did do. However, where, as here, the act complained of namely, failure to repay money or use it as specified at the time of borrowing is as consonant with ordinary commercial default as with criminal conduct, the danger of applying this technique to prove the crime is quite apparent. Business affairs would be materially incumbered by the ever present threat that a debtor might be subjected to criminal penalties if the prosecutor and jury were of the view that at the time of borrowing he was mentally a cheat. The risk of prosecuting one who is guilty of nothing more than a failure or inability to pay his debts is a very real consideration. . . . If we were to accept the government's position the way would be open for every victim of a bad bargain to resort to criminal proceedings to even the score with a judgment proof adversary. No doubt in the development of our criminal law the zeal with which the innocent are protected has provided a measure of shelter for the guilty. However, we do not think it wise to increase the possibility of conviction by broadening the accepted theory of the weight to be attached to the mental attitude of the accused." *Chaplin v. United States*, 157 F.2d 697, 698–699.

We do not find this reasoning persuasive. In this state, and in the majority of American states as well as in England, false promises can provide the foundation of a civil action for deceit. In such actions something more than nonperformance is required to prove the defendant's intent not to perform his promise. Nor is proof of nonperformance alone sufficient in criminal prosecutions based on false promises. In such prosecutions the People must, as in all criminal prosecutions, prove their case beyond a reasonable doubt. Any danger, through the instigation of criminal proceedings by disgruntled creditors, to those who have blamelessly encountered "commercial defaults" must, therefore, be predicated upon the idea that trial juries are incapable of weighing the evidence and understanding the instruction that they must be convinced of the defendant's fraudulent intent beyond a reasonable doubt, or that appellate courts will be derelict in discharging their duty to ascertain that there is sufficient evidence to support a conviction.

The judgment and the order denying the motion for a new trial are affirmed.

Schauer, Justice.

I concur in the judgment solely on the ground that the evidence establishes, with ample corroboration, the making by the defendant of false representations as to existing facts. On that evidence the convictions should be sustained pursuant to long accepted theories of law.

It is unnecessary on the record to make of this rather simple case a vehicle for the revolutionary holding, contrary to the weight of authority in this state and elsewhere, that a promise to pay or perform at a future date, if unfulfilled, can become the basis for a criminal prosecution on the theory that it was a promise made without a present intention to perform it and that, therefore, whatever of value was received for the promise was property procured by a false representation. Accordingly, I dissent from all that portion of the opinion which discusses and pronounces upon the theories which in my view are extraneous to the proper disposition of any issue actually before us.

The majority opinion strikes down a rule of law, relating to the character and competence of proof of crime, which has been almost universally respected for two hundred years and the reasoning which has been advanced for the innovation is that creditors, grand jurors, and prosecutors must not be expected to institute any criminal charges against innocent people, and that even if they do the intelligence of trial jurors and the wisdom of appellate judges can be depended upon to right the wrong, hence the time-honored rule may be scrapped. The unreality of this reasoning and the wisdom of the old rule become obvious on reflection.

In a prosecution for obtaining property by the making of a false promise, knowingly and with intent to deceive, the matter to be proved, as to its criminality, is purely subjective. It is not, like the specific intent in such a crime as burglary, a mere element of the crime; it is, in any significant sense, all of the crime. The proof will necessarily be of objective acts, entirely legal in themselves, from which inferences as to the ultimate illegal subjective fact will be drawn. But, whereas in burglary the proof of the subjective element is normally as strong and reliable as the proof of any objective element, in this type of activity the proof of such vital element can almost never be reliable; it must inevitably (in the absence of confession or something tantamount thereto) depend on inferences drawn by creditors, prosecutors, jurors, and judges from facts and circumstances which by reason of their nature cannot possibly exclude innocence with any certainty, and which can point to guilt only when construed and interpreted by the creditor, prosecutor or trier of fact adversely to the person charged. Such inferences as proof of the alleged crime have long been recognized as so unreliable that they have been excluded from the category of acceptable proof.

As a basis for overturning the rule that proof of the mere making of a promise to perform in the future and of subsequent failure to perform is not proof of a false pretense, the majority opinion first purportedly adheres to the rule by stating that "proof of nonperformance alone (is not) sufficient in criminal prosecutions based on false promises," then argues that "Any danger, through the instigation of criminal proceedings by disgruntled creditors, to those who have blamelessly encountered 'commercial defaults' must, therefore, be predicated upon the idea that trial juries are incapable of weighing the evidence and understanding the instruction that they must be convinced of the defendant's fraudulent intent beyond a reasonable doubt, or that appellate courts will be derelict in discharging their duty to ascertain that there is sufficient evidence to support a conviction." This doctrine, if universally applied, would eliminate all rules governing the quality and sufficiency of proof. The credence to be placed in the testimony of accomplices, or other complaining witnesses, would be left entirely to the sagacity of jurors and the presumed omniscience of appellate judges. I am unwilling to accept as a premise the scholastic redaction of the majority that rules of proof may be set aside because appellate judges will always know when a jury has been misled and the proof is not sufficient. The most important function which courts have to perform in respect to criminal law is not to make easier the conviction of alleged miscreants; it is the protection of the innocent against false conviction. The highest duty which this court has to perform in the cause of justice is to protect the individual person against the power of the state; the most grievous injury it can do to the people is to assist in building a super-state by countenancing encroachments on the rights of individuals and whittling away at the rules which protect them.

The suggestion in the majority opinion that it is inconceivable "that trial juries are incapable of weighing the evidence (impliedly, with omniscient accuracy however inconclusive it be) and understanding the instruction that they must be convinced of the defendant's fraudulent intent beyond a reasonable doubt, or that appellate courts will be derelict (less than omniscient) in discharging their duty" affords no substantial basis for striking down a rule of proof. The opinion naively continues: "If misrepresentations are made innocently or inadvertently, they can no more form the basis for a prosecution for obtaining property by false pretenses than can an innocent breach of contract"!

With the rule that the majority opinion now enunciates, no man, no matter how innocent his intention, can sign a promise to pay in the future, or to perform an act at a future date, without subjecting himself to the risk that at some later date others, in the light of differing perspectives, philosophies and subsequent events, may conclude that, after all, the accused should have known that at the future date he could not perform as he promised and if he, as a "reasonable" man from the point of view of the creditor, district attorney and a grand or trial jury should have known, then, it may be inferred, he did know. And if it can be inferred that he knew, then this court and other appellate courts will be bound to affirm a conviction.

A trial by jury, under circumstances easily to be foreseen, would offer but hazardous protection in such a case. I have faith great faith in our jury system as now constituted. But I have developed that faith through seeing it operate under wise and time-tested regulations and limitations as to the essential characteristics of proof which do not unrealistically assume that any human whether a district attorney or a grand juror or a trial juror or a judge or justice of a court is beyond error.

I think that the judgment should be affirmed but that the highly controversial discussion which is unnecessary to the decision and is aimed at establishing a new rule in California, contrary to the weight of authority here and generally elsewhere, should be eliminated.

Questions and Notes

1. A number of states and the Model Penal Code now adhere to *Ashley*.

2. As a *policy* matter, why should we worry more about state of mind in regard to promises for false pretenses than we do for larceny by trick? In *Blackburn*, for example, Blackburn would not have been guilty of larceny by trick if he rented the horse intending to return her, but subsequently changed his mind. Yet, if the jury misinterpreted his original intent in light of subsequent events, he could have been wrongly convicted. Is there an intelligible difference between the two situations?

3. Does Justice Schauer's opinion bespeak an unwarranted distrust of juries?

4. Consider which judge has the sounder approach in *Nelson*.

Nelson v. United States

227 F.2d 21 (D.C. Cir. 1955)

DANAHER, Circuit judge.

This is an appeal from a conviction for obtaining goods by false pretenses in violation of D.C. Code 22-1301 (1951).[1] Evidence was offered to show that appellant from time to time over a period of months, for purposes of resale, had purchased merchandise from Potomac Distributors of Washington, D.C., Inc. (hereinafter referred to as Potomac Distributors). By September 18, 1952, his account was said to be in arrears more than thirty days. Late that afternoon, appellant sought immediate possession of two television sets and a washing machine, displayed his customers' purchase contracts to support his statement that he had already sold such merchandise and had taken payment therefor, and told one Schneider, secretary-treasurer of Potomac Distributors, "I promised delivery tonight." Appellant was told no further credit could be extended to him because of his overdue indebtedness in excess of $1,800, whereupon appellant offered to give security for the desired items as well as for the delinquent account. He represented himself as the owner of a Packard car for which he had paid $4,260.50 but failed to disclose an outstanding prior indebtedness on the car of $3,028.08 secured by a chattel mortgage in favor of City Bank. Instead, he represented that he owed only one payment of some $55 not then due. Relying upon such representations, Potomac Distributors delivered to appellant two television sets each worth $136, taking in return a demand note for the entire indebtedness, past and present, in the total, $2,047.37, secured by a chattel mortgage on the Packard and the television sets. Appellant promised to make a cash payment on the note within a few days for default of which the holder was entitled to demand full payment. When the promised payment was not forthcoming, Schneider, by

---

1. In pertinent part the section provides: "Whoever, by any false pretense, with intent to defraud, obtains from any person anything of value, or procures the execution and delivery of any instrument of writing or conveyance of real or personal property . . . shall, if the value of the property . . . so obtained . . . is $50 or upward, be imprisoned not less than one year nor more than three years. . . ."

telephone calls and a personal visit to appellant's home, sought to locate appellant but learned be had left town. The Packard about that time was in a collision, incurring damage of about $1,000, and was thereupon repossessed in behalf of the bank which held the prior lien for appellant's car purchase indebtedness.

The foregoing summary of the evidence is sufficient for present purposes. Appellant has not denied the falsity of his representations nor that he received the goods he sought from Potomac Distributors. We have not had the benefit of appellant's explanation, if any, as to why he did not intend Potomac Distributors to rely upon his misrepresentations. His counsel, however, argues that there had been no misrepresentation of a material fact and no evidence that Potomac Distributors was defrauded.

The trial judge in his charge correctly imposed upon the government the burden of proof as to each element necessary to constitute the crime. He broke down the general language of the indictment and with reference to each item, to be proved beyond a reasonable doubt, he particularized in detail:

"First, that the defendant represented to Joseph H. Schneider, an officer of the Potomac Distributors of Washington, D.C. a body corporate, that his Packard automobile was clear except for the final payment of about $55;

"Second, that at the time such representation was made, it was false;

"Third, that the defendant knew such representation was false at the time he made it;

"Fourth, that Joseph H. Schneider relied on such representation, and in so relying upon it, delivered to the defendant two television sets;

"Fifth, that in making such false representations, the defendant intended to defraud Joseph H. Schneider and the Potomac Distributors of Washington, D.C., Inc., a body corporate;

"Sixth, that, relying on such false representation and delivering to the defendant the two television sets, Schneider and the corporation were duly defrauded;

"Seventh, that the transaction, in all its parts, including the making of the false representation by the defendant and the delivery of the two television sets by Schneider to the defendant was had in the District of Columbia on or about September 18, 1952."

Appellant argues that Potomac Distributors could not have been defrauded for the car on September 18, 1952, "had an equity of between $900 and $1,000 and roughly five times the value of the two television sets. That fact is immaterial. This appellant has sold two television sets, and apparently had taken payment therefor although he had no television sets to deliver to his customers. He could not get the sets from Potomac Distributors without offering security for his past due account as well as for his present purchase. In order to get them he lied. He represented that his car acquired at a cost of more than $4,000 required only one further payment of $55. He now complains because his victim believed him when he lied. He argues that the misrepresentations were not material although the victim testified, and the jury could properly find, that he would not have parted with his goods except in reliance upon appellant's statements. "No one can be permitted to say, in respect to his own statements upon a material matter, that he did not expect to be believed; and if they are knowingly false, and willfully made, the fact that they are material is proof of an attempted fraud, because their materiality, in the eye of the law, consists in their tendency to influence the conduct of the party who has an interest in them and to whom they are addressed." *Claflin v. Commonwealth Insurance Co.*, 110 U.S. 81, 95.

He argues that there was no proof of an intent upon his part to defraud his victim. We have sufficiently dealt with the facts. "From these facts the requisite intent to defraud is presumed, and therefore, need not be proven in the absence of countervailing evidence. Materiality and reliance were conclusively established by evidence introduced at the trial, if indeed such proof were needed."

Affirmed.

WILBUR K. MILLER, Circuit Judge (dissenting).

When the essential ingredients of the crime of false pretense have been accurately ascertained, and when irrelevant facts in the evidence have been identified as such and eliminated from consideration, I believe it will be apparent that the Government failed to make out a case for submission to the jury. It will then also appear, I think, that the trial judge erroneously refused to direct a verdict of acquittal, only because he mistakenly attributed significance to the fact that appellant's automobile was damaged in a collision which occurred "early in October" — at least two weeks after September 18, the day he purchased the two television sets and the washing machine from Potomac Distributors.

As to the ingredients of the offense. While our false pretense statute does not in express language require that the person from whom the property is obtained should be defrauded thereby, nevertheless the crime is not complete unless he is in fact defrauded. In order to convict under the statute, the Government must therefore prove that in making a false pretense the defendant intended to defraud the person from whom he obtained property, and that he did thereby defraud him. The trial judge recognized this, and charged the jury accordingly.

Nelson did make a false representation; but the question is whether there was evidence from which the jury could properly be permitted to infer that he intended to defraud, and to conclude that Potomac was thereby defrauded.

Differing definitions of the word "defraud" probably cause the difference in opinion between the majority and me. They seem to think it means, in connection with a purchase, to make a false pretense in the process of obtaining goods even though the purchase price is well secured. I think the word means, in connection with a purchase, to make a false pretense as a result of which the seller is deprived of his goods or of the purchase price. The difference is particularly important in a case like this one where a purchaser is charged with defrauding a seller. A purchaser can be said to have defrauded the seller of his goods only if he intended to defraud him of the purchase price for which the seller was willing to exchange them.

In considering the criminality *vel non* of the false statement, it must be remembered that the past due indebtedness of $1,697.87 is to play no part. That credit had already been extended generally, and with respect to it Potomac parted with nothing on September 18. Nelson was only charged with defrauding Potomac by obtaining through false pretense the articles then delivered, which had a total value of only $349.50.

What was the actual value on September 18 of the property upon which Potomac took a lien, on the strength of which it parted with property worth $349.50? The bank collection manager, testifying for the Government, said that although on September 18 Nelson still owed the bank $3,028.08, he had on that day an equity in the car worth from $900 to $1,000. The mortgaged television sets were, I suppose, worth their price of $272. Adding to this the minimum equity in the automobile proved by the prosecution, it appears that Potomac had a lien on property worth at least $1,172 to protect a debt of $349.50. The proportion was more than three to one.

The reduction in the value of the automobile caused by the collision could not properly be considered by the jury; the question was as to its value September 18, for it was that value which should have been considered in deciding whether Potomac had been defrauded. Had the trial judge observed this distinction, he would have directed a verdict of acquittal, since he was aware of the necessity that there be actual defrauding. The judge made this clear when he said in a bench colloquy: "Until I heard that there had been a wreck and the car had been repossessed I thought maybe there was sufficient equity there to cover the loss sustained; and if that were the case there would be no defrauding." I have demonstrated there was more than sufficient equity September 18 to cover the credit then extended, so there was no defrauding, even though an accident later impaired the margin of protection.

In addition to the irrelevant proof of the collision damage, which should not have been received and without which an acquittal would have been directed, there was another irrelevancy in evidence which may well have played a part in moving the jury to its verdict: the pre-existing indebtedness. Because of Nelson's misrepresentation of his equity in the car, Potomac did not get, as it thought it was getting, security for both old and new debts with a margin of more than two to one. But, as has been shown, Potomac did get more than triple security for the goods which the indictment said were fraudulently obtained. It was therefore of first importance that the jury be told to disregard Potomac's failure to get the security for the preexisting debt which it had been led to believe it was getting, and to consider only whether Potomac had been defrauded out of goods worth $349.50. The jury should also have been told the reason for the distinction, for without it the lay jurors might have concluded-as apparently they did-that on September 18 Nelson defrauded Potomac with respect to the pre-existing indebtedness.

As I have said, Nelson was guilty of a moral wrong in falsely and grossly misrepresenting his debt to the bank, but in the circumstances he should not have been indicted and convicted because of it. The District of Columbia statute under which he was prosecuted does not make mere falsehood felonious; it only denounces as criminal a false pretense which was intended to defraud and which in fact had that result. Even a liar is entitled to the full protection of the law. I am afraid a grave injustice has been done in this case.

Questions and Notes

1. Suppose that Nelson had paid for the television sets (and for that matter even the remainder of his indebtedness), but Potomac had discovered the false pretense by which he had obtained credit. Suppose further that Potomac had insisted (and the prosecutor had been willing) on prosecuting Nelson in order to set an example. Since the fraud occurred when the sets were obtained, would (should) the majority opinion be read to uphold a conviction in the hypothetical situation?

2. Do you agree with Judge Miller that Nelson's prior indebtedness should be immaterial? Why? Why not?

3. Even accepting Judge Miller's premise that adequate security defeats the false pretenses charge, is it clear that Potomac would have accepted a $1,000 uninsured car as adequate security for the television sets?

4. Do we need the criminal law to protect creditors in this situation?

5. How would you have resolved this case? Why? *See* NUTSHELL § 7.05.

6. In addition to embezzlement and false pretenses, the crime of receiving stolen goods is one of the more important. Its importance lies in the role that established "fences" play in encouraging larcenies. The most critical issue for this crime is how much the recipient must know in order to be guilty. Consider in conjunction with *Baker*.

D. Receiving Stolen Property

Commonwealth v. Baker

175 A. 438 (Pa. Super. Ct. 1934)

KELLER, Judge.

Appellant was convicted of having violated the provisions of the Act of April 23, 1909, P.L. 159 (18 PS § 2861)—the offense commonly known as "receiving stolen goods." It will be noted that the act—which is printed in the margin[1]—makes it a

---

1. Be it enacted, etc., That if any person shall buy, have, or receive, within the limits of the Commonwealth of Pennsylvania, any goods, chattels, moneys, or securities, or any other matter or thing, which shall have been stolen or feloniously taken, either in the Commonwealth of Pennsylvania or in any other State or country, knowing the same to have been stolen or feloniously taken,

felony for any person to buy, have, or receive any goods, etc., which shall have been stolen or feloniously taken, *knowing the same to have been stolen or feloniously taken.* The sixth assignment of error complains that the learned trial judge in charging the jury defined the offense as follows: "Now, what is the crime of receiving stolen goods? The law says it is the acquiring of goods knowing them to have been stolen, *or under such circumstances as would lead a man of reasonable prudence to suspect that they were stolen.*" (Italics supplied.)

This was adding to the offense, as defined by the General Assembly, something that was not in the act. It was most material and, in our opinion, requires a reversal of the judgment. The Act of Assembly itself furnishes the best definition of the crime. It differs in form from the statute of June 20, 1919, P.L. 542 (18 PS § 2862), making it a felony to receive or bring into this commonwealth goods, etc., stolen in any other state, in that in the latter act the words used are, "knowing or having reasonable cause to know the [goods] to have been stolen."

The Legislature, in the Act of 1909, *supra,* did not declare it to be a felony for a person to buy, have, or receive stolen goods "under such circumstances as would lead a man of reasonable prudence to suspect that they were stolen," but only, "*knowing* the same to have been stolen." Penal statutes must be strictly construed and cannot be enlarged in scope by the courts, to the prejudice of the accused. The instruction was wrong in two respects: (1) The question at issue was the knowledge of this particular defendant as to the goods having been stolen; not that of a hypothetical man of reasonable prudence; this defendant may, or may not, be a man of reasonable prudence; and (2) the question for the jury was whether this defendant *knew,* not *suspected* that the goods were stolen. Unless they found that he knew they were stolen at the time they were bought, there could be no conviction.

Knowledge is, of course, subjective, and whether a person knows a thing or not is generally, or at least frequently, determined by circumstances. The jury may infer, from circumstances tending to show knowledge on the part of a defendant, that he knew that the goods he was buying were stolen, but in order to find him guilty of the offense charged, they must be satisfied beyond a reasonable doubt that he *knew* they were stolen. It is not sufficient for them to find that the defendant should have suspected they were stolen. In *Commonwealth v. Walter,* 97 Pa. Super. 244, Judge Linn, speaking for this court, said: "The Commonwealth had the burden of proving beyond a reasonable doubt: 1, that the chickens were stolen; 2, that appellant received them; 3, that he received them "knowing the same to be stolen. . . ." The court admitted appellant's own testimony that about a week before he bought the chickens from the thief he had heard rumors that the thief was accused of stealing them. The testimony was properly submitted to the jury because it was sufficient, if believed, to justify the inference by the jury that he knew, at the time that he

---

such person shall be guilty of felony, and, on conviction, suffer the like pains and penalties which are by law imposed upon the person who shall have actually stolen or feloniously carried away the same within the limits of this Commonwealth. (18 PS § 2861.)

received them, that the chickens had been stolen. In such transaction a man's belief is equivalent to knowledge. But the instructions to the jury should continue its consideration of that evidence to the matter of guilty knowledge only—that is, knowledge at the time the chickens were bought. If he did not then know that they had been stolen, the facts (1) that he was so informed sometime after he had completed the purchase, and (2) that he then sold them, will not alone be enough to sustain his conviction of receiving stolen goods knowing them to have been stolen.

We are aware that there is some difference of opinion in other jurisdictions, but the decisions of the appellate courts in this commonwealth do not justify the instruction complained of. The sixth assignment of error is sustained.

The judgment is reversed and a new trial awarded.

Questions and Notes

1. As the opinion suggests, states vary in their approach to this problem. Actual belief is probably the predominant view.

2. Is "believe" different from "know"? How?

3. Is "believe" different from "suspect"? How?

4. In *Baker*, did the court take suspicion ("he had heard rumors that the thief had been accused of stealing them") and upgrade that to belief, and then upgrade belief to knowledge? In short, did it take with one hand what it gave with the other?

5. Why was the court reluctant to adopt the objective standard? If you think that it was merely carrying out the legislative mandate, why do you suppose the legislature was so reluctant? *See* NUTSHELL § 7.07.

6. We now turn to violent theft offenses. In *Patton*, the problem is distinguishing nonviolent pickpockets from violent robbers. Did the court come out on the right side of the line in *Patton*?

E. Identity Theft

We begin our study of aggravated theft with the modern and increasing use of the crime of identity theft. Identity theft is a crime of recent vintage and increasing importance. In the cases that follow (*Presba* and *Allen*) we explore two of the many issues raised by this crime.

State v. Presba

131 Wash. App. 47 (2005)

Cox, C.J.

In 2003, Shyla Dashiell received notice that her automobile insurance rates had significantly increased. Because she had received no tickets and been in no accidents, she inquired of her agent, who referred her to the Department of Licensing (Department). To her surprise, the Department told her that its records indicated that she had been stopped by a state trooper on September 1, 2002, thereafter failed to appear for her court hearings, and, as a result, her driver's license had been suspended. There was also an outstanding warrant for her arrest.

Dashiell contacted a number of people at the court that issued the warrant and eventually used a public disclosure request to obtain a videotape of the traffic stop. Upon viewing the videotape, she recognized the person using her maiden name, birth date, former address, and social security number as a former friend and neighbor, defendant Melissa Presba.

Presba was charged with second degree identity theft, forgery, and third degree driving with a suspended license. Jonathan Lever, the state trooper who had conducted the traffic stop, testified that Presba had given Dashiell's maiden name, date of birth, and social security number with such assurance that he was inclined to believe her. Though the social security number was one digit off from what the Department had for the license record, Presba explained that the Department had always had an incorrect number. Lever was also concerned because the physical appearance notations did not seem to match. But after a half hour of continued discussion he was sufficiently persuaded that Presba was who she said she was that he cited her for the infraction of driving without her license on her person and released her. Presba signed the notice of infraction using Dashiell's maiden name. Presba's actual driving record showed her license was suspended.

Presba did not testify at trial. Her counsel conceded Presba had engaged in all the conduct alleged by the State but argued that the purpose of the identity theft statute was limited to financial crimes. Counsel maintained Presba was guilty only of what she contended was the lesser included offense of criminal impersonation.

The trial court compared the language of the identity theft statute to the criminal impersonation statute and distinguished the two, noting that one could assume a false identity and thus violate the criminal impersonation statute without using the means of identification of a real person that is required to violate the identity theft statute. The court also noted that while it appeared the general impetus for the identity theft statute seemed to be financial crimes, the Legislature had not limited the statute to such circumstances because it was not necessary to use another person's financial information or actually obtain anything of value to violate the statute. The court concluded that a plain reading of the statute showed merely using a real person's means of identification to facilitate any other crime was sufficient, and that was what Presba had done.

Presba appeals.

Presba challenges sufficiency of the evidence. A person challenging the sufficiency of evidence admits the truth of the State's evidence and any reasonable inferences from it. All reasonable inferences from the evidence are drawn in favor of the State and interpreted most strongly against the defendant. Circumstantial and direct evidence are considered equally reliable.

The statutory means of identity theft applied here requires proof only that the defendant used "a means of identification . . . of another person . . . with the intent to commit, or to aid or abet, any crime." Presba was stopped for speeding while driving with a suspended license, offered Dashiell's name, social security number, former address and date of birth all in a temporarily successful effort to thwart the officer's attempt to ascertain her correct identity to enforce the traffic laws. The information Presba used constitutes a "means of identification" and the evidence supports an inference she did so to facilitate both the offense of RCW 9A.76.020, obstructing a police officer, and RCW 46.61.020, giving false information while in charge of a vehicle. The evidence was sufficient.

In each of her arguments, Presba repeats a continuing theme that the State's charging decision creates an absurd result that offends common sense and violates the spirit of the identity theft law. In support of this claim, Presba cites the general statement of intent found in RCW 9.35.001: "The Legislature intends to penalize unscrupulous people for improperly obtaining financial information." But Washington cases "do not permit reliance on a statement of legislative intent to override the unambiguous elements section of a penal statute or to add an element not found there." The charging decision in this case neither created an absurd result nor offended common sense.

Presba further contends the Legislature would not have intended the identity theft statute to turn the actions of defendants attempting to avoid prosecution for misdemeanors into felonies merely because they used another person's identity. The statute, however, expressly carves out a narrow exception for "any person who obtains another person's driver's license or other form of identification for the sole purpose of misrepresenting his or her age." This suggests that, apart from the specific situation described in the prior sentence, the Legislature did indeed mean for acts committed with intent to facilitate misdemeanors to now be treated as felonies when they satisfy the elements of identity theft even if such acts formerly would have been only misdemeanors.

At oral argument, Presba suggested scenarios involving slight culpability that might satisfy the State's reading of the statute. But we deal here only with the case before us, one which constituted a serious offense. Dashiell explained at a sentencing hearing that even after the many hours and multiple trips from Tacoma to Everett required to quash the arrest warrant and reinstate her driver's license, the consequences continued. She had to change her social security number, which in turn caused ongoing difficulties with her financial accounts and credit card files. And the Department had flagged her driving record as having been used for fraudulent purposes, which meant she faced the prospect of additional problems any time her license was checked. These foreseeable consequences of Presba's acts were significant regardless of whether she had in mind only avoiding prosecution for a traffic offense rather than injuring Dashiell.

We affirm the conviction of identity theft.

Questions and Notes

1. Do you think that Presba's behavior should have amounted to identity theft under the statute? Why? Why not?

2. Would the criminal impersonation statute have been (misdemeanor) a more appropriate and fairer charge?

3. Is it fair to convict Presba of a felony when all she was trying to do was avoid being charged with a misdemeanor? Is that a fair way of asking the question?

4. We now look at an identity theft case with jurisdictional overtones.

State v. Allen

336 P.3d 1007 (2014)

VIGIL, Judge.

This is an identity theft case. The question presented is whether Defendant can be prosecuted in New Mexico when he never set foot in New Mexico, and all the acts of using Victim's identity occurred in other states. Concluding that New Mexico has jurisdiction to prosecute Defendant, we affirm.

Background

Victim attempted to obtain a New Mexico driver's license and discovered that someone had used his identifying information to obtain an Arizona driver's license. A police investigation revealed that Defendant used Victim's identity to obtain a driver's license in Arizona, rent cars in Arizona, Nevada, and Georgia, and to provide booking information upon his arrest in Georgia. It is undisputed that none of the acts of using Victim's identity took place in New Mexico and that Victim resided in San Juan County, New Mexico at the time of the transactions. The State charged Defendant with eight counts of identity theft contrary to NMSA 1978, Section 30-16-24.1(A) (2009), which provides:

> Theft of identity consists of willfully obtaining, recording or transferring personal identifying information of another person without the authorization or consent of that person and with the intent to defraud that person or another or with the intent to sell or distribute the information to another for an illegal purpose.

Defendant filed a motion to dismiss for lack of jurisdiction. The motion focused on the fact that the alleged crimes took place in Arizona, Nevada, and Georgia-not New Mexico. He argued that the fact that Victim resides in New Mexico is irrelevant because under the United States and New Mexico constitutions, "[a] crime must be prosecuted in the jurisdiction where it was committed." The State opposed the motion, asserting that Section 30-16-24.1(G) grants New Mexico jurisdiction because under Section 30-16-24.1(G)(1), the crime is deemed to have been committed in the county where the victim resides. Defendant insisted that Section 30-16-24.1(G) is solely a *venue* statute, relevant in cases where New Mexico otherwise has jurisdiction and that Section 30-16-24.1(G) cannot confer New Mexico with jurisdiction to prosecute crimes committed outside of New Mexico. Defendant asserts to interpret Section 30-16-24.1(G) otherwise, would render it unconstitutional.

The district court denied Defendant's motion. The district court did not rely on Section 30-16-24.1(G), ruling instead:

1. If any of the elements of the crime of theft of identity occurred in New Mexico, [the district c]ourt has subject matter jurisdiction.

2. One element of the crime is that the alleged offender used the personal identifying information of another without the authorization of the owner of the personal identifying information.

3. The "without authorization" element of theft of identity can only occur where the owner of the personal identifying information resides.

4. The State alleges that [Victim] did not authorize the use of his personal identifying information by . . . Defendant and that [Victim] resides in San Juan County, New Mexico.

5. If these allegations are proven, the "without authorization" element occurred in New Mexico and [the district c]ourt has subject matter jurisdiction over the alleged crimes and . . . Defendant's *Motion to Dismiss For Lack of Jurisdiction* should be denied.

Thereafter, Defendant plead guilty to two of the counts of identity theft, reserving his right to appeal the denial of the motion to dismiss. This appeal followed.

Defendant argues that the district court erred as a matter of law in ruling that the "without authorization" element of identity theft can only occur where the owner of the personal identifying information resides. Thus, Defendant asserts, the district court erred in concluding that it had jurisdiction because Victim lived in New Mexico, and a New Mexico district court has jurisdiction over the offense if any of the elements of theft identity occurred in New Mexico. It is not necessary for us to determine whether the "without authorization" of the crime must occur where the victim resides because, as discussed below, we conclude that the district court otherwise had jurisdiction. "As a general rule, however, we will uphold the decision of a district court if it is right for any reason."

A. Standard of Review

Our standard of review is de novo for three reasons. First, issues of subject matter jurisdiction are reviewed under a de novo standard. Second, because the pertinent facts are undisputed, we review de novo whether the law was correctly applied to those facts. Finally, to the extent we are required to construe Section 30-16-24.1, our review is de novo.

Evolution of Territorial Jurisdiction

Historically, the concept of territorial jurisdiction was strictly applied. *See Dudley,* 581 S.E.2d at 177 (explaining that "[u]nder the historical strict territorial principle, a state court had jurisdiction only over those crimes which occurred entirely within that state's boundaries; if any essential element occurred in another state, neither possessed jurisdiction over the criminal offense. Under this view of jurisdiction, only one state could have jurisdiction over a particular crime."). Early on, this jurisdictional loophole was addressed legislatively in the context of murders where the stroke was committed in one state and the fatal blow received in another. In *State v. Hall*, 114 N.C. 909, 19 S.E. 602 (1894), the North Carolina Supreme Court noted that in ancient times it was unclear whether a murder should be prosecuted where the fatal blow was struck or where it was received. As a result, states began enacting legislation providing for a prosecution where the blow was received. Such legislation was "never questioned" when applied to acts of murder spanning different counties within a state, "but where its provisions have been extended so as to affect the jurisdiction of the different states, its constitutionality has been vigorously assailed. Such legislation, however, has been very generally, if not, indeed, uniformly, sustained[.] Statutes of this character are founded upon the general power of the legislature, except so far as restrained by the constitution of the commonwealth and the United States, to declare any willful or negligent act which causes an injury to person or property within its territory to be a crime." The court added that the validity of these types of statutes "seems to be undisputed; and, indeed, it has been held in many jurisdictions that such legislation is but in affirmance of the common law."

In *Strassheim v. Daily*, 221 U.S. 280, 31 S.Ct. 558, 55 L.Ed. 735 (1911), the United States Supreme Court expanded the limits of strict territorial jurisdiction in the absence of any legislation. In *Strassheim*, the defendant was indicted in Michigan for bribery and obtaining money from the state of Michigan by false pretenses, based upon his involvement in selling the state used machinery represented as new. He was arrested in Illinois and contested his extradition to Michigan, arguing that Michigan lacked jurisdiction because the alleged acts were completed entirely in Illinois. The defendant argued, and the Court assumed, that none of his acts were committed in Michigan. Nevertheless, the Court opined,

> [T]he usage of the civilized world would warrant Michigan in punishing him, although he never had set foot in the state until after the fraud was complete. Acts done outside a jurisdiction, but intended to produce and producing detrimental effects within it, justify a state in punishing the cause of the harm as if he had been present at the effect, if the state should succeed in getting him within its power.

From *Strassheim* we conclude that if a crime has a detrimental effect in a state, that state has territorial jurisdiction to prosecute the perpetrator notwithstanding that the acts were committed entirely within another state.

Applying the detrimental effects theory, many states have enacted laws that focus on where the effects of a criminal act are felt to establish territorial jurisdiction. *See* 4 Wayne R. LaFave et al. ("A substantial majority of the states today have statutes that adopt an interpretation of the territorial principle substantially more expansive than the traditional common law position[, s]upported by the broad view of the territorial principle set forth by Justice Holmes in . . . *Strassheim* [.]"). The constitutionality of such legislation has been repeatedly assailed and upheld. *See* 4 Wayne R. LaFave et al., *supra,* § 16.4(c), at 855 ("Because such legislation adheres to the territorial principle, it is held not to violate due process.).

C. Section 30-16-24.1(G)

Defendant acknowledges the impact of *Strassheim* in this case but insists that the district court must have been able to point to a specific legislative enactment that encompasses the detrimental effects theory of *Strassheim* and therefore confers New Mexico with jurisdiction. We disagree with Defendant that New Mexico's territorial jurisdiction must be expressed by a statute. The principles recognized by Justice Holmes in *Strassheim* provide the basis for New Mexico's exercise of jurisdiction in the absence of legislation.

Nonetheless, the Legislature enacted Section 30-16-24.1(G). Section 30-16-24.1(G) in its entirety provides:

> G. In a prosecution brought pursuant to this section, the theft of identity or obtaining identity by electronic fraud shall be considered to have been committed in the county:
>
> (1) where the person whose identifying information was appropriated, obtained or sought resided at the time of the offense; or
>
> (2) in which any part of the offense took place, regardless of whether the defendant was ever actually present in the county.

While Section 30-16-24.1(G) necessarily relates to venue, we believe it also has an impact upon territorial jurisdiction. The crime of identity theft necessarily affects the victim, and Section 30-16-24.1(G) expressly provides that the crime is "considered to have been committed" in the county where the victim resides. This language therefore accomplishes a dual purpose. First, it establishes the proper county within New Mexico where the crime may be prosecuted (venue). Second, it sets forth a legislative determination that because the crime has an effect upon the victim in New Mexico, New Mexico has territorial jurisdiction over the offense, even if the acts are committed in another state. *See State v. Ogden,* 1994-NMSC-029, ¶ 24, 118 N.M. 234, 880 P.2d 845 ("The principal command of statutory construction is that the court should determine and effectuate the intent of the [L]egislature, using the plain language of the statute as the primary indicator of legislative intent [.]" (citations omitted)). Here, Victim encountered issues trying to get a driver's license in New Mexico, and Victim was mailed rental car bills in New Mexico that were incurred by Defendant outside of New Mexico. Defendant's extraterritorial actions had detrimental effects upon Victim in New Mexico. Therefore, whether pursuant to Section 30-16-24.1(G), or *Strassheim,* New Mexico had jurisdiction to prosecute Defendant.

Conclusion

The district court order denying Defendant's motion to dismiss for lack of jurisdiction is affirmed.

Questions and Notes

1. What element of the crime was committed in New Mexico?

2. Does it bother you that a person who never set foot in New Mexico can be prosecuted for a crime in that state? Why? Why not?

3. How was New Mexico affected by Allen's conduct?

4. Some theft crimes are aggravated by other factors such as violence or the threat of violence. Robbery is a prime example.

F. Robbery

People v. Patton
389 N.E.2d 1174 (Ill. 1979)

WARD, Justice:

Verdicts of guilty were returned against defendant, Ray Patton, on both counts of an indictment charging robbery and theft from the person arising out of a single incident of "purse snatching." The trial court did not enter judgment on the theft verdict, but entered judgment on the verdict of robbery and sentenced the defendant to a term of 1 year to 6 years. On the defendant's appeal the appellate court, with one justice dissenting, reversed the judgment and remanded the cause to the circuit court of Peoria County with directions to enter a judgment of conviction for the less serious offense of theft from the person. (376 N.E.2d 1099.) We granted the People's petition for leave to appeal.

On June 27, 1976, Rita Alexander, her husband and their four young children were hurrying along a sidewalk toward a church in Peoria Heights, so as not to be late for a 5:30 p.m. service. A few other persons in the immediate vicinity were likewise walking swiftly toward the church entrance. Mrs. Alexander was carrying her purse "(i)n the fingertips of my left hand down at my side." She noticed the defendant cross the street in front of the Alexanders and thought that perhaps he too was going to the service. Instead, the defendant changed direction and walked toward the Alexander family. As he came abreast of Mrs. Alexander, he "swift(ly) grab(bed)" her purse, throwing her arm back "a little bit," she said, and fled. She testified that the purse was gone before she realized what had happened. Once she overcame her momentary shock, Mrs. Alexander screamed, and Mr. Alexander unsuccessfully chased the defendant. He was subsequently apprehended through the tracing of a license plate number on an automobile which witnesses had observed him enter. There was no other evidence offered bearing on the questions of use of force, threat of the imminent use of force, and resistance by or injury to Mrs. Alexander.

The question we consider is whether the simple taking or "snatching" of a purse from the fingertips of its unsuspecting possessor in itself constitutes a sufficient use of force, or threat of the imminent use of force, to warrant a conviction of robbery. It is the People's contention that any amount of physical force whatsoever, employed to overcome the force exerted by the person to maintain control over the object in hand, is sufficient to bring the act of taking within the robbery statute.

Our statute defines robbery:

"A person commits robbery when he takes property from the person or presence of another by the use of force or by threatening the imminent use of force." (Ill. Rev. Stat. 1975, ch. 38, par. 18 1.)

Thus, if no force or threat of imminent force is used in the taking, there is no robbery, although the act may constitute a theft. Mrs. Alexander did not realize what was happening until after the defendant had begun his flight, and it is clear there was no robbery through the "threatening (of) the imminent use of force." The People maintain that the defendant's act of grabbing was a "use of force" such as is contemplated by the robbery statute, and that no minimum amount of force need be shown to constitute robbery under the statute.

In most jurisdictions where the question has been considered it has been held that a simple snatching or sudden taking of property from the person of another does not of itself involve sufficient force to constitute robbery, though the act may be robbery where a struggle ensues, the victim is injured in the taking, or the property is so attached to the victim's person or clothing as to create resistance to the taking.

To illustrate, in *Hall v. People* (1898), 171 Ill. 540, 49 N.E. 495, this court held it was not robbery where the defendant unbuttoned his inebriated drinking companion's vest, "possibly by pulling at it, and took the pocketbook from his inside vest pocket." In distinguishing between private stealing from the person of another and robbery, the court said that "where it appeared that the article was taken without any sensible or material violence to the person, as snatching a hat from the head or a cane or umbrella from the hand of the wearer, rather by sleight of hand and adroitness than by open violence, and without any struggle on his part, it is merely larceny from the person." The court further observed that if the facts of the case were held to constitute robbery, "then no practical distinction between that crime and larceny from the person exists. The two crimes approach each other so closely that cases may arise where it may be doubtful upon which side of the line they should fall. Still, it is the duty of courts, as well as of juries, to resolve such doubts in favor of the accused."

The court in *Klein v. People* (1885), 113 Ill. 596, affirmed a conviction of robbery where the evidence established that the defendant was one of two men who grabbed a handbag "with such force," the prosecuting witness testified, "that it bruised my arm, and it was lame for several days."

Robbery convictions were affirmed in *People v. Campbell* (1908), 234 Ill. 391, 84 N.E. 1035, where the defendants had scuffled with their victim over possession of a diamond stud fastened in his shirt front. The court stated: "In the absence of active opposition, if the article is so attached to the person or clothes as to create resistance, however slight, or if there be a struggle to keep it, the taking is robbery."

In *People v. Jones* (1919), 290 Ill. 603, 125 N.E. 256, the evidence was held insufficient to support a robbery conviction where the defendant had stealthily removed a pocketbook from his intoxicated victim's pocket and transferred it to his own. When the victim, who had observed the transfer, said, "You have my pocket-book," the defendant "hit him over the eye and 'knocked him out.'" The court concluded there was no evidence of a struggle to retain possession, but only an accusation after the theft occurred "which the plaintiff in error resented by assaulting the accuser." His actions were therefore "those of a pick-pocket and not of a highwayman."

Robbery convictions of defendants, who had grabbed a pocketbook from the hand of their victim, were reversed in *People v. O'Connor* (1923), 310 Ill. 403, 141 N.E. 748, for lack of evidence that force or intimidation was used. Although some testimony of violence and threats by the defendants was offered at trial by the complaining witness, the court concluded it appeared to be the "vague remembrance of impressions received while strongly under the influence of alcoholic liquor." And in *People v. Chambliss* (1966), 69 Ill. App. 2d 459, 217 N.E.2d 422, the court sustained a robbery conviction where the necessary force was held to have occurred during the course of a struggle for possession of a wallet immediately after the victim's pocket had been picked.

We have noted that Mrs. Alexander testified her arm was thrown back "a little bit," but "(w)here it is doubtful under the facts whether the accused is guilty of robbery or larceny from the person, it is the duty of the court and the jury to resolve that doubt in favor of the lesser offense." (*People v. Williams* (1961), 23 Ill. 2d 295, 301, 178 N.E.2d 372, 376.) For the reasons given, the judgment of the appellate court is affirmed.

Questions and Notes

1. Given Mrs. Alexander's testimony, shouldn't the jury have been permitted to decide whether she was the victim of force?

2. Are the concepts of: "'resistance, however slight' being sufficient for robbery" and "'doubtful' cases should be resolved against robbery" internally inconsistent? If they are, which one should prevail?

3. Consider the following: Horace, a muscular 6'4" 250-pound mean-looking man, meets Gertrude, a frail-looking 100-pound woman, in a deserted alley. Horace taps Gertrude on the shoulder, stares into her eyes, and says in a no-nonsense voice: "Give me your money!" Gertrude complies. Horace says "Thank you very much," and leaves. Is Horace guilty of robbery? Why? Why not?

4. Robbery is sometimes upgraded to a more serious offense if committed with a firearm. Consider the rationale for this upgrading as you read *Baskerville*.

People v. Baskerville
457 N.E.2d 752 (N.Y. 1983)

MEYER, Judge.

On the morning of Saturday, April 11, 1981, the base exchange at the United States Air Force Base in Plattsburgh was robbed. The robber took nearly $30,000 from the cashier's safe, which he stuffed into a plastic bag taken from a trash can near the cashier's cage. None of the five witnesses to the robbery who testified at defendant's trial could identify the robber, who wore a hooded sweatshirt and used a towel to conceal the lower half of his face. Another towel was wrapped around the robber's arm, but one of the witnesses testified that she saw a black object inside the towel, which she thought was a gun. Another witness testified that when a woman approached the cashier's window in the exchange office, the robber raised his towel-wrapped arm, pointed it at the woman and threatened to kill her.

Within half an hour after the robbery, defendant, an airman at the base, remarked to an acquaintance that the base exchange had been robbed. Less than three hours later, defendant paid a Plattsburgh car dealer almost $6,000 in cash as a down payment on a new car, using money which was still bundled in wrappers that were dated, initiated and stamped with an official seal of the base exchange, and during that weekend spent close to an additional $2,000 on other purchases.

Defendant was arrested the following Monday morning and his locker and dormitory room were searched pursuant to a military warrant. The search turned up an additional $1,100 in defendant's locker and in defendant's room a plastic bag of the type used to carry away the money as well as clothing which matched that described by the witnesses to the robbery, including sneakers with a green stripe. Expert testimony was presented at the trial that the design and wear characteristics of one of defendant's sneakers closely conformed to those of a footprint found in a sandy area adjacent to the exchange shortly after the robbery and that the plastic bag in defendant's room was of the identical formula and manufacturer used by the exchange.

Questioned by investigators after his arrest about the down payment on the car, defendant first said the money had been obtained from the settlement of an accident claim. When confronted with the exchange money wrappers, however, defendant related an entirely different story, which became the theory of his defense at trial. He had, he said, borrowed $5,540 in cash from a loanshark who delivered the money to him behind the gas station on the base during the late morning of the robbery. Although such a loan was consistent with evidence introduced at trial that during the two days preceding the robbery defendant had sought to obtain money from various financial institutions and charities in the Plattsburgh area by stating that he needed the money to ransom his niece, who had purportedly been abducted, he conceded at trial that he had concocted that story in order to obtain money for the down payment on the car.

The Trial Judge charged, over objection, that defendant could not be convicted of robbery in the first degree unless the jury found that he had displayed what appeared to be a firearm but that "It is sufficient . . . if the victim is made to believe the object to be such a weapon or if the defendant holds or wraps the object in such a way as to create the impression that he is holding a pistol, revolver or other firearm." The jury found defendant guilty of robbery in the first degree.

Both subdivision 4 of section 160.15 of the Penal Law, defining robbery in the first degree, and section 160.10 (subd. 2, par. [b]) of the Penal Law, defining robbery in the second degree, require that in the course of forcibly stealing property the perpetrator "[d]isplays what appears to be a pistol, revolver . . . or other firearm". As to the first degree offense, it is, however, an affirmative defense that the object displayed was not an operable firearm and if defendant so proves by a preponderance of the evidence he may only be convicted of robbery in the second degree.

In either case, the Legislature has denominated the display of "what appears to be" a firearm an aggravating factor which increases the degree of the crime over forcible stealing without such a display. The apparent justification for differentiating the situations is the difficulty of proving when no shot was fired that what appeared to be a weapon was in fact a weapon and the effect upon the victim put in fear of his or her life by the display of what appeared to be a weapon. Bearing in mind that provisions of the Penal Law are to be "construed according to the fair import of their terms to promote justice and effect the objects of the law" and the Legislature's purpose in increasing the penalty for displaying what appears to be a firearm, we conclude that display of anything that appears to be such, though held inside a coat or otherwise obscured, is covered by [the statutes].

This does not mean that the test is primarily subjective. The defendant must consciously display something that could reasonably be perceived as a firearm with the intent of compelling an owner of property to deliver it up or for the purpose of preventing or overcoming resistance to the taking. Furthermore, the display must actually be witnessed in some manner by the victim, *i.e.*, it must appear to the victim by sight, touch or sound that he is threatened by a firearm. When both of these requirements are satisfied, however, the true nature of the object displayed is, as concerns criminality, irrelevant. Thus, in *People v. Lockwood*, 52 N.Y.2d 790, 791–792, 436 N.Y.S.2d 703, 417 N.E.2d 1244, *supra*, we recognized that even if defendant's statement that he committed the robbery by holding a toothbrush in his coat pocket to simulate a gun were accepted as true, he could still be guilty of displaying what appears to be a firearm, and would succeed only in reducing his liability from first degree robbery to second degree.

The evidence in the present case that the towel wrapped around the robber's arm concealed a black object that appeared to one of the persons threatened to be a gun, and that the robber raised his arm toward a person and threatened to kill the person his arm was pointed at, was clearly sufficient to establish that the robber displayed what appeared to be a firearm. Nor was there any error in the trial court's charge that the statutory requirement had been satisfied if the object displayed was held or wrapped in such a way as to create the impression that it was a gun.

[Reversed on other grounds.]

Questions and Notes

1. Although Baskerville seems to have behaved in an unbelievably stupid manner, attorneys who have defended robbers have told me that this is not untypical.

2. The propriety of New York's shifting the burden of proof to the defendant is part of an interesting and difficult question that we will explore later. *See* Chapter 16, *infra*.

3. Why does New York make it a more serious offense to have a gun that is actually operational than to have something that only appears to be a gun?

4. Why is carrying a nonoperational (or simulated) gun more serious than unarmed robbery?

5. If a statute merely forbids armed robbery (as many of them do), what factors should determine whether one carrying a simulated weapon is guilty? How should that question be resolved?

6. We now turn to burglary, a crime that usually, though not always, has an element of theft in it.

G. Burglary

People v. Davis

958 P.2d 1083 (Cal. 1998)

GEORGE, Chief Justice.

Defendant was convicted of forgery, receiving stolen property, and burglary, based upon evidence that he presented a stolen and forged check to the teller at a check-cashing business by placing the check in a chute in a walk-up window. Defendant maintains that the burglary conviction must be reversed because he did not enter the check-cashing facility. For the reasons that follow, we agree.

I.

On May 27, 1995, defendant approached the walk-up window of a check-cashing business named the Cash Box and presented a check to the teller by placing the check in a chute in the window. The teller later described the chute as follows: "It has a handle, and it opens out like a flap. It opens out, and they put the check in. They pass the check through." The check was drawn on the account of Robert and Joan Tallman, whose names were imprinted on the check, and was payable in the amount of $274 to Mike Woody, a name defendant sometimes used. The check was signed with the name Robert Tallman.

The teller placed a small, white, oval sticker on the back of the check, passed the check back to defendant, and asked him to place his thumbprint on the sticker and endorse the check. Defendant placed his thumbprint on the sticker, signed the back of the check with the name Michael D. Woody, and passed the check back to the teller, using the chute.

The teller telephoned Robert Tallman, who denied having written the check. Tallman later discovered that a group of checks, including this one, had been stolen from his automobile. The teller placed Tallman on hold and telephoned the police. An officer arrived within minutes and arrested defendant, who still was waiting at the window. At the police station, the police directed defendant to give several examples of his handwriting by repeatedly signing the name "Robert Tallman."

At trial, Tallman testified that neither the signature nor any of the other writing on the check was his.

Defendant was convicted of forgery, burglary, and receiving stolen property. Defendant waived his statutory right to a jury trial as to the truth of the prior prison term allegation, and after a brief hearing the trial court found true the allegation that defendant previously had been convicted of a felony for which he had served a prison term. Defendant was sentenced on the forgery count to the upper term of three years in prison, plus an additional year for the prior prison term enhancement, for a total term of four years in prison. Defendant was sentenced on the burglary count to a concurrent term of three years in prison, and on the receiving stolen property count to a concurrent term of three years in prison. The Court of Appeal affirmed the judgment. We granted review to determine whether there was sufficient evidence to support the conviction for burglary.

II

Under section 459, a person is guilty of burglary if he or she enters any building (or other listed structure) with the intent to commit larceny or any felony. We must determine whether the Legislature intended the term "enter," as used in the burglary statute, to encompass passing a forged check through a chute in a walk-up window of a check-cashing or similar facility.

The burglary statutes do not define the term "enter." In the present case, the Attorney General conceded at oral argument that no part of defendant's body entered the building, but it long has been established that a burglary also can be committed by using an instrument to enter a building.

In his Commentaries on the Laws of England, Sir William Blackstone stated regarding the elements of burglary: "As for the entry, any the least degree of it, with any part of the body, or with an instrument held in the hand, is sufficient; as to step over the threshold, to put a hand or a hook in at a window to draw out goods, or a pistol to demand one's money, are all of them burglarious entries." (4 BLACKSTONE'S COMMENTARIES 227.) But the common law drew a puzzling distinction. An entry by instrument was sufficient for burglary only if the instrument was used to commit the target larceny or felony. Insertion of an instrument for the sole purpose of gaining entry to the building did not constitute burglary.

The common law drew no such distinction if any part of the defendant's body entered the building. As Rollin Perkins observes in his textbook on Criminal Law: "Where it is a part of the body itself, its insertion into the building is an entry, within the rules of burglary, whether the purpose was to complete the felonious design or merely to effect a breaking. Thus, if the miscreant should open a window too small to admit his body, and should insert his hand through this opening merely for the purpose of unlocking a door, through which he intends to gain entrance to the building, he has already made an 'entry' even if he should get no farther. But where a tool or other instrument is intruded, without any part of the person being within the house, it is an entry if the insertion was for the purpose of completing the felony but not if it was merely to accomplish a breaking. If the instrument is inserted in such a manner that it is calculated not only to make a breach but also to accomplish the completion of the felonious design, this constitutes both a breach and an entry." An illustrative case cited by Perkins is *Walker v. State* (1879) 63 Ala. 49, in which the defendant bored a hole through the floor of a corn crib, caught the shelled corn in a sack as it flowed through the hole, then sealed the hole using a corn cob. The entry of the bit of the auger into the corn crib was held to be a sufficient entry for purposes of burglary, because the instrument was used both to effect entry and to accomplish the larceny.

Although many jurisdictions adhere to the rule that entry by means of an instrument is sufficient for burglary only if the instrument was used to commit the intended larceny or felony, the reason for this rule is not clear, and California courts have declined to adopt it.

In *People v. Walters* (1967) 249 Cal. App. 2d 547, 57 Cal. Rptr. 484, the Court of Appeal purported to apply the rule that an entry by instrument must be for the purpose of committing the intended crime, but held nevertheless that a burglarious entry had occurred where the defendants were found on the roof of a market near a vent, the cover of which had been removed and through which a rope had been lowered into the restroom of the market. A grate on the restroom ceiling had been broken, and some tools were found lying on the broken grate, but there was nothing to suggest that these instruments were being used to accomplish the intended larceny. Nevertheless, the Court of Appeal held: "The presence of these items in the market's interior and the discovery of the instruments nearby sustain the inference that hands and tools manipulated by appellants effected an entry which constituted the crime of burglary."

In *People v. Osegueda* (1984) 163 Cal. App. 3d Supp. 25, 210 Cal. Rptr. 182, burglars were apprehended after they had succeeded in creating a small hole in the wall of an electronics store. It reasonably could be inferred that, in creating the hole in the wall, some portion of the tools had entered the building, but that the entry of these implements was not for the purpose of completing the intended larceny. The

Appellate Department of the Los Angeles Superior Court found this was a sufficient entry for purposes of burglary: "We reject the decisions of out-of-state jurisdictions which differentiate between an entry by body and by instrument. We find no plausible reason for holding that an entry by instrument must be for the purpose of removing property. We find no California authority for contrary reasoning."

The Court of Appeal followed *Osegueda* in *People v. Moore* (1994) 31 Cal. App. 4th 489, 37 Cal. Rptr. 2d 104 in holding there was sufficient entry for burglary where the defendant had attempted to pry open the front door of an apartment using a tire iron, and an occupant of the apartment had seen the tip of the tire iron protrude into the apartment.

We agree that a burglary may be committed by using an instrument to enter a building—whether that instrument is used solely to effect entry, or to accomplish the intended larceny or felony as well. Thus, using a tire iron to pry open a door, using a tool to create a hole in a store wall, or using an auger to bore a hole in a corn crib are sufficient entries to support a conviction of burglary. But it does not necessarily follow that the placement of a forged check in the chute of a walk-up window constitutes entering the building within the meaning of the burglary statute, although that conclusion would be compelled were we to follow the decision in *People v. Ravenscroft* (1988) 198 Cal. App. 3d 639, 243 Cal. Rptr. 827, the only California authority to address an analogous question. As we shall explain, we do not find the reasoning in *Ravenscroft* persuasive.

The defendant in that case was convicted of two counts of burglary based upon his conduct of "surreptitiously stealing and inserting the automatic teller machine (ATM) card of his traveling companion, Barbara Ann Lewis, in two ATMs and punching in her personal identification number, which he had previously noted, on the ATM keypads in order to withdraw funds from her account." The Court of Appeal first concluded that an ATM is a structure protected by the burglary statute. The court then turned to the question whether insertion of the ATM card constituted an entry into that structure. The court rejected the defendant's arguments that insertion of the card did not violate the air space of the ATM, and that insertion of the card did not constitute an entry, because the defendant lost control of the card once it entered the ATM: "The insertion of an ATM card to effectuate larcenous intent is no less an entry into the air space of a bank as would be the use of any other tool or instrument. Although the California Penal Code does not define 'entry' for the purpose of burglary, the California courts have found that a burglary is complete upon the slightest partial entry of any kind, with the requisite intent, even if the intended larceny is neither committed nor even attempted. By pushing Lewis's card into an ATM's slot, the defendant completed the crime. Further control of the card is unnecessary."

The Court of Appeal then rejected the defendant's further contention that he did not commit burglary by inserting the ATM card, because this act differed from other examples of entry by instrument:

"Ravenscroft argues that *Walters* and *Osegueda, supra,* should not apply to this case since they involve more traditional violations of air space with more traditional burglars' tools. . . .

The fact that both *Walters* and *Osegueda* involve more traditional methods of burglary is of no moment. The gravamen of burglary is an act of entry, no matter how partial or slight it may be, with an instrument or tool which is appropriate for the particular instance, accompanied by the proper intent."

The appellate court in *Ravenscroft* properly rejected various arguments presented by the defendant, correctly concluding that the card was inserted into the air space of the ATM, that the circumstance that the defendant lost control of the card is not dispositive, and that the rule governing entry by means of an instrument is not limited to traditional burglar tools.[3] Instruments other than traditional burglar tools certainly can be used to commit the offense of burglary. A laser could be used to cut an opening in a wall, a robot could be used to enter a building, or an ATM card could be used to "jimmy" a lock. But it does not necessarily follow from these conclusions that insertion of a stolen card into an ATM constitutes burglary.

The Court of Appeal in *Ravenscroft* appeared to reason that because an entry by means of an instrument is not limited to the use of traditional burglar's tools, there are no limitations within the meaning of the burglary statute on what constitutes entry by means of an instrument. It certainly is within the scope of the burglary statute to recognize that using a cutting tool to breach the walls, doors, or windows of a building constitutes an entry, whether the burglar uses traditional burglar tools or a laser, and that using an instrument to reach into a building and remove property constitutes burglary whether that instrument is a hook or a robot. These are the traditional types of entry prohibited by the burglary statute, even though the entry may be accomplished in new ways.

Inserting a stolen ATM card into the designated opening in an ATM is markedly different from the types of entry traditionally covered by the burglary statute, as is passing a forged check through a chute in a walk-up window. In each situation the defendant causes an object to enter the air space of a building, but it is not apparent that the burglary statute was meant to encompass such conduct. It is important to establish reasonable limits as to what constitutes an entry by means of an instrument for purposes of the burglary statute. Otherwise the scope of the burglary statute could be expanded to absurd proportions. For example, the Attorney General

---

3. In *People v. Montoya* (1994) 7 Cal. 4th 1027, 1041–1042, 31 Cal. Rptr. 2d 128, 874 P.2d 903, we cited the decision in *Ravenscroft*, along with numerous other decisions, in support of the general proposition that "[o]ne may be liable for burglary upon entry with the requisite intent to commit a felony or a theft (whether felony or misdemeanor), regardless of whether the felony or theft is different from that contemplated at the time of entry, or whether any felony or theft actually is committed." Our decision in *Montoya* had no occasion to consider the specific holding or analysis in *Ravenscroft* that is at issue in the present case.

asserted at oral argument that mailing a forged check from New York to a bank in California, or sliding a ransom note under a door, would constitute burglary. A person who mails a forged check to a bank or slides a ransom note under a door causes that forged check or ransom note to enter the building, but it cannot reasonably be argued that these acts constitute burglary. Under the expansive approach to the burglary statute taken by the Attorney General and reflected in the *Ravenscroft* decision, it is difficult to imagine what reasonable limit would be placed upon the scope of the burglary statute. It could be argued similarly that a defendant who, for a fraudulent purpose, accesses a bank's computer from his or her home computer via a modem has electronically entered the bank building and committed burglary.

The crucial issue, not considered by the court in *Ravenscroft*, is whether insertion of the ATM card was the type of entry the burglary statute was intended to prevent. In answering this question, we look to the interest sought to be protected by the burglary statute in general, and the requirement of an entry in particular.

The interest sought to be protected by the common law crime of burglary was clear. At common law, burglary was the breaking and entering of a dwelling in the nighttime. The law was intended to protect the sanctity of a person's home during the night hours when the resident was most vulnerable. As one commentator observed: "The predominant factor underlying common law burglary was the desire to protect the security of the home, and the person within his home. Burglary was not an offense against property, real or personal, but an offense against the habitation, for it could only be committed against the dwelling of another. . . . The dwelling was sacred, but a duty was imposed on the owner to protect himself as well as looking to the law for protection. The intruder had to break and enter; if the owner left the door open, his carelessness would allow the intruder to go unpunished. The offense had to occur at night; in the daytime home-owners were not asleep, and could detect the intruder and protect their homes." The drafters of the Model Penal Code observed: "The notable severity of burglary penalties is accounted for by the fact that the offense was originally confined to violent nighttime assault on a dwelling. The dwelling was and remains each man's castle, the final refuge from which he need not flee even if the alternative is to take the life of an assailant. It is the place of security for his family, as well as his most cherished possessions. Thus, it is perhaps understandable that the offense should have been a capital felony at common law. . . ."

In California, as in other states, the scope of the burglary law has been greatly expanded. There is no requirement of a breaking; an entry alone is sufficient. The crime is not limited to dwellings but includes entry into a wide variety of structures. The crime need not be committed at night. "Of all common law crimes, burglary today perhaps least resembles the prototype from which it sprang. In ancient times it was a crime of the most precise definition, under which only certain restricted acts were criminal; today it has become one of the most generalized forms of crime, developed by judicial accretion and legislative revision. Most strikingly it is a creature of modern Anglo-American law only. The rationale of common law burglary, and of house-breaking provisions in foreign codes, is insufficient to explain it."

More than a century ago, in *People v. Barry* (1892) 94 Cal. 481, 29 P. 1026, this court addressed the subject of what constitutes an entry for purposes of burglary. The defendant in *Barry* entered a grocery store during business hours and attempted to commit larceny. This court, rejecting the contention that a burglary had not occurred because the defendant had entered lawfully as part of the public invited to enter the store, stated: "[A] party who enters with the intention to commit a felony enters without an invitation. He is not one of the public invited, nor is he entitled to enter." *People v. Salemme* (1992) 2 Cal. App. 4th 775, 781, 3 Cal. Rptr. 2d 398 [entering a residence to sell fraudulent securities is an entry within the meaning of the burglary statute].)

In *People v. Gauze* (1975) 15 Cal. 3d 709, 125 Cal. Rptr. 773, 542 P.2d 1365, we clarified our holding in *Barry* and held that a person cannot burglarize his or her own home. We observed that "[a] burglary remains an entry which invades a possessory right in a building." We then discussed the interest protected by the burglary statute: "'Burglary laws are based primarily upon a recognition of the dangers to personal safety created by the usual burglary situation—the danger that the intruder will harm the occupants in attempting to perpetrate the intended crime or to escape and the danger that the occupants will in anger or panic react violently to the invasion, thereby inviting more violence. The laws are primarily designed, then, not to deter the trespass and the intended crime, which are prohibited by others laws, so much as to forestall the germination of a situation dangerous to personal safety.' Section 459, in short, is aimed at the danger caused by the unauthorized entry itself."

Inserting a stolen ATM card into an ATM, or placing a forged check in a chute in the window of a check-cashing facility, is not using an instrument to effect an entry within the meaning of the burglary statute. Neither act violates the occupant's possessory interest in the building as does using a tool to reach into a building and remove property. It is true that the intended result in each instance is larceny. But the use of a tool to enter a building, whether as a prelude to a physical entry or to remove property or commit a felony, breaches the occupant's possessory interest in the building. Inserting an ATM card or presenting a forged check do not. Such acts are no different, for purposes of the burglary statute, from mailing a forged check to a bank or check-cashing facility.

By analogy, a person who returns books to a library by depositing them in a book drop, causing the books to slide down a chute into the library, has not entered the library. It would be unreasonable to characterize the books as "instruments" used to enter the library. But if a person reaches his or her hand into the book drop, or uses a tool, in an attempt to steal books, such an act would constitute burglary.

Our conclusion that the limits of the burglary statute should not be stretched beyond recognition does not leave the public without reasonable protection from criminal conduct, for the Legislature has enacted a variety of penal statutes that apply to the criminal activity involved in cases such as *Ravenscroft* or the present case. The use of an ATM card with intent to defraud, for example, specifically is penalized by section 484g and the Legislature, of course, could enact a similar statute pertaining to check-cashing facilities. Unauthorized entry into a computer system is addressed by sections 502 and 502.01. And in the present case, our reversal of defendant's conviction of burglary does not affect his convictions for forgery and receiving stolen property, or his resulting sentence of four years in prison.[7]

For the reasons discussed above, we conclude that defendant's placement of a forged check in the chute of the walk-up window of the check-cashing facility at issue cannot reasonably be termed an entry into the building for purposes of the burglary statute. Accordingly, the judgment of the Court of Appeal is reversed to the extent it affirms defendant's conviction for burglary, and affirmed in all other respects.

MOSK, KENNARD and WERDEGAR, J.J., concur.

BAXTER, Justice, dissenting.

I respectfully dissent. Defendant's act of passing a forged check through the walk-up security window of the check-cashing facility met the statutory and common law requirement of an "entry" sufficient to sustain his conviction of burglary. Defendant used the forged check as an instrumentality to trick the teller into handing him money back through a chute designed to protect this very type of particularly vulnerable business—a check-cashing facility—and its employee-occupants, from persons with criminal designs such as his. Defendant's use of the forged check served both to *breach* the security system of the business, by tricking the teller into taking the check from him through the security chute, and to gain *entry* into the premises, insofar as the check was literally used as a paper "hook" to enter the air space of the check-cashing facility and effectuate theft of cash on the spot from the business. Such was no less an act of larceny, and no less a breach of the business owner's "possessory interest" in his business premises accomplished through a burglarious entry, than if defendant had reached through an open window or entered through an unlocked door and grabbed his loot.

The majority suggest that conviction of burglary on these facts would unduly expand the scope of the burglary statutes to "absurd proportions." To the contrary, the majority's holding is patently at odds with the approach courts have been taking

---

7. The dissent argues that defendant entered the building by passing the forged check through the chute in the window, but attempts to limit the effects of its proposed holding by creating a new rule: "no burglar at the crime scene, no burglary." The dissent does not explain the genesis of its proposed new rule and does not explore its consequences. Under the dissent's proposed rule, a person who used a remote controlled robot, operated from across the street or across town, to enter a building for the purpose of committing larceny or any felony would not commit burglary, even though such an entry by instrument is simply a modern version of the type of entry the burglary statute was designed to punish.

since the crime of burglary was codified over a century ago—that of moving the law in a direction away from the inflexible restraints that characterized burglary at early common law, and instead adapting the crime, within the confines of its legislative codification, to meet the security needs of a growing, changing, and increasingly crime-ridden modern society.

The majority expressly disapprove *Ravenscroft*, a decision at odds with their analysis. As will be explained, the majority do more than merely disapprove a single decision, for the majority's opinion casts doubt on a well-settled line of authority that dutifully follows this court's teaching in *Gauze* that "burglary remains an entry which invades a *possessory right* in a building" (italics added.) Under settled authorities, the possessory rights of the owners and employees of the check-cashing facility victimized in this case included the right to conduct lawful business through the air space of their security chute; the related right to extend a conditional invitation to only those persons intending to conduct lawful business by inviting such patrons to tender legally valid checks to the teller through the security chute; and the basic right to structure their business operations in a manner that discourages thefts and robberies and protects them from such criminal conduct, namely, through use of a walk-up window and security chute. Defendant's passing of the forged check through the air space of the security chute into the check-cashing facility in an attempt to trick the teller into handing money out to him on the spot violated each of these aspects of the business owners' possessory rights in the business premises.

The majority refuse to recognize as much, and instead effectively redefine the concept of a *possessory right* in premises for purposes of determining whether an entry by tool or instrument constitutes a burglarious entry. The majority seemingly endorse some new test for establishing an unlawful entry by tool or instrument, but it is a nebulous standard that even the majority have difficulty characterizing in concrete terms. The majority first concede, as they must, for the authorities are settled, that "a burglary may be committed by using an instrument to enter a building—whether that instrument is used solely to effect entry, or to accomplish the intended larceny or felony as well." But the majority then go on to require that such an unlawful entry by instrument be one that "[i]t is . . . apparent . . . the burglary statute was meant to encompass. . . ." Exactly how trial courts are to determine this is not clear from the majority's analysis. The trial courts are admonished that "[i]t is important to establish reasonable limits as to what constitutes an entry by means of an instrument for purposes of the burglary statute. Otherwise the scope of the burglary statute could be expanded to absurd proportions." They are also cautioned that "the limits of the burglary statute should not be stretched beyond recognition." A number of farfetched hypotheticals are posed which, under any test, would never constitute burglary. Under the majority's analysis one is ultimately left wondering why defendant's placement of the forged check through the security chute, the functional equivalent of use of a tool or instrument as an extension of the burglar's arm and hand both to *breach* the secured premises and effectuate an *entry* into its air space even under the early common law cases, and an act plainly done with felonious intent, nonetheless does not constitute a burglarious entry.

Whatever be the majority's new test, it sets forth requirements heretofore uncalled for under the present day statutory and prevailing common law definitions of burglary. Confusion in our trial courts will be the result.

I

On appeal defendant contended there was insufficient evidence to sustain his conviction of burglary because evidence that he passed a forged check through the walk-up window or security chute of the check-cashing facility could not establish the element of "entry." The Court of Appeal disagreed.

Since 1892, the courts of this state have recognized that the codification of burglary in Penal Code section 459 shares few elements with the early common law crime of burglary. Presently, any person who "enters any . . . building, . . . with intent to commit . . . larceny or any felony is guilty of burglary." And "[i]t is well settled that an entry occurs for purposes of the burglary statute if any part of the intruder's body, or a tool or instrument wielded by the intruder, is 'inside the premises.'"

Under a straightforward application of the law to the facts of this case, defendant stood at the walk-up window and handed or passed a forged check through the security chute into the check-cashing facility with the intent to steal money from the business. His larcenous intent was a felonious intent. Forgery is also a felony. To the extent defendant passed the check through the chute to perfect and realize gains from his act of forgery, either felonious intent (larceny or forgery) would serve to establish the requisite unlawful specific intent for burglary.

As regards the element of "entry", in this case we are concerned specifically with an entry by "tool or instrument wielded by the [defendant]"—to wit, the forged check. When defendant gave the forged check to the teller through the security chute, at the very least, the paper document he "wielded" in his hand crossed through the outer boundary of the business premises as it was received by the teller.[1] Respondent's misleading and imprudent suggestion at oral argument that mailing a forged check from New York to a bank in California would likewise constitute burglary—and the majority's own hypothetically stated concern that a defendant "who, for a fraudulent purpose, accesses a bank's computer from his or her home computer via a modem [and] has [thereby] electronically entered the bank building" should not be subject to prosecution for burglary—are red herrings. In neither hypothetical

---

1. The majority emphasize respondent's "concession" at oral argument "that no part of defendant's body entered the building" in this case. (Maj. opn., *ante*, at p. 772 of 76 Cal. Rptr. 2d, p. 1085 of 958 P.2d.) I question the propriety of accepting such a factual "concession." Admittedly, the description in the record of the secured window or chute is somewhat vague. However, based on the trial testimony, the jury could have concluded beyond a reasonable doubt that defendant put his hand in the chute. Even if he did not do so when he put the check in the chute the first time, he in probability put at least a finger in it when the teller passed the check back to him for signature and thumbprinting and he took it out of the chute.

has a tool or instrument been wielded by a burglar to serve as an extension of his hand, arm, or body for the purpose of gaining entry into the premises. Simply put: no burglar at the crime scene, no burglary.

The crux of the matter is simply this: can the forged check validly be deemed a "tool or instrument" wielded by defendant and placed or passed through the outer boundary of the business premises (the security chute) for the felonious purpose of burglarizing the establishment?

The majority start out by correctly observing that "the [early] common law drew a puzzling distinction. . . . An entry by instrument was sufficient for burglary only if the instrument was used to commit the target larceny or felony. Insertion of an instrument for the sole purpose of gaining entry to the building did not constitute burglary." In other words, under the early common law, a burglary would have been complete upon the insertion of a hook through a window for the purpose of snagging and pulling out valuables from the burglarized structure. But if the burglary suspect used a crowbar to break through a window or door and then fled before any portion of his body had entered the structure, the insertion of the crowbar into the air space of the building or structure was insufficient to establish a burglarious entry.

The majority further acknowledge, as they must, that unlike several out-of-state jurisdictions, California courts have declined to draw any distinction between the nature or purpose of the "tool or instrument" wielded by the burglar and used to enter the burglarized structure.

In short, it is of no legal consequence in this case that the forged check defendant "wielded" and passed through the check-cashing facility's security chute was not used by him to *forcibly* break or gain entry into the business premises.

In contrast, it is of legal significance to note that defendant used the forged check *both* as a tool or instrument to breach the secured premises of the check-cashing facility (*i.e.*, trick the teller into taking it from him though the air space of the security chute through which all of the business's transactions were conducted), *and* as the means for effectuating his felonious intent to steal (*i.e.*, further trick the teller into cashing the forged check and passing money back out to him through the chute). As Rollin Perkins observes in his textbook on Criminal Law: "If the instrument is inserted in such a manner that it is calculated not only to make a breach but also to accomplish the completion of the felonious design, this constitutes both a breach and an entry." Although either purpose would alone suffice to establish a burglarious entry under California law, here, use of the forged check to gain access into the business premises through the security chute *and* to steal money from the teller within satisfied both. In short, the forged check in this instance served both as a crowbar and a paper "hook."

II

The most commonly recognized test for determining whether an entry sufficient to establish a burglary has occurred is to ascertain whether the defendant, or any tool or instrument wielded by the defendant, has crossed the outer boundary of the "airspace" of the structure or premises.

In *Ravenscroft*, the court concluded that the insertion of an automatic teller card into an automatic teller machine (ATM) installed on the exterior wall of a bank constituted an "entry" within the meaning of section 459. The *Ravenscroft* court reasoned that

> "[t]he insertion of an ATM card to effectuate larcenous intent is no less an entry into the air space of a bank as would be the use of any other tool or instrument. . . .

> The gravamen of burglary is an act of entry, no matter how partial or slight it may be, with an instrument or tool which is appropriate for the particular instance, accompanied by the proper intent. . . . The insertion of a fraudulently obtained ATM card effectuates an entry into a bank's ATM for larceny just as surely as does a crowbar when applied to a vent."

Although not discernible from the majority opinion, a decision directly relevant to the question at issue in this case was handed down the same year as *Ravenscroft*— *People v. Nible* (1988) 200 Cal. App. 3d 838, 247 Cal. Rptr. 396 (*Nible*). Some discussion of *Nible* is pertinent here because, as the Court of Appeal recognized, *Nible* expressly purported to reject the bright line air space test handed down that same year in *Ravenscroft*.

In *Nible*, a woman asleep in her apartment heard a disturbance, investigated, and caught a burglar in the act of removing the screen of an open window of the residence. She slammed the window shut and called her husband, who in turn summoned the police. "There was no evidence defendant touched [the victim's] window or crossed the boundary formed by the window into [her] bedroom." The defendant fled but was quickly apprehended and charged with burglary. Both at trial and on appeal he urged the window was the outer boundary of the apartment, and that he had thus not effectuated a burglarious entry. The trial court instructed the jury they could find an entry if a part of defendant's body or a tool or instrument used by him had penetrated ". . . the area inside where the screen was normally affixed in the window frame in question." The Court of Appeal found the instruction proper and affirmed.

The *Nible* court stated the precise issue before it as follows: "No California authority has considered whether the penetration of a window screen, without penetration of the plane formed by the window beyond, constitutes an entry within the meaning of [section] 459." The defendant in *Nible* actually sought to *invoke* the air space test of *Ravenscroft*, arguing the window, and not the screen, marked the outer boundary of the air space of the victim's apartment. The *Nible* court initially agreed that *Ravenscroft*'s air space test was applicable but concluded it was of no avail to defendant because "it is reasonable to conclude that a window screen contains the outer boundary of a building's air space, especially when, as here, the window was left open."

Unfortunately, the *Nible* court then continued: "However it might be applied here, in our view the 'air space' test, although useful in some situations, *is inadequate as a comprehensive test for determining when a burglarious entry occurs.*" (Italics added.) As a result of that statement, the *Nible* court's ensuing analysis could be mistakenly understood, not merely as a test for determining the outer physical boundary of a burglarized structure's air space, which was the precise factual question before that court, but as a test for redefining the broader concept of what constitutes a burglarious entry generally in all cases. The Court of Appeal in this case astutely recognized this nuance, limited *Nible*'s analysis to its facts, found the air space test of *Ravenscroft* the commonly approved test and the one applicable here for establishing the element of burglarious entry, and further recognized *Ravenscroft* remains good law even though the *Nible* court had gone beyond its own facts in unnecessarily questioning *Ravenscroft*'s rationale.

Given this background, the *Nible* court's analysis must be read, and its holding understood, in light of the facts and limited legal question before that court. *Nible* states that, "the ultimate test of whether a burglarious entry has occurred must focus on the protection the owners or inhabitants of a structure reasonably expect." Under this test, "[t]he proper question is whether the nature of a structure's composition is such that a reasonable person would expect some protection from unauthorized intrusions." The *Nible* court concluded that the penetration of an outer window screen constituted an "entry" under this test because "'the screen door [or window] is a part of the house on which the occupants rely for protection and [the penetration of the screen] is a violation of the security of the dwelling house which is the peculiar gravamen of a burglarious breaking.'"

The Court of Appeal in this case, in discussing and contrasting the holding of *Nible* with the general air space test formulated in *Ravenscroft*, correctly questioned the applicability of *Nible*'s holding "except in cases where the boundaries of the building's air space are difficult to determine." The Court of Appeal went on to conclude that even under the *Nible* test, defendant's actions here constituted a burglarious "entry" because "protection of the cashier is precisely the reason why the structure has a walk-up window and chute, rather than a door, or open window. Although it is expected and authorized to use the chute to pass checks to the cashier, [defendant] passed the check through with felonious intent unknown and unendorsed by the occupants."

I agree with the conclusion of the Court of Appeal that defendant's act of passing the forged check through the security chute plainly established the requisite entry for burglary under the applicable air space test of *Ravenscroft*. As the Court of Appeal aptly observed, "[t]he insertion of a forged check through the chute of a walk-up window is at least as intrusive as inserting an ATM card into a machine." Obviously, the check-cashing facility is a commercial establishment that extends only a conditional invitation to its patrons to transact lawful business through its security chute—*i.e.*, the tendering of valid checks to the teller through the chute for cashing. The facility clearly does not extend an invitation to persons like defendant to pass forged checks through its security chute in an attempt to gain possession of and thereby steal cash from the business.

If we truly had occasion to apply *Nible*'s rationale and holding here—*i.e.*, if defendant was questioning whether the air space of the chute was part-and-parcel of the air space of the check cashing facility premises generally—then it would have to be concluded that the air space of the check-cashing facility *includes* the air space within its security chute, through which it transacts all of its business with patrons who are not invited or permitted to physically enter the business's premises. In short, defendant's burglary conviction on these facts squares with the holding in *Nible*. Nor do I understand defendant to even be arguing that the air space within the security chute is not part of the air space of the check cashing facility, generally speaking. Instead, defendant is seemingly urging that the passing of the forged check into the air space of the chute for some other reason was not the equivalent of the use of a tool or instrument, as an extension of his arm or body, to gain access through the outer boundary of the business premises and effectuate a burglarious entry. Defendant is unable to articulate a convincing basis for this position. The majority fares no better.

The majority's holding today will lead to anomalous results. Under the majority's rationale, if a person inserts a stolen ATM card into an ATM machine affixed to the exterior wall of a bank and succeeds in unlawfully withdrawing money from the cardholder's account, such is *not* burglary because the passing of the ATM card through the ATM machine is "not an unauthorized entry of the sort the burglary statute is designed to prevent." But if that same person *walks into* the bank building with the stolen ATM card in hand, intending to perpetrate the same unlawful transaction at an ATM machine located *inside* the bank lobby, he *has* committed burglary at the moment he crosses the threshold of the building, and he can be arrested for that crime once inside the bank even if he never approaches the ATM or attempts the fraudulent transaction. The same anomalous results would obtain in comparing a business that has a walk-up window or security chute affixed to an external wall of the building, and one that admits patrons into a lobby but then requires them to transact business with their employees through openings in a secured or windowed counter area. In the former type of business, under the majority's rationale, the tendering of a forged check or similar fraudulent document through the external security chute is not burglary even if the suspect makes off with the loot, whereas in the latter business setting, a burglary would be complete when the suspect physically enters the lobby premises with felonious intent, without any further action necessary on his part to perfect his burglarious entry.

Yet another anomalous result that will flow from the majority's holding is that an *incomplete and unsuccessful attempt* at a forcible entry (*i.e.*, inserting a crowbar or other burglar tool into the air space of a window, security chute mechanism, or ATM) will suffice as a legally sufficient entry for burglary, whereas a *completed and successful* nonforcible entry with a "tool or instrument" such as a stolen ATM card or forged check, by which the suspect nets his loot and makes his getaway, will *not*. The irony here is that those very businesses which, by their nature, are particularly vulnerable to theft and burglary, and for that reason protect themselves with anti-crime devices such as walk-up windows, security chutes, or card access machines requiring passwords, will receive less protection in our courts if the burglar is caught and an attempt made to bring him to justice.

The majority find it significant that "in the present case, our reversal of defendant's conviction of burglary does not affect his convictions of forgery and receiving stolen property, or his resulting sentence [therefor]." I fail to see the significance of this observation. The statutes proscribing check forgery and receiving stolen property have as their primary underlying purpose protection of the security interests of the original maker of the check and his bank. Defendant did not make the forged check out to himself, endorse it in his real name, or attempt to deposit it into his own bank account. Under such facts, forgery, and perhaps only forgery, would be his crime. Here, in contrast, defendant made the stolen check out to a fictitious payee and endorsed it with that fictitious name. From a practical standpoint, the forged check, as made out, had no value to defendant other than as a "tool or instrument" useable for the dual purpose of breaching the security system of the check-cashing facility (when it was accepted through the air space of the walk-up security chute) and as a paper "hook" to grab the loot (had the teller been tricked into cashing the forged check and handing money out to him through the chute).

Moreover, lest we forget, *every burglary* by definition has as an integral element the suspect's intent to commit a felony within the targeted premises. It would seem to beg the question to suggest, as does the majority, that conviction of burglary is unnecessary where conviction of the target felony (here forgery and receiving stolen property) is otherwise obtainable. Such circular reasoning would preclude the charging and conviction of burglary in many if not most burglary cases where the target felony (i.e., larceny) has been completed.

In sum, defendant's use of the forged check was no different than if he had "put a hand or a hook in at a window to draw out goods" from the victimized business, a clearly "burglarious entr[y]" even at common law. (See 4 BLACKSTONE'S COMMENTARIES 227.)

I would affirm the judgment of the Court of Appeal in its entirety.

CHIN and BROWN, J.J., concur.

Questions and Notes

1. Burglary, like kidnapping (*see Beatty* in Chapter 4, *supra*) has the potential to allow a multiplicity of charges to emanate from the same offense. And, like kidnapping, can turn on hairline distinctions.

2. If Davis had met the teller in the street, handed her the check, and asked her to bring the proceeds outside, neither the majority nor the dissent would have upheld

a burglary conviction. On the other hand, if Davis had conducted his transaction inside of the bank, both opinions would have upheld a burglary conviction. Which opinion do you think is more anomalous? Why?

3. Under the dissenting opinion's view, why wouldn't a check mailed to the bank constitute burglary?

4. Ideally, should Davis have been convicted of burglary? Should Ravenscroft? Should Nible? Where should the line be drawn? Why?

Chapter 8

Mens Rea

A. In General

The concepts of *mens rea* (guilty mind) and *actus reus* (evil act) are central to the criminal law. Almost nothing can be criminal without the confluence of these basic ingredients. Because of the centrality of these concepts, many casebooks start with them. This book started with specific crimes, not because *mens rea* and *actus reus* are not central, but because they can be better understood by referring to prior cases.

In homicide, for example, we saw that a specific intent to kill was usually necessary for first degree murder. A lesser intent, the intent to inflict serious injury or extreme recklessness, suffices for second degree murder. The even lesser intent of recklessness or gross negligence suffices for involuntary manslaughter.

Similarly, as will become apparent during your reading of the *Morissette* case, theft crimes are paradigm examples of what *mens rea* is all about. As you read this "profoundly insignificant case" think about why it has become a criminal law "classic."

Morissette v. United States
342 U.S. 246 (1952)

Mr. Justice JACKSON delivered the opinion of the Court.

This would have remained a profoundly insignificant case to all except its immediate parties had it not been so tried and submitted to the jury as to raise questions both fundamental and far-reaching in federal criminal law, for which reason we granted certiorari.

On a large tract of uninhabited and untilled land in a wooded and sparsely populated area of Michigan, the Government established a practice bombing range over which the Air Force dropped simulated bombs at ground targets. These bombs consisted of a metal cylinder about forty inches long and eight inches across, filled with sand and enough black powder to cause a smoke puff by which the strike could be located. At various places about the range signs read "Danger—Keep Out—Bombing Range." Nevertheless, the range was known as good deer country and was extensively hunted.

Spent bomb casings were cleared from the targets and thrown into piles "so that they will be out of the way." They were not sacked or piled in any order but were dumped in heaps, some of which had been accumulating for four years or upwards, were exposed to the weather and rusting away.

Morissette, in December of 1948, went hunting in this area but did not get a deer. He thought to meet expenses of the trip by salvaging some of these casings. He loaded three tons of them on his truck and took them to a nearby farm, where they were flattened by driving a tractor over them. After expending this labor and trucking them to market in Flint, he realized $84.

Morissette, by occupation, is a fruit stand operator in summer and a trucker and scrap iron collector in winter. An honorably discharged veteran of World War II, he enjoys a good name among his neighbors and has had no blemish on his record more disreputable than a conviction for reckless driving.

The loading, crushing and transporting of these casings were all in broad daylight, in full view of passers-by, without the slightest effort at concealment. When an investigation was started, Morissette voluntarily, promptly and candidly told the whole story to the authorities, saying that he had no intention of stealing but thought the property was abandoned, unwanted and considered of no value to the Government. He was indicted, however, on the charge that he "did unlawfully, wilfully and knowingly steal and convert" property of the United States of the value of $84, in violation of 18 U.S.C. §641, 18 U.S.C.A. §641, which provides that "whoever embezzles, steals, purloins, or knowingly converts" government property is punishable by fine and imprisonment.[2] Morissette was convicted and sentenced to imprisonment for two months or to pay a fine of $200. The Court of Appeals affirmed, one judge dissenting.

On his trial, Morissette, as he had at all times told investigating officers, testified that from appearances he believed the casings were cast-off and abandoned, that he did not intend to steal the property, and took it with no wrongful or criminal intent. The trial court, however, was unimpressed, and ruled: "(H)e took it because he thought it was abandoned and he knew he was on government property.... That is no defense.... I don't think anybody can have the defense they thought the property was abandoned on another man's piece of property." The court stated: "I will not permit you to show this man thought it was abandoned.... I hold in this case that there is no question of abandoned property." The court refused to submit or to allow counsel to argue to the jury whether Morissette acted with innocent

---

2. 18 U.S.C. §641, 18 U.S.C.A. §641, so far as pertinent, reads:
   "Whoever embezzles, steals, purloins, or knowingly converts to his use or the use of another, or without authority, sells, conveys or disposes of any record, voucher, money, or thing of value of the United States or of any department or agency thereof, or any property made or being made under contract for the United States or any department or agency thereof;
   "Shall be fined not more than $10,000 or imprisoned not more than ten years, or both; but if the value of such property does not exceed the sum of $100, he shall be fined not more than $1,000 or imprisoned not more than one year, or both."

intention. It charged: "And I instruct you that if you believe the testimony of the government in this case, he intended to take it. . . . He had no right to take this property. . . . (A)nd it is no defense to claim that it was abandoned, because it was on private property. . . . And I instruct you to this effect: That if this young man took this property (and he says he did), without any permission (he says he did), that was on the property of the United States Government (he says it was), that it was of the value of one cent or more (and evidently it was), that he is guilty of the offense charged here. If you believe the government, he is guilty. . . . The question on intent is whether or not he intended to take the property. He says he did. Therefore, if you believe either side, he is guilty." Petitioner's counsel contended, "But the taking must have been with a felonious intent." The court ruled, however: "That is presumed by his own act."

The Court of Appeals suggested that "greater restraint in expression should have been exercised," but affirmed the conviction because, "As we have interpreted the statute, appellant was guilty of its violation beyond a shadow of doubt, as evidenced even by his own admissions." Its construction of the statute is that it creates several separate and distinct offenses, one being knowing conversion of government property. The court ruled that this particular offense requires no element of criminal intent.

I.

The contention that an injury can amount to a crime only when inflicted by intention is no provincial or transient notion. It is as universal and persistent in mature systems of law as belief in freedom of the human will and a consequent ability and duty of the normal individual to choose between good and evil.[4] A relation between some mental element and punishment for a harmful act is almost as instinctive as the child's familiar exculpatory "But I didn't mean to," and has afforded the rational basis for a tardy and unfinished substitution of deterrence and reformation in place of retaliation and vengeance as the motivation for public prosecution. Unqualified acceptance of this doctrine by English common law in the Eighteenth Century was indicated by Blackstone's sweeping statement that to constitute any crime there must first be a "vicious will." Common-law commentators of the Nineteenth Century early pronounced the same principle, although a few exceptions not relevant to our present problem came to be recognized.

Crime, as a compound concept, generally constituted only from concurrence of an evil-meaning mind with an evil-doing hand, was congenial to an intense

---

4. For a brief history and philosophy of this concept in Biblical, Greek, Roman, Continental and Anglo-American law see Radin, *Intent, Criminal*, 8 ENCYC. SOC. SCI. 126. For more extensive treatment of the development in English Law, *see* 2 POLLOCK AND MAITLAND, HISTORY OF ENGLISH LAW, 448–511. "Historically, our substantive criminal law is based upon a theory of punishing the vicious will. It postulates a free agent confronted with a choice between doing right and doing wrong and choosing freely to do wrong." Pound, *Introduction to Sayre*, CASES ON CRIMINAL LAW (1927).

individualism and took deep and early root in American soil.[9] As the state codified the common law of crimes, even if their enactments were silent on the subject,
their courts assumed that the omission did not signify disapproval of the principle
but merely recognized that intent was so inherent in the idea of the offense that it
required no statutory affirmation. Courts, with little hesitation or division, found
an implication of the requirement as to offenses that were taken over from the common law. The unanimity with which they have adhered to the central thought that
wrongdoing must be conscious to be criminal is emphasized by the variety, disparity and confusion of their definitions of the requisite but elusive mental element.
However, courts of various jurisdictions, and for the purposes of different offenses,
have devised working formulae, if not scientific ones, for the instruction of juries
around such terms as "felonious intent," "criminal intent," "malice aforethought,"
"guilty knowledge," "fraudulent intent," "wilfulness," "*scienter*," to denote guilty
knowledge, or "*mens rea*," to signify an evil purpose or mental culpability. By use
or combination of these various tokens, they have sought to protect those who were
not blameworthy in mind from conviction of infamous common-law crimes.

Stealing, larceny, and its variants and equivalents, were among the earliest
offenses known to the law that existed before legislation; they are invasions of rights
of property which stir a sense of insecurity in the whole community and arouse
public demand for retribution, the penalty is high and, when a sufficient amount is
involved, the infamy is that of a felony, which, says Maitland, is ". . . as bad a word as
you can give to man or thing." State courts of last resort, on whom fall the heaviest
burden of interpreting criminal law in this country, have consistently retained the
requirement of intent in larceny-type offenses. If any state has deviated, the exception has neither been called to our attention nor disclosed by our research.

Congress, therefore, omitted any express prescription of criminal intent from
the enactment before us in the light of an unbroken course of judicial decision in all
constituent states of the Union holding intent inherent in this class of offense, even
when not expressed in a statute. Congressional silence as to mental elements in an
Act merely adopting into federal statutory law a concept of crime already so well
defined in common law and statutory interpretation by the states may warrant quite
contrary inferences than the same silence in creating an offense new to general law,
for whose definition the courts have no guidance except the Act.

The Government asks us by a feat of construction radically to change the weights
and balances in the scales of justice. The purpose and obvious effect of doing away
with the requirement of a guilty intent is to ease the prosecution's path to conviction, to strip the defendant of such benefit as he derived at common law from innocence of evil purpose, and to circumscribe the freedom heretofore allowed juries.

---

9. HOLMES, THE COMMON LAW, considers intent in the chapter on The Criminal Law, and
earlier makes the pithy observation: "Even a dog distinguishes between being stumbled over and
being kicked." p. 3.

Such a manifest impairment of the immunities of the individual should not be extended to common-law crimes on judicial initiative.

The spirit of the doctrine which denies to the federal judiciary power to create crimes forthrightly admonishes that we should not enlarge the reach of enacted crimes by constituting them from anything less than the incriminating components contemplated by the words used in the statute. And where Congress borrows terms of art in which are accumulated the legal tradition and meaning of centuries of practice, it presumably knows and adopts the cluster of ideas that were attached to each borrowed word in the body of learning from which it was taken and the meaning its use will convey to the judicial mind unless otherwise instructed. In such case, absence of contrary direction may be taken as satisfaction with widely accepted definitions, not as a departure from them.

We hold that mere omission from § 641 of any mention of intent will not be construed as eliminating that element from the crimes denounced.

II.

It is suggested, however, that the history and purposes of § 641 imply something more affirmative as to elimination of intent from at least one of the offenses charged under it in this case. The argument does not contest that criminal intent is retained in the offenses of embezzlement, stealing and purloining, as incorporated into this section. But it is urged that Congress joined with those, as a new, separate and distinct offense, knowingly to convert government property, under circumstances which imply that it is an offense in which the mental element of intent is not necessary.

Congress has been alert to what often is a decisive function of some mental element in crime. It has seen fit to prescribe that an evil state of mind, described variously in one or more such terms as "intentional," "willful," "knowing," "fraudulent" or "malicious," will make criminal an otherwise indifferent act, or increase the degree of the offense or its punishment. Also, it has at times required a specific intent or purpose which will require some specialized knowledge or design for some evil beyond the common-law intent to do injury. The law under some circumstances recognizes good faith or blameless intent as a defense, partial defense, or as an element to be considered in mitigation of punishment. And treason—the one crime deemed grave enough for definition in our Constitution itself—requires not only the duly witnessed overt act of aid and comfort to the enemy but also the mental element of disloyalty or adherence to the enemy. In view of the care that has been bestowed upon the subject, it is significant that we have not found, nor has our attention been directed to, any instance in which Congress has expressly eliminated the mental element from a crime taken over from the common law.

Congress, by the language of this section, has been at pains to incriminate only "knowing" conversions. But, at common law, there are unwitting acts which constitute conversions. In the civil tort, except for recovery of exemplary damages, the defendant's knowledge, intent, motive, mistake, and good faith are generally

irrelevant. If one takes property which turns out to belong to another, his innocent intent will not shield him from making restitution or indemnity, for his well-
meaning may not be allowed to deprive another of his own.

Had the statute applied to conversions without qualification, it would have made
crimes of all unwitting, inadvertent and unintended conversions. Knowledge, of
course, is not identical with intent and may not have been the most apt words of
limitation. But knowing conversion requires more than knowledge that defendant
was taking the property into his possession. He must have had knowledge of the
facts, though not necessarily the law, that made the taking a conversion. In the
case before us, whether the mental element that Congress required be spoken of
as knowledge or as intent, would not seem to alter its bearing on guilt, for it is not
apparent how Morissette could have knowingly or intentionally converted property
that he did not know could be converted, as would be the case if it was in fact abandoned or if he truly believed it to be abandoned and unwanted property. It is said,
and at first blush the claim has plausibility, that, if we construe the statute to require
a mental element as part of criminal conversion, it becomes a meaningless duplica-
tion of the offense of stealing, and that conversion can be given meaning only by
interpreting it to disregard intention. But here again a broader view of the evolution
of these crimes throws a different light on the legislation.

It is not surprising if there is considerable overlapping in the embezzlement,
stealing, purloining and knowing conversion grouped in this statute. What has concerned codifiers of the larceny-type offense is that gaps or crevices have separated
particular crimes of this general class and guilty men have escaped through the
breaches. The books contain a surfeit of cases drawing fine distinctions between
slightly different circumstances under which one may obtain wrongful advantages
from another's property. The codifiers wanted to reach all such instances. Probably
every stealing is a conversion, but certainly not every knowing conversion is a stealing. "To steal means to take away from one in lawful possession without right with
the intention to keep *wrongfully*." (Italics added.) *Irving Trust Co. v. Leff*, 253 N.Y.
359, 364, 171 N.E. 569, 571. Conversion, however, may be consummated without
any intent to keep and without any wrongful taking, where the initial possession by
the converter was entirely lawful. Conversion may include misuse or abuse of property. It may reach use in an unauthorized manner or to an unauthorized extent of
property placed in one's custody for limited use. Money rightfully taken into one's
custody may be converted without any intent to keep or embezzle it merely by com-
mingling it with the custodian's own, if he was under a duty to keep it separate and
intact. It is not difficult to think of intentional and knowing abuses and unauthorized uses of government property that might be knowing conversions but which
could not be reached as embezzlement, stealing or purloining. Knowing conversion
adds significantly to the range of protection of government property without interpreting it to punish unwitting conversions.

The purpose which we here attribute to Congress parallels that of codifiers of
common law in England and in the States and demonstrates that the serious problem

in drafting such a statute is to avoid gaps and loopholes between offenses. It is significant that the English and State codifiers have tried to cover the same type of conduct that we are suggesting as the purpose of Congress here, without, however, departing from the common-law tradition that these are crimes of intendment.

We find no grounds for inferring any affirmative instruction from Congress to eliminate intent from any offense with which this defendant was charged.

III.

As we read the record, this case was tried on the theory that even if criminal intent were essential its presence (a) should be decided by the court (b) as a presumption of law, apparently conclusive, (c) predicated upon the isolated act of taking rather than upon all of the circumstances. In each of these respects we believe the trial court was in error.

Where intent of the accused is an ingredient of the crime charged, its existence is a question of fact which must be submitted to the jury. State court authorities cited to the effect that intent is relevant in larcenous crimes are equally emphatic and uniform that it is a jury issue. The settled practice and its reason are well stated by Judge Andrews in *People v. Flack*, 125 N.Y. 324, 334, 26 N.E. 267, 270, 11 L.R.A. 807:

> "It is alike the general rule of law, and the dictate of natural justice, that to constitute guilt there must be not only a wrongful act, but a criminal intention. Under our system, (unless in exceptional cases) both must be found by the jury to justify a conviction for crime. However clear the proof may be, or however incontrovertible may seem to the judge to be the inference of a criminal intention, the question of intent can never be ruled as a question of law, but must always be submitted to the jury. Jurors may be perverse, the ends of justice may be defeated by unrighteous verdicts; but so long as the functions of the judge and jury are distinct, the one responding to the law, the other to the facts, neither can invade the province of the other without destroying the significance of trial by court and jury. . . ."

It follows that the trial court may not withdraw or prejudge the issue by instruction that the law raises a presumption of intent from an act. It often is tempting to cast in terms of a "presumption" a conclusion which a court thinks probable from given facts. The Supreme Court of Florida, for example, in a larceny case, from selected circumstances which are present in this case, has declared a presumption of exactly opposite effect from the one announced by the trial court here: ". . . But where the taking is open and there is no subsequent attempt to conceal the property, and no denial, but an avowal, of the taking, a strong presumption arises that there was no felonious intent, which must be repelled by clear and convincing evidence before a conviction is authorized. . . ." *Kemp v. State*, 146 Fla. 101, 104, 200 So. 368, 369.

We think presumptive intent has no place in this case. [T]he conclusion supplied by presumption in this instance was one of intent to steal the casings, and it was based on the mere fact that defendant took them. The court thought the only question was, "Did he intend to take the property?" That the removal of them was a conscious and intentional act was admitted. But that isolated fact is not an adequate basis on which the jury should find the criminal intent to steal or knowingly convert, that is, wrongfully to deprive another of possession of property. Whether that intent existed, the jury must determine, nor only from the act of taking, but from that together with defendant's testimony and all of the surrounding circumstances.

Of course, the jury, considering Morissette's awareness that these casings were on government property, his failure to seek any permission for their removal and his self-interest as a witness, might have disbelieved his profession of innocent intent and concluded that his assertion of a belief that the casings were abandoned was an afterthought. Had the jury convicted on proper instructions it would be the end of the matter. But juries are not bound by what seems inescapable logic to judges. They might have concluded that the heaps of spent casings left in the hinterland to rust away presented an appearance of unwanted and abandoned junk, and that lack of any conscious deprivation of property or intentional injury was indicated by Morissette's good character, the openness of the taking, crushing and transporting of the casings, and the candor with which it was all admitted. They might have refused to brand Morissette as a thief. Had they done so, that too would have been the end of the matter.

Reversed.

Questions and Notes

1. Given that Morissette unquestionably appropriated that which he knew was not his, why is the Court so concerned about his state of mind?

2. Would (should) Morissette be convicted on retrial if the evidence shows that he wasn't sure whether the casings were abandoned, but took them anyway?

3. Would (should) *Morissette* have been decided the same way if the statute had forbade "conversion" rather than "knowing conversion"?

4. If you were a juror on retrial, how do you think you would decide the case? Why?

5. Why do you suppose the trial judge's instructions were so pro-prosecution? If you had been the prosecutor, would you have been happy with those instructions?

6. The common law has various imprecise ways of defining *mens rea*. As you read *Pembliton*, think of the multifaceted definitions that can be given to the term "malicious."

Regina v. Pembliton
12 Cox Crim. Cas. 607 (Cr. App. 1874)

Case stated by the recorder of Wolverhampton.

On the night of the 6th of December 1873, the prisoner was drinking with others at a public-house called "The Grand Turk," kept by the prosecutor. About eleven o'clock, p.m., the whole party were turned out of the house for being disorderly, and they then began to fight in the street, and near the prosecutor's window, where a crowd of from forty to fifty persons collected. The prisoner, after fighting some time with persons in the crowd, separated himself from them and removed to the other side of the street, where he picked up a large stone and threw it at the persons he had been fighting with. The stone passed over the heads of those persons and struck a large plate-glass window in the prosecutor's house and broke it, thereby doing damage to the extent of 7l 12s. 9d. The jury, after hearing evidence on both sides, found that the prisoner threw the stone which broke the window, but that he threw it at the people he had been fighting with, intending to strike one or more of them with it, but not intending to break the window, and they returned a verdict of "guilty," whereupon the learned recorder respited the sentence and admitted the prisoner to bail, and prayed the judgment of the Court for Crown Cases Reserved, whether upon the facts stated and the finding of the jury the prisoner was rightly convicted or not.

[The statute provided: "Whosoever shall unlawfully and maliciously commit any damage, injury, or spoil to or upon any real or personal property whatsoever, either of a public or a private nature, for which no punishment is hereinbefore provided, the damage, injury, or spoil being to an amount exceeding five pounds, shall be guilty of a misdemeanour, and being convicted thereof shall be liable at the discretion of the Court to be imprisoned for any term not exceeding two years, with or without hand labour; and in case any such offence shall be committed between the hours of nine of the clock in the evening and six of the clock in the next morning, shall be liable at the discretion of the Court to be kept in penal servitude for any term not exceeding five years, and not less than three, or to be imprisoned for any term not exceeding two years, with or without hard labour."]

Lord Coleridge, C.J. I am of opinion that the conviction should be quashed. The facts of the case are that there was fighting going on in the streets of Wolverhampton near the prosecutor's house, and the prisoner, after fighting some time, separated himself from the crowd and threw a stone, which missed the person he aimed at, but struck and broke a window, doing damage to the extent of upwards of 5l. The question is, whether under an indictment for unlawfully and maliciously injuring the property of the owner of the plate glass window, these facts will support the indictment when coupled with the other facts found by the jury, that the prisoner threw the stone at the people intending to strike one or more of them, but not intending to break a window. I am of opinion that the evidence does not support the conviction. The indictment is under the 24 & 25 Vict. c. 97, s. 51, which deals with malicious injuries to property, and the section expressly says that the act is to be unlawful and malicious. Without saying that if the case had been left to them in a different way the conviction could not have been supported, if, on these facts, the jury had come to a conclusion that the prisoner was reckless of the consequence of his act, and might reasonably have expected that it would result in breaking the window, it is sufficient to say that the jury have expressly found the contrary. I do not say anything to throw doubt on the rule under the common law in cases of murder which has been referred to, but the principles laid down in such case have no application to the offence we have to consider.

BLACKBURN, J. I am of the same opinion. We have not now to consider what would be malice aforethought to bring a given case within the common law definition of murder; here the statute says that the act must be unlawful and malicious, and malice may be defined to be "where any person wilfully does an act injurious to another without lawful excuse." Can this man be considered, on the case submitted to us, as having wilfully broken a pane of glass? The jury might perhaps have found on this evidence that the act was malicious, because they might have found that the prisoner knew that the natural consequence of his act would be to break the glass, and although that was not his wish, yet that he was reckless whether he did it or not; but the jury have not so found, and I think it is impossible to say in this case that the prisoner has maliciously done an act which he did not intend to do.

LUSH, J. I am of the same opinion. On these findings we have no alternative. The jury might have found otherwise, but taking this finding I cannot say that there was an intent either actual or constructive, and "malicious" certainly must be taken to imply an intention either actual or constructive.

Conviction quashed.

Questions and Notes

1. The criminal law has a doctrine called "transferred intent." Under this doctrine, if A throws a stone at B intending to injure him, but she misses B and hits C, a person against whom she had no animus and did not intend to hit, A is guilty of assaulting C. Why didn't this doctrine apply in *Pembliton*?

2. In what sense was Pembliton's behavior not malicious? Throwing a stone at somebody's head certainly meets the dictionary definition of "malicious."

3. Under *Pembliton*, in order to be malicious, is it necessary that the defendant: (a) desire to break the window, (b) know that he is going to break the window, (c) know that there is a substantial probability that he is going to break the window, or (d) ought to know that there is a substantial likelihood that he will break the window?

4. The common (and statutory) law contains an abundance of imprecise terms like "malicious." The MPC sought to simplify the different states of mind (*see* Appendix A, § 2.02) by reducing them to four: purposely (conscious desire to cause result); knowingly (practically certain to cause result); recklessly (consciously disregarding a substantial and unjustifiable risk); and negligently (disregarding a substantial and unjustifiable risk under circumstances manifesting a gross deviation from the standard of care expected from a reasonable person). The MPC further provides that unless otherwise stated, each element of an offense shall require recklessness.

5. The aim of the MPC was to eliminate the imprecision of the common law and clearly indicate to prospective criminals exactly what is expected of them. As you read *Jewell*, consider how well the approach has succeeded.

United States v. Jewell
532 F.2d 697 (9th Cir. 1976)

Before Chambers, Koelsch, Browning, Duniway, Ely, Hufstedler, Wright, Trask, Choy, Goodwin, Wallace, Sneed and Kennedy, Circuit Judges.

Browning, Circuit Judge:

Appellant defines "knowingly" in 21 U.S.C. §§ 841 and 960 to require that positive knowledge that a controlled substance is involved be established as an element of each offense. On the basis of this interpretation, appellant argues that it was reversible error to instruct the jury that the defendant could be convicted upon proof beyond a reasonable doubt that if he did not have positive knowledge that a controlled substance was concealed in the automobile he drove over the border, it was solely and entirely because of the conscious purpose on his part to avoid learning the truth. The majority concludes that this contention is wrong in principle, and has no support in authority or in the language or legislative history of the statute.

It is undisputed that appellant entered the United States driving an automobile in which 110 pounds of marihuana worth $6,250 had been concealed in a secret compartment between the trunk and rear seat. Appellant testified that he did not know the marijuana was present. There was circumstantial evidence from which the jury could infer that appellant had positive knowledge of the presence of the marihuana, and that his contrary testimony was false. On the other hand there was evidence from which the jury could conclude that appellant spoke the truth that although appellant knew of the presence of the secret compartment and had knowledge of facts indicating that it contained marijuana, he deliberately avoided positive knowledge of the presence of the contraband to avoid responsibility in the event of discovery. If the jury concluded the latter was indeed the situation, and if positive knowledge is required to convict, the jury would have no choice consistent with its oath but to find appellant not guilty even though he deliberately contrived his lack of positive knowledge. Appellant urges this view. The trial court rejected the premise that only positive knowledge would suffice, and properly so.

Appellant tendered an instruction that to return a guilty verdict the jury must find that the defendant knew he was in possession of marihuana. The trial judge rejected the instruction because it suggested that "absolutely, positively, he has to know that it's there." The court said, "I think, in this case, it's not too sound an instruction because we have evidence that if the jury believes it, they'd be justified in finding he actually didn't know what it was he didn't because he didn't want to find it."

The court instructed the jury that "knowingly" meant voluntarily and intentionally and not by accident or mistake. The court told the jury that the government must prove beyond a reasonable doubt that the defendant "knowingly" brought the marihuana into the United States. The court continued: The Government can complete their burden of proof by proving, beyond a reasonable doubt, that if the defendant was not actually aware that there was marijuana in the vehicle he was driving when he entered the United States his ignorance in that regard was solely and entirely a result of his having made a conscious purpose to disregard the nature of that which was in the vehicle, with a conscious purpose to avoid learning the truth.

The legal premise of these instructions is firmly supported by leading commentators here and in England. Professor Rollin M. Perkins writes, "One with a deliberate antisocial purpose in mind . . . may deliberately 'shut his eyes' to avoid knowing what would otherwise be obvious to view. In such cases, so far as criminal law is concerned, the person acts at his peril in this regard, and is treated as having 'knowledge' of the facts as they are ultimately discovered to be." J. Ll. J. Edwards, writing in 1954, introduced a survey of English cases with the statement, "For well-nigh a hundred years, it has been clear from the authorities that a person who deliberately shuts his eyes to an obvious means of knowledge has sufficient *mens rea* for an offence based on such words as . . . 'knowingly.'" Professor Glanville Williams states, on the basis both English and American authorities, "To the requirement of actual knowledge there is one strictly limited exception. . . . (T)he rule is that if a party has his suspicion aroused but then deliberately omits to make further enquiries, because he wishes to remain in ignorance, he is deemed to have knowledge." Professor Williams concludes, "The rule that willful blindness is equivalent to knowledge is essential, and is found throughout the criminal law."

The substantive justification for the rule is that deliberate ignorance and positive knowledge are equally culpable. The textual justification is that in common understanding one "knows" facts of which he is less than absolutely certain. To act "knowingly," therefore, is not necessarily to act only with positive knowledge, but also to act with an awareness of the high probability of the existence of the fact in question. When such awareness is present, "positive" knowledge is not required.

This is the analysis adopted in the Model Penal Code. Section 2.02(7) states: "When knowledge of the existence of a particular fact is an element of an offense, such knowledge is established if a person is aware of a high probability of its existence, unless he actually believes that it does not exist." As the Comment to this provision explains, "Paragraph (7) deals with the situation British commentators have denominated 'willful blindness' or 'connivance,' the case of the actor who is aware of the probable existence of a material fact but does not satisfy himself that it does not in fact exist."

"Deliberate ignorance" instructions have been approved in prosecutions under criminal statutes prohibiting "knowing" conduct by the Courts of Appeals of the Second, Sixth, Seventh, and Tenth Circuits. In many other cases, Courts of Appeals reviewing the sufficiency of evidence have approved the premise that "knowingly" in criminal statutes is not limited to positive knowledge, but includes the state of mind of one who does not possess positive knowledge only because he consciously avoided it.

Appellant's narrow interpretation of "knowingly" is inconsistent with the Drug Control Act's general purpose to deal more effectively "with the growing menace of drug abuse in the United States." Holding that this term introduces a requirement of positive knowledge would make deliberate ignorance a defense. It cannot be doubted that those who traffic in drugs would make the most of it. This is evident from the number of appellate decisions reflecting conscious avoidance of positive knowledge of the presence of contraband in the car driven by the defendant or in which he is a passenger, in the suitcase or package he carries, in the parcel concealed in his clothing.

It is no answer to say that in such cases the fact finder may infer positive knowledge. It is probable that many who performed the transportation function, essential to the drug traffic, can truthfully testify that they have no positive knowledge of the load they carry. Under appellant's interpretation of the statute, such persons will be convicted only if the fact finder errs in evaluating the credibility of the witness or deliberately disregards the law.

It begs the question to assert that a "deliberate ignorance" instruction permits the jury to convict without finding that the accused possessed the knowledge required by the statute. Such an assertion assumes that the statute requires positive knowledge. But the question is the meaning of the term "knowingly" in the statute. If it means positive knowledge, then, of course, nothing less will do. But if "knowingly" includes a mental state in which the defendant is aware that the fact in question is highly probable but consciously avoids enlightenment, the statute is satisfied by such proof.

It is worth emphasizing that the required state of mind differs from positive knowledge only so far as necessary to encompass a calculated effort to avoid the sanctions of the statute while violating its substance. A court can properly find wilful blindness only where it can almost be said that the defendant actually knew. In the language of the instruction in this case, the government must prove, "beyond a reasonable doubt, that if the defendant was not actually aware . . . his ignorance in that regard was solely and entirely a result of . . . a conscious purpose to avoid learning the truth."[21]

---

21. We do not suggest that the instruction given in this case was a model in all respects. The jury should have been instructed more directly (1) that the required knowledge is established if the accused is aware of a high probability of the existence of the fact in question, (2) unless he actually believes it does not exist.

The deficiency in the instruction does not require reversal, however. Appellant did not object to the instruction on this ground either below or in this court. Since both of the elements referred to are implied in the instruction, the deficiency in the instructions is not so substantial as to justify reversal for plain error. See *United States v. Dozier*, 522 F.2d 224, 228 (2d Cir. 1975) (on petition for rehearing).

Appellant did not argue below or in this court that the instruction did not require an awareness of a high probability that the controlled substance was present. An objection on this ground would

No legitimate interest of an accused is prejudiced by such a standard, and society's interest in a system of criminal law that is enforceable and that imposes sanctions upon all who are equally culpable requires it.

The conviction is affirmed.

ANTHONY M. KENNEDY, Circuit Judge, with whom ELY, HUFSTEDLER and WALLACE, Circuit Judges, join (dissenting).

The majority opinion justifies the conscious purpose jury instruction as an application of the wilful blindness doctrine recognized primarily by English authorities. A classic illustration of this doctrine is the connivance of an innkeeper who deliberately arranges not to go into his back room and thus avoids visual confirmation of the gambling he believes is taking place. The doctrine is commonly said to apply in deciding whether one who acquires property under suspicious circumstances should be charged with knowledge that it was stolen.

One problem with the wilful blindness doctrine is its bias towards visual means of acquiring knowledge. We may know facts from direct impressions of the other senses or by deduction from circumstantial evidence, and such knowledge is nonetheless "actual." Moreover, visual sense impressions do not consistently provide complete certainty.

---

have little merit. The instruction given (that "(appellant's) ignorance in that regard was solely and entirely the result of his having made a conscious purpose to disregard the nature of that which was in the vehicle") suggests that the accused must be aware of facts making the presence of the contraband will but certain. Only if the accused were aware of such facts could his ignorance of the presence of the marihuana be "*solely* and *entirely*" the result of his conscious purpose to avoid the truth. Under this instruction, neither reckless disregard nor suspicion followed by failure to make full inquiry would be enough.

Nor did appellant suggest in the court below or in this court that the instruction given was deficient because it failed to state specifically (as we think would have been preferable) that appellant could not be convicted if he actually believed there was no controlled substance in the car. The reason appellant does not raise this objection may be, again, that the instruction given includes the limitation by reasonable inference. If appellant were ignorant of the presence of contraband solely and entirely because he "made a conscious purpose to disregard the nature of that which was in the vehicle," as the instruction given requires, it would hardly be a realistic possibility that he might at the same time have entertained a good faith belief that there was no contraband present. Nor did the instruction permit the jury to convict on an "objective" rather than "subjective" theory of the knowledge requirement; that is, on the theory that appellant was chargeable with knowledge because a reasonable man would have inspected the car more thoroughly and discovered the contraband inside. *See United States v. Bright*, 517 F.2d 584, 587–88 (2d Cir. 1975).

The negligence theory was advanced by the government but was rejected by the trial court. The instruction given by the trial court required the jury to find that appellant had a deliberate purpose to avoid the truth. Moreover, the jury was expressly informed that an act was not done "knowingly" within the meaning of the statute if it was done by "mistake or accident or other innocent purpose."

In the circumstances of this case, it was not plain error requiring reversal for the instruction to fail to define knowledge explicitly in terms of an awareness of a high probability of the presence of the contraband and the absence of a belief that the contraband was not present.

Another problem is that the English authorities seem to consider wilful blindness a state of mind distinct from, but equally culpable as, "actual" knowledge. When a statute specifically requires knowledge as an element of a crime, however, the substitution of some other state of mind cannot be justified even if the court deems that both are equally blameworthy.

Finally, the wilful blindness doctrine is uncertain in scope. There is disagreement as to whether reckless disregard for the existence of a fact constitutes wilful blindness or some lesser degree of culpability. Some cases have held that a statute's scienter requirement is satisfied by the constructive knowledge imputed to one who simply fails to discharge a duty to inform himself. There is also the question of whether to use an "objective" test based on the reasonable man, or to consider the defendant's subjective belief as dispositive.

The approach adopted in section 2.02(7) of the Model Penal Code clarifies, and, in important ways restricts, the English doctrine:

> When knowledge of the existence of a particular fact is an element of an offense, such knowledge is established if a person is aware of a high probability of its existence, unless he actually believes that it does not exist.

This provision requires an awareness of a high probability that a fact exists, not merely a reckless disregard, or a suspicion followed by a failure to make further inquiry. It also establishes knowledge as a matter of subjective belief, an important safeguard against diluting the guilty state of mind required for conviction. It is important to note that section 2.02(7) is a definition of knowledge, not a substitute for it.

In light of the Model Penal Code's definition, the "conscious purpose" jury instruction is defective in three respects. First, it fails to mention the requirement that Jewell have been aware of a high probability that a controlled substance was in the car. It is not culpable to form "a conscious purpose to avoid learning the truth" unless one is aware of facts indicating a high probability of that truth. To illustrate, a child given a gift-wrapped package by his mother while on vacation in Mexico may form a conscious purpose to take it home without learning what is inside; yet his state of mind is totally innocent unless he is aware of a high probability that the package contains a controlled substance. Thus, a conscious purpose instruction is only proper when coupled with a requirement that one be aware of a high probability of the truth.

The second defect in the instruction as given is that it did not alert the jury that Jewell could not be convicted if he "actually believed" there was no controlled substance in the car. The failure to emphasize, as does the Model Penal Code, that subjective belief is the determinative factor, may allow a jury to convict on an objective theory of knowledge that a reasonable man should have inspected the car and would have discovered what was hidden inside. One recent decision reversed a jury instruction for this very deficiency failure to balance a conscious purpose instruction with a warning that the defendant could not be convicted if he actually believed to the contrary. *United States v. Bright*, 517 F.2d 584, 586–89 (2d Cir. 1975).

Third, the jury instruction clearly states that Jewell could have been convicted even if found ignorant or "not actually aware" that the car contained a controlled substance. This is unacceptable because true ignorance, no matter how unreasonable, cannot provide a basis for criminal liability when the statute requires knowledge. A proper jury instruction based on the Model Penal Code would be presented as a way of defining knowledge, and not as an alternative to it.

We do not agree with the majority that we can only reverse if the conscious purpose instruction constituted "plain error." Before the instruction was given, the defense counsel objected "strenuously" on the basis that the jury could convict Jewell for failure to make an adequate attempt to check out the car. When the trial judge rejected this argument, the defense counsel further requested that he "add an addendum" to the charge so the jury would understand it properly. The trial court rejected this suggestion as well, and cut off further argument, saying "The record may show your objection."

Although the defense counsel did not fully anticipate our analysis of the conscious purpose instruction, he came close. (1) He gave a reason for his objection that the instruction would allow conviction without proof of the scienter element. (2) He further suggested adding "an addendum" to warn the jury against misinterpreting the instruction. We believe these objections were sufficient to require reversal on appeal unless the deficiencies in the instruction were harmless error.

We do not question the sufficiency of the evidence in this case to support conviction by a properly-instructed jury. As with all states of mind, knowledge must normally be proven by circumstantial evidence. There is evidence which could support a conclusion that Jewell was aware of a high probability that the car contained a controlled substance and that he had no belief to the contrary. However, we cannot say that the evidence was so overwhelming that the erroneous jury instruction was harmless. Accordingly, we would reverse the judgment on this appeal.

Questions and Notes

1. How do the majority and the dissent differ? If you had been on the court, would you have sided with Judge Browning or Judge (future Justice) Kennedy? Why?

2. Does the concept of "willful blindness" reduce "knowingly" to "recklessly"? Is there any real difference between "knowingly" and "recklessly" anyway?

3. Is one who is willfully blind less culpable than another who knows that the vehicle contains drugs and transports them anyway? Assuming that you believe the wilfully blind person to be less culpable, are there nevertheless good reasons to punish him? What are they?

4. Professor Alan Michaels suggested that in a case like *Jewell*, the issue should be whether the government can prove that Jewell was aware of a substantial risk

that the package contained drugs, and would be willing to transport it even if it did. Professor Michaels calls this mental state "acceptance" and contends that it should be both a necessary and sufficient state of mind to justify a conviction in a case like Jewell. *See* Alan C. Michaels, *Acceptance: The Missing Mental State*, 71 S.C. L. Rev. 953 (1998). Do you agree? How is "acceptance" different from recklessness?

5. Although the MPC ordinarily punishes only behavior at least as culpable as reckless, there are times in which it authorizes punishment for negligence. To a lesser extent, it authorizes strict liability—that is, liability without fault. Many jurisdictions support liability without fault to a greater extent than the MPC. The next section focuses upon the issue of faultless and negligent liability, and the rationale therefor.

B. Liability without Fault

One would think that in a system of criminal justice as we know it, the concept of "liability without fault" or "strict liability" would be an oxymoron. Although culpability is not always the only factor or even the most significant factor, it is practically always relevant. Essentially this section is about why the phrase "always relevant" needs to be modified by the word "practically." Once again, the best explanation comes from Justice Jackson's opinion in the "profoundly insignificant" *Morissette* case.

Morissette v. United States
342 U.S. 246 (1952)

Mr. Justice JACKSON delivered the opinion of the Court.

[There are] offenses [that] belong to a category of another character, with very different antecedents and origins. The crimes there involved depend on no mental element but consist only of forbidden acts or omissions. This, while not expressed by the Court, is made clear from examination of a century-old but accelerating tendency, discernible both here and in England, to call into existence new duties and crimes which disregard any ingredient of intent. The industrial revolution multiplied the number of workmen exposed to injury from increasingly powerful and complex mechanisms, driven by freshly discovered sources of energy, requiring higher precautions by employers. Traffic of velocities, volumes and varieties unheard of came to subject the wayfarer to intolerable casualty risks if owners and drivers were not to observe new cares and uniformities of conduct. Congestion of cities and crowding of quarters called for health and welfare regulations undreamed of in simpler times. Wide distribution of goods became an instrument of wide distribution of harm when those who dispersed food, drink, drugs, and even securities, did not comply with reasonable standards of quality, integrity, disclosure and care. Such dangers have engendered increasingly numerous and detailed regulations which heighten the duties of those in control of particular industries, trades, properties or activities that affect public health, safety or welfare.

While many of these duties are sanctioned by a more strict civil liability, lawmakers, whether wisely or not, have sought to make such regulations more effective by invoking criminal sanctions to be applied by the familiar technique of criminal prosecutions and convictions. This has confronted the courts with a multitude of prosecutions, based on statutes or administrative regulations, for what have been aptly called 'public welfare offenses.' These cases do not fit neatly into any of such accepted classifications of common-law offenses, such as those against the state, the person, property, or public morals. Many of these offenses are not in the nature of positive aggressions or invasions, with which the common law so often dealt, but are in the nature of neglect where the law requires care, or inaction where it imposes a duty. Many violations of such regulations result in no direct or immediate injury to person or property but merely create the danger or probability of it which the law seeks to minimize. While such offenses do not threaten the security of the state in the manner of treason, they may be regarded as offenses against its authority, for their occurrence impairs the efficiency of controls deemed essential to the social order as presently constituted. In this respect, whatever the intent of the violator, the injury is the same, and the consequences are injurious or not according to fortuity. Hence, legislation applicable to such offenses, as a matter of policy, does not specify intent as a necessary element. The accused, if he does not will the violation, usually is in a position to prevent it with no more care than society might reasonably expect and no more exertion than it might reasonably exact from one who assumed his responsibilities. Also, penalties commonly are relatively small, and conviction does not grave damage to an offender's reputation. Under such considerations, courts have turned to construing statutes and regulations which make no mention of intent as dispensing with it and holding that the guilty act alone makes out the crime. This has not, however, been without expressions of misgiving.

The pilot of the movement in this country appears to be a holding that a tavernkeeper could be convicted for selling liquor to an habitual drunkard even if he did not know the buyer to be such. *Barnes v. State*, 1849, 19 Conn. 398. Later came Massachusetts holdings that convictions for selling adulterated milk in violation of statutes forbidding such sales require no allegation or proof that defendant knew of the adulteration. Departures from the common-law tradition, mainly of these general classes, were reviewed and their rationale appraised by Chief Justice Cooley, as follows: "I agree that as a rule there can be no crime without a criminal intent, but this is not by any means a universal rule. . . . Many statutes which are in the nature of police regulations, as this is, impose criminal penalties irrespective of any intent to violate them, the purpose being to require a degree of diligence for the protection of the public which shall render violation impossible." *People v. Roby*, 1884, 52 Mich. 577, 579, 18 N.W. 365, 366.

After the turn of the Century, a new use for crimes without intent appeared when New York enacted numerous and novel regulations of tenement houses, sanctioned by money penalties. Landlords contended that a guilty intent was essential to establish a violation. Judge Cardozo wrote the answer: "The defendant asks us to test the meaning of this statute by standards applicable to statutes that govern infamous crimes. The analogy, however, is deceptive. The element of conscious wrongdoing, the guilty mind accompanying the guilty act, is associated with the concept of crimes that are punished as infamous. . . . Even there it is not an invariable element. . . . But in the prosecution of minor offenses there is a wider range of practice and of power. Prosecutions for petty penalties have always constituted in our law a class by themselves. . . . That is true, though the prosecution is criminal in form." *Tenement House Department of City of New York v. McDevitt*, 1915, 215 N.Y. 160, 168, 109 N.E. 88, 90.

Soon, employers advanced the same contention as to violations of regulations prescribed by a new labor law. Judge Cardozo, again for the court, pointed out, as a basis for penalizing violations whether intentional or not, that they were punishable only by fine "moderate in amount," but cautiously added that in sustaining the power so to fine unintended violations "we are not to be understood as sustaining to a like length the power to imprison. We leave that question open." *People ex rel. Price v. Sheffield Farms-Slawson-Decker Co.*, 1918, 225 N.Y. 25, 32–33, 121 N.E. 474, 476, 477.

Thus, for diverse but reconcilable reasons, state courts converged on the same result, discontinuing inquiry into intent in a limited class of offenses against such statutory regulations.

It was not until recently that the Court took occasion more explicitly to relate abandonment of the ingredient of intent, not merely with considerations of expediency in obtaining convictions, nor with the *malum prohibitum* classification of the crime, but with the peculiar nature and quality of the offense. We referred to ". . . a now familiar type of legislation whereby penalties serve as effective means of regulation," and continued, "such legislation dispenses with the conventional requirement for criminal conduct—awareness of some wrongdoing. In the interest of the larger good it puts the burden of acting at hazard upon a person otherwise innocent but standing in responsible relation to a public danger." But we warned: "Hardship there doubtless may be under a statute which thus penalizes the transaction though consciousness of wrongdoing be totally wanting." *United States v. Dotterweich*, 320 U.S. 277, 280–281.

Neither this Court nor, so far as we are aware, any other has undertaken to delineate a precise line or set forth comprehensive criteria for distinguishing between crimes that require a mental element and crimes that do not. We attempt no closed definition, for the law on the subject is neither settled nor static.

Questions and Notes

1. What factors militate in favor of liability without fault?

2. Is it the importance to the public? If so, isn't it more important to be protected from murder or rape than from the sale of alcohol to habitual drunkards?

3. Is the lack of damage to the defendant's reputation important? If we don't want to damage his reputation, why should we call him a criminal at all?

4. Are problems of proof relevant? That is, do we make fault irrelevant so that we won't have to prove fault? If so, why here and not elsewhere in the law?

Problem

In the following problem, consider whether John Park ought to be branded a criminal.

Acme Markets, Inc., is a national retail food chain with approximately 36,000 employees, 874 retail outlets, 12 general warehouses, and four special warehouses. Its headquarters, including the office of the president, respondent Park, who is chief executive officer of the corporation, are located in Philadelphia, Pennsylvania. In a five-count information filed in the United States District Court for the District of Maryland, the Government charged Acme and respondent with violations of the Federal Food, Drug and Cosmetic Act. Each count of the information alleged that the defendants had received food that had been shipped in interstate commerce and that, while the food was being held for sale in Acme's Baltimore warehouse following shipment in interstate commerce, they caused it to be held in a building accessible to rodents and to be exposed to contamination by rodents. These acts were alleged to have resulted in the food's being adulterated within the meaning of 21 U.S.C. §§ 342(a)(3) and (4), in violation of 21 U.S.C. § 331(k).

Acme pleaded guilty to each count of the information. Respondent pleaded not guilty. The evidence at trial demonstrated that in April 1970 the Food and Drug Administration (FDA) advised respondent by letter of insanitary conditions in Acme's Philadelphia warehouse. In 1971 the FDA found that similar conditions existed in the firm's Baltimore warehouse. An FDA consumer safety officer testified concerning evidence of rodent infestation and other insanitary conditions discovered during a 12-day inspection of the Baltimore warehouse in November and December 1971. He also related that a second inspection of the warehouse had been conducted in March 1972. On that occasion the inspectors found that there had been improvement in the sanitary conditions, but that "there was still evidence of rodent activity in the building and in the warehouses and we found some rodent-contaminated lots of food items."

The Government also presented testimony by the Chief of Compliance of the FDA's Baltimore office, who informed respondent by letter of the conditions at the Baltimore warehouse after the first inspection. There was testimony by Acme's Baltimore division vice president, who had responded to the letter on behalf of Acme and respondent and who described the steps taken to remedy the insanitary conditions discovered by both inspections. The Government's final witness, Acme's vice president for legal affairs and assistant secretary, identified respondent as the president and chief executive officer of the company and read a bylaw prescribing the duties of the chief executive officer. He testified that respondent functioned by delegating "normal operating duties," including sanitation, but that he retained "certain things, which are the big, broad, principles of the operation of the company," and had "the responsibility of seeing that they all work together."

At the close of the Government's case in chief, respondent moved for a judgment of acquittal on the ground that the evidence in chief has shown that Mr. Park is not personally concerned in this Food and Drug violation. The trial judge denied the motion.

Respondent was the only defense witness. He testified that, although all of Acme's employees were in a sense under his general direction, the company had an "organizational structure for responsibilities for certain functions" according to which different phases of its operation were "assigned to individuals who, in turn, have staff and departments under them." He identified those individuals responsible for sanitation, and related that upon receipt of the January 1972 FDA letter, he had conferred with the vice president for legal affairs, who informed him that the Baltimore division vice president "was investigating the situation immediately and would be taking corrective action and would be preparing a summary of the corrective action to reply to the letter." Respondent stated that he did not "believe there was anything (he) could have done more constructively than what (he) found was being done."

On cross-examination, respondent conceded that providing sanitary conditions for food offered for sale to the public was something that he was "responsible for in the entire operation of the company," and he stated that it was one of many phases of the company that he assigned to "dependable subordinates." Respondent was asked about and, over the objections of his counsel, admitted receiving, the April 1970 letter addressed to him from the FDA regarding insanitary conditions at Acme's Philadelphia warehouse. He acknowledged that, with the exception of the division vice president, the same individuals had responsibility for sanitation in both Baltimore and Philadelphia. Finally, in response to questions concerning the Philadelphia and Baltimore incidents, respondent admitted that the Baltimore problem indicated the system for handling sanitation "wasn't working perfectly" and that as Acme's chief executive officer he was responsible for "any result which occurs in our company."

At the close of the evidence, respondent's renewed motion for a judgment of acquittal was denied. The relevant portion of the trial judge's instructions to the jury challenged by respondent is set out in the margin.[1] The jury found respondent

---

1. "In order to find the Defendant guilty on any count of the Information, you must find beyond a reasonable doubt on each count. . . ." Thirdly, that John R. Park held a position of authority in the operation of the business of Acme Markets, Incorporated. "However, you need not concern yourselves with the first two elements of the case. The main issue for your determination is only with the third element, whether the Defendant held a position of authority and responsibility in the business of Acme Markets. "The statute makes individuals, as well as corporations, liable for violations. An individual is liable if it is clear, beyond a reasonable doubt, that the elements of the adulteration of the food as to travel in interstate commerce are present. As I have instructed you in this case, they are, and that the individual had a responsible relation to the situation, even though he may not have participated personally.

guilty on all counts of the information, and he was subsequently sentenced to pay a fine of $50 on each count.[2]

Questions and Notes

1. What purpose is served by convicting Park?

2. Is there a better way that the government could serve its purpose?

3. Do you think of Park as a criminal? Would you be alarmed if he moved next door to you? Would you be concerned if your children associated with his children?

4. Park's case went all the way to the Supreme Court. For the result, see *United States v. Park*, 421 U.S. 658 (1975). Given that he was only fined $250 ($50 on each of five counts), why do you suppose he allowed the case to go that far (his legal fees obviously cost more than he could have saved had he been vindicated)?

5. *Park* potentially raises the problem of vicarious liability (liability for the acts of others) as well as strict liability. In fact, the *Park* jury instruction sought to avoid the problem by emphasizing personal duty. Some statutes, however, explicitly provide for both strict and vicarious liability. The extent to which this practice should (must?) be limited is explored in *State v. Guminga*.

State v. Guminga
395 N.W.2d 344 (Minn. 1986)

YETKA, Justice.

On March 29, 1985, in the course of an undercover operation, two investigators for the City of Hopkins entered Lindee's Restaurant, Hopkins, Minnesota, with a 17-year-old woman. All three ordered alcoholic beverages. The minor had never been in Lindee's before, and the waitress did not ask the minor her age or request identification. When the waitress returned with their orders, the minor paid for all the drinks. After confirming that the drink contained alcohol, the officers arrested

---

"The individual is or could be liable under the statute, even if he did not consciously do wrong. However, the fact that the Defendant is pres(id)ent and is a chief executive officer of the Acme Markets does not require a finding of guilt. Though, he need not have personally participated in the situation, he must have had a responsible relationship to the issue. The issue is, in this case, whether the Defendant, John R. Park, by virtue of his position in the company, had a position of authority and responsibility in the situation out of which these charges arose."

2. Sections 303(a) and (b) of the Act, 21 U.S.C. 333(a) and (b), provide:

"(a) Any person who violates a provision of section 331 of this title shall be imprisoned for not more than one year or fined not more than $1,000, or both.

"(b) Notwithstanding the provisions of subsection (a) of this section, if any person commits such a violation after a conviction of him under this section has become final, or commits such a violation with the intent to defraud or mislead, such person shall be imprisoned for not more than three years or fined not more than $10,000, or both."

Respondent's renewed motion for a judgment of acquittal or in the alternative for a new trial, one of the grounds of which was the alleged abuse of discretion in the initiation of the prosecution against him, had previously been denied after argument.

the waitress for serving intoxicating liquor to a minor in violation of Minn. Stat. § 340.73 (1984). The owner of Lindee's, defendant George Joseph Guminga, was subsequently charged with violation of section 340.73 pursuant to Minn. Stat. § 340.941 (1984), which imposes vicarious criminal liability on an employer whose employee serves intoxicating liquor to a minor. The state does not contend that Guminga was aware of or ratified the waitress's actions.

Guminga argues that section 340.941 violates due process as an unjustified and unnecessary invasion of his personal liberties. He maintains that the public interest in prohibiting the sale of liquor to minors does not justify vicarious criminal liability for an employer since there are less burdensome ways to protect the public interest. The state contends that vicarious criminal liability for employers whose employees sell alcohol to minors is a necessary part of liquor control.

We find that criminal penalties based on vicarious liability under Minn. Stat. § 340.941 are a violation of substantive due process and that only civil penalties would be constitutional. A due process analysis of a statute involves a balancing of the public interests protected against the intrusion on personal liberty while taking into account any alternative means by which to achieve the same end. Section 340.941 serves the public interest by providing additional deterrence to violation of the liquor laws. The private interests affected, however, include liberty, damage to reputation and other future disabilities arising from criminal prosecution for an act which Guminga did not commit or ratify. Not only could Guminga be given a prison sentence or a suspended sentence, but, in the more likely event that he receives only a fine, his liberty could be affected by a longer presumptive sentence in a possible future felony conviction. Such an intrusion on personal liberty is not justified by the public interest protected, especially when there are alternative means by which to achieve the same end, such as civil fines or license suspension, which do not entail the legal and social ramifications of a criminal conviction. *See* Model Penal Code § 1.04 comment (b) (1985).[3]

---

3. We agree with the reasoning of the Georgia Supreme Court in *Davis v. City of Peachtree City*, 251 Ga. 219, 304 S.E.2d 701 (1983). *Davis* involved the criminal conviction of the president of a chain of convenience stores whose employee had sold liquor to a minor. The defendant was prosecuted under a city ordinance holding licensees responsible for the acts of their employees and received a $300 fine and a 60-day suspended sentence. The Georgia Supreme Court reversed the conviction, ruling that it was a violation of due process since the public interest did not justify criminal prosecution: In balancing this burden against the public's interests, we find that it cannot be justified under the due process clauses of the Georgia or United States Constitutions, regardless of Peachtree City's admittedly legitimate interests of deterring employers from allowing their employees to break the law and of facilitating the enforcement of these laws. This is especially true, when, as here, there are other, less onerous alternatives which sufficiently promote these interests. The Model Penal Code recommends that civil violations providing civil penalties such as fines or revocation of licenses be used for offenses for which the individual was not morally blameworthy and does not deserve the social condemnation "implicit in the concept 'crime'." Model Penal Code § 1.04(s), Comments, Tent. Draft No. 2, p. 7 (1954). The availability of such sanctions renders the use of criminal sanctions in vicarious liability cases unjustifiable. LaFave & Scott, *supra*, p. 228.

We decline, however, to rewrite section 340.941 by holding that it can be enforced only by civil penalties. That is more properly a legislative function.

[T]he drafters of the MPC were quite explicit in their beliefs on the subject:

> "The liabilities involved are indefensible, unless reduced to terms that insulate conviction from the type of moral condemnation that is and ought to be implicit when a sentence of probation or imprisonment may be imposed. It has been argued, and the argument undoubtedly will be repeated, that strict liability is necessary for enforcement in a number of the areas where it obtains. But if practical enforcement precludes litigation of the culpability of alleged deviation from legal requirements, the enforcers cannot rightly demand the use of penal sanctions for the purpose. Crime does and should mean condemnation and no court should have to pass that judgment unless it can declare that the defendant's act was culpable. This is too fundamental to be compromised. The law goes far enough if it permits the imposition of a monetary penalty in cases where strict liability has been imposed."

Model Penal Code § 2.05, comment 1 (1985).

The dissent argues that vicarious liability is necessary as a deterrent so that an owner will impress upon employees that they should not sell to minors. However, it does not distinguish between an employer who vigorously lectures his employees and one who does not. According to the dissent, each would be equally guilty. We believe it is a deterrent enough that the employee who sells to the minor can be charged under the statute and that the business is subject to fines or suspension or revocation of license.

We specifically and exclusively decide the question under the provisions of the Minnesota Constitution herein cited. We find that, in Minnesota, no one can be convicted of a crime punishable by imprisonment for an act he did not commit, did not have knowledge of, or give expressed or implied consent to the commission thereof.

KELLEY, Justice (dissenting):

> I respectfully dissent. The strong public interest in prohibiting the sale of liquor to minors justifies the imposition of vicarious liability on the bar owner — employer for illegal sales to minors made by an employee. I respectfully suggest that in ruling Minn. Stat. § 340.941 (1984) unconstitutional,

---

Although some commentators and courts have found that vicarious criminal liability does not violate due process in misdemeanor cases which involve as punishment only a slight fine and not imprisonment, we decline to so hold. The damage done to an individual's good name and the peril imposed on an individual's future are sufficient reasons to shift the balance in favor of the individual. The imposition of such a burden on an employer "cannot rest on so frail a reed as whether his employee will commit a mistake in judgment," but instead can be justified only by the appropriate prosecuting officials proving some sort of culpability or knowledge by the employer.

Davis, 304 S.E.2d 703–04 (citations omitted).

the majority has failed to give adequate weight to the clearly expressed, long-standing public policy of this state as reflected in Section 340.941. Imposition of vicarious liability and criminal punishment for sale of intoxicating liquor to minors has been the law in this state since 1905. *See* Minn. Rev. Laws § 1565 (1905).

In explaining the meaning and the purpose of a nearly identical predecessor of this statute, the court in 1913 stated:

> "This language plainly means that the act of the barkeeper is the act of the proprietor, that the proprietor must pay the penalty for sales made by his barkeeper in violation of the law, and that the delinquency of the barkeeper is the only evidence required to prove the guilt of the proprietor. The fact that the sale was made without the knowledge or assent of the proprietor and contrary to his general instructions furnishes no defense. The language of this statute is susceptible of no other construction. The offense is one of the class where proof of criminal intent is not essential. The statute makes the act an offense, and imposes a penalty for violation of the law, irrespective of knowledge or intent.

> "The statute is drastic in its terms, but the Legislature was doubtless of the opinion that drastic measures are required to accomplish the purpose of enforcement of laws regulating the sale of intoxicating liquors. The law was in existence when the offense was committed. It was a notice to every man choosing to follow this line of business that he must control his own business and the men he employs in it, and that he is bound under penalty of the law to employ only men who will not commit crime in his name."

State v. Lundgren, 124 Minn. 167–68, 144 N.W. 752, 754 (1913) (citations omitted). The protection of the morals and general well-being of minors is obviously what the statute aims at. If one operating a place where the vending of intoxicating liquor is the primary objective . . . is to be exonerated from liability because he happens, whether by design or otherwise, to be absent at times when convenient to be away, then assuredly the very purpose of the law is frustrated and made for naught. The very spirit, intent, and purpose of the law, including as well the plain letter of it, repel the notion that any person so conducting his place of business can escape liability by absenting himself therefrom but leaving his servants and agents in charge to do as they please to his financial advantage, but at their own risk if caught in the game of violation.

Furthermore, imposition of vicarious liability and the threat of a short jail, not prison, sentence is reasonably related to the legislative purpose: enforcement of laws prohibiting liquor sales to minors. Without the deterrent of possible personal criminal responsibility and a sentence, the legislature could have rationally concluded that liquor establishment owners will be less likely to impress upon employees the need to require identification of age before serving liquor. Limiting punishment to a fine allows bar owners to view their liability for violations as nothing more than an expense of doing business. The gravity of the problems associated with minors who consume alcoholic beverages justifies the importance by the legislature of harsher punishment on those who help contribute to those problems. The state has the right to impose limited criminal vicarious liability on bar proprietors as a reasonable exchange for the state-granted privilege of a liquor license.

The majority's holding today not only fails to give deference to decades of legislative policy, but it is likewise at odds with rulings of the majority of the courts of our sister jurisdictions. It can be stated as a general rule, that statutes imposing vicarious criminal liability upon the "innocent" employer for the illegal conduct of the employee have been generally upheld as constitutional. *See* Annot., 139 A.L.R. 306 (1942); Annot., 89 A.L.R.3d 1256 (1979). Although somewhat critical of the position of the great majority of the courts, Professor F.B. Sayre writing in Harvard Law Review acknowledged that in this field traditionally vicarious liability has not been considered to infringe on due process rights. Sayre, *Criminal Responsibility for the Acts of Another*, 43 HARV. L. REV. 689 (1930). Likewise, although not necessarily embracing the majority position, and indeed critical of the imposition of vicarious liability in certain areas, LaFave and Scott have summarized the case law noting:

> If the authorized punishment is light — a fine or perhaps a short imprisonment — the statute is likely to be construed to impose vicarious liability on a faultless employer. But if the permitted punishment is severe — a felony or serious misdemeanor — the statute is not apt to be so construed in the absence of an express provision for vicarious responsibility.

HANDBOOK ON CRIMINAL LAW at § 32. The Minnesota statute in question here has an express provision for vicarious liability and permits light punishment. Minn. Stat. § 609.03. Section 340.941 should be upheld as constitutional.

Questions and Notes

1. In regard to the constitutional issue, it is extremely unlikely that the United States Supreme Court would concur. That Court ordinarily invalidates statutes on due process grounds only when the statute is utterly devoid of rationality unless it violates a fundamental right or is unconstitutionally vague. (*See Chicago v. Morales*, Chapter 22, *infra*.) It is probably for that reason that the Minnesota Supreme Court chose to ground its holding on the Minnesota Constitution. You will focus on this issue much more in your constitutional law course.

2. Are there alternatives to criminal liability that would work as well as criminal liability? What are they?

3. Should a distinction be made between a criminal conviction involving imprisonment and one that does not? (*See* footnote 3 of the opinion.) Might that be relevant to the cruel and unusual punishment analysis suggested by *Weitbrecht*?

4. Is (should) *Guminga* (be) applicable to strict as well as vicarious liability? Assume that the defense was being asserted by the waitress at Lindee's, and that her

claim was that the woman appeared to be at least 25 years old. Is there any good reason for Guminga to have a better defense than the waitress?

5. One justification for strict or vicarious liability seems to be that no moral turpitude is involved in the fact of conviction. That is, nobody would tend to shun the convicted perpetrator as a "criminal." In *Garnett*, you will see a strict liability conviction upheld for a crime (statutory rape) that is near the top of the moral turpitude list. Why?

Garnett v. State
632 A.2d 797 (Md. 1993)

MURPHY, Chief Judge.

Maryland's "statutory rape" law prohibiting sexual intercourse with an underage person is codified in Maryland Code (1957, 1992 Repl. Vol.) Art. 27, §463, which reads in full:

"Second degree rape.

(a) *What constitutes.* — A person is guilty of rape in the second degree if the person engages in vaginal intercourse with another person:

(1) By force or threat of force against the will and without the consent of the other person; or

(2) Who is mentally defective, mentally incapacitated, or physically helpless, and the person performing the act knows or should reasonably know the other person is mentally defective, mentally incapacitated, or physically helpless; or

(3) Who is under 14 years of age and the person performing the act is at least four years older than the victim.

(b) *Penalty.* — Any person violating the provisions of this section is guilty of a felony and upon conviction is subject to imprisonment for a period of not more than 20 years."

Subsection (a)(3) represents the current version of a statutory provision dating back to the first comprehensive codification of the criminal law by the Legislature in 1809. Now we consider whether under the present statute, the State must prove that a defendant knew the complaining witness was younger than 14 and, in a related question, whether it was error at trial to exclude evidence that he had been told, and believed, that she was 16 years old.

I

Raymond Lennard Garnett is a young retarded man. At the time of the incident in question he was 20 years old. He has an I.Q. of 52. His guidance counselor from the Montgomery County public school system, Cynthia Parker, described him as a mildly retarded person who read on the third-grade level, did arithmetic on the 5th-grade level, and interacted with others socially at school at the level of someone

11 or 12 years of age. Ms. Parker added that Raymond attended special education classes and for at least one period of time was educated at home when he was afraid to return to school due to his classmates' taunting. Because he could not understand the duties of the jobs given him, he failed to complete vocational assignments; he sometimes lost his way to work. As Raymond was unable to pass any of the State's functional tests required for graduation, he received only a certificate of attendance rather than a high-school diploma.

In November or December 1990, a friend introduced Raymond to Erica Frazier, then aged 13; the two subsequently talked occasionally by telephone. On February 28, 1991, Raymond, apparently wishing to call for a ride home, approached the girl's house at about nine o'clock in the evening. Erica opened her bedroom window, through which Raymond entered; he testified that "she just told me to get a ladder and climb up her window." The two talked, and later engaged in sexual intercourse. Raymond left at about 4:30 a.m. the following morning. On November 19, 1991, Erica gave birth to a baby, of which Raymond is the biological father.

Raymond was tried before the Circuit Court for Montgomery County (Miller, J.) on one count of second degree rape under §463(a)(3) proscribing sexual intercourse between a person under 14 and another at least four years older than the complainant. At trial, the defense twice proffered evidence to the effect that Erica herself and her friends had previously told Raymond that she was 16 years old, and that he had acted with that belief. The trial court excluded such evidence as immaterial, explaining:

> "Under 463, the only two requirements as relate to this case are that there was vaginal intercourse, [and] that . . . Ms. Frazier was under 14 years of age and that . . . Mr. Garnett was at least four years older than she.

> "In the Court's opinion, consent is no defense to this charge. The victim's representation as to her age and the defendant's belief, if it existed, that she was not under age, what amounts to what otherwise might be termed a good faith defense, is in fact no defense to what amount[s] to statutory rape.

> "It is in the Court's opinion a strict liability offense."

The court found Raymond guilty. It sentenced him to a term of five years in prison, suspended the sentence and imposed five years of probation, and ordered that he pay restitution to Erica and the Frazier family. Raymond noted an appeal; we granted certiorari prior to intermediate appellate review by the Court of Special Appeals to consider the important issue presented in the case.

II

In 1975 the Legislative Council of the General Assembly established the Special Committee on Rape and Related Offenses, which proposed a complete revision of Maryland law pertaining to rape and other sex crimes.

The new legislation reformulated the former statutory rape law by introducing the element of a four-year age difference between the accused and the underage complainant. As originally enacted by ch. 573 of the Acts of 1976, sexual intercourse with a person under 14 by an actor more than four years older was classified as rape in the first degree, and carried a maximum penalty of life imprisonment. The Legislature of 1977 reduced the crime to rape in the second degree carrying a maximum sentence of 20 years in prison. Section 463(a)(3) does not expressly set forth a requirement that the accused have acted with a criminal state of mind, or *mens rea*. The State insists that the statute, by design, defines a strict liability offense, and that its essential elements were met in the instant case when Raymond, age 20, engaged in vaginal intercourse with Erica, a girl under 14 and more than 4 years his junior. Raymond replies that the criminal law exists to assess and punish morally culpable behavior. He says such culpability was absent here. He asks us either to engraft onto subsection (a)(3) an implicit *mens rea* requirement, or to recognize an affirmative defense of reasonable mistake as to the complainant's age. Raymond argues that it is unjust, under the circumstances of this case which led him to think his conduct lawful, to brand him a felon and rapist.

III

Raymond asserts that the events of this case were inconsistent with the criminal sexual exploitation of a minor by an adult. As earlier observed, Raymond entered Erica's bedroom at the girl's invitation; she directed him to use a ladder to reach her window. They engaged voluntarily in sexual intercourse. They remained together in the room for more than seven hours before Raymond departed at dawn. With an I.Q. of 52, Raymond functioned at approximately the same level as the 13-year-old Erica; he was mentally an adolescent in an adult's body. Arguably, had Raymond's chronological age, 20, matched his socio-intellectual age, about 12, he and Erica would have fallen well within the four-year age difference obviating a violation of the statute, and Raymond would not have been charged with any crime at all.

The precise legal issue here rests on Raymond's unsuccessful efforts to introduce into evidence testimony that Erica and her friends had told him she was 16 years old, the age of consent to sexual relations, and that he believed them. Thus, the trial court did not permit him to raise a defense of reasonable mistake of Erica's age, by which defense Raymond would have asserted that he acted innocently without a criminal design. At common law, a crime occurred only upon the concurrence of an individual's act and his guilty state of mind. In this regard, it is well understood that generally there are two components of every crime, the *actus reus* or guilty act and the *mens rea* or the guilty mind or mental state accompanying a forbidden act. The requirement that an accused have acted with a culpable mental state is an axiom of criminal jurisprudence. Writing for the United States Supreme Court, Justice Robert Jackson observed:

> "The contention that an injury can amount to a crime only when inflicted by intention is no provincial or transient notion. It is as universal and persistent in mature systems of law as belief in freedom of the human will and a consequent ability and duty of the normal individual to choose between good and evil.

"Crime as a compound concept, generally constituted only from a concurrence of an evil-meaning mind with an evil-doing hand, was congenial to an intense individualism and took deep and early root in American soil."

Morissette.

To be sure, legislative bodies since the mid-19th century have created strict liability criminal offenses requiring no *mens rea*. Almost all such statutes responded to the demands of public health and welfare arising from the complexities of society after the Industrial Revolution. Typically, misdemeanors involving only fines or other light penalties, these strict liability laws regulated food, milk, liquor, medicines and drugs, securities, motor vehicles and traffic, the labeling of goods for sale, and the like. Statutory rape, carrying the stigma of felony as well as a potential sentence of 20 years in prison, contrasts markedly with the other strict liability regulatory offenses and their light penalties.

Modern scholars generally reject the concept of strict criminal liability. Professors LaFave and Scott summarize the consensus that punishing conduct without reference to the actor's state of mind fails to reach the desired end and is unjust:

"It is inefficacious because conduct unaccompanied by an awareness of the factors making it criminal does not mark the actor as one who needs to be subjected to punishment in order to deter him or others from behaving similarly in the future, nor does it single him out as a socially dangerous individual who needs to be incapacitated or reformed. It is unjust because the actor is subjected to the stigma of a criminal conviction without being morally blameworthy. Consequently, on either a preventive or retributive theory of criminal punishment, the criminal sanction is inappropriate in the absence of *mens rea.*"

Dean Singer has articulated other weaknesses of strict criminal liability theory: 1) extensive government civil regulations and strict liability in tort achieve the same deterrent effect; 2) the judicial efficiency of dispatching minor offenses without an inquiry into *mens rea* is attained equally by decriminalizing them, and hearing such cases in a regulatory or administrative forum; 3) the small penalties imposed for most strict liability offenses oblige the public to engage in a pernicious game of distinguishing "real" crime from some lesser form of crime; 4) some strict liability laws may result from careless drafting; and 5) strict liability dilutes the moral force that the criminal law has historically carried. The author concludes that "the predicate for all criminal liability is blameworthiness; it is the social stigma which a finding of guilt carries that distinguishes the criminal [penalty] from all other sanctions. If the predicate is removed, the criminal law is set adrift." Conscious of the disfavor in which strict criminal liability resides, the Model Penal Code states generally as a minimum requirement of culpability that a person is not guilty of a criminal offense unless he acts purposely, knowingly, recklessly, or negligently, *i.e.,* with some degree of *mens rea.* The Model Penal Code generally recognizes strict liability for offenses deemed "violations," defined as wrongs subject only to a fine, forfeiture, or other civil penalty upon conviction, and not giving rise to any legal disability.

The commentators similarly disapprove of statutory rape as a strict liability crime. In addition to the arguments discussed above, they observe that statutory rape prosecutions often proceed even when the defendant's judgment as to the age of the complainant is warranted by her appearance, her sexual sophistication, her verbal misrepresentations, and the defendant's careful attempts to ascertain her true age. Voluntary intercourse with a sexually mature teen-ager lacks the features of psychic abnormality, exploitation, or physical danger that accompanies such conduct with children.

Two sub-parts of the rationale underlying strict criminal liability require further analysis at this point. Statutory rape laws are often justified on the "lesser legal wrong" theory or the "moral wrong" theory; by such reasoning, the defendant acting without *mens rea* nonetheless deserves punishment for having committed a lesser crime, fornication, or for having violated moral teachings that prohibit sex outside of marriage. Maryland has no law against fornication. It is not a crime in this state. Moreover, the criminalization of an act, performed without a guilty mind, deemed immoral by some members of the community rests uneasily on subjective and shifting norms. "[D]etermining precisely what the 'community ethic' actually is [is] not an easy task in a heterogeneous society in which our public pronouncements about morality often are not synonymous with our private conduct." The drafters of the Model Penal Code remarked:

> "[T]he actor who reasonably believes that his partner is above that age [of consent] lacks culpability with respect to the factor deemed critical to liability. Punishing him anyway simply because his intended conduct would have been immoral under the facts as he supposed them to be postulates a relation between criminality and immorality that is inaccurate on both descriptive and normative grounds. The penal law does not try to enforce all aspects of community morality, and any thoroughgoing attempt to do so would extend the prospect of criminal sanctions far into the sphere of individual liberty and create a regime too demanding for all save the best among us."

We acknowledge here that it is uncertain to what extent Raymond's intellectual and social retardation may have impaired his ability to comprehend imperatives of sexual morality in any case.

IV

The legislatures of 17 states have enacted laws permitting a mistake of age defense in some form in cases of sexual offenses with underage persons. In Kentucky, the accused may prove in exculpation that he did not know the facts or conditions relevant to the complainant's age. In Washington, the defendant may assert that he reasonably believed the complainant to be of a certain age based on the alleged victim's own declarations. In some states, the defense is available in instances where the complainant's age rises above a statutorily prescribed level, but is not available when the complainant falls below the defining age. In other states, the availability of the defense depends on the severity of the sex offense charged to the accused.

In addition, the highest appellate courts of four states have determined that statutory rape laws by implication required an element of *mens rea* as to the complainant's age. In the landmark case of *People v. Hernandez*, 61 Cal. 2d 529, 39 Cal. Rptr. 361, 393 P.2d 673 (1964), the California Supreme Court held that, absent a legislative directive to the contrary, a charge of statutory rape was defensible wherein a criminal intent was lacking; it reversed the trial court's refusal to permit the defendant to present evidence of his good faith, reasonable belief that the complaining witness had reached the age of consent. In so doing, the court first questioned the assumption that age alone confers a sophistication sufficient to create legitimate consent to sexual relations: "the sexually experienced 15-year-old may be far more acutely aware of the implications of sexual intercourse than her sheltered cousin who is beyond the age of consent." The court then rejected the traditional view that those who engage in sex with young persons do so at their peril, assuming the risk that their partners are underage:

> "[I]f [the perpetrator] participates in a mutual act of sexual intercourse, believing his partner to be beyond the age of consent, with reasonable grounds for such belief, where is his criminal intent? In such circumstances he has not consciously taken any risk. Instead he has subjectively eliminated the risk by satisfying himself on reasonable evidence that the crime cannot be committed. If it occurs that he has been mislead, we cannot realistically conclude for such reason alone the intent with which he undertook the act suddenly becomes more heinous. . . . [T]he courts have uniformly failed to satisfactorily explain the nature of the criminal intent present in the mind of one who in good faith believes he has obtained a lawful consent before engaging in the prohibited act."

The Supreme Court of Alaska has held that a charge of statutory rape is legally unsupportable unless a defense of reasonable mistake of age is allowed. *State v. Guest*, 583 P.2d 836, 838–839 (Alaska 1978). The Supreme Court of Utah construed the applicable unlawful sexual intercourse statute to mean that a conviction could not result unless the state proved a criminal state of mind as to each element of the offense, including the victim's age. *State v. Elton*, 680 P.2d 727, 729 (Utah 1984) (Utah Criminal Code since amended to disallow mistake of age as a defense to unlawful sexual intercourse). The Supreme Court of New Mexico determined that a defendant should have been permitted at trial to present a defense that his partner in consensual sex told him she was 17, not 15, that this had been confirmed to him by others, and that he had acted under that mistaken belief. Two-fifths of the states, therefore, now recognize the defense in cases of statutory sexual offenses.

V

We think it sufficiently clear, however, that Maryland's second degree rape statute defines a strict liability offense that does not require the State to prove *mens rea*; it makes no allowance for a mistake-of-age defense. The plain language of § 463, viewed in its entirety, and the legislative history of its creation lead to this conclusion. It is well settled that in interpreting a statute to ascertain and effectuate its goal, our first recourse is to the words of the statute, giving them their ordinary and natural import. While penal statutes are to be strictly construed in favor of the defendant, the construction must ultimately depend upon discerning the intention of the Legislature when it drafted and enacted the law in question. To that end, the Court may appropriately look at the larger context, including external manifestations of the legislative purpose, within which statutory language appears.

Section 463(a)(3) prohibiting sexual intercourse with underage persons makes no reference to the actor's knowledge, belief, or other state of mind. As we see it, this silence as to *mens rea* results from legislative design. First, subsection (a)(3) stands in stark contrast to the provision immediately before it, subsection (a)(2) prohibiting vaginal intercourse with incapacitated or helpless persons. In subsection (a)(2), the Legislature expressly provided as an element of the offense that "the person performing the act *knows or should reasonably know* the other person is mentally defective, mentally incapacitated, or physically helpless." Code § 463(a)(2) (emphasis added). In drafting this subsection, the Legislature showed itself perfectly capable of recognizing and allowing for a defense that obviates criminal intent; if the defendant objectively did not understand that the sex partner was impaired, there is no crime. That it chose not to include similar language in subsection (a)(3) indicates that the Legislature aimed to make statutory rape with underage persons a more severe prohibition based on strict criminal liability.

Second, an examination of the drafting history of § 463 during the 1976 revision of Maryland's sexual offense laws reveals that the statute was viewed as one of strict liability from its inception and throughout the amendment process. As originally proposed, Senate Bill 358 defined as a sexual offense in the first degree a sex act committed with a person less than 14 years old by an actor four or more years older. The Senate Judicial Proceedings Committee then offered a series of amendments to the bill. Among them, Amendment # 13 reduced the stipulated age of the victim from less than 14 to 12 or less. Amendment # 16 then added a provision defining a sexual offense in the second degree as a sex act with another "under 14 years of age, which age the person performing the sexual act knows or should know." These initial amendments suggest that, at the very earliest stages of the bill's life, the Legislature distinguished between some form of strict criminal liability, applicable to offenses where the victim was age 12 or under, and a lesser offense with a *mens rea* requirement when the victim was between the ages of 12 and 14.

Senate Bill 358 in its amended form was passed by the Senate on March 11, 1976. The House of Delegates' Judiciary Committee, however, then proposed changes of

---

its own. It rejected the Senate amendments, and defined an offense of rape, without a *mens rea* requirement, for sexual acts performed with someone under the age of 14. The Senate concurred in the House amendments and S.B. 358 became law. Thus the Legislature explicitly raised, considered, and then explicitly jettisoned any notion of a *mens rea* element with respect to the complainant's age in enacting the law that formed the basis of current § 463(a)(3). In the light of such legislative action, we must inevitably conclude that the current law imposes strict liability on its violators.

This interpretation is consistent with the traditional view of statutory rape as a strict liability crime designed to protect young persons from the dangers of sexual exploitation by adults, loss of chastity, physical injury, and, in the case of girls, pregnancy. The majority of states retain statutes which impose strict liability for sexual acts with underage complainants. We observe again, as earlier, that even among those states providing for a mistake-of-age defense in some instances, the defense often is not available where the sex partner is 14 years old or less; the complaining witness in the instant case was only 13. The majority of appellate courts, including the Court of Special Appeals, have held statutory rape to be a strict liability crime.

VI

Maryland's second degree rape statute is by nature a creature of legislation. Any new provision introducing an element of *mens rea*, or permitting a defense of reasonable mistake of age, with respect to the offense of sexual intercourse with a person less than 14, should properly result from an act of the Legislature itself, rather than judicial fiat. Until then, defendants in extraordinary cases, like Raymond, will rely upon the tempering discretion of the trial court at sentencing.

JUDGMENT AFFIRMED, WITH COSTS.

ELDRIDGE, Judge, dissenting:

Both the majority opinion and Judge Bell's dissenting opinion view the question in this case to be whether, on the one hand, Maryland Code Art. 27, § 463(a)(3), is entirely a strict liability statute without any *mens rea* requirement or, on the other hand, contains the requirement that the defendant knew that the person with whom he or she was having sexual relations was under 14 years of age.

The majority takes the position that the statute defines an entirely strict liability offense and has no *mens rea* requirement whatsoever. The majority indicates that the defendant's "knowledge, belief, or other state of mind" is wholly immaterial. The majority opinion at one point states: "We acknowledge here that it is uncertain to what extent Raymond's intellectual and social retardation may have impaired his ability to comprehend imperatives of sexual morality in any case." Nevertheless, according to the majority, it was permissible for the trial judge to have precluded exploration into Raymond's knowledge and comprehension because the offense is entirely one of strict liability.

Judge Bell's dissent, however, argues that, under the due process clauses of the Fourteenth Amendment and the Maryland Declaration of Rights, any "defendant may defend on the basis that he was mistaken as to the age of the prosecutrix." In my view, the issue concerning a *mens rea* requirement in § 463(a)(3) is not limited to a choice between one of the extremes set forth in the majority's and Judge Bell's opinions. I agree with the majority that an ordinary defendant's mistake about the age of his or her sexual partner is not a defense to a prosecution under § 463(a)(3). Furthermore I am not persuaded, at least at the present time, that either the federal or state constitutions require that a defendant's honest belief that the other person was above the age of consent be a defense.[4] This does not mean, however, that the statute contains no *mens rea* requirement at all.

The legislative history of § 463(a)(3), set forth in the majority opinion, demonstrates that the House of Delegates rejected the Senate's proposed requirement that an older person, having sexual relations with another under 14 years of age, know or should know that the other person was under 14. The House of Delegates' version was ultimately adopted. From this, the majority concludes that the enacted version was "without a *mens rea* requirement." The majority's conclusion does not necessarily follow. Although the General Assembly rejected one specific knowledge requirement, it did not decree that any and all evidence concerning a defendant's knowledge and comprehension was immaterial. There are pure strict liability offenses where "the purpose of the penalty is to regulate rather than to punish behavior" and where criminal "liability is imposed regardless of the defendant's state of mind." These "offenses commonly involve light fines or penalties." There are other offenses (also unfortunately often called "strict liability" offenses) where the legislature has dispensed with a knowledge requirement in one respect but has not intended to impose criminal liability regardless of the defendant's state of mind. Such offenses "do require 'fault' ..., in that they 'can be interpreted as legislative judgments that persons who intentionally engage in certain activities and occupy some peculiar or distinctive position of control are to be held accountable for the occurrence of certain consequences.'"

Neither the statutory language nor the legislative history of § 463(a)(3), or of the other provisions of the 1976 and 1977 sexual offense statutes, indicate that the General Assembly intended § 463(a)(3) to define a pure strict liability offense where criminal liability is imposed regardless of the defendant's mental state. The penalty provision for a violation of § 463(a)(3), namely making the offense a felony punishable by a maximum of 20 years imprisonment (§ 463(b)), is strong evidence that the General Assembly did not intend to create a pure strict liability offense.

In the typical situation involving an older person's engaging in consensual sexual activities with a teenager below the age of consent, and the scenario which the

---

4. In this connection, it should be noted that the defendant-appellant, in his opening brief in this Court, made no constitutional argument either directly or by invoking the principle of statutory construction that a statute should be construed so as to avoid a serious constitutional problem. Consequently, the State had no opportunity to brief the constitutional issue discussed in Judge Bell's dissent.

General Assembly likely contemplated when it enacted §§ 463(a)(3), 464A(a)(3), 464B(a)(3), 464C(a)(2), and 464C(a)(3), the defendant knows and intends that he or she is engaging in sexual activity with a young person. In addition, the defendant knows that the activity is regarded as immoral and/or improper by large segments of society. Moreover, the defendant is aware that "consent" by persons who are too young is ineffective. Although in a particular case the defendant may honestly but mistakenly believe, because of representations or appearances, that the other person is above the age of consent, the ordinary defendant in such case is or ought to be aware that there is a risk that the young person is not above the age of consent. As the majority opinion points out, "the traditional view [is] that those who engage in sex with young persons do so at their peril, assuming the risk that their partners are underage. . . ." It seems to me that the above-mentioned knowledge factors, and particularly the mental ability to appreciate that one is taking a risk, constitute the *mens rea* of the offenses defined by §§ 463(a)(3), 464A(a)(3), 464B(a)(3), 464C(a)(2) and 464C(a)(3). In enacting these provisions, the General Assembly assumed that a defendant is able to appreciate the risk involved by intentionally and knowingly engaging in sexual activities with a young person. There is no indication that the General Assembly intended that criminal liability attach to one who, because of his or her mental impairment, was unable to appreciate that risk.

It is unreasonable to assume that the Legislature intended for one to be convicted under § 463(a)(3), or under any of the other statutes proscribing sexual activity with underage persons, regardless of his or her mental state. Suppose, for example, that Raymond Garnett had not had an I.Q. of 52, but rather, had been more severely mentally retarded as was the young woman involved in *Wentzel v. Montgomery Gen. Hosp.*, 293 Md. 685, 447 A.2d 1244, *cert. denied*, 459 U.S. 1147 (1983). The mentally retarded person in *Wentzel* had an I.Q. of 25–30, was physiologically capable of bearing a child, but was unable to comprehend the act of sexual intercourse, or even to understand the difference between the sexes. If someone so disabled, having reached Raymond's chronological age, then had "consensual" sexual intercourse with a person younger than fourteen years of age, I do not believe that he or she would have violated Art. 27, § 463(a)(3). Under the view that §§ 463(a)(3), 464A(a)(3), 464B(a)(3), etc., define pure strict liability offenses without any regard for the defendant's mental state, presumably a 20 year old, who passes out because of drinking too many alcoholic beverages, would be guilty of a sexual offense if a 13 year old engages in various sexual activities with the 20 year old while the latter is unconscious. I cannot imagine that the General Assembly intended any such result.

An impaired mental condition may show the absence of *mens rea*, depending upon the circumstances. In light of the defendant Garnett's mental retardation, and its effect upon his knowledge and comprehension, he may or may not have had the requisite *mens rea*. As previously mentioned, the majority opinion itself acknowledges that it is uncertain to what extent Raymond's intellectual and social retardation may have impaired his ability to comprehend standards of sexual morality. The problem in this case is that the trial judge's view of the statute, which the majority adopts, precluded an exploration into the matter. The majority points out that the trial court would not allow testimony that Erica and her friends had told the defendant that she was 16 years old. The trial court, however, went further. The court would not allow the defendant to testify concerning his knowledge. More importantly, the trial judge took the position that the offense proscribed by § 463(a)(3) is "a strict liability offense" and that the only requirements for conviction were that "the defendant had sexual intercourse with Erica Frazier, that at that time she was 13 years of age, [and] at that time the defendant was more than 4 years older than she. These are the only requirements that the State need prove beyond a reasonable doubt." The trial court's position that the offense lacked any *mens rea* requirement, and that the defendant's mental state was wholly immaterial, was, in my view, erroneous.

I would reverse and remand for a new trial.

ROBERT M. BELL, Judge, dissenting.

"It may be possible to conceive of legislation ... so flagrantly in conflict with natural right, that the courts may set it aside as unwarranted, though no clause of the constitution can be found prohibiting it. But the cases must be rare indeed; and whenever they do occur the interposition of the judicial *veto* will rest upon such foundations of necessity that there can be little or no room for hesitation."

Richard G. Singer, *The Resurgence of Mens Rea: III—The Rise and Fall of Strict Criminal Liability*, 30 B.C. L. REV. 337, 368 (1989), *quoting State v. Clottu*, 33 Ind. 409, 410–11 (1870).

I do not dispute that the legislative history of Maryland Code (1957, 1992 Repl. Vol.), Art. 27, section 463 may be read to support the majority's interpretation that subsection (a)(3) was intended to be a strict liability statute. Nor do I disagree that it is in the public interest to protect the sexually naive child from the adverse physical, emotional, or psychological effects of sexual relations. I do not believe, however, that the General Assembly, in every case, whatever the nature of the crime and no matter how harsh the potential penalty, can subject a defendant to strict criminal liability. To hold, *as a matter of law*, that section 463(a)(3) does not require the State to prove that a defendant possessed the necessary mental state to commit the crime, *i.e.*, knowingly engaged in sexual relations with a female under 14, or that the defendant may not litigate that issue in defense, "offends a principle of justice so rooted in the traditions of conscience of our people as to be ranked as fundamental" and is, therefore, inconsistent with due process.

In the case *sub judice*, according to the defendant, he intended to have sex with a 16, not a 13, year old girl. This mistake of fact was prompted, he said, by the prosecutrix herself; she and her friends told him that she was 16 years old. Because he was mistaken as to the prosecutrix's age, he submits, he is certainly less culpable than the person who knows that the minor is 13 years old, but nonetheless engages in sexual relations with her. Notwithstanding, the majority has construed section 463(a)(3) to exclude any proof of knowledge or intent. But for that construction, the proffered defense would be viable. I would hold that the State is not relieved of its burden to prove the defendant's intent or knowledge in a statutory rape case and, therefore, that the defendant may defend on the basis that he was mistaken as to the age of the prosecutrix.

I. Mens Rea Generally

Generally, a culpable mental state, often referred to as *mens rea*, or intent, is, and long has been, an essential element of a criminal offense. *Morissette*. A crime ordinarily consists of prohibited conduct *and* a culpable mental state; a wrongful act and a wrongful intent must concur to constitute what the law deems a crime, the purpose being to avoid criminal liability for innocent or inadvertent conduct. Historically, therefore, unless the actor also harbored an evil, or otherwise culpable, mind, he or she was not guilty of any crime. More recently, in *Anderson v. State*, 328 Md. 426, 444, 614 A.2d 963, 972 (1992), we held that the trial court improperly convicted the defendant for carrying concealed, a utility knife without considering the intent with which the utility knife was being carried. Noting that the utility knife could be used both as a tool and as a weapon, we rejected the State's argument that no intent was required. We said instead that, when the object is not a dangerous weapon *per se*, to convict a defendant of carrying a concealed dangerous weapon requires proof that the defendant intended to use the object as a weapon.

Although it recognized that Congress could dispense with the intent requirement if it did so specifically, the Court made clear that that power was not without limit. *Morissette*, 342 U.S. at 275, citing *Tot v. United States*, 319 U.S. 463, 467 (1943). Thus, when a legislature wants to eliminate intent as an element of a particular crime, it should expressly so state in the statute. *See* Larry W. Myers, *Reasonable Mistake of Age: A Needed Defense to Statutory Rape*, 64 Mich. L. Rev. 105, 118–19 (1965); *see also People v. Hernandez*, 61 Cal. 2d 529, 536, 39 Cal. Rptr. 361, 365, 393 P.2d 673, 677 (1964) ("in the absence of a legislative direction otherwise, a charge of statutory rape is defensible wherein criminal intent is lacking."); Singer, *supra*, at 397. Legislative imposition of strict criminal liability, however, must be within constitutional limits; it cannot be permitted to violate the Due Process requirement of the Fourteenth Amendment, see *Lambert v. California*, 355 U.S. 225, 227 (1957), or a comparable state constitutional provision. *See infra*.

II. Strict Liability Crimes

Strict liability crimes are recognized exceptions to the "guilty mind" rule in that they do not require the actor to possess a guilty mind, or the *mens rea*, to commit a crime. *See Morissette*. His or her state of mind being irrelevant, the actor is guilty of the crime at the moment that he or she does the prohibited act.

A.

Obviously, and the majority concurs, *see* majority opinion at 801, "statutory rape" is not merely a public welfare offense; it simply does not "fit" the characteristics of such an offense: it is a felony, not a misdemeanor. In striking contrast to "other strict liability regulatory offenses and their light penalties," majority opinion at 801, the potential penalty of 20 years imprisonment is not a light penalty; unlike the "garden variety" strict liability penalty, the penalty under section 463(a)(3), is neither so insignificant that it can be ignored as a criminal sanction, and section 463's primary purpose is to penalize the "rapist", not to correct his or her behavior.

B.

The second class of strict liability offenses, having a different justification than public welfare offenses, consists of narcotic,[6] bigamy,[7] adultery, and statutory rape crimes. The lesser legal wrong theory posits that a defendant who actually intended to do some legal or moral wrong is guilty not only of the crime intended but of a greater crime of which he or she may not have the requisite mental state. The elimination of a *mens rea* element for statutory rape is rationalized by focusing on the defendant's intent to commit a related crime. In other words, if fornication,[8] engaging in sexual intercourse out of wedlock, *see generally* Model Penal Code, § 213.6, Comment at 430–39, is a crime, a defendant intending to engage in sex out of wedlock is made to suffer all of the legal consequences of that act. Statutory rape is such a legal consequence when the other participant is below the age of consent. The theory is premised, in short, upon the proposition that, as to certain crimes, "a 'guilty mind' in a very general sense, should suffice for the imposition of penal sanctions even when the defendant did not intentionally or knowingly engage in the acts proscribed in the statute."

The seminal case in this area is *Regina v. Prince*. There, the defendant was charged with unlawfully taking a girl under the age of 16 out of the possession of the father against his will. The defendant claimed that he acted on the reasonable belief that the girl was 18. The court held that it was no defense that he thought he was committing a different kind of wrong from that which he, in fact, was committing, it being wrong to remove a daughter, even one over 16, from her father's household.

The lesser legal wrong theory does not provide a viable rationale for holding a defendant strictly liable for statutory rape where premarital sex is not criminal. Accordingly, in Maryland, there is no underlying offense from which to transfer intent. Moreover,

> [a] man who engages in consensual intercourse in the reasonable belief that his partner has reached [the age of consent] evidences no abnormality, no

---

6. Maryland does not treat narcotic offenses as strict liability crimes.

7. The Maryland bigamy statute, proscribing the entering into of a marriage ceremony while lawfully married to another, excludes from its coverage individual whose "lawful spouse has been absent from the individual for a continuous period of seven years and who, at the time of the subsequent marriage ceremony, does not know whether or not the spouse is living." The Legislature thus has now recognized the unfairness of convicting a person for remarrying if that person has a *reasonable* belief that his or her former spouse is dead.

8. American penal statutes against fornication are generally unenforced, which may be reflective of the view that such a use of the penal law is improper. *See* Model Penal Code, § 213, Comment at 434.

willingness to take advantage of immaturity, no propensity to corruption of minors. In short, he has demonstrated neither intent nor inclination to violate any of the interests that the law of statutory rape seeks to protect. At most, he has disregarded religious precept or social convention. In terms of mental culpability, his conduct is indistinguishable from that of any other person who engages in fornication. Whether he should be punished at all depends on a judgment about continuing fornication as a criminal offense, but at least he should not be subject to felony sanctions for statutory rape.

Model Penal Code § 213.6, Comment at 415.

C.

In utilizing the moral wrong theory, State legislatures seek to justify strict criminal liability for statutory rape when non-marital sexual intercourse is not a crime on the basis of society's characterization of it as immoral or wrong, *i.e.*, *malum in se*.[12] Reiss, *supra*, at 382. The intent to commit such immoral acts supplies the *mens rea* for the related, but unintended crime; the outrage upon public decency or good morals, not conduct that is wrong only because it is prohibited by legislation, *i.e.*, *malum prohibitum*, is the predicate. There are significant problems with the moral wrong theory. First, it is questionable whether morality should be the basis for legislation or interpretation of the law. Immorality is not synonymous with illegality; intent to do an immoral act does not equate to intent to do a criminal act. Inferring criminal intent from immorality, especially when the accused is not even aware that the act is criminal, seems unjustifiable and unfair. In addition, the values and morals of society are ever evolving. Because sexual intercourse between consenting unmarried adults and minors who have reached the age of consent is not now clearly considered to be immoral, the moral wrong theory does not support strict criminal liability for statutory rape.

Second, classifying an act as immoral, in and of itself, divorced from any consideration of the actor's intention, is contrary to the general consensus of what makes an act moral or immoral.

Third, the assertion that the act alone will suffice for liability without the necessity of proving criminal intent is contrary to the traditional demand of the criminal law that only the act plus criminal intent is sufficient to constitute a crime. "Moral duties should not be identified with criminal duties," and, thus, when fornication is itself not criminal it should not become criminal merely because the defendant has made a reasonable mistake about the age of the girl with whom he has had intercourse.

---

12. An offense *malum in se* is properly defined as one which is naturally evil as adjudged by the sense of a civilized community. Acts *mala in se* have, as a general rule, become criminal offenses by the course and development of common law. BLACK'S LAW DICTIONARY 281 (1984). In comparison, an act *malum prohibitum* is wrong only because made so by statute. *Id. Malum in se* crimes usually include all felonies, injuries to property, adultery, bigamy, indecent acts committed upon underage children, and conduct contributing to the delinquency of a minor.

Therefore, although in the case *sub judice*, the defendant engaged in sexual relations with a girl 13 years old, a minor below the age of consent, his conduct is not *malum in se*, and, so, strict liability is not justified.

III. Mistake of Fact

Generally, a mistake of fact negates the mental state required to establish a material element of the crime. A person who engages in proscribed conduct is relieved of criminal liability if, because of ignorance or mistake of fact, he or she did not entertain the culpable mental state required for the commission of the offense. *Compare Richmond v. State*, 330 Md. 223, 241–42, 623 A.2d 630, 638 (1993) (Bell, J., dissenting) (In case of self-defense, defendant who acts in self-defense is completely exonerated upon findings that he or she subjectively believed that his or her actions were necessary and, viewed objectively, that they were, in fact, necessary; in case of imperfect self-defense, defendant who subjectively believes that his or her actions were necessary, but, objectively, they were not, is not completely exonerated, although lesser sentence is appropriate).

Statutory rape is defined as sexual intercourse, by a person four or more years older, with a person under the age of 14. That statute conclusively presumes that a person under that age is incapable of legally consenting to sexual intercourse. That the female is incapable of consenting means that any act of intercourse in which she engages, even with her consent, is conclusively presumed to have been against her will. Consequently, a person engaging in intercourse with a female, whom he knows to be under 14 may not set up her consent as a defense. This does not mean, however, that one who does not know that the female is under 14 should not be able to set up his mistake of fact as a defense. This is because the closer a minor is to the age of consent, the more the appearance and behavior of that minor can be expected to be consistent with persons who have attained the age of consent. Indeed, one may plausibly mistake a minor 13 years old as being of the statutory age of consent.

A girl 13 years old may appear to be, and, in fact, may represent herself as being, over 16. If she should appear to be the age represented, a defendant may suppose reasonably that he received a valid consent from his partner, whom he mistakenly believes to be of legal age, only to find that her consent is legally invalid. In this situation, the majority holds, his reasonable belief as to the girl's age and consequent lack of criminal intent are no defense; the act alone suffices to establish guilt. But it is when the minor plausibly may represent that she has attained the age of consent that need for a defendant to be able to present a defense based on his or her belief that the minor was of the age to consent is the greatest.

IV. Constitutional Limitations on Strict Criminal Liability

To recognize that a State legislature may, in defining criminal offenses, exclude *mens rea*, is not to suggest that it may do so with absolute impunity, without any limitation whatsoever. The validity of such a statute necessarily will depend on whether it violates any provision of the federal or applicable state constitution. It is ordinarily the due process clause, either of the federal constitution, or the corresponding provision of the appropriate state constitution, which will determine its validity.

Due process, whether pursuant to that clause of the Fourteenth Amendment or the corresponding clause in a state constitution, protects an accused from being convicted of a crime except upon proof beyond a reasonable doubt of every element necessary to constitute the crime with which the accused is charged.

Under our system of justice, a person charged with a crime is presumed innocent until he or she is found guilty beyond a reasonable doubt. That means that he or she may not be found guilty until the State has produced evidence sufficient to convince the trier of fact, to the required extent, of that person's guilt. Moreover, although not required to do so, the defendant may present a defense, in which event the evidence the defendant produces must be assessed along with that of the State in determining whether the State has met its burden. The State's burden is not reduced or changed in any way simply because the defendant elects not to interpose a defense. In those cases, the defendant may still seek to convince the trier of fact that the State has not met its burden of proof by arguing that the inferences to be drawn from the evidence the State has produced simply is not sufficient to support guilt.

The critical issue in a statutory rape case is "the age of the rape victim." That is true because the victim's age serves two related, but distinct purposes: (1) it establishes the victim's capacity to consent and (2) it represents notice to a defendant of proscribed conduct. The Maryland statute seeks irrebuttably to presume not only that the victim could not consent by virtue of age, but also that, when a defendant engages in sexual relations with a minor under the age of 14, he has notice of that fact. Assuming that, based on the victim's age, the Legislature could legitimately exclude consent as an element of the crime,[25] it absolutely should not be able to excuse the State from its obligation to prove the defendant's knowledge of the victim's age or prevent the defendant from producing evidence on that issue. No matter how forcefully it may be argued that there is a rational relationship between the capacity to consent and the age the Legislature selected, given the tremendous difference between individuals, both in appearance and in mental capacity, there

---

25. It is at least arguable that incapacity to consent based on an irrebuttable presumption cannot withstand constitutional scrutiny. For statutory rape to comport with due process, a close correlation between the age of consent specified in the statute and the purpose of the statute—to render minors incapable of consenting to sexual intercourse—is required. It is not necessarily true that a statutory age of consent is a reliable indicator of the capacity of any member of the protected class to understand the nature and consequences of sexual intercourse. Given the variety of cultural factors that can influence a child's acquisition of sexual awareness, it is unlikely that any arbitrary age could do so. While it is reasonable to presume that very young children are naive and incapable of understanding the nature of sexual contact, and, thus, of consenting, an older adolescent's incapacity to consent on this basis seems unreasonable in light of pervasive contemporary sexual mores.

can be no such rational relationship between the proof of the victim's age and the defendant's knowledge of that fact.

The notice element of the crime of statutory rape is different from the consent element, in any event. A defendant who has knowledge that a victim has consented, in fact, to sexual relations, whether the consent is effective or not, is not thereby placed on notice as to the victim's age. Knowledge of consent simply does not equate with knowledge of age, just as intent to engage in sexual relations does not reveal, without more, with whom. Moreover, it is not a crime to engage in sexual relations with a minor who is at least 16 years old; it may be morally wrong, in the minds of most Americans, but it is not a crime. It is only a crime if the defendant engages in such relations with a minor under a specified age, *i.e.*, 14, as in section 463(a)(3), or 14 or 15, as in section 464C. But even when the act engaged in is necessarily a crime, *e.g.*, possession of contraband, knowledge of the illegality—that the contraband is knowingly possessed—is still required. Consequently, where the activity would be legal or, at least, not illegal, but for the ages of the participants, at the very least, the defendant's knowledge of the victim's age must be proven. Otherwise, a defendant who does not know he is acting illegally could be convicted.

A similar result was reached by the Supreme Court of Alaska in *Guest*, involving a charge of statutory rape. Significantly, having held that, under its precedents, a reasonable mistake of age defense was permitted, the court submitted:

> [W]here a particular statute is not a public welfare type of offense, either a requirement of criminal intent must be read into the statute or it must be found unconstitutional. . . . Since statutes should be construed where possible to avoid unconstitutionality, it is necessary here to infer a requirement of criminal intent.

Similarly, the prosecution of statutory rape in Maryland necessarily brings into conflict the State's interests in protecting minors and defendants' due process rights because section 463(a)(3) operates "'to exclude elements of knowledge and diligence from its definition,'" and, thus, removes reasonable ignorance of the girl's age and consequent lack of criminal intent as a defense. The failure of section 463(a)(3) to require proof of a culpable mental state conflicts both with the substantive due process ideal requiring that defendants possess some level of fault for a criminal conviction of statutory rape and the procedural due process ideal requiring that the prosecution overcome the presumption of innocence by proof of the defendant's guilt beyond a reasonable doubt. Notwithstanding the maxim that criminal statutes dispensing with the intent requirement and criminal offenses requiring no *mens rea* have a "generally disfavored status," the rationale of parts V and VI of the majority opinion is that the legislature has absolute authority to create strict liability crimes. For the reasons reviewed, I do not agree. On the contrary, I believe that due process both under the Fourteenth Amendment and under the Declaration of Rights, precludes strict criminal liability for statutory rape. Interpreting section 463(a)(3) as the majority does has the effect of largely relieving the State of its burden of proof and burden of persuasion. By making the defendant's intent, and, hence, blameworthiness, irrelevant, the Legislature has made inevitable, the petitioner's conviction. Moreover, upon conviction of the felony offense of statutory rape under section 463(a)(3), in addition to a substantial penalty of up to 20 years imprisonment, a defendant's reputation will be gravely besmirched. Where there is no issue as to sexual contact, which is more likely than not to be the case in statutory rape prosecutions, proof of the prosecutrix's age is not only proof of the defendant's guilt, it is absolutely dispositive of it and, at the same time, it is fatal to the only defense the defendant would otherwise have. So interpreted, section 463(a)(3) not only destroys absolutely the concept of fault, but it renders meaningless, in the statutory rape context, the presumption of innocence and the right to due process.

I respectfully dissent.

Questions and Notes

1. Although courts are split on the issue raised by *Garnett*, *Garnett* probably reflects the prevailing view.

2. What could motivate a court (or a legislature) to subject a morally innocent human being to the possibility of 20 years' imprisonment for making a reasonable, albeit erroneous, determination of age? Could it be concerned about encouraging "mistakes" or claimed mistakes? Would innocent belief be too easy a defense to fabricate?

3. In regard to Question 2, do you think that the opinion of Judge Eldridge is superior to that of Judge Bell?

4. As between Garnett and Guminga, who do you think had a stronger due process argument?

5. Had you been on the court, would you have concurred with Chief Judge Murphy, Judge Eldridge, or Judge Bell? Why?

6. Suppose Erica were prosecuted as a delinquent for having sex with a retarded man? What result? Why?

7. Would (should) the result be different if Ramona, a 20-year-old female, had sex with Eric, a 13-year-old male?

8. Should it matter that sex between consenting adults is today deemed to be a constitutional right? *See* Loewy, *Statutory Rape in a Post* Lawrence v. Texas *World*, 58 SMU L. Rev. 77 (2005). *See* Nutshell §§ 8.04, 8.05.

C. Mistake of Fact

Classic blackletter law suggests that a mistake of fact will exculpate a defendant if, but only if, it is reasonable. In actuality, that statement is flawed from both directions. If the crime involves strict liability, a reasonable mistake will not help the defendant. *See, e.g., Garnett, supra.* On the other hand, where purpose or knowledge is required for an element of a crime, even an unreasonable mistake will excuse the defendant. For example, if A shoots at what she negligently thinks is a dummy but is in fact B, another person, she cannot be guilty of premeditated murder because she lacked the intent to kill. In other words, her unreasonable mistake of fact would excuse (or more accurately, reduce) her crime.

In the cases that follow (*Morgan* and *Short*), consider whether an unreasonable mistake ought to constitute a defense and why. In both cases, the dissenting opinions probably represent the prevailing view.

D.P.P. v. Morgan

2 All E.R. 365 (1975)

LORD HAILSHAM OF ST. MARYLEBONE.

The appellant Morgan and his three co-defendants, who were all members of the R.A.F., spent the evening of August 15, 1973, in one another's company. The appellant Morgan was significantly older than the other three, and considerably senior to them in rank. He was married to the alleged victim, but not, it seems at the time habitually sleeping in the same bed. At this time, Mrs. Morgan occupied a single bed in the same room as her younger son aged about 11 years, and by the time the appellants arrived at Morgan's house, Mrs. Morgan was already in bed and asleep, until she was awoken by their presence.

According to the version of the facts which she gave in evidence, and which was evidently accepted by the jury, she was aroused from her sleep, frog-marched into another room where there was a double bed, held by each of her limbs, arms and legs apart, by the four appellants, while each of the three young appellants in turn had intercourse with her in the presence of the others, during which time the other two committed various lewd acts upon various parts of her body. When each had finished and had left the room, the appellant Morgan completed the series of incidents by having intercourse with her himself.

All four defendants explained in the witness box that they had spent the evening together in Wolverhampton, and by the time of the alleged offences had had a good deal to drink. Their original intention had been to find some women in the town, but when this failed, Morgan made the surprising suggestion to the others that they should all return to his home and have sexual intercourse with his wife. According to the three younger appellants (but not according to Morgan who described this part of their story as "lying") Morgan told them that they must not be surprised if his wife struggled a bit, since she was "kinky" and this was the only way in which she could get "turned on." However this may be, it is clear that Morgan did invite his three companions home in order that they might have sexual intercourse with his wife, and, no doubt, he may well have led them in one way or another to believe that she would consent to their doing so. This however, would only be matter predisposing them to believe that Mrs. Morgan consented, and would not in any way establish that, at the time, they believed she did consent whilst they were having intercourse. The certified question arises because counsel for the appellants raised the question whether, even if the victim had not consented, the appellants may not have honestly believed that she did. [T]he question was wholly unreal, because if there was reasonable doubt about belief, the same material must have given rise to reasonable doubt about consent, and vice versa. But, presumably because, at that stage, the jury's view of the matter had not been sought, the matter was left to them, as the appellants complain, in a form which implied that they could only acquit if the mistaken belief in consent was reasonable, and it was not enough that it should be honest. This ruling was originally made at the close of the case for the prosecution, but, as it was subsequently embodied in the summing up, it is sufficient to refer to this.

The learned judge said:

> "In the first place, the prosecution have to prove that each defendant intended to have sexual intercourse with this woman without her consent, not merely that he intended to have intercourse with her but he intended to have intercourse without her consent. Therefore if the defendant believed or may have believed that Mrs. Morgan consented to him having sexual intercourse with her, then there would be no such intent in his mind and would be not guilty of the offence of rape, but such a belief must be honestly held by the defendant in the first place. He must really believe that. And, secondly, his belief must be a reasonable belief; such a belief as a reasonable man would entertain if he applied his mind and thought about the matter. It is not enough for a defendant to rely upon a belief, even though he honestly held it, if it was completely fanciful; contrary to every indication which could be given which would carry some weight with a reasonable man. And, of course, the belief must be not a belief that the woman would consent at some time in the future, but a belief that at the time when intercourse was taking place or when it began that she was then consenting to it."

No complaint was made of the judge's first proposition describing the mental element.

It is upon the second proposition about the mental element that the appellants concentrate their criticism. An honest belief in consent, they contend, is enough. It matters not whether it be also reasonable. No doubt a defendant will wish to raise argument or lead evidence to show that his belief was reasonable, since this will support its honesty. No doubt the prosecution will seek to cross-examine or raise arguments or adduce evidence to undermine the contention that the belief is reasonable, because, in the nature of the case, the fact that a belief cannot reasonably be held is a strong ground for saying that it was not in fact held honestly at all. Nonetheless, the appellants contend, the crux of the matter, the *factum probandum*, or rather the fact to be refuted by the prosecution, is honesty and not honesty plus reasonableness. In making reasonableness as well as honesty an ingredient in this "defence" the judge, say the appellants, was guilty of a misdirection.

My first comment upon this direction is that the propositions described "in the first place" and "secondly" in the above direction as to the mental ingredient in rape are wholly irreconcilable. In practice this was accepted by both counsel for the appellants and for the respondent, counsel for the appellants embracing that described as "in the first place" and counsel for the respondent embracing the "secondly," and each rejecting the other as not being a correct statement of the law. In this, in my view, they had no alternative.

If it be true, as the learned judge says "in the first place," that the prosecution have to prove that

> "each defendant intended to have sexual intercourse without her consent, not merely that he intended to have intercourse with her but that he intended to have intercourse without her consent[,]"

The defendant must be entitled to an acquittal if the prosecution fail to prove just that. The necessary mental ingredient will be lacking and the only possible verdict is "not guilty." If, on the other hand, as is asserted in the passage beginning "secondly," it is necessary for any belief in the woman's consent to be "a reasonable belief" before the defendant is entitled to an acquittal, it must either be because the mental ingredient in rape is not "to have intercourse and to have it without her consent" but simply "to have intercourse" subject to a special defence of "honest and reasonable belief," or alternatively to have intercourse without a reasonable belief in her consent. Counsel for the Crown argued for each of these alternatives, but in my view each is open to insuperable objections of principle. No doubt it would be possible, by statute, to devise a law by which intercourse, voluntarily entered into, was an absolute offence, subject to a "defence" of belief whether honest or honest and reasonable, of which the "evidential" burden is primarily on the defence and the "probative" burden on the prosecution. But in my opinion such is not the crime of rape as it has hitherto been understood. The prohibited act in rape is to have intercourse without the victim's consent. The minimum *mens rea* or guilty mind in most common law offenses, including rape, is the intention to do the prohibited act, and that is correctly stated in the proposition stated "in the first place" of the judge's direction. In murder the situation is different, because the murder is only complete when the victim dies, and an intention to do really serious bodily harm has been held to be enough if such be the case.

The only qualification I would make to the direction of the learned judge's "in the first place" is the refinement for which, as I shall show, there is both Australian and English authority, that if the intention of the accused is to have intercourse *nolens volens*, that is recklessly and not caring whether the victim be a consenting party or not, that is equivalent on ordinary principles to an intent to do the prohibited act without the consent of the victim.

The alternative version of the learned judge's direction would read that the accused must do the prohibited act with the intention of doing it without an honest and reasonable belief in the victim's consent. This in effect is the version which took up most of the time in argument, and although I find the Court of Appeal's judgment difficult to understand, I think it the version which ultimately commended itself to that court. At all events I think it the more plausible way in which to state the learned judge's "secondly." In principle, however, I find it unacceptable. I believe that "*mens rea*" means "guilty or criminal mind," and if it be the case, as seems to be accepted here, that mental element in rape is not knowledge but intent, to insist that a belief must be reasonable to excuse is to insist that either the accused is to be found guilty of intending to do that which in truth he did not intend to do, or that his state of mind, though innocent of evil intent, can convict him if it be honest but not rational.

Lord Simon of Glaisdale. (Dissenting in Part):

It remains to consider why the law requires, in such circumstances, that the belief in a state of affairs whereby the actus would not be reus must be held on reasonable grounds. One reason was given by Bridge J. in the Court of Appeal:

> "The rationale of requiring reasonable grounds for the mistaken belief must lie in the law's consideration that a bald assertion of belief for which the accused can indicate no reasonable ground is evidence of insufficient substance to raise any issue requiring the jury's consideration."

I agree; but I think there is also another reason. The policy of the law in this regard could well derive from its concern to hold a fair balance between victim and accused. It would hardly seem just to fob off a victim of a savage assault with such comfort as he could derive from knowing that his injury was caused by a belief, however absurd, that he was about to attack the accused. A respectable woman who has been ravished would hardly feel that she was vindicated by being told that her assailant must go unpunished because he believed, quite unreasonable, that she was consenting to sexual intercourse with him.

I would therefore dismiss the appeal.

Questions and Notes

1. In *Morgan*, the defendants won the battle and lost the war. The court ruled that an unreasonable mistake of fact would exculpate them. It also affirmed the convictions on the ground that, given the verdict as applied to the conflicting stories, there was no way the jury could have found that the defendants honestly believed that Mrs. Morgan was consenting.

2. Why do you suppose that *Morgan* is almost universally rejected in the United States?

3. What are the values in convicting a defendant who did not intend to have sexual intercourse with a nonconsenting woman?

4. Is the question in *Short* different from or the same as that in *Morgan*?

United States v. Short

4 U.S.M.C.A. 437 (1954)

QUINN, Chief Judge:

A general court-martial in Japan convicted the accused of assault with intent to commit rape, and sentenced him to dishonorable discharge, total forfeitures, and confinement at hard labor for ten years. The convening authority modified the sentence by reducing the period of confinement to five years. A board of review affirmed the conviction and the modified sentence. We granted review to consider the correctness of the law officer's general instructions and his denial of certain defense requests for specific instructions.

The events of this case took place on November 28, 1952, in Tokyo. At about 11:30 p.m., two Japanese girls, Yayoi Tomobe and Tukiko Okano, left the shop in which they worked to dispose of some waste paper in a public latrine located across the street. Apparently as the girls were crossing the street, they were approached from behind by the accused and his companion, Private O'Rourke. From their speech, Okano deduced that the 'foreigners' were intoxicated. She was frightened. Calling out to Tomobe to run, Okano ran back to the shop. Tomobe, however, tripped over a stone. As she regained her balance, she was caught under her right arm by the accused. The accused spoke to her in English. Although she had learned some English in school, she was "so scared and . . . surprised" that she did not know what was said, except that there was mention of yen. She was then pulled to the front of the latrine and pushed in. The accused entered and closed the door. Tomobe tried to get away from the accused, but he was "very big." She was "scared" and "had no strength to go out." While the accused did not punch, kick, or otherwise inflict bodily harm upon her, he fondled her person against her protests. She kept saying "no" in Japanese as loudly as she could. She pushed the accused away, but he was "so strong that she was unable to hold him away."

In the meantime, Okano, having seen Tomobe pulled into the latrine, reported to the manager of the shop. He immediately went to the latrine and opened the door. He heard Tomobe saying "no," and he saw the accused holding her. However, just then O'Rourke tapped him on the shoulder and he made no further effort to interfere. Instead, he went to a police box, located approximately forty feet from the latrine, and reported the matter to the Japanese policemen. They hastened to the latrine. One of the policemen opened the door, and in Japanese called out to the accused to stop. In the same language, the accused replied that it was all right. Then he was forcibly removed from the latrine, and taken to the police box.

At the trial, the accused admitted fondling Tomobe, as set out in the specification. However, he denied that he acted unlawfully. He testified that when he saw Tomobe, he thought she was a prostitute since the area was known to be frequented by them. He "propositioned" her, and after some negotiation they agreed on a price of 500 yen. Tomobe showed him the latrine; he previously did not know of its existence. Inside, Tomobe helped him in his efforts to "make love to her." Although he was "under the influence," he was generally aware of what he was doing. When the police entered the latrine, he thought that they wanted to arrest the girl as a prostitute. He told them that it was all right because he was anxious to protect her.

[T]he accused sought to present a defense of mistake of fact. It is axiomatic that, before a failure to instruct on a defense may be alleged as ground for error, the evidence must show that the defense was reasonably raised. We assume for the purposes of this case that sufficient evidence appears in the record from which it may reasonably be inferred the accused believed that Tomobe consented to his "proposition." However, the question still to be answered is whether the instruction requested is legally correct. The accused stresses the similarity of the requested instruction to that in *McQuirk v. State*, 84 Ala. 435, 4 So. 775. In that case the accused was charged with rape. The evidence showed that the prosecutrix was weak-minded. The defendant maintained that he believed she had consented to the act. He requested the following instruction which was denied by the trial judge:

> "if the jury believe, from the evidence, that the conduct of the prosecutrix was such towards the defendant, at the time of the alleged rape, as to create in the mind of the defendant the honest and reasonable belief that she had consented, or was willing for defendant to have connection with her, they must acquit the defendant."

On appeal the conviction was reversed because of the failure of the trial judge to give the requested instruction.

It is immediately apparent that the requested instruction in this case is markedly different from that in *McQuirk*. It fails to qualify the accused's belief by requiring that it be reasonable and honest. *See also United States v. Perruccio*, 4 U.S.M.C.A. 28. This omission is substantial. The requested instruction also assumes too much. When consent is in issue, whether or not it was given is a question of fact for the court. It, not the accused, must determine whether the woman's conduct was such as to lead the accused to believe she had consented to his acts. The accused's personal evaluation of the circumstances is but one factor to be considered by the court; it is not conclusive. The decision of the board of review is affirmed.

BROSMAN, JUDGE (concurring in part and dissenting in part):

Here the evidence seems to me to have raised reasonably the possibility that the accused believed the prosecutrix was acceding to his overtures. The principal opinion suggests that such a belief, to be effective, must be both reasonable and honest. For this its author cites *United States v. Perruccio*, 4 U.S.M.C.A. 28, where an unreasonable — and thus negligent — mistake of fact was deemed no defense to a prosecution for negligent homicide. On the other hand, a mistake of fact may be negligent and yet negate the intent or knowledge required for conviction of certain offenses. Within which category do rape and assault with intent to commit rape fall?

Rape — like unpremeditated murder — has ordinarily been treated as requiring only a general criminal intent. Thus, drunkenness, even in excessive degree, would probably not constitute a defense to this crime — that is, as serving to belie the accused's necessary intent. However, assault with intent to commit rape would seem to occupy a quite different position — since the very designation of the offense indicates the requirement of a specific intent. Clearly, then, drunkenness could operate to negate the intent required for conviction of such an assault. An unreasonable mistake of fact could perhaps not serve to deny criminal liability for a consummated rape. But could it negative the prerequisites for a finding of guilt of assault with intent to commit rape — just as an unreasonable mistake of fact is said to destroy liability for larceny by false pretenses?

Ignorance or mistake of fact — if reasonable — normally provides a defense to an accused. Ignorance of law usually constitutes no excuse — although it may negate the existence of the specific intent required in certain offenses. While consent in some areas may be a matter of law, I would suppose that the type of consent with which we are now dealing is "factual" in nature, and that a mistake as to the woman's attitude would constitute one of fact. Thus, if the accused believed reasonably that the Japanese girl here was consenting to his proposals, he would be exonerated, I should think, even from the crime of assault. On the other hand, an unreasonable mistake on his part would not affect his liability for assault.

But if an assault is to be found here — on the theory there was neither consent nor a reasonable mistake with regard thereto — does not the accused's mistake reenter the picture? One possibility is that the trier of fact may conclude that the girl did not consent, and that no reasonable man would have thought she did, but that the accused — because of drunkenness or some variety of mild sexual complex which destroyed his realism — genuinely believed that she was acquiescent. His purpose simply was to enjoy sexual relations with her under the circumstances presented to him. Those circumstances he unreasonably construed to amount to an invitation on her part. However, he did not intend coitus under any other circumstances. This might be because (a) he did not desire intercourse without full consent; or (b) because he was just not the sort of person who worries about hypothetical problems. When a man fondles a woman against a background of the frame of mind just mentioned, I would suppose him to be wanting in that variety of criminal purpose required for assault with intent to rape. One may well lack an intention to overcome resistance when nothing is present which seems to suggest the possibility of its presence.

It may be regarded as anomalous to conclude that an accused may be exonerated from guilt of assault with intent to commit rape because of an unreasonable mistake, whereas he could have been convicted lawfully of rape had penetration been effected under the same misapprehension. It is to be observed, however, that the anomaly is no greater than that involved in holding that an assault with intent to murder requires a specific intent to kill, whereas the crime of murder may be made out with a lesser intent. The fact of the matter is that a specific intent is, by definition, required for the present finding. The evidence, in my view, raised the possibility that a mistake of fact on the accused's part precluded that intent.

It follows from what has been said that as to mere assault, the accused is not entitled to an instruction on mistake of fact, unless the possibility of a reasonable mistake was raised by the evidence. On the other hand, as to assault with intent to rape, he is so entitled regardless of reasonableness.

I would reverse the decision of the board of review and order a rehearing.

Questions and Notes

1. Which opinion is better reasoned, the majority or the dissent? Why?

2. The dissent is probably the prevailing view in the United States. Is there any good reason for courts to generally accept Judge Brosman's dissenting opinion while at the same time rejecting Lord Hailsham's *Morgan* opinion?

3. Shouldn't the law try to discourage unreasonable "mistakes"?

D. Mistake of Law

Mistake of law problems are somewhat different from mistake of fact. The classic blackletter law says that mistake of law is no defense. As the cases make clear, however, this is something of an overstatement. The first case, *Marrero,* probably represents the prevailing view.

People v. Marrero

507 N.E.2d 1068 (N.Y. 1987)

BELLACOSA, Judge.

The defense of mistake of law (Penal Law § 15.20[2][a], [d]) is not available to a Federal corrections officer arrested in a Manhattan social club for possession of a loaded .38 caliber automatic pistol who claimed he mistakenly believed he was entitled, pursuant to the interplay of CPL 2.10, 1.20 and Penal Law § 265.20, to carry a handgun without a permit as a peace officer.

In a prior phase of this criminal proceeding, defendant's motion to dismiss the indictment upon which he now stands convicted was granted; then it was reversed and the indictment reinstated by a divided Appellate Division; next, defendant allowed an appeal from that order, certified to the Court of Appeals, to lapse and be dismissed (Oct. 22, 1980). Thus, review of that aspect of the case is precluded.

On the trial of the case, the court rejected the defendant's argument that his personal misunderstanding of the statutory definition of a peace officer is enough to excuse him from criminal liability under New York's mistake of law statute. The court refused to charge the jury on this issue and defendant was convicted of criminal possession of a weapon in the third degree. We affirm the Appellate Division order upholding the conviction. Defendant was a Federal corrections officer in Danbury, Connecticut, and asserted that status at the time of his arrest in 1977. He claimed at trial that there were various interpretations of fellow officers and teachers, as well as the peace officer statute itself, upon which he relied for his mistaken belief that he could carry a weapon with legal impunity. The starting point for our analysis is the New York mistake statute as an outgrowth of the dogmatic common-law maxim that ignorance of the law is no excuse. The central issue is whether defendant's personal misreading or misunderstanding of a statute may excuse criminal conduct in the circumstances of this case.

The common-law rule on mistake of law was clearly articulated in *Gardner v. People*, 62 N.Y. 299. In *Gardner*, the defendants misread a statute and mistakenly believed that their conduct was legal. The court insisted, however, that the "mistake of law" did not relieve the defendants of criminal liability. The statute at issue, relating to the removal of election officers, required that prior to removal, written notice must be given to the officer sought to be removed. The statute provided one exception to the notice requirement: "removal . . . shall only be made after notice in writing . . . unless made while the inspector is actually on duty on a day of registration, revision of registration, or election, and for improper conduct" The defendants construed the statute to mean that an election officer could be removed without notice for improper conduct at any time. The court ruled that removal without notice could only occur for improper conduct on a day of registration, revision of registration or election.

In ruling that the defendant's misinterpretation of the statute was no defense, the court said: "The defendants made a mistake of law. Such mistakes do not excuse the commission of prohibited acts. 'The rule on the subject appears to be, that in acts *mala in se*, the intent governs, but in those *mala prohibita*, the only inquiry is, has the law been violated?' The act prohibited must be intentionally done. A mistake as to the fact of doing the act will excuse the party, but if the act is intentionally done, the statute declares it a misdemeanor, irrespective of the motive or intent. . . . The evidence offered [showed] that the defendants were of [the] opinion that the statute did not require notice to be given before removal. This opinion, if entertained in good faith, mitigated the character of the act, but was not a defence [*sic*]." This is to be contrasted with *People v. Weiss*, 276 N.Y. 384, 12 N.E.2d 514 where, in a kidnapping case, the trial court precluded testimony that the defendants acted with the honest belief that seizing and confining the child was done with "authority of law." We held it was error to exclude such testimony since a good-faith belief in the legality of the conduct would negate an express and necessary element of the crime of kidnapping, *i.e.*, intent, without authority of law, to confine or imprison another. Subject to the mistake statute, the instant case, of course, falls within the *Gardner* rationale because the weapons possession statute violated by this defendant imposes liability irrespective of one's intent.

The desirability of the *Gardner*-type outcome, which was to encourage the societal benefit of individuals' knowledge of and respect for the law, is underscored by Justice Holmes' statement: "It is no doubt true that there are many cases in which the criminal could not have known that he was breaking the law, but to admit the excuse at all would be to encourage ignorance where the law-maker has determined to make men know and obey, and justice to the individual is rightly outweighed by the larger interests on the other side of the scales" (HOLMES, THE COMMON LAW, at 48 [1881]).

The revisors of New York's Penal Law intended no fundamental departure from this common-law rule in Penal Law § 15.20, which provides in pertinent part:

"§ 15.20. *Effect of ignorance or mistake upon liability.*

"2. A person is not relieved of criminal liability for conduct because he engages in such conduct under a mistaken belief that it does not, as a matter of law, constitute an offense, unless such mistaken belief is founded upon an official statement of the law contained in (a) a statute or other enactment . . . (d) an interpretation of the statute or law relating to the offense, officially made or issued by a public servant, agency, or body legally charged or empowered with the responsibility or privilege of administering, enforcing or interpreting such statute or law."

This section was added to the Penal Law as part of the wholesale revision of the Penal Law in 1965 (L.1965, ch. 1030). When this provision was first proposed, commentators viewed the new language as codifying "the established common law maxim on mistake of law, while at the same time recognizing a defense when the erroneous belief is founded upon an 'official statement of the law'"

The defendant claims as a first prong of his defense that he is entitled to raise the defense of mistake of law under section 15.20(2)(a) because his mistaken belief that his conduct was legal was founded upon an official statement of the law contained in the statute itself. Defendant argues that his mistaken interpretation of the statute was reasonable in view of the alleged ambiguous wording of the peace officer exemption statute, and that his "reasonable" interpretation of an "official statement" is enough to satisfy the requirements of subdivision (2)(a). However, the whole thrust of this exceptional exculpatory concept, in derogation of the traditional and common-law principle, was intended to be a very narrow escape valve. Application in this case would invert that thrust and make mistake of law a generally applied or available defense instead of an unusual exception which the very opening words of the mistake statute make so clear, *i.e.*, "A person is not relieved of criminal liability for conduct . . . unless" (Penal Law § 15.20). The momentarily enticing argument by defendant that his view of the statute would only allow a defendant to get the issue generally before a jury further supports the contrary view because that consequence is precisely what would give the defense the unintended broad practical application.

The prosecution further counters defendant's argument by asserting that one cannot claim the protection of mistake of law under section 15.20(2)(a) simply by misconstruing the meaning of a statute but must instead establish that the statute relied on actually permitted the conduct in question and was only later found to be erroneous. To buttress that argument, the People analogize New York's official statement defense to the approach taken by the Model Penal Code (MPC). Section 2.04 of the MPC provides:

"Section 2.04. *Ignorance or Mistake.*

"(3) A belief that conduct does not legally constitute an offense is a defense to a prosecution for that offense based upon such conduct when . . . (b) he acts in reasonable reliance upon an official statement of the law, *afterward determined to be invalid or erroneous*, contained in (i) a statute or other enactment" (emphasis added).

Although the drafters of the New York statute did not adopt the precise language of the Model Penal Code provision with the emphasized clause, it is evident and has long been believed that the Legislature intended the New York statute to be similarly construed. In fact, the legislative history of section 15.20 is replete with references to the influence of the Model Penal Code provision.

It was early recognized that the "official statement" mistake of law defense was a statutory protection against prosecution based on reliance of a statute that did *in fact* authorize certain conduct. "It seems obvious that society must rely on some statement of the law, and that conduct which *is in fact* 'authorized' . . . should not be subsequently condemned. The threat of punishment under these circumstances can have no deterrent effect unless the actor doubts the validity of the official pronouncement — *a questioning of authority that is itself undesirable.*" While providing a narrow escape hatch, the idea was simultaneously to encourage the public to read and rely on official statements of the law, not to have individuals conveniently and personally question the validity and interpretation of the law and act on that basis. If later the statute was invalidated, one who mistakenly acted in reliance on the authorizing statute would be relieved of criminal liability. That makes sense and is fair. To go further does not make sense and would create a legal chaos based on individual selectivity.

In the case before us, the underlying statute never *in fact authorized* the defendant's conduct; the defendant only thought that the statutory exemptions permitted his conduct when, in fact, the primary statute clearly forbade his conduct. Moreover, by adjudication of the final court to speak on the subject in this very case, it turned out that even the exemption statute did not permit this defendant to possess the weapon. It would be ironic at best and an odd perversion at worst for this court now to declare that the same defendant is nevertheless free of criminal responsibility.

The "official statement" component in the mistake of law defense in both paragraphs (a) and (d) adds yet another element of support for our interpretation and holding. Defendant tried to establish a defense under Penal Law § 15.20(2)(d) as a second prong. But the interpretation of the statute relied upon must be "officially made or issued by a public servant, agency or body legally charged or empowered with the responsibility or privilege of administering, enforcing or interpreting such statute or law." We agree with the People that the trial court also properly rejected the defense under Penal Law § 15.20(2)(d) since none of the interpretations which defendant proffered meets the requirements of the statute. The fact that there are various complementing exceptions to section 15.20, none of which defendant could bring himself under, further emphasizes the correctness of our view which decides this case under particular statutes with appropriate precedential awareness.

It must also be emphasized that, while our construction of Penal Law § 15.20 provides for narrow application of the mistake of law defense, it does not, as the dissenters contend, "rule out *any* defense based on mistake of law." To the contrary, mistake of law is a viable exemption in those instances where an individual demonstrates an effort to learn what the law is, relies on the validity of that law and, later, it is determined that there was a *mistake in the law itself.*

The modern availability of this defense is based on the theory that where the government has affirmatively, albeit unintentionally, misled an individual as to what may or may not be legally permissible conduct, the individual should not be punished as a result. This is salutary and enlightened and should be firmly supported in appropriate cases. However, it also follows that where, as here, the government is not responsible for the error (for there is none except in the defendant's own mind), mistake of law should not be available as an excuse.

We recognize that some legal scholars urge that the mistake of law defense should be available more broadly where a defendant misinterprets a potentially ambiguous statute not previously clarified by judicial decision and reasonably believes in good faith that the acts were legal. Professor Perkins, a leading supporter of this view, has said: "[i]f the meaning of a statute is not clear, and has not been judicially determined, one who has acted 'in good faith' should not be held guilty of crime if his conduct would have been proper had the statute meant what he 'reasonably believed' it to mean, even if the court should decide later that the proper construction is otherwise." In support of this conclusion Professor Perkins cites two cases: *State v. Cutter,* 36 N.J. Law. 125 and *Burns v. State,* 61 S.W.2d 512, 123 Tex. Cr. R. 611. In both these cases mistake of law was viewed as a valid defense to offenses where a specific intent (*i.e.*, willfully, knowingly, etc.) was an element of the crime charged. In *Burns,* the court recognized mistake of law as a defense to extortion. The statute defining "extortion" made the "willful" doing of the prohibited act an essential ingredient of the offense. The court, holding that mistake of law is a defense only where the mistake negates the specific intent required for conviction, borrowed language from the *Cutter* case: "In *State v. Cutter* . . . the court said: 'The argument goes upon the legal maxim *ignorantia legis neminem excusat.* But this rule, in its application to the law of crimes, is subject . . . to certain important exceptions. Where the act done is *malum in se,* or where the law which has been infringed was settled and plain, the maxim, in its rigor, will be applied; but where the law is not settled, or is obscure, *and where the guilty intention, being a necessary constituent of the particular offence, is dependent on a knowledge of the law, this rule, if enforced, would be misapplied*'" (*Burns v. State,* 123 Tex. Cr. R. at 613, 61 S.W.2d at 513, *supra* [emphasis added]). Thus, while Professor Perkins states that the defense should be available in cases where the defendant claims mistaken reliance on an ambiguous statute, the cases he cites recognize the defense only where the law was ambiguous *and* the ignorance or mistake of law negated the requisite intent (*see also, People v. Weiss, supra*). In this case, the forbidden act of possessing a weapon is clear and unambiguous, and only by the interplay of a double exemption does defendant seek to escape criminal responsibility, *i.e.*, the peace officer statute and the mistake statute.

We conclude that the better and correctly construed view is that the defense should not be recognized, except where specific intent is an element of the offense or where the misrelied-upon law has later been properly adjudicated as wrong. Any broader view fosters lawlessness. It has been said in support of our preferred view in relation to other available procedural protections:

> "A statute ... which is so indefinite that it 'either forbids or requires the doing of an act in terms so vague that men of common intelligence must necessarily guess at its meaning and differ as to its application, violates the first essential of due process of law' and is unconstitutional. If the court feels that a statute is sufficiently definite to meet this test, it is hard to see why a defense of mistake of law is needed. Such a statute could hardly mislead the defendant into believing that his acts were not criminal, if they do in fact come under its ban.... [I]f the defense of mistake of law based on indefiniteness is raised, the court is ... going to require proof ... that the act was sufficiently definite to guide the conduct of reasonable men. Thus, the need for such a defense is largely supplied by the constitutional guarantee."

Strong public policy reasons underlie the legislative mandate and intent which we perceive in rejecting defendant's construction of New York's mistake of law defense statute. If defendant's argument were accepted, the exception would swallow the rule. Mistakes about the law would be encouraged, rather than respect for and adherence to law. There would be an infinite number of mistake of law defenses which could be devised from a good-faith, perhaps reasonable but mistaken, interpretation of criminal statutes, many of which are concededly complex. Even more troublesome are the opportunities for wrongminded individuals to contrive in bad faith solely to get an exculpatory notion before the jury. These are not *in terrorem* arguments disrespectful of appropriate adjudicative procedures; rather, they are the realistic and practical consequences were the dissenters' views to prevail. Our holding comports with a statutory scheme which was not designed to allow false and diversionary stratagems to be provided for many more cases than the statutes contemplated. This would not serve the ends of justice but rather would serve game playing and evasion from properly imposed criminal responsibility.

Accordingly, the order of the Appellate Division should be affirmed.

HANCOCK, Judge (dissenting).

The rule adopted by the majority prohibiting the defense of mistake of law under Penal Law § 15.20(2)(a) in the circumstances here is directly contrary to the plain dictates of the statute and a rejection of the jurisprudential reforms and legislative policies underlying its enactment. For these reasons, as more fully explained herein, we cannot agree with this decision.

I

The basic difference which divides the court may be simply put. Suppose the case of a man who has committed an act which is criminal not because it is inherently wrong or immoral but solely because it violates a criminal statute. He has committed the act in complete good faith under the mistaken but entirely reasonable assumption that the act does not constitute an offense because it is permitted by the wording of the statute. Does the law require that this man be punished? The majority says that it does and holds that (1) Penal Law § 15.20(2)(a) must be construed so that the man is precluded from offering a defense based on his mistake of law and (2) such construction is compelled by prevailing considerations of public policy and criminal jurisprudence. We take issue with the majority on both propositions.

There can be no question that under the view that the purpose of the criminal justice system is to punish blameworthiness or "choosing freely to do wrong,"[1] our supposed man who has acted innocently and without any intent to do wrong should not be punished. Indeed, under some standards of morality he has done no wrong at all. Since he has not knowingly committed a wrong there can be no reason for society to exact retribution. Because the man is law-abiding and would not have acted but for his mistaken assumption as to the law, there is no need for punishment to deter him from further unlawful conduct. Traditionally, however, under the ancient rule of Anglo-American common law that ignorance or mistake of law is no excuse, our supposed man would be punished.

The maxim "*ignorantia legis neminem excusat*" finds its roots in Medieval law when the "actor's intent was irrelevant since the law punished the *act itself*" and when, for example, the law recognized no difference between an intentional killing and one that was accidental. Although the common law has gradually evolved from its origins in Anglo-Germanic tribal law (adding the element of intent [*mens rea*] and recognizing defenses based on the actor's mental state — *e.g.*, justification, insanity and intoxication) the dogmatic rule that ignorance or mistake of law is no excuse has remained unaltered. Various justifications have been offered for the rule, but all are frankly pragmatic and utilitarian — preferring the interests of society (*e.g.*, in deterring criminal conduct, fostering orderly judicial administration, and preserving the primacy of the rule of law)[5] to the interest of the individual in being

---

1. "Historically, our substantive criminal law is based upon a theory of punishing the vicious will. It postulates a free agent confronted with a choice between doing right and doing wrong and choosing freely to do wrong" (Pound, Introduction to Sayre, CASES ON CRIMINAL LAW [1927], quoted in *Morissette*.)

5. The societal interests mentioned in the literature include: facilitating judicial administration, encouraging knowledge and obedience to law and preservation of integrity of legal norms (77 COLUM. L. REV. 775, 787). Justice Holmes, for example, stressed society's interests in deterrence, noting that acceptance of ignorance or mistake of law as a defense would encourage ignorance at the expense of the public good (*see*, HOLMES, THE COMMON LAW, at 48 [1881]; *Ellis v. United States*, 206 U.S. 246, 257). John Austin justified "*ignorantia legis*" on the ground that if the defense were

free from punishment except for intentionally engaging in conduct which he knows is criminal.

Today there is widespread criticism of the common-law rule mandating categorical preclusion of the mistake of law defense. The utilitarian arguments for retaining the rule have been drawn into serious question but the fundamental objection is that it is simply wrong to punish someone who, in good-faith reliance on the wording of a statute, believed that what he was doing was lawful. It is contrary to "the notion that punishment should be conditioned on a showing of subjective moral blameworthiness" In modern times, however, with the profusion of legislation making otherwise lawful conduct criminal (*malum prohibitum*), the "common law fiction that every man is presumed to know the law has become indefensible in fact or logic."

With this background we proceed to a discussion of our disagreement with the majority's construction of Penal Law § 15.20(2)(a) and the policy and jurisprudential arguments made in support of that construction. There are two grounds for our dissent:

> (1) that the majority's construction of Penal Law § 15.20(2)(a) is directly contrary to the plain wording of the statute, renders the statute ineffective and deprives it of any meaning, and superimposes on the language of the statute a limitation found in the language of Model Penal Code § 2.04(3)(b) which the Legislature has specifically rejected; and

> (2) that the policy and jurisprudential reasons advanced by the majority for its rejection of what appears to be the clear intendment of Penal Law § 15.20(2)(a) are the very reasons which the Legislature has considered and rejected in its decision to abandon the unqualified common-law rule in favor of permitting a limited mistake of law defense in the circumstances presented here.

II

Penal Law § 15.20 (effect of ignorance or mistake upon liability), in pertinent part, provides: "2. A person is not relieved of criminal liability for conduct because he engages in such conduct under a mistaken belief that it does not, as a matter of law, constitute an offense, unless such mistaken belief is founded upon an official statement of the law contained in (a) a statute or other enactment."

It is fundamental that in interpreting a statute, a court should look first to the particular words of the statute in question, being guided by the accepted rule that statutory language is generally given its natural and most obvious meaning. Here, there is but one natural and obvious meaning of the statute: that if a defendant can establish that his mistaken belief was "founded upon" his interpretation of "an

---

permitted, the courts would be confronted with questions about defendant's mental state which they could not solve (AUSTIN, LECTURES ON JURISPRUDENCE, at 496–501 [4th ed. 1873]).

official statement of the law contained in . . . statute," he should have a defense. No other natural and obvious meaning has been suggested.

It is difficult to imagine a case more squarely within the wording of Penal Law § 15.20(2)(a) or one more fitted to what appears clearly to be the intended purpose of the statute than the one before us. For this reason it is helpful to discuss the statute and its apparent intended effect in the light of what defendant contends was his mistaken belief founded on an official statement of the law contained in a statute.

Defendant stands convicted after a jury trial of criminal possession of a weapon in the third degree for carrying a loaded firearm without a license (Penal Law § 265.02). He concedes that he possessed the unlicensed weapon but maintains that he did so under the mistaken assumption that his conduct was permitted by law. Although at the time of his arrest he protested that he was a Federal corrections officer and exempt from prosecution under the statute, defendant was charged with criminal possession of a weapon in the third degree. On defendant's motion before trial the court dismissed the indictment, holding that he was a peace officer as defined by CPL 2.10(26) and, therefore, exempted by Penal Law § 265.20 from prosecution under Penal Law § 265.02. The People appealed and the Appellate Division reversed and reinstated the indictment by a 3-2 vote. Defendant's appeal to this court was dismissed for failure to prosecute and the case proceeded to trial. The trial court rejected defendant's efforts to establish a defense of mistake of law under Penal Law § 15.20(2)(a). He was convicted and the Appellate Division has affirmed.

Defendant's mistaken belief that, as a Federal corrections officer, he could legally carry a loaded weapon without a license was based on the express exemption from criminal liability under Penal Law § 265.02 accorded in Penal Law § 265.20(a)(1)(a) to "peace officers" as defined in the Criminal Procedure Law and on his reading of the statutory definition for "peace officer" in CPL 2.10(26) as meaning a correction officer "of *any* penal correctional institution" (emphasis added), including an institution not operated by New York State. Thus, he concluded erroneously that, as a corrections officer in a Federal prison, he was a "peace officer" and, as such, exempt by the express terms of Penal Law § 265.20(a)(1)(a). This mistaken belief, based in good faith on the statute defining "peace officer" (CPL 2.10[26]), is, defendant contends, the precise sort of "mistaken belief . . . founded upon an official statement of the law contained in . . . a statute or other enactment" which gives rise to a mistake of law defense under Penal Law § 15.20(2)(a). He points out, of course, that when he acted in reliance on his belief he had no way of foreseeing that a court would eventually resolve the question of the statute's meaning against him and rule that his belief had been mistaken, as three of the five-member panel at the Appellate Division ultimately did in the first appeal.

The majority, however, has accepted the People's argument that to have a defense under Penal Law § 15.20(2)(a) "a defendant must show that the statute *permitted his conduct,* not merely that he believed it did" (respondent's brief, at 26 [emphasis added]). Here, of course, defendant cannot show that the statute permitted his conduct. To the contrary, the question has now been decided by the Appellate Division and it is settled that defendant was not exempt under Penal Law § 265.20(a)(1)(a). Therefore, the argument goes, defendant can have no mistake of law defense. While conceding that reliance on a statutory provision which is later found to be invalid would constitute a mistake of law defense, the People's flat position is that "one's mistaken reading of a statute, no matter how reasonable or well intentioned, is not a defense."

Nothing in the statutory language suggests the interpretation urged by the People and adopted by the majority: that Penal Law § 15.20(2)(a) is available to a defendant *not* when he has mistakenly read a statute *but only* when he has correctly read and relied on a statute which is later invalidated. Such a construction contravenes the general rule that penal statutes should be construed against the State and in favor of the accused and the Legislature's specific directive that the revised Penal Law should not be strictly construed but "must be construed according to the fair import of [its] terms to promote justice and effect the objects of the law."

More importantly, the construction leads to an anomaly: only a defendant who is *not mistaken* about the law when he acts has a mistake of law defense. In other words, a defendant can assert a defense under Penal Law § 15.20(2)(a) only when his reading of the statute is *correct—not mistaken*. Such construction is obviously illogical; it strips the statute of the very effect intended by the Legislature in adopting the mistake of law defense. The statute is of no benefit to a defendant who has proceeded in good faith on an erroneous but concededly reasonable interpretation of a statute, as defendant presumably has. An interpretation of a statute which produces an unreasonable or incongruous result and one which defeats the obvious purpose of the legislation and renders it ineffective should be rejected.

Finally, the majority's disregard of the natural and obvious meaning of Penal Law § 15.20(2)(a) so that a defendant mistaken about the law is deprived of a defense under the statute amounts, we submit, to a rejection of the obvious legislative purposes and policies favoring jurisprudential reform underlying the statute's enactment.

This reform, like the changes adopted in Model Penal Code § 2.04(3) and those proposed by various legal commentators, was prompted by the prevailing dissatisfaction with the common-law rule accept the general concept that the outright prohibition of the mistake of law defense under the common law should be replaced with a rule permitting "a limited defense based on a reasonable belief on the part of the defendant that the law is such that his conduct does not constitute an offense."

[T]he majority suggests that the Legislature intended that the statute should afford a defense only in cases involving acts *mala in se* such as *People v. Weiss* (involving kidnapping charges), "where specific intent is an element of the offense." Again such construction is at odds with the plain wording of Penal Law § 15.20(2)(a) and finds no support in the statutory history or the literature. There are, moreover, other fundamental objections to such construction which, we believe, rule out any possibility that the Legislature could have intended it. The essential quality of evil or immorality inherent in crimes *mala in se* (murder, robbery, kidnapping, etc.) is incompatible with the notion that the actor could have been operating "under a mistaken belief that [his conduct] [did] not, as a matter of law, constitute an offense" (Penal Law § 15.20[2][a]). There are no policy or jurisprudential reasons for the Legislature to recognize a mistake of law defense to such crimes. On the contrary, it is not with such inherently evil crimes but with crimes which are *mala prohibita i.e.*, "the vast network of regulatory offenses which make up a large part of today's criminal law" where reasons of policy and fairness call for a relaxation of the strict "*ignorantia legis*" maxim to permit a limited mistake of law defense.

III

Any fair reading of the majority opinion, we submit, demonstrates that the decision to reject a mistake of law defense is based on considerations of public policy and on the conviction that such a defense would be bad, rather than on an analysis of CPL 15.20(2)(a) under the usual principles of statutory construction (*see*, majority opn. at 390–391, 515 N.Y.S.2d at 215–217, 507 N.E.2d at 1071–1073). The majority warns, for example, that if the defense were permitted "the exception would swallow the rule"; that "[m]istakes about the law would be encouraged"; that an "infinite number of mistake of law defenses . . . could be devised"; and that "wrong-minded individuals [could] contrive in bad faith solely to get an exculpatory notion before the jury."

These considerations, like the People's argument that the mistake of law defense "'would encourage ignorance where knowledge is socially desired,'" are the very considerations which have been consistently offered as justifications for the maxim "*ignorantia legis.*" That these justifications are unabashedly utilitarian cannot be questioned. It could not be put more candidly than by Justice Holmes in defending the common-law maxim more than 100 years ago: "*Public policy sacrifices the individual to the general good. . . .* It is no doubt true that there are many cases in which the criminal could not have known that he was breaking the law, but to admit the excuse at all would be to encourage ignorance where the lawmaker has determined to make men know and obey, and *justice to the individual is rightly outweighed by the larger interests on the other side of the scales*" (HOLMES, THE COMMON LAW, at 48 [1881]; emphasis added). Regardless of one's attitude toward the acceptability of these views in the 1980's, the fact remains that the Legislature in abandoning the strict "*ignorantia legis*" maxim must be deemed to have rejected them.

We believe that the concerns expressed by the majority are matters which properly should be and have been addressed by the Legislature. We note only our conviction that a statute which recognizes a defense based on a man's good-faith mistaken belief founded on a well-grounded interpretation of an official statement of the law contained in a statute is a just law. The law embodies the ideal of contemporary criminal jurisprudence "that punishment should be conditioned on a showing of subjective moral blameworthiness."

It is no answer to protest that the defense may become a "false and diversionary stratagem[ ], or that "wrongminded individuals [could] contrive" an "infinite number of mistake of law defenses"; for it is the very business of the courts to separate the true claims from the false. Such *in terrorem* arguments should have no more force here than similar objections which doubtless were voiced with equal intensity to the long-accepted defenses of justification, accident, mistake of fact, insanity, entrapment, duress and intoxication. As Justice Holmes wrote in commenting on John Austin's argument that permitting the mistake of law defense would present courts with problems they were not prepared to solve: "If justice requires the fact to be ascertained, the difficulty of doing so is no ground for refusing to try" (HOLMES, THE COMMON LAW, at 48 [1881]).

IV

If defendant's offer of proof is true, his is not the case of a "free agent confronted with a choice between doing right and doing wrong and choosing freely to do wrong." He carried the gun in the good-faith belief that, as a Federal corrections officer, it was lawful for him to do so under the words of the statute. That his interpretation of the statute as exempting corrections officers (whether or not employed in a State facility) was a reasonable one can hardly be questioned. If the statute does not plainly say that corrections officers are exempt, as defendant contends, the statute at the very least is ambiguous and clearly susceptible to that interpretation. Indeed, Supreme Court in dismissing the indictment and two of the five-member panel in the first appeal to the Appellate Division read the statute as it was read by defendant and the police officials and others whose opinions he sought. We believe that under our present Penal Law and the policies underlying its revision this defendant should not be found guilty of violating Penal Law § 265.02 if he can establish that his conduct was based on a good-faith mistake of law founded on the wording of the statute.

We do not believe that permitting a defense in this case will produce the grievous consequences the majority predicts. The unusual facts of this case seem unlikely to be repeated. Indeed, although the majority foresees "an infinite number of mistake of law defenses," New Jersey, which adopted a more liberal mistake of law statute in 1978, has apparently experienced no such adversity (no case construing that law is mentioned in the most recent annotation of the statute). Nor is there any reason to believe that courts will have more difficulty separating valid claims from "diversionary stratagem[s]" in making preliminary legal determinations as to the validity of the mistake of law defense than of justification or any other defense.

But these questions are now beside the point, for the Legislature has given its answer by providing that someone in defendant's circumstances should have a mistake of law defense (Penal Law § 15.20[2][a]). Because this decision deprives defendant of what, we submit, the Legislature intended that he should have, we dissent.

There should be a reversal and defendant should have a new trial in which he is permitted to assert a defense of mistake of law under Penal Law § 15.20(2)(a).

WACHTLER, C.J., and SIMONS and TITONE, J.J., concur with BELLACOSA, J.

HANCOCK, J., dissents and votes to reverse in a separate opinion in which KAYE and ALEXANDER, J.J., concur.

Order affirmed.

Questions and Notes

1. Why was mistake of law a defense in *Weiss*, but not in *Marrero*?

2. Would (should) it make any difference whether Marrero had sought legal advice from a reputable attorney before carrying the gun?

3. On what point do the majority and dissent differ? Whose opinion do you find more persuasive? Why?

4. Should it have mattered that the trial judge and 2/5 of the appellate judges (1/2 of all of the judges that heard the case) thought that Marrero *correctly* read the statute?

5. Sometimes ignorance of the law not only may be recognized, but (as *Lambert* demonstrates) constitutionally must be recognized. As you read *Lambert*, consider the criteria necessary to come within that narrow category.

Lambert v. California
355 U.S. 225 (1957)

Mr. Justice DOUGLAS delivered the opinion of the Court.

Section 52.39 provides that it shall be unlawful for 'any convicted person' to be or remain in Los Angeles for a period of more than five days without registering; it requires any person having a place of abode outside the city to register if he comes into the city on five occasions or more during a 30-day period; and it prescribes the information to be furnished the Chief of Police on registering.

Section 52.43(b) makes the failure to register a continuing offense, each day's failure constituting a separate offense.

Appellant, arrested on suspicion of another offense, was charged with a violation of this registration law. The evidence showed that she had been at the time of her arrest a resident of Los Angeles for over seven years. Within that period, she had been convicted in Los Angeles of the crime of forgery, an offense which California punishes as a felony. Though convicted of a crime punishable as a felony, she had not at the time of her arrest registered under the Municipal Code. At the trial, appellant asserted that § 52.39 of the Code denies her due process of law and other rights under the Federal Constitution, unnecessary to enumerate. The trial court denied this objection. The case was tried to a jury which found appellant guilty.

The court fined her $250 and placed her on probation for three years. Appellant, renewing her constitutional objection, moved for arrest of judgment and a new trial. This motion was denied. On appeal the constitutionality of the Code was again challenged. The Appellate Department of the Superior Court affirmed the judgment, holding there was no merit to the claim that the ordinance was unconstitutional. The case having been argued and reargued, we now hold that the registration provisions of the Code as sought to be applied here violate the Due Process requirement of the Fourteenth Amendment.

The registration provision, carrying criminal penalties, applies if a person has been convicted 'of an offense punishable as a felony in the State of California' or, in case he has been convicted in another State, if the offense 'would have been punishable as a felony' had it been committed in California. No element of willfulness is by terms included in the ordinance nor read into it by the California court as a condition necessary for a conviction.

We must assume that appellant had no actual knowledge of the requirement that she register under this ordinance, as she offered proof of this defense which was refused. The question is whether a registration act of this character violates due process where it is applied to a person who has no actual knowledge of his duty to register, and where no showing is made of the probability of such knowledge.

We do not go with Blackstone in saying that 'a vicious will' is necessary to constitute a crime for conduct alone without regard to the intent of the doer is often sufficient. There is wide latitude in the lawmakers to declare an offense and to exclude elements of knowledge and diligence from its definition. But we deal here with conduct that is wholly passive—mere failure to register. It is unlike the commission of acts, or the failure to act under circumstances that should alert the doer to the consequences of his deed. The rule that 'ignorance of the law will not excuse' is deep in our law, as is the principle that of all the powers of local government, the police power is 'one of the least limitable.' On the other hand, due process places some limits on its exercise. [I]ngrained in our concept of due process is the requirement of notice. Notice is sometimes essential so that the citizen has the chance to defend charges. Notice is required before property interests are disturbed, before assessments are made, before penalties are assessed. Notice is required in a myriad of situations where a penalty or forfeiture might be suffered for mere failure to act. Recent cases illustrating the point are *Mullane v. Central Hanover Bank & Trust Co.*, 339 U.S. 306; *Covey v. Town of Somers*, 351 U.S. 141; *Walker v. City of Hutchinson*, 352 U.S. 112. These cases involved only property in civil litigation. But the principle is equally appropriate where a person, wholly passive and unaware of any wrongdoing, is brought to the bar of justice for condemnation in a criminal case.

Registration laws are common, and their range is wide. Many such laws are akin to licensing statutes in that they pertain to the regulation of business activities. But the present ordinance is entirely different. Violation of its provisions is unaccompanied by any activity whatever, mere presence in the city being the test. Moreover, circumstances which might move one to inquire as to the necessity of registration are completely lacking. At most the ordinance is but a law enforcement technique designed for the convenience of law enforcement agencies through which a list of the names and addresses of felons then residing in a given community is compiled. The disclosure is merely a compilation of former convictions already publicly recorded in the jurisdiction where obtained. Nevertheless, this appellant on first becoming aware of her duty to register was given no opportunity to comply with the law and avoid its penalty, even though her default was entirely innocent. She could but suffer the consequences of the ordinance, namely, conviction with the imposition of heavy criminal penalties thereunder. We believe that actual knowledge of the duty to register or proof of the probability of such knowledge and subsequent failure to comply are necessary before a conviction under the ordinance can stand. As Holmes wrote in THE COMMON LAW, "A law which punished conduct which would not be blameworthy in the average member of the community would be too severe for that community to bear." *Id.* at 50. Its severity lies in the absence of an opportunity either to avoid the consequences of the law or to defend any prosecution brought under it. Where a person did not know of the duty to register and where there was no proof of the probability of such knowledge, he may not be convicted consistently with due process. Were it otherwise, the evil would be as great as it is when the law is written in print too fine to read or in a language foreign to the community.

Reversed.

Mr. Justice BURTON, dissents because he believes that, as applied to this appellant, the ordinance does not violate her constitutional rights.

Mr. Justice FRANKFURTER, whom Mr. Justice HARLAN and Mr. Justice WHITTAKER join, dissenting.

The present laws of the United States and of the forty-eight States are thick with provisions that command that some things not be done and others be done, although persons convicted under such provisions may have had no awareness of what the law required or that what they did was wrongdoing. The body of decisions sustaining such legislation, including innumerable registration laws, is almost as voluminous as the legislation itself. The matter is summarized in *United States v. Balint*, 258 U.S. 250, 252: "Many instances of this are to be found in regulatory measures in the exercise of what is called the police power where the emphasis of the statute is evidently upon achievement of some social betterment rather than the punishment of the crimes as in cases of *mala in se*."

Surely there can hardly be a difference as a matter of fairness, of hardship, or of justice, if one may invoke it, between the case of a person wholly innocent of wrongdoing, in the sense that he was not remotely conscious of violating any law, who is imprisoned for five years for conduct relating to narcotics, and the case of another person who is placed on probation for three years on condition that she pay $250, for failure, as a local resident, convicted under local law of a felony, to register under a law passed as an exercise of the State's "police power."[6] Considerations of hardship often lead courts, naturally enough, to attribute to a statute the requirement of a certain mental element—some consciousness of wrongdoing and knowledge of the law's command—as a matter of statutory construction. Then, too, a cruelly disproportionate relation between what the law requires and the sanction for its disobedience may constitute a violation of the Eighth Amendment as a cruel and unusual punishment, and, in respect to the States, even offend the Due Process Clause of the Fourteenth Amendment.

But what the Court here does is to draw a constitutional line between a State's requirement of doing and not doing. What is this but a return to Year Book distinctions between feasance and nonfeasance—a distinction that may have significance in the evolution of common-law notions of liability, but is inadmissible as a line between constitutionality and unconstitutionality. One can be confident that Mr. Justice Holmes would have been the last to draw such a line. What he wrote about "blameworthiness" is worth quoting in its context:

> "It is not intended to deny that criminal liability, as well as civil, is founded on blameworthiness. Such a denial would shock the moral sense of any civilized community; or, to put it another way, a law which punished conduct which would not be blameworthy in the average member of the community would be too severe for that community to bear." (This passage must be read in the setting of the broader discussion of which it is an essential part. HOLMES, THE COMMON LAW, at 49–50.)

If the generalization that underlies, and alone can justify, this decision were to be given its relevant scope, a whole volume of the United States Reports would be required to document in detail the legislation in this country that would fall or be impaired. I abstain from entering upon a consideration of such legislation, and adjudications upon it, because I feel confident that the present decision will turn out to be an isolated deviation from the strong current of precedents—a derelict on the waters of the law. Accordingly, I content myself with dissenting.

Questions and Notes

1. Isn't the root concept of the "ignorance of law is no excuse" maxim that people are conclusively presumed to know the law? If so, how can there be any unfairness in expecting Lambert to know the registration law?

---

6. This case does not involve a person who, convicted of a crime in another jurisdiction, must decide whether he has been convicted of a crime that 'would have been punishable as a felony' had it been committed in California. Appellant committed forgery in California and was convicted under California law. Furthermore, she was convicted in Los Angeles itself, and there she resided for over seven years before the arrest leading to the present proceedings.

2. As between Marrero and Lambert, who should have a better due process objection to a conviction?

3. Suppose that Lambert had heard of the ordinance and had gone to an attorney to find out if it applied to her and had received the erroneous advice that it did not. Assuming that California followed *Marrero* and affirmed her conviction, would (should) the Supreme Court overturn her conviction?

4. Because *Lambert* is a Supreme Court decision interpreting the United States Constitution, it is binding in all states.

5. Suppose that you have been on vacation for a month. The day that you come home, you water your lawn. While watering your lawn, you are approached by a policeman who informs you that lawn watering is in violation of a recently enacted town ordinance, for which he hands you a citation. At your trial, you raise the *Lambert* defense. What result and why?

E. Mistake of Law and Willfulness: A Lesson in Statutory Interpretation

During the 1990s, the United States Supreme Court had several occasions to deal with the impact of the word "willfully" on the "ignorance of the law is no excuse" maxim. In this section, we examine three such cases, *Cheek, Ratzlaf,* and *Reha.* All of the cases were closely divided. Because these cases do not involve constitutional issues, the Court's analysis is only binding in Federal cases. States are free to construe their statutes as they see fit (subject only to constitutional restraints). In each case, think about which opinion got it right, and why.

Cheek v. United States
498 U.S. 192 (1991)

Justice WHITE delivered the opinion of the Court.

Title 26, § 7201 of the United States Code provides that any person "who willfully attempts in any manner to evade or defeat any tax imposed by this title or the payment thereof" shall be guilty of a felony. Under 26 U.S.C. § 7203, "[a]ny person required under this title . . . or by regulations made under authority thereof to make a return . . . who willfully fails to . . . make such return" shall be guilty of a misdemeanor. This case turns on the meaning of the word "willfully" as used in §§ 7201 and 7203.

I

Petitioner John L. Cheek has been a pilot for American Airlines since 1973. He filed federal income tax returns through 1979 but thereafter ceased to file returns.[1]

---

1. Cheek did file what the Court of Appeals described as a frivolous return in 1982.

He also claimed an increasing number of withholding allowances—eventually claiming 60 allowances by mid-1980—and for the years 1981 to 1984 indicated on his W-4 forms that he was exempt from federal income taxes. In 1983, petitioner unsuccessfully sought a refund of all tax withheld by his employer in 1982. Petitioner's income during this period at all times far exceeded the minimum necessary to trigger the statutory filing requirement.

As a result of his activities, petitioner was indicted for 10 violations of federal law. He was charged with six counts of willfully failing to file a federal income tax return for the years 1980, 1981, and 1983 through 1986, in violation of § 7203. He was further charged with three counts of willfully attempting to evade his income taxes for the years 1980, 1981, and 1983 in violation of 26 U.S.C. § 7201. In those years, American Airlines withheld substantially less than the amount of tax petitioner owed because of the numerous allowances and exempt status he claimed on his W-4 forms. The tax offenses with which petitioner was charged are specific intent crimes that require the defendant to have acted willfully.

At trial, the evidence established that between 1982 and 1986, petitioner was involved in at least four civil cases that challenged various aspects of the federal income tax system. In all four of those cases, the plaintiffs were informed by the courts that many of their arguments, including that they were not taxpayers within the meaning of the tax laws, that wages are not income, that the Sixteenth Amendment does not authorize the imposition of an income tax on individuals, and that the Sixteenth Amendment is unenforceable, were frivolous or had been repeatedly rejected by the courts. During this time period, petitioner also attended at least two criminal trials of persons charged with tax offenses. In addition, there was evidence that in 1980 or 1981 an attorney had advised Cheek that the courts had rejected as frivolous the claim that wages are not income.[4]

Cheek represented himself at trial and testified in his defense. He admitted that he had not filed personal income tax returns during the years in question. He testified that as early as 1978, he had begun attending seminars sponsored by, and following the advice of, a group that believes, among other things, that the federal tax system is unconstitutional. Some of the speakers at these meetings were lawyers who purported to give professional opinions about the invalidity of the federal income tax laws. Cheek produced a letter from an attorney stating that the Sixteenth Amendment did not authorize a tax on wages and salaries but only on gain or profit. Petitioner's defense was that, based on the indoctrination he received from this group and from his own study, he sincerely believed that the tax laws were being unconstitutionally enforced and that his actions during the 1980–1986 period were lawful. He therefore argued that he had acted without the willfulness required for conviction of the various offenses with which he was charged.

---

4. The attorney also advised that despite the Fifth Amendment, the filing of a tax return was required and that a person could challenge the constitutionality of the system by suing for a refund after the taxes had been withheld, or by putting himself "at risk of criminal prosecution."

In the course of its instructions, the trial court advised the jury that to prove "willfulness" the Government must prove the voluntary and intentional violation of a known legal duty, a burden that could not be proved by showing mistake, ignorance, or negligence. The court further advised the jury that an objectively reasonable good-faith misunderstanding of the law would negate willfulness, but mere disagreement with the law would not. The court described Cheek's beliefs about the income tax system[5] and instructed the jury that if it found that Cheek "honestly and reasonably believed that he was not required to pay income taxes or to file tax returns," a not guilty verdict should be returned.

After several hours of deliberation, the jury sent a note to the judge that stated in part:

> "We have a basic disagreement between some of us as to if Mr. Cheek honestly & reasonably believed that he was not required to pay income taxes.

> "Page 32 [the relevant jury instruction] discusses good faith misunderstanding & disagreement. Is there any additional clarification you can give us on this point?"

The District Judge responded with a supplemental instruction containing the following statements:

> "[A] person's opinion that the tax laws violate his constitutional rights does not constitute a good faith misunderstanding of the law. Furthermore, a person's disagreement with the government's tax collection systems and policies does not constitute a good faith misunderstanding of the law."

At the end of the first day of deliberation, the jury sent out another note saying that it still could not reach a verdict because "[w]e are divided on the issue as to if Mr. Cheek honestly & reasonably believed that he was not required to pay income tax." When the jury resumed its deliberations, the District Judge gave the jury an additional instruction. This instruction stated in part that "[a]n honest but unreasonable belief is not a defense and does not negate willfulness," and that "[a]dvice or research resulting in the conclusion that wages of a privately employed person are not income or that the tax laws are unconstitutional is not objectively reasonable and cannot serve as the basis for a good faith misunderstanding of the law defense." The court also instructed the jury that "[p]ersistent refusal to acknowledge the law

---

5. "The defendant has testified as to what he states are his interpretations of the United States Constitution, court opinions, common law and other materials he has reviewed. . . . He has also introduced materials which contain references to quotations from the United States Constitution, court opinions, statutes, and other sources.

"He testified he relied on his interpretations and on these materials in concluding that he was not a person required to file income tax returns for the year or years charged, was not required to pay income taxes and that he could claim exempt status on his W-4 forms, and that he could claim refunds of all moneys withheld. "Among other things, Mr. Cheek contends that his wages from a private employer, American Airlines, does [sic] not constitute income under the Internal Revenue Service laws."

does not constitute a good faith misunderstanding of the law." Approximately two hours later, the jury returned a verdict finding petitioner guilty on all counts.[6]

II

The general rule that ignorance of the law or a mistake of law is no defense to criminal prosecution is deeply rooted in the American legal system. Based on the notion that the law is definite and knowable, the common law presumed that every person knew the law. This common-law rule has been applied by the Court in numerous cases construing criminal statutes.

The proliferation of statutes and regulations has sometimes made it difficult for the average citizen to know and comprehend the extent of the duties and obligations imposed by the tax laws. Congress has accordingly softened the impact of the common-law presumption by making specific intent to violate the law an element of certain federal criminal tax offenses. Thus, the Court almost 60 years ago interpreted the statutory term "willfully" as used in the federal criminal tax statutes as carving out an exception to the traditional rule. This special treatment of criminal tax offenses is largely due to the complexity of the tax laws. In *United States v. Murdock*, 290 U.S. 389 (1933), the Court recognized that:

> "Congress did not intend that a person, by reason of a bona fide misunderstanding as to his liability for the tax, as to his duty to make a return, or as to the adequacy of the records he maintained, should become a criminal by his mere failure to measure up to the prescribed standard of conduct."

The Court held that the defendant was entitled to an instruction with respect to whether he acted in good faith based on his actual belief. In *Murdock*, the Court interpreted the term "willfully" as used in the criminal tax statutes generally to mean "an act done with a bad purpose," or with "an evil motive."

Subsequent decisions have refined this proposition. In *United States v. Bishop*, 412 U.S. 346 (1973), we described the term "willfully" as connoting "a voluntary, intentional violation of a known legal duty," and did so with specific reference to the "bad faith or evil intent" language employed in *Murdock*. Still later, *United States v. Pomponio*, 429 U.S. 10 (1976) (*per curiam*), addressed a situation in which several defendants had been charged with willfully filing false tax returns. The jury was given an instruction on willfulness similar to the standard set forth in *Bishop*. In addition, it was instructed that "[g]ood motive alone is never a defense where the act done or omitted is a crime." The defendants were convicted but the Court of Appeals reversed, concluding that the latter instruction was improper because the statute required a finding of bad purpose or evil motive.

---

6. A note signed by all 12 jurors also informed the judge that although the jury found petitioner guilty, several jurors wanted to express their personal opinions of the case and that notes from these individual jurors to the court were "a complaint against the narrow & hard expression under the constraints of the law." At least two notes from individual jurors expressed the opinion that petitioner sincerely believed in his cause even though his beliefs might have been unreasonable.

We reversed the Court of Appeals, stating that "the Court of Appeals incorrectly assumed that the reference to an 'evil motive' in *Bishop* and prior cases requires proof of any motive other than an intentional violation of a known legal duty." As "the other Courts of Appeals that have considered the question have recognized, willfulness in this context simply means a voluntary, intentional violation of a known legal duty." We concluded that after instructing the jury on willfulness, "[a]n additional instruction on good faith was unnecessary." Taken together, *Bishop* and *Pomponio* conclusively establish that the standard for the statutory willfulness requirement is the "voluntary, intentional violation of a known legal duty."

III

Cheek accepts the *Pomponio* definition of willfulness but asserts that the District Court's instructions and the Court of Appeals' opinion departed from that definition. In particular, he challenges the ruling that a good-faith misunderstanding of the law or a good faith belief that one is not violating the law, if it is to negate willfulness, must be objectively reasonable. We agree that the Court of Appeals and the District Court erred in this respect.

A

Willfulness, as construed by our prior decisions in criminal tax cases, requires the Government to prove that the law imposed a duty on the defendant, that the defendant knew of this duty, and that he voluntarily and intentionally violated that duty. We deal first with the case where the issue is whether the defendant knew of the duty purportedly imposed by the provision of the statute or regulation he is accused of violating, a case in which there is no claim that the provision at issue is invalid. In such a case, if the Government proves actual knowledge of the pertinent legal duty, the prosecution, without more, has satisfied the knowledge component of the willfulness requirement. But carrying this burden requires negating a defendant's claim of ignorance of the law or a claim that because of a misunderstanding of the law, he had a good-faith belief that he was not violating any of the provisions of the tax laws. This is so because one cannot be aware that the law imposes a duty upon him and yet be ignorant of it, misunderstand the law, or believe that the duty does not exist. In the end, the issue is whether, based on all the evidence, the Government has proved that the defendant was aware of the duty at issue, which cannot be true if the jury credits a good-faith misunderstanding and belief submission, whether or not the claimed belief or misunderstanding is objectively reasonable.

In this case, if Cheek asserted that he truly believed that the Internal Revenue Code did not purport to treat wages as income, and the jury believed him, the Government would not have carried its burden to prove willfulness, however unreasonable a court might deem such a belief. Of course, in deciding whether to credit Cheek's good-faith belief claim, the jury would be free to consider any admissible evidence from any source showing that Cheek was aware of his duty to file a return and to treat wages as income, including evidence showing his awareness of the relevant provisions of the Code or regulations, of court decisions rejecting his interpretation of the tax law, of authoritative rulings of the Internal Revenue Service, or of any contents of the personal income tax return forms and accompanying instructions that made it plain that wages should be returned as income.[8]

We thus disagree with the Court of Appeals' requirement that a claimed good-faith belief must be objectively reasonable if it is to be considered as possibly negating the Government's evidence purporting to show a defendant's awareness of the legal duty at issue. Knowledge and belief are characteristically questions for the factfinder, in this case the jury. Characterizing a particular belief as not objectively reasonable transforms the inquiry into a legal one and would prevent the jury from considering it. It would of course be proper to exclude evidence having no relevance or probative value with respect to willfulness; but it is not contrary to common sense, let alone impossible, for a defendant to be ignorant of his duty based on an irrational belief that he has no duty, and forbidding the jury to consider evidence that might negate willfulness would raise a serious question under the Sixth Amendment's jury trial provision. It is common ground that this Court, where possible, interprets congressional enactments so as to avoid raising serious constitutional questions.

It was therefore error to instruct the jury to disregard evidence of Cheek's understanding that, within the meaning of the tax laws, he was not a person required to file a return or to pay income taxes and that wages are not taxable income, as incredible as such misunderstandings of and beliefs about the law might be. Of course, the more unreasonable the asserted beliefs or misunderstandings are, the more likely the jury will consider them to be nothing more than simple disagreement with known legal duties imposed by the tax laws and will find that the Government has carried its burden of proving knowledge.

B

Cheek asserted in the trial court that he should be acquitted because he believed in good faith that the income tax law is unconstitutional as applied to him and thus could not legally impose any duty upon him of which he should have been aware. Such a submission is unsound, not because Cheek's constitutional arguments are not objectively reasonable or frivolous, which they surely are, but because the *Murdock-Pomponio* line of cases does not support such a position. Those cases construed the willfulness requirement in the criminal provisions of the Internal Revenue Code to require proof of knowledge of the law. This was because in "our complex tax system, uncertainty often arises even among taxpayers who earnestly wish to follow the law," and "[i]t is not the purpose of the law to penalize frank

---

8. Cheek recognizes that a "defendant who knows what the law is and who disagrees with it . . . does not have a bona fide misunderstanding defense," but asserts that "a defendant who has a bona fide misunderstanding of [the law] does not 'know' his legal duty and lacks willfulness." The Reply Brief for Petitioner states: "We are in no way suggesting that Cheek or anyone else is immune from criminal prosecution if he knows what the law is, but believes it should be otherwise, and therefore violates it."

difference of opinion or innocent errors made despite the exercise of reasonable care."

Claims that some of the provisions of the tax code are unconstitutional are submissions of a different order.[10] They do not arise from innocent mistakes caused by the complexity of the Internal Revenue Code. Rather, they reveal full knowledge of the provisions at issue and a studied conclusion, however wrong, that those provisions are invalid and unenforceable. Thus in this case, Cheek paid his taxes for years, but after attending various seminars and based on his own study, he concluded that the income tax laws could not constitutionally require him to pay a tax.

We do not believe that Congress contemplated that such a taxpayer, without risking criminal prosecution, could ignore the duties imposed upon him by the Internal Revenue Code and refuse to utilize the mechanisms provided by Congress to present his claims of invalidity to the courts and to abide by their decisions. There is no doubt that Cheek, from year to year, was free to pay the tax that the law purported to require, file for a refund and, if denied, present his claims of invalidity, constitutional or otherwise, to the courts. Also, without paying the tax, he could have challenged claims of tax deficiencies in the Tax Court with the right to appeal to a higher court if unsuccessful. Cheek took neither course in some years, and when he did was unwilling to accept the outcome. As we see it, he is in no position to claim that his good-faith belief about the validity of the Internal Revenue Code negates willfulness or provides a defense to criminal prosecution under §§ 7201 and 7203. Of course, Cheek was free in this very case to present his claims of invalidity and have them adjudicated, but like defendants in criminal cases in other contexts, who "willfully" refuse to comply with the duties placed upon them by the law, he must take the risk of being wrong.

We thus hold that in a case like this, a defendant's views about the validity of the tax statutes are irrelevant to the issue of willfulness and need not be heard by the jury, and, if they are, an instruction to disregard them would be proper. For this purpose, it makes no difference whether the claims of invalidity are frivolous or have substance. It was therefore not error in this case for the District Judge to instruct the jury not to consider Cheek's claims that the tax laws were unconstitutional.

---

10. In *United States v. Murdock*, the defendant Murdock was summoned to appear before a revenue agent for examination. Questions were put to him, which he refused to answer for fear of self-incrimination under state law. He was indicted for refusing to give testimony and supply information contrary to the pertinent provisions of the Internal Revenue Code. This Court affirmed the reversal of Murdock's conviction, holding that the trial court erred in refusing to give an instruction directing the jury to consider Murdock's asserted claim of a good-faith, actual belief that because of the Fifth Amendment he was privileged not to answer the questions put to him. It is thus the case that Murdock's asserted belief was grounded in the Constitution, but it was a claim of privilege not to answer, not a claim that any provision of the tax laws were unconstitutional, and not a claim for which the tax laws provided procedures to entertain and resolve. Cheek's position at trial, in contrast, was that the tax laws were unconstitutional as applied to him.

However, it was error for the court to instruct the jury that petitioner's asserted beliefs that wages are not income and that he was not a taxpayer within the meaning of the Internal Revenue Code should not be considered by the jury in determining whether Cheek had acted willfully.

IV

For the reasons set forth in the opinion above, the judgment of the Court of Appeals is vacated, and the case is remanded for further proceedings consistent with this opinion.

Justice SCALIA, concurring in the judgment.

I concur in the judgment of the Court because our cases have consistently held that the failure to pay a tax in the good-faith belief that it is not legally owing is not "willful." I do not join the Court's opinion because I do not agree with the test for willfulness that it directs the Court of Appeals to apply on remand.

As the Court acknowledges, our opinions from the 1930's to the 1970's have interpreted the word "willfully" in the criminal tax statutes as requiring the "bad purpose" or "evil motive" of "intentional[ly] violat[ing] a known legal duty." It seems to me that today's opinion squarely reverses that long-established statutory construction when it says that a good-faith erroneous belief in the unconstitutionality of a tax law is no defense. It is quite impossible to say that a statute which one believes unconstitutional represents a "known legal duty." *See Marbury v. Madison*, 1 Cranch 137 (1803).

Although the facts of the present case involve erroneous reliance upon the Constitution in ignoring the otherwise "known legal duty" imposed by the tax statutes, the Court's new interpretation applies also to erroneous reliance upon a tax statute in ignoring the otherwise "known legal duty" of a regulation, and to erroneous reliance upon a regulation in ignoring the otherwise "known legal duty" of a tax assessment. These situations as well meet the opinion's crucial test of "reveal[ing] full knowledge of the provisions at issue and a studied conclusion, however wrong, that those provisions are invalid and unenforceable." There is, moreover, no rational basis for saying that a "willful" violation is established by full knowledge of a statutory requirement, but is not established by full knowledge of a requirement explicitly imposed by regulation or order. Thus, today's opinion works a revolution in past practice, subjecting to criminal penalties taxpayers who do not comply with Treasury Regulations that are in their view contrary to the Internal Revenue Code, Treasury Rulings that are in their view contrary to the regulations, and even IRS auditor pronouncements that are in their view contrary to Treasury Rulings. The law already provides considerable incentive for taxpayers to be careful in ignoring any official assertion of tax liability, since it contains civil penalties that apply even in the event of a good-faith mistake. To impose in addition *criminal* penalties for misinterpretation of such a complex body of law is a startling innovation indeed.

I find it impossible to understand how one can derive from the lonesome word "willfully" the proposition that belief in the nonexistence of a textual prohibition excuses liability, but belief in the invalidity (*i.e.*, the legal nonexistence) of a textual prohibition does not. One may say, as the law does in many contexts, that "willfully" refers to consciousness of the act but not to consciousness that the act is unlawful. Or alternatively, one may say, as we have said until today with respect to the tax statutes, that "willfully" refers to consciousness of both the act *and* its illegality. But it seems to me impossible to say that the word refers to consciousness that some legal text exists, without consciousness that that legal text is binding, *i.e.*, with the good-faith belief that it is not a valid law. Perhaps such a test for criminal liability would make sense (though in a field as complicated as federal tax law, I doubt it), but some text other than the mere word "willfully" would have to be employed to describe it—and that text is not ours to write.

Because today's opinion abandons clear and longstanding precedent to impose criminal liability where taxpayers have had no reason to expect it, because the new contours of criminal liability have no basis in the statutory text, and because I strongly suspect that those new contours make no sense even as a policy matter, I concur only in the judgment of the Court.

Justice BLACKMUN, with whom Justice MARSHALL joins, dissenting.

It seems to me that we are concerned in this case not with "the complexity of the tax laws," but with the income tax law in its most elementary and basic aspect: Is a wage earner a taxpayer and are wages income?

The Court acknowledges that the conclusively established standard for willfulness under the applicable statutes is the "'voluntary, intentional violation of a known legal duty.'" That being so, it is incomprehensible to me how, in this day, more than 70 years after the institution of our present federal income tax system with the passage of the Income Tax Act of 1913, any taxpayer of competent mentality can assert as his defense to charges of statutory willfulness the proposition that the wage he receives for his labor is not income, irrespective of a cult that says otherwise and advises the gullible to resist income tax collections. One might note in passing that this particular taxpayer, after all, was a licensed pilot for one of our major commercial airlines; he presumably was a person of at least minimum intellectual competence.

The District Court's instruction that an objectively reasonable and good-faith misunderstanding of the law negates willfulness lends further, rather than less, protection to this defendant, for it adds an additional hurdle for the prosecution to overcome. Petitioner should be grateful for this further protection, rather than be opposed to it.

This Court's opinion today, I fear, will encourage taxpayers to cling to frivolous views of the law in the hope of convincing a jury of their sincerity. If that ensues, I suspect we have gone beyond the limits of common sense.

While I may not agree with every word the Court of Appeals has enunciated in its opinion, I would affirm its judgment in this case. I therefore dissent.

Questions and Notes

1. Why did the Court reverse Cheek's conviction?

2. How does Justice Scalia differ from the Court?

3. How does Justice Blackmun differ from the Court?

4. With whom do you agree? Why?

5. Why should Cheek be more entitled to a mistake of law defense than Marrero?

6. We now turn to *Ratzlaf*, where an even more sharply divided court considered the relationship of the word "willful" to the "ignorance of the law is no excuse" maxim.

Ratzlaf v. United States
510 U.S. 135 (1994)

Justice GINSBURG delivered the opinion of the Court.

Federal law requires banks and other financial institutions to file reports with the Secretary of the Treasury whenever they are involved in a cash transaction that exceeds $10,000. 31 U.S.C. § 5313; 31 CFR § 103.22(a) (1993). It is illegal to "structure" transactions—*i.e.*, to break up a single transaction above the reporting threshold into two or more separate transactions—for the purpose of evading a financial institution's reporting requirement. 31 U.S.C. § 5324. "A person willfully violating" this antistructuring provision is subject to criminal penalties. § 5322. This case presents a question on which Courts of Appeals have divided: Does a defendant's purpose to circumvent a bank's reporting obligation suffice to sustain a conviction for "willfully violating" the antistructuring provision? We hold that the "willfulness" requirement mandates something more. To establish that a defendant "willfully violat[ed]" the antistructuring law, the Government must prove that the defendant acted with knowledge that his conduct was unlawful.

I

On the evening of October 20, 1988, defendant-petitioner Waldemar Ratzlaf ran up a debt of $160,000 playing blackjack at the High Sierra Casino in Reno, Nevada. The casino gave him one week to pay. On the due date, Ratzlaf returned to the casino with cash of $100,000 in hand. A casino official informed Ratzlaf that all transactions involving more than $10,000 in cash had to be reported to state and federal authorities. The official added that the casino could accept a cashier's check for the full amount due without triggering any reporting requirement. The casino helpfully placed a limousine at Ratzlaf's disposal, and assigned an employee to accompany him to banks in the vicinity. Informed that banks, too, are required to report cash transactions in excess of $10,000, Ratzlaf purchased cashier's checks, each for less than $10,000 and each from a different bank. He delivered these checks to the High Sierra Casino.

Based on this endeavor, Ratzlaf was charged with "structuring transactions" to evade the banks' obligation to report cash transactions exceeding $10,000; this conduct, the indictment alleged, violated 31 U.S.C. §§ 5322(a) and 5324(3). The trial judge instructed the jury that the Government had to prove defendant's knowledge of the banks' reporting obligation and his attempt to evade that obligation, but did not have to prove defendant knew the structuring was unlawful. Ratzlaf was convicted, fined, and sentenced to prison.

Ratzlaf maintained on appeal that he could not be convicted of "willfully violating" the antistructuring law solely on the basis of his knowledge that a financial institution must report currency transactions in excess of $10,000 and his intention to avoid such reporting. To gain a conviction for "willful" conduct, he asserted, the Government must prove he was aware of the illegality of the "structuring" in which he engaged. The Ninth Circuit upheld the trial court's construction of the legislation and affirmed Ratzlaf's conviction. We granted certiorari and now conclude that, to give effect to the statutory "willfulness" specification, the Government had to prove Ratzlaf knew the structuring he undertook was unlawful. We therefore reverse the judgment of the Court of Appeals.

II

A

Congress enacted the Currency and Foreign Transactions Reporting Act (Bank Secrecy Act) in 1970, Pub. L. 91-508, Tit. II, 84 Stat. 1118, in response to increasing use of banks and other institutions as financial intermediaries by persons engaged in criminal activity. The Act imposes a variety of reporting requirements on individuals and institutions regarding foreign and domestic financial transactions. The reporting requirement relevant here, § 5313(a), applies to domestic financial transactions. Section 5313(a) reads:

> "When a domestic financial institution is involved in a transaction for the payment, receipt, or transfer of United States coins or currency (or other monetary instruments the Secretary of the Treasury prescribes), in an amount, denomination, or amount and denomination, or under circumstances the Secretary prescribes by regulation, the institution and any other participant in the transaction the Secretary may prescribe shall file a report on the transaction at the time and in the way the Secretary prescribes. . . ."

To deter circumvention of this reporting requirement, Congress enacted an antistructuring provision as part of the Money Laundering Control Act of 1986.[4] Section 5324, which Ratzlaf is charged with "willfully violating," reads:

---

4. The Government does not assert that Ratzlaf obtained the cash used in any of the transactions relevant here in other than a lawful manner.

"No person shall for the purpose of evading the reporting requirements of section 5313(a) with respect to such transaction —

"(3) structure or assist in structuring, or attempt to structure or assist in structuring, any transaction with one or more domestic financial institutions."

The criminal enforcement provision at issue, 31 U.S.C. § 5322(a), sets out penalties for "[a] person willfully violating," *inter alia*, the anti-structuring provision. Section 5322(a) reads:

"A person willfully violating this subchapter [31 U.S.C. § 5311 *et seq.*] or a regulation prescribed under this subchapter shall be fined not more than $250,000, or [imprisoned] for not more than five years, or both."

B

Section 5324 forbids structuring transactions with a "purpose of evading the reporting requirements of section 5313(a)." Ratzlaf admits that he structured cash transactions, and that he did so with knowledge of, and a purpose to avoid, the banks' duty to report currency transactions in excess of $10,000. The statutory formulation (§ 5322) under which Ratzlaf was prosecuted, however, calls for proof of "willful[ness]" on the actor's part. The trial judge in Ratzlaf's case, with the Ninth Circuit's approbation, treated § 5322(a)'s "willfulness" requirement essentially as surplusage — as words of no consequence.[7] Judges should hesitate so to treat statutory terms in any setting, and resistance should be heightened when the words describe an element of a criminal offense.

"Willful," this Court has recognized, is a "word of many meanings," and "its construction [is] often ... influenced by its context." Accordingly, we view §§ 5322(a) and 5324(3) mindful of the complex of provisions in which they are embedded. In this light, we count it significant that § 5322(a)'s omnibus "willfulness" requirement, when applied to other provisions in the same subchapter, consistently has been read by the Courts of Appeals to require both "knowledge of the reporting requirement" *and* a "specific intent to commit the crime," *i.e.,* "a purpose to disobey the law."

The United States urges, however, that § 5324 violators, by their very conduct, exhibit a purpose to do wrong, which suffices to show "willfulness":

"On occasion, criminal statutes — including some requiring proof of 'willfulness' — have been understood to require proof of an intentional violation of a known legal duty, *i.e.,* specific knowledge by the defendant that his conduct is unlawful. But where that construction has been adopted, it has been invoked only to ensure that the defendant acted with a wrongful purpose.

---

7. The United States confirmed at oral argument that, in its view, as in the view of the courts below, "the 5324 offense is just what it would be if you never had 5322."

"The anti-structuring statute, 31 U.S.C. §5324, satisfies the 'bad purpose' component of willfulness by explicitly defining the wrongful purpose necessary to violate the law: it requires proof that the defendant acted with the purpose to evade the reporting requirement of Section 5313(a)."

"[S]tructuring is not the kind of activity that an ordinary person would engage in innocently," the United States asserts. It is therefore "reasonable," the Government concludes, "to hold a structurer responsible for evading the reporting requirements without the need to prove specific knowledge that such evasion is unlawful."

Undoubtedly there are bad men who attempt to elude official reporting requirements in order to hide from Government inspectors such criminal activity as laundering drug money or tax evasion.[11] But currency structuring is not inevitably nefarious. Consider, for example, the small business operator who knows that reports filed under 31 U.S.C. §5313(a) are available to the Internal Revenue Service. To reduce the risk of an IRS audit, she brings $9,500 in cash to the bank twice each week, in lieu of transporting over $10,000 once each week. That person, if the United States is right, has committed a criminal offense, because she structured cash transactions "for the specific purpose of depriving the Government of the information that Section 5313(a) is designed to obtain." Nor is a person who structures a currency transaction invariably motivated by a desire to keep the Government in the dark. But under the Government's construction an individual would commit a felony against the United States by making cash deposits in small doses, fearful that the bank's reports would increase the likelihood of burglary, or in an endeavor to keep a former spouse unaware of his wealth.

Courts have noted "many occasions" on which persons, without violating any law, may structure transactions "in order to avoid the impact of some regulation or tax." This Court, over a century ago, supplied an illustration:

"The Stamp Act of 1862 imposed a duty of two cents upon a bank-check, when drawn for an amount not less than twenty dollars. A careful individual, having the amount of twenty dollars to pay, pays the same by handing to his creditor two checks of ten dollars each. He thus draws checks in payment of his debt to the amount of twenty dollars, and yet pays no stamp duty. . . . While his operations deprive the government of the duties it might reasonably expect to receive, it is not perceived that the practice is open to the charge of fraud. He resorts to devices to avoid the payment of duties, but they are not illegal. He has the legal right to split up his evidences

---

11. On brief, the United States attempted to link Ratzlaf to other bad conduct, describing at some length his repeated failure to report gambling income in his income tax returns. Ratzlaf was not prosecuted, however, for these alleged misdeeds. Nor has the Government ever asserted that Ratzlaf was engaged in other conduct Congress sought principally to check through the legislation in question—not gambling at licensed casinos, but laundering money proceeds from drug sales or other criminal ventures.

of payment, and thus to avoid the tax." *United States v. Isham*, 84 U.S. (17 Wall.) 496 (1873).

In current days, as an *amicus* noted, countless taxpayers each year give a gift of $10,000 on December 31 and an identical gift the next day, thereby legitimately avoiding the taxable gifts reporting required by 26 U.S.C. § 2503(b).

In light of these examples, we are unpersuaded by the argument that structuring is so obviously "evil" or inherently "bad" that the "willfulness" requirement is satisfied irrespective of the defendant's knowledge of the illegality of structuring. Had Congress wished to dispense with the requirement, it could have furnished the appropriate instruction.[16]

C

In § 5322, Congress subjected to criminal penalties only those "willfully violating" § 5324, signaling its intent to require for conviction proof that the defendant knew not only of the bank's duty to report cash transactions in excess of $10,000, but also of his duty not to avoid triggering such a report. There are, we recognize, contrary indications in the statute's legislative history. But we do not resort to legislative history to cloud a statutory text that is clear. Moreover, were we to find § 5322(a)'s "willfulness" requirement ambiguous as applied to § 5324, we would resolve any doubt in favor of the defendant. *Hughey v. United States*, 495 U.S. 411 (1990) (lenity principles "demand resolution of ambiguities in criminal statutes in favor of the defendant"); *Crandon v. United States*, 494 U.S. 152 (1990) ("Because construction of a criminal statute must be guided by the need for fair warning, it is rare that legislative history or statutory policies will support a construction of a statute broader than that clearly warranted by the text.")

We do not dishonor the venerable principle that ignorance of the law generally is no defense to a criminal charge. *See Cheek*. In particular contexts, however, Congress may decree otherwise. That, we hold, is what Congress has done with respect to 31 U.S.C. § 5322(a) and the provisions it controls. To convict Ratzlaf of the crime with which he was charged, violation of 31 U.S.C. §§ 5322(a) and 5324(3), the jury had to find he knew the structuring in which he engaged was unlawful. Because the jury was not properly instructed in this regard, we reverse the judgment of the Ninth Circuit and remand this case for further proceedings consistent with this opinion.

It is so ordered.

Justice BLACKMUN, with whom THE CHIEF JUSTICE, Justice O'CONNOR, and Justice THOMAS join, dissenting.

On October 27, 1988, petitioner Waldemar Ratzlaf arrived at a Nevada casino with a shopping bag full of cash to pay off a $160,000 gambling debt. He told casino

---

16. Congress did provide for civil forfeiture without any "willfulness" requirement in the Money Laundering Control Act of 1986.

personnel he did not want any written report of the payment to be made. The casino vice president informed Ratzlaf that he could not accept a cash payment of more than $10,000 without filing a report.

Ratzlaf, along with his wife and a casino employee, then proceeded to visit several banks in and around Stateline, Nevada, and South Lake Tahoe, California, purchasing separate cashier's checks, each in the amount of $9,500. At some banks the Ratzlafs attempted to buy two checks — one for each of them — and were told that a report would have to be filed; on those occasions they canceled the transactions. Ratzlaf then returned to the casino and paid off $76,000 of his debt in cashier's checks. A few weeks later, Ratzlaf gave three persons cash to purchase additional cashier's checks in amounts less than $10,000. The Ratzlafs themselves also bought five more such checks in the course of a week.

A jury found beyond a reasonable doubt that Ratzlaf knew of the financial institutions' duty to report cash transactions in excess of $10,000 and that he structured transactions for the specific purpose of evading the reporting requirements.

The Court today, however, concludes that these findings are insufficient for a conviction under 31 U.S.C. §§ 5322(a) and 5324(3), because a defendant also must have known that the structuring in which he engaged was illegal. Because this conclusion lacks support in the text of the statute, conflicts in my view with basic principles governing the interpretation of criminal statutes and is squarely undermined by the evidence of congressional intent, I dissent.

I

"The general rule that ignorance of the law or a mistake of law is no defense to criminal prosecution is deeply rooted in the American legal system." *Cheek.* The Court has applied this common-law rule "in numerous cases construing criminal statutes."

Thus, the term "willfully" in criminal law generally "refers to consciousness of the act but not to consciousness that the act is unlawful." ("[T]he word 'willful' . . . means no more than that the person charged with the duty knows what he is doing," not that "he must suppose that he is breaking the law"); American Law Institute, Model Penal Code § 2.02(8) (1985) ("A requirement that an offense be committed wilfully is satisfied if a person acts knowingly with respect to the material elements of the offense, unless a purpose to impose further requirements appears").

As the majority explains, 31 U.S.C. § 5322(a), originally enacted in 1970, imposes criminal penalties upon "person[s] willfully violating this subchapter." The subchapter (entitled "Records and Reports on Monetary Instruments Transactions") contains several different reporting requirements, including § 5313, which requires financial institutions to file reports for cash transactions over an amount prescribed by regulation; § 5314, which requires reports for transactions with foreign financial agencies; and § 5316, which requires reports for transportation of more than $10,000 into or out of the United States. In 1986, Congress added § 5324 to the subchapter to deter rampant evasion by customers of financial institutions' duty to report large cash transactions. The new section provides: "No person shall for the purpose of evading the reporting requirements of section 5313(a) . . . (3) structure . . . any transaction with one or more domestic financial institutions."

Unlike other provisions of the subchapter, the antistructuring provision identifies the purpose that is required for a §5324 violation: "evading the reporting requirements." The offense of structuring, therefore, requires (1) *knowledge* of a financial institution's reporting requirements, and (2) the structuring of a transaction for the *purpose* of evading those requirements. These elements define a violation that is "willful" as that term is commonly interpreted. The majority's additional requirement that an actor have actual knowledge *that structuring is prohibited* strays from the statutory text, as well as from our precedents interpreting criminal statutes generally and "willfulness" in particular.

The Court reasons that the interpretation of the Court of Appeals for the Ninth Circuit, and that of nine other Circuits, renders §5322(a)'s willfulness requirement superfluous. This argument ignores the generality of §5322(a), which sets a single standard—willfulness—for the subchapter's various reporting provisions. Some of those provisions do not themselves define willful conduct, so the willfulness element cannot be deemed surplusage. Moreover, the fact that §5322(a) requires willfulness for criminal liability to be imposed does not mean that each of the underlying offenses to which it applies must involve something less than willfulness. Thus, the fact that §5324 *does* describe a "willful" offense, since it already requires "the purpose of evading the reporting requirements," provides no basis for imposing an artificially heightened scienter requirement. The majority also contends that §5322(a)'s willfulness element, when applied to the subchapter's other provisions, has been read by the Courts of Appeals to require knowledge of and a purpose to disobey the law. In fact, the cases to which the majority refers stand for the more subtle proposition that a willful violation requires knowledge of the pertinent reporting requirements and a purpose to avoid compliance with them. Consistent with and in light of that construction, Congress' 1986 enactment prohibited structuring "for the purpose of evading the reporting requirements." The level of knowledge imposed by the term "willfully" as it applies to all the underlying offenses in the subchapter on reporting requirements is "knowledge of the reporting requirements."[5]

---

5. "Knowledge of the reporting requirements" is easily confused with "knowledge of illegality" because, in the context of the other reporting provisions—§§5313, 5314, and 5316—the entity that can "willfully violate" each provision is also the entity charged with the reporting duty; as a result, a violation with "knowledge of the reporting requirements" necessarily entails the entity's knowledge of the illegality of its conduct (that is, its failure to file a required report). In contrast, §5324 prohibits a customer from purposefully evading a bank's reporting requirements, so knowledge of the reporting requirements does not collapse into actual knowledge that the customer's own conduct is prohibited. Under the cases interpreting the statute as well as fundamental principles of criminal law, it is one's knowledge of the reporting requirements, not "knowledge of the illegality of one's conduct," that makes a violation "willful."

The Court next concludes that its interpretation of "willfully" is warranted because structuring is not inherently "nefarious." It is true that the Court, on occasion, has imposed a knowledge-of-illegality requirement upon criminal statutes to ensure that the defendant acted with a wrongful purpose. *See, e.g., Liparota v. United States*, 471 U.S. 419 (1985). I cannot agree, however, that the imposition of such a requirement is necessary here. First, the conduct at issue—splitting up transactions involving tens of thousands of dollars in cash for the specific purpose of circumventing a bank's reporting duty—is hardly the sort of innocuous activity involved in cases such as *Liparota*, in which the defendant had been convicted of fraud for purchasing food stamps for less than their face value. Further, an individual convicted of structuring is, by definition, aware that cash transactions are regulated, and he cannot seriously argue that he lacked notice of the law's intrusion into the particular sphere of activity. *Cf. Lambert v. California.* By requiring knowledge of a bank's reporting requirements as well as a "purpose of evading" those requirements, the antistructuring provision targets those who knowingly act to deprive the Government of information to which it is entitled. In my view, that is not so plainly innocent a purpose as to justify reading into the statute the additional element of knowledge of illegality. In any event, Congress has determined that purposefully structuring transactions is not innocent conduct.

In interpreting federal criminal tax statutes, this Court has defined the term "willfully" as requiring the "'voluntary, intentional violation of a known legal duty.'" Our rule in the tax area, however, is an "exception to the traditional rule," applied "largely due to the complexity of the tax laws." *Cheek.* The rule is inapplicable here, where, far from being complex, the provisions involved are perhaps among the simplest in the United States Code.[8]

II

Although I believe the statutory language is clear in light of our precedents, the legislative history confirms that Congress intended to require knowledge of (and a purpose to evade) the reporting requirements but not specific knowledge of the illegality of structuring.[9]

---

8. The majority offers examples of tax "avoidance" as further evidence of the apparent "innocence" of structuring transactions to evade the reporting requirements. These examples are inapposite because Congress specifically has prohibited the structuring of transactions to evade the reporting requirements. Indeed, its use of the word "evading" in § 5324 reveals that Congress deemed the intent to circumvent those requirements a "bad purpose." Moreover, the analogy to the tax field is flawed. Tax law involves a unique scheme consisting of myriad categories and thresholds, applied in yearly segments, designed to generate appropriate levels of taxation while also influencing behavior in various ways. Innocent "avoidance" is an established part of this scheme, and it does not operate to undermine the purposes of the tax law. In sharp contrast, evasion of the currency transaction reporting requirements completely deprives the Government of the information that those requirements are designed to obtain, and thus wholly undermines the purpose of the statute.

9. Because the statutory language unambiguously imposes no requirement of knowledge of the illegality of structuring, I would not apply the rule of lenity. Moreover, I am not persuaded that that rule should be applied to defeat a congressional purpose that is as clear as that evidenced here.

Before 1986, the reporting requirements included no provision explicitly prohibiting the structuring of transactions to evade the reporting requirements. The Government attempted to combat purposeful evasion of the reporting requirements through 18 U.S.C. § 1001, which applies to anyone who "knowingly and willfully falsifies, conceals or covers up by any trick, scheme, or device a material fact" within the jurisdiction of a federal agency, and 18 U.S.C. § 2(b), which applies to anyone who "willfully causes an act to be done which if directly performed by him or another would be an offense" under federal law. Some Courts of Appeals upheld application of those criminal statutes where a report would have been filed but for the defendant's purposeful structuring. As the leading case explained, a defendant's willfulness was established if he "knew about the currency reporting requirements and ... purposely sought to prevent the financial institutions from filing required reports ... by structuring his transactions as multiple smaller transactions under $10,000." *Tobon-Builes*, 706 F.2d at 1101.

Other courts rejected imposition of criminal liability for structuring under §§ 1001 and 2(b), concluding either that the law did not impose a duty not to structure or that criminal liability was confined to limited forms of structuring. *See, e.g., United States v. Varbel*, 780 F.2d 758, 760–763 (9th Cir. 1986); *United States v. Denemark*, 779 F.2d 1559, 1561–1564 (11th Cir. 1986); *United States v. Anzalone*, 766 F.2d 676, 679–683 (1st Cir. 1985).

Congress enacted the anti-structuring provision in 1986 "to fill a loophole in the Bank Secrecy Act caused by" the latter three decisions, which "refused to apply the sanctions of [the Act] to transactions 'structured' to evade the act's $10,000 cash reporting requirement." As explained by the Report of the Senate Judiciary Committee:

> "[The anti-structuring provision] would codify *Tobon-Builes* and like cases and would negate the effect of *Anzalone, Varbel* and *Denemark*. It would expressly subject to potential liability a person who causes or attempts to cause a financial institution to fail to file a required report or who causes a financial institution to file a required report that contains material omissions or misstatements of fact. In addition, the proposed amendment would create the offense of structuring a transaction to evade the reporting requirements, without regard to whether an individual transaction is, itself, reportable under the Bank Secrecy Act."

Congress' stated purpose to "codify *Tobon-Builes*" reveals its intent to incorporate *Tobon-Builes*' standard for a willful violation, which required knowledge of the reporting requirements and a purpose to evade them. Nothing in *Tobon-Builes* suggests that knowledge of the illegality of one's conduct is required.

The Senate Report proceeds to explain the intent required under the anti-structuring provision:

> "For example, a person who converts $18,000 in currency to cashier's checks by purchasing two $9,000 cashier's checks at two different banks or on two

different days *with the specific intent that the participating bank or banks not be required to file Currency Transaction Reports for those transactions*, would be subject to potential civil and criminal liability. A person conducting the same transactions for any other reasons or a person splitting up an amount of currency that would not be reportable if the full amount were involved in a single transaction (for example, splitting $2,000 in currency into four transactions of $500 each), would not be subject to liability under the proposed amendment." (emphasis added).

The Committee's specification of the requisite intent as only the intent to prevent a bank from filing reports confirms that Congress did not contemplate a departure from the general rule that knowledge of illegality is not an essential element of a criminal offense.

Finally, it cannot be ignored that the majority's interpretation of § 5324 as a practical matter largely nullifies the effect of that provision. In codifying the currency transaction reporting requirements in 1970, "Congress recognized the importance of reports of large and unusual currency transactions in ferreting out criminal activity." Congress enacted the antistructuring law to close what it perceived as a major loophole in the federal reporting scheme due to easy circumvention. Because requiring proof of actual knowledge of illegality will make prosecution for structuring difficult or impossible in most cases, the Court's decision reopens the loophole that Congress tried to close.

III

The petitioner in this case was informed by casino officials that a transaction involving more than $10,000 in cash must be reported, was informed by the various banks he visited that banks are required to report cash transactions in excess of $10,000, and then purchased $76,000 in cashier's checks, each for less than $10,000 and each from a different bank. Petitioner Ratzlaf, obviously not a person of limited intelligence, was anything but uncomprehending as he traveled from bank to bank converting his bag of cash to cashier's checks in $9,500 bundles. I am convinced that his actions constituted a "willful" violation of the antistructuring provision embodied in 31 U.S.C. § 5324. As a result of today's decision, Waldemar Ratzlaf—to use an old phrase—will be "laughing all the way to the bank."

The majority's interpretation of the antistructuring provision is at odds with the statutory text, the intent of Congress, and the fundamental principle that knowledge of illegality is not required for a criminal act. Now Congress must try again to fill a hole it rightly felt it had filled before. I dissent.

Questions and Notes

1. Do you think that Ratzlaf "will be laughing all the way to the bank"?

2. What is the core difference between the majority and dissent?

3. Do you think that Ratzlaf's behavior was the kind that should have put him on notice that he was violating the law? Explain.

4. Do you think that Ratzlaf's violation of the law was knowing, wilfully blind, reckless, or negligent? Which of those states of mind ought to be sufficient to impose criminal liability?

5. We conclude this section with *Rehaif*, where the Court divided over how specific the defendant's knowledge of the law need be in order to constitute willfulness.

Rehaif v. United States

139 S.Ct. 2191 (2019) (Decided June 21, 2019)

Justice BREYER delivered the opinion of the Court.

A federal statute, 18 U.S.C. § 922(g), provides that "[i]t shall be unlawful" for certain individuals to possess firearms. The provision lists nine categories of individuals subject to the prohibition, including felons and aliens who are "illegally or unlawfully in the United States." A separate provision, § 924(a)(2), adds that anyone who "*knowingly* violates" the first provision shall be fined or imprisoned for up to 10 years. (Emphasis added.)

The question here concerns the scope of the word "knowingly." Does it mean that the Government must prove that a defendant knew both that he engaged in the relevant conduct (that he possessed a firearm) and also that he fell within the relevant status (that he was a felon, an alien unlawfully in this country, or the like)? We hold that the word "knowingly" applies both to the defendant's conduct and to the defendant's status. To convict a defendant, the Government therefore must show that the defendant knew he possessed a firearm and also that he knew he had the relevant status when he possessed it.

I

Petitioner Hamid Rehaif entered the United States on a nonimmigrant student visa to attend university. After he received poor grades, the university dismissed him and told him that his "immigration status" would be terminated unless he transferred to a different university or left the country. Rehaif did neither.

Rehaif subsequently visited a firing range, where he shot two firearms. The Government learned about his target practice and prosecuted him for possessing firearms as an alien unlawfully in the United States. At the close of Rehaif's trial, the judge instructed the jury (over Rehaif's objection) that the "United States is not required to prove" that Rehaif "knew that he was illegally or unlawfully in the United States." The jury returned a guilty verdict, and Rehaif was sentenced to 18 months' imprisonment.

Rehaif appealed. He argued that the judge erred in instructing the jury that it did not need to find that he knew he was in the country unlawfully. The Court of Appeals for the Eleventh Circuit, however, concluded that the jury instruction was correct, and it affirmed. The Court of Appeals believed that the criminal law generally does not require a defendant to know his own status, and further observed that no court of appeals had required the Government to establish a defendant's knowledge of his status in the analogous context of felon-in-possession prosecutions.

We granted certiorari to consider whether, in prosecutions under § 922(g) and § 924(a)(2), the Government must prove that a defendant knows of his status as a person barred from possessing a firearm. We now reverse.

II

Whether a criminal statute requires the Government to prove that the defendant acted knowingly is a question of congressional intent. In determining Congress' intent, we start from a longstanding presumption, traceable to the common law, that Congress intends to require a defendant to possess a culpable mental state regarding "each of the statutory elements that criminalize otherwise innocent conduct." We normally characterize this interpretive maxim as a presumption in favor of "scienter," by which we mean a presumption that criminal statutes require the degree of knowledge sufficient to "mak[e] a person legally responsible for the consequences of his or her act or omission."

We apply the presumption in favor of scienter even when Congress does not specify any scienter in the statutory text. But the presumption applies with equal or greater force when Congress includes a general scienter provision in the statute itself.

A

Here we can find no convincing reason to depart from the ordinary presumption in favor of scienter. The statutory text supports the presumption. The text of § 924(a)(2) says that "[w]hoever knowingly violates" certain subsections of § 922, including § 922(g), "shall be" subject to penalties of up to 10 years' imprisonment. The text of § 922(g) in turn provides that it "shall be unlawful for any person . . . , being an alien . . . illegally or unlawfully in the United States," to "possess in or affecting commerce, any firearm or ammunition."

The term "knowingly" in § 924(a)(2) modifies the verb "violates" and its direct object, which in this case is § 922(g). The proper interpretation of the statute thus turns on what it means for a defendant to know that he has "violate[d]" § 922(g). With some here-irrelevant omissions, § 922(g) makes possession of a firearm or ammunition unlawful when the following elements are satisfied: (1) a status element (in this case, "being an alien . . . illegally or unlawfully in the United States"); (2) a possession element (to "possess"); (3) a jurisdictional element ("in or affecting commerce"); and (4) a firearm element (a "firearm or ammunition").No one here claims that the word "knowingly" modifies the statute's jurisdictional element.

Jurisdictional element aside, however, the text of § 922(g) simply lists the elements that make a defendant's behavior criminal. As "a matter of ordinary English grammar," we normally read the statutory term "'knowingly' as applying to all the subsequently listed elements of the crime." This is notably not a case where the modifier "knowingly" introduces a long statutory phrase, such that questions may reasonably arise about how far into the statute the modifier extends. And everyone agrees that the word "knowingly" applies to §922(g)'s possession element, which is situated after the status element. We see no basis to interpret "knowingly" as applying to the second §922(g) element but not the first.

B

Beyond the text, our reading of §922(g) and §924(a)(2) is consistent with a basic principle that underlies the criminal law, namely, the importance of showing what Blackstone called "a vicious will." As this Court has explained, the understanding that an injury is criminal only if inflicted knowingly "is as universal and persistent in mature systems of law as belief in freedom of the human will and a consequent ability and duty of the normal individual to choose between good and evil." *Morissette*. Scienter requirements advance this basic principle of criminal law by helping to "separate those who understand the wrongful nature of their act from those who do not."

The cases in which we have emphasized scienter's importance in separating wrongful from innocent acts are legion. *Morissette*. We have interpreted statutes to include a scienter requirement even where the statutory text is silent on the question. And we have interpreted statutes to include a scienter requirement even where "the most grammatical reading of the statute" does not support one.

Applying the word "knowingly" to the defendant's status in §922(g) helps advance the purpose of scienter, for it helps to separate wrongful from innocent acts. Assuming compliance with ordinary licensing requirements, the possession of a gun can be entirely innocent. It is therefore the defendant's *status*, and not his conduct alone, that makes the difference. Without knowledge of that status, the defendant may well lack the intent needed to make his behavior wrongful. His behavior may instead be an innocent mistake to which criminal sanctions normally do not attach. Cf. O. Holmes, The Common Law 3 (1881) ("even a dog distinguishes between being stumbled over and being kicked").

We have sometimes declined to read a scienter requirement into criminal statutes. *See United States v. Balint*, 258 U.S. 250, 254 (1922). But we have typically declined to apply the presumption in favor of scienter in cases involving statutory provisions that form part of a "regulatory" or "public welfare" program and carry only minor penalties. See Morissette. The firearms provisions before us are not part of a regulatory or public welfare program, and they carry a potential penalty of 10 years in prison that we have previously described as "harsh." Hence, this exception to the presumption in favor of scienter does not apply.

III

The Government's arguments to the contrary do not convince us that Congress sought to depart from the normal presumption in favor of scienter.

Nor do we believe that Congress would have expected defendants under §922(g) and §924(a)(2) to know their own statuses. If the provisions before us were construed to require no knowledge of status, they might well apply to an alien who was brought into the United States unlawfully as a small child and was therefore unaware of his unlawful status. Or these provisions might apply to a person who was convicted of a prior crime but sentenced only to probation, who does not know that the crime is "punishable by imprisonment for a term exceeding one year." § 922(g)(1) (emphasis added); see also Games-Perez, 667 F.3d at 1138 (defendant held strictly liable regarding his status as a felon even though the trial judge had told him repeatedly—but incorrectly—that he would "leave this courtroom not convicted of a felony"). As we have said, we normally presume that Congress did not intend to impose criminal liability on persons who, due to lack of knowledge, did not have a wrongful mental state. And we doubt that the obligation to prove a defendant's knowledge of his status will be as burdensome as the Government suggests.

The Government also argues that whether an alien is "illegally or unlawfully in the United States" is a question of law, not fact, and thus appeals to the well-known maxim that "ignorance of the law" (or a "mistake of law") is no excuse. *Cheek v. United States.*

This maxim, however, normally applies where a defendant has the requisite mental state in respect to the elements of the crime but claims to be "unaware of the existence of a statute proscribing his conduct." In contrast, the maxim does not normally apply where a defendant "has a mistaken impression concerning the legal effect of some collateral matter and that mistake results in his misunderstanding the full significance of his conduct," thereby negating an element of the offense. Much of the confusion surrounding the ignorance-of-the-law maxim stems from "the failure to distinguish [these] two quite different situations."

We applied this distinction in *Liparota*, where we considered a statute that imposed criminal liability on "whoever knowingly uses, transfers, acquires, alters, or possesses" food stamps "in any manner not authorized by the statute or the regulations.". We held that the statute required scienter not only in respect to the defendant's use of food stamps, but also in respect to whether the food stamps were used in a "manner not authorized by the statute or regulations." We therefore required the Government to prove that the defendant knew that his use of food stamps was unlawful—even though that was a question of law.

This case is similar. The defendant's status as an alien "illegally or unlawfully in the United States" refers to a legal matter, but this legal matter is what the commentators refer to as a "collateral" question of law. A defendant who does not know that he is an alien "illegally or unlawfully in the United States" does not have the guilty state of mind that the statute's language and purposes require.

The Government finally turns for support to the statutory and legislative history. Congress first enacted a criminal statute prohibiting particular categories of persons from possessing firearms in 1938. In 1968, Congress added new categories of persons subject to the prohibition. Then, in 1986, Congress passed the statute at issue here, the Firearms Owners' Protection Act, 100 Stat. 449, note following 18 U.S.C. §921, which reorganized the prohibition on firearm possession and added the language providing that only those who violate the prohibition "knowingly" may be held criminally liable.

The Government says that, prior to 1986, the courts had reached a consensus that the law did not require the Government to prove scienter regarding a defendant's status. And the Government relies on the interpretive canon providing that when particular statutory language has received a settled judicial construction, and Congress subsequently reenacts that "same language," courts should presume that Congress intended to ratify the judicial consensus.

Prior to 1986, however, there was no definitive judicial consensus that knowledge of status was not needed. This Court had not considered the matter. As the Government says, most lower courts had concluded that the statute did not require knowledge of status. But the Sixth Circuit had held to the contrary, specifically citing the risk that a defendant "may not be aware of the fact" that barred him from possessing a firearm. And the Fourth Circuit had found that knowledge of a defendant's status was not needed because the statute "[b]y its terms" did not require knowledge of status.

This last-mentioned circumstance is important. Any pre-1986 consensus involved the statute as it read prior to 1986—without any explicit scienter provision. But Congress in 1986 added a provision clarifying that a defendant could be convicted only if he violated the prohibition on firearm possession "knowingly." This addition, which would serve no apparent purpose under the Government's view, makes it all but impossible to draw any inference that Congress intended to ratify a pre-existing consensus when, in 1986, it amended the statute.

The Government points to the House Report on the legislation, which says that the 1986 statute would require the Government to prove "that the defendant's *conduct* was knowing." H. R. Rep. No. 99-495, p. 10 (1986) (emphasis added). Although this statement speaks of "conduct" rather than "status," context suggests that the Report may have meant the former to include the latter. In any event, other statements suggest that the word "knowingly" was intended to apply to both conduct and status. The Senate Report, for example, says that the proposed amendments sought to exclude "individuals who lack all criminal intent and knowledge," without distinguishing between conduct and status. S. Rep. No. 97-476, p. 15S. Rep. No. 97-476, p. 15 (1982). And one Senate sponsor of the bill pointed out that the absence of a scienter requirement in the prior statutes had resulted in "severe penalties for unintentional missteps."

Thus, assuming without deciding that statutory or legislative history could overcome the longstanding presumption in favor of scienter, that history here is at best inconclusive.

* * *

The Government asks us to hold that any error in the jury instructions in this case was harmless. But the lower courts did not address that question. We therefore leave the question for those courts to decide on remand.

We conclude that in a prosecution under 18 U.S.C. §922(g) and §924(a)(2), the Government must prove both that the defendant knew he possessed a firearm and that he knew he belonged to the relevant category of persons barred from possessing a firearm. We express no view, however, about what precisely the Government must prove to establish a defendant's knowledge of status in respect to other §922(g) provisions not at issue here. See post, at——— ——(ALITO, J., dissenting) (discussing other statuses listed in §922(g) not at issue here). We accordingly reverse the judgment of the Court of Appeals and remand the case for further proceedings consistent with this opinion.

It is so ordered.

[Justice Alito, joined by Justice Thomas, dissented on the ground that under their reading of the statue, "knowingly" did not modify the defendant's status as an unlawful alien]

Questions and Notes

1. If the trial judge hadn't specifically said that knowledge of Rehaif's legal status was unnecessary, but just didn't speak to the question, might the result have been different (Cf. *Morissette*)?

2. What knowledge must the defendant have? Is it necessary that he know of the statute? If not, how are *Cheek* and *Ratzlaf* distinguishable?

3. Is it clear that shooting a gun at a firing range constitutes "possession" of the gun?

4. The Court says that, in the past, it has presumed a scienter requirement even when the most grammatical reading of the statute suggests otherwise. Why is that?

5. In a case like this, how can the Government prove scienter over a defendant's denial?

6. Do you think that the error was in fact harmless? On remand should the Court so hold?

Chapter 9

Actus Reus

A. In General

As previously indicated, most crimes require the concurrence of *mens rea* and *actus reus*. Even crimes that dispense with *mens rea* will rarely, if ever, dispense with *actus reus*. For example, in *Morissette*, even if the lower court opinion in regard to *mens rea* had prevailed, Morissette would have had a defense if someone other than himself had loaded the casings in his truck (assuming of course that the person was not acting at Morissette's direction and that Morissette did not thereafter drive off with the casings). Similarly, in *Garnett*, the defendant would not have been guilty if the girl had engaged in intercourse with Garnett while he was sleeping or unconscious (at least in the absence of his having previously given her permission to do so). *Guminga* in a sense did involve an *actus reus* defense because of his claim that he did not serve the liquor. The court, however, thought that he was responsible for the act of his employee. If, however, the 17-year-old had surreptitiously helped herself to liquor from Guminga's bar, he would not be guilty absent proof that he either permitted or facilitated her conduct.

In short, *actus reus* is even more fundamental or basic to criminal liability than is *mens rea*. The defendant raising an *actus reus* defense is saying "I didn't do it." The *mens rea* defense merely says "I didn't mean it." Much of the difficulty in this area is ascertaining whether a particular defense ought to be conceived of as an *actus reus* or *mens rea* defense.

In this section, we begin with two United States Supreme Court cases, *Robinson v. California* and *Powell v. Texas*, which, taken together, seem to establish that the total elimination of *actus reus* is unconstitutional, but that little else may be required to satisfy the Constitution.

Robinson v. California

370 U.S. 660 (1962)

Mr. Justice STEWART delivered the opinion of the Court.

A California statute makes it a criminal offense for a person to "be addicted to the use of narcotics." This appeal draws into question the constitutionality of that provision of the state law, as construed by the California courts in the present case.

The appellant was convicted after a jury trial in the Municipal Court of Los Angeles. The evidence against him was given by two Los Angeles police officers. Officer

481

Brown testified that he had had occasion to examine the appellant's arms one evening on a street in Los Angeles some four months before the trial. The officer testified that at that time he had observed "scar tissue and discoloration on the inside" of the appellant's right arm, and "what appeared to be numerous needle marks and a scab which was approximately three inches below the crook of the elbow" on the appellant's left arm. The officer also testified that the appellant under questioning had admitted to the occasional use of narcotics.

The trial judge instructed the jury that the statute made it a misdemeanor for a person "either to use narcotics, or to be addicted to the use of narcotics. . . . That portion of the statute referring to the 'use' of narcotics is based upon the 'act' of using. That portion of the statute referring to 'addicted to the use' of narcotics is based upon a condition or status. They are not identical. . . . To be addicted to the use of narcotics is said to be a status or condition and not an act. It is a continuing offense and differs from most other offenses in the fact that (it) is chronic rather than acute; that it continues after it is complete and subjects the offender to arrest at any time before he reforms. The existence of such a chronic condition may be ascertained from a single examination, if the characteristic reactions of that condition be found present."

The judge further instructed the jury that the appellant could be convicted under a general verdict if the jury agreed either that he was of the "status" or had committed the "act" denounced by the statute. "All that the People must show is either that the defendant did use a narcotic in Los Angeles County, or that while in the City of Los Angeles he was addicted to the use of narcotics. . . ."

Under these instructions the jury returned a verdict finding the appellant "guilty of the offense charged." An appeal was taken to the Appellate Department of the Los Angeles County Superior Court, "the highest court of a State in which a decision could be had" in this case. Although expressing some doubt as to the constitutionality of "the crime of being a narcotic addict," the reviewing court in an unreported opinion affirmed the judgment of conviction, citing two of its own previous unreported decisions which had upheld the constitutionality of the statute. We noted probable jurisdiction of this appeal because it squarely presents the issue whether the statute as construed by the California courts in this case is repugnant to the Fourteenth Amendment of the Constitution.

It would be possible to construe the statute under which the appellant was convicted as one which is operative only upon proof of the actual use of narcotics within the State's jurisdiction. But the California courts have not so construed this law. Although there was evidence in the present case that the appellant had used narcotics in Los Angeles, the jury [was] instructed that they could convict him even if they disbelieved that evidence. The appellant could be convicted, they were told, if they found simply that the appellant's "status" or "chronic condition" was that of being "addicted to the use of narcotics." And it is impossible to know from the jury's verdict that the defendant was not convicted upon precisely such a finding.

The instructions of the trial court, implicitly approved on appeal, amounted to "a ruling on a question of state law that is as binding on us as though the precise words had been written" into the statute. We can only take the statute as the state courts read it. Indeed, in their brief in this Court counsel for the State have emphasized that it is "the proof of addiction by circumstantial evidence . . . by the tell-tale track of needle marks and scabs over the veins of his arms, that remains the gist of the section."

This statute, therefore, is not one which punishes a person for the use of narcotics, for their purchase, sale or possession, or for antisocial or disorderly behavior resulting from their administration. It is not a law which even purports to provide or require medical treatment. Rather, we deal with a statute which makes the "status" of narcotic addiction a criminal offense, for which the offender may be prosecuted "at any time before he reforms." California has said that a person can be continuously guilty of this offense, whether or not he has ever used or possessed any narcotics within the State, and whether or not he has been guilty of any antisocial behavior there.

It is unlikely that any State at this moment in history would attempt to make it a criminal offense for a person to be mentally ill, or a leper, or to be afflicted with a venereal disease. A State might determine that the general health and welfare require that the victims of these and other human afflictions be dealt with by compulsory treatment, involving quarantine, confinement, or sequestration. But, in the light of contemporary human knowledge, a law which made a criminal offense of such a disease would doubtless be universally thought to be an infliction of cruel and unusual punishment in violation of the Eighth and Fourteenth Amendments.

We cannot but consider the statute before us as of the same category. In this Court counsel for the State recognized that narcotic addiction is an illness. Indeed, it is apparently an illness which may be contracted innocently or involuntarily. We hold that a state law which imprisons a person thus afflicted as a criminal, even though he has never touched any narcotic drug within the State or been guilty of any irregular behavior there, inflicts a cruel and unusual punishment in violation of the Fourteenth Amendment. To be sure, imprisonment for ninety days is not, in the abstract, a punishment which is either cruel or unusual. But the question cannot be considered in the abstract. Even one day in prison would be a cruel and unusual punishment for the "crime" of having a common cold.

We are not unmindful that the vicious evils of the narcotics traffic have occasioned the grave concern of government. There are, as we have said, countless fronts on which those evils may be legitimately attacked. We deal in this case only with an individual provision of a particularized local law as it has so far been interpreted by the California courts.

Reversed.

Powell v. Texas

392 U.S. 514 (1968)

Mr. Justice MARSHALL announced the judgment of the Court and delivered an opinion in which THE CHIEF JUSTICE, Mr. Justice BLACK, and Mr. Justice HARLAN join.

In late December 1966, appellant was arrested and charged with being found in a state of intoxication in a public place, in violation of Vernon's Ann. Texas Penal Code, Art. 477 (1952), which reads as follows:

> "Whoever shall get drunk or be found in a state of intoxication in any public place, or at any private house except his own, shall be fined not exceeding one hundred dollars."

Appellant was tried in the Corporation Court of Austin, Texas, found guilty, and fined $20. He appealed to the County Court at Law No. 1 of Travis County, Texas, where a trial de novo was held. His counsel urged that appellant was "afflicted with the disease of chronic alcoholism," that "his appearance in public (while drunk was) . . . not of his own volition," and therefore that to punish him criminally for that conduct would be cruel and unusual, in violation of the Eighth and Fourteenth Amendments to the United States Constitution.

Appellant, however, seeks to come within the application of the Cruel and Unusual Punishment Clause announced in *Robinson v. State of California*, 370 U.S. 660 (1962), which involved a state statute making it a crime to "be addicted to the use of narcotics." This Court held there that "a state law which imprisons a person thus afflicted (with narcotic addiction) as a criminal, even though he has never touched any narcotic drug within the State or been guilty of any irregular behavior there, inflicts a cruel and unusual punishment. . . ."

On its face the present case does not fall within that holding, since appellant was convicted, not for being a chronic alcoholic, but for being in public while drunk on a particular occasion. The State of Texas thus has not sought to punish a mere status, as California did in *Robinson*; nor has it attempted to regulate appellant's behavior in the privacy of his own home. Rather, it has imposed upon appellant a criminal sanction for public behavior which may create substantial health and safety hazards, both for appellant and for members of the general public, and which offends the moral and esthetic sensibilities of a large segment of the community. This seems a far cry from convicting one for being an addict, being a chronic alcoholic, being "mentally ill, or a leper. . . ."

Robinson so viewed brings this Court but a very small way into the substantive criminal law. And unless *Robinson* is so viewed it is difficult to see any limiting principle that would serve to prevent this Court from becoming, under the aegis of the Cruel and Unusual Punishment Clause, the ultimate arbiter of the standards of criminal responsibility, in diverse areas of the criminal law, throughout the country.

It is suggested in dissent that *Robinson* stands for the "simple" but "subtle" principle that "(c)riminal penalties may not be inflicted upon a person for being in a condition he is powerless to change." *Post*, at 2171. In that view, appellant's "condition" of public intoxication was "occasioned by a compulsion symptomatic of the disease" of chronic alcoholism, and thus, apparently, his behavior lacked the critical element of *mens rea*. Whatever may be the merits of such a doctrine of criminal responsibility, it surely cannot be said to follow from *Robinson*. The entire thrust of *Robinson*'s interpretation of the Cruel and Unusual Punishment Clause is that criminal penalties may be inflicted only if the accused has committed some act, has engaged in some behavior, which society has an interest in preventing, or perhaps in historical common law terms, has committed some *actus reus*. It thus does not deal with the question of whether certain conduct cannot constitutionally be punished because it is, in some sense, "involuntary" or "occasioned by a compulsion."

We cannot cast aside the centuries-long evolution of the collection of interlocking and overlapping concepts which the common law has utilized to assess the moral accountability of an individual for his antisocial deeds. The doctrines of *actus reus*, *mens rea*, insanity, mistake, justification, and duress have historically provided the tools for a constantly shifting adjustment of the tension between the evolving aims of the criminal law and changing religious, moral, philosophical, and medical views of the nature of man. This process of adjustment has always been thought to be the province of the States.

Affirmed.

Mr. Justice BLACK, whom Mr. Justice HARLAN joins, concurring.

The rule of constitutional law urged by appellant is not required by *Robinson v. California*. In that case we held that a person could not be punished for the mere status of being a narcotics addict. We explicitly limited our holding to the situation where no conduct of any kind is involved, stating:

> "We hold that a state law which imprisons a person thus afflicted as a criminal, *even though he has never touched any narcotic drug within the State or been guilty of any irregular behavior there*, inflicts a cruel and unusual punishment in violation of the Fourteenth Amendment." 370 U.S. at 667. (Emphasis added.)

The argument is made that appellant comes within the terms of our holding in *Robinson* because being drunk in public is a mere status or "condition." Despite this many-faceted use of the concept of "condition," this argument would require converting *Robinson* into a case protecting actual behavior, a step we explicitly refused to take in that decision.

A different question, I admit, is whether our attempt in *Robinson* to limit our holding to pure status crimes, involving no conduct whatever, was a sound one. I believe it was. Although some of our objections to the statute in Robinson are equally applicable to statutes that punish conduct "symptomatic" of a disease, any attempt to explain *Robinson* as based solely on the lack of voluntariness encounters a number of logical difficulties. Other problems raised by status crimes are in no way involved when the State attempts to punish for conduct, and these other problems were, in my view, the controlling aspects of our decision.

Punishment for a status is particularly obnoxious, and in many instances can reasonably be called cruel and unusual, because it involves punishment for a mere propensity, a desire to commit an offense; the mental element is not simply one part of the crime but may constitute all of it. This is a situation universally sought to be avoided in our criminal law; the fundamental requirement that some action be proved is solidly established even for offenses most heavily based on propensity, such as attempt, conspiracy, and recidivist crimes. In fact, one eminent authority has found only one isolated instance, in all of Anglo-American jurisprudence, in which criminal responsibility was imposed in the absence of any act at all.

The reasons for this refusal to permit conviction without proof of an act are difficult to spell out, but they are nonetheless perceived and universally expressed in our criminal law. Evidence of propensity can be considered relatively unreliable and more difficult for a defendant to rebut; the requirement of a specific act thus provides some protection against false charges. *See* 4 BLACKSTONE, COMMENTARIES 21. Perhaps more fundamental is the difficulty of distinguishing, in the absence of any conduct, between desires of the daydream variety and fixed intentions that may pose a real threat to society; extending the criminal law to cover both types of desire would be unthinkable, since "(t)here can hardly be anyone who has never thought evil. When a desire is inhibited it may find expression in fantasy; but it would be absurd to condemn this natural psychological mechanism as illegal."

In contrast, crimes that require the State to prove that the defendant actually committed some proscribed act involve none of these special problems. In addition, the question whether an act is "involuntary" is, as I have already indicated, an inherently elusive question, and one which the State may, for good reasons, wish to regard as irrelevant. In light of all these considerations, our limitation of our *Robinson* holding to pure status crimes seems to me entirely proper.

I would confess the limits of my own ability to answer the age-old questions of the criminal law's ethical foundations and practical effectiveness. I would hold that *Robinson v. California* establishes a firm and impenetrable barrier to the punishment of persons who, whatever their bare desires and propensities, have committed no proscribed wrongful act. But I would refuse to plunge from the concrete and almost universally recognized premises of *Robinson* into the murky problems raised by the insistence that chronic alcoholics cannot be punished for public drunkenness, problems that no person, whether layman or expert, can claim to understand, and with consequences that no one can safely predict. I join in affirmance of this conviction.

Mr. Justice WHITE, concurring in the result.

If it cannot be a crime to have an irresistible compulsion to use narcotics, I do not see how it can constitutionally be a crime to yield to such a compulsion. Punishing an addict for using drugs convicts for addiction under a different name. Distinguishing between the two crimes is like forbidding criminal conviction for being sick with flu or epilepsy but permitting punishment for running a fever or having a convulsion. Unless *Robinson* is to be abandoned, the use of narcotics by an addict must be beyond the reach of the criminal law. Similarly, the chronic alcoholic with an irresistible urge to consume alcohol should not be punishable for drinking or for being drunk.

Powell's conviction was for the different crime of being drunk in a public place. Thus even if Powell was compelled to drink, and so could not constitutionally be convicted for drinking, his conviction in this case can be invalidated only if there is a constitutional basis for saying that he may not be punished for being in public while drunk. The statute involved here, which aims at keeping drunks off the street for their own welfare and that of others, is not challenged on the ground that it interferes unconstitutionally with the right to frequent public places. No question is raised about applying this statute to the nonchronic drunk, who has no compulsion to drink, who need not drink to excess, and who could have arranged to do his drinking in private or, if he began drinking in public, could have removed himself at an appropriate point on the path toward complete inebriation.

Because Powell did not show that his conviction offended the Constitution, I concur in the judgment affirming the Travis County court.

Questions and Notes

1. Do you agree with Justice White (whose vote was necessary for a majority in *Powell*) that punishing an addict for using drugs is like punishing someone with a cold for having a fever? If not, how are the situations different?

2. Is the *Powell* plurality trying to correct the mistake that the Court made in *Robinson*, or is there really a difference between the two situations?

3. At the core, what is wrong with the statute in *Robinson*?

4. In the *actus reus* sense of the term, what does "involuntary" mean? Was Robinson's status acquired involuntarily? Was Powell's condition?

5. Could a state make it a crime to willfully, recklessly, or negligently become addicted to narcotics?

6. After *Powell*, could a state choose to decriminalize public drunkenness, or is it bound by the Supreme Court's decision?

7. States have had their own problems in distinguishing *actus reus* from *mens rea* problems, as you can readily ascertain from reading *Baker*.

State v. Baker

571 P.2d 65 (Kan. Ct. App. 1977)

SPENCER, Judge:

Defendant has appealed his conviction of driving his motor vehicle at a speed of seventy-seven miles per hour in a fifty-five miles per hour zone in violation of K.S.A.1976 Supp. 8-1336(a)(3).

Agreed upon facts are that prior to the trial of this matter to the court, the state moved to suppress evidence offered by the defendant that:

1. Defendant's cruise control stuck in the "accelerate" position causing the car to accelerate beyond the posted speed limit.

2. The defendant attempted to deactivate the cruise control by hitting the off button, and the coast button and tapping the brakes.

3. These actions were not immediately successful in deactivating the cruise control.

4. Subsequent to the date of this incident, the defendant had the defective cruise control repaired.

The trial court sustained the motion, thus precluding the defendant from presenting the proffered evidence as a defense. Because of this ruling, defendant presented no defense and the plaintiff's evidence was uncontradicted and unimpeached. The result was that the defendant was found guilty of driving in excess of the posted speed limit, and, also, that defendant was the "driver" of the car as defined by K.S.A. 8-1416. The sentence of $10 and costs was suspended pending this appeal.

With some eloquence, the defendant states:

"Of all of the beacon principles of criminal liability which have shone bright during the development of Anglo-American Jurisprudence, the necessity of proving two basic elements of a crime have shone brightest. These two elements are: a voluntary act and an evil intention. To constitute a crime, the act must, except as otherwise provided by statute, be accompanied by a criminal intent. . . ."

But defendant readily concedes that a violation of the speeding statute (K.S.A. 1976 Supp. 8-1336) is an absolute liability offense when read in light of the absolute liability statute (K.S.A. 21-3204), which provides:

"A person may be guilty of an offense without having criminal intent if the crime is a misdemeanor and the statute defining the offense clearly indicates a legislative purpose to impose absolute liability for the conduct described. . . ."

Defendant admits that this statute does away with the necessity of proving intent to commit the misdemeanor and, further, that any evidence of the defective cruise control would be inadmissible if introduced merely to negate an intent or culpable state of mind on the part of the motorist. His contention is that the evidence was offered to show that his speeding was not a voluntary act and, therefore, there was no criminal liability. He suggests that the evidence of a defective cruise control goes specifically to whether his speeding was a voluntary act on his part and has nothing to do "with the intent, or state of mind, of the defendant to do the crime to which his act amounted." In sum, the defendant suggests that even though the charge against him was an absolute liability offense per K.S.A. 21-3204, the state must prove that he acted voluntarily.

Defendant directs attention to the Judicial Council comment to K.S.A. 21-3204 which cites *Morissette v. United States*, 342 U.S. 246 (1952), and argues that absolute liability would apply only where the injury does not occur as a result of "fortuity." He says that his act of speeding in this instance was due to fortuity, or chance, and, therefore, he should be allowed to present evidence showing the circumstances of the defective cruise control and that he could not prevent the act which resulted in the charge against him.

On the other hand, the state argues that one should not be allowed to rely on a malfunction of an instrument to which he entrusts control of his automobile, offering as an excuse "fortuitous" circumstances to relieve himself of liability for his acts. It is suggested that "fortuitous" implies circumstances which arise from outside the defendant's vehicle. It is argued that our absolute liability statute (K.S.A. 21-3204) clearly indicates that the state need not prove the defendant acted voluntarily, but rather the defendant must prove that his offense is not within the scope of that statute because he acted involuntarily upon the compulsion of fortuitous circumstances.

Referring again to the Judicial Council comment to K.S.A. 21-3204 and the case of *Morissette v. United States*, supra, we note the following:

"... The accused, if he does not will the violation, usually is in a position to prevent it with no more care than society might reasonably expect and no more exertion than it might reasonably exact from one who assumed his responsibilities. ..."

We have no doubt but that if defendant were able to establish that his act of speeding was the result of an unforeseen occurrence or circumstance, which was not caused by him and which he could not prevent, that such would constitute a valid defense to the charge. But the evidence proffered suggests a malfunction of a device attached to the motor vehicle operated by the defendant over which he had or should have had absolute control. Defendant does not suggest that the operation of the motor vehicle on the day of his arrest was anything but a voluntary act on his part, nor that anyone other than himself activated the cruise control, which may have caused his excessive speed. Nor does he suggest that any occurrence or circumstance existed which required of him more care than society might reasonably expect. Furthermore, as suggested by the state, it appears that defendant was able to bring his vehicle under control and to a stop when directed to do so by the police.

In the New York case of *People v. Shaughnessy*, 66 Misc. 2d 19, 319 N.Y.S.2d 626 (1971), it was held that a defendant could not be found guilty of violating an ordinance prohibiting entry upon private property because the defendant was merely a passenger in the trespassing car and the state's evidence failed to show an overt voluntary act of omission by the defendant. In the case of *State v. Kremer*, 262 Minn. 190, 114 N.W.2d 88 (1962), the Minnesota Supreme Court held that a defendant could not be guilty of violating a city ordinance requiring all traffic to stop at a flashing red light when the evidence showed that defendant's brakes failed with no prior warning to the defendant. Again, the court found no overt voluntary act on the part of the defendant.

Among other cases cited by the defendant are *State v. Binders*, 24 Conn. Supp. 214, 1 Conn. Cir. 506, 189 A.2d 408 (1962), and *State v. Weller*, 4 Conn. Cir. 267, 230 A.2d 242 (1967). In *Binders*, the court on appeal reversed the trial court's conviction of the defendant for failing to drive to the right of a curve. The court stated that the evidence failed to show that the defendant intended to drive on the left side and that all inferences would lead one to believe that the defendant skidded on the ice. The court explained that even if the crime is *malum prohibitum*, in which no specific criminal intent need be proven for conviction, "the only intent requisite to a conviction is the intent or purpose to do the prohibited act." In *Weller*, the Connecticut court stated that the defendant had a valid defense to the speeding charge because the spring which closes the throttle plate broke due to no fault of the defendant. The court reasoned that because "(t)here is not one scintilla of evidence of any intent on the part of the defendant to do the prohibited act ...," the defendant's conviction should be overturned.

In *Kettering v. Greene*, 9 Ohio St. 2d 26, 222 N.E.2d 638 (1966), the Ohio Supreme Court reversed the court of appeals in a per curiam opinion by reinstating the defendant's conviction on a violation of the city ordinance for failing to stop at a stop sign. The court of appeals had previously ruled that the defendant had established a legal excuse for failing to stop because he had no prior warning of any defect in the brakes and because he was, as a city bus driver, not the party responsible for the maintenance of the brakes. The supreme court simply stated that the statutory requirement to stop at a stop sign is mandatory and that brake failure is not a legal excuse.

In support of its position, the state offers the case of *State v. Packin*, 107 N.J. Super. 93, 257 A.2d 120 (1969), wherein the court affirmed the defendant's conviction of speeding and stated that the conviction was not contingent upon a showing that he intended to go sixty-nine miles per hour in a fifty miles per hour zone. This is a case very similar to the case at bar. *Packin* argued that because he had set his cruise control at fifty miles per hour earlier in the day, he could not have had the intent to do the prohibited act. The court stated:

> "... Here defendant was required to drive in conformity with the statutory speed limit and if he was unable to achieve that objective through use of the cruise control, he had but to touch the brake to disengage it and slow the car down." (107 N.J. Super. at 96, 257 A.2d at 121.)

The New Jersey court was therefore unwilling to allow the defendant to assert the defense that he did not have the requisite intent to do the prohibited act because he had set his cruise control at fifty miles per hour, but the cruise control malfunctioned. In that case it was stated:

> "... A motorist who entrusts his car to the control of an automatic device is 'driving' the vehicle and is no less responsible for its operation if the device

fails to perform a function which under the law he is required to perform."
(107 N.J. Super. at 95, 257 A.2d at 121.)

In our view, unexpected brake failure and unexpected malfunction of the throttle on an automobile, both being essential components to the operation of the vehicle, differ significantly from the malfunction of a cruise control device to which the driver has voluntarily delegated partial control of that automobile. We believe it must be said that defendant assumed the full operation of his motor vehicle and when he did so and activated the cruise control attached to that automobile, he clearly was the agent in causing the act of speeding. The safety and welfare of the public require that the motorist operate his vehicle in accordance with the maximum speed limits as set forth in K.S.A. 8-1336, and other rules of the road, and such obligations may not be avoided by delegating a task which he normally would perform to a mechanical device such as a cruise control.

Defendant contends that because of the malfunction of his cruise control he was not then the "driver" of the vehicle in the technical sense because he was not then in "actual physical control" of his vehicle as provided by K.S.A. 8-1416. On the basis of what has previously been said, we consider this argument to be entirely without merit.

Although the proffered evidence might well have been received by the trial court in explanation and mitigation of the offense charged, it was not a defense to that charge and would not have changed the ultimate result of the case. Moreover, in noting the sentence imposed upon the finding of guilt, we must conclude that if any error was committed in sustaining the motion in limine, it was harmless error.

Judgment affirmed.

Questions and Notes

1. How does one distinguish a no *actus reus* case from a no *mens rea* case? Practically every case in which *actus reus* is absent is also devoid of *mens rea*. The converse, however, is not true.

2. Are the Connecticut cases cited in *Baker, Binders*, and *Weller*, analyzed as no *mens rea* cases or no *actus reus* cases? Assuming that they were analyzed as no *mens rea* cases, would the court have reached the same result if those were strict liability crimes in Connecticut?

3. The Minnesota *Kremer* case and the Ohio *Greene* case appear to reach opposite results on the same set of facts. Which court do you think got it right, and why?

4. Are *Baker* and the New Jersey *Packin* case really analogous? If you represented Baker and the judge asked you to distinguish *Packin*, how would you do it?

5. Are you impressed with the distinction between a defective cruise control (defendant's responsibility) and a defective throttle plate (not defendant's responsibility)? What is the difference?

6. Does Baker lose this case because he hadn't alleged enough? Suppose he alleged that the cruise control had never previously stuck? Suppose he had been unable to stop for the policeman and had to eventually crash his car to stop?

7. In *Hinkle*, the court explores some of the conditions that can give rise to a no *actus reus* or automatism defense.

State v. Hinkle
489 S.E.2d 257 (W. Va. 1996)

CLECKLEY, Justice:

I. Factual and Procedural History

On June 12, 1993, the defendant finished his work shift at the Ormet Corporation, an aluminum plant in Hannibal, Ohio, at approximately 4:00 p.m. He obtained a ride to the Village Inn tavern in Paden City, West Virginia. At the tavern, the defendant made several telephone calls attempting to locate someone to give him a ride to his car.[3] The defendant also ordered a can of beer and drank approximately one-third of the beer. While at the tavern, the defendant complained of not feeling well, dizziness, and double vision. The tavern owner's daughter then agreed to take the defendant to retrieve his car. As he was leaving the bar, the defendant took an unopened can of beer with him.

At approximately 7:30 p.m., the defendant was traveling north on Route 2 in St. Mary's, West Virginia. Robert Barrett was driving south on Route 2 with his wife, Charlotte Ann Barrett. It appears the defendant's car gradually crossed the centerline and traveled in a straight line for approximately two hundred yards in the southbound lane before it collided head-on with the Barrett automobile.[5] As a result of the accident, the defendant and Mr. Barrett suffered severe injuries. Mrs. Barrett also sustained serious injuries, and died as a result of those injuries. Eyewitnesses reported the defendant crossed the centerline in a consistent, even fashion without attempting to swerve, brake, change directions, or stop.[6] Witnesses also indicated that both the defendant and Mr. Barrett were traveling at the posted speed limit. A bystander stated the defendant was semi-conscious immediately after the accident, and his breath smelled of alcohol.

An investigation of the defendant's vehicle immediately after the accident revealed one open can of beer, which was one-half full, in the driver's door compartment; several empty beer cans on the passenger's floor; four full beer cans on

---

3. The defendant and his wife recently were separated and were arguing about which of them would retain possession of their automobile. It appears from the record that the defendant parked the car in the locks and dam parking lot in Ohio, across the river from New Martinsville, West Virginia, so his wife would not be able to locate the automobile and take possession of it.

5. Witness accounts indicate Mr. Barrett attempted to avoid the collision by swerving off the road and braking.

6. There was no evidence of skid marks at the accident scene.

the rear floor; three empty beer cans on the driver's floor; and an empty glass, which smelled of beer, on the ground near the car. The defendant was transported to Camden Clark Memorial Hospital where testing revealed he had a blood alcohol level of less than one hundredth of one percent. Officer Charles Templeton of the Pleasants County Sheriff's Department, who investigated the accident, also requested that a blood sample from the defendant be tested by the crime lab. The crime lab found the defendant's blood alcohol level to be less than one thousandth of one percent, well below the statutory definition of intoxication.[7] While treating the defendant's injuries, he was given a Magnetic Resonance Imaging [MRI] scan to determine whether he had sustained any head injuries. The MRI results indicated the defendant had an undiagnosed brain disorder in the portion of his brain that regulates consciousness.

On September 13, 1993, a Pleasants County grand jury returned an indictment charging the defendant with the misdemeanor offense of involuntary manslaughter while driving a motor vehicle in an unlawful manner in violation of W. Va. Code, 61-2-5 (1923). The defendant stood trial, by jury, for this charge in Pleasants County on March 1, 1995. During the trial, the defendant's son testified that the defendant had been having memory loss for several months prior to the accident, and that he believed the defendant had seen a doctor in New Martinsville, West Virginia. Similarly, the tavern owner stated the defendant had complained of feeling ill during the months preceding the collision,[8] and he had complained of dizziness, memory loss, and double vision on the night of the accident. She, too, believed the defendant recently had been treated by a physician.

Defense witness, Ronald Washburn, M.D., reported the defendant's MRI scan showed an undiagnosed brain disorder affecting the reticular activating system of his brain. Dr. Washburn reasoned that because this portion of the brain affects one's consciousness, this disorder could have caused the defendant to suddenly lose

---

7. 7 W. Va. Code, 17C-5-8 (1983), provides, in pertinent part:
   "[U]pon the trial of any civil or criminal action arising out of acts alleged to have been committed by any person driving a motor vehicle while under the influence of alcohol, controlled substances or drugs, evidence of the amount of alcohol in the person's blood at the time of the arrest or of the acts alleged, as shown by a chemical analysis of his blood, breath or urine, is admissible . . . and shall give rise to the following presumptions or have the following effect:
   "(a) Evidence that there was, at that time, five hundredths of one percent or less, by weight, of alcohol in his blood, shall be prima facie evidence that the person was not under the influence of alcohol
   "(b) Evidence that there was, at that time, more than five hundredths of one percent and less than ten hundredths of one percent, by weight, of alcohol in the person's blood shall be relevant evidence, but it is not to be given prima facie effect in indicating whether the person was under the influence of alcohol;
   "(c) Evidence that there was, at that time, ten hundredths of one percent or more, by weight, of alcohol in his blood, shall be admitted as prima facie evidence that the person was under the influence of alcohol[.]" (Emphasis added).
8. The tavern owner indicated the defendant was a regular patron of her establishment.

consciousness immediately before the collision.[10] He also indicated the defendant had developed this brain abnormality approximately four to eight months prior to the accident,[11] and the disease was not caused by chronic alcohol abuse. Testifying further, Dr. Washburn surmised the defendant's prior memory loss was a symptom of his brain disorder, but his other complaints of not feeling well, dizziness, and blurred or double vision were not related to this disease.[12] Concluding his opinion, Dr. Washburn determined the defendant's brain disorder would not have been diagnosed if he had not had an MRI scan after the accident. Finally, both the defendant and Mr. Barrett testified they could not recall any details of the automobile accident.[13]

The trial court denied the defendant's motion to dismiss the indictment; his motion to suppress all evidence obtained immediately after the accident showing the presence of alcoholic beverage containers in or around the defendant's car, and statements indicating the defendant and his car smelled of alcohol; and his motions for a directed verdict of acquittal. Determining that the defendant's blood alcohol level did not establish that he was under the influence of alcohol, the trial court instructed the jury to find the defendant was not intoxicated at the time of the accident. Likewise, the trial court directed the jury to find that the defendant suffered from a brain disorder affecting the consciousness-regulating portion of his brain. The court further instructed the jury:

> "[O]ne who suffers from an as yet undiagnosed disease or defect cannot be convicted of involuntary manslaughter for a death resulting from his operation of an automobile unless the State proves beyond a reasonable doubt that:
>
>> "1. The driver knew or should reasonably have known of the existence of his physical or mental condition, disease or defect; and,
>>
>> "2. The driver should reasonably have foreseen that his condition, disease or defect would impair his ability to drive an automobile to such a degree so as to endanger human life; and,
>>
>> "3. The driver's condition, disease or defect did contribute to the accident resulting in death; and,

---

10. It does not appear the defendant ever had lost consciousness prior to the accident of June 12, 1993.

11. Dr. Washburn based his opinion, in part, on the defendant's medical records from March, 1993.

12. Dr. Washburn attributed the remaining symptoms not associated with the defendant's brain disorder to his chronic sinusitis.

13. During oral arguments before this Court, counsel for the defendant represented that the defendant sustained closed head injuries as a result of the automobile accident. Due to these injuries and his brain disorder, the defendant has not returned to work or driven an automobile since the collision on June 12, 1993.

"4. His decision to drive an automobile at the date and time and in the place set forth in the indictment was negligence so gross, wanton and culpable as to show a reckless disregard of human life; and,

"5. Indicated a conscious indifference to the probable dangerous consequences of driving so impaired.

"If the evidence fails to prove any of these matters beyond a reasonable doubt, then you shall find the defendant, Charles Rhea Hinkle, not guilty of involuntary manslaughter as charged in the indictment.

"If the evidence proves each of these matters beyond a reasonable doubt then you may find the defendant, Charles Rhea Hinkle, guilty of involuntary manslaughter as charged in the indictment."

Following deliberations, the jury, on March 7, 1995, returned a verdict of guilty of involuntary manslaughter. By order dated May 17, 1995, the circuit court denied the defendant's motions for a judgment of acquittal and a new trial and sentenced him to one year in the Pleasants County Jail.

II. Discussion

Despite the additional issues raised, disposition of this appeal begins and ends with an inquiry into whether the jury instructions were inadequate. Thus, the appeal in this case has been limited to one issue: Whether the jury was instructed properly as to the defense of unconsciousness. [T]he State urges the instructions offered were more than adequate to cover the defense of unconsciousness.

[Section A is omitted.]

B. Analysis

The law on the notion of unconsciousness in West Virginia is terribly undeveloped. Indeed, there is only a paucity of American appellate courts that have discussed this defense. With regard to those jurisdictions, Section 44 of Wayne R. LaFave & Austin W. Scott, Jr., CRIMINAL LAW (1972), one of the few treatises that gives this defense any extensive coverage, states: "A defense related to but different from the defense of insanity is that of unconsciousness, often referred to as automatism: one who engages in what would otherwise be criminal conduct is not guilty of a crime if he does so in a state of unconsciousness or semi-consciousness."

Interpreting this defense, the weight of authority in this country suggests that unconsciousness, or automatism as it is sometimes called, is not part of the insanity defense for several reasons. First, unconsciousness does not necessarily arise from a mental disease or defect. Although always containing a mental component in the form of loss of cognitive functioning, the causes and conditions are diverse; examples include epilepsy, concussion, gunshot wounds, somnambulism, coronary episodes, and certain brain disorders, as here. Additionally, these unconscious disorders tend to be acute, unlike most cases of insanity which are typically chronic. Because cases of unconsciousness are temporary, they do not normally call for institutionalization, which is the customary disposition following a successful insanity defense.

Unconsciousness is a separate and distinct defense from insanity. In order to keep this distinction conceptually clear, it is better to view unconsciousness as eliminating the voluntary act requirement rather than negating the mental component of crimes. Thinking of unconsciousness in this conceptual fashion helps to avoid the temptation to collapse it into insanity which, of course, also deals with mental conditions. The defense of unconsciousness should be recognized in a criminal trial and equated with epilepsy rather than insanity. We believe this is the way the claim of unconsciousness should be viewed jurisprudentially in West Virginia.

Accordingly, we hold that unconsciousness (or automatism) is not part of the insanity defense, but is a separate claim which may eliminate the voluntariness of the criminal act.[23] Moreover, the burden of proof on this issue, once raised by the defense, remains on the State to prove that the act was voluntary beyond a reasonable doubt. An instruction on the defense of unconsciousness is required when there is reasonable evidence that the defendant was unconscious at the time of the commission of the crime.[24] In the instant case, it is contended the defendant was, in fact, rendered unconscious at the time of the commission of the crime by reason of an undiagnosed brain disorder affecting the reticular activating system of his brain.

Even if the trier of fact believes the defendant was unconscious at the time of the act, there is another consideration which occasionally arises. If the defendant was sufficiently apprised and aware of the condition and experienced recurring episodes of loss of consciousness, e.g., epilepsy, then operating a vehicle or other potentially destructive implement, with knowledge of the potential danger, might well amount to reckless disregard for the safety of others. Therefore, the jury should be charged that even if it believes there is a reasonable doubt about the defendant's consciousness at the time of the event, the voluntary operation of a motor vehicle with knowledge of the potential for loss of consciousness can constitute reckless behavior.

The next questions are whether the evidence in the present case was sufficient to justify an unconsciousness instruction, and, if so, whether the instruction given by the court was adequate. Finally, we must determine whether the issue regarding the sufficiency of the jury charge was properly preserved below. Jurisdictions appear divided as to whether the defense can be put in issue by only the defendant's testimony. In Starr v. State, 134 Ga. App. 149, 150, 213 S.E.2d 531, 532 (1975), the court

---

23. It has been a long-recognized tenet of criminal jurisprudence that the State punishes only voluntary acts. There also must be some level of intent for a person to be guilty of committing a crime. Thus, under usual circumstances, a person cannot be held responsible for an act he or she commits while unconscious.

24. The defense of unconsciousness must be distinguished from "blackouts" caused by the voluntary ingestion of alcohol or nonprescription drugs. If the evidence indicates that the unconsciousness is due to alcohol or drugs, as we discussed above, the case must be handled as an intoxication defense.

found that additional corroboration was required and, without corroboration, such an instruction was not required. On the other hand, in *People v. Wilson*, 66 Cal. 2d 749, 762, 59 Cal. Rptr. 156, 165, 427 P.2d 820, 829 (1967), the court said because a defendant is entitled to an instruction as to his defense, no matter how incredible his theory is, there need be no corroboration for the instruction to be given. In this case, we need not decide this issue since the defendant's testimony was sufficiently corroborated by expert testimony and other eyewitness testimony.[26] We find the evidence was sufficient to require an unconsciousness instruction. Moreover, in this case the issue appears moot because the trial court not only gave an instruction on the subject but, by such instruction, may very well have decided the issue of unconsciousness as a matter of law.

Four considerations lead us to reverse the defendant's conviction.

[First consideration omitted.]

Second, although the trial court instructed the jury that the defendant was suffering from a brain disorder, no further instruction was given (on insanity or otherwise) which required the jury carefully to focus on how the nature of the defendant's brain disorder related to the elements of the crime. The jury should have been told that, in light of the evidence of the defendant's brain disorder and apparent blackout, he could not be convicted unless the State proved beyond a reasonable doubt that his act was *voluntary and that he acted in reckless disregard of the safety of others.*

The instructions were not wholly wanting in this regard, for the trial court did tell the jury that it could nevertheless convict the defendant, in spite of his brain disorder, if it concluded that he "knew *or should reasonably have known* of the existence of his . . . condition" and he "*should reasonably have foreseen* that his condition, disease or defect would impair his ability to drive an automobile to such a degree as to endanger human life." (Emphasis added.) This portion of the instruction, however, suffers from the infirmity that it is phrased in the language of civil negligence rather than gross negligence or recklessness. Later, in the same instruction, the trial court did refer to "negligence so gross, wanton and culpable as to show a reckless disregard for human life" which "indicated a conscious indifference to the probable consequences." Nevertheless, viewing the instruction as a whole, as we must, the jury may well have been misguided with respect to the appropriate standard by which to measure the defendant's liability. An instruction more faithful to the relevant standard of voluntariness (or recklessness) would require a finding that the defendant *knew* of his condition and *knew* it could impair his ability to drive.

---

26. Even though we decline to address the issue of corroboration head-on, in order to avoid a flood of false and manufactured unconsciousness defenses, an impressive number of jurisdictions seems to favor the corroboration requirement. In these jurisdictions, some substantial corroboration is necessary to trigger the unconsciousness defense. For example, evidence that a defendant does not remember, without other eyewitnesses or expert testimony, is insufficient to carry the issue to the jury. To require otherwise, it is suggested, would place an almost impossible burden on the prosecution to prove the absence of unconsciousness.

Third, irrespective of the foregoing, we would be inclined to reverse the defendant's conviction based on the absence of evidence justifying the "should have known" language in the charge. There is virtually no evidence in the record to indicate that the defendant knew (or reasonably should have known) of the serious nature of his brain disorder or that he knew (or reasonably should have known) that it would impair his ability to drive an automobile so as to endanger human life.[29] We would be inclined to reverse for lack of sufficient evidence, which would bar retrial on double jeopardy grounds, as opposed to the weight of the evidence, which does not bar retrial, except for the fact that the State was not given an adequate opportunity to meet the defendant's unconsciousness claim as we have outlined it above.

Finally, our conclusion about the weight of the evidence is buttressed by the fact that evidence of the presence of alcohol was admitted by the trial court even though contemporaneous blood tests indicated the defendant was clearly not intoxicated, and the trial court so instructed the jury.[30] Under these circumstances, the marginal relevance of alcohol use may have been outweighed substantially by its potential to prejudice the jury and may have obscured the jury's deliberations. On remand, the trial court should consider more carefully the balancing factors under the West Virginia Rules of Evidence and set forth its balancing of the counterfactors on the record.

III. Conclusion

Based on the foregoing, the judgment of the Circuit Court of Pleasants County is reversed, and this case is remanded for a new trial.

Reversed and Remanded.

Questions and Notes

1. Should the following acts qualify as automatistic: (a) acts committed while sleepwalking? (b) acts committed while under a hypnotic trance? (c) reflexive action committed after a gunshot wound? *See generally,* Corrado, *Automatisam and the Theory of Action*, 39 EMORY L.J. 1191 (1990).

2. What was wrong with the instructions given to the jury?

3. Were there any reasons, apart from the jury instructions, for reversing Hinkle's conviction?

4. What should be done with Hinkle, or those like him, who injure people through no voluntary action of their own? Should they be subject to civil commitment? Most courts say no.

---

29. The defendant had suffered from other symptoms such as dizziness and blurred vision, but he had not previously experienced a blackout.

30. The trial court instructed the jury that the defendant "was not under the influence of alcohol at the time of the accident." This Court initially refused to hear this assignment of error on appeal. Our present review of the record indicates this assignment may have substantial merit.

Problem

Supposed Sleepwalker Convicted of Murdering Wife
The Associated Press

PHOENIX-A man who claimed he was sleepwalking when he stabbed his wife 44 times and held her head under water in their swimming pool was convicted of murder Friday and could get the death penalty.

The jury reached its verdict against Scott Falater, 43, after a trial in which dueling experts for the defense and the prosecution disagreed over whether he could have killed in his sleep.

Prosecutors said they will seek the death penalty. The judge will determine the punishment after a series of hearings later this summer. "It's not over yet," Falater said as he left court.

What Falater did the night of Jan. 16, 1997, was never in question: He admitted to stabbing his wife, Yarmila, dragging her to their backyard pool and holding her under water. He did not dispute removing his bloodstained clothes and hiding them and his knife in his Volvo.

But Falater testified he has no memory of any of it.

Two sleep experts cited Falater's family history of sleepwalking, job stress and lack of sleep as reasons for his violent sleepwalking episode.

Prosecutors had an expert witness testify that Falater's actions were too deliberate for him to have been sleepwalking.

The defense painted the former Motorola engineer and his wife of 20 years as happily married, religious couple. Defense attorney Mike Kemerer said Falater had no reason to kill his wife.

But prosecutor Juan Martinez noted that the couple had disputes over Falater's desire to have more children and his wife's waning dedication to the Mormon faith. She was not wearing her wedding ring when her body was found.

Does the defense sound plausible? Why do you suppose that the jury rejected it? Is it possible to engage in criminal activity, and have no memory of it? Do you suppose that is what happened in this case?

Hinkle suggested that a defendant who, while conscious, recklessly creates a dangerous situation may be liable even though he was unconscious at the time the harm occurred. That issue is more fully explored in *Decina*.

People v. Decina
138 N.E.2d 799 (N.Y. 1956)

FROESSEL, Judge.

At about 3:30 p. m. on March 14, 1955, a bright, sunny day, defendant was driving, alone in his car, in a northerly direction on Delaware Avenue in the city of Buffalo. The portion of Delaware Avenue here involved is 60 feet wide. At a point south of an overhead viaduct of the Erie Railroad, defendant's car swerved to the left, across the center line in the street, so that it was completely in the south lane, traveling 35 to 40 miles per hour.

In then veered sharply to the right, crossing Delaware Avenue and mounting the easterly curb at a point beneath the viaduct and continued thereafter at a speed estimated to have been about 50 or 60 miles per hour or more. During this latter swerve, a pedestrian testified that he saw defendant's hand above his head; another witness said he saw defendant's left arm bent over the wheel, and his right hand extended towards the right door.

A group of six schoolgirls were walking north on the easterly sidewalk of Delaware Avenue, two in front and four slightly in the rear, when defendant's car struck them from behind. One of the girls escaped injury by jumping against the wall of the viaduct. The bodies of the children struck were propelled northward onto the street and the lawn in front of a coal company, located to the north of the Erie viaduct on Delaware Avenue. Three of the children, 6 to 12 years old, were found dead on arrival by the medical examiner, and a fourth child, 7 years old, died in a hospital two days later as a result of injuries sustained in the accident.

After striking the children, defendant's car continued on the easterly sidewalk, and then swerved back onto Delaware Avenue once more. It continued in a northerly direction, passing under a second viaduct before it again veered to the right and remounted the easterly curb, striking and breaking a metal lamppost. With its horn blowing steadily apparently because defendant was "stopped over" the steering wheel the car proceeded on the sidewalk until if finally crashed through a 7¼-inch brick wall of a grocery store, injuring at least one customer and causing considerable property damage.

When the car came to a halt in the store, with its horn still blowing, several fires had been ignited. Defendant was stooped over in the car and was "bobbing a little." To one witness he appeared dazed, to another unconscious, lying back with his hands off the wheel.

Various people present shouted to defendant to turn off the ignition of his car, and "within a matter of seconds the horn stopped blowing and the car did shut off."

Defendant was pulled out of the car by a number of bystanders and laid down on the sidewalk. To a policeman who came on the scene shortly he appeared "injured, dazed;" another witness said that "he looked as though he was knocked out, and his arm seemed to be bleeding." An injured customer in the store, after receiving first aid, pressed defendant for an explanation of the accident and he told her: "I blacked out from the bridge."

We turn first to the subject of defendant's [claim] that the indictment here does not charge a crime. The indictment states essentially that defendant, knowing "that he was subject to epileptic attacks or other disorder rendering him likely to lose consciousness for a considerable period of time," was culpably negligent "in that he *consciously* undertook to and *did operate* his Buick sedan on a public highway" (emphasis supplied) and "while so doing" suffered such an attack which caused said automobile "to travel at a fast and reckless rate of speed, jumping the curb and driving over the sidewalk" causing the death of 4 persons. In our opinion, this clearly states a violation of section 1053-a of the Penal Law. The statute does not require that a defendant must deliberately intend to kill a human being, for that would be murder. Nor does the statute require that he knowingly and consciously follow the precise path that leads to death and destruction. It is sufficient, we have said, when his conduct manifests a "disregard of the consequences which may ensue from the act, and indifference to the rights of others. . . ."

Assuming the truth of the indictment, as we must on a demurrer, this defendant knew he was subject to epileptic attacks and seizures that might strike at any time. He also knew that a moving motor vehicle uncontrolled on public highway is a highly dangerous instrumentality capable of unrestrained destruction. With this knowledge, and without anyone accompanying him, he deliberately took a chance by making a conscious choice of a course of action, in disregard of the consequences which he knew might follow from his conscious act, and which in this case did ensue. How can we say as a matter of law that this did not amount to culpable negligence within the meaning of section 1053-a?

To hold otherwise would be to say that a man may freely indulge himself in liquor in the same hope that it will not affect his driving, and if it later develops that ensuing intoxication causes dangerous and reckless driving resulting in death, his unconsciousness or involuntariness at that time would relieve him from prosecution under the statute. His awareness of a condition which he knows may produce such consequences as here, and his disregard of the consequences, renders him liable for culpable negligence, as the courts below have properly held. To have a sudden sleeping spell, an unexpected heart attack or other disabling attack, without any prior knowledge or warning thereof, is an altogether different situation, and there is simply no basis for comparing such cases with the flagrant disregard manifested here.

It is suggested in the dissenting opinion that a new approach to licensing would prevent such disastrous consequences upon our public highways. But would it and how and when? The mere possession of a driver's license is no defense to a prosecution under section 1053-a; nor does it assure continued ability to drive during the period of the license. It may be noted in passing, and not without some significance, that defendant strenuously and successfully objected to the district attorney's offer of his applications for such license in evidence, upon the ground that whether or not he was licensed has nothing to do with the case. Under the view taken by the dissenters, this defendant would be immune from prosecution under this statute even if he were unlicensed. Section 1053-a places a personal responsibility on each driver of a vehicle whether licensed or not and not upon a licensing agency.

Accordingly, the order of the Appellate Division should be affirmed.

DESMOND, Judge (concurring in part and dissenting in part).

I think the indictment should be dismissed because it alleges no crime.

The indictment charges that defendant knowing that "he was subject to epileptic attacks or other disorder rendering him likely to lose consciousness" suffered "an attack and loss of consciousness which caused the said automobile operated by the said defendant to travel at a fast and reckless rate of speed" and to jump a curb and run onto the sidewalk "thereby striking and causing the death" of 4 children. Horrible as this occurrence was and whatever necessity it may show for new licensing and driving laws, nevertheless this indictment charges no crime known to the New York statutes. Our duty is to dismiss it.

Section 1053-a of the Penal Law describes the crime of "criminal negligence in the operation of a vehicle resulting in death." Declared to be guilty of that crime is "A person who operates or drives any vehicle of any kind in a reckless or culpably negligent manner, whereby a human being is killed." The essentials of the crime are, therefore, first, vehicle operation in a culpably negligent manner, and, second, the resulting death of a person. This indictment asserts that defendant violated section 1053-a, but it then proceeds in the language quoted in the next-above paragraph of this opinion to describe the way in which defendant is supposed to have offended against that statute. That descriptive matter (an inseparable and controlling ingredient of the indictment) shows that defendant did not violate section 1053-a. No operation of an automobile in a reckless manner is charged against defendant. The excessive speed of the car and its jumping the curb were "caused," says the indictment itself, by defendant's prior "attack and loss of consciousness." Therefore, what defendant is accused of is not reckless or culpably negligent driving, which necessarily connotes and involves consciousness and volition. The fatal assault by this car was after and because of defendant's failure of consciousness. To say that one drove a car in a reckless manner in that his unconscious condition caused the car to travel recklessly is to make two mutually contradictory assertions. One cannot be "reckless" while unconscious. One cannot while unconscious "operate" a car in a culpably negligent manner or in any other "manner." The statute makes criminal a particular kind of knowing, voluntary, immediate operation. It does not touch at all the involuntary presence of an unconscious person at the wheel of an uncontrolled vehicle. To negative the possibility of applying section 1053-a to these alleged facts we do not even have to resort to the rule that all criminal statutes are closely and strictly construed in favor of the citizen and that no act or omission is criminal unless specifically and in terms so labeled by a clearly worded statute.

Now let us test by its consequences this new construction of section 1053-a. Numerous are the diseases and other conditions of a human being which make it possible or even likely that the afflicted person will lose control of his automobile. Epilepsy, coronary involvements, circulatory diseases, nephritis, uremic poisoning, diabetes, Meniere's syndrome, a tendency to fits of sneezing, locking of the knee, muscular contractions any of these common conditions may cause loss of control of a vehicle for a period long enough to cause a fatal accident. An automobile traveling at only 30 miles an hour goes 44 feet in a second. Just what is the court holding here? No less than this: that a driver whose brief blackout lets his car run amuck and kill another has killed that other by reckless driving. But any such "recklessness" consists necessarily not of the erratic behavior of the automobile while its driver is unconscious, but of his driving at all when he knew he was subject to such attacks. Thus, it must be that such a blackout-prone driver is guilty of reckless driving, Vehicle and Traffic Law, Consol. Laws, c. 71, § 58, whenever and as soon as he steps into the driver's seat of a vehicle. Every time he drives, accident or no accident, he is subject to criminal prosecution for reckless driving or to revocation of his operator's license, Vehicle and Traffic Law, § 71, subd. 3. And how many of this State's 5,000,000 licensed operators are subject to such penalties for merely driving the cars they are licensed to drive? No one knows how many citizens or how many or what kind of physical conditions will be gathered in under this practically limitless coverage of section 1053-a of the Penal Law and section 58 and subdivision 3 of section 71 of the Vehicle and Traffic Law. It is no answer that prosecutors and juries will be reasonable or compassionate. A criminal statute whose reach is so unpredictable violates constitutional rights, as we shall now show.

The manner in which a car is driven may be investigated by a jury, grand or trial, to see whether the manner was such as to show a reckless disregard of consequences. But giving section 1053-a, the new meaning assigned to it permits punishment of one who did not drive in any forbidden manner but should not have driven at all, according to the present theory. No motorist suffering from any serious malady or infirmity can with impunity drive any automobile at any time or place, since no one can know what physical conditions make it "reckless" or "culpably negligent" to drive an automobile. Such a construction of a criminal statute offends against due process and against justice and fairness. The courts are bound to reject such conclusions when, as here, it is clearly possible to ascribe a different but reasonable meaning.

A whole new approach may be necessary to the problem of issuing or refusing drivers' licenses to epileptics and persons similarly afflicted. But the absence of adequate licensing controls cannot in law or in justice be supplied by criminal prosecutions of drivers who have violated neither the language nor the intendment of any criminal law.

Entirely without pertinence here is any consideration of driving while intoxicated or while sleepy, since those are conditions presently known to the driver, not mere future possibilities or probabilities.

The demurrer should be sustained, and the indictment dismissed.

Questions and Notes

1. The majority and dissent seem to agree that if Decina were unaware of his tendency to black out, he would not have been guilty. On what point do they disagree?

2. Under the majority's view, is Decina guilty of reckless driving every time he drives his car to the grocery store alone?

3. If your answer to Question 2 is "no," how can he be guilty in the actual case?

4. Should the state licensing laws and Decina's licensing application have been relevant? If the state forbids epileptics to drive alone and Decina lied on his application, wouldn't the majority clearly be correct? On the other hand, if the state has made a conscious decision to license epileptics, by what right does it now seek to punish Decina?

B. Failure to Act

Although the *actus reus* concept ordinarily implies an affirmative act, there are instances in which one who fails to act under circumstances that call for action can be convicted. The most obvious instance is when a statute calls for a person to act. For example, it is no defense to a charge of willfully failing to file an income tax return that the defendant did not do anything.

More difficult cases occur when the statutes are less explicit. In the cases that follow, think about why the court did or did not impose a duty. Consider also whether there should generally be a duty to aid another when it can be easily done.

Jones v. United States
308 F.2d 307 (D.C. Cir. 1962)

WRIGHT, Circuit Judge.

Appellant, together with one Shirley Green, was tried on a three-count indictment charging them jointly with (1) abusing and maltreating Robert Lee Green (2) abusing and maltreating Anthony Lee Green, and (3) involuntary manslaughter through failure to perform their legal duty of care for Anthony Lee Green, which failure resulted in his death. At the close of evidence, after trial to a jury, the first two counts were dismissed as to both defendants. On the third count, appellant was convicted of involuntary manslaughter. Shirley Green was found not guilty.

Appellant urges several grounds for reversal. We need consider but two. First, appellant argues that there was insufficient evidence as a matter of law to warrant a jury finding of breach of duty in the care she rendered Anthony Lee. Alternatively, appellant argues that the trial court committed plain error in failing to instruct the jury that it must first find that appellant was under a legal obligation to provide food and necessities to Anthony Lee before finding her guilty of manslaughter in failing to provide them. The first argument in without merit. Upon the latter we reverse.

A summary of the evidence, which is in conflict upon almost every significant issue, is necessary for the disposition of both arguments. In late 1957, Shirley Green became pregnant, out of wedlock, with a child, Robert Lee, subsequently born August 17, 1958. Apparently to avoid the embarrassment of the presence of the child in the Green home, it was arranged that appellant, a family friend, would take the child to her home after birth. Appellant did so, and the child remained there continuously until removed by the police on August 5, 1960. Initially appellant made some motions toward the adoption of Robert Lee, but these came to naught, and shortly thereafter it was agreed that Shirley Green was to pay appellant $72 a month for his care. According to appellant, these payments were made for only five months. According to Shirley Green, they were made up to July 1960.

Early in 1959, Shirley Green again became pregnant, this time with the child Anthony Lee, whose death is the basis of appellant's conviction. This child was born October 21, 1959. Soon after birth, Anthony Lee developed a mild jaundice condition, attributed to a blood incompatibility with his mother. The jaundice resulted in his retention in the hospital for three days beyond the usual time, or until October 26, 1959, when, on authorization signed by Shirley Green, Anthony Lee was released by the hospital to appellant's custody. Shirley Green, after a two or three day stay in the hospital, also lived with appellant for three weeks, after which she returned to her parents' home, leaving the children with appellant. She testified she did not see them again, except for one visit in March, until August 5, 1960. Consequently, though there does not seem to have been any specific monetary agreement with Shirley Green covering Anthony Lee's support, appellant had complete custody of both children until they were rescued by the police.

With regard to medical care, the evidence is undisputed. In March 1960, appellant called a Dr. Turner to her home to treat Anthony Lee for a bronchial condition. Appellant also telephoned the doctor at various times to consult with him concerning Anthony Lee's diet and health. In early July 1960, appellant took Anthony Lee to Dr. Turner's office where he was treated for "simple diarrhea." At this time the doctor noted the "wizened" appearance of the child and told appellant to tell the mother of the child that he should be taken to a hospital. This was not done.

On August 2, 1960, two collectors for the local gas company had occasion to go to the basement of appellant's home, and there saw the two children. Robert Lee and Anthony Lee at this time were age two years and ten months respectively. Robert Lee was in a "crib" consisting of a framework of wood, covered with a fine wire screening, including the top which was hinged. The "crib" was lined with newspaper, which was stained, apparently with feces, and crawling with roaches. Anthony Lee was lying in a bassinet and was described as having the appearance of a "small baby monkey." One collector testified to seeing roaches on Anthony Lee.

On August 5, 1960, the collectors returned to appellant's home in the company of several police officers and personnel of the Women's Bureau. At this time, Anthony Lee was upstairs in the dining room in the bassinet, but Robert Lee was still downstairs in his "crib." The officers removed the children to the D. C. General Hospital where Anthony Lee was diagnosed as suffering from severe malnutrition and lesions over large portions of his body, apparently caused by severe diaper rash. Following admission, he was fed repeatedly, apparently with no difficulty, and was described as being very hungry. His death, 34 hours after admission, was attributed without dispute to malnutrition. At birth, Anthony Lee weighed six pounds, fifteen ounces-at death at age ten months, he weighed seven pounds, thirteen ounces. Normal weight at this age would have been approximately 14 pounds.

Appellant argues that nothing in the evidence establishes that she failed to provide food to Anthony Lee. She cites her own testimony and the testimony of a lodger, Mr. Wills, that she did in fact feed the baby regularly. At trial, the defense made repeated attempts to extract from the medical witnesses' opinions that the jaundice, or the condition which caused it, might have prevented the baby from assimilating food. The doctors conceded this was possible but not probable since the autopsy revealed no condition which would support the defense theory. It was also shown by the disinterested medical witnesses that the child had no difficulty in ingesting food immediately after birth, and that Anthony Lee, in the last hours before his death, was able to take several bottles, apparently without difficulty, and seemed very hungry. This evidence, combined with the absence of any physical cause for non-assimilation, taken in the context of the condition in which these children were kept, presents a jury question on the feeding issue.

Moreover, there is substantial evidence from which the jury could have found that appellant failed to obtain proper medical care for the child. Appellant relies upon the evidence showing that on one occasion she summoned a doctor for the child, on another took the child to the doctor's office, and that she telephoned the doctor on several occasions about the baby's formula. However, the last time a doctor saw the child was a month before his death, and appellant admitted that on that occasion the doctor recommended hospitalization. Appellant did not hospitalize the child, nor did she take any other steps to obtain medical care in the last crucial month. Thus, there was sufficient evidence to go to the jury on the issue of medical care, as well as failure to feed.

Appellant also takes exception to the failure of the trial court to charge that the jury must find beyond a reasonable doubt, as an element of the crime, that appellant was under a legal duty to supply food and necessities to Anthony Lee.

The problem of establishing the duty to take action which would preserve the life of another has not often arisen in the case law of this country. The most commonly cited statement of the rule is found in *People v. Beardsley*, 150 Mich. 206, 113 N.W. 1128, 1129:

> The law recognizes that under some circumstances the omission of a duty owed by one individual to another, where such omission results in the death of the one to whom the duty is owing, will make the other chargeable with manslaughter.... This rule of law is always based upon the proposition that the duty neglected must be a legal duty, and not a mere moral obligation. It must be a duty imposed by law or by contract, and the omission to perform the duty must be the immediate and direct cause of death....

There are at least four situations in which the failure to act may constitute breach of a legal duty. One can be held criminally liable: first, where a statute imposes a duty to care for another; second, where one stands in a certain status relationship to another; third, where one has assumed a contractual duty to care for another; and fourth, where one has voluntarily assumed the care of another and so secluded the helpless person as to prevent others from rendering aid.

It is the contention of the Government that either the third or the fourth ground is applicable here. However, it is obvious that in any of the four situations, there are critical issues of fact which must be passed on by the jury-specifically in this case, whether appellant had entered into a contract with the mother for the care of Anthony Lee or, alternatively, whether she assumed the care of the child and secluded him from the care of his mother, his natural protector. On both of these issues, the evidence is in direct conflict, appellant insisting that the mother was actually living with appellant and Anthony Lee, and hence should have been taking care of the child herself, while Shirley Green testified she was living with her parents and was paying appellant to care for both children.

In spite of this conflict, the instructions given in the case failed even to suggest the necessity for finding a legal duty of care. The only reference to duty in the instructions was the reading of the indictment which charged, *inter alia*, that the defendants "failed to perform their legal duty." A finding of legal duty is the critical element of the crime charged and failure to instruct the jury concerning it was plain error.

Questions and Notes

1. Why did the court reverse Jones' conviction?

2. Why didn't the jury finding that Shirley Green was not guilty of manslaughter necessarily include a finding that Jones was contractually liable to care for Anthony Lee?

3. Given the undisputed fact that Jones was living with Anthony Lee, should she be convicted regardless of the resolution of the factual issues?

4. As you read *Davis*, consider how it differs from *Jones*.

Davis v. Commonwealth
335 S.E.2d 375 (Va. 1985)

STEPHENSON, Justice.

In a bench trial, Mary B. Davis was convicted of involuntary manslaughter of her mother, Emily B. Carter, and sentenced to 10 years in the penitentiary. The trial court found that Carter's death resulted from Davis' criminal negligence in failing to provide her mother with heat, food, liquids, and other necessaries.

The principal issues in this appeal are: (1) whether Davis had a legal duty to care for Carter, and if so, (2) whether she breached the duty by conduct constituting criminal negligence. An additional issue involves the admission into evidence of two photographs of the victim taken during the autopsy.

On November 29, 1983, a paramedic with the Lynchburg Fire Department responded to a call at a house located at 1716 Monroe Street in the City of Lynchburg. The house was occupied by Davis and Carter. The paramedic arrived about 5:35 p.m. and found Carter lying on a bed. It was a cold day, and there was no heat in Carter's room. The only source of heat was a tin heater, and it was not being used the only food in the house was two cans oi soup, a can of juice, and an open box of macaroni and cheese. Two trash cans were found behind the house. One contained 11 or 12 empty vegetable cans, and the other was full of empty beer cans. An operable stove, a supply of firewood and a color television were found in Davis' upstairs bedroom.

Carter was admitted to a hospital that evening. According to her treating physician, Carter's vital signs were unstable and she was severely ill. A nurse testified that Carter's "pulse was 35; respiration was 18 ... [,] blood pressure was 148 over nothing ... and her [body] temperature was 80 degrees. ... Carter was at least five to seven percent dehydrated. The doctor diagnosed her principal problems to be low body temperature, severe malnutrition, and bilateral pneumonia. She also had a blood stream infection, a skull laceration, and multiple rib fractures. Carter died in the early hours of December 2.

A forensic pathologist with the Chief Medical Examiner's Office conducted an autopsy on Carter's body. He concluded that the causes of death were "pneumonia and freezing to death due to exposure to cold with a chronic state of starvation." He stated that any one of these conditions alone could have caused her death.

Additionally, the pathologist testified that a body temperature of 80 degrees was extremely low and that, except in rare, isolated cases involving children or young people, "no one survives" such a low body temperature. He estimated that it would take nine hours for a dead body to reach a temperature of 82 degrees in a room temperature of 67 degrees and that a living person would require a longer exposure to the cold to reach that temperature.

The pathologist further testified that when a person's dehydration reaches a five to seven percent range, it suggests that she has received no liquids for at least two days. He described Carter's condition as "bone dry." He also testified that Carter's physical condition at the time of the autopsy indicated that she had eaten "no food whatsoever" for at least 30 days.

For a number of years, Carter had been senile and totally disabled. The attending physician testified that Davis said her mother was "not able to feed herself at all; that she was not able to care for her personal needs and that she had to wear diapers and had to have total care." Moreover, Davis informed a number of people that she was responsible for the total care of Carter.

Carter signed a writing naming Davis her authorized representative to apply for, receive, and use her food stamps. Relying on this document, the Department of Social Services awarded Davis additional food stamp benefits of $75 per month and exempted her from the requirement of registering for outside employment as a requisite to receiving these benefits.

Davis also was the representative payee of Carter's social security benefits in the amount of $310 per month. Davis' household expenses were paid exclusively from Carter's social security. Davis also received $23 per month in food stamps for her mother.

A legal duty is one either "imposed by law, or by contract." When a death results from an omission to perform a legal duty, the person obligated to perform the duty may be guilty of culpable homicide. If the death results from a malicious omission of the performance of a duty, the offense is murder. On the other hand, although no malice is shown, if a person is criminally negligent in omitting to perform a duty, he is guilty of involuntary manslaughter.

Davis acknowledges the accuracy of the foregoing legal principles. She contends, however, that the evidence fails to establish that she had a legal duty to care for her mother, asserting that the evidence proved at most a moral duty. We do not agree.

The evidence makes clear that Davis accepted sole responsibility for the total care of Carter. This became her full-time occupation. In return, Carter allowed Davis to live in her home expense free and shared with Davis her income from social security. Additionally, Carter authorized Davis to act as her food stamp representative, and for this Davis received food stamp benefits in her own right. From this uncontroverted evidence, the trial court reasonably could find the existence of an implied contract. Clearly, Davis was more than a mere volunteer; she had a legal duty, not merely a moral one, to care for her mother.

Finally, we consider whether the evidence is sufficient to support the trial court's finding of criminal negligence. When the sufficiency of the evidence is challenged on appeal, the evidence and all reasonable inferences fairly deducible therefrom shall be viewed in the light most favorable to the Commonwealth, and the court's judgment must be affirmed unless it is plainly wrong or without evidence to support it.

When the proximate cause of a death is simply ordinary negligence, *i.e.*, the failure to exercise reasonable care, the negligent party cannot be convicted of involuntary manslaughter. To constitute criminal negligence essential to a conviction of involuntary manslaughter, an accused's conduct "must be of such reckless, wanton or flagrant nature as to indicate a callous disregard for human life and of the probable consequences of the act."

Davis contends that she cared for her mother as best she could under the circumstances. She points to the testimony of her four sisters and her boyfriend who stated that everything seemed normal and that they observed nothing to suggest that Carter was being neglected. These witnesses stated that the house always was heated properly and that sufficient food was available at all times.

Against this testimony, however, was the scientific evidence that Carter died of starvation and freezing. The evidence indicates that Carter had received no food for at least 30 days. She lay helpless in bed in an unheated room during cold weather. The trial court, as the trier of fact, determines the weight of the evidence and the credibility of the witnesses. Obviously, the court, as it had the right to do, accepted the Commonwealth's evidence and gave little or no weight to the testimony of the defendant and her witnesses. The court reasonably could conclude that Carter could not have starved or frozen to death unless she had been neglected completely for a protracted period of time.

We hold, therefore, that the evidence supports the trial court's finding that Davis' breach of duty was so gross and wanton as to show a callous and reckless disregard of Carter's life and that Davis' criminal negligence proximately caused Carters death. Accordingly, we will affirm the judgment of the trial court.

Affirmed.

Questions and Notes

1. Was Davis held liable because: (1) she was the victim's daughter, (2) she was contractually obligated to care for the victim, or (3) she voluntarily assumed the duty?

2. Is *Davis* consistent with *Jones* in not overturning the conviction? If so, how can you reconcile the decisions?

3. On what theory is Cali held liable in the next case?

Commonwealth v. Cali

141 N.E. 510 (Mass. 1923)

BRALEY, J.

The defendant having been indicted, tried and convicted under G.L. c. 266, § 10, of burning a building in Leominster belonging to Maria Cali, which at the time was insured against loss or damage by fire, with intent to injure the insurer, the case is here on his exceptions to the denial of his motion for a directed verdict, and to rulings at the trial.

The only evidence as to the origin, extent and progress of the fire were the statements of the defendant to the police inspector, and as a witness. The jury who were to determine his credibility and the weight to be given his testimony could find notwithstanding his explanations of its origin as being purely accidental, that when all the circumstances were reviewed he either set it, or after the fire was under way purposely refrained from any attempt to extinguish it in order to obtain the benefit of the proceeds of the policy, which when recovered, would be applied by the mortgagee on his indebtedness. If they so found, a specific intent to injure the insurer had been proved. The motion and the defendant's requests in so far as not given were denied rightly. The instructions to the jury that:

> "If a man does start an accidental fire what is his conduct in regard to it? A question-as if after the fire has started accidentally, and he then has it within his power and ability to extinguish the fire and he realizes and knows that he can, and then he forms and entertains an intent to injure an

insurance company, he can be guilty of this offense. It is not necessary that the intent be formed before the fire is started. . . ."

-also show no error of law. It is true as the defendant contends, that if he merely neglected in the emergency of the moment to act, his negligence was not proof of a purpose to commit the crime charged.

The intention, however, to injure could be formed after as well as before the fire started. On his own admissions the jury were to say whether when considered in connection with all the circumstances, his immediate departure from the premises for his home in Fitchburg, without giving any alarm, warranted the inference of a criminal intent or state of mind, that the building should be consumed.

Questions and Notes

1. If Cali had not started the fire even accidentally, but had simply walked by his building, saw it on fire, and intentionally refrained from reporting the fire so that it would burn and he could collect from the insurance company, would (should) he have been guilty?

2. Should an accident in general give rise to what would otherwise not be a duty? It is generally agreed that one who has not contributed to another's plight has no duty to alleviate it. For example, a six-foot-tall swimmer is not criminally liable for failing to rescue a four-foot-tall child from five feet of water. The rule is the same even if the swimmer personally delights in seeing the child drown. Conversely, if the swimmer negligently pushes the child in the water, he is under a duty to save her. *Cf. Jones v. State*, 43 N.E.2d 1017 (Ind. 1942). What is (should be) the result where a child bounces off the swimmer (while he is sitting on the edge of the pool) and into the five-foot pool, assuming that the swimmer was nonnegligent?

3. Are there any good reasons for not holding the swimmer liable in the classic no-liability situation? What values are served by not criminalizing the swimmer's conduct in callously or obliviously watching a child drown? A few states have attempted to legislate in this area, e.g., Vermont, Minnesota.

See NUTSHELL § 8.05.

Problem

Assume that the state in which your law school is located has the following statutes:

§ 10-10: Any machine that sometimes returns more money than is put into it is a gambling machine.

§ 10-11: It is unlawful to have a gambling machine in one's home.

§ 10-12: It is unlawful to put money into a gambling machine.

§ 10-13: A violation of § 10-11 or § 10-12 shall be punishable by not more than a $200.00 fine, thirty days in jail, or both.

On Monday, January 5, Jimmy Smith, a student at your law school, considered purchasing a slot machine that kept the money put into it until somebody hit the right combination at which point it returned all of the money. It came with a lock and key, however, so that its owner could remove all of the money after each use. Before purchasing the machine, Jimmy checked with his criminal law professor (who is licensed to practice law in your state) to ascertain whether the machine constituted a gambling machine within the meaning of § 10-10. She assured him that, because of the lock and key device, it did not constitute a gambling machine. Upon receiving this advice, Jimmy purchased the machine.

That evening he brought the machine home to his parents' house, where he also lived. He asked his mother, Martha, if he could put his newly purchased machine in the basement. Martha asked him if it was a gambling machine, and Jimmy replied that it was not. Upon hearing this, Martha permitted Jimmy to put it in the basement. Two days later, Jimmy was entertaining his girlfriend, Prudence Virtue, and her father, Police Captain Virtue at the Smith residence. Jimmy invited Prudence to his basement to be the first person to play his new game. Jimmy handed Prudence five nickels to put in the machine. The last nickel proved to be the big winner, returning all five nickels to Prudence.

At that moment, Captain Virtue descended to the basement and demanded to know the nature of the game. Upon hearing the explanation, he arrested Jimmy for violating § 10-11, and, dutiful police officer that he was, arrested his daughter for violating § 10-12. After walking upstairs, Captain Virtue arrested Martha for violating § 10-11. As the four of them walked out of the door, they encountered John Smith, Jimmy's father, who had just returned from a week-long business trip. Captain Virtue arrested him for violating § 10-11.

The trial court convicted all four defendants, and the Court of Appeals affirmed. Their cases are on appeal at the State Supreme Court. Six of the judges are divided three-three on these cases.

The seventh judge, for whom you are employed as a clerk, is uncertain as to how to resolve these cases and would like you to write a memorandum thoroughly exploring all of these issues together with a reasoned judgment of how each of the cases should be resolved.

Chapter 10

Intoxication

Heretofore, we have indirectly looked at the impact of intoxication on the criminal law (*see, e.g., United States v. Short, supra*). Our current focus is on the extent to which intoxication can serve to exculpate a defendant. Intoxication is never a defense in the sense of self-defense. That is, no act is less criminal because the defendant was intoxicated when he perpetrated it. The difficult question is the extent to which one can be criminally liable for possessing a state of mind that she did not possess when the reason she didn't possess it is because of intoxication. The cases in this section are primarily directed to that question.

State v. Coates
735 P.2d 64 (Wash. 1987)

Dore, Justice.

At approximately 11:30 p.m. on September 15, 1984, as Matt Long drove home from his job as a Hanford patrolman, he observed a blue Thunderbird strike another automobile. This second car pulled to the side of the road, but the Thunderbird continued; the officer followed the Thunderbird. Approximately a half mile farther, the Thunderbird's engine died, and it also pulled off to the side of the road. The officer stopped his vehicle behind the car. The defendant exited the driver's side and walked toward the officer's vehicle.

At this juncture, Long identified himself as a police officer and told defendant that he should return to the accident scene. Defendant replied that he was a Navy corpsman and could help if anyone were injured. Defendant returned to his car, spoke briefly with his passenger Dana Soderquist, and then agreed to walk back to the scene of the accident.

As they approached the scene, the officer and defendant observed a police vehicle with emergency lights flashing. Defendant stared at the lights for a few moments, then said that he would not return to the scene. By this time Officer Long had come to question defendant's mental stability, so he agreed that defendant could return to his own car. As they neared the officer's truck, the defendant stabbed Officer Long twice in the back, and then returned to his car.

Shortly thereafter, the state trooper pursuant to his investigation of the accident and DWI charge contacted defendant. The state trooper also requested defendant to take a Breathalyzer test. At first Coates refused, but later agreed. The Breathalyzer

513

test, administered over 4 hours after the accident and assault, showed defendant as having a blood alcohol level of .16 percent.

At trial Long testified to the circumstances of the assault. The subject knife was admitted into evidence. Defendant denied all wrongdoing, testifying that he could not remember the hit-and-run incident or the assault. Defendant stressed that he had consumed a great deal of alcohol that evening.

Upon defense counsel's request, the trial judge instructed the jury on the "intoxication defense" and on the State's burden of proving that defendant's intoxication did not prevent the defendant from forming the particular requisite mental state. Over defense counsel's objection, however, the trial judge instructed the jury that this defense applies only where the mental state is intent, knowledge, or recklessness. The trial judge specifically precluded the jury from considering Coates' intoxication in determining whether he was guilty of the lesser-included offense of third degree (negligent) assault.

The jury found defendant *not guilty* of second-degree assault, but *guilty* of assault in the third degree. Defendant appealed his conviction directly to this court.

The voluntary intoxication statute, RCW 9A.16.090, provides: "No act committed by a person while in a state of voluntary intoxication shall be deemed less criminal by reason of his condition, but whenever the actual existence of any particular mental state is a necessary element to constitute a particular species or degree of crime, the fact of his intoxication may be taken into consideration in determining such mental state."

RCW 9A.16.090 states that voluntary intoxication does not make an act "less criminal," while on the other hand the statute states that intoxication "may be taken into consideration" by the jury in determining whether the defendant acted with the requisite mental state. These provisions indicate how the statute is to be employed. Evidence of voluntary intoxication cannot be employed to make the act "less criminal." This means that such evidence cannot form the basis of an affirmative defense that essentially admits the crime but attempts to excuse or mitigate the actor's criminality. Rather, evidence of voluntary intoxication is relevant to the trier of fact in determining in the first instance whether the defendant acted with a particular degree of mental culpability. The voluntary intoxication statute allows the trier of fact to consider the defendant's intoxication in assessing his mental state; the statute does not require that consideration to lead to any particular result. In this sense the statute describes the manner in which a particular type of evidence is to be employed, in much the same way as neutral instructions describe the use of inferences or circumstantial evidence.

The State always has the burden of proving the defendant acted with the necessary culpable mental state. Generally, evidence of intoxication is relevant to this question, but it is inaccurate to think of intoxication as forming some element that the State must negate, just as it would be erroneous to hold that the State has the burden of proving or disproving circumstantial evidence.

A criminal act committed by a voluntarily intoxicated person is not justified or excused. Intoxication may raise a reasonable doubt as to the mental state element of the offense, thus leading to acquittal or conviction of a lesser included offense, but evidence of intoxication does not add another element to the offense. Thus, the jury was correctly instructed in the language of RCW 9A.16.090 as follows:

> "Intoxication. No act committed by a person while in a state of voluntary intoxication shall be deemed less criminal by reason of his condition, but whenever the actual existence of any particular mental state is a necessary element to constitute a particular species or degree of crime, the fact of his intoxication may be taken into consideration in determining such mental state.

It is unclear how either party can logically be said to have the ultimate burden of proof under RCW 9A.16.090. Also, there does not seem to be any way to convey the burden of proof concept to the jury without implying that intoxication is something the jury must, rather than may, consider. Finally, imposing a burden of proof as to intoxication would seem to ignore the fact that intoxication is not an all-or-nothing proposition. A person can be intoxicated and yet still be able to form the requisite mental state, or he can be so intoxicated as to be unconscious. Under RCW 9A.16.090, it is not the fact of intoxication which is relevant, but the degree of intoxication and the effect it had on the defendant's ability to formulate the requisite mental state. Thus, an instruction which requires one party or the other to prove or disprove the fact of intoxication would be incomplete at best.

In summary, intoxication is not a "defense" to a crime. Evidence of intoxication may bear upon whether the defendant acted with the requisite mental state, but the proper way to deal with the issue is to instruct the jury that it may consider evidence of the defendant's intoxication in deciding whether the defendant acted with the requisite mental state.

Criminal Negligence

Having set forth the proper interpretation of the voluntary intoxication statute, we now turn to how evidence of voluntary intoxication relates particularly to "criminal negligence" as that term is now defined.

When the Legislature adopted the new criminal code, it replaced the concept of general and specific intent with four levels of culpability: intent, knowledge, recklessness, and negligence. At the same time, the Legislature amended the intoxication statute so as to refer to "particular mental state" rather than "purpose, motive, or intent."

Criminal negligence is defined as a person's "[failure] to be aware of a substantial risk that a wrongful act may occur and his failure to be aware of such substantial risk constitutes a gross deviation from the standard of care that a reasonable man would exercise in the same situation." Criminal negligence is the requisite mental state in the crime of assault in the third degree. Because this mental state is based on a reasonable person standard, evidence of defendant's voluntary intoxication cannot work in any way to negate or obviate the mental state. Because of his intoxication, a particular defendant may not act with intent or knowingly inflict grievous bodily harm. Nonetheless, if a reasonable person would have avoided the wrongful act, and the defendant's failure to do so is a gross deviation from this reasonable course of conduct, the defendant has acted with criminal negligence.

In the present case, the "wrongful act" was the stabbing. Defendant's claimed reason for failing to be aware that the victim was being stabbed was evidently defendant's own intoxication. A reasonable person would not have stabbed the victim, and defendant's action was a gross deviation from the reasonable course of conduct. Consequently, defendant was criminally negligent despite his intoxication. This is the proper interpretation to be given the definition of criminal negligence. The trial court did not err in precluding the jury from considering voluntary intoxication as a defense to the charge of third-degree assault.

We affirm the defendant's conviction.

PEARSON, Chief Justice (dissenting).

The majority holds that voluntary intoxication can never be a defense to criminal negligence. The voluntary intoxication statute provides that "whenever the actual existence of *any particular mental state* is a necessary element to constitute a particular species or degree of crime, the fact of [the defendant's] intoxication may be taken into consideration in determining such mental state." (Italics mine.) The defendant contends this defense applies to all four of the particular mental states defined in RCW 9A.08.010; namely, intent, knowledge, recklessness, and criminal negligence. The State argues that public policy considerations require the courts to limit the intoxication defense to the three most culpable mental states, excluding criminal negligence.

As originally enacted, the intoxication statute referred not to "particular mental state," but rather to "particular purpose, motive or intent." This court interpreted this phrase to apply to "specific intent" crimes, but not to "general intent" crimes.

When the Legislature adopted the new criminal code, it replaced the concepts of general and specific intent with four levels of culpability: intent, knowledge, recklessness and criminal negligence. At the same time, the Legislature amended the intoxication statute to refer to "particular mental state" rather than "purpose, motive or intent." [T]hese amendments appear to extend the intoxication defense to all crimes in which one of the four mental states constitutes an element of the crime.

The Court of Appeals understandably was sensitive to the serious public policy considerations raised by the expanded version of the intoxication defense. Under the rule of lenity, however, criminal statutes should be construed strictly against the State and in favor of the accused. If the Legislature desires to limit the scope of RCW 9A.16.090 to crimes involving all mental states other than criminal negligence, it is free to amend the statute to reflect that desire. Until then, a defendant should be entitled to an instruction permitting the jury to determine whether the defendant's intoxication precluded formation of the requisite mental state of criminal negligence.

For the foregoing reasons, I dissent.

Questions and Notes

1. Even if the dissent were correct as a matter of statutory construction, is there any way that intoxication could be relevant as to questions of negligence?

2. Why was the burden of proof issue even relevant if intoxication could not negate negligence?

3. Washington is more generous to drunk defendants than most states. As will be apparent from reading *Cameron* and *Register*, most states do not even allow intoxication to negate recklessness.

State v. Cameron

514 A.2d 1302 (N.J. Sup. Ct. 1986)

CLIFFORD, J.

This appeal presents a narrow, but important, issue concerning the role that a defendant's voluntary intoxication plays in a criminal prosecution. The specific question is whether the evidence was sufficient to require the trial court to charge the jury on defendant's intoxication, as defendant requested. The Appellate Division reversed defendant's convictions, holding that it was error not to have given an intoxication charge.

Defendant, Michele Cameron, age 22 at the time of trial, was indicted for second degree aggravated assault, in violation of N.J.S.A. 2C:12-1(b)(1); possession of a weapon, a broken bottle, with a purpose to use it unlawfully, contrary to N.J.S.A. 2C:39-4(d); and fourth degree resisting arrest, a violation of N.J.S.A. 2C:29-2. A jury convicted defendant of all charges. After merging the possession count into the assault charge, the trial court-imposed sentences aggregating seven years in the custody of the Commissioner of the Department of Corrections, with a three year period of parole ineligibility and certain monetary penalties.

The charges arose out of an incident of June 6, 1981, on a vacant lot in Trenton. The unreported opinion of the Appellate Division depicts the following tableau of significant events:

> The victim, Joseph McKinney, was playing cards with four other men. Defendant approached and disrupted the game with her conduct. The participants moved their card table to a new location within the lot. Defendant followed them, however, and overturned the table. The table was righted and the game resumed. Shortly thereafter, defendant attacked McKinney with a broken bottle. As a result of that attack he sustained an injury to his hand, which necessitated 36 stitches and caused permanent injury.

Defendant reacted with violence to the arrival of the police. She threw a bottle at their vehicle, shouted obscenities, and tried to fight them off. She had to be restrained and handcuffed in the police wagon.

The heart of the Appellate Division's reversal of defendant's conviction is found in its determination that voluntary intoxication is a defense when it negates an essential element of the offense—here, purposeful conduct. We agree with that proposition. Likewise are we in accord with the court below that all three of the charges of which this defendant was convicted—aggravated assault, the possession offense, and resisting arrest—have purposeful conduct as an element of the offense; and that a person acts purposely "with respect to the nature of his conduct or a result thereof if it is his conscious object to engage in conduct of that nature or to cause such a result." We part company with the Appellate Division, however, in its conclusion that the circumstances disclosed by the evidence in this case required that the issue of defendant's intoxication be submitted to the jury.

The court below noted that every witness who testified gave some appraisal of defendant's condition. On the basis of that evidence, the Appellate Division concluded that "defendant's conduct was both bizarre and violent. She had been drinking and could not be reasoned with. The victim thought she was intoxicated, and two police officers thought she was under the influence of something. Not one witness who testified thought that her conduct was normal. Therefore, it was for the jury to determine if she was intoxicated, and if so, whether the element of purposefulness was negated thereby."

The quoted passage reflects a misapprehension of the level of proof required to demonstrate intoxication for purposes of demonstrating an inability to engage in purposeful conduct.

Under the common law intoxication was not a defense to a criminal charge. Rather than being denominated a defense, intoxication was viewed as a "condition of fact," or, in a homicide case, as "a mere circumstance to be considered in determining whether premeditation was present or absent."

Notwithstanding the general proposition that voluntary intoxication is no defense, the early cases nevertheless held that, in some circumstances, intoxication could be resorted to for defensive purposes—specifically, to show the absence of a specific intent.

> The exceptional immunity extended to the drunkard is limited to those instances where the crime involves a specific, actual intent. When the degree of intoxication is such as to render the person incapable of entertaining such intent, it is an effective defence. If it falls short of this it is worthless.

The principle that developed from the foregoing approach—that intoxication formed the basis for a defense to a "specific intent" crime but not to one involving only "general" intent—persisted for about three-quarters of a century, or until this Court's decision in *State v. Maik*, 60 N.J. 203, 287 A.2d 715 (1972). *See, e.g., State v.*

Mack, 86 N.J.L. 233, 235, 90 A. 1120 (E. & A. 1914) ("if defendant was so intoxicated or in such a condition of mind because he was getting over a debauch that his faculties were prostrated and rendered him incapable of forming a specific intent to kill with . . . willful, deliberate and premeditated character, then although it is no defense or justification, his offence would be murder in the second degree").

Eventually the problems inherent in the application of the specific-general intent dichotomy surfaced. In *State v. Maik, supra,* 60 N.J. 203, 287 A.2d 715, this Court dwelt on the elusiveness of the distinction between "specific" and "general" intent crimes, particularly as that distinction determined what role voluntary intoxication played in a criminal prosecution. Chief Justice Weintraub's opinion for the Court restated the original proposition that "a defendant will not be relieved of criminal responsibility because he was under the influence of intoxicants or drugs voluntarily taken," *id* at 214, 287 A.2d 715, and then set forth four exceptions to that rule: (1) the ingestion of drugs for medication, producing unexpected or bizarre results; (2) impairment of mental faculties negating only premeditation or deliberation, to preclude elevation to first degree murder; (3) reduction of felony homicide to second degree murder when the felonious intent is negated; and (4) when insanity results.

Maik, a murder prosecution, was not given a uniform reading. As later pointed out in *State v. Stasio,* 78 N.J. 467, 396 A.2d 1129 (1979), the difference between general and specific intent [is] "not readily ascertainable." [*Stasio* thus] concluded that honoring the distinction would give rise to "incongruous results by irrationally allowing intoxication to excuse some crimes but not others."

Justice Handler's concurrence in *Stasio* took a different approach. Although the concurrence agreed with the majority and with *Maik* that the "attempted differentiation between so-called specific intent and general intent crimes . . . is an unhelpful, misleading and often confusing distinction," *ibid,* and that the "availability of voluntary intoxication as a defense in terms of that distinction . . . has led to anomalous results," it did not accept the proposition that "if the separation between so-called specific and general intent crimes is rejected, voluntary intoxication as a defense must also be rejected." According to the concurrence, "[t]he criminal laws need not be impotent or ineffective when dealing with an intoxicated criminal. The question should always be whether under particular circumstances a defendant ought to be considered responsible for his conduct."

The concurring opinion in *Stasio* took the position that when dealing with the issue of intoxication, the focus at trial should be on the mental state required for the commission of the particular crime charged. In particular, a defendant ought not be considered responsible when the effect of his intoxication reached such a level, operating upon the defendant's mind, . . . as to deprive him of his will to act. . . . I would accordingly require, in order to generate a reasonable doubt as to a defendant's responsibility for his acts, that it be shown he was so intoxicated that he could not think, or that his mind did not function with consciousness or volition.

Justice Pashman's concurrence and dissent likewise would have hinged the success of an intoxication defense on "a showing of such a great prostration of the faculties that the requisite mental state was totally lacking."

We have drawn at such length on the minority opinions in *Stasio* because, as will become apparent, they are much closer to the Code's view of intoxication, and thus to the law governing this appeal, than is the majority opinion in *Stasio*.

Which brings us to the Code.

As indicated, after *Stasio* had been decided, the Code became effective, on September 1, 1979. It in effect displaced the Court's opinion in *Stasio* and in large measure confirmed the approach of the concurring opinions.

[The Code] provided:

a. Except as provided in subsection d. of this section, intoxication of the actor is not a defense unless it negatives an element of the offense.

b. When recklessness establishes an element of the offense, if the actor, due to self-induced intoxication, is unaware of a risk of which he would have been aware had he been sober, such unawareness is immaterial.

c. Intoxication does not, in itself, constitute mental disease within the meaning of chapter 4.

d. Intoxication which (1) is not self-induced or (2) is pathological is an affirmative defense if by reason of such intoxication the actor at the time of his conduct lacks substantial and adequate capacity either to appreciate its wrongfulness or to conform his conduct to the requirement of law.

e. Definitions. In this section unless a different meaning plainly is required:

(1) "Intoxication" means a disturbance of mental or physical capacities resulting from the introduction of substances into the body;

(2) "self-induced intoxication" means intoxication caused by substances which the actor knowingly introduces into his body, the tendency of which to cause intoxication he knows or ought to know, unless he introduces them pursuant to medical advice or under such circumstances as would afford a defense to a charge of crime;

(3) "Pathological intoxication" means intoxication grossly excessive in degree, given the amount of the intoxicant, to which the actor does not know he is susceptible.

As is readily apparent, self-induced intoxication is not a defense unless it negatives an element of the offense. Under the common-law intoxication defense, as construed by the Commission, intoxication could either exculpate or mitigate guilt "if the defendant's intoxication, in fact, prevents his having formed a mental state which is an element of the offense and if the law will recognize the proof of the lack of that mental state." Thus, the Commission recognized that under pre-Code law, intoxication was admissible as a defense to a "specific" intent, but not a "general" intent, crime.

N.J.S.A. 2C:2-8 was modeled after the Model Penal Code (MPC) §2.08. *See* N.J.S.A. 2C:2-8 (Historical Note). The drafters of the MPC, as did the New Jersey Commission, criticized the specific-general intent distinction, MPC Commentaries §2.08 comment at 353–54 and 357–58, and adopted instead the same four states of culpability eventually enacted in the Code. MPC Commentaries §2.02 comment at 230. In the commentary, the drafters of the MPC expressly stated their intention that intoxication be admissible to disprove the culpability factors of purpose or knowledge, but that for crimes requiring only recklessness or negligence, exculpation based on intoxication should be excluded as a matter of law. MPC Commentaries §2.08 comment at 354.

The drafters explicitly determined that intoxication ought to be accorded a significance that is entirely co-extensive with its relevance to disprove purpose or knowledge, when they are the requisite mental elements of a specific crime.... [W]hen the definition of a crime or a degree thereof requires proof of such a state of mind, the legal policy involved will almost certainly obtain whether or not the absence of purpose or knowledge is due to the actor's self-induced intoxication or to some other cause. [*Id.* at 357.]

The policy reasons for requiring purpose or knowledge as a requisite element of some crimes are that in the absence of those states of mind, the criminal conduct would not present a comparable danger, or the actor would not pose as significant a threat. Moreover, the ends of legal policy are better served by subjecting to graver sanctions those who consciously defy legal norms. It was those policy reasons that dictated the result that the intoxication defense should be available when it negatives purpose or knowledge. The drafters concluded: "If the mental state which is the basis of the law's concern does not exist, the reason for its non-existence is quite plainly immaterial." *Id.* at 358.

Thus, when the requisite culpability for a crime is that the person act "purposely" or "knowingly," evidence of voluntary intoxication is admissible to disprove that requisite mental state. The language of N.J.S.A. 2C:2-8 and its legislative history make this unmistakably clear and lend support to *Stasio's* minority opinions.

The foregoing discussion establishes that proof of voluntary intoxication would negate the culpability elements in the offenses of which this defendant was convicted. The charges—aggravated assault, possession of a weapon with a purpose to use it unlawfully and resisting arrest—all require purposeful conduct (aggravated assault uses "purposely" or "knowingly" in the alternative). The question is what level of intoxication must be demonstrated before a trial court is required to submit the issue to a jury. What quantum of proof is required?

The guiding principle is simple enough of articulation. We need not here repeat the citations to authorities already referred to in this opinion that use the language of "prostration of faculties such that defendant was rendered incapable of forming an intent." Justice Depue's instruction to a jury over a century ago, quoted with approval in *State v. Treficanto, supra*, 106 N.J.L. 344, 146 A. 313, remains good law: "You should carefully discriminate between that excitable condition of the mind produced by drink, which is not incapable of forming an intent, but determines to act on a slight provocation, and such prostration of the faculties by intoxication as puts the accused in such a state that he is incapable of forming an intention from which he shall act."

See also Stasio, supra: "[I]t is not the case that every defendant who has had a few drinks may successfully urge the defense. The mere intake of even large quantities of alcohol will not suffice. Moreover, the defense cannot be established solely by showing that the defendant might not have committed the offense had he been sober. What is required is a showing of such a great prostration of the faculties that the requisite mental state was totally lacking. That is, to successfully invoke the defense, an accused must show that he was so intoxicated that he did not have the intent to commit an offense. Such a state of affairs will likely exist in very few cases."

Cases in which evidence of intoxication was deemed sufficient to present a jury question include *State v. Frankland*, 51 N.J. 221, 238 A.2d 680 (1968), in which defendant testified that "he had consumed fifteen drinks of scotch and water and could not remember the events of the evening;"" *State v. Polk*, 164 N.J. Super. 457, 397 A.2d 330 (App. Div. 1977), in which the "question of defendant's consumption of alcoholic beverages permeated [the] entire trial" (defendant drank beer and wine from 9 a.m. until sometime in the afternoon; amount of alcoholic beverages consumed was "substantial;" drinking companion had blood-alcohol concentration of 0.158; defendant acted irrationally, hitting baby with his fist and throwing baby down onto a porch; investigator found beer cans strewn around the scene of the killing; and *State v. Holzman*, 176 N.J. Super. 590, 424 A.2d 454 (Law Div. 1980), in which defendant took four Fiorinal tablets (a mild sedative) with two "Black Russian" drinks prior to her crime; defendant displayed unusual and irrational behavior at the police station and denied all recollection of events occurring one hour prior to her crime. Cases holding that the evidence was insufficient to warrant a jury charge on intoxication are *State v. Selby*, 183 N.J. Super. 273, 443 A.2d 1076 (App. Div. 1981), in which defendant shared with three others a marijuana pipe for about ten minutes, as a result of which he felt "high" and "pretty good;" *State v. Moore*, 178 N.J. Super. 417, 429 A.2d 397 (App. Div. 1981), where defendant shared half of a pint bottle of vodka with her co-defendant, then "had to . . . get another drink to get [her] nerves back up" before joining in the crime, as to the events preceding, during, and following which she had almost total recall; *State v. Kinlaw*, 150 N.J. Super. 70, 374 A.2d 1233 (App. Div. 1977), in which the evidence was that defendant drank beer between 11 a.m. and 2 p.m. and described himself as "drunk;" and *State v. Ghaul*, 132 N.J. Super. 438, 334 A.2d 65 (App. Div. 1975), where defendant testified he had been "drinking all day," police officer detected odor of alcohol on defendant's breath and thought his driving was impaired, but "[d]efendant's own testimony indicated he could think clearly," he could describe the pertinent events, and he had "sufficient presence of mind to take over the driving and to lie to the police. . . ."

From all of the above we conclude that some of the factors pertinent to the determination of intoxication sufficient to satisfy the test of "prostration of faculties"—a shorthand expression used here to indicate a condition of intoxication that renders the actor incapable of purposeful or knowing conduct—are the following: the quantity of intoxicant consumed, the period of time involved, the actor's conduct as perceived by others (what he said, how he said it, how he appeared, how he acted, how his coordination or lack thereof manifested itself), any odor of alcohol or other intoxicating substance, the results of any tests to determine blood-alcohol content, and the actor's ability to recall significant events.

Measured by the foregoing standard and evidence relevant thereto, it is apparent that the record in this case is insufficient to have required the trial court to grant defendant's request to charge intoxication. True, the victim testified that defendant was drunk, and defendant herself said she felt "pretty intoxicated," "pretty bad," and "very intoxicated." But these are no more than conclusory labels, of little assistance in determining whether any drinking produced a prostration of faculties.

More to the point is the fact that defendant carried a quart of wine, that she was drinking (we are not told over what period of time) with other people on the vacant lot, that about a pint of the wine was consumed, and that defendant did not drink this alone but rather "gave most of it out, gave some of it out." Defendant's conduct was violent, abusive, and threatening. But with it all there is not the slightest suggestion that she did not know what she was doing or that her faculties were so beclouded by the wine that she was incapable of engaging in purposeful conduct. That the purpose of the conduct may have been bizarre, even violent, is not the test. The critical question is whether defendant was capable of forming that bizarre or violent purpose, and we do not find sufficient evidence to permit a jury to say she was not.

Defendant's own testimony, if believed, would furnish a basis for her actions. She said she acted in self-defense, to ward off a sexual attack by McKinney and others. She recited the details of that attack and of her reaction to it with full recall and in explicit detail, explaining that her abuse of the police officers was sparked by her being upset by their unfairness in locking her up rather than apprehending McKinney.

Ordinarily, of course, the question of whether a defendant's asserted intoxication satisfies the standards enunciated in this opinion should be resolved by the jury. But here, viewing the evidence and the legitimate inferences to be drawn therefrom in the light most favorable to defendant, the best that can be made of the proof of intoxication is that defendant may have been extremely agitated and distraught. It may even be that a factfinder could conclude that her powers of rational thought and deductive reasoning had been affected. But there is no suggestion in the evidence that defendant's faculties were so prostrated by her consumption of something less than a pint of wine as to render her incapable of purposeful or knowing conduct. The trial court correctly refused defendant's request.

The judgment below is reversed and the cause is remanded to the Appellate Division for further proceedings consistent with this opinion.

Questions and Notes

1. What is the rationale for excluding evidence of intoxication in crimes requiring recklessness? Doesn't intoxication in fact negate recklessness if, for example, Cameron were not aware that she was (or might be) attacking McKinney?

2. Conversely, why should intoxication be a defense to crimes involving purpose or knowledge? Are you persuaded by the court's statement that "[t]he policy reasons for requiring purpose or knowledge . . . are that in the absence of those states of mind, the criminal conduct would not present a comparable danger, or the actor would not pose as significant a threat"?

3. Why does the court require as much evidence of intoxication as it does? Can't somebody be intoxicated without suffering "prostration of faculties"?

4. In the context of cases, what do you understand the terms "general intent" and "specific intent" to mean?

5. Although some have thought that the MPC's rule for intoxication has eliminated the confusion, it left the New York Court of Appeals closely divided in *Register*.

People v. Register
457 N.E.2d 704 (N.Y. 1983)

SIMONS, Judge.

Defendant appeals from an order of the Appellate Division which affirmed a judgment entered after a jury trial convicting him of murder in the second degree [depraved mind murder] and two counts of assault in the first degree. The charges arose from a barroom incident in which defendant shot and killed one man and seriously injured two others. He alleges that the evidence was insufficient to support the murder conviction and that the trial court erred in refusing to instruct the jury that it could consider intoxication evidence to negate an element of the crime of depraved mind murder.

The shootings occurred about 12:30 a.m. on January 15, 1977 in a crowded barroom in downtown Rochester. The evidence established that defendant and a friend, Duval, had been drinking heavily that day celebrating the fact that Duval, through an administrative mixup, would not have to spend the weekend in jail. Sometime between 7:00 p.m. and 8:00 p.m., the two men left home for the bar. Defendant took a loaded pistol with him and shortly after they arrived at the bar, he produced it when he got into an argument with another patron over money owed him. Apparently, the dispute ended without incident and defendant continued his drinking. After midnight another argument developed, this time between Duval and Willie

Mitchell. Defendant took out the gun again, shot at Mitchell but mistakenly injured Lawrence Evans who was trying to stop the fight. He then stepped forward and shot Mitchell in the stomach from close range. At that, the 40 or 50 patrons in the bar started for the doors. Some of the bystanders tried to remove Mitchell to a hospital and while they were doing so, the decedent, Marvin Lindsey, walked by defendant. Lindsey was apparently a friend or acquaintance of defendant although that was the first-time he had seen him that night. For no explained reason, defendant turned and fired his gun killing Lindsey.

Defendant did not contest the shootings. In defense, his counsel elicited evidence during the prosecution's case of defendant's considerable drinking that evening and he called as his only witness a forensic psychiatrist who testified on the debilitating effects of consuming alcoholic beverages. The jury acquitted defendant of intentional murder but convicted him of depraved mind murder and the two assault counts.

The murder conviction must be supported by evidence that defendant "[u]nder circumstances evincing a depraved indifference to human life . . . recklessly engage[d] in conduct which create[d] a grave risk of death to another person, and thereby cause[d] the death of another person." A person acts recklessly when he is aware of and consciously disregards a substantial and unjustifiable risk, but to bring defendant's conduct within the murder statute, the People were required to establish also that defendant's act was imminently dangerous and presented a very high risk of death to others and that it was committed under circumstances which evidenced a wanton indifference to human life or a depravity of mind.

The evidence in the record supports the verdict. Defendant's awareness of and indifference to the attendant risks was established by evidence that he entered a crowded bar with a loaded gun, he said that he was "going to kill somebody tonight," or similar words, several times, and he had brought the gun out in the bar once before during the evening only to be told to put it away. Ultimately, he fired the gun three times in the "packed" barroom, conduct which presented a grave risk of death and did in fact result in the death of Marvin Lindsey. His conduct was well within that defined by the statute.

At the conclusion of the evidence and after the charge, defendant requested the court to instruct the jury on the effect of intoxication. The court complied with the request when discussing the intentional murder and assault counts, but it refused to charge the jury that it could consider defendant's intoxication in determining whether he acted "[u]nder circumstances evincing a depraved indifference to human life" in causing the death of Marvin Lindsey. The court held that the mens rea required for depraved mind murder is recklessness and that subdivision 3 of section 15.05 of the Penal Law precludes evidence of intoxication in defense of reckless crimes because it provides that "[a] person who creates such a risk but is unaware thereof solely by reason of voluntary intoxication also acts recklessly." That ruling is assigned as error by defendant. He contends that depraved mind murder contains a different or additional element of mental culpability, namely "circumstances evincing a depraved indifference to human life," which elevates defendant's conduct from manslaughter to murder and that this additional element may be negated by evidence of intoxication.

The Penal Law does not expressly define the term "element." However, it does set forth what the "elements" of an offense are and identifies them, as does the common law, as a culpable mental state (*mens rea*) and a voluntary act (*actus reus*). Both are required in all but the strict liability offenses. Consistent with that provision, the statutory definition of depraved mind murder includes both a mental element ("recklessly") and a voluntary act ("engaging in conduct which creates a grave risk of death to another person"). Recklessness refers to defendant's conscious disregard of a substantial risk and the act proscribed, the risk creating conduct, is defined by the degree of danger presented. Depraved mind murder resembles manslaughter in the second degree (a reckless killing which includes the requirement that defendant disregard a substantial risk, but the depraved mind murder statute requires in addition not only that the conduct which results in death present a grave risk of death but that it also occur "[u]nder circumstances evincing a depraved indifference to human life." This additional requirement refers to neither the *mens rea* nor the *actus reus*. If it states an element of the crime at all, it is not an element in the traditional sense but rather a definition of the factual setting in which the risk creating conduct must occur — objective circumstances which are not subject to being negated by evidence of defendant's intoxication.

In *People v. Poplis*, 30 N.Y.2d 85, 330 N.Y.S.2d 365, 281 N.E.2d 167, *supra*, we construed the statute and pointed out that depraved mind murder is a crime involving recklessness plus aggravating circumstances. Judge Bergan writing for a unanimous court noted that the new statute eliminated the "psychiatrically complicating" considerations found in the former statute and that it was a distinct improvement over the former statutes which spoke in terms of the operation of defendant's mind. Our holding that depraved mind murder is distinguishable from manslaughter, not by the mental element involved but by the objective circumstances in which the act occurs, finds sound support in that decision.

In sum, the statutory requirement that the homicide result from conduct evincing a depraved indifference to human life is a legislative attempt to qualitatively measure egregiously reckless conduct and to differentiate it from manslaughter. It does not create a new and different *mens rea*, undefined in the Penal Law, or a voluntary act which can be negated by evidence of intoxication. If the objective circumstances under which the crime is committed constitute an element of it, they do so only in the sense that the theft of more than $250 is an element of grand larceny. It is an element which elevates the severity of the offense but it is not an element subject to being negated by evidence of intoxication as may intent or the physical capacity to act.

In conclusion, it is worth noting that at common law intoxication was not a defense or excuse to criminal charges but was viewed instead as an aggravating circumstance which heightened moral culpability. The common-law courts viewed the decision to drink to excess, with its attendant risks to self and others, as an independent culpable act. Despite widespread acceptance of this rule, legal authorities began to recognize that the debilitating impact of voluntarily consuming excessive amounts of alcohol warranted the admission of evidence of intoxication in some cases, particularly to negative proof that defendant possessed the physical capacity to commit the crime, by striking a blow, for example. In New York, the Legislature further modified the common-law rule by permitting the defendant to introduce evidence of intoxication to aid the jury in determining his motive or intent in committing an act.

Notwithstanding this relaxation of the prohibition against use of intoxication evidence, the present statute when enacted in 1967 continued to foreclose the use of intoxication evidence in cases involving recklessness. The rationale is readily apparent: the element of recklessness itself—defined as conscious disregard of a substantial risk—encompasses the risks created by defendant's conduct in getting drunk.

Ultimately, the only intended purpose in permitting the jury to consider intoxication in a reckless crime is to negate defendant's awareness and disregard of the risk. It is precisely that point—the inconsistency of permitting reckless and otherwise aggravating conduct to negate an aspect of the offense—that persuades us that intoxication evidence should be excluded whenever recklessness is an element of the offense (*see, generally,* ALI Model Penal Code [Proposed Official Draft, 1962], § 2.08, subd. [2]). In utilitarian terms, the risk of excessive drinking should be added to and not subtracted from the risks created by the conduct of the drunken defendant for there is no social or penological purpose to be served by a rule that permits one who voluntarily drinks to be exonerated from failing to foresee the results of his conduct if he is successful at getting drunk.

Accordingly, the order of the Appellate Division should be affirmed.

JASEN, Judge (dissenting).

The majority holds that the element of "circumstances evincing a depraved indifference to human life" set forth in subdivision 2 of section 125.25 of the Penal Law is not part of the *mens rea* of murder in the second degree and that evidence of intoxication is, therefore, inadmissible to negate that element. Since I believe the Legislature intended that a defendant's alleged intoxication could be used to negate that element of the crime, I respectfully dissent.

This conclusion finds strong support in a recent decision of this court where it was reasoned that, under the present version of the statute, "circumstances evincing a depraved indifference to human life" plus "recklessness", constitutes conduct of "graver culpability" which involves something more serious than mere recklessness. (*People v. Poplis*, 30 N.Y.2d 85, 88, 330 N.Y.S.2d 365, 281 N.E.2d 167.) [T]his court made it abundantly clear that "depraved indifference" was to be construed as a *mens rea* involving a state of mind more vicious than recklessness but less so than intent. Inasmuch as proof of intoxication is admissible "whenever it is relevant to negative an element of the crime charged," it should have been admitted here to show that defendant did not possess a state of mind sufficiently culpable to warrant a conviction for murder rather than manslaughter.

While the majority correctly states that "[t]he crime differs from intentional murder in that it results not from a specific, conscious intent to cause death, but from an indifference to or disregard of the risks attending defendant's conduct," can there be any doubt that to disregard the risks attending his conduct defendant must have at least been aware of those risks? As stated by Arnold D. Hechtman, Counsel to the Commission on Revision of the Penal Law and Criminal Code, the fatal conduct must be performed with "a depraved kind of wantonness." (Hechtman, Practice Commentaries, McKinney's Cons. Laws of N.Y., Book 39, Penal Law, § 125.25, p. 399.) Wantonness, a term used by the majority in defining what a defendant's conduct must amount to before a conviction for depraved mind murder can be sustained is commonly defined as requiring a conscious doing of some act with knowledge of existing conditions and an awareness of the risks involved.[1] Thus, it should be clear beyond cavil that "depraved indifference' was intended by the Legislature to constitute a culpable state of mind which could be negated by proof that the actor was so intoxicated he was not aware of existing conditions or the risks inherent in his conduct.

The construction which I would give the depraved mind murder statute is not only consistent with the Legislature's intent, the history of the statute and precedent of this court but is also in line with the basic underpinnings of our system of criminal justice. The rule announced by the majority today effectively eviscerates the distinction between manslaughter in the second degree and murder in the second degree with respect to the accused's state of mind. The majority holds that mere recklessness is a sufficient *mens rea* under the depraved mind murder statute if the objective circumstances surrounding the killing "presented a grave risk of death and did in fact result in the death" of another.

Historically, our criminal law is based upon a theory of "punishing the vicious will." It is a deep-rooted part of our jurisprudence that, in the ordinary case, only those offenders who consciously choose to do evil rather than good will be punished. (*Morissette v. United States*, 342 U.S. 246, 250–251.) Under the majority's rule, however, a person who possessed only a reckless state of mind when he caused the death of another could be convicted of depraved mind murder and sentenced to a

---

1. A leading lexicon defines "wantonness" as: "Conscious doing of some act or the omission of some duty with knowledge of existing conditions and consciousness that, from the act or omission, injury will likely result to another. Conscious failure by one charged with a duty to exercise due care and diligence to prevent an injury after the discovery of the peril, or under circumstances where he is charged with a knowledge of such peril and being conscious of the inevitable or probable results of such failure. A reckless or intentional disregard of the property, rights, or safety of others, implying, actively, a willingness to injure and disregard of the consequences to others, and, passively, more than mere negligence, that is, a conscious and intentional disregard of duty." (Citations omitted.) (BLACK's LAW DICTIONARY [5th ed], p. 1419.)

term of 15 years to life imprisonment simply because objective circumstances surrounding the killing presented a "grave risk" of death even though the actor, due to intoxication, was unaware of those circumstances and could not appreciate the risks. The majority would also hold that another person who is fully aware of a "substantial and unjustifiable risk" and consciously disregards that risk can only be found guilty of manslaughter in the second degree and sentenced to as little as one and one-half years in jail. While there may be a technical distinction between a "grave" risk and a "substantial" one, the only real difference is about 15 years in prison. To accept this distinction as justification for the disparate penalties which the respective crimes carry defies basic principles of fairness and logic. I simply cannot agree that the Legislature intended that convictions for murder as opposed to manslaughter would turn upon the nature of the objective surrounding circumstances regardless of whether or not the accused was aware of those circumstances or could appreciate the consequences of his conduct.

In my view, the Legislature purposely distinguished between reckless manslaughter and depraved mind murder, intending that depraved indifference plus recklessness would connote a *mens rea* more culpable than recklessness alone and nearly as culpable as intent. The differences between the mental states set forth in the reckless manslaughter, depraved mind murder and intentional murder statutes are easily delineated, although somewhat difficult to apply. A person acts recklessly in causing the death of another when he is aware of and consciously disregards a substantial and unjustifiable risk. A person intentionally kills another when his "conscious objective" is to cause the death of the victim. A person acts with depraved indifference, however, when he engages in conduct, whereby he does not intend to kill but is so indifferent to the consequences, which he knows with substantial certainty will result in the death of another, as to be willing to kill. It is at this point that reckless homicide becomes knowing homicide and the killing differs so little from an intentional killing that parity of punishment is required. This is so not because the surrounding circumstances happened to create a "grave" as opposed to a "substantial" risk, but because the accused has acted with greater culpability and a wickedness akin to that of one whose conscious objective is to kill.

By this approach, a person who acts without an awareness of the risks involved, due to intoxication or otherwise, will be punished for manslaughter, while a person who acts in a way which he knows is substantially certain to cause death, although not intending to kill, will be treated the same as a person who intentionally kills. It seems to me that this is the far more reasonable approach and the one intended by the Legislature.

Finally, with respect to the majority's statement that "the risk of excessive drinking should be added to and not subtracted from the risks created by the conduct of the drunken defendant for there is no social or penological purpose to be served by a rule that permits one who voluntarily drinks to be exonerated from failing to foresee the results of his conduct if he is successful at getting drunk," I would only note that although this may be an accurate representation of what the majority believes the law should be, the Legislature has decided otherwise and it is this court's responsibility to construe the statute accordingly.

Inasmuch as the legislative history of subdivision 2 of section 125.25 of the Penal Law, prior precedent of this court and basic notions of justice make clear that the element of "depraved indifference" should be construed as a mental state more culpable than recklessness, evidence of defendant's intoxication should have been admitted, pursuant to section 15.25 of the Penal Law, to negate that element of the offense.

Accordingly, I would reverse the conviction and order a new trial.

JONES, WACHTLER and KAYE, J.J., concur with SIMONS, J.

JASEN, J., dissents and votes to reverse in a separate opinion in which COOKE, C.J., and MEYER, J., concur.

Questions and Notes

1. What is the difference in approach between the majority and the dissent?

2. Whose reading of the statute is more persuasive? Why?

3. Assuming that the statute is capable of bearing either reading, who has the better of the policy arguments? Why?

4. We conclude this chapter with several opinions from a sharply divided United States Supreme Court in *Montana v. Egelhoff.*

Montana v. Egelhoff

518 U.S. 37 (1996)

JUSTICE SCALIA announced the judgment of the Court and delivered an opinion, in which THE CHIEF JUSTICE, Justice KENNEDY, and Justice THOMAS join.

We consider in this case whether the Due Process Clause is violated by Montana Code Annotated §45-2-203, which provides, in relevant part, that voluntary intoxication "may not be taken into consideration in determining the existence of a mental state which is an element of [a criminal] offense."

I.

In July 1992, while camping out in the Yaak region of northwestern Montana to pick mushrooms, respondent made friends with Roberta Pavola and John Christenson, who were doing the same. On Sunday, July 12, the three sold the mushrooms they had collected and spent the rest of the day and evening drinking, in bars and at a private party in Troy, Montana. Sometime after 9 p.m., they left the party in Christenson's 1974 Ford Galaxy station wagon. The drinking binge apparently continued, as respondent was seen buying beer at 9:20 p.m. and recalled "sitting on a hill or a bank passing a bottle of Black Velvet back and forth" with Christenson.

At about midnight that night, officers of the Lincoln County, Montana, sheriff's department, responding to reports of a possible drunk driver, discovered Christenson's station wagon stuck in a ditch along U.S. Highway 2. In the front seat were Pavola and Christenson, each dead from a single gunshot to the head. In the rear of the car lay respondent, alive and yelling obscenities. His blood-alcohol content measured .36 percent over one hour later. On the floor of the car, near the brake pedal, lay respondent's .38 caliber handgun, with four loaded rounds and two empty casings; respondent had gunshot residue on his hands.

Respondent was charged with two counts of deliberate homicide, a crime defined by Montana law as "purposely" or "knowingly" causing the death of another human being. Mont. Code Ann. §45-5-102 (1995). A portion of the jury charge, uncontested here, instructed that "[a] person acts purposely when it is his conscious object to engage in conduct of that nature or to cause such a result," and that "[a] person acts knowingly when he is aware of his conduct or when he is aware under the circumstances his conduct constitutes a crime; or, when he is aware there exists the high probability that his conduct will cause a specific result." Respondent's defense at trial was that an unidentified fourth person must have committed the murders; his own extreme intoxication, he claimed, had rendered him physically incapable of committing the murders, and accounted for his inability to recall the events of the night of July 12. Although respondent was allowed to make this use of the evidence that he was intoxicated, the jury was instructed, pursuant to Mont. Code Ann. §45-2-203 (1995), that it could not consider respondent's "intoxicated condition . . . in determining the existence of a mental state which is an element of the offense." The jury found respondent guilty on both counts, and the court sentenced him to 84 years' imprisonment.

The Supreme Court of Montana reversed. It reasoned (1) that respondent "had a due process right to present and have considered by the jury all relevant evidence to rebut the State's evidence on all elements of the offense charged," and (2) that evidence of respondent's voluntary intoxication was "clear[ly] . . . relevant to the issue of whether [respondent] acted knowingly and purposely." Because §45-2-203 prevented the jury from considering that evidence with regard to that issue, the court concluded that the State had been "relieved of part of its burden to prove beyond a reasonable doubt every fact necessary to constitute the crime charged," and that respondent had therefore been denied due process. We granted certiorari.

II.

The cornerstone of the Montana Supreme Court's judgment was the proposition that the Due Process Clause guarantees a defendant the right to present and have considered by the jury *"all relevant evidence* to rebut the State's evidence on all elements of the offense charged." (Emphasis added.) Respondent does not defend this categorical rule; he acknowledges that the right to present relevant evidence "has not been viewed as absolute." That is a wise concession, since the proposition that the Due Process Clause guarantees the right to introduce all relevant evidence is simply indefensible. As we have said: "The accused does not have an unfettered right to offer [evidence] that is incompetent, privileged, or otherwise inadmissible under standard rules of evidence." *Taylor v. Illinois*, 484 U.S. 400 (1988). Relevant evidence may, for example, be excluded on account of a defendant's failure to comply with procedural requirements. And any number of familiar and unquestionably constitutional evidentiary rules also authorize the exclusion of relevant evidence. For example, Federal (and Montana) Rule of Evidence 403 provides: *"Although relevant*, evidence may be excluded if its probative value is substantially outweighed by the danger of unfair prejudice, confusion of the issues, or misleading the jury, or by considerations of undue delay, waste of time, or needless presentation of cumulative evidence" (emphasis added). Hearsay rules, *see* Fed. Rule Evid. 802, similarly prohibit the introduction of testimony which, though unquestionably relevant, is deemed insufficiently reliable.[2] Of course, to say that the right to introduce relevant evidence is not absolute is not to say that the Due Process Clause places *no* limits upon restriction of that right. But it is to say that the defendant asserting such a limit must sustain the usual heavy burden that a due process claim entails:

> "[P]reventing and dealing with crime is much more the business of the States than it is of the Federal Government, and . . . we should not lightly construe the Constitution so as to intrude upon the administration of justice by the individual States. Among other things, it is normally 'within the power of the State to regulate procedures under which its laws are carried out,' . . . and its decision in this regard is not subject to proscription under the Due Process Clause unless 'it offends some principle of justice so rooted in the traditions and conscience of our people as to be ranked as fundamental.'"

Respondent's task, then, is to establish that a defendant's right to have a jury consider evidence of his voluntary intoxication in determining whether he possesses the requisite mental state is a "fundamental principle of justice."

Our primary guide in determining whether the principle in question is fundamental is, of course, historical practice. Here that gives respondent little support. By the laws of England, wrote Hale, the intoxicated defendant "shall have no privilege by this voluntarily contracted madness, but shall have the same judgment as if

---

2. Justice O'CONNOR agrees that "a defendant does not enjoy an absolute right to present evidence relevant to his defense," *post*, at 2026, and does not dispute the validity of the evidentiary rules mentioned above. She contends, however, that Montana's rule is not like these because it "places a blanket exclusion on a *category* of evidence that would allow the accused to negate the offense's mental state element." *Ibid.* (emphasis added). Of course. hearsay is a "category" of evidence as well; what Justice O'CONNOR apparently has in mind is that this particular category relates to evidence tending to prove a particular fact. That is indeed a distinction, but it is hard to understand why it should make a difference. So long as the category of excluded evidence is selected on a basis that has good and traditional policy support, it ought to be valid. We do not entirely understand Justice O'CONNOR's argument that the vice of §45-2-203 is that it excludes evidence "essential to the accused's defense." Evidence of intoxication is not always "essential," any more than hearsay evidence is always "nonessential."

he were in his right senses." 1 M. HALE, PLEAS OF THE CROWN *32–33. According to Blackstone and Coke, the law's condemnation of those suffering from *dementia affectata* was harsher still: Blackstone, citing Coke, explained that the law viewed intoxication "as an aggravation of the offence, rather than an excuse for any criminal misbehaviour." 4 W. BLACKSTONE, COMMENTARIES *25–26. This stern rejection of inebriation as a defense became a fixture of early American law as well. The American editors of the 1847 edition of Hale wrote:

> "Drunkenness, it was said in an early case, can never be received as a ground to excuse or palliate an offence: this is not merely the opinion of a speculative philosopher, the argument of counsel, or the *obiter dictum* of a single judge, but it is a sound and long established maxim of judicial policy, from which perhaps a single dissenting voice cannot be found. But if no other authority could be adduced, the uniform decisions of our own Courts from the first establishment of the government, would constitute it now a part of the common law of the land."

In an opinion citing the foregoing passages from Blackstone and Hale, Justice Story rejected an objection to the exclusion of evidence of intoxication as follows:

> "This is the first time, that I ever remember it to have been contended, that the commission of one crime was an excuse for another. Drunkenness is a gross vice, and in the contemplation of some of our laws is a crime; and I learned in my earlier studies, that so far from its being in law an excuse for murder, it is rather an aggravation of its malignity." *United States v. Cornell*, 25 F. Cas. 650, 657–658 (No. 14,868) (C.C.R.I. 1820).

The historical record does not leave room for the view that the common law's rejection of intoxication as an "excuse" or "justification" for crime would nonetheless permit the defendant to show that intoxication prevented the requisite *mens rea*. Hale, Coke and Blackstone were familiar, to say the least, with the concept of *mens rea*, and acknowledged that drunkenness "deprive[s] men of the use of reason," Hale, *supra*, at *32; *see also* BLACKSTONE, *supra*, at *25. It is inconceivable that they did not realize that an offender's drunkenness might impair his ability to form the requisite intent; and inconceivable that their failure to note this massive exception from the general rule of disregard of intoxication was an oversight. Hale's statement that a drunken offender shall have the same judgment "as if he were in his right senses" must be understood as precluding a defendant from arguing that, because of his intoxication, he could not have possessed the *mens rea* required to commit the crime. And the same must be said of the exemplar of the common-law rule cited by both Hale and Blackstone, which is Serjeant Pollard's argument to the King's Bench in *Reniger v. Fogossa*, 1 Plowd. 1, 19, 75 Eng. Rep. 1, 31 (K.B. 1550): "[I]f a person that is drunk kills another, this shall be Felony, and he shall be hanged for it, and yet he did it through Ignorance, for when he was drunk he had *no Understanding* nor Memory; but inasmuch as that Ignorance was occasioned by his own Act and Folly, and he might have avoided it, he shall not be privileged thereby" (emphasis added). *See also Beverley's Case*, 4 Co. Rep. 123b, 125a, 76 Eng. Rep. 1118, 1123 (K.B. 1603) ("although he who is drunk, is for the time *non compos mentis,* yet his drunkenness does not extenuate his act or offence, *nor turn to his avail*") (emphasis added).

Against this extensive evidence of a lengthy common-law tradition decidedly against him, the best argument available to respondent is the one made by his *amicus* and conceded by the State: Over the course of the 19th century, courts carved out an exception to the common law's traditional across-the-board condemnation of the drunken offender, allowing a jury to consider a defendant's intoxication when assessing whether he possessed the mental state needed to commit the crime charged, where the crime was one requiring a "specific intent." The emergence of this new rule is often traced to an 1819 English case, in which Justice Holroyd is reported to have held that "though voluntary drunkenness cannot excuse from the commission of crime, yet where, as on a charge of murder, the material question is, whether an act was premeditated or done only with sudden heat and impulse, the fact of the party being intoxicated [is] a circumstance proper to be taken into consideration." Justice Park claimed that Holroyd had "retracted his opinion" in *Grindley,* and said "there is no doubt that that case is not law." In this country, as late as 1858 the Missouri Supreme Court could speak as categorically as this:

> "To look for deliberation and forethought in a man maddened by intoxication is vain, for drunkenness has deprived him of the deliberating faculties to a greater or less extent; and if this deprivation is to relieve him of all responsibility or to diminish it, the great majority of crimes committed will go unpunished. This however is not the doctrine of the common law; and to its maxims, based as they obviously are upon true wisdom and sound policy, we must adhere." *State v. Cross,* 27 Mo. 332, 338 (1858).

And as late as 1878, the Vermont Supreme Court upheld the giving of the following instruction at a murder trial:

> "The voluntary intoxication of one who without provocation commits a homicide, although amounting to a frenzy, that is, although the intoxication amounts to a frenzy, does not excuse him from the same construction of his conduct, and the same legal inferences upon the question of premeditation and intent, as affecting the grade of his crime, which are applicable to a person entirely sober." *State v. Tatro,* 50 Vt. 483, 487 (1878).

Eventually, however, the new view won out, and by the end of the 19th century, in most American jurisdictions, intoxication could be considered in determining whether a defendant was capable of forming the specific intent necessary to commit the crime charged.

On the basis of this historical record, respondent's *amicus* argues that "[t]he old common-law rule ... was no longer deeply rooted at the time the Fourteenth Amendment was ratified." That conclusion is questionable, but we need not pursue the point, since the argument of *amicus* mistakes the nature of our inquiry. It is not the State which bears the burden of demonstrating that its rule is "deeply rooted," but rather respondent who must show that the principle of procedure *violated* by the rule (and allegedly required by due process) is "so rooted in the traditions and conscience of our people as to be ranked as fundamental." Thus, even assuming that when the Fourteenth Amendment was adopted the rule Montana now defends was no longer generally applied, this only cuts off what might be called an *a fortiori* argument in favor of the State. The burden remains upon respondent to show that the "new common law" rule—that intoxication may be considered on the question of intent—was so deeply rooted at the time of the Fourteenth Amendment (or perhaps has become so deeply rooted since) as to be a fundamental principle which that Amendment enshrined.

That showing has not been made. Instead of the uniform and continuing acceptance we would expect for a rule that enjoys "fundamental principle" status, we find that fully one-fifth of the States either never adopted the "new common-law" rule at issue here or have recently abandoned it.

It is not surprising that many States have held fast to or resurrected the common-law rule prohibiting consideration of voluntary intoxication in the determination of *mens rea*, because that rule has considerable justification[3]—which alone casts doubt upon the proposition that the opposite rule is a "fundamental principle." A large number of crimes, especially violent crimes, are committed by intoxicated offenders; modern studies put the numbers as high as half of all homicides, for example. Disallowing consideration of voluntary intoxication has the effect of increasing the punishment for all unlawful acts committed in that state, and thereby deters drunkenness or irresponsible behavior while drunk. The rule also serves as a specific deterrent, ensuring that those who prove incapable of controlling violent impulses while voluntarily intoxicated go to prison. And finally, the rule comports with and implements society's moral perception that one who has voluntarily impaired his own faculties should be responsible for the consequences.

There is, in modern times, even more justification for laws such as §45-2-203 than there used to be. Some recent studies suggest that the connection between drunkenness and crime is as much cultural as pharmacological—that is, that

---

3. In his dissent, Justice SOUTER acknowledges that there *may be* valid policy reasons supporting the Montana law, some of which were brought forward by States that appeared as *amici*. He refuses to consider the adequacy of those reasons, however, because they were not brought forward *by Montana's lawyers*. We do not know why the constitutionality of Montana's enactment should be subject to the condition subsequent that its lawyers be able to guess a policy justification that satisfies this Court. Whatever they guess will of course not necessarily be the *real reason* the Montana legislature adopted the provision; Montana's lawyers must speculate about that, just as we must. Our standard formulation has been "Where . . . there are plausible reasons for [the legislature's] action, our inquiry is at an end." Justice SOUTER would change that to "Where there are plausible reasons that counsel for the party supporting the legislation have mentioned." Or perhaps it is "Where there are plausible reasons that counsel for the Government (or State) have mentioned"— so that in this case Hawaii's *amicus* brief would count if a Hawaiian statute were at issue. Either way, it is strange for the constitutionality of a state law to depend upon whether the lawyers hired by the State (or elected by its people) to defend the law happen to hit the right boxes on our bingo-card of acceptable policy justifications.

drunks are violent not simply because alcohol makes them that way, but because they are behaving in accord with their learned belief that drunks are violent. This not only adds additional support to the traditional view that an intoxicated criminal is not deserving of exoneration, but it suggests that juries—who possess the same learned belief as the intoxicated offender—will be too quick to accept the claim that the defendant was biologically incapable of forming the requisite *mens rea*. Treating the matter as one of excluding misleading evidence therefore makes some sense.[5]

In sum, not every widespread experiment with a procedural rule favorable to criminal defendants establishes a fundamental principle of justice. Although the rule allowing a jury to consider evidence of a defendant's voluntary intoxication where relevant to *mens rea* has gained considerable acceptance, it is of too recent vintage, and has not received sufficiently uniform and permanent allegiance to qualify as fundamental, especially since it displaces a lengthy common-law tradition which remains supported by valid justifications today.[6]

* * *

"The doctrines of *actus reus, mens rea*, insanity, mistake, justification, and duress have historically provided the tools for a constantly shifting adjustment of the tension between the evolving aims of the criminal law and changing religious, moral, philosophical, and medical views of the nature of man. This process of adjustment has always been thought to be the province of the States." *Powell v. Texas*, 392 U.S. 514, 535–536 (1968) (plurality opinion). The people of Montana have decided to resurrect the rule of an earlier era, disallowing consideration of voluntary intoxication when a defendant's state of mind is at issue. Nothing in the Due Process Clause prevents them from doing so, and the judgment of the Supreme Court of Montana to the contrary must be reversed.

It is so ordered.

Justice GINSBURG, concurring in the judgment.

The Court divides in this case on a question of characterization. The State's law, Mont. Code Ann. §45-2-203 (1995), prescribes that voluntary intoxication "may not be taken into consideration in determining the existence of a mental state which is an element of [a criminal] offense." For measurement against federal restraints

---

5. These many valid policy reasons for excluding evidence of voluntary intoxication refute Justice O'CONNOR's claim that §45-2-203 has no purpose other than to improve the State's likelihood of winning a conviction.

6. Justice O'CONNOR maintains that "to determine whether a fundamental principle of justice has been violated here, we cannot consider only the historical disallowance of intoxication evidence, but must also consider the 'fundamental principle' that a defendant has a right to a fair opportunity to put forward his defense." What Justice O'CONNOR overlooks, however, is that the historical disallowance of intoxication evidence sheds light upon what our society has understood by a "fair opportunity to put forward [a] defense." That "fundamental principle" has demonstrably not included the right to introduce intoxication evidence.

on state action, how should we type that prescription? If § 45-2-203 is simply a rule designed to keep out "relevant, exculpatory evidence," Justice O'CONNOR maintains Montana's law offends due process. If it is, instead, a redefinition of the mental-state element of the offense, on the other hand, Justice O'CONNOR's due process concern "would not be at issue," for "[a] state legislature certainly has the authority to identify the elements of the offenses it wishes to punish" and to exclude evidence irrelevant to the crime it has defined.

Beneath the labels (rule excluding evidence or redefinition of the offense) lies the essential question: Can a State, without offense to the Federal Constitution, make the judgment that two people are equally culpable where one commits an act stone sober, and the other engages in the same conduct after his voluntary intoxication has reduced his capacity for self-control? For the reasons that follow, I resist categorizing § 45-2-203 as merely an evidentiary prescription, but join the Court's judgment refusing to condemn the Montana statute as an unconstitutional enactment.

Section 45-2-203 does not appear in the portion of Montana's Code containing evidentiary rules (Title 26), the expected placement of a provision regulating solely the admissibility of evidence at trial. Instead, Montana's intoxication statute appears in Title 45 ("Crimes"), as part of a chapter entitled "General Principles of Liability." Mont. Code Ann., Tit. 45, ch. 2 (1995). No less than adjacent provisions governing duress and entrapment, § 45-2-203 embodies a legislative judgment regarding the circumstances under which individuals may be held criminally responsible for their actions.

As urged by Montana and its *amici*, § 45-2-203 "extract[s] the entire subject of voluntary intoxication from the mens rea inquiry," Reply Brief for Petitioner 2, thereby rendering evidence of voluntary intoxication logically irrelevant to proof of the requisite mental state. Thus, in a prosecution for deliberate homicide, the State need not prove that the defendant "purposely or knowingly cause[d] the death of another," Mont. Code Ann. § 45-5-102(a) (1995), in a purely subjective sense. To obtain a conviction, the prosecution must prove only that (1) the defendant caused the death of another with actual knowledge or purpose, *or* (2) that the defendant killed "under circumstances that would otherwise establish knowledge or purpose 'but for' [the defendant's] voluntary intoxication." Accordingly, § 45-2-203 does not "lighte[n] the prosecution's burden to prove [the] mental-state element beyond a reasonable doubt," as Justice O'CONNOR suggests, for "[t]he applicability of the reasonable-doubt standard . . . has always been dependent on how a State defines the offense that is charged," *Patterson v. New York*, 432 U.S. 197 (1977).

Comprehended as a measure redefining *mens rea*, § 45-2-203 encounters no constitutional shoal. States enjoy wide latitude in defining the elements of criminal offenses, particularly when determining "the extent to which moral culpability should be a prerequisite to conviction of a crime." When a State's power to define criminal conduct is challenged under the Due Process Clause, we inquire only whether the law "offends some principle of justice so rooted in the traditions and conscience of our people as to be ranked as fundamental." Defining *mens rea* to eliminate the exculpatory value of voluntary intoxication does not offend a "fundamental principle of justice," given the lengthy common-law tradition, and the adherence of a significant minority of the States to that position today. ("[A] State may so define the mental element of an offense that evidence of a defendant's voluntary intoxication at the time of commission does not have exculpatory relevance and, to that extent, may be excluded without raising any issue of due process.").

Other state courts have upheld statutes similar to §45-2-203, not simply as evidentiary rules, but as legislative redefinitions of the mental-state element. *See State v. Souza*, 72 Haw. 246, 249, 813 P.2d 1384, 1386 (1991) ("("legislature was entitled to redefine the mens rea element of crimes and to exclude evidence of voluntary intoxication to negate state of mind"); *State v. Ramos*, 133 Ariz. 4, 6, 648 P.2d 119, 121 (1982) ("("Perhaps the state of mind which needs to be proven here is a watered down mens rea; however, this is the prerogative of the legislature."); *Commonwealth v. Rumsey*, 309 Pa. Super. 137, 139, 454 A.2d 1121, 1122 (1983). Legislation of this order, if constitutional in Arizona, Hawaii, and Pennsylvania, ought not be declared unconstitutional by this Court when enacted in Montana.

If, as the plurality, Justice O'CONNOR, and Justice SOUTER agree, it is within the legislature's province to instruct courts to treat a sober person and a voluntarily intoxicated person as equally responsible for conduct—to place a voluntarily intoxicated person on a level with a sober person—then the Montana law is no less tenable under the Federal Constitution than are the laws, with no significant difference in wording, upheld in sister States.[7] The Montana Supreme Court did not disagree with the courts of other States; it simply did not undertake an analysis in line with the principle that legislative enactments plainly capable of a constitutional construction ordinarily should be given that construction.

The Montana Supreme Court's judgment, in sum, strikes down a statute whose text displays no constitutional infirmity. If the Montana court considered its analysis forced by this Court's precedent,[8] it is proper for this Court to say what prescriptions federal law leaves to the States, and thereby dispel confusion to which we may have contributed, and attendant state-court misperception.

---

7. Justice BREYER questions the States' authority to treat voluntarily intoxicated and sober defendants as equally culpable for their actions. He asks, moreover, why a legislature concerned with the high incidence of crime committed by individuals in an alcohol-impaired condition would choose the course Montana and several other States have taken. It would be more sensible, he suggests, to "equate voluntary intoxication, [with] knowledge, and purpose," thus dispensing entirely with the *mens rea* requirement when individuals act under the influence of a judgment-impairing substance. It does not seem to me strange, however, that States have resisted such a catch-all approach and have enacted, instead, a measure less sweeping, one that retains a *mens rea* requirement, but "define [s] culpable mental state so as to give voluntary intoxication no exculpatory relevance." Nor is it at all clear to me that "a jury unaware of intoxication would likely infer knowledge or purpose" in the example Justice BREYER provides. It is not only in fiction, *see* J. Thurber, *The Secret Life of Walter Mitty* (1983) (originally published in *The New Yorker* in 1939), but, sadly, in real life as well, that sober people drive while daydreaming or otherwise failing to pay attention to the road.

8. The United States, as *amicus curiae*, so suggested at oral argument.

Justice O'CONNOR, with whom Justice STEVENS, Justice SOUTER, and Justice BREYER join, dissenting.

The Montana Supreme Court unanimously held that Mont. Code Ann. §45-2-203 (1995) violates due process. I agree. Our cases establish that due process sets an outer limit on the restrictions that may be placed on a defendant's ability to raise an effective defense to the State's accusations. Here, to impede the defendant's ability to throw doubt on the State's case, Montana has removed from the jury's consideration a category of evidence relevant to determination of mental state where that mental state is an essential element of the offense that must be proved beyond a reasonable doubt. Because this disallowance eliminates evidence with which the defense might negate an essential element, the State's burden to prove its case is made correspondingly easier. The justification for this disallowance is the State's desire to increase the likelihood of conviction of a certain class of defendants who might otherwise be able to prove that they did not satisfy a requisite element of the offense. In my view, the statute's effect on the criminal proceeding violates due process.

I.

This Court's cases establish that limitations placed on the accused's ability to present a fair and complete defense can, in some circumstances, be severe enough to violate due process. "The right of an accused in a criminal trial to due process is, in essence, the right to a fair opportunity to defend against the State's accusations." Applying our precedent, the Montana Supreme Court held that keeping intoxication evidence away from the jury, where such evidence was relevant to establishment of the requisite mental state, violated the due process right to present a defense, and that the instruction pursuant to §45-2-203 was not harmless error. In rejecting the Montana Supreme Court's conclusion, the Court emphasizes that "any number of familiar and unquestionably constitutional evidentiary rules" permit exclusion of relevant evidence. It is true that a defendant does not enjoy an absolute right to present evidence relevant to his defense. But none of the "familiar" evidentiary rules operates as Montana's does. The Montana statute places a blanket exclusion on a category of evidence that would allow the accused to negate the offense's mental-state element. In so doing, it frees the prosecution, in the face of such evidence, from having to prove beyond a reasonable doubt that the defendant nevertheless possessed the required mental state. In my view, this combination of effects violates due process.

Because the Montana legislature has specified that a person commits "deliberate homicide" only if he "purposely or knowingly causes the death of another human being," Mont. Code Ann. §45-5-102(1)(a) (1995), the prosecution must prove the existence of such mental state in order to convict. That is, unless the defendant is shown to have acted purposely or knowingly, *he is not guilty of the offense of deliberate homicide*. The Montana Supreme Court found that it was inconsistent with the legislature's requirement of the mental state of "purposely" or "knowingly" to prevent the jury from considering evidence of voluntary intoxication, where that category of evidence was relevant to establishment of that mental-state element.

Where the defendant may introduce evidence to negate a subjective mental-state element, the prosecution must work to overcome whatever doubts the defense has raised about the existence of the required mental state. On the other hand, if the defendant may *not* introduce evidence that might create doubt in the factfinder's mind as to whether that element was met, the prosecution will find its job so much the easier. A subjective mental state is generally proved only circumstantially. If a jury may not consider the defendant's evidence of his mental state, the jury may impute to the defendant the culpability of a mental state he did not possess.

The State's brief to this Court enunciates a single reason: due to the well-known risks related to voluntary intoxication, it seeks to prevent a defendant's use of his own voluntary intoxication as basis for exculpation. That is, its interest is to ensure that even a defendant who lacked the required mental-state element—and is therefore not guilty—is nevertheless convicted of the offense. The Court elaborates on reasons *why* Montana might wish to preclude exculpation on the basis of voluntary intoxication, but these reasons—increased punishment and concomitant deterrence for those who commit unlawful acts while drunk, and implementation of society's moral perception that those who become drunk should bear the consequences—merely explain the State's purpose in trying to improve its likelihood of winning convictions. The final justification proffered by the Court on Montana's behalf is that Montana's rule perhaps prevents juries, who might be otherwise be misled, from being "too quick to accept the claim that the [drunk] defendant was biologically incapable of forming the requisite *mens rea*." But this proffered justification is inconsistent with § 45-2-203's exception for persons who are involuntarily intoxicated. That exception makes plain that Montana does *not* consider intoxication evidence misleading—but rather considers it relevant—for the determination of a person's capacity to form the requisite mental state.

A State's placement of a significant limitation on the right to defend against the State's accusations "requires that the competing interest be closely examined." Montana has specified that to prove guilt, the State must establish that the defendant acted purposely or knowingly, but has prohibited a category of defendants from effectively disputing guilt through presentation of evidence relevant to that essential element. And the evidence is indisputably relevant: The Montana Supreme Court held that evidence of intoxication is relevant to proof of mental state, and furthermore, § 45-2-203's exception for involuntary intoxication shows that the legislature does consider intoxication relevant to mental state. Montana has barred the defendant's use of a category of relevant, exculpatory evidence for the express purpose of improving the State's likelihood of winning a conviction against a certain type of defendant. The plurality's observation that all evidentiary rules that exclude exculpatory evidence reduce the State's burden to prove its case is beside the point. The *purpose* of the familiar evidentiary rules is not to alleviate the State's burden, but rather, to vindicate some other goal or value—*e.g.*, to ensure the reliability and competency of evidence or to encourage effective communications within certain relationships. Such rules may or may not help the prosecution, and when they do help, do so only incidentally. While due process does not "ba[r] States from making changes . . . that have the *effect* of making it easier for the prosecution to obtain convictions," an evidentiary rule whose sole *purpose* is to boost the State's likelihood of conviction distorts the adversary process. Montana does not justify its rule on grounds such as that intoxication evidence is unreliable, cumulative, privileged, or irrelevant. The sole purpose for this disallowance is to keep from the jury's consideration a category of evidence that helps the defendant's case and weakens the government's case.

II.

The Court does, however, raise an important argument for the statute's validity: the disallowance, at common law, of consideration of voluntary intoxication where a defendant's state of mind is at issue. Because this disallowance was permitted at common law, the plurality argues, its disallowance by Montana cannot amount to a violation of a "fundamental principle of justice."

From 1551 until its shift in the 19th century, the common-law rule prevailed that a defendant could not use intoxication as an excuse or justification for an offense, or, it must be assumed, to rebut establishment of a requisite mental state. "Early law was indifferent to the defense of drunkenness because the theory of criminal liability was then too crude and too undeveloped to admit of exceptions. . . . But with the refinement in the theory of criminal liability . . . a modification of the rigid old rule on the defense of drunkenness was to be expected." As the plurality concedes, that significant modification took place in the 19th century. Courts acknowledged the fundamental incompatibility of a particular mental state requirement on the one hand, and the disallowance of consideration of evidence that might defeat establishment of that mental state on the other. In the slow progress typical of the common law, courts began to recognize that evidence of intoxication was properly admissible for the purpose of ascertaining whether a defendant had met the required mental-state element of the offense charged.

This recognition, courts believed, was consistent with the common-law rule that voluntary intoxication did not excuse commission of a crime; rather, an element of the crime, the requisite mental state, was not satisfied and therefore the crime had not been committed. As one influential mid-19th century case explained, "Drunkenness is no excuse for crime; yet, in that class of crimes and offences which depend upon guilty knowledge, or the coolness and deliberation with which they shall have been perpetrated, to constitute their commission . . . [drunkenness] should be submitted to the consideration of the Jury"; for, where the crime required a particular mental state, "it is proper to show any state or condition of the person that is adverse to the proper exercise of the mind" in order "[t]o rebut" the mental state or "to enable the Jury to judge rightly of the matter." *Pigman v. State*, 14 Ohio 555, 556–557 (1846); *accord, Cline v. State*, 43 Ohio St. 332, 334, 1 N.E. 22, 23 (1885) ("The rule is well settled that intoxication is not a justification or an excuse for crime. . . . But in many cases evidence of intoxication is admissible with a view to the question whether a crime has been committed; . . . As [mental state], in such case, is of the essence of the offense, it is possible that in proving intoxication you go far to prove that no offense was committed").

Courts across the country agreed that where a subjective mental state was an element of the crime to be proved, the defense must be permitted to show, by reference to intoxication, the absence of that element. One court commented that it seemed "incontrovertible and to be universally applicable" that "where the nature and essence of the crime are made by law to depend upon the peculiar state and condition of the criminal's mind at the time with reference to the act done, drunkenness may be a proper subject for the consideration of the jury, not to excuse or mitigate the offence but to show that it was not committed." *People v. Robinson*, 2 Park. Crim. 235, 306 (N.Y. Sup. Ct. 1855).

With similar reasoning, the Montana Supreme Court recognized the incompatibility of a jury instruction pursuant to §45-2-203 in conjunction with the legislature's decision to require a mental state of "purposely" or "knowingly" for deliberate homicide. It held that intoxication is relevant to formation of the requisite mental state. Unless a defendant is proved beyond a reasonable doubt to have possessed the requisite mental state, he did not commit the offense. Elimination of a critical category of defense evidence precludes a defendant from effectively rebutting the mental-state element, while simultaneously shielding the State from the effort of proving the requisite mental state in the face of negating evidence. It was this effect on the adversarial process that persuaded the Montana Supreme Court that the disallowance was unconstitutional.

The Due Process Clause protects those "principle[s] of justice so rooted in the traditions and conscience of our people as to be ranked as fundamental." At the time the Fourteenth Amendment was ratified, the common-law rule on consideration of intoxication evidence was in flux. The Court argues that rejection of the historical rule in the 19th century simply does not establish that the "new common law" rule is a principle of procedure so "deeply rooted" as to be ranked "fundamental." But to determine whether a fundamental principle of justice has been violated here, we cannot consider only the historical disallowance of intoxication evidence, but must also consider the "fundamental principle" that a defendant has a right to a fair opportunity to put forward his defense, in adversarial testing where the State must prove the elements of the offense beyond a reasonable doubt. As concepts of *mens rea* and burden of proof developed, these principles came into conflict, as the shift in the common law in the 19th century reflects.

III.

Justice Ginsburg concurs in the Court's judgment based on her determination that §45-2-203 amounts to a redefinition of the offense that renders evidence of voluntary intoxication irrelevant to proof of the requisite mental state. The concurrence emphasizes that States enjoy wide latitude in defining the elements of crimes and concludes that, "[c]omprehended as a measure redefining *mens rea*, § 45-2-203 encounters no constitutional shoal."

A state legislature certainly possesses the authority to define the offenses it wishes to punish. If the Montana legislature chose to redefine this offense so as to alter the requisite mental-state element, the due process problem presented in this case would not be at issue.

There is, however, no indication that such a "redefinition" occurred. Justice GINSBURG's reading of Montana law is plainly inconsistent with that given by the Montana Supreme Court, and therefore cannot provide a valid basis to uphold § 45-2-203's operation. "We are, of course, bound to accept the interpretation of [state] law by the highest court of the State." The Montana Supreme Court held that evidence of voluntary intoxication was relevant to the requisite mental state. 272 Mont. at 122, 900 P.2d at 265. And in summing up the court's holding, Justice Nelson's concurrence explains that while the legislature may enact the statutes it chooses, § 45-2-203 "effectively and impermissibly . . . lessens the burden of the State to prove beyond a reasonable doubt an essential element of the offense charged—the mental state element—by statutorily precluding the jury from considering the very evidence that might convince them that the State had not proven that element." The Montana Supreme Court's decision cannot be read consistently with a "redefinition" of the offense.

Because the management of criminal justice is within the province of the States, this Court is properly reluctant to interfere in the States' authority in these matters. Nevertheless, the Court must invalidate those rules that violate the requirements of due process. The Court acknowledges that a reduction of the State's burden through disallowance of exculpatory evidence is unconstitutional if it violates a principle of fairness. I believe that such a violation is present here. Montana's disallowance of consideration of voluntary-intoxication evidence removes too critical a category of relevant, exculpatory evidence from the adversarial process by prohibiting the defendant from making an essential argument and permitting the prosecution to benefit from its suppression. Montana's purpose is to increase the likelihood of conviction of a certain class of defendants, who might otherwise be able to prove that they did not satisfy a requisite element of the offense. The historical fact that this disallowance once existed at common law is not sufficient to save the statute today. I would affirm the judgment of the Montana Supreme Court.

Justice SOUTER, dissenting.

I have no doubt that a State may so define the mental element of an offense that evidence of a defendant's voluntary intoxication at the time of commission does not have exculpatory relevance and, to that extent, may be excluded without raising any issue of due process. I would have thought the statute at issue here (Mont. Code Ann. § 45-2-203 (1995)) had implicitly accomplished such a redefinition, but I read the opinion of the Supreme Court of Montana as indicating that it had no such effect, and I am bound by the state court's statement of its domestic law.

Even on the assumption that Montana's definitions of the purposeful and know-ing culpable mental states were untouched by § 45-2-203, so that voluntary intoxica-tion remains relevant to each, it is not a foregone conclusion that our cases preclude the State from declaring such intoxication evidence inadmissible. A State may typi-cally exclude even relevant and exculpatory evidence if it presents a valid justifica-tion for doing so. There may (or may not) be a valid justification to support a State's decision to exclude, rather than render irrelevant, evidence of a defendant's volun-tary intoxication. Montana has not endeavored, however, to advance an argument to that effect. Rather, the State has effectively restricted itself to advancing undoubt-edly sound reasons for defining the mental state element so as to make voluntary intoxication generally irrelevant (though its own Supreme Court has apparently said the legislature failed to do that) and to demonstrating that evidence of volun-tary intoxication was irrelevant at common law (a fact that goes part way, but not all the way, to answering the due process objection). In short, I read the State Supreme Court opinion as barring one interpretation that would leave the statutory scheme constitutional, while the State's failure to offer a justification for excluding relevant evidence leaves us unable to discern whether there may be a valid reason to support the statute as the State Supreme Court appears to view it. I therefore respectfully dissent from the Court's judgment.

I.

The plurality opinion convincingly demonstrates that when the Fourteenth Amendment's Due Process Clause was added to the Constitution in 1868, the com-mon law as it then stood either rejected the notion that voluntary intoxication might be exculpatory, or was at best in a state of flux on that issue. That is enough to show that Montana's rule that evidence of voluntary intoxication is inadmissible on the issue of culpable mental state contravenes no principle "so rooted in the traditions and conscience of our people," as they stood in 1868, "as to be ranked as fundamen-tal." But this is not the end of the due process enquiry. Justice Harlan's dissenting opinion in *Poe v. Ullman*, 367 U.S. 497 (1961), teaches that the "tradition" to which we are tethered "is a living thing."[1] What the historical practice does not rule out as inconsistent with "the concept of ordered liberty" must still pass muster as rational in today's world.

While I find no apparent constitutional reason why Montana could not render evidence of voluntary intoxication excludable as irrelevant by redefining "knowl-edge" and "purpose," as they apply to the mental state element of its substantive

---

1. "The balance of which I speak is the balance struck by this country, having regard to what history teaches are the traditions from which it developed as well as the traditions from which it broke. That tradition is a living thing. A decision of this Court which radically departs from it could not long survive, while a decision which builds on what has survived is likely to be sound. No formula could serve as a substitute, in this area, for judgment and restraint." *Poe v. Ullman*, 367 U.S. at 542 (Harlan, J., dissenting).

offenses, or by making some other provision for mental state,[2] I do not believe that I am free to conclude that Montana has done so here. Our view of state law is limited by its interpretation in the State's highest court, and I am not able to square the State Supreme Court's opinion in this case with the position advanced by the State here (and supported by the United States, as *amicus curiae*), that Montana's legislature changed the definition of culpable mental states when it enacted § 45-2-203.

A second possible (although by no means certain) option may also be open. Even under a definition of the mental state element that would treat evidence of voluntary intoxication as relevant and exculpatory, the exclusion of such evidence is typically permissible so long as a State presents a "'valid' reason," to justify keeping it out. Hence, I do not rule out the possibility of justifying exclusion of relevant intoxication evidence in a case like this. At the least, there may be reasons beyond those actually advanced by Montana that might have induced a state to reject its prior law freely admitting intoxication evidence going to mental state.

A State (though not necessarily Montana) might, for example, argue that admitting intoxication evidence on the issue of culpable mental state but not on a defense of incapacity (as to which it is widely assumed to be excludable as generally irrelevant[3]) would be irrational since both capacity to obey the law and purpose to accomplish a criminal result presuppose volitional ability. *See* Model Penal Code § 4.01 ("A person is not responsible for criminal conduct if at the time of such conduct as a result of mental disease or defect he lacks substantial capacity . . . to conform his conduct to the requirements of law") and Model Penal Code § 2.02(2)(a)(i) ("A person acts purposely with respect to a material element of an offense when . . . it is his conscious object to engage in conduct of that nature or to cause such a result"). And quite apart from any technical irrationality, a State might think that admitting the evidence in question on culpable mental state but not capacity (when each was a jury issue in a given case) would raise too high a risk of juror confusion. *See* Brief for State of Hawaii et al. as *Amici Curiae* ("[U]se of [intoxication] evidence runs an unacceptable risk of potential manipulation by defendants and [will lead to] confusion of juries, who may not adequately appreciate that intoxication evidence is to be used for the question of mental state, not for purposes of showing an excuse"). While Thomas Reed Powell reportedly suggested that "learning to think like a lawyer is when you learn to think about one thing that is connected to another

2. *See State v. Souza*, 72 Haw. 246, 249, 813 P.2d 1384, 1386 (1991) ("The legislature was entitled to redefine the *mens rea* element of crimes and to exclude evidence of voluntary intoxication to negate state of mind").

3. *See* American Law Institute, Model Penal Code § 2.08(4) (1985), which deems intoxication relevant for this purpose only where by reason of "pathological intoxication" an "actor at the time of his conduct lacks substantial capacity . . . to conform his conduct to the requirements of law." The Model Penal Code further defines "pathological intoxication" as "intoxication grossly excessive in degree, given the amount of the intoxicant, to which the actor does not know he is susceptible." *Id.* § 2.08(5)(c).

without thinking about the other thing it is connected to," Teachout, *Sentimental Metaphors*, 34 UCLA L. Rev. 537, 545 (1986), a State might argue that its law should be structured on the assumption that its jurors typically will not suffer from this facility.[4]

Quite apart from the fact that Montana has made no such arguments for justification here, however, I am not at all sure why such arguments would go any further than justifying redefinition of mental states (the first option above). I do not understand why they would justify the state in cutting the conceptual corner by leaving the definitions of culpable mental states untouched but excluding evidence relevant to this proof. Absent a convincing argument for cutting that corner, *Chambers* and the like constrain us to hold the current Montana statute unconstitutional. I therefore respectfully dissent.

Justice BREYER, with whom Justice STEVENS joins, dissenting.

I join Justice O'CONNOR's dissent. As the dissent says, and as Justice SOUTER agrees, the Montana Supreme Court did not understand Montana's statute to have redefined the mental element of deliberate homicide. In my view, however, this circumstance is not simply happenstance or a technical matter that deprives us of the power to uphold that statute. To have read the statute differently—to treat it as if it had redefined the mental element—would produce anomalous results. A statute that makes voluntary intoxication the legal equivalent of purpose or knowledge *but only where external circumstances would establish purpose or knowledge in the absence of intoxication*, is a statute that turns guilt or innocence not upon state of mind, but upon irrelevant external circumstances. An intoxicated driver stopped at an intersection who unknowingly accelerated into a pedestrian would likely be found guilty, for a jury unaware of intoxication would likely infer knowledge or purpose. An identically intoxicated driver racing along a highway who unknowingly sideswiped another car would likely be found innocent, for a jury unaware of intoxication would likely infer negligence. Why would a legislature want to write a statute that draws such a distinction, upon which a sentence of life imprisonment, or death, may turn? If the legislature wanted to equate voluntary intoxication, knowledge, and purpose, why would it not write a statute that plainly says so, instead of doing so in a roundabout manner that would affect, in dramatically different ways, those whose minds, deeds, and consequences seem identical? I would reserve the question of whether or not such a hypothetical statute might exceed constitutional limits.

---

4. Teachout notes that Powell acknowledged that this concept was not explicitly described in his essay entitled *A Comment on Professor Sabine's "Pragmatic Approach to Politics,"* 81 POL. SCI. Q. 52, 59 (1966), but in a letter wrote:

> If you think you can think about a thing that is hitched to other things without thinking about the things that it is hitched to, then you have a legal mind.

Quoted in Teachout, *Sentimental Metaphors*, 34 UCLA L. Rev. at 545, n.17.

Questions and Notes

1. Assume that you are an attorney for a state legislature that wants to know if it is constitutionally free to eliminate the right to introduce evidence of intoxication to negate specific intent (or knowledge or purpose). What would you advise the legislature? Why?

2. With which opinion would you have agreed? Why?

Chapter 11

Infancy

At early common law, there were a few rules governing infancy. A boy under 14 was conclusively presumed incapable of rape. For other crimes, such as murder, a child under seven was conclusively presumed incapable. Between 7 and 14, there was a rebuttable presumption of incompetence, which became gradually weaker as the child approached 14. Today, most states treat juveniles under 18 as delinquents rather than criminals, and try them in a special court. (*See, e.g., MTS*, Chapter 4, *supra*). However, there are circumstances in which, because of the severity of the crime or other circumstances, a juvenile will be tried in adult court. In *JFB*, *Maddox*, and *Kocher*, we explore the thinking of three courts, acting under somewhat different statutes.

J.F.B. v. State
729 So. 2d 355 (Ala. Crim. App. 1998)

McMILLAN, Judge.

The appellant, J.F.B., was charged with murder made capital because it was committed during a robbery; two counts of first-degree robbery; harassment; and disorderly conduct. He appeals from the juvenile court's order transferring him to circuit court to be prosecuted as an adult.

I.

There was sufficient evidence presented at the transfer hearing to support the juvenile court's finding of probable cause that the appellant committed the alleged acts. At the hearing Antonio Andrade testified that three masked men, one the same height of the appellant and two taller men, entered his house and demanded money from Andrade and his two sons. Andrade had $80 and one of his sons had $800. Andrade identified the appellant as the assailant who shot and killed his son. This evidence was sufficient to support a finding of probable cause that the appellant had committed the offenses of capital murder and robbery. Billy Hooper, the assistant principal at Fort Payne High School, testified at the transfer hearing that the appellant ranted, raved, and cursed at him when Hooper told him to leave the stadium during a fight at a high school football game. Officer Chris Graham also testified that, during the same incident, the appellant got louder and reached back to swing at him when he told him to leave. The testimony of Hooper and Graham was sufficient to show that the appellant had probably committed harassment and disorderly conduct. The State is not required to show at the transfer hearing beyond a reasonable doubt that the defendant committed the act, but rather that "a reasonable man would believe the crime occurred and that the defendant committed it." Andrade's identification of the appellant was sufficient to supply probable cause to believe that the appellant committed the capital murder.

During the dispositional phase, the juvenile court judge must examine the totality of the circumstances to determine whether a transfer is in the best interest of the child or the public. *Williams v. State*, 494 So. 2d 887, 890 (Ala. Cr. App. 1986). Included in this analysis is a review of the six factors listed in § 12-15-34(d), Ala. Code 1975:

> (1) The nature of the present alleged offense.
>
> (2) The extent and nature of the prior delinquency record of the child.
>
> (3) The nature of past treatment efforts and the nature of the response of the child to the effort.
>
> (4) Demeanor.
>
> (5) The extent and nature of the physical and mental maturity of the child.
>
> (6) The interests of the community and of the child requiring that the child be placed under legal restraint or discipline.

Section 12-15-34(d), however, does not limit the inquiry to the above factors but allows the juvenile court judge also to consider other relevant factors. This Court will overturn the juvenile court judge's decision on a transfer order only if it is "clearly erroneous"; that is, if the decision is unsupported by any rational basis and is arbitrary and capricious.

The juvenile court judge's decision to transfer the appellant for criminal prosecution as an adult in this case was not arbitrary and capricious. The appellant concedes that the nature of the present offenses is very serious, and correctly states that a transfer decision cannot be based solely upon the nature of the offense. However, the court's transfer order reveals that it considered more than merely the nature of the offense:

> "[T]he Court having considered all motions by the State and defense counsel, having sworn witnesses and heard the evidence presented and having considered all the relevant factors, makes the following findings relative to the said juvenile:
>
> (1) He was 15 years of age in the cases presented this date.
>
> (2) He is charged with the offense(s) of Disorderly Conduct; Harassment; Capital Murder; Robbery, 1st degree and Robbery, 1st degree.
>
> (3) There are no reasonable grounds to believe that said juvenile is committable to an institution or agency for the mentally retarded or the mentally ill.

(4) The said juvenile cannot be properly disciplined under juvenile law and it would be in the best interest of the community that he be placed under legal restraint and discipline.

(5) There is probable cause for believing the allegations of the petition are true and correct.

In arriving at these findings, the juvenile court considered the appellant's prior juvenile record, including one adjudication of delinquency in Georgia. The appellant argues that the court improperly considered other charges in Georgia in which he was not adjudicated delinquent. Only those charges in which the defendant is adjudicated delinquent can be considered as part of the "prior delinquency record of the child." However, the appellant did not object to the admission into evidence of the record of these charges and there is no indication that the juvenile court placed undue weight on them. There was conflicting evidence regarding the appellant's demeanor, but evidence that he had threatened school and law enforcement officials was sufficient to find that his negative demeanor supported a finding that a transfer was warranted. The juvenile court judge's comments at the conclusion of the transfer hearing and at the hearing on the motion for a new trial indicate that the judge placed heavy weight on the appellant's failure to take advantage of past treatment opportunities. The Georgia charges that did not result in adjudications of delinquency but did result in the appellant's having to serve in "boot camp", being committed to Georgia's Department of Youth Services, and being placed on probation, would be relevant to this issue. Furthermore, the juvenile court judge explicitly stated that he was concerned about the appellant's prior failure to appear in court, which failure occurred at the precise time the crimes involved in the present case were committed. Section 12-15-34(d) does not require that any certain weight be placed on any given factor, but that each case be considered based upon its own individual circumstances. We find that the juvenile court judge's determination that the appellant be transferred for criminal prosecution as an adult was not arbitrary and capricious and is due to be affirmed.

Questions and Notes

1. The standards for transfer, nicely spelled out in *JFB*, are fairly typical. Are there any that seem inappropriate to you?

2. Review *MTS* (Chapter 4, *supra*). Assuming that New Jersey law is similar to Alabama law, should MTS have been tried as a juvenile (as he was) or as an adult?

3. Would it have been an abuse of discretion *not* to try JFB as an adult?

4. Where do you think the presumption lies? What should be sufficient to rebut it?

5. Is it better that the question be governed by flexible standards, or more definite rules? Why?

6. In *Maddox*, we see a court split over the appropriate test.

Maddox v. State

931 S.W.2d 438 (Ark. 1996)

Brown, Justice.

This is a juvenile-transfer case. On October 16, 1995, an information was filed charging appellant Kristy Maddox with criminal mischief in the first degree, a Class C felony. She was accused of intentionally throwing a Mountain Dew bottle from a moving vehicle and striking the victim's automobile, causing damage in excess of $500. Maddox, who was 17 years old at the time of the alleged incident, and who turned 18 on February 4, 1996, moved to have the charge transferred to juvenile court. Her motion was denied. She now appeals that denial.

Only two witnesses testified at the juvenile-transfer hearing. Pamela Maddox, the appellant's mother, related to the court that at the time of the hearing, Maddox was living with her and assisting around the house by doing chores and taking care of her younger siblings. She testified that Maddox was not currently in high school, but that she was working on her G.E.D. and planned to attend college in the Fall. She stated that she had a good relationship with her daughter, but that she did have to call the police on one occasion for an undisclosed "family disturbance." She and the prosecutor agreed that Maddox had no prior criminal history.

Sherry Lynn Kinnamon, the victim, was called as a witness by the prosecution. She testified that on April 20, 1995, she was driving her grandparents from Huntsville to the VA Hospital in Fayetteville when she noticed a red pick-up truck following very closely behind her. She stated that she tapped her brakes a few times to get the driver's attention and slowed so that the truck could pass, but that the driver would not do so. Even when given a straight stretch of road with no cars approaching, the driver of the truck would not pass her. She explained that the driver instead pulled alongside her car several times, and that the driver and two passengers would simply look at her, then drop back behind her car, where they made obscene gestures. She stated that she slowed her car to two-miles-an-hour so that the truck would pass, but that it again would not. Finally, she accelerated, and the truck pulled alongside her car. Maddox hung out of the window on the passenger's side of the truck, held by her belt loops. She was holding a full glass bottle of Mountain Dew, and she and the other occupants of the truck were yelling obscenities at Kinnamon. Kinnamon testified that Maddox then intentionally threw the glass bottle at her car. It dented the front of the hood and cracked the windshield. Kinnamon said that after she regained her composure, she pursued the truck and got its license plate number. No one was injured, but she estimated that the damage to her car was about $800.

The trial court denied the motion to transfer after determining that Maddox's intentional throwing of the Mountain Dew bottle at Kinnamon's car was not only a serious act but a violent one. The court emphasized the harassing nature of the episode and referred to an incident in Oklahoma where a person was killed because an object had been thrown at his vehicle. The court noted that Maddox had no prior criminal record and mentioned that there had been no evidence introduced, one way or the other, with regard to her prospects for rehabilitation.

Maddox claims in her appeal that the trial court clearly erred in retaining jurisdiction of this matter. The Arkansas Juvenile Code provides that the circuit court shall consider the following factors in determining whether to retain jurisdiction or transfer a case to juvenile court:

1) The seriousness of the offense, and whether violence was employed by the juvenile in the commission of the offense;

2) Whether the offense is part of a repetitive pattern of adjudicated offenses which would lead to the determination that the juvenile is beyond rehabilitation under existing rehabilitation programs, as evidenced by past efforts to treat and rehabilitate the juvenile and the response to such efforts; and

3) The prior history, character traits, mental maturity, and any other factor which reflects upon the juvenile's prospects for rehabilitation.

Maddox asserts a twofold challenge to the denial of her motion to transfer. She first urges that the trial court did not recognize the relevance of her mother's testimony and emphasizes that her mother presented sufficient evidence of her character traits to support a positive finding on the issue of her prospects for rehabilitation. She further argues that the charge of criminal mischief is a crime against property which the trial court improperly characterized as "violent" in order to keep the matter in circuit court.

The State responds that criminal mischief is a Class C felony that satisfies the seriousness criterion for purposes of section 9-27-318(e) and that violence was employed in the commission of this offense. The State also questions whether the mother's testimony was really relevant to the criterion of rehabilitation, when there was no showing that Maddox was remorseful or willing to accept responsibility for her actions. Finally, the State contends that the fact Maddox was 18 at the time of her hearing is sufficient, standing alone, to affirm the trial court's ruling.

In recent years, this court has fashioned the following rule in juvenile-transfer cases:

The use of violence in the commission of a serious offense is a factor sufficient in and of itself for a circuit court to retain jurisdiction of a juvenile's case, but the commission of a serious offense without the use of violence is not sufficient grounds to deny the transfer.

In *Green v. State*, this court noted that manslaughter, a Class C felony, was a serious offense: "No doubt the offense charged is serious. Manslaughter is a class C felony. If [the appellant] were convicted he would be sentenced to imprisonment for not less than three nor more than ten years." Criminal mischief in the first degree is also a Class C felony, and it satisfies the seriousness requirement.

The question we next address is whether the trial court was correct in its finding that Maddox committed a violent act. We agree with the trial court that she did.

This is not a case where a juvenile merely committed a crime against property such as we had in *Pennington v. State*, 305 Ark. 312, 807 S.W.2d 660 (1991). In *Pennington*, two 17-year-olds broke about 30 tombstones in a cemetery and were charged with criminal mischief. The circuit court refused to transfer the cases to juvenile court, and we reversed on the basis that the trial court gave too much deference to the prosecutor, after the court acknowledged that violence was not embraced in the young men's actions.

In the instant case, the trial court noted that these facts would likely support an aggravated assault charge as well as a charge of criminal mischief. This court has observed that the crime of aggravated assault is not only serious, but that no violence beyond that necessary to commit aggravated assault is necessary to meet the requirement. We conclude that a violent act lies at the core of the alleged crime in the instant case—the willful throwing of a glass bottle at a moving vehicle containing three passengers, as testified to by Kinnamon. These facts are sufficient to sustain a refusal to transfer in our judgment.

There is, too, the fact that Maddox has now turned 18. Young people over age 18 can no longer be committed to the Division of Youth Services for rehabilitation unless they are already committed at the time they turn 18. The fact that Maddox cannot now be committed to the Division of Youth Services is highly relevant to her prospects for rehabilitation as a juvenile and is a factor that this court considers important in reviewing a trial court's denial of a motion to transfer. This circumstance lends additional support to an affirmance.

Affirmed.

ROAF, J., dissents. [*See* dissenting opinion of Justice Roaf in *Butler v. State*.]

Butler v. State

922 S.W.2d 685 (Ark. 1996)

[The opinion of the Court has been omitted.]

ROAF, Justice, dissenting.

In 1989, the Arkansas General Assembly enacted Act 273 of 1989, which became known as the Arkansas Juvenile Code of 1989. A declaration of purpose for this legislation is found at Ark. Code Ann. § 9-27-302. It is important in the context of this appeal and warrants our reconsideration:

> This subchapter shall be *liberally construed* to the end that its purposes may be carried out:
>
> > (1) To assure that *all juveniles brought to the attention of the courts receive the guidance, care and control, preferably in each juvenile's own home, which will best serve the emotional, mental, and physical welfare of the juvenile and the best interests of the state;*
> >
> > (2) To preserve and strengthen the juvenile's family ties whenever possible, removing him from the custody of his parents only when his

welfare or the safety and protection of the public cannot adequately be safeguarded without such removal; and, when the juvenile is removed nearly as possible equivalent to that which should have been given by his parents; and to assure, in all cases in which a juvenile must be permanently removed from the custody of his parents, that the juvenile be placed in an approved family home and be made a member of the family by adoption;

(3) To protect society more effectively *by substituting for retributive punishment, whenever possible, methods of offender rehabilitation and rehabilitative restitution*, recognizing that the application of sanctions which are consistent with the seriousness of the offense is appropriate in all cases;

(4) To provide means through which the provisions of this subchapter are executed and enforced and in which *the parties are assured a fair hearing and their constitutional and other legal rights recognized and enforced.*

Since 1991, this court has been called upon numerous times to interpret the provisions of the juvenile code dealing with how we treat youth who are charged with criminal offenses. The General Assembly has in turn had the opportunity on several occasions to react to our holdings. I submit that this court and the General Assembly have so woefully failed to consider a significant portion of the stated purposes underpinning the juvenile code that this language has become meaningless.

We have neither liberally construed the statute to the benefit of the emotional, mental, and physical welfare of the juveniles, nor even for the best interests of the state. We have failed to insure that methods of rehabilitation and restitution are substituted wherever possible, for retributive punishment, and we have surely failed to provide that juveniles are assured fair hearings and that their constitutional and other rights provided by this statute are uniformly recognized and enforced. We share this responsibility equally with our elected state representatives.

Today, we once again affirm a trial court's refusal to transfer a criminal case involving a juvenile to juvenile court. The trial court's ruling, and our affirmance, were foregone conclusions because of the prior holdings of this court, because of the weight of stare decisis, and because of the legislature's failure to revisit this legislation in light of our holdings. Children between the ages of 14 and 17 years are paying the price for our failures. We cannot even take comfort in the notion that the best interests of the state are being served, for many of these juveniles will return to our midst as adults, and the opportunity to use our best efforts to rehabilitate, guide and care for them will have been lost.

The landmark case which has led us down this path is, of course, *Walker v. State*, 304 Ark. 393, 803 S.W.2d 502 (1991). In *Walker*, by a 4 to 3 decision, this court reached several significant holdings which have been repeatedly revowed and reaffirmed since *Walker*—that a juvenile movant has the burden of proof when seeking to transfer a case from circuit court to juvenile court—that the trial court need not give equal weight to the three factors that the statute *directs* it to consider in determining whether to transfer a case—that the prosecutor is not even required to introduce proof on each of the three factors that the trial court is *directed* to consider—that the criminal information alone can provide a sufficient basis for the denial of a transfer to juvenile court—that a trial court does not have to make findings of fact or provide a rationale for its decision in a juvenile transfer proceeding.

We have also held that juveniles "ultimately" charged and tried in circuit court are subject to the procedures prescribed for adults, and are not afforded the protections provided by the juvenile code, such as the requirement of parental consent to a waiver of right to counsel.

I am not unmindful of the fact that since 1991, the general assembly has twice amended Ark. Code Ann. § 9-27-318, which deals with waiver and transfer to circuit court, each time to the detriment of juvenile defendants. However, they have not seen fit to amend the stated purposes for the juvenile code. I suggest that they do so at the next opportunity. Until then, our decisions and their inaction are in direct conflict with these purposes.

I dissent.

Questions and Notes

1. Should Maddox have been tried as an adult? Why or why not?

2. Are you persuaded by the distinction attempted between *Maddox* and *Pennington*? If the *Pennington* defendants were 18 at the time of trial, should they be able to get off with no punishment (no adult punishment because the offense was committed as a juvenile, and no adult punishment because juvenile at time acts were committed)?

3. Justice Roaf's *Butler* dissent involved a 15-year-old. Do you think that the statute as written, and construed as he would like it, would be a good idea or a bad idea? Explain.

4. We conclude this section with *Commonwealth v. Kocher*, a case in which age was once again a factor. But this time, we deal with a nine-year-old.

Commonwealth v. Kocher

602 A.2d 1308 (Pa. 1992)

Nix, Chief Justice.

The issue before us is whether the Court of Common Pleas abused its discretion in denying the petition of a nine-year old accused of murder to transfer his case to the juvenile court pursuant to Section 6322(a) of the Juvenile Act, 42 Pa. C.S. § 6322.

The facts of this case require recitation. On the morning of March 6, 1989, a snow holiday from school, Jessica Ann Carr was fatally shot while riding as a passenger on a snowmobile owned by Mr. and Mrs. Richard Ratti, neighbors of the petitioner. On that morning, petitioner had been playing Nintendo at the Rattis' home but stopped playing when Mr. Ratti forbade the children to play because the children had made a mess in the kitchen. Some children, the victim included, started riding snowmobiles but the petitioner returned home. At some point after returning home the petitioner procured the key to his father's locked gun cabinet and removed a hunting rifle equipped with a scope. He loaded the weapon with ammunition, opened a window, removed the screen, and pointed the gun outside. The gun discharged, striking Jessica Ann Carr in the back and fatally wounding her. The scope of the rifle struck the petitioner's forehead and left a visible wound. He returned the rifle to the gun cabinet and hid the empty shell casing.

On March 8, 1989, the petitioner was arrested and charged with criminal homicide in the Court of Common Pleas of Monroe County. After being arraigned, he was released on bail to the custody of his parents.

Petitioner petitioned the court for transfer of the matter to juvenile court pursuant to Section 6322 of the Juvenile Act. The Commonwealth ordered a psychiatric evaluation of the petitioner. The Court of Common Pleas heard testimony on April 20 and 21 and May 25 and 26, 1989. Dr. Harris Rabinowich, a board certified child psychiatrist who had examined the petitioner at the state-ordered evaluation, testified on behalf of the Commonwealth. Psychiatrists Robert Sadoff, M.D., and Marsha Turnberg, M.D., and psychologist Robert G. Chupella, testified on behalf of the petitioner. On June 23, 1989, the Court of Common Pleas rejected petitioner's transfer request.

On July 29 and August 1, 1989, a preliminary hearing was held in which petitioner was bound over for trial on an open charge of criminal homicide, two counts of aggravated assault, and one count of recklessly endangering another person. Petitioner filed a Petition for Review of the Transfer Decision with the Superior Court of Pennsylvania which was denied. In the petition before this Court, petitioner raises six arguments. We need only address petitioner's argument that the lower court's construction of the Juvenile Act creates unreasonable criteria for the transfer of a juvenile from criminal court to juvenile court.[2]

---

2. The other arguments raised by petitioner are:
a. The public policy of the Commonwealth of Pennsylvania and of the United States opposes nine-year-old children being criminally prosecuted for murder.
b. Murder requires a malicious intent which is a uniquely mature, adult moral and mental state not achievable by nine-year olds.
c. In establishing a minimum age of ten for delinquency jurisdiction in Juvenile Court, the Pennsylvania Juvenile Act reflects an implicit legislative intent to establish a minimum age of ten for murder jurisdiction in Criminal Court.
d. Subjecting a nine-year-old to the most severe of adult punishments resulting from a criminal court conviction of murder would be cruel and unusual punishment under the constitutions of Pennsylvania and the United States.
e. The decision of the lower court is not supported by the record.

Because we remand the case for a determination of whether petitioner is amenable to treatment, supervision, and rehabilitation under the Juvenile Act, we need not address the other issues raised by petitioner.

In reviewing the exercise of discretion by the Court of Common Pleas, we are guided by precedent which established that

> [a]n abuse of discretion is not merely an error of judgment, but if in reaching a conclusion the law is overridden or misapplied, or the judgment exercised is manifestly unreasonable or the result of partiality, prejudice, bias, or ill-will as shown by the evidence or the record, discretion is abused.

Applying this test to the instant case, we hold that the trial court abused its discretion when applying the criteria under Section 6355 of the Juvenile Act.

The factors to be considered by the criminal court for transfer are delineated in the following section of the Pennsylvania Juvenile Act:

§ 6355. Transfer of criminal proceedings

(a) General Rule

(4) The court finds:

(iii) that there are reasonable grounds to believe all the following:

(A) that the child is not amenable to treatment, supervision or rehabilitation as a juvenile through available facilities, even though there may not have been a prior adjudication of delinquency. In determining this the court shall consider the following factors:

Age.

Mental capacity.

Maturity.

The degree of criminal sophistication exhibited by the child.

Previous records, if any.

The nature and extent of any prior delinquent history, including the success or failure of any previous attempts by the Juvenile Court to rehabilitate the child.

Whether the child can be rehabilitated prior to the expiration of the Juvenile Court jurisdiction.

Probation or institutional reports, if any.

Any other relevant factor.

The trial court applied these criteria to the facts of the case. We are here called upon to assess the court's application of these provisions.

The Court of Common Pleas found Cameron Kocher to be a normal fourth grader of above-average intelligence with an above-average school record. He was a good student who exhibited occasional inattentiveness. He related well to others in his school, community, and church, and he possessed an average level of maturity and physical development. His home life was stable, close-knit, and supportive. The child exhibited no physical, mental, emotional, or behavioral disorders and had no previous criminal or delinquent history. The trial court considered these factors favorable to his application for transfer.

Conversely, the trial court's analysis of the nature of the crime and the level of criminal sophistication weighed against the petitioner's petition for transfer. When he fired the rifle, he endangered the driver of the snowmobile and the other children playing in the area. His manipulation of the gun and the window, and his dishonesty about the cut on his forehead to his parents and police reflected an adult level of criminal sophistication and knowledge. He appeared to show no remorse for the crime. The petitioner was quoted as saying, "If you don't think about it, you won't be sad," to one of the neighbors' children as the victim lay dying in the Rattis' home. These factors weighed heavily against the petitioner's petition for transfer.

The trial court addressed the issue of the petitioner's capacity to commit the crime in four distinct contexts: first, the overall mental capacity under Section 6355(a)(4)(iii)(A); second, the common law rebuttable presumption that children between the ages of 7 and 14 are not capable of forming the requisite criminal intent to commit a crime; third, the capacity of the child to stand trial competently; and fourth, the petitioner's capability of forming the specific intent to commit murder.

Dr. Rabinowich, a witness for the Commonwealth, testified that the child had the capacity to commit crime, and moreover, specifically to commit murder. He also opined that the petitioner was competent to stand trial. The other doctors all testified that petitioner was "blocking" the causal connection between his actions and the victim's death.

Dr. Sadoff, for the defense, testified that he was not able to render an opinion on whether the petitioner could form the intent to kill. Drs. Chupella and Turnberg testified that petitioner could not. The trial court heard the testimony and ruled that Cameron Kocher was competent to stand trial as an adult, and capable of forming the intent to kill.

The court did not specifically address the common law presumption that children under the age of 14 are not capable of forming the criminal intent necessary to commit a crime. Nonetheless, the court held that petitioner was capable of forming the intent to commit murder.

The Court of Common Pleas then addressed the petitioner's claim that he was amenable to treatment, supervision, and rehabilitation in the juvenile system because he was suffering from an anxiety disorder. The Court of Common Pleas found no merit in that argument. It held that the evidence was clear that the shooting caused the disorder (not vice versa) and that the petitioner was free from any disorder or defect at the time of the shooting. The court stated that if a disease, defect or disorder caused the underlying actions, only then would the child be amenable to treatment, supervision, and rehabilitation under the juvenile system. Conversely, it held that if the shooting was not caused by a defect or disorder, the case would not be transferred. The trial judge stated,

> [I]n short, we believe that there must be some underlying disease or disorder which is causally connected to the homicide in order for transfer to be justified under current law. Thus, since the [petitioner] did not suffer from any defect or impairment at or before the time of the shooting, he has failed to show that he is amenable to treatment, supervision or rehabilitation within the meaning of the law regarding transfer.

Petitioner argues that the Court of Common Pleas erroneously required him to prove that a mental disease or defect caused the killing in order to demonstrate that he is amenable to treatment, supervision, and rehabilitation under the juvenile system. We agree with the petitioner.

In its analysis of the transfer provision of the Juvenile Act, the Court of Common Pleas determined that no child may be transferred from adult criminal court to juvenile proceedings unless he suffers from some disorder or defect which caused the child to commit the murder. Restated, the court held that a mental defect or disorder must cause the criminal action. That requirement contravenes the legislative intent of the amendments to the Juvenile Act that allow transfer of a murder case from criminal to juvenile proceedings. The plain language of the Juvenile Act requires the court to determine that the child is "amenable to treatment, supervision or rehabilitation as a juvenile through available facilities. . . . In determining this, the court shall consider [several] factors. . . ." The trial court's interpretation of the Juvenile Act precludes the weighing of any factors to determine amenability once the court establishes that no disease or defect caused the killing. This contradicts Sections 6355 and 6322, most recently amended in 1986, which allow the child to prove amenability and proscribe the standards to be used in making that determination as those in Section 6355(a)(4)(iii)(A). This particular clause contains no reference to a mental disease or defect.

Our holding does not prohibit discussion of the juvenile's mental state both at the time of the killing and at the time of the transfer petition.

The Court of Common Pleas in its discretion may find that a behavioral disorder is a factor to be considered in determining whether the child is amenable to treatment now; it may also find that a sound mind devoid of any disease or defect at the time of the murder is a factor weighing against transfer of the case to juvenile court. But to find that a lack of mental disorder is dispositive of the entire amenability question is to distort the clear legislative scheme. We therefore hold that the Court of Common Pleas abused its discretion in its denial of petitioner's petition for transfer.

Accordingly, the Order of the Court of Common Pleas is vacated and the matter is remanded for proceedings consistent with this opinion.

FLAHERTY, Justice, concurring.

I join the well reasoned opinion of the majority, but would go further and express that the public policy of Pennsylvania does not allow the criminal prosecution of a nine-year old child for murder. That it was attempted in this instance shocks my conscience.

CAPPY, J., joins this concurring opinion.

PAPADAKOS, Justice, concurring.

It is an understatement to say that this is a difficult case. But it has also often been said that hard cases make bad law. The Chief Justice has written for the majority in a dispassionate way, highlighting the law as expressed by the legislature, and I join in that opinion.

Some of our colleagues, however, cry for the recognition of a public policy that children of the age of nine years and under (how about 10 or 11 or 12 years of age, etc.?) must not be treated as murderers and must not be tried as murderers under any circumstances. Perhaps they are right. But that is a matter better left to the Legislature.

It seems to me that the concurring justices are engaging in oxymoronic dialogue in this case because they do not really agree with the majority opinion or its rationale. On the one hand, they say that a nine-year-old killer should not be tried as an adult killer, yet, on the other hand, by joining the majority opinion they accept the fact as proved by the murderer's own statements and the opinions of the doctors who examined him that he knew exactly what he was doing and they are content to remand to the trial judge to determine in a proper analysis whether this child should be treated as a juvenile or an adult.

The Chief Justice, in the absence of a public policy statement by us or the legislature, concludes for the majority that this matter be remanded to the trial judge to determine, within the parameters of the Juvenile Act, whether this nine-year-old is amenable to treatment, supervision and rehabilitation. But if the propriety of trying a nine-year-old for murder is in doubt then why waste everyone's time by a remand which will only raise more questions. What happens if the trial judge properly concludes that this nine-year-old is not amenable to treatment, supervision and rehabilitation? Do we then try him as an adult for murder of the first degree? And if he is convicted, do we give him the death penalty or mandatory life imprisonment and keep him incarcerated for the next 50, 60 or 70 years or more?

I do not agree with the concurring justices in their attempt to legislate in this matter in the guise of expounding public policy. The law is presently clear and we must apply it. If public policy should be otherwise, then let the legislature come to grips with the problem and change the statute.

LARSEN, Justice, dissenting.

I vigorously and emphatically dissent. The trial judge herein was eminently correct in his interpretation and application of the Juvenile Act, 42 Pa. C.S.A.

§§ 6301–6365, and made a courageous decision that, no doubt, flies in the face of the view taken of the issue by many citizens of this Commonwealth. Whether or not we *personally* find it "shocking" to try a nine-year-old child on a charge of murder in criminal court, this Court does not have the authority to rewrite a statute duly enacted by the Legislature.

Mr. Justice Flaherty, in his concurring opinion, states that it is not the public policy of this Commonwealth to criminally prosecute nine-year-old children for murder. This is simply not true. Murder is a heinous crime, and the Legislature is unquestionably cognizant of this fact. *All* crimes and *all* criminals were tried in "adult" criminal courts prior to the enactment of legislation early in this century requiring the special treatment of juveniles in our courts. There were no juvenile courts until the Legislature created juvenile courts. When the Legislature did so, it explicitly excluded murder from the jurisdiction of the juvenile courts but gave juveniles charged with murder the opportunity to transfer their cases from criminal court to juvenile court if certain prescribed conditions were met. Children were *always* subject to the jurisdiction of the criminal courts of this Commonwealth if they committed murder; in this respect, the law has not changed.

This nine-year-old defendant is not an innocent victim of the tragic instances of accidental shootings occurring in homes where firearms are handled carelessly. He had been repeatedly instructed in the safe handling of firearms, he had shot a rifle while at a gun club to which his parents belonged, and he had gone hunting with his father. The as yet uncontested evidence presented at the hearings on his petition for transfer show that the petitioner, Cameron R. Kocher, in an ill temper, took a key from where it was hidden in the base of a lamp, unlocked a gun cabinet, loaded the proper ammunition into a .35 caliber rifle equipped with a scope, unlocked a bedroom window, removed a screen from the window, and aimed the rifle at a seven-year-old girl, the daughter of two loving parents, as she played, blissfully unaware of the fate about to befall her, with other children in the snow. The rifle, which was in excellent working condition, had a heavy trigger pull and could not accidently discharge under normal circumstances.

The victim, whom the majority seems to forget ever existed, was killed by a bullet deliberately aimed and shot through her back, as she was riding as a passenger on a snowmobile. The bullet pierced her spine and right lung; she collapsed instantly, like a game animal shot by a skilled and experienced hunter and died on the operating table a short time thereafter. The petitioner carefully returned the rifle to the gun cabinet and hid the empty shell casing. When he returned to his neighbor's residence where the victim had been taken after the shooting, he exhibited no emotion on viewing her moribund body and proceeded to play Nintendo as if nothing were amiss. Further, the petitioner, who had received a gash in his forehead when the gun recoiled and the scope struck him, lied about the cause of the gash to his neighbors, his parents and the police. We are not dealing with a guileless boy here and a victimless crime. We do know for certain that an innocent life has been snuffed out with a bullet in the back, delivered by careful aim and followed by a well thought-out cover-up.

The trial court meticulously reviewed and discussed the evidence in light of *every* statutory factor and found that petitioner had proven few factors in favor of granting the transfer request. The petitioner's lack of previous misconduct and his age at the time of the offense were the only factors viewed in petitioner's favor. Significantly, age is only *one* statutory factor that the Legislature permits the courts to consider under section 6322(a) of the Juvenile Act.

Only after the trial court had considered all of the statutory factors, did the trial court consider petitioner's argument that he was suffering from an anxiety disorder that was amenable to treatment as a juvenile. It was solely in response to this assertion that the trial court discussed the meaning and interpretation of the "amenable to treatment" language of section 6355(a)(4)(iii)(A), and concluded that the Legislature could not have intended for defects or disorders arising *after* the commission of the offense to justify a transfer request. The majority herein errs in reading the trial court's opinion as setting forth an absolute criterion for transfer that overrides every other statutory factor, and, indeed, the majority is plain wrong when it implies that the trial court ignored the statutory factors.

Accordingly, I dissent and would affirm the decision of the Court of Common Pleas of Monroe County. Questions about the petitioner's competency to stand trial, capacity to form criminal intent, and possible dispositions in the event of a guilty verdict are all properly matters within the jurisdiction of the *criminal* court where the Legislature has, in its wisdom, bestowed jurisdiction.

Questions and Notes

1. Why did the Pennsylvania Supreme Court reverse the judgment of the Court of Common Pleas?

2. How should the Court of Common Pleas decide this case on remand? Is there more information that you might like to have before making your decision? What kind of information?

3. As between Justice Flaherty and Justice Larsen, which Justice has the better social policy?

4. How should the justice system deal with someone like Cameron Kocher?

Chapter 12

Duress and Necessity

A. Duress

Unlike intoxication, duress, when properly asserted, is a defense. It occurs when a person commits a crime because of extraordinary pressure put upon her by another person. The issues surrounding the defense concern the amount and nature of the pressure necessary to constitute the defense. As you read the cases, consider what factors militate for and against allowing the defense. Ideally, should the courts be generous or parsimonious in allowing the defense?

People v. Carradine
287 N.E.2d 670 (Ill. 1972)

UNDERWOOD, Chief Justice.

The Cook County circuit court found Georgia Carradine to be in direct contempt of court for her refusal to testify, and sentenced her to imprisonment for six months in the Cook County jail. She appealed directly here.

On September 11, 1969, Mrs. Carradine appeared before judge Downing as a State's witness in a criminal prosecution; she had witnessed a homicide and given a statement to an assistant State's Attorney. Having failed to respond to a subpoena, she was in court pursuant to a bench warrant, and after answering certain preliminary questions refused to testify further, indicating that she was in fear of her life and the lives of her children. Her refusal to testify, without claim of fifth-amendment privilege, despite warnings of the consequence of her action and the advice of court-appointed counsel, clearly obstructed the court in its administration of justice.

The more difficult question is the contemnor's request, predicated upon the extenuating circumstances surrounding her refusal to testify, that her punishment be reduced to the two weeks already spent in jail. Those circumstances include the fact that Mrs. Carradine had been separated from her husband for some four years, had six children aged 5 to 18 at home, and was supported by payments from her husband and supplemental welfare funds; that there seems little reason to doubt her refusal to testify resulted solely from her fear of harm to herself and her children if she testified against the defendants who apparently were members of the Blackstone Rangers, a youth gang; that she believed she had been "tricked" and lied to by the assistant State's Attorney to whom she had given a statement, because, as she stated, he told her she would not have to appear and testify and that, absent this assurance, she never would have given him the statement; that she did not believe the law enforcement authorities could protect her from the "Stones" for, as she put it:

> "THE WITNESS: Well, look, judge, I am going to tell you, I live in the middle of the slums, down in the slums. Where I live the police don't even come in there even if we call. I called the police one night about a fight. You'd think they were going to kill one another. But the police don't even come up in there where I live. So how are they going to protect me and my family when they don't even come up in the building where we live?"

Nor does she believe that relocating her family would solve the problems, for the "Stones" were "everywhere."

It is completely clear from the record that Mrs. Carradine understood the likely results of her refusal to testify and deliberately chose to incur imprisonment rather than expose herself and her family to what she considered to be the certainty of serious physical harm or death. The conscientious trial judge appointed counsel for her and patiently, clearly and repeatedly explained the situation, urging her to change her mind and reiterating the offers of protection and relocation; the proceedings were continued on several occasions in order that she might have an opportunity to reconsider her decision.

No useful purpose would be served by prolonged discussion. The reluctance of witnesses to testify is not an uncommon problem, although the circumstances here are particularly distressing. The contempt proceedings were conducted with eminent fairness, and, in our opinion, the judgment and sentence must be affirmed. The fundamental reason therefore was stated by the trial court: "... one of the problems that the Court has is that unless we receive the cooperation of the citizens who see certain alleged events take place these events are not going to be rooted out, nor are perpetrators of these acts going to be brought before the bar of justice unless citizens stand up to be counted, and I think this (fear) is not a valid reason for not testifying. If it's a valid reason then we might as well close the doors."

The judgment of the Cook County circuit court is affirmed.

Questions and Notes

1. What value is served by imprisoning Carradine under these circumstances? *See generally* Dan Cohen, *Decision Rules and Conduct Rules: On Acoustic Separation in Criminal Law*, 97 HARV. L. REV. 625 (1984).

2. Is there a special reason for rejecting duress as a defense under the circumstances of this case?

3. What would you have done had you been in Carradine's position? What should you (or she) do?

4. If the Blackstone Rangers' threats had been more explicit or specific, would (should) it have made a difference?

5. Would Carradine's case be stronger or weaker if her fear had caused her to lie on the witness stand and she had been prosecuted for perjury?

6. As you read *Toscano*, consider whether it is consistent with *Carradine* and, if not, which court had the sounder analysis.

State v. Toscano

378 A.2d 755 (N.J. Sup. Ct. 1977)

PASHMAN, J.

Defendant Joseph Toscano was convicted of conspiring to obtain money by false pretenses in violation of N.J.S.A. 2A:98-1. Although admitting that he had aided in the preparation of a fraudulent insurance claim by making out a false medical report, he argued that he had acted under duress. The trial judge ruled that the threatened harm was not sufficiently imminent to justify charging the jury on the defense of duress. After the jury returned a verdict of guilty, the defendant was fined $500.

We granted certification to consider the status of duress as an affirmative defense to a crime. We hold that duress is an affirmative defense to a crime other than murder, and that it need not be based upon an alleged threat of immediate bodily injury. Under the standard announced today, we find that this defendant did allege sufficient facts to warrant charging the jury on his claim of duress. Accordingly, we reverse his conviction and remand for a new trial.

Dr. Joseph Toscano, a chiropractor, was named as a defendant in the First Count and in two counts alleging a conspiracy to defraud the Kemper Insurance Company (Kemper). Prior to trial, seven of the eleven defendants pleaded guilty to various charges, leaving defendant as the sole remaining defendant charged with the conspiracy to defraud Kemper. Among those who pleaded guilty was William Leonardo, the architect of the alleged general conspiracy and the organizer of each of the separate incidents. Although the First Count was dismissed by the trial judge at the conclusion of the State's case, the evidence did reveal a characteristic *modus operandi* by Leonardo and his cohorts which is helpful in understanding the fraudulent scheme against Kemper. Typically, they would stage an accident or feign a fall in a public place.[2] A false medical report for the "injured" person, together with a false verification of employment and lost wages, would then be submitted to the insurer of the premises. The same two doctors were used to secure the medical reports in every instance except that involving the claim against Kemper. Likewise, the confirmations of employment and lost wages were secured from the same pool of friendly employers. The insurance companies made cash payments to resolve the claims under their "quick settlement" programs, usually within a few weeks after

---

2. The mishaps occurred in supermarkets, discount stores, movie theaters and a factory. On two occasions, Leonardo and others deliberately caused an accident while road testing a used car from a dealer. There were three incidents in 1968, five in 1969, three in 1970 and one in 1971.

the purported accidents. Leonardo took responsibility for dividing the funds to the "victims" of the accidents, to the doctors and employers, taking a substantial portion for himself.

Michael Hanaway, an unindicted co-conspirator who acted. as the victim in a number of these staged accidents, testified that defendant was drawn into this scheme largely by happenstance. On January 6, 1970, Hanaway staged a fall at E.J. Korvette's in Woodridge, New Jersey under the direction of Leonardo and Frank Neri, another defendant who pleaded guilty prior to trial. Dr. Miele, one of the two doctors repeatedly called upon by Leonardo to provide fraudulent medical reports, attested to Hanaway's claimed injuries on a form supplied by the insurer. Hanaway was subsequently paid $975 in settlement of his claim by the Underwriters Adjusting Company on behalf of Korvette's insurer.

In the meantime, however, the same trio performed a similar charade at the R.K.O. Wellmont Theater in Montclair, New Jersey. Kemper, which insured the R.K.O. Theater, was immediately notified of Hanaway's claim, and Dr. Miele was again enlisted to verify Hanaway's injuries on a medical report. However, because the R.K.O. accident occurred on January 8, 1970 only two days after the Korvette's incident Dr. Miele confused the two claims and mistakenly told Kemper's adjuster that he was treating Hanaway for injuries sustained at Korvette's. When Hanaway learned of the claims adjuster's suspicions, he informed William Leonardo who, in turn, contacted his brother Richard (a co-defendant at trial) to determine whether Toscano would agree to verify the treatments.

The State attempted to show that Toscano agreed to fill out the false medical report because he owed money to Richard Leonardo for gambling debts. It also suggested that Toscano subsequently sought to cover up the crime by fabricating office records of nonexistent office visits by Hanaway. Defendant sharply disputed these assertions and maintained that he capitulated to William Leonardo's demands only because he was fearful for his wife's and his own bodily safety. Since it is not our function here to assess these conflicting versions, we shall summarize only those facts which, if believed by the jury, would support defendant's claim of duress.

Defendant first met Richard Leonardo in 1953 as a patient and subsequently knew him as a friend. Defendant briefly encountered the brother, William, in the late 1950's at Caldwell Penitentiary when Toscano served as a prison guard. Although William was an inmate, the doctor did not know him personally. Through conversations with some police officers and William's brother and father, however, he did learn enough about William to know of his criminal record.[4] In particular, Richard told him many times that William was "on junk," that he had a gang, that "they

---

4. Defendant attempted to introduce Williams criminal record into evidence and to establish his unsavory reputation in the community. Although these efforts were not wholly successful, other testimony at trial supported his characterization of William Leonardo as a violent, erratic individual. Hanaway stated that Leonardo "opened Frank Neri's skull with a bat" and often did "off-the-wall things."

can't keep up with the amount of money that they need for this habit," and that he himself stayed away from William.

Thus, when William first called the defendant at his office, asking for a favor, he immediately cut off the conversation on the pretext that he was with a patient. Although William had not specifically mentioned the medical form at that time, defendant testified that he was "nauseated" by "just his name." A few days later, on a Thursday evening, he received another call in his office. This time Leonardo asked defendant to make out a report for a friend in order to submit a bill to a claims adjuster. He was more insistent, stating that defendant was "going to do it," but defendant replied that he would not and could not provide the report. Once again, the doctor ended the conversation abruptly by claiming, falsely, that he was with other persons.

The third and final call occurred on Friday evening. Leonardo was "boisterous and loud" repeating, "You're going to make this bill out for me." Then he said: "Remember, you just moved into a place that has a very dark entrance and you leave there with your wife. . . . You and your wife are going to jump at shadows when you leave that dark entrance."[5] Leonardo sounded "vicious" and "desperate" and defendant felt that he "just had to do it" to protect himself and his wife. He thought about calling the police but failed to do so in the hope that "it would go away and wouldn't bother me anymore."

In accordance with Leonardo's instructions, defendant left a form in his mailbox on Saturday morning for Leonardo to fill in with the necessary information about the fictitious injuries. It was returned that evening and defendant completed it. On Sunday morning he met Hanaway at a pre-arranged spot and delivered a medical bill and the completed medical report. He received no compensation for his services, either in the form of cash from William Leonardo or forgiven gambling debts from Richard Leonardo. He heard nothing more from Leonardo after that Sunday.

Shortly thereafter, still frightened by the entire episode, defendant moved to a new address and had his telephone number changed to an unlisted number in an effort to avoid future contacts with Leonardo. He also applied for a gun permit but was unsuccessful. His superior at his daytime job with the Newark Housing Authority confirmed that the quality of defendant's work dropped so markedly that he was forced to question defendant about his attitude. After some conversation, defendant explained that he had been upset by threats against him and his wife. He also revealed the threats to a co-worker at the Newark Housing Authority.

After defendant testified, the trial judge granted the State's motion to exclude any further testimony in connection with defendant's claim of duress and announced his decision not to charge the jury on that defense. He based his ruling on two decisions by the former Court of Errors and Appeals which referred to the common law

---

5. Defendant described the exit from his office as a "very, very pitch-black alleyway" on the side of the building.

rule that a successful claim of duress required a showing of a "present, imminent and impending" threat of harm. As he interpreted these decisions, the defendant could not satisfy this standard by establishing his own subjective estimate of the immediacy of the harm. Rather, the defendant was obliged to prove its immediacy by an objective standard which included a reasonable explanation of why he did not report the threats to the police. Since Toscano's only excuse for failing to make such a report was his doubts that the police would be willing or able to protect him, the court ruled that his subjective fears were irrelevant.

After stating that the defense of duress is applicable only where there is an allegation that an act was committed in response to a threat of present, imminent and impending death or serious bodily harm, the trial judge charged the jury:

> Now, one who is standing and receiving instructions from someone at the point of a gun is, of course, in such peril. One can describe such threat as being imminent, present and pending, and a crime committed under those circumstances, or rather conduct engaged in under those circumstances, even though criminal in nature, would be excused by reason of the circumstances in which it was committed.

> Now, where the peril is not imminent, present and pending to the extent that the defendant has the opportunity to seek police assistance for himself and his wife as well, the law places upon such a person the duty not to acquiesce in the unlawful demand and any criminal conduct in which he may thereafter engage may not be excused. Now, this principle prevails regardless of the subjective estimate he may have made as to the degree of danger with which he or his wife may have been confronted. Under the facts of this case, I instruct you, as members of the jury, that the circumstances described by Dr. Toscano leading to his implication in whatever criminal activities in which you may find he participated are not sufficient to constitute the defense of duress.

Since New Jersey has no applicable statute defining the defense of duress, we are guided only by common law principles which conform to the purposes of our criminal justice system and reflect contemporary notions of justice and fairness.

At common law the defense of duress was recognized only when the alleged coercion involved a use or threat of harm which is "present, imminent and pending" and "of such a nature as to induce a well-grounded apprehension of death or serious bodily harm if the act is not done."

It was commonly said that duress does not excuse the killing of an innocent person even if the accused acted in response to immediate threats.[7] Aside from this

---

7. The broad assertion that duress is unavailable as a defense to homicide appears repeatedly in the cases and treatises, but several commentators have observed that the decisions have involved murder as opposed to manslaughter. In repeating this adage, moreover, courts have typically gone on to stress the opportunities for resistance or escape. *See* Hitchler, *"Duress as a Defense in Criminal*

exception, however, duress was permitted as a defense to prosecution for a range of serious offenses, *see, e.g., D'Aquino v. United States,* 192 F.2d 338, 358 (9th Cir. 1951) (treason; capital offense); *Gillars v. United States,* 182 F.2d 962, 976, 87 U.S. App. D.C. 16 (D.C. Cir. 1950) (treason); *Shannon v. United States,* 76 F.2d 490 (10th Cir. 1935) (kidnapping); *State v. Ellis,* 232 Or. 461, 374 P.2d 461 (1962) (kidnapping); *Ross v. State,* 169 Ind. 388, 82 N.E. 781 (1907) (arson); and many lesser crimes, *see, e.g., People v. Merhige,* 212 Mich. 601, 180 N.W. 418 (1920) (robbery); *Nall v. Commonwealth,* 208 Ky. 700, 721 S.W. 1059 (1925) (breaking and entering with intent to steal); *People v. Sanders,* 82 Cal. App. 778, 256 P. 251 (1927) (forgery); *Hall v. State,* 136 Fla. 644, 187 So. 392 (1939) (perjury).

To excuse a crime, the threatened injury must induce "such a fear as a man of ordinary fortitude and courage might justly yield to." Although there are scattered suggestions in early cases that only a fear of death meets this test, an apprehension of immediate serious bodily harm has been considered sufficient to excuse capitulation to threats. Thus, the courts have assumed as a matter of law that neither threats of slight injury nor threats of destruction to property are coercive enough to overcome the will of a person of ordinary courage. *See People v. Ricker,* 45 Ill. 2d 562, 262 N.E.2d 456 (1970) (loss of job); *D'Aquino v. United States, supra* (denial of food rations); *Moore v. State,* 23 Ala. App. 432, 127 So. 796 (1929) (loss of job). *Cf. State v. Gann,* N.D., 244 N.W.2d 746 (1976) (economic need); *United States v. Palmer,* 458 F.2d 663 (9th Cir. 1972) (prospect of "financial ruin"). A "generalized fear of retaliation" by an accomplice, unrelated to any specific threat, is also insufficient.

More commonly, the defense of duress has not been allowed because of the lack of immediate danger to the threatened person. When the alleged source of coercion is a threat of "future" harm, courts have generally found that the defendant had a duty to escape from the control of the threatening person or to seek assistance from law enforcement authorities.

Assuming a "present, imminent and impending" danger, however, there is no requirement that the threatened person be the accused. Although not explicitly resolved by the early cases, recent decisions have assumed that concern for the well-being of another, particularly a near relative, can support a defense of duress if the other requirements are satisfied.

A less rigorous standard has been imposed in a few cases involving relatively minor, non-violent crimes. In *Hall v. State,* 136 Fla. 644, 187 So. 392 (1939), for instance, a conviction for perjury was overturned because the trial court failed to charge the jury that the defendant needed only reasonable grounds to believe that danger was imminent. The court did not discuss the possibility that, instead of making false statements, the defendant could have appealed to the trial judge for

---

Cases," 4 Va. L. Rev. 519, 528 (1917); Hall, *General Principles of Criminal Law,* 525 (1947). The Model Penal Code draftsmen point out that duress instructions have sometimes been given in murder cases. Model Penal Code, § 2.09, Comment 1, at 4 it. 24. (Tent. Draft No. 10, 1960).

protection against reprisal. And in *Commonwealth v. Reffitt*, 149 Ky. 300, 148 S.W. 48 (1912) a tenant farmer entered into an illegal transaction after being threatened with physical harm and destruction of his crop. Although there was no clear-cut threat of immediate danger, the court emphasized the inability of the civil and military authorities to prevent acts giving rise to the illegal coercion.

For the most part, however, the same test has been utilized to assess the sufficiency of the defendant's allegations for the purpose of charging the jury, regardless of the nature of the crime.

The insistence under the common law on a danger of immediate force causing death or serious bodily injury may be ascribed to its origins in early cases dealing with treason, to the proclivities of a "tougher-minded age," or simply to judicial fears of perjury and fabrication of baseless defenses. We do not discount the latter concern as a reason for caution in modifying this accepted rule, but we are concerned by its obvious shortcomings and potential for injustice. Under some circumstances, the commission of a minor criminal offense should be excusable even if the coercive agent does not use or threaten force which is likely to result in death or "serious" bodily injury. Similarly, it is possible that authorities might not be able to prevent a threat of future harm from eventually being carried out. The courts have not wholly disregarded the predicament of an individual who reasonably believes that appeals for assistance from law enforcement officials will be unavailing, but there has been no widespread acknowledgment of such an exception. Warnings of future injury or death will be all the more powerful if the prospective victim is another person, such as a spouse or child, whose safety means more to the threatened person than his own well-being. Finally, as the drafters of the Model Penal Code observed, "long and wasting pressure may break down resistance more effectively than a threat of immediate destruction." § 2.09, Comment at 8 (Tent. Draft No. 10, 1960).

Commentators have expressed dissatisfaction with the common law standard of duress. Stephen viewed the defense as a threat to the deterrent function of the criminal law and argued that "it is at the moment when temptation is strongest that the law should speak most clearly and emphatically to the contrary." STEPHEN, 2 HISTORY OF THE CRIMINAL LAW IN ENGLAND 107 (1883). A modern refinement of this position is that the defense should be designed to encourage persons to act against their self-interest if a substantial percentage of persons in such a situation would do so. HALL, GENERAL PRINCIPLES OF CRIMINAL LAW (2 ed. 1960), 446–47. This standard would limit its applicability to relatively minor crimes and exclude virtually all serious crimes unless committed under threat of imminent death.

Others have been more skeptical about the deterrent effects of a strict rule. As the Alabama Supreme Court observed in an early case:

"That persons have exposed themselves to imminent peril and death for their fellow man, and that there are instances where innocent persons have submitted to murderous assaults, and suffered death, rather than take life, is well established; but such self-sacrifice emanated from other motives than the fear of legal punishment." (*Arp v. State*, 97 Ala. at 12, 12 So. at 303.)

Building on this premise, some commentators have advocated a flexible rule which would allow a jury to consider whether the accused actually lost his capacity to act in accordance with "his own desire, or motivation, or will" under the pressure of real or imagined forces. The inquiry here would focus on the weaknesses and strengths of a particular defendant, and his subjective reaction to unlawful demands. Thus, the "standard of heroism" of the common law would give way, not to a "reasonable person" standard, but to a set of expectations based on the defendant's character and situation.

The drafters of the Model Penal Code and the New Jersey Penal Code sought to steer a middle course between these two positions by focusing on whether the standard imposed upon the accused was one with which "normal members of the community will be able to comply. . . . They stated:

> ". . . law is ineffective in the deepest sense, indeed it is hypocritical, if it imposes on the actor who has the misfortune to confront a dilemmatic choice, a standard that his judges are not prepared to affirm that they should and could comply with if their turn to face the problem should arise. Condemnation in such case is bound to be an ineffective threat; what is, however, more significant is that it is divorced from any moral base and is injust. Where it would be both 'personally and socially debilitating' to accept the actor's cowardice as a defense, it would be equally debilitating to demand that heroism be the standard of legality." (Model Penal Code § 2.09, Comment at 7 (Tent. Draft No. 10, 1960), quoting Hart, *The Aims of the Criminal Law*, 23 LAW & CONTEMP. PROB. 401, 414 and n.31 (1958); New Jersey Model Penal Code § 2C:2-9, Commentary at 71 (1970.).

Thus, they proposed that a court limit its consideration of an accused's "situation" to "stark, tangible factors which differentiate the actor from another, like his size or strength or age or health," excluding matters of temperament. They substantially departed from the existing statutory and common law limitations requiring that the result be death or serious bodily harm, that the threat be immediate and aimed at the accused, or that the crime committed be a non-capital offense. While these factors would be given evidential weight, the failure to satisfy one or more of these conditions would not justify the trial judge's withholding the defense from the jury.

Both the Prosecutor and the Attorney General substantially approve of the modifications suggested by the drafters of the model codes. However, they would allow the issue to be submitted to the jury only where the trial judge has made a threshold determination that the harm threatened was "imminent." Defendant, in a rather cryptic fashion, refers us to New York's statutory definition of duress, New York Penal Code § 40.00 (1970), which requires a showing of coercion by the use or threatened imminent use of unlawful force. However, he advocates leaving the question of immediacy to the jury.

For reasons suggested above, a *per se* rule based on immediate injury may exclude valid claims of duress by persons for whom resistance to threats or resort to official protection was not realistic. While we are hesitant to approve a rule which would reward citizens who fail to make such efforts, we are not persuaded that capitulation to unlawful demands is excusable only when there is a "gun at the head" of the defendant. We believe that the better course is to leave the issue to the jury with appropriate instructions from the judge.

Defendant's testimony provided a factual basis for a finding that Leonardo threatened him and his wife with physical violence if he refused to assist in the fraudulent scheme. Moreover, a jury might have found from other testimony adduced at trial that Leonardo's threats induced a reasonable fear in the defendant. Since he asserted that he agreed to complete the false documents only because of this apprehension, the requisite elements of the defense were established. Under the model code provisions, it would have been solely for the jury to determine whether a "person of reasonable firmness in his situation" would have failed to seek police assistance or refused to cooperate, or whether such a person would have been, unlike defendant, able to resist.

Exercising our authority to revise the common law, we have decided to adopt this approach as the law of New Jersey. Henceforth, duress shall be a defense to a crime other than murder if the defendant engaged in conduct because he was coerced to do so by the use of, or threat to use, unlawful force against his person or the person of another, which a person of reasonable firmness in his situation would have been unable to resist. No longer will there be a preliminary judicial determination that the threats posed a danger of "present, imminent and impending" harm to the defendant or to another. In charging the jury, however, the trial judge should advert to this factor of immediacy, as well as the gravity of the harm threatened, the seriousness of the crime committed, the identity of the person endangered, the possibilities for escape or resistance and the opportunities for seeking official assistance. He should also emphasize that the applicable standard for judging the defendant's excuse is the "person of reasonable firmness in (the accused's) situation."

The peculiar nature of duress, which focuses on the reasonableness of the accused's fear and his actual ability to resist unlawful demands, is not completely offset by the "person of reasonable firmness" standard. While the idiosyncrasies of an individual's temperament cannot excuse an inability to withstand such demands, his attributes (age, health, etc.) are part of the "situation" which the jury is admonished to consider. We think that the admittedly open-ended nature of this standard, with the possibility for abuse and uneven treatment, justifies placing the onus on the defendant to convince the jury.

Defendant's conviction of conspiracy to obtain money by false pretenses is hereby reversed and remanded for a new trial.

Questions and Notes

1. If *Carradine* had been decided under the *Toscano* standard, what do you think that the result would (should) have been?

2. Does *Toscano* make it too easy for the Leonardos of the world to recruit cohorts?

3. Shouldn't we have at least required Toscano to have sought the aid of the police first rather than hoping "it would go away and wouldn't bother me anymore"?

4. Does (should) it matter whether Toscano profited from his crime?

5. Is there any disadvantage to leaving the question of duress to a jury under rather amorphous standards?

6. In conjunction with *Tuttle*, consider whether there ought to be different standards when dealing with an escape from prison.

State v. Tuttle

730 P.2d 630 (Utah 1986)

ZIMMERMAN, Justice:

Defendant Wesley Allen Tuttle appeals from a jury conviction on a charge of escaping from official custody while incarcerated at the Utah State Prison. At trial, Tuttle claimed that he was forced to escape because of duress. On appeal, he contends that the trial court's instruction to the jury on the duress defense was improper because in the context of a charge of escape the trial court added three conditions qualifying the statutory defense. We conclude that the trial court properly modified the defense to adapt it to a charge of escape and therefore affirm the conviction.

On August 21, 1984, defendant Wesley Allen Tuttle was incarcerated at the Utah State Prison serving a life sentence for capital homicide. On that day, Tuttle and another inmate, Eugene Brady, were assigned to repair lights in the medium security visiting room. According to Brady, he was informed by an unidentified inmate while he was in the restroom and separated from Tuttle that he and Tuttle would be killed by other inmates if they returned to the main corridor. Brady immediately returned to Tuttle and told him, "We've got big problems."

Tuttle and Brady immediately made their escape, joined by another inmate, Walter Wood. Because the three were dressed as maintenance personnel and had already passed several security checkpoints as part of their work assignment, they had little trouble walking out of the prison unnoticed. Brady and Wood were apprehended later that day, but Tuttle remained at large until he was found in Las Vegas in February of 1985. He was charged with escaping from official custody.[2]

---

2. Tuttle's proposed instruction stated:
    You are instructed that pursuant to the laws of the State of Utah, it is a complete defense to the charge in this case if the Defendant acted under compulsion. Compulsion under the law is when an individual engaged in proscribed conduct because he was coerced to

At trial, Tuttle asserted that he had been forced to escape under duress and offered a jury instruction setting forth nearly verbatim the statutory compulsion defense found in section 76-2:302(l) of the Code, which provides in relevant part:

> (1) A person is not guilty of an offense when he engaged in the proscribed conduct because he was coerced to do so by the use or threatened imminent use of unlawful physical force upon him or a third person, which force or threatened force a person of reasonable firmness in his situation would not have resisted.

The trial court refused Tuttle's proffered instruction on compulsion and instead gave the instruction as it had been suggested by the prosecutor. That instruction qualified the duress defense in an escape case, stating that Tuttle could avail himself of the defense only if the jury found (i) that Tuttle was faced with a specific threat of death or substantial bodily injury, (ii) that there was no time for complaint to the authorities or there was a history of futile complaints, and (iii) that Tuttle immediately reported to authorities after escape. The jury rejected Tuttle's duress defense and convicted him of escape.

On appeal, Tuttle contends that the trial court committed reversible error by qualifying the duress defense in the context of an escape. He contends that in effect the court narrowed the statutory definition and thereby expanded the definition of criminal escape. We disagree.

Before specifically discussing the instruction, a few observations on the development of Utah's criminal code are warranted. The definitions of various common law crimes and defenses evolved over a long period of time as the law adapted to specific fact situations.

In an effort to rationalize, clarify, and improve upon the frequently archaic common law definitions of crimes, the legislature in 1973 repealed wholesale all the prior substantive criminal statutes (including, necessarily, defenses) and enacted a sweeping new penal code that departed sharply from the old common law concepts. As if to emphasize its departure from the old law, the 1973 Code specifically stated that the "common law of crimes is abolished," and it also provided that the old rule that statutes in derogation of the common law shall be narrowly construed should have no application to the new penal code.

Included among the statutes affected by the repeal of criminal statutes that accompanied enactment of the new code was section 76-1-41(9), which had set out the broad common law defense of duress or compulsion. In its place was enacted

---

do so by the use or threatened imminent use of unlawful physical force upon him, or a third person, which force or threatened force a person of reasonable firmness in that individual situation would not have resisted.

Therefore, unless the State proves to your satisfaction and beyond a reasonable doubt that the above elements of compulsion did not exist, it shall be your duty to return a verdict of not guilty.

section 76-2-302, which is modeled after section 209 of the Model Penal Code, although it was quite similar in substance to the pre-code definition of the defense. Neither the old nor the new duress defense as set forth in the Utah statutes discusses how that defense is to be tailored in response to a charge of escape, nor have we been able to locate any Utah cases construing the defense in that context. However, cases from other jurisdictions indicate that when duress was alleged as a defense to an escape charge at common law, the courts added certain conditions to the defense, conditions that were mirrored in the trial court's instruction here, *i.e.*, (i) that Tuttle was faced with a specific threat of death or substantial bodily injury, (ii) that there was no time for complaint to the authorities or there was a history of futile complaints, and (iii) that Tuttle immediately reported to authorities after escape.

The duress defense as enacted in Utah's current criminal code simply states the broadest contours of the defense as it might be raised against a criminal charge. Nothing in the 1973 Utah legislative history or in the commentary to the Model Penal Code indicates that the new code was intended to abolish subtle yet sound common law qualifications upon the defense as it relates to specific crimes that are consistent with its essential nature and that do not otherwise conflict with the provisions or the purposes of the new criminal code.

[W]e have been unable to locate any pre-1973 Utah cases considering the common law defense of duress as it applies to the crime of escape. However, in modifying the defense in this case, the trial court relied on a California case explaining the elements of the common law definition of the duress defense in the context of escape and incorporating them into a statutory duress defense. *See People v. Lovercamp*, 118 Cal. Rptr. at 115. *Lovercamp* appears to correctly state the law and has been widely followed since it was published. Interestingly, courts in Alaska, Arizona, Colorado, Delaware, Hawaii, Illinois, and Louisiana have been faced with the same question presented to us: what are the elements of a compulsion or duress defense when asserted in a case involving an escape charge? In each state, the legislature had, like ours, abolished all common law crimes and enacted a statutory defense of compulsion. None of those statutes included all the common law elements mentioned in *Lovercamp*, yet the courts in all seven states followed *Lovercamp*, finding that their statutes were inadequate to respond to the exigencies of an escape situation. It is especially noteworthy that, like Utah, the Arizona and Colorado statutes were patterned on section 209 of the Model Penal Code. Those courts obviously saw nothing inconsistent between the Model Penal Code and the common law qualifications of the duress defense articulated in *Lovercamp*. In fact, in its most recent commentary on the Model Penal Code, the American Law Institute noted that escape is an "atypical situation" for application of the duress defense, but conceded that the defense might apply and cited the *Lovercamp* decision as an appropriate example of the application of the defense to escape. American Law Institute, Model Penal Code and Commentaries Part I § 2.09 at 377 & n.42 (1980).

With this background in mind, we consider the instant instruction. The first qualification imposed on the defense by the trial court required that the defendant be faced with a specific, imminent threat of death or substantial bodily injury, an element noted by the California court in *Lovercamp*.[5] Although the Utah statute does not require a threat of death or bodily injury, it does require a threat or use of "unlawful physical force ... which ... a person of reasonable firmness ... would not have resisted." Plainly, when the Utah legislature referred to unlawful physical force," it did not intend that minor physical force or incidental bodily injury could justify criminal conduct such as escape. Therefore, we hold that in the context of escape, the threat or use of unlawful physical force alleged in support of a compulsion defense must be at least that which would cause substantial bodily injury. The trial court's instruction also required that the threat of substantial bodily injury be specific. In *State v. Harding*, 635 P.2d 33 (Utah 1981), we found that this qualification comports with the defense. In *Harding*, this Court upheld the trial court's refusal to give a duress defense instruction where the evidence "[did] not support a finding of any threat of imminent use of unlawful force upon the defendant ... [because it lacked] the *specificity* which is necessary to establish the existence of an immediate threat." 635 P.2d at 35 (emphasis added). This part of the trial court's instruction, therefore, is not in error.

The trial court also instructed the jury that the duress defense was not available in response to an escape charge unless there was no time for complaint to the authorities or a history of futile complaints. *Lovercamp* found this to be a common law element of the defense. We find nothing to suggest that it is inconsistent with the legislature's 1973 enactment of the criminal code. In fact, it seems entirely consistent with section 76-2-302(1), which reads: "A person is not guilty of an offense when he engaged in the proscribed conduct because he was *coerced* to do so. . . ." (Emphasis added.) A person obviously cannot be "coerced" to act unlawfully unless there is no reasonable alternative to commission of the crime charged. *Cf. United States v. Bailey*, 444 U.S. 394, 410 (1980) ("("Under [the duress and necessity] defenses one principle remains constant: if there was a reasonable, legal alternative to violating the law, ... the defenses will fail.").

In the context of an escape charge, a reasonable alternative to escape for one incarcerated would always be to complain to authorities in order to remove the threat. Therefore, requiring the jury to find that this alternative was not reasonably

---

5. *Lovercamp* also included forcible sexual assault in its specifications of physical threats and harms. The trial court's instruction here did not; however, that issue was not presented. The inclusion of forcible sexual assault as a physical threat or harm justifying escape seems entirely appropriate. *See Lovercamp* rationale in *People v. Unger*, 66 Ill. 2d at 340, 362 N.E.2d at 322, and *State v. Boleyn*, 328 So. 2d at 97.

The threat of forcible sexual assault is at least as great an assault on the personal integrity of an individual as a threat to commit other bodily injury. We can imagine no reason for permitting the latter to be the foundation for a defense and not the former. Although one incarcerated for a crime must expect confinement under stark conditions, he or she cannot reasonably be expected to bear forcible sexual degradation.

available is entirely consistent with the defense and the concept underlying it. The trial court did not err in reading this qualification into the defense.

Finally, the trial court instructed the jury that duress would not be a defense to an escape charge unless the defendant reported to the authorities immediately after the escape. We find that the importation of this common law requirement into the statute also was proper and consistent with the statute's purpose. The law recognizes that a defendant faced with a serious threat of bodily harm who has no alternative but escape should not, in all fairness, be convicted of a crime for that action. However, while a defendant may be forced to escape a specific threat, the defense does not give an escaped convict a license to remain indefinitely at large. The compulsion defense is certainly not a grant of amnesty. Once the coercion justifying the escape disappears, there is no policy reason to justify the convict in remaining at large. The trial court was correct in concluding that an escapee must make a bona fide effort to surrender himself to the authorities as soon as the specific coercion that forced him to escape is no longer present.

Because the trial court's qualifications on the duress defense were proper, we affirm Tuttle's conviction.

Questions and Notes

1. Isn't the last requirement destructive of the defense? Ordinarily, if a prisoner is threatened with death or rape, does it make sense to require him to turn himself in to be put back in the same situation from which he justifiably extricated himself?

2. Notwithstanding, are there good reasons for retaining this requirement?

3. Should the duress defense be available at all in the "escape" context in view of the prisoner's fault in being incarcerated in the first place?

Problem

The defendant-appellant, Juan Manuel Contento-Pachon, is a native of Bogota, Colombia, and was employed there as a taxicab driver. He asserts that one of his passengers, Jorge, offered him a job as the driver of a privately owned car. Contento-Pachon expressed an interest in the job and agreed to meet Jorge and the owner of the car the next day.

Instead of a driving job, Jorge proposed that Contento-Pachon swallow cocaine-filled balloons and transport them to the United States. Contento-Pachon agreed to consider the proposition. He was told not to mention the proposition to anyone, otherwise he would "get into serious trouble." Contento-Pachon testified that he did not contact the police because he believes that the Bogota police are corrupt and that they are paid off by drug traffickers.

Approximately one week later, Contento-Pachon told Jorge that he would not carry the cocaine. In response, Jorge mentioned facts about Contento-Pachon's personal life, including private details which Contento-Pachon had never mentioned to

Jorge. Jorge told Contento-Pachon that his failure to cooperate would result in the death of his wife and three-year-old child.

The following day the pair met again. Contento-Pachon's life and the lives of his family were again threatened. At this point, Contento-Pachon agreed to take the cocaine into the United States.

The pair met two more times. At the last meeting, Contento-Pachon swallowed 129 balloons of cocaine. He was informed that he would be watched at all times during the trip, and that if he failed to follow Jorge's instruction he and his family would be killed.

After leaving Bogota, Contento-Pachon's plane landed in Panama. Contento-Pachon asserts that he did not notify the authorities there because he believed that the Panamanian police were as corrupt as those in Bogota. He also thought that any such action on his part would place his family in jeopardy.

When he arrived at the customs inspection point in Los Angeles, Contento-Pachon consented to have his stomach x-rayed. The x-rays revealed a foreign substance which was later determined to be cocaine.

At Contento-Pachon's trial, the government moved to exclude the defenses of duress. The motion was granted.

1. On appeal, how should the court resolve this case? Why?

2. Assuming that a duress defense would otherwise be available, should he have been required to turn himself into authorities?

3. Assuming that the court were to impose such a requirement, would consenting to be x-rayed constitute turning himself in?

4. For one resolution of these questions, see *United States v. Contento-Pachon*, 723 F.2d 691 (9th Cir. 1984).

See NUTSHELL § 11.03.

B. Necessity

The defense of necessity bears a surface resemblance to duress. Indeed, a number of cases, most significantly prison escape cases, seem unclear as to which defense *is* more appropriate. Although it is sometimes suggested that the salient differentiating feature is that duress *is* human-impelled whereas necessity is impelled by natural causes, that is not universally true *(see, e.g., Archer, Gerlach,* and *Blake, infra).*

The more significant feature of necessity is that it is a justification and not merely an excuse. The person pleading necessity is saying: "My conduct has made the world better; *you* should rejoice in my actions." Self-defense, which we have previously studied, can and should be analyzed as a species of the necessity defense.

In the cases that follow, we will explore the scope and limitation of the defense. *Archer* adopts an unusually expansive view of the defense. Consider whether this approach ought to commend itself elsewhere.

People v. Archer

537 N.Y.S.2d 726 (City Ct. Rochester 1988)

JOHN MANNING REGAN, Judge.

On Saturday morning, May 21, 1988, at 7:00 a.m., Timothy Archer, Gerald Crawford and 40 others entered Highland Hospital in Rochester, New York, and went at once to the fifth floor, east wing. Upon arrival at that location, all 42 persons sat down in the hallway which led to the examining, and clinical treatment, rooms where nine abortions were scheduled to be performed that day. The group sang hymns, greeted the women who came for abortions, and distributed pro-life literature to them. The Highland Obstetrical Group, a partnership of six physicians, had leased that floor of the east wing of the hospital, for the purpose of performing these abortions, and two members of the partnership, Doctors Wax and Eisenberg, were present that morning, and were anticipating attending to their patients. Around 7:30 a.m., the Director of Security for Highland Hospital notified police of this abortion "sit-in." When the police came, in response to his summons, they found that the 42 people had physically blocked access to the clinic and that no abortions were in progress. Over a period lasting about five hours, the police tried to evacuate these protestors with persuasion, admonition, threats and warnings. These measures having failed, the police resorted, finally, to arrests. They managed to clear the area, and to take all 42 people into custody, about 1:00 p.m. that afternoon.

This episode was free from overt violence to either person or property. The charges which the hospital and the police have filed against the 42 defendants are Criminal Trespass Third-Degree and Resisting Arrest.

The trial of these 42 defendants began November 15, 1988. The People have called about 20 witnesses—mostly police officers—who have testified to the "sit-in" on May 21st on the fifth floor of the hospital, and to the fact that all the defendants resisted arrest because they refused to stand and walk to the "paddy-wagon," and, consequently, the police had to carry them, bodily, or in wheelchairs, to transport vehicles. The Court and jury have also seen a videotape of the event filmed live during the "sit-in."

The evidence so far—particularly the videotape—will support the inferences that the defendants trespassed on hospital premises, and passively resisted their removal from the fifth floor abortion clinic in order to "rescue" the unborn children whom the Highland Obstetrical Group had scheduled for abortions that morning. Further, the evidence for the defendants thus far, offered in cross-examination of the police officers, in their opening address to the jury, and through several of their witnesses in their direct case, strongly suggests that they intend to argue to the jury that the injury they sought to avoid the abortion of the unborn children—clearly outweighs the injury they allegedly committed—i.e., Criminal Trespass and Resisting Arrest.

It is, therefore, at this point, in the midst of the trial, after presentation of the People's case, and during the direct case of the defendants, and prior to submission of the case to the jury for deliberation and verdict, that the statute commands a trial court to rule, as a matter of law, whether these claimed facts and circumstances would, if established, constitute a defense.

For the reasons which follow, the Court denies the motion to preclude the defense of justification, and rules that, as a matter of law, if the claimed facts and circumstances are established, they will constitute a justification defense to the charges of Criminal Trespass and Resisting Arrest.

The Model Penal Code's 6th tentative draft contains the most extensive explanation of its justification defense entitled: "choice of evils." Under the second and third limiting sub-paragraphs (§ 3.02(1)(b) and (c) above) which eliminate the necessity defense whenever the Legislature has specifically spoken on the topic, the commentators explicitly refer to the example of therapeutic abortion as an illustration of the necessity defense at common law. Their example cites an earlier English penal statute which simply prohibited all "unlawful pregnancy terminations"; and points to the case of *Rex v. Bourne*, 1 K.B. 687, 3 All E.R. 615 (1938), which, despite the statute, allowed a pregnancy termination because, in that case, it was a therapeutic abortion (to preserve the life or health of the mother). The decision employed the common law necessity defense as a bar to successful prosecution under that statute.

By contrast, the commentators further advised that a *more specific* statute on abortion—one, for example, that enumerated which pregnancy terminations were legal, and which were not—would pre-empt the defense of justification entirely since "the Legislature had itself canvassed and determined what the choices shall be" . . . and "under this Code, the [Legislature] is always free to do so, and to have its choice prevail." Under the Model Code, whatever was legal, therefore, could not be evil. The Model Code, in other words, precluded the necessity defense whenever the Legislature had legalized conduct.

But what this Court must observe here is that both the Revisors of the New York Penal Law, and the Legislature itself, rejected this limiting language in the Model Code, and adopted, instead, a different standard. They wrote that the "injury . . . to be avoided must . . . *according to ordinary standards of intelligence and morality,* clearly outweigh the injury" the criminal law(s) in question were designed to prevent. The Revisors, therefore, deliberately chose to enlarge the categories of possible evils to include not simply illegal behavior, but any injury which existed "according to ordinary standards of intelligence and morality." In other words, despite the legality of behavior, that behavior could still constitute an "evil" or "injury" to be avoided, so long as, *according to ordinary standards of intelligence and morality,* it could reasonably be classified as such.

What is obvious here is that both the Legislature and the Revisors have recognized, in the New York Penal Law, a different standard of judgment for determining what is an "injury to be avoided", which standard is broader, and more encompassing, than the legal/illegal classifications within the Penal Law itself. Granted what is criminally illegal is, *ipso facto*, an injury to be avoided. But the contrary of that proposition—namely "what is legal is therefore *not* an injury to be avoided" does not follow. In the former case, behavior which is criminally forbidden always violates "ordinary standards of intelligence and morality." But in the latter case, behavior which is permissively legal, does not always comport with ordinary standards of intelligence and morality.

In Nevada, for example, prostitution is legal, but still, immoral. Some type of gambling is almost everywhere legal, but many persons of ordinary intelligence and morality still consider it immoral. Traffic in alcoholic beverages is legal, but its by-product, drunkenness, remains immoral. Divorce is legal, but, in many cases, it is immoral, especially when it affects innocent children of the marriage. Thus, the two ideas—morality and legality—are not the same. Morality is the standard of conduct to which, as good and decent people, we all aspire. Legality is the standard of conduct to which, as members of a civilized society, and under penalty of the criminal sanction, we must all adhere.

The question then, for this Court is whether, under this statutory test of "ordinary standards of intelligence and morality" a jury may find that these nine abortions could have been an "injury to be avoided."

Abortion is still a crime under the New York Penal Code. Ironically, (inasmuch as we are discussing the justification defense) the Legislature, in 1970, created the category of a "Justifiable Abortional Act". That categorization became the method whereby any therapeutic abortion, and any abortion performed with consent within 24 weeks from the commencement of pregnancy, was absolved from criminal responsibility.

This classification of a "Justifiable Abortional Act" became effective July 1, 1970. It antedated the *Roe v. Wade* decision of the U.S. Supreme Court by more than 30 months. One of the principal sponsors of this 1970 legislation, Assemblywoman Constance E. Cook of Ithaca, characterized this amendment, in a memorandum urging its passage, as follows:

> "This legislation is permissive. It would force no one to live under its dictates, or to live in a moral or religious environment foreign to his upbringing or training."

See N.Y. State Legislative Annual, 1970, at p. 242.

This carefully crafted 1970 amendment to the penal abortion laws, therefore, was not authored to establish the morality of abortion. To the contrary, it was intended to alleviate a perceived social crisis of pernicious illegal abortions which were causing death and injury to hundred (*sic*) of thousands of child-bearing women every year. As Assemblywoman Cook said in her memorandum, "illegal abortions are the single largest cause of maternal death" and "hundreds of thousands of illegal abortions are done each year"; yet "virtually no deaths result when an abortion is conducted in accordance with proper medical procedures." *See* New York Legislative Annual, 1970, at p. 240.

Her portrayals of the legislative purpose behind the 1970 amendment illuminate the complex social panorama that both surrounded and spawned the passage of these laws. In effect because the Legislature could not stop illegal abortions, they capitulated to the social reality of it, rather than intensify the enforcement of the then current law. Instead of ameliorating the rigors of the old therapeutic abortion laws, the Legislature leaped from an extreme position at one end of the spectrum, to an equally extreme position at the opposite end. For the "Justifiable Abortional Act" legislation of 1970 did more than modify prior law, it totally eviscerated the criminal sanction(s) for abortion, and replaced a policy of "therapeutic abortion only" with a policy of "abortion on demand."

But, at least, there was no hypocrisy about the morality of what the Legislature did. In characterizing the legislation in terms of justifiability, and *permissiveness*, the lawmakers admitted that they were, in fact, making their own choice among evils. They were admitting that the State was willing to suffer the deplorable social consequences of legalizing abortion rather than the deplorable social consequences of perpetuating illegal abortions. This was an admission of impotency in the face of convincing proof that the then current abortion laws were unable to stem the tide of women resorting to illegal abortion as a remedy for an unwanted pregnancy.

The statutory history of the 1970 amendment is devoid of any hint or suggestion of a moral good to be achieved by legalizing abortion. The supporters all expressed compassion for the loss of maternal lives through illegal abortions and accepted the exigency of legalizing abortion to obviate this social scourge. A statutory history of this kind is not the equivalent of declaring a change in moral values. Tolerance is not approval, although the line between the two is not always easy to find.

In any event, if this change in the law did not propose to compel a citizen "to live in a moral or religious environment foreign to his upbringing," then that citizen remained free to adopt moral values in accordance with "ordinary standards of intelligence and morality," rather than in accordance with the tolerances of the Penal Law. Since that is so, abortion can still constitute a moral "injury to be avoided," under § 35.05 of the Penal Law, because citizens of ordinary intelligence and morality remain free both as individuals and as jurors, to find it so notwithstanding the fact that the Legislature has made most abortions "justifiable" in relation to what would otherwise be a prohibited criminal act.

Moreover, from the evidence in this trial, the practice of abortion-on-demand has at this time — 18 years after the 1970 amendment — far transcended the narrow social evil of maternal deaths due to illegal and unsanitary abortion techniques. Abortion has become simply another birth-control device, or a way to overcome a social inconvenience, or an expedient remedy for conceiving a child of the "wrong" sex. These consequences of "justifying" the abortional act were not envisioned in any of the legislative history behind the 1970 amendment, and it is fair comment to say that these unforeseen and unfortunate circumstances can easily be thought of as "injuries to be avoided" according to ordinary standards of intelligence and morality.

For these reasons, the Court concludes that, despite the 1970 amendment, which made the abortion of a fetus twenty-four weeks or younger "Justifiable Abortional Act", a jury of private citizens is free to decide, under § 35.05 of the Penal Law, that many of those abortions are immoral *"injuries to be avoided"* and that "the urgency of avoiding such injuries clearly outweighs the desirability of avoiding injuries such as Trespassing and Resisting Arrest" which the criminal statutes in issue here are designed to prevent. The jury may weigh the loss of the life of the developing fetus against the property rights the trespass statute protects, and the social order values the arrest statute supports. And if the jury finds that the value of these fetal lives clearly outweighs the competing values of private property and social order, then the Court shall instruct the jury, under § 35.05 of the Penal Law, that they may acquit the defendants.

The codification of the justification defense, and the New York Legislature's adoption of a statutory definition of what comprises "injuries to be avoided" has created a legal framework which allows our courts and juries to decide that abortion, although legal, and whenever performed, can still constitute an "injury to be avoided" There can be no gainsaying that this legal framework, however indirectly, is subject to the criticism that it is a form of state statutory regulation of abortion.

In *Roe v. Wade*, 410 U.S. 113 (1973) the Supreme Court stated:

> ... With respect to the State's important and legitimate interest in the health of the mother, the 'compelling point' ... is at the end of the first trimester."

> ... prior to this "compelling' point, the attending physician, in consultation with his patient, is free to determine, *without regulation by the State*, that, in his medical judgment the patient's pregnancy should be terminated. If that decision is reached, the judgment may be effectuated by an abortion *free of interference by the State.*"

> ... With respect to the State's important and legitimate interest in potential life, the 'compelling point' is at viability." *See* 410 U.S. at p. 163.

(emphasis added).

Succinctly put, the question for this Court, at this point, is: in view of the holding in *Roe*, can § 35.05 of the New York Penal Law be interpreted to allow a jury to find that a first trimester abortion is an "injury to be avoided" which injury may then outweigh the injuries certain of our criminal laws were designed to prevent? Or, is such a finding an indirect form of State regulation of the abortion decision during the first trimester?

The argument for the defendants is that § 35.05 does not actively encourage human behavior of any kind. It stands only as a guideline to define the legal consequences of human behavior after it has happened. The behavior itself is the private action of individuals, not State action under the 14th amendment. Thus, the action of these individual defendants in trespassing in order to prevent first trimester abortions, and the defense of justification the State statute affords them are not forms of forbidden State action under the principles of *Roe v. Wade.*

The argument for the People is that the justification statute (P.L. § 35.05) creates a necessity defense which would otherwise not be available to a law-breaker when it permits a jury to find that a first trimester abortion is an "injury to be avoided." Without that canopy of legal protection, the trespassing demonstrator is subject to criminal and civil liabilities. Moreover, since the decision in *Roe v. Wade,* forbids any state interference with first trimester abortions, the performance of such abortions is more than merely legal, it is a constitutionally protected right of privacy. Since § 35.05 of the Penal Law would, if so interpreted, interfere with that privacy because it would protect and defend intentional interruption of the private abortion decision, the statute would then indirectly regulate the private exercise of abortion rights, during the first trimester, in violation of the 14th amendment.

While the question is by no means free from doubt, there appears to be a body of judicial authority that requires courts to vindicate, in affirmative fashion, constitutionally protected rights of privacy and equality as contrasted with similarly protected due process property rights. For this reason, the Court holds that the decision of *Roe v. Wade,* making the first trimester abortion a constitutionally protected right of privacy, constrains the Court to instruct the jury that § 35.05 cannot classify first trimester abortions as "injuries to be avoided" because neither the statute, nor the Court, nor the jury itself, can intrude upon that constitutionally protected area of privacy. Accordingly, *Roe* prohibits the State statutory necessity defense whenever there are intentional interruptions which interfere with the performance of first trimester abortions.

This Court is aware that decisions in other States have rejected the necessity defense entirely in abortion cases where trespassing is the primary charge. These cases are, however, interpreting State statutes which have, in most cases, enacted the identical language of the Model Penal Code; language which the New York State Legislature did not adopt. Almost all of these cases hold the view that the decision of the Supreme Court in *Roe v. Wade,* has foreclosed any question of whether a jury can find that abortion is an evil or injury to be avoided, because *Roe* has made abortions legal, and that is that *Comm. v. Markum,* 541 A.2d 347 (Pa. Super. 1988) is typical. Applying the Model Penal Code's version of justification almost verbatim, the majority of that Court declares:

> "Appellants cannot use unlawful means in an effort to stop lawful behavior, no matter how morally reprehensible they feel that behavior to be." *See* 541 A.2d at p. 351.

But, unlike the Pennsylvania statute, moral reprehensibility of lawful behavior can be a factor under § 35.05 of the New York Penal Law because our Legislature expanded the concept of "injury to be avoided" to include any conduct which was morally reprehensible according to "ordinary standards of intelligence and morality."

Thus, in cases of moral indignation, the flexibility of the New York statute avoids the chafing attrition of the eternal struggle between what is legal and what is moral. The statute allows a jury to ventilate its displeasure at morally reprehensible conduct regardless of its legality by approving, in a verdict of not guilty, the behavior of those who try, even illegally, to prevent that conduct from happening.

Accordingly, the Court will instruct the Jury that the defendants can present and argue the defense of necessity so long as the jury finds that the Highland Obstetrical Group was about to perform other than first trimester abortions on May 21, 1988.

Epilogue

Under the foregoing instructions, and upon proof from Drs. Eisenberg and Wax that the nine abortions scheduled on May 21st were all during the first trimester, the jury found the 42 defendants guilty of simple Trespass and Resisting Arrest.

Questions and Notes

1. Is the suggestion that necessity can serve as a defense for the prevention of immoral but legal activity one that should be taken seriously? Would we really allow a man who physically restrained his wife from getting what he (and possibly the jury) thought to be an immoral divorce to raise the defense?

2. On the other hand, if morality is the key, how does making abortion a constitutional right change things? Lots of immoral things are protected by the Constitution, e.g., Nazi marches, flag burning, etc.

3. If abortion is special because of the Constitution, why stop at the first trimester? *Roe* upheld the right to abortion through the first two trimesters except where necessary to protect the mother's health. The Court explicitly held that fetal rights were not compelling until the third trimester. Yet Archer and his cohorts were clearly trying to assert fetal rights.

4. Assuming that the first trimester is the cutoff line, shouldn't the issue be whether the defendant thought that some of the abortions were second trimester rather than whether they in fact were?

5. Should one's criminality overtly depend on the moral philosophy of a particular jury?

6. As you read *Gerlach*, consider whether the jury might have reached a different result if it had been instructed in accord with *Archer*.

Gerlach v. State

699 P.2d 358 (Alaska Ct. App. 1985)

SINGLETON, Judge.

Helena Mary Faro Gerlach was convicted of custodial interference in the first degree, a class C felony. Gerlach appeals, arguing that the trial court erred in refusing to permit her to present a defense of necessity to the jury. We affirm.

Robert Faro was originally married to Helena Gerlach's half-sister, Gail. They were divorced and he was awarded custody of their four children. Thereafter, Faro married Gerlach, and they had one child, Angela. In the fall of 1981, Gerlach and Faro separated and commence divorce proceedings. Angela's custody was contested. Faro and Gerlach entered into an agreement under which Robert Faro had temporary custody of Angela and Gerlach had limited visitation rights. The parties were interviewed by the superior court's custody investigator and by a court-appointed psychologist, Dr. James Parsons. Dr. Parsons concluded that both parties were fit custodians for Angela but that permanent custody should be placed with Gerlach. After evaluating the psychologist's report, the parties and counsel met with the custody investigator and entered into a written stipulation that Faro would continue to have temporary custody of Angela pending the final decree of divorce, but that Gerlach's visitation rights would be expanded. Thereafter, Gerlach became concerned that Faro would take Angela outside the state and obtained a court restraining order preventing him from doing so.

On February 2, 1982, three weeks after the modified custody agreement was signed by Gerlach and Faro, Gerlach picked up Angela from her babysitter and flew with her to the State of Washington. Gerlach hid Angela from Faro for over a year. She was finally located and arrested by Washington authorities.

Before trial, Gerlach made the following offer of proof in support of her defense of necessity:

(1) Gerlach would testify that she believed that Faro was not properly caring for Angela, based on Gerlach's discovery that Angela was suffering from a vaginal infection and appeared dirty and unkempt. She would also testify that she knew that Faro's children by his former marriage were slapped, beaten, and verbally abused after visits to their mother. Gerlach would also testify that she had little faith in judicial proceedings as a means for resolving custody disputes. She knew that Faro had more money than she had and feared that she would run out of funds before the custody dispute was resolved. Gerlach was particularly concerned that Judge Carlson had authorized the temporary custody agreement as he had been the judge who ruled in Faro's favor in the earlier *Faro v. Faro* litigation.

(2) Bobby Faro, Gerlach's nephew and Faro's son by his earlier marriage (a fifteen-year-old boy suffering from muscular dystrophy, confined to a wheelchair), would testify that Faro had disciplined his children by beating them with a belt and slapping them, often for things that were not really their fault. Bobby would also testify that Faro slapped Angela when she came home from a visit with Gerlach.

(3) Gerlach's sister Gail would testify that after her own custody dispute with Faro, he abused their children when they returned home from visits with her.

(4) Finally, Dr. Parsons would testify that he saw both Faro and Gerlach at the time of the divorce and recommended that Angela remain with Gerlach.

The purpose of this testimony would have been to show Gerlach's state of mind and her fear of imminent harm to Angela. Superior Court Judge Seaborn J. Buckalew, Jr., held that Gerlach's offer of proof was insufficient as a matter of law. He therefore entered a protective order precluding her from raising the issue of necessity at trial.

Gerlach was convicted of custodial interference in the first degree. Her conviction required the state to prove that she intentionally kept the child from its lawful custodian for a "protracted period," knowing that she had no legal right to do so. Gerlach predicates her "necessity" defense on anticipated harm to her daughter Angela. Specifically, she was concerned that Mr Faro had neglected Angela in permitting her to incur a vaginal infection and had psychologically abused Angela in interrogating her after visitation regarding Gerlach's activities. Gerlach also feared potential physical abuse based upon her experiences in Faro's home and the statements made by Gail and Gerlach's nephew Bobby. However, Gerlach's claims fail.

Gerlach's claim fails to meet the [rule] that the harm caused must not be disproportionate to the harm avoided. There is no question that the harm to Faro from Gerlach's actions was reasonably foreseeable. Faro's contact with his daughter was totally eliminated. It is instructive that if Gerlach's fears of physical abuse had been shown to be well founded and she had been awarded custody or the State Department of Health and Social Services had taken temporary custody of Angela for Angela's protection, Faro would at least have had an opportunity for controlled visitation with Angela. Gerlach's unilateral action denied him any contact with Angela at all. In addition, Gerlach's claim fails because the legislature has made a determination of values in this situation. In establishing procedures for litigating claims of child abuse and neglect and in punishing custodial interference, the legislature addressed Gerlach's fears and rejected her suggested remedy of self-help.

More significantly, Gerlach had ready remedies at law. Even if legislative remedies were not intended to totally preclude self-help, Gerlach should have exhausted them. She was involved in an ongoing custody dispute and was represented by counsel. When she feared that her husband might remove Angela from the state, Gerlach successfully prosecuted a temporary restraining order precluding him from doing so. In addition, Gerlach and Faro had been interviewed by both the superior court's custody investigator and by an independent psychologist appointed by the court who had recommended that Gerlach be given permanent custody. If Gerlach thought Angela was in imminent danger, she should have sought temporary custody rather than stipulating to Faro's continued custody. Gerlach does not contend that her lawyer was incompetent or refused to follow Gerlach's directions.

Finally, it is clear that the legislature views custodial interference to be a continuing offense. The legislature was concerned not only with the initial interference with custody, but also with the duration of the interference. In fact, the offense is committed only where restraint is for a "protracted period" Also, the legislature differentiates between a misdemeanor and a felony based upon whether the interference involves removal of the child from the state. Since custodial interference is a continuing offense, it necessarily follows that one relying on a defense of necessity must offer some evidence justifying the duration of the interference as well as the initial act of interfering. Gerlach's fears might have justified her in temporarily refusing to return Angela to the babysitter chosen by Faro, while Gerlach sought legal or medical advice regarding her fears that Angela was being mistreated or contacted the Department of Health and Social Services to make a child abuse or neglect report. Gerlach's fears could not justify her removing the child from the state in violation of an interim custody order and secreting the child for over a year.

The legislature has recognized the risk of child abuse and neglect and has established remedies to protect vulnerable children. The legislature has also recognized the emotions involved in child custody disputes and has sought to establish procedures for resolving custody disputes to ensure that the child's interest will not be subordinated to vengeful wars between parents. If Gerlach was financially unable to litigate with her husband, she was entitled to obtain funds from him in order to litigate. If Angela's interests were not adequately protected by Gerlach and Faro, Angela was entitled to her own lawyer if necessary, at state expense. To permit a litigant such as Gerlach to use a necessity defense as a means of relitigating a custody determination would not appreciably advance the legislative goals of preventing child abuse and neglect which are adequately protected by existing legislation and would not serve the legislative purposes exhibited in the enactment of the statutes providing a judicial forum to litigate child custody disputes and barring custodial interference. Where the legislature has established procedures for determining custody disputes and separate but complementary procedures for investigating and preventing child abuse and neglect, a person cannot be permitted to ignore those procedures and rely on self-help simply because he or she distrusts lawyers, judges, and social workers. We hold the trial court did not err in denying Gerlach the right to rely on a necessity defense in this case.

The judgment of the superior court is AFFIRMED.

Questions and Notes

1. If Gerlach believed that Angela had been sexually abused by her father, would (should) the case have been decided differently?

2. Are the presence of alternatives critical to the resolution of this case? Suppose all of the courts and agencies had ruled against Gerlach?

3. Although styled a "necessity" case, is the problem substantially similar to that presented in *Carradine*?

4. *Archer* involved a perceived attempt to save many children. *Gerlach* involved an attempt to save one. Other necessity cases, such as *Tate,* have very much of a self-preservation flavor. Consider how lines should be drawn in such a case.

State v. Tate

505 A.2d 941 (N.J. Sup. Ct. 1986)

CLIFFORD, J.

Defendant, Michael Tate, is afflicted with quadriplegia. The spasticity associated with that condition is sometimes so severe as to render defendant completely disabled. He claims that the use of marijuana provides relief. Indicted for possession of over twenty-five grams of marijuana, defendant notified the State of his intention to rely on the defense of "medical necessity." He claims the defense under N.J.S.A. 2C:3-2(a), which provides standards for determining whether conduct that would otherwise constitute a criminal offense is justifiable by reason of necessity.

The trial court denied the State's motion to strike that defense, ruling that under the circumstances presented defendant was not foreclosed from asserting the defense of "necessity" based on justifiable conduct. The Appellate Division affirmed, with one judge dissenting. We granted the State's motion for leave to appeal, and now reverse.

The discretion left to the courts by that statute is governed by criteria specifically set forth therein. The section reads:

"*Necessity.* Conduct which would otherwise be an offense is justifiable by reason of necessity to the extent permitted by law and as to which neither the code nor other statutory law defining the offense provides exceptions or defenses dealing with the specific situation involved and a legislative purpose to exclude the justification claimed does not otherwise plainly appear".

In that one short paragraph the Legislature managed to set forth three limiting criteria governing the defense: (1) conduct is justifiable only to the extent permitted by law, (2) the defense is unavailable if either the Code or other statutory law defining the offense provides exceptions or defenses dealing with the specific situation involved, and (3) the defense is unavailable if a legislative purpose to exclude the justification otherwise plainly appears.

If we follow the mandate to limit the exercise of our discretion in accordance with these governing criteria, the conclusion is inescapable that Michael Tate is not entitled to the defense of "necessity" in this case. First, the conduct is not "permitted by law." Second, other code provisions have dealt with the specific situation involved. And third, legislative intent to exclude the justification urged here does "otherwise plainly appear." Hence, the legislature has made clear its determination that this Court shall not have the discretion to make the "necessity" defense available to this defendant.

Three separate provisions of Title 24 compel the conclusion that Tate is precluded from arguing the defense that he seeks to assert. The first is N.J.S.A. 24:21-5(a), which classifies marijuana as a Schedule I controlled dangerous substance. Its denomination as such means that the legislature has determined that marijuana has "high potential for abuse" and has "no accepted medical use in treatment . . . or lacks accepted safety for use in treatment under medical supervision." The possibility of medical use of marijuana was thus specifically contemplated and specifically rejected.

The legislature nonetheless demonstrated foresight by leaving room for the possibility that scientific developments and advances in knowledge could ultimately render marijuana's Schedule I classification inappropriate: it enacted the second significant provision, N.J.S.A. 24:21-3(a), which granted to the Commissioner of Health the authority to reschedule marijuana (and all scheduled controlled dangerous substances), giving consideration to, *inter alia*, current scientific knowledge. At this juncture the Commissioner has not exercised that authority in respect of marijuana.

The third relevant section, N.J.S.A. 24:2120(a), provides further-and even clearer-evidence that the legislature gave consideration to possible medical uses of controlled dangerous substances. That section defines the offense with which defendant is charged. It provides:

> "It is unlawful for any person, knowingly or intentionally, to obtain, or to possess, actually or constructively, a controlled dangerous substance *unless such substance was obtained directly, or pursuant to a valid prescription or order from a practitioner, while acting in the course of his professional practice,* or except as otherwise authorized by this act. [(Emphasis added.)]

The emphasized language amounts to an exception set forth in the "offense" statute itself—an exception for medically-necessary possession of marijuana. In creating that exception the legislature went so far as to spell out an indispensable condition for possession of a controlled dangerous substance, namely, "a valid prescription or order from a practitioner. . . ." Because defendant did not possess a valid prescription, he cannot claim the protection of this statutory exception. And because the legislature provided this exception dealing with the specific situation presented here, this Court is without authority to fashion an alternative exception for defendant under the Code's "necessity" section, N.J.S.A. 2C:3-2(a).

The foregoing provisions of Title 24 preclude the defense of "necessity" both because they specifically deal with the exception urged and because they evidence a legislative intent to preclude the defense except under the conditions set forth, *i.e.*, with a valid prescription. But there is more. The enactment of the TRA, N.J.S.A. 26:2L-1 to -9, gives further support to the conclusion that the legislature's purpose was to exclude the defense of "necessity" in the circumstances before us. Although scientific and medical knowledge have not yet prompted the rescheduling under N.J.S.A. 24:21-3(a) of marijuana as a non-Schedule I substance, the legislature has recognized marijuana's potential for beneficial medical uses. The TRA provides a way to permit study of and experimentation with those uses while maintaining the protection intended by the Controlled Dangerous Substances Act. Use of a controlled dangerous substance under the auspices of the TRA is not a violation of the criminal provisions regarding use of those substances. N.J.S.A. 26:2L-9.

The judgment of the Appellate Division is reversed. The cause is remanded for further proceedings not inconsistent with this opinion.

HANDLER, Justice, dissenting.

The issue presented in this appeal is the availability of the defense of justification to a criminal indictment for the unlawful possession of marijuana. The defendant is a quadriplegic who asserts that his use of marijuana is a "medical necessity" because it is the only treatment that can ease the pain of severe, recurring spastic contractions. The defense is claimed under the New Jersey Code of Criminal Justice, N.J.S.A. 2C:3-2(a). The Court today rejects the defense. It expresses the view that the Code constitutes a statutory codification that supplants any common-law principles that would otherwise elucidate the meaning of this defense, and, looking to particular provisions of N.J.S.A. 2C:32(a), it rules that medical necessity for the possession of marijuana is not allowed as a justification defense under the Code.

In my opinion the Court misperceives the purpose and effect of the Legislature's codification of the common-law necessity doctrine and errs in discounting the common-law antecedents of the Code justification defense; it also reads the Code much too strictly in interpreting and applying the operative statutory language. I take a different tack and reach a different conclusion. It is my view that under the Code the defense of justification based on medical necessity is available with respect to the use of marijuana in the context of the limited and special circumstances that are present in this case. I therefore dissent from the opinion of the Court.

Defendant here served notice on the Monmouth County Prosecutor that he would rely on the defense of medical necessity at his trial. He contended that he was prepared to present evidence that he uses marijuana because it eases the severity of spastic contractions regularly suffered by quadriplegics and that no other prescribable medication gives him such relief. The trial court accepted this proffer in ruling that the justification defense was available. The court posited four criteria that the defendant must meet to support the claim of medical necessity. It ruled that a defendant who seeks to assert medical necessity as a justification defense must demonstrate by competent evidence that he has a medically recognized condition, that his condition is life- or sense-threatening, that use of an illicit substance ameliorates the condition or relieves the pain, and that no legal, prescribable substance can provide similar relief without deleterious side effects. The court further held that a judge, not the jury, would decide the question of public policy—that is, whether the individual's need outweighs society's interest in enforcing the criminal law. The court also ruled that the defense of necessity was an affirmative defense, which requires that the defendant first produce evidence supporting it, thereby shifting the burden to the State to disprove its existence.

There is some decisional support for this position. In *Washington v. Diana*, 24 Wash. App. 908, 604 P.2d 1312 (1979), the defendant suffered from multiple sclerosis and claimed medical necessity as a defense to a charge of possession of marijuana. The court reversed his earlier conviction and remanded the case to the trial court to give the defendant an opportunity to demonstrate the alleged beneficial effect, if any, of marijuana on his symptoms, and to establish that his use of marijuana was medically necessary and therefore justified his possession. Significantly, the court required defendant to provide corroborating medical testing to support his assertions that he reasonably believed his use of marijuana was necessary to protect his health.

Additionally, in *U.S. v. Randall*, 104 Daily Wash. L. Rtpr. 2249, the defendant grew and used marijuana and was arrested for possession. He raised the defense of medical necessity and provided expert medical testimony that revealed that prescribed glaucoma medications were ineffective and that defendant's experimental use of marijuana neutralized inner-ocular pressure and lessened visual distortion caused by the disease. In determining whether the evil to be avoided by the defendant's act was greater than that inherent in the possession and personal use of marijuana, the court balanced the defendant's interest in preserving his sight against the government's interest in controlling the drug. The court concluded that defendant's right to preserve his sight outweighed the government's interest in outlawing the drug. Special emphasis was placed upon the importance of an individual's right to preserve and protect his own health and body.

Further, in *State v. Bachman*, 61 Hawaii 71, 595 P.2d 287 (1979), the need for adequate expert evidence in support of the defense was particularly emphasized. The court rejected the defense because defendant failed to show by competent medical testimony the beneficial effects upon the defendant's condition of marijuana use, in addition to the absence or ineffectiveness of conventional medical alternatives. The court noted that in the presence of such proof, medical necessity could be asserted as a defense to a charge of unlawful possession of marijuana.

This case law, coupled with the legislative intention to fashion a defense premised upon malleable common-law precepts, is instructive in formulating the standards relevant to the justification defense of medical necessity. Accordingly, I would hold that in order successfully to assert medical necessity as a justification defense in a case involving a controlled dangerous substance, a defendant must meet several criteria. The test would reflect a multi-faceted standard appropriately drawn from the common law. It would require: (1) the defendant must be suffering from a condition that involves intolerable pain, or an immediate, actual, or substantial threat to his life, health, vital senses, or basic physical or mental well-being; (2) the suffering experienced by the defendant from the harmful condition necessitates resort to unlawful conduct involving the prohibited controlled dangerous substance in order to eliminate, avoid, or substantially ameliorate the acuteness of the threatening condition; (3) there must be an absence of any other lawful treatment, substance or procedure that is available to the medical profession for the defendant that could similarly relieve the harmful condition or accomplish the same result as that achieved through the unlawful conduct; (4) it must be demonstrated that the defendant's decision to resort to the unlawful possession or use of the prohibited substance is based on reasonable necessity, which shall include a good-faith effort to relieve the harmful condition through normally accepted medical treatment; (5) competent expert medical evidence must be submitted demonstrating (i) that the harmful condition was medically genuine, (ii) that the unlawful conduct eliminated or materially and substantially relieved the condition, and (iii) that there was no alternative treatment or substance legally available for the harmful condition; (6) it must be shown that the situation precipitating the decision by the defendant to engage in unlawful conduct to alleviate or eliminate the harmful condition was not brought about by any actions of the defendant; and (7) it must appear that from a social standpoint, under the circumstances, the criminal punishment of the defendant for the unlawful conduct is less important than allowing the defendant to obtain relief from the harmful condition.

These standards would impel me to rule in this case that defendant is entitled to demonstrate the availability of the necessity-justification defense.

Questions and Notes

1. Among Tate, Gerlach, and Archer, whose necessity claim has the greatest moral validity?

2. If the legislature had considered and rejected a situation such as Tate's, should Tate necessarily lose?

3. Does the dissent's view of the case create a potential for mischief?

4. In *Blake*, we focus on the difference between a duress (compulsion) defense, which the court gave, and a necessity defense, which it did not give.

People v. Blake

522 N.E.2d 822 (Ill. App. Ct. 1988)

Justice STOUDER delivered the opinion of the court:

The defendant, Levi Q. Blake, was charged with the offenses of home invasion, armed robbery and residential burglary. A jury found him guilty of all three offenses. The trial court entered a judgment of conviction for home invasion and sentenced him to 12 years' imprisonment. The defendant appeals his conviction, arguing, inter alia, that the jury should have been instructed on necessity.

The State presented the following evidence at trial. On February 1, 1987, Mabel Schadt was living at her two-story house at 613 Voris Street in Peoria. Because Schadt had had cataract surgery the previous August, her neighbor, Rosemary Maloney would come to her house at about 7 p.m. each evening and spend the night. On January 31, 1987, the two women went to bed at around 11 p.m. after locking the doors and securing the house. They slept in separate bedrooms on the second floor.

At approximately 6 a.m. on February 1, Schadt was awakened by a noise and saw a young man push open her bedroom door. At approximately the same time, Maloney, who had been awake, saw a different man in the hall. She heard one of the men say "I'm going in and rough her up," and the other man say "I'm going on in her room and have some fun." The man who entered Schadt's room fired a pistol and went through her dresser drawers. After a few minutes, the man left her room and ran downstairs.

Schadt went to Maloney's room to help her. The man in Maloney's room told Schadt to lie down and struck her in the face with a gun. Maloney was already lying on the bed since the same man had put the gun to her head.

The victims remained in the room for about five minutes. The man who had been in Schadt's room returned to that room and ransacked it. He made several quick trips downstairs. At one point the women heard him yell to someone downstairs, referring to him by a number. The women also heard someone downstairs yell to the man upstairs.

In the meantime, the Peoria police were dispatched to 613 Voris. Officer Dale Whitledge arrived first. He inspected the exterior of the residence and saw that the back door had been broken into. He then saw two men appear at the back door. When Whitledge drew his gun and yelled at them to stop, they slammed the door shut, remaining inside.

Officer Jeff Adams saw a man jump through the window of the first-floor dining room and run from the house. Adams pursued the man. When the man pointed a gun and fired a shot at Adams, Adams returned fire, killing the suspect. The deceased, later identified as Willie James Dixon, had a .22 caliber revolver in his hand. The gun had one spent round and five live rounds.

Whitledge saw a man jump out of Schadt's bedroom window, onto the roof of the back porch, and then into a neighbor's yard. Whitledge apprehended the man, Anthony Dixon, nearby. Whitledge found a starter's pistol on the ground near where Anthony had landed. The gun would only fire blanks or caps.

The officers next went into the house to check on the women. Schadt had bruised shoulders and an open wound on her face. The women could not identify the assailants or describe them in detail. A color television set, microwave oven and clock were missing from the house. The officers searched the entire house, including the attic, but found no one.

That same morning, the police found the missing television, microwave oven and clock in an alley a block away. There were two sets of footprints in the snow running from the items toward the general direction of Schadt's residence. Once of the footprints matched a shoe worn by Willie Dixon. A latent thumbprint taken from the clock matched the defendant's left thumbprint.

Around 1:30 p.m. that day, Phillip Berme was inside Schadt's home when he heard a noise upstairs. Berme went to the attic, opened the lid of a cardboard barrel and found the defendant inside. Berme asked the defendant who else was with him and where his gun was. The defendant responded: "My cousins Anthony and James. Man, I don't have no gun. Where's Anthony? Is he in the hospital?" The defendant did not have a weapon.

At trial, the defendant testified on his own behalf. His testimony was as follows. He had known the Dixons for four or five months before February 1, 1987. The defendant had been at Anthony's apartment from morning until 7 p.m. on January 31, 1987. The defendant was drinking malt liquor from a 12-pack which he split with Anthony. The defendant could not recall having the blank gun with him at any time that evening.

Around 7 p.m., the defendant and Anthony went to a party across the street. There, the defendant became intoxicated. Willie later arrived at the party and brought with him some marijuana cigarettes. The defendant smoked the cigarettes, became drowsy and fell asleep at the party. He was awakened later by Anthony. The defendant wanted to sleep but reluctantly went with Anthony to his apartment.

At his apartment the defendant drank some whiskey and fell asleep. He awoke when Willie entered the apartment. Willie argued with Anthony. Anthony then grabbed the defendant and told him he needed fresh air. The defendant said that he was tired and drunk but went outside with the Dixons.

When the defendant stated he was going home, Willie said that it was too late to walk home and that the defendant should go along to Willie's place. The defendant agreed to go with the Dixons if they would walk him home. The defendant stated that he was drunk and confused, and felt as if the Dixons had made the decision where to go for him.

The three men walked past Schadt's house. They then stopped and asked the defendant if he had lived near there. The defendant asked why the Dixons were interested. The Dixons then had a conversation in some sort of "pig Latin" which the defendant could not understand and walked back towards Voris. The defendant, still drunk, foolishly followed. He did not know what the Dixons were going to do.

The Dixons jumped over the backyard fence at 613 Voris. At this point, when the defendant said that he was leaving, Willie pointed a gun at the defendant and ordered him to climb over the fence. The defendant complied and told Willie not to shoot him. The Dixons went over to a basement window, kicked it and then decided to force the back door in. The Dixons went into the house. The defendant remained outside.

The defendant continued to testify that once the Dixons entered the house, he began to walk away. Willie came out of the house and, while holding the gun in his hand, told the defendant he could not leave. The defendant then heard a woman scream inside the house. The defendant told Willie he would do anything so long as the Dixons left the women alone and Willie did not point the gun at him. Willie told the defendant to stay outside. He also told the defendant that if he found that the defendant had left, he would go upstairs and start shooting. According to the defendant, he agreed not to leave because he wanted to save himself and the women.

Willie came back outside with a television set, a microwave oven and a clock. Willie ordered the defendant to help him carry the items. When the defendant balked,

Willie asked the defendant if he wanted to see the women die. The defendant said no and assisted Willie.

The defendant followed Willie to a nearby garage where they left the items. Willie ordered the defendant back to Schadt's home.

Willie told the defendant to come into the house because Willie did not trust the defendant outside. Willie went upstairs after telling the defendant to act as a look-out and saying that he would start shooting if he called down to the defendant and received no response.

After several minutes, the defendant saw the police arrive and begin to inspect the house. At the same time Willie asked Anthony and the defendant if everything was alright, referring to them as "number 2" and "number 3." Only after the defendant saw that the police had surrounded the house did the defendant warn the Dixons, in an effort to get them away from the women. As the Dixons attempted to escape, the defendant hid in the attic. He feared being shot if he revealed himself and had no idea how long he would remain in the attic.

On appeal, the defendant raises two issues. The first is whether the trial court erred in refusing the defendant's instruction on necessity. At the jury instructions conference, the defendant tendered instructions on the defenses of compulsion and necessity. The court accepted the compulsion instruction but refused the instruction on necessity. Rather, the court modified the compulsion instruction to include the concept of threat against another person. The instruction was given as follows:

> "It is a defense to the charges made against the defendant that he acted under the compulsion of threat or menace of the imminent infliction of death or great bodily harm, if he reasonably believed death or great bodily harm would be inflicted upon himself or another if he did not perform the conduct with which he is charged."

The defendant argues first that under the definition of compulsion, a person is not guilty of an offense if: (1) he acts under the threat of imminent death or great bodily harm; and (2) he reasonably believes that death or great bodily harm will be inflicted if he does not perform the conduct which constitutes the offense. The defendant next argues that necessity justifies criminal conduct if: (1) the accused was without blame in developing the situation; and (2) the accused reasonably believed such conduct was necessary to avoid a public or private injury greater than the injury which might result from his own conduct.

From the above, the defendant contends that the court's instruction did not adequately communicate to the jury his theory of defense: that he was acting to prevent a greater injury to the women. The defendant also argues that necessity does not require an imminent threat of harm. The defendant asserts that the jury may have rejected his compulsion defense because he was not imminently threatened while the Dixons were inside the house.

Compulsion is defined in relevant part by the Criminal Code of 1961 in the following manner:

> "A person is not guilty of an offense, other than an offense punishable with death, by reason of conduct which he performs under the compulsion of threat or menace of the imminent infliction of death or great bodily harm, if he reasonably believes death or great bodily harm will be inflicted upon him if he does not perform such conduct." Ill. Rev. Stat., 1985, ch. 38, par. 7–11.

The defense of necessity is defined as follows:

> "Conduct which would otherwise be an offense is justifiable by reason of necessity if the accused was without blame in occasioning or developing the situation and reasonably believed such conduct was necessary to avoid a public or private injury greater than the injury which might reasonably result from his own conduct."

The defense of compulsion generally requires an impending threat of great bodily harm together with a demand that the person perform the specific criminal act for which he eventually is charged. Necessity, on the other hand, justifies illegal conduct if that conduct was the sole reasonable alternative available to the defendant given the circumstances of the case. Necessity involves a choice between two admitted evils where other options are unavailable. It is well settled that only slight evidence is necessary to warrant the giving of appropriate instructions.

In the case at bar, the defendant's testimony, if believed, indicated that he was without blame in occasioning the situation. The defendant stated that he was drunk, that he thought that the Dixons were walking him home, and that Willie ordered him at gunpoint to participate in the robbery. The defendant's testimony further indicates that as the events progressed, he feared that his non-cooperation with the Dixons would cause them to injure the women. If the jury believed his testimony about that fear, it could find that the defendant was forced to choose between the lesser of two admitted evils. The jury instructions given by the court failed to address the possibility that the defendant did not exercise free will, but rather chose to act illegally to avert the injury or death of Schadt and Maloney. We find that the court erred reversibly in refusing to give the defendant's tendered instruction on necessity.

Accordingly, the judgment of the circuit court of Peoria County is reversed. The cause is remanded for further proceedings consistent with this opinion.

Questions and Notes

1. Given that the jury rejected Blake's duress defense, on what basis could it possibly find that he acted from necessity?

2. Is Blake inherently unbelievable? If so, why waste the jury's time with a frivolous defendant?

3. More importantly, why manufacture defenses that encourage criminals to lie?

Problem

Four seamen—Dudley, Stephens, Brooks, and Parker—have been on a life raft for several days more than 1,000 miles from land following a shipwreck disaster. With no immediate hope for or sign of rescue, and all food gone, the men realized that they must sacrifice one of their number as food for the others or all would starve to death.

Because Parker was the weakest and nearest to death, Dudley suggested that he be sacrificed. Stephens agreed, Brooks dissented, and Parker was too weak to express an opinion. Dudley then killed Parker, and the remaining three subsisted on his flesh until they were rescued several days later. At the trial of Dudley and Stephens, it was determined that had they not eaten Parker's flesh all four would have probably perished.

Should Dudley and Stephens have a successful necessity defense? For the court's resolution of this famous case, *see Regina v. Dudley and Stephens*, 15 Cox Crim. Cas. 624 (Q.B. 1884).

See Nutshell § 11.04.

Chapter 13

Entrapment

Entrapment occurs when the government is so excessively involved in encouraging criminal behavior that justice demands an acquittal. As *Sherman*, *Jacobson*, and *Powell* establish, the justification for the defense is far from clear. It is not even certain whether entrapment is a substantive defense such as duress or insanity, or whether it is a procedural defense designed to discipline the police such as the Fourth Amendment's (unreasonable searches and seizures) exclusionary rule. Consider those conflicting rationales as you read *Sherman*.

Sherman v. United States

356 U.S. 369 (1958)

Mr. Chief Justice WARREN delivered the opinion of the Court.

The issue before us is whether petitioner's conviction should be set aside on the ground that as a matter of law the defense of entrapment was established. Petitioner was convicted under an indictment charging three sales of narcotics in violation of 21 U.S.C. § 174, 21 U.S.C.A. § 174.

In late August 1951, Kalchinian, a government informer, first met petitioner at a doctor's office where apparently both were being treated to be cured of narcotics addition. Several accidental meetings followed, either at the doctor's office or at the pharmacy where both filled their prescriptions from the doctor. From mere greetings, conversation progressed to a discussion of mutual experiences and problems, including their attempts to overcome addiction to narcotics. Finally, Kalchinian asked petitioner if he knew of a good source of narcotics. He asked petitioner to supply him with a source because he was not responding to treatment. From the first, petitioner tried to avoid the issue. Not until after a number of repetitions of the request, predicated on Kalchinian's presumed suffering, did petitioner finally acquiesce. Several times thereafter he obtained a quantity of narcotics which he shared with Kalchinian. Each time petitioner told Kalchinian that the total cost of narcotics he obtained was twenty-five dollars and that Kalchinian owed him fifteen dollars. The informer thus bore the cost of his share of the narcotics plus the taxi and other expenses necessary to obtain the drug. After several such sales Kalchinian informed agents of the Bureau of Narcotics that he had another seller for them. On three occasions during November 1951. Government agents observed petitioner give narcotics to Kalchinian in return for money supplied by the Government.

At the trial the factual issue was whether the informer had convinced an otherwise unwilling person to commit a criminal act or whether petitioner was already predisposed to commit the act and exhibited only the natural hesitancy of one acquainted with the narcotics trade. The issue of entrapment went to the jury, and a conviction resulted. Petitioner was sentenced to imprisonment for ten years. The Court of Appeals for the Second Circuit affirmed. We granted certiorari.

In *Sorrells v. United States*, 287 U.S. 435, this Court firmly recognized the defense of entrapment in the federal courts. The intervening years have in no way detracted from the principles underlying that decision. The function of law enforcement is the prevention of crime and the apprehension of criminals. Manifestly, that function does not include the manufacturing of crime. Criminal activity is such that stealth and strategy are necessary weapons in the arsenal of the police officer. However, "A different question is presented when the criminal design originates with the officials of the government, and they implant in the mind of an innocent person the disposition to commit the alleged offense and induce its commission in order that they may prosecute." The stealth and strategy become as objectionable police methods as the coerced confession and the unlawful search. Congress could not have intended that its statutes were to be enforced by tempting innocent persons into violations.

However, the fact that government agents "merely afford opportunities or facilities for the commission of the offense does not" constitute entrapment. Entrapment occurs only when the criminal conduct was "the product of the *creative* activity" of law-enforcement officials. (Emphasis supplied.) To determine whether entrapment has been established, a line must be drawn between the trap for the unwary innocent and the trap for the unwary criminal. The principles by which the courts are to make this determination were outlined in *Sorrells*. On the one hand, at trial the accused may examine the conduct of the government agent; and on the other hand, the accused will be subjected to an "appropriate and searching inquiry into his own conduct and predisposition" as bearing on his claim of innocence.

We conclude from the evidence that entrapment was established as a matter of law. In so holding, we are not choosing between conflicting witnesses, nor judging credibility. Aside from recalling Kalchinian, who was the Government's witness, the defense called no witnesses. We reach our conclusion from the undisputed testimony of the prosecution's witnesses.

It is patently clear that petitioner was induced by Kalchinian. The informer himself testified that, believing petitioner to be undergoing a cure for narcotics addiction, he nonetheless sought to persuade petitioner to obtain for him a source of narcotics. In Kalchinian's own words we are told of the accidental, yet recurring, meetings, the ensuing conversations concerning mutual experiences in regard to narcotics addiction, and then of Kalchinian's resort to sympathy. On request was not enough, for Kalchinian tells us that additional ones were necessary to overcome, first, petitioner's refusal, then has evasiveness, and then his hesitancy in order to achieve capitulation. Kalchinian not only procured a source of narcotics but apparently also induced petitioner to return to the habit. Finally, assured of a catch, Kalchinian informed the authorities so that they could close the net. The Government cannot disown Kalchinian and insist it is not responsible for his actions. Although he was not being paid, Kalchinian was an active government informer who had but recently been the instigatory of at least two other prosecutions. Undoubtedly the impetus for such achievements was the fact that in 1951 Kalchinian was himself under criminal charges for illegally selling narcotics and had not yet been sentenced. It makes no difference that the sales for which petitioner was convicted occurred after a series of sales. They were not independent acts subsequent to the inducement but part of a course of conduct which was the product of the inducement. In his testimony the federal agent in charge of the case admitted that he never bothered to question Kalchinian about the way he had made contact with petitioner. The Government cannot make such use of an informer and then claim disassociation through ignorance.

The Government sought to overcome the defense of entrapment by claiming that petitioner evinced a "ready complaisance" to accede to Kalchinian's request. Aside from a record of past convictions, which we discuss in the following paragraph, the Government's case is unsupported. There is no evidence that petitioner himself was in the trade. When his apartment was searched after arrest, no narcotics were found. There is no significant evidence that petitioner even made a profit on any sale to Kalchinian. The Government's characterization of petitioner's hesitancy to Kalchinian's request as the natural wariness of the criminal cannot fill the evidentiary void.

The Government's additional evidence in the second trial to show that petitioner was ready and willing to sell narcotics should the opportunity present itself was petitioner's record of two past narcotics convictions. In 1942 petitioner was convicted of illegally selling narcotics; in 1946 he was convicted of illegally possessing them. However, a nine-year old sales conviction and a five-year-old possession conviction are insufficient to prove petitioner had a readiness to sell narcotics at the time Kalchinian approached him, particularly when we must assume from the record he was trying to overcome the narcotics habit at the time.

The case at bar illustrates an evil which the defense of entrapment is designed to overcome. The government informer entices someone attempting to avoid narcotics not only into carrying out an illegal sale but also into returning to the habit of use. Selecting the proper time, the informer then tells the government agent. The set-up is accepted by the agent without even a question as to the manner in which the informer encountered the seller. Thus the Government plays on the weaknesses of an innocent party and beguiles him into committing crimes which he otherwise would not have attempted. Law enforcement does not require methods such as this.

The judgment of the Court of Appeals is reversed and the case is remanded to the District Court with instructions to dismiss the indictment.

Reversed and remanded.

Mr. Justice FRANKFURTER, whom Mr. Justice DOUGLAS, Mr. Justice HARLAN, and Mr. Justice BRENNAN join, concurring in the result.

Although agreeing with the Court that the undisputed facts show entrapment as a matter of law, I reach this result by a route different from the Court's.

The first case in which a federal court clearly recognized and sustained a claim of entrapment by government officers as a defense to an indictment was, apparently, *Woo Wai v. United States*, 9 Cir., 223 F. 412. Yet the basis of this defense, affording guidance for its application in particular circumstances, is as much in doubt today as it was when the defense was first recognized over forty years ago, although entrapment has been the decisive issue in many prosecutions. The lower courts have continued gropingly to express the feeling of outrage at conduct of law enforcers that brought recognition of the defense in the first instance, but without the formulated basis in reason that it is the first duty of courts to construct for justifying and guiding emotion and instinct.

Today's opinion does not promote this judicial desideratum and fails to give the doctrine of entrapment the solid foundation that the decisions of the lower courts and criticism of learned writers have clearly shown is needed. Instead it accepts without re-examination the theory espoused in *Sorrells v. United States*, 287 U.S. 435, over strong protest by Mr. Justice Roberts, speaking for Brandeis and Stone, J.J., as well as himself.

It is surely sheer fiction to suggest that a conviction cannot be had when a defendant has been entrapped by government officers or informers because "Congress could not have intended that its statutes were to be enforced by tempting innocent persons into violations." In these cases raising claims of entrapment, the only legislative intention that can with any show of reason be extracted from the statute is the intention to make criminal precisely the conduct in which the defendant has engaged. That conduct includes all the elements necessary to constitute criminality. Without compulsion and "knowingly," where that is requisite, the defendant has violated the statutory command. If he is to be relieved from the usual punitive consequences, it is on no account because he is innocent of the offense described. In these circumstances, conduct is not less criminal because the result of temptation, whether the tempter is a private person or government agent or informer.

The courts refuse to convict an entrapped defendant, not because his conduct falls outside the proscription of the statute, but because, even if his guilt be admitted, the methods employed on behalf of the Government to bring about conviction cannot be countenanced. As Mr. Justice Holmes said in *Olmstead v. United States*, 277 U.S. 438, 470 (dissenting), in another connection, "It is desirable that criminals should be detected, and to that end that all available evidence should be used. It also is desirable that the government should not itself foster and pay for other crimes, when they are the means by which the evidence is to be obtained. . . . (F)or my part I think it a less evil that some criminals should escape than that the government should play an ignoble part." Insofar as they are used as instrumentalities in the administration of criminal justice, the federal courts have an obligation to set their face against enforcement of the law by lawless means or means that violate rationally vindicated standards of justice, and to refuse to sustain such methods by effectuating them. They do this in the exercise of a recognized jurisdiction to formulate and apply "proper standards for the enforcement of the federal criminal law in the federal courts," an obligation that goes beyond the conviction of the particular defendant before the court. Public confidence in the fair and honorable administration of justice, upon which ultimately depends the rule of law, is the transcending value at stake.

The formulation of these standards does not in any way conflict with the statute the defendant has violated, or involve the initiation of a judicial policy disregarding or qualifying that framed by Congress. A false choice is put when it is said that either the defendant's conduct does not fall within the statute or he must be convicted. The statute is wholly directed to defining and prohibiting the substantive offense concerned and expresses no purpose, either permissive or prohibitory, regarding the police conduct that will be tolerated in the detection of crime. A statute prohibiting the sale of narcotics is as silent on the question of entrapment as it is on the admissibility of illegally obtained evidence. It is enacted, however, on the basis of certain presuppositions concerning the established legal order and the role of the courts within that system in formulating standards for the administration of criminal justice when Congress itself has not specifically legislated to that end. Specific statutes are to be fitted into an antecedent legal system.

It might be thought that it is largely an academic question whether the court's finding a bar to conviction derives from the statute or from a supervisory jurisdiction over the administration of criminal justice; under either theory substantially the same considerations will determine whether the defense of entrapment is sustained. But to look to a statute for guidance in the application of a policy not remotely within the contemplation of Congress at the time of its enactment is to distort analysis. It is to run the risk, furthermore, that the court will shirk the responsibility that is necessarily in its keeping, if Congress is truly silent, to accommodate the dangers of overzealous law enforcement and civilized methods adequate to counter the ingenuity of modern criminals. The reasons that actually underlie the defense of entrapment can too easily be lost sight of in the pursuit of a wholly fictitious congressional intent.

The crucial question, not easy of answer, to which the court must direct itself is whether the police conduct revealed in the particular case falls below standards, to which common feelings respond, for the proper use of governmental power. For answer it is wholly irrelevant to ask if the "intention" to commit the crime originated with the defendant or government officers, or if the criminal conduct was the product of "the creative activity" of law-enforcement officials. Yet in the present case the Court repeats and purports to apply these unrevealing tests. Of course in every case of this kind the intention that the particular crime be committed originates with the police, and without their inducement the crime would not have occurred. But it is perfectly clear from such decisions as the decoy letter cases in this Court, *e.g., Grimm v. United States,* 156 U.S. 604, where the police in effect simply furnished the opportunity for the commission of the crime, that this is not enough to enable the defendant to escape conviction.

The intention referred to, therefore, must be a general intention or predisposition to commit, whenever the opportunity should arise, crimes of the kind solicited, and in proof of such a predisposition evidence has often been admitted to show the defendant's reputation, criminal activities, and prior disposition. The danger of prejudice in such a situation, particularly if the issue of entrapment must be submitted to the jury and disposed of by a general verdict of guilty or innocent, is evident. The defendant must either forego the claim of entrapment or run the substantial risk that, in spite of instructions, the jury will allow a criminal record or bad reputation to weigh in its determination of guilt of the specific offense of which he stands charged. Furthermore, a test that looks to the character and predisposition of the defendant rather than the conduct of the police loses sight of the underlying reason for the defense of entrapment. No matter what the defendant's past record and present inclinations to criminality, or the depths to which he has sunk in the estimation of society, certain police conduct to ensnare him into further crime is not to be tolerated by an advanced society. And in the present case it is clear that the Court in fact reverses the conviction because of the conduct of the informer Kalchinian, and not because the Government has failed to draw a convincing picture of petitioner's past criminal conduct. Permissible police activity does not vary according to the particular defendant concerned; surely if two suspects have been solicited at the same time in the same manner, one should not go to jail simply because he has been convicted before and is said to have a criminal disposition. No more does it very according to the suspicions, reasonable or unreasonable, of the police concerning the defendant's activities. Appeals to sympathy, friendship, the possibility of exorbitant gain, and so forth, can no more be tolerated when directed against a past offender than against an ordinary law-abiding citizen. A contrary view runs afoul of fundamental principles of equality under law, and would espouse the notion that when dealing with the criminal classes anything goes. The possibility that no matter what his past crimes and general disposition the defendant might not have committed the particular crime unless confronted with inordinate inducements, must not be ignored. Past crimes do not forever outlaw the criminal and open him to police practices, aimed at securing his repeated conviction, from which the ordinary citizen is protected. The whole ameliorative hopes of modern penology and prison administration strongly counsel against such a view.

This does not mean that the police may not act so as to detect those engaged in criminal conduct and ready and willing to commit further crimes should the occasion arise. Such indeed is their obligation. It does mean that in holding out inducements they should act in such a manner as is likely to induce to the commission of crime only these persons and not others who would normally avoid crime and through self-struggle resist ordinary temptations. This test shifts attention from the record and predisposition of the particular defendant to the conduct of the police and the likelihood, objectively considered, that it would entrap only those ready and willing to commit crime. It is as objective a test as the subject matter permits, and will give guidance in regulating police conduct that is lacking when the reasonableness of police suspicions must be judged or the criminal disposition of the defendant retrospectively appraised. It draws directly on the fundamental intuition that led in the first instance to the outlawing of "entrapment" as a prosecutorial instrument. The power of government is abused and directed to an end for which it was not constituted when employed to promote rather than detect crime and to bring about the downfall of those who, left to themselves, might well have obeyed the law. Human nature is weak enough and sufficiently beset by temptations without government adding to them and generating crime.

What police conduct is to be condemned, because likely to induce those not otherwise ready and willing to commit crime, must be picked out from case to case as new situations arise involving different crimes and new methods of detection. Particularly reprehensible in the present case was the use of repeated requests to overcome petitioner's hesitancy, coupled with appeals to sympathy based on mutual experiences with narcotics addiction. Evidence of the setting in which the inducement took place is of course highly relevant in judging its likely effect, and the court should also consider the nature of the crime involved, its secrecy and difficulty of detection, and the manner in which the particular criminal business is usually carried on.

As Mr. Justice Roberts convincingly urged in the *Sorrells* case, such a judgment, aimed at blocking off areas of impermissible police conduct, is appropriate for the court and not the jury. "The protection of its own functions and the preservation of the purity of its own temple belongs only to the court. It is the province of the court and of the court alone to protect itself and the government from such prostitution of the criminal law. The violation of the principles of justice by the entrapment of the unwary into crime should be dealt with by the court no matter by whom or at what stage of the proceedings the facts are brought to its attention." Equally important is the consideration that a jury verdict, although it may settle the issue of entrapment in the particular case, cannot give significant guidance for official conduct for the future. Only the court, through the gradual evolution of explicit standards in accumulated precedents, can do this with the degree of certainty that the wise administration of criminal justice demands.

Questions and Notes

1. What are the differences between Chief Justice Warren and Justice Frankfurter's approaches to the entrapment issue?

2. Can you think of a case that might come out differently under the two approaches?

3. Had you been on the Court, how would you have voted in *Sherman*? Why?

4. Do you think that it is sheer fiction to believe that congressional intent is relevant here? Does Congress explicitly think about whether it wants its bank robbery statutes enforced against one who performed the robbery under duress?

5. Would (should) Sherman have been convicted if Kalchinian were an ordinary citizen rather than a government employee? Why?

6. In *Jacobson*, the entire Court, at least in form, endorses the non-predisposition requirement. See if you think that the majority retains its substance.

Jacobson v. United States
503 U.S. 540 (1992)

Justice White delivered the opinion of the Court.

On September 24, 1987, petitioner Keith Jacobson was indicted for violating a provision of the Child Protection Act of 1984 (Act), Pub. L. 98-292, 98 Stat. 204, which criminalizes the knowing receipt through the mails of a "visual depiction [that] involves the use of a minor engaging in sexually explicit conduct. . . ." 18 U.S.C. § 2252(a)(2)(A). Petitioner defended on the ground that the Government entrapped him into committing the crime through a series of communications from undercover agents that spanned the 26 months preceding his arrest. Petitioner was found guilty after a jury trial. The Court of Appeals affirmed his conviction, holding that the Government had carried its burden of proving beyond reasonable doubt that petitioner was predisposed to break the law and hence was not entrapped.

Because the Government overstepped the line between setting a trap for the "unwary innocent" and the "unwary criminal," *Sherman*; and as a matter of law failed to establish that petitioner was independently predisposed to commit the crime for which he was arrested, we reverse the Court of Appeals' judgment affirming his conviction.

I

In February 1984, petitioner, a 56-year-old veteran-turned-farmer who supported his elderly father in Nebraska, ordered two magazines and a brochure from a California adult bookstore. The magazines, entitled Bare Boys I and Bare Boys II, contained photographs of nude preteen and teenage boys. The contents of the magazines startled petitioner, who testified that he had expected to receive photographs of "young men 18 years or older." Tr. 425. On cross-examination, he explained his response to the magazines:

"[PROSECUTOR]: You were shocked and surprised that there were pictures of very young boys without clothes on, is that correct?

"[JACOBSON]:Yes, I was.

"[PROSECUTOR]: Were you offended?

"[JACOBSON]: I was not offended because I thought these were a nudist type publication. Many of the pictures were out in a rural or outdoor setting. There was—I didn't draw any sexual connotation or connection with that."

Id. The young men depicted in the magazines were not engaged in sexual activity, and petitioner's receipt of the magazines was legal under both federal and Nebraska law. Within three months, the law with respect to child pornography changed; Congress passed the Act illegalizing the receipt through the mails of sexually explicit depictions of children. In the very month that the new provision became law, postal inspectors found petitioner's name on the mailing list of the California bookstore that had mailed him Bare Boys I and II. There followed over the next 2 1/2 years repeated efforts by two Government agencies, through five fictitious organizations and a bogus pen pal, to explore petitioner's willingness to break the new law by ordering sexually explicit photographs of children through the mail.

The Government began its efforts in January 1985 when a postal inspector sent petitioner a letter supposedly from the American Hedonist Society, which in fact was a fictitious organization. The letter included a membership application and stated the Society's doctrine: that members had the "right to read what we desire, the right to discuss similar interests with those who share our philosophy, and finally that we have the right to seek pleasure without restrictions being placed on us by outdated puritan morality." Petitioner enrolled in the organization and returned a sexual attitude questionnaire that asked him to rank on a scale of one to four his enjoyment of various sexual materials, with one being "really enjoy," two being "enjoy," three being "somewhat enjoy," and four being "do not enjoy." Petitioner ranked the entry "pre-teen sex" as a two, but indicated that he was opposed to pedophilia.

For a time, the Government left petitioner alone. But then a new "prohibited mailing specialist" in the Postal Service found petitioner's name in a file, and in May 1986, petitioner received a solicitation from a second fictitious consumer research company, "Midlands Data Research," seeking a response from those who "believe in the joys of sex and the complete awareness of those lusty and youthful lads and lasses of the neophite [sic] age." The letter never explained whether "neophite" referred to minors or young adults. Petitioner responded: "Please feel free to send me more information, I am interested in teenage sexuality. Please keep my name confidential."

Petitioner then heard from yet another Government creation, "Heartland Institute for a New Tomorrow" (HINT), which proclaimed that it was "an organization founded to protect and promote sexual freedom and freedom of choice. We believe that arbitrarily imposed legislative sanctions restricting your sexual freedom should be rescinded through the legislative process." The letter also enclosed a second survey. Petitioner indicated that his interest in "preteen sex-homosexual" material was above average, but not high. In response to another question, petitioner wrote: "Not only sexual expression but freedom of the press is under attack. We must be ever vigilant to counter attack right wing fundamentalists who are determined to curtail our freedoms."

HINT replied, portraying itself as a lobbying organization seeking to repeal "all statutes which regulate sexual activities, except those laws which deal with violent behavior, such as rape. HINT is also lobbying to eliminate any legal definition of 'the age of consent.'" These lobbying efforts were to be funded by sales from a catalog to be published in the future "offering the sale of various items which we believe you will find to be both interesting and stimulating." HINT also provided computer matching of group members with similar survey responses; and, although petitioner was supplied with a list of potential "pen pals," he did not initiate any correspondence.

Nevertheless, the Government's "prohibited mailing specialist" began writing to petitioner, using the pseudonym "Carl Long." The letters employed a tactic known as "mirroring," which the inspector described as "reflecting whatever the interests are of the person we are writing to." Petitioner responded at first, indicating that his interest was primarily in "male-male items." Record, Government Exhibit 9A. Inspector "Long" wrote back:

> "My interests too are primarily male-male items. Are you satisfied with the type of VCR tapes available? Personally, I like the amateur stuff better if its [sic] well produced as it can get more kinky and also seems more real. I think the actors enjoy it more."

Petitioner responded:

> "As far as my likes are concerned, I like good looking young guys (in their late teens and early 20's) doing their thing together."

Petitioner's letters to "Long" made no reference to child pornography. After writing two letters, petitioner discontinued the correspondence.

By March 1987, 34 months had passed since the Government obtained petitioner's name from the mailing list of the California bookstore, and 26 months had passed since the Postal Service had commenced its mailings to petitioner. Although petitioner had responded to surveys and letters, the Government had no evidence that petitioner had ever intentionally possessed or been exposed to child pornography. The Postal Service had not checked petitioner's mail to determine whether he was receiving questionable mailings from persons—other than the Government—involved in the child pornography industry.

At this point, a second Government agency, the Customs Service, included petitioner in its own child pornography sting, "Operation Borderline," after receiving his name on lists submitted by the Postal Service. Using the name of a fictitious Canadian company called "Produit Outaouais," the Customs Service mailed petitioner a brochure advertising photographs of young boys engaging in sex. Petitioner placed an order that was never filled.

The Postal Service also continued its efforts in the Jacobson case, writing to petitioner as the "Far Eastern Trading Company Ltd." The letter began:

> "As many of you know, much hysterical nonsense has appeared in the American media concerning 'pornography' and what must be done to stop it from coming across your borders. This brief letter does not allow us to give much comments; however, why is your government spending millions of dollars to exercise international censorship while tons of drugs, which makes yours the world's most crime ridden country are passed through easily."

The letter went on to say:

> "We have devised a method of getting these to you without prying eyes of U.S. Customs seizing your mail. . . . After consultations with American solicitors, we have been advised that once we have posted our material through your system, it cannot be opened for any inspection without authorization of a judge."

The letter invited petitioner to send for more information. It also asked petitioner to sign an affirmation that he was "not a law enforcement officer or agent of the U.S. Government acting in an undercover capacity for the purpose of entrapping Far Eastern Trading Company, its agents or customers." Petitioner responded. A catalog was sent and petitioner ordered Boys Who Love Boys, a pornographic magazine depicting young boys engaged in various sexual activities. Petitioner was arrested after a controlled delivery of a photocopy of the magazine.

When petitioner was asked at trial why he placed such an order, he explained that the Government had succeeded in piquing his curiosity:

> "Well, the statement was made of all the trouble and the hysteria over pornography and I wanted to see what the material was. It didn't describe the—I didn't know for sure what kind of sexual action they were referring to in the Canadian letter."

In petitioner's home, the Government found the Bare Boys magazines and materials that the Government had sent to him in the course of its protracted investigation, but no other materials that would indicate that petitioner collected, or was actively interested in, child pornography.

Petitioner was indicted for violating 18 U.S.C. § 2252(a)(2)(A). The trial court instructed the jury on the petitioner's entrapment defense,[1] petitioner was convicted, and a divided Court of Appeals for the Eighth Circuit, sitting en banc, affirmed, concluding that "Jacobson was not entrapped as a matter of law." We granted certiorari.

II

There can be no dispute about the evils of child pornography or the difficulties that laws and law enforcement have encountered in eliminating it. Likewise, there

---

1. The jury was instructed:

As mentioned, one of the issues in this case is whether the defendant was entrapped. If the defendant was entrapped he must be found not guilty. The government has the burden of proving beyond a reasonable doubt that the defendant was not entrapped.

If the defendant before contact with law-enforcement officers or their agents did not have any intent or disposition to commit the crime charged and was induced or persuaded by law-enforcement officers or their agents to commit that crime, then he was entrapped. On the other hand, if the defendant before contact with law-enforcement officers or their agents did have an intent or disposition to commit the crime charged, then he was not entrapped even though law-enforcement officers or their agents provided a favorable opportunity to commit the crime or made committing the crime easier or even participated in acts essential to the crime.

can be no dispute that the Government may use undercover agents to enforce the law. "It is well settled that the fact that officers or employees of the Government merely afford opportunities or facilities for the commission of the offense does not defeat the prosecution. Artifice and stratagem may be employed to catch those engaged in criminal enterprises."

In their zeal to enforce the law, however, Government agents may not originate a criminal design, implant in an innocent person's mind the disposition to commit a criminal act, and then induce commission of the crime so that the Government may prosecute. *Sorrells, supra*, at 442; *Sherman, supra*, at 372. Where the Government has induced an individual to break the law and the defense of entrapment is at issue, as it was in this case, the prosecution must prove beyond reasonable doubt that the defendant was disposed to commit the criminal act prior to first being approached by Government agents.[2]

Thus, an agent deployed to stop the traffic in illegal drugs may offer the opportunity to buy or sell drugs and, if the offer is accepted, make an arrest on the spot or later. In such a typical case, or in a more elaborate "sting" operation involving government-sponsored fencing where the defendant is simply provided with the opportunity to commit a crime, the entrapment defense is of little use because the ready commission of the criminal act amply demonstrates the defendant's predisposition. Had the agents in this case simply offered petitioner the opportunity to order child pornography through the mails, and petitioner—who must be presumed to know the law—had promptly availed himself of this criminal opportunity, it is unlikely that his entrapment defense would have warranted a jury instruction. But

---

2. Inducement is not at issue in this case. The Government does not dispute that it induced petitioner to commit the crime. The sole issue is whether the Government carried its burden of proving that petitioner was predisposed to violate the law before the Government intervened. The dissent is mistaken in claiming that this is an innovation in entrapment law and in suggesting that the Government's conduct prior to the moment of solicitation is irrelevant. The Court rejected these arguments six decades ago in Sorrells when the Court wrote that the Government may not punish an individual "for an alleged offense which is the product of the creative activity of its own officials" and that in such a case the Government "is in no position to object to evidence of the activities of its representatives in relation to the accused. . . ." Indeed, the proposition that the accused must be predisposed prior to contact with law enforcement officers is so firmly established that the Government conceded the point at oral argument, submitting that the evidence it developed during the course of its investigation was probative because it indicated petitioner's state of mind prior to the commencement of the Government's investigation. This long-established standard in no way encroaches upon Government investigatory activities. Indeed, the Government's internal guidelines for undercover operations provide that an inducement to commit a crime should not be offered unless:

(a) There is a reasonable indication, based on information developed through informants or other means, that the subject is engaging, has engaged, or is likely to engage in illegal activity of a similar type; or

(b) The opportunity for illegal activity has been structured so that there is reason for believing that persons drawn to the opportunity, or brought to it, are predisposed to engage in the contemplated illegal activity." Attorney General's Guidelines on FBI Undercover Operations (Dec. 31, 1980), reprinted in S. Rep. No. 97-682, p. 551 (1982).

that is not what happened here. By the time petitioner finally placed his order, he had already been the target of 26 months of repeated mailings and communications from Government agents and fictitious organizations. Therefore, although he had become predisposed to break the law by May 1987, it is our view that the Government did not prove that this predisposition was independent and not the product of the attention that the Government had directed at petitioner since January 1985. *Sorrells, supra,* at 442; *Sherman, supra,* at 372.

The prosecution's evidence of predisposition falls into two categories: evidence developed prior to the Postal Service's mail campaign, and that developed during the course of the investigation. The sole piece of preinvestigation evidence is petitioner's 1984 order and receipt of the Bare Boys magazines. But this is scant if any proof of petitioner's predisposition to commit an illegal act, the criminal character of which a defendant is presumed to know. It may indicate a predisposition to view sexually oriented photographs that are responsive to his sexual tastes; but evidence that merely indicates a generic inclination to act within a broad range, not all of which is criminal, is of little probative value in establishing predisposition.

Furthermore, petitioner was acting within the law at the time he received these magazines. Receipt through the mails of sexually explicit depictions of children for noncommercial use did not become illegal under federal law until May 1984, and Nebraska had no law that forbade petitioner's possession of such material until 1988. Neb. Rev. Stat. § 28-813.01 (1989). Evidence of predisposition to do what once was lawful is not, by itself, sufficient to show predisposition to do what is now illegal, for there is a common understanding that most people obey the law even when they disapprove of it. This obedience may reflect a generalized respect for legality or the fear of prosecution, but for whatever reason, the law's prohibitions are matters of consequence. Hence, the fact that petitioner legally ordered and received the Bare Boys magazines does little to further the Government's burden of proving that petitioner was predisposed to commit a criminal act. This is particularly true given petitioner's unchallenged testimony that he did not know until they arrived that the magazines would depict minors. The prosecution's evidence gathered during the investigation also fails to carry the Government's burden. Petitioner's responses to the many communications prior to the ultimate criminal act were at most indicative of certain personal inclinations, including a predisposition to view photographs of preteen sex and a willingness to promote a given agenda by supporting lobbying organizations. Even so, petitioner's responses hardly support an inference that he would commit the crime of receiving child pornography through the mails.[3]

---

3. We do not hold, as the dissent suggests, that the Government was required to prove that petitioner knowingly violated the law. We simply conclude that proof that petitioner engaged in legal conduct and possessed certain generalized personal inclinations is not sufficient evidence to prove beyond a reasonable doubt that he would have been predisposed to commit the crime charged independent of the Government's coaxing.

Furthermore, a person's inclinations and "fantasies . . . are his own and beyond the reach of government. . . ."

On the other hand, the strong arguable inference is that, by waving the banner of individual rights and disparaging the legitimacy and constitutionality of efforts to restrict the availability of sexually explicit materials, the Government not only excited petitioner's interest in sexually explicit materials banned by law but also exerted substantial pressure on petitioner to obtain and read such material as part of a fight against censorship and the infringement of individual rights. For instance, HINT described itself as "an organization founded to protect and promote sexual freedom and freedom of choice" and stated that "the most appropriate means to accomplish [its] objectives is to promote honest dialogue among concerned individuals and to continue its lobbying efforts with State Legislators." These lobbying efforts were to be financed through catalog sales. Mailings from the equally fictitious American Hedonist Society, and the correspondence from the nonexistent Carl Long, endorsed these themes.

Similarly, the two solicitations in the spring of 1987 raised the spectre of censorship while suggesting that petitioner ought to be allowed to do what he had been solicited to do.

The mailing from the Customs Service referred to "the worldwide ban and intense enforcement on this type of material," observed that "what was legal and commonplace is now an 'underground' and secretive service," and emphasized that "this environment forces us to take extreme measures" to ensure delivery. The Postal Service solicitation described the concern about child pornography as "hysterical nonsense," decried "international censorship," and assured petitioner, based on consultation with "American solicitors," that an order that had been posted could not be opened for inspection without authorization of a judge. It further asked petitioner to affirm that he was not a Government agent attempting to entrap the mail order company or its customers. In these particulars, both Government solicitations suggested that receiving this material was something that petitioner ought to be allowed to do. Petitioner's ready response to these solicitations cannot be enough to establish beyond reasonable doubt that he was predisposed, prior to the Government acts intended to create predisposition, to commit the crime of receiving child pornography through the mails. See Sherman. The evidence that petitioner was ready and willing to commit the offense came only after the Government had devoted 21/2 years to convincing him that he had or should have the right to engage in the very behavior proscribed by law. Rational jurors could not say beyond a reasonable doubt that petitioner possessed the requisite predisposition prior to the Government's investigation and that it existed independent of the Government's many and varied approaches to petitioner. As was explained in Sherman, where entrapment was found as a matter of law, "the Government [may not] play on the weaknesses of an innocent party and beguile him into committing crimes which he otherwise would not have attempted."

Law enforcement officials go too far when they "implant in the mind of an innocent person the *disposition* to commit the alleged offense and induce its commission in order that they may prosecute." *Sorrells* (emphasis added). Like the *Sorrells* Court, we are "unable to conclude that it was the intention of the Congress in enacting this statute that its processes of detection and enforcement should be abused by the instigation by government officials of an act on the part of persons otherwise innocent in order to lure them to its commission and to punish them." When the Government's quest for convictions leads to the apprehension of an otherwise law-abiding citizen who, if left to his own devices, likely would have never run afoul of the law, the courts should intervene. Because we conclude that this is such a case and that the prosecution failed, as a matter of law, to adduce evidence to support the jury verdict that petitioner was predisposed, independent of the Government's acts and beyond a reasonable doubt, to violate the law by receiving child pornography through the mails, we reverse the Court of Appeals' judgment affirming the conviction of Keith Jacobson.

It is so ordered.

Justice O'Connor, with whom The Chief Justice and Justice Kennedy join, and with whom Justice Scalia joins except as to Part II, dissenting.

Keith Jacobson was offered only two opportunities to buy child pornography through the mail. Both times, he ordered. Both times, he asked for opportunities to buy more. He needed no Government agent to coax, threaten, or persuade him; no one played on his sympathies, friendship, or suggested that his committing the crime would further a greater good. In fact, no Government agent even contacted him face to face. The Government contends that from the enthusiasm with which Mr. Jacobson responded to the chance to commit a crime, a reasonable jury could permissibly infer beyond a reasonable doubt that he was predisposed to commit the crime. I agree.

The first time the Government sent Mr. Jacobson a catalog of illegal materials, he ordered a set of photographs advertised as picturing "young boys in sex action fun." He enclosed the following note with his order: "I received your brochure and decided to place an order. If I like your product, I will order more later." For reasons undisclosed in the record, Mr. Jacobson's order was never delivered.

The second time the Government sent a catalog of illegal materials, Mr. Jacobson ordered a magazine called "Boys Who Love Boys," described as: "11-year old and 14-year old boys get it on in every way possible. Oral, anal sex and heavy masturbation. If you love boys, you will be delighted with this." Along with his order, Mr. Jacobson sent the following note: "Will order other items later. I want to be discreet in order to protect you and me."

Government agents admittedly did not offer Mr. Jacobson the chance to buy child pornography right away. Instead, they first sent questionnaires in order to make sure that he was generally interested in the subject matter. Indeed, a "cold call" in such a business would not only risk rebuff and suspicion, but might also shock and offend the uninitiated, or expose minors to suggestive materials. Mr. Jacobson's responses to the questionnaires gave the investigators reason to think he would be interested in photographs depicting preteen sex.

The Court, however, concludes that a reasonable jury could not have found Mr. Jacobson to be predisposed beyond a reasonable doubt on the basis of his responses to the Government's catalogs, even though it admits that, by that time, he was predisposed to commit the crime. The Government, the Court holds, failed to provide evidence that Mr. Jacobson's obvious predisposition at the time of the crime "was independent and not the product of the attention that the Government had directed at petitioner." In so holding, I believe the Court fails to acknowledge the reasonableness of the jury's inference from the evidence, redefines "predisposition," and introduces a new requirement that Government sting operations have a reasonable suspicion of illegal activity before contacting a suspect.

I

This Court has held previously that a defendant's predisposition is to be assessed as of the time the Government agent first suggested the crime, not when the Government agent first became involved. *Sherman.* Until the Government actually makes a suggestion of criminal conduct, it could not be said to have "implanted in the mind of an innocent person the disposition to commit the alleged offense and induce its commission. . . ." Even in *Sherman* in which the Court held that the defendant had been entrapped as a matter of law, the Government agent had repeatedly and unsuccessfully coaxed the defendant to buy drugs, ultimately succeeding only by playing on the defendant's sympathy. The Court found lack of predisposition based on the Government's numerous unsuccessful attempts to induce the crime, not on the basis of preliminary contacts with the defendant.

Today, the Court holds that Government conduct may be considered to create a predisposition to commit a crime, even before any Government action to induce the commission of the crime. In my view, this holding changes entrapment doctrine. Generally, the inquiry is whether a suspect is predisposed before the Government induces the commission of the crime, not before the Government makes initial contact with him. There is no dispute here that the Government's questionnaires and letters were not sufficient to establish inducement; they did not even suggest that Mr. Jacobson should engage in any illegal activity.

If all the Government had done was to send these materials, Mr. Jacobson's entrapment defense would fail. Yet the Court holds that the Government must prove not only that a suspect was predisposed to commit the crime before the opportunity to commit it arose, but also before the Government came on the scene.

The rule that preliminary Government contact can create a predisposition has the potential to be misread by lower courts as well as criminal investigators as requiring that the Government must have sufficient evidence of a defendant's predisposition *before it ever seeks to contact him.* Surely the Court cannot intend to impose such a requirement, for it would mean that the Government must have a reasonable suspicion of criminal activity before it begins an investigation, a condition that we have never before imposed. The Court denies that its new rule will affect run-of-the-mill sting operations, and one hopes that it means what it says. Nonetheless, after this case, every defendant will claim that something the Government agent did before soliciting the crime "created" a predisposition that was not there before. For example, a bribetaker will claim that the description of the amount of money available was so enticing that it implanted a disposition to accept the bribe later offered. A drug buyer will claim that the description of the drug's purity and effects was so tempting that it created the urge to try it for the first time. In short, the Court's opinion could be read to prohibit the Government from advertising the seductions of criminal activity as part of its sting operation, for fear of creating a predisposition in its suspects. That limitation would be especially likely to hamper sting operations such as this one, which mimic the advertising done by genuine purveyors of pornography. No doubt the Court would protest that its opinion does not stand for so broad a proposition, but the apparent lack of a principled basis for distinguishing these scenarios exposes a flaw in the more limited rule the Court today adopts.

The Court's rule is all the more troubling because it does not distinguish between Government conduct that merely highlights the temptation of the crime itself, and Government conduct that threatens, coerces, or leads a suspect to commit a crime in order to fulfill some other obligation. For example, in *Sorrells*, the Government agent repeatedly asked for illegal liquor, coaxing the defendant to accede on the ground that "one former war buddy would get liquor for another." In *Sherman*, the Government agent played on the defendant's sympathies, pretending to be going through drug withdrawal and begging the defendant to relieve his distress by helping him buy drugs.

The Government conduct in this case is not comparable. While the Court states that the Government "exerted substantial pressure on petitioner to obtain and read such material as part of a fight against censorship and the infringement of individual rights," one looks at the record in vain for evidence of such "substantial pressure." The most one finds is letters advocating legislative action to liberalize obscenity laws, letters which could easily be ignored or thrown away. Much later, the Government sent separate mailings of catalogs of illegal materials. Nowhere did the Government suggest that the proceeds of the sale of the illegal materials would be used to support legislative reforms. While one of the HINT letters suggested that lobbying efforts would be funded by sales from a catalog, the catalogs actually sent, nearly a year later, were from different fictitious entities (Produit Outaouais and Far Eastern Trading Company), and gave no suggestion that money would be used for any political purposes. Nor did the Government claim to be organizing a civil disobedience movement, which would protest the pornography laws by breaking them. Contrary to the gloss given the evidence by the Court, the Government's suggestions of illegality may also have made buyers beware, and increased the mystique of the materials offered: "For those of you who have enjoyed youthful material . . . we have devised a method of getting these to you without prying eyes of U.S. Customs seizing your mail." Mr. Jacobson's curiosity to see what "'all the trouble and the hysteria'" was about is certainly susceptible of more than one interpretation. And it is the jury that is charged with the obligation of interpreting it. In sum, the Court fails to construe the evidence in the light most favorable to the Government, and fails to draw all reasonable inferences in the Government's favor. It was surely reasonable for the jury to infer that Mr. Jacobson was predisposed beyond a reasonable doubt, even if other inferences from the evidence were also possible.

II

The second puzzling thing about the Court's opinion is its redefinition of predisposition. The Court acknowledges that "petitioner's responses to the many communications prior to the ultimate criminal act were . . . indicative of certain personal inclinations, including a predisposition to view photographs of preteen sex. . . ." If true, this should have settled the matter; Mr. Jacobson was predisposed to engage in the illegal conduct. Yet, the Court concludes, "petitioner's responses hardly support an inference that he would commit the crime of receiving child pornography through the mails."

The Court seems to add something new to the burden of proving predisposition. Not only must the Government show that a defendant was predisposed to engage in the illegal conduct, here, receiving photographs of minors engaged in sex, but also that the defendant was predisposed to break the law knowingly in order to do so. The statute violated here, however, does not require proof of specific intent to break the law; it requires only knowing receipt of visual depictions produced by using minors engaged in sexually explicit conduct. Under the Court's analysis, however, the Government must prove more to show predisposition than it need prove in order to convict.

The Court ignores the judgment of Congress that specific intent is not an element of the crime of receiving sexually explicit photographs of minors. The elements of predisposition should track the elements of the crime. The predisposition requirement is meant to eliminate the entrapment defense for those defendants who would have committed the crime anyway, even absent Government inducement. Because a defendant might very well be convicted of the crime here absent Government inducement even though he did not know his conduct was illegal, a specific intent requirement does little to distinguish between those who would commit the crime without the inducement and those who would not. In sum, although the fact that Mr. Jacobson's purchases of Bare Boys I and Bare Boys II were legal at the time may have some relevance to the question of predisposition, it is not, as the Court suggests, dispositive.

The crux of the Court's concern in this case is that the Government went too far and "abused" the "'processes of detection and enforcement'" by luring an innocent person to violate the law. Consequently, the Court holds that the Government failed to prove beyond a reasonable doubt that Mr. Jacobson was predisposed to commit the crime. It was, however, the jury's task, as the conscience of the community, to decide whether Mr. Jacobson was a willing participant in the criminal activity here or an innocent dupe. The jury is the traditional "defense against arbitrary law enforcement." Indeed, in *Sorrells*, in which the Court was also concerned about overzealous law enforcement, the Court did not decide itself that the Government conduct constituted entrapment, but left the issue to the jury. There is no dispute that the jury in this case was fully and accurately instructed on the law of entrapment, and nonetheless found Mr. Jacobson guilty. Because I believe there was sufficient evidence to uphold the jury's verdict, I respectfully dissent.

Questions and Notes

1. What is the core difference between Justice White's and Justice O'Connor's opinions?

2. Was Jacobson predisposed before the government first contacted him? Explain.

3. Should the government be allowed to create a predisposition in an individual before it tempts him to commit a crime? Why? Why not?

4. Judge Richard Posner has argued that the purpose of entrapment is to promote police efficiency and that it is efficient to trap somebody who ultimately would have committed the crime without police inducement, but that it is inefficient to entrap somebody who would not have committed the crime, but for police inducement. Posner, *An Economic Theory of the Criminal Law*, 85 COLUM. L. REV. 1193 (1985). If Judge Posner's theory is correct, how should *Jacobson* be resolved?

5. As you read *Powell*, consider whether employing the objective test eliminates the tough questions surrounding entrapment.

State v. Powell
726 P.2d 266 (Haw. 1986)

PER CURIAM.

The question in this appeal by the State of Hawaii is whether the Circuit Court of the First Circuit erred in dismissing with prejudice the charge of Theft in the First Degree brought against Laverne Powell. The charge was dismissed because the circuit court concluded the "drunk decoy" operation that culminated in the commission of theft by the defendant constituted entrapment as a matter of law. The State argues the circuit court erred, but we too conclude the defendant was entrapped.

The incidence of thefts and robberies in the vicinity of the intersection of Wilikina Drive and Kamehameha Highway in Wahiawa prompted a police decision to institute a series of "drunk decoy" operations in the area of the reported crimes. And between November of 1984 and March of 1985 officers of the Honolulu Police

Department organized such operations on eleven occasions and arrested nineteen individuals. Laverne Powell was arrested on March 21, 1985 when she pilfered a wallet containing nine dollars.

The victim on this occasion was a police officer feigning drunkenness. As he lay on his side in a fetal position with a paper bag containing a beer bottle in his hand, a wallet protruded from a rear pocket of his jeans. That the wallet contained money was rendered obvious by the partial exposure of currency. Several other officers stationed themselves at nearby vantage points and awaited possible criminal activity. Shortly after 11:00 p.m., Laverne Powell walked by the officer posing as a helpless drunkard. She then turned back, approached the apparently vulnerable victim, and stole the wallet planted on his person. Two officers who witnessed the theft sprang from cover and apprehended Ms. Powell as she left the scene.

The Grand Jury returned an indictment charging Laverne Powell with Theft in the First Degree. Averring she had been induced by the police to commit the offense, the defendant moved for dismissal of the charge. The circuit court conducted an evidentiary hearing in which the only testimony offered was that of the police sergeant who supervised the "drunk decoy" operation. The court found the dispositive facts were not in dispute, concluded the police conduct in question constituted entrapment as a matter of law, and dismissed the indictment with prejudice.

"Since the defense is not of a constitutional dimension, [the legislature] may address itself to the question and adopt any substantive definition of [entrapment] that it may find desirable. The rationale for providing a defense based on entrapment," in the legislature's view, "does not reside in the fact that entrapped defendants are less culpable or dangerous than those who formulate their intent without outside inducement. . . . The real basis for the defense . . . is a purpose to deter improper conduct on the part of law enforcement officials." HRS § 702-237 (1976), Commentary. The Hawaii Penal Code's definition of "entrapment" therefore focuses not on the [propensities and] predisposition of the defendant to commit the crime charged, but rather . . . on the conduct of . . . law enforcement officials. And by virtue of HRS § 702-237

> [i]n any prosecution, it is an affirmative defense that the defendant engaged in the prohibited conduct or caused the prohibited result because he was induced or encouraged to do so by a law enforcement officer, or by a person acting in cooperation with a law enforcement officer, who, for the purpose of obtaining evidence of the commission of an offense. . . .
>
> (b) Employed methods of persuasion or inducement which created a substantial risk that the offense would be committed by persons other than those who are ready to commit it."

Whether the defendant was entrapped or not ordinarily is a matter for the jury to decide. But when "the evidence is undisputed and . . . clear" entrapment may be established as a matter of law. Here, the circuit court was neither compelled to choose between conflicting witnesses nor judge their credibility. It ruled on the basis of undisputed testimony elicited from the officer who organized the operation in question. Moreover, the findings rendered by the circuit court are not challenged by the State.

The State nonetheless argues a reversal of the court's ruling is in order because the police were "looking to interrupt ongoing criminal activity" and employed means "reasonably tailored to apprehend those involved in stealing from intoxicated persons." But we are convinced from a review of the record that the police "[e]mployed methods of . . . inducement which created a substantial risk that [theft] would be committed by persons other than those who [were] ready to commit it."

That the police were concerned with reports of "thefts and robberies in the area" is not to be disputed. Nor can the decision to organize covert operations be faulted. "Criminal activity is such that stealth and strategy are necessary weapons in the arsenal of the police officer." *Sherman v. United States*, 356 U.S. at 372. Yet as the circuit court found, the reported thefts and robberies did not "involve 'sleeping drunks' or thefts of the same nature as the instant case." We would be hard put to contradict the court's further finding that the "drunk decoy" operations were expressly designed to ensnare anyone who would commit theft when "bait money" is placed in plain view and within easy reach.

The stealth and strategy employed here resulted in the apprehension of nineteen persons, including Laverne Powell, for "rolling drunks." Undeniably, "[t]he function of law enforcement is the prevention of crime and the apprehension of criminals." Yet, what was reported previously as happening in the vicinity were thefts of a different nature, including robberies. "Manifestly, [the law enforcement] function does not include the manufacturing of crime." Under the circumstances, we would have to agree with the circuit court that the "drunk decoy" operation "created a substantial risk that [theft] would be committed by persons other than those who [were] ready to commit it."

Affirmed.

Questions and Notes

1. Do you think that the police scheme in *Powell* created a risk that nonpredisposed people would engage in criminal activity? Explain.

2. Would your answer be different if the police had been concerned about a series of unsolved larcenies from the person of drunks? Why?

3. In the *Grimm* case, cited by Justice Frankfurter in *Sherman*, a postal inspector ordered allegedly obscene pictures from a person that he suspected had been selling them through the mails. If *Grimm* had arisen in Hawaii, would the defendant have been entitled to an acquittal? Should he be?

4. Sometimes the government conduct is so outrageous that it violates due process without regard for the character of the defendant. *Gamble* explores the criteria for ascertaining such a violation.

United States v. Gamble

737 F.2d 853 (10th Cir. 1984)

LOGAN, Circuit Judge.

Defendant, John Gamble, a physician practicing in Kansas City, Kansas, was convicted on four counts of mail fraud, 18 U.S.C. § 1341. The charges against defendant resulted from an elaborate undercover investigation by United States postal inspectors. On appeal, defendant contends that his conviction on all four counts should be overturned because (1) the government failed to prove beyond a reasonable doubt that he committed the crime of mail fraud, and (2) even if he did commit mail fraud, the government's conduct violated his right to due process of law. We also consider whether the government's conduct in this case was so outrageous that defendant's conviction must be overturned under our supervisory power over the administration of criminal justice.

United States postal inspectors concocted two schemes that ultimately involved defendant. In each scheme United States postal inspectors used fictitious names to obtain Missouri driver's licenses. The inspectors then registered automobiles they did not own and obtained insurance for the automobiles under those names. In cooperation with the Kansas City, Missouri, Police Department, the postal inspectors obtained accident reports for collisions that never occurred. The police officer who filled out the fictitious accident reports testified at trial that normally he would face severe sanctions for filling out false reports.

In each of the schemes the police issued a ticket to one of the inspectors and described the accidents in such a way that the inspector cited would be liable for any damages. After receiving the citations, the inspectors appeared in Municipal Court in Kansas City, Missouri, and pleaded guilty before prosecutors and judges who were unaware that the tickets were shams.

The first fictitious accident report, which was filed on May 6, 1980, described a one-car accident in which the driver of the vehicle, in an attempt to miss a stopped vehicle, swerved and struck a post. Postal Inspectors Armstrong and Gillis posed as passengers in the vehicle. Following this fictitious accident the inspectors visited defendant's office, asking him to help them perpetrate a fraud on the insurance company.

Posing as husband and wife, Armstrong and Gillis visited defendant's office seven times. On their first visit the inspectors' temperatures, weights, and blood pressures were checked. They filled out medical information forms, writing "traffic accident" in the blank for type of injury. When Inspector Armstrong met defendant, he told defendant that he had broken his glasses but had suffered no injuries and that he wanted to obtain some funds from the insurance company. Defendant described the procedure for filing claims with the insurance company and then conducted a routine physical examination of each inspector. On each subsequent visit the inspectors' weights, blood pressures, and temperatures apparently were checked. During the second visit defendant asked if he needed to do anything. Inspector Armstrong said no and stated that he had not yet contacted the insurance company. Subsequently, Inspector Armstrong told Jim Amen, an adjuster for State Farm Insurance Company, about injuries in his back and neck.

On the fourth visit the inspectors informed defendant that they had contacted State Farm Insurance Company. Later, Inspector Armstrong spoke with defendant's assistant, who prepared an insurance form and asked several questions. Armstrong told the assistant to write down that he had been unable to work for almost two months. When Inspectors Armstrong and Gillis visited defendant for the last time, they brought a draft from State Farm Insurance Company for $180, the total medical expense reported to the insurer. Defendant calculated that since they had already paid him $104, they owed him $66. (Correctly subtracted the figure was $76. Defendant had previously made the inspectors pay $10 or $12 apiece at each office visit when they saw defendant.) The inspectors gave defendant a $66 money order and kept the draft.

The second undercover operation began with a false accident report filed on July 9, 1980, which described a rear-end collision. Postal Inspectors Robert Bush and Donjette Gilmore posed as husband and wife and claimed to have been in the car that was hit. They visited defendant's office five times. Apparently at each visit the inspectors were given routine tests. When the inspectors first saw defendant, he asked what was wrong. Bush indicated that nothing was wrong but that the person who was responsible was insured and that there was a chance to make some money. Bush affirmed the doctor's stated assumption that they wanted to take advantage of the situation. Defendant then said, "You'll just have to play it up. You can't go out there tell that man ah, I wasn't hurt." Defendant also said, "You gotta have a back injury and you gotta have a neck injury or something. . . . We have to write it up to that effect and you'll make some money out of the deal." Defendant suggested neck and back injuries would be best because they are hard to prove and told them to come back in a few weeks to fill out the insurance papers.

Several weeks later the inspectors informed defendant that they had contacted the insurance company, and they discussed with defendant the insurer's method of handling claims. At a later visit defendant filled out a handwritten bill and put it in an envelope provided by the inspectors that was addressed to Farmers Insurance Group. Defendant handed the envelope back to Inspector Bush and asked him to take care of it. On December 11, 1980, the inspectors brought a draft for $160 from Farmers Insurance Group to defendant's office. A secretary reimbursed them for the $50 they had paid during previous office visits, and the inspectors signed the draft over to defendant.

Defendant contends that the government's conduct in formulating, carrying out, and enmeshing defendant in the mail fraud scheme was so outrageous that defendant's conviction should be overturned as a violation of due process of law. The Supreme Court recognized this defense in *United States v. Russell*, 411 U.S. 423, 431–32 (1973), when it stated, "[W]e may someday be presented with a situation in which the conduct of law enforcement agents is so outrageous that due process principles would absolutely bar the government from invoking judicial processes to obtain a conviction."

When the Supreme Court considered the due process defense three years later in *Hampton v. United States*, 425 U.S. 484 (1976), the eight Justices who participated divided into three groups. The plurality opinion, written by Justice Rehnquist, stated that absent a violation of some protected right of the defendant, the Due Process Clause cannot be invoked to overturn a conviction because of governmental misconduct. Justice Rehnquist wrote, "The remedy of the criminal defendant with respect to the acts of Government agents . . . lies solely in the defense of entrapment." *Id.* at 490. The due process defense survives, however, because a majority of the Justices, two who concurred in the result of the case and three who dissented, rejected the position "that the concept of fundamental fairness inherent in the guarantee of due process would never prevent the conviction of a predisposed defendant, regardless of the outrageousness of police behavior in light of the surrounding circumstances." *Id.* at 492 (Powell, J., concurring). *See also id.* at 497 (Brennan, J., dissenting). Justice Powell added, "I emphasize that the cases, if any, in which proof of predisposition is not dispositive will be rare. Police overinvolvement in crime would have to reach a demonstrable level of outrageousness before it could bar conviction."

The defense that the government's conduct was so outrageous as to require reversal on due process grounds is often raised but is almost never successful. No Supreme Court case and only two circuit court opinions have set aside convictions on that basis. In [one of those cases,] *United States v. Twigg*, 588 F.2d 373 (3d Cir. 1978), a Drug Enforcement Agency (DEA) informant, as part of a plea bargain, involved defendant Neville in establishing a laboratory for the production of a controlled substance, methamphetamine hydrochloride (speed). The government gratuitously supplied about twenty percent of the glassware and an indispensable ingredient, phenyl-2-propanone. The DEA made arrangements with chemical supply houses to facilitate the purchase of the rest of the materials, and the DEA informant, operating under a business name supplied by the DEA, purchased all of the equipment and chemicals with the exception of a separatory funnel. When the participants encountered problems in locating an adequate production site, the government solved the problem by providing an isolated farmhouse. The DEA informant provided the expertise to run the laboratory. Neither Twigg nor Neville knew how to manufacture speed, and each provided only minimal assistance at the specific direction of the informant. The Third Circuit stated, "[W]e are not only concerned with the supply by government agents of necessary ingredients for manufacture, but we also have before us a crime . . . conceived and contrived by government agents." *Id.* at 378. It reversed both convictions. In discussing the government's conduct the court noted in regard to Neville,

> "They [the government] set him up, encouraged him, provided the essential supplies and technical expertise, and when he and Kubica encountered difficulties in consummating the crime, they assisted in finding solutions.

This egregious conduct on the part of government agents generated new crimes by the defendant merely for the sake of pressing criminal charges against him when, as far as the record reveals, he was lawfully and peacefully minding his own affairs. Fundamental fairness does not permit us to countenance such actions by law enforcement officials and prosecution for a crime so fomented by them will be barred." *Id.* at 381 (footnote omitted).

It is important to note that the entrapment defense, which requires an absence of predisposition to commit the crime, is not involved in the instant case. Nevertheless, in a sense, entrapment and the due process defense are on a continuum, because both are based on the principle "that courts must be closed to the trial of a crime instigated by the government's own agents. No other issue, no comparison of equities as between the guilty official and the guilty defendant, has any place in the enforcement of this overruling principle of public policy." *Sorrells v. United States*, 287 U.S. 435, 459 (1932) (Roberts, J., concurring). In stating that until the government provided the means to manufacture speed the *Twigg* defendant Neville was "minding his own affairs," the court notes precisely the point on the entrapment-due process continuum that the two concepts begin to merge. Although the due process defense purportedly ignores the defendant's predisposition to commit the crime charged, the defense nevertheless is concerned with the extent of government involvement in crime and the type of opportunity to become involved with crime that this conduct provides to the unwitting defendant. When the government permits itself to become enmeshed in criminal activity, from beginning to end . . . the same underlying objections which render entrapment repugnant to American criminal justice are operative.

A defendant may not invoke the Due Process Clause, however, unless the government's acts, no matter how outrageous, had a role in inducing the defendant to become involved in the crime:

[T]o be relevant at all, the government's conduct must be postured as connected in some way to the commission of the acts for which the defendant stands convicted. In cases decided since *Russell* . . . this connection has been implicitly acknowledged by reference to the extent to which the government instigated, participated in, or was involved or enmeshed in, the criminal activity itself. Thus, the more immediate the impact of the government's conduct upon the particular defendant, the more vigorously would be applied *Russell's* test for constitutional impropriety.

In the case at bar the government conceived and directed a crime in which defendant participated. The government used fictitious names to obtain driver's licenses, obtained insurance under those names for automobiles they did not own, orchestrated the production of false accident reports, appeared in court and pleaded guilty to traffic violations, and solicited defendant's aid in making false claims against insurance companies. Of the government agencies involved only the Kansas City, Missouri, Police Department knew of the operation. Involved without their knowledge were judges, prosecutors, state licensing authorities, and insurance companies.

The government agents submitted the false claims to the insurance companies and lied to the companies about their injuries.

The government agents in the case before us displayed shocking disregard for the legal system. But these actions did not directly induce defendant to participate in the fraudulent scheme. Perhaps the false statements to state agents and the courts helped the inspectors obtain the medical forms defendant filled out and ultimately secure the settlement check. But defendant did not rely on any display of fictitious credentials or falsified documents; apparently he relied entirely upon what his "patients" told him. Therefore, we must ignore these acts of the government agents in evaluating defendant's due process claim.

Some of the artifices that the government inspectors used in the scheme, however, did directly contribute to defendant's decision to participate. The postal inspectors, with their elaborate machinations, sowed the seeds of criminality and brought defendant into their scheme. This brings the case closer to government manufacture of crime than the sting, Abscam, and other operations in which undercover agents set themselves up as amenable to law-breaking schemes brought to them by others. But did the action of the government agents cross the due process line? We recognize that "because the difficulties in detecting covert crime often warrant secretive investigations, involvement of Government agents must be of the tenor to shock the conscience before a violation of the due process clause will be found." In common with other courts we have struggled to draw the line that defines and identifies what is governmental involvement so outrageous as to warrant finding a due process violation.

The government here enmeshed in criminal schemes fabricated entirely by government agents a black doctor who had no criminal record and with respect to whom the agents had no apparent hint of a predisposition to criminal activity. The government sent agents apparently posing as poor people to a doctor serving a ghetto community to seek to have the doctor help them out financially in appealing circumstances, circumstances in which the doctor might appear callous if he did not cooperate. The record implies that the inspectors pretended to be economically disadvantaged people typical of defendant's patient population. Sympathy based upon economic disadvantage or race may have been played upon as a factor in inducing defendant to join what he informed the inspectors was "the white boys' game." Defendant sought very little profit from his participation, apparently charging only normal office rates for the time he spent with the inspectors.

We must conclude, however, that the government's conduct was insufficient to violate defendant's right to due process. Insurance fraud on a small scale no doubt is very widespread in this country. Many professional or business people may not regard it a serious infraction of society's rules to assist customers or patients in the small scale cheating of insurance companies. Yet, like the Second Circuit in *Myers*, which said it could not accept an "inducement" argument that a proffered bribe was so large a congressman could not be expected to resist, we cannot accept the notion that insurance cheating is so commonplace that it is improper for the government to try to catch and convict citizens who engage in it. We have held that the government need not have a reasonable suspicion of wrongdoing in order to conduct an undercover investigation of a particular person.

Affirmed.

Questions and Notes

1. What do you perceive the difference to be between entrapment and excessive government involvement?

2. As between Gamble and Powell, who do you think was more entitled to raise a defense of either entrapment or excessive government involvement?

3. Do you think that the government did anything wrong in *Gamble*? If so, what? Was Gamble an "otherwise innocent" person?

4. In what sense was Neville (*Twigg* case) victimized more than Gamble by the government?

5. How free should the government be to set traps in cases like this?

Chapter 14

Insanity

In assessing the various tests that have at one time or another been employed for determining insanity, the first question to consider is the function that the insanity defense is designed to serve. What do you perceive that function to be? The earliest test was the "wild beast" test: "He who doth know no more than a wild beast is insane and cannot be convicted." In 1843, the famous M'Naghten right/wrong test was inaugurated. M'Naghten suffered from a delusion that the Prime Minister of England, Sir Robert Peel, intended to kill him. To counteract that, M'Naghten fired a shot at a man in a coach in which Peel ordinarily rode. He killed the man, who turned out to be Sir Edward Drummond, Prime Minister Peel's personal secretary. The Queen's distress at M'Naghten's acquittal on the grounds of insanity impelled her to ask the House of Lords to write an opinion explaining the acquittal. The Lords' opinion provided that insanity was available as a defense only if "at the time of the committing of the act, the party accused was laboring under such a defect of reason from disease of mind, as to not know the nature and quality of the act he was doing, or if he did know it that he did not know he was doing what was wrong." 8 Eng. Rep. 718, 722 (H.L.1843).

M'Naghten remained the primary test for insanity for most of the nineteenth and twentieth centuries, although a substantial minority of jurisdictions supplemented it with something called the irresistible impulse test, i.e., one who understood right from wrong but whose mental disease created an irresistible impulse to do wrong had a valid defense. A short-lived experiment in the District of Columbia called the *Durham* rule [*Durham v. United States*, 214 F.2d 862 [1954]) provided that "an accused is not criminally responsible if his unlawful act was the product of a mental disease or defect." Because of the amorphous character of *Durham*, it never achieved much popularity beyond the circuit that decided it, and eventually was overruled even there (*see United States v. Brawner*, 471 F.2d 969 (D.C. Cir. 1972)).

A test that for a time appeared on the verge of supplanting *M'Naghten* was that adopted by the MPC, which provides: "A person is not responsible for criminal conduct if at the time of such conduct as a result of a mental disease or defect he lacks substantial capacity to either appreciate the criminality of his conduct or to conform his conduct to the requirements of the law." By the early 1980s, most of the Federal Circuits and some of the states had adopted some version of the MPC rule. This trend was abruptly halted by the insanity acquittal of John Hinckley, who attempted to murder President Ronald Reagan.

Because Hinckley was acquitted under the MPC standard, Congress enacted Federal insanity legislation, thereby rendering something akin to *M'Naghten* the rule in all Federal Circuits, including those that had previously adopted the MPC. Its statute provides: "It is an affirmative defense to a prosecution under any federal statute that at the time of the commission of the acts constituting the offense, the defendant, as a result of a severe mental disease or defect, was unable to appreciate the nature and quality or the wrongfulness of his acts. Mental disease or defect does not otherwise constitute a defense." 18 U.S.C. § 20.

Assuming that Hinckley attempted to kill Reagan because of an insane delusion that Jodie Foster would fall in love with him if only he would kill the President, and that M'Naghten attempted to kill Peel only because of an insane delusion that Peel was out to kill him, is there any reason for distinguishing between the two cases? For the most part, the cases in this section build on the preceding background. *Lyons* was decided before the new Federal statute, but after *Hinckley*.

United States v. Lyons

731 F.2d 243, 739 F.2d 994 (5th Cir. 1984)

GEE, Circuit Judge:

Because the concept of criminal responsibility in the federal courts is a congeries of judicially-made rules of decision based on common law concepts, it is usually appropriate for us to reexamine and reappraise these rules in the light of new policy considerations. We last examined the insanity defense in *Blake v. United States*, 407 F.2d 908 (5th Cir. 1969) (en banc), where we adopted the ALI Model Penal Code definition of insanity: that a person is not responsible for criminal conduct if, at the time of such conduct and as a result of mental disease or defect, he lacks substantial capacity either to appreciate the wrongfulness of his conduct or to conform his conduct to the requirements of the law. Following the example of sister circuits, we embraced this standard because we concluded that then current knowledge in the field of behavioral science supported such a result. Unfortunately, it now appears our conclusion was premature—that the brave new world that we foresaw has not arrived.

Reexamining the *Blake* standard today, we conclude that the volitional prong of the insanity defense—a lack of capacity to conform one's conduct to the requirements of the law—does not comport with current medical and scientific knowledge, which has retreated from its earlier, sanguine expectations. Consequently, we now hold that a person is not responsible for criminal conduct on the grounds of insanity only if at the time of that conduct, as a result of a mental disease or defect, he is unable to appreciate the wrongfulness of that conduct.[9]

---

9. We employ the phrase "is unable" in preference to our earlier formulation "lacks substantial capacity" for reasons well stated in the Commentary of the American Bar Association Standing Committee: Finally, it should be pointed out that the standard employs the term "unable" in lieu of

We do so for several reasons. First, as we have mentioned, a majority of psychiatrists now believe that they do not possess sufficient accurate scientific bases for measuring a person's capacity for self-control or for calibrating the impairment of that capacity. Bonnie, *The Moral Basis of the Insanity Defense*, 69 ABA J. 194, 196 (1983). "The line between an irresistible impulse and an impulse not resisted is probably no sharper than between twilight and dusk." American Psychiatric Association Statement on the Insanity Defense, 11 (1982) [APA Statement]. Indeed, Professor Bonnie states: "There is, in short, no objective basis for distinguishing between offenders who were undeterrable and those who were merely undeterred, between the impulse that was irresistible and the impulse not resisted, or between substantial impairment of capacity and some lesser impairment."

In addition, the risks of fabrication and "moral mistakes" in administering the insanity defense are greatest "when the experts and the jury are asked to speculate whether the defendant had the capacity to 'control' himself or whether he could have 'resisted' the criminal impulse." Moreover, psychiatric testimony about volition is more likely to produce confusion for jurors than is psychiatric testimony concerning a defendant's appreciation of the wrongfulness of his act. It appears, moreover, that there is considerable overlap between a psychotic person's inability to understand and his ability to control his behavior. Most psychotic persons who fail a volitional test would also fail a cognitive test, thus rendering the volitional test superfluous for them. Finally, Supreme Court authority requires that such proof be made by the federal prosecutor beyond a reasonable doubt, an all but impossible task in view of the present murky state of medical knowledge.[13]

---

the "substantial capacity" language of the ALI test. This approach has been taken both to simplify the formulation and to reduce the risk that juries will interpret the test too loosely. By using the "substantial capacity" language, the drafters of the ALI standard were trying to avoid the rigidity implicit in the *M'Naughten* formulation. They correctly recognize that it is rarely possible to say that a mentally disordered person was totally unable to "know" what he was doing or to "know" that it was wrong; even a psychotic person typically retains some grasp of reality. However, the phrase "substantial capacity" is not essential to take into account these clinical realities. Sufficient flexibility is provided by the term "appreciate."

13. John Hinckley is the young man who attempted to assassinate President Reagan in order to attract attention to himself and to impress a movie actress whom he admired from a distance. The subsequent proceedings called into question not only the insanity defense but the rationality of our adversarial jury-trial system. After more than a year of expensive pretrial maneuvering and psychiatric examinations, the lawyers jousted for eight weeks of trial, examining and cross-examining expert witnesses who naturally gave conflicting and confusing testimony on whether Hinckley's obviously warped mentality amounted to legal insanity. The judge instructed the jury to return a verdict of not guilty unless they could agree "beyond a reasonable doubt" that Hinckley was sane. If taken literally, the instruction amounted to a directed verdict of not guilty, considering the deadlock of expert opinion and the difficulty of certifying the sanity of a young man who shot the President to impress a movie star. Juries usually ignore such unpopular legal standards, but the *Hinckley* jury surprised everybody by taking the law seriously and finding him not guilty. Hinckley will now be confined to a mental hospital indefinitely because he is "dangerous," although there is no reliable way to predict what he would do if released and no reliable test to determine if he has

One need not disbelieve in the existence of Angels in order to conclude that the present state of our knowledge regarding them is not such as to support confident conclusions about how many can dance on the head of a pin. In like vein, it may be that some day tools will be discovered with which reliable conclusions about human volition can be fashioned.

It appears to be all but a certainty, however, that despite earlier hopes they do not lie in our hands today. When and if they do, it will be time to consider again to what degree the law should adopt the sort of conclusions that they produce. But until then, we see no prudent course for the law to follow but to treat all criminal impulses—including those not resisted—as resistible. To do otherwise in the present state of medical knowledge would be to cast the insanity defense adrift upon a sea of unfounded scientific speculation, with the palm awarded case by case to the most convincing advocate of that which is presently unknown—and may remain so, because unknowable.

ALVIN B. RUBIN, Circuit Judge, with whom TATE, Circuit Judge, joins dissenting. Criminal law punishes the wrongdoer. It attempts to deter others lest they suffer the same fate. If the state punishes a person for conduct that he had no ability to avoid, it imposes punishment without fault. The majority opinion appears to accept these propositions for it recognizes the validity of the plea of insanity for those people who, as a result of a mental disease or defect, lack substantial capacity to appreciate the wrongfulness of their conduct. It denies the plea, however, to those persons who suffer a mental disease or defect that causes them to lack the ability to control their conduct. Therefore, I [can] not join in the decision to draw a line between these two kinds of mental illness. That distinction is constructed on faulty premises and erodes the moral integrity of our criminal justice system.

The majority offers several reasons for its decision both to reexamine and to change the method by which we determine who is criminally responsible. It suggests that "new policy considerations" justify reexamination of the ALI-Model Penal Code test. It expresses concern over the risk of "fabrication" and "moral mistakes" created when experts testify about whether the defendant has the capacity to control his behavior and the risk of confusing juries with psychiatric testimony. Finally, the majority finds reassurance in one doctor's testimony before a congressional committee that the volitional test is "superfluous" for "*most* psychotic persons." (Emphasis supplied.)

The insanity defense reflects the fundamental moral principles of our criminal law. An adjudication of guilt is more than a factual determination that the defendant pulled a trigger, took a bicycle, or sold heroin. It is a moral judgment that the individual is blameworthy. "Our collective conscience does not allow punishment where it cannot impose blame." Our concept of blameworthiness rests on

---

been "cured." Johnson, Book Review, 50 U. CHI. L. REV. 1534, 1536 (1983) (reviewing N. MORRIS, MADNESS AND THE CRIMINAL LAW (1982)).

assumptions that are older than the Republic: "man is naturally endowed with these two great faculties, understanding and liberty of will." "[H]istorically, our substantive criminal law is based on a theory of punishing the vicious will. It postulates a free agent confronted with a choice between doing right and wrong and choosing freely to do wrong." Central, therefore, to a verdict of guilty is the concept of responsibility. Recognition of the insanity defense rests on the conclusion that "it is unjust to punish a person who because of mental illness is without understanding of the nature or quality of his conduct and lacks the capacity to conform his behavior."

An acquittal by reason of insanity is a judgment that the defendant is not guilty because, as a result of his mental condition, he is unable to make an effective choice regarding his behavior.

The majority does not controvert these fundamental principles; indeed, it accepts them as the basis for the defense when the accused suffers from a disease that impairs cognition. It rests its decision to redefine insanity and to narrow the defense on "new policy considerations." The opinion does not fully articulate these considerations, but I discuss what appear to be the principal ones.

The first is the potential threat to society created by the volitional prong of the insanity defense. Public opposition to any insanity-grounded defense is often based, either explicitly or implicitly, on the view that the plea is frequently invoked by violent criminals who fraudulently use it to evade just punishment. Some critics perceive the insanity defense as an opportunity for criminals to use psychiatric testimony to mislead juries. This perception depicts an insanity trial as a "circus" of conflicting expert testimony that confuses a naive and sympathetic jury. And it fears insanity acquittees as offenders who, after manipulating the criminal justice system, are soon set free to prey once again on the community.

Despite the prodigious volume of writing devoted to the plea, the empirical data that are available provide little or no support for these fearsome perceptions and in many respects directly refute them. Both the frequency and the success rate of insanity pleas are grossly overestimated by professionals and lay persons alike; the plea is rarely made, and even more rarely successful. The number of insanity pleas based on control defects, as compared to those based on lack of cognition, must have been almost negligible.

The perception that the defendant who successfully pleads insanity is quickly released from custody is also based only on assumption. Although an acquittal by reason of insanity ends the criminal jurisdiction of federal courts (except in the District of Columbia), and of the courts of a few states, the acquittee is not simply set free. "The truth is that in almost every case, the acquittee is immediately hospitalized and evaluated for dangerousness. Usually, the acquittee remains hospitalized for an extended time."

In sum, the available evidence belies many of the assumptions upon which much popular criticism of the insanity defense are based. The plea is rarely invoked, usually fails, and, when it is successful, the acquittees rarely go free.

Another set of objections to the plea is based on the thesis that factfinders—especially juries—are confused and manipulated by the vagueness of the legal standards of insanity and the notorious "battle of the experts" who present conclusory, superficial, and misleading testimony. These conditions, the argument runs, conspire to produce inconsistent and "inaccurate" verdicts.

Let us first put these objections in perspective. Most cases involving an insanity plea do not go to trial; instead, like most other criminal cases, they are settled by a plea bargain. In many of the cases that do go to trial, psychiatric testimony is presented by deposition, without disagreement among experts, and without opposition by the prosecution. And in the few cases in which a contest does develop, the defendant is usually convicted. Hence the stereotypic "circus tent" may be raised in only a handful of cases.

The manipulated-jury argument is supported largely by declamation, not data. Although there is some evidence to support the assertion that the wording of the insanity defense has little impact on trial outcomes, one major study of jury reactions to criminal cases involving the insanity defense reached conclusions contrary to the assumption that the jury function is usurped by expert testimony. That study found that jurors responsibly and carefully consider the evidence presented, do recognize that the final responsibility for the defendant's fate rests with them, do appreciate the limits and proper use of expert testimony, and do grasp the instructions given them. Although the evidence does not warrant the conclusion that juries function better in insanity trials than in other criminal cases, it certainly does not appear that they function *less* effectively. And no source has been cited to the court to support the conclusion that, as an empirical matter, pleas based upon the volitional prong present an especially problematic task for the jury.

Indeed, the majority opinion does not assert that the insanity defense, particularly the control test, *doesn't* work; it contends that the defense *can't* work. The principal basis for this contention is the belief, held by "a majority of psychiatrists," that they lack "sufficient accurate scientific bases for measuring a person's capacity for self-control or for calibrating the impairment of that capacity." This argument raises practical and important questions regarding the usefulness of expert testimony in determining whether a person has the ability to conform his conduct to law; but the absence of useful expert evidence, if indeed there is none, does not obviate the need for resolving the question whether the defendant ought to be held accountable for his criminal behavior.

Accountability for criminal conduct involves more than mere *actus reus*; it also involves the mental state with which the act is performed. Factfinders are required by law to determine the existence or non-existence of many mental states, for example, whether the defendant was mistaken; acted from necessity, duress, or coercion; acted without willfulness or knowledge or intention; or was unable to appreciate the wrongfulness of his conduct. Our concept of responsibility in this sense is not limited to observable behavior: it embraces *meaningful* choice, and necessarily requires inferences and assumptions regarding the defendant's unobservable mental state. The accompanying external circumstances in cases such as coercion are of course observable; but their effect on the defendant's mental state is inferred, and no more tangible than the mental processes of a defendant pleading the control test. The difference between the concepts of excusing circumstances such as coercion and the insanity defense is that the former is based on objective assumptions about human behavior and is tested against hypothetical-objective standards such as "the reasonable person." "The insanity defense [on the other hand] marks the transition from the adequate man the law demands to the inadequate man he may be."

The majority's fear that the present test invites "moral mistakes" is difficult to understand. The majority opinion concedes that some individuals cannot conform their conduct to the law's requirements. Other writers have concluded that a strictly cognitive insanity test will overlook some individuals who would be covered by a control test. Without citing any data that verdicts in insanity cases decided under a control test are frequently inaccurate, the majority embraces a rule certain to result in the conviction of at least some who are not morally responsible and the punishment of those for whom retributive, deterrent, and rehabilitative penal goals are inappropriate. A decision that virtually ensures undeserved, and therefore unjust, punishment in the name of avoiding moral mistakes rests on a peculiar notion of morality.

Judges are not, and should not be, immune to popular outrage over this nation's crime rate. Like everyone else, judges watch television, read newspapers and magazines, listen to gossip, and are sometimes themselves victims. They receive the message trenchantly described in a recent book criticizing the insanity defense: "Perhaps the bottom line of all these complaints is that *guilty people go free*—guilty people who do not have to accept judgment or responsibility for what they have done and are not held accountable for their actions. . . . These are not cases in which the defendant is *alleged* to have committed a crime. *Everyone knows he did it.*" Although understandable as an expression of uninformed popular opinion, such a viewpoint ought not to serve as the basis for judicial decision making; for it misapprehends the very meaning of guilt.

Guilt is the legal embodiment of moral and philosophical concepts. As discussed above, those concepts presuppose a morally responsible agent to whom guilt can be attributed. By definition, guilt cannot be attributed to an individual unable to refrain from violating the law. When a defendant is properly acquitted by reason of insanity under the control test, the guilty does not go free.

The majority opinion is a radical departure from the established jurisprudence of every federal circuit that has spoken on the issue. It is based only on intuitive reactions and the published recommendations, to which no one has testified, of a few professional groups. We would permit no jury to decide even an unimportant issue on such hearsay. The purposes to be served by this innovation are unclear, for it is doubtful that the decision will make the slightest impact on the enormous problem of crime. Its effect will be felt by only two small groups: a few who otherwise might have made a case for the jury but who will be deprived of a plea that in any event would likely have been bootless, and those few unfortunate persons so afflicted by mental disease that they knew what the law forbade but couldn't control their actions sufficiently to avoid violating it. The nature of their illness makes punishment useless as a means to compel them to behave lawfully; only remission of the disease will permit change. By convicting them we will not deter others who suffer the same mental defect; they too, again by definition, have no ability to obey.

In sum, I cannot join in a decision that, without supporting data, overturns a widely used rule that has not been shown to be working badly in order to adopt a change that will likely produce little or no practical benefit to society as a whole, conflicts with the fundamental moral predicates of our criminal justice system, and may inflict undeserved punishment on a few hapless individuals.

Questions and Notes

1. Is a defendant who invokes an insanity defense saying: "I am not guilty because I lack *mens rea*" or is she saying: "I am not guilty despite having *mens rea*"? What would Judge Rubin say? What would Judge Gee say?

2. Which is more artificial, the insanity defense with a volitional prong or the insanity defense without a volitional prong? Why?

3. If we can't distinguish one who can't resist an impulse from one who won't, can we distinguish one who can't tell right from wrong from one who won't?

4. Consider whether the ability to distinguish right from wrong ought to be limited to an ability to understand what the law forbids in conjunction with *Cameron*.

State v. Cameron

674 P.2d 650 (Wash. 1983)

STAFFORD, Justice.

[O]n the morning of June 9, 1980, petitioner stabbed Marie Cameron in excess of 70 times, leaving the knife sticking in her heart. The body was left in the bathtub with no apparent attempt to conceal it. Later that day a police officer saw petitioner in downtown Shelton wearing only a pair of women's stretch pants, a woman's housecoat, a shirt and no shoes. He was stopped and questioned. After first giving a false name, he corrected it and explained he was dressed that way because "I just grabbed what I could . . . My mother-in-law turned vicious." He also stated he was headed for California. Having no known reason to detain petitioner, the officer released him to continue hitchhiking. The next day petitioner was detained by the Oregon State Police as he wandered along the shoulder of Interstate 5 near Salem. Since he was wearing only the stretch pants and one shoe he was thought to be an escapee from a nearby mental hospital. A check revealed petitioner was wanted in Shelton for the death of Marie Cameron.

In the oral confession petitioner stated generally that he was living in or about the home of his father and stepmother. He left home dressed as he was because his stepmother had become violent. "[S]he's into different types of sorcery. She's just strictly a very evil person . . . and she became very violent with me, with a knife in her hand, and so, uh, I don't deny that I'm the one that did what went on out there." He indicated that when he walked into the bathroom he had not expected her. When he saw her, she had the knife which he was able to take from her easily by bending her wrist back. Then, as he stated: "I took the knife and really stabbed her."

In describing the stabbing, petitioner related: "I just kept stabbing her and stabbing her, because she wasn't feeling . . . it was as if she was laughing . . . as if she was up to something that morning, and I don't know . . . she plays around with witchcraft and that stuff. . . ." The last place he saw her was in the bathtub about which he said "she kept moving and moving and moving, and kind of grabbed me like this, but laughing, as if she was enjoying . . . and it was kind of sickening, but it was really maddening to me, because of her offense towards me, it was like . . . you know, it was almost like she was mechanical . . . I mean, the thing was set up that, that's what she wanted to happen. . . . I feel that deep inside she was asking somebody to put her out of her misery . . . she was very symbolic with the 'Scarlet Whore Beast' she was very much into sorcery very, uh, anti-God, not really anti-God but takes the God's truth and twists it into her sorcery."

Concerning his feelings about the incident petitioner said: "I felt confused . . . I felt no different from the beginning than the end there was no difference . . . legally I know, that it is against the law, but as far as right and wrong in the eye of God, I would say I felt no particular wrong."

When asked further about the incident petitioner responded: "I washed the blood off me, and I changed clothes, and then I looked back at her and she was, uh, she was still moving around, after being stabbed, what I thought was in the heart, and the throat . . . about seven or eight times, and she just . . . she kept moving. It was like, . . . there was a smile on her face, she kept lunging for me, while she was dead . . . I wasn't trying to be vicious . . . it would look that way, but that wasn't the intent, but she kept lunging at me, over and over again, and the nature of her attack, I was, ah, mad enough I wanted to kill her, I felt that I was justified in self defense at that point. . . ." The last petitioner saw of the knife "I tried to stick it in her heart . . . she's some kind of an animal."

Petitioner explained further "she's into a very strong sorcery trip, and that's why so many stab wounds . . . I'm not a goring [sic] person . . . I've never been violent in my life, but for some reason . . . there was some evil spirit behind her that was . . . it was like, it was like there was something within her that, that wasn't really part of her body . . . she was smiling . . . she was almost like enjoying playing and it was disgusting."

When petitioner subsequently gave the written confession, he added: "My attack wasn't a vicious attack the first time. I was trying to stop the spirit that was moving in her. She kept saying, 'Gary, Gary, Gary', as if she was enjoying it." When she stopped moving, he washed himself, changed his clothes and then "My stepmother started moving again as if a spirit was in her. I took the knife and started stabbing her again. When I realized there was something in her that wouldn't stop moving, I started stabbing her in the head and heart. I wanted to kill the spirit that seemed to be attacking my spirit." Once again he changed his clothes but again found her moving and again stabbed her numerous times until all movement stopped. He then changed clothes once more and left.

As with the petitioner's testimony we note the testimony of the psychiatrists and psychologists is not without some disparity. Nevertheless, there is ample evidence which, under a proper insanity instruction, could have been considered by the jury as a matter of defense. Prior to trial, petitioner made a motion to acquit on the ground of insanity pursuant to RCW 10.77.080. Three psychiatrists, Doctors Jarvis, Allison and Bremner and a psychologist, Dr. Trowbridge, were called to testify. They agreed petitioner suffered from paranoid schizophrenia both at the time of the killing and at the time of trial. Although stating it differently, all four appeared to agree that petitioner believed he was an agent of God, required to carry out God's directions. They also agreed that petitioner believed God commanded him to kill his stepmother and that he was therefore obligated to kill the "evil spirit." Consequently, all doctors concurred he was legally insane at the time of the murder. The trial court denied the motion for acquittal and submitted the issue of insanity to the jury. At trial, the four doctors repeated their earlier testimony. All agreed that at the time of the killing, and at the time of trial, petitioner suffered from the mental disease of paranoid schizophrenia. While expressing their views in slightly different ways, they agreed petitioner understood that, as a mechanical thing, he was killing his stepmother and knew it was against the laws of man. They stressed, however, that at the time, he was preoccupied with the delusional belief that his stepmother was an agent of satan who was persecuting him, as were others like Yasser Arafat and the Ayatollah Khomeini. He believed he was being directed by God to kill satan's angel and that by so doing, he was obeying God's higher directive or law. At this time, he believed himself to be a messiah and in fact compared himself with Jesus Christ.

The doctors pointed out, in different ways, that because of his delusional beliefs, petitioner felt God had directed him to send her from this life to another. He had no remorse over the killing. He felt it was justified by God and that he was merely doing a service. "He felt he would generally be protected from any difficulties . . . because 'God would not allow it to happen'."

Concerning the legal tests for insanity the mental health experts opined that while he understood it was against the law to kill, he believed he was responding to God's directive and thus had an obligation to rid the world of this "demon," "sorceress" or "evil spirit." Thus, while technically he understood the mechanical nature of the act, he did not have the capacity to discern between right and wrong with reference to the act. Some of the doctors expressed the clear view that at the time of the killing, he was unable to appreciate the nature and quality of his acts. No doctor contended otherwise.

Concerning petitioner's insanity defense the trial court gave standard WPIC pattern jury instruction 20.01, but, over petitioner's exception, added a last paragraph which defines "right and wrong".

"For a defendant to be found not guilty by reason of insanity you must find that, as a result of mental disease or defect, the defendant's mind was affected to such an extent that the defendant was unable to perceive the nature and quality of the acts with which the defendant is charged or was unable to tell right from wrong with reference to the particular acts with which defendant is charged.

What is meant by the terms "right and wrong" refers to knowledge of a person at the time of committing an act that he was acting contrary to the law." (Italics ours.)

Petitioner, on the other hand, proposed the use of WPIC pattern jury instruction 20.01 which does not contain the last paragraph.

Petitioner argues that the trial court should have left the term "right and wrong" undefined as provided by the Legislature in RCW 9A.12.010. At the very least, it is urged, "right and wrong" should not have been defined in such a way as to exclude from the jury's deliberation the consideration of "right and wrong" in terms of one's ability to understand the moral qualities of the act.

At the time this case was tried, the Court of Appeals had just issued *State v. Crenshaw,* 27 Wash. App. 326, 617 P.2d 1041 (1980) which approved the instruction challenged herein. Subsequent thereto this court affirmed the Court of Appeals opinion in *State v. Crenshaw,* 98 Wash. 2d 789, 659 P.2d 488 (1983).

Insofar as the instant case is concerned, however, our discussion of *Crenshaw* also recognized an exception to the alternative grounds set forth therein. That exception is controlling here: "A narrow exception to the societal standard of moral wrong has been drawn for instances wherein a party performs a criminal act, knowing it is morally and legally wrong, but believing, because of a mental defect, that the act is ordained by God: such would be the situation with a mother who kills her infant child to whom she is devotedly attached, believing that God has spoken to her and decreed the act. Although the woman knows that the law and society condemn the act, it would be unrealistic to hold her responsible for the crime, since her free will has been subsumed by her belief in the deific decree."

Consequently, as we held in *Crenshaw,* one who believes that he is acting under the direct command of God is no less insane because he nevertheless knows murder is prohibited by the laws of man. Indeed, it may actually emphasize his insanity. In the instant case there is considerable evidence (although not unanimous) from which the jury could have concluded that petitioner suffered from a mental disease; that he believed his stepmother was satan's angel or a sorceress; that he believed God directed him to kill his stepmother; that because of the mental disease it was impossible for him to understand that what he was doing was wrong; and that his free will had "been subsumed by [his] belief in the deific decree." The last paragraph of the trial court's challenged instruction precluded the jury's consideration of these factors and thus runs afoul of the *Crenshaw* exception. In short, the instruction prevented the jury from considering those essential relevant facts that formed petitioner's theory of the case. To this extent the trial court erred by adding the definitional paragraph to the instruction.

While we hold the facts of this case fall within the *Crenshaw* exception, we are compelled to observe that the scope of this exception must be determined on a case by case basis.

The cause is reversed and remanded for a new trial consistent with this opinion.

Dore, Justice (concurring).

Last February, we decided *Crenshaw*. Both *Crenshaw* and the subject case were almost factually identical; both involved outrageous, vicious, messy murders.

Crenshaw

Crenshaw stabbed his wife 27 times, one of which stabs was fatal. He later returned and decapitated her and then buried her remains in a hidden place. Cameron committed an equally brutal murder; he stabbed his stepmother 97 times. In *Crenshaw*, there was testimony by medical experts that he had delusions of grandeur, religiosity (including a belief in his possession of special powers), auditory hallucinations, lack of insight, and extreme emotional liability.

A psychiatrist testified that Crenshaw was suffering from a paranoid state and was in remission from former psychotic episodes. He had a history of mental problems. He was hospitalized in his home state of Texas 15 times between 1970 and 1978 where he was diagnosed as a paranoid schizophrenic. Crenshaw testified he knew that if he killed his wife he was violating the law, but he believed he had a duty to do it under the teaching of his Moscovite "religious" beliefs.

Cameron

Medical experts testified that Cameron suffered from paranoid schizophrenia both at the time of the killing and at the time of the trial. Cameron related his feelings about the incident, "I felt confused . . . I felt no different from the beginning than the end there was no difference . . . legally I know, that it is against the law, but as far as right and wrong in the eye of God, I would say I felt no particular wrong." Cameron believed that God commanded him to kill his stepmother and that he was, therefore, obligated to kill the "evil spirit." All doctors agreed that Cameron was legally insane at the time of the murder. Concerning the legal tests for insanity, the mental health experts opined that while Cameron understood it was against the law to kill, he believed he was responding to God's directive and thus had an obligation to rid the world of this "demon," "sorceress" or "evil spirit."

Both *Crenshaw* and *Cameron* came to this court challenging the identical instruction which defined insanity in terms limited to legal right and wrong and rejecting insanity based on moral right and wrong.

Such instruction read as follows:

"What is meant by the terms "right and wrong" refers to knowledge of a person at the time of committing an act that he was acting contrary to the law."

(Italics mine.)

In both cases, it was argued "right and wrong" should not have been defined in such a way as to exclude from the jury's deliberation the consideration of "right and wrong" in terms of one's ability to understand the moral qualities of the act. In *Crenshaw*, the majority rejected Crenshaw's argument and held that the instruction was a proper statement of the law. The issue in both cases pertaining to the subject instruction was whether the terms "right" and "wrong," as used in RCW 9A.12.010(1)(b), should be qualified for the jury. In both cases at trial, the jury was instructed the defendant would not be legally insane if he knew legal right from legal wrong. Both contended the trial court erred in defining right and wrong as legal right and wrong. Contrary to *Crenshaw*, the majority holds that the subject instruction was prejudicial error, saying, "In short, the instruction prevented the jury from considering those essential relevant facts that formed petitioner's theory of the case. To this extent the trial court erred by adding the definitional paragraph to the instruction."

Crenshaw performed his dastardly murder believing he had a duty to do it under the teaching of his Moscovite "religious" beliefs. Cameron committed a very similar, vicious murder on the basis that God commanded him to kill his stepmother and that he was obligated to kill the evil spirit. I, frankly, don't see much or any distinction, however, in carrying out or executing a murder under the direction of God or Crenshaw's Moscovite religious beliefs, or under the beliefs of a prophet, Buddha, etc.

Conclusion

As this case does not reverse *Crenshaw*, which provided prospectively for giving WPIC 20.01 in all future insanity cases, I conclude in the subject case that in all future insanity cases WPIC 20.01 should be given without change or modification and that defendants' defense counsel are free to argue legal and/or moral right and wrong as an affirmative defense.

DIMMICK, Justice (dissenting in part).

In *Crenshaw*, we began the odyssey. Today's majority opinion now leads us further into the Serbonian bog. In *Crenshaw* we recognized that one who knew the illegality of his act was not necessarily "'beyond any of the influences of the criminal law'" and thus not legally insane. We thus found support for upholding an instruction identical to the one given in this case. However, *Crenshaw* contained several alternative holdings. One of which was that "legal" wrong and "moral" wrong were synonymous in that particular case. In explaining this holding, we included as dicta an exception for "deific decrees." The majority in the instant case relies on this exception, holding that this court shall determine the scope of this exception on a case-by-case basis. The majority thus condemns us to review every proffered insanity defense.

The exception itself is inconsistent with a legal definition of wrong. Additionally, what exactly does it entail? Apparently, a person is legally insane if God gives him a direct command, such as the one Mr. Cameron allegedly received. However, a person is not legally insane if God does not directly ordain the act, but the person merely interprets his religious beliefs to require the act. In sum, I predict many problems with this exception.

Thus, I would affirm the Court of Appeals' and trial court's holdings that the insanity instruction was proper in this case. The preferable approach, however, as later suggested in *Crenshaw*, is that the definition of "wrong" should not be included in an instruction in the future.

Questions and Notes

1. Although agreeing on little else, all of the Justices seem to think that the best future course of action is for trial judges to abstain from defining "wrong," thereby leaving it to the judgment of the jurors as to whether "moral wrong" qualifies. Do you see any problems with this approach? If so, what are they?

2. In general, should a defendant who cannot appreciate the moral wrongness of his act be subject to criminal punishment? Why? Why not?

3. Assuming that your answer to Question 2 is "yes," is the Deific exception justified? Why?

4. Assuming that the Deific exception is proper, can *Crenshaw* and *Cameron* be distinguished? In *Crenshaw*, the defendant belonged to a religion that taught that wives who commit adultery should be killed. Crenshaw killed his wife because he believed that she had committed adultery.

5. Should the mother who kills her baby at the command of God be treated any differently from the mother who kills her baby at the suggestion of a hypnotically persuasive cult leader? Why? Why not?

Problem

Cheryl Jones appeals her conviction for indecent liberties. At a bench trial, Mrs. Jones defended on the basis of diminished capacity. She presented expert testimony that she suffers from multiple personality disorder (MPD) and was not conscious of the actions of an alter personality who performed the criminal act. She contends the trial court erred when it determined she acted knowingly because the alter personality was aware of facts described by the statute defining the offense of indecent liberties. The trial court found Mrs. Jones has a form of MPD and at times acts in personalities other than her core personality. The personalities are distinct and have the ability to act knowingly. The personalities sometimes know what happens during the emergence of the various personalities and sometimes do not. In

March 1988, the personality named "Cat" or "Catherine" knowingly touched her three-year-old foster daughter in the vaginal area for the purpose of sexual gratification. The court found the State had not shown that Mrs. Jones knew on the particular occasion at issue what "Cat" or "Catherine" was doing. However, the trial court concluded Mrs. Jones's MPD did not relieve her from criminal responsibility for her acts because the "personality known as 'Cat' or 'Catherine' was able to know, and did know, what she was doing when the events were occurring."

Did the trial court err when it held that Mrs. Jones acted knowingly because her alter personality acted knowingly, even though it also found the State did not prove she knew what her alter personality was doing when it committed the acts in question? For one court's solution, *see State v. Jones*, 920 P.2d 225 (Wash. App. Div. 3 1996). The question of when and how issues of insanity should be relevant was extensively explored by the United States Supreme Court in *Clark v. Arizona*.

Clark v. Arizona
548 U.S. 735 (2006)

Justice SOUTER delivered the opinion of the Court.

The case presents two questions: whether due process prohibits Arizona's use of an insanity test stated solely in terms of the capacity to tell whether an act charged as a crime was right or wrong; and whether Arizona violates due process in restricting consideration of defense evidence of mental illness and incapacity to its bearing on a claim of insanity, thus eliminating its significance directly on the issue of the mental element of the crime charged (known in legal shorthand as the *mens rea*, or guilty mind). We hold that there is no violation of due process in either instance.

I.

In the early hours of June 21, 2000, Officer Jeffrey Moritz of the Flagstaff Police responded in uniform to complaints that a pickup truck with loud music blaring was circling a residential block. When he located the truck, the officer turned on the emergency lights and siren of his marked patrol car, which prompted petitioner Eric Clark, the truck's driver (then 17), to pull over. Officer Moritz got out of the patrol car and told Clark to stay where he was. Less than a minute later, Clark shot the officer, who died soon after but not before calling the police dispatcher for help. Clark ran away on foot but was arrested later that day with gunpowder residue on his hands; the gun that killed the officer was found nearby, stuffed into a knit cap.

Clark was charged with first-degree murder for intentionally or knowingly killing a law enforcement officer in the line of duty. In March 2001, Clark was found incompetent to stand trial and was committed to a state hospital for treatment, but two years later the same trial court found his competence restored and ordered him to be tried. Clark waived his right to a jury, and the case was heard by the court.

At trial, Clark did not contest the shooting and death, but relied on his undisputed paranoid schizophrenia at the time of the incident in denying that he had the specific intent to shoot a law enforcement officer or knowledge that he was doing so, as required by the statute. Accordingly, the prosecutor offered circumstantial evidence that Clark knew Officer Moritz was a law enforcement officer. The evidence showed that the officer was in uniform at the time, that he caught up with Clark in a marked police car with emergency lights and siren going, and that Clark acknowledged the symbols of police authority and stopped. The testimony for the prosecution indicated that Clark had intentionally lured an officer to the scene to kill him, having told some people a few weeks before the incident that he wanted to shoot police officers. At the close of the State's evidence, the trial court denied Clark's motion for judgment of acquittal for failure to prove intent to kill a law enforcement officer or knowledge that Officer Moritz was a law enforcement officer:

> In presenting the defense case, Clark claimed mental illness, which he sought to introduce for two purposes. First, he raised the affirmative defense of insanity, putting the burden on himself to prove by clear and convincing evidence that "at the time of the commission of the criminal act [he] was afflicted with a mental disease or defect of such severity that [he] did not know the criminal act was wrong," Second, he aimed to rebut the prosecution's evidence of the requisite *mens rea*, that he had acted intentionally or knowingly to kill a law enforcement officer.

The trial court ruled that Clark could not rely on evidence bearing on insanity to dispute the *mens rea*. The court cited *State v. Mott*, 187 Ariz. 536, 931 P.2d 1046 (en banc), cert. denied, which "refused to allow psychiatric testimony to negate specific intent," and held that "Arizona does not allow evidence of a defendant's mental disorder short of insanity . . . to negate the *mens rea* element of a crime."[3]

As to his insanity, then, Clark presented testimony from classmates, school officials, and his family describing his increasingly bizarre behavior over the year before the shooting. Witnesses testified, for example, that paranoid delusions led Clark to rig a fishing line with beads and wind chimes at home to alert him to intrusion by invaders, and to keep a bird in his automobile to warn of airborne poison. There was lay and expert testimony that Clark thought Flagstaff was populated with "aliens" (some impersonating government agents), the "aliens" were trying to kill him, and bullets were the only way to stop them. A psychiatrist testified that Clark was suffering from paranoid schizophrenia with delusions about "aliens" when he killed Officer Moritz, and he concluded that Clark was incapable of luring the officer or understanding right from wrong and that he was thus insane at the time of the killing. In rebuttal, a psychiatrist for the State gave his opinion that Clark's paranoid schizophrenia did not keep him from appreciating the wrongfulness of his conduct, as shown by his actions before and after the shooting (such as circling the

---

3. The trial court permitted Clark to introduce this evidence, whether primarily going to insanity or lack of intent, "because it goes to the insanity issue and because we're not in front of a jury." It also allowed him to make an offer of proof as to intent to preserve the issue on appeal.

residential block with music blaring as if to lure the police to intervene, evading the police after the shooting, and hiding the gun).

At the close of the defense case consisting of this evidence bearing on mental illness, the trial court denied Clark's renewed motion for a directed verdict grounded on failure of the prosecution to show that Clark knew the victim was a police officer. The judge then issued a special verdict of first-degree murder, expressly finding that Clark shot and caused the death of Officer Moritz beyond a reasonable doubt and that Clark had not shown that he was insane at the time. The judge noted that though Clark was indisputably afflicted with paranoid schizophrenia at the time of the shooting, the mental illness "did not . . . distort his perception of reality so severely that he did not know his actions were wrong." For this conclusion, the judge expressly relied on "the facts of the crime, the evaluations of the experts, [Clark's] actions and behavior both before and after the shooting, and the observations of those that knew [Clark]." The sentence was life imprisonment without the possibility of release for 25 years.

II.

Clark first says that Arizona's definition of insanity, being only a fragment of the Victorian standard from which it derives, violates due process. The landmark English rule in *M'Naghten's Case*, 10 Cl. & Fin. 200, 8 Eng. Rep. 718 (1843), states that:

> "the jurors ought to be told . . . that to establish a defence on the ground of insanity, it must be clearly proved that, at the time of the committing of the act, the party accused was laboring under such a defect of reason, from disease of the mind, as not to know the nature and quality of the act he was doing; or, if he did know it, that he did not know he was doing what was wrong."

The first part asks about cognitive capacity: whether a mental defect leaves a defendant unable to understand what he is doing. The second part presents an ostensibly alternative basis for recognizing a defense of insanity understood as a lack of moral capacity: whether a mental disease or defect leaves a defendant unable to understand that his action is wrong.

When the Arizona Legislature first codified an insanity rule, it adopted the full *M'Naghten* statement (subject to modifications in details that do not matter here):

> "A person is not responsible for criminal conduct if at the time of such conduct the person was suffering from such a mental disease or defect as not to know the nature and quality of the act or, if such person did know, that such person did not know that what he was doing was wrong."

In 1993, the legislature dropped the cognitive incapacity part, leaving only moral incapacity as the nub of the stated definition. Under current Arizona law, a defendant will not be adjudged insane unless he demonstrates that "at the time of the commission of the criminal act [he] was afflicted with a mental disease or defect of such severity that [he] did not know the criminal act was wrong,"

Clark challenges the 1993 amendment excising the express reference to the cognitive incapacity element. He insists that the side-by-side *M'Naghten* test represents the minimum that a government must provide in recognizing an alternative to criminal responsibility on grounds of mental illness or defect, and he argues that elimination of the *M'Naghten* reference to nature and quality "'offends [a] principle of justice so rooted in the traditions and conscience of our people as to be ranked as fundamental.'"

The claim entails no light burden, and Clark does not carry it. History shows no deference to *M'Naghten* that could elevate its formula to the level of fundamental principle, so as to limit the traditional recognition of a State's capacity to define crimes and defenses.

Even a cursory examination of the traditional Anglo-American approaches to insanity reveals significant differences among them, with four traditional strains variously combined to yield a diversity of American standards. The main variants are the cognitive incapacity, the moral incapacity, the volitional incapacity, and the product-of-mental-illness tests.[7] The first two emanate from the alternatives stated in the *M'Naghten* rule. The volitional incapacity or irresistible-impulse test, which surfaced over two centuries ago, asks whether a person was so lacking in volition due to a mental defect or illness that he could not have controlled his actions. And the product-of-mental-illness test was used as early as 1870, and simply asks whether a person's action was a product of a mental disease or defect. Seventeen States and the Federal Government have adopted a recognizable version of the *M'Naghten* test with both its cognitive incapacity and moral incapacity components. One State has adopted only *M'Naghten's* cognitive incapacity test, and 10 (including Arizona) have adopted the moral incapacity test alone. Fourteen jurisdictions, inspired by the Model Penal Code, have in place an amalgam of the volitional incapacity test and some variant of the moral incapacity test, satisfaction of either (generally by showing a defendant's substantial lack of capacity) being enough to excuse. Three States combine a full *M'Naghten* test with a volitional incapacity formula. And New Hampshire alone stands by the product-of-mental-illness test. The alternatives are multiplied further by variations in the prescribed insanity verdict: a significant number of these jurisdictions supplement the traditional "not guilty by reason of insanity" verdict with an alternative of "guilty but mentally ill." Finally, four States have no affirmative insanity defense,[20] though one provides for a "guilty and mentally ill" verdict. These four, like a number of others that recognize an affirmative

---

7. "Capacity" is understood to mean the ability to form a certain state of mind or motive, understand or evaluate one's actions, or control them.

20. Idaho Code § 18-207 (Lexis 2004); Kan. Stat. Ann. § 22-3220 (1995); Mont. Code Ann. §§ 46-14-102, 46-14-311 (2005); Utah Code Ann. § 76-2-305 (Lexis 2003). We have never held that the Constitution mandates an insanity defense, nor have we held that the Constitution does not so require. This case does not call upon us to decide the matter.

insanity defense, allow consideration of evidence of mental illness directly on the element of *mens rea* defining the offense.

With this varied background, it is clear that no particular formulation has evolved into a baseline for due process, and that the insanity rule, like the conceptualization of criminal offenses, is substantially open to state choice. Indeed, the legitimacy of such choice is the more obvious when one considers the interplay of legal concepts of mental illness or deficiency required for an insanity defense, with the medical concepts of mental abnormality that influence the expert opinion testimony by psychologists and psychiatrists commonly introduced to support or contest insanity claims. For medical definitions devised to justify treatment, like legal ones devised to excuse from conventional criminal responsibility, are subject to flux and disagreement. cf. *Leland*, (no due process violation for adopting the *M'Naghten* standard rather than the irresistible-impulse test because scientific knowledge does not require otherwise and choice of test is a matter of policy). There being such fodder for reasonable debate about what the cognate legal and medical tests should be, due process imposes no single canonical formulation of legal insanity.

We are satisfied that neither in theory nor in practice did Arizona's 1993 abridgment of the insanity formulation deprive Clark of due process.

III.

Clark's second claim of a due process violation challenges the rule adopted by the Supreme Court of Arizona in *State v. Mott*. This case ruled on the admissibility of testimony from a psychologist offered to show that the defendant suffered from battered women's syndrome and therefore lacked the capacity to form the *mens rea* of the crime charged against her. The opinion variously referred to the testimony in issue as "psychological testimony," and "expert testimony," and implicitly equated it with "expert psychiatric evidence," (internal quotation marks omitted), and "psychiatric testimon.,"[25] The state court held that testimony of a professional psychologist or psychiatrist about a defendant's mental incapacity owing to mental disease or defect was admissible, and could be considered, only for its bearing on an insanity defense; such evidence could not be considered on the element of *mens rea*, that is, what the State must show about a defendant's mental state (such as intent or understanding) when he performed the act charged against him.[26]

A.

Understanding Clark's claim requires attention to the categories of evidence with a potential bearing on *mens rea*. First, there is "observation evidence" in the everyday sense, testimony from those who observed what Clark did and heard what he said; this category would also include testimony that an expert witness might give

---

25. We thus think the dissent reads *Mott* too broadly. (opinion of KENNEDY, J.) (no distinction between observation and mental-disease testimony, or lay and expert).

26. The more natural reading of *Mott* suggests to us that this evidence cannot be considered as to *mens rea* even if the defendant establishes his insanity, though one might read *Mott* otherwise.

about Clark's tendency to think in a certain way and his behavioral characteristics. This evidence may support a professional diagnosis of mental disease and in any event is the kind of evidence that can be relevant to show what in fact was on Clark's mind when he fired the gun. Observation evidence in the record covers Clark's behavior at home and with friends, his expressions of belief around the time of the killing that "aliens" were inhabiting the bodies of local people (including government agents),[27] his driving around the neighborhood before the police arrived, and so on. Contrary to the dissent's characterization, observation evidence can be presented by either lay or expert witnesses.

Second, there is "mental-disease evidence" in the form of opinion testimony that Clark suffered from a mental disease with features described by the witness. As was true here, this evidence characteristically but not always[28] comes from professional psychologists or psychiatrists who testify as expert witnesses and base their opinions in part on examination of a defendant, usually conducted after the events in question. The thrust of this evidence was that, based on factual reports, professional observations, and tests, Clark was psychotic at the time in question, with a condition that fell within the category of schizophrenia.

Third, there is evidence we will refer to as "capacity evidence" about a defendant's capacity for cognition and moral judgment (and ultimately also his capacity to form *mens rea*). This, too, is opinion evidence. Here, as it usually does,[29] this testimony came from the same experts and concentrated on those specific details of the mental condition that make the difference between sanity and insanity under the Arizona definition.[30] In their respective testimony on these details the experts disagreed: the defense expert gave his opinion that the symptoms or effects of the

---

27. Clark's parents testified that, in the months before the shooting and even days beforehand, Clark called them "aliens" and thought that "aliens" were out to get him. One night before the shooting, according to Clark's mother, Clark repeatedly viewed a popular film characterized by her as telling a story about "aliens" masquerading as government agents, a story Clark insisted was real despite his mother's protestations to the contrary. And two months after the shooting, Clark purportedly told his parents that his hometown, Flagstaff, was inhabited principally by "aliens," who had to be stopped, and that the only way to stop them was with bullets.

28. This is contrary to the dissent's understanding. (opinion of KENNEDY, J.)

29. In conflict with the dissent's characterization, it does not always, however, come from experts.

30. Arizona permits capacity evidence, *see, e.g., State v. Sanchez*, 117 Ariz. 369, 373, 573 P.2d 60, 64 (1977); *see also* Ariz. Rule Evid. 704 (2006) (allowing otherwise admissible evidence on testimony "embrac[ing] an ultimate issue to be decided by the trier of fact"), though not every jurisdiction permits such evidence on the ultimate issue of insanity. *See, e.g.,* Fed. Rule Evid. 704(b) ("No expert witness testifying with respect to the mental state or condition of a defendant in a criminal case may state an opinion or inference as to whether the defendant did or did not have the mental state or condition constituting an element of the crime charged or a defense thereto. Such ultimate issues are matters for the trier of fact alone"); *United States v. Dixon*, 185 F.3d 393, 400 (C.A.5 1999) (in the face of mental-disease evidence, Rule 704(b) prohibits an expert "from testifying that [the mental-disease evidence] does or does not prevent the defendant from appreciating the wrongfulness of his actions").

disease in Clark's case included inability to appreciate the nature of his action and to tell that it was wrong, whereas the State's psychiatrist was of the view that Clark was a schizophrenic who was still sufficiently able to appreciate the reality of shooting the officer and to know that it was wrong to do that.[31]

B.

It is clear that *Mott* itself imposed no restriction on considering evidence of the first sort, the observation evidence. We read the *Mott* restriction to apply, rather, to evidence addressing the two issues in testimony that characteristically comes only from psychologists or psychiatrists qualified to give opinions as expert witnesses: mental-disease evidence (whether at the time of the crime a defendant suffered from a mental disease or defect, such as schizophrenia) and capacity evidence (whether the disease or defect left him incapable of performing or experiencing a mental process defined as necessary for sanity such as appreciating the nature and quality of his act and knowing that it was wrong).

Mott was careful to distinguish this kind of opinion evidence from observation evidence generally and even from observation evidence that an expert witness might offer, such as descriptions of a defendant's tendency to think in a certain way or his behavioral characteristics; the Arizona court made it clear that this sort of testimony was perfectly admissible to rebut the prosecution's evidence of *mens rea*. Thus, only opinion testimony going to mental defect or disease, and its effect on the cognitive or moral capacities on which sanity depends under the Arizona rule, is restricted.

In this case, the trial court seems to have applied the *Mott* restriction to all evidence offered by Clark for the purpose of showing what he called his inability to form the required *mens rea*, (that is, an intent to kill a police officer on duty, or an understanding that he was engaging in the act of killing such an officer. Thus, the trial court's restriction may have covered not only mental-disease and capacity evidence as just defined, but also observation evidence offered by lay (and expert) witnesses who described Clark's unusual behavior. Clark's objection to the application of the *Mott* rule does not, however, turn on the distinction between lay and expert witnesses or the kinds of testimony they were competent to present.

---

31. Arizona permits evidence bearing on insanity to be presented by either lay or expert witnesses. *See State v. Bay*, 150 Ariz. 112, 116, 722 P.2d 280, 284 (1986). According to *Bay*, "[f]oundationally, a lay witness must have had an opportunity to observe the past conduct and history of a defendant; the fact that he is a lay witness goes not to the admissibility of the testimony but rather to its weight." *Ibid.* (citation omitted); *see also State v. Hughes*, 193 Ariz. 72, 83, 969 P.2d 1184, 1195 (1998). In fact, a defendant can theoretically establish insanity solely via lay testimony. *See Bay*, 150 Ariz., at 116, 722 P.2d, at 284. But cf. *State v. McMurtrey*, 136 Ariz. 93, 100, 664 P.2d 637, 644 (1983) ("[I]t is difficult to imagine how a defendant could place his or her sanity in issue . . . without expert testimony as to the defendant's state of mind at the time of the crime").

C.

There is some, albeit limited, disagreement between the dissent and ourselves about the scope of the claim of error properly before us. To start with matters of agreement, all Members of the Court agree that Clark's general attack on the *Mott* rule covers its application in confining consideration of capacity evidence to the insanity defense.

In practical terms, our agreement on issues presented extends to a second point. Justice KENNEDY understands that Clark raised an objection to confining mental-disease evidence to the insanity issue. As he sees it, Clark in effect claimed that in dealing with the issue of *mens rea* the trial judge should have considered expert testimony on what may characteristically go through the mind of a schizophrenic, when the judge considered what in fact was in Clark's mind at the time of the shooting. He thus understands that defense counsel claimed a right to rebut the State's *mens rea* demonstration with testimony about how schizophrenics may hallucinate voices and other sounds, about their characteristic failure to distinguish the content of their imagination from what most people perceive as exterior reality, and so on. It is important to be clear that this supposed objection was not about dealing with testimony based on observation of Clark showing that he had auditory hallucinations when he was driving around, or failed in fact to appreciate objective reality when he shot; this objection went to use of testimony about schizophrenics, not about Clark in particular. While we might dispute how clearly Clark raised this objection, we have no doubt that the objection falls within a general challenge to the *Mott* rule; we understand that *Mott* is meant to confine to the insanity defense any consideration of characteristic behavior associated with mental disease. We will therefore assume for argument that Clark raised this claim, as we consider the due process challenge to the *Mott* rule.

The point on which we disagree with the dissent, however, is this: did Clark apprise the Arizona courts that he believed the trial judge had erroneously limited the consideration of observation evidence, whether from lay witnesses like Clark's mother or (possibly) the expert witnesses who observed him? This sort of evidence was not covered by the *Mott* restriction, and confining it to the insanity issue would have been an erroneous application of *Mott* as a matter of Arizona law. We think the only issue properly before us is the challenge to *Mott* on due process grounds, comprising objections to limits on the use of mental-disease and capacity evidence.

D.

Clark's argument that the *Mott* rule violates the Fourteenth Amendment guarantee of due process turns on the application of the presumption of innocence in criminal cases, the presumption of sanity, and the principle that a criminal defendant is entitled to present relevant and favorable evidence on an element of the offense charged against him.

1.

The first presumption is that a defendant is innocent unless and until the government proves beyond a reasonable doubt each element of the offense charged. Before the last century, the *mens rea* required to be proven for particular offenses was often described in general terms like "malice," *see, e.g., In re Eckart*, 166 U.S. 481, 17 S.Ct. 638, 41 L.Ed. 1085 (1897); 4 W. Blackstone, Commentaries *21 ("[A]n unwarrant-able act without a vicious will is no crime at all"), but the modern tendency has been toward more specific descriptions, as shown in the Arizona statute defining the murder charged against Clark: the State had to prove that in acting to kill the victim, Clark intended to kill a law enforcement officer on duty or knew that the victim was such an officer on duty. *See* generally Gardner, The *Mens Rea* Enigma: Observations on the Role of Motive in the Criminal Law Past and Present, 1993 Utah L.Rev. 635. As applied to *mens rea* (and every other element), the force of the presumption of innocence is measured by the force of the showing needed to over-come it, which is proof beyond a reasonable doubt that a defendant's state of mind was in fact what the charge states.

2.

The presumption of sanity is equally universal in some variety or other, being (at least) a presumption that a defendant has the capacity to form the *mens rea* nec-essary for a verdict of guilt and the consequent criminal responsibility. This pre-sumption dispenses with a requirement on the government's part to include as an element of every criminal charge an allegation that the defendant had such a capac-ity. The force of this presumption, like the presumption of innocence, is measured by the quantum of evidence necessary to overcome it; unlike the presumption of innocence, however, the force of the presumption of sanity varies across the many state and federal jurisdictions, and prior law has recognized considerable leeway on the part of the legislative branch in defining the presumption's strength through the kind of evidence and degree of persuasiveness necessary to overcome it.[36]

There are two points where the sanity or capacity presumption may be placed in issue. First, a State may allow a defendant to introduce (and a factfinder to con-sider) evidence of mental disease or incapacity for the bearing it can have on the government's burden to show *mens rea*. *See, e.g., State v. Perez*, 882 A.2d 574, 584 (R.I. 2005).[37] In such States the evidence showing incapacity to form the guilty state of mind, for example, qualifies the probative force of other evidence, which consid-ered alone indicates that the defendant actually formed the guilty state of mind. If it is shown that a defendant with mental disease thinks all blond people are robots, he could not have intended to kill a person when he shot a man with blond hair,

---

36. Although a desired evidentiary use is restricted, that is not equivalent to a *Sandstrom* pre-sumption. *See Sandstrom v. Montana*, 442 U.S. 510, 514–524, 99 S.Ct. 2450, 61 L.Ed.2d 39 (1979) (due process forbids use of presumption that relieves the prosecution of burden of proving mental state by inference of intent from an act).

37. In fact, Oregon had this scheme in place when we decided *Leland v. Oregon*, 343 U.S. 790, 794–796, 72 S.Ct. 1002, 96 L.Ed. 1302 (1952). We do not, however, read any part of *Leland* to require as a matter of due process that evidence of incapacity be considered to rebut the *mens rea* element of a crime.

even though he seemed to act like a man shooting another man.[38] In jurisdictions that allow mental-disease and capacity evidence to be considered on par with any other relevant evidence when deciding whether the prosecution has proven *mens rea* beyond a reasonable doubt, the evidence of mental disease or incapacity need only support what the factfinder regards as a reasonable doubt about the capacity to form (or the actual formation of) the *mens rea*, in order to require acquittal of the charge. Thus, in these States the strength of the presumption of sanity is no greater than the strength of the evidence of abnormal mental state that the factfinder thinks is enough to raise a reasonable doubt.

The second point where the force of the presumption of sanity may be tested is in the consideration of a defense of insanity raised by a defendant. Insanity rules like *M'Naghten* and the variants discussed in Part II, are attempts to define, or at least to indicate, the kinds of mental differences that overcome the presumption of sanity or capacity and therefore excuse a defendant from customary criminal responsibility. A State may provide, for example, that whenever the defendant raises a claim of insanity by some quantum of credible evidence, the presumption disappears and the government must prove sanity to a specified degree of certainty (whether beyond reasonable doubt or something less). Or a jurisdiction may place the burden of persuasion on a defendant to prove insanity as the applicable law defines it, whether by a preponderance of the evidence or to some more convincing degree, *see* Ariz.Rev.Stat. Ann. § 13-502(C) (West 2001); *Leland*, 343 U.S., at 798, 72 S.Ct. 1002. In any case, the defendant's burden defines the presumption of sanity, whether that burden be to burst a bubble or to show something more.

3.

The third principle implicated by Clark's argument is a defendant's right as a matter of simple due process to present evidence favorable to himself on an element that must be proven to convict him.[39] As already noted, evidence tending to show

---

38. We reject the State's argument that *mens rea* and insanity, as currently understood, are entirely distinguishable, so that mental-disease and capacity evidence relevant to insanity is simply irrelevant to *mens rea*. Not only does evidence accepted as showing insanity trump *mens rea*, but evidence of behavior close to the time of the act charged may indicate both the actual state of mind at that time and also an enduring incapacity to form the criminal state of mind necessary to the offense charged. *See* Brief for American Psychiatric Association et al. as *Amici Curiae* 12–13; Arenella, The Diminished Capacity and Diminished Responsibility Defenses: Two Children of a Doomed Marriage, 77 Colum. L.Rev. 827, 834–835 (1977); *cf. Powell v. Texas*, 392 U.S. 514, 535–536, 88 S.Ct. 2145, 20 L.Ed.2d 1254 (1968) (plurality opinion) (the "doctrines of *actus reus, mens rea*, insanity, mistake, justification, and duress" are a "collection of interlocking and overlapping concepts which the common law has utilized to assess the moral accountability of an individual for his antisocial deeds").

39. Clark's argument assumes that Arizona's rule is a rule of evidence, rather than a redefinition of mens rea, see *Montana v. Egelhoff*, 518 U.S. 37, 58–59 (1996) (GINSBURG, J., concurring in judgment); *id.*, at 71 (O'Connor, J., dissenting). We have no reason to view the rule otherwise, and on this assumption, it does not violate due process.

that a defendant suffers from mental disease and lacks capacity to form *mens rea* is relevant to rebut evidence that he did in fact form the required *mens rea* at the time in question; this is the reason that Clark claims a right to require the fact-finder in this case to consider testimony about his mental illness and his incapacity directly, when weighing the persuasiveness of other evidence tending to show *mens rea*, which the prosecution has the burden to prove.

As Clark recognizes, however, the right to introduce relevant evidence can be curtailed if there is a good reason for doing that. "While the Constitution . . . prohibits the exclusion of defense evidence under rules that serve no legitimate purpose or that are disproportionate to the ends that they are asserted to promote, well-established rules of evidence permit trial judges to exclude evidence if its probative value is outweighed by certain other factors such as unfair prejudice, confusion of the issues, or potential to mislead the jury." And if evidence may be kept out entirely, its consideration may be subject to limitation, which Arizona claims the power to impose here. State law says that evidence of mental-disease and incapacity may be introduced and considered, and if sufficiently forceful to satisfy the defendant's burden of proof under the insanity rule it will displace the presumption of sanity and excuse from criminal responsibility. But mental-disease and capacity evidence may be considered only for its bearing on the insanity defense, and it will avail a defendant only if it is persuasive enough to satisfy the defendant's burden as defined by the terms of that defense. The mental disease and capacity evidence is thus being channeled or restricted to one issue and given effect only if the defendant carries the burden to convince the factfinder of insanity; the evidence is not being excluded entirely, and the question is whether reasons for requiring it to be channeled and restricted are good enough to satisfy the standard of fundamental fairness that due process requires. We think they are.

E.

1.

The first reason supporting the *Mott* rule is Arizona's authority to define its presumption of sanity (or capacity or responsibility) by choosing an insanity definition, as discussed in Part II, and by placing the burden of persuasion on defendants who claim incapacity as an excuse from customary criminal responsibility. No one, certainly not Clark here, denies that a State may place a burden of persuasion on a defendant claiming insanity (permitting a State, consistent with due process, to require the defendant to bear this burden). And Clark presses no objection to Arizona's decision to require persuasion to a clear and convincing degree before the presumption of sanity and normal responsibility is overcome.

But if a State is to have this authority in practice as well as in theory, it must be able to deny a defendant the opportunity to displace the presumption of sanity more easily when addressing a different issue in the course of the criminal trial. Yet, as we have explained, just such an opportunity would be available if expert testimony of mental disease and incapacity could be considered for whatever a fact-finder might think it was worth on the issue of *mens rea*.[40] As we mentioned, the presumption of sanity would then be only as strong as the evidence a factfinder would accept as enough to raise a reasonable doubt about *mens rea* for the crime charged; once reasonable doubt was found, acquittal would be required, and the standards established for the defense of insanity would go by the boards.

Now, a State is of course free to accept such a possibility in its law. After all, it is free to define the insanity defense by treating the presumption of sanity as a bursting bubble, whose disappearance shifts the burden to the prosecution to prove sanity whenever a defendant presents any credible evidence of mental disease or incapacity. In States with this kind of insanity rule, the legislature may well be willing to allow such evidence to be considered on the *mens rea* element for whatever the factfinder thinks it is worth. What counts for due process, however, is simply that a State that wishes to avoid a second avenue for exploring capacity, less stringent for a defendant, has a good reason for confining the consideration of evidence of mental disease and incapacity to the insanity defense.

It is obvious that Arizona's *Mott* rule reflects such a choice. The State Supreme Court pointed out that the State had declined to adopt a defense of diminished capacity (allowing a jury to decide when to excuse a defendant because of greater than normal difficulty in conforming to the law).[41] The court reasoned that the State's choice would be undercut if evidence of incapacity could be considered for whatever a jury might think sufficient to raise a reasonable doubt about *mens rea*, even if it did not show insanity. In other words, if a jury were free to decide how much evidence of mental disease and incapacity was enough to counter evidence of *mens rea* to the point of creating a reasonable doubt, that would in functional terms be analogous to allowing jurors to decide upon some degree of diminished capacity to obey the law, a degree set by them, that would prevail as a stand-alone defense.[42]

---

40. *Cf.* (KENNEDY, J., dissenting) ("The psychiatrist's explanation of Clark's condition was essential to understanding how he processes sensory data and therefore to deciding what information was in his mind at the time of the shooting. Simply put, knowledge relies on cognition, and cognition can be affected by schizophrenia").

41. Though the term "diminished capacity" has been given different meanings, *see, e.g.*, Morse, Undiminished Confusion in Diminished Capacity, 75 J.Crim. L. & C. 1 (1984) ("The diminished capacity doctrine allows a criminal defendant to introduce evidence of mental abnormality at trial either to negate a mental element of the crime charged, thereby exonerating the defendant of that charge, or to reduce the degree of crime for which the defendant may be convicted, even if the defendant's conduct satisfied all the formal elements of a higher offense"), California, a jurisdiction with which the concept has traditionally been associated, understood it to be simply a "'showing that the defendant's mental capacity was reduced by mental illness, mental defect or intoxication,'" *People v. Berry*, 18 Cal.3d 509, 517, 134 Cal.Rptr. 415, 556 P.2d 777, 781 (1976) (in banc) (quoting *People v. Castillo*, 70 Cal.2d 264, 270, 74 Cal.Rptr. 385, 449 P.2d 449, 452 (1969); emphasis deleted), abrogated by Cal.Penal Code Ann. §§ 25(a), 28(a)–(b), 29 (West 1999 and Supp. 2006).

42. It is beyond question that Arizona may preclude such a defense, *see Fisher v. United States*, 328 U.S. 463, 466–476, 66 S.Ct. 1318, 90 L.Ed. 1382 (1946), and there is no doubt that the Arizona Legislature meant to do so, *see* Ariz.Rev.Stat. Ann. § 13-502(A) (West 2001) ("Mental disease or

2.

A State's insistence on preserving its chosen standard of legal insanity cannot be the sole reason for a rule like *Mott*, however, for it fails to answer an objection the dissent makes in this case. An insanity rule gives a defendant already found guilty the opportunity to excuse his conduct by showing he was insane when he acted, that is, that he did not have the mental capacity for conventional guilt and criminal responsibility. But, as the dissent argues, if the same evidence that affirmatively shows he was not guilty by reason of insanity (or "guilty except insane" under Arizona law also shows it was at least doubtful that he could form *mens rea*, then he should not be found guilty in the first place; it thus violates due process when the State impedes him from using mental-disease and capacity evidence directly to rebut the prosecution's evidence that he did form *mens rea*.

Are there, then, characteristics of mental-disease and capacity evidence giving rise to risks that may reasonably be hedged by channeling the consideration of such evidence to the insanity issue on which, in States like Arizona, a defendant has the burden of persuasion? We think there are: in the controversial character of some categories of mental disease, in the potential of mental-disease evidence to mislead, and in the danger of according greater certainty to capacity evidence than experts claim for it.

To begin with, the diagnosis may mask vigorous debate within the profession about the very contours of the mental disease itself.

Next, there is the potential of mental-disease evidence to mislead jurors (when they are the factfinders) through the power of this kind of evidence to suggest that a defendant suffering from a recognized mental disease lacks cognitive, moral, volitional, or other capacity, when that may not be a sound conclusion at all. Even when a category of mental disease is broadly accepted and the assignment of a defendant's behavior to that category is uncontroversial, the classification may suggest something very significant about a defendant's capacity, when in fact the classification tells us little or nothing about the ability of the defendant to form *mens rea* or to exercise the cognitive, moral, or volitional capacities that define legal sanity.

There are, finally, particular risks inherent in the opinions of the experts who supplement the mental-disease classifications with opinions on incapacity: on whether the mental disease rendered a particular defendant incapable of the cognition necessary for moral judgment or *mens rea* or otherwise incapable of understanding the wrongfulness of the conduct charged. Unlike observational evidence bearing on *mens rea*, capacity evidence consists of judgment, and judgment fraught

---

defect does not include disorders that result from acute voluntary intoxication or withdrawal from alcohol or drugs, character defects, psychosexual disorders or impulse control disorders. Conditions that do not constitute legal insanity include but are not limited to momentary, temporary conditions arising from the pressure of the circumstances, moral decadence, depravity or passion growing out of anger, jealousy, revenge, hatred or other motives in a person who does not suffer from a mental disease or defect or an abnormality that is manifested only by criminal conduct").

with multiple perils: a defendant's state of mind at the crucial moment can be elusive no matter how conscientious the enquiry, and the law's categories that set the terms of the capacity judgment are not the categories of psychology that govern the expert's professional thinking. Although such capacity judgments may be given in the utmost good faith, their potentially tenuous character is indicated by the candor of the defense expert in this very case. Contrary to the State's expert, he testified that Clark lacked the capacity to appreciate the circumstances realistically and to understand the wrongfulness of what he was doing, but he said that "no one knows exactly what was on [his] mind" at the time of the shooting. And even when an expert is confident that his understanding of the mind is reliable, judgment addressing the basic categories of capacity requires a leap from the concepts of psychology, which are devised for thinking about treatment, to the concepts of legal sanity, which are devised for thinking about criminal responsibility.

It bears repeating that not every State will find it worthwhile to make the judgment Arizona has made, and the choices the States do make about dealing with the risks posed by mental-disease and capacity evidence will reflect their varying assessments about the presumption of sanity as expressed in choices of insanity rules.[44] The point here simply is that Arizona has sensible reasons to assign the risks as it has done by channeling the evidence.[45]

F.

Arizona's rule serves to preserve the State's chosen standard for recognizing insanity as a defense and to avoid confusion and misunderstanding on the part of jurors.[46] For these reasons, there is no violation of due process and no cause to claim that channeling evidence on mental disease and capacity offends any "'principle of justice so rooted in the traditions and conscience of our people as to be ranked as fundamental,'"

---

44. A State in which the burden of persuasion as to a defendant's sanity lies with the prosecution might also be justified in restricting mental-disease and capacity evidence to insanity determinations owing to the potential of mental-disease evidence to mislead and the risk of misjudgment inherent in capacity evidence. We need not, in the context of this case, address that issue.

45. Arizona's rule is supported by a further practical reason, though not as weighty as those just considered. As mentioned before, if substantial mental-disease and capacity evidence is accepted as rebutting *mens rea* in a given case, the affirmative defense of insanity will probably not be reached or ruled upon; the defendant will simply be acquitted (or perhaps convicted of a lesser included offense). If an acquitted defendant suffers from a mental disease or defect that makes him dangerous, he will neither be confined nor treated psychiatrically unless a judge so orders after some independent commitment proceeding. But if a defendant succeeds in showing himself insane, Arizona law (and presumably that of every other State with an insanity rule) will require commitment and treatment as a consequence of that finding without more. It makes sense, then, to channel capacity evidence to the issue structured to deal with mental incapacity when such a claim is raised successfully. *See, e.g., Jones*, 463 U.S., at 368, 103 S.Ct. 3043 ("The purpose of commitment following an insanity acquittal . . . is to treat the individual's mental illness and protect him and society from his potential dangerousness").

46. The rule also deals in a practical way with those whose insanity has been shown to make them dangerous to others.

The judgment of the Court of Appeals of Arizona is, accordingly, affirmed.

It is so ordered.

Justice BREYER, concurring in part and dissenting in part.

As I understand the Court's opinion, it distinguishes among three categories of evidence related to insanity: (1) fact-related evidence as to the defendant's specific state of mind at the time of the crime, *e.g.*, evidence that shows he thought the policeman was not a human being; (2) expert opinion evidence that the defendant suffered from a mental disease that would have affected his capacity to form an intent to kill a policeman, *e.g.*, that he suffers from a disease of a kind where powerful voices command the sufferer to kill; and (3) expert opinion evidence that the defendant was legally insane, *e.g.*, evidence that he did not know right from wrong.

I agree with the Court's basic categorization. I also agree that the Constitution permits a State to provide for consideration of the second and third types of evidence solely in conjunction with the insanity defense. A State might reasonably fear that, without such a rule, the types of evidence as to intent would become confused in the jury's mind, indeed that in some cases the insanity question would displace the intent question as the parties litigate both simultaneously.

Nonetheless, I believe the distinction among these kinds of evidence will be unclear in some cases. And though I accept the majority's reading of the record, I remain concerned as to whether the lower courts, in setting forth and applying *State v. Mott*, focused with sufficient directness and precision upon the distinction.

Consequently, I would remand this case so that Arizona's courts can determine whether Arizona law, as set forth in *Mott* and other cases, is consistent with the distinction the Court draws and whether the trial court so applied Arizona law here. I would also reserve the question (as I believe the Court has done) as to the burden of persuasion in a case where the defendant produces sufficient evidence of the second kind as to raise a reasonable doubt that he suffered from a mental illness so severe as to prevent him from forming any relevant intent at all.

For this reason, I dissent only from Parts III-B and III-C of the Court's opinion and the ultimate disposition of this case, and I join the remainder.

Justice KENNEDY, with whom Justice STEVENS and Justice GINSBURG join, dissenting. In my submission the Court is incorrect in holding that Arizona may convict petitioner Eric Clark of first-degree murder for the intentional or knowing killing of a police officer when Clark was not permitted to introduce critical and reliable evidence showing he did not have that intent or knowledge. The Court is wrong, too, when it concludes the issue cannot be reached because of an error by Clark's counsel. Its reasons and conclusions lead me to file this respectful dissent.

Since I would reverse the judgment of the Arizona Court of Appeals on this ground, and the Arizona courts might well alter their interpretation of the State's criminal responsibility statute were my rationale to prevail, it is unnecessary for me to address the argument that Arizona's definition of insanity violates due process.

I.

Clark claims that the trial court erred in refusing to consider evidence of his chronic paranoid schizophrenia in deciding whether he possessed the knowledge or intent required for first-degree murder. Seizing upon a theory invented here by the Court itself, the Court narrows Clark's claim so he cannot raise the point everyone else thought was involved in the case. The Court says the only issue before us is whether there is a right to introduce mental-disease evidence or capacity evidence, not a right to introduce observation evidence. This restructured evidentiary universe, with no convincing authority to support it, is unworkable on its own terms. Even were that not so, however, the Court's tripartite structure is something not addressed by the state trial court, the state appellate court, counsel on either side in those proceedings, or the briefs the parties filed with us. The Court refuses to consider the key part of Clark's claim because his counsel did not predict the Court's own invention. It is unrealistic, and most unfair, to hold that Clark's counsel erred in failing to anticipate so novel an approach. If the Court is to insist on its approach, at a minimum the case should be remanded to determine whether Clark is bound by his counsel's purported waiver.

The Court's error, of course, has significance beyond this case. It adopts an evidentiary framework that, in my view, will be unworkable in many cases. The Court classifies Clark's behavior and expressed beliefs as observation evidence but insists that its description by experts must be mental-disease evidence or capacity evidence. These categories break down quickly when it is understood how the testimony would apply to the question of intent and knowledge at issue here. The most common type of schizophrenia, and the one Clark suffered from, is paranoid schizophrenia. The existence of this functional psychosis is beyond dispute, but that does not mean the lay witness understands it or that a disputed issue of fact concerning its effect in a particular instance is not something for the expert to address. Common symptoms of the condition are delusions accompanied by hallucinations, often of the auditory type, which can cause disturbances of perception. Clark's expert testified that people with schizophrenia often play radios loudly to drown out the voices in their heads. Clark's attorney argued to the trial court that this, rather than a desire to lure a policeman to the scene, explained Clark's behavior just before the killing. The observation that schizophrenics play radios loudly is a fact regarding behavior, but it is only a relevant fact if Clark has schizophrenia.

Even if this evidence were, to use the Court's term, mental-disease evidence, because it relies on an expert opinion, what would happen if the expert simply were to testify, without mentioning schizophrenia, that people with Clark's symptoms often play the radio loudly? This seems to be factual evidence, as the term is defined by the Court, yet it differs from mental-disease evidence only in forcing the witness to pretend that no one has yet come up with a way to classify the set of symptoms being described. More generally, the opinion that Clark had paranoid schizophrenia-an opinion shared by experts for both the prosecution and defense-bears on efforts to determine, as a factual matter, whether he knew he was killing a police officer. The psychiatrist's explanation of Clark's condition was essential to understanding how he processes sensory data and therefore to deciding what information was in his mind at the time of the shooting. Simply put, knowledge relies on cognition, and cognition can be affected by schizophrenia. See American Psychiatric Association, Diagnostic and Statistical Manual of Mental Disorders 299 (4th ed. text rev. 2000) ("The characteristic symptoms of Schizophrenia involve a range of cognitive and emotional dysfunctions that include perception"); *ibid.* (Symptoms include delusions, which are "erroneous beliefs that usually involve a misinterpretation of perceptions or experiences"). The mental-disease evidence at trial was also intertwined with the observation evidence because it lent needed credibility. Clark's parents and friends testified Clark thought the people in his town were aliens trying to kill him. These claims might not be believable without a psychiatrist confirming the story based on his experience with people who have exhibited similar behaviors. It makes little sense to divorce the observation evidence from the explanation that makes it comprehensible.

Assuming the Court's tripartite structure were feasible, the Court is incorrect when it narrows Clark's claim to exclude any concern about observation evidence. In deciding Clark's counsel failed to raise this issue, the Court relies on a series of perceived ambiguities regarding how the claim fits within the Court's own categories. The Court cites no precedent for construing these ambiguities against the claimant and no prudential reason for ignoring the breadth of Clark's claim. It is particularly surprising that the Court does so to the detriment of a criminal defendant asserting the fundamental challenge that the trier of fact refused to consider critical evidence showing he is innocent of the crime charged.

The alleged ambiguities are, in any event, illusory. The evidence at trial addressed more than the question of general incapacity or opinions regarding mental illness; it went further, as it included so-called observation evidence relevant to Clark's mental state at the moment he shot the officer. There was testimony, for example, that Clark thought the people in his town, particularly government officials, were not human beings but aliens who were trying to kill him. The Court recognizes the existence of this essential observation evidence.

The Court holds, nonetheless, that "we cannot be sure" whether the trial court failed to consider this evidence. It is true the trial court ruling was not perfectly clear. Its language does strongly suggest, though, that it did not consider any of this testimony in deciding whether Clark had the knowledge or intent required for first-degree murder. After recognizing that "much of the evidence that [the defense is] going to be submitting, in fact all of it, as far as I know . . . that has to do with the insanity could also arguably be made . . . as to form and intent and his capacity for the intent," the court concluded "we will be focusing, as far as I'm concerned, strictly on the insanity defense." In announcing its verdict, the trial court did not mention any of the mental-illness evidence, observation or otherwise, in deciding Clark's guilt. The most reasonable assumption, then, would seem to be that the trial court did not consider it, and the Court does not hold otherwise.

Clark's objection to this refusal by the trier of fact to consider the evidence as it bore on his key defense was made at all stages of the proceeding. In his post-trial motion to vacate the judgment, Clark argued that "prohibiting consideration of *any* evidence reflecting upon a mentally ill criminal defendant's ability to form the necessary *mens rea* violates due process." He also noted that the trial judge had erred in refusing to consider non-expert testimony-presumably what the Court would call observation evidence-on Clark's mental illness. ("The trial court therefore violated [Clark's] right to present a defense because [the] court refused to consider *any evidence*, including the multiple testimonials of *lay* witnesses . . . in deciding whether he could form the requisite *mens rea*"). The appeals court decided the issue on the merits, holding that the trial court was correct not to consider the evidence of mental illness in determining whether Clark had the *mens rea* for first-degree murder. It offered no distinction at all between observation or mental-disease evidence.

Notwithstanding the appeals court's decision, the Court states that the issue was not clearly presented to the state courts. According to the Court, Clark only raised an objection based on *State v. Mott*, and *Mott's* holding was limited to the exclusion of mental-disease and capacity evidence. The Court is incorrect, and on both counts.

First, Clark's claim goes well beyond an objection to *Mott*. In fact, he specifically attempted to distinguish *Mott* by noting that the trial court in this case refused to consider all evidence of mental illness. The Court notices these arguments but criticizes Clark's counsel for not being specific about the observation evidence he wanted the trial court to consider. There was no reason, though, for Clark's counsel to believe additional specificity was required, since there was no evident distinction in Arizona law between observation evidence and mental-disease testimony.

Second, *Mott's* holding was not restricted to mental-disease evidence. The Arizona Supreme Court did not refer to any distinction between observation and mental-disease evidence, or lay and expert testimony. Its holding was stated in broad terms: "Arizona does not allow evidence of a defendant's mental disorder short of insanity either as an affirmative defense or to negate the *mens rea* element of a crime." ("The legislature's decision . . . evidences its rejection of the use of psychological testimony to challenge the *mens rea* element of a crime"). The Court attempts to divine a fact/opinion distinction in *Mott* based on *Mott's* distinguishing a case, *State v. Christensen*, 129 Ariz. 32, 628 P.2d 580 (1981), where evidence about behavioral tendencies was deemed admissible. *Christensen*, though, also addressed an expert opinion; the difference was that the evidence there concerned a "character trait of acting reflexively in response to stress," not a mental illness. Since the Court recognizes the Arizona Court of Appeals relied on *Mott*, the expansive rule of exclusion in *Mott*-without any suggestion of a limitation depending on the kind of evidence-should suffice for us to reach the so-called observation-evidence issue. Even if, as the Court contends, *Mott* is limited to expert testimony, the Court's categories still do not properly interpret *Mott*, because the Court's own definition of observation evidence includes some expert testimony.

The razor-thin distinction the Court draws between evidence being used to show incapacity and evidence being used to show lack of *mens rea* directly does not identify two different claims. Clark's single claim, however characterized, involves the use of the same mental-illness evidence to decide whether he had the requisite knowledge or intent.

Before this Court Clark framed the issue in broad terms that encompass the question whether the evidence of his mental illness should have been considered to show he did not at the time of the offense have the knowledge or intent to shoot a police officer. See Brief for Petitioner i ("Questions Presented for Review: (1) Whether Arizona's blanket exclusion of evidence and refusal to consider mental disease or defect to rebut the state's evidence on the element of *mens rea* violated Petitioner's right to due process under the United States Constitution, Fourteenth Amendment?").

Clark seeks resolution of issues that can be complex and somewhat overlapping. In the end, however, we must decide whether he had the right to introduce evidence showing he lacked the intent or knowledge the statute itself sets forth in describing a basic element of the crime. Clark has preserved this issue at all stages, including in this Court.

II.

Clark was charged with first-degree murder for the shooting of Officer Jeffrey Moritz. "A person commits first-degree murder if," as relevant here, "[i]ntending or knowing that the person's conduct will cause death to a law enforcement officer, the person causes the death of a law enforcement officer who is in the line of duty." Clark challenges the trial court's refusal to consider any evidence of mental illness, from lay or expert testimony, in determining whether he acted with the knowledge or intent element of the crime.

States have substantial latitude under the Constitution to define rules for the exclusion of evidence and to apply those rules to criminal defendants. *See United States v. Scheffer*, 523 U.S. 303, 308, (1998). This authority, however, has constitutional limits. "Whether rooted directly in the Due Process Clause of the Fourteenth Amendment or in the Compulsory Process or Confrontation Clauses of the Sixth Amendment, the Constitution guarantees criminal defendants "a meaningful opportunity to present a complete defense."

The central theory of Clark's defense was that his schizophrenia made him delusional. He lived in a universe where the delusions were so dominant, the theory was, that he had no intent to shoot a police officer or knowledge he was doing so. It is one thing to say he acted with intent or knowledge to pull the trigger. It is quite another to say he pulled the trigger to kill someone he knew to be a human being and a police officer. If the trier of fact were to find Clark's evidence sufficient to discount the case made by the State, which has the burden to prove knowledge or intent as an element of the offense, Clark would not be guilty of first-degree murder under Arizona law.

The Court attempts to diminish Clark's interest by treating mental-illness evidence as concerning only "judgment," rather than fact. This view appears to derive from the Court's characterization of Clark's claim as raising only general incapacity. This is wrong for the reasons already discussed. It fails to recognize, moreover, the meaning of the offense element in question here. The *mens rea* element of intent or knowledge may, at some level, comprise certain moral choices, but it rests in the first instance on a factual determination. That is the fact Clark sought to put in issue. Either Clark knew he was killing a police officer or he did not.

The issue is not, as the Court insists, whether Clark's mental illness acts as an "excuse from customary criminal responsibility," but whether his mental illness, as a factual matter, made him unaware that he was shooting a police officer. If it did, Clark needs no excuse, as then he did not commit the crime as Arizona defines it. For the elements of first-degree murder, where the question is knowledge of particular facts-that one is killing a police officer-the determination depends not on moral responsibility but on empirical fact. Clark's evidence of mental illness had a direct and substantial bearing upon what he knew, or thought he knew, to be the facts when he pulled the trigger; this lay at the heart of the matter.

The trial court's exclusion was all the more severe because it barred from consideration on the issue of *mens rea* all this evidence, from any source, thus preventing Clark from showing he did not commit the crime as defined by Arizona law.

Arizona's rule is problematic because it excludes evidence no matter how credible and material it may be in disproving an element of the offense.

This is not to suggest all general rules on the exclusion of certain types of evidence are invalid. If the rule does not substantially burden the defense, then it is likely permissible. *See Scheffer*, (upholding exclusion of polygraph evidence in part because this rule "does not implicate any significant interest of the accused"); (KENNEDY, J., concurring in part and concurring in judgment) ("[S]ome later case might present a more compelling case for introduction of the testimony than this one does"). Where, however, the burden is substantial, the State must present a valid reason for its *per se* evidentiary rule.

In the instant case Arizona's proposed reasons are insufficient to support its categorical exclusion. While the State contends that testimony regarding mental illness may be too incredible or speculative for the jury to consider, this does not explain why the exclusion applies in all cases to all evidence of mental illness. "A State's legitimate interest in barring unreliable evidence does not extend to *per se* exclusions that may be reliable in an individual case." *Rock v. Arkansas*, 483 U.S., at 61. States have certain discretion to bar unreliable or speculative testimony and to adopt rules to ensure the reliability of expert testimony. Arizona has done so, and there is no reason to believe its rules are insufficient to avoid speculative evidence of mental illness. This is particularly true because Arizona applies its usual case-by-case approach to permit admission of evidence of mental illness for a variety of other purposes. *See, e.g., State v. Lindsey*, 149 Ariz. 472, 474–475, 720 P.2d 73,

74–75 (1986) (en banc) (psychological characteristics of molestation victims); *State v. Hamilton*, 177 Ariz. 403, 408–410, 868 P.2d 986, 991–993 (App. 1993) (psychological evidence of child abuse accommodation syndrome); *Horan v. Indus. Comm'n*, 167 Ariz. 322, 325–326, 806 P.2d 911, 914–915 (App. 1991) (psychiatric testimony regarding neurological deficits).

The risk of jury-confusion also fails to justify the rule. The State defends its rule as a means to avoid the complexities of determining how and to what degree a mental illness affects a person's mental state. The difficulty of resolving a factual issue, though, does not present a sufficient reason to take evidence away from the jury even when it is crucial for the defense. "We have always trusted juries to sort through complex facts in various areas of law." Even were the risk of jury confusion real enough to justify excluding evidence in most cases, this would provide little basis for prohibiting all evidence of mental illness without any inquiry into its likely effect on the jury or its role in deciding the linchpin issue of knowledge and intent. Indeed, Arizona has a rule in place to serve this very purpose.

Even assuming the reliability and jury confusion justifications were persuasive in some cases, they would not suffice here. It does not overcome the constitutional objection to say that an evidentiary rule that is reasonable on its face can be applied as well to bar significant defense evidence without any rational basis for doing so.

The Court undertakes little analysis of the interests particular to this case. By proceeding in this way it devalues Clark's constitutional rights. The reliability rationale has minimal applicability here. The Court is correct that many mental diseases are difficult to define and the subject of great debate. Schizophrenia, however, is a well-documented mental illness, and no one seriously disputes either its definition or its most prominent clinical manifestations. The State's own expert conceded that Clark had paranoid schizophrenia and was actively psychotic at the time of the killing. The jury-confusion rationale, if it is at all applicable here, is the result of the Court's own insistence on conflating the insanity defense and the question of intent. Considered on its own terms, the issue of intent and knowledge is a straightforward factual question. A trier of fact is quite capable of weighing defense testimony and then determining whether the accused did or did not intend to kill or knowingly kill a human being who was a police officer. True, the issue can be difficult to decide in particular instances, but no more so than many matters juries must confront.

The Court says mental-illness evidence "can easily mislead," and may "tel[l] us little or nothing about the ability of the defendant to form *mens rea*." These generalities do not, however, show how relevant or misleading the evidence in this case would be. As explained above, the evidence of Clark's mental illness bears directly on *mens rea*, for it suggests Clark may not have known he was killing a human being. It is striking that while the Court discusses at length the likelihood of misjudgment from placing too much emphasis on evidence of mental illness, it ignores the risk of misjudging an innocent man guilty from refusing to consider this highly relevant evidence at all. Clark's expert, it is true, said no one could know exactly what was on Clark's mind at the time of the shooting. The expert testified extensively, however, about the effect of Clark's delusions on his perceptions of the world around him, and about whether Clark's behavior around the time of the shooting was consistent with delusional thinking. This testimony was relevant to determining whether Clark knew he was killing a human being. It also bolstered the testimony of lay witnesses, none of which was deemed unreliable or misleading by the state courts.

For the same reasons, the Court errs in seeking support from the American Psychiatric Association's statement that a psychiatrist may be justifiably reluctant to reach legal conclusions regarding the defendant's mental state. In this very case, the American Psychiatric Association made clear that psychiatric evidence plays a crucial role regardless of whether the psychiatrist testifies on the ultimate issue: "Expert evidence of mental disorders, presented by qualified professionals and subject to adversarial testing, is both relevant to the mental-state issues raised by *mens rea* requirements and reliable. . . . Such evidence could not be condemned wholesale without unsettling the legal system's central reliance on such evidence." Brief for American Psychiatric Association et al. as *Amici Curiae* 15.

Contrary to the Court's suggestion, the fact that the state and defense experts drew different conclusions about the effect of Clark's mental illness on his mental state only made Clark's evidence contested; it did not make the evidence irrelevant or misleading. The trial court was capable of evaluating the competing conclusions, as factfinders do in countless cases where there is a dispute among witnesses. In fact, the potential to mislead will be far greater under the Court's new evidentiary system, where jurors will receive observation evidence without the necessary explanation from experts.

The fact that mental-illness evidence may be considered in deciding criminal responsibility does not compensate for its exclusion from consideration on the *mens rea* elements of the crime. The evidence addresses different issues in the two instances. Criminal responsibility involves an inquiry into whether the defendant knew right from wrong, not whether he had the *mens rea* elements of the offense. While there may be overlap between the two issues, "the existence or nonexistence of legal insanity bears no necessary relationship to the existence or nonexistence of the required mental elements of the crime."

Even if the analyses were equivalent, there is a different burden of proof for insanity than there is for *mens rea*. Arizona requires the defendant to prove his insanity by clear and convincing evidence. The prosecution, however, must prove all elements of the offense beyond a reasonable doubt. The shift in the burden on the criminal responsibility issue, while permissible under our precedent, *see Leland v. Oregon*, 343 U.S. 790 (1952), cannot be applied to the question of intent or knowledge without relieving the State of its responsibility to establish this element of the offense. While evidentiary rules do not generally shift the burden impermissibly, where there is a right to have evidence considered on an element of the offense, the right is not respected by allowing the evidence to come in only on an issue for which the defendant bears the burden of proof. By viewing the Arizona rule as creating merely a "presumption of sanity (or capacity or responsibility)," rather than a presumption that the *mens rea* elements were not affected by mental illness, the Court fails to appreciate the implications for *Winship*.

The State attempts to sidestep the evidentiary issue entirely by claiming that its mental-illness exclusion simply alters one element of the crime. The evidentiary rule at issue here, however, cannot be considered a valid redefinition of the offense. Under the State's logic, a person would be guilty of first-degree murder if he knowingly or intentionally killed a police officer or committed the killing under circumstances that would show knowledge or intent but for the defendant's mental illness. To begin with, Arizona law does not say this. And if it did, it would be impermissible. States have substantial discretion in defining criminal offenses. In some instances they may provide that the accused has the burden of persuasion with respect to affirmative defenses. "But there are obviously constitutional limits beyond which the States may not go in this regard." If it were otherwise, States could label all evidentiary exclusions as redefinitions and so evade constitutional requirements. There is no rational basis, furthermore, for criminally punishing a person who commits a killing without knowledge or intent only if that person has a mental illness. *Cf. Robinson v. California*, 370 U.S. 660 (1962). The State attempts to bring the instant case within the ambit of *Montana v. Egelhoff*, 518 U.S. 37 (1996); but in *Egelhoff* the excluded evidence concerned voluntary intoxication, for which a person can be held responsible. Viewed either as an evidentiary rule or a redefinition of the offense, it was upheld because it "comports with and implements society's moral perception that one who has voluntarily impaired his own faculties should be responsible for the consequences." An involuntary mental illness does not implicate this justification.

Future dangerousness is not, as the Court appears to conclude, a rational basis for convicting mentally ill individuals of crimes they did not commit. Civil commitment proceedings can ensure that individuals who present a danger to themselves or others receive proper treatment without unfairly treating them as criminals. The State presents no evidence to the contrary, and the Court ought not to imply otherwise.

While Arizona's rule is not unique, either historically or in contemporary practice, this fact does not dispose of Clark's constitutional argument. While 13 States still impose significant restrictions on the use of mental-illness evidence to negate *mens rea*, a substantial majority of the States currently allow it. The fact that a reasonable number of States restrict this evidence weighs into the analysis, but applying the rule as a *per se* bar, as Arizona does, is so plainly unreasonable that it cannot be sustained.

Putting aside the lack of any legitimate state interest for application of the rule in this case, its irrationality is apparent when considering the evidence that is allowed. Arizona permits the defendant to introduce, for example, evidence of "behavioral tendencies" to show he did not have the required mental state. *See Mott, Christensen*. While defining mental illness is a difficult matter, the State seems to exclude the evidence one would think most reliable by allowing unexplained and uncategorized tendencies to be introduced while excluding relatively well-understood psychiatric testimony regarding well-documented mental illnesses. It is unclear, moreover, what would have happened in this case had the defendant wanted to testify that he thought Officer Moritz was an alien. If disallowed, it would be tantamount to barring Clark from testifying on his behalf to explain his own actions. If allowed, then Arizona's rule would simply prohibit the corroboration necessary to make sense of Clark's explanation. In sum, the rule forces the jury to decide guilt in a fictional world with undefined and unexplained behaviors but without mental illness. This rule has no rational justification and imposes a significant burden upon a straightforward defense: He did not commit the crime with which he was charged.

These are the reasons for my respectful dissent.

Questions and Notes

1. Why do you suppose Clark waived his right to a jury trial? In retrospect, do you think it was a good move on his part?

2. Why was Clark's motion for a directed verdict denied?

3. If the trial court actually heard all of the evidence, should it matter whether it was in regard to the insanity issue, or the *mens rea* issue? Why? Why not?

4. How, if at all, is the Arizona law of insanity stricter than M'Naghten? Do you think it matters? Explain.

5. Should a State be free to abolish the defense of insanity entirely? Should it matter whether it also abolishes evidence of mental illness in regard to *mens rea*? Explain. As this book was going to press, the United States Supreme Court decided *Kahler v. Kansas*, 140 S.Ct. 1021 (Decided March 23, 2020), which upheld a Kansas statute that limited the use of insanity to negating *mens rea*, a position advocated by your author. See Loewy, *Two Faces of Insanity*, 42 Texas Tech L. Rev. 513 (2009).

6. What is Clark's due process argument?

7. Do the majority and dissent differ on the factual question of how much evidence the defendant was allowed to introduce? On the legal question of how much evidence the law must permit him to introduce? Or both? Explain.

8. Where does Justice Breyer come out on these questions?

9. Is the majority being overtechnical in the evidence it is willing to allow?

10. Do you think that, under the majority rule, it is possible to convict somebody of intentionally killing a human being who did not intend to kill a human being? If so, is this (should this be) tolerable?

11. Is Clark's case any different from somebody who thinks he's shooting at dummies for target practice, but is actually shooting a human being?

Problem

Charged with burglary, William Wetmore argued that psychiatric reports showed that, as a result of mental illness, he lacked the specific intent required for conviction of that crime. The trial court reasoned that because the reports described defendant's insanity as well as his diminished capacity, such description of defendant's condition in those reports should not be admitted to prove lack of specific intent. The court found defendant guilty of second degree burglary; subsequently, relying on the psychiatric reports, it found him insane.

The only evidence submitted to the trial court in this case was the testimony of Joseph Cacciatore, the victim of the burglary, at the preliminary hearing, and three psychiatric reports. Cacciatore testified that he left his apartment on March 7, 1975.

When he returned three days later, he discovered defendant in his apartment. Defendant was wearing Cacciatore's clothes and cooking his food. The lock on the front door had been broken; the apartment lay in shambles. Cacciatore called the police, who arrested defendant for burglary. Later Cacciatore discovered that a ring, a watch, a credit card, and items of clothing were missing.[1]

The psychiatric reports submitted to the court explain defendant's long history of psychotic illness, including at least 10 occasions of hospital confinement for treatment. According to the reports, defendant, shortly after his last release from Brentwood Veterans' Hospital, found himself with no place to go. He began to believe that he "owned" property, and was "directed" to Cacciatore's apartment. When he found the door unlocked, he was sure he owned the apartment. He entered, rearranged the apartment, destroyed some advertising he thought was inappropriate, and put on Cacciatore's clothes. When the police arrived, defendant was shocked and embarrassed, and only then understood that he did not own the apartment.

1. How would (should) Wetmore's case be decided?

2. How would it be decided if the court followed the Arizona rule? For one court's solution, see *People v. Wetmore*, 583 P.2d 1308 (Cal. 1978).

We conclude this chapter with *Ford v. Wainwright*, a case dealing with constitutional limitations on the state's power to execute an insane person.

Ford v. Wainwright
477 U.S. 399 (1986)

Justice MARSHALL delivered the opinion of the Court:

---

1. At the preliminary hearing defendant appeared wearing one of Cacciatore's shirts. The magistrate directed the sheriff to provide defendant with a county shirt and admitted Cacciatore's shirt into evidence as an exhibit.

For centuries no jurisdiction has countenanced the execution of the insane, yet this Court has never decided whether the Constitution forbids the practice. Today we keep faith with our common-law heritage in holding that it does.

Alvin Bernard Ford was convicted of murder in 1974 and sentenced to death. There is no suggestion that he was incompetent at the time of his offense, at trial, or at sentencing.

In early 1982, however, Ford began to manifest gradual changes in behavior. They began as an occasional peculiar idea or confused perception, but became more serious over time. After reading in the newspaper that the Ku Klux Klan had held a rally in nearby Jacksonville, Florida, Ford developed an obsession focused upon the Klan. His letters to various people reveal endless brooding about his "Klan work," and an increasingly pervasive delusion that he had become the target of a complex conspiracy, involving the Klan and assorted others, designed to force him to commit suicide. He believed that the prison guards, part of the conspiracy, had been killing people and putting the bodies in the concrete enclosures used for beds. Later, he began to believe that his women relatives were being tortured and sexually abused somewhere in the prison. This notion developed into a delusion that the people who were tormenting him at the prison had taken members of Ford's family hostage. The hostage delusion took firm hold and expanded, until Ford was reporting that 135 of his friends and family were being held hostage in the prison, and that only he could help them. By "day 287" of the "hostage crisis," the list of hostages had expanded to include "senators, Senator Kennedy, and many other leaders." In a letter to the Attorney General of Florida, written in 1983, Ford appeared to assume authority for ending the "crisis," claiming to have fired a number of prison officials. He began to refer to himself as "Pope John Paul, III," and reported having appointed nine new justices to the Florida Supreme Court.

Counsel for Ford asked a psychiatrist who had examined Ford earlier, Dr. Jamal Amin, to continue seeing him and to recommend appropriate treatment. On the basis of roughly 14 months of evaluation, taped conversations between Ford and his attorneys, letters written by Ford, interviews with Ford's acquaintances, and various medical records, Dr. Amin concluded in 1983 that Ford suffered from "a severe, uncontrollable, mental disease which closely resembles 'Paranoid Schizophrenia With Suicide Potential'"—a "major mental disorder . . . severe enough to substantially affect Mr. Ford's present ability to assist in the defense of his life."

Ford subsequently refused to see Dr. Amin again, believing him to have joined the conspiracy against him, and Ford's counsel sought assistance from Dr. Harold Kaufman, who interviewed Ford in November 1983. Ford told Dr. Kaufman that "I know there is some sort of death penalty, but I'm free to go whenever I want because it would be illegal and the executioner would be executed." When asked if he would be executed, Ford replied, "I can't be executed because of the landmark case. I won. *Ford v. State* will prevent executions all over." These statements appeared amidst long streams of seemingly unrelated thoughts in rapid succession. Dr. Kaufman concluded that Ford had no understanding of why he was being executed, made no connection between the homicide of which he had been convicted and the death penalty, and indeed sincerely believed that he would not be executed because he owned the prisons and could control the Governor through mind waves. Dr. Kaufman found that there was "no reasonable possibility that Mr. Ford was dissembling, malingering or otherwise putting on a performance. . . ." The following month, in an interview with his attorneys, Ford regressed further into nearly complete incomprehensibility, speaking only in a code characterized by intermittent use of the word "one," making statements such as "Hands one, face one. Mafia one. God one, father one, Pope one. Pope one. Leader one." Counsel for Ford invoked the procedures of Florida law governing the determination of competency of a condemned inmate, Fla. Stat. §922.07 (1985). Following the procedures set forth in the statute, the Governor of Florida appointed a panel of three psychiatrists to evaluate whether, under §922.07(2), Ford had "the mental capacity to understand the nature of the death penalty and the reasons why it was imposed upon him." At a single meeting, the three psychiatrists together interviewed Ford for approximately 30 minutes. Each doctor then filed a separate two- or three-page report with the Governor, to whom the statute delegates the final decision. One doctor concluded that Ford suffered from "psychosis with paranoia" but had "enough cognitive functioning to understand the nature and the effects of the death penalty, and why it is to be imposed on him." Another found that, although Ford was "psychotic," he did "know fully what can happen to him." The third concluded that Ford had a "severe adaptational disorder," but did "comprehend his total situation including being sentenced to death, and all of the implications of that penalty." He believed that Ford's disorder, "although severe, seem[ed] contrived and recently learned." Thus, the interview produced three different diagnoses, but accord on the question of sanity as defined by state law.

The Governor's decision was announced on April 30, 1984, when, without explanation or statement, he signed a death warrant for Ford's execution. Ford's attorneys unsuccessfully sought a hearing in state court to determine anew Ford's competency to suffer execution.

We begin, then, with the common law. The bar against executing a prisoner who has lost his sanity bears impressive historical credentials; the practice consistently has been branded "savage and inhuman." Blackstone explained:

> "[I]diots and lunatics are not chargeable for their own acts, if committed when under these incapacities: no, not even for treason itself. Also, if a man in his sound memory commits a capital offence, and before arraignment for it, he becomes mad, he ought not to be arraigned for it: because he is not able to plead to it with that advice and caution that he ought. And if, after he has pleaded, the prisoner becomes mad, he shall not be tried: for how can he make his defence? If, after he be tried and found guilty, he loses his senses before judgment, judgment shall not be pronounced; and if, after judgment, he becomes of nonsane memory, execution shall be stayed: for

peradventure, says the humanity of the English law, had the prisoner been of sound memory, he might have alleged something in stay of judgment or execution."

Sir Edward Coke had earlier expressed the same view of the common law of England:

"[B]y intendment of Law the execution of the offender is for example, . . . but so it is not when a mad man is executed, but should be a miserable spectacle, both against Law, and of extream inhumanity and cruelty, and can be no example to others."

As is often true of common-law principles, *see* O. HOLMES, THE COMMON LAW 5 (1881), the reasons for the rule are less sure and less uniform than the rule itself. One explanation is that the execution of an insane person simply offends humanity; another, that it provides no example to others and thus contributes nothing to whatever deterrence value is intended to be served by capital punishment. Other commentators postulate religious underpinnings: that it is uncharitable to dispatch an offender "into another world, when he is not of a capacity to fit himself for it." It is also said that execution serves no purpose in these cases because madness is its own punishment: *furiosus solo furore punitur.* More recent commentators opine that the community's quest for "retribution"—the need to offset a criminal act by a punishment of equivalent "moral quality"—is not served by execution of an insane person, which has a "lesser value" than that of the crime for which he is to be punished. Hazard & Louisdell, *Death, the State, and the Insane: Stay of Execution,* 9 UCLA L. REV. 381, 387 (1962). Unanimity of rationale, therefore, we do not find. "But whatever the reason of the law is, it is plain the law is so." We know of virtually no authority condoning the execution of the insane at English common law.

This ancestral legacy has not outlived its time. Today, no State in the Union permits the execution of the insane. It is clear that the ancient and humane limitation upon the State's ability to execute its sentences has as firm a hold upon the jurisprudence of today as it had centuries ago in England. The various reasons put forth in support of the common-law restriction have no less logical, moral, and practical force than they did when first voiced. For today, no less than before, we may seriously question the retributive value of executing a person who has no comprehension of why he has been singled out and stripped of his fundamental right to life. Similarly, the natural abhorrence civilized societies feel at killing one who has no capacity to come to grips with his own conscience or deity is still vivid today. And the intuition that such an execution simply offends humanity is evidently shared across this Nation. Faced with such widespread evidence of a restriction upon sovereign power, this Court is compelled to conclude that the Eighth Amendment prohibits a State from carrying out a sentence of death upon a prisoner who is insane. Whether its aim be to protect the condemned from fear and pain without comfort of understanding, or to protect the dignity of society itself from the barbarity of exacting mindless vengeance, the restriction finds enforcement in the Eighth Amendment.

Justice Rehnquist, with whom The Chief Justice joins, dissenting.

The Court today holds that the Eighth Amendment prohibits a State from carrying out a lawfully imposed sentence of death upon a person who is currently insane. This holding is based almost entirely on two unremarkable observations. First, the Court states that it "know[s] of virtually no authority condoning the execution of the insane at English common law." Second, it notes that "Today, no State in the Union permits the execution of the insane." *Ibid.* Armed with these facts, and shielded by the claim that it is simply "keep[ing] faith with our common-law heritage," the Court proceeds to cast aside settled precedent and to significantly alter both the common-law and current practice of not executing the insane. It manages this feat by carefully ignoring the fact that the Florida scheme it finds unconstitutional, in which the Governor is assigned the ultimate responsibility of deciding whether a condemned prisoner is currently insane, is fully consistent with the "common law heritage" and current practice on which the Court purports to rely.

The Court places great weight on the "impressive historical credentials" of the common-law bar against executing a prisoner who has lost his sanity. What it fails to mention, however, is the equally important and unchallenged fact that at common law it was the executive who passed upon the sanity of the condemned. So, when the Court today creates a constitutional right to a determination of sanity outside of the executive branch, it does so not in keeping with but at the expense of "our common-law heritage."

Since no State sanctions execution of the insane, the real battle being fought in this case is over what procedures must accompany the inquiry into sanity. The Court reaches the result it does by examining the common law, creating a constitutional right that no State seeks to violate, and then concluding that the common-law procedures are inadequate to protect the newly created but common-law based right. I find it unnecessary to "constitutionalize" the already uniform view that the insane should not be executed, and inappropriate to "selectively incorporate" the common-law practice. I therefore dissent.

Questions and Notes

1. Which, if any, of the rationales for not executing an insane person seem most persuasive?

2. Neither Justice Marshall nor Justice Rehnquist question the propriety or fairness of a rule that allows one who has gone insane pending execution to avoid being executed? Do you agree? If Axel and Basil jointly murder Charles, are jointly tried, convicted, and sentenced to death, is it fair that Axel be executed because he has

remained sane, but Basil be spared because he has gone insane between the time of the sentencing and the time of the scheduled execution?

3. In the Question 2 hypothetical, would it be ethical for a psychiatrist to try to restore Basil's sanity so (or at least knowing) that he will then be executed?

The United States Supreme court has recently reaffirmed and arguably expanded Ford. See *Panetti v. Quarterman*, 551 U.S. 930 (2007).

Problem

Assume that you have just been elected to your state's legislature. The insanity rule currently in effect in your jurisdiction provides: "A person is entitled to be acquitted on the grounds of insanity if at the time of the crime, the person, because of a mental disease or defect, lacked the capacity to appreciate the moral wrongness of his act." There are four bills currently pending in your legislature on this subject:

1. The defense of insanity is abolished. All evidence of insanity shall be irrelevant and inadmissible in any criminal case.

2. The defense of insanity is abolished. Evidence of insanity shall be relevant to the extent that it negates *mens rea* for the offense charged.

3. A person is entitled to be acquitted on the grounds of insanity if at the time of the crime, the person, because of a mental disease or defect, lacked the capacity to understand that his conduct was against the law.

4. A person is entitled to be acquitted on the grounds of insanity if at the time of the crime, the person, because of a mental disease or defect, lacked substantial capacity to appreciate the criminality of his conduct or to conform his conduct to the criminal law.

Which, if any, of these bills should you support? Why?

Chapter 15

Capital Punishment

For most of our constitutional history, capital punishment was not thought to create any special problems. This philosophy was abruptly halted when, in *Furman v. Georgia*, 408 U.S. 238 (1972), five Justices voted to hold capital punishment, as it was then administered, unconstitutional. Only two of the Justices, Brennan and Marshall, thought that the capital punishment was per se a violation of the Eighth Amendment's ban on cruel and unusual punishment. The remaining three members of the majority (Douglas, Stewart, and White) saw the problem in terms of arbitrariness. In their view, the unbridled discretion accorded juries to impose capital punishment or life imprisonment was intolerably arbitrary, and hence unconstitutional.

Following *Furman*, the states that sought to retain capital punishment adopted one of two tacks. One was to adopt the MPC approach of listing a series of aggravating and mitigating circumstances and permitting capital punishment only when the aggravating circumstances outweighed the mitigating ones and warranted the imposition of capital punishment. In *Gregg v. Georgia*, 428 U.S. 153 (1976), the Supreme Court upheld that scheme with only Justices Brennan and Marshall dissenting.

The alternative approach was to render capital punishment mandatory in certain types of cases (e.g., all first degree murders). The states that opted for this approach contended that the element of arbitrariness that invalidated the *Furman* procedures was absent in a mandatory capital punishment scheme. However, in *Woodson v. North Carolina*, 428 U.S. 280 (1976), a companion case to *Gregg*, the Court held that the mandatory nature of the death penalty precluded consideration of individual mitigation and consequently was too harsh to meet evolving standards of decency.

The upshot of *Furman, Gregg*, and *Woodson* is that states are free to retain capital punishment, but only if specified aggravating factors are present, a defendant is permitted to present unlimited evidence of mitigating circumstances, and juries are not permitted to act arbitrarily. The remainder of this section focuses on the difficulties inherent in these standards. We will conclude with the legislative question of whether capital punishment is worth the candle.

In conjunction with *Godfrey*, consider what was lacking in the state's case.

Godfrey v. Georgia

446 U.S. 420 (1980)

Mr. Justice STEWART announced the judgment of the Court and delivered an opinion, in which Mr. Justice BLACKMUN, Mr. Justice POWELL, and Mr. Justice STEVENS joined.

Under Georgia law, a person convicted of murder may be sentenced to death if it is found beyond a reasonable doubt that the offense "was outrageously or wantonly vile, horrible or inhuman in that it involved torture, depravity of mind, or an aggravated battery to the victim." Ga. Code § 27-2534.1(b)(7) (1978).

On a day in early September in 1977, the petitioner and his wife of 28 years had a heated argument in their home. During the course of this altercation, the petitioner, who had consumed several cans of beer, threatened his wife with a knife and damaged some of her clothing. At this point, the petitioner's wife declared that she was going to leave him and departed to stay with relatives. That afternoon she went to a Justice of the Peace and secured a warrant charging the petitioner with aggravated assault. A few days later, while still living away from home, she filed suit for divorce. Summons was served on the petitioner, and a court hearing was set on a date some two weeks later. Before the date of the hearing, the petitioner on several occasions asked his wife to return to their home. Each time his efforts were rebuffed. At some point during this period, his wife moved in with her mother. The petitioner believed that his mother-in-law was actively instigating his wife's determination not to consider a possible reconciliation.

In the early evening of September 20, according to the petitioner, his wife telephoned him at home. Once again, they argued. She asserted that reconciliation was impossible and allegedly demanded all the proceeds from the planned sale of their house. The conversation was terminated after she said that she would call back later. This she did in an hour or so. The ensuing conversation was, according to the petitioner's account, even more heated than the first. His wife reiterated her stand that reconciliation was out of the question, said that she still wanted all proceeds from the sale of their house, and mentioned that her mother was supporting her position. Stating that she saw no further use in talking or arguing, she hung up.

At this juncture, the petitioner got out his shotgun and walked with it down the hill from his home to the trailer where his mother-in-law lived. Peering through a window, he observed his wife, his mother-in-law, and his 11-year-old daughter playing a card game. He pointed the shotgun at his wife through the window and pulled the trigger. The charge from the gun struck his wife in the forehead and killed her instantly. He proceeded into the trailer, striking and injuring his fleeing daughter with the barrel of the gun. He then fired the gun at his mother-in-law, striking her in the head and killing her instantly.

The petitioner then called the local sheriff's office, identified himself, said where he was, explained that he had just killed his wife and mother-in-law, and asked that the sheriff come and pick him up. Upon arriving at the trailer, the law enforcement officers found the petitioner seated on a chair in open view near the driveway. He told one of the officers that "they're dead, I killed them" and directed the officer to the place where he had put the murder weapon. Later the petitioner told a police officer: "I've done a hideous crime, . . . but I have been thinking about it for eight years . . . I'd do it again."

The petitioner was subsequently indicted on two counts of murder and one count of aggravated assault. He pleaded not guilty and relied primarily on a defense of temporary insanity at his trial. The jury returned verdicts of guilty on all three counts.

The sentencing phase of the trial was held before the same jury. No further evidence was tendered, but counsel for each side made arguments to the jury.

Three times during the course of his argument, the prosecutor stated that the case involved no allegation of "torture" or of an "aggravated battery." When counsel had completed their arguments, the trial judge instructed the jury orally and in writing on the standards that must guide them in imposing sentence. Both orally and in writing, the judge quoted to the jury the statutory language of the § (b)(7) aggravating circumstance in its entirety.

The jury imposed sentences of death on both of the murder convictions. As to each, the jury specified that the aggravating circumstance they had found beyond a reasonable doubt was "that the offense of murder was outrageously or wantonly vile, horrible and inhuman."

In accord with Georgia law in capital cases, the trial judge prepared a report in the form of answers to a questionnaire for use on appellate review. One question on the form asked whether or not the victim had been "physically harmed or tortured." The trial judge's response was "No, as to both victims, excluding the actual murdering of the two victims."

The Georgia Supreme Court affirmed the judgments of the trial court in all respects. With regard to the imposition of the death sentence for each of the two murder convictions, the court rejected the petitioner's contention that § (b)(7) is unconstitutionally vague. The court noted that Georgia's death penalty legislation had been upheld in *Gregg v. Georgia*, 428 U.S. 153, and cited its prior decisions upholding § (b)(7) in the face of similar vagueness challenges. The court found no evidence that the sentence had been "imposed under the influence of passion, prejudice, or any other arbitrary factor," held that the sentence was neither excessive nor disproportionate to the penalty imposed in similar cases, and stated that the evidence supported the jury's finding of the § (b)(7) statutory aggravating circumstance. Two justices dissented.

When *Gregg* was decided by this Court in 1976, the Georgia Supreme Court had affirmed two death sentences based wholly on § (b)(7). *See McCorquodale v. State*, 233 Ga. 369, 211 S.E.2d 577 (1974); *House v. State*, 232 Ga. 140, 205 S.E.2d 217 (1974). The homicide in *McCorquodale* was "a horrifying torture-murder." There, the victim had been beaten, burned, raped, and otherwise severely abused before her death by strangulation. The homicide in *House* was of a similar ilk. In that case, the convicted murderer had choked two 7-year-old boys to death after having forced each of them to submit to anal sodomy.

Thus, the validity of the petitioner's death sentences turns on whether, in light of the facts and circumstances of the murders that he was convicted of committing, the Georgia Supreme Court can be said to have applied a constitutional construction of the phrase "outrageously or wantonly vile, horrible or inhuman in that [they] involved . . . depravity of mind. . . ." We conclude that the answer must be no. The petitioner's crimes cannot be said to have reflected a consciousness materially more "depraved" than that of any person guilty of murder. His victims were killed instantaneously. They were members of his family who were causing him extreme emotional trauma. Shortly after the killings, he acknowledged his responsibility and the heinous nature of his crimes. These factors certainly did not remove the criminality from the petitioner's acts. But it is of vital importance to the defendant and to the community that any decision to impose the death sentence be, and appear to be, based on reason rather than caprice or emotion.

That cannot be said here. There is no principled way to distinguish this case, in which the death penalty was imposed, from the many cases in which it was not. Accordingly, the judgment of the Georgia Supreme Court insofar as it leaves standing the petitioner's death sentences is reversed, and the case is remanded to that court for further proceedings.

It is so ordered.

Mr. Justice WHITE, with whom Mr. Justice REHNQUIST joins, dissenting.

The question [is] whether the facts of this case bear sufficient relation to § (b)(7) to conclude that the Georgia Supreme Court responsibly and constitutionally discharged its review function. I believe that they do.

As described earlier, petitioner, in a cold-blooded executioner's style, murdered his wife and his mother-in-law and, in passing, struck his young daughter on the head with the barrel of his gun. The weapon, a shotgun, is hardly known for the surgical precision with which it perforates its target. The murder scene, in consequence, can only be described in the most unpleasant terms. Petitioner's wife lay prone on the floor. Mrs. Godfrey's head had a hole described as "[a]pproximately the size of a silver dollar" on the side where the shot entered, and much less decipherable and more extensive damage on the side where the shot exited. Tr. 259. Pellets that had passed through Mrs. Godfrey's head were found embedded in the kitchen cabinet.

It will be remembered that after petitioner inflicted this much damage, he took out time not only to strike his daughter on the head, but also to reload his single-shot shotgun and to enter the house. Only then did he get around to shooting his mother-in-law, Mrs. Wilkerson whose last several moments as a sentient being must have been as terrifying as the human mind can imagine. The police eventually found her facedown on the floor with a substantial portion of her head missing and her brain, no longer cabined by her skull, protruding for some distance onto the floor. Blood not only covered the floor and table but dripped from the ceiling as well.

The Georgia Supreme Court held that these facts supported the jury's finding of the existence of statutory aggravating circumstance § (b)(7). A majority of this Court disagrees. But this disagreement, founded as it is on the notion that the lower court's construction of the provision was overly broad, in fact reveals a conception of this Court's role in backstopping the Georgia Supreme Court that is itself overly broad. Our role is to correct genuine errors of constitutional significance resulting from the application of Georgia's capital sentencing procedures; our role is not to peer majestically over the lower court's shoulder so that we might second-guess its interpretation of facts that quite reasonably—perhaps even quite plainly—fit within the statutory language.

Who is to say that the murders of Mrs. Godfrey and Mrs. Wilkerson were not "vile," or "inhuman," or "horrible"? In performing his murderous chore, petitioner employed a weapon known for its disfiguring effects on targets, human or other, and he succeeded in creating a scene so macabre and revolting that, if anything, "vile," "horrible," and "inhuman" are descriptively inadequate.

And who among us can honestly say that Mrs. Wilkerson did not feel "torture" in her last sentient moments. Her daughter, an instant ago a living being sitting across the table from Mrs. Wilkerson, lay prone on the floor, a bloodied and mutilated corpse. The seconds ticked by; enough time for her son-in-law to reload his gun, to enter the home, and to take a gratuitous swipe at his daughter. What terror must have run through her veins as she first witnessed her daughter's hideous demise and then came to terms with the imminence of her own. Was this not torture? And if this was not torture, can it honestly be said that petitioner did not exhibit a "depravity of mind" in carrying out this cruel drama to its mischievous and murderous conclusion? I should have thought, moreover, that the Georgia court could reasonably have deemed the scene awaiting the investigating policemen as involving "an aggravated battery to the victim[s]." Ga. Code § 27-2534.1(b)(7) (1978).

The point is not that, in my view, petitioner's crimes were definitively vile, horrible, or inhuman, or that, as I assay the evidence, they beyond any doubt involved torture, depravity of mind, or an aggravated battery to the victims. Rather, the lesson is a much more elementary one, an instruction that, I should have thought, this Court would have taken to heart long ago. Our mandate does not extend to interfering with factfinders in state criminal proceedings or with state courts that are responsibly and consistently interpreting state law, unless that interference is predicated on a violation of the Constitution.

I would affirm the judgment of the Supreme Court of Georgia.

Questions and Notes

1. Did these murders seem "outrageously vile, horrible, or inhuman" to you? Would your answer be any different if you were a close relative of the victims?

2. Why do you suppose the Court* was unwilling to accept the jury's verdict? What principle was it trying to uphold?

3. In addition to carefully circumscribing aggravating circumstances, the Court has vacillated on whether to allow juries to be influenced by nonstatutory aggravating factors, such as victim impact statements. In *Payne*, the Court determined that such statements were not extraneous to the question of capital punishment.

Payne v. Tennessee
501 U.S. 808 (1991)

Chief Justice REHNQUIST delivered the opinion of the Court.

In this case we reconsider our holdings in *Booth v. Maryland*, 482 U.S. 496 (1987), and *South Carolina v. Gathers*, 490 U.S. 805 (1989), that the Eighth Amendment bars the admission of victim impact evidence during the penalty phase of a capital trial.

Petitioner, Pervis Tyrone Payne, was convicted by a jury on two counts of first-degree murder and one count of assault with intent to commit murder in the first degree. He was sentenced to death for each of the murders and to 30 years in prison for the assault.

The victims of Payne's offenses were 28-year-old Charisse Christopher, her 2-year-old daughter Lacie, and her 3-year-old son Nicholas. The three lived together in an apartment in Millington, Tennessee, across the hall from Payne's girl-friend, Bobbie Thomas. On Saturday, June 27, 1987, Payne visited Thomas' apartment several times in expectation of her return from her mother's house in Arkansas but found no one at home. On one visit, he left his overnight bag, containing clothes and other items for his weekend stay, in the hallway outside Thomas' apartment. With the bag were three cans of malt liquor.

Payne passed the morning and early afternoon injecting cocaine and drinking beer. Later, he drove around the town with a friend in the friend's car, each of them taking turns reading a pornographic magazine. Sometime around 3 p.m., Payne returned to the apartment complex, entered the Christophers' apartment, and began making sexual advances towards Charisse. Charisse resisted and Payne became violent. A neighbor who resided in the apartment directly beneath the Christophers heard Charisse screaming, "'Get out, get out,' as if she were telling the children to leave." The noise briefly subsided and then began, "'horribly loud.'" The neighbor called the police after she heard a "blood curdling scream" from the Christophers' apartment. Brief for Respondent.

When the first police officer arrived at the scene, he immediately encountered Payne, who was leaving the apartment building, so covered with blood that he appeared to be "'sweating blood.'" The officer confronted Payne, who responded,

---

* Although technically *Godfrey* was a plurality opinion, I feel comfortable referring to "the Court" because Justices Brennan and Marshall were even less willing to impose death. — Ed.

"'I'm the complainant.'" When the officer asked, "'What's going on up there?'" Payne struck the officer with the overnight bag, dropped his tennis shoes, and fled.

Inside the apartment, the police encountered a horrifying scene. Blood covered the walls and floor throughout the unit. Charisse and her children were lying on the floor in the kitchen. Nicholas, despite several wounds inflicted by a butcher knife that completely penetrated through his body from front to back, was still breathing. Miraculously, he survived, but not until after undergoing seven hours of surgery and a transfusion of 1,700 cc's of blood—400 to 500 cc's more than his estimated normal blood volume. Charisse and Lacie were dead.

Charisse's body was found on the kitchen floor on her back, her legs fully extended. She had sustained 42 direct knife wounds and 42 defensive wounds on her arms and hands. The wounds were caused by 41 separate thrusts of a butcher knife. None of the 84 wounds inflicted by Payne were individually fatal; rather, the cause of death was most likely bleeding from all of the wounds.

Lacie's body was on the kitchen floor near her mother. She had suffered stab wounds to the chest, abdomen, back, and head. The murder weapon, a butcher knife, was found at her feet. Payne's baseball cap was snapped on her arm near her elbow. Three cans of malt liquor bearing Payne's fingerprints were found on a table near her body, and a fourth empty one was on the landing outside the apartment door.

Payne was apprehended later that day hiding in the attic of the home of a former girlfriend. As he descended the stairs of the attic, he stated to the arresting officers, "'Man, I ain't killed no woman.'" According to one of the officers, Payne had "'a wild look about him. His pupils were contracted. He was foaming at the mouth, saliva. He appeared to be very nervous. He was breathing real rapid.'" *Ibid.* He had blood on his body and clothes and several scratches across his chest. It was later determined that the blood stains matched the victims' blood types. A search of his pockets revealed a packet containing cocaine residue, a hypodermic syringe wrapper, and a cap from a hypodermic syringe. His overnight bag, containing a bloody white shirt, was found in a nearby dumpster.

At trial, Payne took the stand and, despite the overwhelming and relatively uncontroverted evidence against him, testified that he had not harmed any of the Christophers. Rather, he asserted that another man had raced by him as he was walking up the stairs to the floor where the Christophers lived. He stated that he had gotten blood on himself when, after hearing moans from the Christophers' apartment, he had tried to help the victims. According to his testimony, he panicked and fled when he heard police sirens and noticed the blood on his clothes. The jury returned guilty verdicts against Payne on all counts.

During the sentencing phase of the trial, Payne presented the testimony of four witnesses: his mother and father, Bobbie Thomas, and Dr. John T. Hutson, a clinical psychologist specializing in criminal court evaluation work. Bobbie Thomas testified that she met Payne at church, during a time when she was being abused by her husband. She stated that Payne was a very caring person, and that he devoted much time and attention to her three children, who were being affected by her marital difficulties. She said that the children had come to love him very much and would miss him, and that he "behaved just like a father that loved his kids." She asserted that he did not drink, nor did he use drugs, and that it was generally inconsistent with Payne's character to have committed these crimes.

Dr. Hutson testified that based on Payne's low score on an IQ test, Payne was "mentally handicapped." Hutson also said that Payne was neither psychotic nor schizophrenic, and that Payne was the most polite prisoner he had ever met. Payne's parents testified that their son had no prior criminal record and had never been arrested. They also stated that Payne had no history of alcohol or drug abuse, he worked with his father as a painter, he was good with children, and he was a good son.

The State presented the testimony of Charisse's mother, Mary Zvolanek. When asked how Nicholas had been affected by the murders of his mother and sister, she responded:

> "He cries for his mom. He doesn't seem to understand why she doesn't come home. And he cries for his sister Lacie. He comes to me many times during the week and asks me, Grandmama, do you miss my Lacie. And I tell him yes. He says, I'm worried about my Lacie."

In arguing for the death penalty during closing argument, the prosecutor commented on the continuing effects of Nicholas' experience, stating:

> But we do know that Nicholas was alive. And Nicholas was in the same room. Nicholas was still conscious. His eyes were open. He responded to the paramedics. He was able to follow their directions. He was able to hold his intestines in as he was carried to the ambulance. So, he knew what happened to his mother and baby sister.
>
> There is nothing you can do to ease the pain of any of the families involved in this case. There is nothing you can do to ease the pain of Bernice or Carl Payne, and that's a tragedy. There is nothing you can do basically to ease the pain of Mr. and Mrs. Zvolanek, and that's a tragedy. They will have to live with it the rest of their lives. There is obviously nothing you can do for Charisse and Lacie Jo. But there is something that you can do for Nicholas.
>
> Somewhere down the road Nicholas is going to grow up, hopefully. He's going to want to know what happened. And he is going to know what happened to his baby sister and his mother. He is going to want to know what type of justice was done. He is going to want to know what happened. With your verdict, you will provide the answer.

In the rebuttal to Payne's closing argument, the prosecutor stated:

> You saw the videotape this morning. You saw what Nicholas Christopher will carry in his mind forever. When you talk about cruel, when you talk

about atrocious, and when you talk about heinous, that picture will always come into your mind, probably throughout the rest of your live. . . .

. . . No one will ever know about Lacie Jo because she never had the chance to grow up. Her life was taken from her at the age of two years old. So, no there won't be a high school principal to talk about Lacie Jo Christopher, and there won't be anybody to take her to her high school prom. And there won't be anybody there—there won't be her mother there or Nicholas' mother there to kiss him at night. His mother will never kiss him good night or pat him as he goes off to bed or hold him and sing him a lullaby.

"[Petitioner's attorney] wants you to think about a good reputation, people who love the defendant and things about him. He doesn't want you to think about the people who love Charisse Christopher, her mother and daddy who loved her. The people who loved little Lacie Jo, the grandparents who are still here. The brother who mourns for her every single day and wants to know where his best little playmate is. He doesn't have anybody to watch cartoons with him, a little one. These are the things that go into why it is especially cruel, heinous, and atrocious, the burden that that child will carry forever."

The jury sentenced Payne to death on each of the murder counts.

We granted certiorari, to reconsider our holdings in *Booth* and *Gathers* that the Eighth Amendment prohibits a capital sentencing jury from considering "victim impact" evidence relating to the personal characteristics of the victim and the emotional impact of the crimes on the victim's family.

In *Booth*, the defendant robbed and murdered an elderly couple. As required by a state statute, a victim impact statement was prepared based on interviews with the victims' son, daughter, son-in-law, and granddaughter. The statement, which described the personal characteristics of the victims, the emotional impact of the crimes on the family, and set forth the family members' opinions and characterizations of the crimes and the defendant, was submitted to the jury at sentencing. The jury imposed the death penalty. The conviction and sentence were affirmed on appeal by the State's highest court.

This Court held by a 5-to-4 vote that the Eighth Amendment prohibits a jury from considering a victim impact statement at the sentencing phase of a capital trial. The Court made clear that the admissibility of victim impact evidence was not to be determined on a case-by-case basis, but that such evidence was *per se* inadmissible in the sentencing phase of a capital case except to the extent that it "related directly to the circumstances of the crime." In *Gathers*, decided two years later, the Court extended the rule announced in *Booth* to statements made by a prosecutor to the sentencing jury regarding the personal qualities of the victim.

The *Booth* Court began its analysis with the observation that the capital defendant must be treated as a "'uniquely individual human being,'" and therefore the Constitution requires the jury to make an individualized determination as to whether the defendant should be executed based on the "'character of the individual and the circumstances of the crime.'" The Court concluded that while no prior decision of this Court had mandated that only the defendant's character and immediate characteristics of the crime may constitutionally be considered, other factors are irrelevant to the capital sentencing decision unless they have "some bearing on the defendant's 'personal responsibility and moral guilt.'" To the extent that victim impact evidence presents "factors about which the defendant was unaware, and that were irrelevant to the decision to kill," the Court concluded, it has nothing to do with the "blameworthiness of a particular defendant." Evidence of the victim's character, the Court observed, "could well distract the sentencing jury from its constitutionally required task [of] determining whether the death penalty is appropriate in light of the background and record of the accused and the particular circumstances of the crime." The Court concluded that, except to the extent that victim impact evidence relates "directly to the circumstances of the crime," the prosecution may not introduce such evidence at a capital sentencing hearing because "it creates an impermissible risk that the capital sentencing decision will be made in an arbitrary manner."

Booth and *Gathers* were based on two premises: that evidence relating to a particular victim or to the harm that a capital defendant causes a victim's family do not in general reflect on the defendant's "blameworthiness," and that only evidence relating to "blameworthiness" is relevant to the capital sentencing decision. However, the assessment of harm caused by the defendant as a result of the crime charged has understandably been an important concern of the criminal law, both in determining the elements of the offense and in determining the appropriate punishment. Thus, two equally blameworthy criminal defendants may be guilty of different offenses solely because their acts cause differing amounts of harm. "If a bank robber aims his gun at a guard, pulls the trigger, and kills his target, he may be put to death. If the gun unexpectedly misfires, he may not. His moral guilt in both cases is identical, but his responsibility in the former is greater." *Booth* (Scalia, J., dissenting). The same is true with respect to two defendants, each of whom participates in a robbery, and each of whom acts with reckless disregard for human life; if the robbery in which the first defendant participated results in the death of a victim, he may be subjected to the death penalty, but if the robbery in which the second defendant participates does not result in the death of a victim, the death penalty may not be imposed.

The principles which have guided criminal sentencing—as opposed to criminal liability—have varied with the times. The book of Exodus prescribes the Lex talionis, "An eye for an eye, a tooth for a tooth." In England and on the continent of Europe, as recently as the 18th century, crimes which would be regarded as quite minor today were capital offenses. Writing in the 18th century, the Italian criminologist Cesare Beccaria advocated the idea that "the punishment should fit the crime." He said that "we have seen that the true measure of crimes is the injury done to society."

Gradually the list of crimes punishable by death diminished, and legislatures began grading the severity of crimes in accordance with the harm done by the criminal. The sentence for a given offense, rather than being precisely fixed by the legislature, was prescribed in terms of a minimum and a maximum, with the actual sentence to be decided by the judge. With the increasing importance of probation, as opposed to imprisonment, as a part of the penological process, some States such as California developed the "indeterminate sentence," where the time of incarceration was left almost entirely to the penological authorities rather than to the courts. But more recently the pendulum has swung back. The Federal Sentencing Guidelines, which went into effect in 1987, provided for very precise calibration of sentences, depending upon a number of factors. These factors relate both to the subjective guilt of the defendant and to the harm caused by his acts.

Wherever judges in recent years have had discretion to impose sentence, the consideration of the harm caused by the crime has been an important factor in the exercise of that discretion:

> "The first significance of harm in Anglo-American jurisprudence is, then, as a prerequisite to the criminal sanction. The second significance of harm—one no less important to judges—is as a measure of the seriousness of the offense and therefore as a standard for determining the severity of the sentence that will be meted out."

Whatever the prevailing sentencing philosophy, the sentencing authority has always been free to consider a wide range of relevant material. In the federal system, we observed that "a judge may appropriately conduct an inquiry broad in scope, largely unlimited either as to the kind of information he may consider, or the source from which it may come." Even in the context of capital sentencing, prior to *Booth* the joint opinion of Justices Stewart, Powell, and Stevens in *Gregg v. Georgia*, 428 U.S. 153, 203–204 (1976), had rejected petitioner's attack on the Georgia statute because of the "wide scope of evidence and argument allowed at presentence hearings." The joint opinion stated:

> "We think that the Georgia court wisely has chosen not to impose unnecessary restrictions on the evidence that can be offered at such a hearing and to approve open and far-ranging argument. . . . So long as the evidence introduced and the arguments made at the presentence hearing do not prejudice a defendant, it is preferable not to impose restrictions. We think it desirable for the jury to have as much information before it as possible when it makes the sentencing decision."

The Maryland statute involved in *Booth* required that the presentence report in all felony cases include a "victim impact statement" which would describe the effect of the crime on the victim and his family. Congress and most of the States have, in recent years, enacted similar legislation to enable the sentencing authority to consider information about the harm caused by the crime committed by the defendant. The evidence involved in the present case was not admitted pursuant to any such enactment, but its purpose and effect were much the same as if it had been. While the admission of this particular kind of evidence—designed to portray for the sentencing authority the actual harm caused by a particular crime—is of recent origin, this fact hardly renders it unconstitutional.

We have held that a State cannot preclude the sentencer from considering "any relevant mitigating evidence" that the defendant proffers in support of a sentence less than death. *Eddings v. Oklahoma*, 455 U.S. 104 (1982). Thus we have, as the Court observed in *Booth*, required that the capital defendant be treated as a "'uniquely individual human bein[g].'" (quoting *Woodson v. North Carolina*). But it was never held or even suggested in any of our cases preceding *Booth* that the defendant, entitled as he was to individualized consideration, was to receive that consideration wholly apart from the crime which he had committed. The language quoted from *Woodson* in the *Booth* opinion was not intended to describe a class of evidence that could not be received, but a class of evidence which must be received. Any doubt on the matter is dispelled by comparing the language in Woodson with the language from *Gregg v. Georgia*, quoted above, which was handed down the same day as Woodson. This misreading of precedent in *Booth* has, we think, unfairly weighted the scales in a capital trial; while virtually no limits are placed on the relevant mitigating evidence a capital defendant may introduce concerning his own circumstances, the State is barred from either offering "a quick glimpse of the life" which a defendant "chose to extinguish," or demonstrating the loss to the victim's family and to society which has resulted from the defendant's homicide.

The *Booth* Court reasoned that victim impact evidence must be excluded because it would be difficult, if not impossible, for the defendant to rebut such evidence without shifting the focus of the sentencing hearing away from the defendant, thus creating a "'minitrial' on the victim's character."

Payne echoes the concern voiced in *Booth*'s case that the admission of victim impact evidence permits a jury to find that defendants whose victims were assets to their community are more deserving of punishment than those whose victims are perceived to be less worthy. As a general matter, however, victim impact evidence is not offered to encourage comparative judgments of this kind—for instance, that the killer of a hardworking, devoted parent deserves the death penalty, but that the murderer of a reprobate does not. It is designed to show instead each victim's "uniqueness as an individual human being," whatever the jury might think the loss to the community resulting from his death might be. The facts of *Gathers* are an excellent illustration of this: The evidence showed that the victim was an out of work, mentally handicapped individual, perhaps not, in the eyes of most, a significant contributor to society, but nonetheless a murdered human being. Under our constitutional system, the primary responsibility for defining crimes against state law, fixing punishments for the commission of these crimes, and establishing procedures for criminal trials rests with the States. The state laws respecting crimes, punishments, and criminal procedure are, of course, subject to the overriding provisions of the United States Constitution. Where the State imposes the death penalty for a particular crime, we have held that the Eighth Amendment imposes special limitations upon that process.

> "First, there is a required threshold below which the death penalty cannot be imposed. In this context, the State must establish rational criteria that narrow the decisionmaker's judgment as to whether the circumstances of a particular defendant's case meet the threshold. Moreover, a societal consensus that the death penalty is disproportionate to a particular offense prevents a State from imposing the death penalty for that offense. Second, States cannot limit the sentencer's consideration of any relevant circumstance that could cause it to decline to impose the penalty. In this respect, the State cannot challenge the sentencer's discretion, but must allow it to consider any relevant information offered by the defendant."

McCleskey v. Kemp, 481 U.S. 279, 305–306 (1987). But, "[b]eyond these limitations . . . the Court has deferred to the State's choice of substantive factors relevant to the penalty determination."

"Within the constitutional limitations defined by our cases, the States enjoy their traditional latitude to prescribe the method by which those who commit murder shall be punished." The States remain free, in capital cases, as well as others, to devise new procedures and new remedies to meet felt needs. Victim impact evidence is simply another form or method of informing the sentencing authority about the specific harm caused by the crime in question, evidence of a general type long considered by sentencing authorities. We think the *Booth* Court was wrong in stating that this kind of evidence leads to the arbitrary imposition of the death penalty. In the majority of cases, and in this case, victim impact evidence serves entirely legitimate purposes. In the event that evidence is introduced that is so unduly prejudicial that it renders the trial fundamentally unfair, the Due Process Clause of the Fourteenth Amendment provides a mechanism for relief. Courts have always taken into consideration the harm done by the defendant in imposing sentence, and the evidence adduced in this case was illustrative of the harm caused by Payne's double murder. We are now of the view that a State may properly conclude that for the jury to assess meaningfully the defendant's moral culpability and blameworthiness, it should have before it at the sentencing phase evidence of the specific harm caused by the defendant. "The State has a legitimate interest in counteracting the mitigating evidence which the defendant is entitled to put in, by reminding the sentencer that just as the murderer should be considered as an individual, so too the victim is an individual whose death represents a unique loss to society and in particular to his family." By turning the victim into a "faceless stranger at the penalty phase of a capital trial," *Booth* deprives the State of the full moral force of its evidence and may prevent the jury from having before it all the information necessary to determine the proper punishment for a first-degree murder.

The present case is an example of the potential for such unfairness. The capital sentencing jury heard testimony from Payne's girlfriend that they met at church; that he was affectionate, caring, and kind to her children; that he was not an abuser of drugs or alcohol; and that it was inconsistent with his character to have committed the murders. Payne's parents testified that he was a good son, and a clinical psychologist testified that Payne was an extremely polite prisoner and suffered from a low IQ. None of this testimony was related to the circumstances of Payne's brutal crimes. In contrast, the only evidence of the impact of Payne's offenses during the sentencing phase was Nicholas' grandmother's description—in response to a single question—that the child misses his mother and baby sister. Payne argues that the Eighth Amendment commands that the jury's death sentence must be set aside because the jury heard this testimony. But the testimony illustrated quite poignantly some of the harm that Payne's killing had caused; there is nothing unfair about allowing the jury to bear in mind that harm at the same time as it considers the mitigating evidence introduced by the defendant. The Supreme Court of Tennessee in this case obviously felt the unfairness of the rule pronounced by *Booth* when it said: "It is an affront to the civilized members of the human race to say that at sentencing in a capital case, a parade of witnesses may praise the background, character and good deeds of Defendant (as was done in this case), without limitation as to relevancy, but nothing may be said that bears upon the character of, or the harm imposed, upon the victims."

In *Gathers*, as indicated above, we extended the holding of *Booth* barring victim impact evidence to the prosecutor's argument to the jury. Human nature being what it is, capable lawyers trying cases to juries try to convey to the jurors that the people involved in the underlying events are, or were, living human beings, with something to be gained or lost from the jury's verdict. Under the aegis of the Eighth Amendment, we have given the broadest latitude to the defendant to introduce relevant mitigating evidence reflecting on his individual personality, and the defendant's attorney may argue that evidence to the jury. Petitioner's attorney in this case did just that. For the reasons discussed above, we now reject the view—expressed in *Gathers*—that a State may not permit the prosecutor to similarly argue to the jury the human cost of the crime of which the defendant stands convicted. We reaffirm the view expressed by Justice Cardozo in *Snyder v. Massachusetts*, 291 U.S. 97 (1934): "Justice, though due to the accused, is due to the accuser also. The concept of fairness must not be strained till it is narrowed to a filament. We are to keep the balance true."

We thus hold that if the State chooses to permit the admission of victim impact evidence and prosecutorial argument on that subject, the Eighth Amendment erects no *per se* bar. A State may legitimately conclude that evidence about the victim and about the impact of the murder on the victim's family is relevant to the jury's decision as to whether or not the death penalty should be imposed. There is no reason to treat such evidence differently than other relevant evidence is treated.

Payne and his amicus argue that despite these numerous infirmities in the rule created by *Booth* and *Gathers*, we should adhere to the doctrine of *stare decisis* and stop short of overruling those cases. *Stare decisis* is the preferred course because it promotes the evenhanded, predictable, and consistent development of legal principles, fosters reliance on judicial decisions, and contributes to the actual and perceived integrity of the judicial process. Adhering to precedent "is usually the wise policy, because in most matters it is more important that the applicable rule of law be settled than it be settled right." Nevertheless, when governing decisions are unworkable or are badly reasoned, "this Court has never felt constrained to follow precedent." *Stare decisis* is not an inexorable command; rather, it "is a principle of policy and not a mechanical formula of adherence to the latest decision." This is particularly true in constitutional cases, because in such cases "correction through legislative action is practically impossible."

Booth and *Gathers* were decided by the narrowest of margins, over spirited dissents challenging the basic underpinnings of those decisions. They have been questioned by Members of the Court in later decisions and have defied consistent application by the lower courts. Reconsidering these decisions now, we conclude, for the reasons heretofore stated, that they were wrongly decided and should be, and now are, overruled.[2] We accordingly affirm the judgment of the Supreme Court of Tennessee.

Affirmed.

Justice O'CONNOR, with whom Justice WHITE and Justice KENNEDY join, concurring.

In my view, a State may legitimately determine that victim impact evidence is relevant to a capital sentencing proceeding. A State may decide that the jury, before determining whether a convicted murderer should receive the death penalty, should know the full extent of the harm caused by the crime, including its impact on the victim's family and community. A State may decide also that the jury should see "a quick glimpse of the life petitioner chose to extinguish," *Mills v. Maryland*, 486 U.S. 367 (1988) (Rehnquist, C.J., dissenting), to remind the jury that the person whose life was taken was a unique human being.

Given that victim impact evidence is potentially relevant, nothing in the Eighth Amendment commands that States treat it differently than other kinds of relevant evidence. "The Eighth Amendment stands as a shield against those practices and punishments which are either inherently cruel or which so offend the moral consensus of this society as to be deemed 'cruel and unusual.'" Certainly there is no strong societal consensus that a jury may not take into account the loss suffered by a victim's family or that a murder victim must remain a faceless stranger at the penalty phase of a capital trial. Just the opposite is true. Most States have enacted legislation enabling judges and juries to consider victim impact evidence. The possibility that this evidence may in some cases be unduly inflammatory does not justify a

---

2. Our holding today is limited to the holdings of *Booth* and *Gathers*, that evidence and argument relating to the victim and the impact of the victim's death on the victim's family are inadmissible at a capital sentencing hearing. *Booth* also held that the admission of a victim's family members' characterizations and opinions about the crime, the defendant, and the appropriate sentence violates the Eighth Amendment. No evidence of the latter sort was presented at the trial in this case.

prophylactic, constitutionally based rule that this evidence may never be admitted. Trial courts routinely exclude evidence that is unduly inflammatory; where inflammatory evidence is improperly admitted, appellate courts carefully review the record to determine whether the error was prejudicial.

We do not hold today that victim impact evidence must be admitted, or even that it should be admitted. We hold merely that if a State decides to permit consideration of this evidence, "the Eighth Amendment erects no *per se* bar." If, in a particular case, a witness' testimony or a prosecutor's remark so infects the sentencing proceeding as to render it fundamentally unfair, the defendant may seek appropriate relief under the Due Process Clause of the Fourteenth Amendment.

That line was not crossed in this case. The State called as a witness Mary Zvolanek, Nicholas' grandmother. Her testimony was brief. She explained that Nicholas cried for his mother and baby sister and could not understand why they did not come home. I do not doubt that the jurors were moved by this testimony—who would not have been? But surely this brief statement did not inflame their passions more than did the facts of the crime: Charisse Christopher was stabbed 41 times with a butcher knife and bled to death; her 2-year-old daughter Lacie was killed by repeated thrusts of that same knife; and 3-year-old Nicholas, despite stab wounds that penetrated completely through his body from front to back, survived—only to witness the brutal murders of his mother and baby sister. In light of the jury's unavoidable familiarity with the facts of Payne's vicious attack, I cannot conclude that the additional information provided by Mary Zvolanek's testimony deprived petitioner of due process.

Nor did the prosecutor's comments about Charisse and Lacie in the closing argument violate the Constitution. The jury had earlier seen a videotape of the murder scene that included the slashed and bloody corpses of Charisse and Lacie. In arguing that Payne deserved the death penalty, the prosecutor sought to remind the jury that Charisse and Lacie were more than just lifeless bodies on a videotape, that they were unique human beings. The prosecutor remarked that Charisse would never again sing a lullaby to her son and that Lacie would never attend a high school prom. In my view, these statements were permissible. "Murder is the ultimate act of depersonalization." It transforms a living person with hopes, dreams, and fears into a corpse, thereby taking away all that is special and unique about the person. The Constitution does not preclude a State from deciding to give some of that back.

I agree with the Court that *Booth* and *Gathers* were wrongly decided. The Eighth Amendment does not prohibit a State from choosing to admit evidence concerning a murder victim's personal characteristics or the impact of the crime on the victim's family and community. *Booth* also addressed another kind of victim impact evidence—opinions of the victim's family about the crime, the defendant, and the appropriate sentence. As the Court notes in today's decision, we do not reach this issue as no evidence of this kind was introduced at petitioner's trial. Nor do we express an opinion as to other aspects of the prosecutor's conduct. As to the victim impact evidence that was introduced, its admission did not violate the Constitution. Accordingly, I join the Court's opinion.

Justice SCALIA, with whom Justice O'CONNOR and Justice KENNEDY join as to Part II, concurring.

I.

The Court correctly observes the injustice of requiring the exclusion of relevant aggravating evidence during capital sentencing, while requiring the admission of all relevant mitigating evidence. I have previously expressed my belief that the latter requirement is both wrong and, when combined with the remainder of our capital sentencing jurisprudence, unworkable. *See Walton v. Arizona* (Scalia, J. concurring in part and concurring in judgment). Even if it were abandoned, however, I would still affirm the judgment here. True enough, the Eighth Amendment permits parity between mitigating and aggravating factors. But more broadly and fundamentally still, it permits the People to decide (within the limits of other constitutional guarantees) what is a crime and what constitutes aggravation and mitigation of a crime.

II.

The response to Justice MARSHALL's strenuous defense of the virtues of *stare decisis* can be found in the writings of Justice MARSHALL himself. That doctrine, he has reminded us, "is not 'an imprisonment of reason.'" *Guardians Assn. v. Civil Service Comm'n of New York City*, 463 U.S. 582, 618 (1983). If there was ever a case that defied reason, it was *Booth v. Maryland*, imposing a constitutional rule that had absolutely no basis in constitutional text, in historical practice, or in logic. *Booth*'s stunning ipse dixit, that a crime's unanticipated consequences must be deemed "irrelevant" to the sentence, conflicts with a public sense of justice keen enough that it has found voice in a nationwide "victims' rights" movement.

Today, however, Justice MARSHALL demands of us some "special justification"— beyond the mere conviction that the rule of *Booth* significantly harms our criminal justice system and is egregiously wrong—before we can be absolved of exercising "power, not reason." I do not think that is fair. In fact, quite to the contrary, what would enshrine power as the governing principle of this Court is the notion that an important constitutional decision with plainly inadequate rational support must be left in place for the sole reason that it once attracted five votes.

It seems to me difficult for those who were in the majority in *Booth* to hold themselves forth as ardent apostles of *stare decisis*. That doctrine, to the extent it rests upon anything more than administrative convenience, is merely the application to judicial precedents of a more general principle that the settled practices and expectations of a democratic society should generally not be disturbed by the courts. It is hard to have a genuine regard for *stare decisis* without honoring that more general principle as well. A decision of this Court which, while not overruling a prior holding, nonetheless announces a novel rule, contrary to long and unchallenged practice, and pronounces it to be the Law of the Land—such a decision, no less than an explicit overruling, should be approached with great caution. It was, I suggest,

Booth, and not today's decision, that compromised the fundamental values under-lying the doctrine of *stare decisis.*

Justice SOUTER, with whom Justice KENNEDY joins, concurring.

I join the Court's opinion addressing two categories of facts excluded from con-sideration at capital sentencing proceedings by *Booth* and *Gathers*: information revealing the individuality of the victim and the impact of the crime on the vic-tim's survivors.[1] As to these two categories, I believe *Booth* and *Gathers* were wrongly decided.

To my knowledge, our legal tradition has never included a general rule that evi-dence of a crime's effects on the victim and others is, standing alone, irrelevant to a sentencing determination of the defendant's culpability. Indeed, as the Court's opinion today, and dissents in *Booth*, make clear, criminal conduct has traditionally been categorized and penalized differently according to consequences not specifi-cally intended, but determined in part by conditions unknown to a defendant when he acted. The majority opinion in *Booth*, nonetheless characterized the consider-ation in a capital sentencing proceeding of a victim's individuality and the conse-quences of his death on his survivors as "irrelevant" and productive of "arbitrary and capricious" results, insofar as that would allow the sentencing authority to take account of information not specifically contemplated by the defendant prior to his ultimate criminal decision. This condemnation comprehends two quite separate elements. As to one such element, the condemnation is merited but insufficient to justify the rule in *Booth*, and as to the other it is mistaken.

Evidence about the victim and survivors, and any jury argument predicated on it, can of course be so inflammatory as to risk a verdict impermissibly based on passion, not deliberation. But this is just as true when the defendant knew of the specific facts as when he was ignorant of their details, and in each case there is a traditional guard against the inflammatory risk, in the trial judge's authority and responsibility to control the proceedings consistently with due process, on which ground defendants may object and, if necessary, appeal. With the command of due process before us, this Court and the other courts of the state and federal systems will perform the "duty to search for constitutional error with painstaking care," an obligation "never more exacting than it is in a capital case."

Booth nonetheless goes further and imposes a blanket prohibition on consider-ation of evidence of the victim's individuality and the consequential harm to survi-vors as irrelevant to the choice between imprisonment and execution, except when such evidence goes to the "circumstances of the crime," and probably then only when the facts in question were known to the defendant and relevant to his deci-sion to kill. This prohibition rests on the belief that consideration of such details

---

1. This case presents no challenge to the Court's holding in *Booth v. Maryland* that a sentencing authority should not receive a third category of information concerning a victim's family members' characterization of and opinions about the crime, the defendant, and the appropriate sentence.

about the victim and survivors as may have been outside the defendant's knowledge is inconsistent with the sentencing jury's Eighth Amendment duty "in the unique circumstance of a capital sentencing hearing . . . to focus on the defendant as a 'uniquely individual human being.'"

Murder has foreseeable consequences. When it happens, it is always to distinct individuals, and, after it happens, other victims are left behind. Every defendant knows, if endowed with the mental competence for criminal responsibility, that the life he will take by his homicidal behavior is that of a unique person, like himself, and that the person to be killed probably has close associates, "survivors," who will suffer harms and deprivations from the victim's death. Just as defendants know that they are not faceless human ciphers, they know that their victims are not valueless fungibles; and just as defendants appreciate the web of relationships and dependencies in which they live, they know that their victims are not human islands, but individuals with parents or children, spouses or friends or dependents. Thus, when a defendant chooses to kill, or to raise the risk of a victim's death, this choice necessarily relates to a whole human being and threatens an association of others, who may be distinctly hurt. The fact that the defendant may not know the details of a victim's life and characteristics, or the exact identities and needs of those who may survive, should not in any way obscure the further facts that death is always to a "unique" individual, and harm to some group of survivors is a consequence of a successful homicidal act so foreseeable as to be virtually inevitable.

I do not, however, rest my decision to overrule wholly on the constitutional error that I see in the cases in question. I must rely as well on my further view that *Booth* sets an unworkable standard of constitutional relevance that threatens, on its own terms, to produce such arbitrary consequences and uncertainty of application as virtually to guarantee a result far diminished from the case's promise of appropriately individualized sentencing for capital defendants. These conclusions will be seen to result from the interaction of three facts. First, although *Booth* was prompted by the introduction of a systematically prepared "victim impact statement" at the sentencing phase of the trial, *Booth*'s restriction of relevant facts to what the defendant knew and considered in deciding to kill applies to any evidence, however derived or presented. Second, details of which the defendant was unaware, about the victim and survivors, will customarily be disclosed by the evidence introduced at the guilt phase of the trial. Third, the jury that determines guilt will usually determine, or make recommendations about, the imposition of capital punishment.

A hypothetical case will illustrate these facts and raise what I view as the serious practical problems with application of the *Booth* standard. Assume that a minister, unidentified as such and wearing no clerical collar, walks down a street to his church office on a brief errand, while his wife and adolescent daughter wait for him in a parked car. He is robbed and killed by a stranger, and his survivors witness his death. What are the circumstances of the crime that can be considered at the sentencing phase under *Booth*? The defendant did not know his victim was a minister, or that he had a wife and child, let alone that they were watching. Under *Booth*, these facts were irrelevant to his decision to kill, and they should be barred from consideration at sentencing. Yet evidence of them will surely be admitted at the guilt phase of the trial. The widow will testify to what she saw, and, in so doing, she will not be asked to pretend that she was a mere bystander. She could not succeed at that if she tried. The daughter may well testify too. The jury will not be kept from knowing that the victim was a minister, with a wife and child, on an errand to his church. This is so not only because the widow will not try to deceive the jury about her relationship, but also because the usual standards of trial relevance afford factfinders enough information about surrounding circumstances to let them make sense of the narrowly material facts of the crime itself. No one claims that jurors in a capital case should be deprived of such common contextual evidence, even though the defendant knew nothing about the errand, the victim's occupation, or his family. And yet, if these facts are not kept from the jury at the guilt stage, they will be in the jurors' minds at the sentencing stage.

Booth thus raises a dilemma with very practical consequences. If we were to require the rules of guilt-phase evidence to be changed to guarantee the full effect of *Booth*'s promise to exclude consideration of specific facts unknown to the defendant and thus supposedly without significance in morally evaluating his decision to kill, we would seriously reduce the comprehensibility of most trials by depriving jurors of those details of context that allow them to understand what is being described. If, on the other hand, we are to leave the rules of trial evidence alone, *Booth*'s objective will not be attained without requiring a separate sentencing jury to be empaneled. This would be a major imposition on the States, however, and I suppose that no one would seriously consider adding such a further requirement.

But, even if *Booth* were extended one way or the other to exclude completely from the sentencing proceeding all facts about the crime's victims not known by the defendant, the case would be vulnerable to the further charge that it would lead to arbitrary sentencing results. In the preceding hypothetical, *Booth* would require that all evidence about the victim's family, including its very existence, be excluded from sentencing consideration because the defendant did not know of it when he killed the victim. Yet, if the victim's daughter had screamed "Daddy, look out," as the defendant approached the victim with drawn gun, then the evidence of at least the daughter's survivorship would be admissible even under a strict reading of *Booth*, because the defendant, prior to killing, had been made aware of the daughter's existence, which therefore became relevant in evaluating the defendant's decision to kill. Resting a decision about the admission of impact evidence on such a fortuity is arbitrary.

Thus, the status quo is unsatisfactory, and the question is whether the case that has produced it should be overruled. In this instance, as in any other, overruling a precedent of this Court is a matter of no small import, for "the doctrine of stare decisis is of fundamental importance to the rule of law." To be sure, *stare decisis* is not an "inexorable command," and our "considered practice [has] not [been] to apply *stare decisis* as rigidly in constitutional [cases] as in nonconstitutional cases." But, even in constitutional cases, the doctrine carries such persuasive force that we have always required a departure from precedent to be supported by some "special justification."

The Court has a special justification in this case. *Booth* promises more than it can deliver, given the unresolved tension between common evidentiary standards at the guilt phase and *Booth's* promise of a sentencing determination free from the consideration of facts unknown to the defendant and irrelevant to his decision to kill. An extension of the case to guarantee a sentencing authority free from the influence of information extraneous under *Booth* would be either an unworkable or a costly extension of an erroneous principle and would itself create a risk of arbitrary results. There is only one other course open to us. We can recede from the erroneous holding that created the tension and extended the false promise, and there is precedent in our *stare decisis* jurisprudence for doing just this. In prior cases, when this Court has confronted a wrongly decided, unworkable precedent calling for some further action by the Court, we have chosen not to compound the original error, but to overrule the precedent. Following this course here has itself the support not only of precedent but of practical sense as well. Therefore, I join the Court in its partial overruling of *Booth* and *Gathers*.

Justice MARSHALL, with whom Justice BLACKMUN joins, dissenting.

Power, not reason, is the new currency of this Court's decision making. Four Terms ago, a five-Justice majority of this Court held that "victim impact" evidence of the type at issue in this case could not constitutionally be introduced during the penalty phase of a capital trial. *Booth v. Maryland*. By another 5-4 vote, a majority of this Court rebuffed an attack upon this ruling just two Terms ago. *South Carolina v. Gathers*. Nevertheless, having expressly invited respondent to renew the attack, today's majority overrules *Booth* and *Gathers* and credits the dissenting views expressed in those cases. Neither the law nor the facts supporting *Booth* and *Gathers* underwent any change in the last four years. Only the personnel of this Court did.

In dispatching *Booth* and *Gathers* to their graves, today's majority ominously suggests that an even more extensive upheaval of this Court's precedents may be in store. Renouncing this Court's historical commitment to a conception of "the judiciary as a source of impersonal and reasoned judgments," the majority declares itself free to discard any principle of constitutional liberty which was recognized or reaffirmed over the dissenting votes of four Justices and with which five or more Justices now disagree. The implications of this radical new exception to the doctrine of *stare decisis* are staggering. The majority today sends a clear signal that scores of established constitutional liberties are now ripe for reconsideration, thereby inviting the very type of open defiance of our precedents that the majority rewards in this case. Because I believe that this Court owes more to its constitutional precedents in general and to *Booth* and *Gathers* in particular, I dissent.

I.

Speaking for the Court as then constituted, Justice Powell and Justice Brennan set out the rationale for excluding victim-impact evidence from the sentencing proceedings in a capital case. As the majorities in *Booth* and *Gathers* recognized, the core principle of this Court's capital jurisprudence is that the sentence of death must reflect an "'individualized determination'" of the defendant's "'personal responsibility and moral guilt'" and must be based upon factors that channel the jury's discretion "'so as to minimize the risk of wholly arbitrary and capricious action.'" The State's introduction of victim-impact evidence, Justice Powell and Justice Brennan explained, violates this fundamental principle. Where, as is ordinarily the case, the defendant was unaware of the personal circumstances of his victim, admitting evidence of the victim's character and the impact of the murder upon the victim's family predicates the sentencing determination on "factors . . . wholly unrelated to the blameworthiness of [the] particular defendant." And even where the defendant was in a position to foresee the likely impact of his conduct, admission of victim-impact evidence creates an unacceptable risk of sentencing arbitrariness. As Justice Powell explained in *Booth*, the probative value of such evidence is always outweighed by its prejudicial effect because of its inherent capacity to draw the jury's attention away from the character of the defendant and the circumstances of the crime to such illicit considerations as the eloquence with which family members express their grief and the status of the victim in the community. I continue to find these considerations wholly persuasive, and I see no purpose in trying to improve upon Justice Powell's and Justice Brennan's exposition of them.

There is nothing new in the majority's discussion of the supposed deficiencies in *Booth* and *Gathers*. Every one of the arguments made by the majority can be found in the dissenting opinions filed in those two cases, and, as I show in the margin, each argument was convincingly answered by Justice Powell and Justice Brennan.[1]

---

1. The majority's primary argument is that punishment in criminal law is frequently based on an "assessment of [the] harm caused by the defendant as a result of the crime charged." Nothing in *Booth* or *Gathers*, however, conflicts with this unremarkable observation. These cases stand merely for the proposition that the State may not put on evidence of one particular species of harm — namely, that associated with the victim's personal characteristics independent of the circumstances of the offense — in the course of a capital murder proceeding. *See Booth*, n.10 (emphasizing that decision does not bar reliance on victim-impact evidence in capital sentencing so long as such evidence "relate[s] directly to the circumstances of the crime"); n.12 (emphasizing that decision does not bar reliance on victim-impact evidence in sentencing for noncapital crimes). It may be the case that such a rule departs from the latitude of sentencers in criminal law generally to "take into consideration the harm done by the defendant." But as the Booth Court pointed out, because this Court's capital-sentencing jurisprudence is founded on the premise that "death is a 'punishment different from all other sanctions,'" it is completely unavailing to attempt to infer from sentencing considerations in noncapital settings the proper treatment of any particular sentencing issue in a capital case.

The majority also discounts Justice Powell's concern with the inherently prejudicial quality of victim-impact evidence. "The mere fact that for tactical reasons it might not be prudent for the defense to rebut victim impact evidence," the majority protests, "makes the case no different than

But contrary to the impression that one might receive from reading the majority's lengthy rehearsing of the issues addressed in *Booth* and *Gathers*, the outcome of this case does not turn simply on who—the *Booth* and *Gathers* majorities or the *Booth* and *Gathers* dissenters—had the better of the argument. Justice Powell and Justice Brennan's position carried the day in those cases and became the law of the land. The real question, then, is whether today's majority has come forward with the type of extraordinary showing that this Court has historically demanded before overruling one of its precedents. In my view, the majority clearly has not made any such showing. Indeed, the striking feature of the majority's opinion is its radical assertion that it need not even try.

II.

The overruling of one of this Court's precedents ought to be a matter of great moment and consequence. Although the doctrine of *stare decisis* is not an "inexorable command," this Court has repeatedly stressed that fidelity to precedent is fundamental to "a society governed by the rule of law."

Consequently, this Court has never departed from precedent without "special justification." *Arizona v. Rumsey*, 467 U.S. 203, 212 (1984). Such justifications include the advent of "subsequent changes or development in the law" that undermine a decision's rationale, the need "to bring [a decision] into agreement with experience and with facts newly ascertained," and a showing that a particular precedent has become a "detriment to coherence and consistency in the law."

---

others in which a party is faced with this sort of a dilemma." Unsurprisingly, this tautology is completely unresponsive to Justice Powell's argument. The *Booth* Court established a rule excluding introduction of victim impact evidence not merely because it is difficult to rebut—a feature of victim-impact evidence that may be "no different" from that of many varieties of relevant, legitimate evidence—but because the effect of this evidence in the sentencing proceeding is unfairly prejudicial: "The prospect of a 'mini-trial' on the victim's character is more than simply unappealing; it could well distract the sentencing jury from its constitutionally required task—determining whether the death penalty is appropriate in light of the background and record of the accused and the particular circumstances of the crime." The law is replete with *per se* prohibitions of types of evidence the probative effect of which is generally outweighed by its unfair prejudice. There is nothing anomalous in the notion that the Eighth Amendment would similarly exclude evidence that has an undue capacity to undermine the regime of individualized sentencing that our capital jurisprudence demands.

Finally, the majority contends that the exclusion of victim-impact evidence "deprives the State of the full moral force of its evidence and may prevent the jury from having before it all the information necessary to determine the proper punishment for a first-degree murder." The majority's recycled contention begs the question. Before it is possible to conclude that the exclusion of victim-impact evidence prevents the State from making its case or the jury from considering relevant evidence, it is necessary to determine whether victim-impact evidence is consistent with the substantive standards that define the scope of permissible sentencing determinations under the Eighth Amendment. The majority offers no persuasive answer to Justice Powell and Justice Brennan's conclusion that victim-impact evidence is frequently irrelevant to any permissible sentencing consideration and that such evidence risks exerting illegitimate "moral force" by directing the jury's attention on illicit considerations such as the victim's standing in the community.

The majority cannot seriously claim that any of these traditional bases for over-ruling a precedent applies to *Booth* or *Gathers*. The majority does not suggest that the legal rationale of these decisions has been undercut by changes or developments in doctrine during the last two years. Nor does the majority claim that experience over that period of time has discredited the principle that "any decision to impose the death sentence be, and appear to be, based on reason rather than caprice or emotion," *Gardner v. Florida*, 430 U.S. 349, 358 (1977) (plurality opinion), the larger postulate of political morality on which *Booth* and *Gathers* rest.

In my view, this impoverished conception of *stare decisis* cannot possibly be reconciled with the values that inform the proper judicial function. Contrary to what the majority suggests, *stare decisis* is important not merely because individuals rely on precedent to structure their commercial activity but because fidelity to precedent is part and parcel of a conception of "the judiciary as a source of impersonal and reasoned judgments."

Carried to its logical conclusion, the majority's debilitated conception of *stare decisis* would destroy the Court's very capacity to resolve authoritatively the abiding conflicts between those with power and those without. If this Court shows so little respect for its own precedents, it can hardly expect them to be treated more respectfully by the state actors whom these decisions are supposed to bind. By signaling its willingness to give fresh consideration to any constitutional liberty recognized by a 5-4 vote "over spirited dissent," the majority invites state actors to renew the very policies deemed unconstitutional in the hope that this Court may now reverse course, even if it has only recently reaffirmed the constitutional liberty in question.

Indeed, the majority's disposition of this case nicely illustrates the rewards of such a strategy of defiance. The Tennessee Supreme Court did nothing in this case to disguise its contempt for this Court's decisions in *Booth* and *Gathers*. Summing up its reaction to those cases, it concluded:

> "It is an affront to the civilized members of the human race to say that at sentencing in a capital case, a parade of witnesses may praise the background, character and good deeds of Defendant (as was done in this case), without limitation as to relevancy, but nothing may be said that bears upon the character of, or harm imposed, upon the victims."

Offering no explanation for how this case could possibly be distinguished from *Booth* and *Gathers*—for obviously, there is none to offer—the court perfunctorily declared that the victim-impact evidence and the prosecutor's argument based on this evidence "did not violate either [of those decisions]." *Ibid*. It cannot be clearer that the court simply declined to be bound by this Court's precedents.

Far from condemning this blatant disregard for the rule of law, the majority applauds it. In the Tennessee Supreme Court's denigration of *Booth* and *Gathers* as "'an affront to the civilized members of the human race,'" the majority finds only confirmation of "the unfairness of the rule pronounced by" the majorities in those cases. It is hard to imagine a more complete abdication of this Court's historic commitment to defending the supremacy of its own pronouncements on issues of constitutional liberty.

I dissent.

Justice STEVENS, with whom Justice BLACKMUN joins, dissenting.

The novel rule that the Court announces today represents a dramatic departure from the principles that have governed our capital sentencing jurisprudence for decades. Justice MARSHALL is properly concerned about the majority's trivialization of the doctrine of *stare decisis*. But even if *Booth* and *Gathers* had not been decided, today's decision would represent a sharp break with past decisions. Our cases provide no support whatsoever for the majority's conclusion that the prosecutor may introduce evidence that sheds no light on the defendant's guilt or moral culpability, and thus serves no purpose other than to encourage jurors to decide in favor of death rather than life on the basis of their emotions rather than their reason.

Until today our capital punishment jurisprudence has required that any decision to impose the death penalty be based solely on evidence that tends to inform the jury about the character of the offense and the character of the defendant. Evidence that serves no purpose other than to appeal to the sympathies or emotions of the jurors has never been considered admissible. Thus, if a defendant, who had murdered a convenience store clerk in cold blood in the course of an armed robbery, offered evidence unknown to him at the time of the crime about the immoral character of his victim, all would recognize immediately that the evidence was irrelevant and inadmissible. Evenhanded justice requires that the same constraint be imposed on the advocate of the death penalty.

I.

As the Court acknowledges today, the use of victim impact evidence "is of recent origin." Insofar as the Court's jurisprudence is concerned, this type of evidence made its first appearance in 1987 in *Booth*. In his opinion for the Court, Justice Powell noted that our prior cases had stated that the question whether an individual defendant should be executed is to be determined on the basis of "'the character of the individual and the circumstances of the crime.'" [T]he Court concluded that unless evidence has some bearing on the defendant's personal responsibility and moral guilt, its admission would create a risk that a death sentence might be based on considerations that are constitutionally impermissible or totally irrelevant to the sentencing process. Evidence that served no purpose except to describe the personal characteristics of the victim and the emotional impact of the crime on the victim's family was therefore constitutionally irrelevant.

Our decision in *Booth* was entirely consistent with the practices that had been followed "both before and since the American colonies became a nation." Our holding was mandated by our capital punishment jurisprudence, which requires any decision to impose the death penalty to be based on reason rather than caprice or emotion. The dissenting opinions in *Booth* and in *Gathers* can be searched in vain for any judicial precedent sanctioning the use of evidence unrelated to the character of the offense or the character of the offender in the sentencing process. Today, however, relying on nothing more than those dissenting opinions, the Court abandons rules of relevance that are older than the Nation itself and ventures into uncharted seas of irrelevance.

II.

Today's majority has obviously been moved by an argument that has strong political appeal but no proper place in a reasoned judicial opinion. Because our decision in *Lockett* recognizes the defendant's right to introduce all mitigating evidence that may inform the jury about his character, the Court suggests that fairness requires that the State be allowed to respond with similar evidence about the *victim*.[1] This argument is a classic *non sequitur*:

> The victim is not on trial; her character, whether good or bad, cannot therefore constitute either an aggravating or a mitigating circumstance.

Even if introduction of evidence about the victim could be equated with introduction of evidence about the defendant, the argument would remain flawed in both its premise and its conclusion. The conclusion that exclusion of victim impact evidence results in a significantly imbalanced sentencing procedure is simply inaccurate. Just as the defendant is entitled to introduce any relevant mitigating evidence, so the State may rebut that evidence and may designate any relevant conduct to be an aggravating factor provided that the factor is sufficiently well defined and consistently applied to cabin the sentencer's discretion.

The premise that a criminal prosecution requires an evenhanded balance between the State and the defendant is also incorrect. The Constitution grants certain rights to the criminal defendant and imposes special limitations on the State designed to

---

1. Justice SCALIA accurately described the argument in his dissent in *Booth*:
"Recent years have seen an outpouring of popular concern for what has come to be known as 'victims' rights'—a phrase that describes what its proponents feel is the failure of courts of justice to take into account in their sentencing decisions not only the factors mitigating the defendant's moral guilt, but also the amount of harm he has caused to innocent members of society. Many citizens have found one-sided and hence unjust the criminal trial in which a parade of witnesses comes forth to testify to the pressures beyond normal human experience that drove the defendant to commit his crime, with no one to lay before the sentencing authority the full reality of human suffering the defendant has produced—which (and not moral guilt alone) is one of the reasons society deems his act worthy of the prescribed penalty."
In his concurring opinion today, Justice SCALIA again relies on the popular opinion that has "found voice in a nationwide 'victims' rights' movement." His view that the exclusion of evidence about "a crime's unanticipated consequences" "significantly harms our criminal justice system," rests on the untenable premise that the strength of that system is to be measured by the number of death sentences that may be returned on the basis of such evidence. Because the word "arbitrary" is not to be found in the constitutional text, he apparently can find no reason to object to the arbitrary imposition of capital punishment.

protect the individual from overreaching by the disproportionately powerful State. Thus, the State must prove a defendant's guilt beyond a reasonable doubt. Rules of evidence are also weighted in the defendant's favor. For example, the prosecution generally cannot introduce evidence of the defendant's character to prove his propensity to commit a crime, but the defendant can introduce such reputation evidence to show his law-abiding nature. Even if balance were required or desirable, today's decision, by permitting both the defendant and the State to introduce irrelevant evidence for the sentencer's consideration without any guidance, surely does nothing to enhance parity in the sentencing process.

III.

Victim impact evidence, as used in this case, has two flaws, both related to the Eighth Amendment's command that the punishment of death may not be meted out arbitrarily or capriciously. First, aspects of the character of the victim unforeseeable to the defendant at the time of his crime are irrelevant to the defendant's "personal responsibility and moral guilt" and therefore cannot justify a death sentence. ("Proportionality requires a nexus between the punishment imposed and the defendant's blameworthiness." "The heart of the retribution rationale is that a criminal sentence must be directly related to the personal culpability of the criminal offender").

Second, the quantity and quality of victim impact evidence sufficient to turn a verdict of life in prison into a verdict of death is not defined until after the crime has been committed and therefore cannot possibly be applied consistently in different cases. The sentencer's unguided consideration of victim impact evidence thus conflicts with the principle central to our capital punishment jurisprudence that, "where discretion is afforded a sentencing body on a matter so grave as the determination of whether a human life should be taken or spared, that discretion must be suitably directed and limited so as to minimize the risk of wholly arbitrary and capricious action." *Gregg v. Georgia*. Open-ended reliance by a capital sentencer on victim impact evidence simply does not provide a "principled way to distinguish [cases], in which the death penalty is imposed, from the many cases in which it is not." *Godfrey v. Georgia* (opinion of Stewart, J.).

The majority attempts to justify the admission of victim impact evidence by arguing that "consideration of the harm caused by the crime has been an important factor in the exercise of [sentencing] discretion." This statement is misleading and inaccurate. It is misleading because it is not limited to harm that is foreseeable. It is inaccurate because it fails to differentiate between legislative determinations and judicial sentencing. It is true that an evaluation of the harm caused by different kinds of wrongful conduct is a critical aspect in legislative definitions of offenses and determinations concerning sentencing guidelines. There is a rational correlation between moral culpability and the foreseeable harm caused by criminal conduct. Moreover, in the capital sentencing area, legislative identification of the special aggravating factors that may justify the imposition of the death penalty is entirely appropriate.[2] But the majority cites no authority for the suggestion that unforeseeable and indirect harms to a victim's family are properly considered as aggravating evidence on a case-by-case basis.

The dissents in *Booth* and *Gathers* and the majority today offer only the recent decision in *Tison v. Arizona*, 481 U.S. 137 (1987), and two legislative examples to support their contention that harm to the victim has traditionally influenced sentencing discretion. *Tison* held that the death penalty may be imposed on a felon who acts with reckless disregard for human life if a death occurs in the course of the felony, even though capital punishment cannot be imposed if no one dies as a result of the crime. The first legislative example is that attempted murder and murder are classified as two different offenses subject to different punishments. The second legislative example is that a person who drives while intoxicated is guilty of vehicular homicide if his actions result in a death but is not guilty of this offense if he has the good fortune to make it home without killing anyone.

These three scenarios, however, are fully consistent with the Eighth Amendment jurisprudence reflected in *Booth* and *Gathers* and do not demonstrate that harm to the victim may be considered by a capital sentencer in the ad hoc and post hoc manner authorized by today's majority. The majority's examples demonstrate only that harm to the victim may justify enhanced punishment if the harm is both foreseeable to the defendant and clearly identified in advance of the crime by the legislature as a class of harm that should in every case result in more severe punishment.

In each scenario, the defendants could reasonably foresee that their acts might result in loss of human life. In addition, in each, the decision that the defendants should be treated differently was made prior to the crime by the legislature, the decision of which is subject to scrutiny for basic rationality. Finally, in each scenario, every defendant who causes the well-defined harm of destroying a human life will be subject to the determination that his conduct should be punished more severely. The majority's scenarios therefore provide no support for its holding, which permits a jury to sentence a defendant to death because of harm to the victim and his family that the defendant could not foresee, which was not even identified until after the crime had been committed, and which may be deemed by the jury, without any rational explanation, to justify a death sentence in one case but not in another. Unlike the rule elucidated by the scenarios on which the majority relies, the majority's holding offends the Eighth Amendment because it permits the sentencer to rely on irrelevant evidence in an arbitrary and capricious manner.

---

2. Thus, it is entirely consistent with the Eighth Amendment principles underlying *Booth* and *Gathers* to authorize the death sentence for the assassination of the President or Vice President, a Congressman, Cabinet official, Supreme Court Justice, or the head of an executive department, or the murder of a policeman on active duty. Such statutory provisions give the potential offender notice of the special consequences of his crime and ensure that the legislatively determined punishment will be applied consistently to all defendants.

The majority's argument that "the sentencing authority has always been free to consider a wide range of *relevant* material," (emphasis added), thus cannot justify consideration of victim impact evidence that is *irrelevant* because it details harms that the defendant could not have foreseen. Nor does the majority's citation of *Gregg v. Georgia* concerning the "wide scope of evidence and argument allowed at presentence hearings" support today's holding. The *Gregg* joint opinion endorsed the sentencer's consideration of a wide range of evidence "so long as the evidence introduced and the arguments made at the presentence hearing do not prejudice a defendant." Irrelevant victim impact evidence that distracts the sentencer from the proper focus of sentencing and encourages reliance on emotion and other arbitrary factors necessarily prejudices the defendant.

The majority's apparent inability to understand this fact is highlighted by its misunderstanding of Justice Powell's argument in *Booth* that admission of victim impact evidence is undesirable because it risks shifting the focus of the sentencing hearing away from the defendant and the circumstances of the crime and creating a "'mini-trial' on the victim's character." *Booth* found this risk insupportable not, as today's majority suggests, because it creates a "tactical" "dilemma" for the defendant, but because it allows the possibility that the jury will be so distracted by prejudicial and irrelevant considerations that it will base its life-or-death decision on whim or caprice.

IV.

The majority thus does far more than validate a State's judgment that "the jury should see 'a quick glimpse of the life petitioner chose to extinguish.'" Instead, it allows a jury to hold a defendant responsible for a whole array of harms that he could not foresee and for which he is therefore not blameworthy. Justice SOUTER argues that these harms are sufficiently foreseeable to hold the defendant accountable because "every defendant knows, if endowed with the mental competence for criminal responsibility, that the life he will take by his homicidal behavior is that of a unique person, like himself, and that the person to be killed probably has close associates, 'survivors,' who will suffer harms and deprivations from the victim's death." (SOUTER, J., concurring). But every juror and trial judge knows this much as well. Evidence about who those survivors are and what harms and deprivations they have suffered is therefore not necessary to apprise the sentencer of any information that was actually foreseeable to the defendant. Its only function can be to "divert the jury's attention away from the defendant's background and record, and the circumstances of the crime."

Arguing in the alternative, Justice SOUTER correctly points out that victim impact evidence will sometimes come to the attention of the jury during the guilt phase of the trial. He reasons that the ideal of basing sentencing determinations entirely on the moral culpability of the defendant is therefore unattainable unless a different jury is empaneled for the sentencing hearing. Thus, to justify overruling *Booth*, he assumes that the decision must otherwise be extended far beyond its actual holding.

Justice SOUTER's assumption is entirely unwarranted. For as long as the contours of relevance at sentencing hearings have been limited to evidence concerning the character of the offense and the character of the offender, the law has also recognized that evidence that is admissible for a proper purpose may not be excluded because it is inadmissible for other purposes and may indirectly prejudice the jury. In the case before us today, much of what might be characterized as victim impact evidence was properly admitted during the guilt phase of the trial and, given the horrible character of this crime, may have been sufficient to justify the Tennessee Supreme Court's conclusion that the error was harmless because the jury would necessarily have imposed the death sentence even absent the error. The fact that a good deal of such evidence is routinely and properly brought to the attention of the jury merely indicates that the rule of *Booth* may not affect the outcome of many cases.

In reaching our decision today, however, we should not be concerned with the cases in which victim impact evidence will not make a difference. We should be concerned instead with the cases in which it will make a difference. In those cases, defendants will be sentenced arbitrarily to death on the basis of evidence that would not otherwise be admissible because it is irrelevant to the defendants' moral culpability. The Constitution's proscription against the arbitrary imposition of the death penalty must necessarily proscribe the admission of evidence that serves no purpose other than to result in such arbitrary sentences.

V.

The notion that the inability to produce an ideal system of justice in which every punishment is precisely married to the defendant's blameworthiness somehow justifies a rule that completely divorces some capital sentencing determinations from moral culpability is incomprehensible to me. Also incomprehensible is the argument that such a rule is required for the jury to take into account that each murder victim is a "unique" human being. The fact that each of us is unique is a proposition so obvious that it surely requires no evidentiary support. What is not obvious, however, is the way in which the character or reputation in one case may differ from that of other possible victims. Evidence offered to prove such differences can only be intended to identify some victims as more worthy of protection than others. Such proof risks decisions based on the same invidious motives as a prosecutor's decision to seek the death penalty if a victim is white but to accept a plea bargain if the victim is black. *See McCleskey v. Kemp*, 481 U.S. 279 (1987) (Stevens, J., dissenting).

Given the current popularity of capital punishment in a crime-ridden society, the political appeal of arguments that assume that increasing the severity of sentences is the best cure for the cancer of crime, and the political strength of the "victims' rights" movement, I recognize that today's decision will be greeted with enthusiasm by a large number of concerned and thoughtful citizens. The great tragedy of the decision, however, is the danger that the "hydraulic pressure" of public opinion that Justice Holmes once described—and that properly influences the deliberations of democratic legislatures—has played a role not only in the Court's decision to hear this case, and in its decision to reach the constitutional question without pausing to consider affirming on the basis of the Tennessee Supreme Court's rationale, but even in its resolution of the constitutional issue involved. Today is a sad day for a great institution.

Questions and Notes

1. *Booth* forbade three types of evidence to come in: (1) evidence of the victim's character, (2) evidence of the loss suffered by the victim's friends and family, and (3) evidence of punishment thought appropriate by the victim's surviving relatives. *Payne* permitted the first two types of evidence to come in, but did not have occasion to reconsider the third.

2. Assume that you are a state legislator considering a bill to allow any of these types of evidence in. Which, if any, will you support? Why? (Note: *Payne* doesn't compel the use of victim impact statements; it only permits them.)

3. Is the issue in *Payne* and *Booth* whether "harm" can count in assessing the death penalty? Or is the issue: "What can count as harm"?

4. Should the defendant be able to put the character of the victim on trial? Suppose it turns out that the murdered clerk at a convenience store regularly terrorized his family (*see, e.g., State v. Norman, supra*, Chapter 6). Should the defendant be able to introduce evidence that by killing J.T. Norman (or somebody like him), he saved the victim's family a lot of grief? Why? Why not?

5. Does equity demand that if Payne's good character is relevant to his defense, the good character of the Christophers should be relevant to the prosecution? Or is that mixing apples and oranges?

6. Why do you suppose the Court compels unlimited use of mitigating circumstances, when it so closely scrutinizes aggravating ones?

Problem

In 1958, respondent Raymond Wallace Shuman was convicted in a Nevada state court of first degree murder for the shooting death of a truck driver during a roadside robbery. He was sentenced to life imprisonment without the possibility of parole under § 200.030 of Nev. Rev. Stat., which at that time provided the jury with sentencing options of the death penalty or of life imprisonment with or without the possibility of parole. In 1975, while serving his life sentence, Shuman was convicted of capital murder for the killing of a fellow inmate. Pursuant to the revised version of § 200.030 then in effect, Shuman's conviction mandated that he be sentenced to death. The Nevada Supreme Court affirmed Shuman's conviction and the imposition of the death penalty. It specifically rejected respondent's claims of error, including his objection that the mandatory imposition of the death sentence violated his rights under the Eighth and Fourteenth Amendments.

How should the Supreme Court resolve this case? Why? *See Sumner v. Shuman*, 483 U.S. 66 (1987).

Problem

Respondent Albert Brown was found guilty by a jury of forcible rape and first degree murder in the death of 15-year-old Susan J. At the penalty phase, the State presented evidence that respondent had raped another young girl some years prior to his attack on Susan J. Respondent presented the testimony of several family members, who recounted respondent's peaceful nature and expressed disbelief that respondent was capable of such a brutal crime. Respondent also presented the testimony of a psychiatrist, who stated that Brown killed his victim because of his shame and fear over sexual dysfunction. Brown himself testified, stating that he was ashamed of his prior criminal conduct and asking for mercy from the jury.

California Penal Code § 190.3 provides that capital defendants may introduce at the penalty phase any evidence "as to any matter relevant to . . . mitigation . . . including, but not limited to, the nature and circumstances of the present offense, . . . and the defendant's character, background, history, mental condition and physical condition." The trial court instructed the jury to consider the aggravating and mitigating circumstances and to weigh them in determining the appropriate penalty. But the court cautioned the jury that it "must not be swayed by mere sentiment, conjecture, sympathy, passion, prejudice, public opinion or public feeling." Respondent was sentenced to death.

On automatic appeal, the Supreme Court of California reversed the sentence of death. Over two dissents on this point, the majority opinion found that the instruction at issue here violates the Federal Constitution: "'Federal constitutional law forbids an instruction which denies a capital defendant the right to have the jury consider any "sympathy factor" raised by the evidence when determining the appropriate penalty. . . . the court ruled that the instruction "is calculated to divert the jury from its constitutional duty to consider 'any [sympathetic] aspect of the defendant's character or record,' whether or not related to the offense for which he is on trial, in deciding the appropriate penalty." We granted certiorari to resolve whether such an instruction violates the United States Constitution.

Assume that the Court is evenly divided on this question, and that you are a law clerk for a Justice who is uncertain as to how to vote. Prepare a memorandum for the Justice indicating all of the arguments on both sides, together with a reasoned opinion as to how the Justice should vote. For the Supreme Court's solution, see *California v. Brown*, 479 U.S. 538 (1987).

Problem

You are an assistant to a legislator who is contemplating introducing a bill to abolish capital punishment. Before doing so, however, she would like a detailed analysis of the advantages and disadvantages of such a bill, along with your reasoned analysis of whether she should go forward with it. What factors should she balance, and would you recommend that she introduce her bill? Why?

Chapter 16

Burden of Proof and Presumptions

A. Burden of Proof

Although nominally a procedural issue, burden of proof says a lot about how we view substantive criminal law. We start with *Winship*, which explains why the state must prove the defendant guilty beyond a reasonable doubt in the first place.

In re Winship

397 U.S. 358 (1970)

Mr. Justice BRENNAN delivered the opinion of the Court.

This case presents the single, narrow question whether proof beyond a reasonable doubt is among the "essentials of due process and fair treatment" required during the adjudicatory stage when a juvenile is charged with an act which would constitute a crime if committed by an adult.

Section 712 of the New York Family Court Act defines a juvenile delinquent as "a person over seven and less than sixteen years of age who does any act which, if done by an adult, would constitute a crime." During a 1967 adjudicatory hearing, conducted pursuant to §742 of the Act, a judge in New York Family Court found that appellant, then a 12-year—old boy, had entered a locker and stolen $112 from a woman's pocketbook. The petition which charged appellant with delinquency alleged that his act, "if done by an adult, would constitute the crime or crimes of Larceny." The judge acknowledged that the proof might not establish guilt beyond a reasonable doubt, but rejected appellant's contention that such proof was required by the Fourteenth Amendment. The judge relied instead on §744(b) of the New York Family Court Act which provides that "(a)ny determination at the conclusion of (an adjudicatory) hearing that a (juvenile) did an act or acts must be based on a preponderance of the evidence."

The requirement that guilt of a criminal charge be established by proof beyond a reasonable doubt dates at least from our early years as a Nation. The "demand for a higher degree of persuasion in criminal cases was recurrently expressed from ancient times, (though) its crystallization into the formula 'beyond a reasonable doubt' seems to have occurred as late as 1798. It is now accepted in common law jurisdictions as the measure of persuasion by which the prosecution must convince the trier of all the essential elements of guilt." Although virtually unanimous adherence to the reasonable-doubt standard in common-law jurisdictions may not conclusively establish it as a requirement of due process, such adherence does "reflect a profound judgment about the way in which law should be enforced and justice administered."

The reasonable-doubt standard plays a vital role in the American scheme of criminal procedure. It is a prime instrument for reducing the risk of convictions resting on factual error. The standard provides concrete substance for the presumption of innocence—that bedrock "axiomatic and elementary" principle whose "enforcement lies at the foundation of the administration of our criminal law." *Coffin v. United States, supra*, 156 U.S. at 453, 15 S. Ct. at 403. As the dissenters in the New York Court of Appeals observed, and we agree, "a person accused of a crime . . . would be at a severe disadvantage, a disadvantage amounting to a lack of fundamental fairness, if he could be adjudged guilty and imprisoned for years on the strength of the same evidence as would suffice in a civil case."

The requirement of proof beyond a reasonable doubt has this vital role in our criminal procedure for cogent reasons. The accused during a criminal prosecution has at stake interest of immense importance, both because of the possibility that he may lose his liberty upon conviction and because of the certainty that he would be stigmatized by the conviction. Accordingly, a society that values the good name and freedom of every individual should not condemn a man for commission of a crime when there is reasonable doubt about his guilt. As we said in *Speiser v. Randall, supra*, 357 U.S. at 525–526; "There is always in litigation a margin of error, representing error in factfinding, which both parties must take into account. Where one party has at stake an interest of transcending value—as a criminal defendant his liberty—this margin of error is reduced as to him by the process of placing on the other party the burden of . . . persuading the factfinder at the conclusion of the trial of his guilt beyond a reasonable doubt. Due process commands that no man shall lose his liberty unless the Government has borne the burden of . . . convincing the factfinder of his guilt." To this end, the reasonable-doubt standard is indispensable, for it "impresses on the trier of fact the necessity of reaching a subjective state of certitude of the facts in issue."

Moreover, use of the reasonable-doubt standard is indispensable to command the respect and confidence of the community in applications of the criminal law. It is critical that the moral force of the criminal law not be diluted by a standard of proof that leaves people in doubt whether innocent men are being condemned. It is also important in our free society that every individual going about his ordinary affairs have confidence that his government cannot adjudge him guilty of a criminal offense without convincing a proper factfinder of his guilt with utmost certainty.

Lest there remain any doubt about the constitutional stature of the reasonable-doubt standard, we explicitly hold that the Due Process Clause protects the accused against conviction except upon proof beyond a reasonable doubt of every fact necessary to constitute the crime with which he is charged.

Reversed.

Mr. Justice Harlan, concurring.

Professor Wigmore, in discussing the various attempts by courts to define how convinced one must be to be convinced beyond a reasonable doubt, wryly observed: "The truth is that no one has yet invented or discovered a mode of measurement for the intensity of human belief. Hence there can be yet no successful method of communicating intelligibly . . . a sound method of self analysis for one's belief," 9 J. Wigmore, Evidence 325 (3d ed. 1940).

Notwithstanding Professor Wigmore's skepticism, we have before us a case where the choice of the standard of proof has made a difference: the juvenile court judge below forthrightly acknowledged that he believed by a preponderance of the evidence, but was not convinced beyond a reasonable doubt, that appellant stole $112 from the complainant's pocketbook. Moreover, even though the labels used for alternative standards of proof are vague and not a very sure guide to decisionmaking, the choice of the standard for a particular variety of adjudication does, I think, reflect a very fundamental assessment of the comparative social costs of erroneous factual determinations.

To explain why I think this so, I begin by stating two propositions, neither of which I believe can be fairly disputed. First, in a judicial proceeding in which there is a dispute about the facts of some earlier event, the factfinder cannot acquire unassailably accurate knowledge of what happened. Instead, all the factfinder can acquire is a belief of what probably happened. The intensity of this belief—the degree to which a factfinder is convinced that a given act actually occurred—can, of course, vary. In this regard, a standard of proof represents an attempt to instruct the factfinder concerning the degree of confidence our society thinks he should have in the correctness of factual conclusions for a particular type of adjudication. Although the phrases "preponderance of the evidence" and "proof beyond a reasonable doubt" are quantitatively imprecise, they do communicate to the finder of fact different notions concerning the degree of confidence he is expected to have in the correctness of his factual conclusions.

A second proposition, which is really nothing more than a corollary of the first, is that the trier of fact will sometimes, despite his best efforts, be wrong in his factual conclusions. In a lawsuit between two parties, a factual error can make a difference in one of two ways. First, it can result in a judgment in favor of the plaintiff when the true facts warrant a judgment for the defendant. The analogue in a criminal case would be the conviction of an innocent man. On the other hand, an erroneous factual determination can result in a judgment for the defendant when the true facts justify a judgment in plaintiff's favor. The criminal analogue would be the acquittal of a guilty man.

The standard of proof influences the relative frequency of these two types of erroneous outcomes. If, for example, the standard of proof for a criminal trial were a preponderance of the evidence rather than proof beyond a reasonable doubt, there would be a smaller risk of factual errors that result in freeing guilty persons, but a far greater risk of factual errors that result in convicting the innocent. Because the standard of proof affects the comparative frequency of these two types of erroneous outcomes, the choice of the standard to be applied in a particular kind of litigation should, in a rational world, reflect an assessment of the comparative social disutility of each.

When one makes such an assessment, the reason for different standards of proof in civil as opposed to criminal litigation becomes apparent. In a civil suit between two private parties for money damages, for example, we view it as no more serious in general for there to be an erroneous verdict in the defendant's favor than for there to be an erroneous verdict in the plaintiff's favor. A preponderance of the evidence standard therefore seems peculiarly appropriate for, as explained most sensibly, it simply requires the trier of fact "to believe that the existence of a fact is more probable than its nonexistence before (he) may find in favor of the party who has the burden to persuade the (judge) of the fact's existence."

In a criminal case, on the other hand, we do not view the social disutility of convicting an innocent man as equivalent to the disutility of acquitting someone who is guilty. In this context, I view the requirement of proof beyond a reasonable doubt in a criminal case as bottomed on a fundamental value determination of our society that it is far worse to convict an innocent man than to let a guilty man go free. It is only because of the nearly complete and long-standing acceptance of the reasonable-doubt standard by the States in criminal trials that the Court has not before today had to hold explicitly that due process, as an expression of fundamental procedural fairness, requires a more stringent standard for criminal trials than for ordinary civil litigation.

Questions and Notes

1. What do we mean by the "presumption of innocence"? Aren't most people who have been indicted and brought to trial probably guilty?

2. Isn't requiring proof beyond a reasonable doubt calculated to maximize error in that it requires a jury that believes the defendant to be probably guilty to return a verdict of not guilty?

3. Who benefits from the beyond a reasonable doubt rule? The accused? Society? The ordinary person who has never committed a crime? How might the ordinary person benefit?

4. Once one determines that the state must prove every element of a crime beyond a reasonable doubt, the question becomes: "What constitutes an element of a crime"? We will consider how the Court assesses that question in conjunction with *Patterson* and *Martin* in Section B, *infra*.

5. In *Victor*, the Court explored what the phrase "beyond a reasonable doubt" means.

Victor v. Nebraska

511 U.S. 1 (1994)

Justice O'CONNOR delivered the opinion of the Court.[1]

The government must prove beyond a reasonable doubt every element of a charged offense. *In re Winship*. Although this standard is an ancient and honored aspect of our criminal justice system, it defies easy explication. In these cases, we consider the constitutionality of two attempts to define "reasonable doubt."

I.

The beyond a reasonable doubt standard is a requirement of due process, but the Constitution neither prohibits trial courts from defining reasonable doubt nor requires them to do so as a matter of course. Indeed, so long as the court instructs the jury on the necessity that the defendant's guilt be proved beyond a reasonable doubt, the Constitution does not require that any particular form of words be used in advising the jury of the government's burden of proof. Rather, "taken as a whole, the instructions [must] correctly conve[y] the concept of reasonable doubt to the jury."

In only one case have we held that a definition of reasonable doubt violated the Due Process Clause. *Cage v. Louisiana*, 498 U.S. 39 (1990) (*per curiam*). There, the jurors were told:

> "'[A reasonable doubt] is one that is founded upon a real tangible substantial basis and not upon mere caprice and conjecture. *It must be such doubt as would give rise to a grave uncertainty*, raised in your mind by reasons of the unsatisfactory character of the evidence or lack thereof. A reasonable doubt is not a mere possible doubt. *It is an actual substantial doubt*. It is a doubt that a reasonable man can seriously entertain. What is required is not an absolute or mathematical certainty, but a *moral certainty*.'" (Emphasis added by this Court in *Cage*).

We held that the highlighted portions of the instruction rendered it unconstitutional:

> "It is plain to us that the words 'substantial' and 'grave,' as they are commonly understood, suggest a higher degree of doubt than is required for acquittal under the reasonable doubt standard. When those statements are then considered with the reference to 'moral certainty,' rather than evidentiary certainty, it becomes clear that a reasonable juror could have interpreted the instruction to allow a finding of guilt based on a degree of proof below that required by the Due Process Clause."

---

1. Justices BLACKMUN and SOUTER join only Part II of this opinion. Justice GINSBURG joins only Parts II, III-B, and IV.

In a subsequent case, we made clear that the proper inquiry is not whether the instruction "could have" been applied in an unconstitutional manner, but whether there is a reasonable likelihood that the jury *did* so apply it. *Estelle v. McGuire*, 502 U.S. 62 (1991). The constitutional question in the present cases, therefore, is whether there is a reasonable likelihood that the jury understood the instructions to allow conviction based on proof insufficient to meet the *Winship* standard. Although other courts have held that instructions similar to those given at petitioners' trials violate the Due Process Clause, both the Nebraska and the California Supreme Courts held that the instructions were constitutional. We granted certiorari and now affirm both judgments.

II.

On October 14, 1984, petitioner Sandoval shot three men, two of them fatally, in a gang-related incident in Los Angeles. About two weeks later, he entered the home of a man who had given information to the police about the murders and shot him dead; Sandoval then killed the man's wife because she had seen him murder her husband. Sandoval was convicted on four counts of first-degree murder. The jury found that Sandoval personally used a firearm in the commission of each offense and found the special circumstance of multiple murder. He was sentenced to death for murdering the woman and to life in prison without possibility of parole for the other three murders. The California Supreme Court affirmed the convictions and sentences.

The jury in Sandoval's case was given the following instruction on the government's burden of proof:

> "A defendant in a criminal action is presumed to be innocent until the contrary is proved, and in case of a reasonable doubt whether his guilt is satisfactorily shown, he is entitled to a verdict of not guilty. This presumption places upon the State the burden of proving him guilty beyond a reasonable doubt.

> "Reasonable doubt is defined as follows: It is *not a mere possible doubt*; because everything relating to human affairs, and *depending on moral evidence*, is open to some possible or imaginary doubt. It is that state of the case which, after the entire comparison and consideration of all the evidence, leaves the minds of the jurors in that condition that they cannot say they feel an abiding conviction, *to a moral certainty*, of the truth of the charge." (Emphasis added.)

The California Supreme Court rejected Sandoval's claim that the instruction, particularly the highlighted passages, violated the Due Process Clause.

The instruction given in Sandoval's case has its genesis in a charge given by Chief Justice Shaw of the Massachusetts Supreme Judicial Court more than a century ago:

> "[W]hat is reasonable doubt? It is a term often used, probably pretty well understood, but not easily defined. It is not mere possible doubt; because

every thing relating to human affairs, and depending on moral evidence, is open to some possible or imaginary doubt. It is that state of the case, which, after the entire comparison and consideration of all the evidence, leaves the minds of jurors in that condition that they cannot say they feel an abiding conviction, to a moral certainty, of the truth of the charge. The burden of proof is upon the prosecutor. All the presumptions of law independent of evidence are in favor of innocence; and every person is presumed to be innocent until he is proved guilty. If upon such proof there is reasonable doubt remaining, the accused is entitled to the benefit of it by an acquittal. For it is not sufficient to establish a probability, though a strong one arising from the doctrine of chances, that the fact charged is more likely to be true than the contrary; but the evidence must establish the truth of the fact to a reasonable and moral certainty; a certainty that convinces and directs the understanding, and satisfies the reason and judgment, of those who are bound to act conscientiously upon it. This we take to be proof beyond reasonable doubt." *Commonwealth v. Webster*, 59 Mass. 295, 320 (1850).

The *Webster* charge is representative of the time when "American courts began applying [the beyond a reasonable doubt standard] in its modern form in criminal cases." In *People v. Strong*, 30 Cal. 151, 155 (1866), the California Supreme Court characterized the *Webster* instruction as "probably the most satisfactory definition ever given to the words 'reasonable doubt' in any case known to criminal jurisprudence." In *People v. Paulsell*, 115 Cal. 6, 12, 46 P. 734 (1896), the court cautioned state trial judges against departing from that formulation. And in 1927, the state legislature adopted the bulk of the *Webster* instruction as a statutory definition of reasonable doubt. Indeed, the California Legislature has directed that "the court may read to the jury section 1096 of this code, and no further instruction on the subject of the presumption of innocence or defining reasonable doubt need be given." The statutory instruction was given in Sandoval's case.

The California instruction was criticized in *People v. Brigham*, 25 Cal.3d 283, 292–316, 599 P.2d 100, 106–121 (1979) (Mosk, J., concurring). Justice Mosk apparently did not think the instruction was unconstitutional, but he "urge[d] the Legislature to reconsider its codification." The California Assembly and Senate responded by requesting the committee on jury instructions of the Los Angeles Superior Court "to study alternatives to the definition of 'reasonable doubt' set forth in Section 1096 of the Penal Code, and to report its findings and recommendations to the Legislature." The committee recommended that the legislature retain the statutory definition unmodified, and § 1096 has not been changed.

A.

Sandoval's primary objection is to the use of the phrases "moral evidence" and "moral certainty" in the instruction. As noted, this part of the charge was lifted verbatim from Chief Justice Shaw's *Webster* decision; some understanding of the historical context in which that instruction was written is accordingly helpful in evaluating its continuing validity.

By the beginning of the Republic, lawyers had borrowed the concept of "moral evidence" from the philosophers and historians of the 17th and 18th centuries. James Wilson, who was instrumental in framing the Constitution and who served as one of the original Members of this Court, explained in a 1790 lecture on law that "evidence . . . is divided into two species—demonstrative and moral."

"Demonstrative evidence has for its subject abstract and necessary truths, or the unchangeable relations of ideas. Moral evidence has for its subject the real but contingent truths and connections, which take place among things actually existing. . . .

"In moral evidence, there not only may be, but there generally is, contrariety of proofs: in demonstrative evidence, no such contrariety can take place. . . . [T]o suppose that two contrary demonstrations can exist, is to suppose that the same proposition is both true and false: which is manifestly absurd. With regard to moral evidence, there is, for the most part, real evidence on both sides. On both sides, contrary presumptions, contrary testimonies, contrary experiences must be balanced."

A leading 19th century treatise observed that "[m]atters of fact are proved by *moral evidence* alone; . . . [i]n the ordinary affairs of life, we do not require demonstrative evidence, . . . and to insist upon it would be unreasonable and absurd." 1 S. GREENLEAF, LAW OF EVIDENCE 3–4 (13th ed. 1876).

The phrase "moral certainty" shares an epistemological pedigree with moral evidence. Moral certainty was the highest degree of certitude based on such evidence. In his 1790 lecture, James Wilson observed:

"In a series of moral evidence, the inference drawn in the several steps is not necessary; nor is it impossible that the premises should be true, while the conclusion drawn from them is false.

". . . In moral evidence, we rise, by an insensible gradation, from possibility to probability, and from probability to the highest degree of moral certainty."

At least one early treatise explicitly equated moral certainty with proof beyond a reasonable doubt:

"Evidence which satisfies the minds of the jury of the truth of the fact in dispute, to the entire exclusion of every reasonable doubt, constitutes full proof of the fact. . . .

"Even the most direct evidence can produce nothing more than such a high degree of probability as amounts to moral certainty. From the highest degree it may decline, by an infinite number of gradations, until it produce in the mind nothing more than a mere preponderance of assent in favour of the particular fact." T. STARKIE, LAW OF EVIDENCE 478 (2d ed. 1833).

Thus, when Chief Justice Shaw penned the *Webster* instruction in 1850, moral certainty meant a state of subjective certitude about some event or occurrence. As the Massachusetts Supreme Judicial Court subsequently explained:

"Proof 'beyond a reasonable doubt' . . . is proof 'to a moral certainty,' as distinguished from an absolute certainty. As applied to a judicial trial for crime, the two phrases are synonymous and equivalent; each has been used by eminent judges to explain the other; and each signifies such proof as satisfies the judgment and consciences of the jury, as reasonable men, and applying their reason to the evidence before them, that the crime charged has been committed by the defendant, and so satisfies them as to leave no other reasonable conclusion possible." *Commonwealth v. Costley*, 118 Mass. 1, 24 (1875).

Indeed, we have said that "[p]roof to a 'moral certainty' is an equivalent phrase with 'beyond a reasonable doubt.'" *Fidelity Mut. Life Assn. v. Mettler*, 185 U.S. 308, 317 (1902).

We recognize that the phrase "moral evidence" is not a mainstay of the modern lexicon, though we do not think it means anything different today than it did in the 19th century. The few contemporary dictionaries that define moral evidence do so consistently with its original meaning.

Moreover, the instruction itself gives a definition of the phrase. The jury was told that "everything relating to human affairs, and depending on moral evidence, is open to some possible or imaginary doubt"—in other words, that absolute certainty is unattainable in matters relating to human affairs. Moral evidence, in this sentence, can only mean empirical evidence offered to prove such matters—the proof introduced at trial.

This conclusion is reinforced by other instructions given in Sandoval's case. The judge informed the jurors that their duty was "to determine the facts of the case from the evidence received in the trial and not from any other source." The judge continued: "Evidence consists of testimony of witnesses, writings, material objects, or anything presented to the senses and offered to prove the existence or non-existence of a fact." The judge also told the jurors that "you must not be influenced by pity for a defendant or by prejudice against him," and that "[y]ou must not be swayed by mere sentiment, conjecture, sympathy, passion, prejudice, public opinion or public feeling." These instructions correctly pointed the jurors' attention to the facts of the case before them, not (as Sandoval contends) the ethics or morality of Sandoval's criminal acts. Accordingly, we find the reference to moral evidence unproblematic.

We are somewhat more concerned with Sandoval's argument that the phrase "moral certainty" has lost its historical meaning, and that a modern jury would understand it to allow conviction on proof that does not meet the beyond a reasonable doubt standard. Words and phrases can change meaning over time: A passage generally understood in 1850 may be incomprehensible or confusing to a modern juror. And although some contemporary dictionaries contain definitions of moral certainty similar to the 19th century understanding of the phrase, *see* WEBSTER'S THIRD NEW INTERNATIONAL DICTIONARY 1468 (1981) ("virtual rather than actual, immediate, or completely demonstrable"); 9 OXFORD ENGLISH DICTIONARY, *supra*, at 1070 ("a degree of probability so great as to admit of no reasonable doubt"), we are willing to accept Sandoval's premise that "moral certainty," standing alone, might not be recognized by modern jurors as a synonym for "proof beyond a reasonable doubt." But it does not necessarily follow that the California instruction is unconstitutional.

Sandoval first argues that moral certainty would be understood by modern jurors to mean a standard of proof lower than beyond a reasonable doubt. In support of this proposition, Sandoval points to contemporary dictionaries that define moral certainty in terms of probability. *E.g.*, WEBSTER'S NEW TWENTIETH CENTURY DICTIONARY, *supra*, at 1168 ("based on strong probability"); RANDOM HOUSE DICTIONARY OF THE ENGLISH LANGUAGE 1249 (2d ed. 1983) ("resting upon convincing grounds of probability"). But the beyond a reasonable doubt standard is itself probabilistic. "[I]n a judicial proceeding in which there is a dispute about the facts of some earlier event, the factfinder cannot acquire unassailably accurate knowledge of what happened. Instead, all the factfinder can acquire is a belief of what *probably* happened." *In re Winship* (Harlan, J., concurring) (emphasis in original). The problem is not that moral certainty may be understood in terms of probability, but that a jury might understand the phrase to mean something less than the very high level of probability required by the Constitution in criminal cases.

Although in this respect moral certainty is ambiguous in the abstract, the rest of the instruction given in Sandoval's case lends content to the phrase. The jurors were told that they must have "an abiding conviction, to a moral certainty, of the truth of the charge." An instruction cast in terms of an abiding conviction as to guilt, without reference to moral certainty, correctly states the government's burden of proof. Accordingly, we reject Sandoval's contention that the moral certainty element of the California instruction invited the jury to convict him on proof below that required by the Due Process Clause.

Sandoval's second argument is a variant of the first. Accepting that the instruction requires a high level of confidence in the defendant's guilt, Sandoval argues that a juror might be convinced to a moral certainty that the defendant is guilty even though the government has failed to *prove* his guilt beyond a reasonable doubt. A definition of moral certainty in a widely used modern dictionary lends support to this argument, *see* AMERICAN HERITAGE DICTIONARY 1173 (3d ed. 1992) ("Based on strong likelihood or firm conviction, rather than on the actual evidence"), and we do not gainsay its force. As we have noted, "[t]he constitutional standard recognized in the *Winship* case was expressly phrased as one that protects an accused against a conviction except on 'proof beyond a reasonable doubt.'" Indeed, in *Cage* we contrasted "moral certainty" with "evidentiary certainty."

But the moral certainty language cannot be sequestered from its surroundings. In the *Cage* instruction, the jurors were simply told that they had to be morally certain of the defendant's guilt; there was nothing else in the instruction to lend meaning to the phrase. Not so here. The jury in Sandoval's case was told that a reasonable doubt is "that state of the case which, *after the entire comparison and consideration of all the evidence,* leaves the minds of the jurors in that condition that they cannot say they feel an abiding conviction, to a moral certainty, of the truth of the charge." The instruction thus explicitly told the jurors that their conclusion had to be based on the evidence in the case. Other instructions reinforced this message. The jury was told "to determine the facts of the case from the evidence received in the trial and not from any other source." The judge continued that "you must not be influenced by pity for a defendant or by prejudice against him. . . . You must not be swayed by mere sentiment, conjecture, sympathy, passion, prejudice, public opinion or public feeling." Accordingly, there is no reasonable likelihood that the jury would have understood moral certainty to be disassociated from the evidence in the case.

We do not think it reasonably likely that the jury understood the words "moral certainty" either as suggesting a standard of proof lower than due process requires or as allowing conviction on factors other than the government's proof. At the same time, however, we do not condone the use of the phrase. As modern dictionary definitions of moral certainty attest, the common meaning of the phrase has changed since it was used in the *Webster* instruction, and it may continue to do so to the point that it conflicts with the *Winship* standard. Indeed, the definitions of reasonable doubt most widely used in the federal courts do not contain any reference to moral certainty. But we have no supervisory power over the state courts, and in the context of the instructions as a whole we cannot say that the use of the phrase rendered the instruction given in Sandoval's case unconstitutional.

B.

Finally, Sandoval objects to the portion of the charge in which the judge instructed the jury that a reasonable doubt is "not a mere possible doubt." The *Cage* instruction included an almost identical reference to "not a mere possible doubt," but we did not intimate that there was anything wrong with that part of the charge. That is because "[a] 'reasonable doubt,' at a minimum, is one based upon 'reason.'" A fanciful doubt is not a reasonable doubt. As Sandoval's defense attorney told the jury: "Anything can be possible. . . . [A] planet could be made out of blue cheese. But that's really not in the realm of what we're talking about." That this is the sense in which the instruction uses "possible" is made clear from the final phrase of the sentence, which notes that everything "is open to some possible or imaginary doubt." We therefore reject Sandoval's challenge to this portion of the instruction as well.

III.

On December 26, 1987, petitioner Victor went to the Omaha home of an 82-year-old woman for whom he occasionally did gardening work. Once inside, he beat her with a pipe and cut her throat with a knife, killing her. Victor was convicted of first degree murder. A three-judge panel found the statutory aggravating circumstances that Victor had previously been convicted of murder and that the murder in this case was especially heinous, atrocious, and cruel. Finding none of the statutory mitigating circumstances, the panel sentenced Victor to death. The Nebraska Supreme Court affirmed the conviction and sentence.

At Victor's trial, the judge instructed the jury that "[t]he burden is always on the State to prove beyond a reasonable doubt all of the material elements of the crime charged, and this burden never shifts." The charge continued:

> "'Reasonable doubt' is such a doubt as would cause a reasonable and prudent person, in one of the graver and more important transactions of life, to pause and hesitate before taking the represented facts as true and relying and acting thereon. It is such a doubt as will not permit you, after full, fair, and impartial consideration of all the evidence, to have an abiding conviction, *to a moral certainty*, of the guilt of the accused. At the same time, absolute or mathematical certainty is not required. You may be convinced of the truth of a fact beyond a reasonable doubt and yet be fully aware that possibly you may be mistaken. You may find an accused guilty upon the *strong probabilities of the case*, provided such probabilities are strong enough to exclude any doubt of his guilt that is reasonable. A reasonable doubt is an *actual and substantial doubt* reasonably arising from the evidence, from the facts or circumstances shown by the evidence, or from the lack of evidence on the part of the State, as distinguished from a doubt arising from mere possibility, from bare imagination, or from fanciful conjecture." (Emphasis added.)

On state postconviction review, the Nebraska Supreme Court rejected Victor's contention that the instruction, particularly the emphasized phrases, violated the Due Process Clause.

A.

Victor's primary argument is that equating a reasonable doubt with a "substantial doubt" overstated the degree of doubt necessary for acquittal. We agree that this construction is somewhat problematic. On the one hand, "substantial" means "not seeming or imaginary"; on the other, it means "that specified to a large degree." Webster's Third New International Dictionary, at 2280. The former is unexceptionable, as it informs the jury only that a reasonable doubt is something more than a speculative one; but the latter could imply a doubt greater than required for acquittal under *Winship*. Any ambiguity, however, is removed by reading the phrase in the context of the sentence in which it appears: "A reasonable doubt is an actual and substantial doubt ... *as distinguished from* a doubt arising from mere possibility, from bare imagination, or from fanciful conjecture." (Emphasis added.)

This explicit distinction between a substantial doubt and a fanciful conjecture was not present in the *Cage* instruction. We did say in that case that "the words 'substantial' and 'grave,' as they are commonly understood, suggest a higher degree of doubt than is required for acquittal under the reasonable doubt standard." But we did not hold that the reference to substantial doubt alone was sufficient to render the instruction unconstitutional. *Cf. Taylor v. Kentucky,* 436 U.S. at 488 (defining reasonable doubt as a substantial doubt, "though perhaps *not in itself reversible error,* often has been criticized as confusing") (emphasis added). Rather, we were concerned that the jury would interpret the term "substantial doubt" in parallel with the preceding reference to "grave uncertainty," leading to an overstatement of the doubt necessary to acquit. In the instruction given in Victor's case, the context makes clear that "substantial" is used in the sense of existence rather than magnitude of the doubt, so the same concern is not present.

In any event, the instruction provided an alternative definition of reasonable doubt: a doubt that would cause a reasonable person to hesitate to act. This is a formulation we have repeatedly approved, *Holland v. United States,* 348 U.S. at 140; *cf. Hopt v. Utah,* 120 U.S. at 439–441, and to the extent the word "substantial" denotes the quantum of doubt necessary for acquittal, the hesitate to act standard gives a common sense benchmark for just how substantial such a doubt must be. We therefore do not think it reasonably likely that the jury would have interpreted this instruction to indicate that the doubt must be anything other than a reasonable one.

B.

Victor also challenges the "moral certainty" portion of the instruction. In another case involving an identical instruction, the Nebraska Supreme Court distinguished *Cage* as follows: "[U]nder the *Cage* instruction a juror is to vote for conviction unless convinced to a moral certainty that there exists a reasonable doubt, whereas under the questioned instruction a juror is to vote for acquittal unless convinced to a moral certainty that no reasonable doubt exists." We disagree with this reading of *Cage.* The moral certainty to which the *Cage* instruction referred was clearly related to the defendant's guilt; the problem in *Cage* was that the rest of the instruction provided insufficient context to lend meaning to the phrase. But the Nebraska instruction is not similarly deficient.

Instructing the jurors that they must have an abiding conviction of the defendant's guilt does much to alleviate any concerns that the phrase "moral certainty" might be misunderstood in the abstract. The instruction also equated a doubt sufficient to preclude moral certainty with a doubt that would cause a reasonable person to hesitate to act. In other words, a juror morally certain of a fact would not hesitate to rely on it; and such a fact can fairly be said to have been proved beyond a reasonable doubt. The jurors were told that they must be convinced of Victor's guilt "after full, fair, and impartial consideration of all the evidence." The judge also told them: "In determining any questions of fact presented in this case, you should be governed solely by the evidence introduced before you. You should not indulge in speculation, conjectures, or inferences not supported by the evidence." There is accordingly no reasonable likelihood that the jurors understood the reference to moral certainty to allow conviction on a standard insufficient to satisfy *Winship,* or to allow conviction on factors other than the government's proof. Though we reiterate that we do not countenance its use, the inclusion of the "moral certainty" phrase did not render the instruction given in Victor's case unconstitutional.

C.

Finally, Victor argues that the reference to "strong probabilities" in the instruction unconstitutionally understated the government's burden. But in the same sentence, the instruction informs the jury that the probabilities must be strong enough to prove the defendant's guilt beyond a reasonable doubt. We upheld a nearly identical instruction in *Dunbar v. United States*, 156 U.S. 185, 199 (1895): "While it is true that [the challenged instruction] used the words 'probabilities' and 'strong probabilities,' yet it emphasized the fact that those probabilities must be so strong as to exclude any reasonable doubt, and that is unquestionably the law." That conclusion has lost no force in the course of a century, and we therefore consider *Dunbar* controlling on this point.

IV.

The Due Process Clause requires the government to prove a criminal defendant's guilt beyond a reasonable doubt, and trial courts must avoid defining reasonable doubt so as to lead the jury to convict on a lesser showing than due process requires. In these cases, however, we conclude that "taken as a whole, the instructions correctly conveyed the concept of reasonable doubt to the jury." There is no reasonable likelihood that the jurors who determined petitioners' guilt applied the instructions in a way that violated the Constitution. The judgments in both cases are accordingly

Affirmed.

Justice KENNEDY, concurring.

It was commendable for Chief Justice Shaw to pen an instruction that survived more than a century, but, as the Court makes clear, what once might have made sense to jurors has long since become archaic. In fact, some of the phrases here in question confuse far more than they clarify.

Though the reference to "moral certainty" is not much better, California's use of "moral evidence" is the most troubling, and to me seems quite indefensible. The derivation of the phrase is explained in the Court's opinion, but even with this help the term is a puzzle. And for jurors who have not had the benefit of the Court's research, the words will do nothing but baffle.

I agree that use of "moral evidence" in the California formulation is not fatal to the instruction here. I cannot understand, however, why such an unruly term should be used at all when jurors are asked to perform a task that can be of great difficulty even when instructions are altogether clear. The inclusion of words so malleable, because so obscure, might in other circumstances have put the whole instruction at risk.

With this observation, I concur in full in the opinion of the Court.

Justice GINSBURG, concurring in part and concurring in the judgment.

I agree with the Court that the reasonable doubt instructions given in these cases, read as a whole, satisfy the Constitution's due process requirement. As the Court observes, the instructions adequately conveyed to the jurors that they should focus exclusively upon the evidence and that they should convict only if they had an "abiding conviction" of the defendant's guilt. I agree, further, with the Court's suggestion that the term "moral certainty," while not in itself so misleading as to render the instructions unconstitutional, should be avoided as an unhelpful way of explaining what reasonable doubt means.

Similarly unhelpful, in my view, are two other features of the instruction given in Victor's case. That instruction begins by defining reasonable doubt as "such a doubt as would cause a reasonable and prudent person, in one of the graver and more important transactions of life, to pause and hesitate before taking the represented facts as true and relying and acting thereon." A committee of distinguished federal judges, reporting to the Judicial Conference of the United States, has criticized this "hesitate to act" formulation

> "because the analogy it uses seems misplaced. In the decisions people make in the most important of their own affairs, resolution of conflicts about past events does not usually play a major role. Indeed, decisions we make in the most important affairs of our lives—choosing a spouse, a job, a place to live, and the like—generally involve a very heavy element of uncertainty and risk-taking. They are wholly unlike the decisions jurors ought to make in criminal cases."

More recently, Second Circuit Chief Judge Jon O. Newman observed:

> "Although, as a district judge, I dutifully repeated [the 'hesitate to act' standard] to juries in scores of criminal trials, I was always bemused by its ambiguity. If the jurors encounter a doubt that would cause them to 'hesitate to act in a matter of importance,' what are they to do then? Should they decline to convict because they have reached a point of hesitation, or should they simply hesitate, then ask themselves whether, in their own private matters, they would resolve the doubt in favor of action, and, if so, continue on to convict?" *Beyond "Reasonable Doubt,"* 68 N.Y.U. L. Rev. 201, 204 (1994) (James Madison Lecture, delivered at New York University Law School, Nov. 9, 1993).

Even less enlightening than the "hesitate to act" formulation is the passage of the *Victor* instruction counseling: "[The jury] may find an accused guilty upon the strong probabilities of the case, *provided such probabilities are strong enough to exclude any doubt of his guilt that is reasonable.*" If the italicized words save this part of the instruction from understating the prosecution's burden of proof, they do so with uninstructive circularity. Jury comprehension is scarcely advanced when a court "defines" reasonable doubt as "doubt . . . that is reasonable."

These and similar difficulties have led some courts to question the efficacy of any reasonable doubt instruction. At least two of the Federal Courts of Appeals have admonished their District Judges not to attempt a definition.[1] This Court, too, has suggested on occasion that prevailing definitions of "reasonable doubt" afford no real aid. *See, e.g., Holland v. United States*, 348 U.S. 121, 140 (1954) ("'[a]ttempts to explain the term "reasonable doubt" do not usually result in making it any clearer to the minds of the jury'") ("The rule may be, and often is, rendered obscure by attempts at definition, which serve to create doubts instead of removing them."). But we have never held that the concept of reasonable doubt is undefinable, or that trial courts should not, as a matter of course, provide a definition. Nor, contrary to the Court's suggestion, have we ever held that the Constitution does not require trial courts to define reasonable doubt.

Because the trial judges in fact defined reasonable doubt in both jury charges we review, we need not decide whether the Constitution required them to do so. Whether or not the Constitution so requires, however, the argument for defining the concept is strong. While judges and lawyers are familiar with the reasonable doubt standard, the words "beyond a reasonable doubt" are not self-defining for jurors. Several studies of jury behavior have concluded that "jurors are often confused about the meaning of reasonable doubt" when that term is left undefined. Thus, even if definitions of reasonable doubt are necessarily imperfect, the alternative — refusing to define the concept at all — is not obviously preferable. *Cf.* Newman, *supra*, at 205–206 ("I find it rather unsettling that we are using a formulation that we believe will become less clear the more we explain it."). Fortunately, the choice need not be one between two kinds of potential juror confusion — on one hand, the confusion that may be caused by leaving "reasonable doubt" undefined, and on the other, the confusion that might be induced by the anachronism of "moral certainty," the misplaced analogy of "hesitation to act," or the circularity of "doubt that is reasonable." The Federal Judicial Center has proposed a definition of reasonable doubt that is clear, straightforward, and accurate. That instruction reads:

> "[T]he government has the burden of proving the defendant guilty beyond a reasonable doubt. Some of you may have served as jurors in civil cases, where you were told that it is only necessary to prove that a fact is more likely true than not true. In criminal cases, the government's proof must be more powerful than that. It must be beyond a reasonable doubt.
>
> "Proof beyond a reasonable doubt is proof that leaves you firmly convinced of the defendant's guilt. There are very few things in this world that we

---

1. See, e.g., United States v. Adkins, 937 F.2d 947, 950 (4th Cir. 1991) ("This circuit has repeatedly warned against giving the jury definitions of reasonable doubt, because definitions tend to impermissibly lessen the burden of proof.... The only exception to our categorical disdain for definition is when the jury specifically requests it."); United States v. Hall, 854 F.2d 1036, 1039 (7th Cir. 1988) (upholding District Court's refusal to provide definition, despite jury's request, because "at best, definitions of reasonable doubt are unhelpful to a jury.... An attempt to define reasonable doubt presents a risk without any real benefit.").

know with absolute certainty, and in criminal cases the law does not require proof that overcomes every possible doubt. If, based on your consideration of the evidence, you are firmly convinced that the defendant is guilty of the crime charged, you must find him guilty. If on the other hand, you think there is a real possibility that he is not guilty, you must give him the benefit of the doubt and find him not guilty." Federal Judicial Center, Pattern Criminal Jury Instructions, at 17–18 (instruction 21).

This instruction plainly informs the jurors that the prosecution must prove its case by more than a mere preponderance of the evidence, yet not necessarily to an absolute certainty. The "firmly convinced" standard for conviction, repeated for emphasis, is further enhanced by the juxtaposed prescription that the jury must acquit if there is a "real possibility" that the defendant is innocent. This model instruction surpasses others I have seen in stating the reasonable doubt standard succinctly and comprehensibly.

I recognize, however, that this Court has no supervisory powers over the state courts and that the test we properly apply in evaluating the constitutionality of a reasonable doubt instruction is not whether we find it exemplary; instead, we inquire only whether there is a "reasonable likelihood that the jury understood the instructio[n] to allow conviction based on proof insufficient to meet" the reasonable doubt standard. On that understanding, I join Parts II, III-B, and IV of the Court's opinion and concur in its judgment.

Justice BLACKMUN, with whom Justice SOUTER joins, concurring in part and dissenting in part.

In *Cage v. Louisiana*, this Court, by a *per curiam* opinion, found a jury instruction defining reasonable doubt so obviously flawed that the resulting state-court judgment deserved summary reversal. The majority today purports to uphold and follow *Cage*, but plainly falters in its application of that case. There is no meaningful difference between the jury instruction delivered at Victor's trial and the jury instruction issued in *Cage*, save the fact that the jury instruction in Victor's case did not contain the two words "grave uncertainty." But the mere absence of these two words can be of no help to the State, since there is other language in the instruction that is equally offensive to due process. I therefore dissent from the Court's opinion and judgment in *Victor v. Nebraska*.

I.

Our democracy rests in no small part on our faith in the ability of the criminal justice system to separate those who are guilty from those who are not. This is a faith which springs fundamentally from the requirement that unless guilt is established beyond all reasonable doubt, the accused shall go free.

Despite the inherent appeal of the reasonable-doubt standard, it provides protection to the innocent only to the extent that the standard, in reality, is an enforceable rule of law. To be a meaningful safeguard, the reasonable-doubt standard must have a tangible meaning that is capable of being understood by those who are required to apply it. It must be stated accurately and with the precision owed to those whose liberty or life is at risk.

Because of the extraordinarily high stakes in criminal trials, "[i]t is critical that the moral force of the criminal law not be diluted by a standard of proof that leaves people in doubt whether innocent men are being condemned."

When reviewing a jury instruction that defines "reasonable doubt," it is necessary to consider the instruction as a whole and to give the words their common and ordinary meaning. It is not sufficient for the jury instruction merely to be susceptible to an interpretation that is technically correct. The important question is whether there is a "reasonable likelihood" that the jury was misled or confused by the instruction, and therefore applied it in a way that violated the Constitution. Any jury instruction defining "reasonable doubt" that suggests an improperly high degree of doubt for acquittal or an improperly low degree of certainty for conviction offends due process. Either misstatement of the reasonable-doubt standard is prejudicial to the defendant, as it "vitiates all the jury's findings" and removes the only constitutionally appropriate predicate for the jury's verdict.

A.

In a Louisiana trial court, Tommy Cage was convicted of first-degree murder and sentenced to death. On appeal to the Supreme Court of Louisiana, he argued, among other things, that the reasonable-doubt instruction used in the guilt phase of his trial violated the Due Process Clause of the Fourteenth Amendment. The instruction in relevant part provided:

> "If you entertain a reasonable doubt as to any fact or element necessary to constitute the defendant's guilt, it is your duty to give him the benefit of that doubt and return a verdict of not guilty. Even where the evidence demonstrates a probability of guilt, if it does not establish such guilt beyond a reasonable doubt, you must acquit the accused. This doubt, however, must be a reasonable one; that is one that is founded upon a real tangible substantial basis and not upon mere caprice and conjecture. It must be such a doubt as would give rise to a *grave uncertainty*, raised in your mind by reasons of the unsatisfactory character of the evidence or lack thereof. A reasonable doubt is not a mere possible doubt. It is an *actual substantial doubt*. It is a doubt that a reasonable man can seriously entertain. What is required is not an absolute or mathematical certainty, but a *moral certainty*." (Second emphasis added; first and third emphases in original.)

The Louisiana Supreme Court affirmed Cage's conviction, reasoning that, although some of the language "might overstate the requisite degree of uncertainty and confuse the jury," the charge as a whole was understandable to "reasonable persons of ordinary intelligence," and therefore constitutional.

We granted certiorari and summarily reversed. The Court noted that some of the language in the instruction was adequate, but ruled that the phrases "actual substantial doubt" and "grave uncertainty" suggested a "higher degree of doubt than is required for acquittal under the reasonable-doubt standard," and that those phrases taken together with the reference to "moral certainty," rather than "evidentiary certainty," rendered the instruction as a whole constitutionally defective.

Clarence Victor also was convicted of first-degree murder and sentenced to death. The instruction in his case reads as follows:

> "'Reasonable doubt' is such a doubt as would cause a reasonable and prudent person, in one of the graver and more important transactions of life, to pause and hesitate before taking the represented facts as true and relying and acting thereon. It is such a doubt as will not permit you, after full, fair, and impartial consideration of all the evidence, to have an abiding conviction, to a *moral certainty*, of the guilt of the accused. At the same time absolute or mathematical certainty is not required. *You may be convinced of the truth of a fact beyond a reasonable doubt and yet be fully aware that possibly you may be mistaken. You may find an accused guilty upon the strong probabilities of the case,* provided such probabilities are strong enough to exclude any doubt of his guilt that is reasonable. A reasonable doubt is an *actual and substantial doubt* reasonably arising from the evidence, from the facts or circumstances shown by the evidence, or from the lack of evidence on the part of the State, as distinguished from a doubt arising from mere possibility, from bare imagination, or from fanciful conjecture." (Emphasis added.)

The majority's attempt to distinguish this instruction from the one employed in *Cage* is wholly unpersuasive. Both instructions equate "substantial doubt" with reasonable doubt, and refer to "moral certainty" rather than "evidentiary certainty." And although Victor's instruction does not contain the phrase "grave uncertainty," the instruction contains language that has an equal potential to mislead, including the invitation to the jury to convict based on the "strong probabilities" of the case and the overt effort to dissuade jurors from acquitting when they are "fully aware that possibly they may be mistaken." Nonetheless, the majority argues that "substantial doubt" has a meaning in Victor's instruction different from that in Cage's instruction, and that the "moral certainty" language is sanitized by its context. The majority's approach seems to me to fail under its own logic.

B.

First, the majority concedes, as it must, that equating reasonable doubt with substantial doubt is "somewhat problematic" since one of the common definitions of "substantial" is "'that specified to a large degree.'" But the majority insists that the jury did not likely interpret the word "substantial" in this manner because Victor's instruction, unlike Cage's instruction, used the phrase "substantial doubt" as a means of distinguishing reasonable doubt from mere conjecture. According to the majority, "[t]his explicit distinction between a substantial doubt and a fanciful conjecture was not present in the *Cage* instruction," and thus, read in context, the use of "substantial doubt" in Victor's instruction is less problematic.

A casual reading of the *Cage* instruction reveals the majority's false premise. The *Cage* instruction plainly states that a reasonable doubt is a doubt "founded upon a real tangible substantial basis and not upon mere caprice and conjecture." The *Cage* instruction also used the "substantial doubt" language to distinguish a reasonable doubt from "a mere possible doubt." ("'A reasonable doubt is not a mere possible doubt. *It is an actual substantial doubt'*"). Thus, the reason the Court condemned the "substantial doubt" language in *Cage* had nothing to do with the absence of appropriate contrasting language; rather, the Court condemned the language for precisely the reason it gave: "[T]he words 'substantial' and 'grave,' as they are commonly understood, suggest a higher degree of doubt than is required for acquittal under the reasonable doubt standard." In short, the majority's speculation that the jury in Victor's case interpreted "substantial" to mean something other than "that specified to a large degree" simply because the word "substantial" is used at one point to distinguish mere conjecture is unfounded and is foreclosed by *Cage* itself.

The majority further attempts to minimize the obvious hazards of equating "substantial doubt" with reasonable doubt by suggesting that, in *Cage*, it was the combined use of "substantial doubt" and "grave uncertainty," "in parallel," that rendered the use of the phrase "substantial doubt" unconstitutional. This claim does not withstand scrutiny. The Court in *Cage* explained that *both* "substantial doubt" and "grave uncertainty" overstated the degree of doubt necessary to acquit, and found that it was the use of those words in conjunction with the misleading phrase "moral certainty" that violated due process. The Court's exact words were:

> "It is plain to us that the words 'substantial' and 'grave,' as they are commonly understood, suggest a higher degree of doubt than is required for acquittal under the reasonable doubt standard. When those statements are then considered with the reference to 'moral certainty,' rather than evidentiary certainty, it becomes clear that a reasonable juror could have interpreted the instruction to allow a finding of guilt based on a degree of proof below that required by the Due Process Clause."

Clearly, the Court was not preoccupied with the relationship between "substantial doubt" and "grave uncertainty." The Court instead endorsed the universal opinion of the Courts of Appeals that equating reasonable doubt with "substantial doubt" is improper and potentially misleading in that it overstates the degree of doubt required for acquittal under the reasonable-doubt standard.[1]

In a final effort to distinguish the use of the phrase "substantial doubt" in this case from its use in *Cage*, the majority states: "In any event, the instruction provided

---

1. Despite the overwhelming disapproval of the use of the phrase "substantial doubt" by appellate courts, some state trial courts continue to employ the language when instructing jurors. *See Bordenkircher*, 718 F.2d at 1279 (dissenting opinion) ("As the majority has forthrightly pointed out, a 'good and substantial doubt' instruction has evoked a 'uniformly disapproving' response from appellate courts. Evidently the slight slaps on the wrist followed by affirmance of the convictions have not served the hoped for end of correction of the error *in futuro*.").

an alternative definition of reasonable doubt: a doubt that would cause a reasonable person to hesitate to act." The Court reasons that since this formulation has been upheld in other contexts, *see Holland v. United States*, this "alternative" statement makes it unlikely that the jury would interpret "substantial" to mean "to a large degree."

To begin with, I note my general agreement with Justice GINSBURG's observation that the "hesitate to act" language is far from helpful, and may in fact make matters worse by analogizing the decision whether to convict or acquit a defendant to the frequently high-risk personal decisions people must make in their daily lives. But even assuming this "hesitate to act" language is in some way helpful to a jury in understanding the meaning of reasonable doubt, the existence of an "alternative" and accurate definition of reasonable doubt somewhere in the instruction does not render the instruction lawful if it is "reasonably likely" that the jury would rely on the faulty definition during its deliberations. *Cage* itself contained proper statements of the law with respect to what is required to convict or acquit a defendant, but this language could not salvage the instruction since it remained reasonably likely that, despite the proper statements of law, the jury understood the instruction to require "a higher degree of doubt than is required for acquittal under the reasonable doubt standard."

In my view, the predominance of potentially misleading language in Victor's instruction made it likely that the jury interpreted the phrase "substantial doubt" to mean that a "large" doubt, as opposed to a merely reasonable doubt, is required to acquit a defendant. It seems that a central purpose of the instruction is to minimize the jury's sense of responsibility for the conviction of those who may be innocent. The instruction goes out of its way to assure jurors that "[y]ou may be convinced of the truth of a fact beyond a reasonable doubt and yet be fully aware that possibly you may be mistaken"; and then, after acquainting jurors with the possibility that their consciences will be unsettled after convicting the defendant, the instruction states that the jurors should feel free to convict based on the "strong probabilities of the case." Viewed as a whole, the instruction is geared toward assuring jurors that although they may be mistaken, they are to make their decision on those "strong probabilities," and only a "substantial doubt" of a defendant's guilt should deter them from convicting.

The majority dismisses the potentially harmful effects of the "strong probabilities" language on the ground that a "nearly identical instruction" was upheld by the Court a century ago. But the instruction in *Dunbar* did not equate reasonable doubt with "substantial doubt," nor did it contain the phrase "moral certainty." As the majority appreciates elsewhere in its opinion, challenged jury instructions must be considered in their entirety. Rather than examining the jury instruction as a whole, the majority parses it, ignoring the relationship between the challenged phrases as well as their cumulative effect.

Considering the instruction in its entirety, it seems fairly obvious to me that the "strong probabilities" language increased the likelihood that the jury understood "substantial doubt" to mean "to a large degree." Indeed, the jury could have a reasonable doubt about a defendant's guilt but still find that the "strong probabilities" are in favor of conviction. Only when a reasonable doubt is understood to be a doubt "to a large degree" does the "strong probabilities" language begin to make sense. A Nebraska Federal District Court recently observed: "The word 'probability' brings to mind terms such as 'chance,' 'possibility,' 'likelihood' and 'plausibility'—none of which appear to suggest the high level of certainty which is required to be convinced of a defendant's guilt 'beyond a reasonable doubt.'" *Morley v. Stenberg,* 828 F. Supp. 1413, 1422 (1993). All of these terms, however, are consistent with the interpretation of "substantial doubt" as a doubt "to a large degree." A jury could have a large and reasonable doubt about a defendant's guilt but still find the defendant guilty on "the strong probabilities of the case," believing it "likely" that the defendant committed the crime for which he was charged.

To be sure, the instruction does qualify the "strong probabilities" language by noting that "the strong probabilities of the case" should be "strong enough to exclude any doubt of his guilt that is reasonable." But this qualification is useless since a "doubt of his guilt that is reasonable" is immediately defined, in the very next sentence, as a "substantial doubt." Thus, the supposed clarification only compounds the confusion by referring the jury to the "substantial doubt" phrase as a means of defining the "strong probabilities" language.

Finally, the instruction issued in Victor's case states that a reasonable doubt "is such a doubt as will not permit you, after full, fair, and impartial consideration of all the evidence, to have an abiding conviction, *to a moral certainty*, of the guilt of the accused." In *Cage,* the Court disapproved of the use of the phrase "moral certainty," because of the real possibility that such language would lead jurors reasonably to believe that they could base their decision to convict upon moral standards or emotion in addition to or instead of evidentiary standards. The risk that jurors would understand "moral certainty" to authorize convictions based in part on value judgments regarding the defendant's behavior is particularly high in cases where the defendant is alleged to have committed a repugnant or brutal crime. In *Cage,* we therefore contrasted "moral certainty" with "evidentiary certainty," and held that where "moral certainty" is used in conjunction with "substantial doubt" and "grave uncertainty," the Due Process Clause is violated.

Just as in *Cage,* the "moral certainty" phrase in Victor's instruction is particularly dangerous because it is used in conjunction with language that overstates the degree of doubt necessary to convict. This relationship between the "moral certainty" language, which potentially understates the degree of certainty required to convict, and the "substantial doubt," "strong probabilities," and "possibly you may be mistaken" language which, especially when taken together, overstates the degree of doubt necessary to acquit, also distinguishes Victor's instruction from the one challenged in *Sandoval v. California.* The jury instruction defining reasonable doubt in *Sandoval* used the phrases "moral certainty" and "moral evidence," but the phrases were not used in conjunction with language of the type at issue here—language that easily may be interpreted as overstating the degree of doubt required to acquit. In other words, in Victor's instruction, unlike Sandoval's, all of the misleading language is mutually reinforcing, both overstating the degree of doubt necessary to acquit and understating the degree of certainty required to convict.

This confusing and misleading state of affairs leads me ineluctably to the conclusion that, in Victor's case, there exists a reasonable likelihood that the jury believed that a lesser burden of proof rested with the prosecution; and, moreover, it prevents me from distinguishing the jury instruction challenged in Victor's case from the one issued in *Cage*. As with the *Cage* instruction, it simply cannot be said that Victor's instruction accurately informed the jury as to the degree of certainty required for conviction and the degree of doubt required for acquittal. Where, as here, a jury instruction attempts but fails to convey with clarity and accuracy the meaning of reasonable doubt, the reviewing court should reverse the conviction and remand for a new trial.

Questions and Notes

1. If you were a trial judge who had a choice of defining or not defining reasonable doubt to a jury, which would you choose? Why?

2. Assuming that you do define reasonable doubt, how would you define it?

3. Do you think that the standard "satisfied to a moral certainty" is less exacting than, more exacting than, or the same as "beyond a reasonable doubt"? Explain.

4. What's an unreasonable doubt?

5. Is "reasonable doubt" quantifiable in percentages (e.g., 70, 80, 90 etc.)? Why? Why not?

6. Had you been on the Court, how would you have resolved (a) *Cage*, (b) *Sandoval*, and (c) *Victor*? Explain.

7. Do you think that Justice O'Connor's description of the defendants as killers rather than alleged killers influenced her opinion?

8. Do you think that failure to take reasonable doubt seriously contributes to convicting the innocent? *See* Loewy, *Taking Reasonable Doubt Seriously* 85 Chi.-Kent L.Rev. 63, 75 (2010).

B. Shifting the Burden

To the extent that we are willing to allow the defendant to be convicted when we are not sure whether some relevant factor was present (e.g., did she kill in self-defense?), we are saying that that factor is relatively unimportant.

In a sense, shifting the burden of proof might be conceived as a halfway house between requiring the state to negate a defense and not allowing the defense at all. For example, if a drunk defendant swings a baseball bat into the head of his victim, we normally don't care whether he thought he was swinging at a baseball rather than a head—he's guilty either way. (*See* Chapter 10, *supra*.) On the other hand, a state might be willing to make the defendant's state of mind relevant so long as it doesn't have to prove it. That is, a state might be willing to allow the defendant to escape liability by proving that he intended to hit a baseball. At the same time, the state might be unwilling to undertake the obligation to prove that the defendant intended to hit a human head.

This section focuses on the extent to which the due process clause of the Constitution permits states to engage in such burden-shifting practices.

Patterson v. New York
432 U.S. 197 (1977)

Mr. Justice WHITE delivered the opinion of the Court.

The question here is the constitutionality under the Fourteenth Amendment's Due Process Clause of burdening the defendant in a New York State murder trial with proving the affirmative defense of extreme emotional disturbance as defined by New York law.

After a brief and unstable marriage, the appellant, Gordon Patterson, Jr., became estranged from his wife, Roberta. Roberta resumed an association with John Northrup, a neighbor to whom she had been engaged prior to her marriage to appellant. On December 27, 1970, Patterson borrowed a rifle from an acquaintance and went to the residence of his father-in-law. There, he observed his wife through a window in a state of semiundress in the presence of John Northrup. He entered the house and killed Northrup by shooting him twice in the head.

Patterson was charged with second-degree murder. In New York there are two elements of this crime: (1) "intent to cause the death of another person"; and (2) "caus(ing) the death of such person or of a third person." Malice aforethought is not an element of the crime. In addition, the State permits a person accused of murder to raise an affirmative defense that he "acted under the influence of extreme emotional disturbance for which there was a reasonable explanation or excuse."

New York also recognizes the crime of manslaughter. A person is guilty of manslaughter if he intentionally kills another person "under circumstances which do not constitute murder because he acts under the influence of extreme emotional disturbance." Appellant confessed before trial to killing Northrup, but at trial he raised the defense of extreme emotional disturbance.

The jury was instructed as to the elements of the crime of murder. Focusing on the element of intent, the trial court charged:

> "Before you, considering all of the evidence, can convict this defendant or anyone of murder, you must believe and decide that the People have established beyond a reasonable doubt that he intended, in firing the gun, to kill either the victim himself or some other human being. . . .

"Always remember that you must not expect or require the defendant to prove to your satisfaction that his acts were done without the intent to kill. Whatever proof he may have attempted, however far he may have gone in an effort to convince you of his innocence or guiltlessness, he is not obliged, he is not obligated to prove anything. It is always the People's burden to prove his guilt, and to prove that he intended to kill in this instance beyond a reasonable doubt."

The jury was further instructed, consistently with New York law, that the defendant had the burden of proving his affirmative defense by a preponderance of the evidence. The jury was told that if it found beyond a reasonable doubt that appellant had intentionally killed Northrup but that appellant had demonstrated by a preponderance of the evidence that he had acted under the influence of extreme emotional disturbance, it had to find appellant guilty of manslaughter instead of murder.

The jury found appellant guilty of murder. Judgment was entered on the verdict, and the Appellate Division affirmed. While appeal to the New York Court of Appeals was pending, this Court decided *Mullaney v. Wilbur*, 421 U.S. 684 (1975), in which the Court declared Maine's murder statute unconstitutional. Under the Maine statute, a person accused of murder could rebut the statutory presumption that he committed the offense with "malice aforethought" by proving that he acted in the heat of passion on sudden provocation. The Court held that this scheme improperly shifted the burden of persuasion from the prosecutor to the defendant and was therefore a violation of due process. In the Court of Appeals appellant urged that New York's murder statute is functionally equivalent to the one struck down in *Mullaney* and that therefore his conviction should be reversed.

The Court of Appeals rejected appellant's argument, holding that the New York murder statute is consistent with due process. The Court distinguished *Mullaney* on the ground that the New York statute involved no shifting of the burden to the defendant to disprove any fact essential to the offense charged since the New York affirmative defense of extreme emotional disturbance bears no direct relationship to any element of murder. This appeal ensued, and we noted probable jurisdiction. We affirm.

II.

It goes without saying that preventing and dealing with crime is much more the business of the States than it is of the Federal Government, and that we should not lightly construe the Constitution so as to intrude upon the administration of justice by the individual States. Among other things, it is normally "within the power of the State to regulate procedures under which its laws are carried out, including the burden of producing evidence and the burden of persuasion," and its decision in this regard is not subject to proscription under the Due Process Clause unless "it offends some principle of justice so rooted in the traditions and conscience of our people as to be ranked as fundamental."

In determining whether New York's allocation to the defendant of proving the mitigating circumstances of severe emotional disturbance is consistent with due process, it is therefore relevant to note that this defense is a considerably expanded version of the common-law defense of heat of passion on sudden provocation and that at common law the burden of proving the latter, as well as other affirmative defenses indeed, "all . . . circumstances of justification, excuse or alleviation" rested on the defendant.

In 1895 the common-law view was abandoned with respect to the insanity defense in federal prosecutions. *Davis v. United States*, 160 U.S. 469 (1895). This ruling had wide impact on the practice in the federal courts with respect to the burden of proving various affirmative defenses, and the prosecution in a majority of jurisdictions in this country sooner or later came to shoulder the burden of proving the sanity of the accused and of disproving the facts constituting other affirmative defenses, including provocation. *Davis* was not a constitutional ruling, however, as *Leland v. Oregon*, 343 U.S. 790 (1952) made clear.

At issue in *Leland* was the constitutionality under the Due Process Clause of the Oregon rule that the defense of insanity must be proved by the defendant beyond a reasonable doubt. Noting that *Davis* "obviously establish(ed) no constitutional doctrine," 343 U.S. at 797, the Court refused to strike down the Oregon scheme, saying that the burden of proving all elements of the crime beyond reasonable doubt, including the elements of premeditation and deliberation, was placed on the State under Oregon procedures and remained there throughout the trial. To convict, the jury was required to find each element of the crime beyond a reasonable doubt, based on all the evidence, including the evidence going to the issue of insanity. Only then was the jury "to consider separately the issue of legal sanity per se. . . ." *Id.* at 795. This practice did not offend the Due Process Clause even though among the 20 States then placing the burden of proving his insanity on the defendant, Oregon was alone in requiring him to convince the jury beyond a reasonable doubt.

In 1970, the Court declared that the Due Process Clause "protects the accused against conviction except upon proof beyond a reasonable doubt of every fact necessary to constitute the crime with which he is charged." *Winship*. Five years later, in *Mullaney v. Wilbur*, 421 U.S. 684 (1975), the Court further announced that under the Maine law of homicide, the burden could not constitutionally be placed on the defendant of proving by a preponderance of the evidence that the killing had occurred in the heat of passion on sudden provocation. The Chief Justice and Mr. Justice Rehnquist, concurring, expressed their understanding that the *Mullaney* decision did not call into question the ruling in *Leland* with respect to the proof of insanity.

Subsequently, the Court confirmed that it remained constitutional to burden the defendant with proving his insanity defense when it dismissed, as not raising a substantial federal question, a case in which the appellant specifically challenged the continuing validity of *Leland*. This occurred in *Rivera v. Delaware*, 429 U.S. 877

(1976), an appeal from a Delaware conviction which, in reliance on *Leland*, had been affirmed by the Delaware Supreme Court over the claim that the Delaware statute was unconstitutional because it burdened the defendant with proving his affirmative defense of insanity by a preponderance of the evidence. The claim in this Court was that *Leland* had been overruled by *Winship* and *Mullaney*. We dismissed the appeal as not presenting a substantial federal question.

We cannot conclude that Patterson's conviction under the New York law deprived him of due process of law. The crime of murder is defined by the statute, which represents a recent revision of the state criminal code, as causing the death of another person with intent to do so. The death, the intent to kill, and causation are the facts that the State is required to prove beyond a reasonable doubt if a person is to be convicted of murder. No further facts are either presumed or inferred in order to constitute the crime. The statute does provide an affirmative defense that the defendant acted under the influence of extreme emotional disturbance for which there was a reasonable explanation which, if proved by a preponderance of the evidence, would reduce the crime to manslaughter, an offense defined in a separate section of the statute. It is plain enough that if the intentional killing is shown, the State intends to deal with the defendant as a murderer unless he demonstrates the mitigating circumstances.

Here, the jury was instructed in accordance with the statute, and the guilty verdict confirms that the State successfully carried its burden of proving the facts of the crime beyond a reasonable doubt. Nothing in the evidence, including any evidence that might have been offered with respect to Patterson's mental state at the time of the crime, raised a reasonable doubt about his guilt as a murderer; and clearly the evidence failed to convince the jury that Patterson's affirmative defense had been made out. It seems to us that the State satisfied the mandate of *Winship* that it prove beyond a reasonable doubt "every fact necessary to constitute the crime with which (Patterson was) charged."

In convicting Patterson under its murder statute, New York did no more than *Leland* and *Rivera* permitted it to do without violating the Due Process Clause. Under those cases, once the facts constituting a crime are established beyond a reasonable doubt, based on all the evidence including the evidence of the defendant's mental state, the State may refuse to sustain the affirmative defense of insanity unless demonstrated by a preponderance of the evidence.

The New York law on extreme emotional disturbance follows this pattern. This affirmative defense, which the Court of Appeals described as permitting "the defendant to show that his actions were caused by a mental infirmity not arising to the level of insanity, and that he is less culpable for having committed them," does not serve to negative any facts of the crime which the State is to prove in order to convict of murder. It constitutes a separate issue on which the defendant is required to carry the burden of persuasion; and unless we are to overturn *Leland* and *Rivera*, New York has not violated the Due Process Clause, and Patterson's conviction must be sustained.

The requirement of proof beyond a reasonable doubt in a criminal case is "bottomed on a fundamental value determination of our society that it is far worse to convict an innocent man than to let a guilty man go free." *Winship* (Harlan, J., concurring). The social cost of placing the burden on the prosecution to prove guilt beyond a reasonable doubt is thus an increased risk that the guilty will go free. While it is clear that our society has willingly chosen to bear a substantial burden in order to protect the innocent, it is equally clear that the risk it must bear is not without limits; and Mr. Justice Harlan's aphorism provides little guidance for determining what those limits are. Due process does not require that every conceivable step be taken, at whatever cost, to eliminate the possibility of convicting an innocent person. Punishment of those found guilty by a jury, for example, is not forbidden merely because there is a remote possibility in some instances that an innocent person might go to jail.

It is said that the common-law rule permits a State to punish one as a murderer when it is as likely as not that he acted in the heat of passion or under severe emotional distress and when, if he did, he is guilty only of manslaughter. But this has always been the case in those jurisdictions adhering to the traditional rule. It is also very likely true that fewer convictions of murder would occur if New York were required to negative the affirmative defense at issue here. But in each instance of a murder conviction under the present law New York will have proved beyond a reasonable doubt that the defendant has intentionally killed another person, an act which it is not disputed the State may constitutionally criminalize and punish. If the State nevertheless chooses to recognize a factor that mitigates the degree of criminality or punishment, we think the State may assure itself that the fact has been established with reasonably certainty. To recognize at all a mitigating circumstance does not require the State to prove its nonexistence in each case in which the fact is put in issue, if in its judgment this would be too cumbersome, too expensive, and too inaccurate.

We thus decline to adopt as a constitutional imperative, operative countrywide, that a State must disprove beyond a reasonable doubt every fact constituting any and all affirmative defenses related to the culpability of an accused. This view may seem to permit state legislatures to reallocate burdens of proof by labeling as affirmative defenses at least some elements of the crimes now defined in their statutes. But there are obviously constitutional limits beyond which the States may not go in this regard. "(I)t is not within the province of a legislature to declare an individual guilty or presumptively guilty of a crime."

Long before *Winship*, the universal rule in this country was that the prosecution must prove guilt beyond a reasonable doubt. At the same time, the long-accepted rule was that it was constitutionally permissible to provide that various affirmative defenses were to be proved by the defendant. This did not lead to such abuses or to such widespread redefinition of crime and reduction of the prosecution's burden that a new constitutional rule was required. This was not the problem to which *Winship* was addressed. Nor does the fact that a majority of the States have now assumed the burden of disproving affirmative defenses for whatever reasons mean that those States that strike a different balance are in violation of the Constitution.

It is urged that *Mullaney* necessarily invalidates Patterson's conviction. In *Mullaney* the charge was murder, which the Maine statute defined as the unlawful killing of a human being "with malice aforethought, either express or implied." The trial court instructed the jury that the words "malice aforethought" were most important because "malice aforethought is an essential and indispensable element of the crime of murder."

Mullaney surely held that a State must prove every ingredient of an offense beyond a reasonable doubt, and that it may not shift the burden of proof to the defendant by presuming that ingredient upon proof of the other elements of the offense. This is true even though the State's practice, as in Maine, had been traditionally to the contrary. Such shifting of the burden of persuasion with respect to a fact which the State deems so important that it must be either proved or presumed is impermissible under the Due Process Clause.

It was unnecessary to go further in *Mullaney*. The Maine Supreme Judicial Court made it clear that malice aforethought, which was mentioned in the statutory definition of the crime, was not equivalent to premeditation and that the presumption of malice traditionally arising in intentional homicide cases carried no factual meaning insofar as premeditation was concerned. Even so, a killing became murder in Maine when it resulted from a deliberate, cruel act committed by one person against another, "suddenly without any, or without a considerable provocation." Premeditation was not within the definition of murder; but malice, in the sense of the absence of provocation, was part of the definition of that crime. Yet malice, *i.e.*, lack of provocation, was presumed and could be rebutted by the defendant only by proving by a preponderance of the evidence that he acted with heat of passion upon sudden provocation. In *Mullaney* we held that however traditional this mode of proceeding might have been, it is contrary to the Due Process Clause as construed in *Winship*.

As we have explained, nothing was presumed or implied against Patterson; and his conviction is not invalid under any of our prior cases. The judgment of the New York Court of Appeals is Affirmed.

Mr. Justice POWELL, with whom Mr. Justice BRENNAN and Mr. Justice MARSHALL join, dissenting.

In the name of preserving legislative flexibility, the Court today drains *Winship* of much of its vitality. Legislatures do require broad discretion in the drafting of criminal laws, but the Court surrenders to the legislative branch a significant part of its responsibility to protect the presumption of innocence.

An understanding of the import of today's decision requires a comparison of the statutes at issue here with the statutes and practices of Maine struck down by a unanimous Court just two years ago in *Mullaney*.

Maine's homicide laws embodied the common-law distinctions along with the colorful common-law language. Murder was defined in the statute as the unlawful killing of a human being "with malice aforethought, either express or implied." Manslaughter was a killing "in the heat of passion, on sudden provocation, without express or implied malice aforethought." Although "express malice" at one point may have had its own significant independent meaning, in practice a finding that the killing was committed with malice aforethought had come to mean simply that heat of passion was absent. Indeed, the trial court in *Mullaney* expressly charged the jury that "malice aforethought and heat of passion on sudden provocation are two inconsistent things." The only inquiry for the jury in deciding whether a homicide amounted to murder or manslaughter was the inquiry into heat of passion on sudden provocation.

Our holding in *Mullaney* found no constitutional defect in these statutory provisions. Rather, the defect in Maine practice lay in its allocation of the burden of persuasion with respect to the crucial factor distinguishing murder from manslaughter. In Maine, juries were instructed that if the prosecution proved that the homicide was both intentional and unlawful, the crime was to be considered murder unless the *defendant* proved by a preponderance of the evidence that he acted in the heat of passion on sudden provocation. Only if the defendant carried this burden would the offense be reduced to manslaughter.

The result, under the Court's holding, is that only the legislature can remedy any defects that come to light as a result of the Court's decision. No matter how clear the legislative intent that defendants bear the burden of persuasion on an issue an ultimate result the Court approves state courts may not effectuate that intent until the right verbal formula appears in the statute book.

New York's present homicide laws had their genesis in lingering dissatisfaction with certain aspects of the common-law framework that this Court confronted in *Mullaney*. Critics charged that the archaic language tended to obscure the factors of real importance in the jury's decision. Also, only a limited range of aggravations would lead to mitigation under the common-law formula, usually only those resulting from direct provocation by the victim himself. It was thought that actors whose emotions were stirred by other forms of outrageous conduct, even conduct by someone other than the ultimate victim, also should be punished as manslaughterers rather than murderers. Moreover, the common-law formula was generally applied with rather strict objectivity. Only provocations that might cause the hypothetical reasonable man to lose control could be considered. And even provocations of that sort were inadequate to reduce the crime to manslaughter if enough time had passed for the reasonable man's passions to cool, regardless of whether the actor's own thermometer had registered any decline.

The American Law Institute took the lead in moving to remedy these difficulties. As part of its commendable undertaking to prepare a Model Penal Code, it endeavored to bring modern insights to bear on the law of homicide. The result was a proposal to replace "heat of passion" with the moderately broader concept of "extreme mental or emotional disturbance." The proposal first appeared in a tentative draft published in 1959, and it was accepted by the Institute and included as § 210.3 of the 1962 Proposed Official Draft.

At about this time the New York Legislature undertook the preparation of a new criminal code, and the Revised Penal Law of 1967 was the ultimate result. The new code adopted virtually word for word the ALI formula for distinguishing murder from manslaughter. The test the Court today establishes allows a legislature to shift, virtually at will, the burden of persuasion with respect to any factor in a criminal case, so long as it is careful not to mention the nonexistence of that factor in the statutory language that defines the crime. The sole requirement is that any references to the factor be confined to those sections that provide for an affirmative defense.[7]

Perhaps the Court's interpretation of *Winship* is consistent with the letter of the holding in that case. But little of the spirit survives. Indeed, the Court scarcely could distinguish this case from *Mullaney* without closing its eyes to the constitutional values for which *Winship* stands. As Mr. Justice Harlan observed in *Winship*, "a standard of proof represents an attempt to instruct the factfinder concerning the degree of confidence our society thinks he should have in the correctness of factual conclusions for a particular type of adjudication." Explaining *Mullaney*, the Court says today, in effect, that society demands full confidence before a Maine factfinder determines that heat of passion is missing a demand so insistent that this Court invoked the Constitution to enforce it over the contrary decision by the State. But we are told that society is willing to tolerate far less confidence in New York's factual determination of precisely the same functional issue. One must ask what possibly could explain this difference in societal demands. According to the Court, it is because Maine happened to attach a name "malice aforethought" to the absence of heat of passion, whereas New York refrained from giving a name to the absence of extreme emotional disturbance.

With all respect, this type of constitutional adjudication is indefensibly formalistic. A limited but significant check on possible abuses in the criminal law now becomes an exercise in arid formalities. What *Winship* and *Mullaney* had sought to teach about the limits a free society places on its procedures to safeguard the liberty of its citizens becomes a rather simplistic lesson in statutory draftsmanship. Nothing in the Court's opinion prevents a legislature from applying this new learning to many of the classical elements of the crimes it punishes. It would be preferable, if the Court has found reason to reject the rationale of *Winship* and *Mullaney*, simply and straightforwardly to overrule those precedents.

The Court understandably manifests some uneasiness that its formalistic approach will give legislatures too much latitude in shifting the burden of

---

7. Although the Court never says so explicitly, its new standards appear to be designed for application to the language of a criminal statute on its face, regardless of how the state court construes the statute. The Court, in explaining *Mullaney*, persistently states that in Maine malice "was part of the definition of that crime (murder)."

persuasion. And so it issues a warning that "there are obviously constitutional limits beyond which the States may not go in this regard." The Court thereby concedes that legislative abuses may occur and that they must be curbed by the judicial branch. But if the State is careful to conform to the drafting formulas articulated today, the constitutional limits are anything but "obvious." This decision simply leaves us without a conceptual framework for distinguishing abuses from legitimate legislative adjustments of the burden of persuasion in criminal cases.

Questions and Notes

1. Are *Patterson* and *Mullaney* consistent? Explain.

2. If they are not consistent, which one is correct? Why?

3. After *Patterson,* could a state define *murder* as being present when another dies, and creating affirmative defenses that either the defendant didn't kill the victim or that the defendant didn't intend to kill the victim?

4. Consider this question in conjunction with *Martin.*

Martin v. Ohio
480 U.S. 228 (1987)

Justice WHITE delivered the opinion of the Court.

The Ohio Code provides that "[e]very person accused of an offense is presumed innocent until proven guilty beyond a reasonable doubt, and the burden of proof for all elements of the offense is upon the prosecution. The burden of going forward with the evidence of an affirmative defense, and the burden of proof by a preponderance of the evidence, for an affirmative defense, is upon the accused." An affirmative defense is one involving "an excuse or justification peculiarly within the knowledge of the accused, on which he can fairly be required to adduce supporting evidence." The Ohio courts have "long determined that self-defense is an affirmative defense," and that the defendant has the burden of proving it.

As defined by the trial court in its instructions in this case, the elements of self-defense that the defendant must prove are (1) that the defendant was not at fault in creating the situation giving rise to the argument; (2) the defendant had an honest belief that she was in imminent danger of death or great bodily harm and that her only means of escape from such danger was in the use of such force; and (3) the defendant must not have violated any duty to retreat or avoid danger. The question before us is whether the Due Process Clause of the Fourteenth Amendment forbids placing the burden of proving self-defense on the defendant when she is charged by the State of Ohio with committing the crime of aggravated murder, which, as relevant to this case, is defined by the Revised Code of Ohio as "purposely, and with prior calculation and design, caus[ing] the death of another."

The facts of the case, taken from the opinions of the courts below, may be succinctly stated. On July 21, 1983, petitioner Earline Martin and her husband, Walter

Martin, argued over grocery money. Petitioner claimed that her husband struck her in the head during the argument. Petitioner's version of what then transpired was that she went upstairs, put on a robe, and later came back down with her husband's gun which she intended to dispose of. Her husband saw something in her hand and questioned her about it. He came at her, she lost her head and fired the gun at him. Five or six shots were fired, three of them striking and killing Mr. Martin. She was charged with and tried for aggravated murder. She pleaded self-defense and testified in her own defense. The judge charged the jury with respect to the elements of the crime and of self-defense and rejected petitioner's Due Process Clause challenge to the charge placing on her the burden of proving self-defense. The jury found her guilty.

Both the Ohio Court of Appeals and the Supreme Court of Ohio affirmed the conviction. Both rejected the constitutional challenge to the instruction requiring petitioner to prove self-defense. The latter court, relying upon our opinion in *Patterson v. New York*, 432 U.S. 197 (1977), concluded that, the State was required to prove the three elements of aggravated murder but that *Patterson* did not require it to disprove self-defense, which is a separate issue that did not require Mrs. Martin to disprove any element of the offense with which she was charged. The court said, "the state proved beyond a reasonable doubt that appellant purposely, and with prior calculation and design, caused the death of her husband. Appellant did not dispute the existence of these elements, but rather sought to justify her actions on grounds she acted in self defense." We granted certiorari and affirm the decision of the Supreme Court of Ohio.

As in *Patterson*, the jury was here instructed that to convict it must find, in light of all the evidence, that each of the elements of the crime of aggravated murder must be proved by the State beyond reasonable doubt and that the burden of proof with respect to these elements did not shift. To find guilt, the jury had to be convinced that none of the evidence, whether offered by the State or by Martin in connection with her plea of self-defense, raised a reasonable doubt that Martin had killed her husband, that she had the specific purpose and intent to cause his death, or that she had done so with prior calculation and design. It was also told, however, that it could acquit if it found by a preponderance of the evidence that Martin had not precipitated the confrontation, that she had an honest belief that she was in imminent danger of death or great bodily harm, and that she had satisfied any duty to retreat or avoid danger. The jury convicted Martin.

We agree with the State and its Supreme Court that this conviction did not violate the Due Process Clause. The State did not exceed its authority in defining the crime of murder as purposely causing the death of another with prior calculation or design. It did not seek to shift to Martin the burden of proving any of those elements, and the jury's verdict reflects that none of her self-defense evidence raised a reasonable doubt about the state's proof that she purposefully killed with prior calculation and design. She nevertheless had the opportunity under state law and the instructions given to justify the killing and show herself to be blameless by proving that she acted in self-defense. The jury thought she had failed to do so, and Ohio is as entitled to punish Martin as one guilty of murder as New York was to punish Patterson.

Petitioner submits that there can be no conviction under Ohio law unless the defendant's conduct is unlawful and that because self-defense renders lawful what would otherwise be a crime, unlawfulness is an element of the offense that the state must prove by disproving self-defense. This argument founders on state law, for it has been rejected by the Ohio Supreme Court and by the Court of Appeals for the Sixth Circuit. It is true that unlawfulness is essential for conviction, but the Ohio courts hold that the unlawfulness in cases like this is the conduct satisfying the elements of aggravated murder—an interpretation of state law that we are not in a position to dispute. The same is true of the claim that it is necessary to prove a "criminal" intent to convict for serious crimes, which cannot occur if self-defense is shown: the necessary mental state for aggravated murder under Ohio law is the specific purpose to take life pursuant to prior calculation and design.

As we noted in *Patterson*, the common law rule was that affirmative defenses, including self-defense, were matters for the defendant to prove. "This was the rule when the Fifth Amendment was adopted, and it was the American rule when the Fourteenth Amendment was ratified." Indeed, well into this century, a number of States followed the common law rule and required a defendant to shoulder the burden of proving that he acted in self-defense. We are aware that all but two of the States, Ohio and South Carolina, have abandoned the common law rule and require the prosecution to prove the absence of self-defense when it is properly raised by the defendant. But the question remains whether those States are in violation of the Constitution; and, as we observed in *Patterson*, that question is not answered by cataloging the practices of other States. We are no more convinced that the Ohio practice of requiring self-defense to be proved by the defendant is unconstitutional than we are that the Constitution requires the prosecution to prove the sanity of a defendant who pleads not guilty by reason of insanity. We have had the opportunity to depart from *Leland v. Oregon* but have refused to do so. *Rivera v. Delaware*, 429 U.S. 877 (1976). These cases were important to the *Patterson* decision and they, along with *Patterson*, are authority for our decision today.

The judgment of the Ohio Supreme Court is accordingly affirmed.

Justice POWELL, with whom Justice BRENNAN and Justice MARSHALL join, and with whom Justice BLACKMUN joins dissenting.

Today the Court holds that a defendant can be convicted of aggravated murder even though the jury may have a reasonable doubt whether the accused acted in self-defense, and thus, whether he is guilty of a crime. Because I think this decision is inconsistent with both precedent and fundamental fairness, I dissent.

Petitioner Earline Martin was tried in state court for the aggravated murder of her husband. Under Ohio law, the elements of the crime are that the defendant have purposely killed another with "prior calculation and design." Martin admitted that she shot her husband but claimed that she acted in self-defense. Because self-defense is classified as an "affirmative" defense in Ohio, the jury was instructed that Martin had the burden of proving her claim by a preponderance of the evidence. Martin apparently failed to carry this burden, and the jury found her guilty.

The Ohio Supreme Court upheld the conviction, relying in part on this Court's opinion in *Patterson*. The Court today also relies on the *Patterson* reasoning in affirming the Ohio decision. If one accepts *Patterson* as the proper method of analysis for this case, I believe that the Court's opinion ignores its central meaning.

The Court significantly, and without explanation, extends the deference granted to state legislatures in this area. Today's decision could be read to say that virtually all state attempts to shift the burden of proof for affirmative defenses will be upheld, regardless of the relationship between the elements of the defense and the elements of the crime. As I understand it, *Patterson* allowed burden-shifting because evidence of an extreme emotional disturbance did not negate the *mens rea* of the underlying offense. After today's decision, however, even if proof of the defense does negate an element of the offense, burden-shifting still may be permitted because the jury can consider the defendant's evidence when reaching its verdict.

I agree, of course, that States must have substantial leeway in defining their criminal laws and administering their criminal justice systems. But none of our precedents suggests that courts must give complete deference to a State's judgment about whether a shift in the burden of proof is consistent with the presumption of innocence. In the past we have emphasized that in some circumstances it may be necessary to look beyond the text of the State's burden-shifting laws to satisfy ourselves that the requirements of *Winship* have been satisfied. In *Mullaney*, we explicitly noted the danger of granting the State unchecked discretion to shift the burden as to any element of proof in a criminal case. The Court today fails to discuss or even cite *Mullaney*, despite our unanimous agreement in that case that this danger would justify judicial intervention in some cases. Even *Patterson*, from which I dissented, recognized that "there are obviously constitutional limits beyond which the States may not go [in labeling elements of a crime as an affirmative defense]." Today, however, the Court simply asserts that Ohio law properly allocates the burdens, without giving any indication of where those limits lie.

Because our precedent establishes that the burden of proof may not be shifted when the elements of the defense and the elements of the offense conflict, and because it seems clear that they do so in this case, I would reverse the decision of the Ohio Supreme Court.

In its willingness to defer to the State's legislative definitions of crimes and defenses, the Court apparently has failed to recognize the practical effect of its decision. Martin alleged that she was innocent because she acted in self-defense, a complete justification under Ohio law. Because she had the burden of proof on this issue, the jury could have believed that it was just as likely as not that Martin's conduct was justified, and yet still have voted to convict. In other words, even though the jury may have had a substantial doubt whether Martin committed a crime, she was found guilty under Ohio law. I do not agree that the Court's authority to review state legislative choices is so limited that it justifies increasing the risk of convicting a person who may not be blameworthy. *See Patterson* (state definition of criminal law must yield when it "offends some principle of justice so rooted in the traditions and conscience of our people as to be ranked as fundamental.") The complexity of the inquiry as to when a state may shift the burden of proof should not lead the Court to fashion simple rules of deference that could lead to such unjust results.

Questions and Notes

1. Does *Martin* present a different problem from *Patterson*? If so, how is it different?

2. Presumably, a state could abolish provocation or extreme emotional excuse as a homicidal factor and punish all intentional and unjustified killers as murderers. Do you think that a state would be justified in making self-defense irrelevant? If not, was *Martin* wrongly decided?

3. Is the only reason that "unlawfulness" is not an element of murder because that element is presumed? Surely a "lawful" killing would not be punished as murder.

4. If a state defined murder as the unlawful killing of another human being, would it be required to shoulder the burden on self-defense? *See Groesbeck v. House-wright*, 657 F. Supp. 798 (D. Nev. 1987). If so, does that exalt form over substance?

5. After *Patterson* and *Martin*, if a legislator asked you whether it would be constitutionally permissible to enact a statute identical to that invalidated in *Mullaney*, what would you advise her?

C. Presumptions

Sandstrom v. Montana

442 U.S. 510 (1979)

Mr. Justice BRENNAN delivered the opinion of the Court.

The question presented is whether, in a case in which intent is an element of the crime charged, the jury instruction, "the law presumes that a person intends the ordinary consequences of his voluntary acts," violates the Fourteenth Amendment's requirement that the State prove every element of a criminal offense beyond a reasonable doubt.

On November 22, 1976, 18-year-old David Sandstrom confessed to the slaying of Annie Jessen. Based upon the confession and corroborating evidence, petitioner was charged on December 2 with "deliberate homicide," in that he "purposely or knowingly caused the death of Annie Jessen." At trial, Sandstrom's attorney informed the jury that, although his client admitted killing Jessen, he did not do so "purposely or knowingly," and was therefore not guilty of "deliberate homicide" but of a lesser crime. The basic support for this contention was the testimony of two court-appointed mental health experts, each of whom described for the jury petitioner's mental state at the time of the incident. Sandstrom's attorney argued that this testimony demonstrated that petitioner, due to a personality disorder aggravated by alcohol consumption, did not kill Annie Jessen "purposely or knowingly."

The prosecution requested the trial judge to instruct the jury that "[t]he law presumes that a person intends the ordinary consequences of his voluntary acts." Petitioner's counsel objected, arguing that "the instruction has the effect of shifting the burden of proof on the issue of" purpose or knowledge to the defense, and that "that is impermissible under the Federal Constitution, due process of law." He offered to provide a number of federal decisions in support of the objection, including this Court's holding in *Mullaney*, but was told by the judge: "You can give those to the Supreme Court. The objection is overruled." The instruction was delivered, the jury found petitioner guilty of deliberate homicide, and petitioner was sentenced to 100 years in prison.

Sandstrom appealed to the Supreme Court of Montana, again contending that the instruction shifted to the defendant the burden of disproving an element of the crime charged, in violation of *Mullaney, Winship*, and *Patterson*. The Montana court conceded that these cases did prohibit shifting the burden of proof to the defendant by means of a presumption, but held that the cases "do not prohibit allocation of *some* burden of proof to a defendant under certain circumstances." Since in the court's view, "[d]efendant's sole burden under [the] instruction was to produce *some* evidence that he did not intend the ordinary consequences of his voluntary acts, not to disprove that he acted 'purposely' or 'knowingly,' . . . the instruction does not violate due process standards as defined by the United States or Montana Constitution. . . ." (Emphasis added.)

The threshold inquiry in ascertaining the constitutional analysis applicable to this kind of jury instruction is to determine the nature of the presumption it describes. That determination requires careful attention to the words actually spoken to the jury, for whether a defendant has been accorded his constitutional rights depends upon the way in which a reasonable juror could have interpreted the instruction.

Respondent argues, first, that the instruction merely described a permissive inference—that is, it allowed but did not require the jury to draw conclusions about defendant's intent from his actions—and that such inferences are constitutional. These arguments need not detain us long, for even respondent admits that "it's possible" that the jury believed they were required to apply the presumption. Sandstrom's jurors were told that "[t]he law presumes that a person intends the ordinary consequences of his voluntary acts." They were not told that they had a choice, or that they might infer that conclusion; they were told only that the law presumed it.

It is clear that a reasonable juror could easily have viewed such an instruction as mandatory.

In the alternative, respondent urges that, even if viewed as a mandatory presumption rather than as a permissive inference, the presumption did not conclusively establish intent but rather could be rebutted. On this view, the instruction required the jury, if satisfied as to the facts which trigger the presumption, to find intent unless the defendant offered evidence to the contrary. Moreover, according to the State, all the defendant had to do to rebut the presumption was produce "some" contrary evidence; he did not have to "prove" that he lacked the required mental state. Thus, "[a]t most, it placed a *burden of production* on the petitioner," but "did not shift to petitioner the *burden of persuasion* with respect to any element of the offense. . . ." Again, respondent contends that presumptions with this limited effect pass constitutional muster.

We need not review respondent's constitutional argument on this point either, however, for we reject this characterization of the presumption as well. Respondent concedes there is a "risk" that the jury, once having found petitioner's act voluntary, would interpret the instruction as automatically directing a finding of intent. Petitioner's jury was told that "[t]he law presumes that a person intends the ordinary consequences of his voluntary acts." They were not told that the presumption could be rebutted, as the Montana Supreme Court held, by the defendant's simple presentation of "some" evidence; nor even that it could be rebutted at all. Given the common definition of "presume" as "to suppose to be true without proof," Webster's New Collegiate Dictionary 911 (1974), and given the lack of qualifying instructions as to the legal effect of the presumption, we cannot discount the possibility that the jury may have interpreted the instruction in either of two more stringent ways.

First, a reasonable jury could well have interpreted the presumption as "conclusive," that is, not technically as a presumption at all, but rather as an irrebuttable direction by the court to find intent once convinced of the facts triggering the presumption. Alternatively, the jury may have interpreted the instruction as a direction to find intent upon proof of the defendant's voluntary actions (and their "ordinary" consequences), unless the defendant proved the contrary by some quantum of proof which may well have been considerably greater than "some" evidence—thus effectively shifting the burden of persuasion on the element of intent. Numerous federal and state courts have warned that instructions of the type given here can be interpreted in just these ways.

We do not reject the possibility that some jurors may have interpreted the challenged instruction as permissive, or, if mandatory, as requiring only that the defendant come forward with "some" evidence in rebuttal. However, the fact that a reasonable juror could have given the presumption conclusive or persuasion-shifting effect means that we cannot discount the possibility that Sandstrom's jurors actually did proceed upon one or the other of these latter interpretations.

Because David Sandstrom's jury may have interpreted the judge's instruction as constituting either a burden-shifting presumption like that in *Mullaney*, or a conclusive presumption, and because either interpretation would have deprived defendant of his right to the due process of law, we hold the instruction given in this case unconstitutional.

Questions and Notes

1. If you had been the prosecutor, would you have encouraged the trial judge to give the presumption? Why? Why not?

2. Why do you suppose that the trial judge was not more receptive to Supreme Court constitutional decisions?

3. What is the difference between a conclusive presumption, a mandatory presumption, and a permissive inference?

4. Would a permissible inference have been allowed in this case? Why? Why not?

5. In another Montana case, *Egelhoff*, the Supreme Court split (4-4) over the meaning of presumptions.

Montana v. Egelhoff

518 U.S. 37 (1996)

[For the facts of this case, *see* page 530, *supra*.]

Justice SCALIA announced the judgment of the Court and delivered an opinion, in which THE CHIEF JUSTICE, Justice KENNEDY, and Justice THOMAS join.

The second line of our cases invoked by the Montana Supreme Court's opinion requires even less discussion. *In re Winship*, announced the proposition that the Due Process Clause requires proof beyond a reasonable doubt of every fact necessary to constitute the charged crime, and *Sandstrom v. Montana*, established a corollary, that a jury instruction which shifts to the defendant the burden of proof on a requisite element of mental state violates due process. These decisions simply are not implicated here because, as the Montana court itself recognized, "the burden is not shifted" The trial judge instructed the jury that "the State of Montana has the burden of proving the guilt of the Defendant beyond a reasonable doubt," and that "[a] person commits the offense of deliberate homicide if he purposely or knowingly causes the death of another human being," Thus, failure by the State to produce evidence of respondent's mental state would have resulted in an acquittal. That acquittal did not occur was presumably attributable to the fact, noted by the Supreme Court of Montana, that the State introduced considerable evidence from which the jury might have concluded that respondent acted "purposely" or "knowingly." For example, respondent himself testified that, several hours before the murders, he had given his handgun to Pavola and asked her to put it in the glove compartment of Christenson's car. That he had to retrieve the gun from the glove compartment before he used it was strong evidence that it was his "conscious object" to commit the charged crimes; as was the execution-style manner in which a single shot was fired into the head of each victim.

Recognizing that Sandstrom is not directly on point, the Supreme Court of Montana described § 45-2-203 as a burden-reducing, rather than burden-shifting, statute. This obviously was not meant to suggest that the statute formally reduced the burden of proof to clear and convincing, or to a mere preponderance; there is utterly no basis for that, neither in the text of the law nor in the jury instruction that was given. What the court evidently meant is that, by excluding a significant line of evidence that might refute *mens rea*, the statute made it easier for the State to meet the requirement of proving mens rea beyond a reasonable doubt — reduced the burden in the sense of making the burden easier to bear. But any evidentiary rule can have that effect. "Reducing" the State's burden in this manner is not unconstitutional, unless the rule of evidence itself violates a fundamental principle of fairness (which, as discussed, this one does not). We have "rejected the view that anything in the Due Process Clause bars States from making changes in their criminal law that have the effect of making it easier for the prosecution to obtain convictions."

Finally, we may comment upon the Montana Supreme Court's citation of the following passage in *Martin v. Ohio*, a case upholding a state law that placed on the defendant the burden of proving self-defense by a preponderance of the evidence:

> "It would be quite different if the jury had been instructed that self-defense evidence could not be considered in determining whether there was a reasonable doubt about the State's case, i. e., that self-defense evidence must be put aside for all purposes unless it satisfied the preponderance standard. Such an instruction would relieve the State of its burden and plainly run afoul of [In re] *Winship's* mandate. The instructions in this case . . . are adequate to convey to the jury that all of the evidence, including the evidence going to self-defense, must be considered in deciding whether there was a reasonable doubt about the sufficiency of the State's proof of the elements of the crime."

This passage can be explained in various ways — e. g., as an assertion that the right to have a jury consider self-defense evidence (unlike the right to have a jury consider evidence of voluntary intoxication) is fundamental, a proposition that the historical record may support. But the only explanation needed for present purposes is the one given in *Kokkonen v. Guardian Life Ins. Co.*, 511 U.S. 375 (1994): "It is to the holdings of our cases, rather than their dicta, that we must attend." If the *Martin* dictum means that the Due Process Clause requires all relevant evidence bearing on the elements of a crime to be admissible, the decisions we have discussed show it to be incorrect.

Justice O'CONNOR, with whom Justice STEVENS, Justice SOUTER, and Justice BREYER join, dissenting.

In *Martin v. Ohio*, 480 U.S. 228 (1987), the Court considered an Ohio statute providing that a defendant bore the burden of proving, by a preponderance of the evidence, an affirmative defense such as self-defense. We held that placing that burden on the defendant did not violate due process. The Court noted in explanation that it would nevertheless have been error to instruct the jury that "self-defense evidence could not be considered in determining whether there was a reasonable doubt about the State's case" where Ohio's definition of the intent element made self-defense evidence relevant to the State's burden. "Such an instruction would relieve the State of its burden and plainly run afoul of *Winship*'s mandate." In other words, the State's right to shift the burden of proving an affirmative defense did not include the power to prevent the defendant from attempting to prove self-defense in an effort to cast doubt on the State's case. Dictum or not, this observation explained our reasoning and is similarly applicable here, where the State has benefited from the defendant's inability to make an argument which, if accepted, could throw reasonable doubt on the State's proof. The placement of the burden of proof for affirmative defenses should not be confused with the use of evidence to negate elements of the offense charged.

Questions and Notes

1. In view of Justice Ginsburg's deciding vote, neither the Scalia four nor the O'Connor four controls this case.

2. Which of the two opinions is more soundly reasoned? Why?

Chapter 17

Attempt

A. Mens Rea

As the materials will indicate, the question of what constitutes an attempt varies widely among jurisdictions. In general terms, however, it can be defined as a substantial, but ineffectual, effort to commit a crime.

Those who attempt crimes are typically subject to substantial criminal penalties, but less than those to which they would have been subjected had they completed the crime. This punishment scheme potentially raises at least two questions. One is: If the defendant failed in bringing about harm, why punish him at all? The other is: If the defendant was as or more culpable in attempting to commit the crime, why should he be subject to less of a punishment?

The first question is the easier of the two. Attempting to murder somebody *is* harmful. Granted, it may not be as harmful as actually murdering somebody, but it is certainly the sort of thing that society can and should deter. Given the defendant's certain culpability, and probable dangerousness, some punishment is clearly appropriate.

In regard to the second question, there is a school of thought that suggests that harm should be irrelevant to the criminal law (*see, e.g.*, Schulhofer, *Harm and Punishment: A Critique of Emphasis on the Results of Conduct in the Criminal Law*, 122 U. Pa. L. Rev. 1497 (1974)). According to this view (partially but not totally adopted by the MPC, *see* §5.05(1) (Appendix A)), one who attempts a crime ought to be punished as severely as another who completes it. It should be apparent from Chapter 3, Causation, that this view has not prevailed. Rather, one who has caused a particular harm is generally treated more seriously than one who has merely tried to cause the same harm.

The major issues in attempt are the defendant's state of mind (did she really mean to do it?) and her proximity to completion (did she go far enough?). Sometimes these issues overlap. Indeed, some of the same cases raise both questions. Nevertheless, they are analytically distinct and will be treated separately, even to the extent of repeating some cases to make different points. We start with a "state of mind" case.

Smallwood v. State

680 A.2d 512 (Md. 1996)

MURPHY, Chief Judge

In this case, we examine the use of circumstantial evidence to infer that a defendant possessed the intent to kill needed for a conviction of attempted murder or assault with intent to murder. We conclude that such an inference is not supportable under the facts of this case.

I

A

On August 29, 1991, Dwight Ralph Smallwood was diagnosed as being infected with the Human Immunodeficiency Virus (HIV). According to medical records from the Prince George's County Detention Center, he had been informed of his HIV-positive status by September 25, 1991. In February 1992, a social worker made Smallwood aware of the necessity of practicing "safe sex" in order to avoid transmitting the virus to his sexual partners, and in July 1993, Smallwood told health care providers at Children's Hospital that he had only one sexual partner and that they always used condoms. Smallwood again tested positive for HIV in February and March of 1994.

On September 26, 1993, Smallwood and an accomplice robbed a woman at gunpoint, and forced her into a grove of trees where each man alternately placed a gun to her head while the other one raped her. On September 28, 1993, Smallwood and an accomplice robbed a second woman at gunpoint and took her to a secluded location, where Smallwood inserted his penis into her with "slight penetration." On September 30, 1993, Smallwood and an accomplice robbed yet a third woman, also at gunpoint, and took her to a local school where she was forced to perform oral sex on Smallwood and was raped by him. In each of these episodes, Smallwood threatened to kill his victims if they did not cooperate or to return and shoot them if they reported his crimes. Smallwood did not wear a condom during any of these criminal episodes.

Based upon his attack on September 28, 1993, Smallwood was charged with, among other crimes, attempted first-degree rape, robbery with a deadly weapon, assault with intent to murder, and reckless endangerment. In separate indictments, Smallwood was also charged with the attempted second-degree murder of each of his three victims. On October 11, 1994, Smallwood pled guilty in the Circuit Court for Prince George's County to attempted first-degree rape and robbery with a deadly weapon.[1] The circuit court (Nichols, J.) also convicted Smallwood of assault with intent to murder and reckless endangerment based upon his September 28, 1993 attack, and convicted Smallwood of all three counts of attempted second-degree murder.

Following his conviction, Smallwood was sentenced to concurrent sentences of life imprisonment for attempted rape, twenty years imprisonment for robbery with a deadly weapon, thirty years imprisonment for assault with intent to murder, and

---

1. In two additional indictments, Smallwood was charged with the rape and robbery of the two women who were attacked on September 26 and September 30. Smallwood pled guilty to attempted first-degree rape and robbery with a deadly weapon in those cases as well, and the judgments entered pursuant to those pleas are not before us on this appeal.

five years imprisonment for reckless endangerment. The circuit court also imposed a concurrent thirty-year sentence for each of the three counts of attempted second-degree murder. The circuit court's judgments were affirmed in part and reversed in part by the Court of Special Appeals.[2] Upon Smallwood's petition, we granted certiorari to consider whether the trial court could properly conclude that Smallwood possessed the requisite intent to support his convictions of attempted second-degree murder and assault with intent to murder.

B

Smallwood asserts that the trial court lacked sufficient evidence to support its conclusion that Smallwood intended to kill his three victims. Smallwood argues that the fact that he engaged in unprotected sexual intercourse, even though he knew that he carried HIV, is insufficient to infer an intent to kill. The most that can reasonably be inferred, Smallwood contends, is that he is guilty of recklessly endangering his victims by exposing them to the risk that they would become infected themselves. The State disagrees, arguing that the facts of this case are sufficient to infer an intent to kill. The State likens Smallwood's HIV-positive status to a deadly weapon and argues that engaging in unprotected sex when one is knowingly infected with HIV is equivalent to firing a loaded firearm at that person.

II

A

As we have previously stated, "the required intent in the crimes of assault with intent to murder and attempted murder is the specific intent to murder, *i.e.*, the specific intent to kill under circumstances that would not legally justify or excuse the killing or mitigate it to manslaughter." "("[T]he intent element of assault with intent to murder requires proof of a specific intent to kill under circumstances such that if the victim had died, the offense would be murder.") Smallwood has not argued that his actions were performed under mitigating circumstances or that he was legally justified in attacking the three women. He was properly found guilty of attempted murder and assault with intent to murder only if there was sufficient evidence from which the trier of fact could reasonably have concluded that Smallwood possessed a specific intent to kill at the time he assaulted each of the three women.

An intent to kill may be proved by circumstantial evidence. "Since intent is subjective and, without the cooperation of the accused, cannot be directly and objectively proven, its presence must be shown by established facts which permit a proper inference of its existence." Therefore, the trier of fact may infer the existence of the required intent from surrounding circumstances such as "the accused's acts, conduct and words." As we have repeatedly stated, "under the proper circumstances, an

---

2. The Court of Special Appeals concluded that Smallwood's conviction for assault with intent to murder should merge into the conviction for attempted second-degree murder based upon the same event. Because we find that the evidence was insufficient to convict Smallwood of either of these two crimes, however, the issue of merger has become moot.

intent to kill may be inferred from the use of a deadly weapon directed at a vital part of the human body."

In *Raines*, we upheld the use of such an inference. In that case, Raines and a friend were traveling on a highway when the defendant fired a pistol into the driver's side window of a tractor trailer in an adjacent lane. The shot killed the driver of the tractor trailer, and Raines was convicted of first-degree murder. The evidence in the case showed that Raines shot at the driver's window of the truck, knowing that the truck driver was immediately behind the window. We concluded that "Raines's actions in directing the gun at the window, and therefore at the driver's head on the other side of the window, permitted an inference that Raines shot the gun with the intent to kill."

The State argues that our analysis in *Raines* rested upon two elements: (1) Raines knew that his weapon was deadly, and (2) Raines knew that he was firing it at someone's head. The State argues that Smallwood similarly knew that HIV infection ultimately leads to death, and that he knew that he would be exposing his victims to the risk of HIV transmission by engaging in unprotected sex with them. Therefore, the State argues, a permissible inference can be drawn that Smallwood intended to kill each of his three victims. The State's analysis, however, ignores several factors.

B

First, we must consider the magnitude of the risk to which the victim is knowingly exposed. The inference drawn in *Raines* rests upon the rule that "it is permissible to infer that 'one intends the natural and probable consequences of his act.'" Before an intent to kill may be inferred based solely upon the defendant's exposure of a victim to a risk of death, it must be shown that the victim's death would have been a natural and probable result of the defendant's conduct. It is for this reason that a trier of fact may infer that a defendant possessed an intent to kill when firing a deadly weapon at a vital part of the human body. When a deadly weapon has been fired at a vital part of a victim's body, the risk of killing the victim is so high that it becomes reasonable to assume that the defendant intended the victim to die as a natural and probable consequence of the defendant's actions.

Death by AIDS is clearly one *natural* possible consequence of exposing someone to a risk of HIV infection, even on a single occasion. It is less clear that death by AIDS from that single exposure is a sufficiently *probable* result to provide the sole support for an inference that the person causing the exposure intended to kill the person who was exposed. While the risk to which Smallwood exposed his victims when he forced them to engage in unprotected sexual activity must not be minimized, the State has presented no evidence from which it can reasonably be concluded that death by AIDS is a probable result of Smallwood's actions to the same extent that death is the probable result of firing a deadly weapon at a vital part of someone's body. Without such evidence, it cannot fairly be concluded that death by

AIDS was sufficiently probable to support an inference that Smallwood intended to kill his victims in the absence of other evidence indicative of an intent to kill.

C

In this case, we find no additional evidence from which to infer an intent to kill. Smallwood's actions are wholly explained by an intent to commit rape and armed robbery, the crimes for which he has already pled guilty. For this reason, his actions fail to provide evidence that he also had an intent to kill. As one commentator noted, in discussing a criminal case involving similar circumstances, "because virus transmission occurs simultaneously with the act of rape, that act alone would not provide evidence of intent to transmit the virus. Some additional evidence, such as an explicit statement, would be necessary to demonstrate the actor's specific intent." Smallwood's knowledge of his HIV-infected status provides the only evidence in this case supporting a conclusion that he intended anything beyond the rapes and robberies for which he has been convicted.

The cases cited by the State demonstrate the sort of additional evidence needed to support an inference that Smallwood intended to kill his victims. The defendants in these cases have either made explicit statements demonstrating an intent to infect their victims or have taken specific actions demonstrating such an intent and tending to exclude other possible intents. In *State v. Hinkhouse*, 139 Ore. App. 446, 912 P.2d 921 (1996), for example, the defendant engaged in unprotected sex with a number of women while knowing that he was HIV positive. The defendant had also actively concealed his HIV-positive status from these women, had lied to several of them by stating that he was not HIV-positive, and had refused the women's requests that he wear condoms. There was also evidence that he had told at least one of his sexual partners that "if he were [HIV-]positive, he would spread the virus to other people." The Oregon Court of Appeals found this evidence to be sufficient to demonstrate an intent to kill, and upheld the defendant's convictions for attempted murder.

In *State v. Caine*, 652 So. 2d 611 (La. App.), a conviction for attempted second degree murder was upheld where the defendant had jabbed a used syringe into a victim's arm while shouting "I'll give you AIDS." The defendant in *Weeks v. State*, 834 S.W.2d 559 (Tex. App. 1992), made similar statements, and was convicted of attempted murder after he spat on a prison guard. In that case, the defendant knew that he was HIV-positive, and the appellate court found that "the record reflects that [Weeks] thought he could kill the guard by spitting his HIV-infected saliva at him." There was also evidence that at the time of the spitting incident, Weeks had stated that he was "going to take someone with him when he went,' that he was 'medical now,' and that he was 'HIV-4.'"

The evidence in *State v. Haines*, 545 N.E.2d 834 (Ind. App. 1989), contained both statements by the defendant demonstrating intent and actions solely explainable as attempts to spread HIV. There, the defendant's convictions for attempted murder were upheld where the defendant slashed his wrists and sprayed blood from them on a police officer and two paramedics, splashing blood in their faces and eyes. Haines attempted to scratch and bite them and attempted to force blood-soaked objects into their faces. During this altercation, the defendant told the officer that he should be left to die because he had AIDS, that he wanted to "give it to him," and that he would "use his wounds" to spray the officer with blood. Haines also "repeatedly yelled that he had AIDS, that he could not deal with it and that he was going to make [the officer] deal with it."

Scroggins v. State, 198 Ga. App. 29, 401 S.E.2d 13, 15 (1990), presents a similar scenario, where the defendant made noises with his mouth as if bringing up spittle and then bit a police officer hard enough to break the skin. Immediately after this incident he informed a nurse that he was HIV-positive and laughed when the police officer asked him if he had AIDS. The Georgia Court of Appeals found that evidence showing that the defendant "sucked up excess "sputum" before biting the officer was "evidence of a deliberate, thinking act" and that in conjunction with the defendant's laughter when asked about AIDS, it provided sufficient evidence of intent to support Scroggins's conviction for assault with intent to kill.

In contrast with these cases, the State in this case would allow the trier of fact to infer an intent to kill based solely upon the fact that Smallwood exposed his victims to the risk that they might contract HIV. Without evidence showing that such a result is sufficiently probable to support this inference, we conclude that Smallwood's convictions for attempted murder and assault with intent to murder must be reversed.

Judgments for attempted murder in the second degree and assault with intent to murder reversed; costs to be paid by the respondent.

Questions and Notes

1. Were the defendants in *Hinkhouse, Caine, Haines*, and *Scroggins* any more likely to kill their victims than Smallwood was?

2. If your answer to Question 1 was "no," why can they be convicted of attempted murder while Smallwood cannot?

3. Should knowledge be sufficient? Suppose that a person attaches a bomb to the ignition of her two-month-old Lemon V-8 automobile, hoping and expecting hoping and expecting that it will explode when the repair shop employee drives it to the repair shop and expecting that the employee will be killed, but hoping that he will not be. If the bomb does not go off, would the defendant be guilty of attempted murder under the *Smallwood* analysis? Should the defendant be guilty? *See* NUT-SHELL § 14.02. Would your answer be any different if the bomb did go off, but the employee was not killed?

4. Although most jurisdictions require specific intent for an attempt, there is a minority view that will permit an attempt on the same state of mind that is necessary for the completed crime. *Thomas* is such a case.

People v. Thomas

729 P.2d 972 (Colo. 1986)

LOHR, Justice

I

On the evening of February 4, 1981, the defendant received a telephone call from a former girlfriend informing him that she had been raped in her apartment by a man who lived in an apartment upstairs. The defendant arrived at the woman's apartment shortly thereafter, armed with a pistol. He went upstairs and gained entrance into the apartment occupied by the alleged assailant by identifying himself as a policeman. The defendant pointed his gun at the man who, believing the defendant was a police officer, accompanied him back down to the woman's apartment. The woman identified the man as the rapist, and the defendant instructed her to call the police. At that time, the man started to flee to his own apartment, and the defendant gave chase. The defendant fired three shots, two of which struck the fleeing man. The defendant testified that he fired the first shot as a warning when the man was going up the stairs, that he fired a second shot accidentally when the man kicked him while on the stairs, and that the third shot was also a warning shot, fired from the outside of the building near the window of the apartment occupied by the alleged rapist. When the police arrived, they found the defendant still waiting outside, holding the gun.

The jury was instructed on the crimes of attempted first degree murder, first degree assault, and the lesser included offenses of attempted second degree murder, attempted reckless manslaughter, attempted heat of passion manslaughter, and second degree assault. The jury returned verdicts of guilty to the charges of first degree assault and attempted reckless manslaughter, and the trial court entered judgment accordingly.

Upon appeal, the court of appeals sustained the conviction for first degree assault, but reversed the attempted reckless manslaughter conviction on the basis that attempted reckless manslaughter is not a legally cognizable offense in Colorado. We granted certiorari to review that latter conclusion and the resulting reversal of the defendant's conviction for attempted reckless manslaughter.

II

A

The language of the relevant statutes provides the framework for our analysis. The crime of reckless manslaughter is defined in section 18-3-104(1)(a), 8B C.R.S. (1986), as follows:

(1) A person commits the crime of manslaughter if:

(a) He recklessly causes the death of another person; . . . .

"Recklessly," the relevant culpable mental state for this crime, is defined in section 18-1-501(8), 8B C.R.S. (1986):

(8) A person acts recklessly when he consciously disregards a substantia and unjustifiable risk that a result will occur or that a circumstance exists.

As applied to the offense of reckless manslaughter, the requisite conscious disregard of a substantial and unjustifiable risk relates to a result, the death of another person.

The inchoate offense of criminal attempt is defined as follows in section 18-2-101(1), 8B C.R.S. (1986):

A person commits criminal attempt if, acting with the kind of culpability otherwise required for commission of an offense, he engages in conduct constituting a substantial step toward the commission of the offense. A substantial step is any conduct, whether act, omission, or possession, which is strongly corroborative of the firmness of the actor's purpose to complete the commission of the offense. . . .

The court of appeals held that "[r]ecklessness is . . . a mental culpability which is incompatible with the concept of an intentional act." This is so, the court held, because the "conscious disregard" with respect to risk of death that is essential to reckless manslaughter cannot be equated with the conscious intent to cause death which the court of appeals implicitly determined to be a necessary element of the offense of criminal attempt in this context. On certiorari review, the defendant supports this analysis, contending that "[o]ne cannot intend to cause a specific result . . . by consciously disregarding the risk that the result will occur." A careful analysis of the elements of criminal attempt and of reckless manslaughter demonstrates, however, that the court of appeals' analysis and the defendant's supporting arguments are misconceived.

In *People v. Frysig*, 628 P.2d 1004 (Colo. 1981), we construed the criminal attempt statute in the context of a charge of attempted first-degree sexual assault. We held that the intent to commit the underlying offense is an essential element of the crime.

More precisely, in order to be guilty of criminal attempt, the actor must act with the kind of culpability otherwise required for commission of the underlying offense and must engage in the conduct which constitutes the substantial step with the further intent to perform acts which, if completed, would constitute the underlying offense.

In order to complete the offense of reckless manslaughter, it is necessary that the actor cause the death of another person by acting in a manner that involves a substantial and unjustifiable risk of death of that other person and that the actor be conscious of that risk and of its nature when electing to act. Attempted reckless manslaughter requires that the accused have the intent to commit the underlying offense of reckless manslaughter. The "intent to commit the underlying "offense" of which *People v. Frysig* speaks is the intent to engage in and complete the risk-producing act or conduct. It does not include an intent that death occur even though the underlying crime, reckless manslaughter, has death as an essential element.[1]

The crime of attempted reckless manslaughter also requires that the risk-producing act or conduct be commenced and sufficiently pursued to constitute a "substantial step toward the commission of the offense." That is, the act or conduct must proceed far enough to be "strongly corroborative of the firmness of the actor's purpose," to complete those acts that will produce a substantial and unjustifiable risk of death of another.

Finally, in order to be guilty of attempted reckless manslaughter the actor must engage in the requisite acts or conduct "with the kind of culpability otherwise required for the commission of the underlying offense," that is, with a conscious disregard of a substantial and unjustifiable risk that the acts or conduct will cause the death of another person. Based upon this analysis, and contrary to the defendant's argument, there is no logical or legal inconsistency involved in the recognition of attempted reckless manslaughter as a crime under the Colorado Criminal Code.

Our analysis of the crime of attempted reckless manslaughter is buttressed by the case of *People v. Castro*, 657 P.2d 932 (Colo. 1983), in which we held that attempted extreme indifference murder is a cognizable crime under the Colorado Criminal Code. In that case, the defendant urged that extreme indifference murder involves an unintentional and inchoate act—apparently referring to the required element of the death of another, which can more accurately be characterized as a result than as an act—and that criminal attempt requires an intent to complete the underlying offense. The latter intent, the argument proceeded, necessarily involves an intent that the death of another result from the actor's conduct. The defendant argued that to intend an unintentional and inchoate act defies logic, so there can be no such crime as attempted extreme indifference murder. We concluded that an essential premise of this argument was fatally flawed. [W]e noted that "the crime of extreme indifference murder, . . . while not requiring a conscious object to kill, necessitates a conscious object to engage in conduct that creates a grave risk of death to another. . . . In this sense the culpability element of extreme indifference murder is akin to what traditionally has been known as 'general intent.'" Therefore, since the intentional state of mind required by the crime of attempted extreme indifference murder relates to the proscribed conduct and not the proscribed result, death of another person, we concluded that there is no logical inconsistency inherent in

1. For some crimes it may be that the intent to perform acts which, if completed, would constitute the underlying offense is the substantial equivalent of a specific intent to commit the underlying offense. *See People v. Frysig*, 628 P.2d 1004 (Colo. 1981) (attempted first-degree sexual assault). For other crimes, however, the purposeful completion of the actor's conduct does not necessarily satisfy all the essential elements of the crime. For instance, in the case of extreme indifference murder, death is an essential element that will not necessarily be satisfied even if all the elements relating to conduct and culpable mental state exist. Reckless manslaughter is analogous to extreme indifference murder in that respect.

charging an attempt to commit extreme indifference murder. This parallels the foregoing analysis and conclusion with respect to the crime of attempted reckless manslaughter to which the present case relates.

B

In *People v. Krovarz*, 697 P.2d 378 (Colo. 1985), we employed a new mode of analysis to determine whether a particular substantive crime can provide a foundation for criminal attempt liability. There, we examined the rationale for imposition of criminal penalties for attempts falling short of accomplishment of a completed substantive crime. We concluded that "culpability for criminal attempt rests primarily upon the actor's purpose to cause harmful consequences," and that "punishment is justified where the actor intends harm because there exists a high likelihood that his 'unspent" intent will flower into harmful conduct at any moment." We held, however, that our criminal attempt statute does not require a conscious purpose to achieve proscribed results as a condition to criminal liability. That is, criminal attempt is not a specific intent offense as such offenses are described in section 18-1-501(5), 8B C.R.S. (1986). Rather, the probability of future dangerousness that has given rise to the justified legislative judgment that criminal attempt liability should be imposed "is equally present when one acts knowingly." "Knowingly" is defined in section 18-1-501(6), 8B C.R.S. (1986), and describes what is commonly referred to as general intent.

In *Krovarz*, we recognized that the underlying offense may consist of elements of conduct, result and circumstance and that where "knowingly" is the culpable mental state attached to each, as it is in the case of the crime of aggravated robbery involved in *Krovarz*, it is necessary to examine that mental state in relation to each type of element to see whether there inheres in each the potential danger that signals the legislative intent to impose criminal attempt liability. The culpable mental state for reckless manslaughter, in contrast, is "recklessly," which is directed only toward result, the death of another person. Under *Krovarz*, therefore, it is necessary to examine the mental state of "recklessly" in relation to the result of death of another in order to see whether it involves the potential danger that justifies the conclusion that attempt liability may be founded on the substantive offense of reckless manslaughter.

One acts recklessly with respect to result when he consciously disregards a substantial and unjustified risk that a result will occur. When one engages in conduct that involves a risk of death that is both substantial and unjustified, and is conscious of the nature and extent of the risk, the actor demonstrates such a disregard for the likelihood that another will die as to evince a degree of dangerousness hardly less threatening to society than if the actor had chosen to cause death. In *Krovarz*, we expressly reserved the issue of whether a substantive crime having recklessness with respect to result as an element could provide the basis for criminal attempt liability.[2]

---

2. In *People v. Hernandez*, 44 Colo. App. 161, 614 P.2d 900 (1980), the court of appeals held that attempted criminally negligent homicide is not a cognizable crime. The analysis in that case

We suggested in *Krovarz* that recklessness might not suffice. We now conclude, however, that it does. The critical inquiry under *Krovarz* is potential for future danger. For this purpose, the awareness of a practical certainty of the prohibited result that is required for knowing conduct cannot be viewed as more dangerous, in any important degree, than the conscious disregard of a substantial and unjustifiable risk that the proscribed result will occur—the hallmark of reckless action. Although a difference in the degree of moral culpability of the actor might be perceived between knowingly achieving a proscribed result and recklessly accomplishing it, we now conclude that the difference in potential for future danger inherent in those two culpable mental states is not significant enough to justify a different result under the *Krovarz* test.[3]

We conclude that the index of dangerousness analysis utilized in *People v. Krovarz* leads to the same result achieved by examining and construing the statutory language under the standards of *Castro* and *Frysig*. Accordingly, we hold that attempted reckless manslaughter is a crime proscribed by the Colorado Criminal Code.

We reverse that part of the court of appeals' judgment overturning the defendant's conviction for attempted reckless manslaughter.

DUBOFSKY, J., specially concurring:

I join the majority opinion under the facts of this case. *People v. Krovarz*, 697 P.2d 378, 381 n.9, suggests that the analysis employed in that case should not be extended to attempted reckless conduct. The footnote in *Krovarz* reflected the concern of a commentator who observed that allowing one to be charged with attempted murder under the wide range of conduct encompassed within "reckless," without a resulting death, may extend criminal liability for harmful conduct to situations such as driving very fast on the wrong side of the road while going around a curve. Enker, *Mens Rea and Criminal Attempt*, 1977 AM. BAR FOUND. RES. J. 845, 854. The conduct is not in fact harmful if there is no traffic coming in the opposite direction. The commentator suggested that where the actor risks harm, rather than intending harm, the conduct should be penalized under a legislative definition of a substantive

---

parallels that of the court of appeals in the present case. Although we have rejected this analysis, we express no opinion concerning the correctness of the result reached by the court of appeals in *People v. Hernandez*.

3. When causing a particular result is an element of the substantive crime, the Model Penal Code requires as an element of criminal attempt that the actor "[do] or [omit] to do anything with the purpose of causing or with the belief that it will cause such result, without further conduct on his part." Model Penal Code § 5.01(1)(b) (Tent. Draft No. 10 1960). We have held, however, that under the different definition of criminal attempt in section 18-2-101(1), 8B C.R.S. (1986), purpose or belief that conduct will cause a proscribed result is not essential to liability. *People v. Castro, People v. Frysig*. Rather, intentional conduct alone will suffice. *People v. Castro*, 657 P.2d at 937–38. Therefore, we conclude that under the Colorado Criminal Code, criminal attempt liability can be predicated on recklessness with respect to result even though it cannot be said, as we did in *People v. Krovarz* with respect to "knowingly," that "recklessly" in effect connotes a choice to create the proscribed result.

crime instead of the common law definition of attempt. Given the facts in this case, however, I am convinced that the defendant came close enough to intending harm that he can be convicted of attempted reckless manslaughter.

Questions and Notes

1. Isn't there a huge difference between the knowing standard of *Krovarz* and recklessness? When one acts knowingly, he knows that the results are practically certain (the Lemon V-8 hypothetical). Recklessness, on the other hand, just means that there is a substantial and unjustifiable risk that the defendant knowingly took.

2. Under the court's view, would every robber be guilty of attempted felony murder on the theory that if death occurred, he had the requisite intent for murder?

3. Under the court's view, what result in Justice Dubofsky's hypothetical about reckless driving when nobody is in fact in harm's way?

4. Suppose Thomas' shots hadn't hit the victim at all (what he says he intended). Could he then be guilty of attempted reckless manslaughter?

5. How should *People v. Hernandez* in footnote 2 of the court's opinion be resolved?

6. Do you prefer the *Smallwood* approach or the *Thomas* approach? Why?

7. As you read *Stewart*, consider the interrelationship of both intent and act in attempt and intent for attempt *vis-à-vis* the completed crime.

State v. Stewart

420 N.W.2d 44 (Wis. 1988)

SHIRLEY S. ABRAHAMSON, Justice.

This is an appeal from an unpublished decision of the court of appeals filed on March 18, 1987, reversing a judgment entered by the circuit court. The court of appeals reversed the conviction of defendant Walter Lee Stewart for attempted robbery.

The only evidence at trial was the testimony of the complainant, Scott Kodanko. The complainant testified that he was waiting for a bus at about 4:30 P.M. on a Saturday, after leaving work. He was alone in a three-sided plexiglass bus shelter open to the street in downtown Milwaukee. Two men, Mr. Moore and the defendant, entered the bus shelter while a third man, Mr. Levy, remained outside.

Moore and the defendant stood one to two feet from the complainant. The complainant was in a corner of the shelter, his exit to the street blocked by the two men. Moore asked the complainant if he wanted to buy some cigarettes. The complainant responded that he did not. Moore then said, "Give us some change." When the complainant refused, the defendant said "Give us some change, man." The defendant repeated this demand in an increasingly loud voice three to four times. The complainant still refused to give the two men change. The defendant then reached into his coat with his right hand at about the waist level, whereupon Moore stated something to the effect of "put that gun away." At that point Levy, who had been waiting outside the bus shelter, entered and said to the defendant and Moore "Come on, let's go." Levy showed the complainant some money, stating, "I don't want your money, I got lots of money."

The three men left the bus shelter together and entered a restaurant across the street. A few minutes later Moore returned and made "small talk" with the complainant. The three men were arrested a short while later. It appears from the record that the complainant did not report the incident to the police. The record does not reveal who called the police.

The complainant testified that he felt threatened throughout the encounter, which lasted less than three minutes. None of the men ever touched him or raised a hand to him, and at no time did he attempt to leave the shelter.

The defendant claims that the state failed to prove beyond a reasonable doubt that he intended to commit the crime of robbery. In *Hamiel v. State*, 285 N.W.2d 639 (1979), this court interpreted sec. 939.32(3) as establishing two elements for the crime of attempt: (1) an intent to commit the crime charged; and (2) sufficient acts in furtherance of the criminal intent to demonstrate unequivocally that it was improbable the accused would desist from the crime of his or her own free will. The *Hamiel* court stated the two elements of attempted robbery as follows:

> "In order for the defendant to be found guilty of attempted robbery pursuant to sec. 943.32 and sec. 939.32(2) (the general attempt statute), Stats., it must only be shown that: (1) the defendant's actions in furtherance of the crime clearly demonstrate, under the circumstances that he had the requisite intent to commit the crime of attempted robbery; and (2) that having formed such intent the defendant had taken sufficient steps in furtherance of the crime so that it was improbable that he would have voluntarily terminated his participation in the commission of the crime."

The defendant argues that viewing the evidence in the light most favorable to the prosecution, this court must conclude that a rational trier of fact could not be convinced beyond a reasonable doubt that he intended to commit robbery. According to the defendant, all of his conduct, including his leaving the bus shelter when he did, demonstrates that he was panhandling, not attempting robbery.

Intent may be inferred from the defendant's conduct, including his words and gestures taken in the context of the circumstances. As we said in *Hamiel*, "[I]n the crime of attempt, it is primarily the acts of the accused which provide evidence of the requisite mental intent. . . . The acts must . . . establish that the accused intended to commit the substantive crime."[2]

---

2. It is difficult sometimes to consider the element of intent apart from the element of conduct because often the sole evidence of intent is the conduct of the accused from which intent must be

The acts of the accused, however, "must not be so few or of such an equivocal nature as to render doubtful the existence of the requisite criminal intent." *State v. Berry*, 280 N.W.2d 204 (1979). When a person desists from acts that appear criminal, the intent of the actor may appear equivocal. Desistance thus raises a factual question relevant to the element of intent. As this court said in *Berry*, "Failure, if and by whatever means the actor's efforts are frustrated, is relevant and significant only insofar as it may negate any inference that the actor did in fact possess the necessary criminal intent to commit the crime in question."

With these principles in mind we examine the record to determine whether the evidence is sufficient for the trier of fact to conclude that the defendant had the requisite intent.

We conclude that the circuit judge as trier of fact could reasonably find that the defendant's repeated statement, "Give us some change," was not merely a request but a demand. Given the setting in which the statement was made, the trier of fact could reasonably find that the demand was backed by threat of force. The circuit judge could find that the defendant's reaching into his coat as Moore said, "Hey, man, put that gun away," demonstrated that the defendant intended to frighten the complainant into handing over his change. The trier of fact could reasonably believe that the defendant exploited the circumstances in order to coerce the complainant into complying with his demand for money.

The trier of fact did not have to accept the inference from the evidence that defense counsel urged, namely, that the defendant was panhandling. We conclude that the evidence adduced, believed and rationally considered by the trier of fact is sufficient to prove beyond a reasonable doubt that the defendant intended to compel the complainant to turn over his money under threat of force. Thus, the evidence satisfies the first element of attempted robbery—intent to commit robbery.

Questions and Notes

1. Is there any difference between the state of mind necessary for robbery and attempted robbery? *Compare People v. Patton, supra*. Would Stewart have been guilty of robbery if Kodanko had given him the money?

2. We will return to *Stewart* when we analyze the question of how far one must go to be guilty of an attempt. First, however, we will examine how far one must go in conjunction with two cases reaching apparently conflicting results, *Rizzo* and *McQuirter*.

---

inferred. The conduct of the actor thus may serve to prove both elements in the attempt statute. First, the conduct may be the basis for proving the actor's intent to commit the crime. Second, the crime of attempt requires sufficient acts in furtherance of the intent.

B. Actus Reus

People v. Rizzo

158 N.E. 888 (N.Y. 1927)

CRANE, J.

The police of the city of New York did excellent work in this case by preventing the commission of a serious crime. It is a great satisfaction to realize that we have such wide-awake guardians of our peace. Whether or not the steps which the defendant had taken up to the time of his arrest amounted to the commission of a crime, as defined by our law, is, however, another matter. He has been convicted of an attempt to commit the crime of robbery in the first degree, and sentenced to state's prison. There is no doubt that he had the intention to commit robbery, if he got the chance. An examination, however, of the facts is necessary to determine whether his acts were in preparation to commit the crime if the opportunity offered, or constituted a crime in itself, known to our law as an attempt to commit robbery in the first degree. Charles Rizzo, the defendant, appellant, with three others, Anthony J. Dorio, Thomas Milo, and John Thomasello, on January 14th planned to rob one Charles Rao of a pay roll valued at about $1,200 which he was to carry from the bank for the United Lathing Company. These defendants, two of whom had firearms, started out in an automobile, looking for Rao or the man who had the pay roll on that day. Rizzo claimed to be able to identify the man, and was to point him out to the others, who were to do the actual holding up. The four rode about in their car looking for Rao. They went to the bank from which he was supposed to get the money and to various buildings being constructed by the United Lathing Company. At last they came to One Hundred and Eightieth street and Morris Park avenue. By this time they were watched and followed by two police officers. As Rizzo jumped out of the car and ran into the building, all four were arrested. The defendant was taken out from the building in which he was hiding. Neither Rao nor a man named Previti, who was also supposed to carry a pay roll, were at the place at the time of the arrest. The defendants had not found or seen the man they intended to rob. No person with a pay roll was at any of the places where they had stopped, and no one had been pointed out or identified by Rizzo. The four men intended to rob the pay roll man, whoever he was. They were looking for him, but they had not seen or discovered him up to the time they were arrested.

Does this constitute the crime of an attempt to commit robbery in the first degree? The Penal Law, § 2, prescribes:

> "An act, done with intent to commit a crime, and tending but failing to effect its commission, is 'an attempt to commit that crime.'"

The word "*tending*" is very indefinite. It is perfectly evident that there will arise differences of opinion as to whether an act in a given case is one tending to commit a crime. "Tending" means to exert activity in a particular direction. Any act in preparation to commit a crime may be said to have a tendency towards its accomplishment. The procuring of the automobile, searching the streets looking for the desired victim, were in reality acts tending toward the commission of the proposed crime. The law, however, had recognized that many acts in the way of preparation are too remote to constitute the crime of attempt. The line has been drawn between those acts which are remote and those which are proximate and near to the consummation. The law must be practical, and therefore considers those acts only as tending to the commission of the crime which are so near to its accomplishment that in all reasonable probability the crime itself would have been committed, but for timely interference. The cases which have been before the courts express this idea in different language, but the idea remains the same. The act or acts must come or advance very near to the accomplishment of the intended crime.

In *Hyde v. U.S.*, 225 U.S. 347, it was stated that the act amounts to an attempt when it is so near to the result that the danger of success is very great. "There must be dangerous promixity to success." Halsbury in his "Laws of England," vol. 9, p. 259, says:

> " "An act in order to be a criminal attempt must be immediately and not remotely connected with and directly tending to the commission of an offense."

Commonwealth v. Peaslee, 177 Mass. 267, 59 N.E. 55, refers to the acts constituting an attempt as coming very near to the accomplishment of the crime.

The method of committing or attempting crime varies in each case, so that the difficulty, if any, is not with this rule of law regarding an attempt, which is well understood, but with its application to the facts. As I have said before, minds differ over proximity and the nearness of the approach.

How shall we apply this rule of immediate nearness to this case? The defendants were looking for the pay roll man to rob him of his money. This is the charge in the indictment. Robbery is defined in section 2120 of the Penal Law as 'the unlawful taking of personal property from the person or in the presence of another, against his will, by means of force, or violence, or fear of injury, immediate or future, to his person." To constitute the crime of robbery, the money must have been taken from Rao by means of force or violence, or through fear. The crime of attempt to commit robbery was committed, if these defendants did an act tending to the commission of this robbery. Did the acts above described come dangerously near to the taking of Rao's property? Did the acts come so near the commission of robbery that there was reasonable likelihood of its accomplishment but for the interference? Rao was not found; the defendants were still looking for him; no attempt to rob him could be made, at least until he came in sight; he was not in the building at One Hundred and Eightieth street and Morris Park avenue. There was no man there with the pay roll for the United Lathing Company whom these defendants could rob. Apparently, no money had been drawn from the bank for the pay roll by anybody at the time of the arrest. In a word, these defendants had planned to commit a crime, and were looking around the city for an opportunity to commit it, but the opportunity fortunately never came. Men would not be guilty of an attempt at burglary if they had planned to break into a building and were arrested while they were hunting about the streets for the building not knowing where it was. Neither would a man be guilty of an attempt to commit murder if he armed himself and started out to find the person whom he had planned to kill but could not find him. So here these defendants were not guilty of an attempt to commit robbery in the first degree when they had not found or reached the presence of the person they intended to rob.

The judgment of the Appellate Division and that of the county court should be reversed, and a new trial ordered.

Questions and Notes

1. Assuming arguendo that the court correctly analyzed the attempt issue, can its praise of the police in its first two sentences be justified? Shouldn't the police be condemned for violating the civil rights of innocent citizens?

2. The most popular tests for attempt are "unequivocal act," "probable desistance," "dangerous proximity," and the MPC's "substantial act" test. (*See* MPC § 5.01(1)(c) (Appendix A)). Which test did the court adopt? Would it have reached a different result under one of the other tests?

3. In an ideal system of jurisprudence, should the defendants in *Rizzo* have been convicted of attempted robbery? Of something else? Consider in conjunction with conspiracy (Chapter 19, *infra*).

4. Consider whether in an ideal system of jurisprudence McQuirter (*McQuirter v. State*) should have been convicted of attempted assault with intent to commit rape.

McQuirter v. State

63 So. 2d 388 (Ala. Ct. App. 1953)

PRICE, Judge.

Appellant, a Negro man, was found guilty of an attempt to commit an assault with intent to rape, under an indictment charging an assault with intent to rape. The jury assessed a fine of $500.

About 8:00 o'clock on the night of June 29, 1951, Mrs. Ted Allen, a white woman, with her two children and a neighbor's little girl, were drinking Coca-Cola at the "Tiny Diner" in Atmore. When they started in the direction of Mrs. Allen's home she noticed appellant sitting in the cab of a parked truck. As she passed the truck appellant said something unintelligible, opened the truck door and placed his foot on the running board.

Mrs. Allen testified appellant followed her down the street and when she reached Suell Lufkin's house she stopped. As she turned into the Lufkin house appellant was within two or three feet of her. She waited ten minutes for appellant to pass. When she proceeded on her way, appellant came toward her from behind a telephone pole. She told the children to run to Mr. Simmons' house and tell him to come and meet her. When appellant saw Mr. Simmons he turned and went back down the street to the intersection and leaned on a stop sign just across the street from Mrs. Allen's home. Mrs. Allen watched him at the sign from Mr. Simmons' porch for about thirty minutes, after which time he came back down the street and appellant went on home.

Mrs. Allen's testimony was corroborated by that of her young daughter. The daughter testified the appellant was within six feet of her mother as she approached the Lufkin house, and this witness said there was a while when she didn't see appellant at the intersection.

Mr. Lewis Simmons testified when the little girls ran up on his porch and said a Negro was after them, witness walked up the sidewalk to meet Mrs. Allen and saw appellant.

Appellant went on down the street and stopped in front of Mrs. Allen's home and waited there approximately thirty minutes.

Mr. Clarence Bryars, a policeman in Atmore, testified that appellant stated after his arrest that he came to Atmore with the intention of getting him a white woman that night.

Mr. W. E. Strickland, Chief of Police of Atmore, testified that appellant stated in the Atmore jail he didn't know what was the matter with him; that he was drinking a little; that he and his partner had been to Pensacola; that his partner went to the "Front" to see a colored woman; that he didn't have any money and he sat in the truck and made up his mind he was going to get the first woman that came by and that this was the first woman that came by. He said he got out of the truck, came around the gas tank and watched the lady and when she started off he started off behind her; that he was going to carry her in the cotton patch and if she hollered he was going to kill her. He testified appellant made the same statement in the Brewton jail.

Mr. Norvelle Seals, Chief Deputy Sheriff, corroborated Mr. Strickland's testimony as to the statement by appellant at the Brewton jail.

Appellant, as a witness in his own behalf, testified he and Bill Page, another Negro, carried a load of junk-iron from Monroeville to Pensacola; on their way back to Monroeville they stopped in Atmore. They parked the truck near the "Tiny Diner" and rode to the "Front," the colored section, in a cab. Appellant came back to the truck around 8:00 o'clock and sat in the truck cab for about thirty minutes. He decided to go back to the "Front" to look for Bill Page. As he started up the street he saw prosecutrix and her children. He turned around and waited until he decided they had gone, then he walked up the street toward the "Front." When he reached the intersection at the telegraph pole he decided he didn't want to go to the "Front" and sat around there a few minutes, then went on to the "Front" and stayed about 25 or 30 minutes, and came back to the truck.

He denied that he followed Mrs. Allen or made any gesture toward molesting her or the children. He denied making the statements testified to by the officers.

He testified he had never been arrested before and introduced testimony by two residents of Monroeville as to his good reputation for peace and quiet and for truth and veracity.

Appellant insists the trial court erred in refusing the general affirmative charge and in denying the motion for a new trial on the ground the verdict was contrary to the evidence.

"'An attempt to commit an assault with intent to rape,'" ... means an attempt to rape which has not proceeded far enough to amount to an assault." *Burton v. State*, 8 Ala. App. 295, 62 So. 394, 396.

Under the authorities in this state, to justify a conviction for an attempt to commit an assault with intent to rape the jury must be satisfied beyond a reasonable doubt that defendant intended to have sexual intercourse with prosecutrix against her will, by force or by putting her in fear.

Intent is a question to be determined by the jury from the facts and circumstances adduced on the trial, and if there is evidence from which it may be inferred that at the time of the attempt defendant intended to gratify his lustful desires against the resistance of the female a jury question is presented.

In determining the question of intention the jury may consider social conditions and customs founded upon racial differences, such as that the prosecutrix was a white woman and defendant was a Negro man.

After considering the evidence in this case we are of the opinion it was sufficient to warrant the submission of the question of defendant's guilt to the jury, and was ample to sustain the judgment of conviction.

Questions and Notes

1. Is intent *simpliciter* enough to sustain an attempt conviction in Alabama? I.e., if the police had arrested McQuirter while he was in his truck and before he had even seen Mrs. Allen, and he had made the same statements at the Atmore and Brewton jails that he allegedly made in this case, could he have been convicted?

2. Assuming arguendo that social conditions of the 1950s could have had some bearing on the issue of Mrs. Allen's consent, how could they possibly be relevant to McQuirter's intent?

3. If McQuirter had been a white male college student, and Allen a white female college student, would McQuirter's conviction have seemed more justified? Why?

4. Given that assault with intent to commit rape is itself an inchoate crime, does the concept of attempted assault with intent to commit rape seem like a *nonsequitur*?

5. Who came closer to completing his crime, Rizzo or McQuirter?

6. Assuming that you believe that ideally someone like Rizzo should be convicted of attempt, but that somebody like McQuirter should not be, can you draft a statute that would accomplish both results? Is the MPC § 5.01 (Appendix A) such a statute? Why or why not?

7. Is the test used in *Stewart* any better?

State v. Stewart

420 N.W. 2d 44 (Wis. 1988)

[The facts and the court's discussion of intent are reproduced
at page {X=REF} *supra.*]

SHIRLEY S. ABRAHAMSON, Justice.

The defendant next argues that the evidence at trial was not sufficient to prove that he had committed sufficient acts in furtherance of the crime of robbery for his conduct to constitute an attempt. The law does not ordinarily punish a person for guilty intentions alone. The attempt statute punishes an individual for acts that further the criminal objective. The most difficult problem in the law of attempts has been to formulate a satisfactory approach or test to describe what constitutes culpable conduct, the second element of the crime of attempt. A significant question in discussing criminal attempt is, what conduct, "when engaged in with a purpose to commit a crime or to advance toward the attainment of a criminal objective, should suffice to constitute a criminal attempt." A.L.I. Model Penal Code, sec. 5.01, comment 1, p. 298 (1985).[3]

Sec. 939.32(3) requires that the accused "does acts toward the commission of the crime which demonstrate unequivocally, under all the circumstances, that he formed that intent and would commit the crime except for the intervention of another person or some other extraneous factor."

The defendant argues that he did not commit sufficient acts in furtherance of the crime to constitute an attempt. He contends that sufficient acts are not committed until the intervention of another person or extraneous factor prevents completion of the crime. If there is no such intervention, the defendant argues, the acts taken toward the criminal end are too few to constitute an attempt. In effect the defendant argues that sec. 939.32 (3) requires the state to prove that "the intervention of another person or some other extraneous "factor" impeded the defendant's completion of the crime.

---

3. The several tests or approaches—such as the preparation theory, the proximity theory, the *locus poenitentiae* or probable desistance theory and the equivocality theory—have been summarized in *Berry v. State*, 90 Wis. 2d at 325, n.7, 280 N.W.2d 204. Under the probable desistance approach, the accused's conduct constitutes an attempt if, in the ordinary and natural course of events, without interruption from an outside source, it will result in the crime intended. Under the *res ipsa loquitur* (or equivocality) test, the accused's acts must demonstrate unequivocally that the accused is unlikely to withdraw voluntarily from the criminal conduct. The test is premised on the assumption that ambiguous acts are the result of an ambiguous intent. ALI Model Penal Code, sec. 5.01, Comment 5(d), (f) (1985); LAFAVE & SCOTT, SUBSTANTIVE CRIMINAL LAW, sec. 6.2(3), pp. 34–36 (1986). The court has stated that sec. 939.32(2) embodies the equivocality test and apparently the *Hamiel* court regards the probable desistance and equivocality tests as similar. Commentators describe the Wisconsin statute as a probable desistance test.

The court of appeals apparently concluded that the complainant's resistance was not an "extraneous factor," and that Levy's entering the bus shelter was not the "intervention of another person," within the meaning of sec. 939.32 (3). Based on that conclusion, the court of appeals reasoned that the defendant's termination of the robbery must have been voluntary because no extraneous factor beyond his control motivated him to desist. Because the defendant did not consummate the robbery, and no force beyond his control prevented him from doing so, the court of appeals concluded there is insufficient evidence to find the defendant would have committed robbery "except for the intervention of another person or some other extraneous factor."

We disagree with the court of appeals interpretation of sec. 939.32(3). This court has concluded that sec. 939.32(3) does not require the state to prove the existence of an extraneous factor as a third element of the crime of attempt.[4]

In *Hamiel*, the court said, "[W]hether another person or some other intervening extrinsic force are present and actually frustrate the accused person's attempt is not material to the inquiry of the defendant's guilt." The court has stated that the statutory language "necessitates a determination whether under all the circumstances it was too late for the person to have repented and withdrawn." The import of sec. 939.32(3) is, according to this court, that "the defendant's conduct must pass that point where most men, holding such an intention as the defendant holds, would think better of their conduct and desist." *Berry*, 280 N.W.2d 204.

The court's interpretation of sec. 939.32(3) as not requiring the state to prove that the accused was actually interrupted by the intervention of another person or an extraneous factor comports with legislative intent. The legislature intended to punish individuals who have exhibited a dangerous propensity toward committing a crime because these individuals are as dangerous as a person who completes the crime contemplated.

Because the legislature intended sec. 939.32(3) to address the accused's manifest dangerousness, we conclude that the legislature did not intend to require an actual interruption of the accused's conduct by intervention of another person or an extraneous factor in order for there to be an attempt under the statute. When the accused's acts demonstrate unequivocally that the accused will continue unless

---

4. Other courts have concluded that the attempt statute does not require proof of a third element. In *People v. Dillon*, 668 P.2d 697 (Cal. 1983), the court wrote: "[P]roperly understood, our reference to interruption by independent circumstances rather than the will of the offender merely clarifies the requirement that the act be unequivocal. It is obviously impossible to be certain that a person will not lose his resolve to commit the crime unless he completes the last act necessary for its accomplishment. But the law of attempts would be largely without function if it could not be invoked until the trigger was pulled, the blow struck or the money seized. If it is not clear from a suspect's acts what he intends to do, an observer cannot reasonably conclude that a crime will be committed; but when the acts are such that any rational person would believe that a crime is about to be consummated absent an intervening force, the attempt is under way, and a last-minute change of heart by the perpetrator should not be permitted to exonerate him."

interrupted, that is, when the acts demonstrate that the accused will probably not desist from the criminal course, then the accused's dangerousness is manifest. Accordingly, we reject defendant's assertion that sec. 939.32(3) requires the state to prove the intervention of another person or an extraneous factor.

The purpose of the language in sec. 939.32(3) relating to intervention of another person and extraneous factor is to denote that the actor must have gone far enough toward completion of the crime to make it improbable that he would change his mind and desist. The conduct element of sec. 939.32(3) is satisfied when the accused engages in conduct which demonstrates that only a circumstance beyond the accused's control would prevent the crime, whether or not such a circumstance actually occurs. An attempt occurs when the accused's acts move beyond the incubation period for the crime, that is, the time during which the accused has formed an intent to commit the crime but has not committed enough acts and may still change his mind and desist. In other words the statute requires a judgment in each case that the accused has committed sufficient acts that it is unlikely that he would have voluntarily desisted from commission of the crime.

The *Hamiel* court suggested that the accused's acts be viewed as a film in which the action is suddenly stopped, so that the audience may be asked to what end the acts are directed. "If there is only one reasonable answer to this question then the accused has done what amounts to an 'attempt' to attain that end. If there is more than one reasonably possible answer, then the accused has not yet done enough." The aim of this "stop the film" test is to determine whether the accused's acts unequivocally demonstrate an intent to commit the crime rendering voluntary desistance from the crime improbable.

If the defendant had been filmed in this case and the film stopped just before Levy entered the bus stop and the three men departed, we conclude that a trier of fact could find beyond a reasonable doubt that the defendant's acts were directed toward robbery. The film would show the defendant demanding money and appearing to reach for a gun. This evidence is sufficient to prove that the defendant had taken sufficient steps for his conduct to constitute an attempted robbery.

In *Jacobs v. State*, 184 N.W.2d 113 (1971), a case involving attempted robbery, the court applied a similar analysis of the accused's acts:

> "The attempt was complete when the defendant, with intent to commit a robbery, took action, to wit, pointing the gun and demanding the money, in furtherance of such intent. Pointing the gun and telling the store proprietor to 'give me that sack' were unequivocal acts, accompanied by intent, sufficient to complete the crime of attempted robbery. The unanticipated set of circumstances, including the store owner stating he had no money and to go ahead and shoot, ... the accomplices suggestion that they leave and his leaving, combined to influence the defendant to abandon the robbery, but *only after attempted armed robbery had been unequivocally completed*. (Emphasis supplied.)"

We conclude that the evidence was sufficient for the trier of fact to find beyond a reasonable doubt that the defendant's conduct in furtherance of the defendant's intent to commit robbery had proceeded far enough toward completion of the crime to make it improbable that the defendant would desist. The state proved the second element of the crime of attempt.

Questions and Notes

1. What test did the court adopt in *Stewart*?

2. Given the finding of intent, is there any conduct test that would not yield liability?

3 If the "stop the film" test had been used in *Rizzo*, what result? *McQuirter*?

4. The MPC, by adopting the substantial act test, sought to make conviction easier. It specifically intended to authorize a conviction in a case like *Rizzo*. In *Still*, the court purported to employ a substantial act test, but it did not exactly work as the MPC had envisioned.

United States v. Still

850 F.2d 607 (9th Cir. 1988)

Brunetti, Circuit Judge:

Reginald Dean Still was convicted of attempted bank robbery of Security Pacific National Bank. Based on this circuit's recent decision in *United States v. Buffington*, 815 F.2d 1292 (9th Cir. 1987), we reverse.

Facts

On August 7, 1985, at about 10:30 a.m., a lay witness saw the defendant putting on a long blonde wig while sitting in a van with the motor running, parked in the Roseville Square Shopping Center. The van was parked approximately 200 feet away from the Security Pacific Bank. The witness notified the police, who arrived in a marked patrol car shortly thereafter. Upon arrival of the police, the defendant put the van in reverse, and drove off. The police caught up with the defendant, who had fled to a nearby camper/trailer. He was arrested for possession of stolen property and taken to the Roseville Police Department.

Following his arrest, the defendant allegedly volunteered the following statements: "You did a good job. You caught me five minutes before I was going to rob a bank. That's what I was putting the wig on for." "The van is stolen. How much do you get for auto theft around here?"

[T]he defendant told the police that he was planning to rob a bank when the marked police vehicle came up to the van he was in. He planned to drive up to the drive-in window of the bank and place a phony bomb, along with a demand note, on the window. The defendant did not specify, by name, the bank he was planning to rob. He described it as a large, two-story building, made of brown or reddish brick. The defendant stated that Security Pacific sounded like the name of the bank he intended to rob. Of the thirty-nine banks within five miles of the Roseville Square Shopping Center, only Security Pacific fits the defendant's description of the bank he was planning to rob.

The defendant told the police that his statements were just "frosting on the cake" because all of the evidence that they needed was located in the van. Inside the van, the police found a hoax bomb which looked like a real bomb, a red pouch with a demand note taped to it, a long blonde wig, a police scanner programmed to the Roseville Police Department, and a notebook containing drafts of demand notes and the radio frequency of the Rocklin Police Department.

Analysis

A conviction for an attempt requires proof of both "culpable "intent" and "conduct constituting a substantial step toward commission of the crime that is in pursuit of that intent." A "substantial "step" is "conduct strongly corroborative of the firmness of the defendant's criminal intent." "Culpable intent" can be inferred from a particular defendant's conduct and from the surrounding circumstances.

In *Buffington*, this court concluded no rational fact finder could find sufficient evidence of the culpable intent necessary to sustain the conviction for attempted bank robbery. In *Buffington*, the government presented the following evidence to establish the defendant's intent to rob a particular bank: assemblage and possession of materials necessary to commit the crime, including two handguns, female clothing and a makeup disguise for one defendant, and a multi-layered clothing disguise for another defendant; two visits to the location before the attempt; actions to carry out the plan, including driving by the bank twice while staring into it, driving to the rear of the bank, one of the defendants staring out of the window of a nearby store toward the bank, and two of the defendants leaving their vehicle armed and standing with their attention directed toward the bank.

This court concluded that the above evidence did not establish the requisite intent because these actions could just as easily indicate an intent to rob another nearby bank or store. The court stated that the fact no defendant came within 50 yards of the bank could produce no more than a suspicion that they intended to rob that particular bank.

However, the court went on to state that there could be sufficient evidence of the requisite intent without actual entry, citing with approval *Rumfelt v. United States*, 445 F.2d 134 (7th Cir.). In *Rumfelt*, the defendant's presence in front of the bank with a ski mask, plus his use of a rifle to intimidate a passerby into trying to open the bank door for him established the requisite intent. The *Buffington* court also stated that a defendant's intent to steal could be inferred from statements of co-conspirators or informants, statements which were excluded in *Buffington*.

In this case, Still's intent to rob the Security Pacific National Bank was clearly established in his statements to the police after his arrest. Without prompting, the defendant stated: "You did a good job. You caught me five minutes before I was going to rob a bank. That's what I was putting the wig on for." After waiving his rights, the defendant stated he intended to use the drive-up window of the bank and place a phony explosive device, along with a note, on that window, to rob a bank. Although the defendant did not state the name of the bank he was planning to rob, he did describe it. Within a five mile area, his description of a large, two-story bank, constructed of brown or reddish color brick fits only the Security Pacific Bank. Additionally, when asked by the police if it was Security Pacific that the defendant intended to rob, he said that Security Pacific sounded like the name of the bank he was going to rob. These statements permit an inference of an unequivocal intent to rob the Security Pacific Bank. Therefore, the first aspect of an attempt, a culpable intent, was established beyond a reasonable doubt.

To establish the second aspect of an attempt, "a substantial step," more than mere preparation must be shown. "[T]here must be some appreciable fragment of the crime committed, it must be in such progress that it will be consummated unless interrupted by circumstances independent of the will of the attempter, and the act must not be equivocal in nature." *United States v. Buffington*, 815 F.2d at 1302, citing with approval *United States v. Mandujano*, 499 F.2d at 376.

In *Buffington*, the court concluded that the defendants' conduct did not cross the line between preparation and attempt. Although the defendants had assembled the disguises and materials necessary to commit the robbery, drove by the bank twice while staring into it, and left their vehicle, armed, and stood with their attention focused on the bank, the court emphasized that none of them made any move toward the bank. Thus, standing alone, the defendants' conduct was too tentative and unfocused to constitute either the requisite "appreciable fragment" of a bank robbery, or a step toward the commission of the crime of such substantiality that, unless frustrated, the crime would have occurred.

The *Buffington* court stopped short of expressly requiring some actual movement toward the bank to show a substantial step toward an attempt. They cited *United States v. Snell* with approval, where this circuit upheld a conviction for attempted robbery without actual movement toward the bank, reasoning that the defendants' entry into the victim's home was analytically similar to entry into a bank.

Our facts do not establish either actual movement toward the bank or actions that are analytically similar to such movement. Before he was apprehended by the police, Still was seen sitting in his van, with the motor running, wearing a long blonde wig, parked approximately 200 feet away from the Security Pacific National Bank. Considering that the *Buffington* defendants' actions went further in manifesting a substantial step than did Still's actions, *Buffington* compels the conclusion that proof of a substantial step toward the attempt was not established beyond a reasonable doubt.

Reversed.

Questions and Notes

1. By adopting the "substantial step strongly corroborative of the defendant's criminal purpose," the MPC hoped to shift focus from what had not been done to what had been done. Does *Still* capture that emphasis?

2. Does *Still* appear to embrace aspects of unequivocality, probable desistance, and/or dangerous proximity? If so, where?

3. Might the *Buffington* court's analysis of the preparation/attempt line have been influenced by the absence of proof of intent in that case? If so, shouldn't the *Still* court be more careful about adopting that reasoning without further analysis?

4. Do you think that Still should have been convicted? Why? Why not?

5. In *Davis*, we will see how the court deals with inchoate criminality when the defendant's intent was to hire another to do his dirty work.

State v. Davis

6 S.W.2d 609 (Mo. 1928)

Davis, C.

Defendant was convicted on May 29, 1926 of an attempt to commit murder in the first degree. The jury returned a verdict fixing his punishment at imprisonment in the penitentiary for a term of eight years, which the trial court reduced to five years, sentencing him to that term. Defendant duly appealed from the judgment entered accordingly.

The evidence submitted on the part of the state warrants the finding that defendant and Alberdina Lourie resided in Kansas City. They were seemingly infatuated with each other, planning and arranging to have Edmon Lourie, the husband of Alberdina, killed so that they could obtain the insurance on his life, aggregating $60,000, as well as cohabit. Edmon Lourie was absent from home the greater part of the time, returning at intervals of two or three weeks. In furtherance of their plan, defendant, acting for himself and Alberdina, arranged to have one Earl Leverton obtain for them the services of an ex-convict to murder Edmon Lourie for hire. Leverton, instead of procuring the services of an ex-convict for that purpose, disclosed the plot to Joel L. Dill, a member of the Kansas City police force, who agreed to pose as an ex-convict to that end. Several meetings were had between defendant, Leverton, and Dill, defendant stating that he and Alberdina were in love, and desired Edmon Lourie killed. He agreed to pay for the execution of the plot. Defendant outlined his plan, offering Dill the sum of $600, with the further agreement that Alberdina, who was to be with her husband at the time of the contemplated assault, would wear diamonds of the value of $3,000. He further arranged for Alberdina and Dill to see each other that each might recognize the other on sight. Defendant, Dill, and Leverton, during January and the early part of February, 1926, held prearranged conferences on the subject. Prior to February 11, 1926, defendant arranged for Dill to go to Chicago to kill Edmon Lourie there, defendant making and giving Dill a map or drawing showing where Lourie could be found, as well as two photographs of him. The arrangements contemplated that, if Dill was unable to locate Lourie, Alberdina would go to Chicago to aid him. The trip to Chicago was to be made about February 12th.

However, Edmon Lourie telegraphed Alberdina that he would return to Kansas City on February 13, 1926, defendant thereupon notifying Leverton, who in turn communicated the fact to Dill. Defendant paid Dill $600, advising him that Alberdina would persuade Edmon to accompany her to a place of amusement, and that she planned to leave their home at 8 o'clock p.m. on February 13, 1926. It was further planned that Alberdina was to carry the diamonds on her person, and that Dill was to shoot Lourie either as they left their home or as they returned, and that Alberdina was to be mussed up and the diamonds taken from her, so that it might appear the result of a robbery. Alberdina was to appear to faint, giving Dill time to make his escape. However, on the night of February 13, 1926, Dill, accompanied by three other police officers, proceeded about 8 o'clock p.m. to the home of Edmon Lourie as arranged. Edmon and Alberdina Lourie were there found dressed and ready to leave, with the diamonds on her person. As Dill and the officers entered the room, she turned her face to the wall as planned. Two officers took charge of Edmon and Alberdina; Dill and the other officer going to the home of defendant, where they arrested him. The defendant had previously informed Dill that he would remain at home in order to have an alibi.

The elements of an attempt are stated in 16 Corpus Juris, p. 113, thus: "An attempt to commit a crime consists of three elements: (1) The intention to commit the crime; (2) performance of some act toward the commission of the crime; and (3) the failure to consummate its commission." The proof adduced advises us that the only debatable question is the presence of sufficient facts to demonstrate the second element. The record develops the presence of the intent to commit the crime and the failure to consummate its commission.

The physical overt act, which with intent and failure to consummate brings the crime of attempt into existence, is distinguishable from solicitation and preparation. An attempt to commit a crime involves an act on the part of the defendant moving directly toward the commission of the offense. With these concepts in mind we proceed to review the solicitations and preparations by defendant to murder Lourie as constituting an overt act.

In *State v. Hayes*, 78 Mo. 307, this court, through Philips, C., said: "It is the recognized law of this country that the solicitation of another to commit a crime is an act toward the commission."

However, the proof in the above case developed, in addition to solicitations, an act on the part of the accused extending beyond solicitation or preparation, that of saturating a portion of the floor with coal oil as well, as the furnishing of plans and an oil can. Conceding that the court reached the proper result in that case, concerning which it is unnecessary to express an opinion, the basic facts there shown extend far beyond the facts here developed. While a few of the courts have treated solicitation to commit a crime as an attempt, the great weight of authority warrants the assertion that mere solicitation, unaccompanied by an act moving directly toward the commission of the intended crime, is not an overt act constituting an element of the crime of attempt. Solicitation of itself is a distinct offense when declared so by law. Therefore, in conformity with the weight of authority, we hold that merely soliciting one to commit a crime does not constitute an attempt.

The state contends that the arrangement of a plan for the accomplishment of the murder of Lourie and the selecting and hiring of the means or instrumentality by which the murder was to be consummated were demonstrated. We take it that the state means by the foregoing declarations that overt acts were shown. To that we do not agree. The evidence goes no further than developing a verbal arrangement with Dill, the selection of Dill as the one to kill Lourie, the delivery of a certain drawing and two photographs of Lourie to Dill, and the payment of a portion of the agreed consideration. These things were mere acts of preparation, failing to lead directly or proximately to the consummation of the intended crime. In this regard we have found no authority which holds that preparations constitute an overt act.

The plans or arrangements amounted to nothing more than mere preparation. The contract of hiring entered into between defendant and Dill also fails to extend beyond mere preparation. In regard to the hiring, the trial court instructed the jury that the payment of money by defendant to Dill to commit the intended crime did not constitute such an overt act as was tantamount to an attempt. The ruling of the court we think was right, for the payment of money was not an act moving directly toward the consummation of the intended crime. The only case we have found involving the actual payment of money to another as the consideration for the proposed crime is *Reg. v. Williams*, 1 Car. & K. 589, 1 Den. C.C. 39. In that case the facts develop the actual delivery of money to the agent who straightway went with the poison given him for that purpose to the home of the intended victims. However, on his arrival he disclosed to them the plan to kill, handing over the poison. The fifteen judges who considered the case on appeal held the conviction erroneous.

The employment of Dill as agent to murder Lourie was not tantamount to an attempt. Dill not only had no intention of carrying out the expressed purpose of defendant, but was guilty of no act directly or indirectly moving toward the consummation of the intended crime. He did nothing more than listen to the plans and solicitations of defendant without intending to act upon them. It was not shown that Dill committed an act that could be construed as an attempt.

Whether it is necessary to make an actual assault before the crime of attempt can be said to come into existence, we need not decide, for the solicitations and preparations upon the part of defendant were not equivalent to an overt act which must take place before the crime of attempt comes into existence.

Our statute, section 3683, Revised Statutes 1919, in prescribing an attempt to commit an offense prohibited by law, is to be interpreted as providing that the doing of any act toward the commission of such offense shall constitute an attempt. The statute, we think, follows and coincides with common law in that respect. There must be an overt act before an attempt exists, and the overt act must move directly in consummation of the crime; in other words, toward the commission of the offense.

It follows from what we have said that the judgment must be reversed, and the defendant discharged. It is so ordered.

WHITE, J. I concur in the conclusion reached in the opinion of DAVIS, C., and in the reasoning by which he reaches it. However, a principle of law, not referred to in the argument or the briefs, I think is decisive of the case. The principle of law is this: Where one hires or incites another person to do a criminal act, he is responsible only for what the other person *does*.

In the argument we were directed to the heinous nature of the crime, where one, who is too cowardly to commit the act himself, employs someone else to do it. That is a serious offense, and no doubt many a crime is committed by a hired agent, but the master minds in the criminal world from whom that danger comes never make mistakes such as Davis made. They know their men, and they employ real killers. Davis was not only a coward, but a fool. The entire plan and preparation showed the want of judgment and discretion. He has no criminal record, and he is not a dangerous criminal. If every person who, at some time in his or her life, entertained a criminal impulse, was put in jail, a small minority of us would be at large.

It is said further that the defendant in this case did all he could do in furtherance of the plan to have this murder committed. This is incorrect. He failed of many things he might have done-things absolutely necessary for the commission of the crime or its attempt. He might have used the weapon himself. He might have used sense enough to solicit a real criminal to commit the deed. He might have taken precaution to find out who the man was that he employed for the purpose. But blindly he picked up the first man who offered his services.

The upshot of the matter is this: The defendant had no intention to kill; that is, to commit the murder himself. Dill had no intention to kill. There can be no crime without a criminal intent, and neither the defendant nor his agent entertained an intent to do the deed. The defendant intended that Dill should do it, but that intent cannot be connected with an act of another which was neither done nor contemplated by the other. The intent to commit the crime must be in the mind of the man who is to commit the crime.

Of course, the defendant was guilty of soliciting another to commit the murder; a serious crime, but he was not charged with that, nor convicted of that offense. We must determine cases upon the law as it is written, and as it has been adjudged for generations.

The judgment is properly reversed.

WALKER, C.J. (dissenting).

The proof of defendant's guilt in the instant case is not limited to solicitations. He and his paramour, the wife of the intended victim, planned and directed with particularity the time, manner, and place of the proposed taking off of her husband. A trip to Chicago was even in contemplation to effect that end, when the husband returned home unexpectedly, and the scene of the proposed tragedy was shifted to Kansas City. When it was to occur, the defendant had it understood that he was to remain at his home so as to afford a basis for a plea of alibi. There he waited expectantly for news of the murder. His paramour—but she is not on trial, and the vocabulary of scorn and contempt need not be wasted on her connection with the contemplated murder of her husband.

The chain of proven facts and properly deducible circumstances cannot be otherwise construed than as conclusive of the defendant's guilt. Of what more avail would it have been as proof of his intent or purpose to have shown that he furnished the detective with the weapon he was to use or the poison or other instrumentality he might employ in committing the murder. The limits of human fancy know no horizon; but it is difficult to conceive what more the defendant could have done than he did do towards the attempt to commit the proposed murder without actually participating in its commission.

Ample proof of the presence of those essentials required by our rulings having been adduced to sustain a conviction, the judgment of the trial court should be affirmed.

Questions and Notes

1. Should solicitation in general be punished? Why?

2. Assuming that your answer to Question 1 is "no," should solicitation to murder be punished? Why?

3. Do you think that Davis was guilty of nothing more than solicitation? Explain.

4. Suppose that Davis had programmed a robot to kill Lourie, and the robot had done all of the things that Dill did but ran out of power when it reached the Lourie residence. On that fact pattern, would (should) Davis have been guilty of attempted murder? How (if at all) is the hypothetical analytically different from *Davis* itself?

5. What test for attempt does the court use? Might it have reached a different result under a different test? *Cf. State v. Molasky*, 765 S.W.2d 597 (Mo. 1989), suggesting that *Davis* would have been decided differently under the MPC test, which Missouri currently employs.

6. Do you agree with Justice White that one who employs a criminal should never be convicted of a more serious crime than that of which his hireling could be convicted? Consider this question in conjunction with *Pendry v. State*, Chapter 18, *infra*.

7. Is the concurring opinion too narrowly focused on the lack of dangerous competence on the part of this particular defendant? To what, if any, general principle is this opinion directed?

8. Is Justice White actually saying that this case involves a *mens rea* problem, i.e., nobody intended to kill Lourie? If so, is it persuasive?

C. Abandonment

When one, with the requisite intent, has gone far enough to attempt a crime and then voluntarily desists from committing it, the courts are split as to whether or not her voluntary abandonment ought to excuse her crime. We will explore that question in the context of two cases with very different criteria for initially finding attempt. We will explore whether the different criteria contributed to the court's willingness to accept abandonment.

State v. Gartlan
512 S.E.2d 74 (N.C. Ct. App. 1999)

Wynn, Judge.

Sometime during the night of 19 August 1996, defendant William Richard Gartlan, an ordained minister with no criminal history, was awakened by his older daughter who informed him that his younger daughter was crying. In fact, the defendant's younger daughter was semiconscious and non-responsive. Additionally, his older daughter was experiencing difficulty breathing, and his son was completely unconscious.

The source of these difficulties was traced to the family's car which was running with the garage door closed. After turning off the car, defendant called 911. The emergency personnel treated them for carbon-monoxide poisoning. They were taken to the hospital and later released.

The next day, while being interviewed at the police station by Detective Bayliff, the defendant cried and confessed to attempting to kill himself and his three children by running his automobile in the closed garage. He stated that he had been depressed and that "he could not kill himself because the kids would be alone and have no one to take care [of] them. This was a way they could all be together." However, the defendant changed his mind after seeing his younger daughter turn blue with breathing difficulty.

The defendant signed a written statement prepared by Detective Saul which included the following concluding remarks:

> I knew the police would eventually ask what happened. I decided I would just tell the event that happened and just leave out the part about who started the car. In closing, I would like to say that I did do this; but, no words can say how sorry I am for it.

Additionally, a social worker called the police station on August 21 after the defendant told her:

> I know that I did this to myself and to the children what I've been accused of by the police and everyone else. But I guess I just wanted to convince myself that I did not do it.

The defendant was indicted for three counts of attempted first-degree murder. Following his conviction of these crimes, he brought this appeal contending that the trial court erred by: (1) failing to give instructions on the defense of abandonment. We find no prejudicial error.

I

The defendant first contends that the trial court erred in denying his written request for jury instructions on the defense of abandonment of the attempted murder crimes. We disagree.

"The elements of an attempt to commit any crime are: (1) an intent to commit the substantive offense, and (2) an overt act done for that purpose which goes beyond mere preparation, but (3) falls short of the completed offense." Specifically, a person commits the crime of attempted first-degree murder if: (1) he or she intends to kill another person unlawfully and (2) acting with malice, premeditation, and deliberation does an overt act calculated to carry out that intent, which goes beyond mere preparation, but falls short of committing murder.

"In North Carolina, an intent does not become an attempt so long as the defendant stops his criminal plan, or has it stopped, prior to the commission of the requisite overt act." An overt act for an attempt crime, must reach far enough towards the accomplishment of the desired result to amount to the commencement of the consummation. It must not be merely preparatory.

Consequently, "[a] defendant can stop his criminal plan short of an overt act on his own initiative or because of some outside intervention. . . . However, once a defendant engages in an overt act, the offense is complete, and it is too late for the defendant to change his mind."

The Court in *Miller* further stated that "an abandonment occurs when an individual voluntarily forsakes his or her criminal plan prior to committing an overt act in furtherance of that plan." Thus, contrary to the defendant's contention, the Court in *Miller* did not abolish the common law defense of abandonment in North Carolina; rather, the Court clarified the limited application of the defense by holding that a person could not abandon an attempt crime once an overt act is committed with the requisite mental intent—a commonsense application because the crime of attempt is at that point already completed.

In the present case, the evidence showed that the defendant intended to kill his children. In furtherance of this purpose, while the children were in their beds at night, he started his car with the garage door closed. As a result, all of the children were exposed to carbon monoxide poisoning. The children exhibited physical symptoms from the exposure—discoloration, difficulty breathing, semiconsciousness, and unconsciousness. Consequently, all of the children required medical treatment for carbon-monoxide poisoning. Only after the defendant observed his younger daughter turning blue did he decide that he could no longer continue with his plan to kill his children.

Certainly, defendant's actions amounted to more than mere preparation to commit murder. Following *Miller*, we conclude that after committing these overt acts, the defendant could not legally abandon the crime of attempted murder. Accordingly, we hold that the trial court did not err in failing to give the instructions on the defense of abandonment.

Questions and Notes

1. Are there any good policy reasons for *not* allowing the defense of abandonment? What are they?

2. In *Stewart, supra*, the Wisconsin Supreme Court, employing reasoning very much like *Gartlan*, refused to allow abandonment as a defense. Was it fair for that court to "stop the film" at the only time that an attempt appeared, and ignore everything that happened before and after? Recall that in *Stewart*, except for the one instantaneous stop point, all of the evidence tended to show no intent to rob.

3. In assessing the wisdom of allowing abandonment as a defense, should it matter what standard the court uses to ascertain attempt in the first place? Should it matter how far the defendant has actually gone?

4. In *Miller*, the defendant had actually killed his robbery victim before panicking and abandoning his robbery attempt. Miller argued that he could not be convicted of attempted robbery (and thus felony-murder) because he had abandoned his robbery attempt. Does (should) the reasoning that rejected Miller's abandonment defense also reject Gartlan's defense?

5. Should it matter that Gartlan not only abandoned his original attempt, but took affirmative steps to ensure that the harm (death of his children) never happened?

6. Will *Gartlan* encourage future Gartlans to go through with their crime, knowing that it is too late to abandon it?

7. If abandonment were available as a defense, of what crime would Gartlan have been guilty?

8. In *Johnson*, the court, without much analysis, allows the defense.

People v. Johnson
750 P.2d 72 (Colo. App. 1987)

PIERCE, Judge.

Defendant, Floyd M. Johnson, appeals the judgment of conviction entered following a jury verdict of guilty of attempted first degree murder. He contends that the evidence was insufficient to sustain a verdict of guilty.

The evidence established that, following a fight with a friend outside a bar where the two had been drinking, defendant walked a mile to his house, retrieved his .22 rifle and ten cartridges, walked back to the bar, and crawled under a pickup truck across the street to wait for the friend. Defendant testified that he, at first, intended to shoot the friend to "pay him back" for the beating he had received in their earlier altercation.

When the owner of the pickup arrived, defendant obtained his keys, instructed him to sit in the pickup, and gave him one or more bottles of beer. Defendant then crawled back under the pickup to resume his wait for his friend. The police were alerted by a passerby and arrested defendant before his friend emerged from the bar. There was also testimony that while he was lying under the pickup truck, defendant sobered up somewhat and began to think through his predicament. He testified that he changed his mind and removed the shells from the rifle, placing them in his pocket. By that time there were two persons in the pickup truck, and he began a discussion with them, telling them his name and address and inviting them to his residence to have a party. The three of them were still there drinking and conversing when the police arrived, at which time the rifle was found to be unloaded and the shells were still in the defendant's pocket.

Defendant contends that while his intent may have been to shoot his friend, no evidence was presented to show that his intent was to cause the friend's death. Absent a showing of intent to kill, he argues, the evidence is insufficient to sustain a conviction of attempted first degree murder. Based on the facts presented, we disagree.

Viewing the evidence in the light most favorable to the prosecution, the court concluded that the defendant's possession of a working rifle and live ammunition and his statements that he intended to shoot the victim were sufficient to submit the case to the jury. We find no error in the trial court's denial of this motion.

Defendant also contends that the trial court erred when it refused his tendered instruction on the affirmative defense of abandonment or renunciation. We agree.

Under the circumstances in this case, there was sufficient evidence to warrant an instruction on the affirmative defense of abandonment or renunciation. Had the tendered instruction been given and the defendant's testimony and other evidence been accepted by the jury, the outcome of this trial could well have been otherwise.

The judgment is reversed and the cause is remanded for a new trial.

Questions and Notes

1. Given that defendant had already attempted to murder his friend, why should his change of heart justify a defense?

2. Although the court never considered how proximate Johnson was to his target crime, his lack of proximity might have influenced the court. Without regard to abandonment, would Johnson have been convicted under *Rizzo? McQuirter? Stewart? Still?* MPC? Would he have been convicted under *Gartlan*? What do these answers suggest in regard to the abandonment defense?

Problem

Appellant appeals from her conviction, after trial without a jury, for attempted taking property without right. Appellant argues that the evidence was insufficient to support her conviction.

At appellant's trial, the shopkeeper of a small clothing store testified to the following events: Appellant, who was visibly pregnant, entered the store where the shopkeeper worked. The shopkeeper was the only employee in the store at that time. Appellant selected two dresses from the racks. One of the dresses, which was blue, was cut "straight from the shoulders to just below the hips," and was "not a dress that a pregnant woman would wear." Appellant asked the shopkeeper if she could go into the dressing room, and the shopkeeper replied that she could. The shopkeeper testified that appellant's request "for some reason . . . drew [her] attention to the outfits that [appellant] had."

Appellant carried the two dresses into a fitting room. The fitting room was covered by a curtain that stopped "about calf-high" from the floor. There was "no obstruction" in the view from where the shopkeeper sat to the fitting room, which was about 10 steps away.

While appellant was inside the fitting room, the shopkeeper "saw the blue dress drop below the curtain and fold." The shopkeeper could see appellant "right up against the curtain," and looking below the curtain and observing appellant's motions, could tell that the dress was being folded into thirds. Appellant did not appear to remove any clothing or to try on either dress. The shopkeeper, suspecting that a shoplifting was in progress, turned the lock on the shop's outer door. She testified that the turning of the lock made a loud noise.

When appellant exited the dressing room, she carried her white sweater draped over one arm and, on a hanger in the other arm, one of the dresses which she had taken into the dressing room. The shopkeeper noticed the second dress, the blue dress, "knotted up" inside the sweater, with only the dress' tags sticking out and part of its sash hanging down about four inches from inside the sweater. The shopkeeper could see the blue dress "quite readily," and was "positive" that it was inside the sweater.

The shopkeeper telephoned her husband to ask him to call the police. Meanwhile, appellant replaced on the rack the dress she had been carrying openly on the hanger, selected two other outfits, and returned to the dressing room. When appellant exited the dressing room a second time, "she had all three dresses back on the hangers." Appellant returned the blue dress, along with the two other items, to the racks. By that time, the shopkeeper's husband and a private security guard had arrived. The police arrived soon afterward, and arrested appellant. Although the cost of the blue dress was $29.99, appellant had only two dollars with her at the time. At no time did appellant attempt to leave the store with any of the items.

At the close of the shopkeeper's testimony, appellant moved for a judgment of acquittal. The court denied the motion, commenting that it would "like to hear what [appellant] was doing by folding the dress up and putting it in the sweater." Both the court and defense counsel acknowledged that appellant's conduct had been ambiguous:

[DEFENSE COUNSEL]:	Your Honor, we would submit that the mere fact that the defendant had this item on her arm with the sweater and she had other items as well she carried into the store is not unusual that she had only two hands [sic]. She had one with one dress in it and another one with another dress in it.
THE COURT:	The first dress was folded up very nicely inside the sweater, why would that be?
[DEFENSE COUNSEL]:	Your Honor, we would surmise it is a reasonable inference that the defendant could have been doing that as one way to carry the sweater around before she left the store.
THE COURT:	And it also could be inferred she was stealing it, right?
[DEFENSE COUNSEL]:	*That could be an inference.*
THE COURT:	That's why your motion is denied, for that reason.

[Emphasis added.]

Appellant testified on her own behalf. According to her, she initially brought three, not two, items inside the dressing room. She lay one of the dresses on a chair because there was no room to hang it up. Appellant testified that she had tried on two of the dresses over the jumpsuit she was wearing by untying its shoulder straps and slipping the dresses on as far as her waist. She did not try on the blue dress, however, because it did not have an elastic waist that would fit over her abdomen.

According to appellant, when she exited the dressing room the first time, she carried her pocketbook in one hand, and all three outfits, along with her sweater, draped over her other arm. At first, appellant testified that the blue dress was not folded up inside the sweater, but rather was across her arm "underneath the rest of the clothes." Later, however, she denied that she had had the blue dress at all during her first trip to the dressing room. Rather, she testified, she had taken and tried on three other items, each of which she returned to the racks. Only then, on her second trip, did she bring the blue dress, along with one or two other outfits, into the dressing room. Appellant denied that she had any intention to take the blue dress, and testified that she had planned to return to the store with a friend who would pay for her purchases.

To find appellant guilty of attempted taking property without right, the finder of fact must have found, beyond a reasonable doubt, that she attempted to (1) take and (2) carry away (3) the property of another (4) without the right to do so.

You are the appellate judge. How would you rule on appeal? Why? For two potential solutions, see the majority and dissenting opinions in *Wormsley v. United States*, 526 A.2d 1373 (D.C. App. 1987).

How would you assess the performance of defendant's counsel in this case?

D. Impossibility

The defense of impossibility is one of the more intriguing criminal defenses. It is raised in situations in which the defendant really wants to commit a crime, but for one reason or another it is impossible to do so. The doctrine causes a great deal of judicial confusion and, as will be apparent from reading the *Booth* case, it is a lot easier to see how courts get the issues confused than it is to figure out how to get them right. We will explore this question by considering *Booth* and the series of questions and notes that follow it.

Booth v. State

398 P.2d 863 (Okla. Ct. App. 1964)

Nix, Judge.

John Fletcher Booth, Jr., was charged by information in the District Court of Oklahoma County with the crime of Receiving Stolen Property, and was found guilty of the lesser crime of Attempt to Receive Stolen Property. The jury assessed his penalty at Two Years in the Oklahoma State Penitentiary, and to pay a fine in the amount of $150.00. From said judgment and sentence the defendant appeals.

The record before this Court reveals that this case arose out of a circumstance as testified to by a self-admitted, well-known thief bearing the name of Charley Stanford, whose FBI "rap sheet" covers 8 pages of arrests extending over a period of 15 years. He was obviously braggadocio about his convictions and related from the witness stand that he had been arrested approximately 300 times on everything in the book, short of murder and rape. He admitted serving 4 terms in the penitentiary, and having been committed to a mental institution twice. He testified, in substance, that in the early morning hours he was walking in the parking lot at the YMCA in Oklahoma City and sighted a topcoat in a parked automobile. That he jimmied the window and removed the coat, took it to his home at 308 N.E. 8th Street, where he retired until about 7:00 at which time he proceeded down to a pay telephone where he called his attorney (the defendant herein). He testified that he advised him he had the coat he had ordered, and agreed to let him have the coat for $20.00. Arrangements were made for the defendant to meet him at the thief's home at approximately 11:00 a.m. where the transfer was to be made. He returned home, and a friend came by and invited him to go get a drink. He started from his house to his friend's car and was arrested by Lt. Anthony of the Oklahoma City Police Department. He was wearing the stolen coat at the time of his arrest. Lt.

Anthony took Stanford to the police station, and asked him where he had gotten the coat and he confessed getting it from the car in the YMCA parking lot.

Lt. Anthony testified, in substance, that he received an anonymous telephone call at approximately 7:00 a.m. on the morning of the day in question, and proceeded to the YMCA and located the owner of the vehicle that had been burglarized. They went then to the vehicle and observed the wing glass had been broken, pried open, and a gray cashmere coat and some shirts were missing. Officer Anthony proceeded to the 300 block on N.E. 8th and saw an ex-convict by the name Charley Stanford leaving his house wearing a gray cashmere coat. Anthony then and there arrested Stanford for Burglary and took him to the police station. He then called Mr. Gothard to the police station, where he identified the coat as his and asked Lt. Anthony for the coat, but was advised that they needed it as evidence. Officer Anthony, Officer Reading and Stanford proceeded to 308 N.E. 8th taking the recovered coat with them. After arriving, they took their position behind a closet door containing "peep-holes" and waited for the arrival of defendant Booth. According to the testimony of Anthony, the following transpired:

> "A. We then went back to the 300 block on 8th Street and I concealed myself in the closet and Mr. Stanford stayed in the other part of the house which was a combination of or the apartment was a combination of a kitchen with a divan on the west side of the room. He laid the overcoat on the divan. And in the door of this clothes closet there was small pin holes and I left the door ajar slightly. Shortly after eleven o'clock Mr. John Booth came to the front door. . . . Booth entered the house, and I heard Charlie say. . . . 'John, I got the coat which you wanted.' 'I need the twenty dollars right away.' And Mr. Booth said, 'This is child support month, Charlie, come to my office later and I will give you a check.'"

There was other conversation.

Q. Was there any other conversation relative to the deal?

A. John Booth and Charlie Stanford. They . . . well, Booth picked up the coat in his arms and there was conversation of and he warned him that the thing was "hot".

Q. Who warned who?

A. Charlie Stanford warned John Booth that the thing was "hot".

Q. That the coat was "hot"?

A. Yes, that's the way he termed it.

Q. What did Mr. Booth say?

A. He said, "well, I know how to handle things like this, don't worry about it, Charlie."

Q. Then what happened?

A. At this point they went into a restroom and what went on in there, I didn't hear. Then they came back out, and Booth went to his car and put the coat in the turtle-back of his car and then returned to the house and that is about all that occurred.

Q. Altogether then Mr. Booth was in Charlie Stanford's house about how long?

A. About ten minutes.

Q. Did he leave?

A. Yes, he left."

After taking Stanford to the police station, Anthony obtained a search warrant and then maintained a surveillance of Booth's house until he arrived. He then entered the premises, arrested Booth, and again recovered the coat.

Though defendant Booth was charged with Receiving Stolen Property, at the conclusion of the evidence and after the state and defendant had rested their case, the trial judge gave the following instruction:

> You are instructed that under the law of this case you are at liberty to consider only the included offense of whether the defendant John Fletcher Booth may be guilty of the crime of Attempt to Receive Stolen Property. In this regard you are instructed, an attempt to commit a crime is defined as being the compound of two elements.
>
> (1) The intent to commit a crime. (2) A direct ineffectual act done towards its commission.
>
> Preparation alone to an attempt to commit a crime is not sufficient. . . .

In view of said instruction, we are justified in assuming that the trial judge and all parties concerned were in agreement. That under the testimony in the instant case, the coat had lost its' [sic] character as stolen property when recovered by the police, and the owner apprised of the recovery and identified the coat as the one taken from him.

The law seems to be clear on this point, leaving the only question to be decided as whether or not the defendant could be convicted of an attempt to receive stolen property in such cases. It is the defendant's contention that if he could not be convicted of the substantive charge, because the coat had lost its character as stolen property; neither could he be convicted of an attempt because the coat was not in the category of stolen property at the time he received it.

The briefs filed in the case, and extensive research has revealed that two states have passed squarely on the question — New York and California. It is definitely one of first impression in Oklahoma.

The New York Court, in passing upon the question, laid down the following rule in the case of *People v. Jaffe*, 78 N.E. 169 on the following facts:

"A clerk stole goods from his employer under an agreement to sell them to accused, but before delivery of the goods the theft was discovered and the goods were recovered. Later the employer redelivered the goods to the clerk to sell to accused, who purchased them for about one-half of their value, believing them to have been stolen.

"Held, that the goods had lost their character as stolen goods at the time defendant purchased them, and that his criminal intent was insufficient to sustain a conviction for an attempt to receive stolen property, knowing it to have been stolen."

The *Jaffe* case was handed down in 1906, and has prevailed as the law in New York state 58 years without modification.

The State of California has passed upon the question several times and up until 1959, they followed the rule laid down in the *Jaffe* case, *supra*. In 1959, in the case of *People v. Camodeca*, 338 P.2d 903, the California Court abandoned the *Jaffe* rationale that a person accepting goods which he believes to have been stolen, but which was not in fact stolen goods, is not guilty of an attempt to receive stolen goods, and imposed a liability for the attempt, overruling its previous holding to the contrary in the above cited cases. The *Camodeca* case, *supra*, was affirmed in *People v. Rojas*, 358 P.2d 921 (1961).

[T]he question of "impossibility" was raised for the first time in *Regina v. McPherson*, *Dears & B.*, 197, 201, (1857), when Baron Bramwell said:

" "... The argument that a man putting his hand into an empty pocket might be convicted of an attempt to steal appeared to me at first plausible; but suppose a man, believing a block of wood to be a man who was his deadly enemy, struck it a blow intending to murder, could he be convicted of attempting to murder the man he took it to be?"

Subsequently, in *Regina v. Collins*, 9 Cox C.C. 497, 169 Eng. Rep. 1477 (1864), the Court expressly held that attempted larceny was not made out by proof that the defendant pickpocket actually inserted his hand into the victim's pocket with intent to steal. Chief Justice Cockburn, declaring, at page 499:

"We think that an attempt to commit a felony can only be made out when, if no interruption had taken place, the attempt could have been carried out successfully, and the felony completed of the attempt to commit which the party is charged."

This very broad language, encompassing as it did all forms of "impossibility", was subsequently rejected by the English courts and it was held that the inability of the pickpocket to steal from an empty pocket did not preclude his conviction of an attempted larceny. *Regina v. Ring*, 17 Cox C.C. 491, 66 L.T. (N.S.) 306 (1892).

In this country it is generally held that a defendant may be charged with an attempt where the crime was not completed because of "physical or factual impossibility", whereas a "legal impossibility" in the completion of the crime precludes prosecution for an attempt.

What is a "legal impossibility" as distinguished from a "physical or factual impossibility" has over a long period of time perplexed our courts and has resulted in many irreconcilable decisions and much philosophical discussion by legal scholars in numerous articles and papers in law school publications and by text writers.

The reason for the "impossibility" of completing the substantive crime ordinarily falls into one of two categories: (1) Where the act if completed would not be criminal, a situation which is usually described as a "legal impossibility", and (2) where the basic or substantive crime is impossible of completion, simply because of some physical or factual condition unknown to the defendant, a situation which is usually described as a "factual impossibility."

The authorities in the various states and the text-writers are in general agreement that where there is a "legal impossibility" of completing the substantive crime, the accused cannot be successfully charged with an attempt, whereas in those cases in which the "factual impossibility" situation is involved, the accused may be convicted of an attempt. Detailed discussion of the subject is unnecessary to make it clear that it is frequently most difficult to compartmentalize a particular set of facts as coming within one of the categories rather than the other. Examples of the so-called "legal impossibility" situations are:

(a) A person accepting goods which he believes to have been stolen, but which were not in fact stolen goods, is not guilty of an attempt to receive stolen goods. (*People v. Jaffe*, 185 N.Y. 497, 78 N.E. 169, 9 L.R.A., N.S., 263.)

(b) It is not an attempt to commit subornation of perjury where the false testimony solicited, if given, would have been immaterial to the case at hand and hence not perjurious. (*People v. Teal*, 196 N.Y. 372, 89 N.E. 1086, 25 L.R.A., N.S., 120.)

(c) An accused who offers a bribe to a person believed to be a juror, but who is not a juror, is not guilty of an attempt to bribe a juror. (*State v. Taylor*, 345 Mo. 325, 133 S.W.2d 336.)

(d) An official who contracts a debt which is unauthorized and a nullity, but which he believes to be valid, is not guilty of an attempt to illegally contract a valid debt. (*Marley v. State*, 58 N.J.L. 207, 33 A. 208.)

(e) A hunter who shoots a stuffed deer believing it to be alive is not guilty of an attempt to shoot a dear out of season. (State v. Guffey, 262 S.W.2d 152 (Mo. App.).)

Examples of cases in which attempt convictions have been sustained on the theory that all that prevented the consummation of the completed crime was a "factual impossibility" are:

(a) The picking of an empty pocket. (*People v. Moran*, 123 N.Y. 254, 25 N.E. 412, 10 L.R.A. 109; *Commonwealth v. McDonald*, 5 Cush. 365 (Mass.); *People v. Jones*, 46 Mich. 441, 9 N.W. 486.)

(b) An attempt to steal from an empty receptacle. (*Clark v. State*, 86 Tenn. 511, 8 S.W. 145) or an empty house. (*State v. Utley*, 82 N.C. 556.)

(c) Where defendant shoots into the intended victim's bed, believing he is there, when in fact he is elsewhere. (*State v. Mitchell*, 170 Mo. 633, 71 S.W. 175.)

(d) Where the defendant erroneously believing that the gun is loaded points it at his wife's head and pulls the trigger. (*State v. Damms*, 9 Wis. 2d 183, 100 N.W.2d 592, 79 A.L.R.2d 1402.)

(e) Where the woman upon whom the abortion operation is performed is not in fact pregnant. (*Commonwealth v. Tibbetts*, 157 Mass. 519, 32 N.E. 910; *People v. Huff*, 339 Ill. 328, 171 N.E. 261; and *Peckham v. United States*, 96 U.S. App. D.C. 312, 266 F.2d 34.)

Your writer is of the opinion that the confusion that exists as a result of the two diverse rationales laid down in the [New York cases] and the [California cases] was brought about by the failure to recognize the distinction between a factual and a legal impossibility to accomplish the crime.

In the case at bar the stolen coat had been recovered by the police for the owner and consequently had, according to the well-established law in this country, lost its character as stolen property. Therefore, a legal impossibility precluded defendant from being prosecuted for the crime of Knowingly Receiving Stolen Property.

It would strain reasoning beyond a logical conclusion to hold contrary to the rule previously stated herein, that,

> " "If all which the accused person intended would, had it been done, constituted no substantive crime, it cannot be a crime under the name 'attempt' to do, with the same purpose, a part of this thing."

If a series of acts together will not constitute an offense, how can it be said that one of the acts alone will constitute an indictable offense? BISHOP CRIM. LAW § 747.

The rule is well stated by the English Court in the case of *R.V. Percy, Ltd.*, 33 Crim. App. R. 102 (1949):

> "Steps on the way to the commission of what would be a crime, if the acts were completed, may amount to attempts to commit that crime, to which, unless interrupted, they would have led; but steps on the way to the doing of something, which is thereafter done, and which is no crime, cannot be regarded as attempts to commit a crime."

Sayre, 41 HARVARD LAW REVIEW 821, 853–54 (1928) states the rationale in this manner:

> "It seems clear that cases (where none of the intended consequences is in fact criminal) cannot constitute criminal attempts. If none of the consequences which the defendant sought to achieve constitute a crime, surely

his unsuccessful efforts to achieve his object cannot constitute a criminal attempt. The partial fulfillment of an object not criminal cannot itself be criminal. If the whole is not criminal, the part cannot be."

The defendant in the instant case leaves little doubt as to his moral guilt. The evidence, as related by the self-admitted and perpetual law violator indicates defendant fully intended to do the act with which he was charged. However, it is fundamental to our law that a man is not punished merely because he has a criminal mind. It must be shown that he has, with that criminal mind, done an act which is forbidden by the criminal law.

Adhering to this principle, the following example would further illustrate the point.

A fine horse is offered to A at a ridiculously low price by B, who is a known horse thief. A, believing the horse to be stolen, buys the same without inquiry. In fact, the horse had been raised from a colt by B and was not stolen. It would be bordering on absurdity to suggest that A's frame of mind, if proven, would support a conviction of an attempt. It would be a 'legal impossibility'.

Our statute provides that defendant must attempt to Knowingly Receive Stolen Property before a conviction will stand. How could one know property to be stolen when it was not? The statute needs to be changed so it would be less favorable to the criminal.

J.C. Smith, a Reader in Law, University of Nottingham, B.A., Cambridge, 1949, LL. Bl, 1950, M. A., 1954, said in an article (70 HARVARD LAW REVIEW 422) supporting the *Jaffe* case, *supra*, and the above reasoning:

> If it appears wrong that the accused should escape unpunished in the particular circumstances, then it may be that there is something wrong with the substantive law and his act ought to be criminal. But the remedy then is to alter the substantive crime. Otherwise "there is no ACTUS REUS because 'the accident has turned up in his favour'" and the accused ought to be acquitted. When a man has achieved all the consequences which he set out to achieve and those consequences do not, in the existing circumstances, amount to an ACTUS REUS it is in accordance both with principle and authority that that man should be held not guilty of any crime.

We earnestly suggest that the Legislature revise the law on Attempts in accordance with The American Law Institute for the adoption of a 'Model Penal Code', which Article 5.01 defines 'Criminal Attempts' in the following manner.

> '(1) DEFINITION OF ATTEMPT. A person is guilty of an attempt to commit a crime if, acting with the kind of culpability otherwise required for commission of the crime, he:
>
> > '(a) purposely engages in conduct which would constitute the crime if the attendant circumstances were as he believes them to be; or,

'(b) When causing a particular result in an element of the crime, does or omits to do anything with the purpose of causing or with the belief that it will cause such result, without further conduct on his part; or,

'(c) purposely does or omits to do anything which, under the circumstances as he believes them to be, is a substantial step in a course of conduct planned to culminate in his commission of the crime.'

The Clerk of this Court is requested to send a copy of this decision to the Legislative Council for consideration, as our Court can only adjudicate, it cannot legislate.

In view of our statutory law, and the decisions herein related, it is our duty to Reverse this case, with orders to Dismiss, and it is so ordered. However, there are other avenues open to the County Attorney which should be explored.

Questions and Notes

1. What is the difference between factual and legal impossibility?

2. Under which category does picking an empty pocket fall?

3. Assuming that you said factual for Question 2, could you construct an argument as defense attorney that the impossibility was really legal?

4. Of the five illustrations of factual impossibility listed by the court, are there any that could not arguably be categorized as legally impossible? If so, which one(s)?

5. In an ideal system of jurisprudence, should Booth have been convicted in this case?

6. Would your answer be any different if Stanford had actually owned the coat, but led Booth to believe that it was stolen (essentially the court's fine horse hypothetical)?

7. In either Question 5 or 6, should it matter that the defendant's purpose is in no way frustrated that the goods are not stolen? I.e., he may not care that the goods were stolen, but he also doesn't care that they were *not* stolen. In essence, he is neutral to that fact.

8. Is there anything wrong with the court's assertion in *Booth* that the substantive law requires one to *know* that the goods were stolen, and that one cannot know that which is not true? Would changing the statute make a difference?

9. We now turn to a modern "impossibility" case in the age of the Internet.

Chen v. State

42 S.W.3d 926 (Tex. Crim. App. 2001)

HOLLAND, J., delivered the opinion of the unanimous Court.

Appellant was convicted in a bench trial of attempted sexual performance by a child, and he was sentenced to seven years confinement and a fine of $1000.

Imposition of the seven years confinement was suspended, and appellant was placed on seven years community supervision. The court of appeals affirmed the conviction We granted appellant's petition for discretionary review to determine "[w]hether a 47 year old male undercover officer posing as a 13 year old female for the purposes of internet communications established evidence that was sufficient, as a matter of law, to support a conviction for the offense of attempted sexual performance by a child." We will affirm the judgment of the court of appeals.

The evidence presented at appellant's bench trial showed that on December 13, 1996, appellant placed an advertisement on an America Online computer bulletin board stating, "A nude dancer needed for discreet pleasure. I am generous and rich. You must be very attractive and young." Detective Steve Nelson, a Dallas Police Officer working on a specialized crime task involving child exploitation, discovered the advertisement. On December 16, 2001, he e-mailed appellant back representing himself as J. Cirello and asking appellant "how young of a nude dancer [he was] looking for." Appellant replied, "I will say between 20 and 30 or as long as you have a young looking face and tender body." Detective Nelson responded that there was no one in that age range and signed the email "J. Cirello."

Appellant e-mailed again and asked, "What age are you in?" Posing as J. Cirello, Detective Nelson wrote, "If you don't care about age I am 13, looking for independence. What are you looking for?" Appellant replied that he was looking for a girl who "dares to be nude and watched by me while I am masturbating." He asked to "get together" and requested her name and location. Detective Nelson e-mailed, stating "My name is Julie." He also wrote that "Julie" had never seen a man masturbate and did not want "her" parents to find out.

During the next few e-mails, appellant asked where Julie lived and when they could get together. He expressed a desire to exchange telephone numbers. He stated that they could get to know each other first and assured Julie that he would not hurt her. "Julie" asked for his description and his phone number and stated that "it might be better if [she] calls [appellant]." "Julie" wrote that "she" had never had sex before and was a little scared. Appellant responded that "sex [a] is wonderful thing." He also later wrote that "sex is not my major object." "Julie" then expressed that "she" was possibly interested in sex "if the right person came along to explain things and help [her]." For a few more weeks, Appellant and "Julie" e-mailed each other, discussing appellant's sexual history, "Julie's" nervousness, and plans to meet in person. Appellant described his van as champagne colored.

On February 6, 1997, appellant and "Julie" began their plan to meet. Appellant assured "Julie" that he would bring protection and lubrication, so that he would not hurt her or get her pregnant. After a series of e-mails, they decided to meet at a Best Western on a Tuesday afternoon (February 11, 1997). Appellant informed Julie that he had a room reserved for that day. "Julie" wrote appellant, stating that she would be outside the lobby between 3:30 and 4:00 pm and described herself as "5-foot one inch tall with long blond hair."

The Garland Police Department set up surveillance at the Best Western. Appellant arrived at the motel in a champagne colored minivan. He initially sat in the minivan for about ten minutes. Eventually, he went in the lobby, stayed for two minutes, then came back out to his vehicle. When he got back into his minivan, the police arrested him. Appellant had a package of condoms and a tube of KY Jelly on the console of his minivan. He later gave a voluntary statement in which he admitted that he was going to show a girl how to have sex.

Detective Nelson admitted on cross-examination that he was a white male and had never been known by the name of Julie Cirello. "Julie" did not exist, and he was the author of the e-mails signed by "Julie." Appellant asked the trial court to render a verdict of "not guilty" because the State failed to prove the elements contained in the indictment. Specifically, appellant argued that the State failed to prove he attempted to induce the named complainant, Julie Cirello, to commit any acts alleged in the indictment. Additionally, he asserted that the State failed to prove that Julie Cirello was a person under the age of 18 and that the proof presented at trial was a fatal variance with the allegation in the indictment. The trial court found appellant guilty beyond a reasonable doubt as charged in the indictment.

On appeal, appellant argued that because Julie Cirello did not exist, it was impossible for the State to prove a "completed" offense. The court of appeals rejected appellant's argument, stating that "[t]he State did . . . prove appellant *attempted* to induce a person, whom he knew as Julie Cirello, a thirteen-year-old child, to have sexual intercourse with him." There was not a variance between the allegations in the indictment and the proof at trial. This Court granted appellant's petition for discretionary review.

In his brief, appellant argues that the court of appeals erred by equating the intent element of the criminal intent statute with the specific intent requirement of the underlying offense. Appellant asserts that the crucial issue in this case is that it is "legally impossible" to commit the underlying offense. Therefore, the evidence in the record is insufficient as a matter of law to support the verdict.

In response, the State argues that this Court should reject the doctrine of legal impossibility as a defense. It states that the defense is not in the Penal Code and has been questioned by members of this Court in the past. Alternatively, the State asks this Court to hold that the impossibility doctrine does not apply to attempt crimes. Even if legal impossibility is a valid defense, the State asserts that appellant's circumstances present a factual impossibility claim, which is not a recognized defense.

The relevant portion of Texas Penal Code . . . states, "A person commits an offense if, knowing the character and content thereof, he employs, authorizes, or induces a child younger than 18 years of age to engage in sexual conduct or a sexual performance[. . .] A person commits an offense, if with specific intent to commit an offense, he does an act amounting to more than mere preparation that tends but fails to effect the commission of the offense intended." Therefore, the offense of attempted sexual performance by a child is committed if: 1) the defendant; 2) with specific intent to commit sexual performance by a child; 3) does an act amounting to more than mere preparation; 4) that tends but fails to effect the commission of sexual performance by a child.

This Court discussed the doctrine of legal impossibility and factual impossibility at length in *Lawhorn v. State*, 898 S.W.2d 886. At that time, we stated that legal impossibility was a valid defense, while factual impossibility was not. In his dissent, Judge Meyers asserted that neither legal nor factual impossibility should be a valid defense to a crime because neither defense is listed in the Texas Penal Code and older common law cases discussing legal impossibility should not survive the enactment of the Texas Penal Code. We find it unnecessary to dispose of the legal impossibility doctrine at this time. While we acknowledge that the line between legal and factual impossibility is sometimes difficult to draw, appellant's case does not involve a legal impossibility scenario. Rather, it presents factual impossibility.

"The distinction between factual and legal impossibility has been characterized as turning on whether the goal of the actor was deemed by the law to be a crime." Legal impossibility exists "where the act if completed would not be a crime, although what the actor intends to accomplish would be a crime." It has also been described as "existing [when] what the actor intends to do would not constitute a crime, or at least the crime charged." On the other hand, factual impossibility exists when "due to a physical or factual condition unknown to the actor, the attempted crime could not be completed." In other words, factual impossibility "refers to a situation in which the actor's objective was forbidden by the criminal law, although the actor was prevented from reaching that objective due to circumstances unknown to him."

This Court has very few cases raising the issues of factual or legal impossibility— especially in the context of attempt crimes. The concept of factual impossibility is well-illustrated in *People v. Grant*, 105 Cal.App.2d 347, 233 P.2d 660 (1951). In *Grant*, the defendant placed a homemade bomb in his suitcase for a family trip to San Diego. The defendant apparently intended for his family to be on the plane when it exploded, leaving him to collect the insurance money on their lives. The bomb discharged before the plane had been filled with people, but it was extinguished before it harmed anyone. At trial, evidence was admitted that showed if the bomb had worked properly, the plane would have crashed into the ocean. In discussing the factual impossibility of the crime, the court noted that the defendant intended to cause the destruction of his family's airplane. Even though the bomb exploded early, the defendant was still guilty of attempted murder. "[W]here a defendant is charged with an attempt to commit a crime it is immaterial whether the attempted crime is impossible of completion if, as in the present case, completion was apparently possible to the defendant who was acting with the intent to commit the crime of murder." *State of New Mexico v. Lopez*, 100 N.M. 291, 669 P.2d 1086, 1087 (1983) (stating that a defendant "should be treated in accordance with the facts as he believe[d] them to be."); *State of North Carolina v. Hageman*, 307 N.C. 1, 296 S.E.2d 433, 441 (1982) (holding that "when a defendant has the specific intent to commit a crime and under the circumstances as he reasonably saw them did the acts necessary to consummate the substantive offense, but, because of facts unknown to him essential elements of the substantive offense were lacking, he may be convicted of an attempt to commit the crime.")

In applying these concepts to the instant case, we initially note that if Julie Cirello had been an actual thirteen-year old, then what appellant intended to accomplish (sexual performance by a child) constituted an actual crime. Appellant's goal was to commit the offense of sexual performance by a child. Because that goal is a crime by law, the doctrine of legal impossibility is not at issue in this case. Rather, this case presents a factual impossibility scenario. Due to a factual condition unknown to appellant (that Julie Cirello did not actually exist), the offense of sexual performance by a child could not be completed. It is true that, as appellant claims, the actual offense of sexual performance by a child would have been impossible for appellant to *complete;* the complainant, Julie Cirello, did not physically exist. But completion of the crime was apparently possible to appellant. He had *specific intent* to commit the offense of sexual performance by a child, and he committed an act amounting to more than mere preparation that tended but failed to effect the commission of the offense. The State presented evidence for each of the necessary elements of attempted sexual performance by a child.

In conclusion, appellant's case does not present the doctrine of legal impossibility. The evidence presented at trial, reviewed in the light most favorable to the verdict, was sufficient for the trier of fact to reasonably conclude that appellant was guilty of attempted sexual performance by a child.

The judgment of the court of appeals is affirmed.

Questions and Notes

1. Do you think that Chen's mistake created a legal or a factual impossibility? Explain. Should it matter?

2. Is *Chen's* characterization of Chen's defense as factual impossibility consistent with *Booth's* conclusion that the impossibility in that case was legal? Is there any difference between the two?

3. Should *Chen* be distinguished from *Grant* on the grounds that the impossibility (if there indeed was any) in *Grant* lay in the means being ineffectual whereas the mistake in *Chen* lay in the question of whether of whether it was impossible by any means to commit the crime that he desired to commit?

4. Even accepting the court's conclusion that the impossibility was factual, why wasn't all of this "mere preparation"?

What should be the result in the following cases?

   (A) In a particular jurisdiction, a boy under age 14 is conclusively presumed to be incapable of rape (which was also the rule at common law). George, a 13-year-old boy forcibly has sexual intercourse at knifepoint with Lucinda, a 24-year-old woman. He is charged with attempted rape.

(B) Merlin, a voodoo practitioner, firmly believes that by sticking pins into a doll representing Marie, his archenemy, Marie, will die. Acting under this belief, Merlin sticks pins into his Marie doll and is charged with attempted murder.

Problem

Tryon Hard has been plotting to kill his ex-girlfriend, Alice. He decided to accomplish his scheme by shooting her through her window and into her bed while she was sleeping. Upon learning of this plan, Alice put a life-size dummy of herself in bed while she slept downstairs in the living room. At midnight, Tryon fired six rifle shots into the dummy, and assumed that he had killed Alice. At 1 a.m., three burglars broke into Alice's house, shot her to death and stole some property. At 2 a.m., Tryon broke into Alice's house to ascertain whether or not he had killed her. Upon seeing her dead body, he determined that she was still alive. Consequently, he decapitated her corpse.

Tryon has been charged with two counts of attempted murder, and the court has appointed you to defend him. What arguments will you make? Do you think that you will succeed? Would it matter whether your jurisdiction followed *Booth* or the MPC?

Chapter 18

Complicity

A. Actus Reus

One of the more intriguing aspects of criminal law is the extent to which an individual can be held criminally responsible for another's conduct. Guilt, of course, ought to be personal, but many crimes are committed with one primary perpetrator and several associates. Nobody suggests that the associates should go free. Indeed, in some cases those who actually do the dirty work may be less culpable than their bosses who remain above it all. We have seen various cases that have raised some aspects of the problem of accessorial liability but have postponed until now a systematized study of the problem.

At common law, the primary perpetrator was called a principal in the first degree. Those with her at the scene of the crime were called principals in the second degree, or aiders and abettors. Those who were active in planning the crime, but who were not present when it was perpetrated, were called accessories before the fact. Today, all three of these categories of criminal are generally punished the same, and it is not necessary for one to be convicted before the other. One who gives aid and comfort to a criminal, knowing that a crime was committed, but having had no part in its perpetration, was called an accessory after the fact and was subject to less severe punishment than the other criminals. *See* Nutshell § 15.01.

How much one must aid in order to be an aider and abettor and the extent to which juries can draw inferences from ambiguous behavior are questions raised in the *Bailey* case.

Bailey v. United States
416 F.2d 1110 (D.C. Cir. 1969)

Spottswood W. Robinson, III, Circuit Judge:

Appellant was tried in the District Court on a single-count indictment charging robbery of an employee of the Center Market Provision Company. The prosecutive theory was that he aided and abetted the principal assailant, who remains unknown, in the commission of the crime. At the close of the Government's case in chief, appellant moved unsuccessfully for a judgment of acquittal on the ground that the proof did not establish a prima facie case against him. The jury returned a verdict finding appellant guilty as charged, and from the conviction this appeal was taken.

Appellant spent some of the afternoon of September 26, 1966, the date of the robbery, in the vicinity of the Center Market Provision Company, a wholesale meat distributor. He was first seen across the street from the company's place of business "shooting craps" with a short, stocky man—the "other man" in the case, who was to become the actual robber. At one point, appellant left the other man but returned minutes later. Appellant subsequently left him again to join several men in a game of "five-and ten-cent crap" on a parking lot in front of the Center Market building. When the game terminated, appellant rejoined the other man, who in the meanwhile had remained across the street, and somewhat later they walked over to the parking lot and stood by a truck owned by Center Market. The offense for which appellant was prosecuted took place shortly thereafter.

Wilson C. Lawson, Jr., a part-time bookkeeper for Center Market, was the victim of the robbery. Each day he checked in the cash receipts of Center Market's drivers and prepared the company's bank deposit. His regular routine was to take the deposit with him when he left and to deliver it to a bank, at which he was employed full-time, on the following day.

As Lawson left Center Market on September 26, he carried a paper bag containing a deposit of approximately $4,200. He noticed appellant and the other man by the truck but attached no significance to that circumstance. While Lawson stood on a loading platform locking the door, a driver whom he recognized came out of another building and conversed with him briefly. A second truck driver was sitting in a car parked facing the platform.

Lawson walked down the platform steps toward his car, which was parked next to the truck where appellant and the other man were. When Lawson reached his car, the other man took the bag with the deposit at gunpoint. Appellant, just prior to the holdup, had walked away from the gunman toward the curb of the street, and was then about ten feet away. The man who had conversed with Lawson yelled "Look, they're robbing him," and both appellant and the other man ran away in the same direction. The two truck drivers attempted to follow but lost them. Appellant was subsequently apprehended, but the other man was never identified or caught.

Appellant's conviction must stand, if at all, on the premise that he aided and abetted the unknown robber, for the record is barren of proof that appellant was an active perpetrator of the offense. And the sufficiency of the Government's evidence to sustain a conviction on that premise became an issue to be tested by familiar rules when the motion for judgment of acquittal was made. "The true rule . . . is that a trial judge, in passing upon a motion for directed verdict of acquittal, must determine whether upon the evidence, giving full play to the right of the jury to determine credibility, weigh the evidence, and draw justifiable inferences of fact, a reasonable mind might fairly conclude guilt beyond a reasonable doubt." For that purpose, the judge "must assume the truth of the Government's evidence and give the Government the benefit of all legitimate inferences to be drawn therefrom." Should the judge determine that prudent jurors might have no such doubt, or might disagree as to its existence, the matter lies within the jury's province and the motion must be denied. But, very importantly, "Guilt, according to a basic principle in our jurisprudence, must be established beyond a reasonable doubt. And, unless that result is possible on the evidence, the judge must not let the jury act; he must not let it act on what would necessarily be only surmise and conjecture, without evidence."

Appellant's conduct, as portrayed in the view most favorable to the Government, amounted to presence at the scene of the crime, slight prior association with the actual perpetrator, and subsequent flight. A sine qua non of aiding and abetting, however, is guilty participation by the accused. "In order to aid and abet another to commit a crime it is necessary that a defendant 'in some sort associate himself with the venture, that he participate in it as in something that he wishes to bring about, that he seek by his action to make it succeed.'" The crucial inquiries in this case relate to the legal capabilities of the evidence to sustain a jury determination that appellant collaborated to that degree in the robbery.

An inference of criminal participation cannot be drawn merely from presence; a culpable purpose is essential. In *Hicks v. United States*, the Supreme Court recognized that the accused's presence is a circumstance from which guilt may be deduced if that presence is meant to assist the commission of the offense or is pursuant to an understanding that he is on the scene for that purpose. And we have had occasion to say that "[mere] presence would be enough if it is intended to and does aid the primary actors." Presence is thus equated to aiding and abetting when it is shown that it designedly encourages the perpetrator, facilitates the unlawful deed — as when the accused acts as a lookout — or where it stimulates others to render assistance to the criminal act. But presence without these or similar attributes is insufficient to identify the accused as a party to the criminality. And this case is devoid of evidence, beyond what the previous associative acts and the subsequent flight might themselves reflect, that appellant's presence on the scene was designed to in any way sanction or promote the robbery.

The Government urges the efficacy of appellant's presence when it is coupled with his association with the perpetrator on the date of and shortly prior to the robbery. But an accused's prior association with one who is to become a criminal offender, even when coupled with the accused's later presence at the scene of the offense, does not warrant an inference of guilty collaboration. Moreover, here the uncontradicted evidence shows that each of appellant's several brief meetings with the eventual robber occurred on the street or the parking lot in the open view of others, including the men with whom appellant fraternized for some time in a dice game — evidence becoming even more eloquent when scrutinized in the light of what was not shown at trial. The Government's proof did not expose appellant as a planner of the robbery, or as an aide or lookout in its consummation,[28] or as one who

---

28. The Government's aiding and abetting theory, as argued to the jury, was that appellant either planned the robbery or functioned as a lookout. But the record is devoid of evidence disclosing circumstances that could give that sort of color to appellant's conduct. There is no trustworthy indication that appellant was a party to the scheme to rob, and the Government did not ask any

shared in its proceeds, or even as one who knew the unidentified robber. In these circumstances, we cannot say that reasonable jurors could find a taint of criminality in appellant's limited association with him.

The Government contends finally that the strength of its case against appellant was enhanced by the fact that appellant fled the scene after the crime was committed. The evidentiary value of flight, however, has depreciated substantially in the face of Supreme Court decisions delineating the dangers inherent in unperceptive reliance upon flight as an indicium of guilt. We no longer hold tenable the notion that "the wicked flee when no man pursueth, but the righteous are as bold as a lion." The proposition that "one who flees shortly after a criminal act is committed or when he is accused of committing it does so because he feels some guilt concerning that act" is not absolute as a legal doctrine "since it is a matter of common knowledge that men who are entirely innocent do sometimes fly from the scene of a crime through fear of being apprehended as the guilty parties, or from an unwillingness to appear as witnesses."

With cautious application in appreciation of its innate shortcomings, flight may under particular conditions be the basis for an inference of consciousness of guilt. But guilt, as a factual deduction, must be predicated upon a firmer foundation than a combination of unelucidated presence and unelucidated flight. Here there was no evidentiary manifestation that the appellant was prompted by subjective considerations related in any wise to the crime.[34] Moreover, as the evidence disclosed, appellant had several convictions prior to the affair in suit, and these might well have dictated what seemed to him to be best. Absent anything more, there was no more basis for attributing his flight to complicity in the robbery than to a purpose consistent with innocence.

If we consider presence, association and flight separately, the Government's case quite obviously did not qualify for submission to the jury. And while "the jury must take the Government's case as a whole and determine whether as a whole it proves guilt beyond a reasonable doubt," any effort to repair the Government's fragmented case still leaves a prosecution constructed from evidence which is pregnant with the probability that appellant was an innocent bystander. After all, it shows only that he openly gambled with the eventual robber, talked to him, and stood with him beside the truck at intermittent periods during the afternoon. Suddenly when the robbery victim appeared on the scene with the bag of money, it was the unidentified man who pointed a gun at him and grabbed the bag. Appellant, prompted by reasons which only random speculation could summon, ran away in the midst

---

of its eyewitnesses to try to elucidate appellant's behavior as he walked away from the unidentified robber immediately before the crime took place.

34. There was no evidence of such things as manifest cooperation, division of the spoils, or the like, activities which have been factors in decisions reaching the contrary conclusion under their particular circumstances.

of shouts that "they" had committed a robbery.[37] The admonition that "innocent people caught in a web of circumstances frequently become terror stricken" carries its usual force here.

In the annals of the case law we find well-reasoned decisions exonerating from conviction persons accused in circumstances not significantly divergent from those appearing here. We hold concordantly that the Government's ambiguous evidence against appellant left too much room for the jury to engage in speculation, with the result that the motion for judgment of acquittal was erroneously denied. The totality of that evidence could only conjecturally support a finding that appellant "[associated] himself with the [criminal] venture, that he [participated] in it as in something that he [wished] to bring about, [and] that he [sought] by his action to make it succeed." The circumstances may arouse suspicions but, as we have counseled, even "grave suspicion is not enough."

We reverse the judgment of appellant's conviction and remand the case to the District Court with direction that a judgment of acquittal be entered.

BASTIAN, Senior Circuit Judge (dissenting):

Carrying a bag which contained about $5,100.00 in cash and checks, a bookkeeper of the Center Market Provision Company left the Company office, intending to deposit the funds in the bank. Appellant and an unidentified man were standing near the Company's truck and the employee's automobile. As the employee was about to put the bag in the trunk of his car, the unidentified man drew his gun and took the bag. Appellant, standing at this time only a short distance away, made no move to run until an eyewitness shouted, "They are robbing him!" Thus alerted by the eyewitness' cry that they were robbing the victim, both the unidentified gunman and appellant ran away together. They were pursued (but kept running together) for some three or four blocks when they outdistanced their pursuers. They did not separate during these three or four blocks. Appellant was later arrested, but the unidentified gunman was never caught, nor was the money recovered. Added to these facts, the record reveals that appellant had been associated with the unidentified gunman for an appreciable period of time immediately preceding the crime. Then appellant was seen joining the robber just before the robbery, and, at the

---

37. Our dissenting colleague emphasizes the word "they" in the shout but we are unable to attach particular significance to it. The witness who made that outcry testified that appellant had walked away from the gunman prior to the holdup and explained appellant's role thusly:

Q. Did Mr. Bailey at any time ever go over to Mr. Lawson?
A. Not as I knows of. Only thing I seen was both running down the street.
Q. You ever *see* Mr. Bailey do anything to Mr. Lawson?
A. No, sir.
Q. You ever *see* Mr. Bailey anytime snatch anything out of Mr. Lawson's hands?
A. No, sir.
Q. The only thing you saw Mr. Bailey do was run up the street?
A. That is all. This coincides with all else said at trial.

moment of the crime, appellant was no more than ten feet from the actual spot of the holdup.

In *Crawford v. United States*, 375 F.2d 332 (1967), we stated that, in order to withstand a motion for acquittal, "the government need only introduce enough evidence to 'sustain' a conviction, *i.e.*, such evidence that reasonable persons *could* find guilt beyond reasonable doubt. It is not a requirement that the evidence compel, but only that it is capable of or sufficient to persuade the jury to reach a verdict of guilt by the requisite standard." Thus does our inquiry focus on the question of whether the government introduced enough evidence to "sustain" a conviction of appellant's aiding and abetting, such evidence, with inferences drawn appropriately in the government's favor, that reasonable persons *could* find guilt of aiding and abetting beyond a reasonable doubt.

Judge Hand's statement in *United States v. Peoni*, 100 F.2d 401, 402 (2d Cir. 1938), on the requirements necessary for one to be an aider and abettor was repeated almost verbatim by the Supreme Court in *Nye & Nissen v. United States*, 336 U.S. 613. There the Court declared, "in order to aid and abet another to commit a crime it is necessary that a defendant 'in some sort associate himself with the venture, that he participate in it as in something that he wishes to bring about, that he seek by his action to make it succeed.'"

In this case, prior to the commission of the crime, appellant was closely associated with the actual perpetrator and was with him immediately before the robbery. Furthermore, appellant was present at the scene of the crime. Finally, he ran away together with the other man after the robbery. Yet, my colleagues decide that only by impermissible conjecture could the evidence support a finding that appellant "in some sort associate himself with the venture, that he participate in it as in something that he wishes to bring about, that he seek by his action to make it succeed."

I, on the other hand, state forcefully that the totality of this evidence, when considered in the light most favorable to the prosecution, is surely adequate, yea, more than adequate, to meet the governing standard, . . . [that] a reasonable mind might fairly conclude guilt beyond a reasonable doubt . . . [and if the trial judge] concludes that either of the two results, a reasonable doubt or no reasonable doubt, is fairly possible, he must let the jury decide the matter."

In the District Court, an experienced trial judge denied appellant's motions for judgment of acquittal and allowed the case to go to the jury. I submit that this was properly done and that the resulting jury verdict should be allowed to stand. I see no justification for my colleagues setting aside appellant's conviction.

So, I dissent.

Questions and Notes

1. Do the majority and dissent purport to apply a different standard of appellate review? If so, what is the difference?

2. Did the court say that Bailey's conduct could never qualify for accessorial liability, or only that it could not qualify in this case? If the latter, why couldn't it apply in this case?

3. If you were the prosecutor, what additional evidence would you have liked to have had in this case?

4. Don't you think that Bailey was probably acting as a lookout?

5. Why wasn't the jury at least allowed to infer that Bailey was so acting?

6. Does the court use Bailey's criminal record as an exculpatory factor? If Bailey had no criminal record but ran anyway, could the jury have considered that to be evidence of guilt?

See NUTSHELL § 15.02.

7. *Bailey* focused primarily on the *actus reus* necessary to be an aider and abettor. In *Beeman* and *Fountain*, we will focus primarily on the *mens rea* necessary for complicity.

B. Mens Rea (Intentional Crimes)

People v. Beeman

674 P.2d 1318 (Cal. 1984)

REYNOSO, J.

Timothy Mark Beeman appeals from a judgment of conviction of robbery, burglary, false imprisonment, destruction of telephone equipment and assault with intent to commit a felony. Appellant was not present during commission of the offenses. His conviction rested on the theory that he aided and abetted his acquaintances James Gray and Michael Burk.

James Gray and Michael Burk drove from Oakland to Redding for the purpose of robbing appellant's sister-in-law, Mrs. Marjorie Beeman, of valuable jewelry, including a 3.5 carat diamond ring. They telephoned the residence to determine that she was home. Soon thereafter Burk knocked at the door of the victim's house, presented himself as a poll taker, and asked to be let in. When Mrs. Beeman asked for identification, he forced her into the hallway and entered. Gray, disguised in a ski mask, followed. The two subdued the victim, placed tape over her mouth and eyes and tied her to a bathroom fixture. Then they ransacked the house, taking numerous pieces of jewelry and a set of silverware. The jewelry included a 3.5 carat, heart shaped diamond ring and a blue sapphire ring. The total value of these two rings was over $100,000. In the course of the robbery, telephone wires inside the house were cut.

Appellant was arrested six days later in Emeryville. He had in his possession several of the less valuable of the stolen rings. He supplied the police with information that led to the arrests of Burk and Gray. With Gray's cooperation appellant assisted police in recovering most of the stolen property.

Burk, Gray and appellant were jointly charged. After the trial court severed the trials, Burk and Gray pled guilty to robbery. At appellant's trial they testified that he had been extensively involved in planning the crime. Burk testified that he had known appellant for two and one-half years. He had lived in appellant's apartment several times. Appellant had talked to him about rich relatives in Redding and had described a diamond ring worth $50,000. According to Burk the feasibility of robbing appellant's relatives was first mentioned two and one-half months before the incident occurred. About one week before the robbery, the discussions became more specific. Appellant gave Burk the address and discussed the ruse of posing as a poll taker. It was decided that Gray and Burk would go to Redding because appellant wanted nothing to do with the actual robbery and because he feared being recognized. On the night before the offense appellant drew a floor plan of the victim's house and told Burk where the diamond ring was likely to be found. Appellant agreed to sell the jewelry for 20 percent of the proceeds.

After the robbery was completed, Burk telephoned appellant to report success. Appellant said that he would call the friend who might buy the jewelry. Burk and Gray drove to appellant's house and showed him the "loot." Appellant was angry that the others had taken so much jewelry, and demanded that his cut be increased from 20 percent to one third.

Gray's testimony painted a similar picture. Gray also had known appellant for approximately two years prior to the incident. Gray said Burk had initially approached him about the robbery, supplied the victim's address, and described the diamond ring. Appellant had at some time described the layout of the house to Gray and Burk and had described to them the cars driven by various members of the victim's family. Gray and Burk, but not appellant, had discussed how to divide the proceeds. Both Gray and Burk owed money to appellant. In addition, Burk owed Gray $3,200.

According to Gray appellant had been present at a discussion three days before the robbery when it was mentioned that appellant could not go because his 6 foot 5 inch, 310 pound frame could be too easily recognized. Two days before the offense, however, appellant told Gray that he wanted nothing to do with the robbery of his relatives. On the day preceding the incident appellant and Gray spoke on the telephone. At that time appellant repeated he wanted nothing to do with the robbery but confirmed that he had told Burk that he would not say anything if the others went ahead.

Gray confirmed that appellant was upset when he saw that his friends had gone through with the robbery and had taken all of the victim's jewelry. He was angered further when he discovered that Burk might easily be recognized because he had not disguised himself. Appellant then asked them to give him all of the stolen goods. Instead Burk and Gray gave appellant only a watch and some rings which they believed he could sell. Gray and Burk then travelled to San Jose where they sold the silverware for $900. Burk used this money to flee to Los Angeles. Sometime later appellant asked for Gray's cooperation in recovering and returning the property to the victim. On several occasions when Burk called them for more money, appellant stalled and avoided questions about the sale of the jewelry.

Appellant Beeman's testimony contradicted that of Burk and Gray as to nearly every material element of his own involvement. Appellant testified that he did not participate in the robbery or its planning. He confirmed that Burk had lived with him on several occasions, and that he had told Burk about Mrs. Beeman's jewelry, the valuable diamond ring, and the Beeman ranch, in the course of day-to-day conversations. He claimed that he had sketched a floor plan of the house some nine months prior to the robbery, only for the purpose of comparing it with the layout of a house belonging to another brother. He at first denied and then admitted describing the Beeman family cars but insisted this never occurred in the context of planning a robbery.

Appellant stated that Burk first suggested that robbing Mrs. Beeman would be easy some five months before the incident. At that time, and on the five or six subsequent occasions when Burk raised the subject, appellant told Burk that his friends could do what they wanted but that he wanted no part of such a scheme.

Beeman admitted Burk had told him of the poll taker ruse within a week before the robbery, and that Burk told him they had bought a cap gun and handcuffs. He further admitted that he had allowed Burk to take some old clothes left at the apartment by a former roommate. At that time Beeman told Burk: "If you're going to do a robbery, you can't look like a bum." Nevertheless, appellant explained that he did not know Burk was then planning to commit this robbery. Further, although he knew there was a possibility Burk and Gray would try to rob Mrs. Beeman, appellant thought it very unlikely they would go through with it. He judged Burk capable of committing the crime but knew he had no car and no money to get to Redding. Appellant did not think Gray would cooperate.

Appellant agreed that he had talked with Gray on the phone two days before the robbery, and said he had then repeated he did not want to be involved. He claimed that Burk called him on the way back from Redding because he feared appellant would report him to the police, but knew appellant would want to protect Gray, who was his closer friend.

Appellant claimed he told the others to come to his house after the robbery and offered to sell the jewelry in order to buy time in which to figure out a way to collect and return the property. He took the most valuable piece to make sure it was not sold. Since Burk had a key to his apartment, appellant gave the diamond ring and a bracelet to a friend, Martinez, for safekeeping.[1] After Burk fled to Los Angeles,

---

1. Martinez corroborated that appellant had given him a diamond ring and other jewelry belonging to appellant's family for this purpose.

appellant showed some of the jewelry to mutual acquaintances in order to lull Burk into believing he was attempting to sell it. During this time Burk called him on the phone several times asking for money and, when appellant told him of plans to return the property, threatened to have him killed.

When confronted with his prior statement to the police that he had given one of the rings to someone in exchange for a $50 loan, appellant admitted making the statement but denied that it was true. He also claimed that his statement on direct examination that "his [Burk's] face was seen. He didn't wear a mask. Didn't do anything he was supposed to do . . ." referred only to the reason Gray had given for wanting to return the victim's property.

Appellant requested that the jury be instructed in accord with *People v. Yarber* (1979) 90 Cal. App. 3d 895 [153 Cal. Rptr. 875] that aiding and abetting liability requires proof of intent to aid. The request was denied.

After three hours of deliberation, the jury submitted two written questions to the court: "We would like to hear again how one is determined to be an accessory and by what actions can he absolve himself"; and "Does inaction mean the party is guilty?" The jury was reinstructed in accord with the standard instructions, CALJIC Nos. 3.00 and 3.01. The court denied appellant's renewed request that the instructions be modified as suggested in *Yarber*, explaining that giving another, slightly different instruction at this point would further complicate matters. The jury returned its verdicts of guilty on all counts two hours later.

Penal Code section 31 provides in pertinent part: "All persons concerned in the commission of a crime . . . whether they directly commit the act constituting the offense, or aid and abet in its commission, or, not being present, have advised and encouraged its commission, . . . are principals in any crime so committed." Thus, those persons who at common law would have been termed accessories before the fact and principals in the second degree as well as those who actually perpetrate the offense, are to be prosecuted, tried and punished as principals in California.[2] The term "aider and abettor" is now often used to refer to principals other than the perpetrator, whether or not they are present at the commission of the offense.

CALJIC No. 3.00 defines principals to a crime to include "Those who, with knowledge of the unlawful purpose of the one who does directly and actively commit or

---

2. The major purpose and effect of this abrogation of the common law distinction between parties to crime apparently has been to alleviate certain procedural difficulties. For instance, at common law an accessory before the fact was punishable where the incitement occurred while the principals were punishable where the offense occurred; one could not be convicted as an accessory if charged as a principal and vice versa; an accessory could not be tried before the principal had been found guilty. *Now*, as at common law, one who is found guilty of the same offense on a theory of aiding and abetting while present at the scene of the crime, or conspiring with the perpetrator beforehand or instigating, encouraging, or advising commission of the crime, is subject to the same punishment as the one who with the requisite criminal intent commits the crime by his or her own acts.

attempt to commit the crime, aid and abet in its commission . . . , or . . . Those who, whether present or not at the commission or attempted commission of the crime, advise and encourage its commission Caljic No. 3.01 defines aiding and abetting as follows: "A person aids and abets the commission of a crime if, with knowledge of the unlawful purpose of the perpetrator of the crime, he aids, promotes, encourages or instigates by act or advice the commission of such crime."

Prior to 1974 Caljic No. 3.01 read: "A person aids and abets the commission of a crime if he knowingly and with criminal intent aids, promotes, encourages or instigates by act or advice, or by act and advice, the commission of such crime."

Appellant asserts that the current instructions, in particular Caljic No. 3.01, substitute an element of knowledge of the perpetrator's intent for the element of criminal intent of the accomplice, in contravention of common law principles and California case law. He argues that the instruction given permitted the jury to convict him of the same offenses as the perpetrators without finding that he harbored either the same criminal intent as they, or the specific intent to assist them, thus depriving him of his constitutional rights to due process and equal protection of the law. Appellant further urges that the error requires reversal because it removed a material issue from the jury and, on this record, it is impossible to conclude that the jury necessarily resolved the same factual question that would have been presented by the missing instruction.

The People argue that the standard instruction properly reflects California law, which requires no more than that the aider and abettor have knowledge of the perpetrator's criminal purpose and do a voluntary act which in fact aids the perpetrator. The People further contend that defendants are adequately protected from conviction for acts committed under duress or which inadvertently aid a perpetrator by the limitation of the liability of an aider and abettor to those acts knowingly aided and their natural and reasonable consequences. Finally, the People argue that the modification proposed by *Yarber, supra,* is unnecessary because proof of intentional aiding in most cases can be inferred from aid with knowledge of the perpetrator's purpose. Thus, respondent argues, it is doubtful that the requested modification would bring about different results in the vast majority of cases.

There is no question that an aider and abettor must have criminal intent in order to be convicted of a criminal offense. Decisions of this court dating back to 1898 hold that "the word 'abet' includes knowledge of the wrongful purpose of the perpetrator and counsel and encouragement in the crime" and that it is therefore error to instruct a jury that one may be found guilty as a principal if one aided or abetted. The act of encouraging or counseling itself implies a purpose or goal of furthering the encouraged result. "An aider and abettor's fundamental purpose, motive and intent is to aid and assist the perpetrator in the latter's commission of the crime."

The essential conflict in current appellate opinions is between those cases which state that an aider and abettor must have an intent or purpose to commit or assist in the commission of the criminal offenses, and those finding it sufficient that the aider and abettor engage in the required acts with knowledge of the perpetrator's criminal purpose.

[T]he weight of authority requires an aider and abettor to have an intent or purpose to commit or assist in commission of the underlying offense. The leading case is *Yarber, supra*, which explained that "[t]he synthesis that intent is inferred from the knowledge by the aider and abettor of the perpetrator's purpose is sound, generally, as a matter of human experience, but we cannot extrapolate therefrom, as a matter of law, that the inference must be drawn. Intent is what must be *proved;* from a person's action with knowledge of the purpose of the perpetrator of a crime, his intent to aid the perpetrator can be *inferred.* In the absence of evidence to the contrary, the intent may be regarded as established. But where a contrary inference is reasonable—where there is room for doubt that a person intended to aid a perpetrator—his knowledge of the perpetrator's purpose will not suffice." (Original italics.)

We agree with the *Yarber* court that the facts from which a mental state may be inferred must not be confused with the mental state that the prosecution is required to prove. Direct evidence of the mental state of the accused is rarely available except through his or her testimony. The trier of fact is and must be free to disbelieve the testimony and to infer that the truth is otherwise when such an inference is supported by circumstantial evidence regarding the actions of the accused. Thus, an act which has the effect of giving aid and encouragement, and which is done with knowledge of the criminal purpose of the person aided, may indicate that the actor intended to assist in fulfillment of the known criminal purpose. However, as illustrated by *Hicks v. U.S.* (1893) 150 U.S. 442 (conviction reversed because jury not instructed that words of encouragement must have been used with the intention of encouraging and abetting crime in a case where ambiguous gesture and remark may have been acts of desperation) and *People v. Bolanger* (1886) 71 Cal. 17 [11 P. 799] (feigned accomplice not guilty because lacks common intent with the perpetrator to unite in the commission of the crime), the act may be done with some other purpose which precludes criminal liability.

If the jury were instructed that the law conclusively presumes the intention of the accused solely from his or her voluntary acts, it would effectively eliminate intent as an ingredient of the offense'" and would "'conflict with the overriding presumption of innocence with which the law endows the accused and which extends to every element of the crime.'" (*Sandstrom v. Montana* (1979) 442 U.S. 510, 522.) Where an appellate court employs the same presumption to support the adequacy of a jury instruction, the reviewing court announces its willingness to permit a conviction to stand regardless of whether the trier of fact has found the required criminal intent. Thus, at the appellate level, the element of criminal intent is effectively eliminated as an ingredient of the offense.

When the definition of the offense includes the intent to do some act or achieve some consequence beyond the *actus reus* of the crime, the aider and abettor must share the specific intent of the perpetrator. By "share" we mean neither that the aider and abettor must be prepared to commit the offense by his or her own act should the perpetrator fail to do so, nor that the aider and abettor must seek to share the fruits of the crime. Rather, an aider and abettor will "share" the perpetrator's specific intent when he or she knows the full extent of the perpetrator's criminal purpose and gives aid or encouragement with the intent or purpose of facilitating the perpetrator's commission of the crime. The liability of an aider and abettor extends also to the natural and reasonable consequences of the acts he knowingly and intentionally aids and encourages.

CALJIC No. 3.01 inadequately defines aiding and abetting because it fails to insure that an aider and abettor will be found to have the required mental state with regard to his or her own act. While the instruction does include the word "abet," which encompasses the intent required by law, the word is arcane and its full import unlikely to be recognized by modern jurors. Moreover, even if jurors were made aware that "abet" means to encourage or facilitate, and implicitly to harbor an intent to further the crime encouraged, the instruction does not *require* them to find that intent because it defines an aider and abettor as one who "aids, promotes, encourages *or* instigates" (italics added). Thus, as one appellate court recently recognized, the instruction would "technically allow a conviction if the defendant knowing of the perpetrator's unlawful purpose, negligently or accidentally aided the commission of the crime."

Both the instruction suggested by *Yarber* ("A person aids and abets the commission of a crime if, with knowledge of the unlawful purpose of the perpetrator of the crime, he intentionally aids, promotes, encourages or instigates by act or advice the commission of such crime") and the version of CALJIC used prior to 1974 ("A person aids and abets the commission of a crime if he knowingly and with criminal intent aids, promotes, encourages or instigates by act or advice, or by act and advice, the commission of such crime") seek to include the required intent element. However, both are sufficiently ambiguous to conceivably permit conviction upon a finding of an intentional act which aids, without necessarily requiring a finding of an intent to encourage or facilitate the criminal offense. We suggest that an appropriate instruction should inform the jury that a person aids and abets the commission of a crime when he or she, acting with (1) knowledge of the unlawful purpose of the perpetrator; and (2) the intent or purpose of committing, encouraging, or facilitating the commission of the offense, (3) by act or advice aids, promotes, encourages or instigates, the commission of the crime.

Respondent argues that the jury clearly found that appellant knew his accomplices' purpose was to rob his sister-in-law and rejected his testimony that he did not in fact assist them. Thus, the only reasonable inference from the evidence was that appellant intentionally aided the actual perpetrators.

We do not agree with respondent's assessment of the effect of the error. Correct instruction on the element of intent was particularly important in this case because appellant's defense focused on the question of his intent more than on the nature of his acts. The prosecution produced considerable evidence which showed that appellant in fact aided the robbery. The prosecution's evidence also sought to show that he had participated extensively in the planning of the robbery and agreed beforehand to sell the jewelry for a percentage of its value, but refused to be present when the offenses were committed.

Appellant did not deny that he had given information to Burk and Gray which aided their criminal enterprise, but he claimed his purposes in doing so were innocent.[5] Appellant admitted that he was at some time made aware of his friends' intent to rob Mrs. Beeman, but insisted that he had repeatedly stated that he wanted nothing to do with a robbery of his relatives. He testified that he didn't think Burk would really go through with the robbery or that Gray would help. Two days before the incident, he again told Gray that he didn't want to be involved. Gray's testimony confirmed that appellant had twice said he did not want to be involved. Finally, appellant claimed to have taken possession of the jewelry and feigned attempts to sell it in order to recover the property and return it to the victims. Thus, the essential point of his defense was that although he acted in ways which in fact aided the criminal enterprise, he did not act with the intent of encouraging or facilitating the planning or commission of the offenses.

The jury certainly could have believed Burk and Gray while disbelieving appellant, and thus found that appellant intentionally aided and encouraged his friends in their crimes. However, the fact that the jury interrupted its deliberations to seek further instruction regarding accomplice liability indicates that the jurors did not dismiss appellant's testimony out of hand. Rather, the questions asked indicate the jury's deliberations were focused on the very issue upon which the defense rested and upon which the court's instructions were inadequate: the elements—including the mental element—of aiding and abetting. When it reinstructed the jury according to the standard instructions and again refused the *Yarber* modification requested by appellant, the court repeated its original mistake.

Under these circumstances, where the defense centered on the very element as to which the jury was inadequately instructed and the jurors' communication to the court indicated confusion on the same point, we cannot find the error harmless.

The convictions are reversed.

Questions and Notes

1. How do the instructions approved by the California Supreme Court differ from the ones actually given by the trial judge? Which do you think states better law? Why?

2. Suppose that Beeman had said to his friends: "I don't want any part of this burglary. But if you want to do it, it's up to you. Here is what the house looks like (drawing a floor plan), and here are where the most valuable jewels can be found."

---

5. He testified that he had mentioned the victim's jewels and car only casually and that he had drawn the floor plan only for the purpose of discussing the design of the house.

Under that scenario, should Beeman be guilty? Would he have been guilty under the trial court's instructions? Would he be guilty under the instructions approved by the supreme court?

3. If Beeman should be guilty under the Question 2 scenario, should he be guilty of as serious an offense as Burk and Gray?

4. Is the fact (if it was a fact) that Beeman tried to return the jewelry relevant to his criminal liability? Why? Why not?

5. The court suggests that "The liability of an aider and abettor extends . . . to the natural and reasonable consequences of the acts he knowingly and intentionally aids and encourages." In conjunction with *Kessler, infra*, we will consider whether such liability is inconsistent with the requirement of a specific criminal intent.

6. As will be apparent from reading *Fountain*, courts will sometimes reject *Beeman* logic, particularly if the crime is serious.

United States v. Fountain
768 F.2d 790 (7th Cir. 1985)

POSNER, Circuit judge.

We have consolidated the appeals in two closely related cases of murder of prison guards in the Control Unit of the federal penitentiary at Marion, Illinois—the maximum security cell block in the nation's maximum-security federal prison—by past masters of prison murder, Clayton Fountain and Thomas Silverstein.

Shortly before these crimes, Fountain and Silverstein, both of whom were already serving life sentences for murder, had together murdered an inmate in the control Unit of Marion, and had again been sentenced to life imprisonment. *See United States v. Silverstein*, 732 F.2d 1338 (7th Cir. 1984). After that, Silverstein killed another inmate, pleaded guilty to that murder, and received his third life sentence. At this point Fountain and Silverstein had each killed three people. (For one of these killings, however, Fountain had been convicted only of voluntary manslaughter. And Silverstein's first murder conviction was reversed for trial error, and a new trial ordered, after the trial in this case.) The prison authorities—belatedly, and as it turned out ineffectually—decided to take additional security measures. Three guards would escort Fountain and Silverstein (separately), handcuffed, every time they left their cells to go to or from the recreation, the law library, or the shower. (Prisoners in Marion's Control Unit are confined, one to a cell, for all but an hour or an hour and a half a day, and are fed in their cells.) But the guards would not be armed; nowadays guards do not carry weapons in the presence of prisoners, who might seize the weapons.

The two murders involved in these appeals took place on the same October day in 1983. In the morning, Silverstein, while being escorted from the shower to his cell, stopped next to Randy Gometzs cell; and while two of the escorting officers were for some reason at a distance from him, reached his handcuffed hands into the cell. The third officer, who was closer to him, heard the clock of the handcuffs being released and saw Gometz raise his shirt to reveal a home-made knife ("shank")—which had been fashioned from the iron leg of a bed—protruding from his waistband. Silverstein drew the knife and attacked one of the guards, Clutts, stabbing him 29 times and killing him. While pacing the corridor after the killing, Silverstein explained that "this is no cop thing. This is a personal thing between me and Clutts. The man disrespected me and I had to get him for it." Having gotten this off his chest he returned to his cell.

Gometz argues that the evidence was insufficient to convict him of aiding and abetting Silverstein in murdering Clutts. This argument requires us to consider the mental element in "aiding and abetting." Under the older cases, illustrated by *Backun v. United States*, 112 F.2d 635, 636–37 (4th Cir. 1940), and *Bacon v. United States*, 127 F.2d 985, 987 (10th Cir. 1942), it was enough that the aider and abettor knew the principal's purpose. Although this is still the test in some states, after the Supreme Court in *Nye & Nissen v. United States*, 336 U.S. 613, 619 (1949), adopted judge Learned Hand's test—that the aider and abettor "in some sort associate himself with the venture, that he participate in it as in something that he wishes to bring about, that he seek by his action to make it succeed," *United States v. Peoni*, 100 F.2d 401, 402 (2d Cir. 1938)—it came to be generally accepted that the aider and abettor must share the principal's purpose in order to be guilty of violating. But as both LaFave & Scott (at p. 509) and Perkins & Boyce (at p. 746) point out, there is support for relaxing this requirement when the crime is particularly grave. The holding of *Backun* itself may have been superseded, but a dictum in *Backun*—"One who sells a gun to another knowing that he is buying it to commit a murder, would hardly escape conviction as an accessory to the murder by showing that he received full price for the gun," makes so compelling an appeal to common sense that Gometz's opening brief in this court, after quoting the dictum, states, "Defendant Gometz has no quarrel with this rule of law."

In *People v. Lauria*, 251 Cal. App. 2d 471, 481, 59 Cal. Rptr. 628, 634 (1967)—not a federal case, but illustrative of the general point—the court, en route to holding that knowledge of the principal's purpose would not suffice for aiding and abetting of just any crime, said it would suffice for "the seller of gasoline who knew the buyer was using his product to make Molotov cocktails for terroristic use." Compare the following hypothetical cases. In the first, a shopkeeper sells dresses to a woman whom he knows to be a prostitute. The shopkeeper would not be guilty of aiding and abetting prostitution unless the prosecution could establish the elements of judge Hand's test. Little would be gained by imposing criminal liability in such a case. Prostitution, anyway a minor crime, would be but trivially deterred, since the prostitute could easily get her clothes from a shopkeeper ignorant of her occupation. In the second case, a man buys a gun from a gun dealer after telling the dealer that he wants it in order to kill his mother-in-law, and he does kill her. The dealer would be guilty of aiding and abetting the murder. This liability would help to deter—and perhaps not trivially given public regulation of the sale of guns—a most serious crime. We hold that aiding and abetting murder is established by proof beyond a reasonable doubt that the supplier of the murder weapon knew the purpose for which it would be used. This interpretation of the federal aider and abettor statute is consistent with though not compelled by precedent.

Gometz argues that there is insufficient evidence that he knew why Silverstein wanted a knife. We disagree. The circumstances make clear that the drawing of the knife from Gometz's waistband was prearranged. There must have been discussions between Silverstein and Gometz. Gometz must have known through those discussions or others that Silverstein had already killed three people in prison — two in Marion — and while this fact could not be used to convict Silverstein of a fourth murder, it could ground an inference that Gometz knew that Silverstein wanted the knife in order to kill someone. If Silverstein had wanted to conceal it on his person in order to take it back to his cell and keep it there for purposes of intimidation, escape, or self-defense (or carry it around concealed for any or all of these purposes), he would not have asked Gometz to release him from his handcuffs (as the jury could have found he had done), for that ensured that the guards would search him. Since the cuffs were off before Silverstein drew the shank from Gometz's waistband, a reasonable jury could find beyond a reasonable doubt that Gometz knew that Silverstein, given his history of prison murders, could have only one motive in drawing the shank and that was to make a deadly assault.

Questions and Notes

1. Is it as clear to you as it was to Judge Posner that Gometz knew why Silverstein wanted a knife? Is it even clear that Gometz knew of Silverstein's homicidal propensities? If not, how much should the jury be permitted to infer?

2. Ought the severity of the crime be relevant to the liability of one who has no true purpose to commit the crime? The Model Penal Code considered such a dichotomy and ultimately rejected it in favor of a standard substantially similar to that adopted by *Beeman*. We will consider the *Lauria* case (Chapter 19, Section B, *infra*) in conjunction with conspiracy.

3. If you represented Gometz, would you have conceded that selling a gun to one whom the seller knew planned to use it for a murder rendered the seller liable for murder? If not, how would you argue against that proposition?

4. *Kessler* focuses on the extent to which a true aider and abettor of one crime can be implicated in another.

People v. Kessler

315 N.E.2d 29 (Ill. 1974)

Mr. Justice Davis delivered the opinion of the court:

In a jury trial in the circuit court of Winnebago County, defendant, Rudolph Louis Kessler, was convicted on one count of burglary and two counts of attempted murder. The appellate court affirmed the burglary conviction and reversed the attempted-murder convictions, and we allowed the People's petition for leave to appeal.

Defendant waited in an automobile outside a tavern while his two unarmed companions entered the building to commit the burglary. While inside the tavern, they were surprised by the owner, and one of the burglars shot and wounded him with a gun taken during the burglary. Later, while defendant's companions were fleeing on foot, one of them fired a shot at a pursuing police officer. At that time defendant was sitting in the automobile.

The evidence established that on the day before the burglary in question, the defendant went to Chicago to *see* Ronald Mass, who introduced him to Rodney Abney. The three men went to a restaurant and drank coffee, where the defendant heard Mass ask another person about obtaining a pistol. The person stated he could not obtain a pistol, but would get a sawed-off shotgun by 8 o'clock that evening.

Later Kessler, Mass and Abney went to a store where Mass purchased a screwdriver while Abney simultaneously shoplifted one. Mass indicated that he had to "put his hands on" $1,800. Kessler told Mass that he recalled seeing quantities of cash at the Anchor Tap, where he had previously been employed.

The three men left Chicago about 8 p.m. and arrived at the Anchor Tap in Rockford about 10:30 p.m. Mass and Abney went into the Tap, had a drink, used the bathroom facilities through which they later gained access to the building, and then returned to Kessler, who had remained in the car. They then went to another bar for a drink and then returned to the Anchor Tap.

Just as they parked the car there, Louis Cotti, a co-owner of the Tap, came out to go home. He drove past the parked car as he left and then returned. He testified that he looked around, saw no one at the front of the tavern, then went to the rear of the building, entered the rear door and saw Abney and Mass up at the bar. He then left the building by the rear door and went across the street to a restaurant to call the police and to get help. Thereupon, Cotti and another man from the restaurant returned to the Tap and entered the rear door. Mass, who had found a pistol at the bar, then shot Cotti in the neck. Mass and Abney then fled from the bar and entered the car where Kessler sat. Mass drove the car from the Tap and was pursued by the police. Mass was forced off the road and into a ditch. Mass and Abney ran from the car. Kessler remained seated. Abney started shooting at the police, who had arrived at the scene. After an exchange of gunfire, one police officer ordered the defendant from the car and frisked him. As the defendant climbed from the car, and before being advised of his rights, the defendant said, "I don't know what's going on all the shooting. I was just hitchhiking." The defendant was then advised of his rights and was taken to Rockford in a squad car where he later at the police station made an inculpatory oral and a written statement.

In reversing the attempted-murder convictions, the appellate court held that "The application of the 'common design' principle is not justified by the language of section 5-2 to hold a defendant accountable for crimes committed by an accomplice which the defendant was not shown to have intended." And, at page 325, the court stated: ". . . the question before us is whether Kessler can be found guilty on accountability principles without proof of his specific intent to commit the attempt murders perpetrated by Mass and Abney." The court further stated that "except in felony-murder cases, the Code does not impose liability on accountability principles for all consequences and further crimes which could flow from participation in the initial criminal venture, absent a specific intent by the accomplice being held accountable to commit, or aid and abet the commission of, such further crimes."

The People argue "that a person is responsible for all criminal violations actually committed by another if he assists another in the commission of a single criminal violation," and that "if the legislature had intended to limit accomplice liability only to further criminal acts which were specifically intended the word 'conduct' would not have been included in the language of section 5-2."

Sections 5-1 and 5-2 of the Criminal Code provide in pertinent part:

"Sec. 5-1. Accountability for *conduct* of another.

A person is responsible for *conduct* which is an element of an offense if the *conduct is* either that of the person himself, or that of another and he is legally accountable for such *conduct* as provided in Section 5-2 or both." (Emphasis added.) Ill. Rev. Stat. 1971, ch. 38, par. 5-1. "Sec. 5-2. When Accountability Exists.

A person is legally accountable for the *conduct* of another when:

(b) The statute defining the offense makes him so accountable; or

(c) Either before or during the commission of *an offense* and with the intent to promote or facilitate such commission, he solicits, aids, abets, agrees or attempts to aid, such other person in the planning or commission of the offense. . . ." (Emphasis added.) (Ill. Rev. Stat. 1971, ch. 38, par. 5-2.)

"*Conduct*" is defined as:

". . . an act or a series of acts, and the accompanying mental state." Ill. Rev. Stat. 1971, ch. 38, par. 2–4.

The People argue that the appellate court disregarded the plain meaning of legal doctrines applied by this court and by the highest courts of other jurisdictions, *i.e.*, that where two or more persons engage in a common criminal design or agreement, any acts in the furtherance thereof committed by one party are considered to be the acts of all parties to the common design and all are equally responsible for the consequences of such further acts; and that the court made an unsound and unwarranted interpretation of section 5-2 of the Illinois accountability statute.

We believe the statute, as it reads, means that where one aids another in the planning or commission of an offense, he is legally accountable for the conduct of the person he aids; and that the word "conduct" encompasses any criminal act done in furtherance of the planned and intended act.

An early application of this rule is found in *Hamilton v. People* (1885), 113 Ill. 34. The defendant and two companions invaded a watermelon patch intending to steal some melons. The owner discovered them and a scuffle or fight ensued during which the owner pinned one of the three to the ground, and when in this position another of the three fired a gun at the owner, but the shot missed the owner and struck the potential watermelon thief, who the owner had thrown to the ground. During this occurrence, the third potential watermelon thief stood by. All three of the putative watermelon thieves were charged and convicted of assault with intent to commit murder. This court stated:

> "The fact is undisputed that the three defendants, one of whom was armed with a pistol, invaded the premises of the prosecuting witness with a criminal purpose. The business upon which the parties had deliberately entered was a hazardous one. They had a right to expect that in the event they were detected in stealing the melons, it would result in violence endangering life or limb, as it actually turned out afterwards. That they were all co-conspirators in a dangerous criminal enterprise, is an undisputed fact. Such being the case, whatever was done by one, in contemplation of law was done by all, and all are therefore equally responsible."

In the case at bar, the record shows a common design to commit a robbery or burglary. Kessler, Mass and Abney sat in on the plan, and Kessler led Mass and Abney to the Anchor Tap where he stated the day's receipts were kept.

In *People v. Cole* (1964), 30 Ill. 2d 375, 196 N.E.2d 375, the court stated:

> "While it is true that mere presence or negative acquiescence is not enough to constitute a person a principal, one may aid and abet without actively participating in the overt act and if the proof shows that a person was present at the commission of the crime without disapproving or opposing it, it is competent for the trier of fact to consider this conduct in connection with other circumstances and thereby reach a conclusion that such person assented to the commission of the crime, lent to it his countenance and approval and was thereby aiding and abetting the crime. Stated differently, circumstances may show there is a common design to do an unlawful act to which all assent, and whatever is done in furtherance of the design is the act of all, making each person guilty of the crime."

A similar conclusion was reached in *People v. Armstrong* (1968), 41 Ill. 2d 390, 243 N.E.2d 825, wherein the court stated as follows:

> "The next contention of defendants involves a request to depart from the long established common-design rule, *i.e.*, that where defendants have a common design to do an unlawful act, then whatever act any one of them does in furtherance of the common design is the act of all and all are equally guilty of whatever crime is committed. We have fully reiterated our support of this rule in recent cases, and we continue to do so in this case. Nor do we accept defendants' argument that the statutorily defined rules

on accountability in any way modify or abrogate the common-design rule. This section provides that a person is legally accountable for the conduct of another when '(c) Either before or during the commission he solicits, aids, abets, or agrees or attempts to aid, such other person in the planning or commission of the offense.

Applying this section to this case the attempted robbery was the offense, which the defendants were jointly committing, and each was legally accountable for the conduct of the other. The result was murder, the killing of an individual without lawful justification while attempting or committing a forcible felony other than voluntary manslaughter."

In applying the rationale of *Armstrong* to the case at bar, the burglary was the offense which the defendant, Mass, and Abney had jointly planned and were jointly committing, and each was legally accountable for the conduct of the other in connection therewith. The result was the offense of attempted murder of Louis Cotti, the tap owner, and of State Trooper Max L. Clevenger, who answered a report of the incident and who tried to apprehend the fleeing parties.

For the foregoing reasons, we affirm the part of the appellate court decision which affirmed the burglary conviction of the defendant, and we reverse the part of its decision which reversed the conviction of the defendant for attempted murder, and we affirm the judgment of the circuit court.

MR. JUSTICE GOLDENHERSH, dissenting:

I dissent. In its well-reasoned opinion, the appellate court correctly reversed defendant's attempt murder convictions and its judgment should be affirmed. The majority opinion is grounded on the assertion that section 5-2 of the Criminal Code "means that where one aids another in the planning or commission of an offense, he is legally accountable for the conduct of the person he aids; and that the word 'conduct' encompasses any criminal act done in furtherance of the planned and intended act." To an extent this interpretation is of course correct, but as will be demonstrated neither the statute nor the cases cited in the opinion support the conclusion reached by the majority. In pertinent part section 5-2 provides:

"A person is legally accountable for the conduct of another when:

(b) The statute defining the offense makes him so accountable; or

(c) Either before or during the commission of an offense and with the intent to promote or facilitate such commission, he solicits, aids, abets, agrees or attempts to aid, such other person in the planning or commission of the offense."

It is clear that defendant's accountability cannot stem from section 5-2(b) for the simple reason that the statute defining the offense of attempt murder does not make him so accountable. In support of its position the majority cites Armstrong, [which is] clearly not in point. [It] involved defendants charged with murder and fall under section 5-2(b) for the reason that section 9-1(3) of the Criminal Code creates the "felony murder" classification and obviates the need of proof of intent.

The majority also quotes from *Hamilton* and *Cole*. In *Hamilton* there was a common design to burglarize a watermelon patch, one of the codefendants was armed, all were present and took part in the fight which followed their being accosted by the farmer whose melons they were stealing and the court applied a common design theory. The rationale of *Cole is* the basis on which the appellate court affirmed, correctly, defendant's conviction on the burglary charge but neither *Cole* nor *Hamilton* can be read so as to stretch the statute to cover the facts of this case. The Committee Comments to section 5-2(c) *inter alia* state:

> "Subsection 5-2(c) is a comprehensive statement of liability based on counseling, aiding and abetting and the like, which includes those situations that, at common law, involve the liability of principals in the second degree and accessories before the fact. It will be observed that liability under this subsection requires proof of an 'intent to promote or facilitate . . . commission' of the substantive offense. Moreover, 'conspiracy' between the actor and defendant is not of itself made the basis of accountability for the actor's conduct, although the acts of conspiring may in many cases satisfy the particular requirements of this subsection." S.H.A., ch. 38, par. 5-2, p. 288.

It should be noted that emphasis is placed on the requirement of proof of an "intent to promote or facilitate . . . commission of the substantive offense" and the Criminal Code provides:

> "A person intends or acts intentionally or with intent, to accomplish a result or engage in conduct described by the statute defining the offense, when his conscious objective or purpose is to accomplish that result or engage in that conduct."

The substantive offense involved is attempt murder and section 84(a) of the Code provides that the requisite elements of the offense of attempt are the intent to commit a specific criminal offense and the doing of an act which constitutes a substantial step toward the commission of that offense. The gist of the crime of attempt murder as defined in the Criminal Code is the specific intent to take life. As pointed out by the appellate court, had either of the intended victims died, the provisions of section 9-1(3) of the Criminal Code would have served to make the defendant accountable, but the attempt statute contains no such provision.

Section 1-3 of the Criminal Code provides that no conduct constitutes an offense unless made so by the Code or another statute and in *People v. Eagle Food Centers, Inc.*, 31 Ill. 2d 535, 202 N.E.2d 473, the court said:

> "By well settled principles of law, a criminal or penal statute is to be strictly construed in favor of an accused, and nothing is to be taken by intendment or implication against him beyond the obvious or literal meaning of such statutes. This is so because 'the penal law is intended to regulate the conduct of people of all grades of intelligence within the scope of responsibility,' and it is therefore, essential to its justice and humanity that it be expressed in language which they can easily comprehend; that it be held obligatory

only in the sense in which all can and will understand it.' And apart from the principle of strict construction, we are, as in the case of civil statutes, bound to the rules which require us to give effect to a legislative intention expressed in clear and unambiguous terms and forbid us from altering the plain meaning of the words employed by forced or subtle construction."

I submit that on this record the defendant was not proved guilty of attempt murder. The evidence is uncontradicted that when his companions embarked on the burglary they were unarmed and that he was not inside the tavern when the shot was fired. Again, when the shot was fired at the pursuing officer, defendant was in the automobile, and under the circumstances neither occurrence is shown to be a consequence of any action of the defendant from which the requisite specific intent could be inferred.

I agree with the appellate court that section 5-2(c) does not impose liability for all consequences which flow from participation in the initial criminal venture and that there is no proof here of the requisite specific intent and would affirm the judgment.

Questions and Notes

1. Under *Beeman*, would Kessler have even been convicted of the burglary?

2. How does the issue in *Kessler* differ from the issue in *Beeman*?

3. How do the majority and dissent differ in their reading of the statutes (§§ 5-1 and 5-2)? Who has the better reading?

4. Who analyzes precedent better, the majority or dissent?

5. The majority apparently would hold Kessler accountable for *any* acts committed in furtherance of the crime. The dissent, like the Model Penal Code, would hold him liable only for those additional crimes that he intended to commit. A third and intermediate view is to hold the defendant liable for the crimes that are natural and probable results of the conduct to which he agreed (*cf. Beeman*). Which of these views is soundest? Why?

See NUTSHELL § 15.03.

6. Unintentional crimes present a special problem for accessorial liability. In theory, one cannot intend an unintentional crime. Yet, in some jurisdictions, one must intend a crime in order to be criminally liable for it. We explore this problem in *McVay* and *Marshall*.

C. Mens Rea (Unintentional Crimes)

State v. McVay
132 A. 439 (R.I. 1926)

BARROWS, J.

Three indictments for manslaughter, each containing four counts, were brought against the captain and engineer of the steamer Mackinac, as principals, and against

Kelly, as accessory before the fact. The steamer carried several hundred passengers from Pawtucket to Newport via Narragansett Bay. The boiler producing the steam by which the vessel was propelled burst near Newport and many lives were lost. The present indictments are for causing the deaths of three persons killed by escaping steam after the explosion of the boiler.

The question is: "May a defendant be indicted and convicted of being an accessory before the fact to the crime of manslaughter arising through criminal negligence as set forth in the indictment?"

That the indictment charges manslaughter against the captain and engineer as a result of criminal negligence connected with the operation of the ship's boiler for present purposes is not disputed. Neither is there dispute as to the meaning of accessory before the fact. He is "one who, being absent at the time the crime is committed, yet procures, counsels, or commands another to commit it." In the first count the negligence charged is the "wanton and willful" creation of any steam in a boiler known to be worn, corroded, defective, and unsafe, as a result whereof an explosion occurred killing a passenger. The charge against Kelley as accessory is that "before said felony and manslaughter was committed" he did, at Pawtucket, "feloniously and maliciously aid, assist, abet, counsel, hire, command and procure the said George W. McVay and John A Grant, the said felony and manslaughter in manner and form aforesaid to do and commit." The latter is substantially the language applied to Kelley as accessory in the other three counts. The second count of the indictment charges knowledge of the strength and capacity of the boiler on the part of the principals and negligence in developing more steam than the boiler could safely hold. The third count charges a lack of reasonable care in generating steam in a boiler known to be so worn, etc., as to be unsafe, and the fourth count charges that defendants, having control of generating steam, and knowing the boiler to be defective, so disregarded their duty that the explosion followed.

The state, substantially adopting the definition of manslaughter as given in WHARTON ON HOMICIDE (3d Ed.) p. 5, defines it as: "The unlawful killing of another without malice either express or implied." The state further refers to the charge in the indictment as "involuntary manslaughter; that is, the killing of another without malice and unintentionally in negligently doing an act lawful in itself and in the negligent omission to perform a legal duty." Because the manslaughter charge is "without malice" and "involuntary" Kelley contends that he cannot be indicted legally as an accessory before the fact. The argument is that manslaughter, being a sudden and unpremeditated crime, inadvertent and unintentional by its very nature, cannot be "maliciously" incited before the crime is committed. Such is the view expressed by [numerous text-writers and cases]. In most of these a charge of murder was under consideration, and the theory was that, after a conviction for manslaughter was had, there could be no accessory before the fact. Some of these authorities state broadly that there can be no accessory before the fact in manslaughter, giving the reasons now urged by Kelley.

While everyone must agree that there can be no accessory before the fact when a killing results from a sudden and unpremeditated blow, we do not think it can be broadly stated that premeditation is inconsistent with every charge of manslaughter. Manslaughter may consist, among other things, of doing an unlawful act resulting in unintentional killing, such as violation of motor vehicle laws or administration of drugs to procure an abortion. Manslaughter is likewise committed if an unintentional killing is occasioned by gross negligence in the doing of an act lawful in itself. There is no inherent reason why, prior to the commission of such a crime, one may not aid, abet, counsel, command, or procure the doing of the unlawful act or of the lawful act in a negligent manner. A premeditated act may be involved in such unlawful homicides. "At common law there may be accessories before the fact to involuntary manslaughter."

Bishop states: "Manslaughter does not commonly admit of an accessory before the fact, because when the killing is of previous malice, it is murder. This is the ordinary doctrine yet probably there may be manslaughter wherein this is not so, as, if one should order a servant to do a thing endangering life yet not so directly as to make a death from the doing murder, it might be manslaughter—then, why should not the matter be an accessory before the fact in homicide?"

"Involuntary," in common parlance, means not in accordance with the actor's will or choice. Webster's New Int. Dict. As applied to charges of manslaughter, it may cover cases of volitionally doing a lawful act wantonly or in a grossly careless manner. "Involuntary," used in connection with manslaughter, characterizes the result of the act, not the doing of the act. It does not mean that volition was not present in the negligent act from which the death resulted.

[Therefore] the present indictment for involuntary manslaughter is not self-contradictory when it charges Kelley to be an accessory before the fact. It was possible for him at Pawtucket to intentionally direct and counsel the grossly negligent act which the indictment charges resulted in the crime. Involuntary manslaughter, as set forth in this indictment, means that defendants exercised no conscious volition to take life, but their negligence was of such a character that criminal intention can be presumed. The crime was consummated when the explosion occurred. The volition of the principals was exercised when they chose negligently to create steam which the boiler could not carry. The doing of the act charged or failure to perform the duty charged was voluntary and intentional in the sense that defendants exercised a choice among courses of conduct. It is obvious that Kelley could participate and is charged with participating in procuring defendants to act in a grossly negligent manner prior to the explosion. Legal precedents based upon facts unlike the present ones do not convince us that he could not have been an accessory before the fact.

We therefore answer the question certified on each indictment in the affirmative. The papers in each case, with this decision certified thereon, are sent back to the superior court for further proceedings.

Questions and Notes

1. Is the court saying that Kelley can be liable for somebody else's negligence? Or is it saying something else? If so, what is it saying?

2. Is Kelley's defense akin to impossibility in attempt? If that is its basis, should it succeed?

3. Is *Marshall* consistent with *McVay*?

People v. Marshall
106 N.W.2d 842 (Mich. 1961)

Smith, J.

At approximately 3 a.m. on the morning of February 4, 1958, a car driven by Neal McClary, traveling in the wrong direction on the Edsel Ford Expressway, crashed head on into another vehicle driven by James Coldiron. The drivers of both cars were killed. Defendant William Marshall has been found guilty of involuntary manslaughter of Coldiron. At the time that the fatal accident took place, he, the defendant William Marshall, was in bed at his place of residence. His connection with it was that he owned the car driven by McClary, and as the evidence tended to prove, he voluntarily gave his keys to the car to McClary, with knowledge that McClary was drunk.

The principal issue in the case is whether, upon these facts, the defendant may be found guilty of involuntary manslaughter. It is axiomatic that "criminal guilt under our law is personal fault." As Sayre puts the doctrine "it is of the very essence of our deep-rooted notions of criminal liability that guilt be personal and individual." This was not always true in our law, nor is it universally true in all countries even today, but for us it is settled doctrine.

The State relies on a case, *Story v. United States*, [16 F.2d 342,] in which the owner, driving with a drunk, permitted him to take the wheel, and was held liable for aiding and abetting him "in his criminal negligence." The owner, said the court, sat by his side and permitted him "without protest so recklessly and negligently to operate the car as to cause the death of another." If defendant Marshall had been by McClary's side an entirely different case would be presented, but on the facts before us Marshall, as we noted, was at home in bed. The State also points out that although it is only a misdemeanor to drive while drunk, yet convictions for manslaughter arising out of drunk driving have often been sustained. It argues from these cases that although it was only a misdemeanor for an owner to turn his keys over to a drunk driver, nevertheless a conviction for manslaughter may be sustained if such driver kills another. This does not follow from such cases as *Story*. In the case before us death resulted from the misconduct of driver. The accountability of the owner must rest as a matter of general principle, upon his complicity in such misconduct. In turning his keys over, he was guilty of a specific offense, for which he incurred a specific penalty. Upon these facts he cannot be held a principal with respect to the fatal accident: the killing of Coldiron was not counseled by him, accomplished by another acting jointly with him, nor did it occur in the attempted achievement of some common enterprise.

This is not to say that defendant is guilty of nothing. He was properly found guilty of violation of paragraph (b) of section 625 of the Michigan vehicle code which makes it punishable for the owner of an automobile knowingly to permit it to be driven by a person "who is under the influence of intoxicating liquor." The State urges that this is not enough, that its manslaughter theory, above outlined, "was born of necessity," and that the urgency of the drunk-driver problem "has made it incumbent upon responsible and concerned law enforcement officials to seek new approaches to a new problem within the limits of our law." What the State actually seeks from us is an interpretation that the manslaughter statute imposes an open-end criminal liability. That is to say, whether the owner may ultimately go to prison for manslaughter or some lesser offense will depend upon whatever unlawful act the driver commits while in the car. Such a theory may be defensible as a matter of civil liability but "It is a basic proposition in a constitutional society that crimes should be defined in advance, and not after action has been taken."[10] We are not unaware of the magnitude of the problem presented, but the new approaches demanded for its solution rest with the legislature, not the courts.

Questions and Notes

1. Is the case against Marshall any weaker than the case against Kelley in *McVay*?

2. Is the prosecution seeking to hold Marshall responsible for his own conduct or for McClary's conduct?

3. If your answer to Question 2 was "McClary's conduct," is there more or less reason to hold Marshall responsible for McClary's conduct than there was to hold Kessler liable for Mass and Abney's conduct?

4. Are there any good reasons for not holding Marshall liable?

See NUTSHELL § 15.05.

5. An issue potentially suggested by both *McVay* and *Marshall is* whether an accessory or aider and abettor can ever be liable for a more serious offense than the principal. For example, if McVay did not know about the boiler's deficiencies but Kelley did, or if Marshall knew that McClary were drunk, but McClary thought that he was sober, could Kelley or Marshall be liable for a more serious offense than the principals? That question is explored in *Pendry*.

_____

10. GELLHORN, AMERICAN RIGHTS, 85, 86.

D. Relationship to Principal's Liability

Pendry v. State
367 A.2d 627 (Del. 1976)

McNEILLY, Justice:

Timothy and Kenneth Pendry appeal from their Superior Court jury convictions and life sentences for first degree murder. Timothy was indicted and tried as principal, Kenneth as his accomplice.

Clifford Faulkner (the victim) was shot and killed by Timothy Pendry following an argument between the victim and defendants concerning defendants' sister, who had lived intermittently with the victim in a stormy relationship, and was, at the time, being held by the victim in her trailer against her will. The defendants went to their sister's trailer, and after some discussion with her, confronted the defendant, ordering him to leave the trailer. They testified that the victim refused to leave, and picked up a whiskey bottle, threatening to kill them. Timothy left the trailer, returned with a shotgun, and fired the three shots which killed the victim.

The defendant Timothy presented some credible evidence of extreme emotional distress at the time of the shooting. [T]he thrust of Timothy's argument is that he was denied the opportunity to be convicted of the lesser included offense of manslaughter. Thus, judgment of manslaughter, included within first degree murder under 11 Del. C. § 206(b)(3), and sentence thereon, will resolve this issue in Timothy's favor.

The resolution of the extreme emotional distress issue raised by Kenneth rests on different grounds. Although the defense, in opening, indicated that both defendants would raise the issue and had psychiatric examinations performed on both defendants, the record shows: (1) psychiatric testimony was introduced as to Timothy's emotional state at the time of the homicide, but not as to Kenneth's; (2) other evidence (the testimony of the defendants' sister) was introduced to prove Timothy's emotional state at the time of the homicide, but was not offered as relevant to Kenneth's; (3) although evidence that the victim had assaulted Kenneth two months before the homicide was introduced, there was no evidence that this factor was operative at the time of the killing; (4) the defense attorney specifically stated that extreme emotional distress was not being raised by Kenneth; (5) no other evidence indicates that Kenneth was subject to extreme emotional distress at the time of the homicide. We conclude, therefore, that the record contains no credible evidence that the issue of extreme emotional distress was raised by Kenneth, leaving him without right to a jury instruction on that issue; and none was given.

But Kenneth also asserts that since his guilt is as an accomplice, he can be convicted of no greater crime than Timothy, the principal. The record shows that

Kenneth's defense was based on this erroneous assumption.[4] Several cases are cited by Kenneth in support of this proposition, but these cases, setting forth the common law rule of accomplice liability, are made inapplicable in Delaware by 11 Del. C. § 272, which "denies a defense in situations in which the old common law, for purely technical reasons, would have been forced to grant an acquittal." Delaware Criminal Code with Commentary, at 50. Section 272 provides in its pertinent part:

> "In any prosecution for an offense in which the criminal liability of the accused is based upon the conduct of another person pursuant to § 271 of this Criminal Code, it is no defense that:
>
> > (1) The other person is not guilty of the offense in question ... because of other factors precluding the mental state required for the commission of the offense; or
> >
> > (2) The other person ... has been convicted of a different offense or in a different degree,"

Under subsection (1) the fact that Timothy's extreme emotional distress negatives the mental state required for conviction of murder in the first degree does not relieve Kenneth from liability for first degree murder, while under subsection (2) Timothy's conviction of manslaughter does not preclude Kenneth's conviction of murder in the first degree.

Reversed and remanded as to Timothy Pendry with directions to strike the judgment of conviction of murder in the first degree and sentence thereon, and to enter a judgment of conviction of manslaughter and to impose an appropriate sentence therefor. Judgment of conviction of murder in the first degree affirmed as to Kenneth Pendry.

Questions and Notes

1. Does it seem fair to you that the aider and abettor was convicted of a more serious offense than the principal perpetrator? Why? Why not?

2. If you had been defense counsel, would (might) you have conducted the defense differently? In what way? How do you assess the overall performance of defense counsel in this case?

Problem

On the evening of February 25, 1973, the defendant's husband, Mr. Richards, left his home in Weymouth in order to go to work. Shortly afterward in a lane not far away, he was attacked by two men who were wearing black balaclavas over their

---

4. The Court: "You are indicating now that that will not be a defense?" Mr. Green: "For Kenny?" The Court : "Yes, as an affirmative defense for Kenny." Mr. Green: "Right. Not that Kenny personally was—he is charged as an accomplice, so he would be an accomplice to whatever Timmy is guilty of. . . ."

heads. He was struck on the back of his head. He tried to escape but was grabbed by the coat sleeves. Eventually he struggled free from his assailants. The medical evidence was that he sustained a laceration on the top of his scalp that required two stitches. There was no need for him to be detained in hospital; it was not a serious injury in fact.

On February 26 the defendant was arrested and at the police station she explained that, according to her, her marriage had been deteriorating. She had become very depressed and started drinking. She was asked if it was at her suggestion that her co-accused Bryant (known as Alan) and Squires (known as Paul) attacked her husband, and to that she replied that she had made the suggestion but in fact she did not want them to hurt him. She said: "All I wanted was for us to get together again. I thought if he was hurt, he would turn to me for affection." But in her statement she admitted in these words: "I told them that I wanted them to beat him up bad enough to put him in hospital for a month." She agreed that she had told them that she would give them five pounds if they would beat up her husband. She also admitted that she had suggested the appropriate time that her husband might be attacked, namely, when he went out to work, and that she would give a signal by putting on the kitchen light in the house where they lived so that those lying in wait would know when he was setting off for work. As it turned out, there was a power cut at the time so she could not put the light on; she had to hold a candle up to the window, but she played her part as she had promised.

Bryant, Squires, and Richards were all charged with unlawful wounding with intent to do grievous bodily harm. Bryant and Squires were each convicted of the lesser offense of unlawful wounding. Richards, however, the accessory before the fact, was convicted of unlawful wounding with intent to do grievous bodily harm. Richards appeals on the ground that she cannot be convicted of a crime more serious than that of the principal defendants.

How should the appellate court resolve the case? For one solution, *see Regina v. Richards*, 1976 Q.B. 776 (1973).

See NUTSHELL §§ 15.06, 15.07.

Chapter 19

Conspiracy

A. The Agreement

The concept of conspiracy interweaves components from the preceding two chapters. Like attempt, conspiracy contains an inchoate component, i.e., it is designed to nip crime in the bud. Like complicity, conspiracy involves problems of the extent to which one's liability might depend on the conduct of another.

The gist (or *actus reus*) of conspiracy is the agreement to engage in unlawful activity. The first series of cases deals with the concept of an "agreement."

Regle v. State
264 A.2d 119 (Md. App. 1970)

MURPHY, C.J., delivered the opinion of the Court.

On September 28, 1968, Sergeant Frank Mazzone, a Maryland State Police officer working under cover, was advised by other police officers that Michael Isele, a police informer, had informed them that he had been invited by the appellant Regle to participate in a robbery. Mazzone immediately contacted Isele, whom he previously knew, and together they went to see the appellant. Isele introduced Mazzone to the appellant as a prospective participant in the planned robbery. After some discussion, the appellant invited Mazzone to participate in the robbery. While appellant did not then specify the place to be robbed, he indicated to Mazzone that Richard Fields had been involved with him in planning the robbery, and that he would also participate in the crime. Appellant, Mazzone, and Isele then met with Fields and the robbery plan was outlined by appellant and Fields. The need for guns was discussed and appellant and Fields spoke of the necessity of killing two employees at O'Donnell's restaurant, the situs of the proposed robbery. The four men then drove in Isele's car to appellant's home where appellant phoned Kent Chamblee for the purpose of purchasing a shotgun. Thereafter, the men drove to Chamblee's home, purchased the gun from him, and tested it in his presence. While Chamblee knew that the shotgun was to be used "for a job," he did not accompany the others when they then drove to the restaurant to perpetrate the robbery. Upon arriving there, Mazzone told appellant that he first wanted to "case" the restaurant. This being agreed, Mazzone and Isele went into the restaurant while appellant and Fields went to a nearby bar to await their return. Once inside the restaurant, Mazzone contacted police headquarters and requested assistance. Thereafter, he and Isele left the restaurant and rejoined appellant and Fields. While several police cars promptly responded to the scene, Mazzone found it necessary, in the interim, to reveal his identity as a police officer and to arrest appellant and Fields at gunpoint. At the same time he also arrested Isele in order "to cover him." After the arrest, appellant made an incriminating statement to the effect that he and Fields had planned the robbery and that he had invited Isele to participate in the crime.

Appellant, Fields, and Chamblee were thereafter jointly indicted for conspiracy to rob with a dangerous and deadly weapon and for carrying a deadly weapon openly with intent to injure. Appellant was separately tried by a jury, found guilty on both counts, and sentenced to twenty years on the conspiracy charge, and two years, concurrent, on the weapons offense.

The docket entries indicated that the conspiracy indictment against Chamblee was *nol prossed* prior to appellant's trial. It also appears that at his trial appellant established through the testimony of a police officer that Fields had been examined by State psychiatrists at the Clifton Perkins State Hospital and found "not guilty by reason of being insane at the time of the alleged crime." The State did not rebut the officer's testimony, although the record indicates that two of the State psychiatrists who had examined Fields were then present in court.

Against this background, appellant contends that since the indictment against Chamblee was *nol prossed*, only he and Fields were charged as conspirators; and that because Fields was found insane at the time of the commission of the crime and thus was not a person legally capable of engaging in a criminal conspiracy, his own conviction cannot stand since one person alone cannot be guilty of the crime of conspiracy.

Conspiracy—a common law misdemeanor in Maryland—is defined as a combination by two or more persons to accomplish a criminal or unlawful act, or to do a lawful act by criminal or unlawful means. The gist of the offense is the unlawful combination resulting from the agreement, rather than the mere agreement itself, and no overt act is required to constitute the crime. Criminal conspiracy is a partnership in crime—"It is the coalition of manpower and human minds enhancing possibilities of achievement aimed at the objective that present a greater threat to society than does a lone offender." In short, it is the existence of the conspiracy which creates the danger.

As one person cannot conspire or form a combination with himself, it is essential in proving the existence of a criminal conspiracy to show "the consent of two or more minds. A formal agreement need not, however, be established; it is sufficient if the minds of the parties meet understandingly, so as to bring about an intelligent and deliberate agreement to do the acts contemplated. As the crime of conspiracy is one requiring a specific intent, and necessarily involves at the least two guilty parties, the required criminal intent must exist in the minds of two or more parties to the conspiracy.

In view of these principles, it is the well settled general rule that one defendant in a prosecution for conspiracy cannot be convicted where all of his alleged co-conspirators, be they one or more, have been acquitted or discharged under circumstances that amount to an acquittal. The rationale underlying the rule appears clear: that it is illogical to acquit all but one of a purported partnership in crime; that acquittal of all persons with whom a defendant is alleged to have conspired is repugnant to the existence of the requisite corrupt agreement; and that regardless of the criminal animus of the one defendant, there must be someone with whom he confected his corrupt agreement, and where all his alleged co-conspirators are not guilty, a like finding as to him must be made.

Generally speaking, it would appear that so long as the disposition of the case against a co-conspirator does not remove the basis for the charge of conspiracy, a single defendant may be prosecuted and convicted of the offense, even though for one reason or another his co-conspirator is either not tried or not convicted. Consistent with this rule, the authorities all agree that the death of one conspirator does not of itself prevent the conviction of the other, where the conspiracy between them is shown by the evidence. In *Hurwitz v. State*, 92 A.2d 575, a case in which all but one of the conspirators were granted immunity from prosecution on a ground not inconsistent with their participation in the conspiracy, the court held that such grant of immunity was not equivalent to acquittal and would not require reversal of the conviction of the one remaining conspirator. The same rule has been applied where one of two conspirators enjoyed diplomatic immunity and therefore could not be prosecuted for the conspiracy. *Farnsworth v. Zerbst*, 98 F.2d 541 (5th Cir.). In *Adams v. State*, 202 Md. 455, 97 A.2d 281, it was held that conviction of one defendant in a conspiracy case was proper despite failure to convict any of the other conspirators where it was alleged and shown that there were persons unknown to the prosecution with whom the convicted defendant had conspired. And while the cases are generally divided on the question whether the entry of a *nolle prosequi* as to one of two alleged conspirators compels an acquittal of the remaining conspirator, the better reasoned view would appear to support the proposition that it does not, at least where the *nolle prosequi* was not entered without the co-conspirator's consent after the trial had begun (which then would have amounted to an acquittal and precluded reindictment).

The State urges that where the acquittal of one of the alleged conspirators is based solely on the fact that he was insane at the time of the crime, the remaining conspirator should nonetheless be held responsible for the offense. The State relies on *Jones v. State*, 19 So. 2d 81 (Ala.), a case in which the defendant, convicted of murder, maintained that the actual killing was done by his brother and that because his brother was insane at the time of the crime, and hence innocent of the offense, he (the defendant) must likewise be exonerated. The court, after characterizing the defendant as "a co-conspirator and an aider and abettor in the homicide;' said: ". . . the insanity [of appellant's brother] would not exculpate the appellant if he conspired with the principal or aided or abetted him in the killing of the deceased. If appellant so conspired or aided or abetted in the homicide, the mental irresponsibility of [his brother] could not be invoked to exonerate said appellant. One may or could use an insane person as the agent of destruction-or conspire with such person to accomplish the homicide-just as guiltily as with a person of sound mind. The fact, if true, that the co-conspirator or principal in the crime is not amenable to justice because of mental irresponsibility does not exempt the other from prosecution."

We think the cases relied upon by the *Jones* court to support its conclusion stand for the proposition that it is no defense to one who participates either as a principal or aider or abettor in the actual commission of the substantive criminal offense that the principal offender was insane at the time of the crime. The principle would appear similar to the rule that a co-conspirator may be convicted of any crime committed by any member of a conspiracy to do an illegal act if the act is done in furtherance of the purpose of the conspiracy. The conspiracy being established, the fact that the member who committed the crime was insane at the time would thus not exonerate the others from complicity in the commission of the substantive offense.

We do not find these cases controlling of the primary question before us, namely, whether *under an indictment for conspiracy,* one conspirator may be convicted of the offense where the only other conspirator was shown to be insane at the time the agreement between them was concluded. Conspiracy to commit a crime is a different offense from the crime that is the object of the conspiracy. One necessarily involves joint action; the other does not. By its nature, conspiracy is a joint or group offense requiring a concert of free wills, and the union of the minds of at least two persons is a prerequisite to the commission of the offense. The essence of conspiracy is, therefore, a mental confederation involving at least two persons; the crime is indivisible in the sense that it requires more than one guilty person; and where the joint intent does not exist, the basis of the charge of conspiracy is necessarily swept away. In short, the guilt of both persons must concur to constitute that of either. It is upon this premise that the authorities all agree that if two persons are charged as conspirators and one is an entrapper, or merely feigns acquiescence in the criminal intent, there is no punishable conspiracy because there was no agreement on the part of the one to engage in a criminal conspiracy.[2] For like reasons, we hold that where only two persons are implicated in a conspiracy, and one is shown to have been insane at the time the agreement was concluded, and hence totally incapable of committing any crime, there is no punishable criminal conspiracy, the requisite joint criminal intent being absent.

Questions and Notes

1. If Regle agreed to commit the crime with Mazzone, Isele, and Fields, why should it matter that they didn't agree with him?

2. Why does Fields' insanity excuse Regle? Is the court saying that because Fields was insane, he lacked the capacity to agree with Regle? If so, do you agree with that conclusion? Why? Why not?

---

2. This would not be true, however, if after elimination of the alleged entrapper, there are at least two other parties to the conspiracy.

3. At retrial, what must the prosecutor prove to obtain a conspiracy conviction?

4. The alternative theories of bilateral and unilateral conspiracies are developed in *Kihnel.*

State v. Kihnel

488 So. 2d 1238 (La. Ct. App. 1986)

Ciaccio, Judge.

After a bench trial the judge found defendant guilty as charged of conspiracy to commit first degree murder, La. R.S. 14:26 and 14:30, and conspiracy to commit aggravated arson, La. R.S. 14:26 and 14:51. Defendant appeals raising a single issue for our consideration: can there be a conspiracy under La. R.S. 14:26 when defendant's only alleged coconspirators are a state informer and an undercover police officer who only pretend to conspire? We answer that there can be no conspiracy. We, therefore, reverse defendant's convictions.

The facts are uncontroverted. Defendant owned at least two pieces of rental property. Defendant employed Steven Brock, a building contractor, to perform renovations on one piece of property. On the morning of October 17, 1984, Mr. Brock met with defendant to secure reimbursement for materials purchased in the renovation. During this meeting defendant indicated that he was having financial problems: the cost of the renovation was exceeding his budget and another piece of rental property which he owned was becoming a financial drain.

Defendant asked Mr. Brock if he would "torch" the property being renovated, or could he find someone who would burn the building. Defendant stated that the arson needed to be accomplished before October 22, 1984, because that was when the insurance expired. He showed Mr. Brock the insurance policy. Defendant further indicated his desire to have other similar tasks performed and requested that Mr. Brock meet him at his house at 6:00 p.m. if he was interested.

Mr. Brock immediately contacted the F.B.I. and the New Orleans Fire Department Arson Squad. He informed them of his meeting with defendant and of defendant's request. Mr. Brock was instructed to meet again with defendant and to tell him that he could secure someone to perform the job.

At 6:00 p.m. Mr. Brock met with defendant. Mr. Brock informed defendant that he could get an individual named Wayne, from Houston, Texas, to carry out defendant's desires. Defendant indicated that he also wanted another piece of property burned and that he wanted someone killed.

Defendant talked about some details in connection with burning the buildings and told Mr. Brock to meet him at the renovation site the next morning to finalize the plans, including the plan for murder. Defendant paid Mr. Brock $400.00 as a downpayment on the agreed price of $800.00 for burning one building and 1,000.00 for burning the other. The price for the murder would be decided later.

Mr. Brock informed the law enforcement agencies of the details of his meeting with defendant. The next morning Mr. Brock avoided meeting with defendant because the police wanted to finalize their plans before the next meeting. An under-cover police officer was to act as the "hit man." That is, he would pretend to be Wayne from Houston prepared to burn the buildings and murder someone.

At 4:15 p.m. from the F.B.I. office in New Orleans, Mr. Brock telephoned defendant and set up a meeting for 6:00 p.m. At the 6:00 p.m. meeting Mr. Brock introduced the undercover officer to defendant. Defendant described to the officer the places he wanted burned, and stressed the importance that they be completely destroyed. Defendant gave Mr. Brock a check for $1,400.00 to cover the remainder due on the agreed total price of $1,800.00.

Defendant then discussed the murder, described the victim, and agreed to a price of $2,000.00 to be paid later plus jewelry worth approximately $3,000.00 which the victim would be carrying in a gym bag at the time of the murder. "Wayne" could keep the jewelry. The buildings were to be burned that night and the murder committed the next morning.

Defendant was arrested later that evening.

Louisiana's criminal code defines criminal conspiracy as follows:

Section 26. Criminal conspiracy

A. Criminal conspiracy is the agreement or combination of two or more persons for the specific purpose of committing any crime; provided that an agreement or combination to commit a crime shall not amount to a criminal conspiracy unless, in addition to such agreement or combination, one or more of such parties does an act in furtherance of the object of the agreement or combination.

If the intended basic crime has been consummated, the conspirators may be tried for either the conspiracy or the completed offense' and a conviction for one shall not bar prosecution for the other.

La. R.S. 14:26. This definition adopts the traditional common-law view of conspiracy as an entirely bilateral or multilateral relationship. This view is inherent in the use of the terms "two or more persons."

Many jurisdictions have elected to follow the American Law Institute's Model Penal Code recommendation that conspiracy be redefined as a "unilateral" crime. (Model Penal Code Section 5.03 (Proposed Official Draft 1962).) The unilateral approach has been criticized as contrary to the historical and theoretical underpinnings of conspiracy law and as potentially abusive of due process. Some state courts adhere to the traditional approach despite statutory reform to the unilateral approach, while in many states the unilateral approach has been rejected both by the language of the statute and by subsequent state law. The federal definition retains the traditional "bilateral" formulation. *See* 18 U.S.C. Sec. 371.

Under a unilateral formulation, the crime of conspiracy is committed when a person agrees to proceed in a prohibited manner; under a bilateral formulation, the crime of conspiracy is committed when two or more persons agree to proceed in such manner. Under either approach, the agreement is all-important to conspiracy. Under the unilateral approach, as distinguished from the bilateral approach, the trier-of-fact assesses the subjective individual behavior of a defendant, rendering irrelevant in determining criminal liability the conviction, acquittal, irresponsibility, or immunity of other co-conspirators.

The federal courts have held that "a conspiracy may be proved even though the link connecting many of the activities of the conspirators is a Government informer." But the courts have also held that "as it takes two to conspire, there can be no indictable conspiracy with a government informer who secretly intends to frustrate the conspiracy." The import of the federal courts' decisions is that there can be no conspiracy when the only other co-conspirator is a government informer.

Although never having directly addressed the issue now before this court, the Louisiana Supreme Court has consistently indicated that "[t]o constitute the crime [of conspiracy], there must be at least two or more conspirators" who form "an agreement to commit a crime." We have found only one reported decision of a Louisiana court which has directly addressed this issue. The Second Circuit Court of Appeal has held that La. R.S. 14:26 "requires criminal intent in the mind [*sic*] of at least two persons. . . ." *State v. Joles*, 485 So. 2d 212 (La. App. 2d Cir. 1986). Thus, the court found that there was no criminal conspiracy between two people when one of those persons, as a state agent, had no intention to commit the crime involved.

Under the bilateral formulation for conspiracy adopted by our legislature when it enacted La. R.S. 14:26, we conclude that in Louisiana there can be no conspiracy when the only supposed co-conspirators are a state informer and an undercover police officer who both only pretend to conspire.

The facts of this case reveal that defendant's only "conspirators" were Steven Brock and an undercover police officer. Steven Brock, immediately upon learning of defendant's desires, contacted law enforcement agencies who instructed him to continue to meet with defendant and to feign agreement. He never agreed to conspire with defendant.

The undercover police officer likewise only pretended to conspire, he never agreed to commit any crime. The intent of both Mr. Brock and the officer was not to conspire with defendant, but secretly to frustrate his plans.

While the actions of Mr. Brock and the involved law enforcement agencies were laudable, and appropriate under the circumstances, under Louisiana law defendant is not guilty of conspiracy.

The possibility of attempted conspiracy has been suggested, but such suggestions have been made in passing and without comment, reason or discussion. Attempt and conspiracy are both inchoate crimes. just as there can be no attempt to commit an attempt, such as "attempted assault" nor can there be an attempt to incite a felony (*See* La.R.S. 14:28, Reporter's Comment), we conclude that under the bilateral formulation of conspiracy there can be no "attempted conspiracy."

As part of the very foundation of criminal law, crimes include both a criminal act (or omission) and a criminal intent. "Attempted conspiracy" suggests a crime formed only of criminal intent, as it is the agreement which constitutes the act. We are not prepared to judicially legislate such a crime.

For the reasons provided, we reverse defendant's conviction and enter a judgment of acquittal as to the charges of conspiracy to commit first degree murder and conspiracy to commit aggravated arson.

REVERSED; JUDGMENT OF ACQUITTAL ENTERED.

Questions and Notes

1. If you were a legislator faced with the choice of adopting a unilateral or bilateral theory of conspiracy, which would you choose? Why?

2. Given the bilateral choice, do you agree with the court's rejection of attempted conspiracy?

3. Of what, if anything, should Kihnel be guilty?

4. As we see in *Gebardi*, some parties are juridically incapable of conspiring to commit a crime.

Gebardi v. United States
287 U.S. 112 (1932)

MR. JUSTICE STONE delivered the opinion of the Court.

This case is here on certiorari, 286 U.S. 539, to review a judgment of conviction for conspiracy to violate the Mann Act (36 Stat. 825; 18 U.S.C. § 397 et seq.). Petitioners, a man and a woman, not then husband and wife, were indicted in the District Court for Northern Illinois, for conspiring together, and with others not named, to transport the woman from one state to another for the purpose of engaging in sexual intercourse with the man. At the trial without a jury there was evidence from which the court could have found that the petitioners had engaged in illicit sexual relations in the course of each of the journeys alleged; that the man purchased the railway tickets for both petitioners for at least one journey, and that in each instance the woman, in advance of the purchase of the tickets, consented to go on the journey and did go on it voluntarily for the specified immoral purpose. There was no evidence supporting the allegation that any other person had conspired. The trial court overruled motions for a finding for the defendants, and in arrest of judgment, and gave judgment of conviction, which the Court of Appeals for the Seventh Circuit affirmed, on the authority of *United States v. Holte*, 236 U.S. 140.

The only question which we need consider here is whether, within the principles announced in that case, the evidence was sufficient to support the conviction. There the defendants, a man and a woman, were indicted for conspiring together that the man should transport the woman from one state to another for purposes of prostitution. In holding the indictment sufficient, the Court said:

"As the defendant is the woman, the District Court sustained a demurrer on the ground that although the offence could not be committed without her she was no party to it but only the victim. The single question is whether that ruling is right. We do not have to consider what would be necessary to constitute the substantive crime under the act of 1910 [the Mann Act], or what evidence would be required to convict a woman under an indictment like this, but only to decide whether it is impossible for the transported woman to be guilty of a crime in conspiring as alleged."

The Court assumed that there might be a degree of cooperation which would fall short of the commission of any crime, as in the case of the purchaser of liquor illegally sold. But it declined to hold that a woman could not under some circumstances not precisely defined, be guilty of a violation of the Mann Act and of a conspiracy to violate it as well. Light is thrown upon the intended scope of this conclusion by the supposititious case which the Court put:

"Suppose, for instance, that a professional prostitute, as well able to look out for herself as was the man, should suggest and carry out a journey within the act of 1910 in the hope of blackmailing the man, and should buy the railroad tickets, or should pay the fare from Jersey City to New York, she would be within the letter of the act of 1910 and we see no reason why the act should not be held to apply. We see equally little reason for not treating the preliminary agreement as a conspiracy that the law can reach, if we abandon the illusion that the woman always is the victim."

In the present case we must apply the law to the evidence; the very inquiry which was said to be unnecessary in *Holte.*

First. Those exceptional circumstances envisaged in *Holte*, as possible instances in which the woman might violate the act itself, are clearly not present here. There is no evidence that she purchased the railroad tickets or that here was the active or moving spirit in conceiving or carrying out the transportation. The proof shows no more than that she went willingly upon the journeys for the purposes alleged.

Section 2 of the Mann Act (18 U.S.C. § 398), violation of which is charged by the indictment here as the object of the conspiracy, imposes the penalty upon "Any person who shall knowingly transport or cause to be transported, or aid or assist in obtaining transportation for, or in transporting in interstate or foreign commerce . . . any woman or girl for the purpose of prostitution or debauchery or for any other immoral purpose. . . ." Transportation of a woman or girl whether with or without her consent, or causing or aiding it, or furthering it in any of the specified ways, are the acts punished, when done with a purpose which is immoral within the meaning of the law.

The Act does not punish the woman for transporting herself; it contemplates two persons-one to transport and the woman or girl to be transported. For the woman to fall within the ban of the statute she must, as the least, "aid or assist" someone else in transporting or in procuring transportation for herself. But such aid and assistance must, as in the case supposed in *Holte*, be more active than mere agreement on her part to the transportation and its immoral purpose. For the statute is drawn to include those cases in which the woman consents to her own transportation. Yet it does not specifically impose any penalty upon her, although it deals in detail with the person by whom she is transported. In applying this criminal statute we cannot infer that the mere acquiescence of the woman transported was intended to be condemned by the general language punishing those who aid and assist the transporter, any more than it has been inferred that the purchaser of liquor was to be regarded as an abettor of the illegal sale. The penalties of the statute are too clearly directed against the acts of the transporter as distinguished from the consent of the subject of the transportation. So it was intimated in *Holte*, and this conclusion is not disputed by the Government here, which contends only that the conspiracy charge will lie though the woman could not commit the substantive offense.

Second. We come thus to the main question in the case, whether, admitting that the woman, by consenting, has not violated the Mann Act, she may be convicted of a conspiracy with the man to violate it. Section 37 of the Criminal Code (18 U.S.C. § 88), punishes a conspiracy by two or more persons "to commit any offense against the United States." The offense which she is charged with conspiring to commit is that perpetrated by the man, for it is not questioned that in transporting her he contravened § 2 of the Mann Act. Hence we must decide whether her concurrence, which was not criminal before the Mann Act, nor punished by it, may, without more, support a conviction under the conspiracy section, enacted many years before.

As was said in the *Holte* case, an agreement to commit an offense may be criminal, though its purpose is to do what some of the conspirators may be free to do alone. Incapacity of one to commit the substantive offense does not necessarily imply that he may with impunity conspire with others who are able to commit it.[5] For it is the collective planning of criminal conduct at which the statute aims. The plan is itself a wrong which, if any act be done to effect 'its object, the state has elected to treat as criminal. And one may plan that others shall do what he cannot do himself.

But in this case, we are concerned with something more than an agreement between two persons for one of them to commit an offense which the other cannot commit. There is the added element that the offense planned, the criminal object of the conspiracy, involves the agreement of the woman to her transportation by the man, which is the very conspiracy charged.

Congress set out in the Mann Act to deal with cases which frequently, if not normally, involve consent and agreement on the part of the woman to the forbidden transportation. In every case in which she is not intimidated or forced into

5. So it has been held repeatedly that one not a bankrupt may be held guilty under § 37 of conspiring that a bankrupt shall conceal property from his trustee. In like manner *Chadwick v. United States*, 141 Fed. 225, sustained the conviction of one not an officer of a national bank for conspiring with an officer to commit a crime which only he could commit.

the transportation, the statute necessarily contemplates her acquiescence. Yet this acquiescence, though an incident of a type of transportation specifically dealt with by the statute, was not made a crime under the Mann Act itself. Of this class of cases we say that the substantive offense contemplated by the statute itself involves the same combination or community of purposes of two persons only which is prosecuted here as conspiracy. If this were the only case covered by the Act, it would be within those decisions which hold, consistently with the theory upon which conspiracies are punished, that where it is impossible under any circumstances to commit the substantive offense without cooperative action, the preliminary agreement between the same parties to commit the offense is not an indictable conspiracy either at common law or under the federal statute. But Criminal transportation under the Mann Act may be effected without the woman's consent, as in cases of intimidation or force (with which we are not now concerned). We assume therefore, for present purposes, as was suggested in the *Holte* case, that the decisions last mentioned do not in all strictness apply. We do not rest our decision upon the theory of those cases, nor upon the related one that the attempt is to prosecute as conspiracy acts identical with the substantive offense. We place it rather upon the ground that we perceive in the failure of the Mann Act to condemn the woman's participation in those transportations which are effected with her mere consent, evidence of an affirmative legislative policy to leave her acquiescence unpunished. We think it a necessary implication of that policy that when the Mann Act and the conspiracy statute came to be construed together, as they necessarily would be, the same participation which the former contemplates as an inseparable incident of all cases in which the woman is a voluntary agent at all, but does not punish, was not automatically to be made punishable under the latter. It would contravene that policy to hold that the very passage of the Mann Act effected a withdrawal by the conspiracy statute of that immunity which the Mann Act itself confers.

It is not to be supposed that the consent of an unmarried person to adultery with a married person, where the latter alone is guilty of the substantive offense, would render the former an abettor or a conspirator, or that the acquiescence of a woman under the age of consent would make her a co-conspirator with the man to commit statutory rape upon herself. *Compare Queen v. Tyrrell*, [1894] 1 Q.B. 710. The principle, determinative of this case, is the same.

On the evidence before us the woman petitioner has not violated the Mann Act and, we hold, is not guilty of a conspiracy to do so. As there is no proof that the man conspired with anyone else to bring about the transportation, the convictions of both petitioners must be Reversed.

Questions and Notes

1. In general, why shouldn't the woman be equally as guilty as the man, if they each agree to engage in the same criminal activity?

2. Would this same issue be raised by a statute that criminalized prostitution, but did not punish a prostitute's customers?

3. If a woman could not be guilty of violating the Mann Act under the circumstances imagined in *Holte*, how could she be guilty of conspiring to violate it?

4. How is *Gebardi* different from the cases cited in footnote 5 of the Court's opinion?

5. Why does the woman's acquittal justify acquitting the man?

6. Why do you suppose the prosecutor brought this case in the first place?

7. The complexity of the concept of agreement is explored in *Macklowitz*.

People v. Macklowitz

514 N.Y.S.2d 883 (N.Y. Sup. Ct. 1987)

IRVING LANG, J.

[The] issue raised by defendant's motion to dismiss the indictment [is whether] the ultimate purchaser of narcotics can be indicted for conspiracy with the sellers to criminally possess a controlled substance.

The People allege that during 1985 (and for several years prior thereto) Jack Buccafusco was in the business of selling cocaine. He stored a large stash of drugs and weapons in a safe secreted in an apartment (known as the studio) located in Staten Island. Buccafusco's right-hand men in this venture were defendants Michael Giammarino and Angelo Tranquillino. Both Giammarino and Tranquillino obtained large amounts of cocaine directly from Buccafusco. Tranquillino's and Giammarino's Staten Island homes were allegedly used as storage and distribution points for the cocaine. With the help of several associates and employees, they either sold cocaine to various smaller scale sellers or sold directly to customer-users.

It is alleged that defendant Michael Macklowitz, an attorney and former Kings County Assistant District Attorney, was one of Jack Buccafusco's steady customers from November 1984 until March 12, 1986, the day of Buccafusco's arrest. Macklowitz allegedly purchased between one-half a gram to one-quarter ounce or more of cocaine on numerous occasions using the code name "Duane" (or "Dwayne" and "Dwane").

Michael Macklowitz is charged with conspiracy in the fourth degree. The People claim that defendant, with the intent that conduct constituting the crime of criminal possession of a controlled substance in the fourth degree be performed, agreed with Jack Buccafusco and others to engage in or cause the performance of such conduct. The prosecutor argues that defendant entered into an agreement with Jack Buccafusco and others, the object of which was the possession of one-eighth ounce or more of cocaine.

Defendant claims that, at best, the evidence presented to the Grand jury shows that Macklowitz was an occasional purchaser and user of cocaine. It is defendant's position that the individual discreet "buys", if they occurred at all, do not establish the requisite shared intent and agreement between defendant and the various code-fendants to engage in an ongoing course of criminal conduct.[1]

Penal Law § 105.10 states that a person is guilty of conspiracy in the fourth degree when, with intent that conduct constituting a class B or class C felony be performed, he agrees with one or more persons to engage in or cause a performance of said conduct and when an overt act is alleged and proved to have been committed by one of the conspirators in furtherance of the conspiracy.

New York embraces the unilateral approach to conspiracy. That is, the focus is upon individual rather than collective liability; the guilt of a particular party is considered independent of that of his co-conspirators. Thus, even if a defendant's sole co-conspirator is legally irresponsible or has feigned agreement, defendant's conviction will stand provided the evidence is otherwise legally sufficient.

The gravamen of conspiracy and an essential element thereof is the agreement to engage in some other substantive crime. The aim is to prevent the commission of the substantive crime by punishing the firm plan to commit it.

The degree of conspiratorial liability hinges upon the seriousness of the object crime sought to be committed. A closely related factor bearing on liability is the scope of the conspiracy—whether a particular defendant can be charged with knowing and joining a criminal enterprise. If sufficient evidence of defendant's knowledge exists, the question then arises whether there is a single indivisible conspiracy with multiple goals (for example, one conspiracy to violate several different statutes), or whether there are distinct multiple conspiracies.

Numerous labels have been used in an effort to categorize different types of conspiracies. Chains, links, wheels, hubs and spokes are just a few of the terms utilized where there are several layers of actors involved with various, albeit related, roles and objectives. The most common distinction made is between wheel conspiracies and chain conspiracies. A wheel conspiracy involves an individual (or small group)—the hub, who transacts illegal dealings with the various other individuals—the spokes. The most common evidentiary issue in a wheel conspiracy is whether the separate transactions between the hub and individual spokes can be merged to form a single conspiracy.

In contrast, the chain conspiracy usually involves several layers of personnel dealing with a single subject matter, as opposed to a specific person. Drug trafficking is often cited as a classic example of a chain conspiracy inasmuch as it is characterized by manufacturing links, wholesaling links and retailing links. A single conspiracy can be proven if each link knew or must have known of the other links

---

1. Defendant was initially charged also with conspiracy in the third degree; conspiracy to sell as well as conspiracy to possess. The People conceded that they could not establish the requisite selling intent of Macklowitz and have abandoned that allegation, thereby eliminating any problem of possible duplicitous pleading.

in the chain, and if each defendant intended to join and aid the larger enterprise. The chain theory of conspiracy has been recognized by New York State courts in a drug distribution case, and in a stolen property fencing scheme.

This structural analysis is not without confusion, as some conspiracies may be classified as chain/spoke combinations. For example, in narcotics trafficking, the links at either end might be comprised of a number of persons "who may have no reason to know that others are performing a role similar to theirs — in other words the extreme links of a chain conspiracy may have elements of the spoke conspiracy."

Perhaps a more accurate way to visualize a complex conspiracy case would be to view it as a three-dimensional organic chemistry molecule with each part interacting continuously with another thereby forming and adhering to the whole, for a common purpose.

The People advance two basic arguments to support the conspiracy charge: (1) they argue that the crime of possession does not require reciprocal cooperation and therefore is not barred from serving as the object crime in a conspiracy count and (2) they claim that the chain theory of conspiracy may be applied to sustain the charge.

The People cite *People v. Jewsbury* (115 AD2d 341 [4th Dept 1985]) and *People v. Potwora* (44 AD2d 207 [4th Dept 1974]) as authority for their position. In *Jewsbury* the court sustained the conspiracy count against defendant se let where the object crimes were criminal sale of a controlled substance in the third degree and criminal possession of a controlled substance in the third degree (possession with intent to sell). In *Potwora*, defendant, a wholesale book distributor, was charged with conspiracy in the third degree and with the substantive crimes of obscenity in the first and second degrees. The indictment was predicated on defendant's sale and distribution of several pornographic publications to two retail book sellers who sold the material to a detective. Defendant in *Potwora* argued that the conspiracy count was defective inasmuch as the substantive crimes involved the mutual cooperation of the wholesaler and retailers and such cooperation similarly served as the foundation for the conspiracy count.

The Fourth Department rejected this argument and upheld the conspiracy charge, stating that where concert between two people is not an *element* of the object crime a conspiracy count is proper. The court observed that, with respect to obscenity in the first and second degrees, the defendant may be found guilty for his individual, singular conduct of knowingly possessing obscene materials totally separate from concert with co-conspirators. *Potwora* distinguished those cases involving bribery and unlawful sale of liquor, where a conspiracy charge would not ordinarily lie in addition to the substantive offense, because concert between the giver and receiver or buyer and seller is an essential element of the object crime.

The People argue that *Potwora* supports the charge of conspiracy to possess one eighth of an ounce or more of cocaine against Macklowitz. They reason that if the Appellate Division found that a wholesaler's distribution of pornographic materials to his retailer purchasers could give rise to a charge of conspiracy to commit obscenity in the first and second degrees on the ground that those crimes do not *necessarily* involve the concerted action of such individuals, then there is no legal impediment to charging a buyer with conspiring with his seller to commit the crime of criminal possession of a controlled substance in the fourth degree because such possession never requires any concerted action. The prosecutor contends that whenever there is a sale of cocaine, both buyer *and* seller become liable for conspiracy to possess the drug because mutual cooperation is not theoretically necessary to commit the crime of possession.

While the People's argument has surface appeal, it does not withstand scrutiny under the facts of this case. Initially, I note that both *Jewsbury* and *Potwora* are easily distinguishable. In *Jewsbury*, the *buyer* was not charged with conspiracy as he is here (there, the defendant was the seller), and the object crime was not naked possession but rather, was *possession with intent to sell*. Similarly, in *Potwora*, the defendant was a *wholesale distributor* of pornography and the charges were based upon possession of obscene materials with *intent to distribute*. In contrast, the evidence before the Grand jury indicates that Macklowitz is, at most, an individual purchaser with *no further criminal objective*. Even accepting the People's tenuous theory that the substantive object crime of possession of narcotics does not necessarily require reciprocal actions of the buyer and seller, that does not alone ratify the conspiracy count. It is axiomatic that conspiracy requires common agreement and intent to *join* with others to commit a substantive crime. As noted by the Supreme Court, the record must be examined for evidence of such intent with special care in a conspiracy case for "charges of conspiracy are not to be made out by piling inference upon inference, thus fashioning . . . a dragnet to draw in all substantive crimes" (*Direct Sales Co. v United States*, 319 US 703, 711 [1943]).

In my view, legally sufficient evidence has not been presented to the Grand Jury to indicate that Macklowitz entered into an agreement with coconspirators Jack Buccafusco, Michael Giammarino and Angelo Tranquillino intending to join the larger criminal enterprise. The evidence, if accepted as true, merely shows that on several occasions Macklowitz purchased cocaine from Buccafusco or Giammarino. The People have not introduced sufficient evidence from which it may logically be inferred that Macklowitz intended or agreed to do anything other than buy and possess cocaine for his own use.

I hold that the ultimate purchaser of cocaine cannot be drawn into the web of a conspiracy when the only evidence submitted to the Grand jury is that on several occasions he bought cocaine for his own use.

The People have cited no authority to the contrary and, indeed, research has failed to uncover a single case where a conspiracy charge has, as its sole foundation, the mere possession of the buyer-user.

Application of the chain theory of conspiracy is of no avail. The People argue that Macklowitz knew or had reason to know that Buccafusco had suppliers and that he had other customers. They claim that all of those individuals shared the intent to possess at least one eighth of an ounce of cocaine[3] and entered into an agreement with Buccafusco, one of the objects of which was the possession of such cocaine.

Simply stated, there comes a point where the conspiracy ends. The People attach significance to the fact that here the evidence established a long-term, routinized arrangement which enabled defendant to purchase cocaine under the code name "Duane" on a regular confidential basis. This does not alter the fact that there was no evidence presented from which the Grand jury could reasonably conclude that Macklowitz intended to do more than merely possess the cocaine. Indeed, an ultimate purchaser may *expect* his supplier to provide the drugs, and may take advantage of the drugs' availability on numerous occasions. These factors do not automatically demonstrate that the buyer *conspired* to bring about that result, and do not render the buyer a coconspirator of the seller. A narcotic conspiracy may begin in the cocaine fields of Peru, continue through processing, transporting, cutting, packaging, wholesaling and retailing. But such an enterprise ends with the person who last obtained it with intent to sell. The ultimate user is not part of this conspiracy.

If the People's argument is to be accepted than every street user becomes a coconspirator with the seller. The prosecutor has made the criminal act itself (sale) as an overt act in the conspiracy (possession). This they cannot do. While the purchase and the sale necessarily involve possession, the ultimate goal of the buyer is to possess while the aim of the seller is to dispossess. The buyer of bootleg whiskey for his own use is not a coconspirator of the seller. Nor is the buyer of drugs molecularly bonded with the purveyor.

I find that the evidence presented to the Grand jury, if accepted as true, shows no more than a series of cocaine purchases by Michael Macklowitz. That is not legally sufficient to sustain a charge of conspiracy with his suppliers. Accordingly, defendant's motion to dismiss that count of the indictment is granted.

Questions and Notes

1. Because New York employs the unilateral theory of conspiracy, could Buccafusco be guilty of conspiring with Macklowitz even though Macklowitz is not guilty of conspiring with Buccafusco?

2. What is the difference between a "chain" conspiracy and a "wheel" conspiracy? Why does it matter?

3. How are *Jewsbury* and *Potwora* different from *Macklowitz*?

4. The court says that conspiracy between a briber and a bribee to take a bribe would not lie. Why not?

---

3. It should be noted that virtually all of the substantive possession counts against defendant involve weights of less than one eighth of an ounce of cocaine.

5. Do you think that Macklowitz ought to be deemed part of the conspiracy? Why? Why not?

See NUTSHELL §§ 16.05, 16.06.

6. The next several cases (*Feola, Lauria, Brown*) focus on the state of mind necessary for conspiratorial liability.

B. Single versus Multiple Conspiracies

State v. Stimpson

807 S.E.2d 603 (N.C. Ct. App. 2017)

TYSON, Judge.

Antonio Lamar Stimpson ("Defendant") appeals from judgments entered after a jury convicted him of discharging a firearm into an occupied property, discharging a firearm into an occupied vehicle, five counts of conspiracy to commit robbery with a firearm, six counts of robbery with a firearm, and two counts of attempted robbery with a firearm. Defendant has abandoned his appeal on all convictions and judgments, except for four of the five conspiracy convictions. We find no error in any of Defendant's convictions and judgments.

I. Factual Background

A. The Crimes

1. Smith

In the early morning hours of 22 March 2014, Debra Smith left a hair salon on Summit Avenue in Greensboro and entered her vehicle. A dark colored Jeep Cherokee vehicle swiftly pulled up and blocked her from leaving. Ms. Smith testified she saw two men exit the Jeep, with one man carrying a pump shotgun. The men wore masks and dark clothing. Ms. Smith was ordered to exit her vehicle and instructed to "give us your money."

Ms. Smith testified she was "scared for her life" when a gunshot was fired near her head. She fell onto the pavement as she exited from her vehicle. Ms. Smith told the men she did not have any money. One of the men with a shotgun began to taunt her. The other man stated, "Come on, man, take the vehicle" and the men got into Ms. Smith's car and drove it away.

2. Eban and Nie

On the same morning at about 5:45 a.m., Kler Eban was watching from the front door of his home on Sunrise Valley Road in Greensboro, as his wife walked to her car to leave for work. He saw three men walk past his house. Mr. Eban testified the men returned and two went behind his wife's car and one came toward the door of his house and shouted at him to open the door. Mr. Eban testified the men's faces were covered. One of the men pointed a gun wrapped in cloth at Mr. Eban.

Mr. Eban heard a gunshot and attempted to get out of the door to assist his wife. Mr. Eban's wife, Lieu Nie, testified a red Jeep was parked behind her car. The men had shot at her through the driver's side window while she was sitting in the driver's seat.

Two shots were also fired in Mr. Eban's direction. Ms. Nie crawled over the front seat and escaped through the rear door. The robbers entered Ms. Nie's car and stole a shopping bag of new cooking utensils. Mr. Eban testified one of the men got into the Jeep and two of them got into his wife's car and drove it away.

3. Nareau

Around 6:30 a.m., John Nareau drove his car into a parking space at his workplace on Norwalk Street in Greensboro. As he exited his vehicle, a male got in front of him and raised what appeared to be a sawed-off shot gun. Mr. Nareau was told "don't try anything. There's two in the back." Mr. Nareau testified the man wore a mask and demanded his wallet and cellphone. After handing over his wallet and phone, Mr. Nareau ran away and watched the men get into a dark colored Jeep and drive away.

4. Tomlin, White, Wilkerson, and Mork

At a little before 7:00 a.m. on the same date, four friends, Elizabeth Tomlin, Brinson White, Clair Wilkerson and Wesley Mork, were loading luggage in the trunk of their rental car, when three men yelled at them "to turn around, mother f—ker;" and "get down mother f—ker." Ms. Tomlin saw the men exit from a red Jeep parked 30–40 feet away. The men wore masks and dark clothing and carried guns. One of the guns appeared to be a sawed-off shotgun. The two women were chased by one man, while Mr. Carter and Mr. Mork were detained on the ground by the other two men from the Jeep. Mr. Mork's wallet and cash were stolen and cash was stolen from Mr. Carter.

During the pursuit, Ms. Tomlin's and Ms. Wilkerson's bags were taken. One of the attackers yelled "get in the car and take the car." The keys to the rental car were not in the vehicle, so all three men ran back to the Jeep and left.

5. Holland

Nicholas Holland was the final victim of the related crimes that occurred that morning. As Mr. Holland left his residence on Tremont Street in Greensboro, he noticed two males walk past the house. Mr. Holland observed a Jeep vehicle quickly pull up in front of his house. A masked male with a handgun demanded, "Give me what you have." Mr. Holland offered his brief case and car keys and attempted to run away. One of the men chased him until the same Jeep pulled up and the man climbed inside. The Jeep sped away.

B. Investigations

In response to the robberies, Greensboro Police Detective Devin Allis received a dispatch with a description of the dark colored Jeep Cherokee being involved.

Detective Allis pursued the Jeep and apprehended the driver, Aaron Spivey, after a chase. Mr. Spivey was arrested with Mr. Mork's wallet in his possession.

After Spivey's arrest, officers located Defendant and LeMarcus McKinnon walking in a nearby area. Defendant and McKinnon ran as the officers approached and had identified themselves. Defendant was apprehended by Lieutenant Larry Patterson. When arrested, Defendant was wearing a dark colored T-shirt, dark blue jeans and grey sneakers. He had cash, Mr. Nareau's cellphone and the keys to Ms. Nie's car in his possession.

When interviewed by police, Defendant initially denied any involvement in the robberies. Eventually Defendant admitted he had been present in the dark Jeep Cherokee with Spivey and McKinnon. Defendant stated he and McKinnon were cousins and were "tight." Defendant acknowledged he had met Spivey the previous week. Defendant also told police he had handled one of the guns a few days before the robberies.

Defendant told police officers he had been a passenger in the Jeep and witnessed the robberies perpetrated by the others. Defendant admitted driving the Jeep from the scene of the robbery of Ms. Nie and to later meeting Spivey and McKinnon for the subsequent robberies.

Officers recovered three pair of gloves, a blue toboggan, a black and grey bandana and a black headband or neckwarmer from inside the passenger area of the Jeep Cherokee. The handbags and briefcase belonging to the various victims were also recovered from inside the Jeep.

* * *

III. Issue

Defendant asserts the trial court erred by failing to dismiss four of the conspiracy charges and argues the State's evidence supported only a single charge.

IV. Standard of Review

"We review the trial court's denial of a motion to dismiss *de novo.*" *State v. Sanders*, 208 N.C. App. 142, 144, 701 S.E.2d 380, 382 (2010). Under a *de novo* standard of review, this Court "considers the matter anew and freely substitutes its own judgment for that of the trial court."

In ruling on a motion to dismiss for insufficiency of the evidence,

> the trial court *must consider the evidence in the light most favorable to the State, drawing all reasonable inferences in the State's favor.* All evidence, competent or incompetent, must be considered. Any contradictions or conflicts in the evidence are resolved in favor of the State, and evidence unfavorable to the State is not considered. . . . [S]o long as the evidence supports a reasonable inference of the defendant's guilt, a motion to dismiss is properly denied even though the evidence also permits a reasonable inference of the

defendant's innocence. The test for sufficiency of the evidence is the same whether the evidence is direct, circumstantial or both.

State v. Bradshaw, 366 N.C. 90, 92–93, 728 S.E.2d 345, 347 (2012) (emphasis supplied) (internal citations and quotation marks omitted).

V. Analysis

A. State's evidence

"A criminal conspiracy is an agreement between two or more persons to do an unlawful act. . . ." The agreement to commit the unlawful act may be established by circumstantial evidence.

A conspiracy ordinarily "ends with the attainment of its criminal objectives. . . . [] The question of whether multiple agreements constitute a single conspiracy or multiple conspiracies is a question of fact for the jury."

The State alleged Defendant, Mr. Spivey and Mr. McKinnon conspired to commit the robberies of Ms. Smith, Ms. Lie, Mr. Nareau, Ms. Tomlin, Ms. Wilkerson, Mr. Mork and Mr. Holland. The State proceeded on five indictments alleging each incident as a separate conspiracy. The State did not offer the testimony of Spivey or McKinnon, Defendant's alleged co-conspirators. The only witnesses called by the State were the victims of the robberies and the police officers involved in the investigation of the crimes.

We all agree the evidence supports the conclusion that Defendant, Spivey and McKinnon conspired to commit the robberies. The State's evidence showed Defendant and his compatriots were all wearing dark clothing. Implements indicating planning in advance and to assist committing robberies were recovered from inside the Jeep: head and face coverings, gloves, and weapons.

Defendant testified concerning his relationship with McKinnon, his cousin, and that he had met Spivey the week prior to the crimes, and had handled a shotgun used in the robberies a few days before the robberies and admitted being present inside the Jeep Cherokee when the crimes occurred. All three men had been together on the afternoon of 21 March 2014. Defendant testified he, Spivey and McKinnon had been drinking and taking drugs together during the evening before and into the morning of the robberies and that all three men had headed out and traveled together in the early morning hours in the Jeep.

B. Single Conspiracy Cases

Defendant argues all of the above facts present only evidence of a single conspiracy to commit robberies on the morning of 22 March 2014. Defendant asserts *State v. Medlin*, and the cases which follow it, control the outcome of his case. We address each in turn.

1. State v. Medlin

In *Medlin*, the defendant and two others were charged with break-ins and thefts of seven retail stores over the period of four months. Defendant—Medlin operated a thrift store where co-conspirators Cox and Williams would "hang out." Cox and Williams testified the break-ins were Medlin's idea. The State's evidence showed all the break-ins occurred in essentially the same manner: Cox and Williams would break a store window, climb through the hole and carry away items. The defendant would drive his truck to the stores to assist the others in carrying away the stolen goods. The participants met after the break-ins to divide the stolen items and to discuss the next break-in. For each of the break-ins, the defendant was charged and convicted under separate indictments for conspiring with Cox and Williams to commit the ten felonious break-ins.

This Court recognized "[w]hen the evidence shows a series of agreements or acts constituting a *single* conspiracy, a defendant cannot be prosecuted on multiple conspiracy indictments consistent with the constitutional prohibition against double jeopardy." While the offense "is complete upon the formation of the unlawful agreement, the offense continues until the conspiracy comes to fruition. . . ."

While there is no simple test for determining whether there was one conspiracy or multiple conspiracies, the Court acknowledged several factors impact the determination of the number of conspiracies, including: "time intervals, participants, objectives, and number of meetings." ("The nature of the agreement or agreements, the objectives of the conspiracies, the time interval between them, the number of participants, and the number of meetings are all factors that may be considered.").

* * *

C. Multiple Conspiracies

The State asserts the facts before us are distinguishable from the line of cases above. Unlike the facts in *State v. Medlin,* no evidence shows any meeting took place between Defendant and the other two robbers subsequent to any of the robberies to plan additional robberies in furtherance of any prior agreement to engage in as many crimes as possible, only that the three men were drinking and doing drugs together the evening and morning before the crimes were committed. There was no evidence that the Defendant and his co-conspirators conspired to engage in as many robberies as they could. They agreed and engaged in random robberies as the opportunities appeared before them.

The dissenting judge asserts the State "impliedly" admits it did not prove five separate agreements. We disagree. On brief, the State acknowledges there was no proof of any meeting about or discussion between Defendant and the other perpetrators *to plan to commit a series of robberies*. Evidence was offered by the State and by Defendant of meetings and interactions with Defendant and the other conspirators, before and between each robbery, but no evidence of the conversations.

The facts in *Wilson* are also dissimilar to the instant case. No evidence shows any meeting being held between Defendant and the other robbers prior to the robberies to discuss or plan the robberies, or the specific property to be stolen during the course of the robberies. Unlike the facts in *Fink* and *Griffin*, there is no evidence of

848 19 · CONSPIRACY

a meeting between Defendant and the other two perpetrators to devise a single plan to engage in a series of robberies.

The dissent finds Defendant's case to be most similar to *Medlin*. However, the State's evidence showed defendant—Medlin initiated the idea and suggested to his co-conspirators the plan to break in and steal the televisions and radios that he could sell in his thrift store. The multiple break-ins were part of a single plan to steal merchandise to be sold at Medlin's thrift store. Here, the crimes were ones of opportunity, where differing victims were accosted and items were stolen from them as Defendant and his co-conspirators happened to come upon them.

No evidence limits Defendant as engaged in a one-time, pre-planned and organized, ongoing and continuing conspiracy to engage in robbery and the other crimes. In particular, the random nature and happenstance of the robberies and related crimes here do not indicate a one-time, pre-planned conspiracy. The victims and property stolen were not connected. The victims and crimes committed arose at random and by pure opportunity. Each of the series of crimes on the various victims was committed and completed before Defendant and his co-conspirators moved on and happened upon and mutually agreed to rob and commit other crimes on their next targets and victims of opportunity. Defendant's argument is overruled.

* * *

2. State v. Glisson

* * *

Considering the totality of the circumstances in the present case, and reviewing the evidence in the light most favorable to the State, sufficient evidence supports a reasonable inference for the jury to consider and conclude that Defendant was involved in five separate conspiracies to commit armed robbery.

While the dissenting opinion sets forth our same standard of review on motions to dismiss, it appears to ignore its application to the motion to dismiss in the case before us. "In 'borderline' or close cases, our courts have consistently expressed a preference for submitting issues to the jury, both in reliance on the common sense and fairness of the twelve and to avoid unnecessary appeals. [] The question of whether multiple agreements constitute a single conspiracy or multiple conspiracies is a question of fact for the jury." The trial court did not err by denying Defendant's motion to dismiss and properly submitted all five conspiracy counts to the jury.

VI. Conclusion

In a motion to dismiss, the trial court must consider the evidence of multiple conspiracies in the light most favorable to the State and give the State every reasonable inference to be draw from the evidence presented. We find no error in Defendant's convictions or the judgments entered thereon. *It is so ordered.*

Judge STROUD concurs.

Judge ELMORE dissents with separate opinion.

ELMORE, Judge, dissenting.

I respectfully disagree with the majority's decision to affirm the trial court's denial of defendant's motions to dismiss four of the five counts of conspiracy to commit robbery with a firearm. The State failed to present substantial evidence of multiple agreements between defendant and his co-conspirators as required to prove more than one conspiracy. Applying the four factors from *State v. Rozier*, the State only proved that defendant engaged in one conspiracy. Accordingly, I respectfully dissent.

I. Standard of Review

A trial court's denial of a motion to dismiss is accorded *de novo* review. A trial court properly denies a defendant's motion to dismiss if "there is substantial evidence (1) of each essential element of the offense charged, . . . and (2) of defendant's being the perpetrator of such offense." Whether evidence is substantial "is a question of law for the court and is reviewed *de novo*. Substantial evidence is relevant evidence that a reasonable mind might accept as adequate to support a conclusion."

* * *

II. Criminal Conspiracy

"A criminal conspiracy is an agreement between two or more people to do an unlawful act. . . . [T]o prove conspiracy, the State need not prove an express agreement; evidence tending to show a mutual, implied understanding will suffice." When the State charges a defendant with two or more conspiracies, "it must prove not only the existence of *at least two agreements* but also that they were *separate.*[] A single conspiracy may, and often does, consist of a series of different offenses." However, a series of different offenses "arising from a single agreement [does] not permit prosecutions for multiple conspiracies."[. . .] "It is the number of separate agreements, rather than the number of substantive offenses agreed upon, which determines the number of conspiracies."

Nevertheless, it is difficult to determine whether a single or multiple conspiracies are involved in a particular case. This Court in *Rozier* established four factors to consider when determining whether a defendant has committed single or multiple conspiracies. Those factors are (1) the time intervals between the crimes, (2) the specific participants involved, (3) the conspiracy's objectives, and (4) the number of meetings among the participants. On appeal, defendant argues that applying the *Rozier* factors to his case reveals a single conspiracy, not five. I agree. To support his argument, defendant cites to four decisions from this Court that applied the *Rozier* factors and found a single conspiracy.

III. Summary of *Rozier* Cases

A. State v. Medlin

In *State v. Medlin*, the State's evidence showed that the defendant participated in ten break-ins of retail stores across Durham from May to August of 1985. The robberies were conducted in a similar manner; various electronics were stolen from each location and the defendant and his co-conspirator, Walter Cox, participated in all ten robberies while a third co-conspirator participated in three. Cox testified that he and the defendant would meet after each break-in to plan the next one. The defendant was convicted of seven counts of conspiracy to break or enter and appealed the judgment, arguing that the State's evidence showed only "a single scheme or plan to commit an ongoing series of felonious breakings or enterings."

The *Medlin* panel, applying the *Rozier* factors, "[found] ample evidence of a single conspiracy." The panel first determined the break-ins were conducted over a short time period of four months, "some within ten days of each other." Second, these crimes were committed by the same three participants, despite the third co-conspirator not being present for some of the robberies. Third, the participants had the common objective to steal televisions and radios from Durham retail stores. Finally, the panel considered the number of meetings among the participants. Although the defendant met with his co-conspirators generally after each break-in, the purpose of the meetings was to "divide the spoils and discuss the next break-in." The panel summarized the fourth *Rozier* factor as follows:

> The gist of the meetings was to plan subsequent break-ins in furtherance of the original unlawful agreement made sometime before the first break-in. We are hard pressed to find facts more clearly telling of an ongoing series of acts in furtherance of a single conspiracy to break or enter. Rather than show ten separate conspiracies to break or enter on ten separate occasions as the State contends, these facts show one unlawful agreement to break or enter as many times as the participants could get away with.

Accordingly, the *Medlin* panel vacated the defendant's seven conspiracy convictions and remanded for entry of a judgment on one conspiracy conviction, with instructions to resentence the defendant on this single conspiracy conviction.

* * *

IV. Analysis

I agree with defendant that the four *Rozier* cases are similar to the present case. Each relevant factor is addressed in turn.

A. Application of *Rozier* Factors

i. Time Intervals

The first *Rozier* factor is the time interval between each crime. It is implied that time is a crucial factor because a short time interval between crimes signifies a low possibility that an agreement can be made between each crime.

The panel in each of the four *Rozier* cases found the respective time intervals to be short. *Medlin* (four months). Although the defendants in the *Rozier* cases had plenty of time to meet or make an agreement in between the crimes, the State did not present evidence of meetings or agreements that occurred in between the crimes in those cases. Moreover, the panels in those cases did not infer the presence of meetings or agreements based on the time intervals.

Here, the time interval in which the five robberies occurred is two to three hours—much shorter than in any of the four *Rozier* cases. Notably, the longest time interval cited by any of the *Rozier* cases is four months, yet the *Medlin* panel still held that application of the *Rozier* factors resulted in a single conspiracy. Nevertheless, the majority fails to credit the time interval of two to three hours in this case.

ii. Participants

The second *Rozier* factor is the specific participants involved in each crime. This factor is significant because when the participants to each crime are completely different, the State must prove separate conspiracies for each crime. However, when the participants are the same, there could potentially be one conspiracy to commit several crimes.

In *Medlin* . . . , the same two individuals participated in each crime, but a third individual participated in some but not all of the crimes. . . .

* * *

iii. Objectives

The third *Rozier* factor is the objective of each alleged conspiracy. 69 N.C. App. at 52, 316 S.E.2d at 902. When the objective of each alleged conspiracy is different, this leans toward separate conspiracies. But when the objective of each alleged conspiracy is same, this leans toward a single conspiracy.

Each panel in the *Rozier* cases determined that the objective of each alleged conspiracy was the same. The *Medlin* panel determined that the conspirators had the common goal to "break or enter as many times as [they] could get away with." ***

Defendant's case is most similar to *Medlin*. Here, the participants committed a string of robberies early one morning over the course of a few hours before they were caught by the police. ***

iv. Meetings

The final *Rozier* factor is the number of meetings among the participants. This factor is crucial to determining the number of conspiracies because it tends to reflect the number of agreements among the participants. To prove a single conspiracy, the State must show an express or implied understanding of an agreement. To prove two or more conspiracies, the State must prove two or more separate agreements. When the State proves multiple separate meetings among the participants, a jury could infer multiple implied understandings, and thus multiple conspiracies.

* * *

As the majority notes, the State "offered no testimony concerning any discussions between the co-participants before, during, or after each robbery". . . . However, there is evidence that defendant spent the evening prior to the robberies with the other two perpetrators. Although this may be enough for a jury to find an implied understanding of an agreement for a single conspiracy, I respectfully disagree with the majority's conclusion that there is no error in defendant's convictions.

The State failed to present substantial evidence of four meetings or agreements among the participants. The State charged defendant with five conspiracies and ... was required to prove five separate meetings or agreements between the participants. Defendant established an implied understanding for one agreement when he testified that he and his fellow perpetrators met the night before the robbery. This single meeting is only enough for the jury to infer a single conspiracy, and the burden was on the State to present evidence of four other separate meetings or agreements. However, the State impliedly admits that it failed to do this by arguing on appeal that "[i]ndeed, there is *no* evidence present that any meetings ever took place between the defendant and any of his fellow perpetrators." (Emphasis added.) Because the State did not present *any* evidence—substantial or not—of the agreement element for four of the five conspiracies, the trial court should have granted defendant's motion to dismiss. The State argues there was an implied understanding to commit each robbery based on the action of committing each robbery. However, the panels in the *Rozier* cases did not find an implied understanding based on the participants' actions, and I believe it would be unwise to depart from that precedent now.

* * *

V. Conclusion

The majority declines to apply *Rozier* and its progeny to this case, effectively overlooking years of precedent from this Court. I, however, would apply the *Rozier* factors to defendant's case. First, the time interval was a few hours—much shorter than in *Medlin*. . . . Second, the participants in the five robberies appear to be the same: defendant and the two men he met earlier that night. Third, the objective of each crime is the same: to commit robbery with a dangerous weapon. Finally, the State presented no evidence of any meetings between defendant and the co-conspirators prior to or during the robberies. Although the jury could find an implied understanding to commit a robbery based on defendant's testimony that he spent the evening prior to the robberies with the other two perpetrators, this only supports one conspiracy conviction; the State failed to present evidence of four other *separate* meetings or agreements. Similar to *Medlin*, the facts here show one agreement to commit as many robberies as possible.

Applying *Rozier*, I believe defendant committed only one conspiracy. I would therefore hold that the trial court erred by failing to dismiss the four other counts of conspiracy to commit robbery with a firearm, and I would vacate four of defendant's five conspiracy convictions and remand for resentencing on the remaining one. I respectfully dissent from the majority's decision to uphold four of defendant's conspiracy convictions.

Questions and Notes

1. The court says that the question of single or multiple conspiracies is a question of fact for the jury. Should that be the case? Isn't the legal significance of the facts that the jury found a question of law?

2. How is this case different from *Medlin*? If *Medlin* only involved one conspiracy, by what logic can *Stimson* involve many?

3. Whose opinion is more persuasive, Tyson's or Elmore's? In regard thereto, is it relevant that Tyson's opinion doesn't even mention *Rozier*?

4. Sometimes, as in this case, the defendant prefers to analyze the case as involving one conspiracy, whereas the government prefers to analyze it as involving many conspiracies. But sometimes the shoe is on the other foot and the defendant would like to argue multiple conspiracies so that he would not be deemed part of a single conspiracy that might be large enough in dollars to get him a larger sentence. *See, e.g., Braverman v. United States*, 317 U.S. 49 (1942)

C. Mens Rea

United States v. Feola

420 U.S. 671 (1975)

MR. JUSTICE BLACKMUN delivered the opinion of the Court.

This case presents the issue whether knowledge that the intended victim is a federal officer is a requisite for the crime of conspiracy to commit an assault upon a federal officer while engaged in the performance of his official duties.

The facts reveal a classic narcotics "rip-off." The details are not particularly important for our present purposes. We need note only that the evidence shows that Feola and his confederates arranged for a sale of heroin to buyers who turned out to be undercover agents for the Bureau of Narcotics and Dangerous Drugs. The group planned to palm off on the purchasers, for a substantial sum, a form of sugar in place of heroin and, should that ruse fail, simply to surprise their unwitting buyers and relieve them of the cash they had brought along for payment. The plan failed when one agent, his suspicions being aroused, drew his revolver in time to counter an assault upon another agent from the rear. Instead of enjoying the rich benefits of a successful swindle, Feola and his associates found themselves charged, to their undoubted surprise, with conspiring to assault, and with assaulting, federal officers.

The Court of Appeals reversed the conspiracy convictions on a ground not advanced by any of the defendants. Although it approved the trial court's instructions to the jury on the substantive charge of assaulting a federal officer, it nonetheless concluded that the failure to charge that knowledge of the victim's official identity must be proved in order to convict on the conspiracy charge amounted to plain error. The court perceived itself bound by a line of cases, commencing with Judge Learned Hand's opinion in *United States v. Crimmins*, 123 F.2d 271 (2d Cir. 1941), all holding that scienter of a factual element that confers federal jurisdiction, while unnecessary for conviction of the substantive offense, is required in order to sustain a conviction for conspiracy to commit the substantive offense. Although the court noted that the *Crimmins* rationale "has been criticized," and, indeed, offered no argument in support of it, it accepted "the controlling precedents somewhat reluctantly."

The Government's plea is for symmetry. It urges that since criminal liability for the offense described does not depend on whether the assailant harbored the specific intent to assault a federal officer, no greater scienter requirement can be engrafted upon the conspiracy offense, which is merely an agreement to commit the act proscribed by [the statute]. Consideration of the Government's contention requires us preliminarily to pass upon its premise, the proposition that responsibility for assault upon a federal officer does not depend upon whether the assailant was aware of the official identity of his victim at the time he acted.

[The Court concluded that the statute's requirement that the victim be a Federal Officer was merely jurisdictional. That is, its function was not to enhance the penalty either because of the defendant's culpability in attacking an officer or because of the harm done to the officer. Rather the victim's status was a *sine qua non* of making the case Federal at all. Consequently, the Court ruled that no state of mind was required in regard to this jurisdictional element. The Court perceived no unfairness to the defendants because they knew that their conduct was criminal. Had the defendants reasonably believed that the Federal officers were intruding burglars bent on harming them, their mistake would have been a defense.]

Our decisions establish that in order to sustain a judgment of conviction on a charge of conspiracy to violate a federal statute, the Government must prove at least the degree of criminal intent necessary for the substantive offense itself. Respondent Feola urges upon us the proposition that the Government must show a degree of criminal intent in the conspiracy count greater than is necessary to convict for the substantive offense; he urges that even though it is not necessary to show that he was aware of the official identity of his assaulted victims in order to find him guilty of assaulting federal officers, the Government nonetheless must show that he was aware that his intended victims were undercover agents, if it is successfully to prosecute him for conspiring to assault federal agents. And the Court of Appeals held that the trial court's failure to charge the jury to this effect constituted plain error.

The general conspiracy statute offers no textual support for the proposition that to be guilty of conspiracy a defendant in effect must have known that his conduct violated federal law. The statute makes it unlawful simply to "conspire ... to commit any offense against the United States." A natural reading of these words would be that since one can violate a criminal statute simply by engaging in the forbidden conduct, a conspiracy to commit that offense is nothing more than an agreement to engage in the prohibited conduct. Then where, as here, the substantive statute does not require that an assailant know the official status of his victim, there is nothing on the face of the conspiracy statute that would seem to require that those agreeing to the assault have a greater degree of knowledge.

We have been unable to find any decision of this Court that lends support to the respondent. With no support on the face of the general conspiracy statute or in this

Court's decisions, respondent relies solely on the line of cases commencing with *Crimmins* for the principle that the Government must prove "antifederal" intent in order to establish liability. In *Crimmins*, the defendant had been found guilty of conspiring to receive stolen bonds that had been transported in interstate commerce. Upon review, the Court of Appeals pointed out that the evidence failed to establish that *Crimmins* actually knew the stolen bonds had moved into the State. Accepting for the sake of argument the assumption that such knowledge was not necessary to sustain a conviction on the substantive offense, Judge Learned Hand nevertheless concluded that to permit conspiratorial liability where the conspirators were ignorant of the federal implications of their acts would be to enlarge their agreement beyond its terms as they understood them. He capsulized the distinction in what has become well known as his "traffic light" analogy:

> "While one may, for instance, be guilty of running past a traffic light of whose existence one is ignorant, one cannot be guilty of conspiring to run past such a light, for one cannot agree to run past a light unless one supposes that there is a light to run past."

Judge Hand's attractive, but perhaps seductive, analogy has received a mixed reception in the Courts of Appeals. The Second Circuit, of course, has followed it; others have rejected it. It appears that most have avoided it by the simple expedient of inferring the requisite knowledge from the scope of the conspiratorial venture. We conclude that the analogy, though effective prose, is, as applied to the facts before us, bad law.[24]

The question posed by the traffic light analogy is not before us, just as it was not before the Second Circuit in *Crimmins*. Criminal liability, of course, may be imposed on one who runs a traffic light regardless of whether he harbored the "evil intent" of disobeying the light's command; whether he drove so recklessly as to be unable to perceive the light; whether, thinking he was observing all traffic rules, he simply failed to notice the light; or whether, having been reared elsewhere, he thought that the light was only an ornament. Traffic violations generally fall into that category of offenses that dispense with a *mens rea* requirement. These laws embody the social judgment that it is fair to punish one who intentionally engages in conduct that creates a risk to others, even though no risk is intended or the actor, through no fault of his own, is completely unaware of the existence of any risk. The traffic light analogy poses the question whether it is fair to punish parties to an agreement to engage intentionally in apparently innocent conduct where the unintended result of engaging in that conduct is the violation of a criminal statute.

---

24. The Government rather effectively exposes the fallacy of the *Crimmins* traffic light analogy by recasting it in terms of a jurisdictional element. The suggested example is a traffic light on an Indian reservation. Surely, one may conspire with others to disobey the light but be ignorant of the fact that it is on the reservation. As applied to a jurisdictional element of this kind the formulation makes little sense.

But this case does not call upon us to answer this question, and we decline to do so. We note in passing, however, that the analogy comes close to stating what has been known as the *"Powell* doctrine;' originating in *People v. Powell*, 63 N.Y. 88 (1875), to the effect that a conspiracy, to be criminal, must be animated by a corrupt motive or a motive to do wrong. Under this principle, such a motive could be easily demonstrated if the underlying offense involved an act clearly wrongful in itself; but it had to be independently demonstrated if the acts agreed to were wrongful solely because of statutory proscription. Interestingly, Judge Hand himself was one of the more severe critics of the *Powell* doctrine.[25]

That Judge Hand should reject the *Powell* doctrine and then create the *Crimmins* doctrine seems curious enough. Fatal to the latter, however, is the fact that it was announced in a case to which it could not have been meant to apply. In *Crimmins*, the substantive offense, namely, the receipt of stolen securities that had been in interstate commerce, proscribed clearly wrongful conduct. Such conduct could not be engaged in without an intent to accomplish the forbidden result. So, too, it is with assault, the conduct forbidden by the substantive statute presently before us. One may run a traffic light "of whose existence one is ignorant," but assaulting another "of whose existence one is ignorant," probably would require unearthly intervention. Thus, the traffic light analogy, even if it were a correct statement of the law, is inapt, for the conduct proscribed by the substantive offense, here assault, is not of the type outlawed without regard to the intent of the actor to accomplish the result that is made criminal. If the analogy has any vitality at all, it is to conduct of the latter variety; that, however, is a question we save for another day. We hold here only that where a substantive offense embodies only a requirement of *mens rea* as to each of its elements, the general federal conspiracy statute requires no more.

Questions and Notes

1. Is there any good reason to require an anti-federal animus for a conspiratorial crime when it is not required for the underlying offense?

2. Does the *Powell* doctrine make any sense?

3. Was Judge Hand consistent in rejecting the *Powell* doctrine and creating the *Crimmins* doctrine?

4. The next case, *Lauria*, has become a classic for both conspiratorial and accessorial liability even though it involved the owner of a telephone answering service, a business that in this day of answering machines is probably as necessary as a buggy whip manufacturing company. Because *Lauria* arose in the context of a conspiracy

---

25. "Starting with *People v. Powell* . . . the anomalous doctrine has indeed gained some footing in the circuit courts of appeals that for conspiracy there must be a 'corrupt motive.' Yet it is hard to see any reason for this, or why more proof should be necessary than that the parties had in contemplation all the elements of the crime they are charged with conspiracy to commit. *United States v. Mack*, 112 F.2d 290, 292 (2d Cir. 1940).

prosecution, it is typically studied in that conjunction. You might consider whether the result would have been any different if Lauria had been prosecuted as an accessory before the fact to prostitution.

People v. Lauria

59 Cal. Rptr. 628 (Cal. App. 1967)

FLEMING, J.

In an investigation of call-girl activity the police focused their attention on three prostitutes actively plying their trade on call, each of whom was using Lauria's telephone answering service, presumably for business purposes.

On January 8, 1965, Stella Weeks, a policewoman, signed up for telephone service with Lauria's answering service. Mrs. Weeks, in the course of her conversation with Lauria's office manager, hinted broadly that she was a prostitute concerned with the secrecy of her activities and their concealment from the police. She was assured that the operation of the service was discreet and "about as safe as you can get." It was arranged that Mrs. Weeks need not leave her address with the answering service, but could pick up her calls and pay her bills in person.

On February 11, Mrs. Weeks talked to Lauria on the telephone and told him her business was modelling and she had been referred to the answering service by Terry, one of the three prostitutes under investigation. She complained that because of the operation of the service she had lost two valuable customers, referred to as tricks. Lauria defended his service and said that her friends had probably lied to her about having left calls for her. But he did not respond to Mrs. Weeks' hints that she needed customers in order to make money, other than to invite her to his house for a personal visit in order to get better acquainted. In the course of his talk he said "his business was taking messages."

On February 15, Mrs. Weeks talked on the telephone to Lauria's office manager and again complained of two lost calls, which she described as a $50 and a $100 trick. On investigation the office manager could find nothing wrong, but she said she would alert the switchboard operators about slip-ups on calls.

On April 1 Lauria and the three prostitutes were arrested. Lauria complained to the police that this attention was undeserved, stating that Hollywood Call Board had 60 to 70 prostitutes on its board while his own service had only 9 or 10, that he kept separate records for known or suspected prostitutes for the convenience of himself and the police. When asked if his records were available to police who might come to the office to investigate call girls, Lauria replied that they were whenever the police had a specific name. However, his service didn't "arbitrarily tell the police about prostitutes on our board. As long as they pay their bills we tolerate them." In a subsequent voluntary appearance before the grand jury Lauria testified he had always cooperated with the police. But he admitted he knew some of his customers were prostitutes, and he knew Terry was a prostitute because he had personally used her services, and he knew she was paying for 500 calls a month.

Lauria and the three prostitutes were indicted for conspiracy to commit prostitution, and nine overt acts were specified. Subsequently the trial court set aside the indictment as having been brought without reasonable or probable cause. The People have appealed, claiming that a sufficient showing of an unlawful agreement to further prostitution was made.

To establish agreement, the People need show no more than a tacit, mutual understanding between co-conspirators to accomplish an unlawful act. Here the People attempted to establish a conspiracy by showing that Lauria, well aware that his codefendants were prostitutes who received business calls from customers through his telephone answering service, continued to furnish them with such service. This approach attempts to equate knowledge of another's criminal activity with conspiracy to further such criminal activity, and poses the question of the criminal responsibility of a furnisher of goods or services who knows his product is being used to assist the operation of an illegal business. Under what circumstances does a supplier become a part of a conspiracy to further an illegal enterprise by furnishing goods or services which he knows are to be used by the buyer for criminal purposes?

The two leading cases on this point face in opposite directions. In *United States v. Falcone*, 311 U.S. 205, the sellers of large quantities of sugar, yeast, and cans were absolved from participation in a moonshining conspiracy among distillers who bought from them, while in *Direct Sales Co. v. United States*, 319 U.S. 703, a wholesaler of drugs was convicted of conspiracy to violate the federal narcotic laws by selling drugs in quantity to a codefendant physician who was supplying them to addicts. The distinction between these two cases appears primarily based on the proposition that distributors of such dangerous products as drugs are required to exercise greater discrimination in the conduct of their business than are distributors of innocuous substances like sugar and yeast.

In the earlier case, *Falcone*, the sellers' knowledge of the illegal use of the goods was insufficient by itself to make the sellers participants in a conspiracy with the distillers who bought from them. Such knowledge fell short of proof of a conspiracy, and evidence on the volume of sales was too vague to support a jury finding that respondents knew of the conspiracy from the size of the sales alone.

In the later case of *Direct Sales*, the conviction of a drug wholesaler for conspiracy to violate federal narcotic laws was affirmed on a showing that it had actively promoted the sale of morphine sulphate in quantity and had sold codefendant physician, who practiced in a small town in South Carolina, more than 300 times his normal requirements of the drug, even though it had been repeatedly warned of the dangers of unrestricted sales of the drug. The court contrasted the restricted goods involved in *Direct Sales* with the articles of free commerce involved in *Falcone*: "All articles of commerce may be put to illegal ends," said the court. "But all do not have inherently the same susceptibility to harmful and illegal use.

... This difference is important for two purposes. One is for making certain that the seller knows the buyer's intended illegal use. The other is to show that by the sale he intends to further, promote, and cooperate in it. This intent, when given effect by overt act, is the gist of conspiracy. While it is not identical with mere knowledge that another purposes unlawful action it is not unrelated to such knowledge.... The step from knowledge to intent and agreement may be taken. There is more than suspicion, more than knowledge, acquiescence, carelessness, indifference, lack of concern. There is informed and interested cooperation, stimulation, instigation. And there is also a 'stake in the venture' which, even if it may not be essential, is not irrelevant to the question of conspiracy." While *Falcone* and *Direct Sales* may not be entirely consistent with each other in their full implications, they do provide us with a framework for the criminal liability of a supplier of lawful goods or services put to unlawful use. Both the element of *knowledge* of the illegal use of the goods or services and the element of *intent* to further that use must be present in order to make the supplier a participant in a criminal conspiracy.

Proof of *knowledge is* ordinarily a question of fact and requires no extended discussion in the present case. The knowledge of the supplier was sufficiently established when Lauria admitted he knew some of his customers were prostitutes and admitted he knew that Terry, an active subscriber to his service, was a prostitute. In the face of these admissions he could scarcely claim to have relied on the normal assumption an operator of a business or service is entitled to make, that his customers are behaving themselves in the eyes of the law. Because Lauria knew in fact that some of his customers were prostitutes, it is a legitimate inference he knew they were subscribing to his answering service for illegal business purposes and were using his service to make assignations for prostitution. On this record we think the prosecution is entitled to claim positive knowledge by Lauria of the use of his service to facilitate the business of prostitution.

The more perplexing issue in the case is the sufficiency of proof of *intent* to further the criminal enterprise. The element of intent may be proved either by direct evidence, or by evidence of circumstances from which an intent to further a criminal enterprise by supplying lawful goods or services may be inferred. Direct evidence of participation, such as advice from the supplier of legal goods or services to the user of those goods or services on their use for illegal purposes, such evidence as appeared in a companion case we decide today, *People v. Roy*, 59 Cal. Rptr. 636, provides the simplest case. When the intent to further and promote the criminal enterprise comes from the lips of the supplier himself, ambiguities of inference from circumstance need not trouble us. But in cases where direct proof of complicity is lacking, intent to further the conspiracy must be derived from the sale itself and its surrounding circumstances in order to establish the supplier's express or tacit agreement to join the conspiracy.

In the case at bench the prosecution argues that since Lauria knew his customers were using his service for illegal purposes but nevertheless continued to furnish it to them, he must have intended to assist them in carrying out their illegal activities. Thus through a union of knowledge and intent he became a participant in a criminal conspiracy. Essentially, the People argue that knowledge alone of the continuing use of his telephone facilities for criminal purposes provided a sufficient basis from which his intent to participate in those criminal activities could be inferred.

In examining precedents in this field we find that sometimes, but not always, the criminal intent of the supplier may be inferred from his knowledge of the unlawful use made of the product he supplies. Some consideration of characteristic patterns may be helpful.

1. Intent may be inferred from knowledge, when the purveyor of legal goods for illegal use has acquired a stake in the venture. For example, in *Regina v. Thomas*, [1957] 2 All Eng. 181, 342, a prosecution for living off the earnings of prostitution, the evidence showed that the accused, knowing the woman to be a convicted prostitute, agreed to let her have the use of his room between the hours of 9 p.m. and 2 a.m. for a charge of three pounds a night. The Court of Criminal Appeal refused an appeal from the conviction, holding that when the accused rented a room at a grossly inflated rent to a prostitute for the purpose of carrying on her trade, a jury could find he was living on the earnings of prostitution.

In the present case, no proof was offered of inflated charges for the telephone answering services furnished the codefendants.

2. Intent may be inferred from knowledge, when no legitimate use for the goods or services exists. The leading California case is *People v. McLaughlin*, 111 Cal. App. 2d 781 [245 P.2d 1076], in which the court upheld a conviction of the suppliers of horse-racing information by wire for conspiracy to promote bookmaking, when it had been established that wire-service information had no other use than to supply information needed by bookmakers to conduct illegal gambling operations.

In *Rex v. Delaval* (1763) 3 Burr. 1434, 97 Eng. Rep. 913, the charge was unlawful conspiracy to remove a girl from the control of Bates, a musician to whom she was bound as an apprentice, and place her in the hands of Sir Francis Delaval for the purpose of prostitution. Lord Mansfield not only upheld the charges against Bates and Sir Francis, but also against Frame, the attorney who drew up the indentures of apprenticeship transferring custody of the girl from Bates to Sir Francis. Fraine, said Lord Mansfield, must have known that Sir Francis had no facilities for teaching music to apprentices so that it was impossible for him to have been ignorant of the real intent of the transaction.

In *Shaw v. Director of Public Prosecutions*, [1962] A.C. 220, the defendant was convicted of conspiracy to corrupt public morals and of living on the earnings of prostitution, when he published a directory consisting almost entirely of advertisements of the names, addresses, and specialized talents of prostitutes. Publication of such a directory, said the court, could have no legitimate use and serve no other purpose than to advertise the professional services of the prostitutes whose advertisements appeared in the directory. The publisher could be deemed a participant in the profits from the business activities of his principal advertisers.

Other services of a comparable nature come to mind: the manufacturer of crooked dice and marked cards who sells his product to gambling casinos; the tipster who furnishes information on the movement of law enforcement officers to known lawbreakers. In such cases the supplier must necessarily have an intent to further the illegal enterprise since there is no known honest use for his goods.

However, there is nothing in the furnishing of telephone answering service which would necessarily imply assistance in the performance of illegal activities. Nor is any inference to be derived from the use of an answering service by women, either in any particular volume of calls, or outside normal working hours. Night-club entertainers, registered nurses, faith healers, public stenographers, photographic models, and free-lance substitute employees, provide examples of women in legitimate occupations whose employment might cause them to receive a volume of telephone calls at irregular hours.

3. Intent may be inferred from knowledge, when the volume of business with the buyer is grossly disproportionate to any legitimate demand, or when sales for illegal use amount to a high proportion of the seller's total business. In such cases an intent to participate in the illegal enterprise may be inferred from the quantity of the business done. For example, in *Direct Sales*, the sale of narcotics to a rural physician in quantities 300 times greater than he would have normal use for provided potent evidence of an intent to further the illegal activity. In the same case the court also found significant the fact that the wholesaler had attracted as customers a disproportionately large group of physicians who had been convicted of violating the Harrison Act. In *Shaw*, almost the entire business of the directory came from prostitutes.

No evidence of any unusual volume of business with prostitutes was presented by the prosecution against Lauria.

Inflated charges, the sale of goods with no legitimate use, sales in inflated amounts, each may provide a fact of sufficient moment from which the intent of the seller to participate in the criminal enterprise may be inferred. In such instances participation by the supplier of legal goods to the illegal enterprise may be inferred because in one way or another the supplier has acquired a special interest in the operation of the illegal enterprise. His intent to participate in the crime of which he had knowledge may be inferred from the existence of his special interest.

Yet there are cases in which it cannot reasonably be said that the supplier has a stake in the venture or has acquired a special interest in the enterprise, but in which he has been held liable as a participant on the basis of knowledge alone. Some suggestion of this appears in *Direct Sales*, where both the knowledge of the illegal use of the drugs and the intent of the supplier to aid that use were inferred. In *Regina v. Bainbridge* (1959) 3 Week. L. 656, a supplier of oxygen cutting equipment to one known to intend to use it to break into a bank was convicted as an accessory to the crime. In *Sykes v. Director of Public Prosecutions* [1962] A.C. 528, one having knowledge of the theft of 100 pistols, 4 submachine guns, and 1,960 rounds of ammunition was convicted of misprision of felony[A] for failure to disclose the theft to the public authorities. It seems apparent from these cases that a supplier who furnishes equipment which he knows will be used to commit a serious crime may be deemed from that knowledge alone to have intended to produce the result. Such proof may justify an inference that the furnisher intended to aid the execution of the crime and that he thereby became a participant. For instance, we think the operator of a telephone answering service with positive knowledge that his service was being used to facilitate the extortion of ransom, the distribution of heroin, or the passing of counterfeit money who continued to furnish the service with knowledge of 'its use, might be chargeable on knowledge alone with participation in a scheme to extort money, to distribute narcotics, or to pass counterfeit money. The same result would follow the seller of gasoline who knew the buyer was using his product to make Molotov cocktails for terroristic use.

Logically, the same reasoning could be extended to crimes of every description. Yet we do not believe an inference of intent drawn from knowledge of criminal use properly applies to the less serious crimes classified as misdemeanors. The duty to take positive action to dissociate oneself from activities helpful to violations of the criminal law is far stronger and more compelling for felonies than it is for misdemeanors or petty offenses. In this respect, as in others, the distinction between felonies and misdemeanors, between more serious and less serious crime, retains continuing vitality. In historically the most serious felony, treason, an individual with knowledge of the treason can be prosecuted for concealing and failing to disclose it. In other felonies, both at common law and under the criminal laws of the United States, an individual knowing of the commission of a felony is criminally liable for concealing it and failing to make it known to proper authority. But this crime, known as misprision of felony, has always been limited to knowledge and concealment of felony and has never extended to misdemeanor. A similar limitation is found in the criminal liability of an accessory, which is restricted to aid in the escape of a principal who has committed or been charged with a felony. We believe the distinction between the obligations arising from knowledge of a felony and those arising from knowledge of a misdemeanor continues to reflect basic human feelings about the duties owed by individuals to society. Heinous crime must be stamped out, and its suppression is the responsibility of all. Venial crime and crime not evil in itself present less of a danger to society, and perhaps the benefits of their suppression through the modern equivalent of the posse, the hue and cry, the informant, and the citizen's arrest, are outweighed by the disruption to everyday life brought about by amateur law enforcement and private officiousness in relatively inconsequential dialects which do not threaten our basic security.

A. An ancient and almost anachronistic crime, whose gravamen consists of a failure to report known criminal activity.

With respect to misdemeanors, we conclude that positive knowledge of the supplier that his products or services are being used for criminal purposes does not, without more, establish an intent of the supplier to participate in the misdemeanors. With respect to felonies, we do not decide the converse, viz., that in all cases of felony knowledge of criminal use alone may justify an inference of the supplier's intent to participate in the crime. The implications of *Falcone* make the matter uncertain with respect to those felonies which are merely prohibited wrongs.

From this analysis of precedent we deduce the following rule: the intent of a supplier who knows of the criminal use to which his supplies are put to participate in the criminal activity connected with the use of his supplies may be established by (1) direct evidence that he intends to participate, or (2) through an inference that he intends to participate based on, (a) his special interest in the activity, or (b) the aggravated nature of the crime itself.

When we review Lauria's activities in the light of this analysis, we find no proof that Lauria took any direct action to further, encourage, or direct the call-girl activities of his codefendants and we find an absence of circumstance from which his special interest in their activities could be inferred. Neither excessive charges for standardized services, nor the furnishing of services without a legitimate use, nor an unusual quantity of business with call girls, are present. The offense which he is charged with furthering is a misdemeanor, a category of crime which has never been made a required subject of positive disclosure to public authority. Under these circumstances, although proof of Lauria's knowledge of the criminal activities of his patrons was sufficient to charge him with that fact, there was insufficient evidence that he intended to further their criminal activities, and hence insufficient proof of his participation in a criminal conspiracy with his codefendants to further prostitution. Since the conspiracy centered around the activities of Lauria's telephone answering service, the charges against his codefendants likewise fail for want of proof.

In absolving Lauria of complicity in a criminal conspiracy we do not wish to imply that the public authorities are without remedies to combat modern manifestations of the world's oldest profession. Licensing of telephone answering services under the police power, together with the revocation of licenses for the toleration of prostitution, is a possible civil remedy. The furnishing of telephone answering service in aid of prostitution could be made a crime. (*Cf.* Pen. Code § 316, which makes it a misdemeanor to let an apartment with knowledge of its use for prostitution.) Other solutions will doubtless occur to vigilant public authorities if the problem of callgirl activity needs further suppression.

The order is affirmed.

Questions and Notes

1. Would *Lauria* have been decided differently if Lauria had been charged as an accessory before the fact to prostitution?

2. Which, if any, of the *Lauria* factors do you think should be relevant? Should any be determinative?

3. Whatever may be said of the *Lauria* factors insofar as accessorial liability is concerned, what relevance do they have to the issue of intent to agree, the requisite *mens rea* for conspiracy?

4. Is there any good reason to prosecute Lauria for conspiracy rather than as an accessory to the crime of prostitution?

5. The differences between accessorial and conspiratorial liability are explored by both Judge Friendly (for the court) and Judge Oakes (in dissent) in *Brown*.

United States v. Brown

776 F.2d 397 (2d Cir. 1985)

FRIENDLY, Circuit Judge:

This is another case, *see United States v. Peterson*, 768 F.2d 64 (2d Cir. 1985), where the federal narcotics laws have been invoked with respect to the New York City Police Department's Operation Pressure Point in Harlem. Here, as in *Peterson*, Officer William Grimball, acting under cover as an addict, procured a "joint" of heroin, and a backup team promptly pounced on those thought to have been involved in the sale.

The indictment, in the District Court for the Southern District of New York, contained two counts. Count One charged appellant Ronald Brown and a codefendant, Gregory Valentine, with conspiring to distribute and to possess with intent to distribute heroin in violation of 21 U.S.C. § 846. Count Two charged them with distribution of heroin in violation of 21 U.S.C. §§ 812, 841(a)(1), 841(b)(1)(A), and 18 U.S.C. § 2. After a three-day trial, the jury convicted Brown on Count One but was unable to reach a verdict on Count Two.[1] After denying motions for entry of judgment of acquittal or a new trial, the judge suspended imposition of sentence on Count One and placed Brown on three years' probation. Count Two was dismissed with the Government's consent. This appeal followed.

Officer Grimball was the Government's principal witness. He testified that early in the evening of October 9, 1984, he approached Gregory Valentine on the corner of 115th Street and Eighth Avenue and asked him for a joint of "D".[2] Valentine asked Grimball whom he knew around the street. Grimball asked if Valentine knew Scott. He did not. Brown "came up" and Valentine said, "He wants a joint, but I don't know him." Brown looked at Grimball and said, "He looks okay to me." Valentine then said, "Okay. But I am going to leave it somewhere and you [meaning Officer

---

1. Valentine was a fugitive at the time of trial.

2. The officer explained that a "joint' is a street term for a Harlem quarter, or $40 worth of heroin, and that "D' is a street term for heroin.

Grimball] can pick it up." Brown interjected, "You don't have to do that. just go and get it for him. He looks all right to me." After looking again at Grimball, Brown said, "He looks all right to me" and I will wait right here."

Valentine then said, "Okay. Come on with me around to the hotel." Grimball followed him to 300 West 116th Street, where Valentine instructed him, "Sit on the black car and give me a few minutes to go up and get it." Valentine requested and received $40, which had been prerecorded, and then said, "You are going to take care of me for doing this for you, throw some dollars my way?," to which Grimball responded, "Yeah."

Valentine then entered the hotel and shortly returned. The two went back to 115th Street and Eighth Avenue, where Valentine placed a cigarette box on the hood of a blue car. Grimball picked up the cigarette box and found a glassine envelope containing white powder, stipulated to be heroin. Grimball placed $5 of prerecorded buy money in the cigarette box, which he replaced on the hood. Valentine picked up the box and removed the $5. Grimball returned to his car and made a radio transmission to the backup field team that "the buy had went down" and informed them of the locations of the persons involved. Brown and Valentine were arrested. Valentine was found to possess two glassine envelopes of heroin and the $5 of prerecorded money. Brown was in possession of $31 of his own money; no drugs or contraband were found on him. The $40 of marked buy money was not recovered, and no arrests were made at the hotel.

The Government sought to qualify Officer Grimball as an expert on the bases that he had made over 30 street buys of small quantities of cocaine in Harlem, had received two 81/2 hours seminars at the Organized Crime Control Bureau "in respect to street value of drugs, safety, integrity," had once been assigned to the Manhattan North Narcotics Division where he had informal seminars with undercover detectives experienced in making street buys in Harlem target area, and had participated in "ghost operations," where he as undercover would be placed "on the set" and would observe an experienced undercover detective in an actual buy operation. The judge having ruled him to be qualified as an expert, he testified that the typical drug buy in the Harlem area involved two to five people." As a result of frequent police sweeps, Harlem drug dealers were becoming so cautious that they employed "people who act as steerers and the steerer's responsibility is basically to determine whether or not you are actually an addict or a user of heroin and they are also used to screen you to see if there is any possibility of you being a cop looking for a bulge or some indication that would give them that you are not actually an addict. And a lot of the responsibility relies [sic] on them to determine whether or not the drug buy is going to go down or not."

In considering the sufficiency of the evidence, we begin with some preliminary observations. One is that, in testing sufficiency, "the relevant question is whether, after viewing the evidence in the light most favorable to the prosecution, *any* rational trier of fact could have found the essential elements of the crime beyond a reasonable doubt." *Jackson v. Virginia*, 443 U.S. 307, 319 (1979) (emphasis in original). The Court also approved our formulation in *United States v. Taylor*, 464 F.2d 240, 243 (2d Cir. 1972) that if reasonable jurors must necessarily have a reasonable doubt as to guilt, the judge must direct a verdict of acquittal. We repeat these familiar quotations because the beyond a reasonable doubt element tends to become blurred by the Government's standard reliance on language in *Glasser v. United States*, 315 U.S. 60, 80 (1942) ("The verdict of a jury must be sustained if there is substantial evidence, taking the view most favorable to the Government, to support it."). Still *Jackson*'s emphasis on "*any*," while surely not going so far as to excise "rational," must be taken as an admonition to appellate judges not to reverse convictions because they would not have found the elements of the crime to have been proved beyond a reasonable doubt when other rational beings might do so.

The second observation is that since the jury convicted on the conspiracy count alone, the evidence must permit a reasonable juror to be convinced beyond a reasonable doubt not simply that Brown had aided and abetted the drug sale but that he had agreed to do so. On the other hand, the jury's failure to agree on the aiding and abetting charge does not operate against the Government; even an acquittal on that count would not have done so.

A review of the evidence against Brown convinces us that it was sufficient, although barely so. Although Brown's mere presence at the scene of the crime and his knowledge that a crime was being committed would not have been sufficient to establish Brown's knowing participation in the conspiracy, the proof went considerably beyond that. Brown was not simply standing around while the exchanges between Officer Grimball and Valentine occurred. He came on the scene shortly after these began and Valentine immediately explained the situation to him. Brown then conferred his seal of approval on Grimball, a most unlikely event unless there was an established relationship between Brown and Valentine. Finally, Brown took upon himself the serious responsibility of telling Valentine to desist from his plan to reduce the risks by not handing the heroin directly to Grimball. A rational mind could take this as bespeaking the authority to command, or at least to persuade. Brown's remark, "Just go and get it for him" permits inferences that Brown knew where the heroin was to be gotten, that he knew that Valentine knew this, and that Brown and Valentine had engaged in such a transaction before.

The mere fact that these inferences were not ineluctable does not mean that they were insufficient to convince a reasonable juror beyond a reasonable doubt. Moreover, pieces of evidence must be viewed not in isolation but in conjunction. When we add to the inferences that can be reasonably drawn from the facts to which Grimball testified about the use of steerers in street sales of narcotics, we conclude that the Government offered sufficient evidence for a reasonable juror to be satisfied beyond a reasonable doubt not only that Brown has acted as a steerer but that he had agreed to do so.

Affirmed.

OAKES, Circuit Judge (dissenting):

> While it is true that this is another $40 narcotics case, *see e.g., United States v. Peterson*, it is also a conspiracy case, and by the majority's own admission one resting on "barely" sufficient evidence. But evidence of what? An agreement—a "continuous and conscious union of wills upon a common undertaking," in the words of Note, *Developments in the Law—Criminal Conspiracy*, 72 HARV. L. REV. 920, 926 (1959)? Not unless an inference that Brown agreed to act as a "steerer" may be drawn from the fact that he said to Valentine (three times) that Grimball "looks okay [all right] to me." as well as "[j]ust go and get it for him." And that inference may [not] be drawn so as to prove guilt beyond a reasonable doubt from Brown's possession, constructive or otherwise, of narcotics or narcotics paraphernalia, his sharing in the proceeds of the street sale, his conversations with others, or even some hearsay evidence as to his "prior arrangements" with Valentine or "an established working relationship between Brown and Valentine," which are inferences that the majority believes may reasonably be drawn and which it draws. There is not a shred of evidence of Brown's "stake in the outcome," *United States v. Falcone*, 109 F.2d 579, 579 580 (2d Cir.), *aff'd*, 311 U.S. 205 (1940); indeed, Brown was apprehended after leaving the area of the crime with only thirty-one of his own dollars in his pocket, and no drugs or other contraband. He did not even stay around for another Valentine sale, though the majority infers, speculatively, that Brown and Valentine had engaged in "such a transaction before."

When, as the majority concedes, numerous other inferences could be drawn from the few words of conversation in which Brown is said to have engaged, I cannot believe that there is proof of conspiracy, or Brown's membership in it, beyond a reasonable doubt, within the meaning of *Jackson v. Virginia*, unless one gives the Court's emphasis on the word "any"—"any rational trier of fact,"—such weight that the word "rational" receives little or no significance at all. Until now, the court has insisted on proof, whether or not by circumstantial evidence, of a specific agreement to deal." If today we uphold a conspiracy to sell narcotics on the street, on this kind and amount of evidence, what conspiracies might we approve tomorrow? The majority opinion will come back to haunt us, I fear.

As for the rule that "[e]ach count in an indictment is regarded as if it was a separate indictment," *Dunn v. United States*, 284 U.S. 390, 393 (1932) so that acquittal on a substantive count is not fatal to a conviction for conspiracy, the verdicts in this case carry the rule to the ultimate extreme. Here the only overt act attributed in the indictment to Brown was the same conversation with Valentine that grounded the substantive charge of aiding and abetting, a charge on which Brown was acquitted. The case appears to me to be the very kind of compromise verdict foreseen by Judge Learned Hand in *Steckler v. United States*, 7 F.2d 59, 60 (2d Cir. 1925), and by Justice Holmes in *Dunn*. It may be that, in a given case, evidence may support a conviction on an aiding and abetting count without supporting a conviction on a conspiracy count. But it is hard to see how, in the case of a completed sale, there can be a conviction of conspiracy but not of aiding and abetting, especially when there is no evidence of a "stake in the outcome."

Accordingly, I dissent.

Questions and Notes

1. Do you think that the case against Brown for aiding and abetting was stronger or weaker than the case against him for conspiracy?

2. If the aiding and abetting charge is stronger and the jury hung on that, how could the court allow the conspiracy conviction to stand?

3. Reconsider *Bailey v. United States* (Chapter 18, Section A, *supra*). Is the division in *Brown* predicated on the same difference as the division in *Bailey*, i.e., one side allowing the jury to draw natural inferences, and the other side demanding direct proof? Is the only difference between the two cases that two out of three judges demanded direct proof in *Bailey*, but only one of the three judges was so demanding in *Brown*?

4. How would *Brown* be decided under the *Lauria* rationale? *See* NUTSHELL § 16.07.

5. The remainder of the conspiracy materials are devoted to various special rules surrounding this crime.

D. Conspiracy and Complicity

Pinkerton v. United States
328 U.S. 640 (1946)

MR. JUSTICE DOUGLAS delivered the opinion of the Court.

Walter and Daniel Pinkerton are brothers who live a short distance from each other on Daniel's farm. They were indicted for violations of the Internal Revenue Code. The indictment contained ten substantive counts and one conspiracy count. The jury found Walter guilty on nine of the substantive counts and on the conspiracy count. It found Daniel guilty on six of the substantive counts and on the conspiracy count. Walter was fined $500 and sentenced generally on the substantive counts to imprisonment for thirty months. On the conspiracy count he was given a two year sentence to run concurrently with the other sentence. Daniel was fined $1,000 and sentenced generally on the substantive counts to imprisonment for thirty months. On the conspiracy count he was fined $500 and given a two year sentence to run concurrently with the other sentence. The judgments of conviction were affirmed by the Circuit Court of Appeals. The case is here on a petition for a writ of certiorari, which we granted because one of the questions presented involved a conflict between the decision below and *United States v. Sall*, 116 F.2d 745, decided by the Circuit Court of Appeals for the Third Circuit.

A single conspiracy was charged and proved. Some of the overt acts charged in the conspiracy count were the same acts charged in the substantive counts. Each of the substantive offenses found was committed pursuant to the conspiracy. Petitioners therefore contend that the substantive counts became merged in the conspiracy count, and that only a single sentence not exceeding the maximum two year penalty provided by the conspiracy statute could be imposed. Or to state the matter differently, they contend that each of the substantive counts became a separate conspiracy count but, since only a single conspiracy was charged and proved, only a single sentence for conspiracy could be imposed. They rely on *Braverman v. United States*, 317 U.S. 49.

In the *Braverman* case the indictment charged no substantive offense. Each of the several counts charged a conspiracy to violate a different statute. But only one conspiracy was proved. We held that a single conspiracy, charged under the general conspiracy statute, however diverse its objects may be, violates but a single statute and no penalty greater than the maximum provided for one conspiracy may be imposed. That case is not apposite here. For the offenses charged and proved were not only a conspiracy but substantive offenses as well.

Nor can we accept the proposition that the substantive offenses were merged in the conspiracy. There are, of course, instances where a conspiracy charge may not be added to the substantive charge. One is where the agreement of two persons is necessary for the completion of the substantive crime and there is no ingredient in the conspiracy which is not present in the completed crime. Another is where the definition of the substantive offense excludes from punishment for conspiracy one who voluntarily participates in another's crime. *Gebardi*. But those exceptions are of a limited character. The common law rule that the substantive offense, if a felony, was merged in the conspiracy, has little vitality in this country. It has been long and consistently recognized by the Court that the commission of the substantive offense and a conspiracy to commit it are separate and distinct offenses. The power of Congress to separate the two and to affix to each a different penalty is well established.

A conviction for the conspiracy may be had though the substantive offense was completed. And the plea of double jeopardy is no defense to a conviction for both offenses.

Moreover, it is not material that overt acts charged in the conspiracy counts were also charged and proved as substantive offenses. "If the overt act be the offense which was the object of the conspiracy, and is also punished, there is not a double punishment of it." The agreement to do an unlawful act is even then distinct from the doing of the act. It is contended that there was insufficient evidence to implicate Daniel in the conspiracy. But we think there was enough evidence for submission of the issue to the jury.

There is, however, no evidence to show that Daniel participated directly in the commission of the substantive offenses on which his conviction has been sustained, although there was evidence to show that these substantive offenses were in fact committed by Walter in furtherance of the unlawful agreement or conspiracy existing between the brothers. The question was submitted to the jury on the theory that each petitioner could be found guilty of the substantive offenses, if it was found at the time those offenses were committed petitioners were parties to an unlawful conspiracy and the substantive offenses charged were in fact committed in furtherance of it.

Daniel relies on *Sall, supra*. That case held that participation in the conspiracy was not itself enough to sustain a conviction for the substantive offense even though it was committed in furtherance of the conspiracy. The court held that, in addition to evidence that the offense was in fact committed in furtherance of the conspiracy, evidence of direct participation in the commission of the substantive offense or other evidence from which participation might fairly be inferred was necessary.

We take a different view. We have here a continuous conspiracy. There is here no evidence of the affirmative action on the part of Daniel which is necessary to establish his withdrawal from it. As stated in that case, "Having joined in an unlawful scheme, having constituted agents for its performance, scheme and agency to be continuous until full fruition be secured, until he does some act to disavow or defeat the purpose he is in no situation to claim the delay of the law. As the offense has not been terminated or accomplished he is still offending. And we think, consciously offending, offending as certainly, as we have said, as at the first moment of his confederation, and consciously through every moment of its existence." And so long as the partnership in crime continues, the partners act for each other in carrying it forward. It is settled that "an overt act of one partner may be the act of all without any new agreement specifically directed to that act The criminal intent to do the act is established by the formation of the conspiracy. Each conspirator instigated the commission of the crime. The unlawful agreement contemplated precisely what was done. It was formed for the purpose. The act done was in execution of the enterprise. The rule which holds responsible one who counsels, procures, or commands another to commit a crime is founded on the same principle. That principle is recognized in the law of conspiracy when the overt act of one partner in crime is attributable to all. An overt act is an essential ingredient of the crime of conspiracy. If that can be supplied by the act of one conspirator, we fail to see why the same or other acts in furtherance of the conspiracy are likewise not attributable to the others for the purpose of holding them responsible for the substantive offense.

A different case would arise if the substantive offense committed by one of the conspirators was not in fact done in furtherance of the conspiracy, did not fall within the scope of the unlawful project, or was merely a part of the ramifications of the plan which could not be reasonably foreseen as a necessary or natural consequence of the unlawful agreement. But as we read this record, that is not this case.

Affirmed.

Mr. Justice Rutledge, dissenting in part.

The judgment concerning Daniel Pinkerton should be reversed. In my opinion it is without precedent here and is a dangerous precedent to establish.

Daniel and Walter, who were brothers living near each other, were charged in several counts with substantive offenses, and then a conspiracy count was added naming those offenses as overt acts. The proof showed that Walter alone committed the substantive crimes. There was none to establish that Daniel participated in them, aided and abetted Walter in committing them, or knew that he had done so. Daniel in fact was in the penitentiary, under sentence for other crimes, when some of Walter's crimes were done.

There was evidence, however, to show that over several years Daniel and Walter had confederated to commit similar crimes concerned with unlawful possession, transportation, and dealing in whiskey, in fraud of the federal revenues. On this evidence both were convicted of conspiracy. Walter also was convicted on the substantive counts on the proof of his committing the crimes charged. Then, on that evidence without more than the proof of Daniel's criminal agreement with Walter and the latter's overt acts, which were also the substantive offenses charged, the court told the jury they could find Daniel guilty of those substantive offenses. They did so.

I think this ruling violates both the letter and the spirit of what Congress did when it separately defined the three classes of crime, namely, (1) completed substantive offenses; (2) aiding, abetting or counseling another to commit them; and (3) conspiracy to commit them. Not only does this ignore the distinctions Congress has prescribed shall be observed. It either convicts one man for another's crime or punishes the man convicted twice for the same offense.

The three types of offense are not identical. Nor are their differences merely verbal. The gist of conspiracy is the agreement; that of aiding, abetting or counseling is in consciously advising or assisting another to commit particular offenses, and thus becoming a party to them; that of substantive crime, going a step beyond mere aiding, abetting, counseling to completion of the offense. These general differences are well understood. But when conspiracy has ripened into completed crime, or has advanced to the stage of aiding and abetting, it becomes easy to disregard their differences and loosely to treat one as identical with the other, that is, for every purpose except the most vital one of imposing sentence. And thus the substance, if not the technical effect, of double jeopardy or multiple punishment may be accomplished. Thus also may one be convicted of an offense not charged or proved against him, on evidence showing he committed another.

The old doctrine of merger of conspiracy in the substantive crime has not obtained here. But the dangers for abuse, which in part it sought to avoid, in applying the law of conspiracy have not altogether disappeared. There is some evidence that they may be increasing. The looseness with which the charge may be proved, the almost unlimited scope of vicarious responsibility for others' acts which follows once agreement is shown, the psychological advantages of such trials for securing convictions by attributing to one proof against another, these and other inducements require that the broad limits of discretion allowed to prosecuting officers in relation to such charges and trials be not expanded into new, wider and more dubious areas of choice. If the matter is not generally of constitutional proportions, it is one for the exercise of this Court's supervisory power over the modes of conducting federal criminal prosecutions.

I think that power should be exercised in this case with respect to Daniel's conviction. If it does not violate the letter of constitutional right, it fractures the spirit. Daniel has been held guilty of the substantive crimes committed only by Walter on proof that he did no more than conspire with him to commit offenses of the same general character. There was no evidence that he counseled, advised or had knowledge of those particular acts or offenses. There was, therefore, none that he aided, abetted or took part in them. There was only evidence sufficient to show that he had agreed with Walter at some past time to engage in such transactions generally. As to Daniel this was only evidence of conspiracy, not of substantive crime.

The Court's theory seems to be that Daniel and Walter became general partners in crime by virtue of their agreement and because of that agreement without more on his part Daniel became criminally responsible as a principal for everything Walter did thereafter in the nature of a criminal offense of the general sort the agreement contemplated, so long as there was not clear evidence that Daniel had withdrawn from or revoked the agreement. Whether or not his commitment to the penitentiary had that effect, the result is a vicarious criminal responsibility as broad as, or broader than, the vicarious civil liability of a partner for acts done by a copartner in the course of the firm's business.

Such analogies from private commercial law and the law of torts are dangerous, in my judgment, for transfer to the criminal field. Guilt there with us remains personal, not vicarious, for the more serious offenses. It should be kept so. The effect of Daniel's conviction in this case, to repeat, is either to attribute to him Walter's guilt or to punish him twice for the same offense, namely, agreeing with Walter to engage in crime. Without the agreement Daniel was guilty of no crime on this record. With it and no more, so far as his own conduct is concerned, he was guilty of two.

Questions and Notes

1. Why does an agreement to violate more than one law constitute only one conspiracy?

2. Do the majority and dissent differ as to whether the crimes committed by Daniel were within the scope of the conspiracy?

3. Did Daniel share in the proceeds of the crime?

4. Would proof that Daniel shared in the proceeds of the crime have affected Justice Rutledge's dissenting opinion?

5. Would proof that Daniel did not share in the proceeds of the crime have affected Justice Douglas's majority opinion?

6. If you had been on the Court, would you have concurred with Justice Douglas or Justice Rutledge? *See* NUTSHELL § 16.03.

7. The Court emphasized Daniel's failure to take steps to withdraw from the conspiracy. There is some difference of opinion among courts as to how much one must do to withdraw, and what the effect of that withdrawal is. These issues are explored in *Read*.

E. Withdrawal

United States v. Read

658 F.2d 1225 (7th Cir. 1981)

BAUER, Circuit Judge.

Defendants-appellants Ralph Read, Ronald E. Spiegel, and Howard Swiger appeal their convictions for conspiracy, mail fraud, and securities fraud. We affirm the judgments of conviction entered for Ralph Read and Howard Swiger in Nos. 80-1017 and 80-1019. We reverse Ronald Spiegel's conviction for conspiracy in No. 80-1018 and remand for a new trial. We affirm Spiegel's conviction on the substantive counts.

The indictment charged a scheme to artificially inflate the year-end inventory of Cenco Medical Health Supply Corporation ("CMH") and thus increase its reported profits. The defendants-appellants were officers of CMH and Cenco, CMH's parent corporation. Ralph Read was president of Cenco and a member of its board of directors; Ronald Spiegel was a vice-president of Cenco, and president of CMH; Howard Swiger was also a vice-president of Cenco and comptroller of CMH. Other defendants—Russell Rabjohns, Bernard Magdovitz, and Jack Carlson—pled guilty to two counts and testified for the government. Another defendant, Robert Smith, was acquitted.

We need only briefly outline the evidence at trial showing defendants' massive manipulation of CMH's finances from 1970 to 1975. The greatest amount of the fraud was accomplished by overstating CMH's inventory. During annual inventory, each CMH branch recorded the amount of every item in stock on computer cards. When the cards were returned to the central Chicago office for processing, some of the defendants, at Spiegel's direction, increased the numbers on the cards. Thousands of cards were altered in this fashion; defendants made additional changes in the computer listings of the inventory that CMH submitted to its auditors. In 1970, defendants increased the reported inventory of CMH by 3.5 million dollars. In each succeeding year, defendants increased the inventory by several millions more and carried the previous years' inflation forward. The overstatement of inventory decreased CMH's cost of sales, which in turn produced greater reported profits, dollar-for-dollar. This practice continued until 1975. Estimates of the total fraud ranged from 20 to 25 million dollars.

Other methods included inflating profits by accruing sales in one year and deferring expenses for those sales until the next fiscal year. The defendants also increased reported sales by listing the sales from August 1972 on computer printouts for March 1973 sales. They also created fake documents showing hundreds of thousands of dollars of non-existent inventory to be in transit between warehouses so that it could not be physically counted.

In 1974, Curtiss-Wright Corporation, a large conglomerate, purchased five percent of Cenco's shares. Curtiss-Wright's accountants, while examining Cenco's finances for a possible loan, found discrepancies in Cenco's inventory records. Alarmed, the defendants sought to create the appearance of $10 million of nonexistent inventory should Curtiss-Wright's auditors physically check the inventory. In order to do so, they ordered the repacking of obsolete inventory in boxes of expensive products. Finally, in 1975, the defendants implemented an inventory destruction program to cover up the fraud. The defendants persuaded Cenco's board of directors to approve the destruction of $16 million of obsolete inventory as part of a supposed tax savings program. Almost all of the "destroyed" inventory existed only on paper.

The ultimate result of the fraud was to overstate the profitability of Cenco, thereby defrauding its board, its stockholders, and the SEC. The prosecution also showed that Read's compensation was linked to the company's profits.

The indictment charged the defendants with conspiracy, mail fraud, and securities fraud. On September 6, 1979, the case proceeded to trial against Read, Spiegel, Swiger, and Smith. On October 29, 1979, following almost eight weeks of testimony, the jury returned guilty verdicts on all counts as to Read, Spiegel, and Swiger. Smith was acquitted. Read, Spiegel, and Swiger appeal their convictions.

Ronald Spiegel's main defense at trial was that he withdrew from the conspiracy more than five years before the indictment was filed. He argued that his prosecution therefore was barred by the statute of limitations. Spiegel argues on appeal that the trial court gave erroneous instructions on the issue of withdrawal.

The trial court instructed the jury:

"Now, we talked about withdrawal. How does a person withdraw from a conspiracy? A person can withdraw from a conspiracy, and in such a case he is not liable for the acts of his former co-conspirators after his withdrawal. A defendant may withdraw by notifying co-conspirators that he will no longer participate in the undertaking. A defendant may also withdraw from a conspiracy by engaging in acts inconsistent with the objects of the conspiracy. These acts or statements need not be known or communicated to all other co-conspirators as long as they are communicated in a manner reasonably calculated to reach some of them. To withdraw from a conspiracy there is no requirement that a conspirator try to convince the other co-conspirators to abandon their undertaking or that he go to public authorities or others to expose the conspiracy or to prevent the carrying out of an act involved in the conspiracy. But a withdrawal defense requires that a defendant completely abandon the conspiracy and that he do so in good faith. If you find that a defendant completely withdrew from the conspiracy before the 24th of April, 1974, you should acquit him. If you find that he was a member on April 24, 1974, and that an overt act was committed while he was still a member, his later withdrawal, if any, standing alone, is not a defense.

"Why do we pick the date 'April 24th, 1974'? We do that because the indictment in this case, as you will see, bears a stamp, the Clerk's stamp that it was filed on April 24th, 1979. There is a five-year statute of limitations for criminal conspiracy and the charge—and the five year statute of limitations runs from the date of the last overt act in the indictment to the date of the filing of the indictment. Accordingly, if you find that an overt act was committed within five years before April 24, 1979—another way of saying that is that if you find that an overt act was committed between April 24th, 1974 and August of 1975, the conspiracy count in its entirety may be considered by you, going all the way back to 1970 or earlier."

Spiegel objected to the above instructions. He attacks the propriety of instructing the jury that the withdrawal must be in good faith. He further asserts that the instruction erroneously allowed the jury to find that he participated in the conspiracy after the limitations date by proof of overt acts not alleged in the indictment.

Spiegel also claims he withdrew before commission of the securities and mail fraud crimes. He complains that the jury was not instructed that his withdrawal was effective if it occurred before the dates of the sales or mailings charged in the indictment.

Withdrawal marks a conspirator's disavowal or abandonment of the conspiratorial agreement. By definition, after a defendant withdraws, he is no longer a member of the conspiracy and the later acts of the conspirators do not bind him. The defendant is still liable, however, for his previous agreement and for the previous acts of his co-conspirators in pursuit of the conspiracy. Withdrawal is not, therefore, a complete defense to the crime of conspiracy. Withdrawal becomes a complete defense only when coupled with the defense of the statute of limitations. A defendant's withdrawal from the conspiracy starts the running of the statute of limitations as to him. If the indictment is filed more than five years after a defendant withdraws, the statute of limitations bars prosecution for his actual participation in the conspiracy. He cannot be held liable for acts or declarations committed in the five years preceding the indictment by other conspirators because his withdrawal ended his membership in the conspiracy. It is thus only the interaction of the two defenses of withdrawal and the statute of limitations which shields the defendant from liability.

We reject Spiegel's objections to the withdrawal instructions. Acts not alleged in the indictment may be proved to show his participation within the statute of limitations. The jury was properly instructed that Spiegel had to withdraw before any act committed within the statute of limitations period.

Good faith may also be required to withdraw. The defendant must put forth some evidence of good faith, although the burden of persuasion is always on the government.

Spiegel also attacks the court's instruction on withdrawal from the securities and mail fraud charges. The judge instructed the jury on the mail fraud counts that "one can withdraw from a scheme to defraud the same way one withdraws from a conspiracy, and you know what has to be shown before you can establish that withdrawal." Spiegel complains that the jury should have been instructed that his withdrawal was effective if he withdrew before the date of the mailings or securities transactions. We reject Spiegel's contention for the more fundamental reason that Spiegel was not entitled to an instruction on withdrawal for the substantive offenses.

A scheme to defraud and conspiracy embrace analogous, but not identical, concepts. The primary analogy between the two crimes is evidentiary. The evidentiary rule that statements and acts of co-conspirators are relevant and admissible against other conspirators applies in mail and securities fraud cases in which an overall scheme to defraud is charged.

The elements of the offenses are, however, different. The predicate for liability for conspiracy is an agreement, and a defendant is punished for his membership in that agreement. Mail and securities fraud, on the other hand, punish the act of using the mails or the securities exchanges to further a scheme to defraud. No agreement is necessary. A party's "withdrawal" from a scheme is therefore no defense to the crime because membership in the scheme is not an element of the offense. Spiegel is liable for mail fraud as a principal or as an aider and abettor, not a conspirator. As an aider and abettor, Spiegel need not agree to the scheme. He need only associate himself with the criminal venture and participate in it.

The evidence here overwhelmingly showed Spiegel's association and participation in the mail and securities frauds. He directed the inventory inflation scheme which largely contributed to the false statements contained in the mailings and disclosure statements. The mailings and sales were an inevitable consequence of his actions. Spiegel "could properly be found to be jointly responsible . . . for setting the scheme in motion . . . and thus causing the mailings by third parties."

Nor is the statute of limitations implicated here. The statute of limitations begins to run from the date of the mailings or stock sales. Like a person who sets a bomb with a timed fuse, Spiegel is responsible from the moment the bomb explodes, even though all his actions occurred before the statutory period. All the mailings and sales occurred within five years of the indictment. Accordingly, the prosecution was timely. Of course, as in any prosecution, proof of conduct prior to the statute of limitations is admissible to show the scheme and intent.

Since we hold that withdrawal is not an available defense to the substantive counts, Spiegel was not entitled to an instruction regarding withdrawal. His conviction on the securities and mail fraud counts was therefore proper.

Questions and Notes

1. What must one do to withdraw from a conspiracy according to *Read?*

2. What ought the criteria to be?

3. What is the significance of withdrawal?

4. Why couldn't Spiegel withdraw from the substantive offenses before they were committed?

5. In Corson, we see an issue somewhat analogous to impossibility in attempt.

United States v. Corson

579 F.3d 804 (7th Cir. 2009)

TINDER, Circuit Judge.

Marcus Corson and Oscar Alvarez were charged with two conspiracies, one to rob a drug stash house and the other to sell what they planned to steal. This seems straightforward enough. But there's a twist. There never was any stash house to rob. Nor were there any drugs. And the two people who introduced **Corson** and Alvarez to the stash house plan never intended to rob anything. That's because one was a government agent and the other a confidential informant ("CI"). This fictitious stash house plot was concocted by law enforcement to entice all-too-eager gangsters to agree to do something illegal.

In the end, there was no robbery, and nobody testified that they saw the defendants with firearms. But the jury convicted on both counts.

Corson and Alvarez appeal their convictions. If judges sat in a policy-making role, perhaps we might have reason to wonder whether this scheme was the right use of law enforcement resources. But directing policy is not within our province. Instead, in this case, our duty is to assess whether the evidence was sufficient for a jury to convict. It's an uphill battle to overturn a jury verdict. Assessing credibility of witnesses and interpreting the evidence are tasks ordinarily left to the jury. After reviewing the record we conclude that there was sufficient evidence for the jury to find guilt beyond a reasonable doubt. We affirm their convictions.

I. Background

The Bureau of Alcohol, Tobacco and Firearms ("ATF") hatched their stash house sting operation in early November 2006. ATF agents met with the CI and asked whether he knew anyone who might be interested in robbing a drug stash house.

The CI identified Marcus Corson and his brother Aaron. (Aaron Corson was also tried and convicted but he withdrew his appeal. To avoid confusion, we will hereafter refer to the Corson brothers by their first names only.) So the ATF instructed the CI to make contact. The CI called Marcus and told him about a "business opportunity." Marcus showed some interest and on November 8 told the CI to meet him at the home of the third defendant, Oscar Alvarez, that day.

The CI showed up to Alvarez's place wearing a body wire, a digital recording device that would capture their conversations. The jury would hear and read a transcription of all of what was said. The CI started to tell Marcus and Alvarez about the plan, describing how he worked security for a guy he met in prison named Loquito, or "Loqs," who worked for a Mexican drug organization. (Of course, there was no Mexican drug organization and "Loquito" was actually an undercover ATF agent.) Before the CI mentioned the robbery, though, Marcus and Alvarez jumped in and asked whether the CI was talking about a "gank" (meaning a heist). When the CI responded affirmatively, Alvarez asked, "How much you talkin'?" to which the CI responded "bricks" of cocaine (the coke, not money, was the target of the robbery). Marcus got excited and Alvarez asked the CI whether he was talking about "runnin and robbin' some niggas" and to "make it clear, the details."

The CI explained the operation: Loquito would not know the location of the stash house until just one hour before the drugs arrived; but once he knew the location, he would call the CI. Then the Corson-Alvarez crew could execute the robbery. Marcus and Alvarez probed the CI for details. Marcus asked if the stash house guards would be "strapped, too," meaning carrying firearms. The CI said they probably would be. But that didn't matter. Marcus and Alvarez said they were in. Marcus: "I'm down, bro. That ain't no thing. I'm down. Ain't a question." Alvarez: "We in it. We in it a hundred percent, bro." As for the guards, Marcus said he wouldn't hesitate to kill them. Marcus then told the CI that his brother Aaron would be involved too and that the three of them had done robberies in the past. They agreed to meet the next day.

During all this Marcus and Alvarez repeatedly expressed their concern-not over whether the plan was real, but whether the drugs would certainly be at the stash house: "if you send us in, the shit gotta be there, bro. He gotta know if it's there." Marcus repeated this ultimatum: "But the only thing is . . . you gotta make sure this shit's there." And so did Alvarez: "But, ya know what I'm sayin', if shit don't go right, nigga, that falls on you and him." The CI assured them the drugs would be there.

* * *

All three repeatedly reconfirmed their commitment to the robbery. Marcus: "you got your squad." Aaron: "I'm ready, man." Loquito said he needed a "professional crew." They reiterated that they were experienced and that they would be the "final crew." Alvarez: "I assured you it straight, so it straight." Aaron: "I'm ready, man"; "Just you do your part. We're gonna do ours, bro." Marcus: "[Y]ou got your squad";

"Man, it's on, dog." Then, one more time, Loquito confirmed the participation of all three . . .

* * *

They finished the conversation discussing how they would split the proceeds or the "chops," as they called it. After some back-and-forth, mostly between Marcus and Alvarez, they settled on an equal share for all five involved. They left with the expectation that Loquito would call when he heard the deal was about to go down. And Loquito could get a hold of them easily, because "we're all a team." As Aaron put it, "You got the president hotline right now, man. That call comes in, everything stops, bro."

On November 27, the CI called Marcus to tell him the robbery might be the next day. On November 28, the CI called Marcus after Marcus got off work and told him that Loquito wanted to talk to them again about the robbery. Marcus responded, "I don't want to see dude again," referring to Loquito. The CI called back a few minutes later and asked whether he was "in or not." Marcus said, "I'm straight." After a few more calls, Marcus agreed to meet up.

Alvarez and the Corsons drove to a shopping mall parking lot to meet the CI and Loquito, who were already there. The CI (wearing the body wire) went over and got in Marcus's car. Marcus expressed some frustration about Loquito. Alvarez asked if Loquito was "just waitin' on the call and shit," and the CI responded affirmatively. Then Marcus complained that the CI and Loquito had parked their car in a way that might stick out to law enforcement. So Marcus started driving around the mall parking lot. (An ATF agent opined at trial that such a tactic is known as a "heat run," where a suspect drives around to see if he's being followed.) Aaron asked whether the Mexican cartel had people following them; the CI said he didn't know. Aaron then asked the CI, "Are you strapped, too, right now or what?" referring to whether the CI was armed. The CI said he had a gun in Loquito's car. Marcus chimed in, "So, it's basically a waiting game, right?" The CI responded, "Yep, Waitin' on that call."

* * *

After the CI took a call from Loquito, the CI started to get out and head back to Loquito's car to check on things. The CI asked the defendants whether he should call them when Loquito got the location on the stash house. Marcus said, "We just gonna go relocate in another spot. . . . as soon as you get the call, just call us, and then we're just gonna be waitin'." The defendants drove away and never came back. Loquito called them several times to try to salvage the sting but to no avail. He asked them to reconfirm their commitment to the robbery but they refused. The sting was over.

The defendants weren't arrested that day, but about two weeks later. A search of defendants' residences revealed little evidence, only a baggie of bullets at Alvarez's apartment. The defendants were indicted on two conspiracy counts: (1) conspiracy to possess with intent to distribute five or more kilograms of cocaine, in violation of 21 U.S.C. §§ 841(a)(1) and 846; and (2) conspiracy to obstruct, delay or affect commerce, and the movement of a commodity in commerce, by means of robbery, in violation of 18 U.S.C. § 1951. After hearing from ATF agents, including "Loquito," as well as hearing the recordings of the conversations picked up over the body wire, the jury convicted the defendants of both counts.

* * *

Only Marcus and Alvarez appeal. They both appeal their convictions, arguing insufficient evidence. . . .

II. Sufficiency of the Evidence (Both Marcus and Alvarez)

Marcus and Alvarez face a "nearly insurmountable hurdle" in this challenge to the sufficiency of the evidence to sustain their convictions. *United States v. Moore*, 572 F.3d 334, 337 (7th Cir.2009) (quotation omitted). To reverse, we must be convinced that even "after viewing the evidence in the light most favorable to the prosecution, no rational trier of fact could have found him guilty beyond a reasonable doubt." *Id.* We will not "weigh the evidence or second-guess the jury's credibility determinations." *United States v. Stevens*, 453 F.3d 963, 965 (7th Cir. 2006) (quotation omitted). Nor will we "overturn a conviction because we would have voted to acquit." *Id.* Rather, "we will overturn a conviction based on insufficient evidence only if the record is devoid of evidence from which a reasonable jury could find guilt beyond a reasonable doubt." *United States v. Farris*, 532 F.3d 615, 618 (7th Cir.) (citation omitted).

The jury convicted Marcus and Alvarez of conspiring to rob a drug stash house and sell their loot. "Conspiracy is agreement to violate some other law." Though it might seem odd, the fact that the stash house, the drugs-indeed the whole plot-was fake is irrelevant. That the crime agreed upon was in fact impossible to commit is no defense to the crime of conspiracy. *United States v. Shively*, 715 F.2d 260, 266 (7th Cir. 1983). The crime of conspiracy is the agreement itself. *See United States v. Shabani*, 513 U.S. 10, 11, 115 S.Ct. 382, 130 L.Ed.2d 225 (1994).

* * *

So in this case, the government must prove just that Marcus and Alvarez agreed to rob the stash house and sell the drugs, and that they "knowingly and intentionally join[ed] the agreement." *United States v. Rollins*, 544 F.3d 820, 835 (7th Cir. 2008). Alone, idle chitchat or mere boasting about one's criminal past is insufficient to establish a conspiracy. Specifically, proof of a drug conspiracy under 21 U.S.C. § 846 requires "substantial evidence that the defendant knew of the illegal objective of the conspiracy and agreed to participate." Yet, "[t]he agreement need not be formal, and the government may establish that agreement, as it may other elements of the charge, through circumstantial evidence[. . .]."

Moreover, an agreement must exist among *coconspirators,* that is, those who actually intend to carry out the agreed-upon criminal plan. A defendant is not liable for conspiring solely with an undercover government agent or a government informant.

Marcus and Alvarez challenge their conspiracy convictions in two ways. First, they contend that they never agreed to violate the law. Instead, they merely boasted and "talked tough," but, they submit, that talk never crystallized to form an agreement to do something illegal. (They assert no claim of entrapment.) Second, they contend that they never agreed with one another. If they agreed with anyone, they argue, they each agreed with the CI or the undercover agent, which is not a conspiracy.

The record proves them wrong on both points. Marcus and Alvarez did much more than talk tough. There was ample evidence to support the jury's finding that the defendants agreed to rob the stash house and sell their loot (keep in mind that the government gets the benefit of all reasonable inferences that can be drawn from the trial evidence,: (1) the defendants met with the CI multiple times to discuss the robbery; (2) during each meeting the defendants sought details about the plan, such as whether the stash house guards were armed, how much coke would be there, and when the robbery would take place; (3) the defendants said they were willing to kill if necessary and indicated they had strong firepower to counter that of the guards; (4) they repeatedly discussed how they would execute the robbery-who would ride with whom, how the defendants would drive to the stash house, how many lookouts to have, and whether to go in quietly or "bum rush" like a "police raid"; (5) they acknowledged the quantity of drugs they expected ("15, 20 keys") and discussed the "chops," or how they would divide up their loot; (6) they repeatedly expressed concern that the coke had to be there; if it wasn't, the defendants made clear that there would be consequences for the CI and "Loquito"; (7) the defendants showed up at the staging location on the day the robbery was to take place; (8) Aaron asked the CI if he was "strapped, too," implying the defendants were armed as well; (9) Marcus said his car was the "getaway ride" and that he didn't want Loquito to see it; (10) Marcus did a "heat run" to avoid police detection and said he felt Loquito had parked too conspicuously; and (11) the defendants time and again reaffirmed their commitment to doing the robbery-"I'm in," "it's gravy," "I'm down," "done deal," "we got the crew," "it's on, dog," "we in it a hundred percent, bro."

All of this evidence showed an intent to carry out the stash house robbery. Moreover, it showed an agreement among the defendants to do so. Accordingly we must conclude that a rational jury could find the defendants guilty of conspiracy beyond a reasonable doubt.

Marcus and Alvarez try to poke holes in this evidence, but to no avail. For instance, they argue that Aaron's "strapped, too" question did not imply that the defendants were armed. This squares with the district court's conclusion at sentencing that the defendants were not armed. This is because, according to the defendants, Aaron actually said "strapped-to," which simply meant "armed," rather than the government's translation "strapped, too," which meant "armed as well." (The government's transcription of the body-wire recording says "strapped, too." The defense did not offer an alternate transcription for the jury.) In support, the defendants point to another occasion when Marcus used the same phrase in asking whether the stash house guards were armed. In that situation, the defendants contend, Marcus couldn't have meant "armed as well" since he wouldn't have been referring to himself, and therefore "strapped, too" should have been understood as "strapped-to."

But the record does not require that conclusion. Even though the district court came to a different conclusion at sentencing, we must view the evidence in a different light. (Remember that on a sufficiency-of-the-evidence challenge, we draw all reasonable inferences in the government's favor.) Why couldn't Marcus have been referring to himself as being armed as well? The defendants repeatedly talked about their own firearms and their willingness to kill when asking about the stash house guards. Moreover, the jury heard the word "strapped" referring to "armed" two more times, without hearing the word "too" (or "-to") along with it. In one instance, Aaron asked if the guards would be "strapped-up." And then later, when discussing how they would enter the stash house, Marcus said, "We could come around the corner, Joe, *strapped*, and get in that door, Joe." (emphasis added). So the contention that the defendants always used the term "strapped-to" to mean "armed" is belied by these other statements. With that, we conclude that the inference that "strapped, too" meant "armed as well" was a reasonable one, and as such, must conclude that Aaron asked the CI whether he, like the defendants, was also carrying firearms.

Likewise, when Marcus told the CI, "I'm straight," on November 28, the day the robbery was to take place, the jury need not necessarily have concluded, as the defendants suggest, that Marcus meant that he didn't want any part of the robbery. Nothing in the record requires that conclusion. In fact, the record suggests the opposite. During the November 20 meeting, Alvarez reconfirmed to Loquito his commitment to the robbery plan by saying, "I assured you it straight, so it straight."

Essentially, the defendants ask us to reweigh the evidence. They argue that the defendants never contacted the CI on their own, the CI always called first; that they met infrequently; that the defendants exhibited an uneasiness about the undercover officer (e.g., "I don't want to see dude again"); that Marcus worked on the day of the robbery, contrary to prior plans; and that despite boasting about being experienced thieves, neither the CI nor the agents saw or found any cash, guns, or anything else typically associated with that activity (indeed, there was some evidence that Alvarez lived on the floor of his mother's apartment-though this might have been construed as an incentive for Alvarez to participate in a lucrative robbery). But these are arguments more appropriate for a jury than for an appellate court-in fact, these *were* the defendants' arguments to the jury in this case.

The fact that the defendants drove away before actually going to the "stash house" falls in this category as well. The agreement—and thus the crime of conspiracy— was already complete. Even if their disappearance from the staging area is viewed as withdrawal, it would not absolve them of all liability. The defendants argue that this is evidence that a conspiracy never existed in the first place. But the jury rejected that interpretation in finding the defendants guilty. We cannot conclude that was an erroneous decision. The evidence was sufficient to establish that the defendants agreed to rob the fictitious stash house.

So was the evidence establishing that the defendants agreed with one another, and not just with the CI or the undercover agent. The defendants bantered back and forth between each other about the plan of attack. They discussed among themselves how they would divide the loot, or the "chop," as they called it. They talked about their prior experience doing robberies together. They showed up to the mall parking lot on the day of the robbery riding in the same car together. And, of course, they each reiterated their willingness to participate, while in each other's company and referring to themselves as a group. They were a "team," a "squad," the "final crew." We conclude that this was sufficient evidence for a rational jury to conclude that the defendants agreed, amongst themselves, to the robbery plan. Accordingly, we affirm the defendants' convictions

Questions and Notes

1. Even if you agree with the court's conclusion that there was sufficient evidence to sustain a conviction for conspiracy to commit robbery, was there also sufficient evidence to sustain a conviction for conspiracy to distribute? Marcus, Aaron, and Alvarez never really cared what the others did with their share of the cocaine once it was stolen, did they?

2. Is the fact that the alleged conspirators never went through with the pretend robbery merely evidence that they withdrew (no defense) or is it also evidence that they were never serious in the first place (valid defense)? Is (should) this be a jury question?

3. Should the defendants have asserted entrapment? If they had, could they have succeeded? Why? Why not?

4. The ubiquitous character of conspiracy is explored in *Krulewitch* (particularly Justice Jackson's famous concurring opinion).

F. Procedural Peculiarities

Krulewitch v. United States
336 U.S. 440 (1949)

MR. JUSTICE BLACK delivered the opinion of the Court.

A federal district court indictment charged in three counts that petitioner and a woman defendant had (1) induced and persuaded another woman to go on October 20, 1941, from New York City to Miami, Florida, for the purpose of prostitution, in violation of 18 U.S.C. § 399 (now § 2422); (2) transported or caused her to be transported from New York to Miami for that purpose, in violation of 18 U.S.C.

§ 398 (now § 2421); and (3) conspired to commit those offenses in violation of 18 U.S.C. § 88 (now § 371). Tried alone, the petitioner was convicted on all three counts of the indictment. We granted certiorari limiting our review to consideration of alleged error in admission of certain hearsay testimony against petitioner over his timely and repeated objections.

The challenged testimony was elicited by the Government from its complaining witness, the person whom petitioner and the woman defendant allegedly induced to go from New York to Florida for the purpose of prostitution. The testimony narrated the following purported conversation between the complaining witness and petitioner's alleged co-conspirator, the woman defendant.

'She asked me, she says, 'You didn't talk yet?' And I says, 'No And she says, 'Well, don't,' she says, 'until we get you a lawyer. 'And then she says, 'Be very careful what you say. 'And I can't put it in exact words. But she said, 'It would be better for us two girls to take the blame than Kay (the defendant) because he couldn't stand it, he couldn't stand to take it.'"

The time of the alleged conversation was more than a month and a half after October 20, 1941, the date the complaining witness had gone to Miami. Whatever original conspiracy may have existed between petitioner and his alleged coconspirator to cause the complaining witness to go to Florida in October 1941, no longer existed when the reported conversation took place in December 1941. For on this latter date the trip to Florida had not only been made-the complaining witness had left Florida, had returned to New York, and had resumed her residence there. Furthermore, at the time the conversation took place, the complaining witness, the alleged co-conspirator, and the petitioner had been arrested. They apparently were charged in a United States District Court of Florida with the offense of which petitioner was here convicted.[1]

It is beyond doubt that the central aim of the alleged conspiracy—transportation of the complaining witness to Florida for prostitution—had either never existed or had long since ended in success or failure when and if the alleged coconspirator made the statement attributed to her. The statement plainly implied that petitioner was guilty of the crime for which he was on trial. It was made in petitioner's absence and the Government made no effort whatever to show that it was made with his authority. The testimony thus stands as an unsworn, out-of-court declaration of petitioner's guilt. This hearsay declaration, attributed to a co-conspirator, was not made pursuant to and in furtherance of objectives of the conspiracy charged in the indictment, because if made, it was after those objectives either had failed or had been achieved. Under these circumstances, the hearsay declaration attributed to the

---

1. The Florida grand jury failed to indict and the cases there were closed without prosecution in February 1942. The New York indictments were not returned until January 1943.

alleged co-conspirator was not admissible on the theory that it was made in further-ance of the alleged criminal transportation undertaking.

Although the Government recognizes that the chief objective of the conspiracy—transportation for prostitution purposes—had ended in success or failure before the reported conversation took place, it nevertheless argues for admissibility of the hearsay declaration as one in furtherance of a continuing subsidiary objective of the conspiracy. Its argument runs this way. Conspirators about to commit crimes always expressly or implicitly agree to collaborate with each other to conceal facts in order to prevent detection, conviction and punishment. Thus the argument is that even after the central criminal objectives of a conspiracy have succeeded or failed, an implicit subsidiary phase of the conspiracy always survives, the phase which has concealment as its sole objective. The Court of Appeals adopted this view. It viewed the alleged hearsay declaration as one in furtherance of this continuing subsidiary phase of the conspiracy, as part of "the implied agreement to conceal." It conse-quently held the declaration properly admitted.

We cannot accept the Government's contention. There are many logical and prac-tical reasons that could be advanced against a special evidentiary rule that permits out-of-court statements of one conspirator to be used against another. But however cogent these reasons, it is firmly established that where made in furtherance of the objectives of a going conspiracy, such statements are admissible as exceptions to the hearsay rule. This prerequisite to admissibility, that hearsay statements by some conspirators to be admissible against others must be made in furtherance of the conspiracy charged, has been scrupulously observed by federal courts. The Gov-ernment now asks us to expand this narrow exception to the hearsay rule and hold admissible a declaration, not made in furtherance of the alleged criminal trans-portation conspiracy charged, but made in furtherance of an alleged implied but uncharged conspiracy aimed at preventing detection and punishment. No federal court case cited by the Government suggests so hospitable a reception to the use of hearsay evidence to convict in conspiracy cases. The Government contention does find support in some but not all of the state court opinions cited in the Government brief. But in none of them does there appear to be recognition of any such broad exception to the hearsay rule as that here urged. The rule contended for by the Gov-ernment could have far-reaching results. For under this rule plausible arguments could generally be made in conspiracy cases that most out-of-court statements offered in evidence tended to shield coconspirators. We are not persuaded to adopt the Government's implicit conspiracy theory which in all criminal conspiracy cases would create automatically a further breach of the general rule against the admis-sion of hearsay evidence.

Reversed.

MR. JUSTICE JACKSON, concurring:

This case illustrates a present drift in the federal law of conspiracy which warrants some further comment because it is characteristic of the long evolution of that elastic, sprawling and pervasive offense. Its history exemplifies the "tendency of a principle to expand itself to the limit of its logic." The unavailing protest of courts against the growing habit to indict for conspiracy in lieu of prosecuting for the substantive offense itself, or in addition thereto, suggests that loose practice as to this offense constitutes a serious threat to fairness in our administration of justice.

The modern crime of conspiracy is so vague that it almost defies definition. Despite certain elementary and essential elements, it also, chameleon-like, takes on a special coloration from each of the many independent offenses on which it may be overlaid. It is always "predominantly mental in composition" because it consists primarily of a meeting of minds and an intent.

The crime comes down to us wrapped in vague but unpleasant connotations. It sounds historical undertones of treachery, secret plotting and violence on a scale that menaces social stability and the security of the state itself. "Privy conspiracy" ranks with sedition and rebellion in the Litany's prayer for deliverance. Conspiratorial movements do indeed lie back of the political assassination, the *coup d'etat*, the *putsch*, the revolution, and seizures of power in modern times, as they have in all history.

But the conspiracy concept also is superimposed upon many concerted crimes having no political motivation. It is not intended to question that the basic conspiracy principle has some place in modern criminal law, because to unite, back of a criminal purpose, the strength, opportunities and resources of many is obviously more dangerous and more difficult to police than the efforts of a lone wrongdoer. It also may be trivialized, as here, where the conspiracy consists of the concert of a loathsome panderer and a prostitute to go from New York to Florida to ply their trade and it would appear that a simple Mann Act prosecution would vindicate the majesty of federal law. However, even when appropriately invoked, the looseness and pliability of the doctrine present inherent dangers which should be in the background of judicial thought wherever it is sought to extend the doctrine to meet the exigencies of a particular case.

Conspiracy in federal law aggravates the degree of crime over that of unconcerted offending. The act of confederating to commit a misdemeanor, followed by even an innocent overt act in its execution, is a felony and is such even if the misdemeanor is never consummated. The more radical proposition also is well-established that at common law and under some statutes a combination may be a criminal conspiracy even if it contemplates only acts which are not crimes at all when perpetrated by an individual or by many acting severally.

Thus, the conspiracy doctrine will incriminate persons on the fringe of offending who would not be guilty of aiding and abetting or of becoming an accessory, for those charges only lie when an act which is a crime has actually been committed.

Attribution of criminality to a confederation which contemplates no act that would be criminal if carried out by any one of the conspirators is a practice peculiar to Anglo-American law. "There can be little doubt that this wide definition of the crime of conspiracy originates in the criminal equity administered in the Star Chamber." In fact, we are advised that "The modern crime of conspiracy is almost entirely the result of the manner in which conspiracy was treated by the court of Star Chamber." The doctrine does not commend itself to jurists of civil-law countries, despite universal recognition that an organized society must have legal weapons for combatting organized criminality. Most other countries have devised what they consider more discriminating principles upon which to prosecute criminal gangs, secret associations and subversive syndicates.

A recent tendency has appeared in this Court to expand this elastic offense and to facilitate its proof. In *Pinkerton*, it sustained a conviction of a substantive crime where there was no proof of participation in or knowledge of it, upon the novel and dubious theory that conspiracy is equivalent in law to aiding and abetting.

Of course, it is for prosecutors rather than courts to determine when to use a scattergun to bring down the defendant, but there are procedural advantages from using it which add to the danger of unguarded extension of the concept.

An accused, under the Sixth Amendment, has the right to trial "by an impartial jury of the State and district wherein the crime shall have been committed." The leverage of a conspiracy charge lifts this limitation from the prosecution and reduces its protection to a phantom, for the crime is considered so vagrant as to have been committed in any district where any one of the conspirators did any one of the acts, however innocent, intended to accomplish its object. The Government may, and often does, compel one to defend at a great distance from any place he ever did any act because some accused confederate did some trivial and by itself innocent act in the chosen district. Circumstances may even enable the prosecution to fix the place of trial in Washington, D.C., where a defendant may lawfully be put to trial before a jury partly or even wholly made up of employees of the Government that accuses him.

When the trial starts, the accused feels the full impact of the conspiracy strategy. Strictly, the prosecution should first establish prima facie the conspiracy and identify the conspirators, after which evidence of acts and declarations of each in the course of its execution are admissible against all. But the order of proof of so sprawling a charge is difficult for a judge to control. As a practical matter, the accused often is confronted with a hodgepodge of acts and statements by others which he may never have authorized or intended or even known about, but which help to persuade the jury of existence of the conspiracy itself. In other words, a conspiracy often is proved by evidence that is admissible only upon assumption that conspiracy existed. The naive assumption that prejudicial effects can be overcome by instructions to the jury, all practicing lawyers know to be unmitigated fiction.

The trial of a conspiracy charge doubtless imposes a heavy burden on the prosecution, but it is an especially difficult situation for the defendant. The hazard from loose application of rules of evidence is aggravated where the Government institutes mass trials.[20] Moreover, in federal practice there is no rule preventing conviction on uncorroborated testimony of accomplices, as there are in many jurisdictions, and the most comfort a defendant can expect is that the court can be induced to follow the "better practice" and caution the jury against "too much reliance upon the testimony of accomplices."

A co-defendant in a conspiracy trial occupies an uneasy seat. There generally will be evidence of wrongdoing by somebody. It is difficult for the individual to make his own case stand on its own merits in the minds of jurors who are ready to believe that birds of a feather are flocked together. If he is silent, he is taken to admit it and if, as often happens, co-defendants can be prodded into accusing or contradicting each other, they convict each other. There are many practical difficulties in defending against a charge of conspiracy which I will not enumerate.

Against this inadequately sketched background, I think the decision of this case in the court below introduced an ominous expansion of the accepted law of conspiracy. The prosecution was allowed to incriminate the defendant by means of the prostitute's recital of a conversation with defendant's alleged co-conspirator, who was not on trial. The conversation was said to have taken place after the substantive offense was accomplished, after the defendant, the coconspirator and the witness had all been arrested, and after the witness and the other two had a falling out. The Court of Appeals sustained its admission upon grounds stated as follows:

> "... We think that implicit in a conspiracy to violate the law is an agreement among the conspirators to conceal the violation after as well as before the illegal plan is consummated. Thus the conspiracy continues, at least for purposes of concealment, even after its primary aims have been accomplished. The statements of the co-conspirator here were made in an effort to protect the appellant by concealing his role in the conspiracy. Consequently, they fell within the implied agreement to conceal and were admissible as evidence against the appellant."

I suppose no person planning a crime would accept as a collaborator one on whom he thought he could not rely for help if he were caught, but I doubt that this fact warrants an inference of conspiracy for that purpose. Of course, if an

---

20. An example is afforded by *Allen v. United States*, 4 F.2d 688. At the height of the prohibition frenzy, seventy-five defendants were tried on charges of conspiracy. A newspaper reporter testified to going to a drinking place where he talked with a woman, behind the bar, whose name he could not give. There was not the slightest identification of her nor showing that she knew or was known by any defendant. But it was held that being back of the bar showed her to be a co-conspirator and, hence, her statements were admissible against all. He was allowed to relate incriminating statements made by her.

understanding for continuous aid had been proven, it would be embraced in the conspiracy by evidence and there would be no need to imply such an agreement. Only where there is no convincing evidence of such an understanding is there need for one to be implied.

It is difficult to see any logical limit to the "implied conspiracy" either as to duration or means, nor does it appear that one could overcome the implication by express and credible evidence that no such understanding existed, nor any way in which an accused against whom the presumption is once raised can terminate the imputed agency of his associates to incriminate him. Conspirators, long after the contemplated offense is complete, after perhaps they have fallen out and become enemies, may still incriminate each other by deliberately harmful, but unsworn declarations, or unintentionally by casual conversations out of court. On the theory that the law will impute to the confederates a continuing conspiracy to defeat justice, one conceivably could be bound by another's unauthorized and unknown commission of perjury, bribery of a juror or witness, or even putting an incorrigible witness with damaging information out of the way.

Moreover, the assumption of an indefinitely continuing offense would result in an indeterminate extension of the statute of limitations. If the law implies an agreement to cooperate in defeating prosecution, it must imply that it continues as long as prosecution is a possibility, and prosecution is a possibility as long as the conspiracy to defeat it is implied to continue.

I do not see the slightest warrant for judicially introducing a doctrine of implied crimes or constructive conspiracies. It either adds a new crime or extends an old one. True, the modern law of conspiracy was largely evolved by the judges. But it is well and wisely settled that there can be no judge-made offenses against the United States and that every federal prosecution must be sustained by statutory authority. No statute authorizes federal judges to imply, presume or construct a conspiracy except as one may be found from evidence. To do so seems to approximate creation of a new offense and one that I would think of doubtful constitutionality even if it were created by Congress. And, at all events, it is one fundamentally and irreconcilably at war with our presumption of innocence.

There is, of course, strong temptation to relax rigid standards when it seems the only way to sustain convictions of evildoers. But statutes authorize prosecution for substantive crimes for most evil-doing without the dangers to the liberty of the individual and the integrity of the judicial process that are inherent in conspiracy charges. We should disapprove the doctrine of implied or constructive crime in its entirety and in every manifestation. And I think there should be no straining to uphold any conspiracy conviction where prosecution for the substantive offense is adequate and the purpose served by adding the conspiracy charge seems chiefly to get procedural advantages to ease the way to conviction.

Although a reversal after four trials is, of course, regrettable, I cannot overlook the error as a harmless one. But I should concur in reversal even if less sure that prejudice resulted, for it is better that the crime go unwhipped of justice than that this theory of implied continuance of conspiracy find lodgment in our law, either by affirmance or by tolerance. Few instruments of injustice can equal that of implied or presumed or constructive crimes. The most odious of all oppressions are those which mask as justice.

Questions and Notes

1. What is the purpose of the hearsay rule?

2. Given that purpose, does the co-conspirator exception make much sense? The Court has recently approved and arguably expanded the rule in *Bourjaily v. United States*, 483 U.S. 171 (1987).

3. If there is to be such an exception, does the *Krulewitch* rule make much sense? If the hearsay statement would have been reliable had the conspiracy been continuing, is there any reason to think it would be less reliable after the crimes contemplated by the conspiracy have been committed?

4. Justice Jackson's opinion raises a number of points. Should a court have the power to dismiss a conspiracy prosecution when the case (like *Krulewitch*) trivializes the concept? *See* NUTSHELL § 16.08.

5. Ought the crime of conspiracy to be abolished? *See* Johnson, *The Unnecessary Crime of Conspiracy*, 61 CAL. L. REV. 1137 (1973).

Chapter 20

RICO

Although some have thought that conspiracy law gave prosecutors an unfair advantage, such thought has been far from universal. The federal government, for example, has concluded that conspiracy laws are not tough enough on criminals. To implement its desire to get tough on criminals, Congress enacted the Racketeer Influenced and Corrupt Organizations Act, known affectionately to prosecutors as RICO. We will now explore the purposes and potential breadth of RICO.

United States v. Turkette

452 U.S. 576 (1981)

JUSTICE WHITE delivered the opinion of the Court.

Chapter 96 of Title 18 of the United States Code, 18 U.S.C. §§ 1961–1968, entitled Racketeer Influenced and Corrupt Organizations (RICO), was added to Title 18 by Title IX of the Organized Crime Control Act of 1970, Pub. L. 91-452, 84 Star. 941. The question in this case is whether the term "enterprise" as used in RICO encompasses both legitimate and illegitimate enterprises or is limited in application to the former. The Court of Appeals for the First Circuit held that Congress did not intend to include within the definition of "enterprise" those organizations which are exclusively criminal.

The indictment described the enterprise as "a group of individuals associated in fact for the purpose of illegally trafficking in narcotics and other dangerous drugs, committing arsons, utilizing the United States mails to defraud insurance companies, bribing and attempting to bribe local police officers, and corruptly influencing and attempting to corruptly influence the outcome of state court proceedings. . . ."

After a 6-week jury trial, in which the evidence focused upon both the professional nature of this organization and the execution of a number of distinct criminal acts, respondent was convicted on all nine counts. He was sentenced to a term of 20 years on the substantive counts, as well as a 2-year special parole term on the drug count. On the RICO conspiracy count he was sentenced to a 20-year concurrent term and fined $20,000.

On appeal, respondent argued that RICO was intended solely to protect legitimate business enterprises from infiltration by racketeers and that RICO does not make criminal the participation in an association which performs only illegal acts and which has not infiltrated or attempted to infiltrate a legitimate enterprise. The Court of Appeals agreed. We reverse.

Section 1962(c) makes it unlawful "for any person employed by or associated with any enterprise engaged in, or the activities of which affect, interstate or foreign commerce, to conduct or participate, directly or indirectly, in the conduct of such enterprise's affairs through a pattern of racketeering activity or collection of unlawful debt." The term "enterprise" is defined as including "any individual, partnership, corporation, association, or other legal entity, and any union or group of individuals associated in fact although not a legal entity." There is no restriction upon the associations embraced by the definition: an enterprise includes any union or group of individuals associated in fact. On its face, the definition appears to include both legitimate and illegitimate enterprises within its scope; it no more excludes criminal enterprises than it does legitimate ones. Had Congress not intended to reach criminal associations, it could easily have narrowed the sweep of the definition by inserting a single word, "legitimate." But it did nothing to indicate that an enterprise consisting of a group of individuals was not covered by RICO if the purpose of the enterprise was exclusively criminal.

[One] reason offered by the Court of Appeals in support of its judgment was that giving the definition of "enterprise" its ordinary meaning would create several internal inconsistencies in the Act. With respect to § 1962(c), it was said: "if 'a pattern of racketeering' can itself be an 'enterprise' for purposes of section 1962(c), then the two phrases 'employed by or associated with any enterprise' and 'the conduct of such enterprise's affairs through [a pattern of racketeering activity]' add nothing to the meaning of the section. The words of the statute are coherent and logical only if they are read as applying to legitimate enterprises." This conclusion is based on a faulty premise. That a wholly criminal enterprise comes within the ambit of the statute does not mean that a "pattern of racketeering activity" is an "enterprise." In order to secure a conviction under RICO, the Government must prove both the existence of an "enterprise" and the connected "pattern of racketeering activity." The enterprise is an entity, for present purposes a group of persons associated together for a common purpose of engaging in a course of conduct. The pattern of racketeering activity is, on the other hand, a series of criminal acts as defined by the statute. The former is proved by evidence of an ongoing organization, formal or informal, and by evidence that the various associates function as a continuing unit. The latter is proved by evidence of the requisite number of acts of racketeering committed by the participants in the enterprise. While the proof used to establish these separate elements may in particular cases coalesce, proof of one does not necessarily establish the other. The "enterprise" is not the "pattern of racketeering activity"; it is an entity separate and apart from the pattern of activity in which it engages. The existence of an enterprise at all times remains a separate element which must be proved by the Government.

It is obvious that §§ 1962(a) and (b) address the infiltration by organized crime of legitimate businesses, but we cannot agree that these sections were not also aimed at preventing racketeers from investing or reinvesting in wholly illegal enterprises and from acquiring through a pattern of racketeering activity wholly illegitimate enterprises such as an illegal gambling business or a loan-sharking operation. There is no inconsistency or anomaly in recognizing that § 1962 applies to both legitimate and illegitimate enterprises. Certainly, the language of the statute does not warrant the Court of Appeals' conclusion to the contrary.

Finally, it is urged that the interpretation of RICO to include both legitimate and illegitimate enterprises will substantially alter the balance between federal and state enforcement of criminal law. This is particularly true, so the argument goes, since included within the definition of racketeering activity are a significant number of acts made criminal under state law. But even assuming that the more inclusive definition of enterprise will have the effect suggested, the language of the statute and its legislative history indicate that Congress was well aware that it was entering a new domain of federal involvement through the enactment of this measure. Indeed, the very purpose of the Organized Crime Control Act of 1970 was to enable the Federal Government to address a large and seemingly neglected problem. The view was that existing law, state and federal, was not adequate to address the problem, which was of national dimensions. That Congress included within the definition of racketeering activities a number of state crimes strongly indicates that RICO criminalized conduct that was also criminal under state law, at least when the requisite elements of a RICO offense are present. As the hearings and legislative debates reveal, Congress was well aware of the fear that RICO would "mov[e] large substantive areas formerly totally within the police power of the State into the Federal realm." In the face of these objections, Congress nonetheless proceeded to enact the measure, knowing that it would alter somewhat the role of the Federal Government in the war against organized crime and that the alteration would entail prosecutions involving acts of racketeering that are also crimes under state law.

Contrary to the judgment below, neither the language nor structure of RICO limits its application to legitimate "enterprises." Applying it also to criminal organizations does not render any portion of the statute superfluous nor does it create any structural incongruities within the framework of the Act. The result is neither absurd nor surprising. On the contrary, insulating the wholly criminal enterprise from prosecution under RICO is the more incongruous position.

Section 904 (a) of RICO, 84 Stat. 947, directs that "[t]he provisions of this Title shall be liberally construed to effectuate its remedial purposes." With or without this admonition, we could not agree with the Court of Appeals that illegitimate enterprises should be excluded from coverage. We are also quite sure that nothing in the legislative history of RICO requires a contrary conclusion.

The judgment of the Court of Appeals is accordingly *Reversed*.

Questions and Notes

1. Is there any good reason to limit the term "enterprise" to legitimate enterprise?

2. Do you believe that the term "enterprise" has the plain meaning attributed to it?

3. Given that a purpose of RICO was to expand federal criminal law and that the statute is to be liberally construed, we turn to the question of just how liberally it is to be construed. Two answers are provided by *Licavoli* and *Teitler.*

United States v. Licavoli
725 F.2d 1040 (6th Cir. 1984)

KENNEDY, Circuit Judge.

The six defendant-appellants were convicted of conspiring to participate in the affairs of an enterprise through a pattern of racketeering activities in violation of RICO following a jury trial, and now appeal those convictions. We affirm the judgments of conviction of all defendants.

In order to sustain a prosecution under RICO the government must establish that defendants engaged in a "pattern of racketeering activity," defined as at least two acts of racketeering activity. 18 U.S.C. § 1961(5). "Racketeering activity" is defined in 18 U.S.C. § 1961(1). The facts elicited by the prosecution at trial to prove the defendants' pattern of racketeering activity are lengthy and complex. Briefly, the government asserts (and we agree) that the evidence, viewed in the light most favorable to it, established the following.

1. Facts

Defendant Licavoli is a leader of organized crime in Cleveland. Liberatore is his second-in-command, and Calandra also holds a position of confidence and responsibility within the organization. Carabbia and Cisternino act for the organization, carrying out the orders of the top men. Ciarcia manages a car dealership and supplies vehicles for the organization's criminal activities and also acts on behalf of the organization in other ways.

In the spring of 1976 Licavoli decided that he needed to have one Danny Greene killed. Greene was the leader of a rival criminal organization which had developed a monopoly on criminal activity in West Cleveland. Licavoli had others in his organization contact Raymond Ferrito regarding his wish to have Greene killed. Ferritto testified that he met at various times with each of the defendants (except Liberatore), sometimes separately, sometimes in groups, to plan Greene's murder. Ferritto stalked Greene for some months without success, sometimes assisted by Cisternino. After Ferritto had been on the job for some time he asked Licavoli for money to cover his expenses, and he was eventually given $5,000 by Carabbia. Licavoli also told Ferritto that he would get a percentage of money derived from gambling in the Warren and Youngstown areas when the murder was accomplished.

Ferritto and Cisternino attempted to bomb Greene's apartment building in order to kill him, but never carried through because of the regular presence of older people in the area. On another occasion they drove to a party attended by Greene intending to kill him. They located Greene's car but found that it was guarded by members of Greene's criminal organization seated in an adjacent car.

Meanwhile Liberatore arranged with two other men, Aratari and Guiles, to kill others in Green's criminal organization, and ultimately to help kill Greene as well. Aratari and Guiles were at times assisted in their efforts by defendants Carabbia, Calandra, Cisternino and Ciarcia. Ciarcia and another man provided Aratari and Guiles with a car and weapons.

Licavoli had Greene's phone tapped in an effort to obtain reliable information regarding Greene's daily activities. Carabbia and Cisternino gave Ferritto the resulting tapes. One tape revealed that Greene was to go to a dentist's appointment at 2:30 p.m. on Thursday, October 6, 1977. Defendants Licavoli, Cisternino and Carabbia played this tape to Ferritto on Monday, October 3.

On Thursday, the day of Greene's dentist appointment, Cisternino and Ferritto built a bomb in an apartment maintained by Cisternino. Ferrito drove to the vicinity of the dentist's office with the bomb in his car, a Plymouth. Carabbia drove a second car to the office, a Nova. This car had a special box mounted on the side in which the bomb was to be placed. Cisternino remained behind at the apartment to listen to a police scanner for calls. A few minutes after Ferritto and Carabbia arrived at the dentist's, Aratari and Guiles arrived in another car, supplied by Ciarcia as the car to be used in "the Danny Greene case." Guiles was armed with a high-powered rifle. The plan was for Guiles to shoot Greene if he had the opportunity. The bomb was to be used as a backup method.

Greene arrived for his appointment, parked his car and entered the office. Guiles apparently had no opportunity to shoot. A few minutes later a parking space opened next to Greene's car. Ferritto placed the bomb in the box on the side of the Nova, parked the Nova next to Greene's car, and activated the bomb. Then he got into the driver's seat of the Plymouth, which was parked down the block. When Greene emerged from the office Ferritto began to drive away, with Carabbia in the back seat. Carabbia then detonated the bomb with a remote control device and Danny Greene was killed.

All six defendants in the present case were tried for Danny Greene's murder in state court. Cisternino, Carabbia and Ciarcia were convicted of Greene's murder.

The RICO prosecution now on appeal also relied on a separate set of events to establish a predicate criminal act. Ms. Geraldine Rabinowitz worked as a file clerk in the Cleveland office of the FBI, while her then-fiance Jeffrey Rabinowitz worked at the car dealership that Ciarcia managed. In the spring of 1977 Ciarcia asked Ms. Rabinowitz to obtain confidential information from the FBI regarding investigations of himself, Liberatore, and Licavoli. Ms. Rabinowitz complied, after some hesitation, and continued to steal confidential information for Ciarcia from time to time throughout the summer of 1977. Ciarcia assured Ms. Rabinowitz that she would in return be "covered" for a downpayment on a new home that she and her fiance planned to buy. On October 12, 1977 the Rabinowitzes met with Liberatore and Ciarcia, and the Rabinowitzes asked for $15,000 for a down payment on the home. Although Liberatore was at first unwilling to comply with this request, the next day he delivered a paper bag to Ms. Rabinowitz containing $15,000 in cash. Counsel for Liberatore characterized this payment as a "loan," but no interest was set, no repayment schedule made, and no collateral specified. The stolen FBI documents were later found at Ciarcia's car dealership. All six defendants were charged with two counts of bribery and one count of conspiracy to commit bribery and were tried in federal court. Ciarcia pleaded guilty to all three counts, and Liberatore was convicted of the conspiracy count and one substantive count.

All six defendants were tried together in federal court for the RICO violation. The jury found all six guilty of having violated RICO. Defendants now raise a large number of issues on appeal.

Murder and Conspiracy To Murder Are Separate Offenses Under Ohio Law and May Both Be Predicate Acts Under RICO

The District Court instructed the jury that there were three possible acts which the jury could find to serve as predicate acts of racketeering for the RICO charge. These were: 1) conspiracy to murder Danny Greene; 2) the murder of Danny Greene; and 3) bribery. The court instructed that the bribery act applied only to defendants Liberatore and Ciarcia. The jury therefore had to find that the other four defendants both conspired to murder, and murdered Danny Greene in order to convict them of the RICO violation. These four defendants (Licavoli, Calandra, Carabbia, Cisternino) now argue that conspiracy to commit murder cannot serve as a predicate act for a RICO conviction, and that their RICO convictions therefore cannot stand.

For a defendant to be convicted under RICO he must have committed more than one act of racketeering activity. In order for a state crime, such as murder or conspiracy to murder to serve as a predicate act, it must be "chargeable under state law and punishable by imprisonment for more than one year" under 18 U.S.C. § 1961(1)(A). Federal law holds that conspiracy to commit a substantive offense and the substantive offense itself are two separate crimes. *See, e.g., Iannelli v. United States*, 420 U.S. 770, 777 (1975). Under Ohio law, conspiracy to murder and murder are also two separate crimes. However, a person convicted of the substantive crime "shall not be convicted of conspiracy involving the same offense." Ohio Rev. Code § 2923.01(G). Thus under Ohio law a person cannot be convicted of or sentenced for both conspiracy to commit murder and the murder crime itself. Defendants argue that the two acts consequently are not both "chargeable under state law and punishable for more than one year."

We disagree, for two reasons. First Ohio law, in both the Ohio Revised Code and the earlier case law, provides that conspiracy to commit a substantive act and the substantive act are separate offenses, both separately chargeable under state law. RICO nowhere indicates that two criminal acts otherwise qualifying as predicate acts may not both constitute predicate acts because under state law a defendant could not be convicted of or sentenced for both crimes.

Secondly, contrary to defendants' contention, it is irrelevant whether these particular defendants could have been charged under Ohio law and imprisoned for more than one year for both conspiracy to murder and murder. This argument has been raised and rejected several times in the context of state statutes of limitations, when the state statute has run on a state crime which is offered as a predicate act for a RICO violation. Courts have held that regardless of the running of the state statute the defendant is still "chargeable" with the state offense within the meaning of 18 U.S.C. § 1961(1)(A). The reference to state law in the statute is simply to define the wrongful conduct, and is not meant to incorporate state procedural law. The Third Circuit noted in *United States v. Frumento*, 563 F.2d 1083, 1087 n.8A (3d Cir. 1977), *cert. denied*, 434 U.S. 1072 (1978):

> Section 1961 requires, in our view, only that the *conduct* on which the federal charge is based be typical of the serious crime dealt with by the state statute, not that the particular defendant be "chargeable under State law" at the time of the federal indictment. (emphasis in original)

We agree and hold that conspiracy to murder and murder may both constitute predicate acts in this case, regardless of the fact that a defendant cannot under Ohio law be separately punished for having committed both crimes. Ohio law does define the two acts as separate crimes, each punishable by imprisonment for more than one year, and this is all that is required under 18 U.S.C. § 1961(1)(A).

Acquittal in State Court of Criminal Acts Does Not Bar Their Use as Predicate Acts for a RICO Conviction

Defendants Licavoli and Calandra were acquitted in state court proceedings of murdering Greene and conspiring to murder Greene. Consequently, they argue, they were not "chargeable" with the murder or conspiracy to commit murder, as required under 18 U.S.C. § 1961(1)(A), and murder and conspiracy to commit murder could not therefore serve as predicate acts for their RICO convictions.

We disagree. *Frumento is* directly on point. Defendants in that case were acquitted in state court on charges of bribery, extortion and conspiracy to accept bribes. They were then convicted in federal court of violating 18 U.S.C. § 1962(c) and (d), with the above crimes as predicate acts. On appeal defendants argued that the conviction was barred by the double jeopardy clause of the fifth amendment. The Third Circuit disagreed. The court said,

> [RICO] forbids "racketeering," not state offenses *per se*. The state offenses referred to in the federal act are definitional only; racketeering, the federal crime, is defined as a matter of legislative draftsmanship by a reference to state law crimes. This is not to say . . . that the federal statute punishes the same conduct as that reached by state law. The gravamen of section 1962 is a violation of federal law and "reference to state law is necessary only to identify the type of unlawful activity in which the defendant intended to engage.

MERRITT, Circuit Judge, concurring.

I concur in the clear and well-reasoned opinion prepared by Judge KENNEDY.

It may seem strange for a federal court to uphold convictions under a federal statute based on two underlying predicate state offenses for which a defendant has either been acquitted at state trials (the murder of Danny Greene) or for which he could not be separately convicted or punished under state law (conspiracy to murder Danny Greene). But RICO is now unique. Although I had earlier believed that normal canons of construction applicable to other criminal statutes should be applied to RICO, *see United States v. Sutton*, 605 F.2d 200 (1979), *reversed en banc*, 642 F.2d 1001, 1042 (6th Cir. 1980) (Merritt, J., dissenting), the Supreme Court has now made it clear that RICO is to be given the broadest and most expansive possible interpretation in order to carry out Congressional intent aimed at eliminating organized crime. *See United States v. Turkette*, 452 U.S. 576 (1981) (RICO not limited to infiltration of a legitimate "enterprise"); *Russello v. United States*, 104 S. Ct. 296 (1983). In *Russello*, a unanimous Supreme Court has pointed to RICO as the only federal criminal statute which should receive this kind of broad and expansive interpretation:

> The legislative history clearly demonstrates that the RICO statute was intended to provide new weapons of unprecedented scope for an assault upon organized crime and its economic roots. . . . Further, Congress directed, by § 904(a) of Pub. L. 91-452, 84 Stat. 947: "The provisions of this title shall be liberally construed to effectuate its remedial purposes." So *far as we have been made aware, this is the only substantive federal criminal statute that contains such a directive*. . . . 104 S. Ct. at 302. (emphasis added).

Thus, RICO, liberally construed as required by the Supreme Court, can reasonably be interpreted, and therefore should be interpreted, so that a defendant can be convicted even though he has already been acquitted or convicted of the two underlying offenses in state court and even though he could not be convicted or punished for both offenses together under state law.

In view of the Supreme Court's decisions in *Turkette* and *Russello*, I therefore agree with our Court's expansive construction of RICO.

Questions and Notes

1. If two separate offenses are a necessary predicate for RICO liability, does it make sense to count murder and conspiracy to commit the same murder as both of them?

2. Even assuming that your answer to Question 1 is yes, does it make sense in Ohio, where it is not possible to convict a defendant of both murder and conspiracy to commit murder?

3. Under the court's reasoning, would it be possible for attempted murder and murder of the same person at the same time to each be a predicate offense?

4. Ought offenses that resulted in acquittal in state court to be barred as predicate offenses? Why weren't they?

5. Does (should) Judge Merritt's analysis of the unique character of RICO affect the answers to Questions 2, 3, or 4?

6. *Teitler* presents yet another illustration of the expansive character of RICO.

United States v. Teitler

802 F.2d 606 (2d Cir. 1986)

PIERCE, Circuit Judge:

Background

Over a number of years, according to the indictment, a law firm in Queens County, New York, defrauded insurance companies by manipulating claims arising out of automobile accidents. Appellants Teitler and Schultz were attorneys at the firm. According to the indictment, the firm itself was the "enterprise" with which the appellants associated and carried out a pattern of racketeering activity. Appellants, along with others, were charged in an indictment alleging twenty-nine "acts of racketeering"—including twenty-eight mail fraud violations, and one count of obstruction of justice. The defendants were Norman Teitler, Morris Teitler, Leo Guise, Ted Dakis, Ismail D'Javid, Jean P Hartman, Jay Teitler, Marc Schultz and Maureen Murphy. Schultz, Murphy and Jay Teitler were tried together. The charges against the other defendants were disposed of separately. The head of the firm, Norman Teitler, pleaded guilty. Jay Teitler was named in two mail fraud counts and Schultz was named in three. Both appellants were named in the RICO and RICO conspiracy counts. Maureen Murphy was named in the obstruction of justice count, one mail fraud count, and in the RICO and RICO conspiracy counts. The counts against Murphy were tried along with the charges against Schultz and Teitier. Neither Schultz nor Teitler was charged with obstruction of justice.

The indictment charged that the method of operation employed by the enterprise included the creation of false documents and the encouragement of perjury by the firm's clients in order to inflate their injuries and expenses so as to obtain better settlements from insurance companies and recover higher damage awards in negligence lawsuits brought by the firm. The government contends that the fraud took several forms—creation of false medical bills, submission of false affidavits to document housekeeping services that were never rendered and lost wages that were never earned; referral of clients to doctors who provided backdated bills and exaggerated medical reports; and procurement of false testimony at trials and examinations before trial (EBTs). Further, when a grand jury investigation was underway, defendants Norman Teitier, head of the firm, and Maureen Murphy, a firm employee, allegedly tried to induce false testimony before the grand jury.

The indictment charged that the firm took advantage of a provision of New York's no-fault law that reimburses a person injured in an automobile accident for medical expenses, lost earnings and up to $25 per day expenses without regard to fault or liability for the accident. The no-fault benefits are limited to $50,000 per person and are paid by the injured driver's insurance company. *Id.* In addition, a person who has been seriously injured may institute a "third party suit" against the other driver to recover compensation for non-economic losses such as pain and suffering and economic losses above the amount paid by no-fault coverage. According to the record evidence, ninety-five percent of such third party suits are settled by the other driver's insurance carrier based on its assessment of the damages sustained. The amount of the settlement is arrived at after consideration of the information provided to the no-fault insurers, including a description of the plaintiffs injuries as described in EBT's, and proof of special damages, *i.e.*, medical bills, lost wages and housekeeping expenses; this information provides an index of the seriousness of the injury and consequently a guideline to gauge the amount of the settlement.

The evidence at trial revealed the manipulation of the no-fault system and third party suits by the law firm. The evidence against appellant Jay Teitler showed that he began working at the firm in 1976, first as a paralegal, then as an associate and finally as a partner of his brother, Norman Teitler. The testimony of government witness Edward Dunbar, a former paralegal at the firm, indicated that Jay Teitler knew of the firm's practices. Dunbar testified that Jay told him that, when signing up clients, Dunbar should encourage them to see doctors often to enhance their chances of large recoveries. Jay Teitler told him, "how we fill up third-party actions [is to] send him to [Dr.] Hartman, and Hartman will send us a report and a bill." In addition, Dunbar testified that Jay Teitler told him that the firm kept a large portion of the housekeeping expenses, which were based on false affidavits, because "the clients won't scream because they're not entitled to it in the first place, and he [Norman Teitler] makes a lot of money on it."

Jay Teitler was charged in two mail fraud counts, which became the predicates for the seventh and eighth acts of racketeering respectively in the indictment. Jay Teitler, Norman Teitler, and Dr. Hartman were charged with mail fraud in connection with the false housekeeping and medical claims made on behalf of one Barbara Brucato. Jay Teitler was the attorney of record for Brucato's personal injury claim filed with the insurance company after her automobile accident on September 26, 1979. The trial evidence showed that Jay Teitler sent Brucato to Dr. Hartman, who recorded nineteen visits by Brucato over the ensuing months in his report; the report also described a knee injury as a "permanent partial disability." Brucato testified that she visited Hartman only five or six times and that her knee was not injured. She further testified that she wanted to stop seeing Hartman, but Jay told her that she should continue because "it didn't look good" if she stopped. Jay gave Brucato an affidavit for her mother to sign as her housekeeper. She returned the form as instructed by Jay—signed, but with the information left blank. The form was completed by Norman Teitler; he described the relationship between Brucato and Brucato's mother as "none," and stated that the latter had been paid $25 per week. The no-fault insurer paid $1,375 in housekeeping benefits, of which Brucato received only $725. After receiving these documents, the third party carrier settled the personal injury claim for $3,500. The jury convicted Jay Teitler of the mail fraud count involving these acts, but was unable to reach a verdict on the second mail fraud count charged, which involved Jay's purported role in filing a false claim on behalf of his father, Morris Teitler. Jay Teitler was also convicted of participating in a RICO conspiracy in violation of 18 U.S.C. § 1962(d), but the jury was unable to reach a verdict on the substantive RICO count.

Discussion

I. Jay Teitler

A. The RICO Conspiracy Count

Appellant Teitler argues that, with respect to his alleged participation in a RICO conspiracy, the trial judge erred in instructing the jury that it need only find an agreement on his part to commit two predicate acts, rather than actual commission of the acts. He also contends that the jury could not, on the evidence before it, find an agreement to commit the predicate acts without first finding that he actually committed the acts. Finally, Teitler posits that the acts of racketeering underlying the RICO conspiracy conviction were insufficient as a matter of law to constitute a pattern of racketeering. We are not persuaded by these arguments.

1. The Sufficiency of the Charged Predicate Acts

Jay Teitler asserts that the two acts with which he was charged will not suffice to establish the requisite pattern of racketeering required by 18 U.S.C. § 1961(5).

Appellant argues that the trial judge improperly charged the jury because he did not instruct the jurors that they had to find *at least* two and possibly more acts of racketeering activity. He contends that this is required by footnote 14 of *Sedirna, S.PR.L. v. Imrex Co.*, 105 S. Ct. 3275 (1985), and points out that justice White stated that the language of 18 U.S.C. § 1961 requires at least two acts, "not that it 'means' two such acts." *Id.* at 3285 n.14. In other words, it is argued that two such acts are required, but will not alone constitute a pattern. Appellant therefore believes that the trial judge erred by refusing to instruct the jury that it had to find at least two and possibly more acts of racketeering activity.

We do not accept appellant's interpretation of footnote 14. Justice White stressed that the number of acts is not crucial: "[W]hile two acts are necessary, they may not be sufficient." *Id.* Instead, the key question is whether the factor of "'*continuity plus relationship*'" shows that the subject acts were not . . . sporadic activity,'" but part of a pattern. *Id.* (quoting S. Rep. No. 617, 91st Cong., 1st Sess. 158 (1969)) (emphasis in original). The most stringent reading of footnote 14 would require that the prosecution show . . . the same or similar purposes, results, participants, victims, or methods of commission. . . .'" *Sedima*, 105 S. Ct. at 3285 n.14. (quoting 18 U.S.C. § 3575(e)). Even if we were to accept this interpretation, Chief Judge Weinstein's charge clearly addressed these concerns:

> "A pattern of racketeering activity is committed if the Defendant committed at least two of the racketeering acts charged against him or her in the indictment. . . . In addition [to proving two racketeering acts], the government must prove beyond a reasonable doubt that the predicate acts constituted part of a larger pattern of activity that characterized each Defendant's conduct of or participation in the affairs of the law firm. That is to say, the predicate acts must have been connected with each other by some common scheme, plan or motive so as to constitute a pattern and not merely a series of disconnected acts.

The second element is that the accused willfully became a member of the conspiracy. . . . This means that in order to meet its burden of proof, the Government must show that the Defendant, knowing the object of the conspiracy, agreed to join with others to achieve those objects, namely the conducting of the affairs of the enterprise through each of them agreeing to commit at least two of the predicate acts identified as the objects of the conspiracy.

A RICO conspiracy conviction requires something more than an ordinary conspiracy. The Defendant must have agreed to assist in at least two of the predicate acts he or she is accused of committing. This means that the Government must prove beyond a reasonable doubt agreement to commit two charged predicate crimes."

This charge certainly reflects Justice White's observations in footnote 14.

The appellant further argues that the record lacked evidence that would permit the jury reasonably to find the required pattern. However, the evidence showed that both of the acts of racketeering charged against the appellant had a similar purpose, namely, defrauding insurance companies; both shared similar success in defrauding such companies; both shared similar participants and similar victims; and both employed similar methods. Further, evidence was presented regarding Jay Teitler's directive role in the operations of the law firm. We conclude that the jury had ample evidence from which it could find that the predicate acts Jay Teitler agreed to perform were part of a RICO pattern.

2. The Trial Court's Charge on the RICO Conspiracy Count

As discussed, the indictment charged Jay Teitler with two counts of mail fraud, which also served as the predicate acts for the RICO conspiracy charges against Teitler. The district judge charged the jury that a defendant could be convicted of participating in a RICO conspiracy if he *agreed* to commit two predicate acts, even if he did not actually carry them out:

> "[T]he Government must prove beyond a reasonable doubt agreement to commit two charged predicate crimes. . . . You do not have to find that any racketeering acts were actually committed by a Defendant to find him or her guilty of a conspiracy."

During its deliberations, the jury inquired as to whether a defendant could be convicted of RICO conspiracy if convicted of only one mail fraud count. The trial judge answered affirmatively and briefly instructed the jury again. Thereafter, the jury returned a verdict convicting Teitler of one mail fraud count and of the RICO conspiracy count. The jury was unable to reach a verdict on the second mail fraud charge.

Teitler argues that this case is governed by *United States v. Ruggiero*, 726 F.2d 913 (2d Cir.), cert. denied, 105 S. Ct. 118 (1984), which requires proof that a defendant at least agreed to commit two predicate acts in order to prove a RICO violation. In *Ruggiero*, defendant Tomasulo was charged with two predicate acts, one of which was a gambling conspiracy—an act legally insufficient to serve as a RICO predicate act. The government argued that no predicate acts were necessary for a RICO conspiracy charge. Instead, it asserted, it was sufficient for the defendant to have conspired with others to engage in an enterprise through a pattern of racketeering acts committed by others. This Court rejected the government's argument and stated that "to convict on a RICO conspiracy [the government] must prove that defendant himself at least agreed to commit two or more predicate crimes."

This case is distinguishable from *Ruggiero*. In that case, the defendant could not be found to be a RICO conspirator since he was charged with conspiring to commit only *one* RICO predicate act—the other act alleged was not a RICO predicate act. Here, Teitler was charged with agreeing to commit *two* RICO predicate acts. Although he was convicted of *committing* only one act, the jury was properly instructed that it could find that Teitler *agreed* to commit the other predicate act as well. Thus, the holding in *Ruggiero is* not governing here.

Teitler further argues that the *Ruggiero* court was compelled to reverse a RICO conspiracy conviction against co-defendant Santora because one of the eight predicate acts with which Santora was charged was not a RICO predicate act and because the record did not show whether the legally insufficient act was relied upon by the jury in returning a RICO conviction. The court suggested that this problem could have been avoided through the use of special verdicts. However, here both RICO predicate acts charged against Teitler were legally sufficient and therefore, once properly instructed, the jury could not have convicted Teitler based on a legally insufficient predicate.

We find no authority for the proposition that a person must commit two predicate acts of racketeering to be convicted of a RICO conspiracy. In accord with *Ruggiero*, Chief Judge Weinstein properly required the jury to determine whether the defendant agreed to commit two predicate acts.

It is fundamental that criminal conspiracy is an agreement among two or more persons to commit a crime. The crime of conspiracy does not require actual commission of the substantive crime. We must not confuse the predicate act requirement of 18 U.S.C. § 1962(d) with the overt act requirement of conspiracy statutes such as 18 U.S.C. § 371.[2] Section 1962(d) does not require proof of overt acts. We therefore conclude that the trial court properly charged the jury with respect to the RICO conspiracy count.

3. Sufficiency of the Evidence of Participation in the RICO Conspiracy

Jay Teitler argues that the jury could not reasonably have convicted him of RICO conspiracy on the evidence presented. He argues that since the jury had no direct evidence of his agreement to participate in the event and deadlocked with respect to the actual commission of it, the evidence could not have shown that he conspired

---

2. Commonly, under a conspiracy statute, it must be shown that the conspirator committed an overt act in furtherance of the conspiracy.

to commit the act charged. However, the jury had before it circumstantial evidence tending to show that Jay Teitler played a role in the fraud. This evidence included his statements made to Dunbar indicating knowledge of wrongdoing, his status as a partner in the Teitler firm, and Dunbar's testimony concerning Jay Teitler's role in the firm. The jury could reasonably infer from this evidence Jay's agreement to participate in the fraud.

As we have noted, during their deliberations the jury sent a note to the judge which asked whether a defendant could be convicted of RICO conspiracy if he was convicted of only one mail fraud count. Appellant asserts that this note is capable of being interpreted in at least two ways, either of which would have required a verdict of acquittal: it could mean that the jury believed that Jay Teitler had no role in a fraud in the father's accident case, or it could mean that the jury found that he agreed to commit fraud, but it did not find enough evidence to convict him of carrying out his planned role in it.

In response to the note, Chief Judge Weinstein explained:

> "A RICO conspiracy conviction requires something more than an ordinary conspiracy. The defendant must have agreed to assist in at least *two* of the predicate acts he or she is accused of committing. This means that the government must prove beyond a reasonable doubt an agreement to commit *two* charged predicate crimes. . . . That is to say that Jay Teitler agreed as part of his conspiratorial agreement to commit *both* acts of mail fraud charged. . . . You do not have to find that any racketeering acts were actually committed by a defendant to find him or her guilty of the conspiracy. . . ." (Emphasis added.)

This explanation made it clear to the jury that Jay Teitler could not be convicted of RICO conspiracy unless it found that he agreed to commit two predicate acts. We hold that the jury was properly charged, and, further, that it had sufficient evidence before it to find Jay Teitler guilty of a RICO conspiracy.

Questions and Notes

1. Is the RICO requirement two predicate acts or a pattern of racketeering activity? Recall that *Licavoli* began its statement of facts by describing the leadership role of the various defendants in organized crime.

2. If Teitler was not convicted of the second fraud count, where was the second predicate offense?

3. If your answer to Question 2 was "an agreement to commit the second fraud"; upon what evidence was that agreement derived? Do you think that this evidence proves the particular agreement?

4. Like conspiracy *(see Brown, Krulewitch, supra)*, RICO can ensnare small fish as well as big ones, such as the petty traffic ticket fixers (Walker and Maynard) in *Sutherland*.

United States v. Sutherland

656 F.2d 1181 (5th Cir. 1981)

RANDALL, Circuit Judge:

In this case three defendants appeal their convictions for conspiracy to violate RICO. The defendants raise a large number of issues, one of which involves an important RICO question: whether and when conspiracies that involve the same enterprise but are otherwise unrelated may be tried together under a single RICO conspiracy count. We consider the defendants' points on appeal seriatim and affirm their convictions.

I. The Facts

Glen Sutherland, Grace Walker and Edward Maynard were indicted in January 1980 for conspiracy to violate [RICO]. The indictment charged, in brief, that the three defendants "did knowingly, wilfully, and unlawfully combine, conspire, confederate, and agree together and with each other," from November 1975 until the date of the indictment, to violate section 1962(c). The conspiracy alleged by the government consisted of an agreement to associate with and to participate in the conduct of an enterprise that affects interstate commerce (the Municipal Court of the City of El Paso) through a pattern of racketeering activity (bribery of a state official in violation of state law).

The alleged conspiracy centers around Sutherland, who at the time of these events was a judge of the Municipal Court. According to the government, the defendants agreed that Maynard and Walker would each collect traffic tickets from his or her friends and associates, along with the amount of the statutory fine plus a small premium ($10); that Maynard and Walker would deliver the tickets to Sutherland, who would have the cases transferred to his docket and would then favorably dispose of them; and that the money collected would in each case be split between Sutherland and whichever other defendant collected and delivered the ticket.

Although the indictment frames the conspiracy as a single agreement among all three defendants, the government did not attempt at trial to prove any agreement between Walker and Maynard. As counsel for the government explained in response to an objection by the defendants to the introduction of co-conspirator hearsay:

MR. BOCK:	. . . It's the government's position that the conspiracy in this case, the hub of it, is the judge [Sutherland], and his activities with these other co-conspirators. And there is absolutely no requirement that they know each other or have knowledge of each other's activities.
THE COURT:	Your theory is that it is a wheel-type conspiracy?
MR. BOCK:	Yes, sir, exactly.
THE COURT:	That there was no one conspiracy but a series of conspiracies?
MR. BOCK:	Yes, sir.

This view of the government's case is consistent with the evidence presented at trial, which we discuss in more detail in Part II of this opinion. Briefly, we find the evidence sufficient to support each of two separate conspiracies, one between Walker and Sutherland and the other between Maynard and Sutherland. In each case the evidence is more than sufficient to establish an agreement to participate in the conduct of the Municipal Court through a pattern of racketeering activity. However, the government has pointed to no evidence in the record (and we have found none) that suggests that either Walker or Maynard knew or should have known of the other's similar agreement with Sutherland. The government's evidence as to these two defendants is entirely unrelated and, in fact, places the two conspiracies at different periods of time: the specific instances of bribery alleged between Walker and Sutherland all took place between 1975 and 1977, while those between Maynard and Sutherland all took place in 1979.

The government does not defend its joint trial in this case on the basis of traditional conspiracy law, *i.e.*, by arguing either that the evidence connected the spokes of a wheel conspiracy by common knowledge or agreement, or that the evidence demonstrates a chain conspiracy. Instead, the government argues that despite the apparent relevance to this case of the traditional multiple conspiracy doctrine, the defendants were properly tried together for a single "enterprise conspiracy" under RICO. The government contends, in brief, that a single conspiracy to violate a substantive RICO provision may be comprised of a pattern of agreements that absent RICO would constitute multiple conspiracies. The government contends that this is so even where, as here, there is no agreement of any kind between the members of the two separate conspiracies. According to the government, these otherwise multiple conspiracies are tied together by the RICO "enterprise:" so long as the object of each conspiracy is participation in the same enterprise in violation of RICO, it matters not that the different conspiracies are otherwise unrelated. Thus, the government argues that it need not demonstrate any connection between Walker and Maynard because the two conspiracies at issue each involved the same RICO enterprise-the Municipal Court of the City of El Paso.

[The court then discussed and limited a prior Fifth Circuit case, *United States v. Elliott*, 571 F.2d 880 (1978) that could have been read so expansively.]

Taken to its logical extreme, a rule allowing the joint trial of otherwise unrelated conspiracies solely on the basis of their relationship to a common enterprise—the rule which the government advocates in this case—leads to ridiculous results: For example, assuming that our own court—the United States Court of Appeals for the Fifth Circuit—was alleged to be the enterprise (as we assume would be proper under our analysis), we question whether an agreement to bribe a court official in El Paso, Texas could be part of the same conspiracy as an unrelated agreement to use a judicial office for illicit profitmaking purposes in Fort Lauderdale, Florida,* when

---

* [At the time of this decision, the Fifth Circuit had not yet been divided into the Fifth and Eleventh Circuits. Fort Lauderdale is currently in the Eleventh Circuit.—Ed.]

neither the El Paso nor the Fort Lauderdale conspirators knew of the existence of the other group.

This extreme hypothetical problem is not fundamentally different from the case now before us. Although both conspiracies in the case at bar involved the same judge, it is not that fact which the government argues ties the two conspiracies together. Rather, it is each conspiracy's relationship to the same enterprise (the Municipal Court of the City of El Paso) that is said to provide the necessary link. Thus, the theory urged by the government would bring together individual conspiracies to bribe different judges on the same court.

In this case the government has not attempted to prove that Walker and Maynard agreed with each other to participate in a bribery scheme with Sutherland, nor has it contended that the nature of each defendant's agreement with Sutherland was such that he or she must necessarily have known that others were also conspiring to commit racketeering offenses in the conduct of the Municipal Court. We must conclude, therefore, that the multiple conspiracy doctrine precluded the joint trial of the two multiple conspiracies involved in this case on a single RICO conspiracy count. [Therefore], we must reverse the defendants' convictions if this error affected their substantial rights.

[The court then concluded that the error did not affect their substantial rights because of the small number of defendants (three) coupled with the extreme unlikelihood of evidence against one being taken as evidence against the other.]

Questions and Notes

1. Does *Sutherland* trivialize RICO? In finding that the municipal court was an enterprise that affected interstate commerce, the court noted that fines assessed by the municipal court were used by the city in making interstate purchases.

2. Even though the court held that Walker and Maynard should not have been subject to the same RICO trial, is the prosecutor likely to take that holding seriously in a similar case, given the affirmation of the convictions?

3. Do you think that the "Fifth Circuit" hypothetical was on point?

4. Why does the court call this a "wheel" type conspiracy? *See* Nutshell § 16.10

Chapter 21

Corporate Criminal Liability

The concept of corporate criminal liability is not difficult to accept. Certainly, cases like *Teitler* demonstrate that organizations that seem most legitimate (in that case a law firm) can engage in criminal activity. Indeed, some kinds of crimes (e.g., antitrust) seem primarily aimed at corporations. When corporate employees act criminally, however, it is sometimes difficult to know whether the corporation can be properly charged with their misconduct. The problem is explored in *Christy Pontiac*.

State v. Christy Pontiac-GMC, Inc.
354 N.W.2d 17 (Minn. 1984)

SIMONETT, J.

We hold that a corporation may be convicted of theft and forgery, which are crimes requiring specific intent, and that the evidence sustains defendant corporation's guilt.

In a bench trial, defendant-appellant Christy Pontiac-GMC, Inc., was found guilty of two counts of theft by swindle and two counts of aggravated forgery and was sentenced to a $1,000 fine on each of the two forgery convictions. Defendant argues that as a corporation it cannot, under our state statutes, be prosecuted or convicted for theft or forgery and that, in any event, the evidence fails to establish that the acts complained of were the acts of the defendant corporation.

Christy Pontiac is a Minnesota corporation, doing business as a car dealership. It is owned by James Christy, a sole stockholder, who serves also as president and as director. In the spring of 1981, General Motors offered a cash rebate program for its dealers. A customer who purchased a new car delivered during the rebate period was entitled to a cash rebate, part paid by GM and part paid by the dealership. GM would pay the entire rebate initially and later charge back, against the dealer, the dealer's portion of the rebate. Apparently, it was not uncommon for the dealer to give the customer the dealer's portion of the rebate in the form of a discount on the purchase price.

At this time Phil Hesli was employed by Christy Pontiac as a salesman and fleet manager. On March 27, 1981, James Linden took delivery of a new Grand Prix for his employer, Snyder Brothers. Although the rebate period on this car had expired on March 19, the salesman told Linden that he would still try to get the $700 rebate for Linden. Later, Linden was told by a Christy Pontiac employee that GM had denied the rebate. Subsequently, it was discovered that Hesli had forged Linden's signature twice on the rebate application form submitted by Christy Pontiac to GM, and that the transaction date had been altered and backdated to March 19 on the buyer's order form. Hesli signed the order form as "Sales Manager or Officer of the Company."

On April 6, 1981, Ronald Gores purchased a new Le Mans, taking delivery the next day. The rebate period for this model car had expired on April 4, and apparently Gores was told he would not be eligible for a rebate. Subsequently, it was discovered that Christy Pontiac had submitted a $500 cash rebate application to GM and that Gores' signature had been forged twice by Hesli on the application. It was also discovered that the purchase order form had been backdated to April 3. This order form was signed by Gary Swandy, an officer of Christy Pontiac.

Both purchasers learned of the forged rebate applications when they received a copy of the application in the mail from Christy Pontiac. Both purchasers complained to James Christy, and in both instances the conversations ended in angry mutual recriminations. Christy did tell Gores that the rebate on his car was "a mistake" and offered half the rebate to "call it even." After the Attorney General's office made an inquiry, Christy Pontiac contacted GM and arranged for cancellation of the Gores rebate that had been allowed to Christy Pontiac. Subsequent investigation disclosed that of 50 rebate transactions, only the Linden and Gores sales involved irregularities.

In a separate trial, Phil Hesli was acquitted of three felony charges but found guilty on the count of theft for the Gores transaction and was given a misdemeanor disposition. An indictment against James Christy for theft by swindle was dismissed, as was a subsequent complaint for the same charge, for lack of probable cause. Christy Pontiac, the corporation, was also indicted, and the appeal here is from the four convictions on those indictments. Before trial, Mr. Christy was granted immunity and was then called as a prosecution witness. Phil Hesli did not testify at the corporation's trial. Christy Pontiac argues on several grounds that a corporation cannot be held criminally liable for a specific intent crime. Minn. Stat. § 609.52, subd. 2 (1982), says "whoever" swindles by artifice, trick or other means commits theft. Minn. Stat. § 609.625, subd. 1 (1982), says "whoever" falsely makes or alters a writing with intent to defraud, commits aggravated forgery. Christy Pontiac agrees that the term "whoever" refers to persons, and it agrees that the term "persons" *may* include corporations, but it argues that when the word "persons" is used here, it should be construed to mean only natural persons. This should be so, argues defendant, because the legislature has defined a crime as "conduct which is prohibited by statute and for which the actor may be sentenced to imprisonment, with or without a fine," and a corporation cannot be imprisoned. Neither, argues defendant, can an artificial person entertain a mental state, let alone have the specific intent required for theft or forgery.

We are not persuaded by these arguments. The Criminal Code is to "be construed according to the fair import of its terms, to promote justice, and to effect its purposes." The legislature has not expressly excluded corporations from criminal liability and, therefore, we take its intent to be that corporations are to be considered persons within the meaning of the Code in the absence of any clear indication to the contrary. *See, e.g.,* Minn. Stat. § 609.055 (1982) (legislative declaration that children under the age of 14 years are incapable of committing a crime). We do not think the statutory definition of a crime was meant to exclude corporate criminal liability; rather, we construe that definition to mean conduct, which is prohibited and, if committed, *may* result in imprisonment. Interestingly, the specific statutes under which the defendant corporation was convicted, sections 609.52 (theft) and 609.625 (aggravated forgery), expressly state that the sentence may be either imprisonment *or* a fine.

Nor are we troubled by any anthropomorphic implications in assigning specific intent to a corporation for theft or forgery. There was a time when the law, in its logic, declared that a legal fiction could not be a person for purposes of criminal liability, at least with respect to offenses involving specific intent, but that time is gone. If a corporation can be liable in civil tort for both actual and punitive damages for libel, assault and battery, or fraud, it would seem it may also be criminally liable for conduct requiring specific intent. Most courts today recognize that corporations may be guilty of specific intent crimes. Particularly apt candidates for corporate criminality are types of crime, like theft by swindle and forgery, which often occur in a business setting.

We hold, therefore, that a corporation may be prosecuted and convicted for the crimes of theft and forgery.

There remains, however, the evidentiary basis on which criminal responsibility of a corporation is to be determined. Criminal liability, especially for more serious crimes, is thought of as a matter of personal, not vicarious, guilt. One should not be convicted for something one does not do. In what sense, then, does a corporation "do" something for which it can be convicted of a crime? The case law, as illustrated by the authorities above cited, takes differing approaches. If a corporation is to be criminally liable, it is clear that the crime must not be a personal aberration of an employee acting on his own; the criminal activity must, in some sense, reflect corporate policy so that it is fair to say that the activity was the activity of the corporation. There must be, as Judge Learned Hand put it, a "kinship of the act to the powers of the officials, who commit it." *United States v. Nearing,* 252 F. 223, 231 (S.D.N.Y. 1918).

We believe, first of all, the jury should be told that it must be satisfied beyond a reasonable doubt that the acts of the individual agent constitute the acts of the corporation. Secondly, as to the kind of proof required, we hold that a corporation may be guilty of a specific intent crime committed by its agent if: (1) the agent was acting within the course and scope of his or her employment, having the authority to act for the corporation with respect to the particular corporate business which was conducted criminally; (2) the agent was acting, at least in part, in furtherance of the corporation's business interests; and (3) the criminal acts were authorized, tolerated, or ratified by corporate management.

This test is not quite the same as the test for corporate vicarious liability for a civil tort of an agent. The burden of proof is different, and, unlike civil liability, criminal guilt requires that the agent be acting at least in part in furtherance of the corporation's business interests. Moreover, it must be shown that corporate management authorized, tolerated, or ratified the criminal activity. Ordinarily, this will be shown by circumstantial evidence, for it is not to be expected that management authorization of illegality would be expressly or openly stated. Indeed, there may be instances where the corporation is criminally liable even though the criminal activity has been expressly forbidden. What must be shown is that from all the facts and circumstances, those in positions of managerial authority or responsibility acted or failed to act in such a manner that the criminal activity reflects corporate policy, and it can be said, therefore, that the criminal act was authorized or tolerated or ratified by the corporation.

Christy Pontiac argues that it cannot be convicted of aiding the very actor whose acts are deemed its own acts; in other words, it argues that it cannot aid itself. Perhaps because it was uncertain of the legal rationale for corporate criminal liability, the state, in each of the four counts of the indictment, alleged that Christy Pontiac "then and there being aided and abetted by another and aiding and abetting another" did commit the crime. We construe the indictment, however, to allege alternatively that Christy Pontiac committed the crimes as a principal or as an aider and abetter. The trial court, without objection, considered the corporation to be prosecuted and convicted as a principal, as do we.

This brings us, then, to the third issue, namely, whether under the proof requirements mentioned above, the evidence is sufficient to sustain the convictions. We hold that it is.

The evidence shows that Hesli, the forger, had authority and responsibility to handle new car sales and to process and sign cash rebate applications.

Christy Pontiac, not Hesli, got the GM rebate money, so that Hesli was acting in furtherance of the corporation's business interests. Moreover, there was sufficient evidence of management authorization, toleration, and ratification. Hesli himself, though not an officer, had middle management responsibilities for cash rebate applications. When the customer Gores asked Mr. Benedict, a salesman, about the then discontinued rebate, Benedict referred Gores to Phil Hesli. Gary Swandy, a corporate officer, signed the backdated retail buyer's order form for the Linden sale. James Christy, the president, attempted to negotiate a settlement with Gores after Gores complained. Not until after the Attorney General's inquiry did Christy contact divisional GM headquarters. As the trial judge noted, the rebate money "was so obtained and accepted by Christy Pontiac and kept by Christy Pontiac until somebody blew the whistle. . . ." We conclude the evidence establishes that the theft by swindle and the forgeries constituted the acts of the corporation. We wish to comment further on two aspects of the proof. First, it seems that the state attempted to prosecute both Christy Pontiac and James Christy, but its prosecution of Mr. Christy failed for lack of evidence. We can imagine a different situation where the corporation is the alter ego of its owner and it is the owner who alone commits the crime, where a double prosecution might be deemed fundamentally unfair. Secondly, it may seem incongruous that Hesli, the forger, was acquitted of three of the four criminal counts for which the corporation was convicted. Still, this is not the first time different trials have had different results. We are reviewing this record, and it sustains the convictions. Affirmed.

Questions and Notes

1. Is there any good reason *not* to hold a corporation liable for a specific intent crime?

2. Analytically, should the corporation be perceived as a principal or as an aider and abetter?

3. Can you think of any way to punish a corporation other than by fine? What other kind of punishment might be appropriate?

4. Are the three criteria developed by the court really equivalent to corporate fraud? Why is tolerating fraud the same as committing it?

5. Is it (ought it to be) relevant that only 2 of the 50 rebate transactions were dishonest and the corporation canceled those upon notification by the attorney general? Should it be relevant that Christy Pontiac itself sent the copies of the applications to the purchasers?

6. Why do you suppose that Hesli was acquitted on three of the four charges against him?

7. Why do you suppose that the indictments against James Christy were dismissed?

8. Corporate liability for homicide will be explored in *Richard Knutson, Inc.*

State v. Richard Knutson, Inc.

537 N.W.2d 420 (Wis. Ct. App. 1995)

ANDERSON, Presiding Judge.

Principles of elementary comparative justice, Wisconsin's tradition of holding corporations criminally liable and persuasive public policy considerations support our conclusion that corporations may be prosecuted for homicide by negligent use of a vehicle. We affirm the conviction of Richard Knutson, Inc. (RKI) holding that it is within the class of perpetrators covered by the statute and that there was sufficient evidence presented at trial to support the jury's verdict.

Facts

In the spring of 1991, RKI undertook the construction of a sanitary sewer line for the City of Oconomowoc. On May 20, 1991, while working in an area adjacent to some Wisconsin Electric Power Company power lines, a work crew attempted to place a section of corrugated metal pipe in a trench in order to remove groundwater.

The backhoe operator misjudged the distance from the boom of the backhoe to the overhead power lines and did not realize he had moved the stick of the boom into contact with the wires. In attempting to attach a chain to the backhoe's bucket, a member of the crew was instantly electrocuted. The State subsequently charged RKI with negligent vehicular homicide under § 940.10, Stats. RKI denied the charge, disputing both the applicability of the negligent vehicular homicide statute to corporations, as well as the substantive allegations themselves. Prior to trial, RKI's motion to dismiss the information was denied. The jury found RKI guilty as charged. The trial court entered judgment, concluding that the evidence was sufficient to support the verdict. RKI appeals.

Construction Of Homicide Statute

RKI raises the same challenges to § 940.10, Stats.,—homicide by negligent operation of a vehicle statute—as it did in the trial court. The trial court held that § 940.10 covered acts by corporations. Reasoning from a series of decisions, including *Vulcan Last Co. v. State*, 217 N.W. 412, 415 (1928), the trial court quoted *Vulcan Last* when it concluded, "'*Prima facie*,' the word 'person,' in a penal statute which is intended to inhibit an act, means 'person in law'; that is, an artificial, as well as a natural, person, and therefore includes corporations, if they are within the spirit and purpose of the statute." The trial court decided that corporate liability was within the spirit of § 940.10, stating, "The purpose of the statute is to protect employees or anyone from the negligent conduct of another which may cause death. It should not matter that the 'another' is a person or corporation as long as the conduct is criminal. . . ."

On appeal, RKI insists that a corporation cannot be held accountable for homicide. RKI argues that "[t]he statute uses the word 'whoever' and the correlative phrase '*another* human being.' In the context of this sentence, 'whoever' necessarily refers to a human being. By its own terms, the statute therefore limits culpability for homicide by operation of a vehicle to natural persons." RKI contends that § 940.10, Stats., is an ambiguous penal statute that must be interpreted in its favor under the rule of lenity.

The State contends that the statute is unambiguous and includes corporations within a broad class of perpetrators. Relying on *Kenosha Unified Sch. Dist. No. 1 v. Kenosha Educ. Ass'n*, 234 N.W.2d 311, 314 (1975), the State argues that when used in the homicide statutes, the word "whoever" refers to natural or corporate persons. The State reasons that either can be liable for taking the life of "another human being."

Our task is to interpret the meaning of the terms "whoever" and "another human being" within the context of the homicide statute. The primary goal of our interpretation of statutory words is to ascertain and give effect to the legislature's intent, and our first resort is to the language of the statute itself. If the statutory language is of uncertain meaning, we will then refer to the canons of statutory construction and consider the scope, history, context, subject matter and object of the statute in order to discover legislative intent.

A statute is ambiguous when it is capable of being interpreted in two or more ways by reasonably well-informed persons. An ambiguity does not exist merely because the parties disagree on a statute's meaning. We must examine the language of the statute to decide if the parties' different views are warranted.

Here, the statute does not provide a definition of "whoever."[2] It is left to the reader to determine if "whoever" should be read expansively to include natural and artificial persons, or should be read narrowly and have its definition gleaned from its reference to the correlative phrase "another human being." We conclude that because reasonably well informed persons could differ as to who might be a perpetrator, the statute is ambiguous.

We will thus employ extrinsic aids to uncover the legislature's intent. RKI reminds us of the rule of lenity; under this rule we are required to construe all penal statutes strictly in favor of the defendant. However, it is also a canon of statutory construction that "[c]onstruction of ambiguous legislation is made in light of the evil sought to be remedied."

Where a penalty is involved it has been said that while such statute must be construed with such strictness as carefully to safeguard the rights of the defendant and at the same time preserve the obvious intention of the legislature, the rule of strict construction is not violated by taking the common-sense view of the statute as a whole and giving effect to the object of the legislature, if a reasonable construction of the words permits it.

The rule of lenity does not require us to give the narrowest possible construction where to do so would be inconsistent with the legislature's intent. The primary goal of statutory construction is to carry out the legislature's intent; the tools of statutory construction, Including the rule of lenity, cannot be used in disregard of the purpose of the statute. In this process, sometimes a strict construction and sometimes a liberal construction of a penal statute are required to carry out the legislative purpose.

Professor James Willard Hurst provides guidance. First, he suggests that the very nature of today's society makes it impossible for the members of the legislature to forecast "the particular condition or set of facts to which someone now suggests applying the statute." According to Hurst, the legislators may well have supplied "sufficient specifications to provide a discernible frame of reference within which the situation now presented quite clearly fits, even though it represents in some degree a new condition of affairs unknown to the lawmakers."

Second, he submits that "as a vital element in the community's life a statute is more than the text we find in the statute book." Hurst argues that the text under

---

2. The statute defines terms applicable to the homicide statutes, and important to this decision, in two different places. First, §939.22(16), Stats., defines "[h]uman being" when used in the homicide sections to mean "one who has been born alive." Second, §990.01(26), Stats., defines "[p]erson" to include "all partnerships, associations and bodies politic or corporate."

judicial analysis gains its vitality from its past "—from the prior state of the law and the shortcomings of that state of law"—and from its future "—from what those charged with applying it do to give it force, not only to promote its objectives but to overcome contrivances to evade its mandates."

Finally, Hurst instructs those interpreting statutes that:

> the content of public policy may grow by accretion of statutory precedents in a fashion analogous to the growth of common law. Statutes dealing with a variety of subjects may begin to cluster around some common value judgment. Recognizing this reality, a court is warranted in finding evidence of legislative intent under a given act by reference to what legislators have done regarding like subjects under other acts.

The homicide statute in question deals exclusively with deaths caused by negligent operation of vehicles.

940.10 Homicide by negligent operation of vehicle. *Whoever* causes the death of *another human being* by the negligent operation or handling of a vehicle is guilty of a Class E felony. [Emphasis added.]

Our task is to ascertain if the legislative intent is to include corporations within the class of perpetrators. This task is made more difficult by the legislature's use of the term "whoever" to identify the perpetrator of a crime and its failure to define that term. Prior to 1955, the comparable provision of the statute encompassing homicide by negligent use of a motor vehicle, described the perpetrator as "any person." The statute defined "[p]erson" to include "all partnerships, associations and bodies politic and corporate." Why, when it rewrote the criminal code in 1955, the legislature chose to describe perpetrators with the ambiguous term "whoever" is an enigma.

Another mystery is the deletion of any statutory language establishing corporate liability for criminal acts. The proposed 1953 version of the criminal code contained a specific provision that held a corporation criminally liable for the acts of its agents when acting within the scope of their authority. This provision was deleted from the 1955 formulation of the criminal code. As explained by William A. Platz, "This was eliminated, upon motion of an advisory committee member who was a house counsel for a large industrial corporation, although it was conceded that the 1953 code correctly stated the rule of law and that its omission from the code would not alter the rule." William A. Platz, *The Criminal Code*, 1956 Wis. L. Rev. 350, 362–63 (footnote omitted).

Prior to adoption of Wisconsin's 1955 criminal code, a corporation could be held criminally liable. *See Vulcan Last*, 217 N.W. at 414–16. *Vulcan Last* was an appeal from a criminal conviction of a corporation for discharging an employee who voted against the corporation's request for a municipal water treatment plant. The supreme court concluded that Wisconsin would follow modern authority and hold corporations liable for criminal acts. RKI attempts to distinguish *Vulcan Last* by arguing that the statute involved described the perpetrator as a "person" defined to include corporations.

RKI's attempt fails because five years later the supreme court explained that "it is now well established that a corporation can be held guilty of crime when it is punishable by a fine. . . ." *State ex rel. Kropf v. Gilbert*, 251 N.W. 478, 484 (1933). *Kropf* was a habeas corpus case in which the petitioners-appellants were challenging the sufficiency of the evidence at a preliminary hearing to support their being bound over for prosecution for embezzlement. The question was whether any of the petitioners-appellants, as agents of a corporation, were parties to the crime of the corporation converting or embezzling funds. The answer turned not on the description and definition of a perpetrator of embezzlement; rather, it turned on whether the perpetrator would be punished by imprisonment or a fine.

We conclude that prior to the enactment of the 1955 criminal code, the well-established rule in Wisconsin was that if a crime was punishable, in part, by a fine, a corporation could be criminally responsible. We are satisfied that it was not the description of the perpetrator as a "person"—defined to include corporations—that governed corporate criminal liability.

We find it significant that in 1955 the legislature did not seek to highlight corporate criminal liability by including a provision as suggested in the 1953 proposed criminal code or by revoking the then-existing rule found in *Vulcan Last* and *Kropf.* The legislature's silence is indicative of its satisfaction with the supreme court's interpretation of the law. As the supreme court has written:

> When determining legislative intent, this court must assume that the legislature knew the law in effect at the time of its actions. Moreover, we presume that the legislature is aware that absent some kind of response this court's interpretation of the statute remains in effect. Legislative silence with regard to new court made decisions indicates legislative acquiescence in those decisions.

> The legislature had another opportunity to consider the reach of the homicide statutes in 1987 when it substantially modified ch. 940, Stats. This consideration came after the decision in *State v. Dried Milk Prods. Co-Op.*, 114 N.W.2d 412 (1962), which reaffirmed the vitality of *Vulcan Last.*

This legislative inaction, in the face of repeated supreme court pronouncements that corporations can be held liable for criminal acts, convinces us that the legislature concurs in the supreme court's decisions. On two separate occasions the legislature significantly revised the homicide statutes; both times it is presumed that the legislature was aware that court decisions have held corporations criminally liable; and on both occasions, the legislature has elected not to undo corporate criminal liability.

Our conclusion conforms to the modern trend of the law. A leading treatise on corporations acknowledges that a corporation may be held to answer for its criminal acts, including homicide. WILLIAM M. FLETCHER, FLETCHER CYCLOPEDIA OF THE LAW OF PRIVATE CORPORATIONS. The Model Penal Code also has several provisions holding corporations accountable for criminal behavior.

LaFave and Scott summarize the persuasive policy considerations supporting corporate criminal liability. Among those considerations is the factor that the corporate business entity has become a way of life in this country and the imposition of criminal liability is an essential part of the regulatory process. Another consideration centers on the premise that it would be unjust to single out one or more persons for criminal punishment when it is the corporate culture that is the origin of the criminal behavior. Also, the size of many corporations makes it impossible to adequately allocate responsibility to individuals.

An additional consideration is the "indirect economic benefits that may accrue to the corporation through crimes against the person. To get these economic benefits, corporate management may shortcut expensive safety precautions, respond forcibly to strikes, or engage in criminal anticompetitive behavior." It has also been suggested that the free market system cannot be depended upon to guide corporate decisions in socially acceptable ways, and the threat of imposition of criminal liability is needed to deter inappropriate (criminal) corporate behavior.

RKI insists that Wisconsin has disregarded the modern trend of criminal law to hold corporations liable for criminal acts. RKI bases its argument on the language of § 940.10, Stats. It argues:

> [T]he only fair reading of [the statute] provides that natural persons alone can be prosecuted for violations of the statute: only "[w]*hoever* causes the death of *another human being* "can be found guilty. . . . Because the statute subjects only human beings to criminal liability for negligent vehicular homicide, RKI does not fall within the scope of [the statute].

RKI's argument ignores reality. A corporation acts of necessity through its agents; therefore, the only way a corporation can negligently cause the death of a human is by the act of its agent—another human. Reading the statute to limit its coverage to perpetrators who are human, as suggested by RKI, skirts around the concepts of vicarious and enterprise liability. If a human was operating a vehicle within the scope of his or her employment when the death occurred, RKI's construction would permit the corporation to escape criminal prosecution simply because it is not a human being.

RKI's attempt to limit the class of perpetrators to natural persons ignores several axioms. First, elementary comparative justice demands that the same criminal liability must be imposed when two relatively similar offenses are committed under similar circumstances. Second, "it is not in virtue of being a person that criminal liability attaches. It is in virtue of possessing the complex relational property of causing harm—voluntarily—with a wrongful state of mind—without excuse." Third, "[f]inding moral responsibility and criminal liability does not depend on first determining whether an entity is a person."

Part of RKI's argument is premised upon a narrow definition of "whoever" that excludes corporations. The supreme court's decision in *Kenosha Unified Sch. Dist.*, 234 N.W.2d at 314, that when the word "whoever" is used in the statute it refers to both natural and corporate persons, appears to be the universal construction of that term. We agree with both FLETCHER AND LAFAVE & SCOTT that if a penal statute is intended to inhibit an act, a corporation is included within the class of perpetrators if to do so is within the spirit and purpose of the act.[10]

Sufficiency of the Evidence

RKI argues that the evidence adduced at trial was insufficient to support its conviction. RKI asserts that the State failed to prove two elements of the offense: (1) that RKI was criminally negligent, in other words, that RKI should have realized that the conduct created a substantial and unreasonable risk of death or great bodily harm to another; and (2) the causal connection between RKI's alleged criminally negligent conduct and the victim's death.

The test for sufficiency of the evidence is whether an appellate court can conclude that a reasonable trier of fact could be convinced of a defendant's guilt beyond a reasonable doubt by the evidence and reasonable inferences that it had a right to believe and accept as true. We follow several guidelines during our review of the evidence. First, evidence is to be considered in a light most favorable to the State and the conviction. Second, the credibility of the witnesses and the resolution of conflicts in the evidence are functions exclusively reserved for the trier of fact. Third, the trier of fact, within the bounds of reason, is free to reject inferences that are consistent with the innocence of the defendant.

Homicide by negligent use of a vehicle has three elements: "(1) that the defendant cause death (2) by criminal negligence (3) in the operation of a vehicle." The core factor of the three elements is that simple negligence is not enough to hold an individual criminally liable. In order for a person to face criminal consequences for a negligent act, his or her negligence must rise to the level of criminal negligence.[12]

---

10. The dissent overlooks Wisconsin's historic adherence to "Mr. Justice HOLMES' epigrammatic direction to 'think things rather than words.'" *Peterson v. Sinclair Refining Co.*, 123 N.W.2d 479, 486 (1963). Although the dissent's use of the rules of grammatical construction to limit the application of § 940.10, Stats., to "persons born alive" is proper application of some of the canons of statutory construction, it does not go far enough. The dissent neglects to consider the prerogative of the courts to disregard grammatical errors or mistakes in statutes in order to give effect to the intent of the legislature. "In other words, if the legislative intent is clear, it must be given effect regardless of inaccuracies of language. . . ." Where there are no other clues to use to discover the legislature's intent, it is appropriate to resort to the rules of grammar. But the employment of the rules of grammar is:

> dependent upon the reasonableness of the interpretation in terms of the subject matter of the statute and whether the interpretation dictated by these ossified rules of construction reaches a workable result. An interpretation reached by relying upon a rule of grammatical construction cannot stand in the face of a conflict revealed in the subject matter under consideration.

12. Of course, by necessity a corporation can only act through its employees, agents or officers; therefore, it is the negligence of the employee that must rise to the level of criminal negligence. In this case, the trial court did instruct the jury on the concepts of corporate vicarious liability using

Criminal negligence differs from ordinary negligence in two respects. First, the risk is more serious—death or great bodily harm as opposed to simple harm. Second, the risk must be more than an unreasonable risk—it must also be substantial. Criminal negligence involves the same degree of risk as criminal recklessness—an unreasonable and substantial risk of death or great bodily harm. The difference between the two is that recklessness requires that the actor be subjectively aware of the risk, while criminal negligence requires only that the actor should have been aware of the risk—an objective standard.

We are satisfied that the evidence and reasonable inferences flowing from the evidence support the jury's conclusion that RKI's conduct created a substantial and unreasonable risk of death or great bodily harm to its employees. RKI's job performance violated general and specific safety requirements. Although RKI did not violate Occupational Safety and Health Act (OSHA) regulations governing working in the vicinity of electrical power lines, it did violate written safety guidelines applying to this job. In addition, RKI's contract for this specific job required it to comply with certain safety guidelines while on property owned by Wisconsin Electric Power Company.

The evidence permits the reasonable inference that RKI neglected to act with due diligence to insure the safety of its employees as they installed sewer pipes in the vicinity of overhead electrical lines. RKI's management took no action to have the power lines de-energized or barriers erected; rather, management elected to merely warn employees about the overhead lines. A finder of fact would be justified in reasonably inferring that RKI had ample notice that the existence of overhead power lines would interfere with the job, and unless there was compliance with safety regulations, working in the vicinity of the overhead lines posed a substantial risk to its employees.

The evidence supports the conclusion that if RKI had enforced the written safety regulations of OSHA, had abided by its own written safety program and had complied with the contract requirements for construction on Wisconsin Electric's property, the electrocution death would likely not have happened. The finder of fact was justified in concluding that RKI operated vehicles in close proximity to the overhead power lines without recognizing the potential hazard to its employees in the vicinity of the vehicles. The jury could reasonably find that RKI's failure to take elementary precautions for the safety of its employees was a substantial cause of the electrocution death.

Judgment affirmed.

BROWN, Judge (dissenting).

I respectfully dissent from the majority decision. I have no quarrel with the general policy considerations favoring corporate criminal liability. And it is indisputable

WISJI—CRIMINAL 430, "Corporate Liability: Acts of Lesser Employees: Other than Strict Liability Cases."

that past Wisconsin cases have made corporations criminally liable for the acts of their agents. But I am convinced that those past cases were based upon statutes with substantially different wording than the statute in this case.

For example, the most often cited illustration favoring corporate criminal liability is *Vulcan Last Co. v. State*. The corporation desired to have the City of Crandon install waterworks so that the plant of the company would have fire protection. An alderman who was an employee of the company voted against the resolution. The plant superintendent held a meeting of employees in which he stated that any person who voted against the company's interest in the upcoming referendum would be discharged; moreover, the alderman was discharged because of his vote at the council meeting. Vulcan Last was charged with attempting to influence the vote of employees by threatening discharge and was convicted. On appeal, one of Vulcan Last's defenses was that, as a corporation, it could not be convicted of a crime. But the supreme court rejected the claim based upon its reading of the statute. The statute at issue stated in pertinent part: "No person shall, by threatening to discharge a person from his employment . . . , attempt to influence a qualified voter. . . ."

The supreme court noted that the statute prohibited any "person" from attempting to influence a voter in the manner prescribed. The court then ruled that the word "person" in a penal statute means "person in law." The court reasoned that a "person in law" included artificial as well as natural persons.

Vulcan Last therefore stands for the proposition that when a statute refers to a "person" or "persons" as the perpetrator, then artificial persons are subject to criminal liability. It also establishes that corporations should be held criminally responsible under a statute employing the words "person" or "persons" unless specifically exempted.

I am satisfied, however, that the instant statute falls outside the *Vulcan Last* rationale. Here, the statute specifically applies to "whoever" causes the death of "another human being" by negligent operation or handling of a vehicle. Clearly, the phrase "another human being" is a referent to the word "whoever." Thus, the pronoun "whoever" is of the same class as its referent—another human being. In my view, the language unambiguously confines the word "whoever" to a natural person, not an artificial person. I am further of the view that this language is an express determination by the legislature that only natural persons, not artificial persons, may be held liable under this statute.

I am influenced by the holding in *People v. Rochester Ry. & Light Co.*, 88 N.E. 22 (1909), cited by Knutson. The court there held that a corporation could not be indicted for homicide where the penal code defined homicide as the "killing of one human being by the act, procurement or omission of another." The court wrote:

> We think that this final word "another" naturally and clearly means a second or additional member of the same kind or class alone referred to by the preceding words, namely, another human being, and that we should not interpret it as appellant asks us to, as meaning another "person," which

might then include corporations. . . . It is true that the term "person" used therein may at times include corporations, but that is not the case here.

I acknowledge that this New York case is old, but so is the English language. What was basic syntactic analysis in 1909 would be unchanged in 1995.

An *American Law Reports* annotation also supports the New York court's reasoning. According to the annotation:

> In jurisdictions where homicide is defined as the killing of a human being by another human being, the definition itself seems to preclude corporate liability for the crime. However, the courts have a more difficult job of analyzing the law in jurisdictions where "person" is used in place of "human being" in the definition of homicide since "person" may include or exclude corporations.

The annotation goes on to cite the reasoning in the New York case as support for commentary. I find all of these authorities persuasive and would adopt them in ruling for Knutson.

The majority opinion dismisses the grammatical distinctions between the statute involved in this case and the statutes in cases like *Vulcan Last* by concluding that it is "not the description of the perpetrator as a 'person'" which governs corporate liability. Rather, it is the public policy of this state to expose corporations to criminal liability whenever a crime is punishable by fine. As I read the majority opinion, what it is saying is that whenever the legislature imposes a fine as one of the alternative methods of punishment, it automatically means to subject corporations to criminal liability no matter what the language of the statute is. The word "fine" is the key to corporate exposure, not any other language of the statute.

The majority gets this idea from its reading of *State ex rel. Kropf v. Gilbert*. The majority cites *Kropf* to say that "it is now well established that a corporation can be held guilty of crime when it is punishable by a fine." But that is not what the case said. What the case really said was:

> Although it is now well established that a corporation can be held guilty of crime when it is punishable by a fine, it has been repeatedly held that when the only punishment prescribed for an offense is imprisonment, which cannot in the nature of things be inflicted upon it, no information or indictment will lie against it because the law does not permit or require that which is futile.

What the *Kropf* court was saying is that while other jurisdictions have generally held that a corporation *can* be held guilty of a crime when it is punishable by a fine, Wisconsin's courts will not hold a corporation guilty if the punishment is imprisonment. This holding is a far cry from ruling that, in Wisconsin, corporations *will* be held liable if a crime is punishable by a fine. The most that can be said about the *Kropf* holding is that when a fine is a form of punishment, it is not a futile exercise for the legislature to expose corporations to criminal liability. In my view, *Kropf* does not resolve the issue in this case; it only begs the question, which is: Did the legislature intend to subject corporations to criminal liability under this statute?

Compounding its error, the majority then reasons that since the supreme court has repeatedly held that corporations can be held liable for criminal acts, and since the legislature's criminal code revisions remained silent about corporate criminal liability, therefore the legislature has acquiesced in the supreme court's pronouncements. But as I have already pointed out, the supreme court has not made the sweeping pronouncement claimed by the majority. The supreme court's judgments regarding corporate liability are no more and no less than what it initially announced in *Vulcan Last*. As I have pointed out, the statute in this case differs substantially from the one in *Vulcan Last* and the reasoning of *Vulcan Last* cannot be applied here.

The majority admits that my use of the canons of statutory construction is "proper," but complains that I have neglected to consider our prerogative to "disregard grammatical errors or mistakes in statutes in order to give effect to the intent of the legislature." I am unaware, however, of any information which would lead me to believe that the language of the instant statute is a "grammatical error [ ] or mistake[ ]." The statutes were substantially modified from the original 1955 laws in 1987 after extended study by the Judicial Council. The Judicial Council is well known for its scholarship and careful attention to detail. I refuse to believe that the language of the present statute is the result of inadvertence or ignorance of the legislative purpose.

What this debate really comes down to is whether it is desirable that a court avoid the literal meaning of this statute. I acknowledge that there exists a tension between the language of the statute and the announced public policy goal by some of our citizenry that corporations be held to criminal liability for negligent deaths. And I reject the notion that we should never search for the "real" rule lying behind the mere words on a printed page. But when the statute's wording is so clear in its contextural rigidity, the statute has therefore generated an answer which excludes otherwise eligible answers from consideration. Unlike the majority, I take the clear wording of the statute seriously. Since the majority has seen fit to quote Justice Oliver Wendell Holmes, Jr., I too quote from a past justice of the nation's highest court. In *United States v. Public Util. Comm'n*, 345 U.S. 295 (1953), Justice Robert Jackson wrote: "I should concur in this result more readily if the Court could reach it by analysis of the statute instead of by psychoanalysis of Congress." My sentiments exactly.

Questions and Notes

1. Where was the negligence? The operator of the backhoe? The corporate official who let the operation occur near a live wire? If it was the driver, is it fair to hold the corporation liable? *Compare Christy Pontiac.* If it was the corporate official, how is the crime "vehicular homicide"?

2. Should the court have been more receptive to the semantic arguments (whoever kills *another* human being)? Should it matter that this statute was a change

from the old statute, which used the term "person," and defined "person" to include a corporation?

3. Do you think that the statute was ambiguous? If not, which side had the better reading?

4. If you had been on the Wisconsin court, with whom would you have agreed? Why?

5. Suppose that the crime (e.g., murder) prescribed a minimum jail term. Would such a provision preclude corporate liability even on proof that the corporate board of directors voted to hire a killer to kill a competitor? Should it?

6. In *Cincotta*, we will explore the interrelationship between corporate and individual liability.

United States v. Cincotta
689 F.2d 238 (1st Cir. 1982)

Coffin, Chief Judge.

Appellant Mystic Fuel Corporation (Mystic) was engaged in the business of delivering heating oil to oil consumers. It did not own or rent oil storage tanks, but it did own several trucks for transporting oil. It used those trucks to earn money in two different ways: it entered delivery contracts whereby oil suppliers without trucks would pay Mystic a commission to deliver oil to the suppliers' customers; and it entered supply contracts whereby oil consumers would buy oil directly from Mystic, which Mystic would then acquire in its own name from suppliers.

Appellant Cincotta was a major stockholder in Mystic, and its Treasurer. He signed all the company's checks, bids, and contracts. Together with appellant Zero, he made all the major decisions of the company, as well as the rules governing its daily operation.

Appellant Zero was also a major stockholder in Mystic, and its dispatcher. He hired the truck drivers, and issued their daily orders on where to pick up and deliver oil. He also supervised Mystic's billing and accounting.

At trial, the government set forth evidence of a scheme through which Mystic would defraud the United States Department of Defense, inducing it to pay for oil that Mystic would sell in its own name to its own clients. The evidence suggested that during fiscal year 1978 (September 1, 1977, through August 31, 1978) Mystic had a delivery contract giving it a commission for delivering "number four oil" (a moderately heavy oil, generally used to heat small industrial buildings, schools, and medium-sized apartment buildings) from the Union Petroleum Corporation (Union) to Fort Devens in Ayer, Massachusetts. The evidence suggested further that on numerous occasions Mystic picked up a shipment of oil at Union, representing that the oil was for delivery to Fort Devens. Then, Mystic would sell the shipment to its own consumer clients. Finally, it would tell the Fort Devens authorities that it had in fact delivered the shipment to Fort Devens, inducing the Department of

Defense to pay Union for the shipment. The net result was that Fort Devens paid for shipments it never received, and Mystic was able to sell oil that it had never paid for.

After a two-week trial, the jury deliberated for ten hours and then found all three defendants guilty of (1) conspiring to defraud the United States in violation of 18 U.S.C. § 371, of (2) wilfully causing seven specific false claims to be made against the United States, in violation of 18 U.S.C. §§ 2, 287, and of (3) knowingly and wilfully making and using seven specific false documents in relation to a matter within the jurisdiction of a United States department, in violation of 18 U.S.C. §§ 2, 1001.

Sufficiency of the Evidence Against Cincotta

Appellant Cincotta contends that the trial judge erred in denying his motion for a judgment of acquittal at the close of the government's case. He argues that the evidence was not sufficient to permit the jury to conclude beyond a reasonable doubt that he personally violated the statutes under which he was convicted. Although he does not contest the sufficiency of the evidence establishing a conspiracy to present false claims, he does contest the sufficiency of the evidence that he was a part of the conspiracy.

Our review of the trial judge's decision on this point is quite limited. We are required to affirm that decision unless the evidence, viewed in the light most favorable to the government, could not have persuaded any rational trier of fact that Cincotta was guilty beyond a reasonable doubt. Moreover, "[p]articipation in a criminal conspiracy need not be proved by direct evidence; a common purpose and plan may be inferred from a 'development and a collocation of circumstances.'" *Glasser v. United States*, 315 U.S. 60, 80 (1942) (citation omitted).

Given this standard of review, we cannot reverse the trial judge's decision. Although there was no "smoking gun" that directly demonstrated Cincotta's sponsorship of the fraudulent conspiracy, there was ample circumstantial evidence. The principal source of that evidence was Elaine Kelly, Cincotta's secretary at Mystic. Mrs. Kelly testified that all major decisions at Mystic were made by either Cincotta or Zero. She testified further that "John Zero and Eddie Cincotta talked over everything that was going on. . . . [W]ho eventually made the final decision I don't know. I would think it would be a mutual thing, or maybe one or the other had a better decision than the other." She also testified that Cincotta "made all the rules . . . for the truck drivers, during the course of the day." Although Zero normally gave the drivers their instructions regarding deliveries to Fort Devens, Cincotta gave them their instructions in Zero's absence. And although Zero and Cincotta mutually handled all company firing decisions, Cincotta alone signed the corporation's checks, contracts, nd bids. Finally, the extent of Cincotta's interest in Mystic's activities is magnified by the fact that his mother and two uncles worked with him in the small company office.

In addition to Mrs. Kelly's testimony there was corroboration in regard to the Fort Devens fraud in the testimony of other witnesses. Frederick Taubert, the Vice President of Marketing at Union Petroleum, testified that he dealt with either Zero or Cincotta on any issues involving the Fort Devens contract, and that he perceived Cincotta to be in charge of the whole operation of Mystic on a day-to-day basis. Patricia Phelan, the supply clerk and ordering officer at Fort Devens, testified that Zero and Cincotta usually came in together twice a week to have her sign the fuel tickets acknowledging delivery of fuel shipments to Fort Devens. She testified further that on those occasions when another Mystic employee brought in the fuel tickets for her signature, if the tickets did not show to what building the oil had allegedly been delivered she would call up Zero or Cincotta and they would give her a building number to fill in. And several truck drivers, including Anthony Carpenter and Brian Esterbrook, referred to the duo collectively, as "John or Eddie", "Zero or Cincotta", in describing the source of their delivery instructions.

In sum, there was sufficient evidence of Cincotta's pervasive involvement in Mystic's operations—both generally and with regard to the Fort Devens deliveries in particular—for a reasonable juror to infer that Cincotta knew of, profited from, and encouraged the conspiracy and each of the individual fraudulent acts that underlay the substantive counts for which he was convicted.

Sufficiency of the Evidence Against Mystic Fuel

A corporation may be convicted for the criminal acts of its agents, under a theory of respondeat superior. But criminal liability may be imposed on the corporation only where the agent is acting within the scope of employment. That, in turn, requires that the agent be performing acts of the kind which he is authorized to perform, and those acts must be motivated—at least in part—by an intent to benefit the corporation. Thus, where intent is an element of a crime (as it is here), a corporation may not be held strictly accountable for acts that could not benefit the stockholders, such as acts of corporate officers that are performed in exchange for bribes paid to the officers personally.

Mystic argues that the trial court erred in denying its motion for acquittal. It contends that the government failed to produce evidence of Cincotta's and/or Zero's intent to benefit the corporation through their scheme to defraud the United States. This argument may be rejected out of hand. The mechanism by which the fraudulent scheme worked required money to pass through Mystic's treasury. When Fort Devens paid Union for the undelivered shipments, the shipments were not resold in Zero's name of Cincotta's name. Rather, they were sold to Mystic's customers in Mystic's name. Mystic—not the individual defendants—was making money by selling oil that it had not paid for.

Other Issues Raised by Appellants

Zero and Cincotta also challenge the trial court's jury instruction on when "conscious avoidance of knowledge" is adequate to demonstrate criminal intent. They argue that there was no evidentiary predicate for the charge. We disagree. There was sufficient evidence that a reasonable juror could have concluded that Cincotta, in bringing delivery tickets to Fort Devens for signature, consciously chose not to know whether the deliveries had been made, when he had reason to believe that they had not been made. The appellants also argue that the charge was deficient because it did not include "balancing language" instructing the jurors that wilfull blindness constitutes knowledge of a fact only where the individual does not subjectively disbelieve the fact. *See United States v. Jewell* [Chapter 8, *supra*]. Although such language may indeed provide useful clarification, the defendants did not ask for it to be included, and the failure to use it is not plain error.

Appellant Zero argues that the instruction raised an unconstitutional presumption of guilt against him when, in attempting to relate the conscious avoidance charge to the facts of the case, the court said, "There has been a great deal of evidence with respect to what was done by the defendant Mr. Zero, but a relatively small amount of evidence with respect to the defendant Mr. Cincotta." Although we can appreciate appellant's point, we believe the trial court nullified any potential prejudice when, only four sentences later, it continued:

> "Now, giving you that instruction I hope you know does not constitute any comment by the Court on the weight of the evidence. The Court is not suggesting that you find that Mr. Cincotta consciously avoided knowledge here of things that were going on, nor does the Court imply that what Mr. Zero did or did not do is a basis for his being either convicted or acquitted. That is what is meant when it says that you are the exclusive judges of the facts."

The judgments of conviction are affirmed.

Questions and Notes

1. Does it make sense to convict a corporation of conspiring with its alter egos? Had Cincotta been acquitted, would a conspiracy between Zero and the corporation lie? Should it?

2. If your answer to the hypothetical in Question 1 is "yes," doesn't that effectively convict Zero of *four* crimes (his substantive crime, his conspiracy, Mystic's substantive crime, Mystic's conspiracy) for every *one* he committed?

3. Whatever may be said for substantive liability predicated on wilfull blindness, does the concept make any sense in the conspiratorial context?

Chapter 22

Fair Notice

One of the most basic notions of criminal law is that before the crime is committed, the defendant has fair notice that her conduct will be deemed criminal. Two basic notions underlie this requirement. First, many of the values of punishment, particularly restraint and deterrence, require that the defendant be aware that the activity she is contemplating is criminal. Second, from a societal perspective, to the extent that the parameters of crime are not clear, the opportunity for arbitrary enforcement is enhanced.

What constitutes adequate notice is explored in *Keeler*.

Keeler v. Superior Court
470 P.2d 617 (Cal. 1970)

Mosk, Justice

In this proceeding for writ of prohibition we are called upon to decide whether an unborn but viable fetus is a "human being" within the meaning of the California statute defining murder (Pen. Code, § 187). We conclude that the Legislature did not intend such a meaning, and that for us to construe the statute to the contrary and apply it to this petitioner would exceed our judicial power and deny petitioner due process of law.

The evidence received at the preliminary examination may be summarized as follows: Petitioner and Teresa Keeler obtained an interlocutory decree of divorce on September 27, 1968. They had been married for 16 years. Unknown to petitioner, Mrs. Keeler was then pregnant by one Ernest Vogt, whom she had met earlier that summer. She subsequently began living with Vogt in Stockton but concealed the fact from petitioner. Petitioner was given custody of their two daughters, aged 12 and 13 years, and under the decree Mrs. Keeler had the right to take the girls on alternate weekends.

On February 23, 1969, Mrs. Keeler was driving on a narrow mountain road in Amador County after delivering the girls to their home. She met petitioner driving in the opposite direction; he blocked the road with his car, and she pulled over to the side. He walked to her vehicle and began speaking to her. He seemed calm, and she rolled down her window to hear him. He said, "I hear you're pregnant. If you are you had better stay away from the girls and from here." She did not reply, and he opened the car door; as she later testified "He assisted me out of the car. . . . [I]t wasn't roughly at this time." Petitioner then looked at her abdomen and became "extremely upset." He said, "You sure are. I'm going to stomp it out of you." He pushed her against the car, shoved his knee into her abdomen, and struck her in the face with several blows. She fainted, and when she regained consciousness, petitioner had departed.

Mrs. Keeler drove back to Stockton, and the police and medical assistance were summoned. She had suffered substantial facial injuries, as well as extensive bruising of the abdominal wall. A Caesarian section was performed and the fetus was examined *in utero.* Its head was found to be severely fractured, and it was delivered stillborn. The pathologist gave as his opinion that the cause of death was skull fracture with consequent cerebral hemorrhaging, that death would have been immediate, and that the injury could have been the result of force applied to the mother's abdomen. There was no air in the fetus' lungs, and the umbilical cord was intact.

Upon delivery the fetus weighed five pounds and was 18 inches in length. Both Mrs. Keeler and her obstetrician testified that fetal movements had been observed prior to February 23, 1969. The evidence was in conflict as to the estimated age of the fetus;[1] the expert testimony on the point, however, concluded "with reasonable medical certainty" that the fetus had developed to the stage of viability, *i.e.,* that in the event of premature birth on the date in question it would have had a 75 percent to 96 percent chance of survival.

An information was filed charging petitioner, in Count I, with committing the crime of murder (Pen. Code, § 187) in that he did "unlawfully kill a human being, to with Baby Girl Vogt, with malice aforethought." In Count II petitioner was charged with willful infliction of traumatic injury upon his wife (Pen. Code § 273d), and in Count III, with assault on Mrs. Keeler by means of force likely to produce great bodily injury (Pen. Code, § 245). His motion to set aside the information for lack of probable cause (Pen. Code, § 995) was denied, and he now seeks a writ of prohibition; as will appear, only the murder count is actually in issue. Pending our disposition of the matter, petitioner is free on bail.

[The court found that at common law and under the California statute a stillborn fetus could not be deemed a homicide victim.]

The People urge, however, that the sciences of obstetrics and pediatrics have greatly progressed since 1872, to the point where with proper medical care a normally developed fetus prematurely born at 28 weeks or more has an excellent chance of survival, *i.e.,* is viable"; that the common law requirement of live birth to prove the fetus had become a "human being" who may be the victim of murder is no

---

1. Mrs. Keeler testified, in effect, that she had no sexual intercourse with Vogt prior to August 1968, which would have made the fetus some 28 weeks old. She stated that the pregnancy had reached the end of the seventh month and the projected delivery date was April 25, 1969. The obstetrician, however, first estimated she was at least 31 1/2 weeks pregnant, then raised the figure to 35 weeks in the light of the autopsy report of the size and weight of the fetus. Finally, on similar evidence an attending pediatrician estimated the gestation period to have been between 34 1/2 and 36 weeks. The average full-term pregnancy is 40 weeks.

longer in accord with scientific fact, since an unborn but viable fetus is now fully capable of independent life; and that one who unlawfully and maliciously terminates such a life should therefore be liable to prosecution for murder under section 187. We may grant the premises of this argument; indeed, we neither deny nor denigrate the vast progress of medicine in the century since the enactment of the Penal Code. But we cannot join in the conclusion sought to be deduced: we cannot hold this petitioner to answer for murder by reason of his alleged act of killing an unborn—even though viable—fetus. To such a charge there are two insuperable obstacles, one "jurisdictional" and the other constitutional.

Penal Code section 6 declares in relevant part that "No act or omission" accomplished after the code has taken effect "is criminal or punishable, except as prescribed or authorized by this Code, or by some of the statutes which it specifies as continuing in force and as not affected by its provisions, or by some ordinance, municipal, county, or township regulation. . . ." This section embodies a fundamental principle of our tripartite form of government, *i.e.*, that subject to the constitutional prohibition against cruel and unusual punishment, the power to define crimes and fix penalties is vested exclusively in the legislative branch. Stated differently, there are no common law crimes in California.

The second obstacle to the proposed judicial enlargement of section 187 is the guarantee of due process of law. Assuming arguendo that we have the power to adopt the new construction of this statute as the law of California, such a ruling, by constitutional command, could operate only prospectively, and thus could not in any event reach the conduct of petitioner on February 23, 1969.

The first essential of due process is fair warning of the act which is made punishable as a crime. "That the terms of a penal statute creating a new offense must be sufficiently explicit to inform those who are subject to it what conduct on their part will render them liable to its penalties, is a well-recognized requirement, consonant alike with ordinary notions of fair play and the settled rules of law." (*Connally v. General Constr. Co.* (1926) 269 U.S. 385, 391.) "No one may be required at peril of life, liberty or property to speculate as to the meaning of penal statutes. All are entitled to be informed as to what the State commands or forbids." (*Lanzetta v. New Jersey* (1939) 306 U.S. 451, 453.)

This requirement of fair warning is reflected in the constitutional prohibition against the enactment of *ex post facto* laws (U.S. Const., art. I, §§ 9, 10; Cal. Const., art I, § 16). When a new penal statute is applied retrospectively to make punishable an act which was not criminal at the time it was performed, the defendant has been given no advance notice consistent with due process. And precisely the same effect occurs when such an act is made punishable under a preexisting statute but by means of an unforeseeable *judicial* enlargement thereof. (*Bouie v. City of Columbia* (1964) 378 U.S. 347.)

In *Bouie* two Negroes took seats in the restaurant section of a South Carolina drugstore; no notices were posted restricting the area to whites only. When the defendants refused to leave upon demand, they were arrested and convicted of violating a criminal trespass statute which prohibited entry on the property of another "after notice" forbidding such conduct. Prior South Carolina decisions had emphasized the necessity of proving such notice to support a conviction under the statute. The South Carolina Supreme Court nevertheless affirmed the convictions, construing the statute to prohibit not only the act of entering after notice not to do so but also the wholly different act of remaining on the property after receiving notice to leave.

The United States Supreme Court reversed the convictions, holding that the South Carolina court's ruling was "unforeseeable" and when an "unforeseeable state-court construction of a criminal statute is applied retroactively to subject a person to criminal liability for past conduct, the effect is to deprive him of due process of law in the sense of fair warning that his contemplated conduct constitutes a crime." Analogizing to the prohibition against retrospective penal legislation, the high court reasoned "Indeed, an unforeseeable judicial enlargement of a criminal statute, applied retroactively, operates precisely like an *ex post facto* law, such as Art. I, § 10, of the Constitution forbids. An *ex post facto* law has been defined by this Court as 'one that makes an action done before the passing of the law, and which was *innocent* when done, criminal; and punishes such action,' or 'that *aggravates a crime*, or makes it *greater* than it was, when committed.' 1 L.Ed. 648, 3 Dall. 386, 390. If a state legislature is barred by the *Ex Post Facto* Clause from passing such a law, it must follow that a State Supreme Court is barred by the Due Process Clause from achieving precisely the same result by judicial construction. The fundamental principle that 'the required criminal law must have existed when the conduct in issue occurred,' must apply to bar retroactive criminal prohibitions emanating from courts as well as from legislatures. If a judicial construction of a criminal statute is 'unexpected and indefensible by reference to the law which had been expressed prior to the conduct in issue,' it must not be given retroactive effect."

Turning to the case law, we find no reported decision of the California courts which should have given petitioner notice that the killing of an unborn but viable fetus was prohibited by section 187. Indeed, the contrary clearly appears from *People v. Eldridge* (1906) 3 Cal. App. 648, 649, 86 P. 832, in which the defendant challenged as uncertain an information which charged him with the murder of "a human being," to wit, the infant child "born to the said Glover H. Eldridge and said Mabel Eldridge on or about said twentieth day of February, 1905." It was urged that "such charge might include the killing before birth, and therefore it cannot be determined from the information whether murder or abortion was intended to be charged." The Court of Appeal rejected the contention, observing that "The only reasonable construction which can be given to the language employed in the information is to say that it charges that a child born to the defendant was by him unlawfully killed and murdered. That it was born is clearly stated; that it could be killed after birth of necessity implies that *it was born alive*, and we think the charge of murder was set forth with the degree of certainty required." (Italics added.)

Properly understood, the often cited case of *People v. Chavez* (1947) 77 Cal. App. 2d 621, 176 P.2d 92, does not derogate from this rule. There the defendant was charged with the murder of her newborn child and convicted of manslaughter. She testified that the baby dropped from her womb into the toilet bowl; that she picked it up two or three minutes later, and cut but did not tie the umbilical cord; that the baby was limp and made no cry; and that after 15 minutes she wrapped it in a newspaper and concealed it, where it was found dead the next day. The autopsy surgeon testified that the baby was a full-term nine-month child, weighing six and one-half pounds and appearing normal in every respect; that the body have very little blood in it, indicating the child had bled to death through the umbilical cord; that such a process would have taken about an hour, and that in his opinion "the child was born alive, based on conditions he found and the fact that the lungs contained air and the blood was extravasated or pushed back into the tissues, indicating heart action."

On appeal, the defendant emphasized that a doctor called by the defense had suggested other tests which the autopsy surgeon could have performed to determine the matter of live birth; on this basis, it was contended that the question of whether the infant was born alive "rests entirely on pure speculation." The Court of Appeal found only an insignificant conflict in that regard, and focused its attention instead on testimony of the autopsy surgeon admitting the possibility that the evidence of heart and lung action could have resulted from the child's breathing "after presentation of the head but before the birth was completed."

The court cited the mid-19th century English infanticide cases, and noted that the decisions had not reached uniformity on whether breathing, heart action, severance of the umbilical cord, or some combination of these or other factors established the status of "human being" for purposes of the law of homicide. The court then adverted to the state of modern medical knowledge, discussed the phenomenon of viability, and held that "a viable child *in the process of being born* is a human being within the meaning of the homicide statutes, whether or not the process has been fully completed. It should at least be considered a human being where it is a living baby and where in the natural course of events *a birth which is already started would naturally be successfully completed*." (Italics added.) Since the testimony of the autopsy surgeon left no doubt in that case that a live birth had at least begun, the court found "the evidence is sufficient here to support the implied finding of the jury that this child *was born alive and became a human being within the meaning of the homicide statutes*." (Italics added.)

Chavez thus stands for the proposition—to which we adhere—that a viable fetus "in the process of being born" is a human being within the meaning of the homicide statutes. But it stands for no more; in particular it does not hold that a fetus, however viable, which is not "in the process of being born" is nevertheless a "human being" in the law of homicide. On the contrary, the opinion is replete with references to the common law requirement that the child be "born alive," however that term is defined, and must accordingly be deemed to reaffirm that requirement as part of the law of California.

We conclude that the judicial enlargement of section 187 now urged upon us by the People would not have been foreseeable to this petitioner, and hence that its adoption at this time would deny him due process of law.

BURKE, Acting Chief Justice (dissenting).

The majority hold that "Baby Girl" Vogt, who, according to medical testimony, had reached the 35th week of development, had a 96 percent chance of survival, and was "definitely' alive and viable at the time of her death, nevertheless was not a "human being" under California's homicide statutes. In my view, in so holding, the majority ignore significant common law precedents, frustrate the express intent of the Legislature, and defy reason, logic and common sense.

We commonly conceive of human existence as a spectrum stretching from birth to death. However, if this court properly might expand the definition of "human being" at one end of that spectrum, we may do so at the other end. Consider the following example: All would agree that "Shooting or otherwise damaging a corpse is not homicide. . . ." (PERKINS, CRIMINAL LAW (2d ed. 1969) ch. 2, § 1, p. 31.) In other words, a corpse is not considered to be a "human being" and thus cannot be the subject of a "killing" as those terms are used in homicide statutes. However, it is readily apparent that our concepts of what constitutes a "corpse" have been and are being continually modified by advances in the field of medicine, including new techniques for life revival, restoration and resuscitation such as artificial respiration, open heart massage, transfusions, transplants, drugs and new surgical methods. Would this court ignore these developments and exonerate the killer of an apparently "drowned" child merely because that child would have been pronounced dead in 1648 or 1850? Obviously not. Whether a homicide occurred in that case would be determined by medical testimony regarding the capability of the child to have survived prior to the defendant's act. And that is precisely the test which this court should adopt in the instant case.

The majority suggest that to do so would improperly create some new offense. However, the offense of murder is no new offense. Contrary to the majority opinion, the Legislature has not "defined the crime of murder in California to apply only to the unlawful and malicious killing one who has been born alive." Instead, the Legislature simply used the broad term "human being" and directed the courts to construe that term according to its "fair import" with a view to effect the objects of the homicide statutes and promote justice. (Pen. Code, § 4.) What justice will be promoted, what objects effectuated, by construing "human being" as excluding Baby Girl Vogt and her unfortunate successors? Was defendant's brutal act of stomping her to death any less an act of homicide than the murder of a newly born baby? No one doubts that the term "human being" would include the elderly or dying persons whose potential for life has nearly lapsed; their proximity to death is deemed immaterial. There is no sound reason for denying the viable fetus, with its unbounded potential for life, the same status.

The majority also suggest that such an interpretation of our homicide statutes would deny defendant "fair warning" that his act was punishable as a crime. Aside from the absurdity of the underlying premise that defendant consulted Coke, Blackstone or Hale before kicking Baby Girl Vogt to death, it is clear that defendant had adequate notice that his act could constitute homicide. Due process only precludes prosecution under a new statute insufficiently explicit regarding the specific conduct prescribed, or under a pre-existing statute "by means of an unforeseeable judicial enlargement thereof."

Our homicide statutes have been in effect in this state since 1850. The fact that the California courts have not been called upon to determine the precise question before us does not render "unforeseeable" a decision which determines that a viable fetus is a "human being" under those statutes. Can defendant really claim surprise that a 5-pound, 18-inch, 34-week-old, living, viable child is considered to be a human being?

Moreover, apart from the common law approach, our Legislature has expressly directed us to construe the homicide statutes in accordance with the fair import of their terms. There is no good reason why a fully viable fetus should not be considered a "human being" under those statutes. To so construe them would not create any new offense and would not deny defendant fair warning or due process since the Chavez case anticipated that construction long ago.

The trial court's denial of defendant's motion to set aside the information was proper, and the peremptory writ of prohibition should be denied.

Questions and Notes

1. Do you think that Keeler consulted Coke, Blackstone, or Hale before stomping Baby Girl Vogt to death? Assuming that your answer is "no," should Keeler nevertheless be able to complain about the prosecutor's attempted deviation from those authorities? Why? Why not?

2. What is an *ex post facto* law? Why are they forbidden?

3. Do *Keeler* and *Bouie v. Columbia* mean that a state court cannot redefine such concepts as "malice" in murder or "intent to steal" in theft? Is so, what role is left for the judiciary?

4. If you were an appellate judge (and thought that you had the power to do so) would you have announced that in the future a viable fetus will be deemed a victim for purposes of the homicide statute? Why? Why not?

5. Subsequent to *Keeler*, California passed legislation rendering fetuses victims for purposes of murder and manslaughter statutes. In *People v. Davis*, 872 P.2d 591 (1994), the California Supreme Court held that a nonviable fetus was also protected

by the statute. But, applying *Keeler* principles, the Court held that its novel construction of the statute* could not be applied to Mr. Davis.

6. As you read *Hall*, think about whether he had more or less notice than *Keeler*.

People v. Hall
557 N.Y.S.2d 879 (N.Y. App. Div. 1990)

Milonas, Justice.

This case concerns a matter of first impression in New York State; specifically, whether an individual can be convicted of the homicide of an infant who succumbs following a premature Caesarean birth necessitated by the shooting of her pregnant mother. In that regard, the facts [adduced] at trial demonstrate the following:

> On the evening of May 16, 1986, defendant Leonard Hall became engaged in a fistfight with Darryl Aaron in a grocery store at Lenox Avenue and 127th Street in Manhattan. After the two men were separated, defendant left to procure a gun. He then returned to the scene of the altercation and waited across the street until Aaron emerged from a corner pool hall. Defendant thereupon opened fire at Aaron, who managed to avoid being hit by ducking for cover. However, two of the bullets hit a passerby, Brigette Garrett, who was on her way to nearby Sylvia's Restaurant, striking her in the arm and the abdomen. Despite being seriously injured, one of the shots having penetrated her uterus and also damaging the intestinal-bowel system, she survived. Garrett was, at the time, some twenty-eight to thirty-two weeks pregnant, and the shot to the stomach also severed the placenta, resulting in a lack of oxygen to the fetus, which mandated an immediate delivery. The baby, Atallia, was born by Caesarean section and lived for some thirty-six hours before expiring from a series of maladies attributed to prematurity and oxygen deprivation.

First, and foremost, [Hall] insists that Garrett's baby was not a "person" as contemplated by Penal Law 125.05(1) and that, therefore, his conviction for manslaughter in the second degree violates certain principles of statutory construction and constitutional proscriptions and, moreover, was not supported by sufficient evidence. In addition, he asserts that his third statement should have been suppressed as the product of a delay in arraignment and that he was improperly sentenced as a second felony offender. There is no merit to any of these arguments.

Earlier Court of appeal cases had held that the statute was limited to viable fetuses.—Ed. The evidence at trial insofar as it relates to the Garrett baby shows that when Brigette Garrett was brought to Harlem Hospital, she was suffering from shock and the consequences of her serious injuries. Abdominal x-rays were taken to ascertain the size and position of her fetus. A sonogram was also performed, and it

---

* Earlier Court of appeal cases had held that the statute was limited to viable fetuses.—Ed.

revealed the presence of a fetal heartbeat. Garrett was then rushed to the operating room where an exploratory laparotomy was undertaken. At this point, it became evident that one bullet had entered her abdomen, passing through the top of her uterus, as well as her flanks, and exited her lower back. Part of the placenta was protruding from the wound. In the view of Dr. David Bateman, the Chief of Newborn Services and attending physician, the wound to Garrett's abdomen necessitated terminating the pregnancy since the bullet had separated the placenta from the womb, thereby cutting off the baby from her mother's oxygen and nutrient supply. According to Dr. Bateman, there would have been no reason for an early delivery by Caesarean section except for the gunshot wound. A team of obstetrical surgeons delivered the baby, which was of some twenty-eight to thirty-two weeks' gestation (the normal period is forty weeks) and turned her over to a team of neonatologists. In the meantime, another group of doctors operated on Garrett.

The infant weighed some two pounds five ounces at birth. Dr. Bateman testified that ninety percent of premature babies of this weight survive. However, Atallia, as a result of her prematurity, compounded by oxygen starvation due to the rupture of the placenta, was very unhealthy at the moment of her removal from her mother's womb. She had an Apgar score of one (the system utilized by hospitals to measure a baby's condition at birth, which assigns a value of from zero to two for each of five variables for a maximum of ten, with a score of zero meaning the absence of life and any positive score reflecting the existence of life) because her heart rate was less than 100 beats per minute, and she was limp. Yet, there was no indication of any congenital malformations or birth defects. Since Atallia's lungs were collapsed at the time of birth, she was immediately placed on a respirator to assist her in breathing. In addition, fluid and sugar were administered intravenously, and she was attached to a cardiac monitor.

Within the first ten minutes after delivery, Atallia's Apgar score had risen to four. Although she was still gravely ill, she had begun circulating blood effectively on her own, and she was making some respiratory effort. At twelve hours of age, Dr. Bateman observed that she was moving her arms and legs, a sign of brain activity. Thereafter, she developed Hyaline Membrane Disease, also known as Respiratory Distress Syndrome, common to premature infants. There was, moreover, testimony that this disease only occurs in a baby who is born alive and that a baby who never breathes or dies in utero never develops the syndrome. Dr. Bateman stated that, in his opinion, the bullet wound to Brigette Garrett, which severed the placenta and deprived the fetus of oxygen, impacted upon Atallia's development of Hyaline Membrane Disease following birth. Dr. Tamara Bloom, an Associate Medical Examiner, agreed that the disease could have been caused by the interruption of the flow of oxygen from the mother to the fetus.

Notwithstanding the efforts made to treat her, Atallia died thirty-six hours after she was born. The ensuing autopsy, which was performed on May 20, 1986, disclosed that the baby's weight had increased by 35 grams, that her lungs were heavy, airless and congested, symptomatic of Hyaline Membrane Disease, and that she had sustained an intraventricular hemorrhage (bleeding in the brain). Dr. Bateman asserted that he believed the hemorrhage to have been formed after birth as a direct consequence of the cutoff of oxygen in the placenta. Dr. Bloom also expressed the view that the hemorrhage was of recent vintage. In any event, while Atallia's circulatory system was adequate, her organs were severely congested, a fact due to an insufficiency of oxygen. The cause of death was described as being "prematurity, Hyaline Membrane Disease and intraventricular hemorrhage in the brain."

All of the doctors who treated or examined the infant were convinced that she was alive at the time of her birth and until she finally succumbed thirty-six hours later. Indeed, the autopsy revealed that her tissues were fresh and well preserved, and, according to Dr. Bloom, the tissues would not have been in this condition if she had been born dead. Similarly, Dr. Bloom explained that there was clear evidence of the baby's having breathed following birth as the duct connecting the major blood vessels and the heart were closed, and closure takes place only after birth. Further, Atallia's birth fits the statutory criteria for being alive. Pursuant to Public Health Law 4130(1):

> Live birth is defined as the complete expulsion or extraction from its mother of a product of conception, irrespective of the duration of pregnancy, which, after, such separation, breathes or shows any other evidence of life such as beating of the heart, pulsation of the umbilical cord, or definite movement of voluntary muscles, whether or not the umbilical cord has been cut or the placenta is attached; each product of such a birth is considered live born.

Since Atallia's birth was a live one under New York law, a birth certificate was filed for her. In contrast, the definition of "fetal death" was certainly not met herein. Pursuant to section 4160(1) of the Public Health Law, fetal death is "death prior to the complete expulsion or extraction from its mother of a product of conception; the death is indicated by the fact that after such separation, the fetus does not breathe or show any other evidence of life such as beating of the heart, pulsation of the umbilical cord, or definitive movement of voluntary muscles." Atallia had been fully expelled from her mother; she was no longer attached to the placenta, had a heartbeat and was capable of independent circulation. She also made respiratory efforts on her own and even showed signs of spontaneous movement. Under these circumstances, there can be no doubt that she was born alive despite defendant's persistent refusal to recognize such an obvious fact. Thus, he unrelentingly refers to Atallia not as a baby or infant or by name, but simply as a fetus, as if by characterizing her as a fetus on enough occasions he can transform her live birth into a miscarriage or a feticide. Defendant, of course, emphasizes that Atallia was in extremely precarious health at birth. In that regard, he points to her having been born limp, to her possessing an Apgar score of only one at the time, her having immediately been placed on a ventilator and to the lack of spontaneous movement at the time of birth.

Defendant, additionally, appears to advance the novel proposition that someone who requires the assistance of modern medical technology to survive, even temporarily, is not really alive. However, it is unclear whether this theory is to be applied only to the newborn or to all people irrespective of age. Perhaps defendant is suggesting that only those persons who have first been the beneficiaries of good health can be considered alive if they subsequently develop medical problems necessitating technological intervention but that sick babies are not fully alive until they recover or their condition improves both significantly and permanently (Atallia did get better before she developed Hyaline Membrane Disease.) In short, defendant seems to claim that although Atallia may not have been completely dead at birth, she was not sufficiently alive to be deemed a "person." This position is untenable. Illness is not equivalent to the absence of life, and the fact that Atallia was very sick at birth scarcely means that she was not alive. Notwithstanding defendant's concerted attempt to depict her as the victim of a feticide, resulting in a miscarriage or stillbirth, she was, by any reasonable measure, born alive.

Defendant was charged with causing the death of a person who had been born and lived after birth, not with causing the death of a fetus, and he was prosecuted under this theory. The trial court never held that a fetus may be considered a "person" under the homicide provisions, nor did the judge instruct the jury that defendant could be found guilty of causing the death of a fetus. Thus, defendant's entire discussion insofar as it pertains to the killing of a fetus is simply irrelevant. It should also be noted that this case does not involve abortion, and any attempt to equate defendant's situation with that of an individual performing or being the recipient of an abortion is unavailing.

Appellate courts in other jurisdictions which have reviewed the issue of whether an individual can be convicted of homicide for injuries inflicted on a fetus that lead to the death of the child after it is born alive have, virtually without exception, decided this question in the affirmative. In *United States v. Spencer*, 839 F.2d 1341 (9th Cir.), defendant kicked and stabbed a pregnant woman in the abdomen, requiring an emergency Caesarean section. The infant lived for ten minutes, yet the court determined that the baby had been born alive so that the infliction of injuries upon the fetus constituted murder under 18 U.S.C. §§ 1153 and 1111. Similarly, in *Williams v. State*, 561 A.2d 216, defendant's arrow struck a pregnant bystander, and her baby was born alive an hour before the mother's death; the child lived for seventeen hours. The court therein upheld defendant's conviction for manslaughter with respect to the infant.

Defendant's claim that his homicide conviction is contrary to due process because the existing penal scheme did not give him proper notice of proscribed conduct and, in addition, contravenes his right to the equal protection of the laws by implementing an irrational classification is totally lacking in substance. A criminal statute violates the prohibition against *ex post facto* law only if it does not furnish a person of ordinary intelligence with fair notice that contemplated actions are forbidden by law (*United States v. Harriss*, 347 U.S. 612). However, it is impossible to perceive how an individual of even less than ordinary intelligence can fail to be aware that standing on a street and firing at someone in a crowd on the other side is not lawful conduct, and, in fact, defendant's behavior after the shooting in immediately divesting himself of the gun and lying low for the next several days clearly indicates that he recognized the criminality involved in his actions.

It is axiomatic that a perpetrator of illegal conduct takes his victims as he finds them, so it is entirely irrelevant whether defendant actually knew or should have known that a pregnant woman was in the vicinity and that her fetus could be wounded as a result of his actions. Clearly, it is the nature of defendant's behavior which is at issue, not the identity of the victim(s), and it is simply ludicrous to suppose that a particular statute fails to provide fair notice of forbidden conduct if it does not expressly anticipate every possible criminal contingency. Since defendant's conduct in firing a loaded gun into a crowd on the street was of such a nature as would enable a rational person to comprehend that it is a gross deviation from the normal standard of behavior, thereby creating a substantial and unjustifiable risk that someone might be shot and injured or killed, it is fatuous for him to complain that he did not receive fair notice that he was acting in a criminal manner. Consequently, the judgment should be affirmed.

Questions and Notes

1. Did Hall have more notice of Atallia Garrett than Keeler had of Baby Girl Vogt?

2. Assuming that your answer to Question 1 was "no," why was Hall convicted and Keeler acquitted?

3. Does the *Keeler/Hall* rule mean that those who kill the fetus more efficiently go free whereas those who merely injures a fetus that dies later are murderers or manslaughterers? If so, does that make any sense?

4. In the next three cases, the United States Supreme Court struggled with the inherently vague concept of "vagueness."

Papachristou v. Jacksonville
405 U.S. 156 (1972)

MR. JUSTICE DOUGLAS delivered the opinion of the Court.

This case involves eight defendants who were convicted in a Florida municipal court of violating a Jacksonville, Florida, vagrancy ordinance.[1] At issue are five

---

1. Jacksonville Ordinance Code § 26-57 provided at the time of these arrests and convictions as follows:

"Rogues and vagabonds, or dissolute persons who go about begging, common gamblers, persons who use juggling or unlawful games or plays, common drunkards, common night walkers, thieves, pilferers or pickpockets, traders in stolen property, lewd, wanton and lascivious persons, keepers of gambling places, common railers and brawlers, persons wandering or strolling around from place to place without any lawful purpose or object, habitual loafers, disorderly persons, persons neglecting all lawful business and habitually spending their time by frequenting houses of ill fame, gaming houses, or places where alcoholic beverages are sold or served, persons able to work but habitually living upon the

consolidated cases. Margaret Papachristou, Betty Calloway, Eugene Eddie Melton, and Leonard Johnson were all arrested early on a Sunday morning, and charged with vagrancy—"prowling by auto."

Jimmy Lee Smith and Milton Henry were charged with vagrancy—"vagabonds." Henry Edward Heath and a codefendant were arrested for vagrancy—"loitering" and "common thief."

Thomas Owen Campbell was charged with vagrancy—"common thief."

Hugh Brown was charged with vagrancy—"disorderly loitering on street" and "disorderly conduct—resisting arrest with violence."

The facts are stipulated. Papachristou and Calloway are white females. Melton and Johnson are black males. Papachristou was enrolled in a job-training program sponsored by the State Employment Service at Florida Junior College in Jacksonville. Calloway was a typing and shorthand teacher at a state mental institution located near Jacksonville. She was the owner of the automobile in which the four defendants were arrested. Melton was a Vietnam war veteran who had been released from the Navy after nine months in a veterans' hospital. On the date of his arrest he was a part-time computer helper while attending college as a full-time student in Jacksonville. Johnson was a tow-motor operator in a grocery chain warehouse and was a lifelong resident of Jacksonville.

At the time of their arrest the four of them were riding in Calloway's car on the main thoroughfare in Jacksonville. They had left a restaurant owned by Johnson's uncle where they had eaten and were on their way to a night club. The arresting officers denied that the racial mixture in the car played any part in the decision to make the arrest. The arrest, they said, was made because the defendants had stopped near a used-car lot which had been broken into several times. There was, however, no evidence of any breaking and entering on the night in question.

Of these four charged with "prowling by auto" none had been previously arrested except Papachristou who had once been convicted of a municipal offense.

Jimmy Lee Smith and Milton Henry (who is not a petitioner) were arrested between 9 and 10 a.m. on a weekday in downtown Jacksonville, while waiting for a friend who was to lend them a car so they could apply for a job at a produce company. Smith was a part-time produce worker and part-time organizer for a Negro

---

earnings of their wives or minor children shall be deemed vagrants and, upon conviction in the Municipal Court shall be punished as provided for Class D offenses."
Class D offenses at the time of these arrests and convictions were punishable by 90 days' imprisonment, $500 fine, or both. Jacksonville Ordinance Code § 1-8 (1965). The maximum punishment has since been reduced to 75 days or $450. § 304.101 (1971). We are advised that that downward revision was made to avoid federal right-to-counsel decisions. The Fifth Circuit case extending right to counsel in misdemeanors where a fine of $500 or 90 days' imprisonment could be imposed is *Harvey v. Mississippi*, 340 F.2d 263 (1965). We are advised that at present the Jacksonville vagrancy ordinance is § 330.107 and identical with the earlier one except that "juggling" has been eliminated.

political group. He had a common-law wife and three children supported by him and his wife. He had been arrested several times but convicted only once. Smith's companion, Henry, was an 18-year-old high school student with no previous record of arrest.

This morning it was cold, and Smith had no jacket, so they went briefly into a dry-cleaning shop to wait but left when requested to do so. They thereafter walked back and forth two or three times over a two-block stretch looking for their friend. The store owners, who apparently were wary of Smith and his companion, summoned two police officers who searched the men and found neither had a weapon. But they were arrested because the officers said they had no identification and because the officers did not believe their story.

Heath and a codefendant were arrested for "loitering" and for "common thief." Both were residents of Jacksonville, Heath having lived there all his life and being employed at an automobile body shop. Heath had previously been arrested but his codefendant had no arrest record. Heath and his companion were arrested when they drove up to a residence shared by Heath's girlfriend and some other girls. Some police officers were already there in the process of arresting another man. When Heath and his companion started backing out of the driveway, the officers signaled to them to stop and asked them to get out of the car, which they did. Thereupon they and the automobile were searched. Although no contraband or incriminating evidence was found, they were both arrested, Heath being charged with being a "common thief" because he was reputed to be a thief. The codefendant was charged with "loitering" because he was standing in the driveway, an act which the officers admitted was done only at their command.

Campbell was arrested as he reached his home very early one morning and was charged with "common thief." He was stopped by officers because he was traveling at a high rate of speed, yet no speeding charge was placed against him.

Brown was arrested when he was observed leaving a downtown Jacksonville hotel by a police officer seated in a cruiser. The police testified he was reputed to be a thief, narcotics pusher, and generally opprobrious character. The officer called Brown over to the car, intending at that time to arrest him unless he had a good explanation for being on the street. Brown walked over to the police cruiser, as commanded, and the officer began to search him, apparently preparatory to placing him in the car. In the process of the search he came on two small packets which were later found to contain heroin. When the officer touched the pocket where the packets were, Brown began to resist. He was charged with "disorderly loitering on street" and "disorderly conduct—resisting arrest with violence." While he was also charged with a narcotics violation, that charge was *nolled*.

This ordinance is void for vagueness, both in the sense that it "fails to give a person of ordinary intelligence fair notice that his contemplated conduct is forbidden by the statute," and because it encourages arbitrary and erratic arrests and convictions. Living under a rule of law entails various suppositions, one of which is that "[all persons] are entitled to be informed as to what the State commands or forbids." *Lanzetta v. New Jersey*, 306 U.S. 451, 453.

The Jacksonville ordinance makes criminal activities which by modern standards are normally innocent. "Nightwalking" is one. Florida construes the ordinance not to make criminal one night's wandering, only the "habitual" wanderer or as the ordinance describes it "common night walkers." We know, however, from experience that sleepless people often walk at night, perhaps hopeful that sleep-inducing relaxation will result.

Persons "wandering or strolling" from place to place have been extolled by Walt Whitman and Vachel Lindsay. The qualification "without any lawful purpose or object" may be a trap for innocent acts. Persons "neglecting all lawful business and habitually spending their time by frequenting . . . places where alcoholic beverages are sold or served" would literally embrace many members of golf clubs and city clubs.

This aspect of the vagrancy ordinance before us is suggested by what this Court said in 1876 about a broad criminal statute enacted by Congress: "It would certainly be dangerous if the legislature could set a net large enough to catch all possible offenders, and leave it to the courts to step inside and say who could be rightfully detained, and who should be set at large." *United States v. Reese*, 92 U.S. 214, 221.

While that was a federal case, the due process implications are equally applicable to the States and to this vagrancy ordinance. Here the net cast is large, not to give the courts the power to pick and choose but to increase the arsenal of the police.

Where the list of crimes is so all-inclusive and generalized as the one in this ordinance, those convicted may be punished for no more than vindicating affronts to police authority: "The common ground which brings such a motley assortment of human troubles before the magistrates in vagrancy-type proceedings is the procedural laxity which permits 'conviction' for almost any kind of conduct and the existence of the House of Correction as an easy and convenient dumping-ground for problems that appear to have no other immediate solution." Foote, *Vagrancy-Type Law and Its Administration*, 104 U. PA. L. REV. 603, 631.[11]

Another aspect of the ordinance's vagueness appears when we focus, not on the lack of notice given a potential offender, but on the effect of the unfettered discretion it places in the hands of the Jacksonville police. Caleb Foote, an early student of this subject, has called the vagrancy-type law as offering "punishment by analogy." *Id.* at 609. Such crimes, though long common in Russia, are not compatible with our constitutional system. We allow our police to make arrests only on "probable cause," a Fourth and Fourteenth Amendment standard applicable to the States as well as to the Federal Government. Arresting a person on suspicion, like arresting

11. Thus, "prowling by auto," which formed the basis for the vagrancy arrests and convictions of four of the petitioners herein, is not even listed in the ordinance as a crime. *But see Hanks v. State*, 195 So. 2d 49, 51, in which the Florida District Court of Appeal construed "wandering or strolling from place to place" as including travel by automobile.

a person for investigation, is foreign to our system, even when the arrest is for past criminality. Future criminality, however, is the common justification for the presence of vagrancy statutes. Florida has, indeed, construed her vagrancy statute "as necessary regulations," *inter alia*, "to deter vagabondage and prevent crimes." *Johnson v. State*, 202 So. 2d 852.

A direction by a legislature to the police to arrest all "suspicious" persons would not pass constitutional muster. A vagrancy prosecution may be merely the cloak for a conviction which could not be obtained on the real but undisclosed grounds for the arrest. A presumption that people who might walk or loaf or loiter or stroll or frequent houses where liquor is sold, or who are supported by their wives or who look suspicious to the police are to become future criminals is too precarious for a rule of law. The implicit presumption in these generalized vagrancy standards— that crime is being nipped in the bud—is too extravagant to deserve extended treatment. Of course, vagrancy statutes are useful to the police. Of course, they are nets making easy the roundup of so-called undesirables. But the rule of law implies equality and justice in its application. Vagrancy laws of the Jacksonville type teach that the scales of justice are so tipped that even-handed administration of the law is not possible. The rule of law, evenly applied to minorities as well as majorities, to the poor as well as the rich, is the great mucilage that holds society together.

The Jacksonville ordinance cannot be squared with our constitutional standards and is plainly unconstitutional.

Questions and Notes

1. Apart from the vagueness doctrine, is there any doctrine that we have studied this semester that would warrant invalidating Jacksonville's ordinance?

2. Should any of the *Papachristou* defendants have been subject to arrest?

3. If you represented Jacksonville's City Council and were asked to draft a vagrancy statute that was not vague, could you do it?

4. Consider California's effort in *Kolender v. Lawson*.

Kolender v. Lawson

461 U.S. 352 (1983)

JUSTICE O'CONNOR delivered the opinion of the Court.

This appeal presents a facial challenge to a criminal statute that requires persons who loiter or wander on the streets to provide a "credible and reliable" identification and to account for their presence when requested by a peace officer under circumstances that would justify a stop under the *Terry v. Ohio*, 392 U.S. 1 (1968)U.S. 1 (1968).[1] We conclude that the statute as it has been construed is unconstitutionally

---

1. [Under *Terry*, the police may stop an individual when there is reasonable suspicion that criminal activity may be afoot. — Ed.] California Penal Code Ann. § 647(e) (West 1970) provides:

vague within the meaning of the Due Process Clause of the Fourteenth Amendment by failing to clarify what is contemplated by the requirement that a suspect provide a "credible and reliable" identification. Accordingly, we affirm the judgment of the court below.

Appellee Edward Lawson was detained or arrested on approximately 15 occasions between March 1975 and January 1977 pursuant to Cal. Penal Code Ann. § 647(e).[2] Lawson was prosecuted only twice and was convicted once. The second charge was dismissed.

Lawson then brought a civil action in the District Court for the Southern District of California seeking a declaratory judgment that § 647(e) is unconstitutional, a mandatory injunction seeking to restrain enforcement of the statute, and compensatory and punitive damages against the various officers who detained him.

As construed by the California Court of Appeal, § 647(e) requires that an individual provide "credible and reliable" identification when requested by a police officer who has reasonable suspicion of criminal activity sufficient to justify a *Terry* detention. *People v. Solomon*, 33 Cal. App. 3d 429, 108 Cal. Rptr. 867. "Credible and reliable" identification is defined by the State Court of Appeal as identification "carrying reasonable assurance that the identification is authentic and providing means for later getting in touch with the person who has identified himself." In addition, a suspect may be required to "account for his presence . . . to the extent that it assists in producing credible and reliable identification. . . ." Under the terms of the statute, failure of the individual to provide "credible and reliable" identification permits the arrest.

Our Constitution is designed to maximize individual freedoms within a framework of ordered liberty. Statutory limitations on those freedoms are examined for substantive authority and content as well as for definiteness or certainty of expression.

As generally stated, the void-for-vagueness doctrine requires that a penal statute define the criminal offense with sufficient definiteness that ordinary people can

---

"Every person who commits any of the following acts is guilty of disorderly conduct, a misdemeanor: . . . (e) Who loiters or wanders upon the streets or from place to place without apparent reason or business and who refuses to identify himself and to account for his presence when requested by any peace officer so to do, if the surrounding circumstances are such as to indicate to a reasonable man that the public safety demands such identification."

2. The District Court failed to find facts concerning the particular occasions on which Lawson was detained or arrested under § 647(e). However, the trial transcript contains numerous descriptions of the stops given both by Lawson and by the police officers who detained him. For example, one police officer testified that he stopped Lawson while walking on an otherwise vacant street because it was late at night, the area was isolated, and the area was located close to a high crime area. Another officer testified that he detained Lawson, who was walking at a late hour is a business area where some businesses were still open and asked for identification because burglaries had been committed by unknown persons in the general area. The appellee states that he has never been stopped by police for any reason apart from his detentions under § 647(e).

understand what conduct is prohibited and in a manner that does not encourage arbitrary and discriminatory enforcement. Although the doctrine focuses both on actual notice to citizens and arbitrary enforcement, we have recognized recently that the more important aspect of the vagueness doctrine "is not actual notice, but the other principal element of the doctrine—the requirement that a legislature establish minimal guidelines to govern law enforcement." Where the legislature fails to provide such minimal guidelines, a criminal statute may permit "a standardless sweep [that] allows policemen, prosecutors, and juries to pursue their personal predilections."

Section 647(e), as presently drafted and as construed by the state courts, contains no standard for determining what a suspect has to do in order to satisfy the requirement to provide a "credible and reliable" identification. As such, the statute vests virtually complete discretion in the hands of the police to determine whether the suspect has satisfied the statute and must be permitted to go on his way in the absence of probable cause to arrest. An individual, whom police may think is suspicious but do not have probable cause to believe has committed a crime, is entitled to continue to walk the public streets "only at the whim of any police officer" who happens to stop that individual under § 647(e).

Section 647(e) is not simply a "stop-and-identify" statute. Rather, the statute requires that the individual provide a "credible and reliable" identification that carries a "reasonable assurance" of its authenticity, and that provides "means for later getting in touch with the person who has identified himself." In addition, the suspect may also have to account for his presence "to the extent it assists in producing credible and reliable identification."

At oral argument, the appellants confirmed that a suspect violates § 647(e) unless "the officer [is] satisfied that the identification is reliable." In giving examples of how suspects would satisfy the requirement, appellants explained that a jogger, who was not carrying identification, could, depending on the particular officer, be required to answer a series of questions concerning the route that he followed to arrive at the place where the officers detained him, or could satisfy the identification requirement simply by reciting his name and address.

It is clear that the full discretion accorded to the police to determine whether the suspect has provided a "credible and reliable" identification necessarily "entrust[s] lawmaking 'to the moment-to-moment judgment of the policeman on his beat.'" Section 647(e) "furnishes a convenient tool for 'harsh and discriminatory enforcement by local prosecuting officials, against particular groups deemed to merit their displeasure,'" *Papachristou*, and "confers on police a virtually unrestrained power to arrest and charge persons with a violation." In providing that a detention under § 647(e) may occur only where there is the level of suspicion sufficient to justify a *Terry* stop, the State ensures the existence of "neutral limitations on the conduct of individual officers." Although the initial detention is justified, the State fails to establish standards by which the officers may determine whether the suspect has complied with the subsequent identification requirement.

Appellants stress the need for strengthened law enforcement tools to combat the epidemic of crime that plagues our Nation. The concern of our citizens with curbing criminal activity is certainly a matter requiring the attention of all branches of government. As weighty as this concern is, however, it cannot justify legislation that would otherwise fail to meet constitutional standards for definiteness and clarity. Section 647(e), as presently construed, requires that "suspicious" persons satisfy some undefined identification requirement, or face criminal punishment. Although due process does not require "impossible standards" of clarity, this is not a case where further precision in the statutory language is either impossible or impractical.

We conclude § 647(e) is unconstitutionally vague on its face because it encourages arbitrary enforcement by failing to describe with sufficient particularity what a suspect must do in order to satisfy the statute. Accordingly, the judgment of the Court of Appeals is affirmed.

Questions and Notes

1. Do you agree with Justice O'Connor that "this is not a case where further precision in the statute is either impossible or impractical"?

2. Would a statute that simply required identification, which presumably would meet the vagueness problem, satisfy California's need for its stop-and-identify statute?

3. In *Morales*, the Court sharply divided over whether Chicago's anti-gang ordinance was unconstitutionally vague.

Chicago v. Morales

119 S. Ct. 1849 (1999)

Justice STEVENS announced the judgment of the Court and delivered the opinion of the Court with respect to Parts I, II, and V, and an opinion with respect to Parts III, IV, and VI, in which Justice SOUTER and Justice GINSBURG join.

In 1992, the Chicago City Council enacted the Gang Congregation Ordinance, which prohibits "criminal street gang members" from "loitering" with one another or with other persons in any public place. The question presented is whether the Supreme Court of Illinois correctly held that the ordinance violates the Due Process Clause of the Fourteenth Amendment to the Federal Constitution.

I.

Before the ordinance was adopted, the city council's Committee on Police and Fire conducted hearings to explore the problems created by the city's street gangs, and more particularly, the consequences of public loitering by gang members. Witnesses included residents of the neighborhoods where gang members are most active, as well as some of the aldermen who represent those areas.

The council found that a continuing increase in criminal street gang activity was largely responsible for the city's rising murder rate, as well as an escalation of

violent and drug related crimes. It noted that in many neighborhoods throughout the city, "the burgeoning presence of street gang members in public places has
intimidated many law-abiding citizens." Furthermore, the council stated that gang
members "establish control over identifiable areas . . . by loitering in those areas
and intimidating others from entering those areas; and . . . [m]embers of criminal
street gangs avoid arrest by committing no offense punishable under existing laws
when they know the police are present. . . ." It further found that "loitering in public places by criminal street gang members creates a justifiable fear for the safety
of persons and property in the area" and that "[a]ggressive action is necessary to
preserve the city's streets and other public places so that the public may use such
places without fear." Moreover, the council concluded that the city "has an interest in discouraging all persons from loitering in public places with criminal gang
members."

The ordinance creates a criminal offense punishable by a fine of up to $500,
imprisonment for not more than six months, and a requirement to perform up to
120 hours of community service. Commission of the offense involves four predicates. First, the police officer must reasonably believe that at least one of the two or
more persons present in a "public place" is a "criminal street gang membe[r]." Second, the persons must be "loitering," which the ordinance defines as "remain[ing]
in any one place with no apparent purpose." Third, the officer must then order "all"
of the persons to disperse and remove themselves "from the area." Fourth, a person
must disobey the officer's order. If any person, whether a gang member or not, disobeys the officer's order, that person is guilty of violating the ordinance.

Two months after the ordinance was adopted, the Chicago Police Department
promulgated General Order 92-4 to provide guidelines to govern its enforcement.[3]
That order purported to establish limitations on the enforcement discretion of
police officers "to ensure that the anti-gang loitering ordinance is not enforced in
an arbitrary or discriminatory way." The limitations confine the authority to arrest
gang members who violate the ordinance to sworn "members of the Gang Crime
Section" and certain other designated officers,[4] and establish detailed criteria for
defining street gangs and membership in such gangs. In addition, the order directs
district commanders to "designate areas in which the presence of gang members has
a demonstrable effect on the activities of law abiding persons in the surrounding
community," and provides that the ordinance "will be enforced only within the designated areas." The city, however, does not release the locations of these "designated
areas" to the public.

----

3. As the Illinois Supreme Court noted, during the hearings preceding the adoption of the ordinance, "representatives of the Chicago law and police departments informed the city counsel that
any limitations on the discretion police have in enforcing the ordinance would be best developed
through police policy, rather than placing such limitations into the ordinance itself."

4. Presumably, these officers would also be able to arrest all nongang members who violate the
ordinance.

II.

During the three years of its enforcement, the police issued over 89,000 dispersal orders and arrested over 42,000 people for violating the ordinance.[7] In the ensuing enforcement proceedings, two trial judges upheld the constitutionality of the ordinance, but eleven others ruled that it was invalid.

III.

The basic factual predicate for the city's ordinance is not in dispute. As the city argues in its brief, "the very presence of a large collection of obviously brazen, insistent, and lawless gang members and hangers-on on the public ways intimidates residents, who become afraid even to leave their homes and go about their business. That, in turn, imperils community residents' sense of safety and security, detracts from property values, and can ultimately destabilize entire neighborhoods." The findings in the ordinance explain that it was motivated by these concerns. We have no doubt that a law that directly prohibited such intimidating conduct would be constitutional,[17] but this ordinance broadly covers a significant amount of additional activity. Uncertainty about the scope of that additional coverage provides the basis for respondents' claim that the ordinance is too vague.

IV.

"It is established that a law fails to meet the requirements of the Due Process Clause if it is so vague and standardless that it leaves the public uncertain as to the conduct it prohibits. . . ." The Illinois Supreme Court recognized that the term "loiter" may have a common and accepted meaning, but the definition of that term in this ordinance — "to remain in any one place with no apparent purpose" — does not. It is difficult to imagine how any citizen of the city of Chicago standing in a public place with a group of people would know if he or she had an "apparent purpose." If she were talking to another person, would she have an apparent purpose?

---

7. The city believes that the ordinance resulted in a significant decline in gang-related homicides. It notes that in 1995, the last year the ordinance was enforced, the gang-related homicide rate fell by 26%. In 1996, after the ordinance had been held invalid, the gang-related homicide rate rose 11%. **However, gang-related homicides fell by 19% in 1997, over a year after the suspension of the ordinance. Given the myriad factors that influence levels of violence, it is difficult to evaluate the probative value of this statistical evidence, or to reach any firm conclusion about the ordinance's efficacy.

17. In fact, the city already has several laws that serve this purpose. *See, e.g.,* Ill. Comp. Stat. ch. 720 §§ 5/12-6 (1998) (Intimidation); 570/405.2 (Streetgang criminal drug conspiracy); 147/1 *et seq.* (Illinois Streetgang Terrorism Omnibus Prevention Act); 5/25-1 (Mob action). Deputy Superintendent Cooper, the only representative of the police department at the Committee on Police and Fire hearing on the ordinance, testified that, of the kinds of behavior people had discussed at the hearing, "90 percent of those instances are actually criminal offenses where people, in fact, can be arrested."

If she were frequently checking her watch and looking expectantly down the street, would she have an apparent purpose?[23]

Since the city cannot conceivably have meant to criminalize each instance a citizen stands in public with a gang member, the vagueness that dooms this ordinance is not the product of uncertainty about the normal meaning of "loitering," but rather about what loitering is covered by the ordinance and what is not. The Illinois Supreme Court emphasized the law's failure to distinguish between innocent conduct and conduct threatening harm.[24] Its decision followed the precedent set by a number of state courts that have upheld ordinances that criminalize loitering combined with some other overt act or evidence of criminal intent.[25] However, state courts have uniformly invalidated laws that do not join the term "loitering" with a second specific element of the crime.[26]

The city's principal response to this concern about adequate notice is that loiterers are not subject to sanction until after they have failed to comply with an officer's order to disperse. "[W]hatever problem is created by a law that criminalizes conduct people normally believe to be innocent is solved when persons receive actual notice from a police order of what they are expected to do." We find this response unpersuasive for at least two reasons.

First, the purpose of the fair notice requirement is to enable the ordinary citizen to conform his or her conduct to the law. "No one may be required at peril of life, liberty or property to speculate as to the meaning of penal statutes." *Lanzetta v. New Jersey*, 306 U.S. 451, 453 (1939). Although it is true that a loiterer is not subject to criminal sanctions unless he or she disobeys a dispersal order, the loitering is the conduct that the ordinance is designed to prohibit. If the loitering is in fact harmless and innocent, the dispersal order itself is an unjustified impairment of liberty. If the police are able to decide arbitrarily which members of the public they will order to disperse, then the Chicago ordinance becomes indistinguishable from the

---

23. The Solicitor General, while supporting the city's argument that the ordinance is constitutional, appears to recognize that the ordinance cannot be read literally without invoking intractable vagueness concerns. "[T]he purpose simply to stand on a corner cannot be an 'apparent purpose' under the ordinance; if it were, the ordinance would prohibit nothing at all."

24. One of the trial courts that invalidated the ordinance gave the following illustration: "Suppose a group of gang members were playing basketball in the park, while waiting for a drug delivery. Their apparent purpose is that they are in the park to play ball. The actual purpose is that they are waiting for drugs. Under this definition of loitering, a group of people innocently sitting in a park discussing their futures would be arrested, while the 'basketball players' awaiting a drug delivery would be left alone."

25. *See, e.g., Tacoma v. Luvene,* 118 Wash. 2d 826, 827 P.2d 1374 (1992) (upholding ordinance criminalizing loitering with purpose to engage in drug-related activities); *People v. Superior Court,* 46 Cal. 3d 381, 394–395, 758 P.2d 1046, 1052 (1988) (upholding ordinance criminalizing loitering for the purpose of engaging in or soliciting lewd act).

26. *See, e.g., State v. Richard,* 108 Nev. 626, 629, 836 P.2d 622, 624, n.2 (1992) (striking down statute that made it unlawful "for any person to loiter or prowl upon the property of another without lawful business with the owner or occupant thereof").

law we held invalid in *Shuttlesworth v. Birmingham*, 382 U.S. 87, 90 (1965).[29] Because an officer may issue an order only after prohibited conduct has already occurred, it cannot provide the kind of advance notice that will protect the putative loiterer from being ordered to disperse. Such an order cannot retroactively give adequate warning of the boundary between the permissible and the impermissible applications of the law.[30]

Second, the terms of the dispersal order compound the inadequacy of the notice afforded by the ordinance. It provides that the officer "shall order all such persons to disperse and remove themselves from the area." This vague phrasing raises a host of questions. After such an order issues, how long must the loiterers remain apart? How far must they move? If each loiterer walks around the block and they meet again at the same location, are they subject to arrest or merely to being ordered to disperse again? As we do here, we have found vagueness in a criminal statute exacerbated by the use of the standards of "neighborhood" and "locality." *Connally v. General Constr. Co.*, 269 U.S. 385 (1926). We remarked in *Connally* that "[b]oth terms are elastic and, dependent upon circumstances, may be equally satisfied by areas measured by rods or by miles."

Lack of clarity in the description of the loiterer's duty to obey a dispersal order might not render the ordinance unconstitutionally vague if the definition of the forbidden conduct were clear, but it does buttress our conclusion that the entire ordinance fails to give the ordinary citizen adequate notice of what is forbidden and what is permitted. The Constitution does not permit a legislature to "set a net large enough to catch all possible offenders and leave it to the courts to step inside and say who could be rightfully detained, and who should be set at large." This ordinance is therefore vague "not in the sense that it requires a person to conform his conduct to an imprecise but comprehensible normative standard, but rather in the sense that no standard of conduct is specified at all."

V.

The broad sweep of the ordinance also violates "the requirement that a legislature establish minimal guidelines to govern law enforcement." There are no such guidelines in the ordinance. In any public place in the city of Chicago, persons who stand or sit in the company of a gang member may be ordered to disperse unless their purpose is apparent. The mandatory language in the enactment directs the police

---

29. "Literally read ... this ordinance says that a person may stand on a public sidewalk in Birmingham only at the whim of any police officer of that city. The constitutional vice of so broad a provision needs no demonstration."

30. As we have noted in a similar context: "If petitioners were held guilty of violating the Georgia statute because they disobeyed the officers, this case falls within the rule that a generally worded statute which is construed to punish conduct which cannot constitutionally be punished is unconstitutionally vague to the extent that it fails to give adequate warning of the boundary between the constitutionally permissible and constitutionally impermissible applications of *Wright v. Georgia*, 373 U.S. 284, 292 (1963). 284, 292 (1963).

to issue an order without first making any inquiry about their possible purposes. It matters not whether the reason that a gang member and his father, for example, might loiter near Wrigley Field is to rob an unsuspecting fan or just to get a glimpse of Sammy Sosa leaving the ballpark; in either event, if their purpose is not apparent to a nearby police officer, she may—indeed, she "shall"—order them to disperse.

Recognizing that the ordinance does reach a substantial amount of innocent conduct, we turn, then, to its language to determine if it "necessarily entrusts lawmaking to the moment-to-moment judgment of the policeman on his beat." *Kolender v. Lawson*, 461 U.S., at 359. As we discussed in the context of fair notice, the principal source of the vast discretion conferred on the police in this case is the definition of loitering as "to remain in any one place with no apparent purpose."

As the Illinois Supreme Court interprets that definition, it "provides absolute discretion to police officers to determine what activities constitute loitering." We have no authority to construe the language of a state statute more narrowly than the construction given by that State's highest court.

Nevertheless, the city disputes the Illinois Supreme Court's interpretation, arguing that the text of the ordinance limits the officer's discretion in three ways. First, it does not permit the officer to issue a dispersal order to anyone who is moving along or who has an apparent purpose. Second, it does not permit an arrest if individuals obey a dispersal order. Third, no order can issue unless the officer reasonably believes that one of the loiterers is a member of a criminal street gang.

Even putting to one side our duty to defer to a state court's construction of the scope of a local enactment, we find each of these limitations insufficient. That the ordinance does not apply to people who are moving—that is, to activity that would not constitute loitering under any possible definition of the term—does not even address the question of how much discretion the police enjoy in deciding which stationary persons to disperse under the ordinance.[32] Similarly, that the ordinance does not permit an arrest until after a dispersal order has been disobeyed does not provide any guidance to the officer deciding whether such an order should issue. The "no apparent purpose" standard for making that decision is inherently subjective because its application depends on whether some purpose is "apparent" to the officer on the scene.

Presumably an officer would have discretion to treat some purposes—perhaps a purpose to engage in idle conversation or simply to enjoy a cool breeze on a warm evening—as too frivolous to be apparent if he suspected a different ulterior motive. Moreover, an officer conscious of the city council's reasons for enacting

---

32. It is possible to read the mandatory language of the ordinance and conclude that it affords the police *no* discretion, since it speaks with the mandatory "shall." However, not even the city makes this argument, which flies in the face of common sense that all police officers must use some discretion in deciding when and where to enforce city ordinances.

the ordinance might well ignore its text and issue a dispersal order, even though an illicit purpose is actually apparent.

It is true, as the city argues, that the requirement that the officer reasonably believe that a group of loiterers contains a gang member does place a limit on the authority to order dispersal. That limitation would no doubt be sufficient if the ordinance only applied to loitering that had an apparently harmful purpose or effect,[33] or possibly if it only applied to loitering by persons reasonably believed to be criminal gang members. But this ordinance, for reasons that are not explained in the findings of the city council, requires no harmful purpose and applies to non-gang members as well as suspected gang members.[34] It applies to everyone in the city who may remain in one place with one suspected gang member as long as their purpose is not apparent to an officer observing them. Friends, relatives, teachers, counselors, or even total strangers might unwittingly engage in forbidden loitering if they happen to engage in idle conversation with a gang member.

Ironically, the definition of loitering in the Chicago ordinance not only extends its scope to encompass harmless conduct, but also has the perverse consequence of excluding from its coverage much of the intimidating conduct that motivated its enactment. As the city council's findings demonstrate, the most harmful gang loitering is motivated either by an apparent purpose to publicize the gang's dominance of certain territory, thereby intimidating nonmembers, or by an equally apparent purpose to conceal ongoing commerce in illegal drugs. As the Illinois Supreme Court has not placed any limiting construction on the language in the ordinance, we must assume that the ordinance means what it says and that it has no application to loiterers whose purpose is apparent. The relative importance of its application to harmless loitering is magnified by its inapplicability to loitering that has an obviously threatening or illicit purpose.

Finally, in its opinion striking down the ordinance, the Illinois Supreme Court refused to accept the general order issued by the police department as a sufficient limitation on the "vast amount of discretion" granted to the police in its enforcement. We agree. That the police have adopted internal rules limiting their enforcement to certain designated areas in the city would not provide a defense to a loiterer who might be arrested elsewhere. Nor could a person who knowingly loitered with a well-known gang member anywhere in the city safely assume that they would not be ordered to disperse no matter how innocent and harmless their loitering might be.

---

33. Justice THOMAS' dissent overlooks the important distinction between this ordinance and those that authorize the police "to order groups of individuals who threaten the public peace to disperse."

34. Not all of the respondents in this case, for example, are gang members. The city admits that it was unable to prove that Morales is a gang member but justifies his arrest and conviction by the fact that Morales admitted "that he knew he was with criminal street gang members." In fact, 34 of the 66 respondents in this case were charged in a document that only accused them of being in the presence of a gang member.

VI.

In our judgment, the Illinois Supreme Court correctly concluded that the ordinance does not provide sufficiently specific limits on the enforcement discretion of the police "to meet constitutional standards for definiteness and clarity." We recognize the serious and difficult problems testified to by the citizens of Chicago that led to the enactment of this ordinance. "We are mindful that the preservation of liberty depends in part on the maintenance of social order." However, in this instance the city has enacted an ordinance that affords too much discretion to the police and too little notice to citizens who wish to use the public streets.

Accordingly, the judgment of the Supreme Court of Illinois is *Affirmed.*

Justice O'CONNOR, with whom Justice BREYER joins, concurring in part and concurring in the judgment.

I agree with the Court that Chicago's Gang Congregation Ordinance, Chicago Municipal Code § 8-4-015 (1992) (gang loitering ordinance or ordinance) is unconstitutionally vague. A penal law is void for vagueness if it fails to "define the criminal offense with sufficient definiteness that ordinary people can understand what conduct is prohibited" or fails to establish guidelines to prevent "arbitrary and discriminatory enforcement" of the law. Of these, "the more important aspect of vagueness doctrine 'is . . . the requirement that a legislature establish minimal guidelines to govern law enforcement.'" I share Justice THOMAS' concern about the consequences of gang violence, and I agree that some degree of police discretion is necessary to allow the police "to perform their peacekeeping responsibilities satisfactorily." A criminal law, however, must not permit policemen, prosecutors, and juries to conduct "a standardless sweep . . . to pursue their personal predilections."

It is important to courts and legislatures alike that we characterize more clearly the narrow scope of today's holding. As the ordinance comes to this Court, it is unconstitutionally vague. Nevertheless, there remain open to Chicago reasonable alternatives to combat the very real threat posed by gang intimidation and violence. For example, the Court properly and expressly distinguishes the ordinance from laws that require loiterers to have a "harmful purpose," from laws that target only gang members, and from laws that incorporate limits on the area and manner in which the laws may be enforced. In addition, the ordinance here is unlike a law that "directly prohibit[s]" the "presence of a large collection of obviously brazen, insistent, and lawless gang members and hangers-on on the public ways," that "intimidates residents." Indeed, as the plurality notes, the city of Chicago has several laws that do exactly this. *See* n.17.

In my view, the gang loitering ordinance could have been construed more narrowly. The term "loiter" might possibly be construed in a more limited fashion to mean "to remain in any one place with no apparent purpose other than to establish control over identifiable areas, to intimidate others from entering those areas, or to conceal illegal activities." Such a definition would be consistent with the Chicago City Council's findings and would avoid the vagueness problems of the ordinance as construed by the Illinois Supreme Court. As noted above, so would limitations that restricted the ordinance's criminal penalties to gang members or that more carefully delineated the circumstances in which those penalties would apply to nongang members.

The Illinois Supreme Court did not choose to give a limiting construction to Chicago's ordinance. To the extent it relied on our precedents, particularly *Papachristou v. Jacksonville*, 405 U.S. 156 (1972), as *requiring* it to hold the ordinance vague in all of its applications because it was intentionally drafted in a vague manner, the Illinois court misapplied our precedents. This Court has never held that the intent of the drafters determines whether a law is vague. Nevertheless, we cannot impose a limiting construction that a state supreme court has declined to adopt. Accordingly, I join Parts I, II, and V of the Court's opinion and concur in the judgment.

Justice KENNEDY, concurring in part and concurring in the judgment.

I join Parts I, II, and V of Justice STEVENS' opinion.

I also share many of the concerns he expresses in Part IV with respect to the sufficiency of notice under the ordinance. As interpreted by the Illinois Supreme Court, the Chicago ordinance would reach a broad range of innocent conduct. For this reason, it is not necessarily saved by the requirement that the citizen must disobey a police order to disperse before there is a violation.

We have not often examined these types of orders. *Cf. Shuttlesworth v. Birmingham*, 382 U.S. 87 (1965). It can be assumed, however, that some police commands will subject a citizen to prosecution for disobeying whether or not the citizen knows why the order is given. Illustrative examples include when the police tell a pedestrian not to enter a building and the reason is to avoid impeding a rescue team, or to protect a crime scene, or to secure an area for the protection of a public official. It does not follow, however, that any unexplained police order must be obeyed without notice of the lawfulness of the order. The predicate of an order to disperse is not, in my view, sufficient to eliminate doubts regarding the adequacy of notice under this ordinance. A citizen, while engaging in a wide array of innocent conduct, is not likely to know when he may be subject to a dispersal order based on the officer's own knowledge of the identity or affiliations of other persons with whom the citizen is congregating; nor may the citizen be able to assess what an officer might conceive to be the citizen's lack of an apparent purpose.

Justice BREYER, concurring in part and concurring in the judgment.

The ordinance before us creates more than a "*minor* limitation upon the free state of nature." (SCALIA, J., dissenting) (emphasis added). The law authorizes a police officer to order any person to remove himself from any "location open to the public, whether publicly or privately owned," *i.e.*, any sidewalk, front stoop, public park, public square, lakeside promenade, hotel, restaurant, bowling alley, bar, barbershop, sports arena, shopping mall, etc., but with two, and only two, limitations: First, that person must be accompanied by (or must himself be) someone police reasonably believe is a gang member. Second, that person must have remained in that public place "with no apparent purpose."

The first limitation cannot save the ordinance. Though it limits the number of persons subject to the law, it leaves many individuals, gang members and non-gang members alike, subject to its strictures. Nor does it limit in any way the range of conduct that police may prohibit. The second limitation is, as Justice STEVENS and Justice O'CONNOR point out, not a limitation at all. Since one always has some apparent purpose, the so-called limitation invites, in fact requires, the policeman to interpret the words "no apparent purpose" as meaning "no apparent purpose except for. . . ." And it is in the ordinance's delegation to the policeman of open-ended discretion to fill in that blank that the problem lies. To grant to a policeman virtually standardless discretion to close off major portions of the city to an innocent person is, in my view, to create a major, not a "minor," "limitation upon the free state of nature."

Nor does it violate "our rules governing facial challenges," (SCALIA, J., dissenting), to forbid the city to apply the unconstitutional ordinance in this case. The reason *why* the ordinance is invalid explains how that is so. As I have said, I believe the ordinance violates the Constitution because it delegates too much discretion to a police officer to decide whom to order to move on, and in what circumstances. And I see no way to distinguish in the ordinance's terms between one application of that discretion and another. The ordinance is unconstitutional, not because a policeman applied this discretion wisely or poorly in a particular case, but rather because the policeman enjoys too much discretion in *every* case. And if every application of the ordinance represents an exercise of unlimited discretion, then the ordinance is invalid in all its applications. The city of Chicago may be able validly to apply some *other* law to the defendants in light of their conduct. But the city of Chicago may no more apply *this* law to the defendants, no matter how they behaved, than could it apply an (imaginary) statute that said, "It is a crime to do wrong," even to the worst of murderers.

Justice SCALIA, dissenting.

The citizens of Chicago were once free to drive about the city at whatever speed they wished. At some point Chicagoans (or perhaps Illinoisans) decided this would not do and imposed prophylactic speed limits designed to assure safe operation by the average (or perhaps even subaverage) driver with the average (or perhaps even subaverage) vehicle. This infringed upon the "freedom" of all citizens but was not unconstitutional.

Similarly, the citizens of Chicago were once free to stand around and gawk at the scene of an accident. At some point Chicagoans discovered that this obstructed traffic and caused more accidents. They did not make the practice unlawful, but they did authorize police officers to order the crowd to disperse, and imposed penalties for refusal to obey such an order. Again, this prophylactic measure infringed upon the "freedom" of all citizens but was not unconstitutional.

Until the ordinance that is before us today was adopted, the citizens of Chicago were free to stand about in public places with no apparent purpose—to engage, that is, in conduct that appeared to be loitering. In recent years, however, the city has been afflicted with criminal street gangs. As reflected in the record before us, these gangs congregated in public places to deal in drugs, and to terrorize the neighborhoods by demonstrating control over their "turf." Many residents of the inner city felt that they were prisoners in their own homes. Once again, Chicagoans decided that to eliminate the problem it was worth restricting some of the freedom that they once enjoyed. The means they took was similar to the second, and more mild, example given above rather than the first: Loitering was not made unlawful, but when a group of people occupied a public place without an apparent purpose and in the company of a known gang member, police officers were authorized to order them to disperse, and the failure to obey such an order was made unlawful. The minor limitation upon the free state of nature that this prophylactic arrangement imposed upon all Chicagoans seemed to them (and it seems to me) a small price to pay for liberation of their streets.

The majority today invalidates this perfectly reasonable measure by ignoring our rules governing facial challenges, by elevating loitering to a constitutionally guaranteed right, and by discerning vagueness where, according to our usual standards, none exists.

III.

I turn to that element of the plurality's facial-challenge formula which consists of the proposition that this criminal ordinance contains no *mens rea* requirement. The first step in analyzing this proposition is to determine what the *actus reus*, to which that *mens rea* is supposed to be attached, consists of. The majority believes that loitering forms part of (indeed, the essence of) the offense, and must be proved if conviction is to be obtained. That is not what the Ordinance provides. The only part of the Ordinance that refers to loitering is the portion that addresses, not the punishable conduct of the defendant, but what the police officer must observe before he can issue an order to disperse; and what he must observe is carefully defined in terms of what the defendant *appears* to be doing, not in terms of what the defendant is *actually* doing. The Ordinance does not require that the defendant have been loitering (*i.e.*, have been remaining in one place with no purpose), but rather that the police officer have observed him remaining in one place without any *apparent* purpose. Someone who in fact *has* a genuine purpose for remaining where he is (waiting for a friend, for example, or waiting to hold up a bank) *can* be ordered to move on (assuming the other conditions of the Ordinance are met), so long as his remaining has no *apparent* purpose. It is likely, to be sure, that the Ordinance will come down most heavily upon those who are *actually* loitering (those who *really* have no purpose in remaining where they are); but that activity is not a condition for issuance of the dispersal order.

The *only* act of a defendant that is made punishable by the Ordinance—or, indeed, that is even mentioned by the Ordinance—is his failure to "promptly obey" an order to disperse. The question, then, is whether that *actus reus* must be accompanied by any wrongful intent — and of course it must. As the Court itself describes the requirement, "a person must *disobey* the officer's order." (emphasis added). No one thinks a defendant could be successfully prosecuted under the Ordinance if he did not hear the order to disperse, or if he suffered a paralysis that rendered his compliance impossible. The willful failure to obey a police order is wrongful intent enough.

IV.

Finally, I address the last of the three factors in the plurality's facial-challenge formula: the proposition that the Ordinance is vague. It is not. A law is unconstitutionally vague if its lack of definitive standards either (1) fails to apprise persons of ordinary intelligence of the prohibited conduct, or (2) encourages arbitrary and discriminatory enforcement.

The plurality relies primarily upon the first of these aspects. Since, it reasons, "the loitering is the conduct that the ordinance is designed to prohibit," and "an officer may issue an order only after prohibited conduct has already occurred," the order to disperse cannot itself serve "to apprise persons of ordinary intelligence of the prohibited conduct." What counts for purposes of vagueness analysis, however, is not what the Ordinance is "designed to prohibit," but what it actually subjects to criminal penalty. As discussed earlier, that consists of nothing but the refusal to obey a dispersal order, as to which there is no doubt of adequate notice of the prohibited conduct. The plurality's suggestion that even the dispersal order *itself* is unconstitutionally vague, because it does not specify *how far to disperse (!)*, scarcely requires a response.[9] If it were true, it would render unconstitutional for vagueness many of the Presidential proclamations issued under that provision of the United States Code which requires the President, before using the militia or the Armed Forces for law enforcement, to issue a proclamation ordering the insurgents to disperse. President Eisenhower's proclamation relating to the obstruction of court-ordered enrollment of black students in public schools at Little Rock, Arkansas, read as follows: "I . . . command all persons engaged in such obstruction of justice to cease and desist therefrom, and to disperse forthwith."

For its determination of unconstitutional vagueness, the Court relies secondarily — and Justice O'CONNOR's and Justice BREYER's concurrences exclusively — upon the second aspect of that doctrine, which requires sufficient specificity to prevent arbitrary and discriminatory law enforcement. In discussing

---

9. I call it a "suggestion" because the plurality says only that the terms of the dispersal order "compound the inadequacy of the notice," and acknowledges that they "might not render the ordinance unconstitutionally vague if the definition of the forbidden conduct were clear." This notion that a prescription ("Disperse!") which is itself not unconstitutionally vague can somehow contribute to the unconstitutional vagueness of the entire scheme is full of mystery — suspending, as it does, the metaphysical principle that nothing can confer what it does not possess (*nemo dat qui non habet*).

whether Chicago's Ordinance meets that requirement, the Justices in the majority hide behind an artificial construct of judicial restraint. They point to the Supreme Court of Illinois' statement that the "apparent purpose" standard "provides absolute discretion to police officers to decide what activities constitute loitering" and protest that it would be wrong to construe the language of the Ordinance more narrowly than did the State's highest court. The "absolute discretion" statement, however, is nothing more than the Illinois Supreme Court's *characterization* of what the language achieved—after that court refused (as I do) to read in any limitations that the words do not fairly contain. It is not a construction of the language (to which we are bound) but a legal conclusion (to which we most assuredly are not bound).

The criteria for issuance of a dispersal order under the Chicago Ordinance could hardly be clearer. First, the law requires police officers to "reasonably believ[e]" that one of the group to which the order is issued is a "criminal street gang member." This resembles a probable-cause standard, and the Chicago Police Department's General Order 92-4 (1992)—promulgated to govern enforcement of the Ordinance—makes the probable cause requirement explicit. Under the Order, officers must have probable cause to believe that an individual is a member of a criminal street gang, to be substantiated by the officer's "experience and knowledge of the alleged offenders" and by "specific, documented and reliable information" such as reliable witness testimony or an individual's admission of gang membership or display of distinctive colors, tattoos, signs, or other markings worn by members of particular criminal street gangs.

Second, the Ordinance requires that the group be "remain[ing] in one place with no apparent purpose." Justice O'CONNOR's assertion that this applies to "any person standing in a public place" is a distortion. The Ordinance does not apply to "standing," but to "remain[ing]"—a term which in this context obviously means "[to] endure or persist." There may be some ambiguity at the margin, but "remain [ing] in one place" requires more than a temporary stop, and is clear in most of its applications, including all of those represented by the facts surrounding the respondents' arrests.

As for the phrase "with no apparent purpose": Justice O'CONNOR again distorts this adjectival phrase, by separating it from the word that it modifies. "[A]ny person standing on the street," her concurrence says, "has a general 'purpose'—even if it is simply to stand," and thus "the ordinance permits police officers to choose which purposes are *permissible*." But Chicago police officers enforcing the Ordinance are not looking for people with no apparent purpose (who are regrettably in oversupply); they are looking for people who "remain in any one place with no apparent purpose"—that is, who remain there without any apparent reason *for remaining there*. That is not difficult to perceive.[11]

---

11. Justice BREYER asserts that "one always has some apparent purpose," so that the policeman must "interpret the words 'no apparent purpose' as meaning 'no apparent purpose except for. . . .'" It is simply not true that "one always has some apparent purpose"—and especially not true that

The Court's attempt to demonstrate the vagueness of the Ordinance produces the following peculiar statement: "The 'no apparent purpose' standard for making [the decision to issue an order to disperse] is inherently subjective because its application depends on whether some purpose is 'apparent' to the officer on the scene." In the Court's view, a person's lack of any purpose in staying in one location is presumably an *objective* factor, and what the Ordinance requires as a condition of an order to disperse—the absence of any *apparent* purpose—is a *subjective* factor. This side of the looking glass, just the opposite is true.

Elsewhere, of course, the Court acknowledges the clear, objective commands of the Ordinance, and indeed relies upon them to paint it as unfair:

> "By its very terms, the ordinance encompasses a great deal of harmless behavior. In any public place in the city of Chicago, persons who stand or sit in the company of a gang member may be ordered to disperse unless their purpose is apparent. The mandatory language in the enactment directs the police to issue an order without first making any inquiry about their possible purposes. It matters not whether the reason that a gang member and his father, for example, might loiter near Wrigley Field is to rob an unsuspecting fan or just to get a glimpse of Sammy Sosa leaving the ballpark; in either event, if their purpose is not apparent to a nearby police officer, she may—indeed, she 'shall'—order them to disperse."

Quite so. And the fact that this clear instruction to the officers "encompasses a great deal of harmless behavior" would be invalidating if that harmless behavior were constitutionally protected against abridgment, such as speech or the practice of religion. Remaining in one place is *not* so protected, and so (as already discussed) it is up to the citizens of Chicago—not us—to decide whether the trade-off is worth it.

The Court also asserts—in apparent contradiction to the passage just quoted—that the "apparent purpose" test is too elastic because it presumably allows police officers to treat *de minimis* "violations" as not warranting enforcement. But such discretion—and, for that matter, the potential for ultra vires action—is no different with regard to the enforcement of this clear ordinance than it is with regard to the enforcement of all laws in our criminal justice system. Police officers (and prosecutors).

V.

The plurality points out that Chicago already has several laws that reach the intimidating and unlawful gang-related conduct the Ordinance was directed at. The problem, of course, well recognized by Chicago's City Council, is that the gang

---

one always has some apparent purpose in remaining at rest, for the simple reason that one often (indeed, perhaps usually) has no *actual* purpose in remaining at rest. Remaining at rest will be a person's normal state, unless he has a purpose which causes him to move. That is why one frequently reads of a person's "wandering aimlessly" (which is worthy of note) but not of a person's "sitting aimlessly" (which is not remarkable at all). And that is why a synonym for "purpose" is "motive": that which causes one *to move.*

members cease their intimidating and unlawful behavior under the watchful eye of police officers but return to it as soon as the police drive away. The only solution, the council concluded, was to clear the streets of congregations of gangs, their drug customers, and their associates.

Justice O'CONNOR's concurrence proffers the same empty solace of existing laws useless for the purpose at hand but seeks to be helpful by suggesting some measures *similar* to this ordinance that *would* be constitutional. It says that Chicago could, for example, enact a law that "directly prohibit[s] the presence of a large collection of obviously brazen, insistent, and lawless gang members and hangers-on on the public ways, that intimidates residents." (If the majority considers the present ordinance too vague, it would be fun to see what it makes of "a large collection of obviously brazen, insistent, and lawless gang members.") This prescription of the concurrence is largely a quotation from the plurality—which itself answers the concurrence's suggestion that such a law would be helpful by pointing out that the city already "has several laws that serve this purpose."

Justice O'CONNOR's concurrence also proffers another cure: "If the ordinance applied only to persons reasonably believed to be gang members, this requirement might have cured the ordinance's vagueness because it would have directed the manner in which the order was issued by specifying to whom the order could be issued." But the Ordinance already specifies to whom the order can be issued: persons remaining in one place with no apparent purpose in the company of a gang member. And if "remain[ing] in one place with no apparent purpose" is so vague as to give the police unbridled discretion in controlling the conduct of non-gang-members, it surpasses understanding how it ceases to be so vague when applied to gang members *alone*. Surely gang members cannot be decreed to be outlaws, subject to the merest whim of the police as the rest of us are not.

The fact is that the present ordinance is entirely clear in its application, cannot be violated except with full knowledge and intent, and vests no more discretion in the police than innumerable other measures authorizing police orders to preserve the public peace and safety. As suggested by their tortured analyses, and by their suggested solutions that bear no relation to the identified constitutional problem, the majority's real quarrel with the Chicago Ordinance is simply that it permits (or indeed requires) too much harmless conduct by innocent citizens to be proscribed. As Justice O'CONNOR's concurrence says with disapprobation, "the ordinance applies to hundreds of thousands of persons who are not gang members, standing on any sidewalk or in any park, coffee shop, bar, or other location open to the public."

But in our democratic system, how much harmless conduct to proscribe is not a judgment to be made by the courts. So long as constitutionally guaranteed rights are not affected, and so long as the proscription has a rational basis, *all sorts* of perfectly harmless activity by millions of perfectly innocent people can be forbidden—riding a motorcycle without a safety helmet, for example, starting a campfire in a national forest, or selling a safe and effective drug not yet approved by the FDA. All of these acts are entirely innocent and harmless in themselves, but because of the *risk* of harm that they entail, the freedom to engage in them has been abridged. The citizens of Chicago have decided that depriving themselves of the freedom to "hang out" with a gang member is necessary to eliminate pervasive gang crime and intimidation—and that the elimination of the one is worth the deprivation of the other. This Court has no business second-guessing either the degree of necessity or the fairness of the trade.

I dissent from the judgment of the Court.

Justice THOMAS, with whom THE CHIEF JUSTICE and Justice SCALIA join, dissenting.

The duly elected members of the Chicago City Council enacted the ordinance at issue as part of a larger effort to prevent gangs from establishing dominion over the public streets. By invalidating Chicago's ordinance, I fear that the Court has unnecessarily sentenced law-abiding citizens to lives of terror and misery. The ordinance is not vague. "[A]ny fool would know that a particular category of conduct would be within [its] reach."

I.

The human costs exacted by criminal street gangs are inestimable. In many of our Nation's cities, gangs have "[v]irtually overtak[en] certain neighborhoods, contributing to the economic and social decline of these areas and causing fear and lifestyle changes among law-abiding residents." Gangs fill the daily lives of many of our poorest and most vulnerable citizens with a terror that the Court does not give sufficient consideration, often relegating them to the status of prisoners in their own homes. "From the small business owner who is literally crippled because he refuses to pay 'protection' money to the neighborhood gang, to the families who are hostages within their homes, living in neighborhoods ruled by predatory drug trafficking gangs, the harmful impact of gang violence . . . is both physically and psychologically debilitating."

The city of Chicago has suffered the devastation wrought by this national tragedy. Last year, in an effort to curb plummeting attendance, the Chicago Public Schools hired dozens of adults to escort children to school. The youngsters had become too terrified of gang violence to leave their homes alone. The children's fears were not unfounded. In 1996, the Chicago Police Department estimated that there were 132 criminal street gangs in the city. Between 1987 and 1994, these gangs were involved in 63,141 criminal incidents, including 21,689 nonlethal violent crimes and 894 homicides. Many of these criminal incidents and homicides result from gang "turf battles," which take place on the public streets and place innocent residents in grave danger.

Before enacting its ordinance, the Chicago City Council held extensive hearings on the problems of gang loitering. Concerned citizens appeared to testify poignantly as to how gangs disrupt their daily lives. Ordinary citizens like Ms. D'Ivory Gordon explained that she struggled just to walk to work:

"When I walk out my door, these guys are out there. . . . They watch you. . . . They know where you live. They know what time you leave, what time you come home. I am afraid of them. I have even come to the point now that I carry a meat cleaver to work with me. . . . I don't want to hurt anyone, and I don't want to be hurt. We need to clean these corners up. Clean these communities up and take it back from them."

Eighty-eight-year-old Susan Mary Jackson echoed her sentiments, testifying, "We used to have a nice neighborhood. We don't have it anymore. . . . I am scared to go out in the daytime . . . you can't pass because they are standing. I am afraid to go to the store. I don't go to the store because I am afraid. At my age if they look at me real hard, I be ready to holler." Another long-time resident testified:

> "I have never had the terror that I feel every day when I walk down the streets of Chicago. . . . I have had my windows broken out. I have had guns pulled on me. I have been threatened. I get intimidated on a daily basis, and it's come to the point where I say, well, do I go out today. Do I put my ax in my briefcase. Do I walk around dressed like a bum, so I am not looking rich or got any money or anything like that."

Following these hearings, the council found that "criminal street gangs establish control over identifiable areas . . . by loitering in those areas and intimidating others from entering those areas." It further found that the mere presence of gang members "intimidate[s] many law abiding citizens" and "creates a justifiable fear for the safety of persons and property in the area." It is the product of this democratic process—the council's attempt to address these social ills—that we are asked to pass judgment upon today.

II

As part of its ongoing effort to curb the deleterious effects of criminal street gangs, the citizens of Chicago sensibly decided to return to basics. The ordinance does nothing more than confirm the well-established principle that the police have the duty and the power to maintain the public peace, and, when necessary, to disperse groups of individuals who threaten it. The plurality, however, concludes that the city's commonsense effort to combat gang loitering fails constitutional scrutiny for two separate reasons—because it infringes upon gang members' constitutional right to "loiter for innocent purposes," and because it is vague on its face. A majority of the Court endorses the latter conclusion. I respectfully disagree.

B

The Court concludes that the ordinance is unconstitutionally vague because it fails to provide adequate standards to guide police discretion and because, in the plurality's view, it does not give residents adequate notice of how to conform their conduct to the confines of the law. I disagree on both counts.

1

At the outset, it is important to note that the ordinance does not criminalize loitering *per se*. Rather, it penalizes loiterers' failure to obey a police officer's order to move along. A majority of the Court believes that this scheme vests too much discretion in police officers. Nothing could be further from the truth. Far from according officers too much discretion, the ordinance merely enables police officers to fulfill one of their traditional functions. Police officers are not, and have never been, simply enforcers of the criminal law. They wear other hats—importantly, they have long been vested with the responsibility for preserving the public peace. Nor is the idea that the police are also *peace officers* simply a quaint anachronism. In most American jurisdictions, police officers continue to be obligated, by law, to maintain the public peace.

In their role as peace officers, the police long have had the authority and the duty to order groups of individuals who threaten the public peace to disperse. The authority to issue dispersal orders continues to play a commonplace and crucial role in police operations, particularly in urban areas. Even the ABA Standards for Criminal Justice recognize that "[i]n day-to-day police experience there are innumerable situations in which police are called upon to order people not to block the sidewalk, not to congregate in a given place, and not to 'loiter.' . . . The police may suspect the loiterer of considering engaging in some form of undesirable conduct that can be at least temporarily frustrated by ordering him or her to 'move on.'"

In order to perform their peace-keeping responsibilities satisfactorily, the police inevitably must exercise discretion. Indeed, by empowering them to act as peace officers, the law assumes that the police will exercise that discretion responsibly and with sound judgment. That is not to say that the law should not provide objective guidelines for the police, but simply that it cannot rigidly constrain their every action. By directing a police officer not to issue a dispersal order unless he "observes a person whom he reasonably believes to be a criminal street gang member loitering in any public place." Chicago's ordinance strikes an appropriate balance between those two extremes. Just as we trust officers to rely on their experience and expertise in order to make spur-of-the-moment determinations about amorphous legal standards such as "probable cause" and "reasonable suspicion," so we must trust them to determine whether a group of loiterers contains individuals (in this case members of criminal street gangs) whom the city has determined threaten the public peace. In sum, the Court's conclusion that the ordinance is impermissibly vague because it "'necessarily entrusts lawmaking to the moment-to-moment judgment of the policeman on his beat'" cannot be reconciled with common sense, longstanding police practice, or this Court's Fourth Amendment jurisprudence.

The illogic of the Court's position becomes apparent when Justice STEVENS opines that the ordinance's dispersal provision "would no doubt be sufficient if the ordinance only applied to loitering that had an apparently harmful purpose or effect, or possibly if it only applied to loitering by persons reasonably believed to be criminal gang members." With respect, if the Court believes that the ordinance is vague as written, this suggestion would not cure the vagueness problem. First, although the Court has suggested that a scienter requirement may mitigate a vagueness problem "with respect to the adequacy of notice to the complainant that his conduct is proscribed," the alternative proposal does not incorporate a scienter requirement. If the statute's prohibition were limited to loitering with "an apparently harmful purpose," the criminality of the conduct would continue to depend on its external appearance, rather than the loiterer's state of mind. For this reason, the proposed alternative would no[t] serve to channel police discretion. Indeed, an ordinance that required officers to ascertain whether a group of loiterers have "an apparently harmful purpose" would require them to exercise *more* discretion, not less.

2

The plurality's conclusion that the ordinance "fails to give the ordinary citizen adequate notice of what is forbidden and what is permitted" is similarly untenable. There is nothing "vague" about an order to disperse. While "we can never expect mathematical certainty from our language," it is safe to assume that the vast majority of people who are ordered by the police to "disperse and remove themselves from the area" will have little difficulty understanding how to comply.

Assuming that we are also obligated to consider whether the ordinance places individuals on notice of what conduct might subject them to such an order, respondents in this facial challenge bear the weighty burden of establishing that the statute is vague in all its applications, "in the sense that no standard of conduct is specified at all." I subscribe to the view of retired Justice White—"If any fool would know that a particular category of conduct would be within the reach of the statute, if there is an unmistakable core that a reasonable person would know is forbidden by the law, the enactment is not unconstitutional on its face." *Kolender* (dissenting opinion). This is certainly such a case. As the Illinois Supreme Court recognized, "persons of ordinary intelligence may maintain a common and accepted meaning of the word 'loiter.'" *Morales*, 177 Ill.2d, at 451, 687 N.E.2d, at 61.

The plurality concludes that the definition of the term loiter—"to remain in any one place with no apparent purpose"—fails to provide adequate notice. "It is difficult to imagine," the plurality posits, "how any citizen of the city of Chicago standing in a public place . . . would know if he or she had an 'apparent purpose.'" The plurality underestimates the intellectual capacity of the citizens of Chicago. Persons of ordinary intelligence are perfectly capable of evaluating how outsiders perceive their conduct, and here "[i]t is self-evident that there is a whole range of conduct that anyone with at least a semblance of common sense would know is [loitering] and that would be covered by the statute." Members of a group standing on the corner staring blankly into space, for example, are likely well aware that passersby would conclude that they have "no apparent purpose." In any event, because this is a facial challenge, the plurality's ability to hypothesize that some individuals, in some circumstances, may be unable to ascertain how their actions appear to outsiders is irrelevant to our analysis. Here, we are asked to determine whether the ordinance is "vague in all of its applications." The answer is unquestionably no.

Today, the Court focuses extensively on the "rights" of gang members and their companions. It can safely do so—the people who will have to live with the consequences of today's opinion do not live in our neighborhoods. Rather, the people who will suffer from our lofty pronouncements are people like Ms. Susan Mary Jackson; people who have seen their neighborhoods literally destroyed by gangs and violence and drugs. They are good, decent people who must struggle to overcome their desperate situation, against all odds, in order to raise their families, earn a living, and remain good citizens. As one resident described, "There is only about maybe one or two percent of the people in the city causing these problems maybe, but it's keeping 98 percent of us in our houses and off the streets and afraid to shop." By focusing exclusively on the imagined "rights" of the two percent, the Court today has denied our most vulnerable citizens the very thing that Justice STEVENS elevates above all else — the "freedom of movement." And that is a shame. I respectfully dissent.

Questions and Notes

1. Is the problem with the Chicago ordinance that it is not clear enough, or that it is too clear? Explain.

2. Does the statute clearly forbid something it can mean? What would Justice Scalia say? What would Justice Breyer say?

3. How can Chicago fix this ordinance? As fixed, would it accomplish its purpose? Would it still be vague? Explain.

Problem

At 2:00 a.m., Mary Jones, a first-year law student, is studying for her criminal law exam. She became somewhat concerned upon noticing a man sitting on a public bench staring at her apartment. At 2:15 a.m., Mary closed the curtains. At 3:00 a.m., she peered through the curtains and noticed that the man was still there, staring at her apartment. At that point she called the police, who arrived on the scene. The police engaged the man in the following dialogue:

Policeman: Who are you?

Man: That's none of your business.

Policeman: What are you doing here?

Man: That's none of your business.

Policeman: Did you know that your upsetting the woman who lives in that apartment?

Man: That's her problem.

Policeman: If you don't start giving me some straight answers, I'm going to arrest you.

Man: So arrest me.

The officer arrested the man and charged him with violating the following statute, predicated on the MPC's model statute:

LOITERING

Whoever loiters or prowls in a place, at a time, or in a manner not usual for law-abiding individuals under circumstances that warrant alarm for the safety of persons or property in the vicinity. Among the circumstances which may be considered in determining whether such alarm is warranted is the fact that the actor takes flight upon appearance of a peace officer, refuses to identify himself, or manifestly endeavors to conceal himself or any object. Unless flight by the actor or other circumstances makes it impracticable, a peace officer shall prior to any arrest for an offense under this section, afford the actor an opportunity to dispel any alarm which would otherwise be warranted, by requesting him to identify himself and explain his presence and conduct. No person shall be convicted of an offense under this section if the peace officer did not comply with the preceding sentence, or if it appears at trial that the explanation given by the actor was true and, if believed by the peace officer at the time, would have dispelled the alarm.

Loitering shall be punishable by not more than a five-hundred-dollar fine.

Under *Papachristou, Kolender,* and *Morales,* is it constitutionally permissible to punish the arrestee under this statute? Should it be permissible to punish him? What should the appropriate police response be in this situation?

Suppose the defendant had said: "My name is Joe Smith." Suppose further that in response to questioning, he said that he had no identification or other means of proving who he was. Suppose that in response to the statement about upsetting the woman in the house, he said: "I'm terribly sorry, but I have a right to be here too." Finally, suppose that when asked to move on, he politely, but firmly, refused, reiterating his right to be there.

Chapter 23

Victimless Crimes

In a sense, the concept of a victimless crime is oxymoronic. The fact that activity is criminalized suggests that the legislature perceives a societal if not an individual victim. Nevertheless, there are clearly some crimes in which the identity of an individual victim is unclear at best. The extent to which the criminal law ought to intervene in the absence of a clearly identifiable individual victim has been subject to considerable debate. We close our study of criminal law by considering the extent to which the criminal law should encompass relatively victimless crimes.

Lawrence v. Texas

539 U.S. 558 (2003)

Justice KENNEDY delivered the opinion of the Court.

Liberty protects the person from unwarranted government intrusions into a dwelling or other private place. In our tradition the State is not omnipresent in the home. And there are other spheres of our lives and existence, outside the home, where the State should not be a dominant presence. Freedom extends beyond spatial bounds. Liberty presumes an autonomy of self that includes freedom of thought, belief, expression, and certain intimate conduct. The instant case involves liberty of the person both in its spatial and in its more transcendent dimensions.

I.

The question before the Court is the validity of a Texas statute making it a crime for two persons of the same sex to engage in certain intimate sexual conduct.

In Houston, Texas, officers of the Harris County Police Department were dispatched to a private residence in response to a reported weapons disturbance. They entered an apartment where one of the petitioners, John Geddes Lawrence, resided. The right of the police to enter does not seem to have been questioned. The officers observed Lawrence and another man, Tyron Garner, engaging in a sexual act. The two petitioners were arrested, held in custody overnight, and charged and convicted before a Justice of the Peace.

The complaints described their crime as "deviate sexual intercourse, namely anal sex, with a member of the same sex (man)."

"Our prior cases make two propositions abundantly clear. First, the fact that the governing majority in a State has traditionally viewed a particular practice as immoral is not a sufficient reason for upholding a law prohibiting the practice.

Second, individual decisions by married persons, concerning the intimacies of their physical relationship, even when not intended to produce offspring, are a form of 'liberty' protected by the Due Process Clause of the Fourteenth Amendment. Moreover, this protection extends to intimate choices by unmarried as well as married persons."

The judgment of the Court of Appeals for the Texas Fourteenth District is reversed, and the case is remanded for further proceedings not inconsistent with this opinion.

Justice SCALIA, with whom THE CHIEF JUSTICE and Justice THOMAS join, dissenting.

The Texas statute undeniably seeks to further the belief of its citizens that certain forms of sexual behavior are "immoral and unacceptable," *Bowers v. Hardwick* 478 U.S. 186 (1986)—the same interest furthered by criminal laws against fornication, bigamy, adultery, adult incest, bestiality, and obscenity. *Bowers* held that this *was* a legitimate state interest. The Court today reaches the opposite conclusion. The Texas statute, it says, "furthers *no legitimate state interest* which can justify its intrusion into the personal and private life of the individual," (emphasis added). The Court embraces instead Justice STEVENS' declaration in his *Bowers* dissent, that "the fact that the governing majority in a State has traditionally viewed a particular practice as immoral is not a sufficient reason for upholding a law prohibiting the practice" This effectively decrees the end of all morals legislation. If, as the Court asserts, the promotion of majoritarian sexual morality is not even a *legitimate* state interest, none of the above-mentioned laws can survive rational-basis review. I dissent.

Questions and Notes

1. Do you agree with the Court that "the fact the governing majority in a State has traditionally viewed a particular practice as immoral is not a sufficient reason for upholding a law prohibiting the practice"? Why? Why not? *See* Loewy, *Morals, Legislation, and the Establishment Clause*, 55 ALA. L. REV. 159 (2003).

2. Is Justice Scalia correct in asserting that the logic of *Lawrence* necessarily invalidates laws against fornication, bigamy, adultery, adult incest, bestiality, and obscenity? Explain.

3. If you think that *Lawrence* was correctly decided, would you also invalidate the other laws listed by Justice Scalia? Why? Why not?

4. If you are inclined toward leaving the criminal law out of conduct such as that involved in *Lawrence*, or that described by Scalia, does your *laissez-faire* attitude extend to the conduct involved in *Samuels*?

People v. Samuels

58 Cal. Rptr. 439 (Cal. App. 1967)

SHOEMAKER, P.J.

Defendant Marvin Samuels was charged with two counts of assault by means of force likely to cause great bodily injury. Defendant pleaded not guilty to all charges.

The jury found him guilty on one charge of aggravated assault and the offense of simple assault included in the other charge of aggravated assault. The simple assault conviction was subsequently dismissed. The court suspended the imposition of sentence, fined defendant $3,000 and placed him on probation for a period of 10 years.

Defendant Samuels, an ophthalmologist, testified that he recognized the symptoms of sadomasochism in himself, and his primary concern became to control and release his sadomasochistic urges in ways which were harmless. Through his hobby of photography, he participated in the production of several films on the east coast. Three of these films depicted bound individuals being whipped. Defendant wielded the whip in two of the films and acted as the cameraman, producer and director for the third film. He testified that the apparent force of the whippings was "faked" and that cosmetics were used to supply the marks of the apparent beating. Defendant produced one of these films at the trial.

Defendant's conviction of aggravated assault was based upon the beating depicted in [one of the films]. Defendant contends that the consent of the victim is an absolute defense to the charge of aggravated assault and that the trial court erred in instructing the jury to the contrary. This argument cannot be sustained.

Although both parties concede that they were unable to find any California case directly in point, consent of the victim is not generally a defense to assault or battery, except in a situation involving ordinary physical contact or blows incident to sports such as football, boxing or wrestling. It is also the rule that the apparent consent of a person without legal capacity to give consent, such as a child or insane person, is ineffective.

It is a matter of common knowledge that a normal person in full possession of his mental faculties does not freely consent to the use, upon himself, of force likely to produce great bodily injury. Even if it be assumed that the victim in the "vertical" film did in fact suffer from some form of mental aberration which compelled him to submit to a beating which was so severe as to constitute an aggravated assault, defendant's conduct in inflicting that beating was no less violative of a penal statute obviously designed to prohibit one human being from severely or mortally injuring another. It follows that the trial court was correct in instructing the jury that consent was not a defense to the aggravated assault charge.

Questions and Notes

1. Is there any good reason why consent should not be a defense in a case like *Samuels*?

2. Is the government ever justified in using the criminal law to protect an adult from his own indiscretions?

3. Is the government justified in punishing: (a) marijuana use, (b) heroin use, (c) cocaine use? Why? Why not?

4. If your answer to any of the hypotheticals in Question 3 was "yes," what about: (a) alcohol use, (b) tobacco use, (c) caffeine use?

5. Even if the libertarian reasons for decriminalizing drug use are unpersuasive, are there any utilitarian reasons for such action? What are they?

6. Which of the following possible crimes do you regard as "victimless": (a) abortion, (b) adultery, (c) aggravated assault on a consenting masochist, (d) drug use, (e) consensual sodomy?

Appendix A

Model Penal Code
(Selected Provisions)[*]
PART I. GENERAL PROVISIONS

---

[*] Model Penal Code © 1985 by the American Law Institute. Reproduced with permission. All rights reserved.

ARTICLE 7. AUTHORITY OF COURT IN SENTENCING

PART II. DEFINITION OF SPECIFIC CRIMES OFFENSES INVOLVING DANGER TO THE PERSON

ARTICLE 210. CRIMINAL HOMICIDE

ARTICLE 211. ASSAULT; RECKLESS ENDANGERING; THREATS

ARTICLE 212. KIDNAPPING AND RELATED OFFENSES; COERCION

ARTICLE 213. SEXUAL OFFENSES

OFFENSES AGAINST THE FAMILY

ARTICLE 230. OFFENSES AGAINST THE FAMILY

OFFENSES AGAINST PUBLIC ADMINISTRATION

ARTICLE 242. OBSTRUCTING GOVERNMENTAL OPERATIONS; ESCAPE

ARTICLE 243. ABUSE OF OFFICE

OFFENSES AGAINST PUBLIC ORDER AND DECENCY

ARTICLE 250. RIOT, DISORDERLY CONDUCT, AND RELATED OFFENSES

Model Penal Code

PART I. GENERAL PROVISIONS
Article 1. Preliminary
Section 1.01.
Title and Effective Date.

(1) This Act is called the Penal and Correctional Code and may be cited as P.C.C. It shall become effective on _____.

(2) Except as provided in Subsections (3) and (4) of this Section, the Code does not apply to offenses committed prior to its effective date and prosecutions for such offenses shall be governed by the prior law, which is continued in effect for that purpose, as if this Code were not in force. For the purposes of this Section, an offense was committed prior to the effective date of the Code if any of the elements of the offense occurred prior thereto.

(3) In any case pending on or after the effective date of the Code, involving an offense committed prior to such date:

(a) procedural provisions of the Code shall govern, insofar as they are justly applicable and their application does not introduce confusion or delay;

(b) provisions of the Code according a defense or mitigation shall apply, with the consent of the defendant;

(c) the Court, with the consent of the defendant, may impose sentence under the provisions of the Code applicable to the offense and the offender.

(4) Provisions of the Code governing the treatment and the release or discharge of prisoners, probationers and parolees shall apply to persons under sentence for offenses committed prior to the effective date of the Code, except that the minimum or maximum period of their detention or supervision shall in no case be increased.

Section 1.02.
Purposes; Principles of Construction.

(1) The general purposes of the provisions governing the definition of offenses are:

(a) to forbid and prevent conduct that unjustifiably and inexcusably inflicts or threatens substantial harm to individual or public interests;

(b) to subject to public control persons whose conduct indicates that they are disposed to commit crimes;

(c) to safeguard conduct that is without fault from condemnation as criminal;

(d) to give fair warning of the nature of the conduct declared to constitute an offense;

(e) to differentiate on reasonable grounds between serious and minor offenses.

(2) The general purposes of the provisions governing the sentencing and treatment of offenders are:

(a) to prevent the commission of offenses;

(b) to promote the correction and rehabilitation of offenders;

(c) to safeguard offenders against excessive, disproportionate or arbitrary punishment;

(d) to give fair warning of the nature of the sentences that may be imposed on conviction of an offense;

(e) to differentiate among offenders with a view to a just individualization in their treatment;

(f) to define, coordinate and harmonize the powers, duties and functions of the courts and of administrative officers and agencies responsible for dealing with offenders;

(g) to advance the use of generally accepted scientific methods and knowledge in the sentencing and treatment of offenders;

(h) to integrate responsibility for the administration of the correctional system in a State Department of Correction [or other single department or agency].

(3) The provisions of the Code shall be construed according to the fair import of their terms but when the language is susceptible of differing constructions it shall

be interpreted to further the general purposes stated in this Section and the special purposes of the particular provision involved. The discretionary powers conferred by the Code shall be exercised in accordance with the criteria stated in the Code and, insofar as such criteria are not decisive, to further the general purposes stated in this Section.

Section 1.03.
Territorial Applicability.

(1) Except as otherwise provided in this Section, a person may be convicted under the law of this State of an offense committed by his own conduct or the conduct of another for which he is legally accountable if:

(a) either the conduct that is an element of the offense or the result that is such an element occurs within this State; or

(b) conduct occurring outside the State is sufficient under the law of this State to constitute an attempt to commit an offense within the State; or

(c) conduct occurring outside the State is sufficient under the law of this State to constitute a conspiracy to commit an offense within the State and an overt act in furtherance of such conspiracy occurs within the State; or

(d) conduct occurring within the State establishes complicity in the commission of, or an attempt, solicitation or conspiracy to commit, an offense in another jurisdiction that also is an offense under the law of this State; or

(e) the offense consists of the omission to perform a legal duty imposed by the law of this State with respect to domicile, residence or a relationship to a person, thing or transaction in the State; or

(f) the offense is based on a statute of this State that expressly prohibits conduct outside the State, when the conduct bears a reasonable relation to a legitimate interest of this State and the actor knows or should know that his conduct is likely to affect that interest.

(2) Subsection (1)(a) does not apply when either causing a specified result or a purpose to cause or danger of causing such a result is an element of an offense and the result occurs or is designed or likely to occur only in another jurisdiction where the conduct charged would not constitute an offense, unless a legislative purpose plainly appears to declare the conduct criminal regardless of the place of the result.

(3) Subsection (1)(a) does not apply when causing a particular result is an element of an offense and the result is caused by conduct occurring outside the State that would not constitute an offense if the result had occurred there, unless the actor purposely or knowingly caused the result within the State.

(4) When the offense is homicide, either the death of the victim or the bodily impact causing death constitutes a "result" within the meaning of Subsection (1)(a),

and if the body of a homicide victim is found within the State, it is presumed that such result occurred within the State.

(5) This State includes the land and water and the air space above such land and water with respect to which the State has legislative jurisdiction.

Section 1.04.
Classes of Crimes; Violations.

(1) An offense defined by this Code or by any other statute of this State, for which a sentence of [death or of] imprisonment is authorized, constitutes a crime. Crimes are classified as felonies, misdemeanors or petty misdemeanors.

(2) A crime is a felony if it is so designated in this Code or if persons convicted thereof may be sentenced [to death or] to imprisonment for a term that, apart from an extended term, is in excess of one year.

(3) A crime is a misdemeanor if it is so designated in this Code or in a statute other than this Code enacted subsequent thereto.

(4) A crime is a petty misdemeanor if it is so designated in this Code or in a statute other than this Code enacted subsequent thereto or if it is defined by a statute other than this Code that now provides that persons convicted thereof may be sentenced to imprisonment for a term of which the maximum is less than one year.

(5) An offense defined by this Code or by any other statute of this State constitutes a violation if it is so designated in this Code or in the law defining the offense or if no other sentence than a fine, or fine and forfeiture or other civil penalty is authorized upon conviction or if it is defined by a statute other than this Code that now provides that the offense shall not constitute a crime. A violation does not constitute a crime and conviction of a violation shall not give rise to any disability or legal disadvantage based on conviction of a criminal offense.

(6) Any offense declared by law to constitute a crime, without specification of the grade thereof or of the sentence authorized upon conviction, is a misdemeanor.

(7) An offense defined by any statute of this State other than this Code shall be classified as provided in this Section and the sentence that may be imposed upon conviction thereof shall hereafter be governed by this Code.

Section 1.05.
All Offenses Defined by Statute; Application of
General Provisions of the Code.

(1) No conduct constitutes an offense unless it is a crime or violation under this Code or another statute of this State.

(2) The provisions of Part I of the Code are applicable to offenses defined by other statutes, unless the Code otherwise provides.

(3) This Section does not affect the power of a court to punish for contempt or to employ any sanction authorized by law for the enforcement of an order or a civil judgment or decree.

Section 1.07.
Method of Prosecution When Conduct Constitutes
More Than One Offense.

(1) *Prosecution for Multiple Offenses; Limitation on Convictions.* When the same conduct of a defendant may establish the commission of more than one offense, the defendant may be prosecuted for each such offense. He may not, however, be convicted of more than one offense if:

(a) one offense is included in the other, as defined in Subsection (4) of this Section; or

(b) one offense consists only of a conspiracy or other form of preparation to commit the other; or

(c) inconsistent findings of fact are required to establish the commission of the offenses; or

(d) the offenses differ only in that one is defined to prohibit a designated kind of conduct generally and the other to prohibit a specific instance of such conduct; or

(e) the offense is defined as a continuing course of conduct and the defendant's course of conduct was uninterrupted, unless the law provides that specific periods of such conduct constitute separate offenses.

(2) *Limitation on Separate Trials for Multiple Offenses.* Except as provided in Subsection (3) of this Section, a defendant shall not be subject to separate trials for multiple offenses based on the same conduct or arising from the same criminal episode, if such offenses are known to the appropriate prosecuting officer at the time of the commencement of the first trial and are within the jurisdiction of a single court.

(3) *Authority of Court to Order Separate Trials.* When a defendant is charged with two or more offenses based on the same conduct or arising from the same criminal episode, the Court, on application of the prosecuting attorney or of the defendant, may order any such charge to be tried separately, if it is satisfied that justice so requires.

(4) *Conviction of Included Offense Permitted.* A defendant may be convicted of an offense included in an offense charged in the indictment [or the information]. An offense is so included when:

(a) it is established by proof of the same or less than all the facts required to establish the commission of the offense charged; or

(b) it consists of an attempt or solicitation to commit the offense charged or to commit an offense otherwise included therein; or

(c) it differs from the offense charged only in the respect that a less serious injury or risk of injury to the same person, property or public interest or a lesser kind of culpability suffices to establish its commission.

(5) *Submission of Included Offense to Jury.* The Court shall not be obligated to charge the jury with respect to an included offense unless there is a rational basis for a verdict acquitting the defendant of the offense charged and convicting him of the included offense.

Section 1.12.
Proof Beyond a Reasonable Doubt; Affirmative Defenses; Burden of Proving Fact When Not an Element of an Offense; Presumptions.

(1) No person may be convicted of an offense unless each element of such offense is proved beyond a reasonable doubt. In the absence of such proof, the innocence of the defendant is assumed.

(2) Subsection (1) of this Section does not:

(a) require the disproof of an affirmative defense unless and until there is evidence supporting such defense; or

(b) apply to any defense that the Code or another statute plainly requires the defendant to prove by a preponderance of evidence.

(3) A ground of defense is affirmative, within the meaning of Subsection (2)(a) of this Section, when:

(a) it arises under a section of the Code that so provides; or

(b) it relates to an offense defined by a statute other than the Code and such statute so provides; or

(c) it involves a matter of excuse or justification peculiarly within the knowledge of the defendant on which he can fairly be required to adduce supporting evidence.

(4) When the application of the code depends upon the finding of a fact that is not an element of an offense, unless the Code otherwise provides:

(a) the burden of proving the fact is on the prosecution or defendant, depending on whose interest or contention will be furthered if the finding should be made; and

(b) the fact must be proved to the satisfaction of the Court or jury, as the case may be.

(5) When the Code establishes a presumption with respect to any fact that is an element of an offense, it has the following consequences:

(a) when there is evidence of the facts that give rise to the presumption, the issue of the existence of the presumed fact must be submitted to the jury, unless the Court is satisfied that the evidence as a whole clearly negatives the presumed fact; and

(b) when the issue of the existence of the presumed fact is submitted to the jury, the Court shall charge that while the presumed fact must, on all the evidence, be proved beyond a reasonable doubt, the law declares that the jury may regard the facts giving rise to the presumption as sufficient evidence of the presumed fact.

(6) A presumption not established by the Code or inconsistent with it has the consequences otherwise accorded it by law.

Section 1.13.
General Definitions.

In this Code, unless a different meaning plainly is required:

(1) "statute" includes the Constitution and a local law or ordinance of a political subdivision of the State;

(2) "act" or "action" means a bodily movement whether voluntary or involuntary;

(3) "voluntary" has the meaning specified In Section 2.01;

(4) "omission" means a failure to act;

(5) "conduct" means an action or omission and its accompanying state of mind, or, where relevant, a series of acts and omissions;

(6) "actor" includes, where relevant, a person guilty of an omission;

(7) "acted" includes, where relevant, "omitted to act";

(8) "person," "he" and "actor" include any natural person and, where relevant, a corporation or an unincorporated association;

(9) "element of an offense" means (i) such conduct or (ii) such attendant circumstances or (iii) such a result of conduct as

(a) is included in the description of the forbidden conduct in the definition of the offense; or

(b) establishes the required kind of culpability; or

(c) negatives an excuse or justification for such conduct; or

(d) negatives a defense under the statute of limitations; or

(e) establishes jurisdiction or venue;

(10) "material element of an offense" means an element that does not relate exclusively to the statute of limitations, jurisdiction, venue, or to any other matter similarly unconnected with (i) the harm or evil, incident to conduct, sought to be prevented by the law defining the offense, or (ii) the existence of a justification or excuse for such conduct;

(11) "purposely" has the meaning specified in Section 2.02 and equivalent terms such as "with purpose," "designed" or "with design" have the same meaning;

(12) "intentionally" or "with intent" means purposely;

(13) "knowingly" has the meaning specified in Section 2.02 and equivalent terms such as "knowing" or "with knowledge" have the same meaning;

(14) "recklessly" has the meaning specified in Section 2.02 and equivalent terms such as "recklessness" or "with recklessness" have the same meaning;

(15) "negligently" has the meaning specified in Section 2.02 and equivalent terms such as "negligence" or "with negligence" have the same meaning;

(16) "reasonably believes" or "reasonable belief" designates a belief that the actor is not reckless or negligent in holding.

Article 2. General Principles of Liability

Section 2.01.
Requirement of Voluntary Act; Omission as Basis of Liability; Possession as an Act.

(1) A person is not guilty of an offense unless his liability is based on conduct that includes a voluntary act or the omission to perform an act of which he is physically capable.

(2) The following are not voluntary acts within the meaning of this Section:

(a) a reflex or convulsion;

(b) a bodily movement during unconsciousness or sleep;

(c) conduct during hypnosis or resulting from hypnotic suggestion;

(d) a bodily movement that otherwise is not a product of the effort or determination of the actor, either conscious or habitual.

(3) Liability for the commission of an offense may not be based on an omission unaccompanied by action unless:

(a) the omission is expressly made sufficient by the law defining the offense; or

(b) a duty to perform the omitted act is otherwise imposed by law.

(4) Possession is an act, within the meaning of this Section, if the possessor knowingly procured or received the thing possessed or was aware of his control thereof for a sufficient period to have been able to terminate his possession.

Section 2.02.
General Requirements of Culpability.

(1) *Minimum Requirements of Culpability.* Except as provided in Section 2.05, a person is not guilty of an offense unless he acted purposely, knowingly, recklessly or negligently, as the law may require, with respect to each material element of the offense.

(2) *Kinds of Culpability Defined.*

(a) *Purposely.* A person acts purposely with respect to a material element of an offense when:

(i) if the element involves the nature of his conduct or a result thereof, it is his conscious object to engage in conduct of that nature or to cause such a result; and

(ii) if the element involves the attendant circumstances, he is aware of the existence of such circumstances or he believes or hopes that they exist.

(b) *Knowingly*. A person acts knowingly with respect to a material element of an offense when:

(i) if the element involves the nature of his conduct or the attendant circumstances, he is aware that his conduct is of that nature or that such circumstances exist; and

(ii) if the element involves a result of his conduct, he is aware that it is practically certain that his conduct will cause such a result.

(c) *Recklessly*. A person acts recklessly with respect to a material element of an offense when he consciously disregards a substantial and unjustifiable risk that the material element exists or will result from his conduct. The risk must be of such a nature and degree that, considering the nature and purpose of the actor's conduct and the circumstances known to him, its disregard involves a gross deviation from the standard of conduct that a law-abiding person would observe in the actor's situation.

(d) *Negligently*. A person acts negligently with respect to a material element of an offense when he should be aware of a substantial and unjustifiable risk that the material element exists or will result from his conduct. The risk must be of such a nature and degree that the actor's failure to perceive it, considering the nature and purpose of his conduct and the circumstances known to him, involves a gross deviation from the standard of care that a reasonable person would observe in the actor's situation.

(3) *Culpability Required Unless Otherwise Provided*. When the culpability sufficient to establish a material element of an offense is not prescribed by law, such element is established if a person acts purposely, knowingly or recklessly with respect thereto.

(4) *Prescribed Culpability Requirement Applies to All Material Elements*. When the law defining an offense prescribes the kind of culpability that is sufficient for the commission of an offense, without distinguishing among the material elements thereof, such provision shall apply to all the material elements of the offense, unless a contrary purpose plainly appears.

(5) *Substitutes for Negligence, Recklessness and Knowledge*. When the law provides that negligence suffices to establish an element of an offense, such element also is established if a person acts purposely, knowingly or recklessly. When recklessness suffices to establish an element, such element also is established if a person acts purposely or knowingly. When acting knowingly suffices to establish an element, such element also is established if a person acts purposely.

(6) *Requirement of Purpose Satisfied if Purpose Is Conditional*. When a particular purpose is an element of an offense, the element is established although such

purpose is conditional, unless the condition negatives the harm or evil sought to be prevented by the law defining the offense.

(7) *Requirement of Knowledge Satisfied by Knowledge of High Probability.* When knowledge of the existence of a particular fact is an element of an offense, such knowledge is established if a person is aware of a high probability of its existence, unless he actually believes that it does not exist.

(8) *Requirement of Willfulness Satisfied by Acting Knowingly.* A requirement that an offense be committed willfully is satisfied if a person acts knowingly with respect to the material elements of the offense, unless a purpose to impose further requirements appears.

(9) *Culpability as to Illegality of Conduct.* Neither knowledge nor recklessness or negligence as to whether conduct constitutes an offense or as to the existence, meaning or application of the law determining the elements of an offense is an element of such offense, unless the definition of the offense or the Code so provides.

(10) *Culpability as Determinant of Grade of Offense.* When the grade or degree of an offense depends on whether the offense is committed purposely, knowingly, recklessly or negligently, its grade or degree shall be the lowest for which the determinative kind of culpability is established with respect to any material element of the offense.

Section 2.03.
Causal Relationship Between Conduct and Result; Divergence Between Result Designed or Contemplated and Actual Result or Between Probable and Actual Result.

(1) Conduct is the cause of a result when:

(a) it is an antecedent but for which the result in question would not have occurred; and

(b) the relationship between the conduct and result satisfies any additional causal requirements imposed by the Code or by the law defining the offense.

(2) When purposely or knowingly causing a particular result is an element of an offense, the element is not established if the actual result is not within the purpose or the contemplation of the actor unless:

(a) the actual result differs from that designed or contemplated, as the case may be, only in the respect that a different person or different property is injured or affected or that the injury or harm designed or contemplated would have been more serious or more extensive than that caused; or

(b) the actual result involves the same kind of injury or harm as that designed or contemplated and is not too remote or accidental in its occurrence to have a [just] bearing on the actor's liability or on the gravity of his offense.

(3) When recklessly or negligently causing a particular result is an element of an offense, the element is not established if the actual result is not within the risk of

which the actor is aware or, in the case of negligence, of which he should be aware unless:

(a) the actual result differs from the probable result only in the respect that a different person or different property is injured or affected or that the probable injury or harm would have been more serious or more extensive than that caused; or

(b) the actual result involves the same kind of injury or harm as the probable result and is not too remote or accidental in its occurrence to have a [just]bearing on the actor's liability or on the gravity of his offense.

(4) When causing a particular result is a material element of an offense for which absolute liability is imposed by law, the element is not established unless the actual result is a probable consequence of the actor's conduct.

Section 2.04.
Ignorance or Mistake.

(1) Ignorance or mistake as to a matter of fact or law is a defense if:

(a) the ignorance or mistake negatives the purpose, knowledge, belief, recklessness or negligence required to establish a material element of the offense; or

(b) the law provides that the state of mind established by such ignorance or mistake constitutes a defense.

(2) Although ignorance or mistake would otherwise afford a defense to the offense charged, the defense is not available if the defendant would be guilty of another offense had the situation been as he supposed. In such case, however, the ignorance or mistake of the defendant shall reduce the grade and degree of the offense of which he may be convicted to those of the offense of which he would be guilty had the situation been as he supposed.

(3) A belief that conduct does not legally constitute an offense is a defense to a prosecution for that offense based upon such conduct when:

(a) the statute or other enactment defining the offense is not known to the actor and has not been published or otherwise reasonably made available prior to the conduct alleged; or

(b) he acts in reasonable reliance upon an official statement of the law, afterward determined to be invalid or erroneous, contained in (i) a statute or other enactment; (ii) a judicial decision, opinion or judgment; (iii) an administrative order or grant of permission; or (iv) an official interpretation of the public officer or body charged by law with responsibility for the interpretation, administration or enforcement of the law defining the offense.

(4) The defendant must prove a defense arising under Subsection (3) of this Section by a preponderance of evidence.

Section 2.05.
When Culpability Requirements Are Inapplicable to Violations and to Offenses Defined by Other Statutes; Effect of Absolute Liability in Reducing Grade of Offense to Violation.

(1) The requirements of culpability prescribed by Sections 2.01 and 2.02 do not apply to:

(a) offenses that constitute violations, unless the requirement involved is included in the definition of the offense or the Court determines that its application is consistent with effective enforcement of the law defining the offense; or

(b) offenses defined by statutes other than the Code, insofar as a legislative purpose to impose absolute liability for such offenses or with respect to any material element thereof plainly appears.

(2) Notwithstanding any other provision of existing law and unless a subsequent statute otherwise provides:

(a) when absolute liability is imposed with respect to any material element of an offense defined by a statute other than the Code and a conviction is based upon such liability, the offense constitutes a violation; and

(b) although absolute liability is imposed by law with respect to one or more of the material elements of an offense defined by a statute other than the Code, the culpable commission of the offense may be charged and proved, in which event negligence with respect to such elements constitutes sufficient culpability and the classification of the offense and the sentence that may be imposed therefor upon conviction are determined by Section 1.04 and Article 6 of the Code.

Section 2.06.
Liability for Conduct of Another; Complicity.

(1) A person is guilty of an offense if it is committed by his own conduct or by the conduct of another person for which he is legally accountable, or both.

(2) A person is legally accountable for the conduct of another person when:

(a) acting with the kind of culpability that is sufficient for the commission of the offense, he causes an innocent or irresponsible person to engage in such conduct; or

(b) he is made accountable for the conduct of such other person by the Code or by the law defining the offense; or

(c) he is an accomplice of such other person in the commission of the offense.

(3) A person is an accomplice of another person in the commission of an offense if:

(a) with the purpose of promoting or facilitating the commission of the offense, he

(i) solicits such other person to commit it, or

(ii) aids or agrees or attempts to aid such other person in planning or committing it, or

(iii) having a legal duty to prevent the commission of the offense, fails to make proper effort so to do; or

(b) his conduct is expressly declared by law to establish his complicity.

(4) When causing a particular result is an element of an offense, an accomplice in the conduct causing such result is an accomplice in the commission of that offense if he acts with the kind of culpability, if any, with respect to that result that is sufficient for the commission of the offense.

(5) A person who is legally incapable of committing a particular offense himself may be guilty thereof if it is committed by the conduct of another person for which he is legally accountable, unless such liability is inconsistent with the purpose of the provision establishing his incapacity.

(6) Unless otherwise provided by the Code or by the law defining the offense, a person is not an accomplice in an offense committed by another person if:

(a) he is a victim of that offense; or

(b) the offense is so defined that his conduct is inevitably incident to its commission; or

(c) he terminates his complicity prior to the commission of the offense and

(i) wholly deprives it of effectiveness in the commission of the offense; or

(ii) gives timely warning to the law enforcement authorities or otherwise makes proper effort to prevent the commission of the offense.

(7) An accomplice may be convicted on proof of the commission of the offense and of his complicity therein, though the person claimed to have committed the offense has not been prosecuted or convicted or has been convicted of a different offense or degree of offense or has an immunity to prosecution or conviction or has been acquitted.

Section 2.07.
Liability of Corporations, Unincorporated Associations and Persons Acting, or Under a Duty to Act, in Their Behalf.

(1) A corporation may be convicted of the commission of an offense if:

(a) the offense is a violation or the offense is defined by a statute other than the Code in which a legislative purpose to impose liability on corporations plainly appears and the conduct is performed by an agent of the corporation acting in behalf of the corporation within the scope of his office or employment, except that if the law defining the offense designates the agents for whose conduct the corporation is accountable or the circumstances under which it is accountable, such provisions shall apply; or

(b) the offense consists of an omission to discharge a specific duty of affirmative performance imposed on corporations by law; or

(c) the commission of the offense was authorized, requested, commanded, performed or recklessly tolerated by the board of directors or by a high managerial agent acting in behalf of the corporation within the scope of his office or employment.

(2) When absolute liability is imposed for the commission of an offense, a legislative purpose to impose liability on a corporation shall be assumed, unless the contrary plainly appears.

(3) An unincorporated association may be convicted of the commission of an offense if:

(a) the offense is defined by a statute other than the Code that expressly provides for the liability of such an association and the conduct is performed by an agent of the association acting in behalf of the association within the scope of his office or employment, except that if the law defining the offense designates the agents for whose conduct the association is accountable or the circumstances under which it is accountable, such provisions shall apply; or

(b) the offense consists of an omission to discharge a specific duty of affirmative performance imposed on associations by law.

(4) As used in this Section:

(a) "corporation" does not include an entity organized as or by a governmental agency for the execution of a governmental program;

(b) "agent" means any director, officer, servant, employee or other person authorized to act in behalf of the corporation or association and, in the case of an unincorporated association, a member of such association;

(c) "high managerial agent" means an officer of a corporation or an unincorporated association, or, in the case of a partnership, a partner, or any other agent of a corporation or association having duties of such responsibility that his conduct may fairly be assumed to represent the policy of the corporation or association.

(5) In any prosecution of a corporation or an unincorporated association for the commission of an offense included within the terms of Subsection (1)(a) or Subsection(3)(a) of this Section, other than an offense for which absolute liability has been imposed, it shall be a defense if the defendant proves by a preponderance of evidence that the high managerial agent having supervisory responsibility over the subject matter of the offense employed due diligence to prevent its commission. This paragraph shall not apply if it is plainly inconsistent with the legislative purpose in defining the particular offense.

(6) (a) A person is legally accountable for any conduct he performs or causes to be performed in the name of the corporation or an unincorporated association or in its behalf to the same extent as if it were performed in his own name or behalf.

(b) Whenever a duty to act is imposed by law upon a corporation or an unincorporated association, any agent of the corporation or association having primary responsibility for the discharge of the duty is legally accountable for a reckless omission to perform the required act to the same extent as if the duty were imposed by law directly upon himself.

(c) When a person is convicted of an offense by reason of his legal accountability for the conduct of a corporation or an unincorporated association, he is subject to the sentence authorized by law when a natural person is convicted of an offense of the grade and the degree involved.

Section 2.08.
Intoxication.

(1) Except as provided in Subsection (4) of this Section, intoxication of the actor is not a defense unless it negatives an element of the offense.

(2) When recklessness establishes an element of the offense, if the actor, due to self-induced intoxication, is unaware of a risk of which he would have been aware had he been sober, such unawareness is immaterial.

(3) Intoxication does not, in itself, constitute mental disease within the meaning of Section 4.01.

(4) Intoxication that (a) is not self-induced or (b) is pathological is an affirmative defense if by reason of such intoxication the actor at the time of his conduct lacks substantial capacity either to appreciate its criminality [wrongfulness] or to conform his conduct to the requirements of law.

(5) *Definitions.* In this Section unless a different meaning plainly is required:

(a) "intoxication" means a disturbance of mental or physical capacities resulting from the introduction of substances into the body;

(b) "self-induced intoxication" means intoxication caused by substances that the actor knowingly introduces into his body, the tendency of which to cause intoxication he knows or ought to know, unless he introduces them pursuant to medical advice or under such circumstances as would afford a defense to a charge of crime;

(c) "pathological intoxication" means intoxication grossly excessive in degree, given the amount of the intoxicant, to which the actor does not know he is susceptible.

Section 2.09.
Duress.

(1) It is an affirmative defense that the actor engaged in the conduct charged to constitute an offense because he was coerced to do so by the use of, or a threat to use, unlawful force against his person or the person of another, that a person of reasonable firmness in his situation would have been unable to resist.

(2) The defense provided by this Section is unavailable if the actor recklessly placed himself in a situation in which it was probable that he would be subjected to duress. The defense is also unavailable if he was negligent in placing himself in such a situation, whenever negligence suffices to establish culpability for the offense charged.

(3) It is not a defense that a woman acted on the command of her husband, unless she acted under such coercion as would establish a defense under this Section. [The presumption that a woman acting in the presence of her husband is coerced is abolished.]

(4) When the conduct of the actor would otherwise be justifiable under Section 3.02, this Section does not preclude such defense.

Section 2.10.
Military Orders.

It is an affirmative defense that the actor, in engaging in the conduct charged to constitute an offense, does no more than execute an order of his superior in the armed services that he does not know to be unlawful.

Section 2.11.
Consent.

(1) *In General.* The consent of the victim to conduct charged to constitute an offense or to the result thereof is a defense if such consent negatives an element of the offense or precludes the infliction of the harm or evil sought to be prevented by the law defining the offense.

(2) *Consent to Bodily Injury.* When conduct is charged to constitute an offense because it causes or threatens bodily injury, consent to such conduct or to the infliction of such injury is a defense if:

(a) the bodily injury consented to or threatened by the conduct consented to is not serious; or

(b) the conduct and the injury are reasonably foreseeable hazards of joint participation in a lawful athletic contest or competitive sport or other concerted activity not forbidden by law; or

(c) the consent establishes a justification for the conduct under Article 3 of the Code.

(3) *Ineffective Consent.* Unless otherwise provided by the Code or by the law defining the offense, assent does not constitute consent if:

(a) it is given by a person who is legally incompetent to authorize the conduct charged to constitute the offense; or

(b) it is given by a person who by reason of youth, mental disease or defect or intoxication is manifestly unable or known by the actor to be unable to make a reasonable judgment as to the nature or harmfulness of the conduct charged to constitute the offense; or

(c) it is given by a person whose improvident consent is sought to be prevented by the law defining the offense; or

(d) it is induced by force, duress or deception of a kind sought to be prevented by the law defining the offense.

Section 2.12.
De Minimis Infractions.

The Court shall dismiss a prosecution if, having regard to the nature of the conduct charged to constitute an offense and the nature of the attendant circumstances, it finds that the defendant's conduct:

(1) was within a customary license or tolerance, neither expressly negatived by the person whose interest was infringed nor inconsistent with the purpose of the law defining the offense; or

(2) did not actually cause or threaten the harm or evil sought to be prevented by the law defining the offense or did so only to an extent too trivial to warrant the condemnation of conviction; or

(3) present such other extenuations that it cannot reasonably be regarded as envisaged by the legislature in forbidding the offense.

The Court shall not dismiss a prosecution under Subsection (3) of this Section without filing a written statement of its reasons.

Section 2.13.
Entrapment.

(1) A public law enforcement official or a person acting in cooperation with such an official perpetrates an entrapment if for the purpose of obtaining evidence of the commission of an offense, he induces or encourages another person to engage in conduct constituting such offense by either:

(a) making knowingly false representations designed to induce the belief that such conduct is not prohibited; or

(b) employing methods of persuasion or inducement that create a substantial risk that such an offense will be committed by persons other than those who are ready to commit it.

(2) Except as provided in Subsection (3) of this Section, a person prosecuted for an offense shall be acquitted if he proves by a preponderance of evidence that his conduct occurred in response to an entrapment. The issue of entrapment shall be tried by the Court in the absence of the jury.

(3) The defense afforded by this Section is unavailable when causing or threatening bodily injury is an element of the offense charged and the prosecution is based

on conduct causing or threatening such injury to a person other than the person perpetrating the entrapment.

Article 3. General Principles of Justification

Section 3.01.
Justification an Affirmative Defense; Civil Remedies Unaffected.

(1) In any prosecution based on conduct that is justifiable under this Article, justification is an affirmative defense.

(2) The fact that conduct is justifiable under this Article does not abolish or impair any remedy for such conduct that is available in any civil action.

Section 3.02.
Justification Generally: Choice of Evils.

(1) Conduct that the actor believes to be necessary to avoid a harm or evil to himself or to another is justifiable, provided that:

(a) the harm or evil sought to be avoided by such conduct is greater than that sought to be prevented by the law defining the offense charged; and

(b) neither the Code nor other law defining the offense provides exceptions or defenses dealing with the specific situation involved; and

(c) a legislative purpose to exclude the justification claimed does not otherwise plainly appear.

(2) When the actor was reckless or negligent in bringing about the situation requiring a choice of harms or evils or in appraising the necessity for his conduct, the justification afforded by this Section is unavailable in a prosecution for any offense for which recklessness or negligence, as the case may be, suffices to establish culpability.

Section 3.03.
Execution of Public Duty.

(1) Except as provided in Subsection (2) of this Section, conduct is justifiable when it is required or authorized by:

(a) the law defining the duties or functions of a public officer or the assistance to be rendered to such officer in the performance of his duties; or

(b) the law governing the execution of legal process; or

(c) the judgment or order of a competent court or tribunal; or

(d) the law governing the armed services or the lawful conduct of war; or

(e) any other provision of law imposing a public duty.

(2) The other sections of this Article apply to:

(a) the use of force upon or toward the person of another for any of the purposes dealt with in such sections; and

(b) the use of deadly force for any purpose, unless the use of such force is otherwise expressly authorized by law or occurs in the lawful conduct of war.

(3) The justification afforded by Subsection (1) of this Section applies:

(a) when the actor believes his conduct to be required or authorized by the judgment or direction of a competent court or tribunal or in the lawful execution of legal process, notwithstanding lack of jurisdiction of the court or defect in the legal process; and

(b) when the actor believes his conduct to be required or authorized to assist a public officer in the performance of his duties, notwithstanding that the officer exceeded his legal authority.

Section 3.04.
Use of Force in Self-Protection.

(1) *Use of Force Justifiable for Protection of the Person.* Subject to the provisions of this Section and of Section 3.09, the use of force upon or toward another person is justifiable when the actor believes that such force is immediately necessary for the purpose of protecting himself against the use of unlawful force by such other person on the present occasion.

(2) *Limitations on Justifying Necessity for Use of Force.*

(a) The use of force is not justifiable under this Section:

(i) to resist an arrest that the actor knows is being made by a peace officer, although the arrest is unlawful; or

(ii) to resist force used by the occupier or possessor of property or by another person on his behalf, where the actor knows that the person using the force is doing so under a claim of right to protect the property, except that this limitation shall not apply if:

(A) the actor is a public officer acting in the performance of his duties or a person lawfully assisting him therein or a person making or assisting in a lawful arrest; or

(B) the actor has been unlawfully dispossessed of the property and is making a re-entry or recaption justified by Section 3.06; or

(C) the actor believes that such force is necessary to protect himself against death or serious bodily injury.

(b) The use of deadly force is not justifiable under this Section unless the actor believes that such force is necessary to protect himself against death, serious bodily injury, kidnapping or sexual intercourse compelled by force or threat; nor is it justifiable if:

(i) the actor, with the purpose of causing death or serious bodily injury, provoked the use of force against himself in the same encounter; or

(ii) the actor knows that he can avoid the necessity of using such force with complete safety by retreating or by surrendering possession of a thing to a person asserting a claim of right thereto or by complying with a demand that he abstain from any action that he has no duty to take, except that:

(A) the actor is not obliged to retreat from his dwelling or place of work, unless he was the initial aggressor or is assailed in his place of work by another person whose place of work the actor knows it to be; and

(B) a public officer justified in using force in the performance of his duties or a person justified in using force in his assistance or a person justified in using force in making an arrest or preventing an escape is not obliged to desist from efforts to perform such duty, effect such arrest or prevent such escape because of resistance or threatened resistance by or on behalf of the person against whom such action is directed.

(c) Except as required by paragraphs (a) and (b) of this Subsection, a person employing protective force may estimate the necessity thereof under the circumstances as he believes them to be when the force is used, without retreating, surrendering possession, doing any other act that he has no legal duty to do or abstaining from any lawful action.

(3) *Use of Confinement as Protective Force.* The justification afforded by this Section extends to the use of confinement as protective force only if the actor takes all reasonable measures to terminate the confinement as soon as he knows that he safely can, unless the person confined has been arrested on a charge of crime.

Section 3.05.
Use of Force for the Protection of Other Persons.

(1) Subject to the provisions of this Section and of Section 3.09, the use of force upon or toward the person of another is justifiable to protect a third person when:

(a) the actor would be justified under Section 3.04 in using such force to protect himself against the injury he believes to be threatened to the person whom he seeks to protect; and

(b) under the circumstances as the actor believes them to be, the person whom he seeks to protect would be justified in using such protective force; and

(c) the actor believes that his intervention is necessary for the protection of such other person.

(2) Notwithstanding Subsection (1) of this Section:

(a) when the actor would be obliged under Section 3.04 to retreat, to surrender the possession of a thing or to comply with a demand before using force in self-protection, he is not obliged to do so before using force for the protection of another person, unless he knows that he can thereby secure the complete safety of such other person; and

(b) when the person whom the actor seeks to protect would be obliged under Section 3.04 to retreat, to surrender the possession of a thing or to comply with a demand if he knew that he could obtain complete safety by so doing, the actor is obliged to try to cause him to do so before using force in his protection if the actor knows that he can obtain complete safety in that way; and

(c) neither the actor nor the person whom he seeks to protect is obliged to retreat when in the other's dwelling or place of work to any greater extent than in his own.

Section 3.06.
Use of Force for Protection of Property.

(1) *Use of Force Justifiable for Protection of Property.* Subject to the provisions of this Section and of Section 3.09, the use of force upon or toward the person of another is justifiable when the actor believes that such force is immediately necessary:

(a) to prevent or terminate an unlawful entry or other trespass upon land or a trespass against or the unlawful carrying away of tangible, movable property, provided that such land or movable property is, or is believed by the actor to be, in his possession or in the possession of another person for whose protection he acts; or

(b) to effect an entry or re-entry upon land or to retake tangible movable property, provided that the actor believes that he or the person by whose authority he acts or a person from whom he or such other person derives title was unlawfully dispossessed of such land or movable property and is entitled to possession, and provided, further, that:

(i) the force is used immediately or on fresh pursuit after such dispossession; or

(ii) the actor believes that the person against whom he uses force has no claim of right to the possession of the property and, in the case of land, the circumstances, as the actor believes them to be, are of such urgency that it would be an exceptional hardship to postpone the entry or re-entry until a court order is obtained.

(2) *Meaning of Possession.* For the purposes of Subsection (1) of this Section:

(a) a person who has parted with the custody of property to another who refuses to restore it to him is no longer in possession, unless the property is movable and was and still is located on land in his possession;

(b) a person who has been dispossessed of land does not regain possession thereof merely by setting foot thereon;

(c) a person who has a license to use or occupy real property is deemed to be in possession thereof except against the licensor acting under claim of right.

(3) *Limitations on Justifiable Use of Force.*

(a) *Request to Desist.* The use of force is justifiable under this Section only if the actor first requests the person against whom such force is used to desist from his interference with the property, unless the actor believes that:

(i) such request would be useless; or

(ii) it would be dangerous to himself or another person to make the request; or

(iii) substantial harm will be done to the physical condition of the property that is sought to be protected before the request can effectively be made.

(b) *Exclusion of Trespasser.* The use of force to prevent or terminate a trespass is not justifiable under this Section if the actor knows that the exclusion of the trespasser will expose him to substantial danger of serious bodily injury.

(c) *Resistance of Lawful Re-entry or Recaption.* The use of force to prevent an entry or reentry upon land or the recaption of movable property is not justifiable under this Section, although the actor believes that such re-entry or recaption is unlawful, if:

(i) the re-entry or recaption is made by or on behalf of a person who was actually dispossessed of the property; and

(ii) it is otherwise justifiable under Subsection (1)(b) of this Section.

(d) *Use of Deadly Force.* The use of deadly force is not justifiable under this Section unless the actor believes that:

(i) the person against whom the force is used is attempting to dispossess him of his dwelling otherwise than under a claim of right to its possession; or

(ii) the person against whom the force is used is attempting to commit or consummate arson, burglary, robbery or other felonious theft or property destruction and either:

(A) has employed or threatened deadly force against or in the presence of the actor; or

(B) the use of force other than deadly force to prevent the commission or the consummation of the crime would expose the actor or another in his presence to substantial danger of serious bodily injury.

(4) *Use of Confinement as Protective Force.* The justification afforded by this Section extends to the use of confinement as protective force only if the actor takes all reasonable measures to terminate the confinement as soon as he knows that he can do so with safety to the property, unless the person confined has been arrested on a charge of crime.

(5) *Use of Device to Protect Property.* The justification afforded by this Section extends to the use of a device for the purpose of protecting property only if:

(a) the device is not designed to cause or known to create a substantial risk of causing death or serious bodily injury; and

(b) the use of the particular device to protect the property from entry or trespass is reasonable under the circumstances, as the actor believes them to be; and

(c) the device is one customarily used for such a purpose or reasonable care is taken to make known to probable intruders the fact that it is used.

(6) *Use of Force to Pass Wrongful Obstructor.* The use of force to pass a person whom the actor believes to be purposely or knowingly and unjustifiably obstructing the actor from going to a place to which he may lawfully go is justifiable, provided that:

(a) the actor believes that the person against whom he uses force has no claim of right to obstruct the actor; and

(b) the actor is not being obstructed from entry or movement on land that he knows to be in the possession or custody of the person obstructing him, or in the possession or custody of another person by whose authority the obstructor acts, unless the circumstances, as the actor believes them to be, are of such urgency that it would not be reasonable to postpone the entry or movement on such land until a court order is obtained; and

(c) the force used is not greater than would be justifiable if the person obstructing the actor were using force against him to prevent his passage.

Section 3.07.
Use of Force in Law Enforcement.

(1) *Use of Force Justifiable to Effect an Arrest.* Subject to the provisions of this Section and of Section 3.09, the use of force upon or toward the person of another is justifiable when the actor is making or assisting in making an arrest and the actor believes that such force is immediately necessary to effect a lawful arrest.

(2) *Limitations on the Use of Force.*

(a) The use of force is not justifiable under this Section unless:

(i) the actor makes known the purpose of the arrest or believes that it is otherwise known by or cannot reasonably be made known to the person to be arrested; and

(ii) when the arrest is made under a warrant, the warrant is valid or believed by the actor to be valid.

(b) The use of deadly force is not justifiable under this Section unless:

(i) the arrest is for a felony; and

(ii) the person effecting the arrest is authorized to act as a peace officer or is assisting a person whom he believes to be authorized to act as a peace officer; and

(iii) the actor believes that the force employed creates no substantial risk of injury to innocent persons; and

(iv) the actor believes that:

(A) the crime for which the arrest is made involved conduct including the use or threatened use of deadly force; or

(B) there is a substantial risk that the person to be arrested will cause death or serious bodily injury if his apprehension is delayed.

(3) *Use of Force to Prevent Escape from Custody.* The use of force to prevent the escape of an arrested person from custody is justifiable when the force could justifiably have been employed to effect the arrest under which the person is in custody, except that a guard or other person authorized to act as a peace officer is justified in using any force, including deadly force, that he believes to be immediately necessary to prevent the escape of a person from a jail, prison, or other institution for the detention of persons charged with or convicted of a crime.

(4) *Use of Force by Private Person Assisting an Unlawful Arrest.*

(a) A private person who is summoned by a peace officer to assist in effecting an unlawful arrest, is justified in using any force that he would be justified in using if the arrest were lawful, provided that he does not believe the arrest is unlawful.

(b) A private person who assists another private person in effecting an unlawful arrest, or who, not being summoned, assists a peace officer in effecting an unlawful arrest, is justified in using any force that he would be justified in using if the arrest were lawful, provided that (i) he believes the arrest is lawful, and (ii) the arrest would be lawful if the facts were as he believes them to be.

(5) *Use of Force to Prevent Suicide or the Commission of a Crime.*

(a) The use of force upon or toward the person of another is justifiable when the actor believes that such force is immediately necessary to prevent such other person from committing suicide, inflicting serious bodily injury upon himself, committing or consummating the commission of a crime involving or threatening bodily injury, damage to or loss of property or a breach of the peace, except that:

(i) any limitations imposed by the other provisions of this Article on the justifiable use of force in self-protection, for the protection of others, the protection of property, the effectuation of an arrest or the prevention of an escape from custody shall apply notwithstanding the criminality of the conduct against which such force is used; and

(ii) the use of deadly force is not in any event justifiable under this subsection unless:

(A) the actor believes that there is a substantial risk that the person whom he seeks to prevent from committing a crime will cause death or serious bodily injury to another unless the commission or the consummation of the crime is prevented and that the use of such force presents no substantial risk of injury to innocent persons; or

(B) the actor believes that the use of such force is necessary to suppress a riot or mutiny after the rioters or mutineers have been ordered to disperse and warned, in any particular manner that the law may require, that such force will be used if they do not obey.

(b) The justification afforded by this Subsection extends to the use of confinement as preventive force only if the actor takes all reasonable measures to terminate the confinement as soon as he knows that he safely can, unless the person confined has been arrested on a charge of crime.

Section 3.08.
Use of Force by Persons with Special Responsibility for Care, Discipline or Safety of Others.

The use of force upon or toward the person of another is justifiable if:

(1) the actor is the parent or guardian or other person similarly responsible for the general care and supervision of a minor or a person acting at the request of such parent, guardian or other responsible person and:

(a) the force is used for the purpose of safeguarding or promoting the welfare of the minor, including the prevention or punishment of his misconduct; and

(b) the force used is not designed to cause or known to create a substantial risk of causing death, serious bodily injury, disfigurement, extreme pain or mental distress or gross degradation; or

(2) the actor is a teacher or a person otherwise entrusted with the care or supervision for a special purpose of a minor and:

(a) the actor believes that the force used is necessary to further such special purpose, including the maintenance of reasonable discipline in a school, class or other group, and that the use of such force is consistent with the welfare of the minor; and

(b) the degree of force, if it had been used by the parent or guardian of the minor, would not be unjustifiable under Subsection (1)(b) of this Section; or

(3) the actor is the guardian or other person similarly responsible for the general care and supervision of an incompetent person and:

(a) the force is used for the purpose of safeguarding or promoting the welfare of the incompetent person, including the prevention of his misconduct, or, when such incompetent person is in a hospital or other institution for his care and custody, for the maintenance of reasonable discipline in such institution; and

(b) the force used is not designed to cause or known to create a substantial risk of causing death, serious bodily injury, disfigurement, extreme or unnecessary pain, mental distress, or humiliation; or

(4) the actor is a doctor or other therapist or a person assisting him at his direction and:

(a) the force is used for the purpose of administering a recognized form of treatment that the actor believes to be adapted to promoting the physical or mental health of the patient; and

(b) the treatment is administered with the consent of the patient or, if the patient is a minor or an incompetent person, with the consent of his parent or guardian or other person legally competent to consent in his behalf, or the treatment is administered in an emergency when the actor believes that no one competent to consent can be consulted and that a reasonable person, wishing to safeguard the welfare of the patient, would consent; or

(5) the actor is a warden or other authorized official of a correctional institution and:

(a) he believes that the force used is necessary for the purpose of enforcing the lawful rules or procedures of the institution, unless his belief in the lawfulness of the rule or procedure sought to be enforced is erroneous and his error is due to ignorance or mistake as to the provisions of the Code, any other provision of the criminal law or the law governing the administration of the institution; and

(b) the nature or degree of force used is not forbidden by Article 303 or 304 of the Code; and

(c) if deadly force is used, its use is otherwise justifiable under this Article; or

(6) the actor is a person responsible for the safety of a vessel or an aircraft or a person acting at his direction and:

(a) he believes that the force used is necessary to prevent interference with the operation of the vessel or aircraft or obstruction of the execution of lawful order, unless his belief in the lawfulness of the order is erroneous and his error is due to ignorance or mistake as to the law defining his authority; and

(b) if deadly force is used, its use is otherwise justifiable under this Article; or

(7) the actor is a person who is authorized or required by law to maintain order or decorum in a vehicle, train or other carrier or in a place where others are assembled, and:

(a) he believes that the force used is necessary for such purpose; and

(b) the force used is not designed to cause or known to create a substantial risk of causing death, bodily injury, or extreme mental distress.

Section 3.09.
Mistake of Law as to Unlawfulness of Force or Legality of Arrest, Reckless or Negligent Use of Otherwise Justifiable Force; Reckless or Negligent Injury or Risk of Injury to Innocent Persons.

(1) The justification afforded by Sections 3.04 to 3.07, inclusive, is unavailable when:

(a) the actor's belief in the unlawfulness of the force or conduct against which he employs protective force or his belief in the lawfulness of an arrest that he endeavors to effect by force is erroneous; and

(b) his error is due to ignorance or mistake as to the provisions of the Code, any other provision of the criminal law or the law governing the legality of an arrest or search.

(2) When the actor believes that the use of force upon or toward the person of another is necessary for any of the purposes for which such belief would establish a justification under Sections 3.03 to 3.08 but the actor is reckless or negligent in having such belief or in acquiring or failing to acquire any knowledge or belief that is material to the justifiability of his use of force, the justification afforded by those Sections is unavailable in a prosecution for an offense for which recklessness or negligence, as the case may be, suffices to establish culpability.

(3) When the actor is justified under Sections 3.03 to 3.08 in using force upon or toward the person of another but he recklessly or negligently injures or creates a risk of injury to innocent persons, the justification afforded by those Sections is unavailable in a prosecution for such recklessness or negligence towards innocent persons.

Section 3.10.
Justification in Property Crimes.

Conduct involving the appropriation, seizure or destruction of, damage to, intrusion on or interference with property is justifiable under circumstances that would establish a defense of privilege in a civil action based thereon, unless:

(1) the Code or the law defining the offense deals with the specific situation involved; or

(2) a legislative purpose to exclude the justification claimed otherwise plainly appears.

Section 3.11.
Definitions.

In this Article, unless a different meaning plainly is required:

(1) "unlawful force" means force, including confinement, that is employed without the consent of the person against whom it is directed and the employment of which constitutes an offense or actionable tort or would constitute such offense or tort except for a defense (such as the absence of intent, negligence, or mental capacity; duress; youth; or diplomatic status) not amounting to a privilege to use the force. Assent constitutes consent, within the meaning of this Section, whether or not it otherwise is legally effective, except assent to the infliction of death or serious bodily injury.

(2) "deadly force" means force that the actor uses with the purpose of causing or that he knows to create a substantial risk of causing death or serious bodily injury. Purposely firing a firearm in the direction of another person or at a vehicle in which another person is believed to be constitutes deadly force. A threat to cause death or serious bodily injury, by the production of a weapon or otherwise, so long as the

actor's purpose is limited to creating an apprehension that he will use deadly force if necessary, does not constitute deadly force.

(3) "dwelling" means any building or structure, though movable or temporary, or a portion thereof, that is for the time being the actor's home or place of lodging.

Article 4. Responsibility

Section 4.01.
Mental Disease or Defect Excluding Responsibility.

(1) A person is not responsible for criminal conduct if at the time of such conduct as a result of mental disease or defect he lacks substantial capacity either to appreciate the criminality [wrongfulness] of his conduct or to conform his conduct to the requirements of law.

(2) As used in this Article, the terms "mental disease or defect" do not include an abnormality manifested only by repeated criminal or otherwise antisocial conduct.

Section 4.02.
Evidence of Mental Disease or Defect Admissible When Relevant to Element of the Offense[; Mental Disease or Defect Impairing Capacity as Ground for Mitigation of Punishment in Capital Cases].

(1) Evidence that the defendant suffered from a mental disease or defect is admissible whenever it is relevant to prove that the defendant did or did not have a state of mind that is an element of the offense.

[(2) Whenever the jury or the Court is authorized to determine or to recommend whether or not the defendant shall be sentenced to death or imprisonment upon conviction, evidence that the capacity of the defendant to appreciate the criminality [wrongfulness] of his conduct or to conform his conduct to the requirements of law was impaired as a result of mental disease or defect is admissible in favor of sentence of imprisonment.]

Section 4.03.
Mental Disease or Defect Excluding Responsibility Is Affirmative Defense; Requirement of Notice; Form of Verdict and Judgment When Finding of Irresponsibility Is Made.

(1) Mental disease or defect excluding responsibility is an affirmative defense.

(2) Evidence of mental disease or defect excluding responsibility is not admissible unless the defendant, at the time of entering his plea of not guilty or within ten days thereafter or at such later time as the Court may for good cause permit, files a written notice of his purpose to rely on such defense.

(3) When the defendant is acquitted on the ground of mental disease or defect excluding responsibility, the verdict and the judgment shall so state.

Section 4.04.
Mental Disease or Defect Excluding Fitness to Proceed.

No person who as a result of mental disease or defect lacks capacity to understand the proceedings against him or to assist in his own defense shall be tried, convicted or sentenced for the commission of an offense so long as such incapacity endures.

Section 4.05.
Psychiatric Examination of Defendant with Respect to
Mental Disease or Defect.

(1) Whenever the defendant has filed a notice of intention to rely on the defense or defect excluding responsibility, or there is reason to doubt his fitness to proceed, or reason to believe that mental disease or defect of the defendant will otherwise become an issue in the cause, the Court shall appoint at least one qualified psychiatrist or shall request the Superintendent of the Hospital to designate at least one qualified psychiatrist, which designation may be or include himself, to examine and report upon the mental condition of the defendant. The Court may order the defendant to be committed to a hospital or other suitable facility for the purpose of the examination for a period of not exceeding sixty days or such longer period as the Court determines to be necessary for the purpose and may direct that a qualified psychiatrist retained by the defendant be permitted to witness and participate in the examination.

(2) In such examination any method may be employed that is accepted by the medical profession for the examination of those alleged to be suffering from mental disease or defect.

(3) The report of the examination shall include the following: (a) a description of the nature of the examination; (b) a diagnosis of the mental condition of the defendant; (c) if the defendant suffers from a mental disease or defect, an opinion as to his capacity to understand the proceedings against him and to assist in his own defense; (d) when a notice of intention to rely on the defense of irresponsibility has been filed, an opinion as to the extent, if any, to which the capacity of the defendant to appreciate the criminality [wrongfulness] of his conduct or to conform his conduct to the requirements of law was impaired at the time of the criminal conduct charged; and (e) when directed by the Court, an opinion as to the capacity of the defendant to have a particular state of mind that is an element of the offense charged.

If the examination cannot be conducted by reason of the unwillingness of the defendant to participate therein, the report shall so state and shall include, if possible, an opinion as to whether such unwillingness of the defendant was the result of mental disease or defect.

The report of the examination shall be filed [in triplicate] with the clerk of the Court, who shall cause copies to be delivered to the district attorney and to counsel for the defendant.

Section 4.06.
Determination of Fitness to Proceed; Effect of Finding of Unfitness; Proceedings if Fitness Is Regained[; Post-Commitment Hearing].

(1) When the defendant's fitness to proceed is drawn in question, the issue shall be determined by the Court. If neither the prosecuting attorney nor counsel for the defendant contests the finding of the report filed pursuant to Section 4.05, the Court may make the determination on the basis of such report. If the finding is contested, the Court shall hold a hearing on the issue. If the report is received in evidence upon such hearing, the party who contests the finding thereof shall have the right to summon and to cross-examine the psychiatrists who joined in the report and to offer evidence upon the issue.

(2) If the Court determines that the defendant lacks fitness to proceed, the proceeding against him shall be suspended, except as provided in Subsection (3) [Subsections (3) and (4)] of this Section, and the Court shall commit him to the custody of the Commissioner of Mental Hygiene [Public Health or Correction] to be placed in an appropriate institution of the Department of Mental Hygiene [Public Health or Correction] for so long as such unfitness shall endure. When the Court, on its own motion or upon the application of the Commissioner of Mental Hygiene [Public Health or Correction] or the prosecuting attorney, determines, after a hearing if a hearing is requested, that the defendant has regained fitness to proceed, the proceeding shall be resumed. If, however, the Court is of the view that so much time has elapsed since the commitment of the defendant that it would be unjust to resume the criminal proceeding, the Court may dismiss the charge and may order the defendant to be discharged or, subject to the law governing the civil commitment of persons suffering from mental disease or defect, order the defendant to be committed to an appropriate institution of the Department of Mental Hygiene [Public Health].

(3) The fact that the defendant is unfit to proceed does not preclude any legal objection to the prosecution that is susceptible of fair determination prior to trial and without the personal participation of the defendant.

[Alternative: (3) At any time within ninety days after commitment as provided in Subsection (2) of this Section, or at any later time with permission of the Court granted for good cause, the defendant or his counsel or the Commissioner of Mental Hygiene [Public Health or Correction] may apply for a special post-commitment hearing. If the application is made by or on behalf of a defendant not represented by counsel, he shall be afforded a reasonable opportunity to obtain counsel, and if he lacks funds to do so, counsel shall be assigned by the Court. The application shall be granted only if counsel for the defendant satisfies the Court by affidavit or otherwise that as an attorney he has reasonable grounds for a good faith belief that his client has, on the facts and the law, a defense to the charge other than mental disease or defect excluding responsibility.

[(4) If the motion for a special post-commitment hearing is granted, the hearing shall be by the Court without a jury. No evidence shall be offered at the hearing by either party on the issue of mental disease or defect as a defense to, or in mitigation of, the crime charged. After hearing, the Court may in an appropriate case quash the indictment or other charge, or find it to be defective or insufficient, or determine that it is not proved beyond a reasonable doubt by the evidence, or otherwise terminate the proceedings on the evidence or the law. In any such case, unless all defects in the proceedings are promptly cured, the Court shall terminate the commitment ordered under Subsection (2) of this Section and order the defendant to be discharged or, subject to the law governing the civil commitment of persons suffering from mental disease or defect, order the defendant to be committed to an appropriate institution of the Department of Mental Hygiene [Public Health].]

Section 4.07.
Determination of Irresponsibility on Basis of Report;
Access to Defendant by Psychiatrist of His Own Choice;
Form of Expert Testimony When Issue of Responsibility Is Tried.

(1) If the report filed pursuant to Section 4.05 finds that the defendant at the time of the criminal conduct charged suffered from a mental disease or defect that substantially impaired his capacity to appreciate the criminality [wrongfulness] of his conduct or to conform his conduct to the requirements of law, and the Court, after a hearing if a hearing is requested by the prosecuting attorney or the defendant, is satisfied that such impairment was sufficient to exclude responsibility, the Court on motion of the defendant shall enter judgment of acquittal on the ground of mental disease or defect excluding responsibility.

(2) When, notwithstanding the report filed pursuant to Section 4.05, the defendant wishes to be examined by a qualified psychiatrist or other expert of his own choice, such examiner shall be permitted to have reasonable access to the defendant for the purposes of such examination.

(3) Upon the trial, the psychiatrists who reported pursuant to Section 4.05 may be called as witnesses by the prosecution, the defendant or the Court. If the issue is being tried before a jury, the jury may be informed that the psychiatrists were designated by the Court or by the Superintendent of the Hospital at the request of the Court, as the case may be. If called by the Court, the witness shall be subject to cross-examination by the prosecution and by the defendant. Both the prosecution and the defendant may summon another qualified psychiatrist or other expert to testify, but no one who has not examined the defendant shall be competent to testify to an expert opinion with respect to the mental condition or responsibility of the defendant, as distinguished from the validity of the procedure followed by, or the general scientific propositions stated by, another witness.

(4) When a psychiatrist or other expert who has examined the defendant testifies concerning his mental condition, he shall be permitted to make a statement as to the nature of his examination, his diagnosis of the mental condition of the defendant at the time of the commission of the offense charged and his opinion as to the

extent, if any, to which the capacity of the defendant to appreciate the criminality [wrongfulness] of his conduct or to conform his conduct to the requirements of law or to have a particular state of mind that is an element of the offense charged was impaired as a result of mental disease or defect at that time. He shall be permitted to make any explanation reasonably serving to clarify his diagnosis and opinion and may be cross-examined as to any matter bearing on his competency or credibility or the validity of his diagnosis or opinion.

Section 4.08.

Legal Effect of Acquittal on the Ground of Mental Disease or Defect Excluding Responsibility; Commitment; Release or Discharge.

(1) When a defendant is acquitted on the ground of mental disease or defect excluding responsibility, the Court shall order him to be committed to the custody of the Commissioner of Mental Hygiene [Public Health] to be placed in an appropriate institution for custody, care and treatment.

(2) If the Commissioner of Mental Hygiene [Public Health] is of the view that a person committed to his custody, pursuant to Subsection (1) of this Section, may be discharged or released on condition without danger to himself or to others, he shall make application for the discharge or release of such person in a report to the Court by which such person was committed and shall transmit a copy of such application and report to the prosecuting attorney of the county [parish] from which the defendant was committed. The Court shall thereupon appoint at least two qualified psychiatrists to examine such person and to report within sixty days, or such longer period as the Court determines to be necessary for the purpose, their opinion as to his mental condition. To facilitate such examination and the proceedings thereon, the Court may cause such person to be confined in any institution located near the place where the Court sits, which may hereafter be designated by the Commissioner of Mental Hygiene [Public Health] as suitable for the temporary detention of irresponsible persons.

(3) If the Court is satisfied by the report filed pursuant to Subsection (2) of this Section and such testimony of the reporting psychiatrists as the Court deems necessary that the committed person may be discharged or released on condition without danger to himself or others, the Court shall order his discharge or his release on such conditions as the Court determines to be necessary. If the Court is not so satisfied, it shall promptly order a hearing to determine whether such person may safely be discharged or released. Any such hearing shall be deemed a civil proceeding and the burden shall be upon the committed person to prove that he may safely be discharged or released. According to the determination of the Court upon the hearing, the committed person shall thereupon be discharged or released on such conditions as the Court determines to be necessary, or shall be recommitted to the custody of the Commissioner of Mental Hygiene [Public Health], subject to discharge or release only in accordance with the procedure prescribed above for a first hearing.

(4) If, within [five] years after the conditional release of a committed person, the Court shall determine, after hearing evidence, that the conditions of release have not been fulfilled and that for the safety of such person or for the safety of others his conditional release should be revoked, the Court shall forthwith order him to be recommitted to the Commissioner of Mental Hygiene [Public Health], subject to discharge or release only in accordance with the procedure prescribed above for a first hearing.

(5) A committed person may make application for his discharge or release to the Court by which he was committed, and the procedure to be followed upon such application shall be the same as that prescribed above in the case of an application by the Commissioner of Mental Hygiene [Public Health]. However, no such application by a committed person need be considered until he has been confined for a period of not less than [six months] from the date of the order of commitment, and if the determination of the Court be adverse to the application, such person shall not be permitted to file a further application until [one year] has elapsed from the date of any preceding hearing on an application for his release or discharge.

Section 4.09.
Statements for Purposes of Examination or Treatment Inadmissible Except on Issue of Mental Condition.

A statement made by a person subjected to psychiatric examination or treatment pursuant to Sections 4.05, 4.06 or 4.08 for the purpose of such examination or treatment shall not be admissible in evidence against him in any criminal proceeding on any issue other than that of his mental condition but it shall be admissible upon that issue, whether or not it would otherwise be deemed a privileged communication[, unless such statement constitutes an admission of guilt of the crime charged].

Section 4.10
Immaturity Excluding Criminal Conviction; Transfer of Proceedings to Juvenile Court.

(1) A person shall not be tried for or convicted of an offense if:

(a) at the time of the conduct charged to constitute the offense he was less than sixteen years of age[, in which case the Juvenile Court shall have exclusive jurisdiction*]; or

(b) at the time of the conduct charged to constitute the offense he was sixteen or seventeen years of age, unless:

(i) the Juvenile Court has no jurisdiction over him, or

(ii) the Juvenile Court has entered an order waiving jurisdiction and consenting to the institution of criminal proceedings against him.

---

* The bracketed words are unnecessary if the Juvenile Court Act so provides or is amended accordingly.

(2) No court shall have jurisdiction to try or convict a person of an offense if criminal proceedings against him are barred by Subsection (1) of this Section. When it appears that a person charged with the commission of an offense may be of such an age that criminal proceedings may be barred under Subsection (1) of this Section, the Court shall hold a hearing thereon, and the burden shall be on the prosecution to establish to the satisfaction of the Court that the criminal proceeding is not barred upon such grounds. If the Court determines that the proceeding is barred, custody of the person charged shall be surrendered to the Juvenile Court, and the case, including all papers and processes relating thereto, shall be transferred.

Article 5. Inchoate Crimes
Section 5.01.
Criminal Attempt.

(1) *Definition of Attempt.* A person is guilty of an attempt to commit a crime if, acting with the kind of culpability otherwise required for commission of the crime, he:

(a) purposely engages in conduct that would constitute the crime if the attendant circumstances were as he believes them to be; or

(b) when causing a particular result is an element of the crime, does or omits to do anything with the purpose of causing or with the belief that it will cause such result without further conduct on his part; or

(c) purposely does or omits to do anything that, under the circumstances as he believes them to be, is an act or omission constituting a substantial step in a course of conduct planned to culminate in his commission of the crime.

(2) *Conduct That May Be Held Substantial Step Under Subsection (1)(c).* Conduct shall not be held to constitute a substantial step under Subsection (1)(c) of this Section unless it is strongly corroborative of the actor's criminal purpose. Without negativing the sufficiency of other conduct, the following, if strongly corroborative of the actor's criminal purpose, shall not be held insufficient as a matter of law:

(a) lying in wait, searching for or following the contemplated victim of the crime;

(b) enticing or seeking to entice the contemplated victim of the crime to go to the place contemplated for its commission;

(c) reconnoitering the place contemplated for the commission of the crime;

(d) unlawful entry of a structure, vehicle or enclosure in which it is contemplated that the crime will be committed;

(e) possession of materials to be employed in the commission of the crime, that are specially designed for such unlawful use or that can serve no lawful purpose of the actor under the circumstances;

(f) possession, collection or fabrication of materials to be employed in the commission of the crime, at or near the place contemplated for its commission, if such possession, collection or fabrication serves no lawful purpose of the actor under the circumstances;

(g) soliciting an innocent agent to engage in conduct constituting an element of the crime.

(3) *Conduct Designed to Aid Another in Commission of a Crime*. A person who engages in conduct designed to aid another to commit a crime that would establish his complicity under Section 2.06 if the crime were committed by such other person, is guilty of an attempt to commit the crime, although the crime is not committed or attempted by such other person.

(4) *Renunciation of Criminal Purpose*. When the actor's conduct would otherwise constitute an attempt under Subsection (1)(b) or (1)(c) of this Section, it is an affirmative defense that he abandoned his effort to commit the crime or otherwise prevented its commission, under circumstances manifesting a complete and voluntary renunciation of his criminal purpose. The establishment of such defense does not, however, affect the liability of an accomplice who did not join in such abandonment or prevention.

Within the meaning of this Article, renunciation of criminal purpose is not voluntary if it is motivated, in whole or in part, by circumstances, not present or apparent at the inception of the actor's course of conduct, that increase the probability of detection or apprehension or that make more difficult the accomplishment of the criminal purpose.

Renunciation is not complete if it is motivated by a decision to postpone the criminal conduct until a more advantageous time or to transfer the criminal effort to another but similar objective or victim.

Section 5.02.
Criminal Solicitation.

(1) *Definition of Solicitation*. A person is guilty of solicitation to commit a crime if with the purpose of promoting or facilitating its commission he commands, encourages or requests another person to engage in specific conduct that would constitute such crime or an attempt to commit such crime or would establish his complicity in its commission or attempted commission.

(2) *Uncommunicated Solicitation*. It is immaterial under Subsection (1) of this Section that the actor fails to communicate with the person he solicits to commit a crime if his conduct was designed to effect such communication.

(3) *Renunciation of Criminal Purpose*. It is an affirmative defense that the actor, after soliciting another person to commit a crime, persuaded him not to do so or otherwise prevented the commission of the crime, under circumstances manifesting a complete and voluntary renunciation of his criminal purpose.

Section 5.03.
Criminal Conspiracy.

(1) *Definition of Conspiracy.* A person is guilty of conspiracy with another person or persons to commit a crime if with the purpose of promoting or facilitating its commission he:

(a) agrees with such other person or persons that they or one or more of them will engage in conduct that constitutes such crime or an attempt or solicitation to commit such crime; or

(b) agrees to aid such other person or persons in the planning or commission of such crime or of an attempt or solicitation to commit such crime.

(2) *Scope of Conspiratorial Relationship.* If a person guilty of conspiracy, as defined by Subsection (1) of this Section, knows that a person with whom he conspires to commit a crime has conspired with another person or persons to commit the same crime, he is guilty of conspiring with such other person or persons, whether or not he knows their identity, to commit such crime.

(3) *Conspiracy with Multiple Criminal Objectives.* If a person conspires to commit a number of crimes, he is guilty of only one conspiracy so long as such multiple crimes are the object of the same agreement or continuous conspiratorial relationship.

(4) *Joinder and Venue in Conspiracy Prosecutions.*

(a) Subject to the provisions of paragraph (b) of this Subsection, two or more persons charged with criminal conspiracy may be prosecuted jointly if:

(i) they are charged with conspiring with one another; or

(ii) the conspiracies alleged, whether they have the same or different parties, are so related that they constitute different aspects of a scheme of organized criminal conduct.

(b) In any joint prosecution under paragraph (a) of this Subsection:

(i) no defendant shall be charged with a conspiracy in any county [parish or district] other than one in which he entered into such conspiracy or in which an overt act pursuant to such conspiracy was done by him or by a person with whom he conspired; and

(ii) neither the liability of any defendant nor the admissibility against him of evidence of acts or declarations of another shall be enlarged by such joinder; and

(iii) the Court shall order a severance or take a special verdict as to any defendant who so requests, if it deems it necessary or appropriate to promote the fair determination of his guilt or innocence, and shall take any other proper measures to protect the fairness of the trial.

(5) *Overt Act.* No person may be convicted of conspiracy to commit a crime, other than a felony of the first or second degree, unless an overt act in pursuance of

such conspiracy is alleged and proved to have been done by him or by a person with whom he conspired.

(6) *Renunciation of Criminal Purpose.* It is an affirmative defense that the actor, after conspiring to commit a crime, thwarted the success of the conspiracy, under circumstances manifesting a complete and voluntary renunciation of his criminal purpose.

(7) *Duration of Conspiracy.* For purposes of Section 1.06(4):

(a) conspiracy is a continuing course of conduct that terminates when the crime or crimes that are its object are committed or the agreement that they be committed is abandoned by the defendant and by those with whom he conspired; and

(b) such abandonment is presumed if neither the defendant nor anyone with whom he conspired does any overt act in pursuance of the conspiracy during the applicable period of limitation; and

(c) if an individual abandons the agreement the conspiracy is terminated as to him only ii and when he advises those with whom he conspired of his abandonment or he informs the law enforcement authorities of the existence of the conspiracy and of his participation therein.

Section 5.04.
Incapacity, Irresponsibility or Immunity of Party
to Solicitation or Conspiracy.

(1) Except as provided in Subsection (2) of this Section, it is immaterial to the liability of a person who solicits or conspires with another to commit a crime that:

(a) he or the person whom he solicits or with whom he conspires does not occupy a particular position or have a particular characteristic that is an element of such crime, if he believes that one of them does; or

(b) the person whom he solicits or with whom he conspires is irresponsible or has an immunity to prosecution or conviction for the commission of the crime.

(2) It is a defense to a charge of solicitation or conspiracy to commit a crime that if the criminal object were achieved, the actor would not be guilty of a crime under the law defining the offense or as an accomplice under Section 2.06(5) or 2.06(6) (a) or (6)(b).

Section 5.05.
Grading of Criminal Attempt, Solicitation and Conspiracy; Mitigation
in Cases of Lesser Danger; Multiple Convictions Barred.

(1) *Grading.* Except as otherwise provided in this Section, attempt, solicitation and conspiracy are crimes of the same grade and degree as the most serious offense that is attempted or solicited or is an object of the conspiracy. An attempt, solicitation or conspiracy to commit a [capital crime or a] felony of the first degree is a felony of the second-degree.

(2) *Mitigation.* If the particular conduct charged to constitute a criminal attempt, solicitation or conspiracy is so inherently unlikely to result or culminate in the commission of a crime that neither such conduct nor the actor presents a public danger warranting the grading of such offense under this Section, the Court shall exercise its power under Section 6.12 to enter judgment and impose sentence for a crime of lower grade or degree or, in extreme cases, may dismiss the prosecution.

(3) *Multiple Convictions.* A person may not be convicted of more than one offense defined by this Article for conduct designed to commit or to culminate in the commission of the same crime.

Section 5.06.
Possessing Instruments of Crime; Weapons.

(1) *Criminal Instruments Generally.* A person commits a misdemeanor if he possesses any instrument of crime with purpose to employ it criminally. "Instrument of crime" means:

(a) anything specially made or specially adapted for criminal use; or

(b) anything commonly used for criminal purposes and possessed by the actor under circumstances that do not negative unlawful purpose.

(2) *Presumption of Criminal Purpose from Possession of Weapon.* If a person possesses a firearm or other weapon on or about his person, in a vehicle occupied by him, or otherwise readily available for use, it is presumed that he had the purpose to employ it criminally, unless:

(a) the weapon is possessed in the actor's home or place of business;

(b) the actor is licensed or otherwise authorized by law to possess such weapon; or

(c) the weapon is of a type commonly used in lawful sport. "Weapon" means anything readily capable of lethal use and possessed under circumstances not manifestly appropriate for lawful uses it may have; the term includes a firearm that is not loaded or lacks a clip or other component to render it immediately operable, and components that can readily be assembled into a weapon.

(3) *Presumptions as to Possession of Criminal Instruments in Automobiles.* If a weapon or other instrument of crime is found in an automobile, it is presumed to be in the possession of the occupant if there is but one. If there is more than one occupant, it is presumed to be in the possession of all, except under the following circumstances:

(a) it is found upon the person of one of the occupants;

(b) the automobile is not a stolen one and the weapon or instrument is found out of view in a glove compartment, car trunk, or other enclosed customary depository, in which case it is presumed to be in the possession of the occupant or occupants who own or have authority to operate the automobile;

(c) in the case of a taxicab, a weapon or instrument found in the passengers' portion of the vehicle is presumed to be in the possession of all the passengers, if there are any, and, if not, in the possession of the driver.

Section 5.07.
Prohibited Offensive Weapons.

A person commits a misdemeanor if, except as authorized by law, he makes, repairs, sells, or otherwise deals in, uses, or possesses any offensive weapon. "Offensive weapon" means any bomb, machine gun, sawed-off shotgun, firearm specially made or specially adapted for concealment or silent discharge, any blackjack, sandbag, metal knuckles, dagger, or other implement for the infliction of serious bodily injury that serves no common lawful purpose. It is a defense under this Section for the defendant to prove by a preponderance of evidence that he possessed or dealt with the weapon solely as a curio or in a dramatic performance, or that he possessed it briefly in consequence of having found it or taken it from an aggressor, or under circumstances similarly negativing any purpose or likelihood that the weapon would be used unlawfully. The presumptions provided in Section 5.06(3)are applicable to prosecutions under this Section.

Article 6. Authorized Disposition of Offenders
Section 6.01.
Degrees of Felonies.

(1) Felonies defined by this Code are classified, for the purpose of sentence, into three degrees, as follows:

(a) felonies of the first degree;

(b) felonies of the second degree;

(c) felonies of the third degree.

A felony is of the first or second degree when it is so designated by the Code. A crime declared to be a felony, without specification of degree, is of the third degree.

(2) Notwithstanding any other provision of law, a felony defined by any statute of this State other than this Code shall constitute, for the purpose of sentence, a felony of the third degree.

Section 6.02.
Sentence in Accordance with Code; Authorized Dispositions.

(1) No person convicted of an offense shall be sentenced otherwise than in accordance with this Article.

[(2) The Court shall sentence a person who has been convicted of murder to death or imprisonment, in accordance with Section 210.6.]

(3) Except as provided in Subsection (2) of this Section and subject to the applicable provisions of the Code, the Court may suspend the imposition of sentence on

a person who has been convicted of a crime, may order him to be committed in lieu of sentence, in accordance with Section 6.13, or may sentence him as follows:

(a) to pay a fine authorized by Section 6.03; or

(b) to be placed on probation[, and, in the case of a person convicted of a felony or misdemeanor to imprisonment for a term fixed by the Court not exceeding thirty days to be served as a condition of probation]; or

(c) to imprisonment for a term authorized by Section 6.05, 6.06, 6.07, 6.08, 6.09, or 7.06; or

(d) to fine and probation or fine and imprisonment, but not to probation and imprisonment[, except as authorized in paragraph (b) of this Subsection].

(4) The Court may suspend the imposition of sentence on a person who has been convicted of a violation or may sentence him to pay a fine authorized by Section 6.03.

(5) This Article does not deprive the Court of any authority conferred by law to decree a forfeiture of property, suspend or cancel a license, remove a person from office, or impose any other civil penalty. Such a judgment or order may be included in the sentence.

Section 6.03.
Fines.

A person who has been convicted of an offense may be sentenced to pay a fine not exceeding:

(1) $10,000, when the conviction is of a felony of the first or second degree;

(2) $5,000, when the conviction is of a felony of the third degree;

(3) $1,000, when the conviction is of a misdemeanor;

(4) $500, when the conviction is of a petty misdemeanor or a violation;

(5) any higher amount equal to double the pecuniary gain derived from the offense by the offender;

(6) any higher amount specifically authorized by statute.

Section 6.04.
Penalties Against Corporations and Unincorporated Associations; Forfeiture of Corporate Charter or Revocation of Certificate Authorizing Foreign Corporation to Do Business in the State.

(1) The Court may suspend the sentence of a corporation or an unincorporated association that has been convicted of an offense or may sentence it to pay a fine authorized by Section 6.03.

(2) (a) The [prosecuting attorney] is authorized to institute civil proceedings in the appropriate court of general jurisdiction to forfeit the charter of a corporation organized under the laws of this State or to revoke the certificate authorizing

a foreign corporation to conduct business in this State. The Court may order the charter forfeited or the certificate revoked upon finding

(i) that the board of directors or a high managerial agent acting in behalf of the corporation has, in conducting the corporation's affairs, purposely engaged in a persistent course of criminal conduct and

(ii) that for the prevention of future criminal conduct of the same character, the public interest requires the charter of the corporation to be forfeited and the corporation to be dissolved or the certificate to be revoked.

(b) When a corporation is convicted of a crime or a high managerial agent of a corporation, as defined in Section 2.07, is convicted of a crime committed in the conduct of the affairs of the corporation, the Court, in sentencing the corporation or the agent, may direct the [prosecuting attorney] to institute proceedings authorized by paragraph (a) of this Subsection.

(c) The proceedings authorized by paragraph (a) of this Subsection shall be conducted in accordance with the procedures authorized by law for the involuntary dissolution of a corporation or the revocation of the certificate authorizing a foreign corporation to conduct business in this State. Such proceedings shall be deemed additional to any other proceedings authorized by law for the purpose of forfeiting the charter of a corporation or revoking the certificate of a foreign corporation.

Section 6.06.
Sentence of Imprisonment for Felony; Ordinary Terms.

A person who has been convicted of a felony may be sentenced to imprisonment, as follows:

(1) in the case of a felony of the first degree, for a term the minimum of which shall be fixed by the Court at not less than one year nor more than ten years, and the maximum of which shall be life imprisonment;

(2) in the case of a felony of the second degree, for a term the minimum of which shall be fixed by the Court at not less than one year nor more than three years, and the maximum of which shall be ten years;

(3) in the case of a felony of the third degree, for a term the minimum of which shall be fixed by the Court at not less than one year nor more than two years, and the maximum of which shall be five years.

Alternative Section 6.06.
Sentence of Imprisonment for Felony; Ordinary Terms.

A person who has been convicted of a felony may be sentenced to imprisonment, as follows:

(1) in the case of a felony of the first degree, for a term the minimum of which shall be fixed by the Court at not less than one year nor more than ten years, and the maximum at not more than twenty years or at life imprisonment;

(2) in the case of a felony of the second degree for a term the minimum of which shall be fixed by the Court at not less than one year nor more than three years, and the maximum at not more than ten years;

(3) in the case of a felony of the third degree, for a term the minimum of which shall be fixed by the Court at not less than one year nor more than two years, and the maximum at not more than five years.

No sentence shall be imposed under this Section of which the minimum is longer than one half the maximum, or, when the maximum is life imprisonment, longer than ten years.

Section 6.07.
Sentence of Imprisonment for Felony; Extended Terms.

In the cases designated in Section 7.03, a person who has been convicted of a felony may be sentenced to an extended term of imprisonment, as follows:

(1) in the case of a felony of the first degree, for a term the minimum of which shall be fixed by the Court at not less than five years nor more than ten years, and the maximum of which shall be life imprisonment;

(2) in the case of a felony of the second degree, for a term the minimum of which shall be fixed by the Court at not less than one year nor more than five years, and the maximum of which shall be fixed by the Court at not less than ten years nor more than twenty years;

(3) in the case of a felony of the third degree, for a term the minimum of which shall be fixed by the Court at not less than one year nor more than three years, and the maximum of which shall be fixed by the Court at not less than five years nor more than ten years.

Section 6.08.
Sentence of Imprisonment for Misdemeanors and Petty Misdemeanors; Ordinary Terms.

A person who has been convicted of a misdemeanor or a petty misdemeanor may be sentenced to imprisonment for a definite term which shall be fixed by the Court and shall not exceed one year in the case of a misdemeanor or thirty days in the case of a petty misdemeanor.

Section 6.09.
Sentence of Imprisonment for Misdemeanors and Petty Misdemeanors; Extended Terms.

(1) In the cases designated in Section 7.04, a person who has been convicted of a misdemeanor or a petty misdemeanor may be sentenced to an extended term of imprisonment, as follows:

(a) in the case of a misdemeanor, for a term the minimum of which shall be fixed by the Court at not more than one year and the maximum of which shall be three years;

(b) in the case of a petty misdemeanor, for a term the minimum of which shall be fixed by the Court at not more than six months and the maximum of which shall be two years.

(2) No such sentence for an extended term shall be imposed unless:

(a) the Director of Correction has certified that there is an institution in the Department of Correction, or in a county or city [or other appropriate political subdivision of the State] that is appropriate for the detention and correctional treatment of such misdemeanants or petty misdemeanants, and that such institution is available to receive such commitments; and

(b) the [Board of Parole] [Parole Administrator] has certified that the Board of Parole is able to visit such institution and to assume responsibility for the release of such prisoners on parole and for their parole supervision.

Section 6.12.
Reduction of Conviction by Court to Lesser Degree of
Felony or to Misdemeanor.

If, when a person has been convicted of a felony, the Court, having regard to the nature and circumstances of the crime and to the history and character of the defendant, is of the view that it would be unduly harsh to sentence the offender in accordance with the Code, the Court may enter judgment of conviction for a lesser degree of felony or for a misdemeanor and impose sentence accordingly.

Section 6.13.
Civil Commitment in Lieu of Prosecution or of Sentence.

(1) When a person prosecuted for a [felony of the third degree,] misdemeanor or petty misdemeanor is a chronic alcoholic, narcotic addict[, prostitute] or person suffering from mental abnormality and the Court is authorized by law to order the civil commitment of such person to a hospital or other institution for medical, psychiatric or other rehabilitative treatment, the Court may order such commitment and dismiss the prosecution. The order of commitment may be made after conviction, in which event the Court may set aside the verdict or judgment of conviction and dismiss the prosecution.

(2) The Court shall not make an order under Subsection (1) of this Section unless it is of the view that it will substantially further the rehabilitation of the defendant and will not jeopardize the protection of the public.

Article 7. Authority of Court in Sentencing

Section 7.01.
Criteria for Withholding Sentence of Imprisonment and for
Placing Defendant on Probation.

(1) The Court shall deal with a person who has been convicted of a crime without imposing sentence of imprisonment unless, having regard to the nature and circumstances of the crime and the history, character and condition of the defendant,

it is of the opinion that his imprisonment is necessary for protection of the public because:

(a) there is undue risk that during the period of a suspended sentence or probation the defendant will commit another crime; or

(b) the defendant is in need of correctional treatment that can be provided most effectively by his commitment to an institution; or

(c) a lesser sentence will depreciate the seriousness of the defendant's crime.

(2) The following grounds, while not controlling the discretion of the Court, shall be accorded weight in favor of withholding sentence of imprisonment:

(a) the defendant's criminal conduct neither caused nor threatened serious harm;

(b) the defendant did not contemplate that his criminal conduct would cause or threaten serious harm;

(c) the defendant acted under a strong provocation;

(d) there were substantial grounds tending to excuse or justify the defendant's criminal conduct, though failing to establish a defense;

(e) the victim of the defendant's criminal conduct induced or facilitated its commission;

(f) the defendant has compensated or will compensate the victim of his criminal conduct for the damage or injury that he sustained;

(g) the defendant has no history of prior delinquency or criminal activity or has led a law-abiding life for a substantial period of time before the commission of the present crime;

(h) the defendant's criminal conduct was the result of circumstances unlikely to recur;

(i) the character and attitudes of the defendant indicate that he is unlikely to commit another crime;

(j) the defendant is particularly likely to respond affirmatively to probationary treatment;

(k) the imprisonment of the defendant would entail excessive hardship to himself or his dependents.

(3) When a person who has been convicted of a crime is not sentenced to imprisonment, the Court shall place him on probation if he is in need of the supervision, guidance, assistance or direction that the probation service can provide.

Section 7.02.
Criteria for Imposing Fines.

(1) The Court shall not sentence a defendant only to pay a fine, when any other disposition is authorized by law, unless having regard to the nature and circumstances

of the crime and to the history and character of the defendant, it is of the opinion that the fine alone suffices for protection of the public.

(2) The Court shall not sentence a defendant to pay a fine in addition to a sentence of imprisonment or probation unless:

(a) the defendant has derived a pecuniary gain from the crime; or

(b) the Court is of opinion that a fine is specially adapted to deterrence of the crime involved or to the correction of the offender.

(3) The Court shall not sentence a defendant to pay a fine unless:

(a) the defendant is or will be able to pay the fine; and

(b) the fine will not prevent the defendant from making restitution or reparation to the victim of the crime.

(4) In determining the amount and method of payment of a fine, the Court shall take into account the financial resources of the defendant and the nature of the burden that its payment will impose.

Section 7.03.
Criteria for Sentence of Extended Term of Imprisonment; Felonies.

The Court may sentence a person who has been convicted of a felony to an extended term of imprisonment if it finds one or more of the grounds specified in this Section. The finding of the Court shall be incorporated in the record.

(1) The defendant is a persistent offender whose commitment for an extended term is necessary for protection of the public.

The Court shall not make such a finding unless the defendant is over twenty-one years of age and has previously been convicted of two felonies or of one felony and two misdemeanors, committed at different times when he was over [insert Juvenile Court age] years of age.

(2) The defendant is a professional criminal whose commitment for an extended term is necessary for protection of the public.

The Court shall not make such a finding unless the defendant is over twenty-one years of age and:

(a) the circumstances of the crime show that the defendant has knowingly devoted himself to criminal activity as a major source of livelihood; or

(b) the defendant has substantial income or resources not explained to be derived from a source other than criminal activity.

(3) The defendant is a dangerous, mentally abnormal person whose commitment for an extended term is necessary for protection of the public.

The Court shall not make such a finding unless the defendant has been subjected to a psychiatric examination resulting in the conclusions that:

(a) his mental condition is gravely abnormal;

(b) his criminal conduct has been characterized by a pattern of repetitive or compulsive behavior or by persistent aggressive behavior with heedless indifference to consequences; and

(c) such condition makes him a serious danger to others.

(4) The defendant is a multiple offender whose criminality was so extensive that a sentence of imprisonment for an extended term is warranted.

The Court shall not make such a finding unless:

(a) the defendant is being sentenced for two or more felonies, or is already under sentence of imprisonment for felony, and the sentences of imprisonment involved will run concurrently under Section 7.06; or

(b) the defendant admits in open court the commission of one or more other felonies and asks that they be taken into account when he is sentenced; and

(c) the longest sentences of imprisonment authorized for each of the defendant's crimes, including admitted crimes taken into account, if made to run consecutively would exceed in length the minimum and maximum of the extended term imposed.

Section 7.04.
Criteria for Sentence of Extended Term of Imprisonment; Misdemeanors and Petty Misdemeanors.

The Court may sentence a person who has been convicted of a misdemeanor or petty misdemeanor to an extended term of imprisonment if it finds one or more of the grounds specified in this Section. The finding of the Court shall be incorporated in the record.

(1) The defendant is a persistent offender whose commitment for an extended term is necessary for protection of the public.

The Court shall not make such a finding unless the defendant has previously been convicted of two crimes, committed at different times when he was over [insert Juvenile Court age] years of age.

(2) The defendant is a professional criminal whose commitment for an extended term is necessary for protection of the public.

The Court shall not make such a finding unless:

(a) the circumstances of the crime show that the defendant has knowingly devoted himself to criminal activity as a major source of livelihood; or

(b) the defendant has substantial income or resources not explained to be derived from a source other than criminal activity.

(3) The defendant is a chronic alcoholic, narcotic addict, prostitute or person of abnormal mental condition who requires rehabilitative treatment for a substantial period of time.

The Court shall not make such a finding unless, with respect to the particular category to which the defendant belongs, the Director of Correction has certified that there is a specialized institution or facility that is satisfactory for the rehabilitative treatment of such persons and that otherwise meets the requirements of Section 6.09(2).

(4) The defendant is a multiple offender whose criminality was so extensive that a sentence of imprisonment for an extended term is warranted.

The Court shall not make such a finding unless:

(a) the defendant is being sentenced for a number of misdemeanors or petty misdemeanors or is already under sentence of imprisonment for crimes of such grades, or admits in open court the commission of one or more such crimes and asks that they be taken into account when he is sentenced; and

(b) maximum fixed sentences of imprisonment for each of the defendant's crimes, including admitted crimes taken into account, if made to run consecutively, would exceed in length the maximum period of the extended term imposed.

Section 7.06.
Multiple Sentences; Concurrent and Consecutive Terms.

(1) *Sentences of Imprisonment for More Than One Crime.* When multiple sentences of imprisonment are imposed on a defendant for more than one crime, including a crime for which a previous suspended sentence or sentence of probation has been revoked, such multiple sentences shall run concurrently or consecutively as the Court determines at the time of sentence, except that:

(a) a definite and an indefinite term shall run concurrently and both sentences shall be satisfied by service of the indefinite term; and

(b) the aggregate of consecutive definite terms shall not exceed one year; and

(c) the aggregate of consecutive indefinite terms shall not exceed in minimum or maximum length the longest extended term authorized for the highest grade and degree of crime for which any of the sentences was imposed; and

(d) not more than one sentence for an extended term shall be imposed.

(2) *Sentences of Imprisonment Imposed at Different Times.* When a defendant who has previously been sentenced to imprisonment is subsequently sentenced to another term for a crime committed prior to the former sentence, other than a crime committed while in custody:

(a) the multiple sentences imposed shall so far as possible conform to Subsection (1) of this Section; and

(b) whether the Court determines that the terms shall run concurrently or consecutively, the defendant shall be credited with time served in imprisonment on the prior sentence in determining the permissible aggregate length of the term or terms remaining to be served; and

(c) when a new sentence is imposed on a prisoner who is on parole, the balance of the parole term on the former sentence shall be deemed to run during the period of the new imprisonment.

(3) *Sentence of Imprisonment for Crime Committed While on Parole.* When a defendant is sentenced to imprisonment for a crime committed while on parole in this State, such term of imprisonment and any period of reimprisonment that the Board of Parole may require the defendant to serve upon the revocation of his parole shall run concurrently, unless the Court orders them to run consecutively.

(4) *Multiple Sentences of Imprisonment in Other Cases.* Except as otherwise provided in this Section, multiple terms of imprisonment shall run concurrently or consecutively as the Court determines when the second or subsequent sentence is imposed.

(5) *Calculation of Concurrent and Consecutive Terms of Imprisonment.*

(a) When indefinite terms run concurrently, the shorter minimum terms merge in and are satisfied by serving the longest minimum term and the shorter maximum terms merge in and are satisfied by discharge of the longest maximum term.

(b) When indefinite terms run consecutively, the minimum terms are added to arrive at an aggregate minimum to be served equal to the sum of all minimum terms and the maximum terms are added to arrive at an aggregate maximum equal to the sum of all maximum terms.

(c) When a definite and an indefinite term run consecutively, the period of the definite term is added to both the minimum and maximum of the indefinite term and both sentences are satisfied by serving the indefinite term.

(6) *Suspension of Sentence or Probation and Imprisonment; Multiple Terms of Suspension and Probation.* When a defendant is sentenced for more than one offense or a defendant already under sentence is sentenced for another offense committed prior to the former sentence:

(a) the Court shall not sentence to probation a defendant who is under sentence of imprisonment [with more than thirty days to run] or impose a sentence of probation and a sentence of imprisonment[, except as authorized by Section 6.02(3)(b)]; and

(b) multiple periods of suspension or probation shall run concurrently from the date of the first such disposition; and

(c) when a sentence of imprisonment is imposed for an indefinite term, the service of such sentence shall satisfy a suspended sentence on another count or a prior suspended sentence or sentence to probation; and

(d) when a sentence of imprisonment is imposed for a definite term, the period of a suspended sentence on another count or a prior suspended sentence or sentence to probation shall run during the period of such imprisonment.

(7) *Offense Committed While Under Suspension of Sentence or Probation.* When a defendant is convicted of an offense committed while under suspension of sentence or on probation and such suspension or probation is not revoked:

(a) if the defendant is sentenced to imprisonment for an indefinite term, the service of such sentence shall satisfy the prior suspended sentence or sentence to probation; and

(b) if the defendant is sentenced to imprisonment for a definite term, the period of the suspension or probation shall not run during the period of such imprisonment; and

(c) if sentence is suspended or the defendant is sentenced to probation, the period of such suspension or probation shall run concurrently with or consecutively to the remainder of the prior periods, as the Court determines at the time of sentence.

PART II. DEFINITION OF SPECIFIC CRIMES OFFENSES INVOLVING DANGER TO THE PERSON
Article 210. Criminal Homicide
Section 210.0.
Definitions.

In Articles 210–213, unless a different meaning plainly is required:

(1) "human being" means a person who has been born and is alive;

(2) "bodily injury" means physical pain, illness or any impairment of physical condition;

(3) "serious bodily injury" means bodily injury which creates a substantial risk of death or which causes serious, permanent disfigurement, or protracted loss or impairment of the function of any bodily member or organ;

(4) "deadly weapon" means any firearm or other weapon, device, instrument, material or substance, whether animate or inanimate, which in the manner it is used or is intended to be used is known to be capable of producing death or serious bodily injury.

Section 210.1.
Criminal Homicide.

(1) A person is guilty of criminal homicide if he purposely, knowingly, recklessly or negligently causes the death of another human being.

(2) Criminal homicide is murder, manslaughter or negligent homicide.

Section 210.2.
Murder.

(1) Except as provided in Section 210.3(1)(b), criminal homicide constitutes murder when:

(a) it is committed purposely or knowingly; or

(b) it is committed recklessly under circumstances manifesting extreme indifference to the value of human life. Such recklessness and indifference are presumed if the actor is engaged or is an accomplice in the commission of, or an attempt to commit, or flight after committing or attempting to commit robbery, rape or deviate sexual intercourse by force or threat of force, arson, burglary, kidnapping or felonious escape.

(2) Murder is a felony of the first degree [but a person convicted of murder may be sentenced to death, as provided in Section 210.6].

Section 210.3.
Manslaughter.

(1) Criminal homicide constitutes manslaughter when:

(a) it is committed recklessly; or

(b) a homicide which would otherwise be murder is committed under the influence of extreme mental or emotional disturbance for which there is reasonable explanation or excuse. The reasonableness of such explanation or excuse shall be determined from the viewpoint of a person in the actors situation under the circumstances as he believes them to be.

(2) Manslaughter is a felony of the second degree.

Section 210.4.
Negligent Homicide.

(1) Criminal homicide constitutes negligent homicide when it is committed negligently.

(2) Negligent homicide is a felony of the third degree.

Section 210.5.
Causing or Aiding Suicide.

(1) *Causing Suicide as Criminal Homicide.* A person may be convicted of criminal homicide for causing another to commit suicide only if he purposely causes such suicide by force, duress or deception.

(2) *Aiding or Soliciting Suicide as an Independent Offense.* A person who purposely aids or solicits another to commit suicide is guilty of a felony of the second degree if his conduct causes such suicide or an attempted suicide, and otherwise of a misdemeanor.

Section 210.6.
Sentence of Death for Murder; Further Proceedings
to Determine Sentence.

(1) *Death Sentence Excluded.* When a defendant is found guilty of murder, the Court shall impose sentence for a felony of the first degree if it is satisfied that:

(a) none of the aggravating circumstances enumerated in Subsection (3) of this Section was established by the evidence at the trial or will be established if further proceedings are initiated under Subsection (2) of this Section; or

(b) substantial mitigating circumstances, established by the evidence at the trial, call for leniency; or

(c) the defendant, with the consent of the prosecuting attorney and the approval of the Court, pleaded guilty to murder as a felony of the first degree; or

(d) the defendant was under 18 years of age at the time of the commission of the crime; or

(e) the defendant's physical or mental condition calls for leniency; or

(f) although the evidence suffices to sustain the verdict, it does not foreclose all doubt respecting the defendant's guilt.

(2) *Determination by Court or by Court and Jury.* Unless the Court imposes sentence under Subsection (1) of this Section, it shall conduct a separate proceeding to determine whether the defendant should be sentenced for a felony of the first degree or sentenced to death. The proceeding shall be conducted before the Court alone if the defendant was convicted by a Court sitting without a jury or upon his plea of guilty or if the prosecuting attorney and the defendant waive a jury with respect to sentence. In other cases it shall be conducted before the Court sitting with the jury which determined the defendant's guilt or, if the Court for good cause shown discharges that jury, with a new jury empaneled for the purpose.

In the proceeding, evidence may be presented as to any matter that the Court deems relevant to sentence, including but not limited to the nature and circumstances of the crime, the defendant's character, background, history, mental and physical condition and any of the aggravating or mitigating circumstances enumerated in Subsections (3) and (4) of this Section. Any such evidence, not legally privileged, which the Court deems to have probative force, may be received, regardless of its admissibility under the exclusionary rules of evidence, provided that the defendant's counsel is accorded a fair opportunity to rebut such evidence. The prosecuting attorney and the defendant or his counsel shall be permitted to present argument for or against sentence of death.

The determination whether sentence of death shall be imposed shall be in the discretion of the Court, except that when the proceeding is conducted before the Court sitting with a jury, the Court shall not impose sentence of death unless it submits to the jury the issue whether the defendant should be sentenced to death or to imprisonment and the jury returns a verdict that the sentence should be death. If the jury is unable to reach a unanimous verdict, the Court shall dismiss the jury and impose sentence for a felony of the first degree.

The Court, in exercising its discretion as to sentence, and the jury, in determining upon its verdict, shall take into account the aggravating and mitigating circumstances enumerated in Subsections (3) and (4) and any other facts that it deems relevant, but it shall not impose or recommend sentence of death unless it finds one of the aggravating circumstances enumerated in Subsection (3) and further finds that there are no mitigating circumstances sufficiently substantial to call for leniency. When the issue is submitted to the jury, the Court shall so instruct and also shall inform the jury of the nature of the sentence of imprisonment that may be imposed, including its implication with respect to possible release upon parole, if the jury verdict is against sentence of death.

Alternative formulation of Subsection (2):

(2) *Determination by Court.* Unless the Court imposes sentence under Subsection (1) of this Section, it shall conduct a separate proceeding to determine whether the defendant should be sentenced for a felony of the first degree or sentenced to death. In the proceeding, the Court, in accordance with Section 7.07, shall consider the report of the pre-sentence investigation and, if a psychiatric examination has been ordered, the report of such examination. In addition, evidence may be presented as to any matter that the Court deems relevant to sentence, including but not limited to the nature and circumstances of the crime, the defendant's character, background, history, mental and physical condition and any of the aggravating or mitigating circumstances enumerated in Subsections (3) and (4) of this Section. Any such evidence, not legally privileged, which the Court deems to have probative force, may be received, regardless of its admissibility under the exclusionary rules of evidence, provided that the defendant's counsel is accorded a fair opportunity to rebut such evidence. The prosecuting attorney and the defendant or his counsel shall be permitted to present argument for or against sentence of death.

The determination whether sentence of death shall be imposed shall be in the discretion of the Court. In exercising such discretion, the Court shall take into account the aggravating and mitigating circumstances enumerated in Subsections (3) and (4) and any other facts that it deems relevant but shall not impose sentence of death unless it finds one of the aggravating circumstances enumerated in Subsection (3) and further finds that there are no mitigating circumstances sufficiently substantial to call for leniency.

(3) Aggravating Circumstances.

(a) The murder was committed by a convict under sentence of imprisonment.

(b) The defendant was previously convicted of another murder or of a felony involving the use of threat of violence to the person.

(c) At the time the murder was committed the defendant also committed another murder.

(d) The defendant knowingly created a great risk of death to many persons.

(e) The murder was committed while the defendant was engaged or was an accomplice in the commission of, or an attempt to commit, or flight after committing or attempting to commit robbery, rape or deviate sexual intercourse by force or threat of force, arson, burglary or kidnapping.

(f) The murder was committed for the purpose of avoiding or preventing a lawful arrest or effecting an escape from lawful custody.

(g) The murder was committed for pecuniary gain.

(h) The murder was especially heinous, atrocious or cruel, manifesting exceptional depravity.

(4) Mitigating Circumstances.

(a) The defendant has no significant history of prior criminal activity.

(b) The murder was committed while the defendant was under the influence of extreme mental or emotional disturbance.

(c) The victim was a participant in the defendant's homicidal conduct or consented to the homicidal act.

(d) The murder was committed under circumstances which the defendant believed to provide a moral justification or extenuation for his conduct.

(e) The defendant was an accomplice in a murder committed by another person and his participation in the homicidal act was relatively minor.

(f) The defendant acted under duress or under the domination of another person.

(g) At the time of the murder, the capacity of the defendant to appreciate the criminality [wrongfulness] of his conduct or to conform his conduct to the requirements of law was impaired as a result of mental disease or defect or intoxication.

(h) The youth of the defendant at the time of the crime.]

Article 211. Assault; Reckless Endangering; Threats

Section 211.0.
Definitions.

In this Article, the definitions given in Section 210.0 apply unless a different meaning plainly is required.

Section 211.1.
Assault.

(1) *Simple Assault.* A person is guilty of assault if he:

(a) attempts to cause or purposely, knowingly or recklessly causes bodily injury to another; or

(b) negligently causes bodily injury to another with a deadly weapon; or

(c) attempts by physical menace to put another in fear of imminent serious bodily injury.

Simple assault is a misdemeanor unless committed in a fight or scuffle entered into by mutual consent, in which case it is a petty misdemeanor.

(2) *Aggravated Assault.* A person is guilty of aggravated assault if he:

(a) attempts to cause serious bodily injury to another, or causes such injury purposely, knowingly or recklessly under circumstances manifesting extreme indifference to the value of human life; or

(b) attempts to cause or purposely or knowingly causes bodily injury to another with a deadly weapon.

Aggravated assault under paragraph (a) is a felony of the second degree; aggravated assault under paragraph (b) is a felony of the third degree.

Section 211.2.
Recklessly Endangering Another Person.

A person commits a misdemeanor if he recklessly engages in conduct which places or may place another person in danger of death or serious bodily injury. Recklessness and danger shall be presumed where a person knowingly points a firearm at or in the direction of another, whether or not the actor believed the firearm to be loaded.

Section 211.3.
Terroristic Threats.

A person is guilty of a felony of the third degree if he threatens to commit any crime of violence with purpose to terrorize another or to cause evacuation of a building, place of assembly, or facility of public transportation, or otherwise to cause serious public inconvenience, or in reckless disregard of the risk of causing such terror or inconvenience.

Article 212. Kidnapping and Related Offenses; Coercion

Section 212.0.
Definitions.

In this Article, the definitions given in Section 210.0 apply unless a different meaning plainly is required.

Section 212.1.
Kidnapping.

A person is guilty of kidnapping if he unlawfully removes another from his place of residence or business, or a substantial distance from the vicinity where he is found, or if he unlawfully confines another for a substantial period in a place of isolation, with any of the following purposes:

(a) to hold for ransom or reward, or as a shield or hostage; or

(b) to facilitate commission of any felony or flight thereafter; or

(c) to inflict bodily injury on or to terrorize the victim or another; or

(d) to interfere with the performance of any governmental or political function.

Kidnapping is a felony of the first degree unless the actor voluntarily releases the victim alive and in a safe place prior to trial, in which case it is a felony of the second degree. A removal or confinement is unlawful within the meaning of this Section if it is accomplished by force, threat or deception, or, in the case of a person who is under the age of 14 or incompetent, if it is accomplished without the consent of a parent, guardian or other person responsible for general supervision of his welfare.

Section 212.2.
Felonious Restraint.

A person commits a felony of the third degree if he knowingly:

(a) restrains another unlawfully in circumstances exposing him to risk of serious bodily injury; or

(b) holds another in a condition of involuntary servitude

Section 212.3.
False Imprisonment.

A person commits a misdemeanor if he knowingly restrains another unlawfully so as to interfere substantially with his liberty.

Section 212.4.
Interference with Custody.

(1) *Custody of Children.* A person commits an offense if he knowingly or recklessly takes or entices any child under the age of 18 from the custody of its parent, guardian or other lawful custodian, when he has no privilege to do so. It is an affirmative defense that:

(a) the actor believed that his action was necessary to preserve the child from danger to its welfare; or

(b) the child, being at the time not less than 14 years old, was taken away at its own instigation without enticement and without purpose to commit a criminal offense with or against the child.

Proof that the child was below the critical age gives rise to a presumption that the actor knew the child's age or acted in reckless disregard thereof. The offense is a misdemeanor unless the actor, not being a parent or person in equivalent relation to the child, acted with knowledge that his conduct would cause serious alarm for the child's safety, or in reckless disregard of a likelihood of causing such alarm, in which case the offense is a felony of the third degree.

(2) *Custody of Committed Persons.* A person is guilty of a misdemeanor if he knowingly or recklessly takes or entices any committed person away from lawful custody when he is not privileged to do so. "Committed person" means, in addition to anyone committed under judicial warrant, any orphan, neglected or delinquent child, mentally defective or insane person, or other dependent or incompetent person entrusted to another's custody by or through a recognized social agency or otherwise by authority of law.

Section 212.5.
Criminal Coercion.

(1) *Offense Defined.* A person is guilty of criminal coercion if, with purpose unlawfully to restrict another's freedom of action to his detriment, he threatens to:

(a) commit any criminal offense; or

(b) accuse anyone of a criminal offense; or

(c) expose any secret tending to subject any person to hatred, contempt or ridicule, or to impair his credit or business repute; or

(d) take or withhold action as an official, or cause an official to take or withhold action.

It is an affirmative defense to prosecution based on paragraphs (b), (c) or (d) that the actor believed the accusation or secret to be true or the proposed official action justified and that his purpose was limited to compelling the other to behave in a way reasonably related to the circumstances which were the subject of the accusation, exposure or proposed official action, as by desisting from further misbehavior, making good a wrong done, refraining from taking any action or responsibility for which the actor believes the other disqualified.

(2) *Grading.* Criminal coercion is a misdemeanor unless the threat is to commit a felony or the actor's purpose is felonious, in which cases the offense is a felony of the third degree.

Article 213. Sexual Offenses

Section 213.0.
Definitions.

In this Article, unless a different meaning plainly is required:

(1) the definitions given in Section 210.0 apply;

(2) "Sexual intercourse" includes intercourse per os or per anum, with some penetration however slight; emission is not required;

(3) "Deviate sexual intercourse" means sexual intercourse per os or per anum between human beings who are not husband and wife, and any form of sexual intercourse with an animal.

Section 213.1.
Rape and Related Offenses.

(1) *Rape.* A male who has sexual intercourse with a female not his wife is guilty of rape if:

(a) he compels her to submit by force or by threat of imminent death, serious bodily injury, extreme pain or kidnapping, to be inflicted on anyone; or

(b) he has substantially impaired her power to appraise or control her conduct by administering or employing without her knowledge drugs, intoxicants or other means for the purpose of preventing resistance; or

(c) the female is unconscious; or

(d) the female is less than 10 years old. Rape is a felony of the second degree unless (i) in the course thereof the actor inflicts serious bodily injury upon anyone, or (ii) the victim was not a voluntary social companion of the actor upon the occasion of the crime and had not previously permitted him sexual liberties, in which cases the offense is a felony of the first degree.

(2) *Gross Sexual Imposition.* A male who has sexual intercourse with a female not his wife commits a felony of the third degree if:

(a) he compels her to submit by any threat that would prevent resistance by a woman of ordinary resolution; or

(b) he knows that she suffers from a mental disease or defect which renders her incapable of appraising the nature of her conduct; or

(c) he knows that she is unaware that a sexual act is being committed upon her or that she submits because she mistakenly supposes that he is her husband.

Section 213.2.
Deviate Sexual Intercourse by Force or Imposition.

(1) By *Force or Its Equivalent.* A person who engages in deviate sexual intercourse with another person, or who causes another to engage in deviate sexual intercourse, commits a felony of the second degree if:

(a) he compels the other person to participate by force or by threat of imminent death, serious bodily injury, extreme pain or kidnapping, to be inflicted on anyone; or

(b) he has substantially impaired the other person's power to appraise or control his conduct, by administering or employing without the knowledge of the other person drugs, intoxicants or other means for the purpose of preventing resistance; or

(c) the other person is unconscious; or

(d) the other person is less than 10 years old.

(2) By *Other Imposition.* A person who engages in deviate sexual intercourse with another person, or who causes another to engage in deviate sexual intercourse, commits a felony of the third degree if:

(a) he compels the other person to participate by any threat that would prevent resistance by a person of ordinary resolution; or

(b) he knows that the other person suffers from a mental disease or defect which renders him incapable of appraising the nature of his conduct; or

(c) he knows that the other person submits because he is unaware that a sexual act is being committed upon him.

Section 213.3.
Corruption of Minors and Seduction.

(1) *Offense Defined.* A male who has sexual intercourse with a female not his wife, or any person who engages in deviate sexual intercourse or causes another to engage in deviate sexual intercourse, is guilty of an offense if:

(a) the other person is less than [16] years old and the actor is at least [four] years older than the other person; or

(b) the other person is less than 21 years old and the actor is his guardian or otherwise responsible for general supervision of his welfare; or

(c) the other person is in custody of law or detained in a hospital or other institution and the actor has supervisory or disciplinary authority over him; or

(d) the other person is a female who is induced to participate by a promise of marriage which the actor does not mean to perform.

(2) *Grading.* An offense under paragraph (a) of Subsection (1) is a felony of the third degree. Otherwise an offense under this section is a misdemeanor.

Section 213.4.
Sexual Assault.

A person who has sexual contact with another not his spouse, or causes such other to have sexual conduct with him, is guilty of sexual assault, a misdemeanor, if:

(1) he knows that the contact is offensive to the other person; or

(2) he knows that the other person suffers from a mental disease or defect which renders him or her incapable of appraising the nature of his or her conduct; or

(3) he knows that the other person is unaware that a sexual act is being committed; or

(4) the other person is less than 10 years old; or

(5) he has substantially impaired the other person's power to appraise or control his or her conduct, by administering or employing without the other's knowledge drugs, intoxicants or other means for the purpose of preventing resistance; or

(6) the other person is less than [16] years old and the actor is at least [four] years older than the other person; or

(7) the other person is less than 21 years old and the actor is his guardian or otherwise responsible for general supervision of his welfare; or

(8) the other person is in custody of law or detained in a hospital or other institution and the actor has supervisory or disciplinary authority over him.

Sexual contact is any touching of the sexual or other intimate parts of the person for the purpose of arousing or gratifying sexual desire.

Section 213.5.
Indecent Exposure.

A person commits a misdemeanor if, for the purpose of arousing or gratifying sexual desire of himself or of any person other than his spouse, he exposes his genitals under circumstances in which he knows his conduct is likely to cause affront or alarm.

Section 213.6.
Provisions Generally Applicable to Article 213.

(1) *Mistake as to Age.* Whenever in this Article the criminality of conduct depends on a child's being below the age of 10, it is no defense that the actor did not know the child's age, or reasonably believed the child to be older than 10. When criminality depends on the child's being below a critical age other than 10, it is a defense for the actor to prove by a preponderance of the evidence that he reasonably believed the child to be above the critical age.

(2) *Spouse Relationships.* Whenever in this Article the definition of an offense excludes conduct with a spouse, the exclusion shall be deemed to extend to persons living as man and wife, regardless of the legal status of their relationship. The exclusion shall be inoperative as respects spouses living apart under a decree of judicial separation. Where the definition of an offense excludes conduct with a spouse or conduct by a woman, this shall not preclude conviction of a spouse or woman as accomplice in a sexual act which he or she causes another person, not within the exclusion, to perform.

(3) *Sexually Promiscuous Complainants.* It is a defense to prosecution under Section 213.3 and paragraphs (6), (7) and (8) of Section 213.4 for the actor to prove by a preponderance of the evidence that the alleged victim had, prior to the time of the offense charged, engaged promiscuously in sexual relations with others.

(4) *Prompt Complaint.* No prosecution may be instituted or maintained under this Article unless the alleged offense was brought to the notice of public authority within [3] months of its occurrence or, where the alleged victim was less than [16] years old or otherwise incompetent to make complaint, within [3] months after a parent, guardian or other competent person specially interested in the victim learns of the offense.

(5) *Testimony of Complainants.* No person shall be convicted of any felony under this Article upon the uncorroborated testimony of the alleged victim. Corroboration may be circumstantial.

In any prosecution before a jury for an offense under this Article, the jury shall be instructed to evaluate the testimony of a victim or complaining witness with special care in view of the emotional involvement of the witness and the difficulty of determining the truth with respect to alleged sexual activities carried out in private.

OFFENSES AGAINST PROPERTY
Article 220. Arson, Criminal Mischief, and
Other Property Destruction
Section 220.1.
Arson and Related Offenses.

(1) *Arson.* A person is guilty of arson, a felony of the second degree, if he starts a fire or causes an explosion with the purpose of:

(a) destroying a building or occupied structure of another; or

(b) destroying or damaging any property, whether his own or another's, to collect insurance for such loss. It shall be an affirmative defense to prosecution under this paragraph that the actor's conduct did not recklessly endanger any building or occupied structure of another or place any other person in danger of death or bodily injury.

(2) *Reckless Burning or Exploding.* A person commits a felony of the third degree if he purposely starts a fire or causes an explosion, whether on his own property or another's, and thereby recklessly:

(a) places another person in danger of death or bodily injury; or

(b) places a building or occupied structure of another in danger of damage or destruction.

(3) *Failure to Control or Report Dangerous Fire.* A person who knows that a fire is endangering life or a substantial amount of property of another and fails to take reasonable measures to put out or control the fire, when he can do so without substantial risk to himself, or to give a prompt fire alarm, commits a misdemeanor if:

(a) he knows that he is under an official, contractual, or other legal duty to prevent or combat the fire; or

(b) the fire was started, albeit lawfully, by him or with his assent, or on property in his custody or control.

(4) *Definitions.* "Occupied structure" means any structure, vehicle or place adapted for overnight accommodation of persons, or for carrying on business therein, whether or not a person is actually present. Property is that of another, for the purposes of this section, if anyone other than the actor has a possessory or proprietary interest therein. If a building or structure is divided into separately occupied units, any unit not occupied by the actor is an occupied structure of another.

Section 220.2.
Causing or Risking Catastrophe.

(1) *Causing Catastrophe.* A person who causes a catastrophe by explosion, fire, flood, avalanche, collapse of building, release of poison gas, radioactive material or other harmful or destructive force or substance, or by any other means of causing

potentially widespread injury or damage, commits a felony of the second degree if he does so purposely or knowingly, or a felony of the third degree if he does so recklessly.

(2) *Risking Catastrophe.* A person is guilty of a misdemeanor if he recklessly creates a risk of catastrophe in the employment of fire, explosives or other dangerous means listed in Subsection (1).

(3) *Failure to Prevent Catastrophe.* A person who knowingly or recklessly fails to take reasonable measures to prevent or mitigate a catastrophe commits a misdemeanor if:

(a) he knows that he is under an official, contractual or other legal duty to take such measures; or

(b) he did or assented to the act causing or threatening the catastrophe.

Section 220.3.
Criminal Mischief.

(1) *Offense Defined.* A person is guilty of criminal mischief if he:

(a) damages tangible property of another purposely, recklessly, or by negligence in the employment of fire, explosives, or other dangerous means listed in Section 220.2(1); or

(b) purposely or recklessly tampers with tangible property of another so as to endanger person or property; or

(c) purposely or recklessly causes another to suffer pecuniary loss by deception or threat.

(2) *Grading.* Criminal mischief is a felony of the third degree if the actor purposely causes pecuniary loss in excess of $5,000, or a substantial interruption or impairment of public communication, transportation, supply of water, gas or power, or other public service. It is a misdemeanor if the actor purposely causes pecuniary loss in excess of $100, or a petty misdemeanor if he purposely or recklessly causes pecuniary loss in excess of $25. Otherwise criminal mischief is a violation.

Article 221. Burglary and Other Criminal Intrusion
Section 221.0.
Definitions.

In this Article, unless a different meaning plainly is required:

(1) "occupied structure" means any structure, vehicle or place adapted for overnight accommodation of persons, or for carrying on business therein, whether or not a person is actually present.

(2) "night" means the period between thirty minutes past sunset and thirty minutes before sunrise.

Section 221.1.
Burglary.

(1) *Burglary Defined.* A person is guilty of burglary if he enters a building or occupied structure, or separately secured or occupied portion thereof, with purpose to commit a crime therein, unless the premises are at the time open to the public or the actor is licensed or privileged to enter. It is an affirmative defense to prosecution for burglary that the building or structure was abandoned.

(2) *Grading.* Burglary is a felony of the second degree if it is perpetrated in the dwelling of another at night, or if, in the course of committing the offense, the actor:

(a) purposely, knowingly or recklessly inflicts or attempts to inflict bodily injury on anyone; or

(b) is armed with explosives or a deadly weapon.

Otherwise, burglary is a felony of the third degree. An act shall be deemed "in the course of committing" an offense if it occurs in an attempt to commit the offense or in flight after the attempt or commission.

(3) *Multiple Convictions.* A person may not be convicted both for burglary and for the offense which it was his purpose to commit after the burglarious entry or for an attempt to commit that offense, unless the additional offense constitutes a felony of the first or second degree.

Section 221.2.
Criminal Trespass.

(1) *Buildings and Occupied Structures.* A person commits an offense if, knowing that he is not licensed or privileged to do so, he enters or surreptitiously remains in any building or occupied structure, or separately secured or occupied portion thereof. An offense under this Subsection is a misdemeanor if it is committed in a dwelling at night. Otherwise it is a petty misdemeanor.

(2) *Defiant Trespasser.* A person commits an offense if, knowing that he is not licensed or privileged to do so, he enters or remains in any place as to which notice against trespass is given by:

(a) actual communication to the actor; or

(b) posting in a manner prescribed by law or reasonably likely to come to the attention of intruders; or

(c) fencing or other enclosure manifestly designed to exclude intruders.

An offense under this Subsection constitutes a petty misdemeanor if the offender defies an order to leave personally communicated to him by the owner of the premises or other authorized person. Otherwise it is a violation.

(3) *Defenses.* It is an affirmative defense to prosecution under this Section that:

(a) a building or occupied structure involved in an offense under Subsection (1) was abandoned; or

(b) the premises were at the time open to members of the public and the actor complied with all lawful conditions imposed on access to or remaining in the premises; or

(c) the actor reasonably believed that the owner of the premises, or other person empowered to license access thereto, would have licensed him to enter or remain.

Article 222. Robbery
Section 222.1.
Robbery.

(1) *Robbery Defined.* A person is guilty of robbery if, in the course of committing a theft, he:

(a) inflicts serious bodily injury upon another; or

(b) threatens another with or purposely puts him in fear of immediate serious bodily injury; or

(c) commits or threatens immediately to commit any felony of the first or second degree.

An act shall be deemed "in the course of committing a theft" if it occurs in an attempt to commit theft or in flight after the attempt or commission.

(2) *Grading.* Robbery is a felony of the second degree, except that it is a felony of the first degree if in the course of committing the theft the actor attempts to kill anyone, or purposely inflicts or attempts to inflict serious bodily injury.

Article 223. Theft and Related Offenses
Section 223.0.
Definitions.

In this Article, unless a different meaning plainly is required:

(1) "deprive" means: (a) to withhold property of another permanently or for so extended a period as to appropriate a major portion of its economic value, or with intent to restore only upon payment of reward or other compensation; or (b) to dispose of the property so as to make it unlikely that the owner will recover it.

(2) "financial institution" means a bank, insurance company, credit union, building and loan association, investment trust or other organization held out to the public as a place of deposit of funds or medium of savings or collective investment.

(3) "government" means the United States, any State, county, municipality, or other political unit, or any department, agency or subdivision of any of the foregoing, or any corporation or other association carrying out the functions of government.

(4) "movable property" means property the location of which can be changed, including things growing on, affixed to, or found in land, and documents although

the rights represented thereby have no physical location; "immovable property" is all other property.

(5) "obtain" means: (a) in relation to property, to bring about a transfer or purported transfer of a legal interest in the property, whether to the obtainer or another; or (b) in relation to labor or service, to secure performance thereof.

(6) "property" means anything of value, including real estate, tangible and intangible personal property, contract rights, choses-in-action and other interests in or claims to wealth, admission or transportation tickets, captured or domestic animals, food and drink, electric or other power.

(7) "property of another" includes property in which any person other than the actor has an interest which the actor is not privileged to infringe, regardless of the fact that the actor also has an interest in the property and regardless of the fact that the other person might be precluded from civil recovery because the property was used in an unlawful transaction or was subject to forfeiture as contraband. Property in possession of the actor shall not be deemed property of another who has only a security interest therein, even if legal title is in the creditor pursuant to a conditional sales contract or other security agreement.

Section 223.1.
Consolidation of Theft Offenses; Grading; Provisions
Applicable to Theft Generally.

(1) *Consolidation of Theft Offenses.* Conduct denominated theft in this Article constitutes a single offense. An accusation of theft may be supported by evidence that it was committed in any manner that would be theft under this Article, notwithstanding the specification of a different manner in the indictment or information, subject only to the power of the Court to ensure fair trial by granting a continuance or other appropriate relief where the conduct of the defense would be prejudiced by lack of fair notice or by surprise.

(2) *Grading of Theft Offenses.*

(a) Theft constitutes a felony of the third degree if the amount involved exceeds $500, or if the property stolen is a firearm, automobile, airplane, motorcycle, motorboat, or other motorpropelled vehicle, or in the case of theft by receiving stolen property, if the receiver is in the business of buying or selling stolen property.

(b) Theft not within the preceding paragraph constitutes a misdemeanor, except that if the property was not taken from the person or by threat, or in breach of a fiduciary obligation, and the actor proves by a preponderance of the evidence that the amount involved was less than $50, the offense constitutes a petty misdemeanor.

(c) The amount involved in a theft shall be deemed to be the highest value, by any reasonable standard, of the property or services which the actor stole or attempted to steal. Amounts involved in thefts committed pursuant to one scheme or course of conduct, whether from the same person or several persons, may be aggregated in determining the grade of the offense.

(3) *Claim of Right.* It is an affirmative defense to prosecution for theft that the actor:

(a) was unaware that the property or service was that of another; or

(b) acted under an honest claim of right to the property or service involved or that he had a right to acquire or dispose of it as he did; or

(c) took property exposed for sale, intending to purchase and pay for it promptly, or reasonably believing that the owner, if present, would have consented.

(4) *Theft from Spouse.* It is no defense that theft was from the actor's spouse, except that misappropriation of household and personal effects, or other property normally accessible to both spouses, is theft only if it occurs after the parties have ceased living together.

Section 223.2.
Theft by Unlawful Taking or Disposition.

(1) *Movable Property.* A person is guilty of theft if he unlawfully takes, or exercises unlawful control over, movable property of another with purpose to deprive him thereof.

(2) *Immovable Property.* A person is guilty of theft if he unlawfully transfers immovable property of another or any interest therein with purpose to benefit himself or another not entitled thereto.

Section 223.3.
Theft by Deception.

A person is guilty of theft if he purposely obtains property of another by deception. A person deceives if he purposely:

(1) creates or reinforces a false impression, including false impressions as to law, value, intention or other state of mind; but deception as to a person's intention to perform a promise shall not be inferred from the fact alone that he did not subsequently perform the promise; or

(2) prevents another from acquiring information which would affect his judgment of a transaction; or

(3) fails to correct a false impression which the deceiver previously created or reinforced, or which the deceiver knows to be influencing another to whom he stands in a fiduciary or confidential relationship; or

(4) fails to disclose a known lien, adverse claim or other legal impediment to the enjoyment of property which he transfers or encumbers in consideration for the property obtained, whether such impediment is or is not valid, or is or is not a matter of official record.

The term "deceive" does not, however, include falsity as to matters having no pecuniary significance, or puffing by statements unlikely to deceive ordinary persons in the group addressed.

Section 223.4.
Theft by Extortion.

A person is guilty of theft if he purposely obtains property of another by threatening to:

(1) inflict bodily injury on anyone or commit any other criminal offense; or

(2) accuse anyone of a criminal offense; or

(3) expose any secret tending to subject any person to hatred, contempt or ridicule, or to impair his credit or business repute; or

(4) take or withhold action as an official, or cause an official to take or withhold action; or

(5) bring about or continue a strike, boycott or other collective unofficial action, if the property is not demanded or received for the benefit of the group in whose interest the actor purports to act; or

(6) testify or provide information or withhold testimony or information with respect to another's legal claim or defense; or

(7) inflict any other harm which would not benefit the actor.

It is an affirmative defense to prosecution based on paragraphs (2), (3) or (4) that the property obtained by threat of accusation, exposure, lawsuit or other invocation of official action was honestly claimed as restitution or indemnification for harm done in the circumstances to which such accusation, exposure, lawsuit or other official action relates, or as compensation for property or lawful services.

Section 223.5.
Theft of Property Lost, Mislaid, or Delivered by Mistake.

A person who comes into control of property of another that he knows to have been lost, mislaid, or delivered under a mistake as to the nature or amount of the property or the identity of the recipient is guilty of theft if, with purpose to deprive the owner thereof, he fails to take reasonable measures to restore the property to a person entitled to have it.

Section 223.6.
Receiving Stolen Property.

(1) *Receiving.* A person is guilty of theft if he purposely receives, retains, or disposes of movable property of another knowing that it has been stolen, or believing that it has probably been stolen, unless the property is received, retained, or disposed with purpose to restore it to the owner. "Receiving" means acquiring possession, control or title, or lending on the security of the property.

(2) *Presumption of Knowledge.* The requisite knowledge or belief is presumed in the case of a dealer who:

(a) is found in possession or control of property stolen from two or more persons on separate occasions; or

(b) has received stolen property in another transaction within the year preceding the transaction charged; or

(c) being a dealer in property of the sort received, acquires it for a consideration which he knows is far below its reasonable value. "Dealer" means a person in the business of buying or selling goods including a pawnbroker.

Section 223.7.
Theft of Services.

(1) A person is guilty of theft if he purposely obtains services which he knows are available only for compensation, by deception or threat, or by false token or other means to avoid payment for the service. "Services" includes labor, professional service, transportation, telephone or other public service, accommodation in hotels, restaurants or elsewhere, admission to exhibitions, use of vehicles or other movable property. Where compensation for service is ordinarily paid immediately upon the rendering of such service, as in the case of hotels and restaurants, refusal to pay or absconding without payment or offer to pay gives rise to a presumption that the service was obtained by deception as to intention to pay.

(2) A person commits theft if, having control over the disposition of services of others, to which he is not entitled, he knowingly diverts such services to his own benefit or to the benefit of another not entitled thereto.

Section 223.8.
Theft by Failure to Make Required Disposition of Funds Received.

A person who purposely obtains property upon agreement, or subject to a known legal obligation, to make specified payment or other disposition, whether from such property or its proceeds or from his own property to be reserved in equivalent amount, is guilty of theft if he deals with the property obtained as his own and fails to make the required payment or disposition. The foregoing applies notwithstanding that it may be impossible to identify particular property as belonging to the victim at the time of the actor's failure to make the required payment or disposition. An officer or employee of the government or of a financial institution is presumed: (i) to know any legal obligation relevant to his criminal liability under this Section, and (ii) to have dealt with the property as his own if he fails to pay or account upon lawful demand, or if an audit reveals a shortage or falsification of accounts.

Section 223.9.
Unauthorized Use of Automobiles and Other Vehicles.

A person commits a misdemeanor if he operates another's automobile, airplane, motorcycle, motorboat, or other motor-propelled vehicle without consent of the owner. It is an affirmative defense to prosecution under this Section that the actor reasonably believed that the owner would have consented to the operation had he known of it.

Article 224. Forgery And Fraudulent Practices

Section 224.0.
Definitions.

In this Article, the definitions given in Section 223.0 apply unless a different meaning plainly is required.

Section 224.1.
Forgery.

(1) *Definition.* A person is guilty of forgery if, with purpose to defraud or injure anyone, or with knowledge that he is facilitating a fraud or injury to be perpetrated by anyone, the actor:

(a) alters any writing of another without his authority; or

(b) makes, completes, executes, authenticates, issues or transfers any writing so that it purports to be the act of another who did not authorize that act, or to have been executed at a time or place or in a numbered sequence other than was in fact the case, or to be a copy of an original when no such original existed; or

(c) utters any writing which he knows to be forged in a manner specified in paragraphs (a) or (b)."Writing" includes printing or any other method of recording information, money, coins, tokens, stamps, seals, credit cards, badges, trademarks, and other symbols of value, right, privilege, or identification.

(2) *Grading.* Forgery is a felony of the second degree if the writing is or purports to be part of an issue of money, securities, postage or revenue stamps, or other instruments issued by the government, or part of an issue of stock, bonds or other instruments representing interests in or claims against any property or enterprise. Forgery is a felony of the third degree if the writing is or purports to be a will, deed, contract, release, commercial instrument, or other document evidencing, creating, transferring, altering, terminating, or otherwise affecting legal relations. Otherwise forgery is a misdemeanor.

Section 224.2.
Simulating Objects of Antiquity, Rarity, Etc.

A person commits a misdemeanor if, with purpose to defraud anyone or with knowledge that he is facilitating a fraud to be perpetrated by anyone, he makes, alters or utters any object so that it appears to have value because of antiquity, rarity, source, or authorship which it does not possess.

Section 224.3.
Fraudulent Destruction, Removal or Concealment
of Recordable Instruments.

A person commits a felony of the third degree if, with purpose to deceive or injure anyone, he destroys, removes or conceals any will, deed, mortgage, security instrument or other writing for which the law provides public recording.

Section 224.4.
Tampering with Records.

A person commits a misdemeanor if, knowing that he has no privilege to do so, he falsifies, destroys, removes or conceals any writing or record, with purpose to deceive or injure anyone or to conceal any wrongdoing.

Section 224.5.
Bad Checks.

A person who issues or passes a check or similar sight order for the payment of money, knowing that it will not be honored by the drawee, commits a misdemeanor. For the purpose of this Section as well as in any prosecution for theft committed by means of a bad check, an issuer is presumed to know that the check or order (other than a post-dated check or order) would not be paid, if:

(1) the issuer had no account with the drawee at the time the check or order was issued; or

(2) payment was refused by the drawee for lack of funds, upon presentation within 30 days after issue, and the issuer failed to make good within 10 days after receiving notice of that refusal.

Section 224.6.
Credit Cards.

A person commits an offense if he uses a credit card for the purpose of obtaining property or services with knowledge that:

(1) the card is stolen or forged; or

(2) the card has been revoked or cancelled; or

(3) for any other reason his use of the card is unauthorized by the issuer.

It is an affirmative defense to prosecution under paragraph (3) if the actor proves by a preponderance of the evidence that he had the purpose and ability to meet all obligations to the issuer arising out of his use of the card. "Credit card" means a writing or other evidence of an undertaking to pay for property or services delivered or rendered to or upon the order of a designated person or bearer. An offense under this Section is a felony of the third degree if the value of the property or services secured or sought to be secured by means of the credit card exceeds $500; otherwise it is a misdemeanor.

Section 224.7.
Deceptive Business Practices.

A person commits a misdemeanor if in the course of business he:

(1) uses or possesses for use a false weight or measure, or any other device for falsely determining or recording any quality or quantity; or

(2) sells, offers or exposes for sale, or delivers less than the represented quantity of any commodity or service; or

(3) takes or attempts to take more than the represented quantity of any commodity or service when as buyer he furnishes the weight or measure; or

(4) sells, offers or exposes for sale adulterated or mislabeled commodities. "Adulterated" means varying from the standard of composition or quality prescribed by or pursuant to any statute providing criminal penalties for such variance, or set by established commercial usage. "Mislabeled" means varying from the standard of truth or disclosure in labeling prescribed by or pursuant to any statute providing criminal penalties for such variance, or set by established commercial usage; or

(5) makes a false or misleading statement in any advertisement addressed to the public or to a substantial segment thereof for the purpose of promoting the purchase or sale of property or services; or

(6) makes a false or misleading written statement for the purpose of obtaining property or credit; or

(7) makes a false or misleading written statement for the purpose of promoting the sale of securities, or omits information required by law to be disclosed in written documents relating to securities.

It is an affirmative defense to prosecution under this Section if the defendant proves by a preponderance of the evidence that his conduct was not knowingly or recklessly deceptive.

Section 224.8.
Commercial Bribery and Breach of Duty to Act Disinterestedly.

(1) A person commits a misdemeanor if he solicits, accepts or agrees to accept any benefit as consideration for knowingly violating or agreeing to violate a duty of fidelity to which he is subject as:

(a) partner, agent, or employee of another;

(b) trustee, guardian, or other fiduciary;

(c) lawyer, physician, accountant, appraiser, or other professional adviser or informant;

(d) officer, director, manager or other participant in the direction of the affairs of an incorporated or unincorporated association; or

(e) arbitrator or other purportedly disinterested adjudicator or referee.

(2) A person who holds himself out to the public as being engaged in the business of making disinterested selection, appraisal, or criticism of commodities or services commits a misdemeanor if he solicits, accepts or agrees to accept any benefit to influence his selection, appraisal or criticism.

(3) A person commits a misdemeanor if he confers, or offers or agrees to confer, any benefit the acceptance of which would be criminal under this Section.

Section 224.9.
Rigging Publicly Exhibited Contest.

(1) A person commits a misdemeanor if, with purpose to prevent a publicly exhibited contest from being conducted in accordance with the rules and usages purporting to govern it, he:

(a) confers or offers or agrees to confer any benefit upon, or threatens any injury to a participant, official or other person associated with the contest or exhibition; or

(b) tampers with any person, animal or thing.

(2) *Soliciting or Accepting Benefit for Rigging.* A person commits a misdemeanor if he knowingly solicits, accepts or agrees to accept any benefit the giving of which would be criminal under Subsection (1).

(3) *Participation in Rigged Contest.* A person commits a misdemeanor if he knowingly engages in, sponsors, produces, judges, or otherwise participates in a publicly exhibited contest knowing that the contest is not being conducted in compliance with the rules and usages purporting to govern it, by reason of conduct which would be criminal under this Section.

Section 224.10.
Defrauding Secured Creditors.

A person commits a misdemeanor if he destroys, removes, conceals, encumbers, transfers or otherwise deals with property subject to a security interest with purpose to hinder enforcement of that interest.

Section 224.11.
Fraud in Insolvency.

A person commits a misdemeanor if, knowing that proceedings have been or are about to be instituted for the appointment of a receiver or other person entitled to administer property for the benefit of creditors, or that any other composition or liquidation for the benefit of creditors has been or is about to be made, he:

(1) destroys, removes, conceals, encumbers, transfers, or otherwise deals with any property with purpose to defeat or obstruct the claim of any creditor, or otherwise to obstruct the operation of any law relating to administration of property for the benefit of creditors; or

(2) knowingly falsifies any writing or record relating to the property; or

(3) knowingly misrepresents or refuses to disclose to a receiver or other person entitled to administer property for the benefit of creditors, the existence, amount or location of the property, or any other information which the actor could be legally required to furnish in relation to such administration.

Section 224.12.
Receiving Deposits in a Fading Financial Institution.

An officer, manager or other person directing or participating in the direction of a financial institution commits a misdemeanor if he receives or permits the receipt of a deposit, premium payment or other investment in the institution knowing that:

(1) due to financial difficulties the institution is about to suspend operations or go into receivership or reorganization; and

(2) the person making the deposit or other payment is unaware of the precarious situation of the institution.

Section 224.13.
Misapplication of Entrusted Property and Property of
Government or Financial Institution.

A person commits an offense if he applies or disposes of property that has been entrusted to him as a fiduciary, or property of the government or of a financial institution, in a manner which he knows is unlawful and involves substantial risk of loss or detriment to the owner of the property or to a person for whose benefit the property was entrusted. The offense is a misdemeanor if the amount involved exceeds $50; otherwise it is a petty misdemeanor.

"Fiduciary" includes trustee, guardian, executor, administrator, receiver and any person carrying on fiduciary functions on behalf of a corporation or other organization which is a fiduciary.

Section 224.14.
Securing Execution of Documents by Deception.

A person commits a misdemeanor if by deception he causes another to execute any instrument affecting, purporting to affect, or likely to affect the pecuniary interest of any person.

OFFENSES AGAINST THE FAMILY
Article 230. Offenses Against the Family
Section 230.1.
Bigamy and Polygamy.

(1) *Bigamy.* A married person is guilty of bigamy, a misdemeanor, if he contracts or purports to contract another marriage, unless at the time of the subsequent marriage:

(a) the actor believes that the prior spouse is dead; or

(b) the actor and the prior spouse have been living apart for five consecutive years throughout which the prior spouse was not known by the actor to be alive; or

(c) a Court has entered a judgment purporting to terminate or annul any prior disqualifying marriage, and the actor does not know that judgment to be invalid; or

(d) the actor reasonably believes that he is legally eligible to remarry.

(2) *Polygamy.* A person is guilty of polygamy, a felony of the third degree, if he marries or cohabits with more than one spouse at a time in purported exercise of the right of plural marriage. The offense is a continuing one until all cohabitation and claim of marriage with more than one spouse terminates. This section does not apply to parties to a polygamous marriage, lawful in the country of which they are residents or nationals, while they are in transit through or temporarily visiting this State.

(3) *Other Party to Bigamous or Polygamous Marriage.* A person is guilty of bigamy or polygamy, as the case may be, if he contracts or purports to contract marriage with another knowing that the other is thereby committing bigamy or polygamy.

Section 230.2.
Incest.

A person is guilty of incest, a felony of the third degree, if he knowingly marries or cohabits or has sexual intercourse with an ancestor or descendant, a brother or sister of the whole or half blood [or an uncle, aunt, nephew or niece of the whole blood]. "Cohabit" means to live together under the representation or appearance of being married. The relationships referred to herein include blood relationships without regard to legitimacy, and relationship of parent and child by adoption.

Section 230.3.
Abortion.

(1) *Unjustified Abortion.* A person who purposely and unjustifiably terminates the pregnancy of another otherwise than by a live birth commits a felony of the third degree or, where the pregnancy has continued beyond the twenty-sixth week, a felony of the second degree.

(2) *Justifiable Abortion.* A licensed physician is justified in terminating a pregnancy if he believes there is substantial risk that continuance of the pregnancy would gravely impair the physical or mental health of the mother or that the child would be born with grave physical or mental defect, or that the pregnancy resulted from rape, incest, or other felonious intercourse. All illicit intercourse with a girl below the age of 16 shall be deemed felonious for purposes of this subsection. Justifiable abortions shall be performed only in a licensed hospital except in case of emergency when hospital facilities are unavailable. [Additional exceptions from the requirement of hospitalization may be incorporated here to take account of situations in sparsely settled areas where hospitals are not generally accessible.]

(3) *Physicians' Certificates; Presumption from Non-Compliance.* No abortion shall be performed unless two physicians, one of whom may be the person performing the abortion, shall have certified in writing the circumstances which they believe to

justify the abortion. Such certificate shall be submitted before the abortion to the hospital where it is to be performed and, in the case of abortion following felonious intercourse, to the prosecuting attorney or the police. Failure to comply with any of the requirements of this Subsection gives rise to a presumption that the abortion was unjustified.

(4) *Self-Abortion.* A woman whose pregnancy has continued beyond the twenty-sixth week commits a felony of the third degree if she purposely terminates her own pregnancy otherwise than by a live birth, or if she uses instruments, drugs or violence upon herself for that purpose. Except as justified under Subsection (2), a person who induces or knowingly aids a woman to use instruments, drugs or violence upon herself for the purpose of terminating her pregnancy otherwise than by a live birth commits a felony of the third degree whether or not the pregnancy has continued beyond the twenty-sixth week.

(5) *Pretended Abortion.* A person commits a felony of the third degree if, representing that it is his purpose to perform an abortion, he does an act adapted to cause abortion in a pregnant woman although the woman is in fact not pregnant, or the actor does not believe she is. A person charged with unjustified abortion under Subsection (1) or an attempt to commit that offense may be convicted thereof upon proof of conduct prohibited by this Subsection.

(6) *Distribution of Abortifacients.* A person who sells, offers to sell, possesses with intent to sell, advertises, or displays for sale anything specially designed to terminate a pregnancy, or held out by the actor as useful for that purpose, commits a misdemeanor, unless:

(a) the sale, offer or display is to a physician or druggist or to an intermediary in a chain of distribution to physicians or druggists; or

(b) the sale is made upon prescription or order of a physician; or

(c) the possession is with intent to sell as authorized in paragraphs (a) and (b); or

(d) the advertising is addressed to persons named in paragraph (a) and confined to trade or professional channels not likely to reach the general public.

(7) *Section Inapplicable to Prevention of Pregnancy.* Nothing in this Section shall be deemed applicable to the prescription, administration or distribution of drugs or other substances for avoiding pregnancy, whether by preventing implantation of a fertilized ovum or by any other method that operates before, at or immediately after fertilization.

Section 230.4.
Endangering Welfare of Children.

A parent, guardian, or other person supervising the welfare of a child under 18 commits a misdemeanor if he knowingly endangers the child's welfare by violating a duty of care, protection or support.

OFFENSES AGAINST PUBLIC ADMINISTRATION
Article 242. Obstructing Governmental Operations; Escape
Section 242.2.
Resisting Arrest or Other Law Enforcement.

A person commits a misdemeanor if, for the purpose of preventing a public servant from effecting a lawful arrest or discharging any other duty, the person creates a substantial risk of bodily injury to the public servant or anyone else, or employs means justifying or requiring substantial force to overcome the resistance.

Section 242.3.
Hindering Apprehension or Prosecution.

A person commits an offense if, with purpose to hinder the apprehension, prosecution, conviction or punishment of another for crime, he:

(1) harbors or conceals the other; or

(2) provides or aids in providing a weapon, transportation, disguise or other means of avoiding apprehension or effecting escape; or

(3) conceals or destroys evidence of the crime, or tampers with a witness, informant, document or other source of information, regardless of its admissibility in evidence; or

(4) warns the other of impending discovery or apprehension, except that this paragraph does not apply to a warning given in connection with an effort to bring another into compliance with law; or

(5) volunteers false information to a law enforcement officer.

The offense is a felony of the third degree if the conduct which the actor knows has been charged or is liable to be charged against the person aided would constitute a felony of the first or second degree. Otherwise it is a misdemeanor.

Section 242.4.
Aiding Consummation of Crime.

A person commits an offense if he purposely aids another to accomplish an unlawful object of a crime, as by safeguarding the proceeds thereof or converting the proceeds into negotiable funds. The offense is a felony of the third degree if the principal offense was a felony of the first or second degree. Otherwise it is a misdemeanor.

Section 242.5.
Compounding.

A person commits a misdemeanor if he accepts or agrees to accept any pecuniary benefit in consideration of refraining from reporting to law enforcement authorities the commission or suspected commission of any offense or information relating to an offense. It is an affirmative defense to prosecution under this Section that the pecuniary benefit did not exceed an amount which the actor believed to be due as restitution or indemnification for harm caused by the offense.

Section 242.6.
Escape.

(1) *Escape.* A person commits an offense if he unlawfully removes himself from official detention or fails to return to official detention following temporary leave granted for a specific purpose or limited period. "Official detention" means arrest, detention in any facility for custody of persons under charge or conviction of crime or alleged or found to be delinquent, detention for extradition or deportation, or any other detention for law enforcement purposes; but "official detention" does not include supervision of probation or parole, or constraint incidental to release on bail.

(2) *Permitting or Facilitating Escape.* A public servant concerned in detention commits an offense if he knowingly or recklessly permits an escape. Any person who knowingly causes or facilitates an escape commits an offense.

(3) *Effect of Legal Irregularity in Detention.* Irregularity in bringing about or maintaining detention, or lack of jurisdiction of the committing or detaining authority, shall not be a defense to prosecution under this Section if the escape is from a prison or other custodial facility or from detention pursuant to commitment by official proceedings. In the case of other detentions, irregularity or lack of jurisdiction shall be a defense only if:

(a) the escape involved no substantial risk of harm to the person or property of anyone other than the detainee; or

(b) the detaining authority did not act in good faith under color of law.

(4) *Grading of Offenses.* An offense under this Section is a felony of the third degree where:

(a) the actor was under arrest for or detained on a charge of felony or following conviction of crime; or

(b) the actor employs force, threat, deadly weapon or other dangerous instrumentality to effect the escape; or

(c) a public servant concerned in detention of persons convicted of crime purposely facilitates or permits an escape from a detention facility.

Otherwise an offense under this Section is a misdemeanor.

Article 243. Abuse of Office

Section 243.1.
Official Oppression.

A person acting or purporting to act in an official capacity or taking advantage of such actual or purported capacity commits a misdemeanor if, knowing that his conduct is illegal, he:

(1) subjects another to arrest, detention, search, seizure, mistreatment, dispossession, assessment, lien or other infringement of personal or property rights; or

(2) denies or impedes another in the exercise or enjoyment of any right, privilege, power or immunity.

OFFENSES AGAINST PUBLIC ORDER AND DECENCY
Article 250. Riot, Disorderly Conduct, and Related Offenses
Section 250.1.
Riot; Failure to Disperse.

(1) *Riot.* A person is guilty of riot, a felony of the third degree, if he participates with [two] or more others in a course of disorderly conduct:

(a) with purpose to commit or facilitate the commission of a felony or misdemeanor;

(b) with purpose to prevent or coerce official action; or

(c) when the actor or any other participant to the knowledge of the actor uses or plans to use a firearm or other deadly weapon.

(2) *Failure of Disorderly Persons to Disperse upon Official Order.* Where [three] or more persons are participating in a course of disorderly conduct likely to cause substantial harm or serious inconvenience, annoyance or alarm, a peace officer or other public servant engaged in executing or enforcing the law may order the participants and others in the immediate vicinity to disperse. A person who refuses or knowingly fails to obey such an order commits a misdemeanor.

Section 250.2.
Disorderly Conduct.

(1) *Offense Defined.* A person is guilty of disorderly conduct if, with purpose to cause public inconvenience, annoyance or alarm, or recklessly creating a risk thereof, he:

(a) engages in fighting or threatening, or in violent or tumultuous behavior; or

(b) makes unreasonable noise or offensively coarse utterance, gesture or display, or addresses abusive language to any person present; or

(c) creates a hazardous or physically offensive condition by any act which serves no legitimate purpose of the actor. "Public" means affecting or likely to affect persons in a place to which the public or a substantial group has access; among the places included are highways, transport facilities, schools, prisons, apartment houses, places of business or amusement, or any neighborhood.

(2) *Grading.* An offense under this section is a petty misdemeanor if the actor's purpose is to cause substantial harm or serious inconvenience, or if he persists in disorderly conduct after reasonable warning or request to desist. Otherwise disorderly conduct is a violation.

Section 250.3.
False Public Alarms.

A person is guilty of a misdemeanor if he initiates or circulates a report or warning of an impending bombing or other crime or catastrophe, knowing that the report or warning is false or baseless and that it is likely to cause evacuation of a building, place of assembly, or facility of public transport, or to cause public inconvenience or alarm.

Section 250.4.
Harassment.

A person commits a petty misdemeanor if, with purpose to harass another, he:

(1) makes a telephone call without purpose of legitimate communication; or

(2) insults, taunts or challenges another in a manner likely to provoke violent or disorderly response; or

(3) makes repeated communications anonymously or at extremely inconvenient hours, or in offensively coarse language; or

(4) subjects another to an offensive touching; or

(5) engages in any other course of alarming conduct serving no legitimate purpose of the actor.

Section 250.5.
Public Drunkenness; Drug Incapacitation.

A person is guilty of an offense if he appears in any public place manifestly under the influence of alcohol, narcotics or other drug, not therapeutically administered, to the degree that he may endanger himself or other persons or property, or annoy persons in his vicinity. An offense under this Section constitutes a petty misdemeanor if the actor has been convicted hereunder twice before within a period of one year. Otherwise the offense constitutes a violation.

Section 250.6.
Loitering or Prowling.

A person commits a violation if he loiters or prowls in a place, at a time, or in a manner not usual for law-abiding individuals under circumstances that warrant alarm for the safety of persons or property in the vicinity. Among the circumstances which may be considered in determining whether such alarm is warranted is the fact that the actor takes flight upon appearance of a peace officer, refuses to identify himself, or manifestly endeavors to conceal himself or any object. Unless flight by the actor or other circumstance makes it impracticable, a peace officer shall prior to any arrest for an offense under this section afford the actor an opportunity to dispel any alarm which would otherwise be warranted, by requesting him to identify himself and explain his presence and conduct. No person shall be convicted of an offense under this Section if the peace officer did not comply with the preceding sentence, or if it appears at trial that the explanation given by the actor was true and, if believed by the peace officer at the time, would have dispelled the alarm.

Section 250.7.
Obstructing Highways and Other Public Passages.

(1) A person, who, having no legal privilege to do so, purposely or recklessly obstructs any highway or other public passage, whether alone or with others,

commits a violation, or, in case he persists after warning by a law officer, a petty misdemeanor. "Obstructs" means renders impassable without unreasonable inconvenience or hazard. No person shall be deemed guilty of recklessly obstructing in violation of this Subsection solely because of a gathering of persons to hear him speak or otherwise communicate, or solely because of being a member of such a gathering.

(2) A person in a gathering commits a violation if he refuses to obey a reasonable official request or order to move:

(a) to prevent obstruction of a highway or other public passage; or

(b) to maintain public safety by dispersing those gathered in dangerous proximity to a fire or other hazard.

An order to move, addressed to a person whose speech or other lawful behavior attracts an obstructing audience, shall not be deemed reasonable if the obstruction can be readily remedied by police control of the size or location of the gathering.

Section 250.8.
Disrupting Meetings and Processions.

A person commits a misdemeanor if, with purpose to prevent or disrupt a lawful meeting, procession or gathering, he does any act tending to obstruct or interfere with it physically, or makes any utterance, gesture or display designed to outrage the sensibilities of the group.

Section 250.9.
Desecration of Venerated Objects.

A person commits a misdemeanor if he purposely desecrates any public monument or structure, or place of worship or burial, if he purposely desecrates the national flag or any other object of veneration by the public or a substantial segment thereof in any public place. "Desecrate" means defacing, damaging, polluting or otherwise physically mistreating in a way that the actor knows will outrage the sensibilities of persons likely to observe or discover his action.

Section 250.10.
Abuse of Corpse.

Except as authorized by law, a person who treats a corpse in a way that he knows would outrage ordinary family sensibilities commits a misdemeanor.

Section 250.11.
Cruelty to Animals.

A person commits a misdemeanor if he purposely or recklessly:

(1) subjects any animal to cruel mistreatment; or

(2) subjects any animal in his custody to cruel neglect; or

(3) kills or injures any animal belonging to another without legal privilege or consent of the owner.

Subsections (1) and (2) shall not be deemed applicable to accepted veterinary practices and activities carried on for scientific research.

Section 250.12.
Violation of Privacy.

(1) *Unlawful Eavesdropping or Surveillance.* A person commits a misdemeanor if, except as authorized by law, he:

(a) trespasses on property with purpose to subject anyone to eavesdropping or other surveillance in a private place; or

(b) installs in any private place, without the consent of the person or persons entitled to privacy there, any device for observing, photographing, recording, amplifying or broadcasting sounds or events in such place, or uses any such unauthorized installation; or

(c) installs or uses outside a private place any device for hearing, recording, amplifying or broadcasting sounds originating in such place which would not ordinarily be audible or comprehensible outside, without the consent of the person or persons entitled to privacy there. "Private place" means a place where one may reasonably expect to be safe from casual or hostile intrusion or surveillance, but does not include a place to which the public or a substantial group thereof has access.

(2) *Other Breach of Privacy of Messages.* A person commits a misdemeanor if, except as authorized by law, he:

(a) intercepts without the consent of the sender or receiver a message by telephone, telegraph, letter or other means of communicating privately; but this paragraph does not extend to (i) overhearing of messages through a regularly installed instrument on a telephone party line or on an extension, or (ii) interception by the telephone company or subscriber incident to enforcement of regulations limiting use of the facilities or incident to other normal operation and use; or

(b) divulges without the consent of the sender or receiver the existence or contents of any such message if the actor knows that the message was illegally intercepted, or if he learned of the message in the course of employment with an agency engaged in transmitting it.

Article 251. Public Indecency

Section 251.1.
Open Lewdness.

A person commits a petty misdemeanor if he does any lewd act which he knows is likely to be observed by others who would be affronted or alarmed.

Section 251.2.
Prostitution and Related Offenses.

(1) *Prostitution.* A person is guilty of prostitution, a petty misdemeanor, if he or she:

(a) is an inmate of a house of prostitution or otherwise engages in sexual activity as a business; or

(b) loiters in or within view of any public place for the purpose of being hired to engage in sexual activity.

"Sexual activity" includes homosexual and other deviate sexual relations. A "house of prostitution" is any place where prostitution or promotion of prostitution is regularly carried on by one person under the control, management or supervision of another. An "inmate" is a person who engages in prostitution in or through the agency of a house of prostitution. "Public place" means any place to which the public or any substantial group thereof has access.

(2) *Promoting Prostitution.* A person who knowingly promotes prostitution of another commits a misdemeanor or felony as provided in Subsection (3). The following acts shall without limitation of the foregoing, constitute promoting prostitution:

(a) owning, controlling, managing, supervising or otherwise keeping, alone or in association with others, a house of prostitution or a prostitution business; or

(b) procuring an inmate for a house of prostitution or a place in a house of prostitution for one who would be an inmate; or

(c) encouraging, inducing, or otherwise purposely causing another to become or remain a prostitute; or

(d) soliciting a person to patronize a prostitute; or

(e) procuring a prostitute for a patron; or

(f) transporting a person into or within this state with purpose to promote that person's engaging in prostitution, or procuring or paying for transportation with that purpose; or

(g) leasing or otherwise permitting a place controlled by the actor, alone or in association with others, to be regularly used for prostitution or the promotion of prostitution, or failure to make reasonable effort to abate such use by ejecting the tenant, notifying law enforcement authorities, or other legally available means; or

(h) soliciting, receiving, or agreeing to receive any benefit for doing or agreeing to do anything forbidden by this Subsection.

(3) *Grading of Offenses Under Subsection (2).* An offense under Subsection (2) constitutes a felony of the third degree if:

(a) the offense falls within paragraph (a) (b) or (c) of Subsection (2); or

(b) the actor compels another to engage in or promote prostitution; or

(c) the actor promotes prostitution of a child under 16, whether or not he is aware of the child's age; or

(d) the actor promotes prostitution of his wife, child, ward or any person for whose care, protection or support he is responsible. Otherwise the offense is a misdemeanor.

(4) *Presumption from Living off Prostitutes.* person, other than the prostitute or the prostitutes minor child or other legal dependent incapable of self-support, who is supported in whole or in substantial part by the proceeds of prostitution is presumed to be knowingly promoting prostitution in violation of Subsection *(2).*

(5) *Patronizing Prostitutes.* A person commits a violation if he hires a prostitute to engage in sexual activity with him, or if he enters or remains in a house of prostitution for the purpose of engaging in sexual activity.

(6) *Evidence.* On the issue whether a place is a house of prostitution the following shall be admissible evidence: its general repute; the repute of the persons who reside in or frequent the place; the frequency, timing and duration of visits by nonresidents. Testimony of a person against his spouse shall be admissible to prove offenses under this Section.

Section 251.3.
Loitering to Solicit Deviate Sexual Relations.

A person is guilty of a petty misdemeanor if he loiters in or near any public place for the purpose of soliciting or being solicited to engage in deviate sexual relations.

Section 251.4.
Obscenity.

(1) *Obscene Defined.* Material is obscene if, considered as a whole, its predominant appeal is to prurient interest, that is, a shameful or morbid interest, in nudity, sex or excretion, and if in addition it goes substantially beyond customary limits of candor in describing or representing such matters. Predominant appeal shall be judged with reference to ordinary adults unless it appears from the character of the material or the circumstances of its dissemination to be designed for children or other specially susceptible audience. Undeveloped photographs, molds, printing plates, and the like, shall be deemed obscene notwithstanding that processing or other acts may be required to make the obscenity patent or to disseminate it.

(2) *Offenses.* Subject to the affirmative defense provided in Subsection (3), a person commits a misdemeanor if he knowingly or recklessly:

(a) sells, delivers or provides, or offers or agrees to sell, deliver or provide, any obscene writing, picture, record or other representation or embodiment of the obscene; or

(b) presents or directs an obscene play, dance or performance, or participates in that portion thereof which makes it obscene; or

(c) publishes, exhibits or otherwise makes available any obscene material; or

(d) possesses any obscene material for purposes of sale or other commercial dissemination; or

(e) sells, advertises or otherwise commercially disseminates material, whether or not obscene, by representing or suggesting that it is obscene. A person who disseminates or possesses obscene material in the course of his business is presumed to do so knowingly or recklessly.

(3) *Justifiable and Non-Commercial Private Dissemination.* It is an affirmative defense to prosecution under this Section that dissemination was restricted to:

(a) institutions or persons having scientific, educational, governmental or other similar justification for possessing obscene material; or

(b) non-commercial dissemination to personal associates of the actor.

(4) *Evidence; Adjudication of Obscenity.* In any prosecution under this Section evidence shall be admissible to show:

(a) the character of the audience for which the material was designed or to which it was directed;

(b) what the predominant appeal of the material would be for ordinary adults or any special audience to which it was directed, and what effect, if any, it would probably have on conduct of such people;

(c) artistic, literary, scientific, educational or other merits of the material;

(d) the degree of public acceptance of the material in the United States;

(e) appeal to prurient interest, or absence thereof, in advertising or other promotion of the material; and

(f) the good repute of the author, creator, publisher or other person from whom the material originated.

Expert testimony and testimony of the author, creator, publisher or other person from whom the material originated, relating to factors entering into the determination of the issue of obscenity, shall be admissible. The Court shall dismiss a prosecution for obscenity if it is satisfied that the material is not obscene.

Appendix B

Culpability, Dangerousness and Harm: Balancing the Factors on Which Our Criminal Law Is Predicated[*]

Arnold H. Loewy

Classically, criminal law is thought to be predicated upon two factors, *mens rea* and *actus reus*, which literally mean "evil mind" and "bad act" respectively. The thesis of this Article is that three factors—culpability, dangerousness, and harm—rather than two—*mens rea* and *actus reus*—need to be balanced in order to assess one's criminal liability. Culpability, which is substantially subjective, refers to the defendant's moral blame, worthiness or state of mind. Dangerousness, which is more objective, focuses on the likelihood of harm emanating from the defendant's conduct. Harm is the actual negative consequence occasioned by the conduct. Although culpability and harm roughly approximate *mens rea* and *actus reus*, dangerousness has no corresponding Latin term. Yet, as this Article will establish, dangerousness is frequently the decisive factor in assessing criminal liability.

In the typical case there is no conflict among these factors. For example, when *A*, with the intent to kill, shoots *B* in the heart, killing *B*, *A* has manifested a culpable mind and a dangerous capacity by willfully inflicting the forbidden harm. More complex issues, however, divide judges, legislators, and theorists. Often, these involve nothing more than deciding how much weight ought to be given to each factor, when reliance on one factor would yield a result different from reliance on another factor.

The crime of assault is an ideal paradigm for demonstrating the relevance of each of these factors in assessing the seriousness of the crime. Consider the following eight hypotheticals:

(1) Alan intentionally pushes Barbara. Barbara hits the ground and suffers a few scratches.

(2) Carl intentionally pushes Deidra. Deidra's head hits the ground, causing brain damage.

---

[*] Originally published at 66 N.C. L. REV. 283 (1988). Reprinted with permission.

(3) Edna throws Frank out of the window, intending to seriously injure Frank. Frank suffers only a few minor scratches.

(4) Gertrude stabs Harold's leg with a knife. Harold suffers a minor cut.

(5) Iris stabs James' leg with a knife. James goes into shock and is hospitalized for a month.

(6) Kristen throws a knife at Linda's chest, intending to seriously injure Linda. Linda ducks and is not hit.

(7) Mark throws Norman out of the window, intending to seriously injure Norman. Norman suffers two broken legs and is confined to a wheelchair for three months.

(8) Olivia throws a knife at Paul's chest, intending to seriously injure Paul. Paul's lung is perforated.

In most jurisdictions, Alan's simple non-aggravated assault would be deemed the least serious assault.[1] Many jurisdictions would convict Carl, Edna, and Gertrude of aggravated assault.[2] Carl's assault differs from Alan's only in the amount of harm it caused. Carl is not more culpable than Alan, nor is he more dangerous.[3] Nevertheless, Carl is subject to condemnation for a more heinous offense, carrying a more severe sanction. Similarly, Edna, because of a culpable intent to cause serious injury, and Gertrude, by using a dangerous weapon, are subject to aggravated penalties. Because Gertrude's crime is aggravated by manifest dangerousness rather than culpability or harm, the fact that Gertrude intended and succeeded in inflicting on Harold the same harm that Alan inflicted on Barbara will not reduce Gertrude's criminal liability to Alan's level.

Iris, Kristen, and Mark each have committed assaults aggravated by two of the three factors. Iris' crime is aggravated by dangerousness and harm, Kristen's by dangerousness and culpability, and Mark's by culpability and harm. In some jurisdictions, the multiplicity of factors aggravate these crimes beyond the single aggravating factor present in Carl, Edna, and Gertrude's crimes.[4] Even in those juris-

---

1. The Model Penal Code deems mutual combat to be even less serious, classifying it as a petty misdemeanor. MODEL PENAL CODE § 211.1(1) (1962).

2. *See, e.g.,* D.C. CODE ANN. § 22-501 (1981); N.Y. PENAL LAW § 120. 10 (McKinney 1975); N.C. GEN. STAT. § 14-33 (b)(1) (1986); MODEL PENAL CODE § 211.1(2)(a), (b) (1962).

3. It would be possible for Deidra's brain damage to have been caused by Carl's unusual strength, which would make Carl more dangerous and — assuming that Carl knew of this strength — more culpable. This hypothetical, as well as the statutes that aggravate penalties for assaults on the basis of resulting injury, make no such assumption.

4. *See, e.g.,* KY. REV. STAT. ANN. §§ 508.010 to -.040 (Michie/Bobbs-Merrill 1 1986). N.C. GEN. STAT. § 14-32 (1981) provides:

(a) Any person who assaults another person with a deadly weapon with intent to kill and inflicts serious injury shall be punished as a Class F felon.

(b) Any person who assaults another person with a deadly weapon and inflicts serious injury shall be punished as a Class H felon.

dictions that maintain only one crime of aggravated assault, the presence of multiple factors is likely to exert an upward influence on the penalty imposed.[5] Olivia's crime, involving serious injury, dangerousness, and culpability, is likely to be punished most seriously either by statute or judicial discretion.

I. The Relevance of the Three Factors
A. Culpability

Hardly any theorist questions the relevance of culpability to criminality. One partial exception is Lady Barbara Wootton, a nonlawyer magistrate in England. In Lady Wootton's view the function of the criminal law ought to be preventive rather than punitive.[6] Consequently, she perceives culpability as relevant only insofar as it sheds light on dangerousness, the elimination or reduction of which she views as the overarching goal of the criminal law. Even under this approach, culpability is not altogether irrelevant. A defendant who is culpably bent on mischief—who, for example, kills another person—will take longer to "cure" than one who inadvertently does the same thing.[7] Nevertheless, this approach, which no court or legislature has adopted, would limit the relevancy of culpability to its impact on dangerousness.[8]

Although courts and legislatures usually require at least minimal culpability, such as criminal negligence, there are exceptions. The most common of these are public welfare offenses, such as marketing impure food or drugs. Eliminating the

---

(c) Any person who assaults another person with a deadly weapon with intent to kill shall be punished as a Class H felon.

Assaults aggravated by only one of the factors are punished less severely. N.C. Gen. Stat. § 14-33(b)(1) (1986) provides that a person is guilty of a misdemeanor punishable by a fine or imprisonment for not more than two years or both if, in the course of an assault, the person "[i]nflicts, or attempts to inflict, serious injury upon another person or uses a deadly weapon." An unaggravated simple assault in North Carolina is a "misdemeanor punishable by a fine not to exceed fifty dollars ($50.00) or imprisonment for not more than 30 days." *Id.* § 14-33(a).

5. *See, e.g.,* Ill. Rev. Stat. ch. 38, para. 12–2 (1982). In *People v. Simms,* 38 Ill. App. 3d 703, 348 N.E.2d 478 (1976), the Appellate Court of Illinois acknowledged that "[w]hile aggravated battery is a class III felony for which a minimum term of one year's imprisonment would be proper, the trial judge may set a longer term if, in his discretion, the nature and circumstances of the offense and the history and character of the defendant so warrant." *Id.* at 708, 348 N.E.2d at 482 (citations omitted). The appellate court found that the trial court did not abuse its discretion in setting a three-year sentence for an aggravated battery. Defendant, who used a deadly weapon, inflicted a serious injury and threatened to kill the victim. *Id.* at 708–09, 348 N.E.2d at 482–83; *see also People v. Holt,* 7 Ill. App. 3d 646, 656, 288 N.E.2d 245, 253 (1972) (trial court did not abuse discretion in sentencing defendant with no prior felony convictions to a term of one to ten years on an aggravated battery conviction, when defendant used a deadly weapon, inflicted serious injury, and manifested viciousness).

6. B. Wootton, Crime and The Criminal Law 40–41 (1963).

7. *Id.* at 49.

8. *Id.* at 58. For a critique of Lady Wootton's view, see Kadish, *The Decline of Innocence,* 26 Cambridge L.J. 273 (1968).

requirement of culpability is thought to be justified by the great harm that these substances cause, coupled with the relatively minor penalties authorized.[9] In short, concern for harm is so predominant in these crimes that culpability is rendered irrelevant. The Model Penal Code (M.P.C.) accepts strict liability under these circumstances only insofar as the offense is called a "violation" rather than a "crime" and has a penalty limited to a fine.[10] The M.P.C. would permit such "violations" to be treated as "crimes" when the State is able to establish at least minimal culpability beyond a reasonable doubt.[11]

Although no other type of crime entirely lacks the culpability requirement, some elements of crimes are defined exclusively in terms of harm or dangerousness, thereby rendering culpability irrelevant. For example, grand larceny may be defined as the theft of property worth at least five hundred dollars. Under such a statute, it is no defense that the thief acted on the reasonable belief that the property was worth less than five hundred dollars.[12] Similarly, a nighttime burglar who acts on the honest and reasonable but mistaken belief that it is daytime will be convicted of nighttime burglary.[13] In these cases, the subordination of culpability to harm (larceny) or dangerousness (burglary) is deemed proper because of the culpability inherent in the basic larcenous or burglarious state of mind. Essentially, this type of case is analytically identical to assault inflicting serious injury—that is, a crime aggravated by harm rather than culpability.

The victim's age in statutory rape is a much more dubious element from which to eliminate culpability. In many jurisdictions, one need only have sexual intercourse with a person who is a minor to be convicted for statutory rape.[14] The only intent required is the intent to have intercourse. The age of the minor is merely a circumstance, like the amount stolen or the time of the burglary in the above hypotheticals. So long as sex outside of marriage is criminal, a rough sort of analogy to these hypotheticals is plausible. When such sex is not criminal, and arguably not even immoral,[15] it seems impossible to condemn an intent to have consensual sex with an

---

9. *See Morrissette v. United States*, 342 U.S. 246 (1952).

10. MODEL PENAL CODE §2.05(2)(a) (1962).

11. *Id.* §2.05(2)(b). For a discussion of the burden of proof problem, see *infra* notes 41–50 and accompanying text.

12. "[I]t is the value of the property taken, not the thief's estimate of its worth, which governs." W. LAFAVE & A. SCOTT, CRIMINAL LAW §8.4, at 719 (2d ed. 1986). Thus, one who steals a valuable necklace believing it to be costume jewelry is guilty of grand larceny. *Id.* at 719 n.17; *see Hedge v. State*, 89 Tex. Crim. 236, 229 S.W. 862 (1921). The *Hedge* court, in affirming a larceny conviction, stated that "the degree of guilt is determined by the value of the property actually taken, not by what he thought or intended as to its value or the amount so taken." *Id.* at 240, 229 S.W. at 864; *cf. People v. Earle*, 222 Cal. App. 2d 476, 35 Cal. Rptr. 265 (1963) (defendant's knowledge of money bag contents at time he took it held not necessary for grand theft conviction).

13. W. LAFAVE & A. SCOTT, *supra* note 12, §8.13(d).

14. *E.g., Commonwealth v. Murphy*, 165 Mass. 66, 42 N.E. 504 (1895).

15. According to Kinsey, nearly 50% of the females and 85% of the males surveyed in 1951 had had coitus before marriage. A. KINSEY, W. POMEROY, C. MARTIN & P. GEBHARD, SEXUAL BEHAVIOR

adult as a culpable state of mind. Some modern statutes excuse those who honestly and reasonably believe they are copulating with an adult.[16] The statutes that do not must either be predicated on the immorality of nonmarital sex, thereby requiring such "deviants" to ensure absolutely that their age assessment of each partner is correct,[17] or be rationalized as strict liability statutes with extraordinarily stringent penalties.[18]

The willingness of some states to focus entirely on harm to the exclusion of culpability in bigamy prosecutions[19] is even harder to explain. The law usually regards the intent of a single person to marry as honorable.[20] Thus, a person who honestly and reasonably believes her spouse to be divorced or deceased when contracting the bigamous marriage has acted with praiseworthy intentions. One rationale for excluding culpability seems to be that the integrity of marriage is so fundamental that when it is compromised by bigamy, we cannot pause to consider such matters as intent.[21] Another rationale is that so long as a person was once married, that person is aware of the possibility that the prior spouse is not divorced or deceased.[22] For this reason, even courts that impose strict liability for bigamous marriages will not impose such liability on the previously unmarried partner who was unaware that her apparent spouse ever had a different spouse.[23] Needless to say, such small regard for culpability in bigamy cases has not met with universal approval.[24]

IN THE HUMAN FEMALE 286 (1953). There is no reason to believe that these figures have diminished since the time of that survey.

16. *E.g.*, KY. REV. STAT. ANN. § 510.030 (Michie/Bobbs-Merrill 1985); *cf. People v. Hernandez*, 61 Cal. 2d 529, 535–36, 393 P.2d 673, 677–78, 39 Cal. Rptr. 361, 365 (1964) (judicial rejection of liability when defendant made an honest and reasonable mistake of age).

17. *Cf. Regina v. Prince*, 13 Cox Crim. Cas. (Crim. App. 1875) (no defense to abduction charge that defendant reasonably and in good faith believed abducted girl was older than 16).

18. *See, e.g., Commonwealth v. Murphy*, 165 Mass. 66, 69, 42 N.E. 504, 504 (1895) (court defers to legislative intent of treating statutory rape as a strict liability offense and providing a punishment as severe as that for second degree murder).

19. *See, e.g., Turner v. State*, 212 Miss. 590, 55 So. 2d 228 (1951).

20. The United States Supreme Court has referred to marriage "as creating the most important relation in life, as having more to do with the morals and civilization of a people than any other institution. . . ." *Maynard v. Hill*, 125 U.S. 190, 205 (1888).

21. *State v. Goonan*, 89 N.H. 528, 529, 3 A.2d 105, 106 (1938). The New Hampshire Supreme Court opined that "had it been the intention of the Legislature to include in the list of exceptions any person entertaining a reasonable belief that he has been legally divorced, it is unlikely, in view of 'the public concern for the stability of marriage,' that such legislative purpose would have been left to implication." *Id.* (quoting *Heath v. Heath*, 85 N.H. 419, 428, 159 A. 418, 422 (1932)).

22. *See Braun v. State*, 230 Md. 82, 185 A.2d 905 (1962).

23. *See, e.g.*, State v. Audette, 81 Vt. 400, 404, 70 A. 833, 834 (1908).

24. *E.g.*, IOWA CODE ANN. § 726.1 (West 1979); KY. REV. STAT. ANN. § 30.010(2) (Michie/Bobbs-Merrill 1985); ME. REV. STAT. ANN. tit. 17-A, § 51 (1964); MICH. STAT. ANN. §§ 28.694, 28.695 (Callaghan 1982); NEV. REV. STAT. § 201.170 (1979); *see also People v. Vogel*, 46 Cal. 2d 798, 801, 299 P.2d 850, 852–53 (1956) (wrongful intent required for bigamy conviction).

B. Dangerousness

So long as culpability is present, most authorities regard dangerousness as an aggravating factor. There is virtually no support, however—Lady Wootton excepted[25]—for convicting a dangerous but not culpable offender. To take the M.P.C.'s classic hypothetical, a man who, through no fault of his own, believed he was squeezing lemons rather than his wife's neck would not be guilty of murder.[26] He would, of course, be subject to civil commitment. When a mentally deranged, but not legally insane, defendant commits a crime, there is some question as to whether his condition mitigates or aggravates his liability. Some statutes, relying on diminished culpability, mitigate liability.[27] Others, including the M.P.C., rely on dangerousness to aggravate liability.[28]

C. Harm

The relevance of harm is probably the most disputed of the three criteria. Most statutes vary criminal liability greatly according to whether and what kind of harm occurred.[29] The M.P.C., with considerable vacillation, sometimes regards harm as relevant[30] and sometimes does not.[31] Professor Paul Robinson believes that harm is a *sine qua non* of criminal liability.[32] Professor Steven Schulhofer, on the other hand,

---

25. *See* B. Wootton, *supra* note 6, at 54; *supra* text accompanying notes 6–8.

26. Model Penal Code § 4.01 comment at 156 (Tent. Draft No. 4, 1953); *id.* § 4.01 comment at 166 (1962).

27. *See, e.g.*, Fla. Stat. § 921.141(2)(b) (1984); N.C. Gen. Stat. § 15A-1340.4(2)(e) (1984); Pa. Cons. Stat. § 971 l(e)(2), (3) (1986).

28. Model Penal Code § 4.01 (1962); *see, e.g.*, Ill. Ann. Stat. ch. 38, para. 6-2 (SmithHurd 1972 & Supp. 1986) (following Model Penal Code rule).

29. For example, an attempt is usually punished less severely than a completed crime. In Alabama, felonies are classified as A, B, or C. The sentence for class A felonies is life or not more than 99 years or less than 10 years; for class B, not more than 20 years or less than two years; for class C, not more than 10 years or less than one year and a day. Ala. Code § 13A-5-6 (1982). Alabama law provides that the attempted crime is punishable as one class lower than that of the crime itself. Id. § 13A-4-2 (1975). Other states have similar statutes. *See, e.g.*, Ky. Rev. Stat. Ann. § 56.010 (Michie/Bobbs-Merrill 1985); Ohio Rev. Code Ann. § 2923.02(E) (Anderson 1982 & Supp. 1986).

30. For instance, reckless endangerment (recklessly engaging in conduct that places another person in danger of death or serious bodily injury) is a misdemeanor. Model Penal Code § 211.2 (1962). If such conduct actually causes death, however, it is punished as a second-degree felony. *Id.* § 210.3. Risking catastrophe is a misdemeanor, *id.* § 220.2(2), but actually causing catastrophe is a second-degree felony. *Id.* § 220.2(l).

31. The Model Penal Code establishes a general rule that attempt, solicitation, and conspiracy are crimes of the same degree of the most serious offense that is attempted or solicited or is an object of the conspiracy. *Id.* § 5.05(l). Importantly, the Code does not distinguish between conspiracies that are actually carried out and those that are not, or between solicitation that actually results in the commission of a crime and solicitation that does not. *Id.* §§ 5.02–5.03. As an exception to the general rule, the Code provides that an attempt, solicitation, or conspiracy to commit a felony of the first degree is a felony of the second degree. *Id.* § 5.05(l).

32. Robinson, A *Theory of Justification: Societal Harm as a Prerequisite Criminal Liability*, 23 UCLA L. Rev. 266, 266–75 (1975).

contends that harm never should be relevant in assessing criminal liability.[33] As one might suspect, neither of these views has been completely embraced by the courts.

According to Professor Robinson, one never ought to be liable for an evil mind or dangerous behavior, so long as the end result was justifiable. For example, assume that *A*, a Ku Klux Klan member, devises a plan to burn the farms of twenty-five farmers (*B* through *Z*), all of whom are black. Upon his arrest for burning *B*'s farm, a diary containing the plan for burning the remaining farms is discovered. It is also discovered that, unbeknownst to *A*, the burning of *B*'s farm was necessary to start a backfire which successfully contained a raging forest fire that would have destroyed the farms of *C* through *Z*, had it not been contained. Because burning *B*'s farm in order to save the other twenty-four is justifiable, Robinson would not allow *A* to be convicted of arson.[34]

Although most authorities would impose liability in the above hypothetical,[35] they do so on the ground that harmful physical consequence actually occurred—*i.e.*, *B*'s farm was burned. In cases in which the unknown factor totally negates harm, liability usually is not imposed. Thus, if *C* takes *D*'s car, not knowing that *D* already has transferred the car to *C*'s name, *C* will not be convicted of larceny.[36] Similarly, if *E* surreptitiously enters *F*'s room while *F* is sleeping and has sexual intercourse with *F*, which much to *E*'s surprise pleases *F*, *E* will not be guilty of rape.[37] Consequently, Robinson's view of the indispensability of harm is only slightly overstated.

Professor Schulhofer's view that harm should be irrelevant to criminality is almost universally rejected, at least by the courts.[38] According to this view, one who intentionally pushes another, thereby causing brain damage, should be treated identically with one who pushes another causing a few scratches.[39] Similarly, one who throws a knife at another intending to inflict serious injury should receive the same treatment whether the knife perforates the victim's lung, misses entirely, or kills the

---

33. Schulhofer, *Harm and Punishment: A Critique of Emphasis on the Results of Conduct in the Criminal Law*, 122 U. PA. L. REV. 1497 (1974).

34. Robinson, *supra* note 32, at 272. Robinson's hypothetical is not embellished with racial motivation. He leaves open the possibility of attempt liability but seems to oppose it.

35. Even Robinson concedes this point. Robinson, *supra* note 32, at 288. According to LaFave and Scott, lack of knowledge of the justifying circumstances will bar a defense of justification. *See* W. LAFAVE & A. SCOTT, *supra* note 12, §3.6(a), at 230; *id.* §5.4(d), at 446.

36. *See* Fletcher, *The Right Deed for the Wrong Reason: A Reply to Mr. Robinson*, 23 UCLA L. REV. 293, 295 (1976).

37. He may, however, be guilty of attempted rape depending on the jurisdiction's view of impossibility. *Compare United States v. Thomas*, 13 C.M.A. 278, 32 C.M.R. 27 (1962) (fact that female with whom defendants had sexual intercourse was dead at the time of intercourse is no bar to conviction of attempted rape) *with State v. Guffey*, 262 S.W.2d 152 (Mo. Ct. App. 1953) (as basis for its holding that defendants who shot stuffed deer in field could not be convicted of attempt to take deer out of season, court noted that it is no crime to attempt to murder a human corpse because a corpse cannot be murdered).

38. Indeed, Schulhofer wrote the article to change the law. *See* Schulhofer, *supra* note 33, at 1503.

39. This hypothetical assumes that the pushes were equally hard and with the same intent.

victim. The rationale for this punishment apportionment scheme is the fortuity of harm occurring and its consequent irrelevance to culpability.[40]

To the extent that culpability ought to be the sole criterion in assessing criminality, Schulhofer would undoubtedly be correct. At bottom, the question is one of fairness. Is it fair to allow a factor unrelated to culpability to affect one's liability? Unfortunately, there is no *a priori* answer. One could just as easily ask whether fairness permits a punishment differential on the basis of culpability or dangerousness when two people cause identical harm—for example, one person causes brain damage with a push while another causes brain damage by a blow to the head with a rock. Few, if any, jurisdictions are troubled by aggravating a crime for any of these reasons.

One factor supporting the persistent retention of harm as a relevant factor in criminal sanctions may be that it mirrors life. Consider the following hypotheticals: A calls his boss, B, a jerk; B fires A. C calls D, her boss, a jerk; D starts a dialogue with C to find the reason for C's opinion. Ultimately D develops different characteristics and promotes C. E uses cocaine and dies from it. F uses cocaine and has a pleasant evening. Obviously, the list could be multiplied.

Suffice it to say, the world is full of instances in which equally culpable people wind up very differently. Consequently, it should not be surprising that one who chances driving while drunk and kills somebody will be dealt with more harshly than a drunk who wins his gamble and gets home safely or is stopped for drunk driving before a victim is killed. Similarly, one whose thrown knife kills another simply loses as compared to a similar knife thrower who misses the victim.

II. Problems of Proof

Having introduced the relevance of the three factors—culpability, dangerousness, and harm—I will shortly explore how many of the most divisive issues in criminal law involve a balancing of these factors, and how one's ultimate view of the correct resolution will depend on the relative importance attached to each of these factors.[41] First, I will focus on the problem of proof of facts, a problem which often silently underlies criminal law doctrine.

Frequently, we are convinced beyond a reasonable doubt that a particular defendant caused substantial harm, but are not convinced beyond a reasonable doubt that the defendant acted with a culpable state of mind. Under classic Anglo-American jurisprudence, such a defendant should be acquitted. Hardly any principle is more dear to the hearts of those who defend our criminal justice system than our willingness to acquit a guilty person rather than convict one who is innocent.

---

40. *See* Schulhofer, *supra* note 33, at 1577–80.

41. *See infra* notes 51–185 and accompanying text.

Consequently, our Constitution forbids conviction unless the State can prove every element of the crime beyond a reasonable doubt.[42]

Ascertaining what constitutes an element is an exercise in constitutional schizophrenia. For example, we believe that one should not be convicted of a crime without a culpable state of mind. We also believe that insanity, however defined, negates culpability.[43] Yet the Supreme Court permits insanity to be treated as a defense rather than an element, thereby allowing the burden of proof to be shifted to the defendant.[44] Most states have chosen to shift the burden on this issue,[45] thereby rendering it possible to convict a person even when the jury is not satisfied that the person possesses the requisite culpability for the crime.

The Supreme Court's criteria for permitting the burden of proof to be shifted is unclear at best and downright bizarre at worst.[46] For this and other reasons, certain aspects of culpability are sometimes made irrelevant. For example, such matters as insufficient sobriety to know what one is doing,[47] reasonable belief that one's sex partner is an adult,[48] and extreme care to prevent the distribution of impure food[49] usually will not exculpate the defendant. Even if the burden could be shifted on these issues,[50] some states would disallow the defense for at least two reasons. First, there is a danger that the jury would believe the defense even if it were not true. For example, if a drunk who could not remember the incident testified to that lack of

---

42. *Mullaney v. Wilbur*, 421 U.S. 684 (1975); *In re Winship*, 397 U.S. 358 (1970).

43. *See infra* notes 51-82 and accompanying text.

44. *See, e.g.*, Rivera v. Delaware, 429 U.S. 877 (1976); Leland v. Oregon, 343 U.S. 790 (1952).

45. *E.g.*, ILL. REV. STAT. ch. 38, para. 6-2(e) (1986); IND. CODE § 35-41-4-1 (1985); WIS. STAT. § 971.15(3) (1985).

46. In *Mullaney*, 421 U.S. 684 (1975), the Court held that because Maine defined malice aforethought as an essential element of murder, the prosecution must prove the absence of provocation beyond a reasonable doubt. In *Patterson v. New York*, 432 U.S. 197 (1977), the Court held that in New York the prosecution did not have to prove the lack of extreme emotional disturbance, which is the mitigating factor for manslaughter in New York. Commentators, regardless of persuasion, find the two cases inconsistent because the laws in the two cases are substantively equivalent. Some commentators contend that the State should be required to prove every element, including the absence of any mitigating, excusing, or justifying factors. *E.g.*, Underwood, *The Thumb on the Scales of Justice: Burdens of Persuasion in Criminal Cases*, 86 YALE L.J. 1299 (1976). To allow convictions on less would violate the presumption of innocence. Other commentators contend that the State should only be required to prove all factors necessary to establish a constitutionally sufficient basis to convict and punish the defendant, and that if the State wishes to provide a defense beyond what is constitutionally required it should be allowed to shift the burden of proof to the defendant on that issue. *E.g.*, Allen, *The Restoration of In re Winship: A Comment on Burdens of Persuasion in Criminal Cases After* Patterson v. New York, 76 MICH. L. REV. 30 (1977); *see* Jeffries & Stephan, *Defenses, Presumptions, and Burden of Proof in the Criminal Law*, 88 YALE L.J. 1325 (1979). Underwood supports *Mullaney* and opposes *Patterson*, while Allen supports *Patterson* and opposes *Mullaney*.

47. *See infra* notes 83-101 and accompanying text.

48. *See supra* notes 14–18 and accompanying text.

49. *See supra* text accompanying notes 9–11.

50. There is good reason to think that the burden could be shifted. *See Martin v. Ohio*, 107 S. Ct. 1098 (1987); *Patterson v. New York*, 432 U.S. 197, 207–09 (1977); *supra* note 45 (citing statutes).

memory, a jury might wrongly conclude that absence of memory was tantamount to absence of intent. To prevent this possibility of error, such issues simply are made irrelevant. Second, apart from jury error, the mere possibility of a defense may encourage some to be less careful in the mistaken belief they will be able to persuade a jury that they acted with due care. A man who has sex with an under-age girl may think he can persuade a jury that he reasonably believed her to be of age, and a woman who fails to inspect the purity of the food her company sells may believe she can persuade a jury that she made the requisite inspections. Even if these beliefs are false, the presence of the defense coupled with the uncertainty of the fact-ascertainment process creates something of an incentive to take the risk. Consequently, by withdrawing the defense, this incentive is also withdrawn.

III. Balancing the Factors

This section will explore nine of the most controversial issues in substantive criminal law today: insanity, intoxication, state of mind necessary for rape, state of mind necessary for assault with intent to commit rape, self-defense, provocation, unintentional killings, felony murder, and inchoate criminality. Each section will focus on the conflict among the three factors, and the reasons for placing decisive weight on one factor over another.

A. Insanity

Insanity, which is seldom employed in cases other than murder,[51] balances dangerousness and harm on the one side against culpability on the other. In the extreme case, the resolution is easy. The M.P.C.'s "lemon squeezer"[52] would not be convicted. Despite the extraordinary dangerousness of a person who cannot tell the difference between a lemon and his wife's neck, the total absence of culpability in such a case precludes resort to the criminal law. Such cases, however, are extremely rare. Few psychiatrists have ever seen a "lemon squeezer."[53] Even if we found one, it is unlikely that such a person would be mentally competent to stand trial.[54]

In the real world, the killer knows the difference between a lemon and his wife's neck, and knows that by squeezing her neck he will kill her. His defense usually is that he did not know it was wrong (M'Naghten),[55] he had an irresistible impulse to do it,[56] or he lacked substantial capacity either to appreciate the criminality of his conduct or to conform his conduct to the criminal law (M.P.C.).[57] In each of these cases, the defendant, by intentionally killing another human being, has manifested

---

51. *See* S. HALLECK, PSYCHIATRY AND THE DILEMMAS OF CRIME 216 (1967).
52. MODEL PENAL CODE § 4.01 comment at 156 (Tent. Draft No. 4, 1953); *id.* § 4.01 comment at 166 (1957); *see supra* text accompanying note 26.
53. *See* S. HALLECK, *supra* note 51, at 213.
54. This would not be the case, of course, if the person regained sanity prior to trial.
55. M'Naghten's Case, 8 Eng. Rep. 718 (1843).
56. *United States v. Kunak*, 5 C.M.A. 346 (1954).
57. MODEL PENAL CODE § 4.01(l) (1962).

some culpability to accompany his dangerousness and harm. Consequently, some jurisdictions have abolished the insanity defense entirely—except for those who, like the "lemon squeezer," lack the intent to kill[58]—or added a verdict of guilty but mentally ill.[59]

Jurisdictions that retain the insanity defense differ in the amount of culpability required for criminal liability, and range from a strict reading of *M'Naghten's Case*[60] to an expansive reading of the M.P.C. Under the most stringent view of *M'Naghten*, only those individuals who totally lack the capacity to understand that the law forbids murder would have a defense. These individuals are very nearly as scarce as "lemon squeezers" and just about as likely to be incompetent to stand trial.[61] The only practical difference between jurisdictions with such a stringent test and those that have abolished the insanity defense entirely is that the strict *M'Naghten* jurisdictions give the jury the opportunity to nullify the law by acquitting a defendant in what it perceives to be an especially compelling case.[62] As the test becomes more liberal, defendants with relatively more culpability will be acquitted.[63] The question becomes: How much culpability should we demand before a dangerous killer can be condemned as a murderer?

One means of liberalizing the strict *M'Naghten* test is to limit liability to those defendants who are capable of emotionally appreciating the illegality of their conduct as opposed to those whose capacities are limited to an intellectual understanding of it.[64] Another closely related device is to limit liability to those who can understand or appreciate the moral, as opposed to legal, wrongness of their acts.[65] Under this standard, one who appreciates the illegality of killing his wife, but because of an insane delusion believes that God commanded him to kill her, would not be guilty of any crime. Those supporting such expansions of the defense argue that unless one appreciates the moral wrongness of one's conduct, culpability is insufficient to impose criminal sanctions.[66] Those opposed contend that such highly dangerous people, who are not deterred by a common sense of morality, need

---

58. *E.g.*, IDAHO CODE § 18-207 (Supp. 1987).

59. *E.g.*, ALASKA STAT. § 12.47.030(a) (1984); GA. CODE ANN. § 17-7-131-(c)(2) (Supp. 1987); MICH. STAT. ANN. § 28.1059 (Callaghan 1985).

60. 8 Eng. Rep. 718 (1843).

61. *See* Diamond, *Criminal Responsibility of the Mentally Ill*, 14 STAN. L. REV. 59, 60–61 (1961).

62. Examples include killings which run contrary to our expectations, such as a mother killing her child. This ethic may explain in part the success of the defense in political killings or attempted killings from *Regina v. Hadfield*, 2 All E.R. 765 (1954), and *M'Naghten*, 8 Eng. Rep. 718 (1843), through United *States v. Hinckley*, 525 F. Supp. 1342 (D.D.C. 1981), in which the court held that [o]nly an insane person would want to kill our President." Hinckley, however, was exculpated under a very different test. *See infra* text accompanying notes 69–72.

63. This result assumes that jurors will follow instructions. Some evidence indicates that they do not. H. KALVEN & H. ZEISEL, THE AMERICAN JURY (1966).

64. *See* Zilboorg, *Misconceptions of Legal Insanity*, 9 AM. J. ORTHOPSYCHIATRY 540, 552 (1939).

65. *Id.*

66. *See* J. SMITH & B. HOGAN, CRIMINAL LAW 175 (5th ed. 1983).

to know that their failure to adhere to the criminal law (which they intellectually understand) will result in severe sanctions.[67]

Under *M'Naghten*, in any form, one who fully understands the immorality of his conduct but lacks capacity to control it has no defense. Much of the criticism of *M'Naghten* is predicated on this total emphasis on cognition.[68] Some jurisdictions responded by superimposing on *M'Naghten* an irresistible impulse test under which one who knew right from wrong but had an irresistible impulse to do wrong could not be punished.[69] Some think that this test still convicts too many nonculpable or marginally culpable people, because in some forms it is only available to those who would have acted the same "with a policeman at the elbow."[70] Others contend that the test potentially could free too many dangerous and culpable defendants, and argue that it is essentially circular because the only measure of the irresistibility of the impulse is whether or not it was resisted.[71] Obviously, this problem is exacerbated in those jurisdictions that require the State to prove resistibility beyond a reasonable doubt. For one or the other of these reasons, most jurisdictions currently reject the irresistible impulse test in favor of either the more stringent *M'Naghten* test or the more liberal standards of the M.P.C.[72]

Support for the M.P.C. test, requiring substantial capacity both to appreciate the criminality of one's conduct and to conform such conduct to the criminal law, comes from those who believe that too many nonculpable people are convicted under the other tests. Those opposed to the test worry about the number of highly dangerous and somewhat culpable people who may totally escape liability under it, particularly when the Government must prove substantial capacity beyond a reasonable doubt. As Seymour Halleck once mused in reference to the *Hinckley* case, which was decided in a jurisdiction that required the Government to prove substantial capacity beyond a reasonable doubt: "How can anyone prove the substantial capacity to control anything of a defendant who believes that Jodie Foster will fall in love with him if only he would assassinate the President?"[73]

All of these tests are complicated by at least two factors. The first is the all-or-nothing nature of the insanity defense: the killer is either on one side of the line

---

67. *See* W. LaFave & A. Scott, *supra* note 12, § 4.1 (c)(4).

68. *See Durham v. United States*, 214 F.2d 862, 875–76 (1954); Model Penal Code § 4.01 comment at 156–57 (Tent. Draft No. 4, 1953); *id.* § 4.01 comment at 166–67 (1962).

69. *See, e.g.*, Colo. Rev. Stat. § 16-8-101 (1973) (amended to strict *M'Naghten* rule in 1986); Ga. Code Ann. § 16-3-2 to -3 (1984).

70. *United States v. Kunak*, 5 C.M.A. 346, 359 (1954).

71. Waite, *Irresistible Impulse and Criminal Liability*, 23 Mich. L. Rev. 443, 454 (1925).

72. Model Penal Code § 4.01 & commentaries at 168 (1962). Colorado now applies the strict *M'Naghten* test, which inquires whether the defendant is "incapable of distinguishing right from wrong." Colo. Rev. Stat. § 16-8-101 (1986). Delaware rejected the irresistible impulse test in favor of the liberal M.P.C. test, which inquires whether "the accused lacked substantial capacity to appreciate

73. Dr. Seymour Halleck, Remarks at the University of North Carolina School of Law (Nov. 4, 1986). Dr. Halleck credits Dr. Allen Stone as the inspiration for his remark.

in which case there is no liability, or on the other side in which case there is full liability.[74] In fact, most people who kill without justification are probably somewhat mentally disturbed. Indeed, increasing evidence indicates that such behavior frequently can be traced to such physical abnormalities as the XYY chromosome,[75] premenstrual syndrome,[76] or a brain with a damaged frontal lobe.[77] Consequently, any but the most stringent insanity tests tend to make a monumental decision rest on a microscopic distinction.[78]

The other complicating factor is the uncertainty of extensive civil commitment. A convicted murderer who is not executed usually will receive life imprisonment. Although parole is sometimes possible, the public is guaranteed the protection of a substantial prison term. Civil commitment of the insanity acquittee is less certain. Many jurisdictions require civil commitment,[79] but some do not.[80] Even if incarcerated, a civil detainee, because she has not been convicted of a crime, is entitled to release after convincing a court that she is no longer the wrongfulness of his conduct or lacked sufficient willpower to choose whether he would do the act or refrain from doing it." DEL. CODE. ANN. tit. 11, §401 (1974).[81] Consequently, the public knows that a person who has been found beyond a reasonable doubt to have intentionally killed another human being can be freed as soon as the killer or his smart lawyer can persuade a judge that the killer is no longer dangerous. Although statistics seem to indicate this problem is more theoretical than real,[82] a populace concerned with even this theoretical possibility is not likely to turn dangerous killers away from the apparent certainty of the criminal justice system. This factor, along with the *Hinckley* acquittal, may explain the current trend towards minimizing the insanity defense.

---

74. In some jurisdictions, insanity may be relevant to prove lack of premeditation. However, unless premeditation has to be meaningful and mature—as it once was in California, *see* People v. Wolff, 61 Cal. 2d 795, 394 P.2d 959, 40 Cal. Rptr. 271 (1964), but no longer is, *see* CAL. PENAL CODE § 189 (West 1970 & Supp. 1986)—it is not likely to make much difference. In any event, if the defendant actually did premeditate, his mental condition would be irrelevant to that issue. If he did not premeditate, he would not be guilty of premeditated murder anyway. Indeed, those jurisdictions that do not permit insanity to negate premeditation when it in fact does negate it actually use insanity to aggravate liability.

75. W. LAFAVE & A. SCOTT, *supra* note 12, §4.8, at 377–82.

76. Press, *Pre-Menstrual Stress Syndrome as a Defense in Criminal Cases*, 1983 DUKE L.J. 176.

77. Krieger, *What Makes People Kill?*, CHAPEL HILL NEWSPAPER, July 6, 1986, at 9E, col. I (originally printed in SAN FRANCISCO EXAMINER).

78. This consequence perhaps explains Lady Wootton's willingness to abolish principles of culpability entirely. *See supra* text accompanying notes 6–8.

79. *E.g.*, COLO. REV. STAT. § 16-8-105 (4) (1978); DEL. CODE ANN. tit. 11, §403 (1984); ME. REV. STAT. ANN. tit. 15, § 103 (1964).

80. *E.g.*, ALA. CODE § 15-16-41 (1975); MICH. STAT. ANN. § 14.800 (1050) (Callaghan 1980).

81. *E.g.*, COLO. REV. STAT. § 16-8-120 (1978); DEL. CODE ANN. tit. 11, §403 (1984); ME. REV. STAT. ANN. tit. 15, § 104 (1964).

82. S. SHAW, W. CURRAN & L. McGARRY, CRIMINAL RESPONSIBILITY IN FORENSIC PSYCHOLOGY AND PSYCHOLOGY EXHIBITS 186–87 (1986).

B. Intoxication

Intoxication, like insanity, balances dangerousness and harm against culpability. Even more than with insanity, courts facing an intoxication defense tend to subordinate culpability to dangerousness. For example, a defendant who kills another while so inebriated or drugged that he thinks he is squeezing a lemon rather than a human neck will usually be guilty of murder[83] or manslaughter.[84] Similarly, a drunk who swings a baseball bat at another's head, either unaware of what he is doing or believing the head to be a baseball, will be convicted of assault.[85] Only those who become intoxicated involuntarily are likely to escape liability.[86]

Usually such expansive liability is predicated on the concept of general intent crimes. Black-letter law classically provides that intoxication, regardless of how extreme, cannot negate general intent.[87] Frequently, instead of defining general intent, courts use it simply as an epithet to justify convicting the lemon squeezer or baseball batter.[88] Courts that do attempt a definition often define a general intent crime as one requiring no particular state of mind.[89] As a consequence, because there is no particular state of mind to be negated, it matters not that the defendant thought he was squeezing lemons, hitting home runs, or not thinking at all. The difficulty with such analysis, of course, is that it simply is not correct. Although jurisdictions vary with regard to the state of mind required for murder, manslaughter, or assault, they all require some sort of culpability. For example, no jurisdiction would convict a golfer of assault if the golf ball he hit accidentally hit a passerby whose presence was not reasonably apparent to the golfer. Thus, it follows that some particular state of mind is required even for general intent crimes.

Justice Traynor of the California Supreme Court developed a somewhat more plausible theory to explain the irrelevance of intoxication to a crime such as assault with a dangerous weapon. Traynor opined that a drunk man is capable of forming

---

83. *See State v. Hall*, 214 N.W.2d 205 (Iowa 1974) (defendant found guilty despite drug-induced hallucination that he was shooting dog).

84. *See, e.g., Regina v. Lipman*, 3 All E.R. 410 (1969) (defendant convicted of manslaughter after killing victim while "tripping" on LSD).

85. *D.P.P. v. Majewski*, 2 All E.R. 142 (1976); People v. Hood, 1 Cal. 3d 444, 462 P.2d 370, 82 Cal. Rptr. 618 (1969).

86. Involuntary intoxication occurs when the defendant is unaware that he has ingested an intoxicant or has been forced to ingest it. Sometimes pathological intoxication is deemed involuntary. Pathological intoxication occurs when a person without knowledge of any peculiar susceptibility becomes grossly more intoxicated than would normally occur from the amount of intoxicant ingested.

87. W. LaFave & A. Scott, *supra* note 12, §4.10(a), at 389–90.

88. *See, e.g., State v. Brough*, 112 N.H. 182, 291 A.2d 618 (1972). The Supreme Court of New Hampshire held that "[t]he offense with which this defendant was charged [aggravated assault] was a 'general intent crime' and his intent could be inferred from the evidence of his conduct. Under this view, the defendant's intoxication could be no defense." *Id.* at 185, 291 A.2d at 621 (citations omitted).

89. *See, e.g., Kane v. United States*, 399 F.2d 730, 736 (9th Cir. 1968) (drunkenness irrelevant in general intent crimes because no particular state of mind is required).

an intent to do something simple, such as strike another, unless he is so drunk that he has reached the stage of unconsciousness. What he is not as capable as a sober man of doing is exercising judgment about the social consequences of his acts or controlling his impulses towards anti-social acts. He is more likely to act rashly and impulsively and to be susceptible to passion and anger. It would therefore be anomalous to allow evidence of intoxication to relieve a man of responsibility for the crimes of assault with a deadly weapon or simple assault, which are frequently committed in just such a manner.[90]

Without question, Justice Traynor's analysis accurately describes most intoxication cases that come before experienced judges. Indeed, in the very case before the California court, the defendant had questioned a police officer, the ultimate victim of the assault, about his lack of a warrant.[91] Such concern for legal niceties is not the hallmark of one whose intoxication is so extreme that he cannot understand what he is doing. Nevertheless, Traynor's analysis is unsatisfactory in those unusual cases in which an intoxicated or drugged defendant really does not know what he is doing.

The M.P.C., not without some internal difference of opinion,[92] chose to retain the traditional rule for intoxication. The rule provides that "[w]hen recklessness establishes an element of the offense, if the actor, due to self-induced intoxication, is unaware of a risk of which he would have been aware had he been sober, such unawareness is immaterial."[93] Under this test, the inebriated or drugged lemon squeezer would be guilty of murder. Although he was unaware of the risk that his "lemon" might have been a human neck, he would have been aware of that risk had he been sober. The M.P.C. makes reckless homicide murder when "it is committed recklessly under circumstances manifesting extreme indifference to the value of human life,"[94] certainly an apt description of one who is squeezing a human neck.

Part of the M.P.C.'s rationale for this rule is that awareness of the potential consequences of excessive drinking on the capacity of human beings to gauge the risks incident to their conduct is by now so dispersed in our culture that [it is not unfair] to postulate a general equivalence between the risks created by the conduct of the drunken actor and the risks created by his conduct in becoming drunk.[95]

This effort to postulate an equivalence between getting drunk and attacking, let alone strangling, another human being simply will not wash. One who willfully gets drunk or drugged to excess, while culpable, is not nearly as culpable as one who willfully or recklessly harms another person—unless, of course, the drunk or drugged person knew of his propensity to cause injury while drunk.

---

90. *People v. Hood*, 1 Cal. 3d 444, 458, 462 P.2d 370, 379, 82 Cal. Rptr. 618, 627 (1969).

91. *Id.* at 448, 462 P.2d at 371, 82 Cal. Rptr. at 619.

92. MODEL PENAL CODE § 2.08 commentary at 350–56 (1962).

93. *Id.* § 2.08(2).

94. *Id.* § 2.10 (2).

95. *Id.* § 2.08 commentary at 359.

The M.P.C.'s other reasons for adopting its rule are more persuasive. One is the problem of proof. In an overwhelmingly high percentage of cases the drunk will have the requisite state of mind; he knows the difference between a head and a baseball. Yet he usually cannot remember his state of mind or anything else surrounding the incident. Consequently, it is difficult for a jury to ascertain his state of mind at the time. By making the question irrelevant, the jury need not worry about it. Even though this might seem harsh in a legal system dedicated to the presumption of innocence, it is less harsh than the irrelevancy of a number of other questions, such as awareness of the age of a statutory rape victim. Many states believe that protecting minors is so important that one who has sex with a minor will be deemed a rapist even if he reasonably believed her to be an adult.[96] Similarly, a drunk is required to comply with the law while drunk, not because drunkenness is culpable, but because it is dangerous.

Ultimately, the bottom line is that insofar as intoxication is concerned, we regard dangerousness as more important than culpability. This sentiment was most apparent in *D.P.P. v. Majewski*,[97] a case in which the English House of Lords, despite impressive academic criticism, continued to reject the intoxication defense.[98] The critics argued that it was illogical and unjust to obtain an assault conviction against one who was too drunk to know that he was assaulting another person. The Lords' objections to the academic critics was best summarized by Lord Russell, who argued that [t]he ordinary citizen who is badly beaten up would rightly think little of the criminal law as effective protection if, because his attacker had deprived himself of ability to know what he was doing by getting himself drunk or going on a trip with drugs, the attacker is to be held innocent of any crime in the assault.[99]

This placing of dangerousness and harm above culpability is not so illogical as the English academics claim. Their arguments seem to be predicated on the assumption that criminal liability ought to be proportionate to culpability. Once one accepts the notion that criminal liability can vary markedly according to dangerousness and harm so long as minimal culpability is present,[100] it is entirely logical to hold a drunk liable for a more serious crime than the one he thought he was committing. Furthermore, given that an appallingly high percentage of crimes are committed under the influence of an intoxicant,[101] it may well be good policy to continue to do so.

---

96. *See supra* text accompanying notes 14–16.

97. 2 All E.R. 142 (1976).

98. *See, e.g.,* J. SMITH & B. HOGAN, *supra* note 66, at 193 ("*Majewski*, itself, fails to reveal any consistent principle.").

99. *Majewski*, 2 All E.R. at 171.

100. All of the academics concede that getting too drunk to know what one is doing results in at least minimal culpability. *See, e.g.,* J. SMITH & B. HOGAN, *supra* note 66, at 192–93 (discussing effect of intoxication on specific intent).

101. Shupe, *Alcohol and Crime*, 44 J. CRIM. L. & CRIMINOLOGY 661, 661–64 (1954).

C. Mens Rea of Rape

Much of the argument for and against an expansive intoxication defense applies to the *mens rea* requirement for rape. The problem arises when a man who forces an unwilling woman to have sexual intercourse with him claims that he thought she had consented. The resolution of this issue, like intoxication, involves balancing culpability on the one hand, against dangerousness and harm on the other. Indeed, in most such cases, the rapist *vel non*'s misperception is due, at least in part, to intoxication.

In the United States, the resolution of this issue is fairly simple: an honest and reasonable mistake will excuse the defendant.[102] As a practical matter, this normally will mean little to the defendant. Unless the unwilling victim manifests substantial resistance, except when the defendant's threats make resistance useless, she will be deemed to have consented.[103] Because a court need not reach the mistake issue unless it has found nonconsent, the same substantial resistance that defeated the nonconsent claim should also defeat any claim based on *reasonable* belief.[104]

In England, however, even an unreasonable belief in consent precludes a conviction for rape. The House of Lords made this ruling in the celebrated case of *D.P.P v. Morgan.*[105] Exalting culpability as the primary criterion, Lord Hailsham for the majority opined that to insist that a belief must be reasonable to excuse [rape] is to insist that either the accused be found guilty of intending to do that which in truth he did not intend to do, or that his state of mind, though innocent of evil intent, can convict him if he be honest but not rational.[106]

Much to the delight of most British academics,[107] Lord Hailsham refused to so hold. Instead he held that only a defendant who believes his victim is not consenting or who acts "recklessly and not caring whether the victim be a consenting party or not" can be convicted.[108] Lord Hailsham gave no example of what he meant by "recklessly and not caring," but presumably he was thinking of a defendant who

---

102. *See* W. LaFave & A. Scott, *supra* note 12, § 5.1, at 408–10. Some jurisdictions, however, do not allow even a reasonable mistake to exculpate the defendant. *See, e.g.*, State v. Reed, 479 A.2d 1291, 1296 (Me. 1984) ("The legislature, by carefully defining the sex offenses in the criminal code, and by making no reference to a culpable state of mind for rape, clearly indicated that rape compelled by force or threat of force requires no culpable state of mind.").

103. *See, e.g.*, State v. Dizon, 47 Haw. 444, 451, 390 P.2d 759, 764 (1964) ("the resistance must be in good faith, real, active, and not feigned or pretended").

104. *But see* People v. Mayberry, 15 Cal. 3d 143, 158, 542 P.2d 1337, 1346–47, 125 Cal. Rptr. 745, 754 (1975) (jury found no implied consent, but factual issue of whether defendant reasonably believed victim consented left unresolved).

105. 2 All E.R. 365 (1975).

106. *Id.* at 367.

107. *See* S. Kadish, S. Schulhofer & M. Paulsen, Criminal Law and its Processes 290–91 (4th ed. 1983); London Times, May 7, 1975, at 15 (letter from Professor J.C. Smith); *id.* May 8, 1975, at 15 (letter from Professor Glanville Williams).

108. *Morgan*, 2 All E.R. at 367.

forcibly overpowered a woman without bothering to find out what her desires were. After much furor,[109] Parliament codified the *Morgan* result.[110]

From the perspective of harm and dangerousness, there is much to commend the American view. Focusing on harm in his dissenting opinion in *Morgan*, Lord Simon said: "A respectable woman who has been ravished would hardly feel that she was vindicated by being told that her assailant must go unpunished because he believed, quite unreasonably, that she was consenting to sexual intercourse with him."[111] Regarding dangerousness, it cannot be denied that one who cannot tell that a kicking and screaming woman is not consenting is extraordinarily dangerous. Furthermore, for any such defense to have the remotest plausibility of being believed, the defendant would have to be extremely intoxicated. Thus, all of the problems of proof discussed in the immediately preceding section are again relevant. Moreover, the presence of such a defense might encourage a mildly intoxicated defendant to ravish a woman whom he knows is resisting in the belief that he will be able to persuade a jury that he did not know. Consequently, *Morgan is* not likely to be followed on this side of the Atlantic.[112]

D. Mens Rea for Assault With Intent to Commit Rape

The *mens rea* issue in assault with intent to commit rape can arise in a case identical to *Morgan*, except that the defendant's attempt to have sexual intercourse is thwarted. A paradigm case from the Court of Military Appeals, *United States v. Short*,[113] involved a drunken soldier who attempted to have sexual intercourse with a woman whom he claimed to have mistaken for a consenting prostitute. Such a defendant is as dangerous as the *Morgan* defendants.[114] Unlike them, however, he has caused less harm. Consequently, considerations of both harm and culpability seem to call for an acquittal, while dangerousness alone seems to call for conviction. The courts are split on this issue. In *Short*, the defense was disallowed, but the prevailing view is probably to the contrary.[115]

---

109. In response to the *Morgan* holding, one concerned commentator stated, "As a consequence of this regrettable judgment we can expect an increase in rape and decrease in the percentage of proceedings against rapists. . . . Waiting to see if the judgment becomes a 'rapist's charter' is indefensible. And the introduction of emergency legislation to reverse this ruling is indispensable." LONDON TIMES, May 12, 1975, at 15 (letter from Jack Ashley) (quoted in S. KADISH, S. SCHULHOFER & M. PAULSEN, *supra* note 107, at 292).

110. Sexual Offenses (Amendment) Act, 1976, ch. 82, § 1(b).

111. *Morgan*, 2 All E.R. at 367.

112. *Morgan* continues to be criticized in England as well, largely on the ground that it ignores dangerousness. *See* Wells, *Swatting the Subjective Bug*, 1982 CRIM. L. REV. 209, 212–14.

113. 4 C.M.A. 436 (1979).

114. A defendant is as dangerous as the *Morgan* defendants when, as in *Short*, he was thwarted only because of the arrival of a policeman who arrested him. Conceivably, a defendant who tries to overcome his victim's resistance but eventually desists would be less dangerous.

115. *See, e.g., Michael v. State*, 1 Md. App. 243, 229 A.2d 145 (1967) (per curiam); *People v. Guillett*, 342 Mich. 1, 69 N.W.2d 140 (1955); *State v. Adams*, 214 N.C. 501, 199 S.E. 716 (1938).

Those courts, which allow the defense, emphasize that assault with intent to rape is a crime requiring specific intent, which can be negated by intoxication. In this context, specific intent means an intent to cause more harm than occurred. In Short, the harm that actually occurred was the assault, whereas the intended harm allegedly was the rape. Because the defendant did not intend the additional harm in that, as the dissent stated, "he did not desire intercourse without full consent . . . or . . . was just not the sort of person who worries about hypothetical problems,"[116] he cannot be convicted of assault with intent to commit rape. Of course, the defendant still would be guilty of simple assault, a crime which merely requires general intent.[117] Courts that disallow the defense do so either because in their jurisdictions intoxication cannot negate even specific intent,[118] or simply because they apparently are unaware of the problem.[119]

One's assessment of these views depends on the importance attached to each of the three factors. If one views assault with intent to commit rape as an assault aggravated by culpability, the defense should be allowed. The defendant is guilty of assault for causing harm under an unreasonable belief that the victim desired to be touched. He does not, however, have the further intent to have intercourse with the victim against her will. Just as one who assaults another without intending to inflict serious injury cannot be convicted of assault intending to inflict serious injury, one who assaults without intending to rape should not be convicted of assault with intent to rape. Those wishing to uphold the conviction exalt dangerousness above culpability. Under such a view, a drunken defendant whose efforts to force himself on a screaming woman are thwarted only by an alert policeman is every bit as dangerous as a would-be rapist who knows that his victim is not consenting. Perhaps there ought to be crime aggravated by harm or dangerousness, such as assault putting a person in fear of rape, or assault creating a danger of rape. So long as these are not aggravating factors, however, and the aggravating factor purports to be only culpability, defendants such as Short, who do not have the requisite culpability, should not be convicted of the aggravated crime.

E. Self-Defense

As with rape and assault with intent to commit rape, a major issue surrounding self-defense is what to do with the person who in self-defense employs such force that a reasonable person would know is not necessary. Classically, one who employs such force is guilty of an assault, which can be aggravated if serious injury is inflicted or intended, or if a deadly weapon is used.[120] If such unreasonable defen-

---

116. *Short*, 4 C.M.A. at 446 (Brosman, J., dissenting).

117. *See supra* notes 87–89 and accompanying text.

118. *E.g.*, *Chittum v. Commonwealth*, 211 Va. 12, 174 S.E.2d 779 (1970).

119. *E.g.*, *Short*, 4 C.M.A. at 446.

120. *See, e.g.*, *State v. Manis*, 95 Ariz. 27, 29–30, 386 P.2d 77, 78 (1963); *People v. Bramlett*, 194 Colo. 205, 210, 573 P.2d 94, 97 (1977) (en banc), *cert. denied*, 435 U.S. 956 (1978).

sive force causes death, some jurisdictions deem the act to be murder,[121] while most of the remainder call it manslaughter.[122] A few jurisdictions reject the classic view by exculpating those who kill in self-defense, even when objectively unreasonable.[123]

Before assessing the factors relied on by the classic and minority jurisdictions, it is helpful to analyze the characteristics of three types of self-defense defendants: (a) those who correctly assess the necessity for defensive force; (b) those who erroneously but reasonably believe in the necessity of defensive force; and (c) those who erroneously and unreasonably believe in the necessity of defensive force. A type (a) defendant is clean on all counts, being neither culpable, dangerous, nor the cause of harm.[124] A type (b) defendant, although no more culpable or dangerous than a type (a) defendant, has caused more harm, namely the *unnecessary* injury or death of her apparent attacker. Nevertheless, because harm alone is not enough to convict, type (b) defendants are universally excused.[125] Type (c) defendants, whose liability is at issue, are slightly more culpable than type (b) defendants in that they are at least negligent. More importantly, they are substantially more dangerous.

Those jurisdictions that acquit type (c) defendants believe that negligence in the face of perceived danger simply is not culpable enough to justify conviction for an intentional crime. The M.P.C., accepting this principle, would allow a type (c) defendant to be convicted only of a crime for which negligence is sufficient, such as negligent homicide.[126] The case for more serious liability is predicated on dangerousness. One who cannot act reasonably before killing or injuring another human being is extraordinarily dangerous. Such a person poses the same kind of threat to the populace as the sexually aggressive individual who cannot understand that his kicking and screaming victim is not consenting.[127]

The negligent self-defender arguably is less culpable than the negligent rapist in that circumstances sometimes compel him to make a split-second decision regarding the necessity of force, whereas the rapist usually spends more time completing the sex act with his victim. Furthermore, society may be more tolerant towards one whose life or safety is at stake than one who merely seeks sexual gratification.[128]

---

121. *See, e.g., Saylors v. State*, 251 Ga. 735, 737, 309 S.E.2d 796, 797–98 (1983); *Lloyd v. State*, 448 N.E.2d 1062, 1071 (Ind. Ct. App. 1983).

122. *E.g.*, Ill. Rev. Stat. ch. 38, para. 9–2 (1979); Pa. Cons. Stat. Ann. § 2503 (Purdon 1983).

123. *See, e.g., Gunn v. State*, 174 Ind. App. 26, 365 N.E.2d 1234 (1977). The Court in *Gunn* held that "the question of the existence or appearance of danger to the defendant, the necessity of defending himself, and the amount of force necessary must be determined from the standpoint of the accused at the time and under the existing circumstances." *Id.* at 34, 365 N.E.2d at 1240; *see* W. LaFave & A. Scott, *supra* note 12, § 5.7(c), at 457.

124. Killing or injuring one who otherwise would unjustifiably kill or injure the actor is not harmful; it is a consequence the law desires to prevent.

125. *See supra* notes 29-40 and accompanying text.

126. Model Penal Code § 3.04(1) and commentaries at 36 (1962).

127. *See supra* notes 102-12 and accompanying text.

128. Many, perhaps most, rapists seek domination over and humiliation of their victims rather than sexual gratification. One who believes his victim has consented, however, is not in that category.

Perhaps for this reason, most jurisdictions that convict unreasonable self-defenders reduce a killing so committed to voluntary manslaughter.[129] Nevertheless, because of the dangerousness of such a person—coupled with the difficulty of proving one's subjective state of mind, as well as the temptation to falsely raise the defense[130]—it is unlikely that a large number of jurisdictions will reject the classic reasonableness requirement of self-defense.[131]

F. Provocation

Classically, voluntary manslaughter has been defined as an intentional killing committed pursuant to provocation sufficient to cause both the defendant and a hypothetical reasonable person to act in the heat of passion.[132] Occasionally a court will define the necessary provocation as that which is sufficient to justify the violence used by the killer.[133] Obviously, if this were the correct standard, manslaughterers would be no more culpable or dangerous than the ordinary reasonable person in society, and presumably should not be criminally liable at all.[134] Of course, such a standard would not help anybody because as several commentators have noted: "[T]he reasonable man, however greatly provoked he may be, does not kill."[135] The correct theory, of course, is that the killing is mitigated, not justified. One who kills only when a reasonable person would be governed by passion is less culpable and less dangerous than another who would kill under less provocative circumstances.

Whether the provocation ought to be sufficient to inflame a reasonable person is a question frequently rethought by commentators. Arguably one who kills in the heat of passion engendered by objectively inadequate provocation is less culpable than one who coolly and calmly kills another.[136] Nevertheless, such a person is probably more culpable than one who is reasonably provoked.[137] More importantly, such a person is considerably more dangerous. A potential victim can conduct herself by not doing anything to antagonize an ordinary person. There is no way that one can

---

129. Some cases have mitigated the charge to involuntary manslaughter on the M.P.C. gross negligence theory. The more sound rationale, however, is voluntary manslaughter because the killing is intentional, but is mitigated to manslaughter because of fear. *See infra* notes 132–45 and accompanying text.

130. *See supra* notes 41–50 and accompanying text.

131. *See, e.g., State v. Simon*, 231 Kan. 572, 646 P.2d 1119 (1982).

132. *Austin v. United States*, 382 F.2d 129, 137 (D.C. Cir. 1967); W. LaFave & A. Scott, *supra* note 12, at § 7.10, at 653.

133. *See, e.g., Bedder v. D.P.P.*, 2 All E.R. 801, 802 (1954).

134. In a few jurisdictions this is thought to be the case when one catches a spouse in the act of adultery. *See, e.g.,* N.M. Stat. Ann. § 30-2-5 (1978).

135. W. LaFave & A. Scott, *supra* note 12, § 7.10(b), at 654; *see* Michael & Wechsler, A *Rationale of the Law of Homicide*, 37 Colum. L. Rev. 1261, 1281–82 (1937).

136. For this reason, many jurisdictions that retain the premeditation-deliberation formula for first degree murder would convict such a defendant of second-degree murder. *See, e.g., People v. Caruso*, 246 N.Y. 437, 159 N.E. 390 (1927).

137. Of course, a whole host of factors, from background to genetics, might have to be explored in any given case.

avoid antagonizing a person who is subject to irrational fits of anger. If reasonableness were not required, a man who flew into a rage and killed a woman for refusing to have sex with him would be guilty of nothing more than manslaughter. Furthermore, when the law rewards irrational behavior, it encourages people to feign irrationality. Thus, if the man in the above hypothetical had coolly decided to kill the woman as punishment for her refusal, he would be encouraged to feign rage in order to mitigate his crime.

Some jurisdictions are so concerned about the potential abuse of the provocation mitigation that they have restricted it to certain categories, called legally sufficient provocation. In such jurisdictions, no provocation, however reasonable, can mitigate murder to manslaughter unless it is one of the specifically enumerated categories such as adultery[138] or battery.[139] Along these same lines, many jurisdictions specifically preclude "words alone, however insulting" from reducing murder to manslaughter.[140] Under this view, a jury's ability to mitigate murder to manslaughter, arbitrarily or otherwise, is severely circumscribed.[141]

The M.P.C. would mitigate to manslaughter "a homicide . . . committed under the influence of extreme mental or emotional disturbance for which there is reasonable explanation or excuse. The reasonableness of such explanation or excuse shall be determined from the viewpoint of a person in the actor's situation under the circumstances as he believes them to be."[142] This test, a remarkable hybrid of subjectivity and objectivity, has been adopted by a growing minority of jurisdictions.[143] Although retaining elements of objectivity, the test focuses much more on culpability and less on dangerousness than the classic reasonable person provocation test. This focus seems justified. Unlike a dangerous defendant who seeks exculpation on the ground of insanity[144] or intoxication,[145] a defendant who successfully invokes a provocation argument will be convicted of voluntary manslaughter, a serious felony. Moreover, the grand criterion classically distinguishing murder from manslaughter is "malice aforethought," a term which appears to be concerned more with culpability than dangerousness.[146] These factors, coupled with the M.P.C.'s retention of significant elements of objectivity, render this test a reasonable concession to human frailty without unduly compromising the public safety.

---

138. *E.g., State v. Davis*, 328 SW.2d 706, 709 (Mo. 1959).

139. *E.g., State v. Young*, 51 N.M. 77, 83–86, 178 P.2d 592, 596–98 (1947).

140. *State v. King*, 37 N.J. 285, 299, 181 A.2d 158, 165 (1962).

141. *See, e.g., Freddo v. State*, 127 Tenn. 376, 155 S.W. 170 (1913).

142. Model Penal Code § 210.3(l)(b) (1962).

143. *See, e.g.,* Conn. Gen. Stat. § 53a-55(a)(2) (1972); Ky. Rev. Stat. Ann. § 507.030(b) (Michie/Bobbs-Merrill 1985); N.Y. Penal Law § 125.20(2) (McKinney 1975); Or. Rev. Stat. § 163.118(l)(b) (1983).

144. *See supra* notes 51–82 and accompanying text.

145. *See supra* notes 83–101 and accompanying text.

146. Interestingly, the Model Penal Code avoids the term "malice aforethought." Nevertheless, it generally seems to focus on culpability rather than dangerousness to a much greater extent than the common-law courts.

G. Unintentional Killings

The harm involved in an unintentional killing almost always exceeds the culpability of the killer. Unintentional killings can range in severity from excusable homicide to murder, depending on two variables: culpability and dangerousness. Culpability runs the gamut from reasonable unawareness of a homicidal risk to complete awareness of an extreme risk. Dangerousness, which focuses on the magnitude of the risk, varies from a slight risk that somebody will be killed to an outrageously high risk that a large number of people will be killed. Dangerousness also varies according to the justification for the risk. A person driving ninety miles per hour through town creates the same risk of death whether she is transporting a heart attack victim or simply joy riding. Nevertheless, the law would deem the former instance less dangerous because the risk is balanced by the possibility of saving a life.

To the framers of the M.P.C., culpability is the overarching criterion. Absent at least a subjective awareness of the risk, the most serious homicidal crime to which a person can be subjected is negligent homicide. Even this crime is possible only when dangerousness reaches a fairly high level: "The risk must be of such a nature and degree that the actor's failure to perceive it . . . involves a gross deviation from the standard of care that a reasonable person would observe in the actor's situation."[147] When the actor is aware of such a risk and takes it anyway, she is guilty of manslaughter. In some jurisdictions, dangerousness is more important than culpability. Such jurisdictions do not require subjective awareness of the risk for manslaughter[148] or even murder.[149]

All jurisdictions, including those that have adopted the M.P.C., vary liability with the degree of dangerousness. Unintentional killings that are committed with an "abandoned and malignant heart,"[150] or committed "under circumstances manifesting extreme indifference to the value of human life"[151] have been condemned as murder. Some jurisdictions require that the risk endanger more than one person to constitute murder,[152] but most do not. Some jurisdictions purport to distinguish manslaughter from reckless, negligent, or vehicular homicide on the basis of the magnitude of the risk. Candor compels acknowledging that such distinctions tend to be more tautological than real, and that their only legitimate purpose is to provide juries with a lesser offense to convict dangerous drivers who may be perceived

---

147. MODEL PENAL CODE § 2.02(2)(d) (1962).

148. *See, e.g., United States v. Bradford*, 344 A.2d 208, 215 (D.C. 1975); *Commonwealth v. Garcia*, 474 Pa. 449, 463–64, 378 A.2d 1199, 1206–07 (1977).

149. *See, e.g., Commonwealth v. Malone*, 354 Pa. 180, 47 A.2d 445 (1946).

150. *Welch v. State*, 254 Ga. 603, 607, 331 S.E.2d 573, 577 (1985).

151. MODEL PENAL CODE § 210.2(l)(b) (1962).

152. *E.g., Northington v. State*, 413 So. 2d 1169 (Ala. Crim. App. 1981).

as less culpable.[153] A few jurisdictions subordinate culpability to dangerousness by convicting of manslaughter those who kill with ordinary negligence.[154]

H. Felony Murder

Although felony murder is a type of unintentional killing, it can be better analyzed separately. The theoretical rationale for felony murder is that the intent to commit the underlying felony—typically arson, burglary, kidnapping, robbery, or rape[155]—provides the "malice aforethought" required for murder. Frequently, the doctrine is defended on the ground that these felonies are potentially dangerous to human life.[156] The M.P.C. accepts the doctrine only to the extent of creating a rebuttable presumption that a killing perpetrated during one of the enumerated felonies was committed with the requisite recklessness and extreme indifference to human life necessary for murder. Some states, including a few that have revised their criminal laws to comport substantially with the M.P.C., do not accept the M.P.C.'s limitation on felony murder.[157] Undoubtedly, problems of proof[158] contribute to the persistence of the felony murder rule in this country.[159] We know that most armed robbers kill their victims either intentionally or with extreme indifference to human life, but we believe that without the felony murder rule, some of these murderers would be able to successfully claim that the killing was accidental.[160]

Problems of proof alone would not permit a first-degree murder conviction, which is the usual conviction under felony murder. Why then should a felon who has not created an outrageously reckless risk of death be treated as or more harshly than a nonfelon who has? The answer is culpability. Although a robber whose victim dies of a heart attack may not have created an outrageous risk of death,[161] his culpability in committing the robbery differentiates him from another who simply created the same risk.[162] If culpability is the key, why should the robber not be treated the same as any other robber? The reason is harm. Crimes such as robbery and

---

153. *See Cichos v. Indiana*, 385 U.S. 76 (1966).

154. *See, e.g., State v. Williams*, 4 Wash. App. 908, 484 P.2d 1167 (1971).

155. Some statutes have an *ejusdem generis* clause. *See, e.g.,* N.M. STAT. ANN. § 30-2-1(A)(2) (1978); PA. STAT. ANN. tit. 18, § 2502(b) (Purdon 1983). Other statutes include other dangerous crimes, such as forcible deviate sexual intercourse and felonious escape. *See, e.g.,* N.Y. PENAL LAW § 125.25 (McKinney 1975); N.D. CENT. CODE § 12.1-16-01 (1985); OKLA. STAT. tit. 21, § 701.7(B) (1983); PA. STAT. ANN. tit. 18, § 2502(d) (Purdon 1983); R.I. GEN. LAWS § 11-23-1 (1981); TEX. PENAL CODE ANN. § 19.03(a)(4) (Vernon 1974).

156. *See* W. LAFAVE & A. SCOTT, *supra* note 12, § 7.5(b), at 624.

157. *See, e.g.,* N.J. STAT. ANN. § 2C-11-3(a)(3) (West 1982 & Supp. 1986).

158. *See supra* notes 42–50 and accompanying text.

159. The felony murder rule has been abolished where it was created, in England. English Homicide Act of 1957, 5 & 6 Eliz. 2, ch. 11, § 1.

160. *See* Crump & Crump, *In Defense of the Felony Murder Doctrine*, 8 HARV. J.L. & PUB. POL'Y 359, 376 (1985).

161. *See People v. Stamp*, 2 Cal. App. 3d 203, 82 Cal. Rptr. 598 (1969), *cert. denied*, 400 U.S. 819 (1970).

162. Even without the aggravation of the underlying robbery, such a person probably would be guilty of at least manslaughter. For example, if a movie director decided to stage a robbery against

the other underlying felony murder crimes, unaggravated by additional harm, are usually punished almost as severely as murder.[163] If the crime were called robbery inflicting death, life imprisonment would not seem to be a disproportionate penalty.[164] Consequently, by viewing felony murder as an aggravated form of the felony, principles of culpability plus harm can justify its retention.

I. Inchoate Criminality

Inchoate crimes—attempt, conspiracy, and solicitation—are the mirror images of unintentional killings other than felony murders. Although unintentional killings are relatively low in culpability and high in harm, inchoate crimes by definition are high in culpability, requiring an intent to commit the crime,[165] and low in harm; if the harm had occurred, the crime would not be inchoate. Dangerousness then emerges as the factor determining the criminality of culpable people who have not caused harm. In the easiest case, one who deeply desires the murder of his enemy but is unprepared to carry it out is not dangerous enough to be guilty. One who solicits another to commit a crime for him is obviously more dangerous than one who merely desires the crime. Nevertheless, because the danger is not solidified until acceptance—at which point there would probably be a conspiracy[166]—many

a real victim in order to film his reactions as he was robbed, the director's recklessness should be sufficient to warrant a manslaughter conviction if the victim dies of fright.

163. In North Carolina, arson is punishable by a maximum of 40 years and a presumptive sentence of 12 years, and first-degree rape is punished by life imprisonment. N.C. GEN. STAT. §§ 1427.2, 14-1.1, 14-87, 15A-1340.4 (1986). In Illinois, armed robbery, aggravated sexual assault, and aggravated arson are all class X felonies punishable by 6 to 30 years. ILL. REV. STAT. ch. 38, paras. 1005-8-1, -12-14, -18-2, -20-1.1 (1982 & Supp. 1987). In Washington, armed robbery, first degree rape, first degree assault, kidnapping, and arson are punished by imprisonment for a maximum term of not less than 20 years. WASH. REV. CODE §§ 9A.56.200, 9A.36.010, 9A.40.20, 9A.48.020, 9A.20.20 (1977). In Texas, armed robbery, aggravated kidnapping, and aggravated sexual assault are punishable by not more than 99 years and not less than 5. TEX. PENAL CODE ANN. §§ 12.32, 20.04, 22.02, 29.03 (Vernon 1974). Alabama includes first degree kidnapping and forcible rape as class A felonies, punishable by not more than 99 years and not less than 10. ALA. CODE §§ 13A-5-6, 13A-6-43, 13A-6-61 (1982).

164. Accomplice liability in felony murder, without more, is constitutionally inadequate to support the death penalty. See Enmund v. Florida, 458 U.S. 782 (1981); cf. Tison v. Arizona, 107 S. Ct. 1676 (1987) (allowing possibility of capital punishment for felony murder accomplices under certain circumstances); infra text accompanying notes 198–204 (discussing Enmund and Tison). Not all jurisdictions merge the felony with the murder. In those jurisdictions, liability for both the robbery and murder is arguably disproportionate. Fortunately, most jurisdictions do merge the crimes. W. LAFAVE & A. SCOTT, supra note 12, at § 7.5(g)(3).

165. In traditional jurisdictions, inchoate crimes are still said to require a specific intent. Consequently, even outrageously reckless conduct will not suffice for attempt. E.g., Free v. State, 455 So. 2d 137, 147 (Ala. Crim. App. 1984); State v. Huff, 469 A.2d 1251, 1253 (Me. 1984). The M.P.C. suggests that knowing as well as purposeful conduct will suffice. As a practical matter this makes little difference and in any event involves substantial culpability. MODEL PENAL CODE § 5.01 and commentary at 304–05 (1962).

166. The State still may need to prove an overt act. See infra text accompanying note 181. Of course, if the crime required two people, Wharton's rule might preclude conviction. F. WHARTON, CRIMINAL LAW § 218 (12th ed. 1932).

jurisdictions do not generally punish solicitation.[167] Most of these jurisdictions do punish solicitation selectively, *e.g.*, solicitation to murder.[168] In such cases, the severity of the potential harm is so great that even the remoteness of the solicitation to the crime does not sufficiently negate the danger to preclude criminal liability. Because of the remoteness of the danger, however, these jurisdictions usually punish solicitation far less severely than the completed crime or even an unsuccessful attempt.[169] The M.P.C., focusing more on culpability than dangerousness, usually punishes solicitation to commit any crime as severely as it would punish the completed crime.[170]

The various tests for attempt are designed to measure dangerousness. The "dangerous proximity" test obviously speaks for itself[171] "Probable desistance" is simply a more precise manner of explaining dangerous proximity.[172] Jurisdictions adopting the "unequivocality" test desire objective evidence that the defendant really is dangerous.[173] The M.P.C.'s "substantial step" test requires less dangerousness than any of the others.[174] This is in accord with the M.P.C.'s usual emphasis on culpability. Given proof of culpability, the M.P.C. finds dangerous proximity simply unnecessary.

---

167. *See* W. Lafave & A. Scott, *supra* note 12, § 6.1(a), at 487; *see, e.g.*, Okla. Stat. Ann. tit. 21, § 701.16 (West 1987).

168. *See, e.g.*, Cal. Penal Code § 653f (West 1970 & 1986 Supp.); Okla. Stat. Ann. tit. 21, § 701.16 (West 1987).

169. *See, e.g.*, Cal. Penal Code § 653f (West 1970 & 1986 Supp.); Okla. Stat. Ann. tit. 21, § 701.16 (West 1987).

170. Model Penal Code §§ 5.02, 5.05 (1962). Section 5.05 limits solicitation to commit a capital crime or a felony in first degree to felony in second degree.

171. Model Penal Code § 5.01 and commentaries at 322 (1985). Under this approach, the question is whether the defendant's act was dangerously proximate to the intended crime. W. Lafave & A. Scott, *supra* note 12, § 6.2(d)(1), at 504–05; *see, e.g.*, *People v. Bracey*, 41 N.Y.2d 296, 360 N.E.2d 1094 (1977) (to constitute attempt to commit crime, act need not be final one toward completion of offense, but it must carry project forward with dangerous proximity to criminal end to be obtained).

172. The probable desistance test provides that for an act to be a criminal attempt, it must be one that would result in the commission of the crime but for the intervention of some extraneous factor. W. Lafave & A. Scott, *supra* note 12, § 6.2(d)(2), at 506–07; *see, e.g.*, *People v. Buffam*, 40 Cal. 2d 709, 256 P.2d 317 (1953); West v. State, 437 So. 2d 1212 (Miss. 1983); *Hamiel v. State*, 92 Wis. 2d 656, 285 NW.2d 639 (1979).

173. J. Salmond, Jurisprudence 404 (7th ed. 1924); *see* Salmond's discussion of theory in King v. Barker, 1924 N.Z.L.R. 865; Turner, *Attempts to Commit Crimes*, 5 Cambridge L.J. 230 (1934). Expressing the unequivocality approach, Salmond states: "An attempt is an act of such a nature that it is itself evidence of the criminal intent with which it was done. A criminal attempt bears a criminal intent upon its face." J. Salmond, *supra*, at 404.

174. The "substantial step" test provides: A person is guilty of an attempt to commit a crime if acting with the kind of culpability otherwise required for commission of the crime, he . . . purposely does or omits to do anything that, under the circumstances as he believes them to be, is an act or omission constituting a substantial step in a course of conduct planned to culminate in his commission of the crime. Model Penal Code § 5.01(1)(c) (1962). The M.P.C. states that only conduct "strongly corroborative of the actor's criminal purpose will be held to constitute a substantial step." *Id.* § 5.01(2).

The recurrent question of legally impossible attempts basically boils down to a question of objective versus subjective measurement of dangerousness.[175] For example, consider *People* v. *Jaffe*,[176] the classic case in which defendant purchased goods that he wrongly believed were stolen. Those who would acquit defendant for attempting to receive stolen goods emphasize that he has taken no steps which objectively brought him close to receiving stolen goods.[177] Those who would convict him emphasize that subjectively he did everything he could to bring about the crime. As one might suspect, the M.P.C., with its emphasis on culpability, adopts the subjective perspective and supports conviction.[178] Jurisdictions that allow abandonment as a defense attempt do so on the ground that the requisite dangerousness has been dissipated.[179] Involuntary abandonment, such as the arrival of a policeman, is never a defense because the failure to proceed under those circumstances does nothing to negate the already manifested dangerousness. Indeed, even when the defendant desists only because the circumstances turn out to be different from his expectations, such as his prospective rape victim's being pregnant, abandonment is not allowed.[180]

The crime of conspiracy permits criminal liability to be imposed at a significantly earlier stage of the planning than is possible under attempt. All that is required for conspiracy is an agreement to commit a crime, and in some jurisdictions an overt act in furtherance of the agreement.[181] The act does not have to be substantial, and certainly does not have to be dangerously proximate to completion.[182] The reason for such liability is that the agreement of more than one person renders it more likely that the crime will actually be committed. One person's thoughts, without more, may not be sufficiently dangerous to concern the law. But the prospect of a

---

175. The term "legal impossibility" as used in this Article, refers to situations in which what the defendant thinks he is doing is against the law, but what he is in fact doing is lawful—for example, "stealing" one's own suitcase. This situation can be distinguished from "true legal" impossibility. in which what the defendant thinks he is doing, as well as what he is in fact doing. is not forbidden by the law. *See, e.g.,* Elkind, *Impossibility in Criminal Attempts: A Theorist's Headache,* 54 Va. L. Rev. 20, 26 (1968); Enker, *Impossibility in Criminal Attempts—Legality and the Legal Process.* 53 Minn. L. Rev. 665, 676–87 (1969).

176. 185 N.Y. 497, 78 N.E. 169 (1906).

177. *See* G. Fletcher, Rethinking Criminal Law 182 (1978).

178. Model Penal Code § 5.01(l) and commentaries at 307–20 (1962). The Code rejects the defense of impossibility by providing that defendant's conduct should be measured according to the circumstances as he believes them to be rather than the circumstances as they may have existed in fact. *Id.* at 307. In accordance, the commentary explicitly states that "[the] *Jaffe* case . . . would result in a conviction under the Code because the defendant would have purposely engaged in conduct that would constitute the crime if the attendant circumstances were as he believed them to be." *Id.* at 317.

179. *See, e.g., id.* § 5.01 and commentary at 359.

180. *See, e.g., Hamiel v. State,* 92 Wis. 2d 656, 661, 285 NW.2d 639, 646 (1979); *see Lebarron v. State,* 32 Wis. 2d 294, 297, 145 NW.2d 79, 82 (1966).

181. *See* Minn. Stat. Ann. § 609.175(2)(2) (West 1964 & Supp. 1986); N.J. Rev. Stat. § 2c: 5-2d (1982).

182. *Kaplan v. United States,* 7 F.2d 594, 596 (2d Cir. 1925).

multiparty agreement resulting in crime is thought to be so much more dangerous that intervention of the criminal law is justified.

Because conspiracy is sufficiently dangerous to warrant such early intervention only because of the multiparty agreement, most jurisdictions will not allow a conspiracy conviction unless both parties are actually agreeing to commit the crime. Thus, if one of two parties is merely feigning agreement, neither will be liable for conspiracy because the one would-be conspirator has nobody with whom to conspire.[183] The M.P.C., on the other hand, defines conspiracy in terms of one person agreeing with another.[184] Thus, the person who actually agreed with another to commit a crime is guilty even though her cohort did not agree with her. The M.P.C. concedes that the play-along conspirator probably has decreased rather than increased the danger of success. Nevertheless, the M.P.C. justifies liability on the ground that the play-along conspirator's phoniness does nothing to diminish the culpability of the real conspirator.[185]

IV. Punishment and the Three Factors

Focusing on the most relevant of the three factors can assist a legislature or judge in apportioning punishment. The significance of deterrence, retribution, restraint, rehabilitation, and compensation can vary substantially depending on the most important factor in the particular case. When culpability is paramount, considerations of deterrence and retribution are most important. Restraint and rehabilitation are especially important when dealing with dangerous defendants. Finally, compensation should be paramount when harm is the principal reason for the severity of the crime. Although many cases involve more than one of the factors, it is often possible to allocate punishment in accordance with the most significant factor in the case.

A. Culpability

Crimes involving significant willfulness and premeditation seem especially amenable to deterrence. One acting on the emotions of the moment is relatively unlikely to be deterred by the prospect of substantial punishment. On the other hand, one who, Benthamlike,[186] coolly and calmly calculates the benefits and detriments to be obtained from criminal behavior is more likely to be deterred by such an unpleasant prospect. Furthermore, to the extent that retribution is deemed appropriate, such a

---

183. *State v. Kilinel*, 488 So. 2d 1238 (La. Ct. App. 1986).

184. MODEL PENAL CODE § 5.03(1) (1962). The Code provides: A person is guilty of conspiracy with another person or persons to commit a crime if with the purpose of promoting or facilitating its commission he: a) agrees with such other person or persons that they or one or more of them will engage in conduct that constitutes such crime or an attempt or solicitation to commit such crime; or b) agrees to aid such other person or persons in the planning or commission of such crime or an attempt or solicitation to commit such crime. *Id.*

185. *Id.* § 5.03 and commentary at 400.

186. *See* J. BENTHAM, *Specimen of a Penal Code, in* TEN WORKS OF JEREMY BENTHAM 469 (1843).

person is a prime candidate for it. When deterrence and retribution are overarching concerns, mandatory minimum sentences are most appropriate.

Armed robbery is a good illustration. Although armed robbers are undoubtedly dangerous and harmful, which may provide a basis for additional penalties, the calculated nature of such a crime has caused many states to adopt mandatory minimum sentences.[187] Many merchants in such states post signs in their windows stating the mandatory minimum sentence in order to maximize the deterrent effect of the statute. For such an approach to be effective, other factors need to be overlooked. Thus, even if a particular defendant can establish that this was an isolated occurrence and that he would not be a danger to society if released on probation, he could not receive less than the minimum sentence. Although such an approach subordinates the defendant's best interest to the larger societal goal of deterring others from implementing their culpable thoughts, the subordination is appropriate because it follows in direct response to the defendant's own manifested culpability.

B. Dangerousness

Defendants who have manifested themselves as dangerous frequently warrant flexible maximum sentences. To the extent that the criminal law is viewed as a societal protection device, it is desirable to keep such defendants restrained until they are no longer dangerous.[188] When such a defendant's dangerousness is caused by a mental abnormality—thereby minimizing culpability—a flexible minimum also seems appropriate. For such a defendant, an indeterminate sentence ought to be available.

A psychologically unstable, but not legally insane, child molester is such a person. Because child molestation is not usually deterred by the prospect of punishment,[189] a guaranteed mandatory minimum sentence such as an armed robber might receive is not likely to have much deterrence value. Moreover, because a psychologically unstable defendant is less culpable than one who is simply evil, retribution—punishment for its own sake—is not particularly important. What is critical is restraint while necessary and rehabilitation if possible. If such a defendant can be

---

187. *See, e.g.,* FLA. STAT. ANN. § 775.087(2) (West 1984) (three-year minimum term of imprisonment for selected crimes); ME. REV. STAT. ANN. tit. 17-A, § 1252(5) (1964) (minimum imprisonment of one to four years for conviction of certain classes of crimes); N.C. GEN. STAT. § 14-87(d) (1985) (minimum seven-year sentence for armed robbery conviction); 42 PA. CONS. STAT. ANN. § 9712(a) (Purdon 1983) (five-year minimum sentence for certain crimes).

188. Defendants should be restrained at least to the extent that the sentence is not disproportionate to the crime. For example, a defendant with a history of inebriation and minor property crime, whenever free, may be substantially certain to continue on such a path. Nevertheless, life imprisonment without the possibility of parole constitutes cruel and unusual punishment for such a person. *See* Solem v. Helm, 463 U.S. 277, 296–303 (1983).

189. *Cf.* Curran, *Commitment of the Sex Offender in Massachusetts,* 37 MASS. L.Q. 58, 61 (1952) (stating lack of deterrent effect of criminal punishment on persons with "uncontrollable" sexual desires).

rehabilitated quickly, limited incapacitation should be sufficient. On the other hand, if he cannot be rehabilitated, lengthy incarceration should be a possible sentence.

One difficulty with this approach is the uncertainty of rehabilitation. If a defendant is wrongly deemed rehabilitated, he can be released to perpetrate more atrocities on innocent children. If he is wrongly believed to be unrehabilitated, however, he can languish unnecessarily in prison, possibly to his and society's detriment. Given that the defendant's wrongful act, coupled with sufficient culpability to be accountable for his crime, is responsible for his predicament, it seems reasonable to require him to prove his rehabilitation as a condition of release.[190] On the other hand, his burden should not be so great as to render an early or moderate release date practically impossible.

C. Harm

Activity that is criminal primarily because of the harm caused involves different penological considerations. When culpability and dangerousness are relatively insignificant, the rationale for deterrence, retribution, restraint, and rehabilitation is concomitantly diminished. Of increasing significance in such a case is the emerging concept of victim or societal compensation.[191] This concept, which literally focuses on the defendant's debt to society, can be categorized as a "tort plus" punishment as opposed to more traditional criminal sanctions which leave compensation to civil courts. Illustrations of "tort plus" punishment include uncompensated community service and payment of the victim's medical bills.

Strict liability crimes are ideal candidates for such an approach. A bartender who serves liquor to a minor in jurisdictions in which this conduct is criminal without fault could perform several hours of service in an alcoholic rehabilitation center. Similarly, one who sells misbranded drugs could be sentenced to pay the medical costs of anybody harmed by them, or to perform uncompensated public service in a hospital that treats victims of such drugs. This approach tailors the punishment to the harm, which in these cases is the only justification for imposing criminal liability.

The same approach may be appropriate in cases of involuntary manslaughter by automobile. Although such drivers are somewhat culpable and manifest more than a little dangerousness, the principal reason for their punishment is the harm they have caused.

Involuntary manslaughter is usually regarded much more seriously than driving while intoxicated. Of course, such individuals do need to be restrained, but from cars and/or liquor, not from society in general. They are not dangerous if so restrained. Consequently, an appropriate sentence might include substantial community service and/or compensation to the victim's family, coupled with suspended

---

190. This assumes that the defendant's maximum sentence is not cruelly disproportionate to his crime. *See supra* note 188.

191. *See* Sugarman, *Doing Away with Tort Law*, 73 CALIF. L. REV. 558, 591–96 (1985).

imprisonment on the condition that the defendant neither drive nor drink. Violation of these conditions would, of course, show the ineffectiveness of the restraint in the particular case and mandate the reinstitution of the suspended imprisonment.

V. Capital Punishment and the Three Factors

The constitutional key to capital punishment is proportion. Unless aggravating circumstances sufficiently preponderate over mitigating circumstances, the death penalty may not be imposed.[192] Because of the uniqueness of the death penalty, it may not be imposed if any of the three factors warrant a lesser punishment.

A. Harm

Absent sufficient harm, usually murder,[193] a state may not impose the death penalty. Regardless of how dangerous or culpable a defendant may be, if he causes insufficient harm to warrant the death penalty, he may not be executed. A good example of such a defendant is Ehrlich Coker, the petitioner in *Coker v. Georgia*.[194] While serving three sentences for life, two for twenty years, and one for eight years—all of which were to run consecutively—for the rape and murder of one young woman and the rape, kidnapping, and assault of another, Coker escaped from prison. Before being apprehended, he broke into the home of a young couple, robbed them at knifepoint, raped the sixteen-year old wife in the presence of her husband, kidnapped the wife, and threatened them both with death. Fortunately, he was recaptured before implementing his threat.

In terms of dangerousness, it is hard to imagine a stronger case for capital punishment. Coker demonstrated an extraordinary propensity for all sorts of violence, including indiscriminate murder. Moreover, by virtue of his escape, he showed himself to be one of the few people who cannot be adequately restrained by prison walls. Just as drunk drivers who violate a court order against further driving may need to be imprisoned, violent criminals who escape from prison to commit more violence arguably need to suffer the ultimate restraint. Notwithstanding these appeals to considerations of dangerousness, appeals which persuaded the dissenting Justices,[195] the Court held that unless the harm was more serious than the rob-

---

192. *Cf. Gregg v. Georgia*, 428 U.S. 153, 193 (1976) (citing Model Penal Code § 201.6 comment 3, at 71 (Tent. Draft No. 9, 1959), with approval for its approach of weighing aggravating and mitigating circumstances against each other).

193. It is theoretically possible that some other harm might suffice, such as treason. *Cf. Rosenberg v. United States*, 346 U.S. 273, 287–88 (1953) (vacating stay of execution for espionage conspiracy). No decision since *Gregg*, however, has upheld the death penalty for a crime other than murder.

194. 433 U.S. 584 (1977).

195. *Id.* at 606–07, 610–11 (Burger, J., dissenting).

bery, rape, and kidnapping perpetrated during Coker's most recent escapade,[196] no amount of aggravating circumstances could justify execution.[197]

B. Culpability

In *Enmund v. Florida*,[198] the Supreme Court limited the instances in which one convicted of felony murder can be executed. Emphasizing the importance of personal culpability as a *sine qua non* of capital punishment, the Court held that the death penalty could not be imposed "on one such as Enmund who aids and abets a felony in the course of which a murder is committed by others but who himself does not kill, attempt to kill, or intend that a killing take place or that lethal force will be employed."[199] Enmund, who drove the getaway car, was never proven to have intended such violence. Without this personal culpability in regard to the killing, the Court held that no amount of aggravating circumstances—in this case Enmund planned the robbery and previously had been convicted of a crime of violence—or absence of mitigating circumstances could justify execution.[200]

Enmund was limited by *Tison v. Arizona*,[201] which upheld the possibility of capital punishment for two brothers, aged nineteen and twenty, who were convicted of felony murder, notwithstanding that they did not kill, attempt to kill, intend that a killing take place, or intend lethal force to be employed. The Tison brothers had armed themselves and their imprisoned father, along with another prisoner, in a successful attempt to escape from prison.[202] After escaping, the armed defendants flagged down a car, kidnapping and robbing its four occupants, whereupon the escaped prisoners, apparently to the surprise and disappointment of the defendants, killed all four victims. In the Court's view, the Tisons' major role in the felony, coupled with their reckless indifference towards human life,[203] constituted sufficient culpability to warrant the death penalty. As the Court stated, "These facts not only indicate that the Tison brothers participation in the crime was anything but minor, they also would clearly support a finding that they both subjectively appreciated that their acts were likely to result in the taking of innocent life."[204] Although the Court in *Tison* emphasized its continuing requirement of a high degree of culpability as a *sine qua non* of capital punishment, the extraordinary level of dangerousness

---

196. Coker probably was also guilty of burglary in that he broke into and entered his victim's house. *See id.* at 587. For reasons that do not appear in the record, however, he was not charged with burglary.

197. *Id.* at 598.

198. 458 U.S. 782 (1981).

199. *Id.* at 797, 801.

200. *Id.*

201. 107 S. Ct. 1676 (1987).

202. The defendants' liability for murder was not predicated on their role in the prison break, but on their role in the subsequent kidnapping and robbery. *Id.* at 1679–80.

203. Their father had killed a prison guard during an earlier escape attempt. *Id.* at 1678.

204. *Id.* at 1685.

inherent in the defendants' conduct may have persuaded the Court to reduce the necessary level of culpability from intentionally causing death to reckless indifference.

Any possibility that *Tison* portended the subordination of culpability to harm in capital cases was dashed a few weeks later by *Booth v. Maryland*.[205] The Court in *Booth* held that a victim impact statement describing the goodness of the murder victims and the impact of the murder on their family could not be introduced by the State to justify capital punishment. Rejecting the relevance of such factors, the Court emphasized that "[t]hese factors may be wholly unrelated to the blameworthiness of a particular defendant."[206]

The dissenting Justices — Rehnquist, White, O'Connor, and Scalia — in opinions by White and Scalia, emphasized the relevance of harm as an aggravating factor. As Scalia wrote: "It seems to me, however — and, I think, to most of mankind — that the amount of harm one causes does bear upon the extent of his 'personal responsibility.'"[207] He then illustrated his point by comparing the fate of the reckless driver who kills somebody with the equally reckless driver who does not, and the bank robber who fails in his attempt to kill the bank guard with the robber who succeeds.

On the surface, the dissenters appear to "have the better of the argument." Harm is unquestionably relevant in capital as well as other cases. For example, one could hardly doubt that an arsonist who burns down a house, killing two people in the process, is more likely to receive the death penalty than an otherwise similar arsonist who kills only one person. Consequently, the Court's opinion lacks intellectual coherence to the extent it implies that additional harm, unrelated to culpability, can never be relevant to imposing capital punishment. Another dimension to the *Booth* Court's opinion, however, is the question of what can constitute harm for purposes of capital punishment. It is one thing to say that killing two people is more serious than killing one. It is quite another to say that killing a good person is more harmful than killing a bad one. Although the status of a murder victim might sometimes make a difference (*e.g.*, a police officer in the line of duty),[208] the reluctance of the Court to allow the victim's character to make a difference is understandable.[209]

Apart from the goodness of his victims, the only additional harm inflicted by Booth was the suffering of his victims' family and friends. The Court found this harm to be too attenuated to have a just bearing on capital punishment. Had the victim impact statement focused on special suffering of the murder victims themselves — for example, torture — rather than the suffering of their relatives, there is no reason to believe the Court would have found it to be constitutionally irrelevant. In sum, *Booth* holds that unless some harm beyond the killing itself is imposed

---

205. 107 S. Ct. 2529 (1987).
206. *Id.* at 2534.
207. *Id.* at 2541 (Scalia, J., dissenting).
208. *See id.* at 2540 n.2 (White, J., dissenting).
209. *Cf.* McCleskey v. Kemp, 107 S. Ct. 1756 (1987).

directly on the victim, some form of aggravated culpability normally will be required to justify capital punishment.

C. Dangerousness

Although no Supreme Court decision has ever explicitly required dangerousness as a condition of capital punishment, decisions such as *Coker, Enmund*, and *Tison* ensure that only the most dangerous criminals will be executed. Although one certainly can be dangerous without causing harm[210] or being culpable,[211] it is not possible to culpably inflict death without being dangerous.

VI. Conclusion

The purpose of this Article is not so much to answer questions as to ask them. When culpability should prevail over dangerousness is a question that can and should engender disagreement. It is, however, a question that must be asked unless the factors which really influence judges are to remain unanalyzed. The classic criminal concepts of *mens rea* and *actus reus* can perhaps roughly translate to culpability and harm. Neither of these concepts encompass dangerousness, a factor that successfully influences everything from intoxication to self-defense. Besides aiding analysis of several of the most controversial issues in the criminal law, including the nine topics explored in Section III, a proper focus on culpability, dangerousness, and harm can assist judges and legislatures in making difficult decisions concerning punishment.[212]

My challenge to judges, legislatures, and other commentators is simply to be aware of the importance that the criminal law traditionally has attached to each of these concepts and to consider each of them when analyzing criminal doctrine.

---

210. For a discussion of inchoate criminality, see *supra* notes 165–85 and accompanying text.

211. For a discussion of the insanity defense, see *supra* notes 51–82 and accompanying text.

212. *See supra* notes 186–91 and accompanying text.

Index

[References are to page numbers.]